Inside Microsoft® Exchange Server 2007 Web Services

David Sterling
Ben Spain
Michael Mainer
Mark Taylor
Huw Upshall

PUBLISHED BY
Microsoft Press
A Division of Microsoft Corporation
One Microsoft Way
Redmond, Washington 98052-6399

Library of Congress Control Number: 2007934740

Printed and bound in the United States of America.

1 2 3 4 5 6 7 8 9 QWT 2 1 0 9 8 7

Distributed in Canada by H.B. Fenn and Company Ltd.

A CIP catalogue record for this book is available from the British Library.

Microsoft Press books are available through booksellers and distributors worldwide. For further information about international editions, contact your local Microsoft Corporation office or contact Microsoft Press International directly at fax (425) 936-7329. Visit our Web site at www.microsoft.com/mspress. Send comments to mspinput@microsoft.com.

Acquisitions Editor: Ben Ryan
Developmental Editor: Devon Musgrave
Project Editor: Victoria Thulman
Editorial Production: Custom Editorial Productions, Inc.
Technical Reviewers: Christopher Simison and Bob Dean

Body Part No. X14-06310

Contents at a Glance

Table of Contents

What do you think of this book? We want to hear from you!

Microsoft is interested in hearing your feedback so we can continually improve our books and learning resources for you. To participate in a brief online survey, please visit:

www.microsoft.com/learning/booksurvey

What do you think of this book? We want to hear from you!

Microsoft is interested in hearing your feedback so we can continually improve our books and learning resources for you. To participate in a brief online survey, please visit:

www.microsoft.com/learning/booksurvey

Acknowledgments

From David   There are many people who have contributed to this book or to my own personal enrichment. First, to Him who is worthy to "receive power, and riches, and wisdom, and strength, and honour, and glory, and blessing" (Rev 5:12), I am ever indebted to You for You redeemed me and called me Your own, not by my merit but for Your glory. I would also like to thank my children: Caleb, Gavin, Paris, Haley, and Evelyn for bearing with me while I finished working on the book. We will have a tickle-monster and popcorn night when this is over!

To my fellow authors, thanks for all the time and effort you put into writing the content for this book. It was demanding and above and beyond your normal workload at Microsoft. You will never look at a Word document with change tracking in the same way again!

I want to thank my technical reviewers, Chris Simison and Bob Dean. Chris, you did an excellent (and exceedingly thorough) job of reviewing this book. You were a true advocate for the reader and this book is MUCH better as a result of your hard work. Thanks for taking on the project and sticking with it! Bob, thanks for coming onboard to keep the schedule from slipping.

This book was indeed quite an undertaking, but more so was the Exchange Web Service software that this book is about. As such, I want to thank the Exchange Web Services team for your friendship, teamwork, and the innovation that you poured into the product (ordered by first name): Ben Spain, Bob Congdon, Chris Simison, David Claux, Gauri Deshpande, Henrik Jensen, Huw Upshall, Ilya Smirnov, James Shen, Jason Henderson, John Gibbon, John Merrill, Kumarswamy Valegerepura, Mark Taylor, Michael Mainer, Rahul Dhar , Raz Mathias, Rebecca Zou, Rob McCann, and Robin Thomas. Karim Batthish, you have a vast amount of technical knowledge in your head—thanks for answering my questions and taking time to explain things so thoroughly. Elena Kharitidi, thank you for putting up with my frequent e-mails about the ASMX framework and serialization; you are spoken of fondly by the Exchange Web Services team for your prompt, kind, and thorough explanations.

To the editing team, your kind attention to both the big and small details has made the end product much better than the drafts I submitted: Victoria Thulman, Devon Musgrave, Megan Smith-Creed, Jan Clavey, and Sarah Wales McGrath. Ben Ryan, thanks for looking at and taking the book proposal through the approval process in the first place!

I want to thank all the people who reviewed early drafts of the chapters: Roosevelt Sheriff, Henrik Jensen, Kumarswamy Valegerepura, John Gibbon, Wilson Li, Jaya Matthew, Ilya Smirnov, David Claux, and Karim Batthish. And lastly, I would like to thank my keyboard and coffee maker for bearing with the extra load during this time.

From Ben   To my fellow authors, David, Mark, Michael, and Huw, this has been a terrific ride. To our technical reviewer, Chris, you truly went the extra mile and I could not have made it sound like I knew anything without your help.

From Michael   First, I want to thank Martin Tracy for inspiring choices that eventually led me to this book. Thank you, Martin. Next, I want to thank David Sterling for putting this book project together. He has valiantly led the development of this content. He is such a valuable asset to any project. I also want to thank my co-authors, editor, technical reviewers, the people at Microsoft Press, Microsoft Corporation, and any other person or organization that has contributed to the creation of this book. Most importantly, I want to acknowledge the customer. Without the customers, without our partners, this book would be a meaningless undertaking. It is the customers and their desire to succeed that fuels works like this. Thank you.

From Mark   I would like to thank all those who reviewed my material, including my fellow authors and other colleagues. Your time and diligence helped me improve my explanations and remove those silly mistakes.

Introduction

One mid-year day in 2006, as the Exchange Web Services team was finishing work on Exchange 2007, David Sterling walked into Chris Simison's office and said, "You might think this is crazy, but what would you think if I wrote a book on Exchange Web Services?"[1] Chris was his manager at the time and mentioned that the thought was not actually crazy and that several others had tossed the idea back and forth, but nothing had been decided yet. So began the story of this year-long endeavor to take the information from the collective brain of the Exchange Web Services team and put it in writing.

The need for such a book was well established, being that Exchange Web Services was a completely new application programming interface (API) for Exchange. The material that needed to be covered was certainly there, as can be seen by the size of this book. However, what we had not yet determined was *how* to present the material and *who* the intended audience would be. You see, a Web Service by nature deals with Simple Object Access Protocol (SOAP) XML messages, which can be created and consumed on any operating system that knows how to deal with text. So the natural way to talk about a Web Service API is to talk about the XML schema that defines the structure of the request and response messages and to show examples of compliant XML instance documents representing those messages. Such a presentation appeals to us since we spend so much time dealing with raw XML. In addition, since SOAP messages represent the "native" way to communicate with Web Services, such a presentation could be understood by those developing on non-Microsoft platforms as there are no Microsoft-specific constructs that get in the way.

However, we also went with the assumption that many of our readers would be developing applications on the Microsoft platform, and most of those would be using Visual Studio 2003 or 2005 as their development environment. As you will see in Chapter 1, Visual Studio simplifies Web Service communication by creating auto-generated proxy classes that deal with XML generation and parsing under the covers. However, the proxy generator used by Visual Studio is not the only proxy generator available. In fact, with the advent of Windows Communication Foundation (WCF) in the Microsoft .NET 3.0 framework, Microsoft has released another utility (svcutil.exe) that generates a *different* set of auto-generated proxy classes that can be used to talk to a Web Service. And of course, there are proxy generators for other platforms such as Axis for Java.

Although talking about the XML message structure is convenient for instruction, in practice most developers will be using auto-generated proxy classes to manage their communication with Exchange Web Services. But *which* set of proxy classes should we use when writing this book? In the end, we decided that the most used proxy generator for talking with Exchange

---

[1] Chris Simison was the primary technical reviewer for this book.

Web Services would be the one used by Visual Studio 2003 or 2005.[2] As such, in addition to discussing the raw XML structure of the SOAP messages passed between a client application and Exchange Web Services, we also include a number of examples of how to program using the auto-generated proxy classes.

So, the general pattern in the book is that we first present the concept using XML and XML schema and then make that concept more concrete by writing proxy class code to show the concept at work.

What Does This Book Cover?

This book is divided into five parts. Each part contains chapters that are in some way related (very loosely in some cases). The parts are as follows:

Part I: The Basics

While it would have been nice for a given chapter to be able to stand on its own, Chapter 4 through Chapter 22 assume that the reader has a good understanding of the content in Part I, which contains Chapter 1 through Chapter 3. As such, we strongly recommend that you spend some time on the first three chapters before skipping around. Part I covers such concepts as the following:

- Using Visual Studio to generate the proxy classes for talking to Exchange Web Services (Chapter 1)

- Understanding the schema and WSDL files that define the Exchange Web Services contract (Chapter 1)

- Understanding item and folder identifiers (Chapter 2)

- Understanding property paths and response shapes (Chapter 3)

Part II: Things in Your Mailbox

A mailbox isn't very interesting if there is nothing in it. As such, Part II covers all of the item and folder types that can exist in a mailbox (with the exception of search folders, which are covered in Part III, Chapter 15). Part II covers Folders (Chapter 4), Items (Chapter 5), Contacts and Distribution Lists (Chapter 6), Messages (Chapter 7), Calendar related items (Chapter 8 through Chapter10), Tasks (Chapter 11), and Attachments (Chapter 12). Part II concludes with an indepth discussion of accessing native MAPI properties using Exchange Web Services extended properties, which is an important chapter since you will see extended properties used throughout the book (Chapter 13).

---

[2] At least until the next version of Visual Studio is officially released.

Part III: Searching

Part III discusses the restriction architecture in Exchange Web Services. Restrictions provide a way for Exchange Web Service consumers to search for items or folders that meet a certain set of criteria (Chapter 14). In addition, advance searching functionality such as paging, grouping, and search folders are discussed (Chapter 15).

Part IV: Keeping You in the Loop

Part IV covers the Exchange Web Service functionality used to alert you of changes to the content of a Mailbox. The Synchronization (Chapter 16) and Notification (Chapter 17) chapters discuss the features of each and when you would choose one over the other.

Part V: Advanced Topics

The last section of the book covers various and sundry topics that defied categorization.

Chapter 18 covers error handling in Exchange Web Services. Exchange Web Services is a batching API, and therefore errors are reported in a slightly different fashion than you may be used to. In addition, you will encounter SOAP faults, which are a by-product of communicating via SOAP messages.

Chapter 19 discusses Server to Server (S2S) authentication, which allows properly configured accounts to perform work on behalf of another account. S2S authentication enables Exchange Web Services to be leveraged as part of a more elaborate work process without having to set up a complex single-sign-on solution or Windows Kerberos Constrained Delegation.

Chapter 20 covers Autodiscover, which enables callers to determine the correct Client Access Server to use when talking to Exchange Web Services. In fact, Microsoft Office Outlook 2007 uses Autodiscover to automatically configure new Exchange 2007 mailbox accounts.

Chapter 21 and Chapter 22 cover the three Availability Web methods. *GetUserAvailability* is useful when trying to determine the best time to schedule a meeting. *GetUserOofSettings* and *SetUserOofSettings* allow you to retrieve and set (respectively) the Out of Office (OOF) configuration for a mailbox account.

Who Is This Book For?

This book is primarily aimed at developers who will be writing applications that use Exchange Web Services to talk to Exchange Server 2007. We assume that the reader is comfortable with the Microsoft .NET 2.0 framework and the C# programming language. For instance, many of the C# examples in this book make use of partial class extensions and generics. In addition, we assume a basic familiarity with XML. We do not, however, assume that the reader has had any exposure to programming against Exchange using any other API.

Companion Web Site

On the companion Web site, you'll find four tastefully appointed appendices that will prove useful in your Exchange Web Service development experience.

Appendix A "Response Codes," provides the error response codes that are defined in the Exchange Web Services schema, what they mean, and what Web methods you may encounter them from.

Appendix B, "Calendaring Supplementals," provides additional source code to aid in calendaring development.

Appendix C, "Mapping to MAPI Properties," talks about the property paths exposed in Exchange Web Services, the MAPI properties that each maps to (if applicable), and the operations that can be performed on each property.

Appendix D, "SP1 Feature Review," offers a quick view of the Exchange Web Service features that are expected to be released in Exchange 2007 Service Pack 1. Note that this book does not cover SP1 features.

All the code samples discussed in this book can be downloaded from the book's companion Web page at the following address:

http://www.microsoft.com/mspress/companion/9780735623927

System Requirements

To use Microsoft Exchange 2007 Web Services, you must have access to an Exchange 2007 Client Access Server. Several chapters cover topics that require administrative privileges in Exchange and the Active Directory. However, in such cases, you can simply follow along in the book if you do not have administrative privileges on your Exchange Server.

If you are using the auto-generated proxy classes or coding using one of the .NET languages, then the following is required:

- Microsoft .NET 2.0 framework SDK (included with all versions of Visual Studio 2005)

The C# examples in this book were written and compiled in Visual Studio 2005 Professional edition, although you can also use another text editor and compile them using the command-line C# compiler (csc.exe) included with the Microsoft .NET 2.0 framework SDK.

Support for This Book

Microsoft Press provides support for books and companion content at the following Web site:

http://www.microsoft.com/learning/support/books/

Questions and Comments

If you have comments, questions, or ideas regarding the book or the companion content, or questions that are not answered by visiting the sites just listed, please send them to Microsoft Press via e-mail to

mspinput@microsoft.com

Or via postal mail to

Microsoft Press
Attn: Inside Microsoft Exchange Server 2007 Web Services
One Microsoft Way
Redmond, WA 98052-6399

Please note that Microsoft software product support is not offered through the above addresses.

Part I
The Basics

Chapter 1
Welcome to Exchange Web Services

Believe it or not, this is the last chapter that we wrote for the book. We figured that it would be better to write all of the other chapters first so as to know what to introduce rather than introducing one thing and then writing about another.[1] The book that is before you is an exhaustive look at the Microsoft Exchange Server 2007 Web Services (EWS) application programming interface (API). Throughout this book, we've tried to give you an understanding of why the Exchange Web Services development team did things the way they did. You see, developing software is a process. The consumer will typically see the end product as if it magically popped out of thin air. But it didn't magically appear. There were meetings, specs, coding sessions, coffee, code reviews, debugging sessions, coffee, testing, explanations, eureka moments, coffee, and so on that constitute the API covered by this book. The API grew out of these experiences—the experiences of the developers, testers, program managers, documenters, and other members that make up the Exchange Web Services team. It is our goal that you will not only understand how to program on Exchange using Exchange Web Services, but also why the Exchange Web Services team designed it the way they did.

What Is Exchange Web Services?

So what precisely is Exchange Web Services? First and foremost, Exchange Web Services is an application programming interface that third-party developers can use to communicate with Microsoft Exchange 2007. This interface is exposed as a Simple Object Access Protocol (SOAP)-based Web service, which means that callers must send their requests to Exchange Web Services as SOAP+XML messages contained in an HTTP POST request. Exchange Web Services itself will respond with SOAP+XML messages in the HTTP response. Exchange Web Services is exposed on an Exchange Client Access Server (CAS) through an ASP.NET 2.0 Web service named Exchange.asmx.

Apart from its physical aspects, Exchange Web Services provides a way for consumers to interact with Exchange mailboxes in a Microsoft Office Outlook- and Outlook Web Access (OWA)–compatible manner. In fact, under the covers, Outlook Web Access and Exchange Web Services use the same business logic layer for accessing, creating, modifying, and deleting mailbox data.

What Does It Cover?

Exchange Web Services surfaces functionality that is primarily of interest to mailbox owners or accounts that want to do something on behalf of mailbox owners. This means that you will

---

[1] This book was originally supposed to be about house framing, so we are indeed glad that we postponed writing this chapter until everything else was done.

find methods to manipulate private mailbox database information such as folders, messages, calendar items, contacts, and tasks. What Exchange Web Services covers is the subject of this book.

What Features Are Missing?

The RTM version of Exchange Web Services offers a great deal of functionality. However, several significant areas are missing.

- Folder Associated Information (FAI) messages
- Most delegate access scenarios
- Public Folder support
- Administrative functionality (managing Exchange)
- Folder access control lists (ACLs)
- Delegate management

Rest assured that the Exchange Web Services team is working on these issues and more. If you need such functionality, you will have to continue using your legacy APIs until this functionality is provided by Exchange Web Services. We encourage you to visit the TechNet forums and let the Exchange Web Services developers know which legacy features you want to appear in Exchange Web Services. The development forum is located here:[2]

http://forums.microsoft.com/TechNet/ShowForum.aspx?ForumID=838&SiteID=17

Which APIs Is It Meant to Replace?

Microsoft has been extremely generous with their APIs, especially when it comes to Exchange. In fact, if you include API version updates and extensions, you'll realize that Microsoft has shipped several dozen APIs, as shown in Figure 1-1, that overlap in many places.

---

[2] And yes, coffee-infused members of the EWS team do indeed read and respond to these, but only if you are very, very polite. ☺

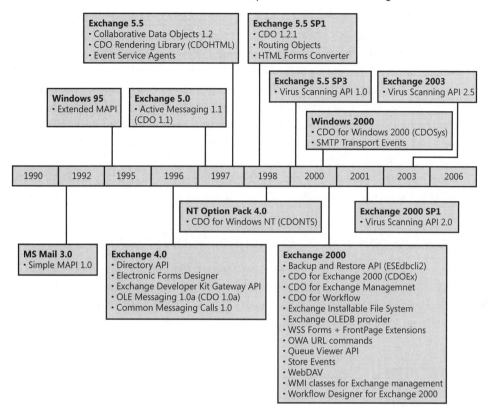

FIGURE 1-1 Shipping APIs for Exchange

Unfortunately, such a myriad of APIs paints a confusing picture for developers, especially those developers who are new to Exchange programming. So, the Exchange Web Services team stepped up to offer a solution—another API. Ah, yes. Yet, there is a method to their madness. Before Exchange Web Services, which API you talked to depended on your location (intranet or Internet), your development language of choice, your platform, and how much Outlook interoperability business logic you wanted to implement yourself. Refer to the grid in Figure 1-2.

		Outlook interop responsibility	
		Developer	Microsoft
Remote access from	Intranet	MAPI	CDO 1.2.1
	Internet	WebDAV	Exchange Web Services

FIGURE 1-2 The API grid

Prior to Exchange 2007, there was nothing in the lower right-hand box of this grid. If Microsoft could provide a full-featured API that could be called regardless of location and platform *and* offer Outlook and Outlook Web Access interoperability, then many of the disparate, partial APIs could be deprecated. In fact, the end goal is to have a single API for accessing Exchange mailbox data. "What about Windows PowerShell and the Edge Extensibility API?" you ask. Windows PowerShell, which is exposed in Exchange 2007 as the Exchange Management Shell, provides an excellent scripting environment for performing administrative tasks. However, it is not geared toward mailbox owner actions, such as sending meeting invitations. The Edge Extensibility API is geared toward developers who want to insert themselves into the mail receiving and sending pipeline. In the end, a single API for everything is unlikely. However, the overlap between APIs will be insignificant if not non-existent.

How Do You Talk to Exchange Web Services?

Because Exchange Web Services is a SOAP-based Web service, all communication must be over HTTP with an XML body. There are two primary ways to get there. First, die-hard programmers might indeed manually create XML and send it over HTTP explicitly. If you are using the .NET Framework, you can use a class such as *HttpWebRequest* to do this as shown in Figure 1-3.[3]

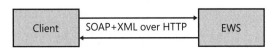

FIGURE 1-3 Client talking SOAP+XML to Exchange Web Services

However, the vast majority of developers will choose to program through an *autogenerated proxy*.

Most Web services publish a "contract" of sorts that tells those on the outside what the service can do and how to talk to it. Exchange Web Services exposes this contract as a standard Web Services Description Language (WSDL) document named Services.wsdl that is located in the same directory as the Web service. Feel free to take a look at it, although it really isn't intended for human consumption. Typically, the path to this document will be

https://*yourserver*/ews/Services.wsdl

where "yourserver" is the hostname of the Exchange CAS.

We like to think of the WSDL file as a poorly written user's manual. Although we don't suggest it, you could delete the WSDL file off the server and the Web service would work just fine. Think of it this way: You just received a new digital camera that you ordered. The camera itself has no need for the user's manual that came in the box. It already knows what it can do and doesn't know how to read anyway. However, as a digital camera *consumer*, you do need

---

[3] You will see an example of this shortly.

the manual if you are going to figure out how to set the date, turn off the flash, format the memory card, and so on.

Now, this WSDL file is indeed a poor user's manual, but it is exactly what proxy generator tools need to create the autogenerated proxies that most of you use when talking to Exchange Web Services. You see, the WSDL file is itself an XML file that lists all of the methods that can be called, the particular input and output types, the protocols that are supported, and things of that nature.[4] As a consumer, you point your proxy generator of choice to the Services.wsdl file, and the proxy generator magically creates numerous classes with methods and properties that enable you to talk to Exchange Web Services without requiring you to know the first thing about SOAP and XML.[5]

However, it is important to keep in mind that while you are talking to this fancy autogenerated proxy, the proxy is talking SOAP+XML over HTTP to Exchange Web Services. And Exchange Web Services responds with SOAP+XML, which the proxy then takes and converts into your method response. If you consider Figure 1-3, the client box can actually contain anything as long as it sends out and consumes XML. Take Figure 1-4 as an example.

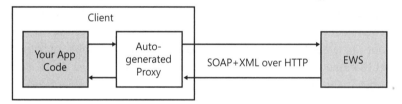

FIGURE 1-4 Inside the client box

In Figure 1-4, your application code is talking to the proxy using normal .NET property accessors and method calls, while the proxy talks SOAP+XML over HTTP to Exchange Web Services. Exchange Web Services is blissfully unaware of this arrangement within your client application.

Just be aware of two things:

1. **Proxy generators are your friend.** Manually creating and parsing XML is not something that most people do for fun. If this task can be delegated to a tool, that is a good thing.

2. **Performance implications to making Web service calls are hidden by the use of a proxy.** When you make a method call on the proxy class, the resulting request is being serialized, sent over the wire to the Exchange Web Services server, processed, sent back to the proxy, and then deserialized into the response. Make sure that you understand the performance implications of such proxy calls during your design phase.

---

[4] If you are familiar with the Component Object Model (COM), an Interface Definition Lanaguge (IDL) file is to a COM object as a WSDL file is to a Web service.

[5] Okay, so you had to know enough to pass the WSDL file to the proxy generator.

Development Environment

Given that Exchange Web Services is a standards-based SOAP Web service, you can call it from any platform that knows how to make HTTP POST requests. Of course, given that most of you will be using autogenerated proxies and that most of those autogenerated proxies will be for Visual Studio .NET users, we will take some time to discuss how to set up your development environment so that you can use Visual Studio to talk to Exchange Web Services. Even if you are on a different platform, we encourage you to read over this material because we might slip in a suggestion here and there that is applicable to other environments.

Generating the Proxy in Visual Studio 2005

There are two main methods to generate an Exchange Web Services proxy. The first of these is to use the "Add Web Reference" feature within Visual Studio to generate the proxy and add it to an existing project. As a general rule, we do not like the idea of adding a Web reference to an existing project because the generated proxy source code files reside in the same project as the code that uses the proxy. Why would we be of this persuasion? Every project that you want to talk to Exchange Web Services will have to go through this same step, which means that each project will contain the same generated code files. If you decide to modify or extend the autogenerated proxies, you will need to do this in a number of places—once for each project that references Exchange Web Services. In this book, we will indeed make numerous changes to the autogenerated proxies through partial class extension to make your life easier.

What we do recommend is to generate the proxy classes into their own class library project, compile that class library, and then reuse the resulting assembly dynamic-link library (DLL) in all of your projects that need to talk with Exchange Web Services. The great thing about this method is that any modifications or partial class extensions that you make in the autogenerated code will be available to all applications that consume your proxy DLL. Code in one place—that is a good thing.

So, let's do this. We are using Microsoft Visual Studio 2005 Professional Edition here, but this should also work in Microsoft Visual Studio 2003 (with minor changes).

STEP 1: Create a New Class Library Project

To do this, simply choose File, choose New, and then choose Project from the main menu. You are greeted by the New Project dialog box as shown in Figure 1-5.

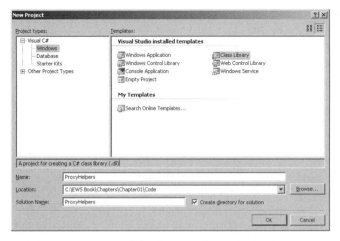

FIGURE 1-5 New Project dialog box in Visual Studio 2005

We will call our class library "ProxyHelpers." Make sure that you choose "Class Library" under the templates section. Set the location and solution name to whatever you want it to be, and click OK.

Visual Studio 2005 kindly creates your class library project and even provides a new, empty class file named Class1.cs. Of course, we will snub this empty class and cast it forth from our project by selecting the file in the Solution Explorer and pressing Delete.[6] Now, the Solution Explorer should look like the image shown in Figure 1-6.

FIGURE 1-6 Solution Explorer for our newly created class library

STEP 2: Add a Web Reference to Your Project

If you right-click your project in the Solution Explorer, one of the options on the pop-up menu is "Add Web Reference." Note that you can also do this from the main menu by choosing Project and then Add Web Reference. Either way, you are greeted by the Add Web Reference dialog box as shown in Figure 1-7.

---

[6] Also known as "deleting" the file.

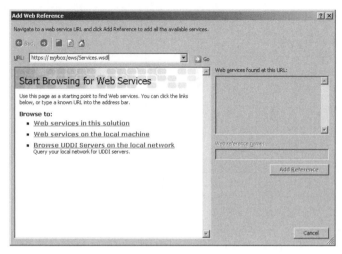

FIGURE 1-7 Adding a Web reference to your project

When you see the phrase "Add Web Reference," you should instead think "create a set of proxy classes for calling this Web service." Of course, the former is much easier to say and fits better on a menu. Now, in the URL text box, type the URL of an Exchange CAS in your organization. The URL will be something like the following:

https://*yourserver*/ews/Services.wsdl

You can also use

https://*yourserver*/ews/Exchange.asmx?wsdl

The latter involves more typing and simply returns the Services.wsdl file, so there is really no need to use that version unless you enjoy typing question marks in your URLs. Now click Go next to the URL text box. Your server might require you to supply your credentials, so go ahead and do so if prompted.

Certificate Issues on Client Access Servers

Depending on the nature of the certificate that the Exchange CAS provides to Visual Studio, Visual Studio might complain that the certificate is untrusted and therefore disable the Add Reference button. If that occurs, you can use Internet Explorer to help you in your cause.

Start Internet Explorer (we are using Internet Explorer 7 in this case), and type **https://yourserver/ews/Services.wsdl** in the address bar. You will likely see some complaints about the certificate. In fact, to the right of the address bar, you will see the flamingo pink Certificate Error button as shown in Figure 1-8.[7]

---

[7] My wife suggested that it is really "baby pink" rather than flamingo pink. Apparently, flamingo pink is more flourescent.

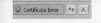

FIGURE 1-8 Flamingo pink Certificate Error button

The next step is to install this certificate so that the machine trusts it. If you click the Certificate Error button, a pop-up appears indicating that the certificate is not trusted. However, at the bottom of the pop-up is a link for viewing the certificate. Click that link to bring up the Certificate dialog box as shown in Figure 1-9.

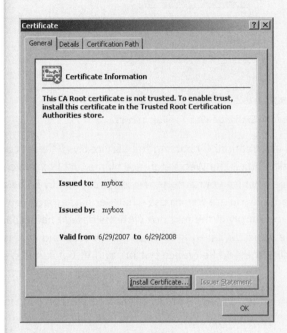

FIGURE 1-9 Viewing the certificate

Click the Install Certificate button, and step through the Certificate Import Wizard by using all of the default values. After the wizard indicates its success, close out all dialog boxes and close out Internet Explorer 7.

You should now be able to add the Web reference in Visual Studio 2005.

At this point, the Add Web Reference dialog box should be updated to include a list of the Web methods available for the Web service on your server as shown in Figure 1-10.

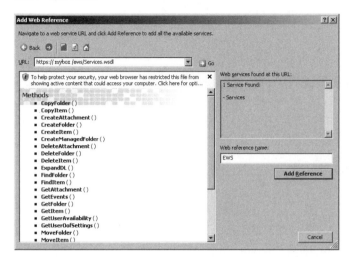

FIGURE 1-10 Web methods exposed by the Exchange Web Services service

Where did Visual Studio get this information? By parsing the Services.wsdl file, of course.[8] Near the bottom right of the dialog box is the Web Reference Name text box, which is actually used to define the namespace in which your autogenerated proxy will live. The example uses *EWS* as the namespace, although you are free to use whatever namespace you want. Visual Studio prefixes the value you supply in the text box with the default namespace of your project. Because the sample project is called ProxyHelpers, the resulting namespace is *ProxyHelpers.EWS*. Once done, click the Add Reference button, and Visual Studio generates your proxy classes for you.

Your project now has a new entry under Web References called EWS as shown in Figure 1-11.

FIGURE 1-11 Exchange Web Services Web reference displayed in the Solution Explorer

So, where are your autogenerated proxy classes? They are hiding! To display them, click the Show All Files button at the top of the Solution Explorer and then expand EWS and References.map. Within the numerous datasource files is a file named Reference.cs. Double-

---

8 Interestingly enough, some ASP.NET Web services do not expose an explicit WSDL file for their service, but rather rely on the "SomeService.asmx?wsdl" URL format. Doing so actually causes a WSDL file to be autogenerated by reflecting across the classes within the Web service and emitting the relevant information into the Web response. This is not how EWS handles it. We hand-coded our WSDL file, and Exchange.asmx?wsdl simply returns the physical Services.wsdl file.

click that file to open it in Visual Studio. This significantly long file contains your autogenerated proxy classes and is the only file that you really need to be able to talk to Exchange Web Services through the proxies.

STEP 3: Compile the Library

Compiling the library creates a DLL assembly that you can now use in other projects.[9]

Generating Proxies by Using wsdl.exe

Another method for generating the proxy is to use the wsdl.exe command line tool that comes with the .NET Framework 2.0 software development kit (SDK). It is also included by default when you install Visual Studio 2003 or 2005 on your machine. To access this tool, you need to run the Visual Studio Command Prompt, which is typically reached by going to the Start menu and choosing All Programs, choose Microsoft Visual Studio 2005, choose Visual Studio Tools, and then choose Visual Studio 2005 Command Prompt.[10] This opens a console window with the proper path and environment variables set so that you can use the wsdl. exe tool. To see the myriad settings you might pass to wsdl.exe, type **wsdl /?**. The command shown in Listing 1-1 will serve the example's purposes quite well.

LISTING 1-1 Using wsdl.exe to generate the proxy for C#

```
wsdl https://yourServer/ews/Services.wsdl /username:yourUsername
/password:yourPassword /domain:yourDomain /language:CS
/namespace:ProxyHelpers.EWS
```

When you press Enter, wsdl.exe chugs away for a moment and then displays the following to indicate that the proxy has been generated.

```
Microsoft (R) Web Services Description Language Utility
Microsoft (R) .NET Framework, Version 2.0.50727.42]
Copyright (C) Microsoft Corporation. All rights reserved.
Writing file 'C:\Program Files\Microsoft Visual Studio 8\VC\output.cs'.
```

There are several things to notice about the wsdl.exe command in Listing 1-1. First, you had to authenticate against Exchange Web Services to retrieve the WSDL file. Second, you specified C# as the language in which the proxy generator should create the proxy. In reality, you didn't need to add the "/language" parameter because wsdl.exe generates the proxy in C# by default. However, if you want to generate a VB.net or C++ proxy, you need to supply "VB" or "CPP," respectively.

---

[9] We ran into a strange situation once in which the library would not build, but Visual Studio wouldn't tell us why. We saved the project, closed and reopened Visual Studio, and then loaded and built the project. It worked fine. We're not sure exactly what caused it, but this is something to try if you run into the same situation.

[10] Of course, if you are running Visual Studio 2003, this will be slightly different.

For C++ proxies, you may need to make a slight modification to the wsdl.exe command. If you make the above request and replace the language tag with CPP, you might get the following error:[11]

```
Error: Failed to generate output file
'C:\Program Files\Microsoft Visual Studio8\VC\output.h'
  - Indexed property cannot have an empty parameter list:
  'System.CodeDom.CodeMemberProperty' Parameter name: e
```

To fix this, you add the */fields* flag that generates fields rather than properties. This really isn't a problem because there is no business logic within the autogenerated property getters and setters anyway—they simply access the private members.[12] The slightly modified command is shown in Listing 1-2.

LISTING 1-2 Using wsdl.exe to generate a proxy in C++

```
wsdl https://yourServer/ews/Services.wsdl /username:yourUsername
/password:yourPassword /domain:yourDomain /language:CPP
/namespace:ProxyHelpers.EWS /fields
```

Looking again at the listings (Listing 1-1 or Listing 1-2), the third thing to notice is that you told the proxy generator the namespace within which to generate the proxy classes. If this parameter is omitted, the resulting proxy classes are created in the global namespace, which is not a good idea. The last thing to note is that the proxy generator created a single source code file containing your generated proxy classes. In the C# case, the created file is named output.cs. If you want wsdl.exe to generate a file with a different name, simply add the *"/out: filename.cs"* parameter to the wsdl call.

Now that you have this file, what do you do with it?

Creating a Class Library

Open Visual Studio and create a new class library project. In the Solution Explorer, right-click your project, choose Add, then choose Existing Item, and file your output.cs file that you generated with wsdl.exe. Click Add (or Add As Link as you see fit), and your project is updated to include this single file. If you try to compile your project, it fails with the following error message:

The type or namespace name 'Services' does not exist in the namespace 'System.Web' (are you missing an assembly reference?)

---

[11] There was another team member who did not seem to have this problem. If it works for you without the */fields* flag, then feel free to go either way.

[12] As a matter of principle, we would recommend against surfacing public member variables in classes that you design. However, the */fields* parameter does indeed get around this issue when generating C++ proxies.

Ah, yes. By default, Visual Studio projects do not reference the various Web-related assemblies, so you need to add those references manually. Not a problem. Simply right-click your project in the Solution Explorer and choose Add Reference, which brings up the Add Reference dialog box.[13] On the .NET tab, scroll down to System.Web.Services, select it, and click OK. You should then be able to compile your project.

Schema Files

We have talked a bit about Services.wsdl, but it has some friends. If you are brave enough to look inside the Services.wsdl file, you will notice that it imports a file named messages.xsd.

```
<wsdl:types>
  <xs:schema xmlns:xs="http://www.w3.org/2001/XMLSchema">
    <xs:import namespace="…/messages" schemaLocation="messages.xsd"/>
  </xs:schema>
</wsdl:types>
```

The types section of a WSDL file defines the various custom types that will be exposed by the service. Rather than embedding these types directly into the WSDL file, we chose to keep them separate and import them into the WSDL file. Now, although messages.xsd is the only schema file that is listed here, messages.xsd actually references another schema file named types.xsd. These two schema files define all of the types exposed by Exchange Web Services.

We mentioned earlier that Exchange Web Services does not use the WSDL file. In contrast, Exchange Web Services does indeed use types.xsd and messages.xsd. Every request that comes across the wire is schema validated against these files before processing begins. Requests must adhere to the structure defined in these two schema files. Given that, we highly recommend that you become acquainted with how schema files are structured and what the various constructs mean. You can certainly code against Exchange Web Services without such an understanding, but it will do you a world of good if you do put forth some effort into reading XSD files.

The examples demonstrated how the proxy generator can consume the WSDL file to generate the proxy classes, right? Well, in actuality, it used the WSDL file to create what is known as the binding and used the imported XSD files to create all of the other various types that are passed into and out of the Web service.

One thing that might take a little getting used to is the fact that "messages" are king when dealing with Web services. Regardless of how fancy your proxy classes are, you are ultimately sending a request message over to Exchange Web Services and Exchange Web Services responds with a response message. Now, the proxy classes expose such methods as *CreateFolder* and *SendItem*, and you call them with the thought that you are performing the corresponding action. In reality, you are not creating a folder—you are sending a CreateFolder message to Exchange Web Services. This might not seem like much, but it will help you understand the schema a little better.

---

[13] Note that this is NOT Add Web Reference.

Messages.xsd

For the most part, messages.xsd contains the actual Web method request and response types for each surfaced Web method. Every Web method that you call takes one of these request types as its single argument and returns one of these response types. Each is named according to the Web method that uses it. For example, the *GetFolder* Web method takes a *GetFolderType* instance and returns a *GetFolderResponseType* instance. The request types are the name of the Web method with "Type" appended to them, while the response types are the name of the Web method with "ResponseType" appended to them.

Messages.xsd also includes all of the response codes that can be returned to indicate success or failure of items within a call. We will be discussing response codes in depth throughout this book.

Types that are defined within the messages.xsd schema file are all exposed through the "messages" namespace. The URL of this namespace is *http://schemas.microsoft.com/exchange/ services/2006/messages*. Because this is relatively long, we will shorten this in the book to *.../messages*.

A namespace in XML is nothing magical. In fact, you could have used *"abc"* for the messages namespace, although that probably would not have passed code review. Also, to make things a bit more readable, XML supports the concept of prefixes, which are shorthand ways to refer to a given namespace. You will see namespace prefixes defined like the following:

```
xmlns:m="http://schemas.microsoft.com/exchange/services/2006/messages"
```

Anywhere within the scope of that declaration, you can use the m: prefix to indicate that the type we are referring to is the one that is defined in the messages namespace. For instance:

```
<soap:Body xmlns:m=".../messages">
  <m:GetFolder>
     <!-- other stuff -->
  </m:GetFolder>
</soap:Body>
```

You can also declare the default namespace for the current scope by leaving off the ":m" after the xmlns. In doing so, anything listed within that scope that does not have a prefix is treated as if it was defined in the default namespace for that scope. You will see both approaches in the XML examples in this book. Of course, this book isn't intended to be a primer on XML or XML schema. If you need more background in this area, a number of great books on this topic are available, such as *XML Schema* by Eric van der Vlist (O'Reilly Media, Inc., 2002).

Types.xsd

While messages.xsd contains all of the request and response types and response codes, types.xsd contains everything else. In fact, each request and response type in messages.xsd has members that are defined in types.xsd. The types within types.xsd have a different namespace:

```
http://schemas.microsoft.com/exchange/services/2006/types
```

This does introduce some quirkiness in how elements need to be prefixed, although once you get the hang of it, you shouldn't have any trouble. Before we scare you off, note that this will only affect you if you are manually building XML requests. If you are using the auto-generated proxy classes, the namespace prefixes are taken care of behind the scenes. As an example, *GetItemType* in messages.xsd defines the request element that is passed into a *GetItem* call. The schema definition for *GetItemType* is shown in Listing 1-3.

LISTING 1-3 GetItemType in the schema

```
<xs:complexType name="GetItemType">
  <xs:complexContent>
    <xs:extension base="m:BaseRequestType">
      <xs:sequence>
        <xs:element name="ItemShape" type="t:ItemResponseShapeType"/>
        <xs:element name="ItemIds"
                    type="t:NonEmptyArrayOfBaseItemIdsType"/>
      </xs:sequence>
    </xs:extension>
  </xs:complexContent>
</xs:complexType>
```

Listing 1-3 shows that the type is called *GetItemType* and contains two child elements: *ItemShape* and *ItemIds*. If you look at the type attribute on each of these elements, you notice that they are both prefixed with "t:" suggesting that both *ItemResponseShapeType* and *NonEmptyArrayOfBaseItemIdsType* are defined in types.xsd.[14]

You might be surprised then that the following is *schema invalid*:

```
<CreateItem xmlns=".../messages" xmlns:t=".../types">
  <t:ItemShape …
  <t:ItemIds …
</CreateItem>
```

Why would this be? Although *ItemResponseShapeType* and *NonEmptyArrayOfBaseItemIdsType* are both defined in the types namespace, the "*ItemShape*" and "*ItemIds*" *instances* of these types are defined within the *GetItemType* schema type—which is in what namespace? Messages!

It makes a little more sense if you consider it from a normal object-oriented programming (OOP) viewpoint. Imagine that the type is the class definition. Ignoring static classes for a moment, in order to do something to a class, you must first instantiate it. Consider a class as shown in Listing 1-4.

---

[14] More accurately, they are defined within the types namespace.

LISTING 1-4 Example class for namespace discussion

```
namespace SomeNamespace
{
  public class MyClass
  {
    public string Prop;
  }
}
```

Now, you know that the *String* class is defined in the *System* namespace, right? However, Prop is an *instance* of *System.String*, but the Prop *instance* is defined in the *SomeNamespace* namespace.[15] This is similar to how XML element instances work. The corrected *CreateItem* instance should look like this:

```
<CreateItem xmlns="…/messages" xmlns:t="…/types" xmlns:m="…/messages">
  <m:ItemShape …
  <m:ItemIds …
</CreateItem>
```

Or, better yet, messages is the default namespace in this scope (see the xmlns="…"), and you can therefore get rid of the prefixes.

```
<CreateItem xmlns="…/messages" xmlns:t="…/types">
  <ItemShape …
  <ItemIds …
</CreateItem>
```

Moving on a bit further, *ItemIds* is a collection of *BaseItemIdType* instances, which again is defined in the types namespace. The *NonEmptyArrayOfBaseItemIdsType* schema type is shown in Listing 1-5.

LISTING 1-5 *NonEmptyArrayOfBaseItemIdsType*

```
<xs:complexType name="NonEmptyArrayOfBaseItemIdsType">
  <xs:choice minOccurs="1" maxOccurs="unbounded">
    <xs:element name="ItemId" type="t:ItemIdType"/>
    <xs:element name="OccurrenceItemId" type="t:OccurrenceItemIdType"/>
    <xs:element name="RecurringMasterItemId"
                type="t:RecurringMasterItemIdType"/>
  </xs:choice>
</xs:complexType>
```

Listing 1-5 shows that *NonEmptyArrayOfBaseItemIdsType* can contain an element named *ItemId* OR *OccurrenceItemId* OR *RecurringMasterItemId*. When you look at the element

```
<xs:element name="ItemId" type="t:ItemIdType"/>
```

---

[15] *SomeNamespace.MyClass* if you want to consider the class as part of the "namespace."

you should automatically think that an instance of *ItemIdType* is being created with a name of "*ItemId*." So, *ItemIdType* itself is defined in the types namespace, but where is the "*ItemId*" instance being created? Well, it is being created within *NonEmptyArrayOfBase ItemIdsType*, which is in the *types* namespace. Therefore, *ItemId*, *OccurenceItemId*, and *RecurringMasterItemId* all have the "t:" prefix.

If you add an *ItemId* element to the example XML, it looks like the following:

```
<CreateItem xmlns="…/messages" xmlns:t="…/types">
  <ItemShape …
  <ItemIds>
    <t:ItemId …/>
  </ItemIds>
</CreateItem>
```

Because the "*ItemId*" *instance* is defined in the types namespace, it MUST be prefixed accordingly.

Therefore, as you are reading the schema, always ask yourself "What namespace is this *instance* defined in?" instead of "What namespace is this *type* defined in?"

Schema, Meet Proxy

If you were to create your own Web service in Visual Studio, you would not be required to deal with schema files at all. In fact, the "standard way" to do Web service programming in Visual Studio is to decorate your classes and methods with the various XML serialization attributes and allow the .NET Framework to handle the generation of the XSD and WSDL files when necessary, which really only occurs when a consumer makes a YourService.asmx?wsdl call.

The Exchange Web Services development team, however, took a "contract first" approach and actually wrote the XSD and WSDL files by hand. There are some wonderful things and some not-so-wonderful things about doing this.

Pros

- XML schema is very expressive.
- You can add comments in the schema.
- You can explicitly validate requests against the schema.
- You can define the contract in an industry standard language and then create a .NET Web service to generate instance documents that are compliant.

Cons

- XML schema is very expressive.

Having an extremely expressive language with which to generate contracts is very nice while you are defining the contract. However, it is so expressive that you can create types that are not easily expressed in .NET languages, such as C#. Not only that, things that make perfect sense in schema translate into beastly constructs in code. Unfortunately, the "contract first" approach did result in some "interesting" artifacts being surfaced in the autogenerated proxies.

Choice Elements

XML schema exposes the idea of a "choice" in which a given slot within an instance document can contain one[16] of the items defined by the choice. As an example, consider the schema in Listing 1-6.

LISTING 1-6 Choice schema example

```
<xs:complexType name="FamilyType">
  <xs:choice maxOccurs="unbounded">
    <xs:element name="Brother" type="BrotherType"/>
    <xs:element name="Sister" type="SisterType"/>
  </xs:choice>
</xs:complexType>
```

With the type in Listing 1-6, both of the following are valid instance documents:

```
<Family>
  <Brother/>
</Family>

<Family>
  <Sister/>
</Family>
```

If you generate a proxy class for this type, you have an issue to contend with. First, the choice really represents a single slot in the schema, *not* two different properties. The proxy generator could treat this as two properties, but then one of them would always be null. Or, it could create a single property with a type that is a common base class for both BrotherType and SisterType. That would work great except for one *minor* issue: what exactly should the proxy generator *name* this property? In the XML instance document, it could be named either "Brother" or "Sister," but you don't have the flexibility to change property names on the fly in a language such as C#. Because the proxy generator can't determine what to name it, it simply calls the property "Item."

---

[16] Or more, depending on the *maxOccurs* attribute set on the choice element. However, in EWS, you do not use choices that allow for more than one item, so ignore that "feature" right now.

As you have seen, choice elements make sense when dealing with schema and XML instance documents directly. However, they cause problems for proxy users. A better way to do this is to get rid of the choice altogether and instead have a single element as shown in Listing 1-7.

LISTING 1-7 Polymorphic element with a sensible name

```
<xs:complexType name="FamilyType">
  <xs:element name="Sibling" type="SiblingType" maxOccurs="unbounded"/>
</xs:complexType>
```

Assuming for a moment that *BrotherType* and *SisterType* both derive from *SiblingType*, the proxy creates a property called *"Sibling"* that can either contain a Brother instance or a Sister instance. Of course, because the element name no longer identifies which type it is, an XML instance document must provide additional information regarding the type, which it can do via the *xsi:type* attribute.

```
<Family>
  <Sibling xsi:type="BrotherType"/>
  <Sibling xsi:type="SisterType"/>
  <!-- more… -->
</Family>
```

When the the proxy sends such a document to the Web service, each sibling element is deserialized to the correct Brother or Sister type according to the *xsi:type* attribute. Now, Exchange Web Services does not currently define its schemas in this way. So, why are we telling you this? So that if you ever create your own Web service, you will avoid choice elements and lean toward well-named elements of the base type in question. Exchange Web Services developers expect that future versions of Exchange Web Services will lean in this direction. In the meantime, you will have to contend with property names that the autogenerated proxies create such as Item, Item1, and so forth.

There is one feature that choice elements provide that is not possible with "polymorphic" elements. In choice elements, the possible choices need not be related in any way. However, with polymorphic elements, only types that derive from the base element type can be used.

*Specified Flags

Types fall into two general categories in .NET: value types and reference types. We won't go into depth distinguishing between these two because there are a number of excellent books available that do a much better job. For the purposes of this book, value types cannot have a null value, whereas reference types can.

Now, XML schema allows you to define optional elements and attributes within a type. An instance document does not have to include these optional elements or attributes to be schema compliant. Proxy classes indicate that an optional value is missing for value and reference types in distinct ways. For reference types, the proxy can simply use a null value to indicate that the instance document did not include that element or attribute. However, if the element or attribute represents a value type (such as int, bool, or DateTime), you have a problem because value types cannot have a null value.

With .NET 2.0, the proxy generator could have used nullable types to represent these optional value type elements and attributes, but alas, it is solved in another way. For every optional element and attribute in the schema, the proxy generates a second property named <PropertyName>Specified. For example, if the element in question is named "DateTimeReceived," the proxy generator creates two properties:

```
public DateTime DateTimeReceived {get; set;}
```

```
public bool DateTimeReceivedSpecified {get; set;}
```

One ugly thing about this method is that when a client sets the *DateTimeReceived* property, the DateTimeReceived*Specified* property is *not* automatically set to true. We can almost guarantee that this will bite you at least once—it certainly has caught us off guard a time or two. Setting the *DateTimeReceived* property without setting the *DateTimeReceivedSpecified* property to true results in that property *not* being emitted into your request. It is as if you didn't set it at all. If you set a value type property, you *must* set the corresponding *Specified property to true.

Only Default Constructors

Generated proxy classes all have the default constructor, which is required for the XML serializer to deserialize an instance of that class. If you do any significant amount of coding against Exchange Web Services using the proxy classes, you will most certainly want to add constructor overloads that take various parameters. Now, when you define an overloaded constructor, the type no longer has the implicit default constructor. This makes the XML serializer quite upset with you and generates a runtime error when it tries to deserialize an instance of that class. If you are going to provide an overloaded constructor, you must explicitly provide the default constructor so that the XML serializer continues to work properly. As an example, a proxy class that you will use often is *DistinguishedFolderIdType*, which allows you to identify well-known folders, such as the Inbox or Sent Items. By default, you need to instantiate one of these and then set the id to point to the folder type of interest. For example, to identify the Inbox, you would do the following:

```
DistinguishedFolderIdType myInbox = new DistinguishedFolderIdType();
myInbox.Id = DistinguishedFolderIdNameType.inbox;
```

Of course, if you want to refer to someone else's Inbox, you also must add a *Mailbox* element as follows:

```
DistinguishedFolderIdType inbox = new DistinguishedFolderIdType();
inbox.Id = DistinguishedFolderIdNameType.inbox;
inbox.Mailbox = new EmailAddressType();
inbox.Mailbox.EmailAddress = "john@contoso.com";
```

This process might not seem bad, but if you do it a few times, you notice that the pattern is always the same. This reduces to a single line. Isn't this better?

```
DistinguishedFolderIdType inbox = new DistinguishedFolderIdType(
                               DistinguishedFolderIdNameType.inbox,
                               "john@contoso.com");
```

Therefore, you simply extend the class via partial class extension and add the new constructor. However, because you are overloading the default constructor, you need to explicitly add it back so that the XML serializer continues to work as shown in Listing 1-8.

LISTING 1-8 Partial class extension of *DistinguishedFolderIdType*

```
/// <summary>
/// Partial class extension of DistinguishedFolderIdType
/// </summary>
public partial class DistinguishedFolderIdType
{
  /// <summary>
  /// Default constructor needed for Xml serialization
  /// </summary>

  public DistinguishedFolderIdType() { }
  /// <summary>
  /// Constructor for sanity's sake
  /// </summary>
  /// <param name="folderName">Folder id enum to indicate which
  /// distinguished folder we are dealing with</param>
  ///
  public DistinguishedFolderIdType
          (DistinguishedFolderIdNameType folderName)
  {
    this.idField = folderName;
  }


  /// <summary>
  /// Constructor for sanity's sake
  /// </summary>
  /// <param name="folderName">Folder id enum to indicate which
  /// distinguished folder we are dealing with</param>
  /// <param name="primarySmtpAddress">Primary Smtp Address of the mailbox
  /// we are trying to access</param>
  ///
  public DistinguishedFolderIdType(
                  DistinguishedFolderIdNameType folderName,
                  string primarySmtpAddress) : this(folderName)
  {
    this.mailboxField = new EmailAddressType();
    this.mailboxField.EmailAddress = primarySmtpAddress;
  }
}
```

> **Important** If you are going to provide overloaded constructors in your proxy classes, make sure to provide an explicit default constructor so that XML serialization continues to work.

Name Mangling on enum Values

XML schema allows you to include some strange characters in your enum values. For instance, "item:Subject" is a completely acceptable enum value in an XML schema. However, that is *not* a valid enum value in languages such as C#. So, when the proxy generator creates proxy classes based on a schema that includes such strange enum values, it must mangle the names to make them valid for that language. The mangling isn't horrible—it simply removes the inappropriate characters. Therefore, "item:Subject" becomes "itemSubject" (notice the missing colon). This isn't a big deal, although you will have to contend with it when parsing SOAP fault detail elements in Chapter 18, "Errors Never Happen."

Array Length Restrictions Lost

XML schema allows you to specify both a minimum and maximum number of items that can occur within an "array." For instance, the element defined in Listing 1-9 indicates that you must have at least two but not more than ten instances of the *Sibling* element to be schema compliant.

LISTING 1-9 Array type with upper and lower limits

```
<xs:element name="Sibling"
            type="SiblingType"
            minOccurs="2"
            maxOccurs="10"/>
```

How does that translate into the proxy class? Well, simply, as an array. All of the bounds limits are lost, which means that you can create a non-schema–compliant document by creating an array of siblings with only a single item—or twenty. The proxy class happily complies, although once the request gets over the Web service and is schema validated, the server returns a SOAP fault indicating that the request is schema invalid.

It is important to know that while the proxy classes do an honorable job of "protecting" you from the schema, there are times when you really do need to know what the schema says to get the proxy to work properly.

Some Simple Type Restrictions Lost

Along the same lines as array length restrictions, other XSD constructs, such as regex patterns, lists and unions, are lost when proxy classes are generated. For instance, *PathToExtendedFieldUriType* surfaces an element named *PropertyTag* that has the following definition:

```
<xs:simpleType name="PropertyTagType">
  <xs:annotation>
    <xs:documentation>
       This type represents the property tag (MINUS the type part).

       There are two options for representation:
       1.  Hex ==> 0x3fa4
       2.  Decimal ==> 0-65535
    </xs:documentation>
  </xs:annotation>
  <xs:union memberTypes ="xs:unsignedShort">
    <xs:simpleType id="HexPropertyTagType">
      <xs:restriction base="xs:string">
        <xs:pattern value="(0x|0X)[0-9A-Fa-f]{1,4}"/>
      </xs:restriction>
    </xs:simpleType>
  </xs:union>
</xs:simpleType>
```

For an instance document containing a property tag to be schema compliant, the value for that property tag *must* match the regex pattern in the schema type. When the proxy generator creates the proxy class, it simply marks the *PropertyTag* property as a string, which of course is much more permissive than the regex pattern.

Certain Reference Type Elements Are No Longer Required

Earlier in the chapter, we discussed value types and the *Specified property. The reverse problem occurs with reference types. Although the proxy generator provides additional *Specified properties to show which value type elements/attributes are optional, it loses the concept of which reference type elements/attributes are required and which are optional. You are free to set any reference type properties on the proxy class instances to null, although doing so for required properties causes you to encounter a schema validation SOAP fault. This is another case in which familiarity with the schema is a good thing and will save you hours of pain down the line. Perhaps the proxy generator should create classes that throw when you set required properties to null.

Coding by Using Raw XML

Most consumers will bypass this option, but the most earthy and natural way to talk to Exchange Web Services is through raw SOAP+XML messages over HTTP. Well, natural for the Web service at least. There are any number of ways to do this, and we will show you one way here.

Knowing that Web service requests to Exchange Web Services are made via HTTP POST calls, the *HttpWebRequest* class in the *System.Web* namespace is your friend. Listing 1-10 provides a general-purpose method for sending XML SOAP requests to Exchange Web Services.

LISTING 1-10 Sending raw SOAP over HTTP

```
/// <summary>
/// Makes a raw soap request
/// </summary>
/// <param name="url">URL of server to talk to</param>
/// <param name="userName">UserName</param>
/// <param name="password">Password</param>
/// <param name="domain">User's domain</param>
/// <param name="EWSRequestString">The contents of the soap body (minus the
/// body element)</param>
/// <param name="headers">PARAMS any soap headers to add</param>
/// <returns>DOM wrapper around the response</returns>
///
public static XmlDocument MakeRawSoapRequest(
                                    string url,
                                    string userName,
                                    string password,
                                    string domain,
                                    string EWSRequestString,
                                    params string[] headers)
{
  HttpWebRequest request = (HttpWebRequest)HttpWebRequest.Create(url);
  request.Method = "POST";
  request.ContentType = "text/xml;utf-8";
  request.Credentials = new NetworkCredential(userName, password, domain);

  StringBuilder builder = new StringBuilder();
  builder.AppendLine("<?xml version=\"1.0\" encoding=\"utf-8\"?>");
  builder.AppendLine("<soap:Envelope xmlns:xsi=\"http://www.w3.org" +
                  "/2001/XMLSchema-instance\"");
  builder.AppendLine(
        "xmlns:xsd=\"http://www.w3.org/2001/XMLSchema\"");
  builder.AppendLine(
        "xmlns:soap=\"http://schemas.xmlsoap.org/soap/envelope/\"");
  builder.AppendLine("xmlns=\"http://schemas.microsoft.com/exchange/" +
        "services/2006/messages\"");
  builder.AppendLine("xmlns:t=\"http://schemas.microsoft.com/exchange/" +
        "services/2006/types\">");

  // Add the soap headers if present
  //
  if ((headers != null) && (headers.Length > 0))
  {
    builder.AppendLine("<soap:Header>");
    foreach (string header in headers)
    {
      builder.Append(header);
    }
    builder.AppendLine("</soap:Header>");
  }
  builder.AppendLine("<soap:Body>");
  // Add the passed request
  //

  builder.Append(EWSRequestString);
```

```
  builder.AppendLine("</soap:Body>");
  builder.AppendLine("</soap:Envelope>");

  // Grab the request as a byte array
  //
  byte[] requestBytes = Encoding.UTF8.GetBytes(builder.ToString());

  request.ContentLength = requestBytes.Length;

  // Write our request bytes to the web request
  //
  using (Stream requestStream = request.GetRequestStream())
  {
    requestStream.Write(requestBytes, 0, requestBytes.Length);
    requestStream.Flush();
    requestStream.Close();
  }
  HttpWebResponse response;
  try
  {
    // Try to get the response
    //
    response = request.GetResponse() as HttpWebResponse;
  }
  catch (WebException webException)
  {
    HttpWebResponse httpResponse = webException.Response as
            HttpWebResponse;
    using (Stream responseStream = httpResponse.GetResponseStream())
    {
      using (StreamReader reader = new StreamReader(responseStream))
      {
        throw new Exception(reader.ReadToEnd());
      }
    }
  }

  // Read the response stream
  //
  string responseString;
  using (Stream responseStream = response.GetResponseStream())

  {
    using (StreamReader reader = new StreamReader(responseStream))
    {
      responseString = reader.ReadToEnd();
    }
  }

  // Now we have our response.  Load it into the DOM
  //
  XmlDocument doc = new XmlDocument();
  int xmlStartIndex = responseString.IndexOf("<?xml");
  doc.LoadXml(responseString.Substring(xmlStartIndex));
  return doc;
}
```

Now, admittedly, that isn't terribly pretty, although it works quite well. In fact, it is easy enough to put together a "SOAP tester" application that uses the above method to send SOAP messages to your Exchange Web Services server. Listing 1-11 shows how to make a simple GetFolder call with this method.

LISTING 1-11 Making a raw GetFolder request using the request sender

```
StringBuilder request = new StringBuilder();
request.AppendLine("<GetFolder>");
request.AppendLine("    <FolderShape>");
request.AppendLine("        <t:BaseShape>AllProperties</t:BaseShape>");
request.AppendLine("    </FolderShape>");
request.AppendLine("    <FolderIds>");
request.AppendLine("        <t:DistinguishedFolderId Id=\"inbox\"/>");
request.AppendLine("    </FolderIds>");
request.AppendLine("</GetFolder>");

XmlDocument doc = MakeRawSoapRequest(
                    @"https://yourserver/ews/Exchange.asmx",
                    "username",
                    "yourPassword",
                    "yourDomain",
                    request.ToString());
```

To be honest, using raw XML is a way to educate yourself on the structure of requests and responses and to try out new techniques. However, you will need to build and parse the results, meaning that you will likely end up creating your own proxy classes of sorts. With that in mind, it might make more sense to use the autogenerated proxies and modify them to suit your needs.

Summary

Exchange Server 2007 Web Services is an exciting, new, platform-agnostic API for talking to Exchange 2007. In this chapter, we covered some basics of Web services and how to build the autogenerated proxy classes that you use when talking to Exchange Web Services. We also discussed some of the "gotchas" that you might encounter when using the proxy classes due to the differences between XSD and C# classes. We finished the chapter by showing you how to make raw SOAP+XML calls using *HttpWebRequest*. In the next chapter, we will begin discussions on how to identify mailboxes and the items contained therein.

Chapter 2
May I See Your Id?

It's Saturday morning. You wake up early, completely aware of the large task before you. It is time to clean out and organize the garage. You toil, sweat, whine, and eventually the garage is in pristine condition. As you stand back to appreciate your work, you realize that you just cleaned out your neighbor's garage. Appreciative as your neighbor is, it would have been prudent to identify your garage before you began working on it.

Although the Microsoft Exchange Server 2007 Information Store is smart enough to keep you from touching things that you do not have rights to touch, it is still worthwhile to consider how to identify the mailbox that you are working with as well as the items within it—which, coincidentally, is the subject of this chapter.

Accessing Your Own Mailbox

Every Web service request that comes across the wire to an Exchange Client Access Server (CAS) box must be authenticated by ASP.NET before it gets to Exchange Web Services. This means that by the time the request arrives, we already know the identity of the caller.[1] Using this identity, we can perform an Active Directory lookup to determine which mailbox is associated with the caller's account. As such, there is no need to add any mailbox-identifying data within the request if the caller is trying to access his or her own mailbox.

It is worthwhile noting that there is a difference between the caller's *primary* mailbox and any other mailbox to which the caller has owner rights. By definition, a given mailbox user account can only be associated with a single mailbox because the user object within the Active Directory has a single mailbox globally unique identifier (GUID) that points to the mailbox in question. The account can be thought of as the mailbox and the mailbox as the account. If user A is a mailbox user account, there will be a corresponding user A mailbox. User A can certainly give user B "owner rights" to user A's mailbox, but user A's mailbox is still associated with user A.

To access a non-primary mailbox to which you might have rights, you need to use delegate access, which is discussed later in this chapter.

---

[1] Anonymous access is not permitted in EWS.

Exchange Web Services Indentifiers

Usually, the mailbox itself isn't terribly interesting. However, the contents of the mailbox are. Each item or folder within a mailbox must have a way to distinguish it from another item or folder within the mailbox (and even outside of the mailbox). You make this distinction by using identifiers, of which there are three basic categories in Exchange Web Services: folder, item, and attachment ids. Each of these identifiers uniquely identifies its related object.

Folder Ids

Not surprisingly, a folder id identifies a folder within a mailbox. Most mailboxes have some well-known folders such as the Inbox, Sent Items, and Deleted Items. Due to their ubiquitous nature, these folders seem a bit more "distinguished" than their less common relatives. Therefore, the Exchange Web Services developers provided a special way to refer to these well-known folders by calling them "distinguished folders." They are exposed in the schema via the *DistinguishedFolderIdType* schema type.

Distinguished Folder Ids

Distinguished folder ids are used to identify well-known folders in a given mailbox. Fifteen such folders are shown in Table 2-1.

TABLE 2-1 Distinguished Folder Id Enumeration Values

Folder	*DistinguishedFolderIdNameType* Value	Comments
Calendar	calendar	The default calendar folder
Contacts	contacts	The default contacts folder
Deleted Items	deleteditems	The deleted items folder; holds deleted items/folders
Drafts	drafts	The drafts folder; holds messages and meeting requests that have not yet been sent
Inbox	inbox	The Inbox: the location where all inbound mail is placed
Journal	journal	The Journal folder
Notes	notes	The Notes folder
Outbox	outbox	The Outbox: the location where outbound mail sits until transport takes it away
Sent Items	sentitems	The Sent Items folder: holds copies of messages that have been sent
Tasks	tasks	The default tasks folder

Folder	DistinguishedFolderIdNameType Value	Comments
Top of Information Store	msgfolderroot	The root folder for the displayable portion of the mailbox; sometimes called the *Inter-Personal Message (IPM) subtree*
Root	root	The absolute root folder of the mailbox that holds all sorts of wonderful folders such as msgfolderroot, finder (search folders), and others; sometimes called the *Non-IPM subtree*
Junk E-mail	junkemail	The location where inbound e-mail identified as "junk" is placed
Search Folders	searchfolders	The Finder folder that is located in root; houses all the search folders that are visible to Microsoft Outlook
Voice Mail	voicemail	The folder that holds voice mail messages; not created by the server until the first voice mail has been received

Besides making your requests look cleaner, distinguished folder ids offer a starting point for mailbox access and can be used anywhere that folder ids are accepted in the schema. With that being said, Exchange Web Services does not permit you to move or delete distinguished folders.

A distinguished folder id has the following basic layout:

```
<t:DistinguishedFolderId Id="DistinguishedFolderIdNameType"
                         ChangeKey="OptionalChangeKey">
   <!-- Optional mailbox element.  This is discussed in the
        delegate access section-->
   <t:Mailbox/>
</t:DistinguishedFolderId>
```

The *Id* attribute must contain one of the values from the *DistinguishedFolderIdNameType* enumeration shown in Table 2-1.[2] Whereas the *Id* attribute identifies the folder without respect to time, the *ChangeKey* provides a "snapshot in time" identifier that allows the server to know whether the folder you are referring to has been modified on the server. Any folder modifications that are sent to the server cause a new change key to be generated for the folder. Since it is atypical to make modifications to folders, the *ChangeKey* attribute is not very useful for distinguished folders, nor folders in general, although including it will increase performance.[3] Following are two distinguished folder id representations based on the information presented so far:

---

[2] *DistinguishedFolderIdNameType* can be found in types.xsd.

[3] Refer to Chapter 3, "Property Paths and Response Shapes," concerning the reasons for this performance boost.

```
<t:DistinguishedFolderId Id="inbox"/>
<t:DistinguishedFolderId Id="contacts" ChangeKey="AAA=="/>
```

Using the Inbox distinguished folder id in the previous code, you can send a *GetFolder* request that allows you to obtain data about the folder in question as shown in Listing 2-1. Don't worry about the structure of *GetFolder* at this point, for we will discuss the operation in more detail in Chapter 4, "Folders."

LISTING 2-1 GetFolder with a distinguished folder id

```
<GetFolder xmlns="...\messages"
           xmlns:t="...\types">
  <FolderShape>
    <t:BaseShape>Default</t:BaseShape>
  </FolderShape>
  <FolderIds>
    <t:DistinguishedFolderId Id="inbox"/>
  </FolderIds>
</GetFolder>
```

Do you notice the distinguished folder id in Listing 2-1, nestled between the opening and closing *FolderIds* elements? Making the request gives back the following response:

```
<GetFolderResponse xmlns:m=".../messages"
                   xmlns:t=".../types"
                   xmlns=".../messages">
  <m:ResponseMessages>
    <m:GetFolderResponseMessage ResponseClass="Success">
      <m:ResponseCode>NoError</m:ResponseCode>
        <m:Folders>
          <t:Folder>
            <t:FolderId
Id="AAAtAEFklaXbWaN0cmF0b3JAZmxodnJmLWRvbS51eHRlc3QubWljcm9zb2ZDLmNvbQAuAAAAAAAhdFx6Ltv4
TI5MEbECyQlaAQDMSJn1HSrXS6DhxFUMEZdPAAAChG6fAAA="
ChangeKey="AQAAABYAAADMSJn1HSrXS6DhxFUMEZdPAAAChHDm"/>
              <t:DisplayName>Inbox</t:DisplayName>
              <t:TotalCount>0</t:TotalCount>
              <t:ChildFolderCount>0</t:ChildFolderCount>
              <t:UnreadCount>0</t:UnreadCount>
          </t:Folder>
        </m:Folders>
      </m:GetFolderResponseMessage>
  </m:ResponseMessages>
</GetFolderResponse>
```

The response contains a *FolderId* element with an alphabet soup *Id* attribute. The change key is also there. This *Id* attribute contains the actual id for the distinguished folder that was requested. The distinguished folder id format is actually just a moniker that makes life a little easier when referring to the more common folders. To confirm that these ids are interchangeable, you can make the same request but replace the *DistinguishedFolderId* element with the *FolderId* element that you just received as shown in Listing 2-2.

LISTING 2-2 GetFolder with a *FolderId*

```
<GetFolder xmlns=".../messages"
           xmlns:t=".../types">
  <FolderShape>
    <t:BaseShape>Default</t:BaseShape>
  </FolderShape>
  <FolderIds>
    <t:FolderId
Id="AAAtAEFklaXbWaNOcmFOb3JAZmxodnJmLWRvbS5leHRlc3QubWljcm9zb2ZOLmNvbQAuAAAAAAAhd
Fx6Ltv4TI5MEbECyQlaAQDMSJn1HSrXS6DhxFUMEZdPAAAChG6fAAA=" ChangeKey="AQAAABYAAADMSJn1HS
rXS6DhxFUMEZdPAAAChHDm"/>
  </FolderIds>
</GetFolder>
```

And the result?

```
<GetFolderResponse xmlns:m=".../messages"
                   xmlns:t=".../types"
                   xmlns=".../messages">
  <m:ResponseMessages>
    <m:GetFolderResponseMessage ResponseClass="Success">
      <m:ResponseCode>NoError</m:ResponseCode>
      <m:Folders>
        <t:Folder>
          <t:FolderId Id="AAAtAEdfadrX0FOb3JAZmxodnJmLWRvbS5leHRlc3QubWljcm9zb2ZOLmNvbQAuAAAA
AAAAhdFx6Lt
v4TI5MEbECyQlaAQDMSJn1HSrXS6DhxFUMEZdPAAAChG6fAAA=" ChangeKey="AQAAABYAAADMSJn1HSrXS6DhxFUME
ZdPAAAChHDm"/>
          <t:DisplayName>Inbox</t:DisplayName>
          <t:TotalCount>0</t:TotalCount>
          <t:ChildFolderCount>0</t:ChildFolderCount>
          <t:UnreadCount>0</t:UnreadCount>
        </t:Folder>
      </m:Folders>
    </m:GetFolderResponseMessage>
  </m:ResponseMessages>
</GetFolderResponse>
```

You see that in both cases the Inbox is returned.

Fear the *DisplayName*

The *DisplayName* element returned by *GetFolder* shows the name of the returned folder. This might tempt some people to write code that makes business decisions based on the text value of the *DisplayName* element. We would like to discourage you from doing that. The display names of distinguished folders end up being localized based on the language that is first used to connect to the mailbox. If you connect to a brand new mailbox for the first time by using the French culture, all of your distinguished folder names will be localized in French. That would break any code that expects the display name for the Inbox to be in US English.

A better way to make distinguished folder comparisons is to request and cache the *FolderId* for each distinguished folder of interest and make comparisons based on the *Id* attribute of the folder in question. You can request the *FolderIds* for all distinguished folders by using a single *GetFolder* call as shown in Listing 2-3.

LISTING 2-3 Retrieving *FolderIds* for all distinguished folders

```
<GetFolder xmlns=".../messages"
           xmlns:t=".../types">
  <FolderShape>
    <t:BaseShape>IdOnly</t:BaseShape>
  </FolderShape>
  <FolderIds>
    <t:DistinguishedFolderId Id="calendar"/>
    <t:DistinguishedFolderId Id="contacts"/>
    <t:DistinguishedFolderId Id="deleteditems"/>
    <t:DistinguishedFolderId Id="drafts"/>
    <t:DistinguishedFolderId Id="inbox"/>
    <t:DistinguishedFolderId Id="journal"/>
    <t:DistinguishedFolderId Id="notes"/>
    <t:DistinguishedFolderId Id="outbox"/>
    <t:DistinguishedFolderId Id="sentitems"/>
    <t:DistinguishedFolderId Id="tasks"/>
    <t:DistinguishedFolderId Id="msgfolderroot"/>
    <t:DistinguishedFolderId Id="root"/>
    <t:DistinguishedFolderId Id="junkemail"/>
    <t:DistinguishedFolderId Id="searchfolders"/>
    <t:DistinguishedFolderId Id="voicemail"/>
  </FolderIds>
</GetFolder>
```

The response contains the *FolderId* for each of the distinguished folders in the order request-ed. The following response shows results for only the last two distinguished folders (search-folders and voicemail). The mailbox on which this request was made had not received voice mail messages yet, and thus the voice mail folder did not exist. In Figure 2-1, notice that the *ResponseCode* returned for the voice mail folder indicates that an error was encountered.

```
                        <!-- previous xml omitted for brevity -->
                          <m:GetFolderResponse Message ResponseClass="Success">
                            <m:ResponseCode>NoError</m:ResponseCode>
    Response for            <m:Folders>
    search folders            <t:Folder>
                                <t:FolderId Id="AAtAEFk..."/>
                              </t:Folder>
                            </m:Folders>
                          </m:GetFolderResponseMessage>
                          <m:Get FolderResponseMessage ResponseClass="Error">
                            <m:MessageText>The specified folder could not be found
    Response for               in the store.</m:MessageText>
    non-existent            <m:ResponseCode>ErrorFolderNotFound</m:ResponseCode>
    voice mail folder       <m:DescriptiveLinkKey>0</m:DescriptiveLinkKey>
                            <m:Folders/>
                          </m:GetFolderResponseMessage>
                        </m:ResponseMessages>
```

FIGURE 2-1 *GetFolder* response

By using proxy objects, you can take advantage of the *Enum* class to simplify your request.
Listing 2-4 shows a method named *GetAllDistinguishedFolderIdsForRequest* that grabs
all of the values from the *DistinguishedFolderIdNameType* enum and creates an array of
BaseFolderIdType, with one entry for each distinguished folder.

LISTING 2-4 Retrieving all distinguished folder ids using the proxy classes

```
/// <summary>
/// Returns an array of BaseFolderIdType representing all of the supported
/// distinguished folders in a mailbox
/// </summary>
/// <returns>Array of BaseFolderIdType</returns>
///
public static BaseFolderIdType[] GetAllDistinguishedFolderIdsForRequest()
{
  Array enumValues =
    Enum.GetValues(typeof(DistinguishedFolderIdNameType));

  BaseFolderIdType[] result = new BaseFolderIdType[enumValues.Length];
  for (int folderIndex = 0; folderIndex<enumValues.Length; folderIndex++)
  {
    DistinguishedFolderIdType id = new DistinguishedFolderIdType();
    id.Id = (DistinguishedFolderIdNameType)
                  enumValues.GetValue(folderIndex);
    result[folderIndex] = id;
  }

  return result;
}
```

You can take this a step further and create a mapping of distinguished folder enum name to the
actual folder id for that distinguished folder. This enables you to easily check whether a given
folder is the Inbox without having to perform *DisplayName* comparisons as shown in Listing 2-5.

LISTING 2-5 Creating mapping of distinguished folder names to folder ids

```
/// <summary>
/// Creates a mapping of distinguished folder name to the actual folder id
/// for that distinguished folder.
/// </summary>
/// <param name="binding">The service binding to use to make the actual
/// SOAP calls.</param>
/// <returns>Dictionary mapping distinguished folder enum name to actual
/// folder id</returns>
/// <remarks>Note that the folder Id will be null if the response for that
/// folder gave us an error.  Mainly this will happen with voicemail since
/// the folder is created lazily when the first voice mail is received
/// </remarks>
///
public static Dictionary<DistinguishedFolderIdNameType, FolderIdType>
            GetAllDistinguishedFolderIds(ExchangeServiceBinding binding)
{
  // Prepare the request
  //
  GetFolderType getFolderRequest = new GetFolderType();
  getFolderRequest.FolderIds = GetAllDistinguishedFolderIdsForRequest();
  getFolderRequest.FolderShape = new FolderResponseShapeType();

  // We only want the id.  See chapter 3 for details
  //
  getFolderRequest.FolderShape.BaseShape = DefaultShapeNamesType.IdOnly;

  // Make the call
  //
  GetFolderResponseType response = binding.GetFolder(getFolderRequest);
  ResponseMessageType[] responseMessages =
                    response.ResponseMessages.Items;

  Dictionary<DistinguishedFolderIdNameType, FolderIdType> result =
            new Dictionary<DistinguishedFolderIdNameType, FolderIdType>();

  Array enumValues =
            Enum.GetValues(typeof(DistinguishedFolderIdNameType));

  // For each response message, we want to create a dictionary entry
  // mapping the distinguished folder id name to the actual folder id for
  // the folder.
  // Remember that responses always match the order of the request so
  // we can just iterate across the enum values and they should match up.
  //
  for (int folderIndex = 0;
       folderIndex < responseMessages.Length;
       folderIndex++)
  {
    FolderInfoResponseMessageType folderInfoMessage =
        responseMessages[folderIndex] as FolderInfoResponseMessageType;
    FolderIdType folderId = null;
    if (folderInfoMessage.ResponseClass == ResponseClassType.Success)
    {
```

```
            // Note that each response message will always hold zero or one
            // folders.
            //
            folderId = folderInfoMessage.Folders[0].FolderId;
        }

        // If we encounter a failure for a distinguished folder, just add a
        // null if in the map.  For real applications, we should probably
        // throw or at least trace out a debug message.
        //
        result.Add(
            (DistinguishedFolderIdNameType)enumValues.GetValue(folderIndex),
            folderId);
    }
    return result;
}
```

And, of course, you can test the code from Listing 2-5. Figure 2-2 displays the results.

```
static void Main(string[] args)
{

    // Create our service binding
    //
    ExchangeServiceBinding binding = new ExchangeServiceBinding();
    binding.Url = @"https://yourserver/ews/exchange.asmx";
    binding.Credentials = new NetworkCredential("username", "password", "domain");

    Dictionary<DistinguishedFolderIdNameType, FolderIdType> mapping;

    // Now call our shiny new method to get the mapping for username's
    // distinguished folders
    //
    mapping = GetAllDistinguishedFolderIds(binding);
    Console.WriteLine("The Id of the inbox is: \r\n" +
                mapping[DistinguishedFolderIdNameType.inbox].Id);
    Console.WriteLine();
    Console.WriteLine("The Id of sentitems is: \r\n" +
                mapping[DistinguishedFolderIdNameType.sentitems].Id);
}
```

FIGURE 2-2 Testing distinguished folder ids

> **Important** The preceding code maintains a collection of distinguished folder name enumeration values to the folder ids contained *within the caller's mailbox*. You *cannot* use this mapping for someone else's mailbox. If you are writing code that deals with multiple mailboxes, we suggest that you keep a mapping per mailbox.

To determine whether a given folder id refers to one of the distinguished folders, just compare the *Id* attribute of the folder in question to the *Id* attribute of the distinguished folder. The id values are simply strings.

Normal Folder Ids

All folders within an Exchange mailbox have a *FolderId* representation, whereas only the 15 distinguished folders have a distinguished folder id representation. Looking at the *FolderId* element structure, you see two attributes (attribute values are shortened for readability).

```
<t:FolderId Id="AAAtAEFkbW1uaXN0cm...=" ChangeKey="AQAAABYAAADMSJn..."/>
```

The *Id* attribute holds a poetically challenged identifier that is unique to that folder regardless of the changes that are made to that folder. Not only does the folder mentioned in the preceding code refer to the Inbox, but it refers to the Inbox in a *specific* mailbox. The *FolderId* for user Jane Dow's Inbox folder will have a different value than the *FolderId* for user Ken Malcolmson's Inbox folder. If you copy a folder (via CopyFolder), the copy will of course be a new folder and have a different id than the original folder.

As mentioned earlier, the *ChangeKey* attribute represents an opaque versioning mechanism that really isn't intended to be useful for the end user.[4] The Exchange Store uses this value to determine whether you are dealing with an out-of-date copy of a folder.

Folder change keys are required only for *UpdateFolder* operations. However, even in the cases in which they are not required, folder change keys must be correct if you supply them. You can't simply set the attribute to a garbage value and expect things to go through smoothly.

Item Ids

As the name suggests, item ids are identifiers for items. What is an item? An item is anything that descends from *ItemType* including messages, contacts, calendar items, distribution lists, tasks, meeting messages, meeting requests, meeting responses, and meeting cancellations.[5] In contrast to folder ids, there is no distinguished item id type, which makes sense because there are no well-known items.

---

4 We will discuss change keys in more depth in Chapter 5, "Items."

5 There are also some *ResponseObject* types that derive from *ItemType*, but you will never encounter an id for these. They are therefore omitted from the list.

The format of an item id is quite similar to that of a folder id.

```
<t:ItemId Id="RequiredIdentifier" ChangeKey="OptionalChangeKey"/>
```

As in the folder id case, the required *Id* attribute identifies the item in question and the optional *ChangeKey* attribute is used for opaque version control as shown in the following example:

```
<t:ItemId
Id="AAAtAEFkdrafs0b3mF0b3JAZmxodnJmLWRvbS5leHRlc3QubWljcm9zb2Z0LmNvbQBGAAAAAAAhdFx6Ltv4T
I5MEbECyQlaBwDMSJn1HSrXS6DhxFUMEZdPAAAChCejAADMSJn1HSrXS6DhxFUMEZdPAAAChHTxAAA="
ChangeKey="CQAAABYAAADMSJn1HSrXS6DhxFUMEZdPAAAChHb0"/>
```

Pretty, isn't it? Makes you really appreciate GUIDs and Security Identifiers (SIDs). Up-to-date change keys are required for *UpdateItem*, *SendItem*, and *CreateItem* when performing a calendar cancellation or suppressing a read receipt. This might seem inconsistent because several other Web methods modify the item (*MoveItem*, *CopyItem*, *CreateAttachment*, and *DeleteAttachment*). This is actually an Exchange Web Services-imposed restriction rather than an Exchange Store restriction.

The reasoning for requiring change keys for only *UpdateItem*, *SendItem*, and *CreateItem* went along these lines. For *SendItem*, you want to make sure you know what you are sending. If for some reason the message that you are working on has changed beneath you, it could be a career-limiting move to blindly send that message without seeing what has changed. As such, you must supply an up-to-date change key when calling *SendItem*. If your change key is stale (out-of-date), you encounter an *ErrorStaleObject* response code. If you do not provide a change key, you encounter *ErrorChangeKeyRequiredForWriteOperations*.

In the *UpdateItem case*, if someone has changed an item underneath you, you might be overwriting data that should not be overwritten. That just will not do. As a result, if the data is stale, you must obtain an up-to-date change key so that you know you are dealing with an up-to-date item. What's important here isn't really that the item or folder state is up to date, but that you are aware that changes have been made underneath you. You are free to ignore whatever changes have been made to the state (possibly to your own peril). This awareness is indicated by the value of your change key.

With this in mind, you will run into situations in which you need an up-to-date change key. This can easily be done by making a *GetItem* request using the *Id* that you already have. It doesn't matter that you have an old or missing change key because *GetItem* returns the item with an up-to-date change key. To assist with this process, you could write a method as shown in Listing 2-6.

LISTING 2-6 Retrieving an up-to-date change key for an item

```
/// <summary>
/// Returns an up to date Id and change key for the specified item
/// </summary>
/// <param name="binding">ExchangeServiceBinding used to make the
/// requests</param>
/// <param name="oldId">The Id that you have and wish to update</param>
/// <returns>The shiny new, up to date id and changekey</returns>
///
public ItemIdType GetCurrentChangeKey(
                        ExchangeServiceBinding binding,
                        ItemIdType oldId)
{
  // Create the request type itself and set the response shape.  All we
  // need is the Id.
  //
  GetItemType getItemRequest = new GetItemType();
  getItemRequest.ItemShape = new ItemResponseShapeType();
  getItemRequest.ItemShape.BaseShape = DefaultShapeNamesType.IdOnly;
  // Set the single Id that we wish to look up
  //
  getItemRequest.ItemIds = new BaseItemIdType[] { oldId };
  // Make the actual web request
  //
  GetItemResponseType response = binding.GetItem(getItemRequest);
  // Get the appropriate message.
  //
  ItemInfoResponseMessageType responseMessage =
      response.ResponseMessages.Items[0] as ItemInfoResponseMessageType;

  // If we succeeded, the response class will be success
  //
  if (responseMessage.ResponseClass == ResponseClassType.Success)
  {
    return responseMessage.Items.Items[0].ItemId;
  }
  else
  {
    throw new ArgumentException(
      String.Format(
            "Item not found in mailbox.  Error Code: {0}",
            responseMessage.ResponseCode.ToString()),
        "oldId");
  }
}
```

Attachment Ids

Attachment ids identity file or item attachments that are tied to items within a mailbox. They will be discussed in depth in Chapter 12, "Attachments."

Id Caching

The idea of id caching came up several times during the development of Exchange Web Services. It is quite acceptable to store ids for long periods of time. Certainly, your local cache of ids might get out of sync with the data within the mailbox, but that is easily rectified by utilizing the Sync and Notification mechanisms provided by Exchange Web Services. Just keep your ids in a cool, dry place and avoid prolonged exposure to sunlight.

Delegate Access

It is entirely possible that a caller does not have a mailbox on the system. In this case, the caller must *explicitly* specify the mailbox that is being accessed because there is no way of determining this from the authenticated caller's identity. Such access is considered *delegate* access, in which the primary owner of a mailbox has *delegated* certain rights to another account. Note that this could include "owner" rights to the mailbox as mentioned earlier.

Consider the garage-cleaning scenario from the beginning of the chapter. You are standing on Greenbriar Lane, but you do not live on Greenbriar Lane. Someone else on the scene, John, gives a command: "Clean out the garage." He needs to provide you with more information. Which garage on Greenbriar Lane? If John lived on this street, you could implicitly determine which garage he was talking about. But, alas, you cannot. Maybe John is the local property manager and has rights to clean out all of the garages on Greenbriar Lane. John further qualifies his request: "Clean out the garage at 123 Greenbriar Lane." Good. Assuming that John has the rights to enter and clean out the identified garage, you can fulfill such a request on his behalf.

Now let's apply this to Exchange Web Services. You can use delegate access to access any mailbox on the system to which you have rights, whether you have a primary mailbox on the system or not. If you do not have a mailbox on the system, delegate access is your only choice. However, if you have a mailbox on the system and you do not explicitly indicate which mailbox you would like to access, Exchange Web Services will assume that you want to access your own mailbox.

When making a delegate access request, you specify the mailbox to access by using the *Mailbox* child element of DistinguishedFolderIdType as shown in Listing 2-7.

LISTING 2-7 GetFolder using delegate access

```
<GetFolder xmlns=".../messages"
           xmlns:t=".../types">
  <FolderShape>
    <t:BaseShape>AllProperties</t:BaseShape>
  </FolderShape>
  <FolderIds>
    <t:DistinguishedFolderId Id="inbox">
```

```
      <t:Mailbox>
        <t:Name>123 Greenbriar Lane</t:Name>
        <t:EmailAddress>jane.dow@contoso.com</t:EmailAddress>
        <t:RoutingType>SMTP</t:RoutingType>
      </t:Mailbox>
    </t:DistinguishedFolderId>
  </FolderIds>
</GetFolder>
```

You can also do this via the proxy objects:

```
// Create the distinguished folder id type
//
DistinguishedFolderIdType distinguishedFolderId = new
                                DistinguishedFolderIdType();
EmailAddressType mailbox = new EmailAddressType();

// Note that Name and RoutingType are optional
//
mailbox.Name = "123 Greenbriar Lane";
mailbox.EmailAddress = "jane.dow@contoso.com";
mailbox.RoutingType = "SMTP";

// Set the mailbox to access on the distinguished folder id.
//
distinguishedFolderId.Mailbox = mailbox;
```

You may have noticed that there is no *Mailbox* child element on *FolderId* or *ItemId* elements. Can you guess why? Well, the folder and item ids just happen to know the mailbox with which they are associated. In fact, if you make the *GetFolder* call in the preceding code, the *FolderId* that is returned will be the Inbox folder id associated with the *jane.dow@contoso. com* mailbox. You can persist this id and use it at a later date to get back to that particular Inbox. Of course, you must have the appropriate rights to access the mailbox to which the id refers. As a result, you can use a single request to retrieve data from multiple mailboxes. The following request in Listing 2-8 returns the Inbox folders of Jane and Ken as well as the folder identified by the folder *Id* element (let's say this is Janusz's Inbox).

LISTING 2-8 *GetFolder* accessing folders from different mailboxes via delegate access

```
<GetFolder xmlns=".../messages"
           xmlns:t=".../types">
  <FolderShape>
    <t:BaseShape>AllProperties</t:BaseShape>
  </FolderShape>
  <FolderIds>
    <t:DistinguishedFolderId Id="inbox">
      <t:Mailbox>
        <t:EmailAddress>jane.dow@contoso.com</t:EmailAddress>
      </t:Mailbox>
    </t:DistinguishedFolderId>
```

```
    <t:DistinguishedFolderId Id="inbox">
      <t:Mailbox>
        <t:EmailAddress>ken.malcolmson@contoso.com</t:EmailAddress>
      </t:Mailbox>
    </t:DistinguishedFolderId>
    <t:FolderId Id="AAAtAEFkbWluaXNOcmF..."/>
  </FolderIds>
</GetFolder>
```

If the *DistinguishedFolderId* form with the *Mailbox* subelement refers to a specific mailbox, what does the form without the *Mailbox* element refer to? If you specify a distinguished folder id without a *Mailbox* subelement, then Exchange Web Services assumes that you are trying to access your own mailbox. It is as if you added a *Mailbox* element with your own primary SMTP address within.[6] As a result, if you do not have a mailbox on the system, the *Mailbox* element *must* be supplied or you encounter an error with a response code of *ErrorMissingEmailAddress*.

> **Important** *FolderId* and *ItemId* point to a specific mailbox. You cannot, however, look at a given id and determine which mailbox the id is referring to because these ids are opaque.

Primary SMTP Addresses

Exchange Web Services identifies a mailbox by using the primary SMTP address of the mailbox owner. Primary SMTP addresses are unique within an organization (in theory)[7]. An account can also have additional proxy addresses that could be SMTP addresses, but might also include X400 and addresses with other routing types. Exchange Web Services does not allow you to refer to a mailbox by using anything other than the primary SMTP address. If you do so, Exchange Web Services returns the *ErrorNonPrimarySmtpAddress* response code.

```
<m:GetFolderResponseMessage ResponseClass="Error">
  <m:MessageText>You must specify the primary SMTP address when
                 referencing a mailbox.</m:MessageText>
  <m:ResponseCode>ErrorNonPrimarySmtpAddress</m:ResponseCode>
  <m:DescriptiveLinkKey>0</m:DescriptiveLinkKey>
  <m:MessageXml>
    <t:Value Name="Primary">jane.dow@corp.contoso.com</t:Value>
  </m:MessageXml>
  <m:Folders/>
</m:GetFolderResponseMessage>
```

---

6 We will discuss the significance of primary SMTP addresses in the next section.

7 In reality, the Active Directory does not enforce this. As such, you can have accounts with duplicate primary and/or proxy addresses as a result of tampering with the Active Directory. If this is the case, you receive an ErrorMailboxConfiguration error from EWS. This condition is reported via the normal Microsoft Operations Manager (MOM) alerts mechanism so that your Exchange administrator can rectify the situation.

Notice that the *MessageXml* element gives you the primary SMTP address that you should use. Previous APIs allowed you to use the "Legacy Exchange DN" to identify a mailbox, which is not permitted in Exchange Web Services.

Culture and Your Mailbox

When you make an Exchange Web Services request to access a given mailbox, that mailbox by default opens in the language of the Exchange CAS. This may or may not be what you want to do. The language used to open the mailbox governs how certain message properties are emitted, such as To, From, and Subject prefix, as well as the language in which error messages are returned within responses. In addition, the first time a mailbox is opened, the distinguished folders, such as Inbox or Sent Items, and so on, are localized in the language that is used to open the mailbox.[8] You specify the culture to use in an Exchange Web Services call via the *MailboxCulture* SOAP header. Listing 2-9 provides the general structure of the header.

LISTING 2-9 MailboxCulture SOAP header

```
<soap:Header>
  <t:MailboxCulture>en-US</t:MailboxCulture>
</soap:Header>
```

When dealing with proxy classes, SOAP headers are exposed as properties on the *ExchangeServiceBinding* type. Listing 2-10 demonstrates how you would set the language by using proxy classes.

LISTING 2-10 Setting the MailboxCulture by using proxy classes

```
/// <summary>
/// Sets the mailbox culture based on the passed culture info
/// </summary>
/// <param name="binding">Binding to set the culture on</param>
/// <param name="info">CultureInfo to use</param>
///
public static void SetMailboxCulture(
                    ExchangeServiceBinding binding,
                    CultureInfo info)
{
  binding.MailboxCulture = new language();
  binding.MailboxCulture.Text = new string[] { info.Name };
}
```

Do you notice anything strange about Listing 2-10? The language is set as a string array, which is a strange side effect of the proxy generator. It is not valid to pass in multiple items to

---

8 With the exception of the voice mail folder.

this array, so don't try it. If you do, the culture identifiers will be concatenated together and produce an invalid culture. Because Exchange Web Services is not able to resolve the identifier to a supported culture, it falls back to use the default server culture.

Of course, you can also modify the autogenerated proxy to make it a string instead of a string[ ] as shown in Listing 2-11. The property name is changed from "Text" to "CultureName" to make it easier for you to detect what is happening.

LISTING 2-11 Changing the language SOAP header to contain a single string

```
public partial class language : System.Web.Services.Protocols.SoapHeader
{
  private string textField;

  /// <remarks/>
  [System.Xml.Serialization.XmlTextAttribute()]
  public string CultureName
  {
    // code elided...
```

With this change, you can get rid of the string array creation as shown in Listing 2-12.

LISTING 2-12 Setting the MailboxCulture using the corrected language proxy

```
/// <summary>
/// Sets the mailbox culture based on the passed culture info
/// </summary>
/// <param name="binding">Binding to set the culture on</param>
/// <param name="info">CultureInfo to use</param>
///
public static void SetMailboxCulture(
                    ExchangeServiceBinding binding,
                    CultureInfo info)
{
  binding.MailboxCulture = new language();
  binding.MailboxCulture.CultureName = info.Name;
}
```

We don't know about you, but the version in Listing 2-12 seems much more natural to us.

Client Cultures versus Server Cultures

Internally, Exchange Web Services maintains the concept of client cultures and server cultures. Client cultures are used for things such as subject prefixes, reply/forward headers, and so on. There is a set of supported client cultures and there is a set of supported server cultures with some overlap. Error messages generated by Exchange Web Services are limited to the supported set of server cultures.

When an Exchange Web Services call comes in with a *MailboxCulture* SOAP header, Exchange Web Services tries to match the passed-in culture to both a supported client culture and a supported server culture. If the passed-in culture is not directly supported, it falls back to the passed-in culture's parent culture and checks again.[9] It continues to do this until it finds a match or reaches the invariant culture, at which point it silently falls back to the installed server culture. Because the set of client cultures intersects with but is not an exact match of the set of server cultures, you might encounter a situation in which Exchange Web Services finds a match for the client culture, but fails to find a match for the server culture. In that case, error codes will be returned in the installed culture of the server rather than the supplied culture while values derived from the client culture will match the supplied culture.

Table 2-2 provides the list of supported client cultures, and Table 2-3 provides the list of supported server cultures. Although the list of supported cultures are shown in region-neutral format, you should pass in the specific culture that you want to use. Thus, it is better to use "vi-VN" instead of "vi."

TABLE 2-2 Supported Client Cultures

Ar	bg	ca	cs
Da	el	en	es
Et	eu	fa	fi
Fr	he	hr	hu
Id	is	it	ja
Kk	lt	lv	ms
Nl	no	pl	pt
pt-pt	ro	ru	sk
Sl	sr	sr-latn-cs	sv
Th	tr	uk	ur
Vi	zh-chs	zh-cht	zh-hk

TABLE 2-3 Supported Server Cultures

De	en	es
Fr	lt	ja
Ko	pt	ru
zh-chs	zh-cht	

Even though the cultures listed in Table 2-2 and Table 2-3 are all neutral cultures, it doesn't mean that only neutral cultures are supported. Due to the fallback mentioned earlier, any culture that "derives" from the cultures in Table 2-2 are supported. Therefore, fr-FR is completely acceptable because its parent culture is fr.

---

[9] For more information on cultures and culture "hierarchies," refer to the *CultureInfo* class documentation at *http://msdn2.microsoft.com/en-us/library/system.globalization.cultureinfo(VS.71).aspx.*

Given that the supported client culture list is a superset of the supported server cultures, if you pass in a MailboxCulture of "vi-VN" (Vietnamese - Vietnam), the client culture ends up using vi-VN because it is a child of "vi." However, the server culture falls back to the installed server culture (such as en-US). So, when you reply to a message, you have localized subject prefixes in Vietnamese, but any error messages you get back are in English. Since, typically, error messages are geared toward developers, this dichotomy should not pose any serious issues, but it is something for you to keep in mind.

Summary

Exchange Web Services allows you to access your own mailbox as well as any other mailbox to which you have rights. When accessing your own mailbox, there is no need for additional mailbox identifiers because Exchange Web Services is able to determine which mailbox to access based on the authenticated user's identity. When accessing another mailbox as a delegate, you must specify the primary SMTP address of the mailbox in the *Mailbox* subelement of *DistinguishedFolderId*. Normal *FolderIds* and *ItemIds* uniquely identify folders and items, respectively, and are tied to a given mailbox so that a *Mailbox* subelement is not needed. whereas they are required for *UpdateItem* and *SendItem* operations. Of course, you should use the change key if it is available because it will increase performance.

Chapter 3
Property Paths and Response Shapes

Standard object-oriented programming (OOP) methods focus on objects, hence the name. At the proxy class level, Exchange Web Services programming has *ItemType* objects, *MessageType* objects, and the like. Although it is certainly true that you are dealing with objects, some interesting things are going on behind the scenes of which you should be aware.

An Item by Any Other Name

The Microsoft Exchange Server 2007 Store manages one or more databases. A single database has an item table that contains all items within the mailboxes managed by that database. Consider Table 3-1.[1]

TABLE 3-1 Conceptual Item Table

	Item Class	Parent Id	Subject	Date Sent	Home Phone
Message	IPM.Note	Fjldsajfdklsa	Here it is!	01/02/2004	NULL
Contact	IPM.Contact	Jfkdlajfd	Jane Dow	NULL	123-456-7890

The item table contains two items: a message and a contact. Notice that each row of the table has the *potential* to have data in each of its cells, which becomes interesting when you consider that each row has a "nature" to it. A message is conceptually different than a contact, and a contact is conceptually different than a meeting request. From the Exchange Store's viewpoint, this distinction is made by the Item Class property assigned to each item in the database. Ignoring constraints and such, you could turn a message into a contact by simply updating the Item Class field from IPM.Note to IPM.Contact. But what happens when you do that? Well, all of the other properties stay the same. You now have a contact that has a Date Sent. Maybe that isn't too weird. But go in the other direction. Change the contact into a message. Poof! Now, you have a message that has a home phone number. Weird.

To rectify this, you can do one of the following:

- Treat each row as a collection of properties and ignore the fact that the rows represent messages, contacts, and so forth. This is essentially the approach that Web Distributed Authoring and Versioning (WebDAV) takes.

---

1 This simplistic explanation does not reflect the actual workings within a database. However, it is sufficient for the purposes of this chapter and removes details that are not pertinent to our current discussion.

- Use business logic and force an object paradigm on top of the table so that data is validated going both into and out of the table. As such, a message could never have a home phone number and would be considered "corrupt" if it did.

- Compromise and take a hybrid approach in which you have both of the following:

  - Well-formed business logic that treat rows as specific item types and performs validation on read and write

  - A flexible data collection view in which rows are just a collection of any properties you throw at it.

Although all three options have their good and bad points, the development team chose the third option for Exchange Web Services. Let's look at the results.

In Exchange Web Services, Properties Are King

Properties in Exchange Web Services take on a significant role, even outside of the objects on which they reside. When we refer to a property, we are talking about one of the columns in the item table, such as the subject. A property as an entity can be referenced by using a *property path*. A property path has nothing to do with any specific value on any specific item. The property is simply a piece of metadata. Comparing it with standard OOP principles, a property path is to a property as a class is to an instance. Comparing it with relational databases, a property path is to a property as a column definition is to a specific value within that column.

Exchange Web Services exposes several different types of property paths as shown in Table 3-2.

TABLE 3-2 Property Paths in Exchange Web Services

Property Path Type	Schema Type	Comments
FieldURI	*PathToUnindexedFieldType*	A property path that is seen as a single entity; might contain multiple values. Examples are the subject, the date an item was created, and so on.
IndexedFieldURI	*PathToIndexedFieldType*	A property path that is seen as a collection of related properties; requires a "key" to determine exactly which property within the collection is being referred to. Examples are a contact's e-mail addresses, phone numbers, and physical addresses.

Property Path Type	Schema Type	Comments
ExtendedFieldURI	*PathToExtendedFieldType*	A property path that refers to a MAPI property using MAPI naming constructs such as property tags. Extended property paths are used to access properties that are not exposed through the schema.
ExceptionFieldURI	*PathToExceptionFieldType*	A property path that is used only in responses to indicate properties within error XML.

Unindexed Property Paths

An unindexed property path is the most common property path type that you will encounter. The property that a given unindexed property path refers to is specified within the schema by the *UnindexedFieldURIType* enumeration, meaning that there is a predefined, limited, and nonextensible set of properties that can be referenced as an unindexed property path. In addition, the enumeration value is sufficient to determine exactly what property is being referenced, which is in contrast to indexed property paths that require both an enumeration value and a key to determine which property is being referenced.[2]

Although the schema type for an unindexed property path is *PathToUnindexedFieldType*, you usually encounter it within XML by the name of its global instance, *FieldURI*.

```
<t:FieldURI FieldURI="UnindexedFieldURIType enumeration value" />
```

The *FieldURI* element has a single attribute called *FieldURI* that must contain a value from the *UnindexedFieldURIType* enumeration. Appendix C, "MAPI Property Mapping," contains a detailed list of all of these values along with notes underlying such things as MAPI properties.

Here are some examples:

```
<t:FieldURI FieldURI="item:Subject"/>
<t:FieldURI FieldURI="folder:DisplayName"/>
<t:FieldURI FieldURI="message:IsRead"/>
<t:FieldURI FieldURI="calendar:Start"/>
<t:FieldURI FieldURI="task:DueDate"/>
<t:FieldURI FieldURI="contacts:FileAs"/>
```

Each enumeration value is prefixed by the type to which it applies. That prefix helps you quickly determine which enumeration value to use in your unindexed property path for the item type in question. That being said, a class hierarchy does exist among item types.

---

2 We will discuss indexed property paths in the next section.

Descendant classes can typically use unindexed property paths that are applicable to their parents. Refer to the item class hierarchy shown in Figure 3-1.

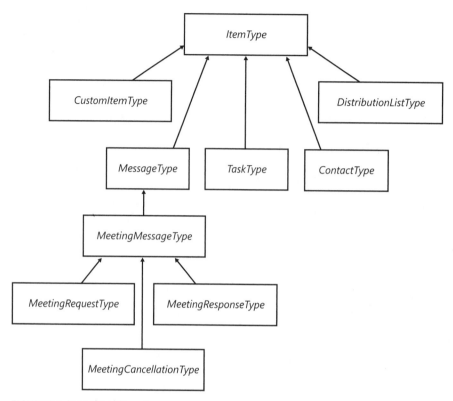

FIGURE 3-1 Item class hierarchy

The class hierarchy in Figure 3-1 shows that any property with an "item:" prefix should be applicable to any item type descendant. However, because both *MessageType* and *CalendarItemType* are peers, properties with a "message:" prefix cannot be used on calendar items, and properties with a "calendar:" prefix cannot be used on a message. Refer to the folder class hierarchy shown in Figure 3-2.

The unindexed property paths for folders break the nicely defined relationship described earlier. If you examine the schema in types.xsd, you notice that all unindexed property paths for folder properties start with the "folder:" prefix, suggesting that only *FolderType*, *SearchFolderType*, and *TasksFolderType* can use those properties. However, this is not the case. In reality, all except two of the "folder:" prefixed properties are applicable to *BaseFolderType* and therefore to all descendant types. The two exceptions are folder:UnreadCount and folder:SearchParameters.

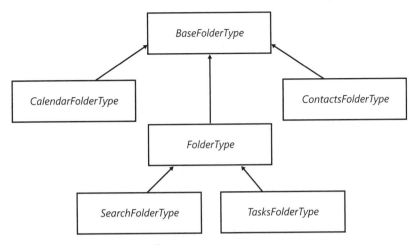

FIGURE 3-2 Folder class hierarchy

The concept of an unread count, which represents the number of items within the folder that have not yet been read, makes good sense for a normal folder (*FolderType*), search folder (*SearchFolderType*), and, to a lesser extent, tasks folder (*TasksFolderType*). However, it doesn't make any sense for a calendar folder (*CalendarFolderType*) or contacts folder (*ContactsFolderType*). Therefore, Exchange Web Services developers created the *BaseFolderType* type that surfaces all folder properties except folder:UnreadCount and places the unread count on *FolderType*. To be consistent, Exchange Web Services developers should have prefixed the other properties with "basefolder:", but alas, they did not.

Table 3-3 provides the list of folder property enumeration values and the folder classes to which they apply.

TABLE 3-3 Folder Property Path Applicability

Enumeration Name	Acts as if it was	Applicable to
folder:FolderId	basefolder:FolderId	*BaseFolderType*
folder:ParentFolderId	basefolder:ParentFolderId	*BaseFolderType*
folder:DisplayName	basefolder:DisplayName	*BaseFolderType*
folder:UnreadCount	The only one that is correct!	*FolderType*
folder:TotalCount	basefolder:TotalCount	*BaseFolderType*
folder:ChildFolderCount	basefolder:ChildFolderCount	*BaseFolderType*
folder:FolderClass	basefolder:FolderClass	*BaseFolderType*
folder:SearchParameters	searchfolder:SearchParameters	*SearchFolderType*
folder:ManagedFolderInformation	basefolder:managedFolderInformation	*BaseFolderType*

If you use proxy classes to talk to Exchange Web Services, it is useful to add an overloaded constructor to the *PathToUnindexedFieldType* class so that you can assign the enumeration value when you create the unindexed property path.

```
/// <summary>
/// Extension of the unindexed field uri type
/// </summary>
public partial class PathToUnindexedFieldType
{
  /// <summary>
  /// Constructor
  /// </summary>
  /// <param name="propertyUriEnumValue">enum value that indicates which
  /// property we are dealing with</param>
  ///
  public PathToUnindexedFieldType(UnindexedFieldURIType propertyUriEnumValue)
  {
    this.fieldURIField = propertyUriEnumValue;
  }

  /// <summary>
  /// Default constructor needed for serialization to work³
  /// </summary>
  ///
  public PathToUnindexedFieldType() { }
}
```

This simplifies things slightly. As a result, you can define unindexed property paths in a single line (ignoring word wrap):

```
PathToUnindexedFieldType subject = new
              PathToUnindexedFieldType(UnindexedFieldURIType.itemSubject);
```

If you didn't make this change, it would require two lines.

```
PathToUnindexedFieldType subject = new PathToUnindexedFieldType();
subject.FieldURI = UnindexedFieldURIType.itemSubject;
```

Every little bit helps.

Notice that the enumeration value names in the proxy class are missing the colon between the applicable class and the property. Therefore, "item:Subject" becomes "itemSubject" and so forth. This is reasonable because colons are not allowed as part of identifiers.

---

3 The auto-generated proxies do not include a default constructor since there were no other constructors. Since a non-default constructor is being added, the implicit default constructor "magically" disappears and you *must* explicitly add the default constructor so that the XML serializer has a way to instantiate the type during deserialization.

Indexed Property Paths

An indexed property path is a property path that identifies a single property from within a related set of properties. While an unindexed property path is identified using a single value from the *UnindexedFieldURIType* enumeration, an indexed property path requires two pieces of information to properly identify the property being referenced. One piece identifies the "scope" or group of related properties, and another piece identifies a specific property within that scope.

To explain indexed property paths, we will begin with an illustration. Let's say a family contains individuals and they all share a last name. This last name would be the "scope" that identifies them as a unit distinct from other units with individuals. This is shown in Figure 3-3.

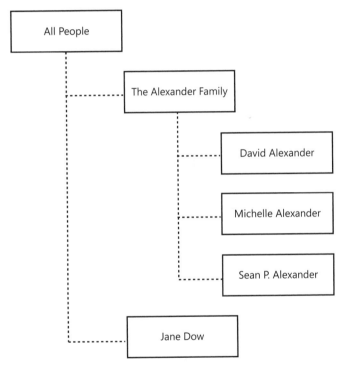

FIGURE 3-3 The family tree

This scoping is more convenient when considering relationships. In a similar way, some item and folder properties seem more related than others, depicting a common ground that does not exist between other properties. To emphasize this relationship, such properties are grouped together, and their group is identified by an enumeration value. The actual property within that group is identified by a key. The combination of the enumeration value and the key is surfaced as an indexed property path, which is sometimes called a dictionary property path. The schema type for an indexed property path is *PathToIndexedFieldType*, but you will most often refer to it in XML by its global name, *IndexedFieldURI*.

As with unindexed property paths, indexed property paths have an enumeration that identifies the property path family being referenced. This enumeration is surfaced through the *DictionaryURIType* in the schema. *DictionaryURIType* provides the "scope," but to determine precisely which property within the scope is being referenced, you need to add an additional identifier known as the key or field index. Each *DictionaryURIType* has a different set of keys just like each family scope has a different set of family members. Table 3-4 presents the list of indexed properties along with their key types, and Table 3-5 lists the indexed key types and their values.

TABLE 3-4 Indexed Properties and Their Key Types

DictionaryURIType	Related key type
item:InternetMessageHeader	*String.* (Keyed off of header name; headers are extensible)
contacts:ImAddress	*ImAddressKeyType*
contacts:PhysicalAddress:Street	*PhysicalAddressKeyType*
contacts:PhysicalAddress:City	*PhysicalAddressKeyType*
contacts:PhysicalAddress:State	*PhysicalAddressKeyType*
contacts:PhysicalAddress:PostalCode	*PhysicalAddressKeyType*
contacts:PhysicalAddress:CountryOrRegion	*PhysicalAddressKeyType*
contacts:PhoneNumber	*PhoneNumberKeyType*
contacts:EmailAddress	*EmailAddressKeyType*

TABLE 3-5 Indexed Key Types and Their Values

Key Types	Values
ImAddressKeyType	*ImAddress1, ImAddress2, ImAddress3*
PhysicalAddressKeyType	*Business, Home, Other*
PhoneNumberKeyType	*AssistantPhone, BusinessFax, BusinessPhone, BusinessPhone2, Callback, CarPhone, CompanyMainPhone, HomeFax, HomePhone, HomePhone2, Isdn, MobilePhone, OtherFax, OtherTelephone, Pager, PrimaryPhone, RadioPhone, Telex, TtyTddPhone*
EmailAddressKeyType	*EmailAddress1, EmailAddress2, EmailAddress3*

If you wanted to refer to the home street address, you would use a combination of the *contacts:PhysicalAddress:Street* value from the *DictionaryURIType* enumeration to identify the scope, and the *PhysicalAddressKey:Home* value from the *PhysicalAddressKeyType* enumeration to identify the key. For the business street address, it would be the *contacts: PhysicalAddress:Street DictionaryURIType* value for the scope and the *PhysicalAddressKey: Business PhysicalAddressKeyType* value for the key. Listing 3-1 shows how this would look within an XML document.

LISTING 3-1 Using Indexed Field URIs

```
<t:IndexedFieldURI FieldURI="contacts:PhysicalAddress:Street"
                   FieldIndex="Home"/>
<t:IndexedFieldURI FieldURI="contacts:PhysicalAddress:Street"
                   FieldIndex="Business"/>
```

Notice that "PhysicalAddressKey:" is not inserted before home and business in Listing 3-1 because the property path for indexed properties has a *FieldIndex* attribute of type *String* and not of those listed in Table 3-4. The key types in the schema serve two purposes. First, they tell you what applicable values can be entered in the *FieldIndex* attribute for your given indexed property path. Second, the key types are used in the actual item properties. This topic will be discussed in subsequent chapters corresponding to the item types in question.

The schema could have been defined using the key types explicitly rather than using strings. Because attributes in a schema must be simple types, this would have derived a new *PathToIndexedFieldType* descendant type for each of the key types. In other words, there would be additional types, such as *PathToEmailAddressIndexedFieldType* and *PathToPhoneNumberIndexedFieldType*, instead of the single *PathToIndexedFieldType*. That might not have been a bad decision in hindsight, but nevertheless, the Exchange Web Services developers chose the direction that they did.

This introduces a little weirdness when dealing with the proxy classes. Because the *FieldIndex* attribute is defined as an *xs:string* in the schema, the proxy class surfaces this as a *String*. You cannot set this property using the enumeration values without first converting the enumeration value to a *String*.

```
PathToIndexedFieldType field = new PathToIndexedFieldType();
field.FieldURI = DictionaryURIType.contactsEmailAddress;

// FieldIndex is a string, so we need to explictly convert our key type to string.
//
field.FieldIndex = EmailAddressKeyType.EmailAddress1.ToString();
```

If you are going to do a lot of proxy coding, it may be worthwhile to add a few factory methods to remove the need to call *ToString()* on the enumeration value. You can do that by extending *PathToIndexedFieldType* using partial classes as shown in Listing 3-2.

LISTING 3-2 Extending *PathToIndexedFieldType* to help with key types

```
/// <summary>
/// Extension the the PathToIndexedFieldType to increase usability and
/// subsequently decrease programmer irritability.
/// </summary>
public partial class PathToIndexedFieldType
```

```csharp
{
    /// <summary>
    /// Enum to expose only the physical address field uris
    /// </summary>
    public enum PhysicalAddressPart
    {
        Street = DictionaryURIType.contactsPhysicalAddressStreet,
        City = DictionaryURIType.contactsPhysicalAddressCity,
        State = DictionaryURIType.contactsPhysicalAddressState,
        PostalCode = DictionaryURIType.contactsPhysicalAddressPostalCode,
        CountryOrRegion =
            DictionaryURIType.contactsPhysicalAddressCountryOrRegion,
    }


    /// <summary>
    /// Constructor required for XML serialization    /// </summary>
    public PathToIndexedFieldType()
    { }


    /// <summary>
    /// Constructor
    /// </summary>
    /// <param name="fieldURI">Dictionary FieldURI to use</param>
    /// <param name="fieldIndex">Key or index to use</param>
    ///
    public PathToIndexedFieldType(
                    DictionaryURIType fieldURI,
                    string fieldIndex)
    {
        this.FieldURI = fieldURI;
        this.FieldIndex = fieldIndex;
    }


    /// <summary>
    /// Factory method for creating an email address dictionary field uri
    /// </summary>
    /// <param name="fieldIndex">Email address field index</param>
    /// <returns>Indexed Field URI</returns>
    ///
    public static PathToIndexedFieldType
        CreateEmailAddress(EmailAddressKeyType fieldIndex)
    {
        return new PathToIndexedFieldType(
                    DictionaryURIType.contactsEmailAddress,
                    fieldIndex.ToString());
    }


    /// <summary>
    /// Factory method for creating an Im address dictionary field uri
    /// </summary>
    /// <param name="fieldIndex">Im address field index</param>
    /// <returns>Indexed field uri</returns>
    ///
    public static PathToIndexedFieldType CreateImAddress(
```

```
                            ImAddressKeyType fieldIndex)
{
    return new PathToIndexedFieldType(
                DictionaryURIType.contactsImAddress,
                fieldIndex.ToString());
}


/// <summary>
/// Factory method for creating a physical address part field uri
/// </summary>
/// <param name="part">Indicates which part of a physical address to
/// use</param>
/// <param name="fieldIndex">Indicates the address category (home,
/// business, etc...)</param>
/// <returns>Indexed field uri</returns>
///
public static PathToIndexedFieldType CreatePhysicalAddress(
                            PhysicalAddressPart part,
                            PhysicalAddressKeyType fieldIndex)
{
    // Since we defined our enum to have the same values as the
    // corresponding dictionary
    // uris, we can just cast our enum value here.
    //
    return new PathToIndexedFieldType(
                (DictionaryURIType)part,
                fieldIndex.ToString());
}


/// <summary>
/// Factory method for creating a phone number dictionary field uri
/// </summary>
/// <param name="fieldIndex">Indicates the type of phone number</param>
/// <returns>Indexed field uri</returns>
///
public static PathToIndexedFieldType
                CreatePhoneNumber(PhoneNumberKeyType fieldIndex)
{
    return new PathToIndexedFieldType(
                DictionaryURIType.contactsPhoneNumber,
                fieldIndex.ToString());
}
}
```

Using these additional methods makes the code a little cleaner and helps reveal any issues as compile time problems rather than run-time errors.

```
PathToIndexedFieldType homeCity =
        PathToIndexedFieldType.CreatePhysicalAddress(
                PathToIndexedFieldType.PhysicalAddressPart.City,
                PhysicalAddressKeyType.Home);
PathToIndexedFieldType emailAddress1 =
        PathToIndexedFieldType.CreateEmailAddress(
                EmailAddressKeyType.EmailAddress1);
```

Extended Property Paths

Extended properties as a whole will be addressed in Chapter 13, "Extended Properties." However, when writing this book, we found it necessary to use extended properties in several of the examples in the first half of the book. Without a basic grounding in what extended properties are, such examples may be difficult to follow. Since we could not get rid of the first half of the book, it seems prudent for us to give you an overview of extended properties here.

The Exchange Store doesn't know anything about property paths. All properties contained within a mailbox database are identified by a *property tag*, which is an unsigned 32-bit integer. Every property path presented so far has a corresponding property tag that the Exchange Store uses to identify the property. For example, the *item:Subject* unindexed property path has a property tag of 0x0037001E.[4] When you send a request to Exchange Web Services and ask for the *item:Subject*, Exchange Web Services maps that into a Exchange Store request for 0x0037001E.

A property tag actually contains two pieces of information. The left-most four digits of the property tag (excluding the 0x hexadecimal identifier) provide the actual property identifier while the right-most four digits of the property tag indicate the data type of the property. So, for the item:Subject example, the actual property identifier is "0037" (hex) and the data type is "001E", which indicates that this is a *String*.

All properties whose identifiers are below 0x7FFF are considered "standard" MAPI properties, meaning that they are the same across all databases. Property tags whose identifiers are from 0x7FFF and above are considered "custom" MAPI properties. Such property tag assignments are *not* constant across all databases.

Given that properties that have identifiers in the custom property range are not consistent across databases, you need a consistent way to identify such custom properties. Exchange Web Services prohibits you from referencing MAPI properties in the custom range by property tag. Rather than using the property tag, you can identify custom MAPI properties using their *property set*, which defines a namespace and either a name or integer identifier, which is sometimes called a dispatch identifier.

Extended property paths are exposed in the XML schema through the *PathToExtendedFieldType* schema type, although you will typically encounter them in XML instance documents by the global instance named *ExtendedFieldURI*.

Given this information, there are three ways to refer to a MAPI property: property tag, property set with name, and property set with dispatch identifier.

---

[4] Subject also has a "friendly" name of PR_SUBJECT, but EWS doesn't deal with such friendly names.

Property Tag

Given that a property tag represents two pieces of information, the *PathToExtendedFieldType* type surfaces two corresponding attributes: *PropertyTag* and *PropertyType*. The *PropertyTag* attribute holds either the decimal or hexadecimal property identifier while the *PropertyType* attribute holds values from the *MapiPropertyTypeType* enumeration. For example, the *item:Subject* unindexed property path from above can be expressed as an extended property as follows:

```
<t:ExtendedFieldURI PropertyTag="0x0037" PropertyType="String"/>
```

Property Set with Name

For MAPI properties in the custom range that have an associated name, you need to identify both the property set id as well as the name of the property. Exchange Web Services surfaces a set of well-known property sets via the *DistinguishedPropertySetType* enumeration.

```
<t:ExtendedFieldURI DistinguishedPropertySetId="PublicStrings"
                    Name="MyProperty"
                    PropertyType="String"/>
```

For custom properties defined in property sets that are not listed in the *DistinguishedPropertySetType* enumeration, you must specify the actual property set id GUID.

```
<t:ExtendedFieldURI PropertySetId="00020329-0000-0000-C000-000000000046"
                    Name="MyOtherProperty"
                    PropertyType="String"/>
```

Property Set with Dispatch Identifier

For MAPI properties in the custom range that have an associated dispatch identifier, you need to identify both the property set id as well as the dispatch id of the property.

```
<t:ExtendedFieldURI DistinguishedPropertySetId="PublicStrings"
                    PropertyId="2"
                    PropertyType="String"/>

<t:ExtendedFieldURI PropertySetId="00020329-0000-0000-C000-000000000046"
                    PropertyId="3"
                    PropertyType="String"/>
```

As mentioned earlier, we will cover extended property paths in more detail in Chapter 13. The previous discussion should give you enough to get through the book until that point. If this section was so exhilarating that you cannot bear to part with extended property paths at this point, feel free to skip ahead to Chapter 13. Just don't forget to come back.

Exception Property Paths

Exception property paths are used to report errors. As such, you will never have a need to create one yourself. You can find exception property paths within the *MessageXml* element of an error response message, and the only place you encounter these is when dealing with calendar recurrence definitions. (Calendar item recurrence is discussed in Chapter 9, "Recurring Appointments and Time Zones.") The exception property path indicates which property was in error.

Get in Shape

So far, we discussed property paths as independent entities outside of the scope of any items or folders. You can consider these property paths to be metadata or "data about data." Property paths allow you to indicate the property to which you are referring. However, if you ever want to deal with the actual property data, you must consider the intersection of property paths and items/folders.

When you consider a standard .NET object, such as *System.String*, you always get a fully formed object when you create it. Of course, there might be properties that are null or set to a default value, but the actual state of that instance is fully represented by that object. Moving over to the database world, if you take a table containing three columns (A, B, and C) and then perform a query to retrieve two of the columns, you have a *partial* representation of the row. More data exists in the database, but you simply didn't ask for it.

Exchange Web Services surfaces a hybrid mix of the "fully formed" and "only-what-you-need" models. How is that possible? Well, in the standard "only-what-you-need" model, data comes back as a result set in which the focus is on the collection of properties and not on what those properties represent. For instance, all ActiveX Data Objects (ADO) queries return a *RecordSet* interface regardless of the table you are querying. In Exchange Web Services, you can specify which properties you are interested in, but rather than receiving a generic collection of properties, you receive a strongly typed object containing only those properties you requested. The upside of this is that you can reduce network traffic by requesting only those properties that are of interest to you. The downside is that you can fool yourself into thinking a property is empty when, in fact, there is data in the Exchange Store for it that you just didn't request.

For example, if you make a request such as "Give me Message Q with properties DateCreated, Size, and Id," you would receive the requested item, but in the proxy class instance, Q's subject would be null. Why? Because you didn't ask for the subject. In practice, this has never been an issue.[5] As a general rule, make sure you request any properties that you want to use.

---

[5] Well, we did run into it once, but we figured it out pretty quickly.

The set of properties that are returned for an item or folder is determined by the item or folder *shape* that is specified in the request.[6] You as the caller determine how your objects will be "shaped" when they are returned to you. Response shape parameters appear in any request that returns items or folders as part of a response.

Base Shapes

Before we start talking in depth about response shapes, we need to discuss base shapes. Rather than requiring you to specify every property that you want whenever you make a request, Exchange Web Services defines common sets of properties that make sense for each item and folder type. Three base shapes are available, and you must specify a single base shape as part of a request. You can always add to the set of properties that are to be returned, but you cannot remove properties from the set. The three base shapes are *IdOnly*, *Default*, and *AllProperties*.

IdOnly

The *IdOnly* base shape returns a single property for each item within a response: the id. It is surprising how useful this shape is, especially considering that you can add to the list of properties to be returned.

Default

The *Default* base shape returns the set of properties that are considered common or standard for the item or folder type in question, meaning that the default set of properties returned for a message is different than the default set of properties returned for a contact. Typically, default properties follow the inheritance model. If a property is in the default set for a base class, it is in the default set for a descendant class. As an example, *item:Subject* is in the default shape for *ItemType*. Because both *MessageType* and *CalendarItemType* derive from *ItemType*, *item:Subject* is also in their default shapes.[7]

AllProperties

This will be a surprise for some, but the *AllProperties* base shape does not return *every* property that is set on an item or folder in the Exchange Store. *AllProperties* returns all properties that Exchange Web Services has categorized as *applicable* to the object type in question. So, if you have a message in the Exchange Store that for some strange reason has a start time set on it, you do not get start time by specifying the *AllProperties* base shape when requesting

---

[6] Note that there is also the concept of an attachment shape, although it behaves differently than item and folder shapes. Attachment shapes will be discussed in Chapter 12, "Attachments."

[7] The properties returned for each item/folder type and base shape combination are listed in Appendix C, available on the companion Web page.

the message. If you know the properties that you are looking for, you can certainly get them by *explicitly* specifying the property paths of interest. This will bother some, but Exchange Web Services does not provide a way to get every property on an item.[8]

Item Shapes

Item shapes appear in *GetItem*, *FindItem*, and *SyncFolderItems* Web requests. Following is the general structure of an item response shape:

```
<m:ItemShape>9
    <t:BaseShape>base shape enum value</t:BaseShape>
    <t:IncludeMimeContent>True/False(Default)</t:IncludeMimeContent>
    <t:BodyType>Best, Html, Text or if omitted (Best)</t:BodyType>
    <t:AdditionalProperties>
        <!-- Any additional properties go here -->
    </t:AdditionalProperties>
</m:ItemShape>
```

The trivial form of an item shape is sufficient for most purposes, whereby only the *BaseShape* child element is required. The following example uses an item shape to request the *Default* properties for any items returned in the response.

```
<m:ItemShape>
    <t:BaseShape>Default</t:BaseShape>
</m:ItemShape>
```

BaseShape

As mentioned earlier, the *BaseShape* subelement can contain one of three values: *IdOnly*, *Default*, or *AllProperties*.

IncludeMimeContent

The optional *IncludeMimeContent* element allows you to request the Base64-encoded Multipurpose Internet Mail Extensions (MIME) content for the item in question. Because the MIME content can be quite large, the default setting for this optional element is false. This means that if you request an item and specify a base shape of *AllProperties*, but omit the *IncludeMimeContent* element, you do *not* get MIME for the returned items. To indicate that MIME should be returned, simply add the *IncludeMimeContent* child element with a value of true. MIME content can only be retrieved for messages and calendar items.[10]

---

8 This might very well change in future versions of the product.

9 Notice that *ItemShape* is prefixed with *m:*, which is indicative of the messages namespace. Although *ItemResponseShapeType* is defined in the types namespace, you will usually deal with element *instances* defined in the messages namespace.

10 *FindItem* does not allow you to specify the *IncludeMimeContent* element in the item shape.

```
<GetItem xmlns=".../messages"
         xmlns:t=".../types">
   <ItemShape>
      <t:BaseShape>IdOnly</t:BaseShape>
      <t:IncludeMimeContent>true</t:IncludeMimeContent>
   </ItemShape>
   <ItemIds>
      <t:ItemId Id="AAAeAGRhdnNOZXJAZXhjaGFuZ..." ChangeKey="CQAAABYA..."/>
   </ItemIds>
</GetItem>
```

In the response, you can see the additional *MimeContent* node. The Base64-encoded content is shortened for readability.

```
<GetItemResponse xmlns:m=".../messages"
                 xmlns:t=".../types"
                 xmlns=".../messages">
  <m:ResponseMessages>
    <m:GetItemResponseMessage ResponseClass="Success">
      <m:ResponseCode>NoError</m:ResponseCode>
      <m:Items>
        <t:Message>
          <t:MimeContent CharacterSet="UTF-8">Q29udG...</t:MimeContent>
          <t:ItemId Id="AAAeAGRhdnNOZX..." ChangeKey="CQAAABYAAADc..."/>
        </t:Message>
      </m:Items>
    </m:GetItemResponseMessage>
  </m:ResponseMessages>
</GetItemResponse>
```

BodyType

The optional *BodyType* element allows you to specify the format of the message body to be returned. We will cover this in detail in Chapter 5, "Items."

AdditionalProperties

The optional *AdditionalProperties* element allows you to indicate specific properties that you want to be returned in addition to those properties that are associated with the base shape. One important caveat here is that you can only request properties that are applicable to the type of item for which you are requesting them. For example, if you have the id for a message and try to request *calendar:Start* as an additional property, you are greeted by the *ErrorInvalidPropertyRequest* response code indicating that the property you requested is not applicable to the item in question.[11]

---

[11] Extended property paths provide a mechanism to get around this restriction for native MAPI properties. See Chapter 13 for more details.

In our own coding, we mainly use the *AdditionalProperties* element in conjunction with the *IdOnly* base shape, although you are free to use it with *Default* and *AllProperties*, too. All items within the *AdditionalProperties* element must be in the property path format. Unindexed, indexed, and extended property path formats are all allowed.

LISTING 3-3 Specifying additional properties in a request shape

```
<GetItem xmlns=".../messages"
         xmlns:t=".../types">
  <ItemShape>
    <t:BaseShape>IdOnly</t:BaseShape>
    <t:AdditionalProperties>
      <t:FieldURI FieldURI="item:Subject"/>
      <t:IndexedFieldURI FieldURI="item:InternetMessageHeader"
                         FieldIndex="Thread-Index"/>
      <t:IndexedFieldURI FieldURI="item:InternetMessageHeader"
                         FieldIndex="Thread-Topic"/>
    </t:AdditionalProperties>
  </ItemShape>
  <ItemIds>
    <t:ItemId Id="AAAeAGRhdnNOZ..."/>
  </ItemIds>
</GetItem>
```

The code in Listing 3-3 asks for the id (as indicated by the base shape), the subject, and then two named Internet message headers. The response returns precisely what is requested.

```
<GetItemResponse xmlns:m=".../messages"
                 xmlns:t=".../types"
                 xmlns=".../messages">
  <m:ResponseMessages>
    <m:GetItemResponseMessage ResponseClass="Success">
      <m:ResponseCode>NoError</m:ResponseCode>
      <m:Items>
        <t:Message>
          <t:ItemId Id="AAAeAGRhdnN..." ChangeKey="CQAAABY..."/>
          <t:Subject>RE: Here is an email with some internet
                     message headers</t:Subject>
          <t:InternetMessageHeaders>
            <t:InternetMessageHeader HeaderName="Thread-Index">
                    AcbjLvNF...</t:InternetMessageHeader>
            <t:InternetMessageHeader HeaderName="Thread-Topic">Here is an
                    email with some internet message headers
            </t:InternetMessageHeader>
          </t:InternetMessageHeaders>
        </t:Message>
      </m:Items>
    </m:GetItemResponseMessage>
  </m:ResponseMessages>
</GetItemResponse>
```

If the requested property does not exist on the item, then the requested property is not emitted into the resulting XML.

To demonstrate, the following request is the same except it asks for the Large-Elephant Internet message header, which, in theory, should not exist.

```
<!-- Additional XML omitted for brevity -->
<ItemShape>
   <t:BaseShape>IdOnly</t:BaseShape>
   <t:AdditionalProperties>
      <t:FieldURI FieldURI="item:Subject"/>
      <t:IndexedFieldURI FieldURI="item:InternetMessageHeader"
                         FieldIndex="Large-Elephant"/>
   </t:AdditionalProperties>
</ItemShape>
```

As you can see in the response, the id and subject are returned, but there is no element for the Large-Elephant Internet message header.

```
<!-- Additional XML omitted for brevity -->
<m:Items>
   <t:Message>
      <t:ItemId Id="AAAeAGRhdnN0ZXJA..." ChangeKey="CQAAABYA..."/>
      <t:Subject>RE: Some email</t:Subject>
   </t:Message>
</m:Items>
```

Folder Shapes

You can specify the properties that you would like returned for folders by using folder response shapes. Folder shapes appear in *GetFolder*, *FindFolder*, and *SyncFolderHierarchy* requests. Folder shapes are much simpler than item shapes as seen in Listing 3-4

LISTING 3-4 Basic structure of a folder shape

```
<m:FolderShape>
    <t:BaseShape>IdOnly or Default or AllProperties</t:BaseShape>
    <t:AdditionalProperties>
       <!-- Optional additional properties -->
    </t:AdditionalProperties>
</m:FolderShape>
```

Because the folder response shape follows the same format as the item shape, only a single example is provided here. It calls *GetFolder* on a search folder and requests the search parameters that define which items appear in the folder.

```
<GetFolder xmlns=".../messages"
           xmlns:t=".../types">
  <FolderShape>
    <t:BaseShape>IdOnly</t:BaseShape>
    <t:AdditionalProperties>
      <t:FieldURI FieldURI="folder:SearchParameters"/>
```

```
        </t:AdditionalProperties>
      </FolderShape>
    <FolderIds>
      <t:FolderId Id="AAAeAGRhdnN0ZXJA..." ChangeKey="BwAAA..."/>
    </FolderIds>
</GetFolder>
```

In the response, you can see both the folder id and the search parameters for the folder in question.

```
<t:SearchFolder>
    <t:FolderId Id="AAAeAGRhdnN0ZXJ..." ChangeKey="BwAAABYAA..."/>
    <t:SearchParameters Traversal="Shallow">
        <t:Restriction>
            <t:Exists>
                <t:FieldURI FieldURI="item:Subject"/>
            </t:Exists>
        </t:Restriction>
        <t:BaseFolderIds>
            <t:FolderId Id="AAAeAGRhdnN0ZXJ..." ChangeKey="AQAAAA=="/>
        </t:BaseFolderIds>
    </t:SearchParameters>
</t:SearchFolder>
```

Now, search parameters are only applicable to search folders. If you try to request *folder:SearchParameters* on the Inbox, you get an *ErrorInvalidPropertyRequest* error indicating that the "Property is not valid for this object type." Of course, if the *AdditionalProperties* element is ommitted, just the folder id is returned because a base shape of *IdOnly* was requested.

Folder properties that are actually returned for each shape are discussed in Chapter 4, "Folders."

Useful Proxy Class Extensions

It might not seem obvious right now, but dealing with response shape types in proxy code can be very repetitive. The pattern is always the same: create the response shape, set the base shape, and, if necessary, add additional properties. It makes perfect sense to centralize the repetitive code in one location. Listing 3-5 presents this extension for both folder and item response shapes.

LISTING 3-5 Partial class extension for item and folder response shape types

```
/// <summary>
/// Partial class extension of ItemResponseShapeType to include useful
/// constructor overloads.
/// </summary>
public partial class ItemResponseShapeType
{
    /// <summary>
    /// Default constructor needed for XML serialization
    /// </summary>
```

```csharp
    public ItemResponseShapeType() { }

  /// <summary>
  /// Constructor
  /// </summary>
  /// <param name="baseShape">BaseShape associated with this response
  /// shape</param>
  /// <param name="additionalProperties">OPTIONAL list of additional
  /// properties for this shape</param>
  ///
  public ItemResponseShapeType(
          DefaultShapeNamesType baseShape,
          params BasePathToElementType[] additionalProperties)
  {
    this.BaseShape = baseShape;
    if ((additionalProperties != null) &&
        (additionalProperties.Length > 0))
    {
      this.AdditionalProperties = additionalProperties;
    }
  }
}

/// <summary>
/// Partial class extension of FolderResponseShapeType to include useful
/// constructor overloads.
/// </summary>
public partial class FolderResponseShapeType
{
  /// <summary>
  /// Default constructor needed for XML serialization
  /// </summary>
  public FolderResponseShapeType() { }

  /// <summary>
  /// Constructor
  /// </summary>
  /// <param name="baseShape">BaseShape associated with this response
  /// shape</param>
  /// <param name="additionalProperties">OPTIONAL list of additional
  /// properties for this shape</param>
  ///
  public FolderResponseShapeType(
          DefaultShapeNamesType baseShape,
          params BasePathToElementType[] additionalProperties)
  {
    this.BaseShape = baseShape;

    if ((additionalProperties != null) &&
        (additionalProperties.Length > 0))
    {
      this.AdditionalProperties = additionalProperties;
    }
  }
}
```

This might not seem terribly exciting now, but you will thank us for it in time.

Relating Property Paths to Instance Element Names

On one hand, you have property paths that identify properties you want to request, and on the other hand, you have child elements that contain the actual data as shown in Figure 3-4.

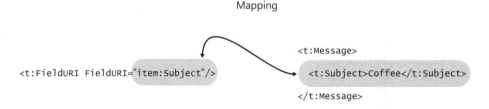

FIGURE 3-4 Mapping property paths to instance elements

You make a request, adding property paths as additional property elements. However, in the response, the corresponding property values come back as instance elements. The question that comes to mind is, "How do I map from what I requested to what I received?" Unfortunately, there is no single line solution for this. Certainly, most properties can be mapped by inspection, although that requires human involvement, and it is hard to put people on an install CD. As a result, this mapping must be created by you, the ever-patient Exchange Web Services programmer. If you are dealing with XML as opposed to proxy objects, it is relatively easy to create a mapping from an *UnindexedFieldURIType* enumeration value to an XPath query, although this needs to be done for each and every property.

Why do you need to do this? Well, certain errors come back and identify the offending property by using a property path. In some cases, these erroneous values come directly or indirectly from an end user, so you might wish to display a dialog box telling them which property is naughty.

As an example, Exchange Web Services does not allow you to create a folder with a display name that starts with spaces. If you try to do this, you get the following error response:

```
<CreateFolderResponse xmlns:m=".../messages"
                      xmlns:t=".../types"
                      xmlns=".../messages">
  <m:ResponseMessages>
    <m:CreateFolderResponseMessage ResponseClass="Error">
      <m:MessageText>The folder save operation failed due to invalid
                     property values.</m:MessageText>
      <m:ResponseCode>ErrorFolderSavePropertyError</m:ResponseCode>
      <m:DescriptiveLinkKey>0</m:DescriptiveLinkKey>
      <m:MessageXml>
        <t:FieldURI FieldURI="folder:DisplayName"/>
      </m:MessageXml>
      <m:Folders/>
    </m:CreateFolderResponseMessage>
  </m:ResponseMessages>
</CreateFolderResponse>
```

Your program receives the preceding error message. What do you do with this? You probably should not show a dialog box like that shown in Figure 3-5.

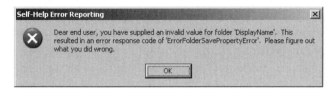

FIGURE 3-5 Unacceptable Error dialog box

Instead, you need to parse the response code and turn it into an intelligent error message.

You also need to perform this mapping when making requests for an item or folder with a response shape that has additional properties. You certainly get the additional properties back, but you must know what to look for in your response. The fact of the matter is, you either need to hard-code in your expectations when parsing the response or maintain your own reusable mapping table. The second is preferable if you are doing any extensive programming using Exchange Web Services, which is essentially what the development team ended up doing within the Exchange Web Services code.

In Chapter 18, "Errors Never Happen," we touch on a way to do mapping programmatically by building up mapping tables using reflection.

Change Keys and Shapes

In Chapter 2, "May I See Your Id?," we indicated that including the change key increases performance. We could leave it at that and have everyone scratching their heads in wonder. Instead, we will tell you why *and* leave you scratching your head in wonder.

When Exchange Web Services receives a folder or item id that it needs to open, an interesting situation arises. Exchange Web Services knows the response shape that the caller has requested (for example, IdOnly, Default) along with the additional properties and so on, but that final list of properties is a function of the type of item or folder to which Exchange Web Services is binding. If a request comes in *without a change key*, Exchange Web Services blindly opens the item and determines the type of item (such as message, calendar item) to which the id refers. Using that information, Exchange Web Services can then determine the actual properties that it needs to fetch from the Exchange Store. The result is that Exchange Web Services incurs two remote procedure call (RPC) calls (at a minimum) when it binds to an item *without* the change key.

To remedy this situation, one thing that Exchange Web Services embeds in the change key is the type of object that the id represents. With that information, it can expand the response shape into the list of properties *up front* and thereby reduce the RPC count by one. This is a far distant relative of branch prediction, twice removed. Now, after Exchange Web Services receives the item or folder from the Exchange Store, Exchange Web Services verifies the assumption that it really is what the change key said it was. If the change key indicator is incorrect, Exchange Web Services treats it as if the object does not exist. For example, a request comes in for a calendar item with id xyz. Exchange Web Services grabs item xyz and sees that it is actually a message. Well, the Exchange Store doesn't have a *calendar item* with that id, and therefore the calendar item doesn't exist. Of course, you should never run into this situation unless:

1. Someone changed the item or folder type from under you by using another client access application programming interface, such as MAPI or DAV, such that the change key you have refers to the old object type, or

2. You are mucking with the change keys just to see what happens, in which case you owe us a cup of coffee if it works as expected and we owe you a cup of coffee if it doesn't.

Important Microsoft is not publishing the layout of the change key and reserves the right to change both the data contained within the change key as well as the performance implications surrounding whether to supply the change key. We figured it would be beneficial to help you understand why it is a good idea in the current release to pass the change key in if you have it. Some might question why Exchange Web Services developers didn't throw the object type into the id itself. They did consider that, but there are some specific reasons why that was not prudent, and therefore it found a home in the change key.

Summary

This chapter introduced two new concepts: property paths and shapes. They arose as a result of the hybrid nature of items and folders exposed through Exchange Web Services. Really, these concepts aren't that new but are simply concepts brought over from the relational database world. Property paths represent a way to refer to a property as a piece of metadata, independent of the objects that hold the values for that property. If you say, "Give me the list of people that this message was sent to," the "list of people" is a property path that turns into a value when the request is fulfilled. This chapter also touched on response shapes and how they affect the data that is returned for both items and folders.

Part II
Things in Your Mailbox

Chapter 4
Folders

Just like their physical counterparts, mailbox folders hold items. Unlike physical folders, it is common for mailbox folders to hold other folders. In this chapter, we will discuss folders and how they fit into the mailbox structure. We will cover the various types of folders, their properties, and the operations that apply to them. Although the depth of your folder tree appears to be a function of personal obsessiveness, this has not been scientifically proven.

Mailbox Structure

Most users are blissfully unaware that there is a lot of stuff in their mailboxes that they never actually see. The vast majority of folders that appear in client applications, such as Microsoft Office Outlook, are actually children of a folder called the Inter-Personal Message (IPM) Subtree. Interesting. Let's look at the general folder structure of a mailbox as shown in Figure 4-1 before digging into what you can actually do with folders.

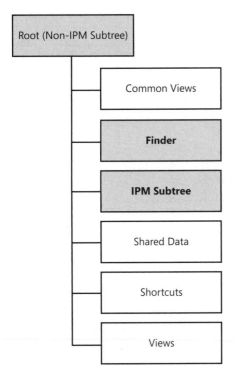

FIGURE 4-1 General folder structure of a mailbox

A single root folder exists in any folder hierarchy. The root folder has no parent. In Microsoft Exchange Server 2007 Web Services (EWS), this root folder is called "root" (quite ingenious, eh?). Root contains several folders, although we are interested in only two for now. The others contain configuration information that should not be interesting to the user. The first folder of interest is the aforementioned IPM Subtree that contains the well-known Inbox, Sent Items, and other folders that users know and love. The second folder of interest, Finder, is the parent of all search folders that are visible to Office Outlook. Now, being in the Finder folder is not the only requirement for Office Outlook visibility, but it certainly is a fundamental one. In Office Outlook, users see the Finder folder indirectly by the name of "Search Folders." We will discuss search folders at length in Chapter 15, "Advanced Searching."

Folder Types

As mentioned briefly in Chapter 3, "Property Paths and Response Shapes," you encounter several different types of folders when dealing with Exchange Web Services. These folder types and their relationship to each other are shown in Figure 4-2.

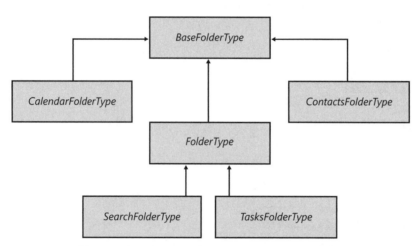

FIGURE 4-2 Folder types in Exchange Web Services

BaseFolderType

The base schema type for all folder types supported by Exchange Web Services is *BaseFolderType*. The schema identifies *BaseFolderType* as an abstract type. Several properties are exposed on *BaseFolderType*, and by the nature of schema derivation, these properties are also available on all derived types.[1] Refer to Table 4-1 for a listing of *BaseFolderType* properties.

---

[1] These properties are listed in detail in Appendix C, "Mapping to MAPI Properties," available on the companion Web page.

TABLE 4-1 *BaseFolderType* **Properties**

Property Name	Type	Comment
FolderId	t:FolderIdType	The identifier for the folder.
ParentFolderId	t:FolderIdType	The identifier for the folder's parent; only the root (Non-IPM Subtree) folder does not have a parent.
FolderClass	string	Identifies the class of folder.*
DisplayName	string	The name used for folder display.
TotalCount	int	The number of items contained directly in this folder; does not include child folders.
ChildFolderCount	int	The number of child folders contained directly in this folder.
ExtendedProperty	t:ExtendedPropertyType	Any number of extended properties set on the folder; can be a plurality of these elements on a given folder.
ManagedFolderInformation	t:ManagedFolderInformation	Information regarding the managed status of the folder; if not a managed folder, then this property is not present.

*FolderClass updates are restricted to changes that preserve the fundamental type of the folder.

A couple of these properties need some explanation.

FolderClass Property

What determines whether a given folder is a contacts folder, a calendar folder, or a search folder? For *most* folders, the type is determined by its folder class (also known as the container class).[2] Surprisingly, the folder class has little to do with the actual folder and is really a hint about the intended *contents* of a folder. We say "intended" because there is nothing in the Exchange Store to keep you from storing contacts in a calendar folder, for example.[3] Certainly, these contacts do not appear in clients, such as Office Outlook or Microsoft Office Outlook Web Access, but nonetheless, they are lurking around your appointments. There are many standard folder classes such as IPF.Note (general message folder), IPF.Contact (contacts), and IPF.Tasks (tasks). Class determination for these folders is based on the folder class *prefix*. For instance, any folder class that starts with IPF.Contact, plus an additional dot, is considered a contacts folder. Therefore, a folder with a folder class of IPF.Contact.Contoso is just as much a contacts folder as one with a folder class of IPF.Contact. This scoping mechanism

---

2 Search folders are a bit different. The *FolderClass* property is not considered when determining whether a folder is a search folder. Search folders are discussed in Chapter 15.

3 That being said, EWS tries very hard to keep you from shooting yourself in the foot. So, trying to do this through EWS results in an error code, such as *ErrorCannotCreateContactInNonContactFolder*.

allows you to define folder class "inheritance" for your own purposes, although using extended properties may be a better solution.

Please note that if you update the folder class, you must maintain the nature of the folder (for instance, it must remain a contact folder). In other words, you must maintain the same folder class prefix. It is completely unacceptable to change the folder class so that the nature of the folder is changed (for instance, updating the folder class from IPF.Contact to IPF.Tasks). However, there is a special case, and that is the folder class IPF.Note. IPF.Note represents a generic folder, although any folder class for which Exchange Web Services has no specific mapping is also considered a generic folder. Essentially, Exchange Web Services treats all such folders as if their folder class *is* IPF.Note. This means that you can take a folder with a folder class of IPF.Note and change it to "I_AM_A_SPECIAL_FOLDER_CLASS," and EWS is more than happy to comply. Why? Because you start with a generic folder and end with a generic folder. On the other hand, if you take a contacts folder (IPF.Contact) and try to change its folder class to "I_AM_A_SPECIAL_FOLDER_CLASS," you encounter an error (*ErrorObjectTypeChanged*). Why? Because you started with a contacts folder and tried to change it to a generic folder.

When you create a folder through Exchange Web Services, you have the option to set the folder class to whatever you want it to be. You can indicate your desired folder class implicity by specifying the type of folder you want during the creation (*ContactsFolder*) and let Exchange Web Services assign the folder class under the covers.

```
<t:ContactsFolder>
  <t:DisplayName>My contacts folder</t:DisplayName>
</t:ContactsFolder>
```

Alternatively, you can indicate your desired folder class explicitly by specifying a generic folder type (*Folder*) and providing the *FolderClass* value yourself.

```
<t:Folder>
  <t:FolderClass>IPF.Contact</t:FolderClass>
  <t:DisplayName>My contacts folder</t:DisplayName>
</t:Folder>
```

Or, you can make it a little more specialized, such as:

```
<t:Folder>
  <t:FolderClass>IPF.Contact.Friendly</t:FolderClass>
  <t:DisplayName>Friendly Contacts</t:DisplayName>
</t:Folder>
```

As a result, you end up with a contacts folder that will always be a contacts folder until it is old and gray and its bits are finally returned to the Great Bit Bucket.

It should be obvious from the preceding discussion that using the following code to create a folder will fail, considering that you are trying to create a contacts folder and then change it to a generic folder.

```
<t:ContactsFolder>
  <t:FolderClass>IPF.Note</t:FolderClass>
  <t:DisplayName>My sort-of contacts folder</t:DisplayName>
</t:ContactsFolder>
```

What might not be obvious is that if you specify a non-generic folder element, such as *ContactsFolder*, you cannot add a *FolderClass* element even if it is correctly set to IPF.Contact.

```
<!-- This will fail.  You cannot specify the FolderClass element when creating a non-
generic folder -->
<t:ContactsFolder>
  <t:FolderClass>IPF.Contact</t:FolderClass>
  <t:DisplayName>Not a chance</t:DisplayName>
</t:ContactsFolder>
```

Two other quick points about the folder class include:

■   You cannot delete the folder class.

■   The folder class cannot be in excess of 255 characters.

DisplayName Property

The *DisplayName* property represents the name that users will likely see when interacting with the folder. For instance, the Inbox folder has a display name of "Inbox" when localized in US English.

A few limitations surround the display name property:

■   You cannot delete the display name.

■   The display name cannot be in excess of 255 characters.[4]

■   The display name cannot begin with a space character.

CalendarFolderType

CalendarFolderType descends from *BaseFolderType*, but adds no additional properties. Calendar Folders are intended to house appointments. In fact, Exchange Web Services does not allow you to create non-calendar items inside of a calendar folder.[5] It should be noted that the process of responding to meeting requests places appointments in the distinguished calendar folder only. Exchange Web Services does not support automatic interaction with non-distinguished calendar folders. Calendar folders are encountered as *CalendarFolder* elements and have a folder class that begins with IPF.Appointment. *CalendarFolderType* will be discussed at length in Chapter 8, "Working with Calendars."

---

[4]   If there is an existing folder with a display name in excess of 255 characters, EWS still returns the entire folder display name. You cannot, however, use EWS to create or update a folder so that its display name exceeds 255 characters.

[5]   You can get around this by moving an existing non-calendar item into a calendar folder, but why would you want to do that?

FolderType

FolderType represents the base class for both search and tasks folders. However, *FolderType* is interesting in itself because it is used to represent all generic folders.[6] *FolderType* adds a single property named *UnreadCount*. The unread count represents the number of items contained directly within the folder that have not been read by the current user. Note that the Exchange Store maintains unread status information on a per-user basis. As such, assuming that user A and user B both have access to a given mailbox, the unread count may be different depending on who is accessing the mailbox. Generic folders are encountered in XML documents as *Folder* elements. Exchange Web Services maintains a mapping of folder class to the appropriate Exchange Web Services folder type. You saw in the previous section that calendar folders have a folder class that begins with the prefix IPF.Appointment. Most generic folders that you encounter will have a folder class of IPF.Note. However, if Exchange Web Services encounters a folder that has a folder class that does not map to an Exchange Web Services folder type, it will also treat that folder as a generic folder.

Most distinguished folders are represented as generic folders: Deleted Items, Drafts, Inbox, Journal, Notes, Outbox, Sent Items, Message Folder Root (IPM Subtree), Root (Non-IPM Subtree), Junk Email, and Voice Mail.

ContactsFolderType

ContactsFolderType represents a folder that is intended to house contacts and distribution lists. In fact, Exchange Web Services does not allow you to create non-contact items inside of a contacts folder. Contact folders are encountered in XML documents as *ContactsFolder* elements and have a folder class that begins with IPF.Contact. As you will see in Chapter 6, "Contacts and Distribution Lists," contact folders are the only folders to which you can apply a *ContactsView* paging mechanism and still live to tell about it.

SearchFolderType

Search folders are folders in which the contents are determined by a restriction, which uses a filter to determine which items will appear in the search folder and which will not. In other words, a search folder is really a logical folder because the items "contained" within actually reside elsewhere. Search folders cannot contain subfolders. As such, *ChildFolderCount* is always zero. No limitations exist on the types of items that can be logically contained within a search folder. Search folders are encountered in XML documents as *SearchFolder* elements. We discussed the folder class in depth as it pertains to determining the type of a folder. Concerning search folders, the folder class is irrelevant, superfluous, even wanton, if

---

[6] A generic folder has a folder class of either *IPF.Note* or a non-mapped value such as "fdhjkalfhjdksahfdjksaf."

you will. A search folder can only be created by specifying a *SearchFolder* element during a *CreateFolder* call.

Search folders expose one additional property: *SearchParameters*. This property will be discussed at length in Chapter 15. At this point, it is sufficient to say that the *SearchParameters* property defines the restriction that all items must pass into to show up in the search folder.

TasksFolderType

Last, but not least, is the tasks folder. A task represents a work item that needs to be completed. A tasks folder is intended to contain tasks. As with contacts and contact folders, Exchange Web Services does not allow you to create non-task items inside of a tasks folder. Tasks folders are encountered within XML documents as *TasksFolder* elements and have a folder class that is prefixed by *IPF.Task*.

Folder Operations

Folders wouldn't be very interesting if you couldn't do anything with them. And there wouldn't be a need for a book if folders were not interesting. So, in order to write a book, the Exchange Web Services team had to add folder operations.

GetFolder

The *GetFolder* Web method allows you to get information about an existing folder. Of course, you need a way to identify a folder to be able to access it, and folder ids serve this purpose quite nicely.[7] Unless your application is caching ids in offline mode, you typically start your mailbox access by specifying one of the distinguished folder ids. Let's look at the structure of a *GetFolder* request.

The *GetFolder* operation is exposed through the messages namespace, as are all operations surfaced by Exchange Web Services.[8] *GetFolder* is a relatively simple operation that exposes two elements as shown in Listing 4-1.

LISTING 4-1 *GetFolder* request structure

```
<GetFolder xmlns=".../messages">
  <FolderShape/>
  <FolderIds/>
</GetFolder>
```

---

[7] See Chapter 2, "May I See Your Id?" for an in-depth discussion of folder ids.

[8] The messages namespace is defined in .../messages.

The first of these, as discussed in Chapter 3, is *FolderShape*. The folder shape determines what properties of each folder are returned in the response. The second child element, *FolderIds*, contains a plurality of folder ids (either *DistinguishedFolderId* or *FolderId* elements). If you remember back to the folder id section, a given folder id not only identifies the folder to retrieve, but also identifies the mailbox. As such, you can access folders from multiple mail-boxes within a single *GetFolder* call.

The following is a request for the default properties for both the Inbox and Deleted Items folders.

```
<GetFolder xmlns=".../messages" xmlns:t=".../types">
  <FolderShape>
    <t:BaseShape>Default</t:BaseShape>
  </FolderShape>
  <FolderIds>
    <t:DistinguishedFolderId Id="inbox"/>
    <t:DistinguishedFolderId Id="deleteditems"/>
  </FolderIds>
</GetFolder>
```

And this response is:

```
<GetFolderResponse xmlns:m=".../messages"
                   xmlns:t=".../types"
                   xmlns=".../messages">
  <m:ResponseMessages>
    <m:GetFolderResponseMessage ResponseClass="Success">
      <m:ResponseCode>NoError</m:ResponseCode>
      <m:Folders>
        <t:Folder>
          <t:FolderId Id="AQAtAEFkbWluaX..." ChangeKey="AQAAABYAAA..."/>
          <t:DisplayName>Inbox</t:DisplayName>
          <t:TotalCount>0</t:TotalCount>
          <t:ChildFolderCount>0</t:ChildFolderCount>
          <t:UnreadCount>0</t:UnreadCount>
        </t:Folder>
      </m:Folders>
    </m:GetFolderResponseMessage>
    <m:GetFolderResponseMessage ResponseClass="Success">
      <m:ResponseCode>NoError</m:ResponseCode>
      <m:Folders>
        <t:Folder>
          <t:FolderId Id="AQAtAEFkbWluaX..." ChangeKey="AQAAABYAA..."/>
          <t:DisplayName>Deleted Items</t:DisplayName>
          <t:TotalCount>0</t:TotalCount>
          <t:ChildFolderCount>0</t:ChildFolderCount>
          <t:UnreadCount>0</t:UnreadCount>
        </t:Folder>
      </m:Folders>
    </m:GetFolderResponseMessage>
  </m:ResponseMessages>
</GetFolderResponse>
```

Because the request does not include *Mailbox* subelements for the distinguished folder ids, this operation accesses the caller's own mailbox.

Of course, if you have the actual *FolderId* values for the Inbox and Deleted Items, you can do the same thing using those ids instead.

```
<GetFolder xmlns=".../messages" xmlns:t=".../types">
  <FolderShape>
    <t:BaseShape>Default</t:BaseShape>
  </FolderShape>
  <FolderIds>
    <t:FolderId Id="AQAtAEFkbWluaXN0cmF0..." ChangeKey="AQAAABYAAAAhniO..."/>
    <t:FolderId Id="AQAtAEFkbluaXN0cmF0b..." ChangeKey="AQAAABYAAAAh9R..."/>
  </FolderIds>
</GetFolder>
```

And the response (which presumably is the same) is:

```
<GetFolderResponse xmlns:m=".../messages"
                   xmlns:t=".../types"
                   xmlns=".../messages">
  <m:ResponseMessages>
    <m:GetFolderResponseMessage ResponseClass="Success">
      <m:ResponseCode>NoError</m:ResponseCode>
      <m:Folders>
        <t:Folder>
          <t:FolderId Id="AQAtAEFkbWlu..." ChangeKey="AQAAABYAi..."/>
          <t:DisplayName>Inbox</t:DisplayName>
          <t:TotalCount>0</t:TotalCount>
          <t:ChildFolderCount>0</t:ChildFolderCount>
          <t:UnreadCount>0</t:UnreadCount>
        </t:Folder>
      </m:Folders>
    </m:GetFolderResponseMessage>
    <m:GetFolderResponseMessage ResponseClass="Success">
      <m:ResponseCode>NoError</m:ResponseCode>
      <m:Folders>
        <t:Folder>
          <t:FolderId Id="AQAtAEFkmF0b..." ChangeKey="AQAniO..."/>
          <t:DisplayName>Deleted Items</t:DisplayName>
          <t:TotalCount>0</t:TotalCount>
          <t:ChildFolderCount>0</t:ChildFolderCount>
          <t:UnreadCount>0</t:UnreadCount>
        </t:Folder>
      </m:Folders>
    </m:GetFolderResponseMessage>
  </m:ResponseMessages>
</GetFolderResponse>
```

Listing 4-2 demonstrates how this operation would look in proxy code.

LISTING 4-2 *GetFolder* via proxy classes

```
/// <summary>
/// Returns the inbox and deleted items folders
/// </summary>
/// <param name="binding">Binding which is used to call the EWS web
/// service</param>
/// <returns>Array containing the inbox and deleted items folders</returns>
///
public BaseFolderType[] GetInboxAndDeletedItemsFolders(ExchangeServiceBinding⁹
binding)
{
    // Create our request object and set the response shape
    //
    GetFolderType request = new GetFolderType();
    request.FolderShape = new FolderResponseShapeType();
    request.FolderShape.BaseShape = DefaultShapeNamesType.Default;

    // Set the folders that we wish to request
    //
    DistinguishedFolderIdType inboxId = new DistinguishedFolderIdType();
    inboxId.Id = DistinguishedFolderIdNameType.inbox;
    DistinguishedFolderIdType deletedItemsId = new DistinguishedFolderIdType();
    deletedItemsId.Id = DistinguishedFolderIdNameType.deleteditems;
    request.FolderIds = new BaseFolderIdType[] { inboxId, deletedItemsId };

    // Now make the actual request
    //
    GetFolderResponseType response = binding.GetFolder(request);

    // There should be two response messages - one for each folder we requested
    //
    Debug.Assert(response.ResponseMessages.Items.Length == 2);
    BaseFolderType[] result = new BaseFolderType[2];
    FolderInfoResponseMessageType firstFolderResponse =
        (FolderInfoResponseMessageType)response.ResponseMessages.Items[0];
    result[0] = firstFolderResponse.Folders[0];

    FolderInfoResponseMessageType secondFolderResponse =
        (FolderInfoResponseMessageType)response.ResponseMessages.Items[1];
    result[1] = secondFolderResponse.Folders[0];
    return result;
}
```

Dealing with Response Messages

The previous proxy example brings up an interesting point. The response comes back with an array of *ResponseMessageType* instances. Some interesting items can be found on a *ResponseMessageType* instance (such as the response code and message), but the data you are really interested in (the folders) is not there. Due to the way that the schema is defined, all

---

⁹ Chapter 1, "Welcome to Exchange Web Services" discusses how to create an *ExchangeServiceBinding* instance that references your EWS installation.

responses come back in the same fashion. The actual type of each message is a function of the Web method that is called. *ResponseMessageType* is the base class for all response message types.

Unfortunately, you just have to know what the actual type is. You could certainly call *GetType()* on the response message instance to figure out what the type really is, but it is easier to simply familiarize yourself with the relationship between Web methods and their associated response message types. For instance, in all cases, *CreateFolder*, *GetFolder*, and *UpdateFolder* return response messages of type *FolderInfoResponseMessageType*. *CreateItem*, *GetItem*, and *UpdateItem* always return response messages of *ItemInfoResponseMessageType*. We will identify each of the response message types as we progress through the various Web methods.

The previous example called *GetFolder* and therefore all response messages are of type *FolderInfoResponseMessageType*.

The proxy code in Listing 4-2 specifies that the default shape be returned. What determines the properties that are actually returned? Well, we discussed this in principle in Chapter 3, but we never provided a definitive list of properties for each folder type. Table 4-2 gives the breakdown. Note that if a given property does not exist on a folder, that property is not returned even if it is "in" the shape.

TABLE 4-2 Folder Properties by Type and Shape

Folder type	Default	All Properties
CalendarFolderType	*FolderId, DisplayName, ChildFolderCount*	*FolderId, ParentFolderId, FolderClass, DisplayName, TotalCount, ChildFolderCount*
FolderType	*FolderId, DisplayName, UnreadCount, TotalCount, ChildFolderCount*	*FolderId, ParentFolderId, FolderClass, DisplayName, TotalCount, ChildFolderCount, UnreadCount, ManagedFolderInformation*
ContactsFolderType	*FolderId, DisplayName, TotalCount, ChildFolderCount*	Same as *CalendarFolderType*
SearchFolderType	*FolderId, DisplayName, UnreadCount, TotalCount*	*FolderId, ParentFolderId, FolderClass, DisplayName, TotalCount, ChildFolderCount, UnreadCount, SearchParameters*
TasksFolderType	Same as *FolderType*	*FolderId, ParentFolderId, FolderClass, DisplayName, TotalCount, ChildFolderCount, UnreadCount*

So, what happens if something goes wrong? Well, different errors can be returned depending on the condition at hand (Exchange Store is down, access denied, folder not found).[10] The important thing is that Exchange Web Services attempts to fulfill as much of the request as it can. If you request two folders (one "good" and one "bad"), you should get results for the good one and an error for the bad one as shown in the next example.

---

[10] Errors are discussed in more detail in Chapter 18, "Errors Never Happen."

```
<GetFolder xmlns=".../messages"
           xmlns:t=".../types">
  <FolderShape>
    <t:BaseShape>Default</t:BaseShape>
  </FolderShape>
  <FolderIds>
    <t:FolderId Id="AQAtAEFkbWluaXN0..." ChangeKey="AQAAABY..."/>
    <t:FolderId Id="Blah, blah blah!" ChangeKey="AQAAABY..."/>
  </FolderIds>
</GetFolder>
```

Listing 4-3 displays the response. Notice that the second response message indicates a response code of *ErrorInvalidIdMalformed*.

LISTING 4-3 Failures within a batched operation

```
<GetFolderResponse xmlns:m=".../messages"
                   xmlns:t=".../types"
                   xmlns=".../messages">
  <m:ResponseMessages>
    <m:GetFolderResponseMessage ResponseClass="Success">
      <m:ResponseCode>NoError</m:ResponseCode>
      <m:Folders>
        <t:Folder>
          <t:FolderId Id="AQAtAEFkbWluaXN0..." ChangeKey="AQAAABYAA..."/>
          <t:DisplayName>Inbox</t:DisplayName>
          <t:TotalCount>0</t:TotalCount>
          <t:ChildFolderCount>0</t:ChildFolderCount>
          <t:UnreadCount>0</t:UnreadCount>
        </t:Folder>
      </m:Folders>
    </m:GetFolderResponseMessage>
    <m:GetFolderResponseMessage ResponseClass="Error">
      <m:MessageText>Id is malformed.</m:MessageText>
      <m:ResponseCode>ErrorInvalidIdMalformed</m:ResponseCode>
      <m:DescriptiveLinkKey>0</m:DescriptiveLinkKey>
      <m:Folders/>
    </m:GetFolderResponseMessage>
  </m:ResponseMessages>
</GetFolderResponse>
```

There are limitations to this "fulfill as much as possible" approach. First, if the request is schema invalid, the entire request fails since Exchange Web Services performs schema validation on all requests. In addition, if Exchange Web Services encounters what it considers to be a "batch stop" error, it does not attempt to process any remaining parts within the request.[11]

Moving on, you can access several different mailboxes in a single call as long as you have access to the mailboxes in question as shown in Listing 4-4.

---

[11] "Batch stop" errors are discussed in Chapter 18.

LISTING 4-4 Accessing folders in other mailboxes

```
<GetFolder xmlns=".../messages"
           xmlns:t=".../types">
  <FolderShape>
    <t:BaseShape>AllProperties</t:BaseShape>
  </FolderShape>
  <FolderIds>
    <t:DistinguishedFolderId Id="inbox">
      <t:Mailbox>
        <t:EmailAddress>jane.dow@contoso.com</t:EmailAddress>
      </t:Mailbox>
    </t:DistinguishedFolderId>
    <t:DistinguishedFolderId Id="inbox">
      <t:Mailbox>
        <t:EmailAddress>ken.malcolmson@contoso.com</t:EmailAddress>
      </t:Mailbox>
    </t:DistinguishedFolderId>
  </FolderIds>
</GetFolder>
```

In this example, assuming that you have access to each mailbox specified in the request, the response returns information for both Jane's and Ken's mailboxes. It is important to note that a given Client Access Server (CAS) can service requests only for mailboxes within the Active Directory forest containing that CAS server. If you want to access mailboxes from a different forest, you need to make a request to Exchange Web Services running on a CAS within that forest. This is true even in cross-forest trust scenarios.

CreateFolder

To create a new folder within a mailbox, you use the *CreateFolder* request. The basic structure of *CreateFolder* is shown in Listing 4-5.

LISTING 4-5 Basic structure of *CreateFolder*

```
<CreateFolder xmlns=".../messages"
  <ParentFolderId/>
  <Folders/>
</CreateFolder>
```

The *ParentFolderId* element must contain one and only one folder identifier that represents where the new folder will live. Either a distinguished folder id or normal folder id will do. Because a given folder id identifies not only a folder but also the mailbox containing that folder, the folder id also determines in which mailbox the new folder resides. As a result, assuming that you have the rights to another mailbox, you can use the *CreateFolder* call to create a folder in another mailbox.

The second child element, *Folders*, specifies an array of folders to be created in the destination specified by *ParentFolderId*. To be clear, you can create multiple folders in a single call, but all of those folders end up in the same parent folder. To create folders in different parents, you must make one call per destination folder.

What Does Your New Folder Look Like?

The contents of the *Folders* element are the actual folders that you want created. What kind of folder will it be? Do you want to create a normal folder, search folder, or contacts folder? What will its name be? The *Folders* element is where you specify all of this information. Earlier in this chapter, we discussed each folder type and the properties available on each. Any of the writeable properties can be specified during a *CreateFolder* call. Certain properties are required, although you cannot determine that by looking at the schema, where all are "optional." In addition, properties must be in schema order. For instance, consider *BaseFolderType* defined in types.xsd:

```
<!-- Basic information in a folder definition -->
<xs:complexType name="BaseFolderType" abstract ="true">
    <xs:sequence>
        <xs:element name="FolderId" type="t:FolderIdType" minOccurs="0"/>
        <xs:element name="ParentFolderId" type="t:FolderIdType"
                    minOccurs="0"/>
        <xs:element name="FolderClass" type="xs:string" minOccurs="0"/>
        <xs:element name="DisplayName" type="xs:string" minOccurs="0"/>
        <xs:element name="TotalCount" type="xs:int" minOccurs="0"/>
        <xs:element name="ChildFolderCount" type="xs:int" minOccurs="0"/>
        <xs:element name="ExtendedProperty" type="t:ExtendedPropertyType"
                    minOccurs="0" maxOccurs="unbounded"/>
        <xs:element name="ManagedFolderInformation"
                    type="t:ManagedFolderInformationType"
                    minOccurs="0"/>
    </xs:sequence>
</xs:complexType>
```

The schema expects that, in all cases, the *FolderClass* element occurs before the *DisplayName* element if it exists.[12]

To illustrate, you can try a really basic *CreateFolder* call and see what happens. The following example provides an empty *Folder* element with no defined properties.

```
<CreateFolder xmlns=".../messages"
              xmlns:t=".../types">
  <ParentFolderId>
    <t:DistinguishedFolderId Id="inbox"/>
  </ParentFolderId>
  <Folders>
```

---

[12] An understanding of XML schema is not required to communicate with EWS, but you will be well served if you can learn to read XML schema. The schema defines the public contract for communicating with EWS and, as a result, it dictates the structure of all request and response messages.

```
      <t:Folder/>
   </Folders>
</CreateFolder>
```

Here is the response:

```
<CreateFolderResponse xmlns:m=".../messages"
                      xmlns:t=".../types"
                      xmlns=".../messages">
  <m:ResponseMessages>
    <m:CreateFolderResponseMessage ResponseClass="Error">
      <m:MessageText>The folder save failed due to invalid property
                     values.</m:MessageText>
      <m:ResponseCode>ErrorFolderSavePropertyError</m:ResponseCode>
      <m:DescriptiveLinkKey>0</m:DescriptiveLinkKey>
      <m:MessageXml>
        <t:FieldURI FieldURI="folder:DisplayName"/>
      </m:MessageXml>
      <m:Folders/>
    </m:CreateFolderResponseMessage>
  </m:ResponseMessages>
</CreateFolderResponse>
```

Ah, yes—an error. Why? Because Exchange Web Services requires that you specify a display name for the folder you are creating. Why, then, is *DisplayName* marked as optional in the schema? Because Exchange Web Services uses the same type definitions for both request and response documents. Since Exchange Web Services allows you to retrieve only the folder id using operations such as *GetFolder* and *FindFolder*, it cannot require the *DisplayName* element in the schema without returning non-compliant documents in the responses. A number of types have this same issue. In such cases, properly structured elements are validated by a mixture of schema validation and business logic.

Here is the same code with a display name added.

```
<CreateFolder xmlns=".../messages"
              xmlns:t=".../types">
  <ParentFolderId>
    <t:DistinguishedFolderId Id="inbox"/>
  </ParentFolderId>
  <Folders>
    <t:Folder>
      <t:DisplayName>My First Folder</t:DisplayName>
    </t:Folder>
  </Folders>
</CreateFolder>
```

And the response is:

```
<CreateFolderResponse xmlns:m=".../messages"
                      xmlns:t=".../types"
                      xmlns=".../messages">
  <m:ResponseMessages>
```

```
        <m:CreateFolderResponseMessage ResponseClass="Success">
          <m:ResponseCode>NoError</m:ResponseCode>
          <m:Folders>
            <t:Folder>
              <t:FolderId Id="AAAeAGRhdnu..." ChangeKey="AQAAAB..."/>
            </t:Folder>
          </m:Folders>
        </m:CreateFolderResponseMessage>
      </m:ResponseMessages>
</CreateFolderResponse>
```

That is much better. The response from *CreateFolder* returns the id of the previously created folder. You can see from the response XML why *DisplayName* had to be marked as an
optional element in the schema—the *Folder* element in the response XML does not include a
DisplayName element! Exchange Web Services can't be handing back a non-schema-compliant
response now, can it?

Listing 4-6 does the same thing using the proxy classes. Assume that there is already a Web
service binding object (*ExchangeServiceBinding*). If you need to see how this is done, refer to
Chapter 1.

LISTING 4-6 *CreateFolder* using the proxy

```
// Create our request
//
CreateFolderType createRequest = new CreateFolderType();
createRequest.ParentFolderId = new TargetFolderIdType();

// Set the parent folder that we want to create our new folder in.
//
DistinguishedFolderIdType parentId = new DistinguishedFolderIdType();
parentId.Id = DistinguishedFolderIdNameType.inbox;
createRequest.ParentFolderId.Item = parentId;

// Define the structure of our new folder.
//
FolderType folderToCreate = new FolderType();
folderToCreate.DisplayName = "My First Proxy Folder";

// Set the folder on our request
//
createRequest.Folders = new BaseFolderType[] { folderToCreate };

// Make the call using the service binding instance
//
CreateFolderResponseType response = binding.CreateFolder(createRequest);
// Since we created a single item, we can expect a single response message.
// The response message will be of type FolderInfoResponseMessageType.  We
// must cast it appropriately.
//
FolderInfoResponseMessageType responseMessage =
        response.ResponseMessages.Items[0] as FolderInfoResponseMessageType;
if (responseMessage.ResponseCode == ResponseCodeType.NoError)
```

```
{
    Console.WriteLine("New folder id is :" +
            responseMessage.Folders[0].FolderId.Id);
}
else
{
    Console.WriteLine("Hmmm.  CreateFolder failed.  Error code: " +
            responseMessage.ResponseCode.ToString());
}
```

Creating Strongly Typed Folders

The easiest way to create non-generic folders, such as calendar folders or contact folders, is to specify the appropriate element in your request. In other words, if you want to create a contacts folder, say so.

```
<CreateFolder xmlns=".../messages"
              xmlns:t=".../types">
  <ParentFolderId>
    <t:DistinguishedFolderId Id="inbox"/>
  </ParentFolderId>
  <Folders>
    <t:ContactsFolder>
      <t:DisplayName>My Contacts Folder</t:DisplayName>
    </t:ContactsFolder>
  </Folders>
</CreateFolder>
```

As you see by the response, Exchange Web Services is happy to comply.

```
<CreateFolderResponse xmlns:m=".../messages"
                      xmlns:t=".../types"
                      xmlns=".../messages">
  <m:ResponseMessages>
    <m:CreateFolderResponseMessage ResponseClass="Success">
      <m:ResponseCode>NoError</m:ResponseCode>
      <m:Folders>
        <t:ContactsFolder>
          <t:FolderId Id="AAAeAGRhdnN..." ChangeKey="AwAAABYAA..."/>
        </t:ContactsFolder>
      </m:Folders>
    </m:CreateFolderResponseMessage>
  </m:ResponseMessages>
</CreateFolderResponse>
```

In fact, Exchange Web Services does this for all non-generic folders. Let's look at another example that creates several non-generic folders. For fun, the following example adds a search folder for all items in the Inbox whose size is greater than 100,000 bytes.[13]

---

[13] Search folders are covered in Chapter 15.

```
<CreateFolder xmlns=".../messages"
              xmlns:t=".../types">
  <ParentFolderId>
    <t:DistinguishedFolderId Id="inbox"/>
  </ParentFolderId>
  <Folders>
    <t:ContactsFolder>
      <t:DisplayName>My Contacts Folder?</t:DisplayName>
    </t:ContactsFolder>
    <t:CalendarFolder>
      <t:DisplayName>My Calendar Folder?</t:DisplayName>
    </t:CalendarFolder>
    <t:TasksFolder>
      <t:DisplayName>My Tasks Folder?</t:DisplayName>
    </t:TasksFolder>
    <t:SearchFolder>
      <t:DisplayName>My Search Folder?</t:DisplayName>
      <t:SearchParameters>
        <t:Restriction>
          <t:IsGreaterThan>
            <t:FieldURI FieldURI="item:Size"/>
            <t:FieldURIOrConstant>
              <t:Constant Value="100000"/>
            </t:FieldURIOrConstant>
          </t:IsGreaterThan>
        </t:Restriction>
        <t:BaseFolderIds>
          <t:DistinguishedFolderId Id="inbox"/>
        </t:BaseFolderIds>
      </t:SearchParameters>
    </t:SearchFolder>
  </Folders>
</CreateFolder>
```

The response shows that all of the folders are created and are the types of folders that were requested.

```
<CreateFolderResponse xmlns:m=".../messages"
                      xmlns:t=".../types"
                      xmlns=".../messages">
    <m:ResponseMessages>
      <m:CreateFolderResponseMessage ResponseClass="Success">
        <m:ResponseCode>NoError</m:ResponseCode>
        <m:Folders>
          <t:ContactsFolder>
            <t:FolderId Id="AAAeAGR..." ChangeKey="AwAAABYAAADcPi..."/>
          </t:ContactsFolder>
        </m:Folders>
      </m:CreateFolderResponseMessage>
      <m:CreateFolderResponseMessage ResponseClass="Success">
        <m:ResponseCode>NoError</m:ResponseCode>
        <m:Folders>
          <t:CalendarFolder>
            <t:FolderId Id="AAAeA..." ChangeKey="AgAAABYAAAD..."/>
          </t:CalendarFolder>
```

```
      </m:Folders>
    </m:CreateFolderResponseMessage>
    <m:CreateFolderResponseMessage ResponseClass="Success">
      <m:ResponseCode>NoError</m:ResponseCode>
      <m:Folders>
        <t:TasksFolder>
          <t:FolderId Id="AAAeAGRh..." ChangeKey="BAAAABYAA..."/>
        </t:TasksFolder>
      </m:Folders>
    </m:CreateFolderResponseMessage>
    <m:CreateFolderResponseMessage ResponseClass="Success">
      <m:ResponseCode>NoError</m:ResponseCode>
      <m:Folders>
        <t:SearchFolder>
          <t:FolderId Id="AAAeAGRh..." ChangeKey="BwAAABYAAADcP..."/>
        </t:SearchFolder>
      </m:Folders>
    </m:CreateFolderResponseMessage>
  </m:ResponseMessages>
</CreateFolderResponse>
```

MoveFolder

Sometimes you need to move a folder from one location to another. Doing so moves not only the folder in question, but all of the subfolders and items contained within that folder. It is worthy to note that moving a search folder does nothing to the items "contained" within the search folder because those items are present based on the filter evaluation for the search folder. However, you cannot move distinguished folders.

Look at the structure of *MoveFolder* shown in Listing 4-7.

LISTING 4-7 *MoveFolder* structure

```
<MoveFolder xmlns=".../messages">
  <ToFolderId/>
  <FolderIds/>
</MoveFolder>
```

MoveFolder is defined in the messages namespace. The first child element within *MoveFolder* is *ToFolderId*, which contains a single folder id representing the destination for the folder(s) that are to be moved. You can use either a distinguished or a normal folder id. The second child element, *FolderIds*, represents an array of folder ids that are to be moved into the folder identified by the *ToFolderId* element. You can specify a plurality of folder ids, although all specified folders are moved to the same destination. Should you need to move folders to different destinations, you need to make multiple *MoveFolder* calls—one for each destination. Note that you cannot move a folder from one mailbox to another; moves must occur within the confines of a single mailbox.

The following is a *MoveFolder* call that moves a newly created folder to the Sent Items folder.

```
<MoveFolder xmlns=".../messages"
            xmlns:t=".../types">
   <ToFolderId>
     <t:DistinguishedFolderId Id="sentitems"/>
   </ToFolderId>
   <FolderIds>
     <t:FolderId Id="AAAeAGRhdnNOZXJAZX..." ChangeKey="AQAAABYAAAD..."/>
   </FolderIds>
</MoveFolder>
```

The response is:

```
<MoveFolderResponse xmlns:m=".../messages"
                    xmlns:t=".../types"
                    xmlns=".../messages">
   <m:ResponseMessages>
      <m:MoveFolderResponseMessage ResponseClass="Success">
         <m:ResponseCode>NoError</m:ResponseCode>
         <m:Folders>
            <t:Folder>
               <t:FolderId Id="AAAeAGRhdnN..." ChangeKey="AQAAABYAAA..."/>
            </t:Folder>
         </m:Folders>
      </m:MoveFolderResponseMessage>
   </m:ResponseMessages>
</MoveFolderResponse>
```

Listing 4-8 demonstrates how to do this by using the proxy classes.

LISTING 4-8 Moving a folder by using the proxy classes

```
MoveFolderType moveRequest = new MoveFolderType();
moveRequest.ToFolderId = new TargetFolderIdType();

// Set the parent folder that we want to move our folder to.
//
DistinguishedFolderIdType destinationId = new DistinguishedFolderIdType();
destinationId.Id = DistinguishedFolderIdNameType.sentitems;
moveRequest.ToFolderId.Item = destinationId;

// Set the folder to move.  The GetFolderToMove() implementation is not provided
// here.
BaseFolderIdType folderIdToMove = GetFolderToMove();

moveRequest.FolderIds = new BaseFolderIdType[] { folderIdToMove };

// Make the call.  Note that binding is an instance of ExchangeServiceBinding.
//
MoveFolderResponseType response = binding.MoveFolder(moveRequest);

// Since we moved a single item, we can expect a single response message.
// The response message will be of type FolderInfoResponseMessageType.  We
```

```
// must cast it appropriately if we want to get the folder
// id that the web method returns.
//
FolderInfoResponseMessageType responseMessage =
        response.ResponseMessages.Items[0] as
                FolderInfoResponseMessageType;

if (responseMessage.ResponseCode == ResponseCodeType.NoError)
{
    Console.WriteLine("Folder moved successfully!  FolderId: " +
        responseMessage.Folders[0].FolderId.Id);}
else
{
    Console.WriteLine("Hmmm.  MoveFolder failed.  Error code: " +
        responseMessage.ResponseCode.ToString());
}
```

Notice that the basic structure of proxy programming is the same for all requests we have covered so far. You will get the hang of it pretty quickly. As with *GetFolder* and *CreateFolder*, *MoveFolder* returns *FolderInfoResponseMessageType* instances.

When you move a folder from one place to another, its folder id remains the same. Thus, in reality, you *don't* need to get the *FolderId* from the response. In addition, any folders and items contained within the moved folder also retain their original ids.

MoveFolder and Delegate Access

As discussed briefly in Chapter 2, delegate access allows a caller to access a mailbox that is not his/her primary mailbox. Of course, the caller must have permission to access that mailbox. Calls, such as *MoveFolder*, introduce a slight twist in delegate access. Let's work through an example. Jane has delegate rights to Ken's mailbox. Jane wants to create a folder in Ken's mailbox, so she makes a call like this:

```
<CreateFolder xmlns=".../messages"
              xmlns:t=".../types">
  <ParentFolderId>
    <t:DistinguishedFolderId Id="inbox">
      <t:Mailbox>
        <t:EmailAddress>ken.malcolmson@contoso.com</t:EmailAddress>
      </t:Mailbox>
    </t:DistinguishedFolderId>
  </ParentFolderId>
  <Folders>
    <t:Folder>
      <t:DisplayName>Folder created by Jane for Ken</t:DisplayName>
    </t:Folder>
  </Folders>
</CreateFolder>
```

You know from Chapter 2 that this creates the folder in the Inbox of the *ken.malcolmson@contoso.com* mailbox and returns an id that points to the newly created folder. Now, Jane tries to move it to the Sent Items folder.

```
<MoveFolder xmlns=".../messages"
            xmlns:t=".../types">
   <ToFolderId>
     <t:DistinguishedFolderId Id="sentitems"/>
   </ToFolderId>
   <FolderIds>
      <t:FolderId Id="AAAeAGRhdnNOZXJAZX..." ChangeKey="AQAAABYAAAD..."/>
   </FolderIds>
</MoveFolder>
```

Remember, this call is coming from Jane, and the folder we are moving is in Ken's mailbox. So, here is a trick question: Where does the folder end up? The Sent Items folder, right? The Sent Items folder in *which* mailbox? You *think* it would be Ken's mailbox, right? But recall that, in Chapter 2, we discussed how the absence of the *Mailbox* subelement in a *DistinguishedFolderId* element suggests that the distinguished folder is coming from the *caller's* mailbox. And who is the caller? Jane. The implication is that this *MoveFolder* call moves the folder in Ken's mailbox to Jane's Sent Items folder. That is actually what it *tries* to do, but of course, it fails because cross-mailbox moves are not supported in Exchange Web Services.

So, how does Jane fix this request? She needs to be explicit about where she wants to put the folder. Listing 4-9 shows the correct way to make this request.

LISTING 4-9 Delegate access and moving folders

```
<MoveFolder xmlns=".../messages"
            xmlns:t=".../types">
   <ToFolderId>
     <t:DistinguishedFolderId Id="sentitems">
       <t:Mailbox>
         <t:EmailAddress>ken.malcolmson@contoso.com</t:EmailAddress>
       </t:Mailbox>
     </t:DistinguishedFolderId>
   </ToFolderId>
   <FolderIds>
     <t:FolderId Id="AAAeAGRhdnNOZXJAZX..." ChangeKey="AQAAABYAAAD..."/>
   </FolderIds>
</MoveFolder>
```

Because the folder that Jane is attempting to move is in Ken's mailbox, she must ensure that the destination folder is also in Ken's mailbox. Of course, if Ken is making this call instead of Jane, he does not need to add the *Mailbox* element because the missing *Mailbox* element suggests that he is dealing with the caller's Sent Items folder, which in this case is Ken's.

Important This distinguished folder delegate access issue crops up in a number of places such as *MoveFolder*, *CopyFolder*, *MoveItem*, *CopyItem*, *SendItem*, and *CreateItem* (for forward, reply, accept item, etc.)—really, anywhere that you are dealing with an existing item and have the ability to reference a destination to be used during the operation.

CopyFolder

CopyFolder is almost identical to *MoveFolder* with two small exceptions.

1. You make the call using the *CopyFolder* element instead of *MoveFolder*.

2. The copied folder has a different id than the source folder. In addition, all folders and items contained within the copied folder have different ids than their source counterparts.

Rather than rehash what we discussed for *MoveFolder*, here is an example:

```
<CopyFolder xmlns=".../messages"
            xmlns:t=".../types">
   <ToFolderId>
      <t:DistinguishedFolderId Id="msgfolderroot"/>
   </ToFolderId>
   <FolderIds>
      <t:FolderId Id="AAAeAGRhdnN0ZXJJAZ..." ChangeKey="AQAAABYAAA..."/>
   </FolderIds>
</CopyFolder>
```

And the response is:

```
<CopyFolderResponse xmlns:m=".../messages"
                    xmlns:t=".../types"
                    xmlns=".../messages">
   <m:ResponseMessages>
      <m:CopyFolderResponseMessage ResponseClass="Success">
         <m:ResponseCode>NoError</m:ResponseCode>
         <m:Folders>
            <t:Folder>
               <t:FolderId Id="AAAeAGRhdnN..." ChangeKey="AQAAABYAA..."/>
            </t:Folder>
         </m:Folders>
      </m:CopyFolderResponseMessage>
   </m:ResponseMessages>
</CopyFolderResponse>
```

Like its close relative *MoveFolder*, *CopyFolder* returns *FolderInfoResponseMessageType* instances—one for each folder that is copied.

One interesting situation arises when you consider operations that relocate folders. What happens if you try to move or copy a folder into itself or one of its subfolders? It would be neat if it created a black hole, but that didn't pass the first review of the design document. Legal considered that the liability concerns outweighed the "neat-o" factor. In addition, black holes don't have a public constructor, so developers were out of luck. If you do try such a thing, you get the extremely descriptive response code *ErrorMoveCopyFailed*. No black hole for you!

FindFolder

FindFolder is a versatile operation. With *FindFolder*, you can

- Find all of the folders within a parent folder or group of parent folders (both shallow and deep traversal).
- Return paged views of such folders so that you only retrieve the portions of the view that you wish to deal with at that point. This is useful for large result sets.
- Find all such folders that have properties that pass a filter.

Listing 4-10 depicts the structure of a *FindFolder* request.

LISTING 4-10 *FindFolder* request structure

```
<FindFolder Traversal="Shallow | Deep"
            xmlns=".../messages">
  <FolderShape/>
  <IndexedPageFolderView/> | <FractionalPageFolderView/>
  <Restriction/>
  <ParentFolderIds/>
</FindFolder>
```

Note that the *Restriction* element is discussed in Chapter 14 and the *IndexedPageFolderView* and *FractionalPageFolderView* elements are discussed in Chapter 15.

Traversal

The *Traversal* attribute identifies the type of traversal you wish to perform in your request. This attribute must be specified. There is no default value. Three valid values for the traversal attribute are shown in Table 4-3.

TABLE 4-3 Traversal Attribute Values

Traversal value	Description
Shallow	Consider only folders that are direct children of the parent folder(s) in question
Deep	Consider both direct children as well as all subfolders contained within those children as well as the children's children, etc.
SoftDeleted	Consider only those items that are soft deleted from the parent folders specified

We will cover soft deleting shortly, but the general idea is that when you soft-delete an item or folder, you are not actually moving that object to the Deleted Items folder. You are simply marking it for deletion, but the object stays where it is. If you wish to find a folder that you soft-deleted from the Inbox, you do a search on the Inbox with a traversal type of *SoftDeleted*. If you conduct a *FindFolder* request on the Deleted Items folder with a traversal type of *SoftDeleted*, you do not find that folder. Why? Because it is still in the Inbox, but is just hiding. Shhhh!

The following is an example:

```
<FindFolder xmlns=".../messages" Traversal="Shallow">
  <!-- child nodes omitted for brevity -->
</FindFolder>
```

Using the proxy objects, you simply set the appropriate property on the request object.

```
FindFolderType request = new FindFolderType();
request.Traversal = FolderQueryTraversalType.Shallow;14
```

ParentFolderIds

The required *ParentFolderIds* element contains an array of parent folder ids from which to perform the search. Either distinguished or normal folder ids are permissible. The response contains a node for each supplied parent folder id in the same order as they are supplied. Listing 4-11 is a simple *FindFolder* on both the Inbox and the Drafts distinguished folders.[15]

LISTING 4-11 Parent folder ids in *FindFolder*

```
<FindFolder xmlns=".../messages"
            xmlns:t=".../types"
            Traversal="Shallow">
   <FolderShape>
      <t:BaseShape>Default</t:BaseShape>
   </FolderShape>
   <ParentFolderIds>
      <t:DistinguishedFolderId Id="inbox"/>
      <t:DistinguishedFolderId Id="drafts"/>
   </ParentFolderIds>
</FindFolder>
```

The response contains two *FindFolderResponseMessage* elements, one for each parent folder that was specified.

---

[14] Note that although *Traversal* is a value type, no *TraversalSpecified* property needs to be set because *Traversal* is a required attribute.

[15] Before making the request in Listing 4-11, we created a folder in the Inbox and another in the Drafts folder so that we had data to return.

```
<FindFolderResponse xmlns:m=".../messages"
                    xmlns:t=".../types"
                    xmlns=".../messages">
    <m:ResponseMessages>
        <m:FindFolderResponseMessage ResponseClass="Success">
            <m:ResponseCode>NoError</m:ResponseCode>
            <m:RootFolder TotalItemsInView="1" IncludesLastItemInRange="true">
                <t:Folders>
                    <t:Folder>
                        <t:FolderId Id="AQAtAEX..." ChangeKey="AQAAABY..."/>
                        <t:DisplayName>Subfolder of the inbox</t:DisplayName>
                        <t:TotalCount>0</t:TotalCount>
                        <t:ChildFolderCount>0</t:ChildFolderCount>
                        <t:UnreadCount>0</t:UnreadCount>
                    </t:Folder>
                </t:Folders>
            </m:RootFolder>
        </m:FindFolderResponseMessage>
        <m:FindFolderResponseMessage ResponseClass="Success">
            <m:ResponseCode>NoError</m:ResponseCode>
            <m:RootFolder TotalItemsInView="1" IncludesLastItemInRange="true">
                <t:Folders>
                    <t:Folder>
                        <t:FolderId Id="AQAtAEF..." ChangeKey="AQAAABYA..."/>
                        <t:DisplayName>Subfolder of drafts</t:DisplayName>
                        <t:TotalCount>0</t:TotalCount>
                        <t:ChildFolderCount>0</t:ChildFolderCount>
                        <t:UnreadCount>0</t:UnreadCount>
                    </t:Folder>
                </t:Folders>
            </m:RootFolder>
        </m:FindFolderResponseMessage>
    </m:ResponseMessages>
</FindFolderResponse>
```

You can make this same request by using proxy classes as shown in Listing 4-12.

LISTING 4-12 Calling *FindFolder* on two parent folders by using the proxy

```
// Create the request, set the traversal and the folder response shape
//
FindFolderType request = new FindFolderType();
request.Traversal = FolderQueryTraversalType.Shallow;
request.FolderShape = new FolderResponseShapeType();
request.FolderShape.BaseShape = DefaultShapeNamesType.Default;

// Set the root folders from which to perform the search
//
DistinguishedFolderIdType inbox = new DistinguishedFolderIdType();
inbox.Id = DistinguishedFolderIdNameType.inbox;
DistinguishedFolderIdType drafts = new DistinguishedFolderIdType();
drafts.Id = DistinguishedFolderIdNameType.drafts;
request.ParentFolderIds = new BaseFolderIdType[] {inbox, drafts};
```

```
// Make the request
//
FindFolderResponseType response = binding.FindFolder(request);

// Iterate over the results
//
for (int folderIndex = 0;
     folderIndex<response.ResponseMessages.Items.Length;
     folderIndex++)
{
    FindFolderResponseMessageType message =
          response.ResponseMessages.Items[folderIndex] as
              FindFolderResponseMessageType;
    Console.WriteLine(
            "Root Folder #{0} contained {1} subfolders",
            folderIndex,
            message.RootFolder.TotalItemsInView);

    // For each parent folder, let's write out the names of the child
    // folders.
    //
    foreach (FolderType folder in message.RootFolder.Folders)
    {
        Console.WriteLine("                  Folder: " + folder.DisplayName);
    }
}
```

As you can see in Figure 4-3, the proxy implementation yields the same result as the XML request.

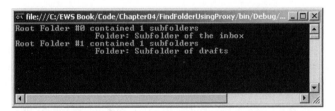

FIGURE 4-3 Console window results for proxy example

FindFolder is the first method you run into that doesn't return *FolderInfoResponseMessageType* instances. You must deal with *FindFolderResponseMessageType* when examining *FindFolder* responses. The main difference between these two response message types is that the *FindFolder* version includes information about paging operations, which we will discuss in Chapter 15.

DeleteFolder

You don't want a certain folder anymore? Well, delete it. *DeleteFolder* is used to get rid of folders that you no longer need. Listing 4-13 shows the basic structure.

LISTING 4-13 *DeleteFolder* structure

```
<DeleteFolder xmlns=".../messages "
              DeleteType="HardDelete | SoftDelete | MoveToDeletedItems">
  <FolderIds>
    <!-- List of folder ids to delete -->
  </FolderIds>
</DeleteFolder>
```

The *FolderIds* element contains the ids for all of the folders you wish to delete. The schema allows you to pass in distinguished folder ids, but any such attempt is futile and is greeted by the *ErrorDeleteDistinguishedFolder* response code. You can supply one or more folders for deletion. These folder ids can even come from different mailboxes (assuming, of course, that you have the appropriate access).

DeleteType Attribute

The required *DeleteType* attribute can be set to one of three values: *HardDelete*, *SoftDelete*, or *MoveToDeletedItems*.

HardDelete   When you hard-delete a folder, it is gone. It does not appear in the Deleted Items folder. All items contained within that folder are also hard deleted.[16]

SoftDelete   You might think that soft-deleting a folder moves it to the Deleted Items folder, but you would be mistaken. Soft-deleting a folder puts it in a strange state. The deleted folder has not changed its parentage; rather, it is flagged so that it no longer "appears" as a subfolder. We mentioned earlier that the only way to see these folders is to make a *FindFolder* call with a *SoftDeleted* traversal.

A problem exists with soft-deleted folders, however. Although the delete works fine, once the folder is in that state, you can't do anything to it. You can't hard delete it, get it, move it, or copy it. The only thing you can do is find it via *FindFolder*. At this point, soft deleting is something you should probably avoid through Exchange Web Services.

MoveToDeletedItems   When most people think of deleting a folder using a client such as Outlook Web Access or Office Outlook, they assume that it ends up in the Deleted Items folder. Really, there is no difference between calling *DeleteFolder* with a *DeleteType* of *MoveToDeletedItems* and simply calling *MoveFolder* and moving it to the Deleted Items folder.

---

[16] Search folders are an exception to this. The items are not really "contained" within a search folder and therefore are not deleted when the search folder is deleted, regardless of the *DeleteType* value.

Listing 4-14 displays an example of calling *DeleteFolder*. In this case, it is a hard delete.

LISTING 4-14 *DeleteFolder* call example (XML)

```
<DeleteFolder xmlns=".../messages"
              xmlns:t=".../types"
              DeleteType="HardDelete">
   <FolderIds>
      <t:FolderId Id="AQAtAEFkbW..." ChangeKey="AQAAABYAAAAZ/..."/>
   </FolderIds>
</DeleteFolder>
```

And the response is:

```
<DeleteFolderResponse xmlns:m=".../messages"
                      xmlns:t=".../types"
                      xmlns=".../messages">
   <m:ResponseMessages>
      <m:DeleteFolderResponseMessage ResponseClass="Success">
         <m:ResponseCode>NoError</m:ResponseCode>
      </m:DeleteFolderResponseMessage>
   </m:ResponseMessages>
</DeleteFolderResponse>
```

Notice that the response indicates simply whether the operation succeeded or not. As mentioned in the discussion of *DeleteType* values, if you use a *DeleteType* of *SoftDelete* or *MoveToDeletedItems*, the folder isn't really gone. In fact, the folder id is still quite valid (with the exception of the *SoftDelete* issues mentioned earlier). You can call *GetFolder* on a folder that was deleted with a *DeleteType* of *MoveToDeletedItems* and it happily complies.

Here is a *DeleteFolder* call with the proxy classes.

```
/// <summary>
/// Delete a folder using the proxy classes
/// </summary>
/// <param name="binding">ExchangeServiceBinding to use for the call</param>
/// <param name="folderToDelete">Id of the folder to delete</param>
///
public static void DeleteFolder(ExchangeServiceBinding binding, FolderIdType
folderToDelete)
{
  DeleteFolderType request = new DeleteFolderType();
  request.DeleteType = DisposalType.HardDelete;
  request.FolderIds = new BaseFolderIdType[] { folderToDelete };
  DeleteFolderResponseType response = binding.DeleteFolder(request);

  // We deal directly with ResponseMessageType here.  There is no derived class.
  //
  ResponseMessageType responseMessage = response.ResponseMessages.Items[0];
  Console.WriteLine("Response was: " + responseMessage.ResponseCode.ToString());
}
```

Users associate the Deleted Items folder with the ability to "empty" that folder of its contents. If you want to empty the contents of the Deleted Items folder, you need to perform a hard delete on the items contained therein. This would imply four calls:

1. *FindFolder* on the Deleted Items folder to retrieve all folders

2. *FindItem* on the Deleted Items folder to retrieve all items

3. *DeleteFolder* (*HardDelete*) using the ids returned in step 1

4. *DeleteItem* (*HardDelete*) using the ids returned in step 2

UpdateFolder

The *UpdateFolder* operation is used whenever you want to add, modify, or delete a property on a given folder. *UpdateFolder* has an interesting structure that may take a little time to get used to. Look at the structure of the *UpdateFolder* call shown in Listing 4-15.

LISTING 4-15 *UpdateFolder* structure

```
<UpdateFolder xmlns=".../messages.xsd"
              xmlns:t=".../types.xsd">
  <FolderChanges>
    <t:FolderChange>
      <t:FolderId/> | <t:DistinguishedFolderId/>
      <t:Updates/>
    </t:FolderChange>
  </FolderChanges>
</UpdateFolder>
```

First, notice that *UpdateFolder* exposes the *FolderChanges* element. The plural nature of this name suggests that you can perform multiple changes within a single request. The *FolderChanges* element contains *FolderChange* instances, one for each folder that you want to update.

Looking at a given *FolderChange* element, you notice another plural element called *Updates*. The *Updates* element contains one child element for each property of a given folder that you wish to create, modify, append, or delete. So, you have five properties that you want to modify on a given folder? Then you need to supply five child elements in the *Updates* collection, each of which indicates the type of update you are performing for that property.

```
<t:FolderChange>
  <t:FolderId/> | <t:DistinguishedFolderId/>
  <t:Updates>
    <t:SetFolderField/> |
    <t:DeleteFolderField/> |
    <t:AppendToFolderField/>
  </t:Updates>
</t:FolderChange>
```

What are these child elements that you need to add to the *Updates* node? Three differ-ent update operations can be performed on folder properties, and, therefore, there are three different folder field update types. Each of these ultimately derives from the abstract *ChangeDescriptionType* schema type as shown in Figure 4-4. Item updates also follow the same pattern, but these are discussed in Chapter 5, "Items."

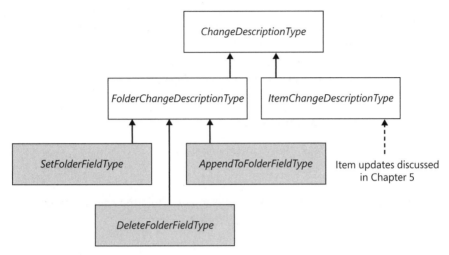

FIGURE 4-4 Change Description hierarchy

SetFolderFieldType

The first of the three folder field change types that we will discuss is *SetFolderFieldType*. You use *SetFolderFieldType* instances whenever you want to add or update a property on a given folder. If the property in question already has a value, the set operation replaces the existing value. If the property does not exist on the folder, then the property is added. You specify a *SetFolderFieldType* instance in an XML document using the *SetFolderField* element.[17] The *SetFolderField* element has the following structure:

```
<SetFolderField>
  <t:FieldURI/> | <t:IndexedFieldURI/> | <t:ExtendedFieldURI/>
  <t:Folder> | <t:CalendarFolder> | <t:ContactsFolder> |
      <t:SearchFolder> | <t:TasksFolder>
</SetFolderField>
```

The first element that appears in *SetFolderField* is the property path you wish to update. Remember that a property path does not represent the value of the property, but merely identifies the property that is to be modified. This is a singular path, meaning that you need to provide one *SetFolderField* for each property that you want to update on a given folder. Let's say you want to update the display name for the folder. You would use the property path for the *folder:DisplayName* as follows:

---

[17] However, if you are dealing with auto-generated proxies, you do not have to concern yourself with the local ele-ment names of request. You simply deal with the *SetFolderFieldType* class.

```
<t:SetFolderField>
  <t:FieldURI FieldURI="folder:DisplayName"/>
  <!-- more to come -->
</t:SetFolderField>
```

You can specify the property to update using a *FieldURI*, *IndexedFieldURI*, or *ExtendedFieldURI* element.[18]

The second element you need to supply within *SetFolderField* is the actual folder state that you wish to update. Here, you can use *Folder*, *CalendarFolder*, *ContactsFolder*, *SearchFolder*, or *TasksFolder*. If, as in the example, you are updating the display name of the folder, the only state element that the folder can contain is the display name.

```
<t:SetFolderField>
  <t:FieldURI FieldURI="folder:DisplayName"/>
  <t:Folder>
    <t:DisplayName>New Display Name</t:DisplayName>
  </t:Folder>
</t:SetFolderField>
```

In fact, if you try to add more than one child element within the *Folder* element, you encounter a response code of *ErrorIncorrectUpdatePropertyCount*.

```
<t:SetFolderField>
  <t:FieldURI FieldURI="folder:DisplayName"/>
  <t:Folder>
    <!-- Can't have two state elements.  This will result
         in an error. -->
    <t:FolderClass>IPF.Note.Contoso</t:FolderClass>
    <t:DisplayName>New Display Name</t:DisplayName>
  </t:Folder>
</t:SetFolderField>
```

In addition, the property path and folder element for which you are specifying a value must match. If they do not, you receive an error code of *ErrorUpdatePropertyMismatch*. For example, the following *SetFolderField* element has a disagreement between the property path and the folder state. Notice that the property path is for the display name, but the folder state specifies the *FolderClass* property.

```
<t:SetFolderField>
  <t:FieldURI FieldURI="folder:DisplayName"/>
  <t:Folder>
    <!-- property disagreement -->
    <t:FolderClass>IPF.Note.Contoso</t:FolderClass>
  </t:Folder>
</t:SetFolderField>
```

So, what if you wanted to set two properties on a given folder in a single call? To do this, simply use two *SetFolderField* elements as shown in Figure 4-5.

---

[18] *ExtendedFieldURI* is discussed in detail in Chapter 13, "Extended Properties."

```
<t:FolderChange>
  <t:FolderId Id="AQAtAEFkbW…" ChangeKey="AQAAABYA…"/>
  <t:Updates>
```

```
    <t:SetFolderField>
      <t:FieldURI FieldURI="folder:DisplayName"/>
      <t:Folder>
        <t:DisplayName>My New DisplayName</t:DisplayName>
      </t:Folder>
    </t:SetFolderField>
```
← *DisplayName* update

```
    <t:SetFolderField>
      <t:FieldURI FieldURI="folder.FolderClass"/>
      <t:Folder>
        <t:FolderClass>IPF.Note.Custom</t:FolderClass>
      </t:Folder>
    </t:SetFolderField>
```
← *FolderClass* update

```
  </t:Updates>
</t:FolderChange>
```

FIGURE 4-5 Setting two properties within a single call

Why Only One Property Change Per Change Description?

At first glance, it might seem easier if the Exchange Web Services schema got rid of the property path in *SetFolderField* and just allowed you to set all of the properties of interest within the *Folder* element. While that would have some advantages, it would introduce a subtle constraint that could prove undesirable. Based on the way that the Exchange Web Services schema is written, the order of elements within a given *Folder* instance must match the order specified within the schema for it to be schema valid. For instance, although *FolderClass* and *DisplayName* are both valid child elements of *FolderType*, *FolderClass* must *always* come before *DisplayName* if both exist. The following would be schema invalid:

```
<t:Folder>
  <t:DisplayName>Schema Invalid Folder</t:DisplayName>
  <t:FolderClass>IPF.Note.Contoso</t:FolderClass>
</t:Folder>
```

Now, hypothetically, what if the outcome of setting *FolderClass* before *DisplayName* is different than the outcome of setting *DisplayName* before *FolderClass*? Well, if the schema required you to specify all of the properties of interest within a single *Folder* element, you would be out of luck. To be fair, developers could provide a hybrid approach in which you either combine property changes into one *SetFolderField* element if you don't care about order or list them individually if you do. Yet, that approach seems to increase the complexity of an already complex operation, and therefore is cast forth, vanquished, and otherwise removed from consideration.

Considering the multiple property update scenario, you can stick this all together into a complete call, which is shown in Listing 4-16.

LISTING 4-16 Updating multiple properties in a single call

```
<UpdateFolder xmlns=".../messages"
              xmlns:t=".../types">
  <FolderChanges>
    <t:FolderChange>
      <t:FolderId Id="AQAtAEFkbWlu..." ChangeKey="AQAAABYAAABO..."/>
      <t:Updates>
        <t:SetFolderField>
          <t:FieldURI FieldURI="folder:DisplayName"/>
          <t:Folder>
            <t:DisplayName>My New DisplayName</t:DisplayName>
          </t:Folder>
        </t:SetFolderField>
        <t:SetFolderField>
          <t:FieldURI FieldURI="folder:FolderClass"/>
          <t:Folder>
            <t:FolderClass>IPF.Note.Contoso</t:FolderClass>
          </t:Folder>
        </t:SetFolderField>
      </t:Updates>
    </t:FolderChange>
  </FolderChanges>
</UpdateFolder>
```

The preceding call sets *both* the display name and the folder class on a single folder, in that order. It is interesting to note that these operations are atomic, meaning that if one of the property set operations fails, all of them fail.

Of course, you can also do this through the proxy classes as demonstrated by Listing 4-17.

LISTING 4-17 Setting two folder properties using a single *UpdateFolder* call

```
public static void UpdateFolderSet(
                ExchangeServiceBinding binding,
                FolderIdType folderIdToChange)
{
    // Create the request
    //
    UpdateFolderType request = new UpdateFolderType();

    // Create our single folder change element (we are only updating a
    // single folder)
    //
    FolderChangeType folderChange = new FolderChangeType();

    // Here is another "Item" property.  This one is for the folder id to
```

```
// update
//
folderChange.Item = folderIdToChange;

// We are updating two properties
//
folderChange.Updates = new FolderChangeDescriptionType[2];

// Now let's fill in the info for the display name update
//
SetFolderFieldType displayNameUpdate = new SetFolderFieldType();

// Set the path first
//
PathToUnindexedFieldType displayNamePath = new
                            PathToUnindexedFieldType();
displayNamePath.FieldURI = UnindexedFieldURIType.folderDisplayName;
displayNameUpdate.Item = displayNamePath;

// Now set the state
//
FolderType folderDisplayNameState = new FolderType();

// Remember that we can only set a single property and it must match our
// path from above
//

folderDisplayNameState.DisplayName = "New Folder Name";

// That's exciting, now we have an Item1 too!  This one refers to the
// Folder state to update
//
displayNameUpdate.Item1 = folderDisplayNameState;

// And again for the FolderClass (less comments this time)
//
SetFolderFieldType folderClassUpdate = new SetFolderFieldType();
PathToUnindexedFieldType folderClassPath = new
                             PathToUnindexedFieldType();
folderClassPath.FieldURI = UnindexedFieldURIType.folderFolderClass;
folderClassUpdate.Item = folderClassPath;

FolderType folderClassState = new FolderType();
folderClassState.FolderClass = "IPF.Note.Contoso";
folderClassUpdate.Item1 = folderClassState;

// Now add the two field changes that we just created to the updates
// array
//
folderChange.Updates[0] = displayNameUpdate;
folderChange.Updates[1] = folderClassUpdate;

// Let's take the single folder change which contains updates to two
// properties
```

```
    // and assign it to the FolderChanges property on our request
    //
    request.FolderChanges = new FolderChangeType[] { folderChange };

    // Make the call and extract the response
    //
    UpdateFolderResponseType response = binding.UpdateFolder(request);
    FolderInfoResponseMessageType responseMessage =
        response.ResponseMessages.Items[0] as FolderInfoResponseMessageType;

    Console.WriteLine(responseMessage.Folders[0].FolderId.ToString());
}
```

OK, that was a *lot* of code just to make a simple *UpdateItem* call. Of course, this could be greatly simplified by adding a few overloaded constructors to the autogenerated proxy classes, which we touched on in Chapter 2 and Chapter 3.

Notice that the response message type for *UpdateFolder* is *FolderInfoResponseMessageType*. This is the same response message type that *CreateFolder*, *GetFolder*, and others return.

When using *SetFolderFieldType* in proxy objects, you notice that odd *"Item"* property rearing its head again. But wait! There is *another* one called *Item1*. As mentioned in Chapter 1, the proxy generator has no way to name these properties and therefore makes up names. Because two "choice" types are found within *SetFolderFieldType*, you end up with two *"Item"* fields. Of course, you can always modify the autogenerated proxy to provide better property names. Just know that if you need to regenerate the proxy, you overwrite your updated property names.[19]

DeleteFolderFieldType

If there is a property on a folder that you no longer want, you can delete it using the *DeleteFolderFieldType*. Deleting a property does not null or zero out a property, but instead removes the actual property. It's gone. Bye bye, property. *DeleteFolderFieldType* is the simplest of the three folder update actions. All that is required is the property path that you wish to delete, and there is no need for folder data elements. You specify a *DeleteFolderFieldType* instance in an XML document using the *DeleteFolderField* element. The structure of *DeleteFolderField* is shown in Listing 4-18.

LISTING 4-18 Basic structure of *DeleteFolderField*

```
<t:DeleteFolderField>
  <t:FieldURI/> | <t:IndexedFieldURI/> | <t:ExtendedFieldURI/>
</t:DeleteFolderField>
```

---

[19] Partial classes are a way around this, although in that case you are adding properties rather than replacing them.

So, let's delete some properties. Let's try the display name:

```
<UpdateFolder xmlns=".../messages">
   <FolderChanges>
      <t:FolderChange>
         <t:FolderId Id="AQAtAEFkbWluaX..." ChangeKey="AQAAA..."/>
         <t:Updates>
            <t:DeleteFolderField>
               <t:FieldURI FieldURI="folder:DisplayName"/>
            </t:DeleteFolderField>
         </t:Updates>
      </t:FolderChange>
   </FolderChanges>
</UpdateFolder>
```

Running this gives... oops! An error.

```
<UpdateFolderResponse xmlns:m=".../messages"
                      xmlns:t=".../types"
                      xmlns=".../messages">
   <m:ResponseMessages>
      <m:UpdateFolderResponseMessage ResponseClass="Error">
         <m:MessageText>The folder save operation failed due to invalid
                        property values.</m:MessageText>
         <m:ResponseCode>ErrorFolderSavePropertyError</m:ResponseCode>
         <m:DescriptiveLinkKey>0</m:DescriptiveLinkKey>
         <m:MessageXml>
            <t:FieldURI FieldURI="folder:DisplayName"/>
         </m:MessageXml>
         <m:Folders/>
      </m:UpdateFolderResponseMessage>
   </m:ResponseMessages>
</UpdateFolderResponse>
```

So, what happened? A missing display name is an invalid value for the display name. You can't get rid of the display name. In fact, you can't get rid of any of the standard folder properties. To demonstrate let's consider an example where a new property is created and then deleted. This will set up a quintessential example for *DeleteFolderField*. Because you have *SetFolderField* under your belt, the example uses that to add a new property to the folder first. Also, the following code adds a *ShoeSize* property using extended properties because there is no standard *ShoeSize* property for folders.[20]

```
<UpdateFolder xmlns=".../messages"
              xmlns:t=".../types">
   <FolderChanges>
      <t:FolderChange>
         <t:FolderId Id="AQAtAEFkbWluaXN0cmF0..." ChangeKey="AQAAABYAA..."/>
         <t:Updates>
            <t:SetFolderField>
               <t:ExtendedFieldURI
                     DistinguishedPropertySetId="PublicStrings"
```

---

[20] Extended properties are discussed in Chapter 13.

```
                    PropertyName="ShoeSize"
                    PropertyType="Double"/>
          <t:Folder>
            <t:ExtendedProperty>
             <t:ExtendedFieldURI
                  DistinguishedPropertySetId="PublicStrings"
                  PropertyName="ShoeSize"
                  PropertyType="Double"/>
             <t:Value>10.5</t:Value>
            </t:ExtendedProperty>
          </t:Folder>
        </t:SetFolderField>
      </t:Updates>
    </t:FolderChange>
  </FolderChanges>
</UpdateFolder>
```

Is the *ShoeSize* property there? Listing 4-19 calls *GetFolder* and explicitly asks for the *ShoeSize*
property.

LISTING 4-19 Retrieving the *ShoeSize* property using *GetFolder*

```
<GetFolder xmlns=".../messages"
           xmlns:t=".../types">
  <FolderShape>
    <t:BaseShape>IdOnly</t:BaseShape>
    <t:AdditionalProperties>
      <t:ExtendedFieldURI
                 DistinguishedPropertySetId="PublicStrings"
                 PropertyName="ShoeSize"
                 PropertyType="Double"/>
    </t:AdditionalProperties>
  </FolderShape>
  <FolderIds>
    <t:FolderId Id="AQAtAEFkbWluaX..." ChangeKey="AQAAABYAA..."/>
  </FolderIds>
</GetFolder>
```

Yes, there it is.

```
<GetFolderResponse xmlns:m=".../messages" xmlns:t=".../types"
                   xmlns=".../messages">
    <m:ResponseMessages>
      <m:GetFolderResponseMessage ResponseClass="Success">
        <m:ResponseCode>NoError</m:ResponseCode>
        <m:Folders>
          <t:Folder>
            <t:FolderId Id="AQAtAEF..." ChangeKey="AQAAABY..."/>
            <t:ExtendedProperty>
              <t:ExtendedFieldURI
                     DistinguishedPropertySetId="PublicStrings"
                     PropertyName="ShoeSize"
                     PropertyType="Double"/>
```

```
            <t:Value>10.5</t:Value>
          </t:ExtendedProperty>
        </t:Folder>
      </m:Folders>
    </m:GetFolderResponseMessage>
  </m:ResponseMessages>
</GetFolderResponse>
```

Next, the following code deletes the property.

```
<UpdateFolder xmlns=".../messages" xmlns:t=".../types">
  <FolderChanges>
    <t:FolderChange>
      <t:FolderId Id="AQAtAEFkbWluaX..." ChangeKey="AQAAABYAAAB..."/>
      <t:Updates>
        <t:DeleteFolderField>
          <t:ExtendedFieldURI
                    DistinguishedPropertySetId="PublicStrings"
                    PropertyName="ShoeSize"
                    PropertyType="Double"/>
        </t:DeleteFolderField>
      </t:Updates>
    </t:FolderChange>
  </FolderChanges>
</UpdateFolder>
```

And, it should be gone. If you repeat the same *GetFolder* call from Listing 4-19, and what is the result? No shoe size.

```
<GetFolderResponse xmlns:m=".../messages"
                   xmlns:t=".../types"
                   xmlns=".../messages">
  <m:ResponseMessages>
    <m:GetFolderResponseMessage ResponseClass="Success">
      <m:ResponseCode>NoError</m:ResponseCode>
      <m:Folders>
        <t:Folder>
          <t:FolderId Id="AQAtAEFkbWlu..." ChangeKey="AQAAABY..."/>
        </t:Folder>
      </m:Folders>
    </m:GetFolderResponseMessage>
  </m:ResponseMessages>
</GetFolderResponse>
```

AppendToFolderFieldType

In theory, *AppendToFolderFieldType* should allow you to take the existing value of a folder property and append additional data to it. Currently, no folder properties exist that support the append operation.[21] Therefore, you cannot use *AppendToFolderField*Type currently in Exchange Web Services. To "mimic" an append, you can fetch the current data for the prop-

---

[21] This includes extended properties. While it might seem acceptable to append to array-typed extended properties, that is currently not supported.

erty in question, append the data within your client application, and then use a *SetFolderField* to set the new data.

Application Operations for Properties

We have covered the three update operations that can be performed on folder properties. Can you set, delete, and append to all folder properties?[22] Well, no. The applicable operations are a function of the property in question. For instance, you can certainly retrieve a *FolderId*, but you cannot set, delete, or append to a *FolderId* because it is read only. You have also seen that you can't append to any folder properties. Appendix C (available on the companion Web page) lists each folder property and the update folder changes that can be performed on each.

At this point, it is sufficient to say that if you try to perform an operation on a property that does not support the proposed action, you receive an error indicating that the property in question does not support the proposed action. The action to error code mapping can be seen in Table 4-4. It is possible to encounter other errors while trying to update properties (as in the failed delete *folder:DisplayName* example), but as a general rule, the mappings below are what you will see.

TABLE 4-4 Invalid Folder Action Error Codes

Update folder action	Error code
SetFolderFieldType	ErrorInvalidPropertySet
AppendFolderFieldType	ErrorInvalidPropertyAppend
DeleteFolderFieldType	ErrorInvalidPropertyDelete

Managed Folders

Let's say that Jane works in the legal department of Contoso Ltd. Specifically, Jane works in the Intellectual Property department and is responsible for submitting new patents as well as handling patent infringement cases. Due to law XYZ.12345.abc-2-bc-long, information related to patent filings needs to be maintained for one year and three days. Due to law XYZ.12345.efg-2-bc-longer, information related to patent infringement cases needs to be maintained for three years and one day.[23]

One morning, Jane gets two e-mails. One has to do with a patent filing and the other with an ongoing infringement case. How is Jane going to comply with the retention policies mandated by law? Well, Jane will just stick each e-mail into a specific folder that has the applicable

---

[22] Well, two if you ignore *AppendToFolderType*.

[23] These are fictitious numbers. No legal advice is being given here.

retention policy attached to it. So, she moves the patent filing e-mail into the Patent Filings folder and the infringement e-mail into the Case 123 Infringement folder.

Great! So, how did those folders get there in the first place? Ah, that was Ken's job. You see, Ken is an Exchange Administrator. The legal department defined the policies that are applicable to Contoso Ltd., and Ken took those requirements and defined "managed folders" within the Exchange Management Console to meet those retention policies. In reality, Ken didn't create actual folders, but instead created folder *definitions* that reside in the Active Directory. The set of managed folder definitions that Ken defined now make up a menu of managed folders from which users can choose to add to their mailboxes.[24]

When Jane was hired into the legal department, Ken added the Patent Filings managed folder *instance* to Jane's mailbox. Remember, the folder definition for Patent Filings was already in the Active Directory. When Jane opened Outlook, the Patent Filings managed folder was there, right under the Managed Folders folder.

Later, when Jane was assigned to the Case 123 infringement project, she used her company's Opt-In folder application[25] to add the "Case 123 Infringement" opt-in folder to her mailbox. Remember, the folder definition for "Case 123 Infringement" was already in the Active Directory.

Thus, Jane has two managed folders that reside within her mailbox, but these managed folders point back to their definitions within the Active Directory to determine their retention policies. Not to belabor the point, but it should be clear by now that Jane cannot have any managed folders in her mailbox *unless* there is a corresponding managed folder definition in the Active Directory.

How does this all fit into Exchange Web Services? First, Exchange Web Services does *not* provide any functionality for creating managed folder definitions or defining the retention policies attached to such folders. Such operations are considered administrative duties and are currently outside of the scope of Exchange Web Services. What it does provide is a way to

- subscribe to existing managed folders,
- determine which managed folders are currently within a given mailbox, and
- examine some of the metadata information assigned to a managed folder instance within a given mailbox.

Although we will not discuss the administration of managed folders, we will show you how to create one of them using the Exchange Management Console. The first thing to do is navigate to the *Mailbox* node under Organizational Configuration in the tree view as shown in Figure 4-6.

---

[24] Users who have owner rights to the mailbox in question can choose from the menu.

[25] A custom in-house application that was most likely built using a combination of Active Directory calls and EWS.

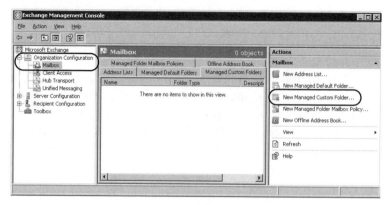

FIGURE 4-6 *Mailbox* tree node in the Exchange Management Console

The tab of interest is "Managed Custom Folders."

To create a new managed folder, click "New Managed Custom Folder" on the Actions panel. Doing so presents the New Managed Custom Folder Wizard as shown in Figure 4-7.

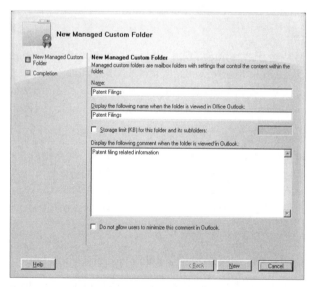

FIGURE 4-7 A new managed custom folder

After entering the information, click New as shown in Figure 4-8.

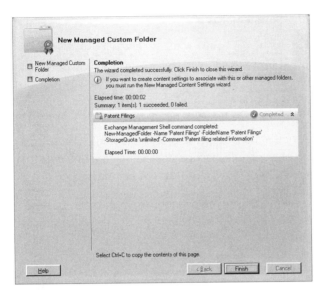

FIGURE 4-8 Creation of a managed custom folder

After the folder is created, you can set the retention policy on the folder by creating the content settings for the folder.[26] Now that the managed folder definition is created in the directory, we can return our focus to Exchange Web Services.

Creating Managed Folder Instances in Exchange Web Services

When you "create" a managed folder in Exchange Web Services, you are really creating only an *instance* of a managed folder definition within your mailbox. To do this, you use the *CreateManagedFolder* Web method.[27] This operation has the structure shown in Listing 4-20.

LISTING 4-20 *CreateManagedFolder* structure

```
<CreateManagedFolder xmlns=".../messages.xsd" xmlns:t=".../types.xsd">
    <FolderNames/>
    <!-- Optional mailbox element -->
    <Mailbox/>
</CreateManagedFolder>
```

CreateManagedFolder has two child elements that are described in Table 4-5.

---

[26] We don't show the content settings here because EWS doesn't concern itself with policy settings. It is as simple as selecting your folder, clicking the New Managed Content Settings option in the Actions panel, and then filling in the pertinent information. Of course this example uses two managed folders. You should be able to create the second folder definition by repeating the steps used to create the first managed folder definition.

[27] It might have been clearer if EWS developers had called this *AddManagedFolder*. Hopefully, you get the idea though.

TABLE 4-5 *CreateManagedFolder* **Subelements**

Child element	Description
FolderNames	Holds a collection of *FolderName* elements, one for each managed folder definition you want to add to the mailbox. This element is required.
Mailbox	Indicates the mailbox in which to add the managed folders. This element is optional, and if omitted, the managed folders are added to the *caller's* mailbox.

Regardless of whether you specify the *Mailbox* element or not, a single *CreateManagedFolder* call can add managed folders to only a *single* mailbox. To add managed folders to multiple mailboxes, you must make a single *CreateManagedFolder* call *per* mailbox.

The following call uses Jane's credentials from the previous example, so there is no need to specify the *Mailbox* element because Exchange Web Services uses the caller's mailbox (Jane's, in this case) unless the *Mailbox* element is specified.[28]

```
<CreateManagedFolder xmlns=".../messages" xmlns:t=".../types">
   <FolderNames>
     <t:FolderName>Case 123 Infringement</t:FolderName>
   </FolderNames>
</CreateManagedFolder>
```

The response returns the id of the newly created folder.

```
<CreateManagedFolderResponse xmlns:m=".../messages"
                             xmlns:t=".../types"
                             xmlns=".../messages">
   <m:ResponseMessages>
     <m:CreateManagedFolderResponseMessage ResponseClass="Success">
        <m:ResponseCode>NoError</m:ResponseCode>
        <m:Folders>
           <t:Folder>
             <t:FolderId Id="AQAtAEFkbW..." ChangeKey="AQAAAB..."/>
           </t:Folder>
        </m:Folders>
     </m:CreateManagedFolderResponseMessage>
   </m:ResponseMessages>
</CreateManagedFolderResponse>
```

If you wanted to make this call using an account other than Jane's, you would have to use an account that has *owner* rights to Jane's mailbox.[29] The following code adds Jane's primary SMTP address in the *Mailbox* element so that Exchange Web Services knows in which mailbox to add the managed folder.

```
<!-- Assuming the call is coming from Ken, we need to add the mailbox element -->
<CreateManagedFolder xmlns=".../messages"
                     xmlns:t=".../types">
   <FolderNames>
```

---

[28] This information is discussed in Chapter 2.

[29] Ken would have this right because he is an administrator. Of course, you don't have to be an administrator to have owner rights to a mailbox. For example, Jane would simply need to grant the rights to her mailbox to another account and then this call will succeed.

```
          <t:FolderName>Case 123 Infringement</t:FolderName>
    </FolderNames>
    <Mailbox>
        <t:EmailAddress>jane.dow@contoso.com</t:EmailAddress>
    </Mailbox>
</CreateManagedFolder>
```

So, the Case 123 Infringement managed folder has been added to Jane's mailbox. In this scenario, Ken already added the Patent Filings managed folder. You can use Outlook Web Access to see whether there is anything of interest in your mailbox. Figure 4-9 shows the results from the current example.[30]

FIGURE 4-9 Viewing managed folders with Outlook Web Access

You see that both of the managed folders have been added under Managed Folders.

Finding the Managed Folder Root

At some point, you may want to find managed folder instances within a given mailbox. Currently, there is no way in Exchange Web Services to return the "menu" of available managed folder definitions that exist in the Active Directory.[31]

As you see in Figure 4-9, the managed folders from the previous example exist under a folder named "Managed Folders." So, how would you get to the "Managed Folders" folder programmatically? It would be very nice to have a distinguished folder id for the managed folder root, but unfortunately, this distinguished folder id does not exist. Therefore, you have a problem. In Chapter 2, we warned against the use of the folder display name for business logic decisions. Although it might *seem* that the only way to determine the managed folder root is to look for a folder named "Managed Folders," there is a better way.

Managed folders expose a special property named *ManagedFolderInformation*. You can do look at all of the folders to see which ones have this property. If a folder has the property, it is a managed folder. If it doesn't, it is not a managed folder. All managed folder instances created in Exchange Web Services will reside in the Managed Folder folder.[32] In practice, this folder lives under the IPM Subtree (msgfolderroot), so you can look at all of the folders directly under msgfolderroot and see whether there is anything of interest. To look specifically for managed folders, you add *ManagedFolderInformation* to your response shape.

---

[30] OWA is a component of an Exchange 2007 Client Access Server that allows you to access your mailbox through a Web browser. This assumes, of course, that your administrator has not turned off this feature.

[31] This must be done on the server using the *Get-ManagedFolder* PowerShell cmdlet or by querying the Active Directory using *System.DirectoryServices* or another Active Directory access API.

[32] Note that this is an EWS restriction. A mailbox can certainly contain managed folders that live outside of the Managed Folders folder, and you can use EWS to look at the contents of these folders. You just cannot use EWS to create managed folder instances outside of the Managed Folder folder.

```
<FindFolder xmlns=".../messages"
            xmlns:t=".../types"
            Traversal="Shallow">
  <FolderShape>
    <t:BaseShape>IdOnly</t:BaseShape>
    <t:AdditionalProperties>
      <t:FieldURI FieldURI="folder:ManagedFolderInformation"/>
    </t:AdditionalProperties>
  </FolderShape>
  <ParentFolderIds>
    <t:DistinguishedFolderId Id="msgfolderroot"/>
  </ParentFolderIds>
</FindFolder>
```

To save space, most of the boilerplate *FindFolder* response has been ommitted. The response information of interest is shown in Listing 4-21.

LISTING 4-21 Finding managed folders

```
<!-- Previous XML omitted for brevity -->
<t:Folder>
      <t:FolderId Id="AQAtAEFkbWluaX..." ChangeKey="AQAAABYAAA..."/>
</t:Folder>
<t:Folder>
      <t:FolderId Id="AQAtAEFkbWluaXN..." ChangeKey="AQAAABYA..."/>
      <t:ManagedFolderInformation>
          <t:CanDelete>false</t:CanDelete>
          <t:CanRenameOrMove>false</t:CanRenameOrMove>
          <t:MustDisplayComment>false</t:MustDisplayComment>
          <t:HasQuota>false</t:HasQuota>
          <t:IsManagedFoldersRoot>true</t:IsManagedFoldersRoot>
      </t:ManagedFolderInformation>
</t:Folder>
<t:Folder>
      <t:FolderId Id="AQAtAEFkbWlua..." ChangeKey="BQAAABY..."/>
</t:Folder>
<!-- additional response elements omitted -->
```

The full response contains 11 folders. Regardless, you see that one of the folders in the response does indeed contain the *ManagedFolderInformation* property. That is the managed folder root. Note that only one such root can exist within a mailbox. You can write a little method to get this by using the proxy classes as shown in Listing 4-22.

LISTING 4-22 Retrieving the managed folder root via proxy classes

```
public static FolderIdType GetManagedFolderRootUsingProperty(
                               ExchangeServiceBinding binding)
{
  FindFolderType findRequest = new FindFolderType();
  findRequest.Traversal = FolderQueryTraversalType.Shallow;
  findRequest.FolderShape = new FolderResponseShapeType();
  findRequest.FolderShape.BaseShape = DefaultShapeNamesType.IdOnly;
```

```
        // we also want to grab the managed folder information
        //
        PathToUnindexedFieldType managedFolderProp = new
                                    PathToUnindexedFieldType();
        managedFolderProp.FieldURI =
                    UnindexedFieldURIType.folderManagedFolderInformation;

        findRequest.FolderShape.AdditionalProperties = new
                        BasePathToElementType[] { managedFolderProp };

        // we want to look in msgfolderroot (IPM subtree) as that is where
        // the managed folder root resides.
        //
        DistinguishedFolderIdType msgFolderRoot = new
                        DistinguishedFolderIdType();
        msgFolderRoot.Id = DistinguishedFolderIdNameType.msgfolderroot;
        findRequest.ParentFolderIds = new BaseFolderIdType[] { msgFolderRoot };

        // make the call and parse the response
        //
        FindFolderResponseType response = binding.FindFolder(findRequest);
        FindFolderResponseMessageType responseMessage =
            response.ResponseMessages.Items[0] as FindFolderResponseMessageType;

        if (responseMessage.ResponseCode != ResponseCodeType.NoError)
        {
          throw new Exception("FindFolder failed with error code " +
                    responseMessage.ResponseCode.ToString());
        }

        // iterate across each folder in our response and see if it has the
        // managed folder property set.  If so, then it is our managed folder
        // root.
        //
        foreach (BaseFolderType folder in
                        responseMessage.RootFolder.Folders)
        {
            if ((folder.ManagedFolderInformation != null) &&
                (folder.ManagedFolderInformation.IsManagedFoldersRoot))
            {
              return folder.FolderId;
            }
        }
    }
    // We didn't find a managed folder root.  That most likely means that
    // there are no managed folders in the mailbox and therefore no root.
    //
    return null;
}
```

Simply repeat this process to find all of the managed folders contained within the managed folder root, but use the managed folder root id as the parent folder from which to perform the search. Of course, for managed folders that are not inside the root managed folder folder, you will likely need to perform a deep traversal *FindFolder* and only return those folders whose *ManagedFolderInformation* is set. In Chapter 13, we discuss how you can use extended MAPI properties with *FindFolder* to return only those folders that match a certain set of criteria such as those with the *ManagedFolderInformation* property set.

Updating Managed Folder Information

Can you update the *ManagedFolderInformation* property? No, you can't. So, why did we put this section here? We just wanted to reiterate that managed folders are governed by their definitions within the Active Directory. For the most part, you can't modify the instance that is in a given mailbox.[33] You can certainly delete it, as described in the next section.[34] In addition, you cannot move a managed folder. Attempting to move a managed folder gives you the extremely descriptive *ErrorMoveCopyFailed* error code.

Deleting Managed Folders

Just as you can opt in to managed folders, you can opt out of them by calling *DeleteFolder* and passing in the *FolderId* of the managed folder. As with unmanaged folders, all of the contents of the folder are deleted. The request is shown in Listing 4-23.

LISTING 4-23 Deleting managed folder instances

```
<DeleteFolder xmlns=".../messages"
              xmlns:t=".../types"
              DeleteType="HardDelete">
   <FolderIds>
      <t:FolderId Id="AQAtAEFkbWluaXN0..." ChangeKey="AQAAABYAAA..."/>
   </FolderIds>
</DeleteFolder>
```

Summary

We are actually surprised at how much information there is about folders. You will see more information in Chapter 14 and Chapter 15. In this chapter, we covered the folder structure of the mailbox and met the various types of folders that you encounter there. In addition, we discussed in detail the operations that are applicable to folders and examined the difference between generic and typed folders and how folders cannot have their type changed after creation. The chapter concluded with both the rationale behind managed folders as well as the various Web methods that can be used to create, read, and delete them.

---

[33] You can set custom properties on a managed folder instance, but the standard folder properties cannot be set using EWS.

[34] If you are using Office Outlook, you can delete a managed folder using SHIFT+DELETE on the keyboard.

Chapter 5
Items

An item is any non-folder that resides within a folder.[1] Users do not typically see "items" as such, but instead see one of the descendant types such as a message, calendar item, meeting request, or contact. This chapter covers the features that are common to all item types. The finer nuances of each descendant type will be handled in Chapter 6 (contacts), Chapter 7 (messages), Chapter 8 through Chapter 10 (calendar-related items), and Chapter 11 (tasks).

What Is an Item?

An item is anything that exists within the message table in the Exchange Store. Like folders, items are represented as a collection of properties. As far as the Store is concerned, all properties are applicable to all items. It is completely acceptable to have a home phone number on a message or a collection of "To" recipients on a contact. Of course, those are meaningless things in principle. As mentioned in Chapter 3, "Property Paths and Response Shapes," Microsoft Exchange Server 2007 Web Services (EWS) uses a hybrid approach of tightening the reins on which properties are exposed on a given item type while providing a mechanism for circumventing these restrictions as the need arises. You saw Figure 5-1 back in Chapter 3 (as Figure 3-1), but it seems prudent to re-introduce it here.

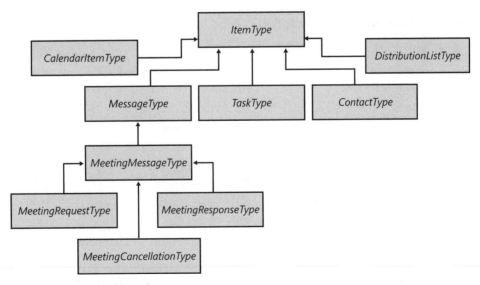

FIGURE 5-1 Item type hierarchy

---

1 In other words, a folder is not an item.

When we discussed folders in Chapter 4, "Folders," you saw that the base type (*BaseFolderType*) never appears in instance documents. A different situation is in effect with items. The base type, *ItemType*, is *not* abstract and can certainly appear in instance documents. A reasonable view is that *FolderType* is to folders as *ItemType* is to items.

Determining the Type of an Item

So what makes a message a message? You saw in Chapter 3 that you can view a mailbox database as having an item table where each row represents an item within that database. Any type classification for a given item within the item table must come from the data *within* the corresponding row. In other words, a given item's own state reveals its type. While Chapter 4 showed that Exchange Web Services looks at the PR_CONTAINER_CLASS "column" within the folder table in order to determine the type of folder you are dealing with, Exchange Web Services looks at the PR_MESSAGE_CLASS "column" within the item table in order to determine the type of item you are dealing with. Both PR_CONTAINER_CLASS and PR_MESSAGE_CLASS are Messaging Application Programming Interface (MAPI) properties, which are surfaced as the *folder:FolderClass* and *item:ItemClass* unindexed property paths, respectively. Going forward, we will refer to PR_MESSAGE_CLASS using its Exchange Web Services property name on *ItemType*, *ItemClass*.[2] Two primary operations that return existing item data within a mailbox, *GetItem* and *FindItem*. In most cases, these two operations agree in their type classification of items; however, there are some edge cases where these two methods disagree. Table 5-1 displays an item-by-item breakdown and demonstrates how the *ItemClass* property value is used to determine type in a *FindItem* operation.

TABLE 5-1 Determining the Item Type[3]

Item Type	ItemClass	Matching
MeetingRequestType	IPM.Schedule.Meeting.Request	Exact
MeetingCancellationType	IPM.Schedule.Meeting.Canceled	Exact
MeetingResponseType	IPM.Schedule.Meeting.Resp.	Prefix
CalendarItemType	IPM.Appointment.	Prefix
CalendarItemOccurrenceExceptionType	IPM.OLE.CLASS.{00061055-0000-0000-C000-000000000046}	Exact
ContactType	IPM.Contact.	Prefix
DistributionListType	IPM.DistList.	Prefix
MessageType	IPM.Note.	Prefix
TaskType	IPM.Task.	Prefix

---

[2] You might be wondering why the Exchange Web Services team didn't call the property *MessageClass*. The reason is that not all items are "messages" and so *MessageClass* would be somewhat of a misnomer.

[3] You might notice in the schema that a *MeetingMessageType* can appear in a number of places. In reality, *MeetingMessageType* serves simply as a base class for *MeetingRequest*, *MeetingResponse*, and *MeetingCancellation* types and never occurs in an instance document.

Item Type	*ItemClass*	Matching
DeliveryReport *(MessageType)*	Prefix: REPORT.IPM.Note. Suffix: .DR	Prefix/Suffix
Non-Delivery Report *(MessageType)*	Prefix: REPORT.IPM.Note. Suffix: .NDR	Prefix/Suffix
Read Receipt *(MessageType)*	Prefix: REPORT.IPM.Note. Suffix: .IPNRN	Prefix/Suffix
Non-Read Receipt *(MessageType)*	Prefix: REPORT.IPM.Note. Suffix: .IPNNRN	Prefix/Suffix

In Table 5-1, you see three different matching modes specified in the Matching column. "Exact" matching is an exact match of the message class against the target strings. For example, if *FindItem* encounters an item with an *ItemClass* of "IPM.Schedule.Meeting. Request.*ABC,*" it is *not* considered to be a *MeetingRequest*, but instead falls back to *ItemType*. This is a known issue within Exchange Web Services. In fact, there is currently no need to perform an exact matching on *ItemClass*. Rather, Exchange Web Services should be performing prefix matching in those cases. This situation might be rectified in a future release. Of course, this affects only items whose *ItemClass* starts with one of the "exact match" values and ends with a custom value. You can consider such *ItemClass* values to be "specializations" of the well-known or standard *ItemClass* values listed in Table 5-1. This is where *FindItem* and *GetItem* have their aforementioned disagreement. If *FindItem* encounters a meeting request, response, or cancellation whose *ItemClass* exactly matches the pattern described in Table 5-1, it returns the correct element instead of falling back to *ItemType*. In contrast, *GetItem* always returns the correct item element even when dealing with specialized meeting types.

For prefix matching, an item is classified according to the *ItemClass* prefix. For example, if *FindItem* or *GetItem* encounters an item with an *ItemClass* of IPM.Contact.*ABC*, it is classified as a *Contact* because the message class bears a prefix of IPM.Contact.

Prefix/suffix matching is both a prefix match and a suffix match. What occurs in the middle of the *ItemClass* doesn't really matter as long as it starts with the known prefix and ends with the known suffix. For example, REPORT.IPM.Note.*I_Am_A_Delivery_Report*.DR is classified as a delivery report because it starts with "REPORT.IPM.Note." and ends with ".DR".

So what happens when the pattern is not matched? In those cases, the item type classification falls back to *ItemType*. If Exchange Web Services encounters an *ItemClass* of "I_AM_JUST_A_GENERIC_ITEM," then it treats it as a generic item.

Now that you have a general idea of what an item is, let's look at how to retrieve one from a given mailbox.

Item Operations

GetItem

The standard way to retrieve an item from a mailbox in Exchange Web Services is to call the *GetItem* Web method. Let's look at the structure of a *GetItem* call as shown in Listing 5-1.

LISTING 5-1 Basic structure of a *GetItem* call

```
<GetItem xmlns=".../messages"
         xmlns:t=".../types">
   <t:ItemShape/>
   <t:ItemIds/>
</GetItem>
```

GetItem exposes two child elements. The first of these, *ItemShape*, defines the set of properties that you want to retrieve on each item that is returned. We discussed response shapes at length in Chapter 3. To reiterate, it is prudent to request only those properties that you need rather than over-using the *AllProperties* base shape. Get in the habit of using *IdOnly* and explicitly listing out the properties you need under the *AdditionalProperties* element. Your Exchange administrators will love you for it.

The next child element is *ItemIds*. Its name implies that you can pass a plurality of ids to this Web method. In fact, you can. Because this is a collection of *ItemId* instances, it is obvious that you need to know the id of the item you are trying to fetch before you can fetch it. If you want to fetch an item using some other means, you need to use *FindItem*, which we discuss later.

Let's view an example of *GetItem* as shown in Listing 5-2.

LISTING 5-2 The first *GetItem* call

```
<GetItem xmlns=".../messages"
         xmlns:t=".../types">
   <ItemShape>
      <t:BaseShape>Default</t:BaseShape>
   </ItemShape>
   <ItemIds>
      <t:ItemId Id="AAAtAEFkbWlua..." ChangeKey="AAAAA..."/>
   </ItemIds>
</GetItem>
```

Listing 5-2 demonstrates an attempt to retrieve a single item (only one *ItemId* is listed in the collection) along with the default properties associated with the type of item. As mentioned in Chapter 2, "May I See Your Id?" the change key is optional here, but is suggested for performance reasons. The response contains a single item with the default properties associated with the type of item in question. In this case, a generic item is retrieved because that is the type of item created for this example. You can tell it is a generic item by looking at the XML element name within the *Items* node, which is *"Item"* in the following example.

```
<GetItemResponse xmlns:m=".../messages"
                 xmlns:t=".../types"
                 xmlns=".../messages">
   <m:ResponseMessages>
      <m:GetItemResponseMessage ResponseClass="Success">
         <m:ResponseCode>NoError</m:ResponseCode>
         <m:Items>
            <t:Item>
               <t:ItemId Id="AAAtAEFkbWlu..." ChangeKey="AAAAA..."/>
               <t:HasAttachments>false</t:HasAttachments>
               <t:Culture>en-US</t:Culture>
            </t:Item>
         </m:Items>
      </m:GetItemResponseMessage>
   </m:ResponseMessages>
</GetItemResponse>
```

Assuming that the item actually exists, the results of *GetItem* always include the *ItemId* of the item with an up-to-date change key. This current change key is essential when performing *UpdateItem* and *SendItem* calls, as you will see shortly. Now, if you request an item using an id that no longer exists, you receive an error indicating that the item is not found.

```
<GetItemResponse xmlns:m=".../messages"
                 xmlns:t=".../types"
                 xmlns=".../messages">
  <m:ResponseMessages>
    <m:GetItemResponseMessage ResponseClass="Error">
      <m:MessageText>The specified object was not found in the store.</m:MessageText>
      <m:ResponseCode>ErrorItemNotFound</m:ResponseCode>
      <m:DescriptiveLinkKey>0</m:DescriptiveLinkKey>
      <m:Items/>
    </m:GetItemResponseMessage>
  </m:ResponseMessages>
</GetItemResponse>
```

Listing 5-3 demonstrates how to get the item using the proxy classes.

LISTING 5-3 *GetItem* using the proxy classes

```
/// <summary>
/// Binds to an item and returns the item with its default shape
/// </summary>
/// <param name="binding">Binding to use</param>
/// <param name="id">Id of item to bind to</param>
/// <returns>ItemType instance or null if error</returns>
///
public static ItemType SimpleGetItem(
```

```
                           ExchangeServiceBinding binding,
                           ItemIdType id)
{
    // Create our request type
    //
    GetItemType getItemRequest = new GetItemType();

    // Set our single id on our request
    //
    getItemRequest.ItemIds = new ItemIdType[] { id };

    // Build up the response shape (the properties we want back)
    //
    getItemRequest.ItemShape = new ItemResponseShapeType();
    getItemRequest.ItemShape.BaseShape = DefaultShapeNamesType.Default;

    // Now make the call
    //
    GetItemResponseType getItemResponse = binding.GetItem(getItemRequest);

    // GetItem returns ItemInfoResponseMessages.  Since we only requested
    // one item, we should only get back one response message.
    //
    ItemInfoResponseMessageType getItemResponseMessage =
            getItemResponse.ResponseMessages.Items[0] as
                    ItemInfoResponseMessageType;

    // Like all good, happy and compliant developers, we should check our
    // response code...
    //
    if (getItemResponseMessage.ResponseCode == ResponseCodeType.NoError)
    {
        return getItemResponseMessage.Items.Items[0];
    }
    else
    {
        throw new Exception(
                "Failed to get the item.  ResponseCode: " +
                    getItemResponseMessage.ResponseCode.ToString());
    }
}
```

CreateItem

Before you can retrieve items from a mailbox, you need to have items there in the first place. Items typically appear in a mailbox after inbound mail is delivered by Exchange, but you can also explicitly create items within your mailbox. Certainly, messages and meeting requests that you send need to be explicitly created.

Listing 5-4 shows the basic structure of a *CreateItem* request.

LISTING 5-4 Basic *CreateItem* structure

```
<CreateItem xmlns=".../messages"
            xmlns:t=".../types"
            MessageDisposition="SaveOnly | SendOnly | SendAndSaveCopy"
            SendMeetingInvitations="SendToNone | SendOnlyToAll |
                    SendToAllAndSaveCopy">
    <SavedItemFolderId/>
    <Items/>
</CreateItem>
```

MessageDisposition Attribute

The *MessageDisposition* attribute is optional...sometimes. When you create any type of item that descends from *MessageType*, you must specify the *MessageDisposition* attribute. If you create any other type of item, the *MessageDisposition* attribute is ignored. We will postpone discussion of the *MessageDisposition* attribute until Chapter 7, "Messages."

SendMeetingInvitations Attribute

The *SendMeetingInvitations* attribute is also optional... sometimes. When you create any type of item that is classified as a *CalendarItemType*, you must specify the *SendMeetingInvitations* attribute. If you create any other type of item, the *SendMeetingInvitations* attribute is ignored. Just like the *MessageDisposition* attribute, *SendMeetingInvitations* provides additional information about your request in an attempt to reduce the number of Web method calls.

The *SendMeetingInvitations* attribute is of type *CalendarItemCreateOrDeleteOperationType*, which is an enumeration with three valid values: *SendToNone*, *SendOnlyToAll*, and *SendToAllAndSaveCopy*. These will be discussed in detail in Chapter 8, "Working with Calendars."

SavedItemFolderId Element

The *SavedItemFolderId* element is an optional element that indicates the folder in which the created items should be saved. If this element is omitted, the created items are saved to the default folder that is applicable to the type of item created. This default mapping is shown in Table 5-2.

TABLE 5-2 **Default Folders for Various Item Types**

Item Type	Default Folder
ItemType	Drafts
MessageType (and descendants)	Drafts
CalendarItemType (and descendants)	Calendar
TaskType	Tasks
DistributionListType	Contacts
Contact	Contacts

Certain item types cannot be created explicitly. For example, a meeting response is only created when an attendee responds to a meeting request.

The *SavedItemFolderId* element is of type *TargetFolderIdType*, which means that the actual folder id occurs as a child element of *SavedItemFolderId*. For example:

```
<SavedItemFolderId>
    <t:FolderId Id="AAAeAGRhd..." ChangeKey="AAAAA..."/>
</SavedItemFolderId>
```

Of course, you can also use distinguished folder ids:

```
<SavedItemFolderId>
    <t:DistinguishedFolderId Id="drafts"/>
</SavedItemFolderId>
```

Limitations exist, however. Messages and items can be saved to any folder. It is completely acceptable (albeit strange) to create a message in a calendar folder. Calendar items can be created only in a calendar folder (default or user created). Trying to save a calendar item to any other folder results in one of the longest-named response codes being returned: *ErrorCannotCreateCalendarItemInNonCalendarFolder*. Similarly, tasks can be created only in a tasks folder, and both contacts and distribution lists are limited to contacts folders. Why such restrictions? Because creating strongly typed objects in the wrong folder type is atypical and is most likely an error. If you really need to store strongly typed items in atypical folders, you can create the item first and then call *MoveItem* to move it to the folder of choice.

Items Element

Due to the plural nature of the *Items* element, it is correct to assume that it allows a plurality of items to be presented. You must, of course, specify at least one item because it would be silly to call *CreateItem* and not specify any items to create.[4] So, what goes into the *Items* element? Well, the items that you want to create. Because the item does not yet exist, you need to give Exchange Web Services as much information as you can about the item. That being said, Exchange Web Services uses default values for many properties if they are not specified. Listing 5-5 shows what happens when you create an item without specifying properties.

LISTING 5-5 Creating an item with no properties

```
<CreateItem xmlns=".../messages"
            xmlns:t=".../types">
  <Items>
    <t:Item/>
  </Items>
</CreateItem>
```

---

4   This would also produce a schema validation error.

Listing 5-6 shows the response.

LISTING 5-6 *CreateItem* response

```
<CreateItemResponse xmlns:m=".../messages"
                    xmlns:t=".../types"
                    xmlns=".../messages">
  <m:ResponseMessages>
    <m:CreateItemResponseMessage ResponseClass="Success">
      <m:ResponseCode>NoError</m:ResponseCode>
      <m:Items>
        <t:Item>
          <t:ItemId Id="AAAtAEFkbWl..." ChangeKey="AAAAA..."/>
        </t:Item>
      </m:Items>
    </m:CreateItemResponseMessage>
  </m:ResponseMessages>
</CreateItemResponse>
```

CreateItem always gives response messages of type *ItemInfoResponseMessageType*. In the case of *CreateItem*, the only property that is ever returned is the *ItemId* of the newly created item. That's fine. But what happens if you call *GetItem* and ask for *AllProperties*? The response is shown in Listing 5-7.

LISTING 5-7 *GetItem* response on the empty item

```
<GetItemResponse xmlns:m=".../messages"
                 xmlns:t=".../types"
                 xmlns=".../messages">
  <m:ResponseMessages>
    <m:GetItemResponseMessage ResponseClass="Success">
      <m:ResponseCode>NoError</m:ResponseCode>
      <m:Items>
        <t:Item>
          <t:ItemId Id="AAAtAEFkbWl..." ChangeKey="AAAAA..."/>
          <t:ParentFolderId Id="AQAtAEFkbWl..." ChangeKey="AAAAA..."/>
          <t:ItemClass/>
          <t:Sensitivity>Normal</t:Sensitivity>
          <t:Body BodyType="Text"/>
          <t:DateTimeReceived>2006-12-27T15:18:35Z</t:DateTimeReceived>
          <t:Size>134</t:Size>
          <t:Importance>Normal</t:Importance>
          <t:IsSubmitted>false</t:IsSubmitted>
          <t:IsDraft>true</t:IsDraft>
          <t:IsFromMe>false</t:IsFromMe>
          <t:IsResend>false</t:IsResend>
          <t:IsUnmodified>false</t:IsUnmodified>
          <t:DateTimeSent>2006-12-27T15:18:35Z</t:DateTimeSent>
          <t:DateTimeCreated>2006-12-27T15:18:35Z</t:DateTimeCreated>
          <t:DisplayCc/>
          <t:DisplayTo/>
          <t:HasAttachments>false</t:HasAttachments>
```

```
            <t:Culture>en-US</t:Culture>
          </t:Item>
        </m:Items>
      </m:GetItemResponseMessage>
    </m:ResponseMessages>
  </GetItemResponse>
```

Now, that is quite a bit of information considering that nothing is initially specified in Listing 5-5.

Listing 5-8 shows how the item is created through the proxy classes.

LISTING 5-8 Calling *CreateItem* through the proxy classes

```
/// <summary>
/// Create an item with no properties set
/// </summary>
/// <param name="binding">Binding to use for web method call</param>
/// <returns>Id of newly created item or NULL if failure</returns>
///
public static ItemIdType SimpleCreateItem(ExchangeServiceBinding binding)
{
  // Create our request
  //
  CreateItemType request = new CreateItemType();
  request.Items = new NonEmptyArrayOfAllItemsType();

  // We want to create a single, empty item (no properties set)
  //
  request.Items.Items = new ItemType[] { new ItemType() };

  // Make the call...
  //
  CreateItemResponseType response = binding.CreateItem(request);

  // Parse the result.  CreateItem returns ItemInfoResponseMessageType
  // instances
  //
  ItemInfoResponseMessageType responseMessage =
      response.ResponseMessages.Items[0] as ItemInfoResponseMessageType;
  if (responseMessage.ResponseCode == ResponseCodeType.NoError)
  {
    return responseMessage.Items.Items[0].ItemId;
  }
  else
  {
    throw new Exception("Failed to create the item. Response code: " +
          responseMessage.ResponseCode.ToString());
  }
}
```

Although it can certainly be done, an item containing all default properties is not terribly interesting. You should therefore at least set the subject.

```
<CreateItem xmlns=".../messages"
            xmlns:t=".../types">
  <Items>
    <t:Item>
      <t:Subject>Here is my item subject</t:Subject>
    </t:Item>
  </Items>
</CreateItem>
```

Even though numerous properties are presented on an *Item* (or any descendant type for that matter), not all of them are settable. Refer to Appendix C, "Mapping to MAPI Properties," on the companion Web page to see which operations are applicable to which properties.

Of course, for the settable properties, you must make sure to set the right type. For example, *Sensitivity* is of type *SensitivityChoicesType*, which the schema defines as an enumeration with four acceptable values: *Normal*, *Personal*, *Private*, and *Confidential*. If you try to create an item and set *Sensitivity* to "true," you get a schema validation error for raw XML requests and a compile time error for proxy class requests. How do you create multiple items in a single call? Simple—just list out multiple items under the *Items* element as shown in Listing 5-9.

LISTING 5-9 Creating multiple items in a single call

```
<CreateItem xmlns=".../messages"
            xmlns:t=".../types">
  <Items>
    <t:Item>
      <t:Subject>Item #1</t:Subject>
    </t:Item>
    <t:Item>
      <t:Subject>Item #2</t:Subject>
    </t:Item>
    <t:Item>
      <t:Subject>Item #3</t:Subject>
      <t:Sensitivity>Private</t:Sensitivity>
    </t:Item>
  </Items>
</CreateItem>
```

Listing 5-9 includes three items, and there is no reason that you cannot have a mixture of *Items*, *Messages*, *CalendarItems*, and so forth.

What is interesting is the response as shown in Listing 5-10.

LISTING 5-10 *CreateItem* with multiple results

```
<CreateItemResponse xmlns:m=".../messages"
                    xmlns:t=".../types"
                    xmlns=".../messages">
  <m:ResponseMessages>
    <m:CreateItemResponseMessage ResponseClass="Success">
      <m:ResponseCode>NoError</m:ResponseCode>
      <m:Items>
        <t:Item>
          <t:ItemId Id="AAAtAEFkbWlu..." ChangeKey="AAAAA..."/>
        </t:Item>
      </m:Items>
    </m:CreateItemResponseMessage>
    <m:CreateItemResponseMessage ResponseClass="Success">
      <m:ResponseCode>NoError</m:ResponseCode>
      <m:Items>
        <t:Item>
          <t:ItemId Id="AAAtAEFkbWl..." ChangeKey="AAAAA..."/>
        </t:Item>
      </m:Items>
    </m:CreateItemResponseMessage>
    <m:CreateItemResponseMessage ResponseClass="Success">
      <m:ResponseCode>NoError</m:ResponseCode>
      <m:Items>
        <t:Item>
          <t:ItemId Id="AAAtAEFkbWl..." ChangeKey="AAAAA..."/>
        </t:Item>
      </m:Items>
    </m:CreateItemResponseMessage>
  </m:ResponseMessages>
</CreateItemResponse>
```

Notice that the result contains three *CreateItemResponseMessage* elements. It just so happens that this number corresponds to the number of items created in Listing 5-9. What is a bit strange is that each response message contains an *Items* element. The name suggests that there might be more than one, but in reality, you never encounter more than one item within the *Items* element when dealing with *ItemInfoResponseMessageType* instances.[5]

So, why is there an *Items* element at all? It seems more prudent to vanquish the *Items* element and simply have the *Item* as a direct child of the *CreateItemResponseMessage* element, which would have been a great idea. As history has it, however, there was a time during the development of Exchange Web Services when a *CreateItem* request returned a single response message containing all of the items that were created. Yet, that did not allow Exchange Web Services to indicate success or failure on an item-by-item basis. Therefore, the developers restructured the responses so that a response message would be emitted for each item processed. Unfortunately, the *Items* element was not eradicated and therefore

---

[5] *ItemInfoResponseMessageType* is also returned by *CopyItem*, *MoveItem*, *UpdateItem*, *SendItem*, and *DeleteItem*.

found a permanent home in the schema. Note that whenever you are dealing with *ItemInfoResponseMessageType* instances, there is always either zero or one item contained in the array.[6]

The value of individual response messages can be seen when you create multiple items and one of them fails. Two items are created in Listing 5-11, one of which has a really long item class name.[7]

LISTING 5-11 Creating multiple items in which one fails

```
<CreateItem xmlns=".../messages"
            xmlns:t=".../types">
  <Items>
    <t:Item>
      <t:Subject>Item #4</t:Subject>
    </t:Item>
    <t:Item>
      <t:ItemClass>Here is a really long item class.Here is a really long item
class.Here is a really long item class.Here is a really long item class.Here is a
 really long item class.Here is a really long item class.Here is a really long
item class.Here is a really long item class.Here is a really long item class.Here
is a really long item class.Here is a really long item class.Here is a really long
 item class.Here is a really long item class.Here is a really long item class.Here
 is a really long item class.Here is a really long item class.Here is a really
long item class.Here is a really long item class.Here is a really long item class.Here
is a really long item class.Here is a really long item class.Here is a
 really long item class.Here is a really long item class.Here is a really long
item class.Here is a really long item class.Here is a really long item class.Here
 is a really long item class.Here is a really long item class.Here is a really
long item class.Here is a really long item class.Here is a really long item
class.Here is a really long item class.Here is a really long item class.Here is a
really long item class.Here is a really long item class.Here is a really long
item class.</t:ItemClass>
      <t:Subject>This should fail</t:Subject>
    </t:Item>
  </Items>
</CreateItem>
```

The response contains two response messages. The first succeeds and the second fails.

```
<CreateItemResponse xmlns:m=".../messages"
                    xmlns:t=".../types"
                    xmlns=".../messages">
  <m:ResponseMessages>
    <m:CreateItemResponseMessage ResponseClass="Success">
      <m:ResponseCode>NoError</m:ResponseCode>
      <m:Items>
        <t:Item>
```

---

[6] The array contains zero in the case of an error.

[7] *ItemClass* is limited to 255 characters.

```
        <t:ItemId Id="AAAtAEFkbWlu..." ChangeKey="AAAAA..."/>
      </t:Item>
    </m:Items>
  </m:CreateItemResponseMessage>
  <m:CreateItemResponseMessage ResponseClass="Error">
    <m:MessageText>Data is corrupt.</m:MessageText>
    <m:ResponseCode>ErrorCorruptData</m:ResponseCode>
    <m:DescriptiveLinkKey>0</m:DescriptiveLinkKey>
    <m:Items/>
  </m:CreateItemResponseMessage>
 </m:ResponseMessages>
</CreateItemResponse>
```

Remember the *SavedItemFolderId* element? Because *SavedItemFolderId* can house a single target folder id, it should be clear that all items within the *CreateItem* call end up in the same destination folder. There is a caveat to this statement, however. If you omit the *SavedItemFolderId* element, then each item within the *CreateItem* call is saved to the default location specified in Table 5-2. If you need to create several items and explicitly dictate where each item goes, you need to make one *CreateItem* call for each destination folder.

CopyItem

The *CopyItem* operation allows you to copy one or more items into a single destination folder. Like with folders, cross-mailbox operations are *not* permitted. Let's look at the structure of the *CopyItem* request. As can be seen in Listing 5-12, *CopyItem* is a relatively simple operation.

LISTING 5-12 *CopyItem* operation structure

```
<CopyItem xmlns=".../messages">
  <ToFolderId/>
  <ItemIds/>
</CopyItem>
```

ToFolderId Element

The *ToFolderId* element is of type *TargetFolderIdType*. This element holds a single destination folder. You can specify a distinguished folder id:

```
<ToFolderId>
  <t:DistinguishedFolderId Id="inbox "/>
</ToFolderId>
```

Or, you can specify a normal folder id:

```
<ToFolderId>
  <t:FolderId Id="AAAtAEFkbWl..." ChangeKey="AAAAA..."/>
</ToFolderId>
```

This element is required.

ItemIds Element

As you can see by the plural nature of the element name, *ItemIds* can contain one or more item identifiers to move to the destination folder. The destination folder *must* be in the same mailbox as each of the items you wish to copy. While *ItemIds* can contain a plethora of item identifiers, it goes without mentioning that all listed items are copied into the same place because there is a single destination folder. If you need to copy items into several different locations, you need to make one *CopyItem* call for each destination folder.

Let's view an example. First, an item is created in the Drafts folder.

```
<CreateItem xmlns=".../messages"
            xmlns:t=".../types">
  <Items>
    <t:Item>
      <t:Subject>Item for Copy/Move</t:Subject>
    </t:Item>
  </Items>
</CreateItem>
```

Great. Now that we have this, let's copy it into the Inbox.

```
<CopyItem xmlns=".../messages"
          xmlns:t=".../types">
  <ToFolderId>
    <t:DistinguishedFolderId Id="inbox"/>
  </ToFolderId>
  <ItemIds>
    <t:ItemId Id="AAAtAEFkbWl..." ChangeKey="AAAAA..."/>
  </ItemIds>
</CopyItem>
```

Listing 5-13 shows the response.

LISTING 5-13 *CopyItem* response

```
<CopyItemResponse xmlns:m=".../messages"
                  xmlns:t=".../types"
                  xmlns=".../messages">
  <m:ResponseMessages>
    <m:CopyItemResponseMessage ResponseClass="Success">
      <m:ResponseCode>NoError</m:ResponseCode>
      <m:Items/>
    </m:CopyItemResponseMessage>
  </m:ResponseMessages>
</CopyItemResponse>
```

You probably noticed something abnormal about the preceding response. The response contains an empty *Items* element. Let's reason this out for a bit. As discussed in Chapter 2, identifiers are unique across mailboxes. Because this is a copy operation and therefore the original does not change, the new copy must have a new id. Yet, the response does not contain the id. What is going on here?

This behavior occurs by design. At one point during the development process, *CopyItem* returned the identifiers for the copied items. The problem that emerged was that the Web method was very slow. The underlying application programming interfaces (APIs) that service Exchange Web Services did not provide the new identifiers as a result of the copy operation, so Exchange Web Services had to perform a search based on other criteria to get the new item and its id. A distinct search was being performed for *each* copied item. This is not terribly noticeable when copying single items, but try copying 100 items into another folder using this approach and you soon see that it is quite unacceptable.[8]

When you copy an item, you typically don't really care about the new id of the item. In these cases, the copy operation is the end of the line. It doesn't make sense to tax the common case by requiring the additional lookup. However, if you really do need the id of the item you just copied, you can get a unique piece of information about the item (the MAPI PR_SEARCH_KEY property, for instance), copy the item, and then do a search in the destination folder for the item that has that unique piece of information.[9] To that end, Listing 5-14 shows the *CopyItemEx* method that returns the new id after the copy is complete. Hopefully, you can see why developers decided to strip this from the standard code path in Exchange Web Services.

LISTING 5-14 New version of *CopyItem* that returns the ids of copied items[10]

```
/// <summary>
/// Copy items to a destination folder and return the new ids for these
/// items.
/// </summary>
/// <param name="binding">Exchange binding to use for the call</param>
/// <param name="destinationFolderId">Destination for the items</param>
/// <param name="itemsToCopy">Items to copy</param>
/// <returns>List of new item ids</returns>
///
public static List<ItemIdType> CopyItemEx(
                    ExchangeServiceBinding binding,
                    BaseFolderIdType destinationFolderId,
                    List<BaseItemIdType> itemsToCopy)
{
  // STEP 1:  First, we need to retrieve some unique information about
  // each item.  Let's use the PR_SEARCH_KEY.  Note that extended properties are
```

---

8 Not to mention the load on the mailbox server that 100 explicit searches produces.

9 Actually, the search key is not guaranteed to be unique. In fact, if you make multiple copies of an item within the same destination folder, you will have multiple items with the same search key. In that case, your best bet is to sort the results based on the *item:DateTimeCreated* property path and grab the first matching item. We discuss such filtering in Chapter 14, "Searching the Mailbox."

10 This example uses extended properties and searching techniques that are detailed in Chapter 13, "Extended Properties," and Chapter 14, respectively.

```
// discussed in Chapter 13, "Extended Properties"
//
GetItemType getSearchKeyRequest = new GetItemType();
PathToExtendedFieldType searchKeyPath = new PathToExtendedFieldType();
searchKeyPath.PropertyTag = "0x300B";
searchKeyPath.PropertyType = MapiPropertyTypeType.Binary;
// Use ItemResponseShapeType overload from chapter 3. We want the Id and the
// search key
//
ItemResponseShapeType idAndSearchKeyShape = new ItemResponseShapeType(
                        DefaultShapeNamesType.IdOnly,
                        searchKeyPath);
getSearchKeyRequest.ItemShape = idAndSearchKeyShape;
getSearchKeyRequest.ItemIds = itemsToCopy.ToArray();

// Get the items
//
GetItemResponseType getSearchKeyResponse =
          binding.GetItem(getSearchKeyRequest);
List<string> base64SearchKeys = new List<string>(
            getSearchKeyResponse.ResponseMessages.Items.Length);

// For each item, add the search keys to our list
//
foreach (ItemInfoResponseMessageType searchKeyMessage in
              getSearchKeyResponse.ResponseMessages.Items)
{
  ExtendedPropertyType searchKeyProperty =
        searchKeyMessage.Items.Items[0].ExtendedProperty[0];
  base64SearchKeys.Add((string)searchKeyProperty.Item);
}

// Now we have a list of the search keys for the items that we want to
// copy.
// STEP 2:  Perform the copy

CopyItemType copyItemRequest = new CopyItemType();
copyItemRequest.ToFolderId = new TargetFolderIdType();
copyItemRequest.ToFolderId.Item = destinationFolderId;

// Just copy the array from our GetItem request rather than building a
// new one.
//
copyItemRequest.ItemIds = getSearchKeyRequest.ItemIds;
CopyItemResponseType copyResponse = binding.CopyItem(copyItemRequest);

// Now, we know that we do not get new ids from the above request, but
// we (read: you) SHOULD check the response code for each of the copies
// operations.
//
// STEP 3:  For each successful copy, we want to find the items by
// search key.
//
FindItemType findBySearchKey = new FindItemType();
```

```
findBySearchKey.ItemShape = idAndSearchKeyShape;
findBySearchKey.ParentFolderIds = new BaseFolderIdType[] {
        destinationFolderId };
findBySearchKey.Traversal = ItemQueryTraversalType.Shallow;
findBySearchKey.Restriction = new RestrictionType();

// Here we need to build up our query.  Rather than issuing several
// FindItem calls, let's build up a single OR restriction here with a
// bunch of items. Note that EWS restricts filter depths, so we
// might need to break this up depending on how many items we are
// copying...
//
if (base64SearchKeys.Count > 1)
{
  OrType or = new OrType();
  List<IsEqualToType> orChildren = new List<IsEqualToType>();
  foreach (string searchKey in base64SearchKeys)
  {
    // Note that CreateIsEqualToSearchKey is implemented below
    //
    IsEqualToType isEqualTo = CreateIsEqualToSearchKey(
          searchKeyPath, searchKey);
    orChildren.Add(isEqualTo);
  }
  or.Items = orChildren.ToArray();

  findBySearchKey.Restriction.Item = or;
}
else
{
  // we only have one item.  No need for the OR clause
  //
  IsEqualToType isEqualTo = CreateIsEqualToSearchKey(
                searchKeyPath, base64SearchKeys[0]);
  findBySearchKey.Restriction.Item = isEqualTo;
}

FindItemResponseType findResponse = binding.FindItem(findBySearchKey);

// Since we searched in a single target folder, we will have a single
// response message
//
FindItemResponseMessageType findResponseMessage =
    findResponse.ResponseMessages.Items[0] as FindItemResponseMessageType;
ItemType[] foundItems = (findResponseMessage.RootFolder.Item as
                        ArrayOfRealItemsType).Items;
List<ItemIdType> newIds = new List<ItemIdType>();
foreach (ItemType item in foundItems)
{
  newIds.Add(item.ItemId);
}
return newIds;
}
```

```
/// <summary>
/// Creates an IsEqualTo clause for our search key
/// </summary>
/// <param name="searchKeyPath">Search key path</param>
/// <param name="value">base64 search key to look for</param>
/// <returns>IsEqualTo clause</returns>
///
public static IsEqualToType CreateIsEqualToSearchKey(
                    PathToExtendedFieldType searchKeyPath,
                    string value)
{
  IsEqualToType isEqualTo = new IsEqualToType();
  isEqualTo.Item = searchKeyPath;
  isEqualTo.FieldURIOrConstant = new FieldURIOrConstantType();
  ConstantValueType constant = new ConstantValueType();
  constant.Value = value;
  isEqualTo.FieldURIOrConstant.Item = constant;
  return isEqualTo;
}
```

MoveItem

The *MoveItem* call is identical in structure to the *CopyItem* call. In fact, in the schema, both *MoveItem* and *CopyItem* are instances of *BaseMoveCopyItemType*. As a result, all of the concepts that pertain to *CopyItem* pertain to *MoveItem*. You might be surprised to find that the id of the item changes when you move it to another folder. Just for reference, a *MoveItem* call is shown in Listing 5-15.

LISTING 5-15 A token *MoveItem* call

```
<MoveItem xmlns=".../messages"
        xmlns:t=".../types">
  <ToFolderId>
    <t:DistinguishedFolderId Id="sentitems"/>
  </ToFolderId>
  <ItemIds>
    <t:ItemId Id="AAAtAEFkbW..." ChangeKey="AAAAA..."/>
  </ItemIds>
</MoveItem>
```

The response is quite similar to the *CopyItem* response shown in Listing 5-13 (note the empty *Items* element).

```
<MoveItemResponse xmlns:m=".../messages"
                xmlns:t=".../types"
                xmlns=".../messages">
  <m:ResponseMessages>
    <m:MoveItemResponseMessage ResponseClass="Success">
```

```
      <m:ResponseCode>NoError</m:ResponseCode>
      <m:Items/>
    </m:MoveItemResponseMessage>
  </m:ResponseMessages>
</MoveItemResponse>
```

DeleteItem

When you want to delete an item, you call the aptly named *DeleteItem* Web method. Listing 5-16 shows the basic structure of a *DeleteItem* call.

LISTING 5-16 Structure of *DeleteItem*

```
<DeleteItem xmlns=".../messages.xsd"
            xmlns:t=".../types.xsd"
    DeleteType="HardDelete | SoftDelete | MoveToDeletedItems"
    SendMeetingCancellations="SendToNone | SendOnlyToAll | SendToAllAndSaveCopy"
    AffectedTaskOccurrences="AllOccurrences | SpecifedOccurrenceOnly">
  <ItemIds/>
</DeleteItem>
```

DeleteItem is light on the child elements and heavy on the attributes. Let's look at each of these in turn.

ItemIds Element

The *ItemIds* element contains one or more *ItemId* child elements that identify the items you wish to delete. The change key is not required when deleting an item, but feel free to include it if you have one.

DeleteType Attribute

The required *DeleteType* attribute allows you to specify just how much you dislike the item you are deleting. You saw these values in Chapter 4 in the *DeleteFolder* operation. Rather than rehash them here in detail, Table 5-3 displays a brief summary of each value and its implications.

TABLE 5-3 *DeleteType* Values for *DeleteItem*

DeleteType Value	Comments
HardDelete	Deletes the item irrevocably. Does not move the item to the Deleted Items folder.
SoftDelete	"Deletes" the item so that it is no longer visible in the folder, but actually still exists there. Avoid using this because there is nothing that you can do with soft-deleted items from EWS aside from finding them.
MoveToDeletedItems	Doesn't actually delete the item, but instead simply moves it to the Deleted Items folder.

Note that calling *DeleteItem* with a *DeleteType* of *MoveToDeletedItems* is really the same thing as calling *MoveItem* and moving the item to the Deleted Items folder explicitly.

SendMeetingCancellations Attribute

This attribute is only required when you are trying to delete calendar items, which is an unfortunate side effect of trying to incorporate too much functionality into a single method.[11] If you specify this attribute when deleting non-calendar items, it is ignored. This attribute will be discussed in detail in Chapter 8.

Note that if you do end up setting this attribute via the proxy classes, you must also set the *SendMeetingCancellationsSpecified* property to true because this is an optional value type.

AffectedTaskOccurrences Attribute

This attribute is only required when you are trying to delete task items. If you specify this attribute when deleting non-task items, it is ignored. This attribute will be discussed in detail in Chapter 9, "Recurring Appointments and Time Zones."

Note that if you do end up setting this attribute via the proxy classes, you must also set the *AffectedTaskOccurrencesSpecified* property to true because this is an optional value type.

Now that you understand the attributes, let's view an example of a *DeleteItem* call. Listing 5-17 details a single *DeleteItem* call with two ids specified.

LISTING 5-17 *DeleteItem* call

```
<DeleteItem xmlns=".../messages"
            xmlns:t=".../types"
            DeleteType="HardDelete">
   <ItemIds>
      <t:ItemId Id="AAAtAEF..." ChangeKey="AAAAA..."/>
      <t:ItemId Id="AAAtAFG..." ChangeKey="AAAAA..."/>
   </ItemIds>
</DeleteItem>
```

The response is about as exciting as a response can be—there's a response code for each deleted item.

```
<DeleteItemResponse xmlns:m=".../messages"
                    xmlns:t=".../types"
                    xmlns=".../messages">
  <m:ResponseMessages>
    <m:DeleteItemResponseMessage ResponseClass="Success">
      <m:ResponseCode>NoError</m:ResponseCode>
```

---

[11] Don't be surprised if EWS comes out with a *CancelCalendarItem* Web method down the line.

```
    </m:DeleteItemResponseMessage>
    <m:DeleteItemResponseMessage ResponseClass="Success">
      <m:ResponseCode>NoError</m:ResponseCode>
    </m:DeleteItemResponseMessage>
  </m:ResponseMessages>
</DeleteItemResponse>
```

How would this look using the proxy classes? Refer to Listing 5-18.

LISTING 5-18 Calling *DeleteItem* via the proxy classes

```
/// <summary>
/// Delete items passed in and write results to console
/// </summary>
/// <param name="binding">binding to use for web method call</param>
/// <param name="deleteType">Delete type to use</param>
/// <param name="itemsToDelete">params array of items to delete</param>
///
public static void DeleteItems(
                      ExchangeServiceBinding binding,
                      DisposalType deleteType,
                      params ItemIdType[] itemsToDelete)
{
  DeleteItemType request = new DeleteItemType();
  request.DeleteType = deleteType;
  request.ItemIds = itemsToDelete;
  DeleteItemResponseType response = binding.DeleteItem(request);

  // Since there really isn't anything interesting in our response
  // messages, we can just use the base class for the response messages.
  // Of course, if we really want to deal with the actual class,
  // DeleteItem returns ItemInfoResponseMessageType -- of course, the
  // Items collection will always be empty.
  //
  int index = 0;
  foreach (ResponseMessageType responseMessage in
                      response.ResponseMessages.Items)
  {
    Console.WriteLine("Item #{0} - result: {1}", index++,
              responseMessage.ResponseCode.ToString());
  }
}
```

Remember the approach to retrieving the new id for items that are moved or copied? Because calling *DeleteItem* with a *DeleteType* of *MoveToDeletedItems* is really just a move operation, you can use this same approach to retrieve the new id of the "deleted item."

FindItem

The *FindItem* Web method returns all of the items within a set of folders that match a given set of criteria. It is quite versatile, but with that versatility comes some complexity. A number of features can be found within *FindItem* that will be addressed in Chapter 15, "Advanced Searching." For starters, let's look at the basic structure of a *FindItem* Web method call as shown in Listing 5-19.

LISTING 5-19 Basic structure of *FindItem*

```
<FindItem xmlns=".../messages"
          xmlns:t=".../types"
          Traversal="Shallow | SoftDeleted">
  <ItemShape/>
  <IndexedPageView/> | <FractionalPageView/> | <CalendarView/> | <ContactsView/>
  <GroupBy/> | <DistinguishedGroupBy/>
  <Restriction/>
  <SortOrder/>
  <ParentFolderIds/>
</FindItem>
```

Traversal Attribute

The required *Traversal* attribute specifies the scope of the search. This attribute's values are defined by the *ItemQueryTraversalType* enumeration in the schema. Although it is very close to the *Traversal* enumeration for *FindFolder*, there is one notable omission. *FindItem* does not allow deep traversal searches. If you want to mimic a deep traversal search, you need to either drill down a folder hierarchy and call *FindItem* on each subfolder or create a *SearchFolder* to do the work for you.[12]

A *Shallow* traversal causes the *FindItem* operation to look directly in the folders that are specified in the *ParentFolderIds* element. No subfolders are considered. A traversal value of *SoftDeleted* causes the *FindItem* operation to consider only soft-deleted items that are contained in the folders specified in the *ParentFolderIds* element.[13] Again, no subfolders are considered.

When setting the *Traversal* attribute via the proxy classes, there is no corresponding *TraversalSpecified* property because this is a required attribute. You simply set the value to the enumeration value of interest:

```
FindItemType findItem = new FindItemType();
findItem.Traversal = ItemQueryTraversalType.Shallow;
```

ItemShape Element

The *ItemShape* element is used to designate which properties should be returned for each item that passes the query. *ItemShape* is of type *ItemResponseShapeType* and can be used in

---

[12] *SearchFolders* do allow deep traversal to be specified. *SearchFolders* are covered in Chapter 15.

[13] See the *FindFolder* operation in Chapter 4 for a more detailed description of *SoftDeleted* traversals.

the same manner as the *ItemShape* within a *GetItem* call—with one noteworthy exception. Exchange Web Services will complain if you try to specify calculated properties within the response shape of a *FindItem* call. Of course, this information won't do you any good until you understand calculated properties.

Calculated Properties

Exchange Web Services supports two kinds of properties. The distinction between these property types is not exposed to the user, but it is important to know that they are there and have limitations surrounding them. The first type, MAPI properties, represents the bulk of the properties that are accessible through Exchange Web Services. For each MAPI property, a column exists in the Exchange Store that contains that value. Like a piece of data in a relational database table, the property value can be retrieved directly without knowing anything else about the item on which the property resides.

Both *FindItem* and *FindFolder* perform queries on the Exchange Store. The result of this query is a flat result set of data rather than a well-formed item or message object. Exchange Web Services makes some intelligent decisions about this flat set of data and transforms it into the XML representation of an item, message, and so on.

The second type of property is known as a *calculated* property, which implies that the property does not exist in a native format, but instead is generated using additional data. In some cases, this additional data is simply other native properties, but in other cases, internal business logic, such as queries, must be executed in order to generate this extra data.

As an example, Exchange Web Services exposes a calendar property named *AdjacentMeetingCount*. This property value is not persisted anywhere in the Exchange Store. As such, Exchange Web Services business logic must perform an internal query to determine which meetings are next to the meeting in question. *FindItem* and *FindFolder* operations deal with result sets containing raw data and do not have access to this internal business logic. The cost associated with building the internal item representations for each row that would be necessary to access this business logic is too high. As a result, calculated properties are not accessible via *FindItem* and *FindFolder*.

Another example is the *Body* of an item. Although there are underlying native MAPI properties for the body of an item, the *Body* property introduces another limitation present in *FindItem* and *FindFolder*—the maximum size of a property returned by *FindItem* and *FindFolder* is 512 bytes. Property values that are larger than 512 bytes are truncated. Often, e-mail bodies will greatly exceed this limit. As such you cannot include the *item:Body* property path in the response shape of a *FindItem* call.[14]

---

[14] You can, however, use *FindItem* to request the "preview text" of a message using the extender property tag 0x3FD9, Property Type: String. This will give you the first 256 unicode characters (512 bytes) of the item body.

Appendix C on the companion Web page lists all of the properties exposed through Exchange Web Services and whether each can be specified in the response shape of a *GetItem/GetFolder* or *FindItem/FindFolder* call. Should you need to access calculated properties for items returned from a *FindItem* or *FindFolder* call, you need to explicitly call *GetItem* or *GetFolder* yourself.

Paging Elements

Paging allows you to request a specific subset of the matching items rather than retrieving a potentially large set of data in one shot. Four mutually exclusive paging elements can be specified in a *FindItem* call. *IndexedPageView* and *FractionalPageView* will be covered in detail in Chapter 15. *ContactsView* will be covered in Chapter 6, "Contacts and Distribution Lists," and *CalendarView* will be covered in Chapter 8. Paging is optional and so none of these elements will be used in this chapter.

Grouping Elements

Two mutually exclusive grouping elements provide a way to group resulting items based on property similarity. Grouping will be covered in Chapter 15. As with paging, grouping is optional and so none of these elements will be used in this chapter.

Restriction Element

The *Restriction* element allows you to specify a set of conditions that potential items must meet to be included in the result set. The restriction architecture allows you to create arbitrarily complex filters using a combination of filter expressions.[15] Restrictions and filtering expressions are covered in detail in Chapter 14. The *Restriction* element is optional and if omitted, all items in the specified scope are returned in the result set. In this chapter, the *Restriction* element is omitted.

SortOrder Element

The *SortOrder* element allows you to specify an ordered list of property paths to be used for sorting as well as a direction in which to sort the corresponding property values. The *SortOrder* element is of type *NonEmptyArrayOfFieldOrdersType*, whose name implies that you can provide a plurality of these items. *NonEmptyArrayOfFieldOrdersType* holds one or more *FieldOrder* elements of type *FieldOrderType*. Listing 5-20 demonstrates the basic structure of *FieldOrderType*.

---

[15] Within reason of course. See Chapter 14 for more details.

LISTING 5-20 Basic structure of *FieldOrderType*

```
<FieldOrder xmlns=".../types" Order="Ascending | Descending">
  <FieldURI> | <IndexedFieldURI> | <ExtendedFieldURI>
</FieldOrder>
```

Thus, a given *FieldOrder* element defines a single property path along with a direction in which to sort. For example, you can specify that you want to sort by the subject in ascending order with the following code.

```
<t:FieldOrder Order="Ascending ">
  <t:FieldURI FieldURI="item:Subject"/>
</t:FieldURI>
```

Actual sorting depends on the comparison algorithm used for the type of data represented by the property path. For instance, Subject is a string property, and therefore sorting is based on the character ordering for the current request culture.[16] On the other hand, item size is an integer property and therefore follows the normal value ordering of integer types. This shouldn't be a problem, but it can cause you grief if you store integer data in a string field, for instance.

Because the type of the *SortOrder* element is actually an array, how are multiple *FieldOrder* elements reconciled when generating a single sorted result set? *FieldOrder* elements are applied in the order specified. Let's look at a simple example of two *FieldOrder* elements within a single sort.

First, the six items in Table 5-4 are created.

TABLE 5-4 Various Messages for *SortOrder*

Subject	Importance	*DateTimeCreated*
Message A	Low	2007-01-14T07:13:54Z
Message B	High	2007-01-14T07:14:17Z
Message C	Low	2007-01-14T07:14:30Z
Message D	High	2007-01-14T07:14:39Z
Message E	Low	2007-01-14T07:14:06Z
Message F	High	2007-01-14T07:13:40Z

Now, given the sort shown in Listing 5-21, how do you think the *FindItem* will respond?

---

[16] As mentioned in Chapter 2, the current request culture is governed by the *MailboxCulture* SOAP header if present and by the default server culture if the SOAP header is missing.

LISTING 5-21 *SortOrder* example #1

```
<SortOrder>
  <t:FieldOrder Order="Ascending">
    <t:FieldURI FieldURI="item:Importance"/>
  </t:FieldOrder>
  <t:FieldOrder Order="Descending">
    <t:FieldURI FieldURI="item:DateTimeCreated"/>
  </t:FieldOrder>
</SortOrder>
```

The first *FieldOrder* element concerns itself with the *Importance* property path and is sorting in ascending order, so you would expect all of the low-importance items to come first followed by the high-importance items. The second *FieldOrder* element concerns itself with the *DateTimeCreated* property. Here, the element is sorting in descending order, which means that within the low-importance group, you would expect Message C to appear first because it was the last low-importance item to be created. You would then expect Message E in the middle and Message A to take up the rear. It doesn't matter that Message D was created after Message C because Message D is a high-importance item and, therefore, not in consideration at this point. Listing 5-22 displays the results.[17]

LISTING 5-22 Sorting example response

```
<FindItemResponse xmlns:m=".../messages"
                  xmlns:t=".../types"
                  xmlns=".../messages">
  <m:ResponseMessages>
    <m:FindItemResponseMessage ResponseClass="Success">
      <m:ResponseCode>NoError</m:ResponseCode>
      <m:RootFolder TotalItemsInView="6"
                    IncludesLastItemInRange="true">
        <t:Items>
          <t:Item>
            <t:ItemId Id="AAAtAEFk..." ChangeKey="AAAAA..."/>
            <t:Subject>Message C</t:Subject>
            <t:Importance>Low</t:Importance>
            <t:DateTimeCreated>2007-01-14T07:14:30Z</t:DateTimeCreated>
          </t:Item>
          <t:Item>
            <t:ItemId Id="AAAtAEFkbWl..." ChangeKey="AAAAA..."/>
            <t:Subject>Message E</t:Subject>
            <t:Importance>Low</t:Importance>
            <t:DateTimeCreated>2007-01-14T07:14:06Z</t:DateTimeCreated>
          </t:Item>
          <t:Item>
            <t:ItemId Id="AAAtAEFkbWl..." ChangeKey="AAAAA..."/>
            <t:Subject>Message A</t:Subject>
            <t:Importance>Low</t:Importance>
```

---

[17] We will discuss the *FindItem* response structure shortly.

```
                    <t:DateTimeCreated>2007-01-14T07:13:54Z</t:DateTimeCreated>
                </t:Item>
                <t:Item>
                  <t:ItemId Id="AAAtAEFkbW1..." ChangeKey="AAAAA..."/>
                  <t:Subject>Message D</t:Subject>
                  <t:Importance>High</t:Importance>
                  <t:DateTimeCreated>2007-01-14T07:14:39Z</t:DateTimeCreated>
                </t:Item>
                <t:Item>
                  <t:ItemId Id="AAAtAEFkbW..." ChangeKey="AAAAA..."/>
                  <t:Subject>Message B</t:Subject>
                  <t:Importance>High</t:Importance>
                  <t:DateTimeCreated>2007-01-14T07:14:17Z</t:DateTimeCreated>
                </t:Item>
                <t:Item>
                  <t:ItemId Id="AAAtAEFkbW..." ChangeKey="AAAAA..."/>
                  <t:Subject>Message F</t:Subject>
                  <t:Importance>High</t:Importance>
                  <t:DateTimeCreated>2007-01-14T07:13:40Z</t:DateTimeCreated>
                </t:Item>
              </t:Items>
            </m:RootFolder>
          </m:FindItemResponseMessage>
        </m:ResponseMessages>
      </FindItemResponse>
```

What happens if you try to sort by a property that doesn't exist for one or more items? Let's see.[18]

```
<SortOrder>
  <t:FieldOrder Order="Descending">
    <t:ExtendedFieldURI DistinguishedPropertySetId="Common"
                        PropertyName="Sort_I_Dont_Exist"
                        PropertyType="Integer"/>
  </t:FieldOrder>
  <t:FieldOrder Order="Ascending">
    <t:FieldURI FieldURI="item:Importance"/>
  </t:FieldOrder>
</SortOrder>
```

The results come back in the following order: A, E, C, F, B, D. Interesting. It looks like Exchange Web Services ignored the non-existent property for sorting and simply went to the next property path to sort by. In fact, Exchange Web Services did "sort" based on the non-existent property. It just so happens that all of the records have the same value (missing), and therefore the sort clause is effectively ignored.

---

[18] We use extended properties here because we want to ensure that the property in question doesn't exist. Extended properties are covered in Chapter 13.

For proxy coding, setting the sort order can be simplified by extending *FieldOrderType*. Oddly enough, the proxy generator does not create a type for the *NonEmptyArrayOfFieldOrdersType*, which is actually a nice omission. As such, you can merely add an overload to the constructor of *FieldOrderType* as shown in Listing 5-23.

LISTING 5-23 Partial class extension to *FieldOrderType*

```
/// <summary>
/// Partial class extension of the FieldOrderType
/// </summary>
public partial class FieldOrderType
{
  /// <summary>
  /// Default constructor.  Since we are providing an overload below, we
  /// must explicitly declare the default constructor so that XML
  /// serialization will be happy.
  /// </summary>
  public FieldOrderType() { }

  /// <summary>
  /// Convenience constructor
  /// </summary>
  /// <param name="sortDirection">Direction of the sort</param>
  /// <param name="propertyPath">Property path used for this field
  /// order</param>
  ///
  public FieldOrderType(
          SortDirectionType sortDirection,
          BasePathToElementType propertyPath)
  {
    this.orderField = sortDirection;
    this.itemField = propertyPath;
  }
}
```

You see how this overloaded constructor can be used in Listing 5-24, where the importance and date time created sort is shown.

LISTING 5-24 Proxy example for sorting

```
/// <summary>
/// Sort items by importance and date time created
/// </summary>
/// <param name="binding">binding to use for FindItem call</param>
///
public static void SortItems(ExchangeServiceBinding binding)
{
  FindItemType request = new FindItemType();
  request.ItemShape = new ItemResponseShapeType();
  request.ItemShape.BaseShape = DefaultShapeNamesType.AllProperties;
  DistinguishedFolderIdType drafts = new
      DistinguishedFolderIdType(DistinguishedFolderIdNameType.drafts);
```

```
    request.ParentFolderIds = new BaseFolderIdType[] { drafts };

    // create our sort order using our handy overloaded FieldOrderType
    // constructor
    //
    request.SortOrder = new FieldOrderType[] {
      new FieldOrderType(
        SortDirectionType.Ascending,
        new PathToUnindexedFieldType(
                UnindexedFieldURIType.itemImportance)),
      new FieldOrderType(
        SortDirectionType.Descending,
        new PathToUnindexedFieldType(
                UnindexedFieldURIType.itemDateTimeCreated))
    };

    FindItemResponseType response = binding.FindItem(request);
    FindItemResponseMessageType responseMessage =
            response.ResponseMessages.Items[0] as
                    FindItemResponseMessageType;

    ItemType[] items = (responseMessage.RootFolder.Item as
            ArrayOfRealItemsType).Items;
    foreach (ItemType item in items)
    {
      Console.WriteLine("Subject: " + item.Subject);
    }
  }
```

If you are going to do any amount of proxy class coding against Exchange Web Services, we strongly recommend that you write some partial class extensions or wrappers to reduce the amount of work you must do. Simply adding a few constructor overloads saves a significant amount of work.

ParentFolderIds Element

The *ParentFolderIds* element holds a collection of folder identifiers that are used as the starting point for the search. The response contains a collection of resulting items for each supplied parent folder. In other words, the resulting items are broken out into parent folder-specific collections rather than amassed into a single resulting collection. You must specify at least one parent folder id. Either *DistinguishedFolderId* or *FolderId* elements are permissible.

To specify parent folders, simply emit the corresponding folder id element as a child of *ParentFolderIds*.

```
<ParentFolderIds>
  <t:DistinguishedFolderId Id="inbox"/>
  <t:FolderId Id="AAAtAEFkbW..." ChangeKey="AAAAA..."/>
</ParentFolderIds>
```

Dealing with the *FindItem* Response

FindItem responses follow a pattern similar to other response messages. However, instead of containing *ItemInfoResponseMessageType* instances, a *FindItem* response contains *FindItemResponseMessageType* instances.

The response returns a *FindItemResponseMessageType* instance for each parent folder id that is passed in. If you pass in a single parent folder id, you can expect a single *FindItemResponse MessageType* instance. In that case, you can do a single cast using the *as* operator.

```
FindItemResponseType response = binding.FindItem(request);
FindItemResponseMessageType responseMessage =
        response.ResponseMessages.Items[0] as FindItemResponseMessageType;
```

On the other hand, if you make a request with multiple parent folder ids, you get back a *FindItemResponseMessageType* for each parent folder id. As such, you will probably want to process the results in a loop. The *foreach* operation works well for this.

```
FindItemResponseType response = binding.FindItem(request);
foreach (FindItemResponseMessageType responseMessage in
            response.ResponseMessages.Items)
{
  // do something
}
```

The cool thing about *foreach* is that it automatically performs the cast for you so that you don't have to use the *as* operator. Of course, if you try to grab the wrong type during the *foreach* operation, you get a *System.InvalidCastException*.

You can see that the *FindItemResponseMessageType* differs in structure from the other response message types. Aside from the normal *ResponseCode* property and friends, there is an additional property named *RootFolder*. *RootFolder* is of type *FindItemParentType*. The "Parent" part of this name derives from the idea that the *RootFolder* is related to the "parent" folder that you pass into the request.

If you look at the proxy class for *FindItemParentType*, you see that there are many properties related to offsets and fractions and so forth. We will cover those properties in detail in Chapter 15. For now, we are interested in the ubiquitous *Item* property. Unfortunately, this property is of type *System.Object*. Looking at the proxy class itself, however, gives a clue as to what the property might contain as shown in Listing 5-25.

LISTING 5-25 *FindItemParentType.Item* property

```
/// <remarks/>
[System.Xml.Serialization.XmlElementAttribute("Groups",
        typeof(ArrayOfGroupedItemsType))]
[System.Xml.Serialization.XmlElementAttribute("Items",
        typeof(ArrayOfRealItemsType))]
public object Item
// ...
```

You see that the *Item* property can be either an *ArrayOfGroupedItemsType* or an *ArrayOfRealItemsType*. The actual type that is returned is a function of the element name that comes back in the response. In other words, if the XML serializer encounters a response that has a *Groups* element in it, it instantiates an *ArrayOfGroupedItemsType* object in the response proxy class instance. If the XML serializer encounters a response that has an *Items* element in it, it instantiates an *ArrayOfRealItemsType* object in the response proxy class instance.

How you do determine which type you get? Thankfully, it is quite predictable. If you perform a *FindItem* request and include a grouping construct, you receive a response with a *Groups* element and therefore an *ArrayOfGroupedItemsType* instance in your proxy class. If you perform a *FindItem* request and *omit* the grouping construct, you receive a response with an *Items* element and therefore an *ArrayOfRealItemsType* instance in your proxy class.

Because we haven't covered grouped queries yet (to be covered in Chapter 15), all of the examples in this chapter come back with *ArrayOfRealItemsType* instances. You can do a simple cast using the *as* operator as shown in Listing 5-26.

LISTING 5-26 Casting as *ArrayOfRealItemsType*

```
FindItemResponseType response = binding.FindItem(request);
FindItemResponseMessageType responseMessage =
        response.ResponseMessages.Items[0] as FindItemResponseMessageType;
ItemType[] items = (responseMessage.RootFolder.Item as
        ArrayOfRealItemsType).Items;
```

Because this is a frequent cast, it makes sense to add it to the proxy classes via partial class extension. You can add a *GetNormalResults()* method that does the appropriate cast and returns the array of items. Although we will touch on grouping in Chapter 15, it is reasonable to also add a *GetGroupedResults()* method here that does the appropriate cast and returns the grouped results as shown in Listing 5-27.

LISTING 5-27 Partial class extension of *FindItemParentType*

```
/// <summary>
/// Partial class extension of FindItemParentType proxy class
/// </summary>
public partial class FindItemParentType
{
  /// <summary>
  /// Returns the normal (non-grouped) results from a FindItem query for
  /// this RootFolder
  /// </summary>
  /// <returns>Array of items</returns>
  ///
  public ItemType[] GetNormalResults()
  {
    ArrayOfRealItemsType realItems = this.Item as ArrayOfRealItemsType;
```

```
    return realItems.Items;
  }


  /// <summary>
  /// Returns the grouped result from a FindItem query for this RootFolder
  /// </summary>
  /// <returns>Array of groups</returns>
  ///
  public GroupedItemsType[] GetGroupedResults()
  {
    ArrayOfGroupedItemsType groupedItems = this.Item as
        ArrayOfGroupedItemsType;

    return groupedItems.Items;
  }
}
```

Reconsidering Listing 5-26, you can see the new method in action as follows:

```
FindItemResponseType response = binding.FindItem(request);
FindItemResponseMessageType responseMessage =
      response.ResponseMessages.Items[0] as FindItemResponseMessageType;
ItemType[] items = responseMessage.RootFolder.GetNormalResults();
```

It doesn't reduce much of the typing, but it does make things a bit clearer.

SendItem

SendItem is used to submit messages to transport for delivery. *SendItem* will be covered in detail in Chapter 7. Note that only *MessageType* and its descendants can be "sent," which causes a problem in some cases. Exchange Web Services considers anything that is either "IPM.Note" or starts with "IPM.Note." to be a message to the exclusion of everything else. For instance, if you have an item with an item class of IPM.Sharing, you cannot send it through Exchange Web Services. Therefore, Microsoft Office Outlook features, such as calendar sharing requests, cannot currently be duplicated using solely Exchange Web Services. We say solely because there are ways outside of Exchange Web Services in which this can be handled. This is a known issue and will likely be addressed in a service pack or future version of Exchange Web Services.

UpdateItem

To make modifications to an existing item, you use the *UpdateItem* Web method. *UpdateItem* follows a similar structure as *UpdateFolder*, although there are some new attributes and a new element to consider. Let's look at the structure of an *UpdateItem* call as shown in Listing 5-28.

LISTING 5-28 *UpdateItem* structure

```
<UpdateItem xmlns=".../messages.xsd"
            xmlns:t=".../types.xsd"
            ConflictResolution="NeverOverwrite | AutoResolve | AlwaysOverwrite"
            MessageDisposition="[See Chapter 6]"
            SendMeetingInvitationsOrCancellations="[See Chapter 8]">
  <SavedItemFolderId/>
  <ItemChanges/>
</UpdateItem>
```

First, you see that *UpdateItem* exposes three attributes. Two of these (*MessageDisposition* and *SendMeetingInvitationsOrCancellations*) will be discussed in Chapter 7 and Chapter 8, respectively. The third attribute needs a little explanation.

ConflictResolution Attribute

It is commonly known that conflict resolution is an important people skill. Yet, conflict resolution in Exchange Web Services has nothing to do with anger, but instead deals with stale data. From a schema standpoint, there are three valid values for the *ConflictResolution* attribute: *NeverOverwrite*, *AutoResolve*, and *AlwaysOverwrite*. These values are defined by the *ConflictResolutionType* enumeration. Their names are fairly descriptive as shown in Table 5-5.

TABLE 5-5 *ConflictResolution* **Enumeration Values**

Enumeration Value	Comments
NeverOverwrite	The call never overwrites data that has changed underneath you.
AutoResolve	If stale data issues can be resolved, they are; otherwise the request fails.
AlwaysOverwrite	Ignores changes that occurred underneath you; last writer wins.

But what *is* conflict resolution? It is conceivable that two entities can be working on a given item in a mailbox at the same "time." We emphasize time with quotation marks because it is possible to store local copies of an item so that the period of time between the initial retrieval of the item and a subsequent update to that item can be hours, days, or even longer.

Imagine that you are writing to an e-mail client using Exchange Web Services.[19] The client fetches the new items in his mailbox so that there is a local copy on his machine (think Send and Receive). In the meantime, an automatic e-mail stamping agent runs every 15 minutes on the mailbox server and stamps all new E-mails with some legal disclaimer. Several hours later, the client opens an existing item and makes some changes (let's say he changes the subject). This means that the copy of the item that your client has stored locally and is in the process of updating is stale. The client does not have the latest version that include the stamping agent changes.

---

[19] We did this internally. One of our test leads affectionately called it OLAF (Outlook Look And Feel).

Let's set this up just to see what happens. First, the following code creates a message in the Inbox as if it just came into the mailbox as new mail.

```
<CreateItem xmlns=".../messages"
            xmlns:t=".../types"
            MessageDisposition="SaveOnly">
  <Items>
    <t:Message>
      <t:Subject>Just received this email</t:Subject>
    </t:Message>
  </Items>
</CreateItem>
```

The response returns the id of the newly created item. What is of interest is the change key:

```
ChangeKey="CQAAABYAAACztoUHyjkrQrFZTji77KwvAAADTMim"
```

Now, imagine that the client application pulls down this new item, including the id and change key. A few minutes later, the stamping agent opens the mailbox and stamps all new mail messages by appending a legal disclaimer to the message body. If you fetch the item using *GetItem*, you see something interesting—the returned item has a different change key!

Original ChangeKey	CQAAABYAAACztoUHyjkrQrFZTji77KwvAAADTMi**m**
New ChangeKey	CQAAABYAAACztoUHyjkrQrFZTji77KwvAAADTMi**s**

Of course, this isn't surprising because this is exactly what the change key was designed to do and why it was so named. In this case, only the last letter changed. However, don't count on that. You should treat change keys as opaque blobs. Anyway, the client's cached change key does not match the new change key. Let's say that the client wants to update the item by changing the subject, as mentioned earlier.[20] An *UpdateItem* call is made—this time from the client. But remember, the client is passing in the *old* change key. Listing 5-29 shows this call.

LISTING 5-29 *UpdateItem* and conflict resolution

```
<UpdateItem MessageDisposition="SaveOnly"
            ConflictResolution="AutoResolve"
            xmlns=".../messages"
            xmlns:t=".../types">
  <ItemChanges>
    <t:ItemChange>
      <t:ItemId Id="AAAtAEFkbWlu..."
                ChangeKey="CQAAABYAAACztoUHyjkrQrFZTji77KwvAAADTMim"/>
      <t:Updates>
        <t:SetItemField>
          <t:FieldURI FieldURI="item:Subject"/>
          <t:Message>
```

---

[20] In this case, it is reasonable to think that there won't be any conflict because the two parties are changing two unrelated properties on the item in question.

```
            <t:Subject>I have been changed!</t:Subject>
          </t:Message>
        </t:SetItemField>
      </t:Updates>
    </t:ItemChange>
  </ItemChanges>
</UpdateItem>
```

In the client's *UpdateItem* call, the *ConflictResolution* mode is set to *"AutoResolve."* This *implies* that Exchange Web Services will intelligently resolve whatever it can. Unfortunately, an error is returned.

```
<m:UpdateItemResponseMessage ResponseClass="Error">
   <m:MessageText>The send or update operation could not be performed because the
change key passed in the request does not match the current change key for the
item.</m:MessageText>
   <m:ResponseCode>ErrorIrresolvableConflict</m:ResponseCode>
   <m:DescriptiveLinkKey>0</m:DescriptiveLinkKey>
   <m:Items/>
</m:UpdateItemResponseMessage>
```

Notice that the failure message doesn't indicate that it can't resolve the discrepancies, but instead indicates that the change keys don't match. Now, you might expect that behavior with a conflict resolution of *NeverOverwrite*, but *AutoResolve* should be more flexible than that.[21] In fact, the error message isn't entirely accurate. In the *AutoResolve* case, it *isn't* the fact that the change keys don't match that causes the failure. It is the fact that the internal automatic conflict resolution engine detects an irreconcilable difference. But the changes don't seem at odds with each other, so why the failure?

There are two main types of properties that cannot be auto-resolved. The first class are called "streamable" properties. A property is considered "streamable" if fetching the property from the Store *might* require you to open a stream and read the data for that property. In fact, any string, binary, or array type property is considered streamable. Why? Because such property values *can* be large and therefore require streaming from the Exchange Store to the Client Access Server (CAS) box. The *Body* of a message is one such property because it can, by its nature, be a very large property. It doesn't matter whether the property is large enough to require you to open a stream—it is the fact that it is possible. A *Body* property that is a single character long is still considered streamable.

The second class of properties are those that touch the recipient or attachment tables within an item.

---

[21] Indeed, if you retry the request with a conflict resolution of *NeverOverwrite*, you get back the same error (*ErrorIrresolvableConflict*).

Surprisingly, it isn't actually the stamping agent's modification of the streamable *Body* property that causes problems in our example. It is the client's attempt to modify another streamable property—the *Subject*. Yes, the *Subject*! Remember, any string, binary, or array type property is considered streamable. If, in this example, the client sets the *Sensitivity* (enumeration) instead of the *Subject*, the *UpdateItem* call with *AutoResolve* succeeds even though the stamping agent modifies the *Body* property. What do you think might happen if that's reversed? What if the stamping agent changes the *Sensitivity* and then the client tries to change the *Body* with a stale change key? Yes, the call fails because the client with the stale change key is trying to set a streamable property.

This limitation surrounding streamable properties and the recipient and attachment tables is a function of what the *caller with the stale change key is doing* rather than the type of change that occurrs underneath the client.

So, what can you do in a situation like this? You have a few options. First, you can go in the direction of the ultra-paranoid and use *NeverOverwrite*. In this case, the change key fails if it is stale, streamable changes or not. Next, the *AutoResolve* option is interesting in theory, but because string, binary, and array props are not resolvable and the recipient and attachment tables are no-nos, it's hard to really make a case for using automatic conflict resolution. Lastly, you can simply ignore conflict resolution altogether and make all of your *UpdateItem* calls with *AlwaysOverwrite*. The "last writer wins" approach isn't always a bad thing. Because updates write only "dirty" properties back to the Store rather than replacing the entire item, you won't be clobbering someone else's update unless you change the same property. Feel free to go in any direction you want.

SavedItemFolderId Element

The *SavedItemFolderId* element comes to life when calling *UpdateItem* on messages. Therefore, we will defer discussion of this element until Chapter 7.

ItemChanges Element

What good is an *UpdateItem* call if there is no way to let Exchange Web Services know what properties you want to update? Thankfully, the *ItemChanges* element can help in this matter. By reading Chapter 4, you already know how this all works. Why? Because the structure of the *ItemChanges* element is exactly the same as the *FolderChanges* element. Nevertheless, it is worthwhile to review the basic structure here.

Due to the plural nature of *ItemChanges*, you can correctly assume that the element allows one or more changes to be contained therein. The *ItemChanges* element is of type *NonEmptyArrayOfItemChangesType*, which is simply an unbounded sequence of *ItemChangeType* instances. So, you can visualize something like the following at this point:

```
<ItemChanges>
  <t:ItemChange/>
  <t:ItemChange/>
  <t:ItemChange/>
  <t:ItemChange/>
  <!-- more... -->
</ItemChanges>
```

Each *ItemChange* element is of type *ItemChangeType*, which is only slightly more interesting. The general structure of *ItemChangeType* is shown in Listing 5-30.

LISTING 5-30 *ItemChangeType* general structure

```
<t:ItemChange>
  <t:ItemId/> | <t:OccurrenceItemId/> | <t:RecurringMasterItemId/>
  <t:Updates/>
</t:ItemChange>
```

First, you see that a given *ItemChange* element is tied to a single item in a mailbox. You can determine this based on the fact that you have a choice of either an *ItemId*, *OccurrenceItemId*, or *RecurringMasterItemId*.[22] Then, there is the *Updates* element, which is of type *NonEmpty ArrayOfItemChangeDescriptionsType*. At this point, you see that *UpdateItem* has a collection of *ItemChange* elements, each of which is tied to a single item. Each *ItemChange* element has a list of *"ItemChangeDescriptions"* within the *Updates* element. So, how about these *ItemChangeDescription* objects? If you look at the *NonEmptyArrayOfItemChangeDescriptionsType* in the schema, you see that it is an unbound sequence of *AppendToItemField*, *SetItemField*, and/ or *DeleteItemField* elements. Listing 5-31 shows the structure.

LISTING 5-31 The ongoing saga of the *ItemChange* structure

```
<t:ItemChange>
  <t:ItemId Id="AAA==" ChangeKey="AAA=="/>
  <t:Updates>
    <t:AppendToItemField/> | <t:SetItemField/> | <t:DeleteItemField/>
    <t:AppendToItemField/> | <t:SetItemField/> | <t:DeleteItemField/>
    <t:AppendToItemField/> | <t:SetItemField/> | <t:DeleteItemField/>
    <!-- more... -->
  </t:Updates>
</t:ItemChange>
```

These three operations have a common base class as shown in Figure 5-2.

---

[22] We will discuss *OccurrenceItemIds* and *RecurringMasterItemIds* in the Chapter 9.

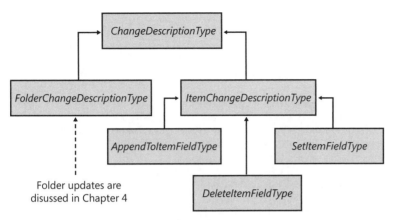

FIGURE 5-2 *ItemChangeDescription* hierarchy

If Figure 5-2 looks familiar, you must have read Chapter 4. We are now filling in the "items" side of the equation. The *ChangeDescription* type at the top of the tree introduces a single element that identifies the path of the property that you want to update. This can be a single *FieldURI*, *IndexedFieldURI*, or *ExtendedFieldURI* element. For instance, if you want to "set" the subject, you can simply include the path for the subject like this:

```
<t:Updates>
  <t:SetItemField>
    <t:FieldURI FieldURI="item:Subject"/>
    <!-- more -->
  </t:SetItemField>
</t:Updates>
```

The structure also implies that there is a one-to-one correspondence between *Set/Append/ Delete* elements and the number of paths that you want to update. You have three properties that you want to update on an item? Well then, you *must* have three corresponding change descriptions in your request. Let's look at each of these change descriptions in turn.

SetItemFieldType   The *SetItemFieldType* is used whenever you want to replace an existing value for a property on an item or add a new property to an item where one does not yet exist. No distinction exists between these cases in the syntax. If the property already exists, it is overwritten with the new value. If the property doesn't yet exist, it is added to the item. *SetItemFieldType* adds a single element to the mix. The element name and type depends on the type of item you are modifying. In other words, if you are modifying an item, you supply an *Item* element. If you are modifying a *CalendarItem*, you supply a *CalendarItem* element and so on. The valid types for *UpdateItem* are detailed in types.xsd and repeated here in Listing 5-32.

LISTING 5-32 *SetItemFieldType* schema type

```
<xs:complexType name="SetItemFieldType">
  <xs:complexContent>
    <xs:extension base="t:ItemChangeDescriptionType">
      <xs:choice>
        <xs:element name="Item" type="t:ItemType"/>
        <xs:element name="Message" type="t:MessageType"/>
        <xs:element name="CalendarItem" type="t:CalendarItemType"/>
        <xs:element name="Contact" type="t:ContactItemType"/>
        <xs:element name="DistributionList"
                    type="t:DistributionListType"/>
        <xs:element name="MeetingMessage" type="t:MeetingMessageType"/>
        <xs:element name="MeetingRequest"
                    type="t:MeetingRequestMessageType"/>
        <xs:element name="MeetingResponse"
                    type="t:MeetingResponseMessageType"/>
        <xs:element name="MeetingCancellation"
                    type="t:MeetingCancellationMessageType"/>
        <xs:element name="Task" type="t:TaskType"/>
      </xs:choice>
    </xs:extension>
  </xs:complexContent>
</xs:complexType>
```

You can expect to see something like the following code when using *SetItemFieldType*:

```
<t:SetItemField>
  <t:FieldURI FieldURI="item:Subject"/>
  <t:Message...
</t:SetItemField>
```

According to the schema, this item element that can occur within *SetItemField* can have many properties set on it. In fact, these are exactly the same types that you pass into *CreateItem* as you saw earlier in this chapter. Of course, if you specify more than one property when performing a *SetItem* change, you will be sorely disappointed. Listing 5-33 shows this in action.

LISTING 5-33 Attempting to set more than one property within a change description

```
<!-- previous xml elided -->
  <t:SetItemField>
    <t:FieldURI FieldURI="item:Subject"/>
    <t:Message>
      <t:Subject>Change the subject</t:Subject>
      <t:Sensitivity>Private</t:Sensitivity>
    </t:Message>
  </t:SetItemField>
<!-- xml elided -->
```

Listing 5-33, shows an attempt to set the subject and the sensitivity in one shot. Submitting this request returns the following error:

```
<UpdateItemResponse xmlns:m=".../messages"
                    xmlns:t=".../types"
                    xmlns=".../messages">
  <m:ResponseMessages>
    <m:UpdateItemResponseMessage ResponseClass="Error">
      <m:MessageText>An object within a change description must contain one and only
                     one property to modify.</m:MessageText>
      <m:ResponseCode>ErrorIncorrectUpdatePropertyCount</m:ResponseCode>
      <m:DescriptiveLinkKey>0</m:DescriptiveLinkKey>
      <m:Items/>
    </m:UpdateItemResponseMessage>
  </m:ResponseMessages>
</UpdateItemResponse>
```

This shouldn't surprise you based on the fact that change descriptions include only a single property path element. Even though the schema allows you to specify multiple properties, the Exchange Web Services business logic forbids it. As a result, you must supply a single property within the item.

```
<UpdateItem MessageDisposition="SaveOnly"
            ConflictResolution="AutoResolve"
            xmlns=".../messages"
            xmlns:t=".../types">
  <ItemChanges>
    <t:ItemChange>
      <t:ItemId Id="AAAtAEFkb..." ChangeKey="AAAAA..."/>
      <t:Updates>
        <t:SetItemField>
          <t:FieldURI FieldURI="item:Subject"/>
          <t:Message>
            <t:Subject>Change the subject</t:Subject>
          </t:Message>
        </t:SetItemField>
      </t:Updates>
    </t:ItemChange>
  </ItemChanges>
</UpdateItem>
```

Note that the property path and the object property must match, as we touched on in Chapter 4. For example, if you use the property path for the subject but use the *Sensitivity* property within the message element, the call fails.

```
<t:SetItemField>
  <t:FieldURI FieldURI="item:Subject"/>
  <t:Message>
    <t:Sensitivity>Private</t:Sensitivity>
  </t:Message>
</t:SetItemField>
```

And the failure?

```
<m:UpdateItemResponseMessage ResponseClass="Error">
  <m:MessageText>Property for update does not match property in object.</m:MessageText>
```

```
<m:ResponseCode>ErrorUpdatePropertyMismatch</m:ResponseCode>
<m:DescriptiveLinkKey>0</m:DescriptiveLinkKey>
<m:MessageXml>
   <t:FieldURI FieldURI="item:Subject"/>
</m:MessageXml>
<m:Items/>
</m:UpdateItemResponseMessage>
```

It should be clear that whenever you are updating a property, you must include both the property path representation as well as the property element with the actual value you want to update. In hindsight, Exchange Web Services probably could do without the property path within the change description. But, alas, it is there and you must contend with it. Of course, you can simplify things a little bit by using the proxy classes. Listing 5-34 shows how the *SetItemFieldType* class can be extended so that you can pass in both the path and the item in the constructor.

LISTING 5-34 Partial class extension for *SetItemFieldType*

```
/// <summary>
/// Partial class extension for the SetItemFieldType proxy class
/// </summary>
public partial class SetItemFieldType
{
  /// <summary>
  /// Constructor needed for XML serialization
  /// </summary>
  public SetItemFieldType() { }

  /// <summary>
  /// Constructor
  /// </summary>
  /// <param name="propertyPath">PropertyPath for this single
  /// change</param>
  /// <param name="itemWithChange">The item along with the change</param>
  ///
  public SetItemFieldType(BasePathToElementType propertyPath,
                          ItemType itemWithChange)
  {
    this.Item = propertyPath;
    this.Item1 = itemWithChange;
  }
}
```

Now, changing the subject field in the example is a little easier.

```
ItemType myItem = new ItemType();
myItem.Subject = "Here is a changed subject";

SetItemFieldType setItem = new SetItemFieldType(
        new PathToUnindexedFieldType(UnindexedFieldURIType.itemSubject),
        myItem);
```

Of course, the overloaded constructor is also used for *PathToUnindexedFieldType*. These small additional constructors can make your life much easier.

Let's tie this all together into an *UpdateItem* call via the proxy classes as shown in Listing 5-35.

LISTING 5-35 *UpdateItem* call via the proxy classes

```
/// <summary>
/// Update the subject of the supplied item
/// </summary>
/// <param name="binding">Binding to use for the UpdateItem call</param>
/// <param name="itemIdToChange">ItemId of the item to update</param>
/// <param name="newSubject">The new subject to use</param>
/// <returns>The updated id and change key</returns>
///
public static ItemIdType UpdateItemSubject(
                        ExchangeServiceBinding binding,
                        ItemIdType itemIdToChange,
                        string newSubject)
{
  UpdateItemType request = new UpdateItemType();
  request.ConflictResolution = ConflictResolutionType.AlwaysOverwrite;

  // Since we are updating an item rather than a message, we do not need
  // to include the MessageDisposition attribute.  Just remember that if
  // you ARE dealing with a Message or descendant, you must include
  // this attribute.  Of course, including it here wouldn't cause
  // problems, it would just be ignored.
  //

  // Let's create our item that will hold the changed subject.  Remember,
  // we can only set a single property.
  //
  ItemType myItem = new ItemType();
  myItem.Subject = newSubject;

  // Now, create our change description using our handy overloaded
  // constructor
  //
  SetItemFieldType setItem = new SetItemFieldType(
        new PathToUnindexedFieldType(UnindexedFieldURIType.itemSubject),
        myItem);

  // The change description lives within an ItemChange
  //
  ItemChangeType itemChange = new ItemChangeType();
  itemChange.Item = itemIdToChange;
  itemChange.Updates = new ItemChangeDescriptionType[] { setItem };

  // Now set our single item change on the request
  //
  request.ItemChanges = new ItemChangeType[] { itemChange };

  UpdateItemResponseType response = binding.UpdateItem(request);
```

```
    // UpdateItem gives us back ItemInfoResponseMessageType instances.  All
    // it gives us, however, is the id of the item.

    ItemInfoResponseMessageType responseMessage =
              response.ResponseMessages.Items[0] as
                            ItemInfoResponseMessageType;
    if (responseMessage.ResponseCode == ResponseCodeType.NoError)
    {
      return responseMessage.Items.Items[0].ItemId;
    }
    else
    {
      throw new Exception("Error trying to update item:  ResponseCode: " +
            responseMessage.ResponseCode);
    }
}
```

As mentioned in Listing 5-35, *UpdateItem* responses contain *ItemInfoResponseMessageType* instances. This type is also used in *GetItem* responses to return all properties of interest. In the *UpdateItem* case, however, you get only the updated *ItemId*. For example

```
<UpdateItemResponse xmlns:m=".../messages"
                    xmlns:t=".../types"
                    xmlns=".../messages">
  <m:ResponseMessages>
    <m:UpdateItemResponseMessage ResponseClass="Success">
        <m:ResponseCode>NoError</m:ResponseCode>
        <m:Items>
          <t:Message>
            <t:ItemId Id="AAAtAEFkbW1uaX..." ChangeKey="AAAAA..."/>
          </t:Message>
        </m:Items>
    </m:UpdateItemResponseMessage>
  </m:ResponseMessages>
</UpdateItemResponse>
```

Why do you need the id? Don't you already have that? Yes, you do, but remember that the change key changes as a result of an *UpdateItem* call. While the id portion remains the same, the change key is different and therefore might be of interest to you if you do further updates.

Are all properties settable? Nope. If you try to set a read-only property, you get back an *ErrorInvalidPropertySet* response code indicating that the property you tried to update does not support the "set" operation. Refer to Appendix C on the companion Web page to determine which operations are applicable to which properties.

DeleteItemFieldType   Deleting a property from an item is much simpler than setting or appending to a property. In fact, all that is necessary is the property path of the property that you want to delete. For instance, if you want to delete the body of an e-mail, put the following in your *Updates* element and you are good to go.[23]

```
<DeleteItemField>
  <t:FieldURI FieldURI="item:Body"/>
</DeleteItemField>
```

Again, to make things a little easier, you can add an overloaded constructor for *DeleteItemField* so that you can pass in the property path during construction. We will leave that as an exercise for you. Without the overload, creating a *DeleteItem* change description looks like the following:

```
DeleteItemFieldType deleteItem = new DeleteItemFieldType();
deleteItem.Item = new
        PathToUnindexedFieldType(UnindexedFieldURIType.itemBody);
```

Not much to it.

AppendItemFieldType   In Chapter 4, we discussed that the *AppendFolderFieldType* is a vestigial element. Luckily for you, there are actually properties that you can append to in items—but not many, mind you. In fact, they are so few that we feel compelled to list them here.

- *calendar:OptionalAttendees*

- *calendar:RequiredAttendees*

- *calendar:Resources*

- *item:Body*

- *message:ToRecipients*

- *message:CcRecipients*

- *message:BccRecipients*

- *message:ReplyTo*

If you try to append to any other property, you get an *ErrorInvalidPropertyAppend* response code indicating that you cannot append to the property in question. Actually, the syntax for *AppendItemField* is the same as *SetItemField*. You list out the property path you want to change and then add the object with the property value that you want to append. So, if you want to append to the body of an item, you can do the following:

```
<t:AppendToItemField>
   <t:FieldURI FieldURI="item:Body"/>
   <t:Message>
      <t:Body BodyType="Text">Some additional text to append</t:Body>
   </t:Message>
</t:AppendToItemField>
```

---

[23] Normally, *DeleteItemField* removes a property from an item. *Body* is special, however. Deleting the body clears out its contents, but the property is still there.

Pretty simple. Now, there is a slight "gotcha" to consider when appending to the body of an item. You must append the same body type that is already present on the item. For example, if your existing message has an HTML body, you cannot append a text body to it. You must append HTML. Likewise, if your existing message has a text body, you cannot append an HTML body to it. You must append text. If you try to append the wrong body type, you get a slightly confusing response code: *ErrorInvalidPropertyAppend*. Actually, the response code makes sense, but the error message does not. The error message implies that the *Body* property does not support the append operation, which is incorrect. It doesn't support your attempt to append disparate body types, so keep this in mind when trying to append to the body. What if you don't know the existing body type? You must call *GetItem* to determine the body type before calling *UpdateItem*.

How about appending recipients?[24] Same idea. Just list out the values to append. For example, if you want to add two more recipients to your message, you can do the following:

```
<t:AppendToItemField>
    <t:FieldURI FieldURI="message:ToRecipients"/>
    <t:Message>
      <t:ToRecipients>
        <t:Mailbox>
          <t:EmailAddress>jane.dow@contoso.com</t:EmailAddress>
        </t:Mailbox>
        <t:Mailbox>
          <t:EmailAddress>ken.malcolmson@contoso.com</t:EmailAddress>
        </t:Mailbox>
      </t:ToRecipients>
    </t:Message>
</t:AppendToItemField>
```

Notice that although multiple values are specified here (two mailbox elements), only a single property is updated. Don't confuse the property path count with multi-valued properties.

What if the property to which you want to append doesn't support append? In that case, you can fetch the existing property, perform the append yourself, and then set the property. For instance, let's say that you want to append some string to the subject of a message. Subject does not support the append operation. Therefore, you need to first get the item, do the append yourself, and then set the subject as shown in Listing 5-36.

LISTING 5-36 Simulating append operations on non-appendable properties

```
/// <summary>
/// Simulate an AppendItemField operation on the subject
/// </summary>
/// <param name="binding">Binding to use for EWS calls</param>
/// <param name="itemIdToChange">ItemId of item to append subject
/// to</param>
```

---

[24] Recipients will be covered in Chapter 7. However, because we are talking about the append operation, it makes sense to show how you can append to multi-valued properties.

```
/// <param name="subjectSuffix">Suffix to append to subject</param>
/// <returns>Updated id of item</returns>
///
public static ItemIdType AppendToSubject(
                ExchangeServiceBinding binding,
                ItemIdType itemIdToChange,
                string subjectSuffix)
{
  // First, get the item using GetItem
  //
  GetItemType getRequest = new GetItemType();
  getRequest.ItemShape = new ItemResponseShapeType(
        DefaultShapeNamesType.IdOnly,
        new PathToUnindexedFieldType(UnindexedFieldURIType.itemSubject));
  getRequest.ItemIds = new BaseItemIdType[] { itemIdToChange };

  GetItemResponseType getItemResponse = binding.GetItem(getRequest);
  ItemInfoResponseMessageType itemInfoMessage =
  getItemResponse.ResponseMessages.Items[0] as
            ItemInfoResponseMessageType;

  if (itemInfoMessage.ResponseCode != ResponseCodeType.NoError)
  {
    throw new Exception("Error getting item :" +
            itemInfoMessage.ResponseCode.ToString());
  }

  ItemType item = itemInfoMessage.Items.Items[0];

  // Note that the subject CAN be null.  If we encounter this, just set
  // the subject to be the suffix
  //
  string newSubject = (item.Subject == null) ? subjectSuffix :
        item.Subject + subjectSuffix;

  // Now call our UpdateItemSubject method from listing 5-37

  return UpdateItemSubject(binding, item.ItemId, newSubject);
}
```

What If You Specify the Wrong Type?

Notice that in both *SetItemField* and *AppendItemField*, it is you, the caller, who determines the local name that is used for the item to update. Let's say you are trying to update a contact, but you include a *CalendarItem* element in the *SetItemField*. For instance

```
<t:SetItemField>
  <t:FieldURI FieldURI="calendar:Start"/>
  <t:CalendarItem>
    <t:Start>2006-07-12T17:31:49Z</t:Start>
  </t:CalendarItem>
</t:SetItemField>
```

Well, the behavior of *UpdateItem* here depends on whether the property in question makes sense on the actual item you are trying to update. For instance, in the preceding snippet, the start time does not make sense on a contact. As such, you get an *ErrorInvalidPropertyRequest* response code and the call fails. However, what if you alter your change description to the following?

```
<t:SetItemField>
   <t:FieldURI FieldURI="item:Subject"/>
   <t:CalendarItem>
     <t:Subject>Hey!  I am not a calendarItem!</t:Subject>
   </t:CalendarItem>
</t:SetItemField>
```

In this case, the call goes through just fine because a contact does have a subject. Strange. We suggest keeping away from such silliness and always using the correct types. For instance, if you are dealing with common properties, such as *item:Subject*, it is completely acceptable to use *ItemType* as the local name when updating your contact. Why? Because a contact *is* an item.

Thus, the item element name determines which child properties you can define, but it is the child properties that determine the applicability of the updated property to the actual item in question.

ItemType Properties

As you saw in Chapter 3, descendant types "inherit" the schema properties of their base types. Properties that are exposed on *ItemType* are available on *MessageType*, *ContactType*, *MeetingResponseType*, and so forth. As a result, these *ItemType* properties are encountered quite often. All of the properties available on *ItemType* are shown in Table 5-6, and we will expound on those requiring extra clarification.

TABLE 5-6   Properties on *ItemType*

Property Name	Type	Comments
MimeContent	*MimeContentType*	Base64-encoded contents of the MIME stream for an item
ItemId	*ItemIdType*	Unique identifier for an item
ParentFolderId	*FolderIdType*	Unique identifier for the folder that contains an item
ItemClass	*ItemClassType*	PR_MESSAGE_CLASS MAPI property for an item
Subject	String	Subject of an item

Property Name	Type	Comments
Sensitivity	*SensitivityChoicesType*	Enumeration indicating the sensitive nature of an item; valid values are *Normal, Personal, Private*, and *Confidential*
Body	*BodyType*	Body content of an item
Attachments	*NonEmptyArrayOfAttachmentsType*	Metadata about the attachments on an item
DateTimeReceived	*DateTime*	Date/Time an item was received
Size	Integer	Size in bytes of an item
Categories	*ArrayOfStringsType*	Categories associated with an item
Importance	*ImportanceChoicesType*	Enumeration indicating the importance of an item; valid values are *Low, Normal*, and *High*
InReplyTo	String	Taken from PR_IN_REPLY_TO_ID MAPI property
IsSubmitted	Boolean	True if an item has been submitted for delivery
IsDraft	Boolean	True if an item is a draft
IsFromMe	Boolean	True if an item is from you
IsResend	Boolean	True if an item is a re-send
IsUnmodified	Boolean	True if an item is unmodified
InternetMessageHeaders	*NonEmptyArrayOfInternetHeadersType*	Collection of Internet message headers associated with an item
DateTimeSent	*DateTime*	Date/Time an item was sent
DateTimeCreated	*DateTime*	Date/Time an item was created
ResponseObjects	*NonEmptyArrayOfResponseObjectsType*	Applicable actions for an item
ReminderDueBy	*DateTime*	Due date of an item; used for reminders
ReminderIsSet	Boolean	True if a reminder has been set on an item
ReminderMinutesBeforeStart	*ReminderMinutesBeforeStartType*	Number of minutes before the due date that a reminder should be shown to the user
DisplayCc	String	Concatenated string of the display names of the Cc recipients of an item; each recipient is separated by a semicolon
DisplayTo	String	Concatenated string of the display names of the To recipients of an item; each recipient is separated by a semicolon

Property Name	Type	Comments
HasAttachments	Boolean	True if an item has non-hidden attachments
ExtendedProperty*	*ExtendedPropertyType* (unbounded)	List of zero or more extended properties that are requested for an item
Culture	*xs:language*	Culture name associated with the body of an item

*Extended properties are so special that we have dedicated an entire chapter to them (Chapter 13).

ItemType Properties and Shapes

As discussed in Chapter 3, the properties that are returned for a given item type are determined by the supplied response shape and the type of item in question. For *ItemType*, an *IdOnly* base shape returns only the *ItemId* of the item. The *Default* base shape returns the *ItemId*, *Attachments*, *ResponseObjects*, *HasAttachments*, and *Culture* properties. The *AllProperties* base shape returns all of the properties listed in Table 5-2 with the exception of *ExtendedProperties*. You must explicitly ask for extended properties by using the *AdditionalProperties* child element within the response shape.

Of course, if a given property is not set on an item, then the property cannot be returned, even if the property is spelled out in the response shape.

Now, let's touch on some of the properties that need a little more explanation.

MimeContent Property

Multipurpose Internet Mail Extensions (MIME) is a standard way to encode e-mails to support such things as binary attachments and non-ASCII character sets. You can think of the MIME content as a way to extract a given item out of the Exchange Store. You can also create items in a mailbox by setting the *MimeContent* property to be the contents of a MIME stream during a *CreateItem* call, which you will see shortly.

Retrieving MIME Content   For starters, let's make a *GetItem* call on a message and request the MIME content. As seen in Chapter 3, you must explicitly ask for the MIME content by setting the *IncludeMimeContent* element in the item response shape to true.

```
<GetItem xmlns=".../messages"
         xmlns:t=".../types">
  <ItemShape>
    <t:BaseShape>IdOnly</t:BaseShape>
    <t:IncludeMimeContent>true</t:IncludeMimeContent>
  </ItemShape>
  <ItemIds>
    <t:ItemId Id="AAAtAEFkbWlu..." ChangeKey="AAAAA..."/>
  </ItemIds>
</GetItem>
```

Because *MimeContent* is emitted as a child element of the item, it seems inconsistent with the other property paths to have to use the *IncludeMimeContent* optional element. Why can't you simply request *MimeContent* as an additional property and forget about the *IncludeMimeContent* optional element? It turns out that you can as shown in Listing 5-37.

LISTING 5-37 Requesting *MimeContent* using additional properties

```
<GetItem xmlns=".../messages"
         xmlns:t=".../types">
  <ItemShape>
    <t:BaseShape>IdOnly</t:BaseShape>
    <t:AdditionalProperties>
      <t:FieldURI FieldURI="item:MimeContent"/>
    </t:AdditionalProperties>
  </ItemShape>
  <ItemIds>
    <t:ItemId Id="AAAtAEFkbWlua..." ChangeKey="AAAAA..."/>
  </ItemIds>
</GetItem>
```

The response is shown in Listing 5-38.

LISTING 5-38 *GetItem* response with *MimeContent*

```
<GetItemResponse xmlns:m=".../messages"
                 xmlns:t=".../types"
                 xmlns=".../messages">
  <m:ResponseMessages>
    <m:GetItemResponseMessage ResponseClass="Success">
      <m:ResponseCode>NoError</m:ResponseCode>
      <m:Items>
        <t:Message>
          <t:MimeContent CharacterSet="UTF-8">Q29udGVudC1DbG...</t:MimeContent>
          <t:ItemId Id="AAAtAEFkbWlua..." ChangeKey="AAAAA..."/>
        </t:Message>
      </m:Items>
    </m:GetItemResponseMessage>
  </m:ResponseMessages>
</GetItemResponse>
```

Notice that the *MimeContent* element contains a *CharacterSet* attribute. Because MIME is a string-based encoding, it's important to know how the string is encoded. In this case, the string is UTF-8 encoded. To access the original MIME text, you can decode the Base64 string into a byte array and then decode the bytes using the UTF-8 decoder as shown in Listing 5-39.

LISTING 5-39 Decoding the MIME stream

```
/// <summary>
/// Returns the UTF-8 MIME string contents from the Base64 encoded string
/// </summary>
/// <param name="base64MimeContent">Base64 encoded content</param>
/// <returns>MIME string</returns>
///
public static string GetMimeText(string base64MimeContent)
{
    // Content is Base64 encoded.  We need the byte[]
    //
    byte[] bytes = System.Convert.FromBase64String(base64MimeContent);

    // Of course, for other encodings, you would replace the UTF8 singleton
    // reference here accordingly.
    //
    return Encoding.UTF8.GetString(bytes);
}
```

After running the new method and writing out the results, the conversion is successful.

```
Content-Class: urn:content-classes:message
Date: Mon, 25 Dec 2006 07:45:07 -0800
Subject: Here is a message for MIME examples
Thread-Topic: Here is a message for MIME examples
Thread-Index: AQHHKDun6JwzcJa8uk6m7NwioIaraw==
Message-ID:
 <A546EB021E35734B8AC94A7AEDE11D98784E2D@someserver.com>
Accept-Language: en-US
Content-Language: en-US
X-MS-Has-Attach:
X-MS-TNEF-Correlator:
Content-Type: text/plain; charset="us-ascii"
Content-Transfer-Encoding: quoted-printable
MIME-Version: 1.0
```

Of course, you can also retrieve the MIME content via the proxy classes as shown in Listing 5-40. Here, the handy *GetMimeText()* method from Listing 5-39 is used to decode the stream.

LISTING 5-40 Retrieving the MIME string via the proxy classes

```
/// <summary>
/// Retrieves the MIME string from the item
/// </summary>
/// <param name="binding">Binding to use for calls</param>
/// <param name="itemId">Id of the item to retrieve MIME text for</param>
/// <returns>Mime string</returns>
///
public static string GetMimeTextViaProxy(
                        ExchangeServiceBinding binding,
                        ItemIdType itemId)
```

```
{
  GetItemType request = new GetItemType();

  // Let's use some of our handy partial class extenstions to build up our
  // shape so that this example is a bit shorter :)  Here we just want the
  // Id along with the mime content so the mime content will be specified
  // as an additional property.
  //
  PathToUnindexedFieldType mimeContent = new
        PathToUnindexedFieldType(UnindexedFieldURIType.itemMimeContent);
  request.ItemShape = new
        ItemResponseShapeType(DefaultShapeNamesType.IdOnly, mimeContent);

  request.ItemIds = new BaseItemIdType[] { itemId };

  GetItemResponseType response = binding.GetItem(request);
  ItemInfoResponseMessageType responseMessage =
        response.ResponseMessages.Items[0] as ItemInfoResponseMessageType;
  if (responseMessage.ResponseCode == ResponseCodeType.NoError)
  {
    ItemType item = responseMessage.Items.Items[0];
    if (item.MimeContent != null)
    {
      return GetMimeText(item.MimeContent.Value);
    }
    else
    {
      return null;
    }
  }
  else
  {
    throw new InvalidOperationException(
        "Failed to get Mime Content.  Error " +
            responseMessage.ResponseCode);
  }
}
```

Although you can retrieve the MIME in two ways (via the *IncludeMimeContent* and *AdditionalProperties* elements), our personal preference is to use the additional properties approach and ignore the *IncludeMimeContent* element. There is no performance improvement either way, but we opt for this approach for consistency.

Just for reference, MIME content can be retrieved only for descendants of *Post* (IPM.Post), *Message*, and *CalendarItems*. This might change in future versions to include other item types (hopefully, all).

Creating an Item from MIME   You might need to create an item given the MIME content.[25] A typical example is when you have an electronic mail (.EML) file containing the message. Because the *MimeContent* property is read/write, you are able to set this in a *CreateItem* call as shown in Listing 5-41.

LISTING 5-41 Creating an item given the MIME content

```
<CreateItem xmlns=".../messages"
            xmlns:t=".../types" MessageDisposition="SaveOnly">
  <Items>
    <t:Message>
      <t:MimeContent CharacterSet="UTF-8">Q29udGVudC1Dzczo... </t:MimeContent>
    </t:Message>
  </Items>
</CreateItem>
```

That is pretty easy. Given that the MIME content holds a great deal of properties about an item, what happens if you set some properties at the same time that you create an item from MIME? For example, the original example message has a subject of "Here is a message for MIME examples." Let's create an item given the MIME content, but also set a new subject.

```
<CreateItem xmlns=".../messages"
            xmlns:t=".../types"
            MessageDisposition="SaveOnly">
  <Items>
    <t:Message>
      <t:MimeContent CharacterSet="UTF-8">Q29udGVudC1D...</t:MimeContent>
      <t:Subject>This is a replacement subject</t:Subject>
    </t:Message>
  </Items>
</CreateItem>
```

What should you expect the results to be? First, it succeeds. Second, the explicit subject replaces the subject embedded in the MIME content. Why is that? Well, during a *CreateItem* call, properties are processed on a first-come, first-served basis. You first create an empty message, set the contents from the MIME, and *then* set the explicit subject. As such, the MIME subject is overwritten by the explicit subject. This really isn't a problem in practice, although it has some interesting implications. The schema mandates a specific ordering of elements within item instances. In other words, trying to put the subject before the *MimeContent* property results in a schema validation error. Therefore, which property overwrites which is dictated by the ordering as defined in the schema. The only other time that you encounter two competing properties is with extended properties, whereby you can set a property such as the subject, and then overwrite it with an extended property that points to the MAPI subject property. But as a matter of practice, you should not write conflicting properties to an item.

---

[25] Although you can create an item from MIME, you cannot update the MIME content of an existing item. The *MimeContent* property does not support update or append operations.

Body Property

The *Body* property exposes the body of a message. Two different kinds of bodies are supported by Exchange Web Services: text and HTML. As seen in Chapter 3, the *ItemResponseShapeType* exposes the *BodyType* optional element that you can specify to indicate the type of body you want to retrieve. The type of this element is *BodyTypeResponseType*, which exposes three valid enumeration values: *Text*, *HTML*, and *Best*.

Before getting too far, let's put a message in the mailbox with an HTML body to have something to play with. Note that HTML markup must be wrapped in a character data (CDATA) block so that valid XML is passed as shown in Listing 5-42.

LISTING 5-42 Creating an item with an HTML body

```
<CreateItem xmlns=".../messages"
            xmlns:t=".../types"
            MessageDisposition="SaveOnly">
  <Items>
    <t:Message>
      <t:Subject>Message with an HTML body</t:Subject>
      <t:Body BodyType="HTML"><![CDATA[<b>Here is some HTML</b>]]></t:Body>
    </t:Message>
  </Items>
</CreateItem>
```

The *CreateItem* call returns the *ItemId* of the newly created item. You can try to retrieve the item just created after adding the *BodyType* element to the item response shape as shown in Listing 5-43.

LISTING 5-43 Trying (in vain) to retrieve the HTML body

```
<GetItem xmlns=".../messages"
         xmlns:t=".../types">
  <ItemShape>
    <t:BaseShape>IdOnly</t:BaseShape>
    <t:BodyType>HTML</t:BodyType>
  </ItemShape>
  <ItemIds>
    <t:ItemId Id="AAAeAGXJAZXhjaG..." ChangeKey="CQAAABYAAADcPi2fp..."/>
  </ItemIds>
</GetItem>
```

And the response is:

```
<GetItemResponse xmlns:m=".../messages"
                 xmlns:t=".../types"
                 xmlns=".../messages">
  <m:ResponseMessages>
    <m:GetItemResponseMessage ResponseClass="Success">
```

```
        <m:ResponseCode>NoError</m:ResponseCode>
        <m:Items>
          <t:Message>
            <t:ItemId Id="AAAeAGRhdnNOZX..." ChangeKey="CQAAABYAAA..."/>
          </t:Message>
        </m:Items>
      </m:GetItemResponseMessage>
    </m:ResponseMessages>
</GetItemResponse>
```

Well, that's exciting. Sort of an "out-of-body" experience. (Sorry.) Where did it go? Well, the *BodyType* element in the response shape should have been named *"BodyTypeIfYouActually RequestTheBody."* But, alas, that was considered too long. Since the request asks for a *BaseShape* of *IdOnly* and doesn't explicitly ask for the body, there is no body to format. This *BodyType* element in the response shape is simply metadata about the *Body* property.

Following is another example, but this time the request asks for the item with the *Default* shape, which happens to include the *Body* property when you are dealing with messages.

```
<ItemShape>
    <t:BaseShape>Default</t:BaseShape>
    <t:BodyType>HTML</t:BodyType>
</ItemShape>
```

And the response (just the message element) is:

```
<t:Message>
    <t:ItemId Id="AAAeAGRhdnN..." ChangeKey="CQAAABYAAADcP..."/>
    <t:Subject>Message with an HTML body</t:Subject>
    <t:Sensitivity>Normal</t:Sensitivity>
    <t:Body BodyType="HTML"><html> <head> <meta http-equiv="Content-Type"
            content="text/html; charset=utf-8"> </head> <body>
            <b>Here is some HTML</b></body> </html></t:Body>
    <t:Size>228</t:Size>
    <t:DateTimeSent>2006-09-22T20:01:19Z</t:DateTimeSent>
    <t:DateTimeCreated>2006-09-22T20:01:19Z</t:DateTimeCreated>
    <t:ResponseObjects>
        <t:ForwardItem/>
    </t:ResponseObjects>
    <t:HasAttachments>false</t:HasAttachments>
    <t:IsReadReceiptRequested>false</t:IsReadReceiptRequested>
    <t:IsDeliveryReceiptRequested>false</t:IsDeliveryReceiptRequested>
    <t:IsRead>true</t:IsRead>
</t:Message>
```

Of course, if you want only the body element, you can save a few bytes by specifying the *IdOnly* base shape and explicitly asking for the *Body* property via the *AdditionalProperties* element. This is our preference because you really don't need the other properties.

```
<!-- Request -->
<ItemShape>
    <t:BaseShape>IdOnly</t:BaseShape>
    <t:BodyType>HTML</t:BodyType>
    <t:AdditionalProperties>
        <t:FieldURI FieldURI="item:Body"/>
    </t:AdditionalProperties>
</ItemShape>
```

The response (just the message element) is:

```
<t:Message>
    <t:ItemId Id="AAAeAGRhdnN0ZXJ..." ChangeKey="CQAAABYAAA..." />
    <t:Body BodyType="HTML"><html> <head> <meta http-equiv="Content-Type"
        content="text/html; charset=utf-8"> </head>
        <body> <b>Here is some HTML</b> </body> </html></t:Body>
</t:Message>
```

When the message is created, it is explicitly given an HTML body. So far, the examples have retrieved the body as HTML. What if you just want the text (no mark up) content? Simply change the *BodyType* to *Text* and your wish is granted.[26]

```
<ItemShape>
    <t:BaseShape>IdOnly</t:BaseShape>
    <t:BodyType>Text</t:BodyType>
    <t:AdditionalProperties>
        <t:FieldURI FieldURI="item:Body"/>
    </t:AdditionalProperties>
</ItemShape>
```

And the response is

```
<t:Message>
    <t:ItemId Id="AAAeAGRhdnN0ZXJAZ..." ChangeKey="CQAAABYAAADcP..."/>
    <t:Body BodyType="Text">Here is some HTML</t:Body>
</t:Message>
```

If the *BodyType* element is omitted from the response shape, the body is returned in whatever format it was created in.[27] In other words, if you create an item with a text body and then call *GetItem* with an item shape that omits the *BodyType* element, you get back a text body. If you perform the same call on an item that was created with an HTML body, you get back an HTML body. Setting *BodyType* to "Best" is the same as omitting it entirely.

As mentioned earlier in this chapter, the *item:Body* property path cannot be requested during *FindItem* operations as the *Body* can be large and properties returned by *FindItem* are truncated to 512 bytes.

---

[26] Of course, if you have a text body and want it converted to HTML, you can request a *BodyType* of HTML and EWS will convert the body for you.

[27] There is an exception to this. If the item has an RTF body, it will be converted to HTML.

Attachments Property

In Exchange Web Services, an item can have zero or more attachments. The *Attachments* property exposes metadata about the attachments, but does not expose the attachments themselves. To add, get, or delete the actual attachments, you must use the *CreateAttachment*, *GetAttachment*, and *DeleteAttachment* Web methods, respectively.[28] You might question the value of the *Attachments* property if it doesn't provide the actual attachment content. Well, it actually is quite useful. You might want to retrieve the contents of a message along with information about the attachments, but defer the loading of the attachments until the user actually wants to view the attachments.

Attachments will be covered in depth in Chapter 12.

Categories Property

The *Categories* property exposes the idea that items can be "grouped" together based on certain user-defined characteristics. Each category is represented as a string, and a given item can be assigned to zero or more categories. By default, an item has no categories. In the schema, the *Categories* property is an *ArrayOfStringsType*, which is simply an unbounded sequence of *String* elements. For example, the following code is a perfectly acceptable categories instance.

```
<t:Categories>
  <t:String>Blue</t:String>
  <t:String>Fuzzy</t:String>
  <t:String>Creature</t:String>
</t:Categories>
```

Setting or updating categories is as simple as using the preceding code within an *Item* element of a *CreateItem* or *UpdateItem* call as shown in Listing 5-44.

LISTING 5-44 Creating an item with categories

```
<CreateItem xmlns=".../messages"
            xmlns:t=".../types">
  <Items>
    <t:Item>
      <t:Subject>Item With Categories</t:Subject>
      <t:Categories>
        <t:String>Blue</t:String>
        <t:String>Fuzzy</t:String>
        <t:String>Creature</t:String>
      </t:Categories>
    </t:Item>
  </Items>
</CreateItem>
```

---

[28] All of which are discussed in Chapter 12.

In proxy code, you might be pleasantly surprised that *Categories* is surfaced as an actual string array rather than an *ArrayOfStringType* wrapper class. As such, setting categories is as simple as creating a new string array.

```
ItemType item = new ItemType();
item.Categories = new string[] { "Blue", "Fuzzy", "Creature" };
```

InternetMessageHeaders Property

Internet message headers provide information about a given message in the form of name-value pairs. There are a number of standard headers defined in RFC 822, RFC 1123, and RFC 2822, and users are free to define new ones as they see fit. Many of the standard header values get promoted to individual properties on the item by the Store, but custom headers do not. It is often necessary to dig into the Internet message headers if your application transmits pertinent data within the Internet message headers of an item.

Internet message headers conform to a pattern that you have seen, and will see, in several places in Exchange Web Services—the metadata/data pattern. Because Internet message headers can contain a great deal of data, the data is not returned by default. Exchange Web Services does, however, return the header names. You can call *GetItem* with the *Default* base shape, but because the response will be fairly large, it's simpler to ask for the id and the headers explicitly as shown in Listing 5-45.

LISTING 5-45 *GetItem* with *item:InternetMessageHeaders* property path

```
<GetItem xmlns=".../messages"
         xmlns:t=".../types">
  <ItemShape>
    <t:BaseShape>IdOnly</t:BaseShape>
    <t:AdditionalProperties>
      <t:FieldURI FieldURI="item:InternetMessageHeaders"/>
    </t:AdditionalProperties>
  </ItemShape>
  <ItemIds>
    <t:ItemId Id="AAAeAGRhdn..." ChangeKey="AAAAA..."/>
  </ItemIds>
</GetItem>
```

Listing 5-46 displays the response.

LISTING 5-46 *GetItem* response with *InternetMessageHeaders*

```
<GetItemResponse xmlns:m=".../messages"
                 xmlns:t=".../types"
                 xmlns=".../messages">
  <m:ResponseMessages>
    <m:GetItemResponseMessage ResponseClass="Success">
      <m:ResponseCode>NoError</m:ResponseCode>
      <m:Items>
        <t:Message>
          <t:ItemId Id="AAAeAGRh...
          <t:InternetMessageHeaders>
            <t:InternetMessageHeader HeaderName="Received"/>
            <t:InternetMessageHeader HeaderName="Content-Type"/>
            <t:InternetMessageHeader
                    HeaderName="Content-Transfer-Encoding"/>
            <t:InternetMessageHeader HeaderName="From"/>
            <t:InternetMessageHeader HeaderName="To"/>
            <t:InternetMessageHeader HeaderName="Date"/>
            <t:InternetMessageHeader HeaderName="Subject"/>
            <t:InternetMessageHeader HeaderName="Thread-Topic"/>
            <t:InternetMessageHeader HeaderName="Thread-Index"/>
            <t:InternetMessageHeader HeaderName="Message-ID"/>
            <t:InternetMessageHeader HeaderName="References"/>
            <t:InternetMessageHeader HeaderName="In-Reply-To"/>
            <t:InternetMessageHeader HeaderName="Accept-Language"/>
            <t:InternetMessageHeader HeaderName="Content-Language"/>
            <t:InternetMessageHeader HeaderName="X-MS-Has-Attach"/>
            <t:InternetMessageHeader
                  HeaderName="X-MS-Exchange-Organization-SCL"/>
            <t:InternetMessageHeader HeaderName="X-MS-TNEF-Correlator"/>
            <t:InternetMessageHeader HeaderName="MIME-Version"/>
          </t:InternetMessageHeaders>
        </t:Message>
      </m:Items>
    </m:GetItemResponseMessage>
  </m:ResponseMessages>
</GetItemResponse>
```

Wow! That's a lot of headers. You can see some familiar ones in there such as From, To, Subject, and so forth. Yet, there are also some unfamiliar ones, such as Content-Language and MIME-Version. It's great that you can see which headers are on the item, but how do you get the actual header values?

Notice that Listing 5-46 asks for the property path *item:InternetMessageHeaders* (plural) in the response shape. A corresponding dictionary property path is named *item:InternetMessageHeader* (singular). Now, since this is a dictionary property, you must supply both the *FieldURI* identifier as well as the "Value" or *FieldIndex* within the property path. Let's say you want to get the Date message header. You can request it in the response shape as shown in Listing 5-47.

LISTING 5-47 Asking for a specific header in the response shape

```
<ItemShape>
  <t:BaseShape>IdOnly</t:BaseShape>
  <t:AdditionalProperties>
    <t:IndexedFieldURI FieldURI="item:InternetMessageHeader"
                       FieldIndex="Date"/>
  </t:AdditionalProperties>
</ItemShape>
```

This response shows only the message element to save space.

```
<t:Message>
  <t:ItemId Id="AAAeAGRhdnN...
  <t:InternetMessageHeaders>
    <t:InternetMessageHeader HeaderName="Date">
        Sun, 14 Jan 2007 21:01:04 -0800</t:InternetMessageHeader>
  </t:InternetMessageHeaders>
</t:Message>
```

It is interesting to note that the Date header is returned within the *InternetMessageHeaders* parent element, even though *item:InternetMessageHeaders* (plural) is not requested in the response shape. Also notice that, due to the absence of *item:InternetMessageHeaders* (plural), none of the other header names show up. What happens if you ask for two?

```
<ItemShape>
  <t:BaseShape>IdOnly</t:BaseShape>
  <t:AdditionalProperties>
    <t:IndexedFieldURI FieldURI="item:InternetMessageHeader"
                       FieldIndex="Date"/>
    <t:IndexedFieldURI FieldURI="item:InternetMessageHeader"
                       FieldIndex="Subject"/>
  </t:AdditionalProperties>
</ItemShape>
```

Again, only the message element of the response is displayed.

```
<t:Message>
  <t:ItemId Id="AAAeAGRhdnNOZ..." ChangeKey="AAAAA..."/>
  <t:InternetMessageHeaders>
    <t:InternetMessageHeader HeaderName="Date">
        Sun, 14 Jan 2007 21:01:04 -0800</t:InternetMessageHeader>
    <t:InternetMessageHeader HeaderName="Subject">
        RE: Cheese and crackers</t:InternetMessageHeader>
  </t:InternetMessageHeaders>
</t:Message>
```

Ah, now you see that both requested headers reside within the *InternetMessageHeaders* parent element. What do you think would happen if you added *item:InternetMessageHeaders* (plural) to the request?

```
<ItemShape>
  <t:BaseShape>IdOnly</t:BaseShape>
  <t:AdditionalProperties>
    <t:FieldURI FieldURI="item:InternetMessageHeaders"/>
    <t:IndexedFieldURI FieldURI="item:InternetMessageHeader"
                       FieldIndex="Date"/>
    <t:IndexedFieldURI FieldURI="item:InternetMessageHeader"
                       FieldIndex="Subject"/>
  </t:AdditionalProperties>
</ItemShape>
```

The response in Listing 5-48 is somewhat interesting.

LISTING 5-48 *GetItem* response with both header names and specific headers

```
<t:Message>
  <t:ItemId Id="AAAeAGR..." ChangeKey="AAA..."/>
  <t:InternetMessageHeaders>
   <t:InternetMessageHeader HeaderName="Received"/>
   <t:InternetMessageHeader HeaderName="Content-Type"/>
   <t:InternetMessageHeader HeaderName="Content-Transfer-Encoding"/>
   <t:InternetMessageHeader HeaderName="From"/>
   <t:InternetMessageHeader HeaderName="To"/>
   <t:InternetMessageHeader HeaderName="Thread-Topic"/>
   <t:InternetMessageHeader HeaderName="Thread-Index"/>
   <t:InternetMessageHeader HeaderName="Message-ID"/>
   <t:InternetMessageHeader HeaderName="References"/>
   <t:InternetMessageHeader HeaderName="In-Reply-To"/>
   <t:InternetMessageHeader HeaderName="Accept-Language"/>
   <t:InternetMessageHeader HeaderName="Content-Language"/>
   <t:InternetMessageHeader HeaderName="X-MS-Has-Attach"/>
   <t:InternetMessageHeader HeaderName="X-MS-Exchange-Organization-SCL"/>
   <t:InternetMessageHeader HeaderName="X-MS-TNEF-Correlator"/>
   <t:InternetMessageHeader HeaderName="MIME-Version"/>
   <t:InternetMessageHeader HeaderName="Date">
        Sun, 14 Jan 2007 21:01:04 -0800</t:InternetMessageHeader>
   <t:InternetMessageHeader HeaderName="Subject">
        RE: Cheese and crackers</t:InternetMessageHeader>
  </t:InternetMessageHeaders>
</t:Message>
```

Notice that the results of *item:InternetMessageHeaders* (plural) and the specific header values are combined into one collection.

So, how about retrieving the headers via the proxy classes? Listing 5-49 does this and a bit more. The method in Listing 5-49 fetches the headers and all their values.

LISTING 5-49 Retrieve all Internet message headers via the proxy classes

```
/// <summary>
/// Returns an item along with all of its internet message header values
/// </summary>
/// <param name="binding">Binding to use for calls</param>
/// <param name="id">Id of item to get</param>
/// <returns>ItemType instance</returns>
///
public static ItemType GetItemAndAllHeaders(
                    ExchangeServiceBinding binding,
                    ItemIdType id)
{
  // First, we need to get all the header names and then build up another
  // request to fetch each header explicitly.
  //
  GetItemType firstGetRequest = new GetItemType();
  firstGetRequest.ItemShape = new ItemResponseShapeType(
            DefaultShapeNamesType.IdOnly,
            new PathToUnindexedFieldType(
                UnindexedFieldURIType.itemInternetMessageHeaders));

  firstGetRequest.ItemIds = new ItemIdType[] { id };

  GetItemResponseType firstGetResponse = binding.GetItem(firstGetRequest);
  ItemInfoResponseMessageType firstMessage =
            firstGetResponse.ResponseMessages.Items[0] as
                ItemInfoResponseMessageType;
  if (firstMessage.ResponseCode != ResponseCodeType.NoError)
  {
    throw new Exception("First get failed with error code: " +
            firstMessage.ResponseCode.ToString());
  }

  // Now, we need to cycle through all the headers to get the names so we
  // can make our second request for the header values.
  //
  ItemType item = firstMessage.Items.Items[0];
  BasePathToElementType[] additionalProps = new
          BasePathToElementType[item.InternetMessageHeaders.Length];
  int index = 0;
  foreach (InternetHeaderType headerName in item.InternetMessageHeaders)
  {
    PathToIndexedFieldType headerPath = new PathToIndexedFieldType(
        DictionaryURIType.itemInternetMessageHeader,
        headerName.HeaderName);

    additionalProps[index++] = headerPath;
  }

  // Now that we have the additional props set up, make our second
  // request.
  //
  GetItemType secondGetRequest = new GetItemType();
  secondGetRequest.ItemShape = new ItemResponseShapeType(
```

```
                    DefaultShapeNamesType.IdOnly,
                    additionalProps);

    secondGetRequest.ItemIds = new ItemIdType[] { id };
    GetItemResponseType secondGetResponse =
            binding.GetItem(secondGetRequest);
    ItemInfoResponseMessageType secondMessage =
            secondGetResponse.ResponseMessages.Items[0] as
                    ItemInfoResponseMessageType;
    if (secondMessage.ResponseCode != ResponseCodeType.NoError)
    {
      throw new Exception("Second get failed with error code: " +
            secondMessage.ResponseCode.ToString());
    }

    return secondMessage.Items.Items[0];
}
```

Be advised that it is possible for a header to be on a message, but for the value for that header to be empty. In these cases, the value is returned as null when using the proxy classes.

One reasonable question that might arise is how to set/update the headers for a given message. Well, you can't accomplish this through Exchange Web Services.

Some issues surrounding Internet message header retrieval need to be brought to your attention. Without going into too much detail, when a message arrives, some of the Internet message headers get promoted into individual properties on a message. The original MIME header block also gets persisted as MAPI property (PR_TRANSPORT_MESSAGE_HEADERS). It is important to note that the promoted headers are a *subset* of the headers contained within the original header block. Why is this important? Because the collection property (*item:InternetMessageHeaders*) deals with the original header block, whereas the individual headers deal with the promoted properties.

Although you can get a list of all of the header names associated with a message, you can only get header values from promoted headers. If you truly need to get values for all headers, you need to get the header block and decode it yourself.[29] This, of course, means that you can't get all of your header values through *FindItem* because *FindItem* truncates all large values to 512 bytes, which is likely smaller than your Internet message header block.

The Internet message header block can be obtained by using extended properties with the MAPI property tag for the PR_TRANSPORT_MESSAGE_HEADERS as shown in the following item response shape.

---

[29] In Exchange Server 2007 Service Pack 1, this has been changed so that the *InternetMessageHeaders* collection always returns the header values.

```
<ItemShape>
  <t:BaseShape>IdOnly</t:BaseShape>
    <t:AdditionalProperties>
      <t:ExtendedFieldURI PropertyTag="0x007D" PropertyType="String"/>
    </t:AdditionalProperties>
</ItemShape>
```

Once you have the data, you need to parse it to obtain the header values that are of interest to you.

ResponseObjects Property

In Exchange Web Services, there are "items" that are not *really* items. For better or worse, the Exchange Web Services team decided to keep the number of Web methods small and over-load their functionality based on the data passed in. Therefore, performing an action such as forwarding a message is not accomplished, as you might think, by calling a *ForwardItem* Web method (which doesn't exist). Instead, you call *CreateItem* and pass in a "virtual" item named *ForwardItem*. This can be seen as creating a forwarded item.

During the development of Exchange 2007 Web Services, these actions were called "virtual items." However, virtual items are created in *response* to another item. As such, rather than calling them by the nebulous term "virtual items," such items are called *response objects*. In fact, you can notice in the schema that there are references to "real" items (for instance, *ArrayOfRealItemsType*). Real items are persisted as an item in the Store. Virtual items are not real items, but rather are actions that you pass to *CreateItem* that might or might not gener-ate an item as a result of the action. It is a little strange to pass these response actions into *CreateItem*, but that is how things work at this point.

The *ResponseObjects* property tells you which operations can be applied in response to the item in question. As mentioned above, you "apply" these actions by calling *CreateItem* with the corresponding action. The *ResponseObjects* property is exposed on *ItemType* in both the *Default* and *AllProperties* shapes. In addition, you can ask for it via the *item:ResponseObjects* property path. We will discuss response objects in more detail in Chapter 7 and in the calen-daring chapters (Chapter 8 through Chapter 10). We will simply say here that the following items are the only actions you will ever encounter within a *ResponseObjects* property.

- *ReplyToItemType*

- *ReplyAllToItemType*

- *ForwardItemType*

- *SuppressReadReceiptType*

- *AcceptItemType*

- *TentativelyAcceptItemType*

- *DeclineItemType*

- *CancelCalendarItemType*

- *RemoveItemType*

This list is generated by looking at the *NonEmptyArrayOfResponseObjectsType* schema type in types.xsd.

The types returned within this collection are the actual types that need to be used for the corresponding action. For example, if you are sent a meeting request and *AcceptItem* is a valid response for this meeting request, you can grab the instance from the *ResponseObjects* collection, fill it in, and pass it off to *CreateItem*.[30] This could, in theory, be useful in some cases, but we can't think of such a time off the top of our heads.

It is possible for the *ResponseObjects* collection to be empty. And, of course, *ResponseObjects* is read-only.

Culture Property

The *Culture* property identifies the culture that best describes the body content of the item. When the caller sets the culture for an item, both the PR_MESSAGE_LOCALE_ID and PR_MESSAGE_CODEPAGE MAPI properties are internally set to the appropriate values. When reading the *Culture* property, Exchange Web Services first tries to get the PR_MESSAGE_LOCALE_ID MAPI property. If that fails, it tries to get the PR_INTERNET_CPID MAPI property. If that fails, it tries to get the PR_MESSAGE_CODEPAGE MAPI property. Finally, if that fails, it tries to get the "preferred culture" associated with the owner of the mailbox in question.

This property is used in several ways by both Exchange and Office Outlook for:

- Creating the Content-Language MIME header when converting to MIME

- Word breaking for content indexing

- Personal name parsing for virtual information card (VCARD) reading

- Generation of friendly Delivery Status Notification (DSN) bodies

In general, you should set the *Culture* property for any message you create if you want to guarantee that the listed features work as desired. This property is exposed in the schema as an xs:language and as a string in the proxy classes. You should use RFC 1766 naming for these culture identifiers. The general structure for these identifiers is:

```
<languagecode>-<country/regioncode>
```

For example:

```
<t:Culture>en-US</t:Culture>
```

---

[30] Meeting requests will be covered in Chapter 10, "Scheduling Meetings."

Refer to the *System.Globalization.CultureInfo* class in the MSDN library or the RFC 1766 document for more information.

Summary

In Exchange Web Services, everything is either an item or a folder. *ItemType* is the absolute base class for all objects that are contained within a folder. Objects such as messages, items, contacts, calendar items, and so forth are all items. In this chapter we discussed the difference between response objects and real items, although the details of response objects will have to wait until Chapter 7 for the message-related response objects and Chapter 8 through Chapter 10 for the calendaring-related response objects. We covered the various operations that are dedicated to items and their descendants. We finished with a discussion of the properties that are exposed on an Item.

Because *ItemType* is the base class for all items, there are a number of elements and attributes that we didn't expound on in this chapter because they are applicable only to certain *ItemType* descendants. Don't worry—we will cover them in due time.

Chapter 6
Contacts and Distribution Lists

They say it's all in who you know. Of course, unless you have a really good memory, it is prudent to store personal contact information somewhere. Little black books have been replaced by little "bit" books, and there is no better bit-book than a Microsoft Exchange Server 2007 Mailbox. With Exchange, you have a central Store for your contacts regardless of whether you access them through your mobile device, over the Web with Outlook Web Access (OWA), in the rich Microsoft Office Outlook client, or through the quite dashing Exchange Web Services application programming interface (API). In this chapter, we will discuss contacts as seen through Exchange Web Services and describe how to manipulate them to your heart's content.[1]

What Is a Contact?

So what exactly is a contact? Well, that depends. Every item type that you have seen up to this point resides in the Mailbox. Certainly, contacts can reside in the Mailbox, but contacts can also reside in the Microsoft Active Directory directory service.[2]

Store Contacts

A Store contact is simply an item in the Store with an *ItemClass* that begins with IPM.Contact. That being said, Exchange Web Services exposes a whole slew of properties on a contact. Remember, the Store enables any property to be set on any item. Exchange Web Services tries to make sense of this mess by exposing properties in a more orderly fashion. Exchange Web Services presents Store contacts using the *ContactItemType* type in the schema, and this is where all these "contact" properties are exposed.

You can perform a number of operations on Store contacts—they are just items after all. We will discuss these operations in detail shortly.

Directory Contacts

Directory contacts are objects that exist within the Active Directory. Active Directory contacts are read-only through Exchange Web Services. You cannot create, modify, or delete them. In fact, you can't even retrieve them, at least not like you can with Store contacts. What are they

---

[1] It should be clear that we are referring to manipulation of the items within the Store. Whether you manipulate the individuals represented by your contacts is up to you (although we don't recommend it).

[2] This is where things can get quite confusing. A specific type in the Active Directory is called a *Contact*, but here we are just referring generically to organizational persons, users, contacts, and the like as *Contacts*.

good for then? Two Active Directory-friendly Web methods enable you to access directory contact information. These Web methods are *ResolveNames* and *ExpandDL*, both of which will be covered later in this chapter.

What Is a Distribution List?

A distribution list (DL) is a convenient way to group users and/or contacts together so that the list can be referenced as a single entity. For example, the Exchange Web Service team has distribution lists for its development, test, and triage teams. A given contact can reside in zero, one, or more distribution lists. These groupings can exist within Active Directory as distribution lists, security groups, or the Exchange specific "dynamic" distribution lists, where membership is evaluated dynamically based on certain attributes.[3] In addition, the Exchange Store also surfaces its own concept of a distribution list, which is known as a *private* distribution list. Such distribution lists are considered private because they are defined within a given mailbox and are therefore only accessible to accounts that have access to the mailbox in question.

Both Store and directory distribution lists are read-only through Exchange Web Services.

Creating a Contact

Before you can do anything of interest to a contact, your Mailbox must have a contact. Certainly you could create your contacts through client applications such as Office Outlook or Outlook Web Access, but it is much more fun to do this using Exchange Web Services.

Because a contact is simply an item with a personality, you can create one using the ever-familiar *CreateItem* call. The only change is that you pass in a *Contact* element rather than an item or message. Look at the request in Listing 6-1.

LISTING 6-1 Creating a Contact

```
<CreateItem xmlns=".../messages"
            xmlns:t=".../types">
  <Items>
    <t:Contact>
      <t:GivenName>Jane</t:GivenName>
      <t:Surname>Dow</t:Surname>
    </t:Contact>
  </Items>
</CreateItem>
```

---

[3] A security group is really just a distribution list with a security identifier (SID).

One thing to notice in Listing 6-1 is that the friendly *MessageDisposition* attribute is missing, and Exchange Web Services is agreeable to that omission. Why is that? A contact is not a message and the *MessageDisposition* attribute is applicable only to message-derived types. Of course, you could add that attribute back in, but it will be ignored.

Listing 6-2 shows the response to Listing 6-1. It follows the same pattern as any other *CreateItem* call—the id of the newly created item is returned.

LISTING 6-2 Response after creating a contact

```
<CreateItemResponse xmlns:m=".../messages"
                    xmlns:t=".../types"
                    xmlns=".../messages">
  <m:ResponseMessages>
    <m:CreateItemResponseMessage ResponseClass="Success">
      <m:ResponseCode>NoError</m:ResponseCode>
      <m:Items>
        <t:Contact>
          <t:ItemId Id="AAAtAEFkbWlu..." ChangeKey="AAAAA..."/>
        </t:Contact>
      </m:Items>
    </m:CreateItemResponseMessage>
  </m:ResponseMessages>
</CreateItemResponse>
```

One other thing to notice about the response in Listing 6-2 is that the returned item element has a local name of *Contact*.

Where is the new contact is saved? Newly created contacts will be saved in the default contacts folder. If you try to save the new contact in a non-contacts folder such as the Inbox or Drafts folder, you will encounter an error response code of *ErrorCannotCreateContactInNonContactFolder*. Why is that? Mainly because the action is so atypical that it is probably not what you intended. Contacts don't typically reside in non-contact folders. It is kind of like pouring orange juice in your cereal. If you really do need a contact to live within a non-contact folder, you should first create the contact in the contacts folder and then move it to its final resting place by using the *MoveItem* call.[4]

Of course, you are free to save your contacts in any contact folder, not just the default one. You saw in Chapter 4, "Folders," that you can create a new contacts folder by calling *CreateFolder* and passing in a *ContactsFolder* element for the folder to create.

---

[4] If you do so, comment your code *really* well so that others know why you are doing such an odd thing.

Other Common Operations

Because a contact is a descendant of *ItemType*, all of the standard operations that you can perform on an item can be performed on a contact. As a result, we will not go over those operations explicitly here. Instead, let's look at the many properties that are available on *ContactItemType*.

Contact Properties

Aside from the properties inherited from *ItemType*, *ContactItemType* includes the properties shown in Table 6-1. Following the table, we will discuss a number of them in more detail.

TABLE 6-1 *ContactItemType* **Properties**

Property	Type	Comment
FileAs	String	How the name should be filed for display/sorting purposes
FileAsMapping	*FileAsMappingType*	How the various parts of a contact's information interact to form the *FileAs* property value
DisplayName	String	The name to display for a contact
GivenName	String	The name by which a person is known; often referred to as a person's first name
Initials	String	Initials for the contact
MiddleName	String	The middle name for the contact
Nickname	String	Another name by which the contact is known
CompleteName	*CompleteNameType*	A combination of several name fields in one convenient place
CompanyName	String	The company that the contact is affiliated with
EmailAddresses	*EmailAddressDictionaryType*	A collection of e-mail addresses for the contact
PhysicalAddresses	*PhysicalAddressDictionaryType*	A collection of mailing addresses for the contact
PhoneNumbers	*PhoneNumberDictionaryType*	A collection of phone numbers for the contact
AssistantName	String	The name of the contact's assistant
Birthday	*DateTime*	The contact's birthday
BusinessHomePage	String	Web page for the contact's business; typically a URL

Property	Type	Comment
Children	ArrayOfStringsType	A collection of children's names associated with the contact
Companies*	ArrayOfStringsType	A collection of companies that a contact is associated with
ContactSource	ContactSourceType	Indicates whether this is a directory or a Store contact
Department	String	The department name that the contact is in
Generation	String	Sr, Jr, I, II, III, and so on
ImAddresses	ImAddressDictionaryType	A collection of instant messaging addresses for the contact
JobTitle	String	The job title for the contact
Manager	String	The name of the contact's manager
Mileage	String	The distance that the contact resides from some reference point.
OfficeLocation	String	Location of the contact's office.
PostalAddressIndex	PhysicalAddressIndexType	The physical addresses in the *PhysicalAddresses* collection that represents the mailing address for the contact
Profession	String	Occupation or discipline of the contact
SpouseName	String	Name of the contact's spouse
Surname	String	The family name of the contact; usually considered the last name
WeddingAnniversay	DateTime	Date that the contact was married

*You can include the *CompanyName* property when generating the *FileAs* string from *FileAsMapping* (that is, *FirstLastCompany*), whereas you cannot include the *Companies* property. *FileAs* and *FileAsMapping* are discussed shortly.

You can use a number of the properties here in any way that you want. For example, you are free to fill in the mileage for your contact in any format you want. You might assume this property indicates the distance that the contact is from the office. But maybe it indicates how efficient the contact's car is (miles per gallon). Maybe you want to be creative and store the distance that your contact runs each day for exercise. Or maybe you are guessing when your contact will retire, and you can interpret this as YTR (years to retirement) instead of miles. The possibilities are endless. A number of properties *do* have explicit semantics that need to be observed. The schema helps in most cases, but it never hurts to have an understanding of what is going on with these properties and their relationship to other properties.

FileAs and FileAsMapping

FileAs seems like a relatively simple property. If you retrieve this property from an existing contact that has been created in a client such as Office Outlook, you will typically get a string formatted as [first name last name] or possibly [last name, first name]. You can set this property yourself to whatever you want. For example, you can file a person by a nickname, as shown in Listing 6-3.

LISTING 6-3 Setting the *FileAs* property for a contact

```
<CreateItem xmlns=".../messages"
            xmlns:t=".../types">
  <Items>
    <t:Contact>
      <t:FileAs>Jane "Janie" Dow</t:FileAs>
      <t:GivenName>Jane</t:GivenName>
      <t:Surname>Dow</t:Surname>
    </t:Contact>
  </Items>
</CreateItem>
```

If you look at the newly created contact through Outlook Web Access, you will see that the *FileAs* from Listing 6-3 is respected (Figure 6-1).

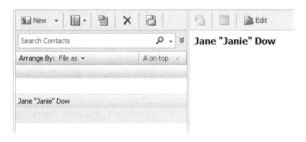

FIGURE 6-1 The new contact arranged by *FileAs*

If you bring up the properties for the contact, you see something a little interesting (Figure 6-2).

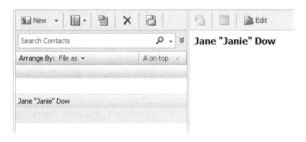

FIGURE 6-2 *FileAsMapping*, as shown in Outlook Web Access

Notice that the *File As* field is listed as *Last, First* even though *FileAs* has a custom value. To figure out what is going on here, let's look at *FileAsMapping* and how it interacts with *FileAs*.

The *FileAsMapping* property is defined by the *FileAsMappingType* schema type in types.xsd. For example, assuming the contact's name is Jane Dow II and that she works for Contoso Ltd.,

Table 6-2 includes the enumeration values for *FileAsMappingType* and how the resulting name should be rendered.

TABLE 6-2 *FileAsMappingType* **Values and Examples**

Enumeration name	Example
None	[No mapping]
LastCommaFirst	Dow, Jane
FirstSpaceLast	Jane Dow
Company	Contoso Ltd.
LastCommaFirstCompany	Dow, Jane Contoso Ltd.
CompanyLastFirst	Contoso Ltd. Dow Jane
LastFirst	Dow Jane
LastFirstCompany	Dow Jane Contoso Ltd.
CompanyLastCommaFirst	Contoso Ltd. Dow, Jane
LastFirstSuffix	Dow, Jane II
LastSpaceFirstCompany	Dow Jane Contoso Ltd.
CompanyLastSpaceFirst	Contoso Ltd. Dow Jane
LastSpaceFirst	Dow Jane

But where do the last, first, suffix, and company names come from? From the appropriate properties on the *Contact* object, of course. The *FileAsMapping* property simply tells client applications which properties were used to render the *FileAs* string. However, as you saw in Listing 6-3, you can explicitly set the *FileAs* property to a value that doesn't follow any of the *FileAsMapping* enumeration values. But more on that in a minute. To continue the discussion, let's create a new contact with a first and last name and a *FileAsMapping*, but no *FileAs*. Note that the first name is covered by the *GivenName* property, and the last name is covered by the *Surname* property. This is shown in Listing 6-4.

LISTING 6-4 Creating a contact with a *FileAsMapping*

```
<CreateItem xmlns=".../messages"
            xmlns:t=".../types">
  <Items>
    <t:Contact>
      <t:FileAsMapping>LastCommaFirst</t:FileAsMapping>
      <t:GivenName>Jane</t:GivenName>
      <t:Surname>Dow</t:Surname>
    </t:Contact>
  </Items>
</CreateItem>
```

Notice that the *FileAs* property is not set here. Outlook Web Access respects the *FileAsMapping* as shown in Figure 6-3.

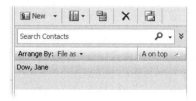

FIGURE 6-3 Outlook Web Access respects the *FileAsMapping*

Interesting. It *looks* like in the first case, Outlook Web Access used what was explicitly set through the *FileAs* property and in the second case, it used what was explicitly set through the *FileAsMapping* property. Actually, Outlook Web Access doesn't make that distinction at all. To see what values are stored on the contact, you can make a *GetItem* call on the contact from Listing 6-4 and explicitly ask for the *FileAs* and *FileAsMapping* properties, as shown here:

```
<GetItem xmlns=".../messages"
         xmlns:t=".../types">
  <ItemShape>
    <t:BaseShape>IdOnly</t:BaseShape>
    <t:AdditionalProperties>
      <t:FieldURI FieldURI="contacts:FileAs"/>
      <t:FieldURI FieldURI="contacts:FileAsMapping"/>
    </t:AdditionalProperties>
  </ItemShape>
  <!-- contents elided -->
</GetItem>
```

The response shows something quite interesting.

```
<t:Contact>
    <t:ItemId Id="AAAtAEFkbWlu..." ChangeKey="AAAAA..."/>
    <t:FileAs>Dow, Jane</t:FileAs>
    <t:FileAsMapping>LastCommaFirst</t:FileAsMapping>
</t:Contact>
```

The *FileAs* property is filled in! When you create the contact and set the *FileAsMapping* property, Exchange Web Services automatically fills in the *FileAs* property based on the mapping and the first and last names of the contact. What do you think would happen if you updated the contact's *FileAsMapping* property? Would it correct the *FileAs* property? Let's see.

```
<UpdateItem ConflictResolution="AutoResolve"
            xmlns=".../messages"
            xmlns:t=".../types">
  <!-- contents elided -->
  <t:SetItemField>
    <t:FieldURI FieldURI="contacts:FileAsMapping"/>
    <t:Contact>
      <t:FileAsMapping>FirstSpaceLast</t:FileAsMapping>
    </t:Contact>
  </t:SetItemField>
  <!-- contents elided -->
</UpdateItem>
```

If *FileAs* is automatically updated based on the *FileAsMapping*, you would expect *FileAs* to be *Jane Dow* here instead of *Dow, Jane*. After fetching the updated contact, the response shows that this is the case.

```
<t:Contact>
    <t:ItemId Id="AAAtAEFkbWlu..." ChangeKey="AAAAA..."/>
    <t:FileAs>Jane Dow</t:FileAs>
    <t:FileAsMapping>FirstSpaceLast</t:FileAsMapping>
</t:Contact>
```

So, changing the *FileAsMapping* property at any point updates the *FileAs* property accordingly. Note that the reverse is *not* true. In this example, the *FileAs* could be explicitly set back to *Dow, Jane*, but the *FileAsMapping* would remain as *FirstSpaceLast*. We recommend that if you are going to set the *FileAs* property directly, you should also set *FileAsMapping* to *None*.

There is one last slight "gotcha" to consider: what happens when you set both the *FileAs* and *FileAsMapping* during a *CreateItem* call?

```
<CreateItem xmlns=".../messages"
            xmlns:t=".../types">
  <Items>
    <t:Contact>
      <t:FileAs>Jane "Janie" Dow</t:FileAs>
      <t:FileAsMapping>LastCommaFirst</t:FileAsMapping>
      <t:GivenName>Jane</t:GivenName>
      <t:Surname>Dow</t:Surname>
    </t:Contact>
  </Items>
</CreateItem>
```

Because properties are applied in an ordered fashion, it would be reasonable to think that Exchange Web Services would first set the *FileAs* to *Jane "Janie" Dow* and then, when it sees the *FileAsMapping*, it would overwrite the *FileAs* property with *Dow, Jane*. That would be accurate *if* the *FileAsMapping* modifications were applied when the property is set. In reality, they are evaluated at the time when the contact is saved. So, in this case, *FileAs* is set to *Jane "Janie" Dow* and *FileAsMapping* is set to *LastCommaFirst*. When the contact is saved, however, the underlying API sees that *FileAs* was explicitly set and therefore does not update the *FileAs* property based on the *FileAsMapping*.

As a general rule, you should avoid setting both the *FileAs* and *FileAsMapping* properties unless you are setting *FileAsMapping* to *None*.[5]

---

[5] That being said, there is a "feature" in OWA where contacts with a *FileAsMapping* of *None* will show a mapping of *Last, First* on the Contacts property page. However, the *FileAs* string will be correct.

Subject and *DisplayName*

Something that might be a little confusing is whether to set the *Subject* or the *DisplayName* properties on contacts. *Subject* is inherited from *ItemType,* and *DisplayName* is explicitly surfaced on *ContactItemType.* We have touched on this in several places already; but remember, as far as the Store is concerned, a contact, an item, and a message are all just bags of properties. Any property can appear on any row in the message table. Two of the standard properties are *DisplayName* (prop tag 0x3001001F) and *Subject* (prop tag 0x0037001F). In other words, both of these standard properties are "available" for use on a contact in the Store.

When you create a contact through a client application like Office Outlook, it will typically fill in *both* the subject and the display name. In fact, it fills in a number of properties. This is where your good friend Outlook Spy comes in handy. Using Office Outlook 2007, if you create a contact with only the *FullName* field filled in, then click the IMessage Outlook Spy button for that contact, you would see that a number of fields are filled in (shown in the following list with their property tags).[6]

- *FileAs (PropertySetId:*[7] *{00062004-0000-0000-C000-000000000046}, PropertyId:* 0x8005
- *ConversationTopic* (0x0070001E)
- *Display Name* (0x3001001E)
- *Initials* (0x3A0A001E)
- *Normalized Subject* (0x0E1D001E)
- *Subject* (0x0037001E)
- *Surname* (0x3A11001E)

So what happens when you create a contact through Exchange Web Services and specify the display name? And how about the subject? Table 6-3 makes things a little clearer.

TABLE 6-3 Contacts Created with *Subject* vs. *DisplayName*

Property	Outlook	EWS with *Subject*	EWS with *DisplayName*
FileAs	X		
Conversation Topic	X		
DisplayName	X		X
Initials	X		
Normalized Subject	X	X	
Subject	X	X	
Surname	X		

---

[6] This is by no means an exhaustive list. We present it to show you that Office Outlook is doing a lot behind the scenes.

[7] *PropertySetId* is discussed in depth in Chapter 13, "Extended Properties."

If you create a contact through Exchange Web Services and set only the subject, that contact will be displayed without a name in Office Outlook! Remember, Exchange Web Services is an API, whereas Office Outlook and Outlook Web Access are client applications. Exchange Web Services will do exactly what you tell it to, even if what you are telling it to do isn't the best idea. In contrast, client applications will often have concrete business logic and side effects that are well defined for that application. Although Exchange Web Services does wrap up quite a bit of business logic for you, it is your responsibility as the application developer to ensure that all the necessary properties for your client application are filled in.

So, Office Outlook appears to concern itself with *DisplayName* for display purposes, but it fills in the subject for completeness. As a result, it is probably prudent to set *both* the subject and the display name to the same value when creating a contact through Exchange Web Services if you are expecting clients to view your custom contacts through Office Outlook.

Actually, as you saw in the discussion of *FileAs* and *FileAsMapping*, you can (and probably should) fill in a number of "name" properties.

CompleteName

The read-only *CompleteName* property surfaces all of the name-related properties in one class. The *CompleteName* property is defined by the *CompleteNameType* schema type in types.xsd. All of the child elements of *CompleteNameType* are optional strings, as shown in Listing 6-5.

LISTING 6-5 *CompleteNameType* schema type

```
<xs:complexType name="CompleteNameType">
  <xs:sequence>
    <xs:element name="Title" type="xs:string" minOccurs="0" />
    <xs:element name="FirstName" type="xs:string" minOccurs="0" />
    <xs:element name="MiddleName" type="xs:string" minOccurs="0" />
    <xs:element name="LastName" type="xs:string" minOccurs="0" />
    <xs:element name="Suffix" type="xs:string" minOccurs="0" />
    <xs:element name="Initials" type="xs:string" minOccurs="0" />
    <xs:element name="FullName" type="xs:string" minOccurs="0" />
    <xs:element name="Nickname" type="xs:string" minOccurs="0" />
    <xs:element name="YomiFirstName" type="xs:string" minOccurs="0" />
    <xs:element name="YomiLastName" type="xs:string" minOccurs="0" />
  </xs:sequence>
</xs:complexType>
```

How do you retrieve the *CompleteName* property? *CompleteName* will be returned in both the *Default* and *AllProperties* shapes when calling *GetItem*.[8] Of course, before retrieving a contact's *CompleteName* property, it would make sense to put a contact in the Store that has many of these properties set. But that is a bit of a problem. First, *CompleteName* is read-only. Second, *FullName*, *FirstName*, *LastName*, and several other name properties exposed on *CompleteNameType* don't seem to appear on the *Contact* type in the schema. Most of them are actually there—they are just masquerading as other properties. Table 6-4 shows a mapping of *CompleteName* property names to properties on *ContactItemType*. Note that MAPI properties are discussed in Chapter 13, "Extended Properties."

TABLE 6-4 *CompleteName* **Property to Underlying Property Mapping**

CompleteName Property	*ContactItemType* or MAPI Property
Title	MAPI property tag 0x3A45 (14917 in decimal)
FirstName	GivenName
MiddleName	MiddleName
LastName	Surname
Suffix	Generation
Initials	Initials
FullName	DisplayName
Nickname	Nickname
YomiFirstName	MAPI Property: Property Set: Address *PropertyId*: 0x802C (32812 in decimal)
YomiLastName	MAPI Property: Property Set: Address *PropertyId*: 0x802D (32813 in decimal)
YomiCompanyName	MAPI Named Property: Property Set: Address *PropertyId*: 0x802E (32814 in decimal)

Given this mapping list, you should be able to set all of these properties and then fetch them via the *CompleteName* property. Listing 6-6 shows the *CreateItem* call. Don't worry if you don't understand the *ExtendedProperty* elements—we will cover them in detail in Chapter 13. For now, just understand that they are used to access native MAPI properties on an item or folder.

---

[8] Note that *CompleteName* is a calculated property and therefore is not available via *FindItem*.

LISTING 6-6 Creating an item with all the *CompleteName* properties set

```xml
<CreateItem xmlns=".../messages"
            xmlns:t=".../types">
  <Items>
    <t:Contact>
      <t:ExtendedProperty>
        <t:ExtendedFieldURI PropertyTag="0x3A45"
                            PropertyType="String"/>
        <t:Value>Title</t:Value>
      </t:ExtendedProperty>
      <t:ExtendedProperty>
        <t:ExtendedFieldURI DistinguishedPropertySetId="Address"
                            PropertyId="32812"
                            PropertyType="String"/>
        <t:Value>YomiFirstName</t:Value>
      </t:ExtendedProperty>
      <t:ExtendedProperty>
        <t:ExtendedFieldURI DistinguishedPropertySetId="Address"
                            PropertyId="32813"
                            PropertyType="String"/>
        <t:Value>YomiLastName</t:Value>
      </t:ExtendedProperty>
      <t:DisplayName>FullName</t:DisplayName>
      <t:GivenName>FirstName</t:GivenName>
      <t:Initials>Initials</t:Initials>
      <t:MiddleName>MiddleName</t:MiddleName>
      <t:Nickname>Nickname</t:Nickname>
      <t:Generation>Suffix</t:Generation>
      <t:Surname>LastName</t:Surname>
    </t:Contact>
  </Items>
</CreateItem>
```

When you call *GetItem* on the returned id and ask for the *CompleteName* property, you see that the mappings were correct.

```xml
<t:Contact>
  <t:ItemId Id="AAAtAEFkbWlu..." ChangeKey="AAAAA..."/>
  <t:CompleteName>
    <t:Title>Title</t:Title>
    <t:FirstName>FirstName</t:FirstName>
    <t:MiddleName>MiddleName</t:MiddleName>
    <t:LastName>LastName</t:LastName>
    <t:Suffix>Suffix</t:Suffix>
    <t:Initials>Initials</t:Initials>
    <t:FullName>FullName</t:FullName>
    <t:Nickname>Nickname</t:Nickname>
    <t:YomiFirstName>YomiFirstName</t:YomiFirstName>
    <t:YomiLastName>YomiLastName</t:YomiLastName>
  </t:CompleteName>
</t:Contact>
```

CompleteName was originally intended to be a dynamic, culture-dependent display name. For example, if the culture assigned to the contact was Japanese, the *GivenName* would be mapped to *LastName* and *Surname* to *FirstName*. Unfortunately, cultural-dependent functionality in *CompleteName* has not yet been implemented in Exchange Web Services.

Wouldn't it be great if *CompleteName* was writeable? Let it be so. Listing 6-7 shows a partial class extension for the *ContactItemType* proxy class. Note that you could easily put this on *ExchangeServiceBinding* instead. This method does use some of the overloads defined elsewhere in this book (namely Chapter 3, "Property Paths and Response Shapes," Chapter 5, "Items," and Chapter 13, "Extended Properties").

LISTING 6-7 Adding the *SetCompleteName* static method to *ContactItemType*

```
/// <summary>
/// Partial class extension on ContactItemType
/// </summary>
public partial class ContactItemType
{
  // Let's set up our property paths.  Note that the BuildPropertyTag static method
  // on PathToExtendedFieldType is defined in Chapter 13, "Extended Properties".
  //
  private static readonly PathToExtendedFieldType TitlePath =
        PathToExtendedFieldType.BuildPropertyTag(14917,
                    MapiPropertyTypeType.String);
  private static readonly PathToUnindexedFieldType GivenNamePath = new
        PathToUnindexedFieldType(UnindexedFieldURIType.contactsGivenName);
  private static readonly PathToUnindexedFieldType MiddleNamePath = new
      PathToUnindexedFieldType(UnindexedFieldURIType.contactsMiddleName);
  private static readonly PathToUnindexedFieldType SurnamePath = new
      PathToUnindexedFieldType(UnindexedFieldURIType.contactsSurname);
  private static readonly PathToUnindexedFieldType GenerationPath = new
      PathToUnindexedFieldType(UnindexedFieldURIType.contactsGeneration);
  private static readonly PathToUnindexedFieldType InitialsPath = new
      PathToUnindexedFieldType(UnindexedFieldURIType.contactsInitials);
  private static readonly PathToUnindexedFieldType DisplayNamePath = new
      PathToUnindexedFieldType(UnindexedFieldURIType.contactsDisplayName);
  private static readonly PathToUnindexedFieldType NicknamePath = new
      PathToUnindexedFieldType(UnindexedFieldURIType.contactsNickname);
  private static readonly PathToExtendedFieldType YomiFirstNamePath =
      PathToExtendedFieldType.BuildGuidId(
              DistinguishedPropertySetType.Address, 32812,
              MapiPropertyTypeType.String);
  private static readonly PathToExtendedFieldType YomiLastNamePath =
      PathToExtendedFieldType.BuildGuidId(
          DistinguishedPropertySetType.Address, 32813,
          MapiPropertyTypeType.String);


  /// <summary>
  /// Helper method for setting the underlying fields represented by the
  /// CompleteName property
  /// </summary>
```

```
/// <param name="binding">ExchangeServiceBinding to use for the
/// call</param>
/// <param name="contactId">Id and change key of the contact to
/// update</param>
/// <param name="completeName">The complete name to set on the
/// contact</param>
/// <returns>ItemInfoResponse message due to UpdateItem call</returns>
///
public static ItemInfoResponseMessageType SetCompleteName(
                              ExchangeServiceBinding binding,
                              ItemIdType contactId,
                              CompleteNameType completeName)
{
  // Create our request.  We will do a single UpdateItem call with a
  // bunch of change descriptions.
  //
  UpdateItemType updateRequest = new UpdateItemType();

  // We are updating a single item
  //
  ItemChangeType itemChange = new ItemChangeType();
  itemChange.Item = contactId;
  updateRequest.ItemChanges = new ItemChangeType[] { itemChange };

  // We will only set those props that are not null in the complete
  // name.  So right now, we don't know how many that will be, so let's
  // create a list to hold the change descriptions.
  //
  List<ItemChangeDescriptionType> changeList = new
              List<ItemChangeDescriptionType>();

  // Now, for each possible property, let's check to make sure it is
  // not null, then we will set the value on a ContactItem instance
  // needed for our change description and add it to our change list.
  //
  // Title
  if (completeName.Title != null)
  {
    ContactItemType titleContact = new ContactItemType();
    ExtendedPropertyType titleProp = new ExtendedPropertyType(
                    TitlePath,
                    completeName.Title);
    titleContact.ExtendedProperty = new ExtendedPropertyType[] {
                    titleProp };
    changeList.Add(new SetItemFieldType(TitlePath, titleContact));
  }

  // GivenName
  if (completeName.FirstName != null)
  {
    ContactItemType givenNameContact = new ContactItemType();
    givenNameContact.GivenName = completeName.FirstName;
    changeList.Add(
        new SetItemFieldType(
```

```
                GivenNamePath,
                givenNameContact));
}


// MiddleName
if (completeName.MiddleName != null)
{
  ContactItemType middleNameContact = new ContactItemType();
  middleNameContact.MiddleName = completeName.MiddleName;
  changeList.Add(
          new SetItemFieldType(
                  MiddleNamePath,
                  middleNameContact));
}


// Surname
if (completeName.LastName != null)
{
  ContactItemType surnameContact = new ContactItemType();
  surnameContact.Surname = completeName.LastName;
  changeList.Add(
          new SetItemFieldType(SurnamePath, surnameContact));
}


// Generation
if (completeName.Suffix != null)
{
  ContactItemType generationContact = new ContactItemType();
  generationContact.Generation = completeName.Suffix;
  changeList.Add(
        new SetItemFieldType(
                GenerationPath,
                generationContact));
}


// Initials
if (completeName.Initials != null)
{
  ContactItemType initialsContact = new ContactItemType();
  initialsContact.Initials = completeName.Initials;
  changeList.Add(
          new SetItemFieldType(
                InitialsPath,
                initialsContact));
}


// DisplayName
if (completeName.FullName != null)
{
  ContactItemType displayNameContact = new ContactItemType();
  displayNameContact.DisplayName = completeName.FullName;
  changeList.Add(
          new SetItemFieldType(
                  DisplayNamePath,
```

```
                              displayNameContact));
}

// Nickname
if (completeName.Nickname != null)
{
  ContactItemType nicknameContact = new ContactItemType();
  nicknameContact.Nickname = completeName.Nickname;
  changeList.Add(
          new SetItemFieldType(
                  NicknamePath,
                  nicknameContact));
}

// YomiFirstName
if (completeName.YomiFirstName != null)
{
  ContactItemType yomiFirstContact = new ContactItemType();
  ExtendedPropertyType yomiFirstProp = new ExtendedPropertyType(
                  YomiFirstNamePath,
                  completeName.YomiFirstName);

  yomiFirstContact.ExtendedProperty = new ExtendedPropertyType[] {
              yomiFirstProp };
  changeList.Add(new SetItemFieldType(YomiFirstNamePath,
              yomiFirstContact));
}

// YomiLastName
if (completeName.YomiLastName != null)
{
  ContactItemType yomiLastContact = new ContactItemType();
  ExtendedPropertyType yomiLastProp = new ExtendedPropertyType(
                  YomiLastNamePath,
                  completeName.YomiLastName);
  yomiLastContact.ExtendedProperty = new ExtendedPropertyType[] {
                  yomiLastProp };
  changeList.Add(
          new SetItemFieldType(
                      YomiLastNamePath,
                      yomiLastContact));
}

// If they passed in a CompleteName with all NULL props, we should
// fail.
//
if (changeList.Count == 0)
{
  throw new ArgumentException("No parts of CompleteName were set",
                  "completeName");
}

itemChange.Updates = changeList.ToArray();
updateRequest.ConflictResolution =
```

```
              ConflictResolutionType.AlwaysOverwrite;

    // Make the call and return the response message
    //
    return binding.UpdateItem(updateRequest).ResponseMessages.Items[0] as
              ItemInfoResponseMessageType;
}
```

Now, that was a whole bunch of code, but using it is quite easy. For instance, if you wanted to set the first and last name for one of your contacts, you can do that in a couple of lines.

```
CompleteNameType completeName = new CompleteNameType();
completeName.FirstName = "New First Name";
completeName.LastName = "New Last Name";

ItemInfoResponseMessageType response = ContactItemType.SetCompleteName(
          binding, id, completeName);
ItemIdType newid = response.Items.Items[0].ItemId;
```

Using the code from Listing 6-7, it is relatively easy to add a *CreateContactWithCompleteName* static method that does the same thing using a *CreateItem* call.

EmailAddresses

The *EmailAddresses* property is a collection of three e-mail addresses that can be set on a contact. *EmailAddresses* is defined in the schema as an instance of *EmailAddressDictionaryType*. *EmailAddressDictionaryType* surfaces a single unbounded array where each element is called *Entry,* which—as you will see in a moment—is a bit strange. Each of these *Entry* elements are of type *EmailAddressDictionaryEntryType,* which is essentially a key-value pair with the following format:

```
<t:Entry Key="The Key Value">someone@contoso.com</t:Entry>
```

The *Key* attribute is represented by the *EmailAddressKeyType* enumeration in the schema. This has three valid values: *EmailAddress1, EmailAddress2,* and *EmailAddress3.* So, combining all the information that you know, the following would be a valid *EmailAddresses* property:

```
<t:EmailAddresses>
  <t:Entry Key="EmailAddress1">email1@contoso.com</t:Entry>
  <t:Entry Key="EmailAddress3">email3@contoso.com</t:Entry>
</t:EmailAddresses>
```

Notice that address 2 is intentionally skipped here just to show you that they don't have to all be listed. In addition, the keys can come in any order, the e-mail address values can be duplicated, or they can be syntactically invalid Simple Mail Transfer Protocol (SMTP) addresses. You must have at least one entry in the *EmailAddresses* element. An empty *EmailAddresses* element will result in a schema validation error. As such, if a contact doesn't have any e-mail addresses defined, then the *EmailAddresses* element will never be returned. In addition, you can actually duplicate the keys within the *EmailAddresses* collection. For example, Exchange Web Services allows you to supply two or more elements with a *Key* value of *EmailAddress1*. In that case, the entries are processed in order and the last value will overwrite the previous values. Such duplication is not suggested.

As we mentioned before, having an unbounded array of *Entry* elements is strange. Since only three distinct keys can occur in the collecton, the schema *should* have indicated a maxOccurs of three rather than unbounded.

Listing 6-8 details how to create a contact with two e-mail addresses.

LISTING 6-8 Creating a contact with e-mail addresses

```
<CreateItem xmlns=".../messages"
            xmlns:t=".../types">
  <Items>
    <t:Contact>
      <t:FileAsMapping>LastCommaFirst</t:FileAsMapping>
      <t:DisplayName>Jane Dow</t:DisplayName>
      <t:GivenName>Jane</t:GivenName>
      <t:EmailAddresses>
        <t:Entry Key="EmailAddress1">email1@contoso.com</t:Entry>
        <t:Entry Key="EmailAddress3">email3@contoso.com</t:Entry>
      </t:EmailAddresses>
      <t:Surname>Dow</t:Surname>
    </t:Contact>
  </Items>
</CreateItem>
```

So, now you see how to use the three e-mail address keys, but why does Exchange Web Services limit you to three addresses? Office Outlook uses three e-mail address properties, and they are the properties that Exchange Web Services uses. Interestingly, for each of these three e-mail addresses, there are also two related address properties that are not exposed through Exchange Web Services, and that might be of interest.[9] The first of these is the display name for the e-mail address, and the second is the routing type for the associated e-mail address.

---

9 These must be accessed using extended properties, which are covered in Chapter 13.

TABLE 6-5 MAPI E-Mail Address Properties in *DistinguishedPropertySetType.Address*

	EmailAddress1 PropertyId	EmailAddress2 PropertyId	EmailAddress3 PropertyId
EmailAddress Property	0x8083 (32899 decimal)	0x8093 (32915 decimal)	0x80A3 (32931 decimal)
DisplayName Property	0x8084 (32900 decimal)	0x8094 (32916 decimal)	0x80A4 (32932 decimal)
RoutingType Property	0x8082 (32898 decimal)	0x8192 (33170 decimal)	0x80A2 (32930 decimal)

Just to round out this section, let's create a contact and set the e-mail address, e-mail address display name, and routing type.

```
public static ItemIdType CreateContactWithEmailAddresses(
                            ExchangeServiceBinding binding)
{
  CreateItemType request = new CreateItemType();
  request.Items = new NonEmptyArrayOfAllItemsType();

  ContactItemType newContact = new ContactItemType();
  // Set all the appropriate name fields
  //
  newContact.GivenName = "Jane";
  newContact.Surname = "Dow";
  newContact.FileAsMapping = FileAsMappingType.FirstSpaceLast;
  newContact.FileAsMappingSpecified = true;
  newContact.DisplayName = "Jane Dow";
  newContact.Subject = "Jane Dow";

  // Set up our single email address.
  //
  EmailAddressDictionaryEntryType address = new
          EmailAddressDictionaryEntryType();
  address.Key = EmailAddressKeyType.EmailAddress1;
  address.Value = "jane.dow@contoso.com";
  newContact.EmailAddresses = new EmailAddressDictionaryEntryType[] {
          address };

  // Now let's also set the email address display name and routing type
  // The BuildGuidId static method is defined in Chapter 13, "Extended Properties"
  //
  PathToExtendedFieldType emailDisplayPath =
        PathToExtendedFieldType.BuildGuidId(
              DistinguishedPropertySetType.Address,
              32900,
              MapiPropertyTypeType.String);
  PathToExtendedFieldType emailRoutingPath =
        PathToExtendedFieldType.BuildGuidId(
              DistinguishedPropertySetType.Address,
              32898,
              MapiPropertyTypeType.String);
  ExtendedPropertyType emailDisplayProp = new ExtendedPropertyType(
```

```
                emailDisplayPath,
                "Janie >> jane.dow@contoso.com");
    ExtendedPropertyType emailRoutingProp = new ExtendedPropertyType(
                emailRoutingPath,
                "SMTP");

    newContact.ExtendedProperty = new ExtendedPropertyType[] {
                emailDisplayProp, emailRoutingProp };

    request.Items.Items = new ItemType[] { newContact };

    // Now make the call
    //
    ItemInfoResponseMessageType responseMessage =
            binding.CreateItem(request).ResponseMessages.Items[0] as
                ItemInfoResponseMessageType;
    return responseMessage.Items.Items[0].ItemId;
}
```

Figure 6-4 shows the new contact in Office Outlook 2007. You see that the e-mail display name was accepted. Also notice in Figure 6-5, when you compose a new e-mail and add the contact to as a recipient you will see the nice display name.[10]

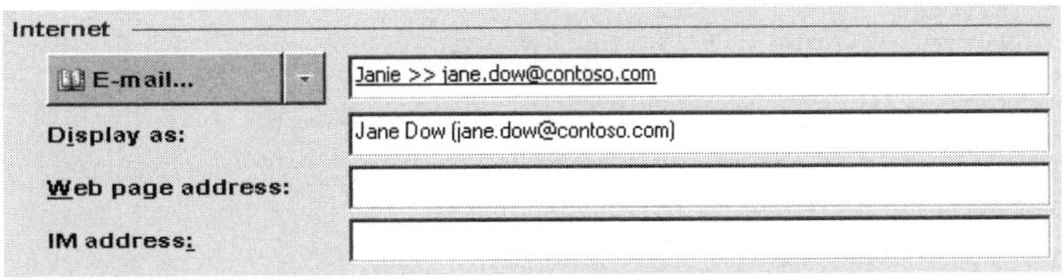

FIGURE 6-4 Contacts property page in Office Outlook showing the e-mail display name

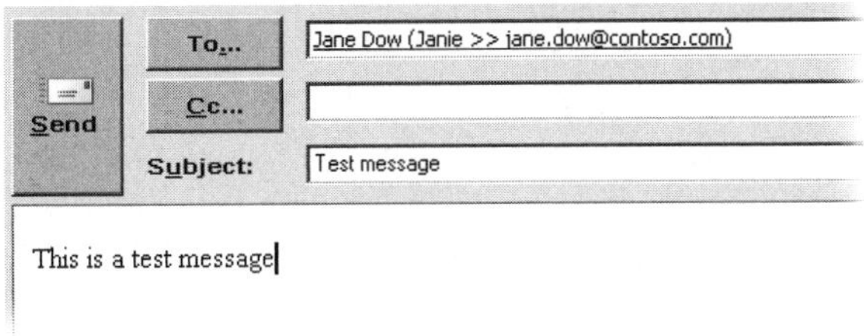

FIGURE 6-5 New e-mail showing the e-mail display name in the To line

---

[10] Of course, that depends on how you add the recipient to the message. If you use the AutoComplete in Office Outlook, then you won't see the display name in this format. If you browse your contacts and select your recipient directly, you will.

The *contacts:EmailAddresses* Property Path

If you dig through the schema a bit, you might find a property path value called *contacts: EmailAddresses* (plural). This is currently unused in Exchange Web Services. The original intent was two-fold:

- To enable *UpdateItem* calls to specify the entire *EmailAddresses* collection for update
- To enable you to make *GetItem* calls and request the collection as an additional property

But, alas, it never made it into the product.[11] Instead, for operations that require property paths, you must use the dictionary property path *contact:EmailAddress* (singular) and specify via the *KeyIndex* attribute which e-mail address you are dealing with. So, if you want to call *GetItem* and explicitly fetch all of the e-mail addresses for a given contact, you need to list three additional properties—one for each of the possible e-mail address indices.

For example, you could perform a *FindItem* call and explicitly ask for the individual e-mail addresses in the response shape.

```
<FindItem xmlns=".../messages"
          xmlns:t=".../types"
          Traversal="Shallow">
  <ItemShape>
    <t:BaseShape>IdOnly</t:BaseShape>
    <t:AdditionalProperties>
      <t:IndexedFieldURI FieldURI="contacts:EmailAddress"
                         FieldIndex="EmailAddress1"/>
      <t:IndexedFieldURI FieldURI="contacts:EmailAddress"
                         FieldIndex="EmailAddress2"/>
      <t:IndexedFieldURI FieldURI="contacts:EmailAddress"
                         FieldIndex="EmailAddress3"/>
    </t:AdditionalProperties>
  </ItemShape>
  <ParentFolderIds>
    <t:DistinguishedFolderId Id="contacts"/>
  </ParentFolderIds>
</FindItem>
```

Notice that the *FieldIndex* values correspond to the e-mail address *Entry* keys used during contact creation earlier in the chapter.

Listing 6-9 shows the response.

LISTING 6-9 *FindItem* response with e-mail address dictionary fields

```
<FindItemResponse xmlns:m=".../messages"
                  xmlns:t=".../types"
                  xmlns=".../messages">
```

---

[11] There were other difficulties surrounding replacing/merging existing data. It wasn't simply an oversight.

```
<!-- contents elided -->
    <t:Contact>
        <t:ItemId Id="AAAtAEFkbWlu..." ChangeKey="AAAAA..."/>
        <t:EmailAddresses>
            <t:Entry Key="EmailAddress1">jane.dow@contoso.com</t:Entry>
            <t:Entry Key="EmailAddress2">janie@consolidatedmessenger.com</t:Entry>
            <t:Entry Key="EmailAddress3">jdow@corp.contoso.com</t:Entry>
        </t:EmailAddresses>
    </t:Contact>
<!-- contents elided -->
</FindItemResponse>
```

Deleting E-Mail Addresses

What if you wanted to delete one of the e-mail addresses in a collection? Simply supply the dictionary property path for the e-mail address index that you want to delete. The updates portion of an *UpdateItem* call is shown in Listing 6-10.

LISTING 6-10 Deleting an e-mail address from a collection

```
<!-- UpdateItem contents elided -->
<t:Updates>
  <t:DeleteItemField>
   <t:IndexedFieldURI FieldURI="contacts:EmailAddress"
                      FieldIndex="EmailAddress1"/>
   </t:DeleteItemField>
</t:Updates>
```

PhysicalAddresses and *PostalAddressIndex*

The *PhysicalAddresses* property is similar to the *EmailAddresses* collection in many ways. It is defined in the schema by the *PhysicalAddressDictionaryType* schema type and is, similar to the e-mail address dictionary type, an unbounded collection of *Entry* elements where each entry is an instance of *PhysicalAddressDictionaryEntryType*. Listing 6-11 shows the basic structure of this entry type.

LISTING 6-11 Basic structure of the *PhysicalAddressDictionaryEntryType* schema type

```
<t:Entry Key="[address key type]">
  <t:Street>One Microsoft Way</t:Street>
  <t:City>Redmond</t:City>
  <t:State>WA</t:State>
  <t:CountryOrRegion>USA</t:CountryOrRegion>
  <t:PostalCode>98052</t:PostalCode>
</t:Entry>
```

Notice that the local name of the *PhysicalAddressDictionaryEntryType* is *Entry*. This is how you normally see it in an instance document. Now, you saw in the case of the e-mail addresses collection that each entry was associated with a key of *EmailAddress1*, *EmailAddress2*, or *EmailAddress3*. How are the physical address entries keyed? By another enumeration, of course.

The *PhysicalAddressKeyType* enumeration provides three keys to use for the addresses. Once again, this shows the strangeness of allowing an unbounded sequence of address entries—you can have a maximum of three. The valid values for this enumeration are:

- *Business*
- *Home*
- *Other*

Of course, "other" can be anything you want it to be. What if your contact has four or more addresses? Then either that contact is part of the witness protection program and shouldn't be in your address book, or the contact has far too much money and should be buying more development books and fewer houses. In any case, you need to store those "extra" addresses elsewhere. Office Outlook and Outlook Web Access clients support only three addresses. You could create more than one contact for your e-mail address inundated friend or you could create a single contact and store these additional addresses using extended MAPI properties and write your own Office Outlook plug-in to display them, but that is outside of the scope of this book.

So putting this all together, the following *Entry* collection is valid.

```
<t:PhysicalAddresses>
  <t:Entry Key="Home">
    <t:Street>One Microsoft Way/t:Street>
    <t:City>Redmond</t:City>
    <t:State>WA</t:State>
    <t:CountryOrRegion>USA</t:CountryOrRegion>
    <t:PostalCode>98052</t:PostalCode>
  </t:Entry>
  <t:Entry Key="Business">
    <t:Street>Two Microsoft Way</t:Street>
    <t:City>Redmond</t:City>
    <t:State>WA</t:State>
    <t:CountryOrRegion>USA</t:CountryOrRegion>
    <t:PostalCode>98052</t:PostalCode>
  </t:Entry>
</t:PhysicalAddresses>
```

You are not required to fill in any of the entry's child elements, although it would be a bit strange to supply an empty address.

Physical Address Property Paths

There are actually a number of physical address property paths to consider. First, there is the *contacts:PhysicalAddresses* that suffers from the same shortcomings as the *contacts: EmailAddresses* property path. You cannot use this property path for anything. It may become useful in a future release.

Whereas a contact's e-mail addresses are accessible through a single dictionary property path (*contacts:EmailAddress*), physical addresses are accessible through five distinct property paths. Why five? Because there are five distinct pieces of information about a physical address. These correspond to the five child elements in an entry. The property paths of interest are

- *contacts:PhysicalAddress:Street*

- *contacts:PhysicalAddress:City*

- *contacts:PhysicalAddress:State*

- *contacts:PhysicalAddress:CountryOrRegion*

- *contacts:PhysicalAddress:PostalCode*

You use these like any other dictionary property path. For instance, if you wanted to retrieve the home city and state for a given contact, you would add two dictionary property paths to the *AdditionalProperties* element in the response shape.

```
<GetItem xmlns=".../messages"
         xmlns:t=".../types">
  <ItemShape>
    <t:BaseShape>IdOnly</t:BaseShape>
    <t:AdditionalProperties>
      <t:IndexedFieldURI FieldURI="contacts:PhysicalAddress:City"
                         FieldIndex="Home"/>
      <t:IndexedFieldURI FieldURI="contacts:PhysicalAddress:State"
                         FieldIndex="Home"/>
    </t:AdditionalProperties>
  </ItemShape>
  <ItemIds>
    <t:ItemId Id="AAAtAE...
  </ItemIds>
</GetItem>
```

Of course, such information can be retrieved by using the *Default* or *AllProperties* response shapes, but we wanted to illustrate that they can be explicitly specified via property paths in the response shape as shown in Listing 6-12.

LISTING 6-12 Using physical address property paths via the proxy classes

```
/// <summary>
/// Retrieve a contact by Id and return two physical address properties.
/// </summary>
/// <param name="binding">Binding to use for the call</param>
```

```
/// <param name="contactId">Id of contact to retrieve</param>
/// <returns>The contact</returns>
///
public static ContactItemType GetContactWithPhysicalAddresses(
                             ExchangeServiceBinding binding,
                             ItemIdType contactId)
{
  // Create our request
  //
  GetItemType request = new GetItemType();

  // Build our response shape using our handy overloaded constructor from Chapter 3.
  // Note that we are only interested in the two address property paths.
  //
  request.ItemShape = new ItemResponseShapeType(
                          DefaultShapeNamesType.IdOnly,
                          new PathToIndexedFieldType(
                              DictionaryURIType.contactsPhysicalAddressCity,
                              PhysicalAddressKeyType.Home.ToString()),
                          new PathToIndexedFieldType(
                              DictionaryURIType.contactsPhysicalAddressState,
                              PhysicalAddressKeyType.Home.ToString()));
  request.ItemIds = new BaseItemIdType[] { contactId };

  // Make the request
  //
  GetItemResponseType response = binding.GetItem(request);
  ItemInfoResponseMessageType responseMessage =
         binding.GetItem(request).ResponseMessages.Items[0] as
             ItemInfoResponseMessageType;

  if (responseMessage.ResponseCode != ResponseCodeType.NoError)
  {
    throw new Exception("GetItem failed with response code: " +
          responseMessage.ResponseCode.ToString());
  }
  else
  {
    // Cast the item as a contact item.
    //
    return responseMessage.Items.Items[0] as ContactItemType;
  }
}
```

For *UpdateItem* requests, you do the same thing. Of course, because each part of an address has a property path, if you wanted to update all five parts of the home address, you would need to specify five *SetItemField* change descriptions within your *UpdateItem* call. But then, what do you put within the *Contact* element of your *UpdateItem* request? Just make sure that the *PhysicalAddresses* entry you supply matches the property path in your *ItemChange*. This is shown in Listing 6-13.

LISTING 6-13 Updating the physical addresses of a contact

```
<UpdateItem ConflictResolution="AutoResolve"
            xmlns=".../messages"
            xmlns:t=".../types">
  <ItemChanges>
    <t:ItemChange>
      <t:ItemId Id="AAAtAEFkbWlu..." ChangeKey="AAAAA..."/>
      <t:Updates>
        <t:SetItemField>
          <t:IndexedFieldURI FieldURI="contacts:PhysicalAddress:City"
                             FieldIndex="Home"/>
          <t:Contact>
            <t:PhysicalAddresses>
              <t:Entry Key="Home">
                <t:City>Seattle</t:City>
              </t:Entry>
            </t:PhysicalAddresses>
          </t:Contact>
        </t:SetItemField>
      </t:Updates>
    </t:ItemChange>
  </ItemChanges>
</UpdateItem>
```

If the *FieldIndex* in your property path does not match the *Entry* key in your contact, you are greeted by *ErrorUpdatePropertyMismatch*. And of course, you can only update the single address component that agrees with your property path. Unfortunately, if the physical address part doesn't agree with the property path *FieldURI*, you get an Internal Server Error.[12] We recommend avoiding this.

PhoneNumbers

Ah yes, another dictionary type! The *PhoneNumbers* property follows closely in the footsteps of the *EmailAddresses* property. Each entry has a single value (the phone number). However, while e-mail addresses have three possible keys, there are 19 different phone number keys. The key values are defined by the *PhoneNumberKeyType* enumeration in the schema. The valid values are shown in Table 6-6.

TABLE 6-6 Phone Number Keys

AssistantPhone	*HomeFax*	*Pager*
BusinessFax	*HomePhone*	*PrimaryPhone*
BusinessPhone	*HomePhone2*	*RadioPhone*
BusinessPhone2	*Isdn*	*Telex*
Callback	*MobilePhone*	*TtyTddPhone*
CarPhone	*OtherFax*	
CompanyMainPhone	*OtherTelephone*	

---

[12] This is a known issue and should be addressed in a future release.

So, the following is a schema valid list of phone numbers:

```
<t:PhoneNumbers>
  <t:Entry Key="HomePhone">123-456-7890</t:Entry>
  <t:Entry Key="MobilePhone">456-789-0123</t:Entry>
  <t:Entry Key="BusinessPhone">Same as Jane's</t:Entry>
</t:PhoneNumbers>
```

The third entry was added so that you would realize that Exchange Web Services doesn't do any validation of the format of a given phone number. If you need to force a phone number format, you should do that yourself before calling Exchange Web Services.

Phone Number Property Paths

There are two phone number property paths, which are divided into two categories. The first category contains the property path that doesn't work at all, *contacts:PhoneNumbers*. This property path should be avoided along with its two brothers, *contacts:EmailAddresses* and *contacts:PhysicalAddresses*. The second, abundantly more useful category contains the property path that actually does work, *contacts:PhoneNumber*. This property is a dictionary property and can be used to fetch a specific phone number by key directly. Of course, it is also necessary for any phone number updates you might do via *UpdateItem,* as shown in Listing 6-14.

LISTING 6-14 Updating a contact's phone number by using *UpdateItem*

```
<UpdateItem ConflictResolution="AutoResolve"
            xmlns=".../messages"
            xmlns:t=".../types">
  <ItemChanges>
    <t:ItemChange>
      <t:ItemId Id="AAAtAEFkbWlu..." ChangeKey="AAAAA..."/>

      <t:Updates>
        <t:SetItemField>
          <t:IndexedFieldURI FieldURI="contacts:PhoneNumber"
                             FieldIndex="BusinessPhone"/>
          <t:Contact>
            <t:PhoneNumbers>
              <t:Entry Key="BusinessPhone">789-112-3456</t:Entry>
            </t:PhoneNumbers>
          </t:Contact>
        </t:SetItemField>
      </t:Updates>
    </t:ItemChange>
  </ItemChanges>
</UpdateItem>
```

ImAddresses

We won't go into detail on the *ImAddresses* property. Once again, it follows the example of the *EmailAddresses* property. The three valid key values are defined by the *ImAddressKeyType* enumeration and have the values *ImAddress1, ImAddress2,* and *ImAddress3.* As expected, the *contacts:ImAddresses* property path is useless. You should instead use the *contacts:ImAddress* dictionary property with the appropriate field index.

Dictionary Property Paths and the Proxy Classes

We would be remiss if we failed to draw your attention back to some helper methods defined in Chapter 3. If you find yourself using indexed properties a lot, these helper methods simplify your life quite a bit and keep you from having to convert enumeration values to strings in order to set your property path field indices. For example, creating a physical address property path is as simple as calling the *CreatePhysicalAddress* factory method from Chapter 3.

```
PathToIndexedFieldType homeCityPath =
        PathToIndexedFieldType.CreatePhysicalAddress(
            PathToIndexedFieldType.PhysicalAddressPart.City,
            PhysicalAddressKeyType.Home);
```

Aside from looking cleaner, passing strongly typed enumeration arguments to the helper methods causes compile time exceptions to be thrown for invalid values, whereas allowing keys to be specified as strings causes schema violations to be returned at runtime.

Children and *Companies*

Children and *Companies* are both exposed as instances of *ArrayOfStringsType* in the schema. *ArrayOfStringsType* is an unbounded sequence of *String* elements. As such, the following are valid instances:

```
<t:Children>
  <t:String>Bill</t:String>
  <t:String>Karim</t:String>
</t:Children>

<t:Companies>
  <t:String>Microsoft Corporation</t:String>
  <t:String>Contoso Ltd.</t:String>
</t:Companies>
```

It should be noted that neither of these properties supports the append change description. As a result, if you want to add new children or companies, you need to read the existing state, add your own to it, and then write back the combined list by using a *SetItemField* change description in *UpdateItem.*

ContactSource

The read-only *ContactSource* property tells you the data store that the contact comes from. Up until now, the items and folders that you have encountered all reside in the Store. Contacts, however, can also come from the Active Directory. There are two valid values for *ContactSource*: *ActiveDirectory* and *Store*. This will become more important in the discussion of the *ResolveNames* and *ExpandDL* Web methods later in this chapter.

Creating a Distribution List

Exchange Web Services does not currently support the creation of Active Directory or Store distribution lists. Such functionality may be available in a future release. However, Exchange Web Services does support interacting with both Active Directory and Store-based distribution lists, as we will now discuss.

Distribution List Properties

In the schema, a distribution list is exposed by the *DistributionListType* schema type, which derives from *ItemType*. As such, all of the properties that are exposed on *ItemType* are available on *DistributionListType*. In addition to these inherited properties, *DistributionListType* adds three other properties, all of which were also exposed on *ContactItemType*. These properties are shown in Table 6-7.

TABLE 6-7 *DistributionList* Properties

Property name	Type	Comments
DisplayName	*String*	*DisplayName* of the distribution list, maps to MAPI property *PR_DISPLAY_NAME*
FileAs	*String*	*FileAs* property; notice that there is no corresponding *FileAsMapping*
ContactSource	*ContactSourceType*	Enumeration value with two valid values: *ActiveDirectory* and *Store*; indicates where the contact originated

Finding Store Contacts and Distribution Lists

Finding contacts and distribution lists is as simple as making a *FindItem* call against the contacts folder of interest. Of course, if that was all there was to it, we wouldn't be talking about it in this chapter. You can indeed make a *FindItem* call and get contacts and distribution lists back, but Exchange Web Services exposes a contact-specific paging mechanism that is intended to make your life a bit easier.

Say you want to provide an address book user interface (UI) view of all of the contacts in a user's contacts folder. A reasonable approach is to break contacts into alphabetical pages so that all the contacts whose last name starts with *A* are on one page and those with *B* are on the next page. Similar to Office Outlook, imagine that you have the alphabet on the user form so that users can click a letter and jump to that page. Certainly you could fetch all of the contacts up front and break them apart on the client side, but it is better to populate each page as it is accessed so that your application doesn't perform work that it doesn't have to. Such performance optimizations will increase the responsiveness of your application. Most likely, the end-user will not navigate to each and every page.

To help with this, *FindItem* takes an optional paging mechanism called *ContactsView*. *ContactsView* is of type *ContactsViewType* as defined in types.xsd. It derives from *BasePagingType* and therefore inherits the *MaxEntriesReturned* attribute. Let's look at the basic structure of a *ContactsView* instance.

```
<m:ContactsView MaxEntriesReturned="50"
                InitialName="Adams"
                FinalName="Axford"/>
```

Continuing with the address book example, what if your application has room for only 50 names on the user interface? The optional *MaxEntriesReturned* attribute enables you to specify the maximum number of contacts that you want to be returned for a given *FindItem* call. You can set *MaxEntriesReturned* appropriately so that you will never be given excess contacts.

The optional *InitialName* attribute enables you to specify an inclusive name that defines the alphabetical beginning of your filter. If you do not specify the *InitialName* attribute, your view will have no lower alphabetical bound to the contacts returned. If present, the *InitialName* attribute gets converted into a "greater than or equal to" MAPI restriction against the *DisplayName* of the contact.

The optional *FinalName* attribute enables you to specify an inclusive name to define the alphabetical end of your filter. If you do not specify the *FinalName* attribute, your view will have no upper alphabetical bound to the contacts returned. If present, the *FinalName* attribute gets converted into a "less than or equal to" MAPI restriction against the *DisplayName* of the contact.

Because all of the attributes are optional, you could submit a *FindItem* request with a trivial *ContactsView* paging element, *<ContactsView/>*, but doing so yields the same results as omitting the element and is a fruitless and somewhat silly endeavor.

Notice that with both the *InitialName* and *FinalName* attributes, it is the *DisplayName* property that is used in the filter. It doesn't matter what *GivenName* or *Surname* is set to, nor the *FileAs* value. Unfortunately, that limits the usefulness of *ContactsView*. Given that the *InitialName* and *FinalName* attributes are converted into restrictions, you can reproduce the behavior of *ContactsView* by specifying your own restrictions in *FindItem*. In fact, this gives you a lot more functionality because you can determine whether you want to filter on the first name, last name, file as, or any other property of interest. We will cover restrictions in Chapter 14, "Searching the Mailbox," but Listing 6-15 gives you a taste of doing a pseudo-contacts view by using the *FileAs* property. In addition, it provides the ability to do something that the *ContactsView* cannot do—exclusive rather than inclusive boundaries. Exclusive boundaries are accomplished by the use of the *IsLessThanType* search expression instead of the *IsLessThanOrEqualToType* search expression.

LISTING 6-15 A more flexible *ContactsView*

```
<FindItem xmlns=".../messages"
          xmlns:t=".../types"
          Traversal="Shallow">
  <ItemShape>
    <t:BaseShape>Default</t:BaseShape>
  </ItemShape>
  <Restriction>
    <t:And>
      <t:IsGreaterThanOrEqualTo>
        <t:FieldURI FieldURI="contacts:FileAs"/>
        <t:FieldURIOrConstant>
          <t:Constant Value="A"/>
        </t:FieldURIOrConstant>
      </t:IsGreaterThanOrEqualTo>
      <t:IsLessThan>
        <t:FieldURI FieldURI="contacts:FileAs"/>
        <t:FieldURIOrConstant>
          <t:Constant Value="B"/>
        </t:FieldURIOrConstant>
      </t:IsLessThan>
    </t:And>
  </Restriction>
  <ParentFolderIds>
    <t:DistinguishedFolderId Id="contacts"/>
  </ParentFolderIds>
</FindItem>
```

Of course, by omitting the *ContactsView* element, you lose the *MaxEntriesReturned* attribute. That isn't a problem, though—you can just use the *IndexedPageView* element instead if you need to specify a limit to the number of items you want returned.[13]

To make Listing 6-15 a little more general and reusable, Listing 6-16 provides the *SuperContactsView* method.

---

[13] Discussed in Chapter 15, "Advanced Searching."

LISTING 6-16 The *SuperContactsView* method

```
/// <summary>
/// A new, improved ContactsView method
/// </summary>
/// <param name="binding">Binding to use for the call</param>
/// <param name="folderId">Folder to perform FindItem on</param>
/// <param name="responseShape">ResponseShape for returned contacts</param>
/// <param name="pathForRestriction">The property path to compare
/// against</param>
/// <param name="lowerBounds">lower bounds string (inclusive)</param>
/// <param name="upperBounds">upper bounds string (exclusive)</param>
/// <param name="offset">For indexed paging, the offset into the result set
/// to start at. If you are not using paging, set to zero</param>
/// <param name="maxEntries">Max entries to return for each page.  Zero for
/// unbounded</param>
/// <returns>FindItemResponseMessageType</returns>
///
public FindItemResponseMessageType SuperContactsView(
                        ExchangeServiceBinding binding,
                        BaseFolderIdType folderId,
                        ItemResponseShapeType responseShape,
                        BasePathToElementType pathForRestriction,
                        string lowerBounds,
                        string upperBounds,
                        int offset,
                        int maxEntries)
{
  FindItemType request = new FindItemType();
  request.ItemShape = responseShape;

  // If maxEntries > 0, use indexed paging to limit the
  // results (see Chapter 15)
  //
  if (maxEntries > 0)
  {
    IndexedPageViewType paging = new IndexedPageViewType();
    paging.BasePoint = IndexBasePointType.Beginning;
    paging.Offset = offset;
    paging.MaxEntriesReturned = maxEntries;
    paging.MaxEntriesReturnedSpecified = true;
    request.Item = paging;
  }

  request.ParentFolderIds = new BaseFolderIdType[] { folderId };
  request.Traversal = ItemQueryTraversalType.Shallow;

  // Build up our restriction
  //
  IsGreaterThanOrEqualToType lowerBoundsFilter = new IsGreaterThanOrEqualToType();
  lowerBoundsFilter.Item = pathForRestriction;
  lowerBoundsFilter.FieldURIOrConstant = new FieldURIOrConstantType();
  ConstantValueType lowerBoundsValue = new ConstantValueType();
  lowerBoundsValue.Value = lowerBounds;
  lowerBoundsFilter.FieldURIOrConstant.Item = lowerBoundsValue;
```

```
        IsLessThanType upperBoundsFilter = new IsLessThanType();
        upperBoundsFilter.Item = pathForRestriction;
        upperBoundsFilter.FieldURIOrConstant = new FieldURIOrConstantType();
        ConstantValueType upperBoundsValue = new ConstantValueType();
        upperBoundsValue.Value = upperBounds;
        upperBoundsFilter.FieldURIOrConstant.Item = upperBoundsValue;

        AndType and = new AndType();

        and.Items = new SearchExpressionType[] { lowerBoundsFilter,
                upperBoundsFilter };
        request.Restriction = new RestrictionType();
        request.Restriction.Item = and;

        // Make the request
        //
        FindItemResponseType response = binding.FindItem(request);
        return response.ResponseMessages.Items[0] as
                FindItemResponseMessageType;
    }
```

Using this method is pretty easy. To perform a contacts view against *FileAs* and return a maximum of 20 contacts per page for all contacts in the *A* range, do the following:

```
FindItemResponseMessageType response = SuperContactsView(
    binding,
    new DistinguishedFolderIdType(DistinguishedFolderIdNameType.contacts),
    new ItemResponseShapeType(DefaultShapeNamesType.Default),
    new PathToUnindexedFieldType(UnindexedFieldURIType.contactsFileAs),
    "A" /* lower bounds (inclusive) */,
    "B" /* upper bounds (exclusive) */,
    0 /* offset */,
    20 /* max records*/);
```

ResolveNames

If you have ever done any work with the Lightweight Directory Access Protocol (LDAP) and the Active Directory, you may have run into ambiguous name resolution (ANR). Essentially, ANR is a partial name search against entities in the Active Directory, and the *ResolveNames* Web method is your access to ANR through Exchange Web Services. In addition to searching the Active Directory, *ResolveNames* also searches the default contacts folder in your Mailbox. Note that there is no way to search any non-default contacts folders. Contacts, distribution lists, and mail-enabled public folders are considered during resolution. Also, the only way to search someone else's Mailbox with *ResolveNames* is to use Exchange Impersonation, which is probably overkill.[14]

---

[14] Exchange Impersonation is discussed in Chapter 19, "Server to Server Authentication."

Let's look at the basic structure of a *ResolveNames* request, as shown in Listing 6-17.

LISTING 6-17 Basic structure of the *ResolveNames* Web method

```
<ResolveNames xmlns=".../messages.xsd"
              xmlns:m=".../message.xsd"
              xmlns:t=".../types.xsd"
              ReturnFullContactData="true | false ">
  <UnresolvedEntry>John</UnresolvedEntry>
</ResolveNames>
```

Yippee! A relatively simple Web method! Yes, there isn't much to the *ResolveNames* request. Let's look at the various and sundry parts.

UnresolvedEntry Element

We will get to the *ReturnFullContactData* attribute later on, but first let's talk about the *UnresolvedEntry* element. *ResolveNames* exposes a single *UnresolvedEntry* element. This element is simply a non-empty string. So, putting in an empty *UnresolvedEntry* is a schema violation—you must have at least one character. So, what do you put into *UnresolvedEntry*? Part of a name you are searching for.

Resolving Directory Contacts

Assume you have the following Mailbox users defined in the Active Directory:[15]

- Tina Makovec
- Ken Malcolmson
- Alfredo Maldonado Guerra
- Janusz Malgorzaciak

After these contacts have been created through the Exchange Management Console, you can go into Active Directory Users and Computers to set some other information on them such as office location, phone numbers, and so on.

Listing 6-18 shows a simple request for *mako*.

LISTING 6-18 The *ResolveNames* request

```
<ResolveNames xmlns=".../messages"
              ReturnFullContactData="false">
  <UnresolvedEntry>mako</UnresolvedEntry>
</ResolveNames>
```

---

[15] For the example, we created these accounts by using the Microsoft Exchange Server 2007 Management Console.

The *UnresolvedEntry* string is insensitive both to case and diacritical marks. In addition, leading and trailing whitespace characters are ignored.[16]

Submitting the request in Listing 6-18 returns a single record.

```
<ResolveNamesResponse xmlns:m="../messages"
                      xmlns:t="../types"
                      xmlns="../messages">
  <m:ResponseMessages>
    <m:ResolveNamesResponseMessage ResponseClass="Success">
      <m:ResponseCode>NoError</m:ResponseCode>
      <m:ResolutionSet TotalItemsInView="1"
                       IncludesLastItemInRange="true">
        <t:Resolution>
          <t:Mailbox>
            <t:Name>Tina Makovec</t:Name>
            <t:EmailAddress>tina.makovec@contoso.com</t:EmailAddress>
            <t:RoutingType>SMTP</t:RoutingType>
            <t:MailboxType>Mailbox</t:MailboxType>
          </t:Mailbox>
        </t:Resolution>
      </m:ResolutionSet>
    </m:ResolveNamesResponseMessage>
  </m:ResponseMessages>
</ResolveNamesResponse>
```

Here you see that *ResolveNames* matched the expected user. Guess what? You would also get the same results if you searched on *Tina*. And also *Tin Mak* (notice the space). However, if you supplied *ina*, you would come out empty-handed. What does this show? Well, first, *ResolveNames* must be looking at more than one property to determine its matches. Second, only prefix matches are considered.

So what properties does *ResolveNames* look at? It is important to keep in mind that ANR is simply delegated to an LDAP call.[17] Therefore, how Active Directory ANR works through LDAP calls is how it will behave through Exchange Web Services. As such, the following attributes are considered when performing ANR lookups:[18]

- *Display-Name*
- *Given-Name*[19]
- *Legacy-Exchange-DN*

---

[16] For Active Directory ANR, the first embedded space breaks up the search phrase, each part is searched, and the results are combined using the AND logical operation. Subsequent spaces are ignored. This is standard ANR behavior.

[17] By the way, only objects in the Active Directory that have the *ShowInAddressLists* attribute set appropriately will be considered. If this value is not set, then the object does not belong to any address lists and therefore should not show up in a Global Address List (GAL) search. This is an additional EWS constraint, not an ANR constraint.

[18] Refer to MSDN regarding the meaning and usage of each of these Active Directory attributes.

[19] Hey, look at that! So that is where the *GivenName* and *Surname* property names actually came from.

- *Physical-Delivery-Office-Name*
- *Proxy-Address*
- *RDN*
- *SAM-Account-Name*
- *Surname*

Based on the information entered for Tina, you could also find her by searching on her mail nickname (tina.makovec), her e-mail address, and so on. It is worth mentioning that when performing *ResolveNames* against the Active Directory, the *QueryBaseDN* for the caller is taken into consideration. The *QueryBaseDN* directory attribute specifies the root organizational container that can be set by administrators on a user-by-user basis. Results are then limited to items contained within that organizational unit. As one might imagine, this is extremely important in hosted Exchange scenarios where a given Exchange installation services two or more unaffiliated companies. In hosted scenarios, one company should not have access to another company's address lists.

Resolving Store Contacts

Having discussed how Active Directory contacts are resolved, it is time to consider Store contacts. When you call *ResolveNames*, how do Store contacts fit into the picture?

You saw that Active Directory ANR uses the first space to separate partial strings that need to be matched, and it combines the results using a logical ANDs operation. However, Store ANR uses space, dash, and comma to separate partial strings. A Store ANR name is valid if it is not empty and contains something other than a space, dash or comma. For instance, *Tina,* is a valid value whereas a single comma (i.e., ",") is not. Also, Store ANR is not limited to a single separator—you can supply as many as you like. Note that doing so modifies your results for Active Directory matches, so it is best to stay with a single separator if you care about Active Directory results.

As with Active Directory ANR, Store ANR performs an AND operation between partial string matches. Let's define a couple of Store contacts to use in the examples. To make the responses a little more understandable, we will add (Store) to the last name of each of these contacts to distinguish them from Active Directory contacts. Notice that these are the same names that were added to the Active Directory.

- Tina Makovec (Store)
- Ken Malcolmson (Store)
- Alfredo Maldonado Guerra (Store)
- Janusz Malgorzacia (Store)

Just for sanity's sake, the following is a *ResolveNames* call requesting *Makovec*. This should return two records—one for the Active Directory and one for the Store.

```
<ResolveNames xmlns="...­/messages"
              ReturnFullContactData="false">
  <UnresolvedEntry>Makovec</UnresolvedEntry>
</ResolveNames>
```

Hmmm. The response contains a single record—the record for the Active Directory contact. So, what happened to the Store contact? Well, the way that Store ANR is implemented, only those contacts that have one or more e-mail addresses are considered in an ANR call. To show the importance that Store ANR places on e-mail addresses, we'll update Tina Makovec to have two e-mail addresses: tina.makovec_store1@contoso.com and tina.makovec_store2@contoso.com. If the *ResolveNames* request is reissued, *three* matches will be returned—one for the Active Directory contact and one for *each* e-mail address for the matching Store contact. This means that if Tina had three e-mail addresses, then there would be four total matches (including the Active Directory contact). In addition, the "name" of the matched contact is not the display name of the contact, but rather the display name for the e-mail address in question.

```
<m:ResolutionSet TotalItemsInView="3" IncludesLastItemInRange="true">
  <!-- directory contact elided -->
  <t:Resolution>
    <t:Mailbox>
      <t:Name>Tina's first email address</t:Name>
      <t:EmailAddress>tina.makovec_store1@contoso.com</t:EmailAddress>
      <t:RoutingType>SMTP</t:RoutingType>
      <t:MailboxType>Contact</t:MailboxType>
      <t:ItemId Id="AQAtAEFkb…
    </t:Mailbox>
  </t:Resolution>
  <t:Resolution>
    <t:Mailbox>
      <t:Name>Tina's second email address</t:Name>
      <t:EmailAddress>tina.makovec_store2@contoso.com</t:EmailAddress>
      <t:RoutingType>SMTP</t:RoutingType>
      <t:MailboxType>Contact</t:MailboxType>
      <t:ItemId Id="AQAtAEFkb…
    </t:Mailbox>
  </t:Resolution>
</m:ResolutionSet>
```

One option for dealing with the expansion of a Store contact's e-mail addresses is to walk through your response and combine these matches based on the value of the *ItemId* element, which will be the same for all the e-mail addresses for a given Store contact. Of course, that doesn't help you with the display name weirdness. Your only option there is to bind to the contact by using *GetItem* and then retrieve the *DisplayName* or *CompleteName* properties from there.

Maybe this isn't as strange as it first looks. An Active Directory user object contains a reference to only one Mailbox. The primary SMTP address is sufficient to send e-mail to that user.

The other proxy addresses are optional, although when used, mail will still be delivered to the same Mailbox.[20]

A Store contact can have up to three e-mail addresses that are not necessarily alternative addresses for the same mailbox. A given contact might have a home e-mail address, a business e-mail address, and a shared e-mail address as a representative of a non-profit organization, for example.

During name resolution, if a Store contact is matched, and that contact has more than one e-mail address, it makes sense to warn the user that the same person has more than one e-mail address. This is especially true if the sender is going to transmit confidential information to the contact and doesn't want to send it to a shared e-mail address.

Of course, if you also consider the schema, *ResolveNames* returns a *Mailbox* element, which can contain at most one e-mail address. To be schema-compliant, *ResolveNames* would have to either eliminate the additional e-mail addresses or supply different *Mailbox* elements for each e-mail address on a given Store contact.

If a person needs to have more than one Mailbox, an Exchange administrator must create two or more user accounts with the same "regular" contact data—names, phones, physical addresses—but different logon/account ids. In such a case, ANR will return two results—the two Mailboxes for the user in the Active Directory—and therefore follow more in the footsteps of its Store-based cousin.

So what happens if there is more than one match returned for a given unresolved entry? In our example, if you search for *Malcolmson*, then Ken Malcolmson will be returned twice—once for the Active Directory contact and once for the Store contact. This response is shown in Listing 6-19.

LISTING 6-19 ResolveNames response for multiple matches

```
<ResolveNamesResponse xmlns:m=".../messages"
                      xmlns:t=".../types"
                      xmlns=".../messages">
  <m:ResponseMessages>
    <m:ResolveNamesResponseMessage ResponseClass="Warning">
      <m:MessageText>Multiple results were found.</m:MessageText>
      <m:ResponseCode>ErrorNameResolutionMultipleResults</m:ResponseCode>
      <m:DescriptiveLinkKey>0</m:DescriptiveLinkKey>
      <m:ResolutionSet TotalItemsInView="2" IncludesLastItemInRange="true">
        <t:Resolution>
          <t:Mailbox>
            <t:Name>Ken Malcolmson</t:Name>
            <t:EmailAddress>ken.malcolmson@contoso.com</t:EmailAddress>
            <t:RoutingType>SMTP</t:RoutingType>
            <t:MailboxType>Mailbox</t:MailboxType>
          </t:Mailbox>
```

---

[20] These proxy addresses are not necessarily SMTP addresses either.

```
        </t:Resolution>
        <t:Resolution>
          <t:Mailbox>
            <t:Name>ken.malcolmson_store@contoso.com</t:Name>
            <t:EmailAddress>ken.malcolmson_store@contoso.com</t:EmailAddress>
            <t:RoutingType>SMTP</t:RoutingType>
            <t:MailboxType>Contact</t:MailboxType>
            <t:ItemId Id="AAAtAEFkbWlu..." ChangeKey="AAAAA..."/>
          </t:Mailbox>
        </t:Resolution>
      </m:ResolutionSet>
    </m:ResolveNamesResponseMessage>
  </m:ResponseMessages>
</ResolveNamesResponse>
```

The result contains two matches, as expected. What is interesting, however, is that the
ResponseClass attribute is not *Success*, but rather it is *Warning*. In addition, the *ResponseCode*
is not *NoError*, but rather it is *ErrorNameResolutionMultipleResults*. Despite the response code
prefix, this is not an "error" per se, but rather something that should be noted. The idea behind ANR is that you are taking an ambiguous reference to a user and having that reference
resolved into a concrete user. Unfortunately, the resolution is still somewhat ambiguous because there was more than one match. Listing 6-20 shows this call made through the proxy.

LISTING 6-20 *ResolveNames* through the proxy classes

```
/// <summary>
/// Resolve the given ambiguous name
/// </summary>
/// <param name="binding">Binding to use for call</param>
/// <param name="name">Ambiguous name to resolve</param>
/// <param name="returnFullContactData">If true will return full contact
/// data</param>
///
public static void ResolveNames(
                    ExchangeServiceBinding binding,
                    string name,
                    bool returnFullContactData)
{
    ResolveNamesType request = new ResolveNamesType();
    request.ReturnFullContactData = returnFullContactData;

    // Set the ambiguous name we want to resolve
    //
    request.UnresolvedEntry = name;

    // Make the call
    //
    ResolveNamesResponseType response = binding.ResolveNames(request);
    ResolveNamesResponseMessageType responseMessage =
        response.ResponseMessages.Items[0] as
                ResolveNamesResponseMessageType;
```

```
  // Remember that ErrorNameResolutionMultipleResults is not necessarily
  // an error
  //
  if ((responseMessage.ResponseCode == ResponseCodeType.NoError) ||
      (responseMessage.ResponseCode ==
          ResponseCodeType.ErrorNameResolutionMultipleResults))
  {
    // The response message holds an array of ResolutionType instance -
    // one for each matched name
    //
    foreach (ResolutionType entry in
              responseMessage.ResolutionSet.Resolution)
    {
      // do something with each result
    }
  }
}
```

Dealing with the Response

The *ResolveNames* response structure follows the standard *Response/ResponseMessage* structure. However, once you get down to a given response message, you run into some interesting features. *ResolveNamesResponseMessageType* exposes a single element called *ResolutionSet,* which is of type *ArrayOfResolutionType.* As the name suggests, *ArrayOfResolutionType* holds one or more resolution type instances. Listing 6-21 shows this type as defined in types.xsd.

LISTING 6-21 *ArrayOfResolutionType* from types.xsd

```
<xs:complexType name="ArrayOfResolutionType">
   <xs:sequence>
      <xs:element name="Resolution"
                  type="t:ResolutionType"
                  minOccurs="0"
                  maxOccurs="100" />
   </xs:sequence>
   <xs:attributeGroup ref="t:FindResponsePagingAttributes" />
</xs:complexType>
```

ArrayOfResolutionType exposes a *bounded* array of *Resolution* elements. If you notice the *maxOccurs* attribute, it is set to 100, which limits the possible number of responses to 100.[21] What happens if there are more than 100 matches? Well, you won't get all of them. In fact, if you try, your response will contain the following XML:

```
<m:ResolutionSet TotalItemsInView="100"
                 IncludesLastItemInRange="false">
```

---

[21] Note that OWA also uses this 100-contact limit when resolving e-mail addresses.

The *IncludesLastItemInRange* attribute tells you that more data is available. However, there really is no way to get it. *ResolveNames* does not support paging. The developer responsible for *ResolveNames* has said that if there are more than 100 responses, it's likely that the string is way too ambiguous and the request should be repeated with a more appropriate string.

Since *ResolveNames* searches both the Active Directory and the default contacts folder, it is worthwhile to note that the Active Directory is searched first and then the default contacts folder. If there are 75 matches in both the Active Directory and the Store, then your response will contain 75 entries from the Active Directory but only 25 from the Store. In fact, if there are 100 or more matches from the Active Directory, your response will contain no matches from the Store, even if more matches were found.

Of interest is the fact that *ArrayOfResolutionType* exposes the attribute group *FindResponsePagingAttributes*. This is the same attribute group used by *FindItem* and *FindFolder* to return values for future paging requests. Although this looks promising, the attributes are never filled in the responses. Even if they were used, there is no mechanism to pass these values into a *ResolveNames* request. As such we recommend that you ignore them.

Let's look a little closer at this response. What is contained in *ResolutionType*? See Listing 6-22 for the answer.

LISTING 6-22 *ResolutionType* schema definition from types.xsd

```
<xs:complexType name="ResolutionType">
  <xs:sequence>
    <xs:element name="Mailbox" type="t:EmailAddressType" />
    <xs:element name="Contact" type="t:ContactItemType" minOccurs="0" />
  </xs:sequence>
</xs:complexType>
```

ResolutionType exposes two elements. The first of these, *Mailbox,* is of type *EmailAddressType* and will always be present in a response. We will discuss *EmailAddressType* in more detail in Chapter 7, "Messages;" however, there are two child elements that are of particular interest to at this point.

```
<xs:complexType name="EmailAddressType">
    <xs:complexContent>
      <xs:extension base="t:BaseEmailAddressType">
        <xs:sequence>
          <xs:element name="Name" type="xs:string" minOccurs="0"/>
          <xs:element name="EmailAddress" type="t:NonEmptyStringType"
                                          minOccurs="0"/>
          <xs:element name="RoutingType" type="t:NonEmptyStringType"
                                          minOccurs="0"/>
          <xs:element name="MailboxType" type="t:MailboxTypeType"
                                          minOccurs="0" />
          <!-- for private DL (CDL) only-->
          <xs:element name="ItemId" type="t:ItemIdType" minOccurs="0" />
```

```
        </xs:sequence>
      </xs:extension>
    </xs:complexContent>
  </xs:complexType>
```

The *MailboxType* element is an instance of the *MailboxTypeType* type and tells you what kind of creature this resolved entity is.[22] The valid values for *MailboxTypeType* are listed in Table 6-8.

TABLE 6-8 *MailboxTypeType* Values

MailboxTypeType	Comments
Mailbox	An Active Directory Mailbox owner, Mailbox user or public folder
PublicDL	An Active Directory distribution list, which covers both distribution and security groups as well as "dynamic" distribution groups
PrivateDL	A Store distribution list; it is called private because it came from a personal Mailbox
Contact	Either an Active Directory contact object or a normal Store contact; both are represented by the *ContactItemType* schema type

The second "new" element is *ItemId*. Notice the friendly comment that was included in the schema—"for private DL (CDL) only."[23] This would imply that you encounter this element only with Store distribution lists. Well, that's wrong. You also encounter this element for Store contacts. Consider, for example, an Office Outlook-generated distribution list called Some Team in your Mailbox, with the four Store contacts from our example added. In addition, imagine a contact named "Some Person". Running *ResolveNames* against "Some" gives the following:

```
<m:ResolutionSet TotalItemsInView="2" IncludesLastItemInRange="true">
   <t:Resolution>
      <t:Mailbox>
         <t:Name>Some Team</t:Name>
         <t:RoutingType>MAPIPDL</t:RoutingType>
         <t:MailboxType>PrivateDL</t:MailboxType>
         <t:ItemId Id="AAAtAEFkbWlu..." ChangeKey="AAAAA..."/>
      </t:Mailbox>
   </t:Resolution>
   <t:Resolution>
      <t:Mailbox>
         <t:Name>some.person@contoso.com</t:Name>
         <t:EmailAddress>some.person@contoso.com</t:EmailAddress>
         <t:RoutingType>SMTP</t:RoutingType>
         <t:MailboxType>Contact</t:MailboxType>
         <t:ItemId Id="AAAtAEFkbWlu..." ChangeKey="AAAAA..."/>
      </t:Mailbox>
   </t:Resolution>
</m:ResolutionSet>
```

---

[22] One of the authors wanted to use a sentence with multiple occurrences of the word "Type" in rapid succession ever since he read a similar construct from Dino Esposito's most excellent book, *Applied XML Programming for .NET*. Dino referred to the *XmlAttributeAttribute* attribute, which still amuses our author to this day.

[23] CDL stands for Contact Distribution List or Contact folder Distribution List. It is really just a private distribution list, but because private and public DLs would have the same acronym, CDL was chosen. Maybe SDL (Store Distribution List) would have been better?

Looking back at the *ResolutionType* from Listing 6-21, you see the second element is *Contact*. *Contact* will be present only if the *ResolveNames* request had its *ReturnFullContactData* attribute set to true.

ReturnFullContactData Attribute

If the *ReturnFullContactData* attribute is set to true, Active Directory contacts will be filled in with as much information as is provided in the Active Directory. Oddly enough, the *Contact* element is never present for Store contacts. Why is this? Because to fill in this data, *ResolveNames* would need to bind to each contact in turn to retrieve such contact data. Such an operation is cost prohibitive by default. If you do need such information, you need to use *GetItem* and pass in the item ids for the contacts or distribution lists you want to return. As another option, you could perform a *FindItem* on the contacts folder if you don't care about retrieving the calculated properties (such as, *CompleteName*).

ExpandDL

ResolveNames returns matching distribution lists, but it is often desirable to retrieve the members of a distribution list. This is where the *ExpandDL* Web method comes into play. Let's look at the basic structure of an *ExpandDL* request, as shown in Listing 6-23.

LISTING 6-23 Basic structure of *ExpandDL*

```
<ExpandDL xmlns=".../messages"
  <Mailbox/>
</ExpandDL>
```

Another simple Web method. You can expand one single distribution list at a time, as can be seen by the single *Mailbox* element. Now, what may not be clear is that you can expand both Store and Active Directory distribution lists. The secret to this lies in the *Mailbox* element.

If the *EmailAddress* element is filled in, then you are trying to expand an Active Directory distribution list. If the *ItemId* element is filled in, then you are trying to expand a Store distribution list. What happens if you fill in both? The code first checks to see if the e-mail address is filled in. If it is, it doesn't even check the *ItemId*. So, it will always think it is an Active Directory distribution list in that case. This really isn't too big of a deal. Why? Because a Store distribution list never has an e-mail address. This is apparent when you consider that the routing type for private distribution lists is *MAPIPDL* instead of *SMTP*.[24] So, you should be able to pass a *Mailbox* entry obtained from *ResolveNames* directly into *ExpandDL*.

---

[24] MAPIPDL = MAPI Private Distribution List

You cause an Active Directory distribution list expansion if you pass in something like this:

```
<Mailbox>
  <t:EmailAddress>sales@contoso.com25</t:EmailAddress>
</Mailbox>
```

And you cause a Store distribution list expansion if you pass in something like this:

```
<Mailbox>
  <t:ItemId Id="AAAtAEFkbWlu..." ChangeKey="AAAAA..."/>
</Mailbox>
```

All the other *Mailbox* child elements are ignored during *ExpandDL*. You are free to leave them in there.

Expanding Store (Private) Distribution Lists

Earlier in the chapter, we showed a private distribution list called Some Team that had four Store contacts as members. You can get the item id for this distribution list by calling *ResolveNames* against Some Team.[26] The *ResolveNames* call returns the following *Mailbox* element:

```
<t:Mailbox>
   <t:Name>Some Team</t:Name>
   <t:RoutingType>MAPIPDL</t:RoutingType>
   <t:MailboxType>PrivateDL</t:MailboxType>
   <t:ItemId Id="AAAtAEFkbWlu..." ChangeKey="AAAAA..."/>
</t:Mailbox>
```

Listing 6-24 shows this entire element handed off to *ExpandDL*.

LISTING 6-24 Expanding a private DL

```
<ExpandDL xmlns=".../messages"
        xmlns:t=".../types">
   <Mailbox>
      <t:Name>Some Team</t:Name>
      <t:RoutingType>MAPIPDL</t:RoutingType>
      <t:MailboxType>PrivateDL</t:MailboxType>
      <t:ItemId Id="AAAtAEFkbWlu..." ChangeKey="AAAAA..."/>
   </Mailbox>
</ExpandDL>
```

Listing 6-25 shows the response.

---

[25] You can also pass in a DL alias, name, display name, simple display name, X500, X400, or legacy DN address.

[26] You could also call *FindItem* on the contacts folder, but because we just talked about *ResolveNames*, we figured this would be a good choice.

LISTING 6-25 Expand DL response for a private DL

```
<ExpandDLResponse xmlns:m=".../messages"
                  xmlns:t=".../types"
                  xmlns=".../messages">
  <m:ResponseMessages>
    <m:ExpandDLResponseMessage ResponseClass="Success">
      <m:ResponseCode>NoError</m:ResponseCode>
      <m:DLExpansion TotalItemsInView="4" IncludesLastItemInRange="true">
        <t:Mailbox>
          <t:Name>Tina Makovec</t:Name>
          <t:EmailAddress>tina.makovec@contoso.com</t:EmailAddress>
          <t:RoutingType>SMTP</t:RoutingType>
          <t:MailboxType>Mailbox</t:MailboxType>
        </t:Mailbox>
        <t:Mailbox>
          <t:Name>Ken Malcolmson</t:Name>
          <t:EmailAddress>ken.malcolmson@contoso.com</t:EmailAddress>
          <t:RoutingType>SMTP</t:RoutingType>
          <t:MailboxType>Mailbox</t:MailboxType>
        </t:Mailbox>
        <t:Mailbox>
          <t:Name>Alfredo Maldonado Guerra</t:Name>
          <t:EmailAddress>alfredom@contoso.com</t:EmailAddress>
          <t:RoutingType>SMTP</t:RoutingType>
          <t:MailboxType>Mailbox</t:MailboxType>
        </t:Mailbox>
        <t:Mailbox>
          <t:Name>Janusz Malgorzacia</t:Name>
          <t:EmailAddress>janusz.malgorzacia@contoso.com</t:EmailAddress>
          <t:RoutingType>SMTP</t:RoutingType>
          <t:MailboxType>Mailbox</t:MailboxType>
        </t:Mailbox>
      </m:DLExpansion>
    </m:ExpandDLResponseMessage>
  </m:ResponseMessages>
</ExpandDLResponse>
```

Eariler, you saw that in *ResolveNames*, an entry was returned for each e-mail address of a given contact. In *ExpandDL*, a single entry is returned for each contact regardless of the number of e-mail addresses each has. Also, the Mailbox name returned by *ExpandDL* is the actual display name for the contact rather than the display name for the e-mail address.

Expanding Directory (Public) Distribution Lists

Expanding public distribution lists follows a similar pattern except that the *Mailbox* element that you pass into *ExpandDL* contains *EmailAddress* instead of *ItemId*. Take, for example, a distribution list called *My Public DL* created through the Exchange Management Console with some Active Directory contacts added to it. Calling *ResolveNames* on *My Public DL* gives the following entry:

```
<t:Mailbox>
   <t:Name>My Public DL</t:Name>
   <t:EmailAddress>MyPublicDL@contoso.com</t:EmailAddress>
   <t:RoutingType>SMTP</t:RoutingType>
   <t:MailboxType>PublicDL</t:MailboxType>
</t:Mailbox>
```

Listing 6-26 shows a *ExpandDL* call made with the previous entry.

LISTING 6-26 Expanding a public DL

```
<ExpandDL xmlns=".../messages"
          xmlns:t=".../types">
   <Mailbox>
      <t:Name>My Public DL</t:Name>
      <t:EmailAddress>MyPublicDL@contoso.com</t:EmailAddress>
      <t:RoutingType>SMTP</t:RoutingType>
      <t:MailboxType>PublicDL</t:MailboxType>
   </Mailbox>
</ExpandDL>
```

As mentioned previously, *ResolveNames* and *ExpandDL* work only with visible, *mail-enabled* contacts and public distribution lists. If *My Public DL* has five mail-enabled contacts and three contacts that are *not* mail-enabled, then expanding the public DL will return only the five mail-enabled members. This is also true of nested distribution lists. If a mail-enabled distribution list contains another distribution list that is *not* mail-enabled, the nested public DL is not returned. However, if you go into the Exchange Management Console and mail-enable the nested DL, then it will appear the next time you expand your outer distribution list. Doing so results in a response like the one shown in Listing 6-27.

LISTING 6-27 Public DL expansion with nested DL

```
<ExpandDLResponse xmlns:m=".../messages"
                  xmlns:t=".../types"
                  xmlns=".../messages">
<m:ResponseMessages>
  <m:ExpandDLResponseMessage ResponseClass="Success">
    <m:ResponseCode>NoError</m:ResponseCode>
    <m:DLExpansion TotalItemsInView="5" IncludesLastItemInRange="true">
      <t:Mailbox>
         <t:Name>Tina Makovec</t:Name>
         <t:EmailAddress>tina.makovec@contoso.com</t:EmailAddress>
         <t:RoutingType>SMTP</t:RoutingType>
         <t:MailboxType>Mailbox</t:MailboxType>
      </t:Mailbox>
      <t:Mailbox>
         <t:Name>Ken Malcolmson</t:Name>
         <t:EmailAddress>ken.malcolmson@contoso.com</t:EmailAddress>
         <t:RoutingType>SMTP</t:RoutingType>
         <t:MailboxType>Mailbox</t:MailboxType>
      </t:Mailbox>
```

```
    <t:Mailbox>
      <t:Name>Alfredo Maldonado Guerra</t:Name>
      <t:EmailAddress>alfredom@contoso.com</t:EmailAddress>
      <t:RoutingType>SMTP</t:RoutingType>
      <t:MailboxType>Mailbox</t:MailboxType>
    </t:Mailbox>
    <t:Mailbox>
      <t:Name>Janusz Malgorzacia</t:Name>
      <t:EmailAddress>janusz.malgorzacia@contoso.com</t:EmailAddress>
      <t:RoutingType>SMTP</t:RoutingType>
      <t:MailboxType>Mailbox</t:MailboxType>
    </t:Mailbox>
    <t:Mailbox>
      <t:Name>My Nested DL</t:Name>
      <t:EmailAddress>MyNestedDL@contoso.com</t:EmailAddress>
      <t:RoutingType>SMTP</t:RoutingType>
      <t:MailboxType>PublicDL</t:MailboxType>
    </t:Mailbox>
   </m:DLExpansion>
  </m:ExpandDLResponseMessage>
 </m:ResponseMessages>
</ExpandDLResponse>
```

Notice that the response does indeed include the nested public distribution list. You can tell that it is a distribution list by looking at its *MailboxType* element, which in this case is *PublicDL*. If you want, you can then take this Mailbox element and pass it off to *ExpandDL* once again to retrieve its mail-enabled members.

A Proxy Class Example

To round out this section, we present a proxy example that takes a given name, resolves it using *ResolveNames*, and then, for each match, either writes out the mailbox information for a contact or expands the DL recursively. The main entry point for Listing 6-28 is the *ResolveAndExpand* static method. It calls the other two methods as necessary.

LISTING 6-28 Proxy example combining *ResolveNames* and *ExpandDL*

```
/// <summary>
/// Resolves the passed partialName and prints out contacts and expands
/// DLs.
/// </summary>
/// <param name="binding">Binding to use for calls</param>
/// <param name="partialName">Ambiguous name to match</param>
///
public static void ResolveAndExpand(
                    ExchangeServiceBinding binding,
                    string partialName)
{
   ResolveNamesType resolveRequest = new ResolveNamesType();
```

```
resolveRequest.ReturnFullContactData = false;
resolveRequest.UnresolvedEntry = partialName;
ResolveNamesResponseType resolveResponse =
            binding.ResolveNames(resolveRequest);

ResolveNamesResponseMessageType resolveMessage =
        resolveResponse.ResponseMessages.Items[0] as
                ResolveNamesResponseMessageType;
int offset = 0;

// For each match we either write out the contact or expand the DL
//
foreach (ResolutionType singleMatch in
            resolveMessage.ResolutionSet.Resolution)
{
  // Always write out the info (contact or DL)
  //
  WriteOutMailbox(offset, singleMatch.Mailbox);
  if ((singleMatch.Mailbox.MailboxType == MailboxTypeType.PrivateDL) ||
      (singleMatch.Mailbox.MailboxType == MailboxTypeType.PublicDL))
  {
    // It's a DL, so expand it
    //
    ExpandDL(binding, offset, singleMatch.Mailbox);
  }
 }
}


/// <summary>
/// Expands the passed DL and writes out its membership
/// </summary>
/// <param name="binding">Binding to use for the call</param>
/// <param name="offset">Offset number of tabs for printing</param>
/// <param name="dlToExpand">Mailbox for DL to expand</param>
///
private static void ExpandDL(
            ExchangeServiceBinding binding,
            int offset,
            EmailAddressType dlToExpand)
{
  // increment the offset so we show nesting when we print out the
  // results.
  //
  offset++;
  ExpandDLType expandRequest = new ExpandDLType();
  expandRequest.Mailbox = dlToExpand;
  ExpandDLResponseType expandResponse = binding.ExpandDL(expandRequest);

  ExpandDLResponseMessageType expandMessage =
            expandResponse.ResponseMessages.Items[0] as
                ExpandDLResponseMessageType;

  // If there are no mail-enabled contacts in the DL, the DL expansion will
  // come back empty so check for null.
```

```csharp
    //
    if (expandMessage.DLExpansion.Mailbox != null)
    {
       foreach (EmailAddressType mailbox in
                     expandMessage.DLExpansion.Mailbox)
       {
          WriteOutMailbox(offset, mailbox);
          if ((mailbox.MailboxType == MailboxTypeType.PrivateDL) ||
              (mailbox.MailboxType == MailboxTypeType.PublicDL))
          {
             // recursive expansion of DLs
             //
             ExpandDL(binding, offset, mailbox);
          }
       }
    }
}


/// <summary>
/// Writes the mailbox info out to the console
/// </summary>
/// <param name="offset">offset to use for tabbing</param>
/// <param name="mailbox">Mailbox to write out</param>
///
private static void WriteOutMailbox(int offset, EmailAddressType mailbox)
{
  StringBuilder sb = new StringBuilder();
  for (int pad = 0; pad < offset; pad++)
  {
    sb.Append("\t");
  }
  string padding = sb.ToString();
  Console.WriteLine(
        "{0}Name: {1}\r\n{2}Email: {3}\r\n{4}Type:{5}\r\n" +
        "{6}RoutingType:{7}\r\n{8}ItemId:{9}\r\n--------------------",
        padding,
        mailbox.Name == null ? "<NULL>" : mailbox.Name,
        padding,
        mailbox.EmailAddress == null ? "<NULL>" : mailbox.EmailAddress,
        padding,
        mailbox.MailboxType.ToString(),
        padding,
        mailbox.RoutingType == null ? "<NULL>" : mailbox.RoutingType,
        padding,
        mailbox.ItemId == null ? "<NULL>" : mailbox.ItemId.Id);
}
```

Summary

This chapter began with a discussion of Store contacts and distribution lists and the various properties that are surfaced on each. We discussed the *ContactsView* paging mechanism and why it should be replaced with something better. And of course, we provided something that was better—*SuperContactsView*. Having our fill of Store-related activities, we discussed the *ResolveNames* and *ExpandDL* Web methods, both of which can touch the Active Directory. Remember, only mail-enabled contacts and distribution lists are considered by these two Web methods.

Chapter 7
Messages

When one thinks of messages, many different meanings come to mind. In elementary school, children used to write little notes and fold them up to be passed over to a friend while the teacher was not looking. When they felt exceptionally brave, they would wad them up and send them sailing across the room while the teacher was writing on the chalkboard. "Man-in-the-middle" attacks were perpetrated by the students sitting between the thrower and receiver. They would try to swat the note out of the air before it reached its intended target. These days, pupils simply text message each other, which takes all the fun out of it.

Although technology has done much to advance the method of communication between pupils in a classroom setting, there are striking similarities between words scrawled on a piece of paper and the stream of bytes passed between text-messaging devices.

- Both are intended as a form of communication between one sending entity and one or more recipient entities.

- Both can be considered a payload of information to be delivered *even before* that information is transported to the recipient entities.

For the sake of this chapter, let's take the first similarity and use it as a basis for our definition of a message.

A message as a discrete and finite set of information that can be passed from one sending entity to one or more recipient entities.

Although this definition suggests that the message will actually be sent to the recipient entities at some point in time, it allows you to declare the set of information to be a message even before it has been sent.

With the above definition of message in mind, this chapter will discuss what makes a message a message and how these unique characteristics of a message come into play when interacting with Exchange Server 2007 Web Services (EWS).

What Exactly *Is* a Message?

Our definition of message implies that there must be a way to designate the *sender* as well as the *recipients* of the message. In Chapter 5, "Items," we covered the *ItemType* class in depth. However, no such sender or recipient properties were found there. This would imply that *ItemType* does not have the necessary properties to be a message. A contact, as seen in

Chapter 6, "Contacts and Distribution Lists," may look promising, but alas, although a contact may represent *either* the sending entity *or* a receiving entity, it certainly doesn't represent the communication *between* the sending and receiving entities.

To combat the inability of *ItemType* and *ContactItemType* to function as messages, Exchange Web Services introduces *MessageType*, which descends from *ItemType*. *MessageType* inherits all *ItemType* properties while also adding a number of message-specific properties.

As discussed in Chapter 5, the type of an item is determined by its *ItemClass* property value. Most notably, in Table 5-1, you saw that an *ItemClass* value of exactly "IPM.Note" or a value that is prefixed with "IPM.Note." is considered to be a message.[1] When an item is encountered within a mailbox that has such an *ItemClass* value, Exchange Web Services returns this item as a *MessageType* instance.

What Exactly *Is* a Recipient?

We have been throwing around the term "recipient" quite loosely, and before we go any further, we need to define what we mean by this term. First, you may have noticed that we have gone to great lengths in this chapter to avoid using the word "person" when discussing recipients. We have, however, used the word "entities" since it can be applied to animate and inanimate objects, to single individuals as well as groups of individuals. There was good reasons for this avoidance. A recipient can be

- An individual person like Ken Malcolmson
- All of the people within the sales team at Contoso, Ltd
- A piece of software
- A conference room

Of course, the above list is not exhaustive. Although we have been avoiding the use of people when talking about recipients, we will relax a bit so that we can offer an illustration.

Jane Dow needs to talk to Ken Malcolmson about the company meeting that is scheduled for the following week. However, Ken is hiding behind the vending machines in the break room because he has not yet ordered the materials he was supposed to order several weeks ago. Although Jane wants to initiate communication with Ken, she cannot until she locates him. Yet, is that really true? Jane could simply go back to her desk and write out a note and tape it to the door of Ken's office. Ken's office door is a "holding place" for such messages. Jane

---

[1] Notice the "." at the end of IPM.Note. For prefix matching this is essential because "IPM.Note.Custom" is a valid *ItemClass* value for a message while "IPM.NoteCustom" (no dot between the Note and Custom) is not. Going forward, we will simply refer to this as an "IPM.Note prefix". While it is true that any item with an *ItemClass* of exactly "IPM.Note" or an *ItemClass* that is prefixed by "IPM.Note." is considered a message, such phrasing is far too unwieldy to state more than once. Oops—that was twice.

believes that at some point, Ken will return to his office and will read the note that is taped to his door.

However, Ken found out from the supplier that because of his tardiness, the material would not arrive in time for the company meeting. So, Ken has planned his great escape. He purchased an airline ticket out of the country so that he can avoid Jane's wrath. Ken is waiting behind the vending machine until Jane goes upstairs so that he can bolt out the door. You see, Ken is not planning to return to his office.

Unfortunately, this is not the first time that Ken has performed below expectations. Nor is this the first time that Ken has hid to avoid Jane's wrath. Knowing this, Jane returns to her office and dials Ken's cell phone, the same phone that Ken forgot to turn off when planning his hasty escape.[2]

We have just identified two methods that Jane could use to get in touch with Ken. In fact, there are many more. She could send him a postal letter, which would be addressed to his house. She could have someone go out and post a note on his car windshield in the parking lot. She could contact his wife. All of these approaches are attempts to contact Ken. But Ken's office is not Ken, nor is his car, nor is his wife. These "end points" *represent* Ken, and are where Jane's messages actually arrive. They are the actual "recipients" of Jane's messages. The messages then wait in their various forms at the end points for Ken to read.

As we will use the term, a *recipient address* embodies one way to refer to an end point. In the soap-opera example above, a recipient address for Ken's office endpoint might be "Building 34, Office 1234." A recipient address for Ken's car endpoint might be "Front parking lot, Row A, Space 12." However, there may be more than one way to reference a given endpoint. Ken's car might also have a recipient address of "The red station wagon with license plate 123-456." In this case, not only is the car one way to access Ken, but there are two addresses that actually refer to the same endpoint. Figure 7-1 shows the distinction between addresses, endpoints, and Ken.

---

[2] This is much too exciting for a development book. We can amuse ourselves with the thought that Ken's cell phone is both loud and that the ringer is set to a polka tune, and that the new recruits just happen to be getting a tour of the breakroom. We may continue this story later.

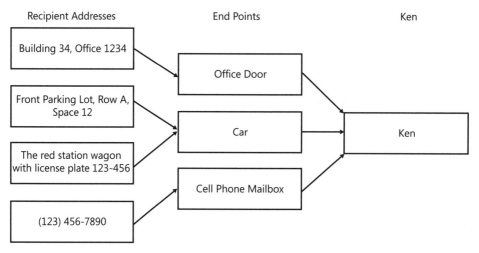

FIGURE 7-1 Addresses, endpoints, and Ken

In the Exchange Web Services world, an endpoint is typically a mailbox, that mailbox is identified by a recipient address, and Ken would be the mailbox owner.

Recipient Addresses

When delivering a message, the "message bearer" needs to know where to deliver the message to. If Jane tries to call Ken on the phone, she must use a phone number with a well defined format (such as 123-456-7890) so that the phone system knows how to connect to Ken's phone. If Jane asks her colleague Alfredo Maldonado Guerra to put a note on Ken's car, telling him it is "the red station wagon in the front parking lot" will be helpful, however, giving Alfredo Ken's phone number will not. Exchange Web Services commonly refers to recipient addresses using the Simple Mail Transfer Protocol (SMTP) e-mail address format. However, there are additional formats for recipient addresses that Exchange Web Services permits which we will discuss shortly.

The *EmailAddressType*

Exchange Web Services expresses recipient addresses within *EmailAddressType* instances. *EmailAddressType* is defined in the schema as shown in Listing 7-1.

LISTING 7-1 *EmailAddressType* schema definition

```
<xs:complexType name="EmailAddressType">
 <xs:complexContent>
  <xs:extension base="t:BaseEmailAddressType">
   <xs:sequence>
    <xs:element name="Name" type="xs:string" minOccurs="0"/>
    <xs:element name="EmailAddress" type="t:NonEmptyStringType" minOccurs="0"/>
```

```
        <xs:element name="RoutingType" type="t:NonEmptyStringType" minOccurs="0"/>
        <xs:element name="MailboxType" type="t:MailboxTypeType" minOccurs="0" />
        <!-- for private DL (CDL) only-->
        <xs:element name="ItemId" type="t:ItemIdType" minOccurs="0" />
      </xs:sequence>
    </xs:extension>
  </xs:complexContent>
</xs:complexType>
```

Note that although the type is called *EmailAddressType*, you will encounter it in XML instance documents and on proxy class properties by the name *Mailbox*. For instance, Ken Malcolmson's e-mail address is shown here:

```
<t:Mailbox>
  <t:Name>Ken Malcolmson</t:Name>
  <t:EmailAddress>ken.malcomson@contoso.com</t:EmailAddress>
  <t:RoutingType>SMTP</t:RoutingType>
<t:Mailbox>
```

Looking back at Listing 7-1, one thing that might be a little strange is that none of the elements are actually required. You can tell this by the presence of the *minOccurs* attribute on all of the elements within the type. In practice, however, an empty *EmailAddressType* instance is both useless and invalid. In order for an *EmailAddressType* instance to be valid, it must have either its *EmailAddress* or *ItemId* elements filled in.[3] As discussed in Chapter 6, the *MailboxType* element indicates the source of the recipient address and is outbound only, meaning that you will not need to set this element in any of your requests. We touched briefly on the *ItemId* element in Chapter 6, but will cover its significance in more detail later in this chapter. Let's look at the three other elements.

The *Name* element   The *Name* element is optional and provides a descriptive name for the recipient address. Note that we did not say "a descriptive name for the endpoint or for the mailbox owner." Why the distinction? Because it is perfectly reasonable to have multiple recipient addresses for a given mailbox endpoint. For instance

```
<t:Mailbox>
  <t:Name>Ken at home</t:Name>
  <t:EmailAddress>kmalcomson123@consolidatedmessenger.com</t:EmailAddress>
  <t:RoutingType>SMTP</t:RoutingType>
</t:Mailbox>

<t:Mailbox>
  <t:Name>Ken at work</t:Name>
  <t:EmailAddress>ken.malcomson@contoso.com</t:EmailAddress>
  <t:RoutingType>SMTP</t:RoutingType>
</t:Mailbox>
```

---

[3] If you are dealing with the proxy classes, these will be properties on *EmailAddressType*.

Although both of the recipient addresses refer to and endpoint owned by Ken Malcolmson, the *Name* describes the recipient *address*, and can be any string value, including those with amusing qualities.

```
<t:Mailbox>
  <t:Name>Super-K-Man</t:Name>
  <t:EmailAddress>kmalcomson124@consolidatedmessenger.com</t:EmailAddress>
  <t:RoutingType>SMTP</t:RoutingType>
</t:Mailbox>
```

It should be noted that Ken's recipient addresses could all be pointing to the same mailbox endpoint (in which case they would be *proxy addresses)* or to different mailbox endpoints.

The *EmailAddress* and *RoutingType* elements   The *EmailAddress* element is required except when dealing with private distribution lists, in which case the *ItemId* element is used instead. The value of this element is closely tied to the value of the *RoutingType* element. The *RoutingType* element defines the format or, "protocol," that is to be used when evaluating the address in the *EmailAddress* element. Just as Jane shouldn't use a phone number to tell Alfredo the location of Ken's car in the parking lot, your *EmailAddress* value should agree with the *RoutingType* specified.

Although the SMTP routing type is the most common format you will encounter, there are other e-mail address formats. For instance, the EX routing type, which is commonly referred to as the Legacy Exchange Distinguished Name (LegDN) has the following format:

```
/O=CONTOSO/OU=FIRST ADMINISTRATIVE GROUP/CN=RECIPIENTS/CN=KEN.MALCOLMSON
```

Exchange uses the LegDN internally to route e-mails between mailboxes in the same organization. Given Ken's LegDN address, it could be expressed within a *Mailbox* element like this:

```
<t:Mailbox>
  <t:Name>Ken's LegDN address</t:Name>
  <t:EmailAddress>/O=CONTOSO/OU=FIRST ADMINISTRATIVE GROUP/CN=RECIPIENTS/CN=KEN.MALCOLMSON
  </t:EmailAddress>
  <t:RoutingType>EX</t:RoutingType>
</t:Mailbox>
```

Exchange Web Services goes to great measure to convert LegDN addresses to SMTP addresses when they are encountered. As such, you will rarely encounter LegDN addresses when using Exchange Web Services.[4]

If the *RoutingType* element is missing, Exchange Web Services will attempt to infer the *RoutingType* by examining the value of the *EmailAddress*.

---

[4] You can specify LegDN addresses when sending messages and/or meeting requests to recipients. However, there are other areas, such as Exchange Impersonation, that accept only SMTP e-mail addresses. As such, use of the LegDN format is not suggested.

Although we have discussed both the SMTP and EX address formats, this list is extensible. In addition, there can be multiple address representations within a given routing type. For instance, Ken might have more than one recipient SMTP address that refers to the same mailbox endpoint.

ken.malcolmson@contoso.com
ken.malcolmson@northamerica.contoso.com

Assuming that both of these addresses are configured for Ken's mailbox, an e-mail sent to either of these addresses will end up in the same mailbox. In Exchange, these various recipient address formats that point to the same mailbox endpoint, as well as the alternate representations within a given routing type, are referred to as *proxy addresses* . A given mailbox within Exchange can have many proxy addresses as long as they are unique within the organization.

You will encounter *EmailAddressType* instances so often in Exchange Web Services programming that it is prudent to provide some overloaded constructors to make your experience more palatable. A partial class extension of *EmailAddressType* is offered in Listing 7-2.

LISTING 7-2 Partial class extension of *EmailAddressType*

```
/// <summary>
/// Partial class extension of EmailAddressType for ease of use
/// </summary>
public partial class EmailAddressType
{
  /// <summary>
  /// Constructor needed for xml serialization
  /// </summary>
  public EmailAddressType() { }

  /// <summary>
  /// Constructor that takes an email address
  /// </summary>
  /// <param name="emailAddress">email address of recipient</param>
  ///
  public EmailAddressType(string emailAddress)
  {
    this.emailAddressField = emailAddress;
  }

  /// <summary>
  /// Constructor that takes all three properties
  /// </summary>
  /// <param name="name">Name for the recipient address</param>
  /// <param name="emailAddress">email address of the recipient</param>
  /// <param name="routingType">routing type for the email address</param>
  ///
  public EmailAddressType(string name, string emailAddress, string routingType)
  {
    this.nameField = name;
    this.emailAddressField = emailAddress;
```

```
        this.routingTypeField = routingType;
    }

    /// <summary>
    /// Constructor that takes the ItemId of a private DL
    /// </summary>
    /// <param name="privateDLItemId">Id of a private DL</param>
    ///
    public EmailAddressType(ItemIdType privateDLItemId)
    {
        this.itemIdField = privateDLItemId;
    }
}
```

Now, *MessageType* doesn't directly expose instances of *EmailAddressType*. Instead, it surfaces two innocuous wrappers: *SingleRecipientType* and *ArrayOfRecipientsType*. The *SingleRecipientType* type contains a single child element called *Mailbox*, which just happens to be an *EmailAddressType* instance as shown in Listing 7-3.

LISTING 7-3 *SingleRecipientType*

```
<xs:complexType name="SingleRecipientType">
    <xs:choice>
        <xs:element name="Mailbox" type="t:EmailAddressType"/>
    </xs:choice>
</xs:complexType>
```

The second recipient wrapper type is *ArrayOfRecipientsType*, which contains zero or more *EmailAddressType* instances, each of which is expressed within a *Mailbox* element. The schema definition for *ArrayOfRecipientsType* is shown in Listing 7-4.

LISTING 7-4 *ArrayOfRecipientsType*

```
<xs:complexType name="ArrayOfRecipientsType">
    <xs:choice minOccurs="0" maxOccurs="unbounded">
        <xs:element name="Mailbox" type="t:EmailAddressType"/>
    </xs:choice>
</xs:complexType>
```

The Disposition of a Message

Is your message good-natured? Or is it a "flame mail?" Fortunately, such classifications are outside of the scope of Exchange Web Services behavior. However, there is a curious *MessageDisposition* attribute exposed on both *CreateItemType* and *UpdateItemType* that we have skillfully avoided until now. The *MessageDisposition* value has little to do with the message itself, but rather indicates actions to be performed on that message when creation or modification is complete. The available actions are shown in Table 7-1.

TABLE 7-1 *MessageDispositionType* **Enumeration Values**

MessageDispositionType value	Comments
SaveOnly	Saves the message in the folder specified in the *SavedItemFolderId* node. If no folder is specified, the Drafts folder is used.
SendOnly	Sends the message and does not save a copy of the message in the sender's mailbox.
SendAndSaveCopy	Sends the message and also puts a copy of the message in the specified parent folder. If no folder is specified in the *SavedItemFolderId* node, the Sent Items folder is used.

Both *CreateItem* and *UpdateItem* require you to set the *MessageDisposition* attribute when dealing with *MessageType* instances. If *MessageDisposition* is omitted, you will encounter a response code of *ErrorMessageDispositionRequired*. Listing 7-5 shows an example of setting the *MessageDisposition* attribute for a *CreateItem* call.

LISTING 7-5 Creating a message with a *MessageDisposition*

```
<CreateItem xmlns=".../messages"
            xmlns:t=".../types"
            MessageDisposition="SaveOnly">
  <Items>
    <t:Message>
      <t:Subject>Here is a message with a happy disposition</t:Subject>
    </t:Message>
  </Items>
</CreateItem>
```

Listing 7-6 shows the same thing for an *UpdateItem* call.

LISTING 7-6 Updating a message with a *MessageDisposition*

```
<UpdateItem MessageDisposition="SaveOnly"
            ConflictResolution="AutoResolve"
            xmlns=".../messages"
            xmlns:t=".../types">
  <ItemChanges>
    <t:ItemChange>
      <t:ItemId Id="AQAtAEF..." ChangeKey="CQAAABYA..."/>
      <t:Updates>
        <t:SetItemField>
          <t:FieldURI FieldURI="item:Subject"/>
          <t:Message>
            <t:Subject>The message was happier than I originally thought</t:Subject>
          </t:Message>
```

```
        </t:SetItemField>
      </t:Updates>
    </t:ItemChange>
  </ItemChanges>
</UpdateItem>
```

You can think of the *MessageDisposition* attribute as being "value-added" functionality to perform after the *CreateItem* or *UpdateItem* operation has completed.

Now, remember, when executing an *UpdateItem* call, you are touching an item that already exists and already has a home within a folder in the mailbox. In what situation does an update require a destination folder? You cannot change the parent folder of a given item using *UpdateItem* because *item:ParentFolderId* is read only.

This *SavedItemFolderId* element is actually related to the *MessageDisposition* attribute value.[5] If the attribute value is *SaveOnly*, this element does nothing, which seems really backward. But, as mentioned previously, the item already has a home, so it doesn't make sense to save it somewhere else. If the *MessageDisposition* attribute value is *SendAndSaveCopy*, then this element suddenly comes to life. Sending a message is an asynchronous operation. As part of submitting the message to the Exchange Store, you supply a folder identifier so that, once the message is sent, Exchange can save a copy of the sent message to the supplied folder. This element probably should have been named "*SentItemFolderId*" or "*FolderForSentItem*," but it was not.

So, the *SavedItemFolderId* element indicates the folder to which to save a copy of the message *if* the *MessageDisposition* attribute is *SendAndSaveCopy*. Otherwise, it is ignored. If you use *SendAndSaveCopy* but omit the *SavedItemFolderId* element, then the sent item is copied to the Sent Items folder, which is probably where you want it anyway.

As suggested by the name, a *MessageDisposition* value of *SendAndSaveCopy* will cause the message to be sent to the intended recipients and a copy of the message will also be saved to the Sent Items folder which is the default folder for *sent* items. Of course, if you provide an alternate folder in the *SavedItemFolderId* element, a copy of the sent message will be saved to your designated folder instead of the Sent Items folder.

Listing 7-7 shows a message created with a *MessageDisposition* of *SendAndSaveCopy*. Notice you must supply at least one recipient in the *ToRecipient* collection or you will encounter a response code of *ErrorInvalidRecipients*.

---

[5] *SavedItemFolderId* is also used by the *SendMeetingInvitationsAndCancellations* attribute in the same manner.

LISTING 7-7 Creating a message with *SendAndSaveCopy*

```
<CreateItem xmlns=".../messages"
            xmlns:t=".../types"
            MessageDisposition="SendAndSaveCopy">
  <Items>
    <t:Message>
      <t:Subject>Read this!</t:Subject>
      <t:ToRecipients>
        <t:Mailbox>
          <t:EmailAddress>ken.malcolmson@contoso.com</t:EmailAddress>
        </t:Mailbox>
      </t:ToRecipients>
    </t:Message>
  </Items>
</CreateItem>
```

Listing 7-8 shows the response.

LISTING 7-8 *CreateItem* response for *SendAndSaveCopy MessageDisposition*

```
<m:CreateItemResponse xmlns:t=".../types"
                      xmlns:m=".../messages">
  <m:ResponseMessages>
    <m:CreateItemResponseMessage ResponseClass="Success">
      <m:ResponseCode>NoError</m:ResponseCode>
      <m:Items/>
    </m:CreateItemResponseMessage>
  </m:ResponseMessages>
</m:CreateItemResponse>
```

The response did not return the *ItemId* of the newly created message! The *Items* element is empty. Contrast this to the response returned when the same call was made with a *MessageDisposition* value of *SaveOnly* as shown in Listing 7-9.

LISTING 7-9 *CreateItem* response for *SaveOnly MessageDisposition*

```
<m:CreateItemResponse xmlns:t=".../types"
                      xmlns:m=".../messages">
  <m:ResponseMessages>
    <m:CreateItemResponseMessage ResponseClass="Success">
      <m:ResponseCode>NoError</m:ResponseCode>
      <m:Items>
        <t:Message>
          <t:ItemId Id="AQAtAEFkbWlua..." ChangeKey="CQAAABYA..."/>
        </t:Message>
      </m:Items>
    </m:CreateItemResponseMessage>
  </m:ResponseMessages>
</m:CreateItemResponse>
```

Interesting. Not only is the *ItemId* element missing in the response when *SendAndSaveCopy* is used, but the entire *Message* element is gone. Perhaps it is hiding behind the vending machines with Ken. Such a search would be fruitless, so let's turn our attention to the real reason for this behavior.

If you look at the word ordering in the term *SendAndSaveCopy*, you will see that *send* is listed first. This ordering is intentional because it actually describes a timeline of events in processing your message. When Exchange Web Services encounters a *CreateItem* or *UpdateItem* call on a message with a *MessageDisposition* of either *SendAndSaveCopy* or *SendOnly*, the message is *submitted* for transmission to the recipients asynchronously and then Exchange Web Services returns your response. No where in the previous sentence does it say that Exchange Web Services ever saves the message to your folder of choice. The reason for this is that when Exchange Web Serivces submits the message for transmission, it also tells the Exchange Store where a copy of the message should be saved. Once the Store has transmitted the message, the Store, *rather* than Exchange Web Services, will save a copy of the message to the folder specified when the message was submitted. In other words, by the time Exchange Web Services returns, the message copy does not yet exist, so there *is* no *ItemId* available to be returned in the response. We will discuss how to retrieve the saved copy of the sent message later in this chapter.

The *SendOnly MessageDisposition* behaves like *SendAndSaveCopy* except that the Store is instructed that it should not save a copy of the sent message.

If you create a message with a *MessageDisposition* of *SaveOnly*, the only way to send such a message is to either call the *SendItem* Web method or call *UpdateItem* with a *MessageDisposition* of *SendOnly* or *SendAndSaveCopy*. Of course, calling *UpdateItem* would imply that you are changing values on the message, so if you only need to send an existing message, you would use *SendItem*.

Now that we have discussed recipient types and set the groundwork for making *CreateItem* and *UpdateItem* calls on *MessageType*, we are ready to turn our attention to the properties exposed on a message.

Message Properties

In addition to the properties inherited from *ItemType*, *MessageType* exposes its own set of properties as listed Table 7-2.

TABLE 7-2 **First-Class Properties on *MessageType***

Property name	Type	Comments
ConversationIndex	*base64Binary*	An identifier that is used to link multiple messages together into a single conversation. All messages that have the same *ConversationIndex* property value are considered to be in the same conversation.
ConversationTopic	String	Describes the overall topic of a conversation. For most scenarios, the value of the *Subject* property is an appropriate value for the *ConversationTopic*.
From	*SingleRecipientType*	This is the recipient information for who sent the message.
InternetMessageId	String	Represents the Internet message identifier of a particular message. This property is further explained in RFC 2822 section 3.6.4.
IsDeliveryReceiptRequested	Boolean	Indicates whether the sender of an item requests a delivery receipt.
IsRead	Boolean	Indicates whether a message has been read.
IsReadReceiptRequested	Boolean	Indicates whether the sender of an item requests a read receipt.
References	String	Represents the Internet message header used to correlate replies with their original messages. This is further explained in RFC 2822 section 3.6.4.
IsResponseRequested	Boolean	Indicates whether the sender of an item requests a response to the message.
ReplyTo	*ArrayOfRecipientsType*	Contains an array of recipients to whom replies to this message should be sent.
Sender	*SingleRecipientType*	The recipient information for the sender of the message.
ToRecipients	*ArrayOfRecipientsType*	Contains an array of recipients for an item.
CcRecipients	*ArrayOfRecipientsType*	A collection of recipients who will receive a copy of the message.
BccRecipients	*ArrayOfRecipientsType*	A collection of recipients who will receive a blind copy of the message. *ToRecipients* and *CcRecipients* will not be able to discover any recipients in this collection.

Recipient Collection Properties

At the beginning of this chapter, we defined a message as *a discrete and finite set of informa-tion that can be passed from one sending entity to one or more recipient entities*. Of course, this definition implies that there must be some way to indicate both the sending entity as well as the recipient entities. We will discuss setting the sending entity later in this chapter. Right now we will deal with the recipient entities.

MessageType exposes three recipient collections that indicate where the message should be delivered. The *ToRecipients* collection contains the addresses of the primary recipients of the message and has an unindexed property path of *message:ToRecipients*. The *CcRecipients* col-lection contains the addresses of the recipients that are to be copied on the message and has an unindexed property path of *message:CcRecipients*. The *BccRecipients* collection contains the addresses of the recipients that are to be blind copied on the message, meaning that the identity of the *BccRecipients* are not available to the other recipients on the message. *BccRecipients* has an unindexed property path of *message:BccRecipients*.

All three recipient collections are of type *ArrayOfRecipientsType*, and, therefore, each col-lection can contain zero or more recipients. In order for a message to be sent, at least one recipient must be defined in the *ToRecipients* collection. You are, however, free to omit the *CcRecipients* and *BccRecipients*. You can also include an empty collection, although doing so is the same as omitting the collection element and is therefore discouraged.

For example, Jane decides that in addition to posting a note on Ken's door, she will also send him an e-mail. The *ToRecipients* collection Jane builds is shown in Listing 7-10.

LISTING 7-10 Creating a message with recipients

```
<CreateItem xmlns=".../messages"
            xmlns:t=".../types"
            MessageDisposition="SaveOnly">
  <Items>
    <t:Message>
      <t:Subject>You are hiding again, aren't you?</t:Subject>
      <t:ToRecipients>
        <t:Mailbox>
          <t:Name>Ken Malcolmson</t:Name>
          <t:EmailAddress>ken.malcolmson@contoso.com</t:EmailAddress>
          <t:RoutingType>SMTP</t:RoutingType>
        </t:Mailbox>
      </t:ToRecipients>
    </t:Message>
  </Items>
</CreateItem>
```

Notice that the *MessageDisposition* attribute is set to *SaveOnly*. As such, once Jane creates this message, it will be stored in the Drafts folder, which is the default folder for unsent messages. It will not, however, be sent. Now, let's assume that Jane would also like to add Tina Makovec and Janusz Malgorzaciak from the Human Resources department to the message to alert them of the fact that Ken is missing again. Since the message is not directed to Tina or Janusz, Jane adds them to the *CcRecipients* collection as shown in Listing 7-11.

LISTING 7-11 A message with *CcRecipients*

```
<!-- previous xml elided -->
<t:Message>
  <t:Subject>You are hiding again, aren't you?</t:Subject>
  <t:ToRecipients>
    <t:Mailbox>
      <t:Name>Ken Malcolmson</t:Name>
      <t:EmailAddress>ken.malcolmson@contoso.com</t:EmailAddress>
      <t:RoutingType>SMTP</t:RoutingType>
    </t:Mailbox>
  </t:ToRecipients>
  <t:CcRecipients>
    <t:Mailbox>
      <t:EmailAddress>tina.makovec@contoso.com</t:EmailAddress>
    </t:Mailbox>
    <t:Mailbox>
      <t:EmailAddress>janusz.malgorzaciak@contoso.com</t:EmailAddress>
    </t:Mailbox>
  </t:CcRecipients>
</t:Message>
```

Notice in Listing 7-11 that the *Mailbox* element containing Tina's and Janusz' recipient addresses omit the *Name* and *RoutingType* elements because they are optional. If, however, the *EmailAddress* element was omitted, the response would be the response code *ErrorMissingInformationEmailAddress,* indicating that either the *EmailAddress* or the *ItemId* must be filled in when specifying a recipient address.

Updating the Recipient Collection Properties

The *CreateItem* call in the previous section returns the *ItemId* of Jane's draft message, which waits impatiently in her Drafts folder. What if Jane decided that she wanted to add yet another recipient address? In fact, let's make this more interesting and say that she wants to remove Tina from the *CcRecipient* collection and add Alfredo Maldonado Guerra instead. This introduces an interesting problem. You saw in Chapter 5 how to call *UpdateItem* with the *AppendToItemFieldType* change description to add an item to a collection, but how can you remove an item from such a collection?

You might be tempted to call *UpdateItem* with the *DeleteItemFieldType* change description to remove Tina from the *CcRecipients* collection. However, doing so will actually clear out the entire *CcRecipients* collection on the message. Yet, there is a way to "delete" recipients from these collections. You can mimic a delete operation by calling *UpdateItem* with a *SetItemFieldType* change description and "overwrite" the existing collection with only those recipients that you wish to remain in the collection. Although this might seem elementary, Exchange Web Services performs some special processing in this case.

Let's first look at the structure of the *UpdateItem* call in Listing 7-12 and then talk about how Exchange Web Services acts on the request.

LISTING 7-12 Updating the *CcRecipients* collection

```
<UpdateItem MessageDisposition="SaveOnly"
            ConflictResolution="AutoResolve"
            xmlns=".../messages"
            xmlns:t=".../types">
  <ItemChanges>
    <t:ItemChange>
      <t:ItemId Id="AQAtAEFkbW..." ChangeKey="CQAAABY..."/>
      <t:Updates>
        <t:SetItemField>
          <t:FieldURI FieldURI="message:CcRecipients"/>
          <t:Message>
            <t:CcRecipients>
              <t:Mailbox>
                <t:EmailAddress>janusz.malgorzaciak@contoso.com</t:EmailAddress>
              </t:Mailbox>
              <t:Mailbox>
                <t:EmailAddress>alfredom@contoso.com</t:EmailAddress>
              </t:Mailbox>
            </t:CcRecipients>
          </t:Message>
        </t:SetItemField>
      </t:Updates>
    </t:ItemChange>
  </ItemChanges>
</UpdateItem>
```

At first glance, it would appear that the *SetItemFieldType* operation in Listing 7-12 would simply overwrite the *CcRecipients* collection with the two recipient addresses listed in the *UpdateItem* request. However, that is not what actually happens. When Exchange Web Services encounters such a request, it will iterate over the supplied recipients and perform the following actions:

■ If there is a recipient in the *SetItemFieldType* change description that is already in the recipient collection on the message, it will leave that recipient alone.

■ If there is a recipient in the *SetItemFieldType* change description that is not in the recipient collection on the message, it will add that recipient to the collection.

■ If there is a recipient that is currently on the message, but is *not* in the *SetItemFieldType* change description, it will remove that recipient from the collection.

The first bullet point is significant because during the lifetime of a message, additional information can be associated with a recipient on a message.[6] If Exchange Web Services simply overwrote existing recipients with the contents of the *SetItemFieldType* change description, any additional information would be lost.

Of course, if Jane wanted to add Tina back to the e-mail, she could call *UpdateItem* with an *AppendToItemFieldType* change description as shown in Listing 7-13.

LISTING 7-13 Appending to the *CcRecipients* collection

```xml
<UpdateItem MessageDisposition="SaveOnly"
            ConflictResolution="AutoResolve"
            xmlns=".../messages">
  <ItemChanges>
    <t:ItemChange>
      <t:ItemId Id="AQAtAEFkb..." ChangeKey="CQAAABYAA..."/>
      <t:Updates>
        <t:AppendToItemField>
          <t:FieldURI FieldURI="message:CcRecipients"/>
          <t:Message>
            <t:CcRecipients>
              <t:Mailbox>
                <t:EmailAddress>tina.makovec@contoso.com</t:EmailAddress>
              </t:Mailbox>
            </t:CcRecipients>
          </t:Message>
        </t:AppendToItemField>
      </t:Updates>
    </t:ItemChange>
  </ItemChanges>
</UpdateItem>
```

Retrieving the Recipient Collection Properties

The *ToRecipients*, *CcRecipients*, and *BccRecipient* collections are available in the *Default* and *AllProperties* response shapes for messages. However, you can also explicitly ask for them by their corresponding property paths. For instance, Listing 7-14 shows how you can specify the *CcRecipients* property path in the *AdditionalProperties* element of a *GetItem* request. Of course, since the recipient collection properties are included in the *Default* and *AllProperties* shapes, *IdOnly* is the only base shape that makes sense when explicitly listing the recipient collection property paths in the *AdditionalProperties* element.

---

6   This is more significant when considering recipients at the MAPI level since entries in the MAPI recipient table can have arbitrary properties set on them. EWS does not expose such properties. However, this does become more significant when dealing with meeting attendees in Chapter 10, "Scheduling Meetings."

LISTING 7-14 *GetItem* with *CcRecipients*

```
<GetItem xmlns=".../messages"
         xmlns:t=".../types">
  <ItemShape>
    <t:BaseShape>IdOnly</t:BaseShape>
    <t:AdditionalProperties>
      <t:FieldURI FieldURI="message:CcRecipients"/>
    </t:AdditionalProperties>
  </ItemShape>
  <ItemIds>
    <t:ItemId Id="AQAtAEFkb..." ChangeKey="CQAAABY..."/>
  </ItemIds>
</GetItem>
```

Jane's e-mail should have three recipients in the *CcRecipients* collection, and the response in Listing 7-15 confirms this.

LISTING 7-15 *GetItem* response containing *CcRecipients*

```
<m:GetItemResponse xmlns:t=".../types"
                   xmlns:m=".../messages">
  <m:ResponseMessages>
    <m:GetItemResponseMessage ResponseClass="Success">
      <m:ResponseCode>NoError</m:ResponseCode>
      <m:Items>
        <t:Message>
          <t:ItemId Id="AQAtAEFkbWlu..." ChangeKey="CQAAABYA..."/>
          <t:CcRecipients>
            <t:Mailbox>
              <t:Name>janusz.malgorzaciak@contoso.com</t:Name>
              <t:EmailAddress>janusz.malgorzaciak@contoso.com</t:EmailAddress>
              <t:RoutingType>SMTP</t:RoutingType>
            </t:Mailbox>
            <t:Mailbox>
              <t:Name>alfredom@contoso.com</t:Name>
              <t:EmailAddress>alfredom@contoso.com</t:EmailAddress>
              <t:RoutingType>SMTP</t:RoutingType>
            </t:Mailbox>
            <t:Mailbox>
              <t:Name>tina.makovec@contoso.com</t:Name>
              <t:EmailAddress>tina.makovec@contoso.com</t:EmailAddress>
              <t:RoutingType>SMTP</t:RoutingType>
            </t:Mailbox>
          </t:CcRecipients>
        </t:Message>
      </m:Items>
    </m:GetItemResponseMessage>
  </m:ResponseMessages>
</m:GetItemResponse>
```

IsRead Property

The *IsRead* boolean property indicates whether a given entity has read a message or not. Did you notice that we avoided the word "recipient" in the previous sentence? There is good reason for this. Of course, the recipients of a message can read their copies of the message, but so can any other account that has access to one or more of the recipient's mailboxes. In addition, the value of the *IsRead* property is a function of which entity is looking at the message. Let's assume for a moment that Robert Lyon has the rights to read Ken Malcolmson's mailbox. The value of the *IsRead* property that Robert sees when he retrieves a given message from Ken's mailbox can be different than the value that Ken sees. Marking Robert's view of the message as having been read does not affect the value of *IsRead* for Ken's view of the message.

Exchange Web Services does not mark messages as read implicitly. In order to mark a message as read, you must explicitly call *UpdateItem* with a *SetItemFieldType* change description and set the *IsRead* property to true.

The *IsRead* property is also quite influential when considering read receipts, as discussed next. We will also present an example of setting the *IsRead* property using *UpdateItem*.

Creating and Suppressing Read Receipts

If you would like to know when a recipient in the *ToRecipients* collection has read a message, you can request a *read receipt* before sending your message. Requesting a read receipt is accomplished by setting the boolean *IsReadReceiptRequested* element to true when creating or updating a message.

```
<t:Message>
  <t:Subject>Read this!</t:Subject>
  <t:IsReadReceiptRequested>true</t:IsReadReceiptRequested>
</t:Message>
```

But when is a message considered read? If we can defer to precedence, client applications such as Office Outlook do not mark a message as read until the user actually clicks on the message in the user interface.[7] In the same way, Exchange Web Services requires you to explicitly mark a message as read using *UpdateItem* with a *SetItemFieldType* change description. When a received message is marked as read through *UpdateItem,* Exchange Web Services checks to see if the message has a read receipt requested on it. If such a request is present, Exchange Web Services will generate and send a read notification message back to the sender of the message.[8] That is, of course, unless the client application *suppresses* the read receipt, in which case a read receipt is not generated for the sender. If you want to suppress

---

[7] And even then the behavior is configurable.

[8] If the message is in the Junk Mail folder, Exchange Web Services will not generate a read receipt, even if the sender requested that a read receipt be generated.

the read receipt, you must do this *before* you mark the message as read. You cannot suppress a read receipt on a message that does not have a read receipt requested.

There are two ways to determine if a given message has a read receipt request on it. First, you can look at the *IsReadReceiptRequested* element on the received message. If the value is true, then a read receipt has been requested. This approach works in both *GetItem* and *FindItem* calls. The second approach, which works only with *GetItem,*[9] is to look for the presence of the *SuppressReadReceipt* response object in the *ResponseObjects* collection that is returned from a *GetItem* call. Since the *ResponseObjects* property is a calculated property, it is not available in *FindItem* requests.

LISTING 7-16 The *SuppressReadReceipt* response object

```
<m:GetItemResponse xmlns:t=".../types"
                   xmlns:m=".../messages">
  <m:ResponseMessages>
    <m:GetItemResponseMessage ResponseClass="Success">
      <m:ResponseCode>NoError</m:ResponseCode>
      <m:Items>
        <t:Message>
<!-- some message elements elided -->
          <t:ItemId Id="AQAtAEFkbWlu..." ChangeKey="CQAAABYAAAC9V..."/>
          <t:ResponseObjects>
            <t:ReplyToItem/>
            <t:ReplyAllToItem/>
            <t:ForwardItem/>
            <t:SuppressReadReceipt/>
          </t:ResponseObjects>
          <t:IsReadReceiptRequested>true</t:IsReadReceiptRequested>
        </t:Message>
      </m:Items>
    </m:GetItemResponseMessage>
  </m:ResponseMessages>
</m:GetItemResponse>
```

Notice that the *GetItemResponse* in Listing 7-16 indicates that the *SuppressReadReceipt* response object is applicable to this message. If a read receipt was not requested for this message, then *SuppressReadReceipt* would not be present in the *ResponseObjects* collection.

In order to suppress a read receipt, the recipient must call *CreateItem* and pass in a *SuppressReadReceipt* response object that references the message that should not generate a read receipt. The *SuppressReadReceiptType* has the general structure shown in Listing 7-17.

---

[9] The *ResponseObjects* property is calculated and is therefore not available on *FindItem*.

LISTING 7-17 General structure of *SuppressReadReceiptType*

```
<t:SuppressReadReceipt>
  <t:ReferenceItemId Id="AQAtAEFkbWlua..." ChangeKey="CQAAABYA..."/>
</t:SuppressReadReceipt>
```

The *ReferenceItemId* element contains the *ItemId* of the message that you want read receipts to be suppressed for. Listing 7-18 shows what *SuppressReadReceipt* looks like inside a *CreateItem* call.

LISTING 7-18 *CreateItem* with *SuppressReadReceipt*

```
<CreateItem xmlns=".../messages"
            xmlns:t=".../types">
  <Items>
    <t:SuppressReadReceipt>
      <t:ReferenceItemId Id="AQAtAEFkbWlua..." ChangeKey="CQAAABYA..."/>
    </t:SuppressReadReceipt>
  </Items>
</CreateItem>
```

Once a read receipt has been suppressed, the value of *IsReadReceiptRequested* will be false and the *SuppressReadReceipt* response object will no longer be present in the collection of applicable *ResponseObjects* for the message. In fact, if you try to call *CreateItem* with a *SuppressReadReceipt* for such a message, you will encounter a response code of *ErrorReadReceiptNotPending*.

To put this all together, the steps for creating a message with a read receipt and a suppression of that read receipt are as follows:

1. Sender generates a message with a *MessageDisposition* of *SendAndSaveCopy* and sets the *IsReadReceiptRequested* property to true. This sends the message to the recipient.

```
<CreateItem xmlns=".../messages"
            xmlns:t=".../types"
            MessageDisposition="SendAndSaveCopy">
  <Items>
    <t:Message>
      <t:Subject>Read this!</t:Subject>
      <t:ToRecipients>
        <t:Mailbox>
          <t:EmailAddress>ken.malcolmson@contoso.com</t:EmailAddress>
        </t:Mailbox>
      </t:ToRecipients>
      <t:IsReadReceiptRequested>true</t:IsReadReceiptRequested>
    </t:Message>
  </Items>
</CreateItem>
```

2. Recipient retrieves the message by looking in the inbox. Since the recipient does not know the *ItemId* of the received message, *FindItem* must be used.

```
<FindItem xmlns=".../messages"
          xmlns:t=".../types"
          Traversal="Shallow">
  <ItemShape>
    <t:BaseShape>AllProperties</t:BaseShape>
  </ItemShape>
  <ParentFolderIds>
    <t:DistinguishedFolderId Id="inbox"/>
  </ParentFolderIds>
</FindItem>
```

3. Recipient examines the message to see if read receipts are requested. Since this was a *FindItem* response, this can be accomplished only by looking at the *IsReadReceiptRequested* element.

```
<m:FindItemResponse xmlns:t=".../types"
                    xmlns:m=".../messages">
  <m:ResponseMessages>
    <m:FindItemResponseMessage ResponseClass="Success">
      <m:ResponseCode>NoError</m:ResponseCode>
      <m:RootFolder TotalItemsInView="1" IncludesLastItemInRange="true">
        <t:Items>
          <t:Message>
            <t:ItemId Id="AQAtAEFkbWlua..." ChangeKey="CQAAABYA..."/>
      <!-- some properties elided -->
            <t:IsReadReceiptRequested>true</t:IsReadReceiptRequested>
            <t:IsRead>false</t:IsRead>
          </t:Message>
        </t:Items>
      </m:RootFolder>
    </m:FindItemResponseMessage>
  </m:ResponseMessages>
</m:FindItemResponse>
```

4. If desired, the recipient suppresses the read receipt.

```
<CreateItem xmlns=".../messages"
            xmlns:t=".../types">
  <Items>
    <t:SuppressReadReceipt>
      <t:ReferenceItemId Id="AQAtAEFkbWlua..." ChangeKey="CQAAABYA..."/>
    </t:SuppressReadReceipt>
  </Items>
</CreateItem>
```

5. Recipient marks the message as read.

```
<UpdateItem MessageDisposition="SaveOnly"
            ConflictResolution="AutoResolve"
            xmlns=".../messages"
            xmlns:t=".../types">
  <ItemChanges>
```

```
    <t:ItemChange>
      <t:ItemId Id="AQAtAEFkbWlua..." ChangeKey="CQAAABYAA..."/>
      <t:Updates>
        <t:SetItemField>
          <t:FieldURI FieldURI="message:IsRead"/>
          <t:Message>
            <t:IsRead>true</t:IsRead>
          </t:Message>
        </t:SetItemField>
      </t:Updates>
    </t:ItemChange>
  </ItemChanges>
</UpdateItem>
```

IsDeliverReceiptRequested Property

You can request that a delivery receipt be generated for a message by setting the *IsDeliverReceiptRequested* property to true before sending the message. While Exchange Web Services is involved in generating read receipt notifications, it is not involved in generating delivery receipts. As such, there is no notion of suppressing delivery receipts. The Exchange Store is responsible for generating and sending delivery receipts.

ReplyTo Property

The *ReplyTo* property holds a collection of recipients that any responses should be directed to. There is no automatic functionality surrounding this property—this collection is just a suggestion. In other words, if you receive a message and reply to that message, your reply will not automatically be sent to the recipients in the *ReplyTo* property. Although *ReplyTo* is an *ArrayOfRecipientType* just like the *To*, *Cc*, and *Bcc* recipient collections, *ReplyTo* does not provide the special *SetItemFieldType* behavior of the other recipient collections. In other words, if you call *UpdateItem* with a *SetItemFieldType* change description for *ReplyTo*, Exchange Web Services will clear out the *ReplyTo* property and replace it with the new collection passed into *UpdateItem*.

From and *Sender* Properties

Looking back at the definition of message at the beginning of the chapter, you see that a message as a discrete and finite set of information that can be passed from one sending entity to one or more recipient entities. We showed that you can set the *To*, *Cc*, and *Bcc* recipient collections to include the recipient address you would like the message to be delivered to. However, those collections represent only half of the communication pattern. At first glance it seems that the sender of the message is implied. If Jane's account is used to generate the message through *CreateItem* it is reasonable to assume that the message should be stamped as if it came from Jane. Such behavior is indeed the default. However, Exchange Web Services exposes two properties: the *From* and *Sender* properties, both of which point to the initiating end of the conversation. Why two? Which one should you use?

Be assured that there is a reason for two similar-looking properties. We will start with the *Sender* property as it is the simpler of the two. The *Sender* property simply returns the account that was used to generate the message. If Jane's account was used to create and send the message, then Jane will be the sender. What is a little suprising is that Exchange Web Services does not complain if you try to set the *Sender* property when creating a message. Thankfully, this is a fruitless endeavor as the *Sender* is intiailized with the correct information when the message is sent.

The innocent looking *From* property needs some more attention. Tina Makovec has an administrative assistant, Phyllis Harris, who handles Tina's alarmingly complex calendar and extraordinarily full mailbox. Since Tina is often helping Jane in their search for the ever-elusive Ken, Phyllis has been given rights to send mail for Tina. Now, Tina can delegate this responsibility to Phyllis by making her a *delegate* through a client applicaton such as Office Outlook. Note that the management of delegates is handled by the mailbox owner.[10] Assuming that Phyllis has been given delegate rights to Tina's mailbox, Phyllis can make the *CreateItem* call shown in Listing 7-19. Notice that the *From* element is set to Tina's e-mail address.

LISTING 7-19 *CreateItem* with the *From* element set

```
<CreateItem xmlns=".../messages"
            xmlns:t=".../types"
            MessageDisposition="SendAndSaveCopy">
  <Items>
    <t:Message>
      <t:Subject>Where are you???</t:Subject>
      <t:ToRecipients>
        <t:Mailbox>
          <t:EmailAddress>ken.malcolmson@contoso.com</t:EmailAddress>
        </t:Mailbox>
      </t:ToRecipients>
      <t:From>
        <t:Mailbox>
          <t:EmailAddress>tina.makovec@contoso.com</t:EmailAddress>
        </t:Mailbox>
      </t:From>
    </t:Message>
  </Items>
</CreateItem>
```

Listing 7-20 shows a *GetItem* call on Ken's inbox and reveals what the *From* and *Sender* properties contain.

---

[10] Exchange Web Services does not offer delegate management functionality. Configuring delegate access through Office Outlook is beyond the scope of this book.

LISTING 7-20 Retrieving the *From* and *Sender* properties on a delegated message

```
<GetItem xmlns=".../messages"
         xmlns:t="http://schemas.microsoft.com/exchange/services/2006/types">
  <ItemShape>
    <t:BaseShape>IdOnly</t:BaseShape>
    <t:AdditionalProperties>
      <t:FieldURI FieldURI="message:From"/>
      <t:FieldURI FieldURI="message:Sender"/>
    </t:AdditionalProperties>
  </ItemShape>
  <ItemIds>
    <t:ItemId Id="AQAuAGtlbi5tYWxjb..." ChangeKey="CQAAABYAAA..."/>
  </ItemIds>
</GetItem>
```

The response is show in Listing 7-21.

LISTING 7-21 *GetItem* response for a delegate-sent message

```
<m:GetItemResponse xmlns:t=".../types"
                   xmlns:m=".../messages">
  <m:ResponseMessages>
    <m:GetItemResponseMessage ResponseClass="Success">
      <m:ResponseCode>NoError</m:ResponseCode>
      <m:Items>
        <t:Message>
          <t:ItemId Id="AAAuAGtlbi5tYW..." ChangeKey="CQAAABYAA..."/>
          <t:Sender>
            <t:Mailbox>
              <t:Name>Phyllis Harris</t:Name>
              <t:EmailAddress>phyllis.harris@contoso.com</t:EmailAddress>
              <t:RoutingType>SMTP</t:RoutingType>
            </t:Mailbox>
          </t:Sender>
          <t:From>
            <t:Mailbox>
              <t:Name>Tina Makovec</t:Name>
              <t:EmailAddress>tina.makovec@contoso.com</t:EmailAddress>
              <t:RoutingType>SMTP</t:RoutingType>
            </t:Mailbox>
          </t:From>
        </t:Message>
      </m:Items>
    </m:GetItemResponseMessage>
  </m:ResponseMessages>
</m:GetItemResponse>
```

Notice that the response in Listing 7-21 indicates that the message is *from* Tina but the *sender* is Phyllis. If Ken looks at this message through Outlook Web Access, he will see that the message came from "Phyllis Harris on behalf of Tina Makovec" as shown in Figure 7-2.

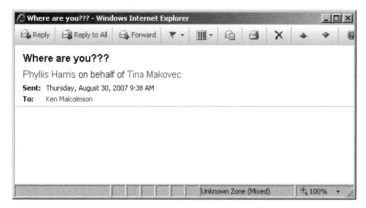

FIGURE 7-2 Delegated message as seen through Outlook Web Access

Another way to allow Phyllis to send e-mails on behalf of Tina is to give Phyllis *SendAs* rights on Tina's Active Directory user account. Note that while delegate access to Tina's mailbox is administered by Tina, *SendAs* rights are administered by an Exchange Administrator. You can set this right using the Active Directory Users and Computers tool, or you can set the right through the Exchange Management Shell. Listing 7-22 shows how to grant *SendAs* rights using the Add-ADPermission cmdlet in the Shell.

LISTING 7-22 Granting *SendAs* rights using the Exchange Management Shell

```
Add-ADPermission -Identity "Tina Makovec" -User phyllis.harris -AccessRights
extendedright -ExtendedRights "send as"
```

The *Identity* parameter indicates the mailbox that you want to grant access to and the *User* parameter indicates the account that you want to give delegate rights to. As such, Listing 7-22 gives Phyllis Harris "send as" rights on Tina Makovec's user object (and therefore her mailbox).

With this right in place, if you repeat the *CreateItem* call as Phyllis from Listing 7-19, and the *GetItem* call as Ken from Listing 7-20, the *From* and *Sender* elements will both be set to Tina as shown in Listing 7-23.

LISTING 7-23 *GetItem* response for a message sent with *SendAs* rights

```
<m:GetItemResponse xmlns:t=".../types"
                   xmlns:m=".../messages">
  <m:ResponseMessages>
    <m:GetItemResponseMessage ResponseClass="Success">
      <m:ResponseCode>NoError</m:ResponseCode>
      <m:Items>
        <t:Message>
          <t:ItemId Id="AQAuAGtlbi5tYW..." ChangeKey="CQAAABYAAA..."/>
          <t:Sender>
```

```
            <t:Mailbox>
              <t:Name>Tina Makovec</t:Name>
              <t:EmailAddress>tina.makovec@contoso.com</t:EmailAddress>
              <t:RoutingType>SMTP</t:RoutingType>
            </t:Mailbox>
          </t:Sender>
          <t:From>
            <t:Mailbox>
              <t:Name>Tina Makovec</t:Name>
              <t:EmailAddress>tina.makovec@contoso.com</t:EmailAddress>
              <t:RoutingType>SMTP</t:RoutingType>
            </t:Mailbox>
          </t:From>
        </t:Message>
      </m:Items>
    </m:GetItemResponseMessage>
  </m:ResponseMessages>
</m:GetItemResponse>
```

If Ken looks at this message through Outlook Web Access, he will see that the message came from Tina Makovec as shown in Figure 7-3. There is no mention of Phyllis' involvement.

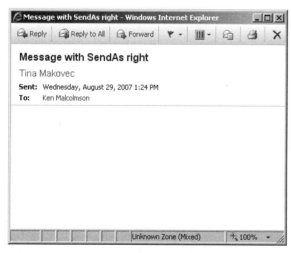

FIGURE 7-3 A message sent with *SendAs* rights

Message Flags

When you use Exchange Web Services to create a draft message, the message appears in your mailbox, but clients such as Outlook Web Access and Office Outlook will indicate that the message has not yet been sent. There may be times where you want to create a message in the inbox that you never intend to send, and you would rather not have clients suggesting that the message should be sent. Underneath the covers, Office Outlook looks at a special MAPI property to determine if a message is a draft. Exchange Web Services surfaces this MAPI property via the *IsDraft* first-class property, which happens to be read-only.

Now, you can resort to extended MAPI properties to clear the *IsDraft* flag, although there is a catch. According to MSDN, the *MSGFLAG_UNSENT* message flag is read-write only *before* the message is first saved.[11] After that, the flag is read-only. What this means is that if you are going to modify the message flags for a message, you must do it when you first call *CreateItem*. You cannot clear this flag on an existing message.

The MAPI property of interest is *PR_MESSAGE_FLAGS,* which has a property tag value of 0x0E070003. Two of the most interesting message flags are *IsDraft* and *IsRead*. Listing 7-14 shows an example of creating messages with the flags set to different values.

LISTING 7-14 Creating a message with various message flags

```
<CreateItem xmlns=".../messages"
        xmlns:t=".../types"
        MessageDisposition="SaveOnly">
 <Items>
  <t:Message>
   <t:Subject>I have been "sent" and read</t:Subject>
   <t:ExtendedProperty>
    <t:ExtendedFieldURI PropertyTag="0x0E07" PropertyType="Integer"/>
    <t:Value>1</t:Value>
   </t:ExtendedProperty>
  </t:Message>
  <t:Message>
   <t:Subject>I have been "sent" and unread</t:Subject>
   <t:ExtendedProperty>
    <t:ExtendedFieldURI PropertyTag="0x0E07" PropertyType="Integer"/>
    <t:Value>0</t:Value>
   </t:ExtendedProperty>
  </t:Message>
  <t:Message>
   <t:Subject>I have not been sent and am unread</t:Subject>
   <t:ExtendedProperty>
    <t:ExtendedFieldURI PropertyTag="0x0E07" PropertyType="Integer"/>
    <t:Value>8</t:Value>
   </t:ExtendedProperty>
  </t:Message>
 </Items>
</CreateItem>
```

Figure 7-4 shows the effects of creating messages with various message flags.

---

[11] *http://msdn2.microsoft.com/en-us/library/ms527629.aspx*

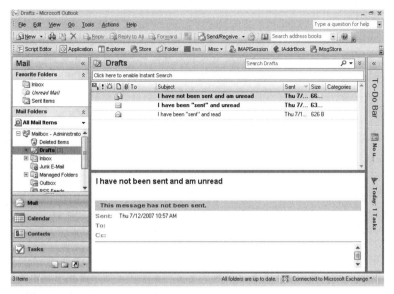

FIGURE 7-4 Messages and message flags

Sending Messages

The *SendItem* Web Method

Up to this point in the chapter, the *CreateItem* and *UpdateItem* Web methods have been used to send messages to their recipients. Sending was accomplished by setting the *MessageDisposition* attribute to *SendOnly* or *SendAndSaveCopy* when making the Web method call. However, there may be times when you want to send an existing draft message without making modifications to it. *CreateItem* will not work in such a case since it always generates a new message. *UpdateItem* will work, but you must also specify a property to change as part of the call.

To cover this scenario, Exchange Web Services offers the *SendItem* Web method. Listing 7-25 shows the basic structure of a *SendItem* call.

LISTING 7-25 Basic structure of *SendItem*

```
<SendItem xmlns=".../messages"
          xmlns:t=".../types"
          SaveItemToFolder="true | false">
  <ItemIds/>
  <SavedItemFolderId/>
</SendItem>
```

ItemIds Element

The required *ItemIds* element contains one or more message identifiers that you would like Exchange Web Services to send. The *ItemId* contained therein must refer to a valid message.[12] If you specify the *ItemId* of another type of item, you will encounter a response code of *ErrorInvalidItemForOperationSendItem*.

SavedItemFolderId and *SaveItemToFolder*

The *SavedItemFolderId* element and the *SaveItemToFolder* attribute are related, so it makes sense to discuss them at the same time. The required *SaveItemToFolder* attribute indicates whether a copy of the sent message should be saved *somewhere*. If *SaveItemToFolder* is set to false, then the message will be sent, but no copy will be saved to your mailbox. This setting behaves like *CreateItem* with a *MessageDisposition* of *SendOnly*.

If *SaveItemToFolder* is true, then a copy of the message will be saved *somewhere*. The actual folder that the sent message is saved in is a function of the presence and the value of the *SavedItemFolderId* element. Table 7-3 provides the various combinations of *SaveItemToFolder* and *SavedItemFolderId* and the resulting behavior of each.

TABLE 7-3 *SaveItemToFolder* and *SavedItemFolderId* Relationship

SaveItemToFolder attribute	*SavedItemFolderId* element	Result
True	Missing	Save message in Sent Items folder
True	Present	Save message in specified folder
False	Missing	Do not save message
False	Present	Error response code *ErrorInvalidSendItemSaveSettings*

If present, *SavedItemFolderId* must contain a single *FolderId* or *DistinguishedFolderId* that indicates which folder a copy of the message should be saved in. Once the message has been sent, the draft message that was referenced will be deleted by Exchange Web Services.

When calling *CreateItem* or *UpdateItem* with a *MessageDisposition* of *SendAndSaveCopy*, the *ItemId* of the copied message is not returned because message submission is an asynchronous operation. The same is true for *SendItem*. As such, the response returned from a *SendItem* call contains nothing more than an indication of whether the call succeeded or not.

```
<m:SendItemResponse xmlns:t=".../types"
                    xmlns:m=".../messages">
  <m:ResponseMessages>
    <m:SendItemResponseMessage ResponseClass="Success">
```

---

[12] By valid we mean any item in the mailbox with an ItemClass that starts with IPM.Note.

```
        <m:ResponseCode>NoError</m:ResponseCode>
      </m:SendItemResponseMessage>
    </m:ResponseMessages>
  </m:SendItemResponse>
```

Resending Messages

To resend a message to its original recipients, all you need to do is to call *SendItem* with the *ItemId* of the message that you wish to resend. However, sometimes it is necessary to resend a message to different recipients. To do this, you must call *UpdateItem* and modify the recipients of the message accordingly. The resulting updated message will be sent automatically if the *MessageDisposition* value in the *UpdateItem* call is either *SendOnly* or *SendAndSaveCopy*.

One slight drawback with this resending approach is that the original message that is referenced in the *UpdateItem* call is deleted once it is sent. That isn't a problem when sending the first e-mail because you typically do not want the draft hanging around after you send it. However, if you send the message first to Ken, retrieve the saved copy out of the Sent Items folder, update it, and send it to Tina, then the copy of the message that was sent to Ken will be deleted after it is sent to Tina. As such, when you look in your Sent Items folder, you have only a single e-mail in there—a copy of the one you sent to Tina. If that behavior is unpalatable, we suggest duplicating the message that was sent to Ken and updating that duplicate to send to Tina. In that case, it is the explicit duplicate that is deleted rather than the copy that was sent to Ken, which is likely what you wanted in the first place.

So why would you ever update and send a copy of the message? Let's say you want to send an e-mail with a large attachment to ten different people, but you want the message to look as if each person were the only recipient. You could call *CreateItem* ten times, but that would also mean you would have to call *CreateAttachment* with the same large attachment ten times. That is a lot of network traffic. Instead, you can create the message once, add the attachment once, and then go through a loop of *CopyItem/UpdateItem(SendAndSaveCopy)*, once for each of the recipients you want to send it to.

Sending to a Store Distribution List

At the beginning of the chapter, we indicated that the *ItemId* property of *EmailAddressType* would be explored in greater detail, and explore it we will. As discussed in Chapter 6, a Store distribution list is a grouping of Store contacts and/or other Store distributions lists. Since a Store distribution list is simply an item within a given mailbox, it has an *ItemId* that can be used to identify it. What a Store distribution list does *not* have, however, is an e-mail address that can be used to send messages to that distribution list. Yet, sending messages to a Store distribution list is a very valuable feature to have. When you think about it, a distribution list is simply an unexpanded collection of recipient addresses. The real recipients of a message sent to a distribution list are the recipients resulting from a full expansion of that distribution list. Don't worry, I am not suggesting that you should manually expand a Store distribution list in order to mimic sending mail to it. However, that is precisely what is done under the covers.

To send a message to a Store distribution list, simply provide the *ItemId* of that distribution list in the *ItemId* element of the *EmailAddressType* recipient address.

```
<t:Mailbox>
  <t:ItemId Id="AQAsAHRp..." ChangeKey="EgAAABQA.../>
</t:Mailbox>
```

Listing 7-26 shows a *CreateItem* call that will send a message to a Store distribution list as well as a normal recipient.

LISTING 7-26 Sending a message to a Store distribution list

```
<CreateItem xmlns=".../messages"
            xmlns:t=".../types"
            MessageDisposition="SendAndSaveCopy">
  <Items>
    <t:Message>
      <t:Subject>Message to send to DL</t:Subject>
      <t:ToRecipients>
        <t:Mailbox>
          <t:ItemId Id="AQAsAHRpbmEu..." ChangeKey="EgAAABQA..."/>
        </t:Mailbox>
        <t:Mailbox>
          <t:EmailAddress>ken.malcolmson@contoso.com</t:EmailAddress>
        </t:Mailbox>
      </t:ToRecipients>
    </t:Message>
  </Items>
</CreateItem>
```

This example shows the message sent using Tina's account. The Store distribution list used for this example had three store contacts in it—Ken, Tina, and Phyllis. Listing 7-27 shows how this message looks as seen by one of the recipients.

LISTING 7-27 Recipient's view of message sent to Store distribution list

```
<m:GetItemResponse xmlns:t=".../types"
                   xmlns:m=".../messages">
  <m:ResponseMessages>
    <m:GetItemResponseMessage ResponseClass="Success">
      <m:ResponseCode>NoError</m:ResponseCode>
      <m:Items>
        <t:Message>
          <t:ItemId Id="AQAuAGtlbi5tYWxjb..." ChangeKey="CQAAABYAA..."/>
          <t:ToRecipients>
```

```
            <t:Mailbox>
              <t:Name>Ken Malcolmson</t:Name>
              <t:EmailAddress>ken.malcolmson@contoso.com</t:EmailAddress>
              <t:RoutingType>SMTP</t:RoutingType>
            </t:Mailbox>
            <t:Mailbox>
              <t:Name>Ken Malcolmson</t:Name>
              <t:EmailAddress>ken.malcolmson@contoso.com</t:EmailAddress>
              <t:RoutingType>SMTP</t:RoutingType>
            </t:Mailbox>
            <t:Mailbox>
              <t:Name>Phyllis Harris</t:Name>
              <t:EmailAddress>phyllis.harris@contoso.com</t:EmailAddress>
              <t:RoutingType>SMTP</t:RoutingType>
            </t:Mailbox>
            <t:Mailbox>
              <t:Name>Tina Makovec</t:Name>
              <t:EmailAddress>tina.makovec@contoso.com</t:EmailAddress>
              <t:RoutingType>SMTP</t:RoutingType>
            </t:Mailbox>
          </t:ToRecipients>
        </t:Message>
      </m:Items>
    </m:GetItemResponseMessage>
  </m:ResponseMessages>
</m:GetItemResponse>
```

Notice that the contents of the *ToRecipients* collection have been expanded to the individual recipients. In fact, Ken is listed twice—once because he was explicitly listed as a *ToRecipient* and once because he is a member of the Store distribution list that the message was sent to. Interestingly, if you were to examine the copy of the message that was saved in Tina's Sent Items folder, you would see the same list of *ToRecipients*. The expansion of Store distribution lists is done by the Store right before the message is actually sent out. Since the copy that appears in the Sent Items folder is placed there by the Store *after* the message is submitted, it is easy to see why the *ToRecipients* collection contains the expanded list of recipients rather than the *ItemId* of the Store distribution list.

You can optionally set the *RoutingType* property when using an *EmailAddressType* object to represent a private distribution list. However, if you do wish to set the value, it must be set to "MAPIPDL."

Replying To and Forwarding Messages

After a recipient reads a message that they receive, it is common to either reply or forward the message to somebody else. To programmatically reply to a message in previous versions of Exchange, several things had to be done. First, a new empty message had to be created, then all of the important properties had to be copied from the original message to the newly created one. Only after this had been done could the reply body be added and the message sent. When replying to or forwarding a message, client applications such as Outlook Web Access and Office Outlook insert a header block of text between the original body of the message and the newly added text. This header contains information about the original message such as the sender, date sent, recipients, and subject. Instead of requiring you to write the necessary code to be able to produce this header, Exchange Web Services includes this header by default when replying to or forwarding messages.

The three most common operations that apply to received messages are

- Replying to the sender of the message
- Replying to the sender and all recipients
- Forwarding the message

It should not be suprising, therefore, to learn that these three operation each have a corresponding response object: *ReplyToItem*, *ReplyAllToItem*, and *ForwardItem*.

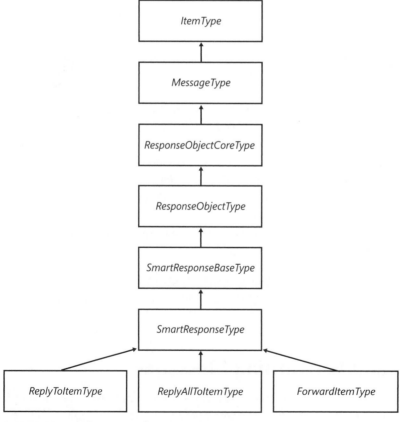

FIGURE 7-5 Partial *ResponseObject* hierarchy

Figure 7-5 shows that *ReplyToItemType*, *ReplyAllToItemType*, and *ForwardItemType* all follow the same derivation path. In fact, none of the three introduce their own properties. As such, the properties that they expose are inherited from their common base classes. However, if you examine the schema files, you will notice that *SmartResponseBaseType* is a *restriction* of its parent type rather than an *extension*. Schema restrictions allow you to remove properties that were present in the parent class. While such functionality allows you to have more flexibility in defining data structures, it has no mapping to languages such as C#. As such, the proxy classes that descend from *SmartResponseBaseType* will have properties exposed on them that you are not allowed to use. Rather than telling you which properties you cannot use, Table 7-4 provides a list of the properties that are available for use on *ReplyToItemType*, *ReplyAllToItemType*, and *ForwardItemType*. If you try to set the other inherited properties, you will be greeted by a schema validation error when submitting your request.

TABLE 7-4 Available *SmartResponseType* Properties

Property	Type	Comments
Subject	String	Sets the subject of the new message generated by the response object
Body	BodyType	Access to the entire body of the old message
ToRecipients	ArrayOfRecipientsType	Recipients that the new message generated by the response object should be addressed to
CcRecipients	ArrayOfRecipientsType	Recipients that should receive a "carbon copy" of the new message generated by the response object
BccRecipients	ArrayOfRecipientsType	Recipients that should receive a "blind carbon copy" of the new message generated by the response object
IsReadReceiptRequested	Boolean	Indicates whether a read receipt should be generated for the new message
IsDeliveryReceiptRequested	Boolean	Indicates whether a delivery receipt should be generated for the new message
ReferenceItemId	ItemIdType	Indicates the original message that should be used as a basis for this response object, for instance, the *ItemId* of the message being forwarded
NewBodyContent	BodyType	The new body content to append to prefix the old body content with

Most of these properties have either been discussed before or are self explanatory. However three of them need more explanation. In the following discussion, we will use the *ForwardItemType* response object exclusively. Note, however, that this discussion is just as applicable to both *ReplyToItemType* and *ReplyAllToItemType*.

ReferenceItemId Property

The *ReferenceItemId* property holds the *ItemId* of the message you are replying to or forwarding. The response object action you are trying to create must be applicable to the message you are referencing. If the response object action is not applicable to the item in question, you will encounter a response code of *ErrorInvalidReferenceItem*. A little later you will see how to programmatically determine the applicability of a response object action for a given item. Since the *ReferenceItemId* property is of type *ItemIdType*, the format will look very familiar.

```
<t:ForwardItem>
  <t:ReferenceItemId Id="AQAsAHRpbmE..." ChangeKey="CQAAAB..."/>
</t:ForwardItem>
```

Body and *NewBodyContent* Properties

The *Body* and *NewBodyContent* properties are both instances of *BodyType*. The *Body* property holds the original body of the message to be replied to or forwarded. Typically, you will leave the original body of the message intact when replying to or forwarding a message. For example, Listing 7-28 shows the original message that Tina sends to Phyllis.

LISTING 7-28 Original message with body

```
<CreateItem xmlns=".../messages"
            xmlns:t=".../types"
            MessageDisposition="SendAndSaveCopy">
  <Items>
    <t:Message>
      <t:Subject>Original Message</t:Subject>
      <t:Body BodyType="Text">Here is the original body of the message</t:Body>
      <t:ToRecipients>
        <t:Mailbox>
          <t:EmailAddress>phyllis.harris@contoso.com</t:EmailAddress>
        </t:Mailbox>
      </t:ToRecipients>
    </t:Message>
  </Items>
</CreateItem>
```

After receiving this message, Phyllis decides to forward this to Ken without modifying the body at all. She does this by calling *CreateItem* with a *ForwardItem* response object as shown in Listing 7-29.

LISTING 7-29 Creating a forwarded item

```
<CreateItem xmlns=".../messages"
            xmlns:t=".../types"
```

```
                    MessageDisposition="SendAndSaveCopy">
    <Items>
      <t:ForwardItem>
        <t:ToRecipients>
          <t:Mailbox>
            <t:EmailAddress>ken.malcolmson@contoso.com</t:EmailAddress>
          </t:Mailbox>
        </t:ToRecipients>
        <t:ReferenceItemId Id="AAAuAHBoeWxsaX..." ChangeKey="CQAAABYAAAC..."/>
      </t:ForwardItem>
    </Items>
  </CreateItem>
```

The message that Ken receives is shown in Listing 7-30.

LISTING 7-30 The received forwarded message

```
<m:GetItemResponse xmlns:t=".../types" xmlns:m=".../messages">
  <m:ResponseMessages>
    <m:GetItemResponseMessage ResponseClass="Success">
      <m:ResponseCode>NoError</m:ResponseCode>
      <m:Items>
        <t:Message>
          <t:ItemId Id="AQAuAGtlbi..." ChangeKey="CQAAABYAAAC..."/>
          <t:ItemClass>IPM.Note</t:ItemClass>
          <t:Subject>FW: Original Message</t:Subject>
          <t:Body BodyType="Text">


          _____

          From: Tina Makovec
          Sent: Friday, August 31, 2007 1:23:09 PM
          To: Phyllis Harris
          Subject: Original Message

          Here is the original body of the message
          </t:Body>
          <t:InReplyTo>&lt;BD5619DC2027534...</t:InReplyTo>
          <t:ConversationIndex>AQHH69ITmwz...</t:ConversationIndex>
          <t:ConversationTopic>Original Message</t:ConversationTopic>
        </t:Message>
      </m:Items>
    </m:GetItemResponseMessage>
  </m:ResponseMessages>
</m:GetItemResponse>
```

The request to forward the message in Listing 7-29 identified who should receive it (the recipient) and included a reference to the actual message to be forwarded. Yet, there are many more goodies in the forwarded message that Ken received in Listing 7-30, all of which came for free!

First notice that the forwarded message is simply a normal message. You can see that by the presence of the *Message* element name as well as the *ItemClass* value of IPM.Note. Second, notice that the original subject was preserved, *but* was also prefixed by the string "FW:".[13] Third, notice that Exchange Web Services added an intelligent header block of text at the beginning of the message body that indicated who the original message was from, the date sent, the to recipient list, as well as the original subject. Below this header is the original body text. Fourth, the forwarded message includes the *InReplyTo*, *ConversationIndex*, and *ConversationTopic* properties, which tie the forwarded message back to the original message.

Figure 7-6 shows how this message appears in Outlook Web Access.

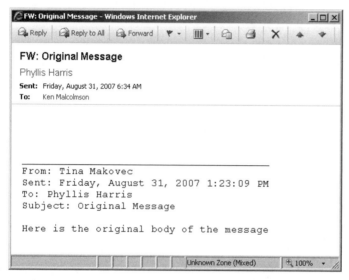

FIGURE 7-6 Forwarded message with no body modificiations

While Phyllis is free to forward the message without modifying the two body properties, there may be times when she would like to replace the original body with a modified version or erase it completely. Listing 7-30 shows another forward where the old message body is erased. This is accomplished by providing an empty *Body* element.

LISTING 7-31 Erasing the old body and supplying a new body

```
<CreateItem xmlns=".../messages"
            xmlns:t=".../types" MessageDisposition="SendAndSaveCopy">
  <Items>
    <t:ForwardItem>
      <t:Body BodyType="Text"/>
      <t:ToRecipients>
        <t:Mailbox>
```

---

[13] This prefix string is localized based on the culture passed in the *MailboxCulture* SOAP header as discussed in Chapter 2, "May I See Your ID?"

```
                <t:EmailAddress>ken.malcolmson@contoso.com</t:EmailAddress>
            </t:Mailbox>
        </t:ToRecipients>
        <t:ReferenceItemId Id="AAAuAHB..." ChangeKey="CQAAABYAAAC..."/>
      </t:ForwardItem>
    </Items>
  </CreateItem>
```

Figure 7-7 shows how this message looks in Outlook Web Access.

FIGURE 7-7 Forwarded message with old *Body* cleared out

There are several *Body* and *NewBodyContent* combinations as shown in Table 7-5.

TABLE 7-5 *Body* and *NewBodyContent* Combinations

Body	NewBodyContent	Result
Omitted	Omitted	The original message contents will be presented to the recipients of the forwarded message along with information header block.
Omitted	Provided	The contents of the *NewBodyContents* will appear above the information header block. The original message contents will be presented after the header block.
Provided	Omitted	Neither the original message contents nor the information header block will be presented to the recipient of the forwarded message. The contents of the *Body* property value from the *ForwardItem* response object will be presented instead.

Body	NewBodyContent	Result
Provided	Provided	Neither the original message contents nor the information header block will be presented to the recipient of the forwarded message. The contents of the *Body* property value from the *ForwardItem* response object will be presented instead. The *NewBodyContent* value will be ignored.

If you provide the *Body* property in a *ForwardItem, ReplyToItem,* or *ReplyAllToItem* response object:

- The original body will be removed

- No header information block will be provided

- Any *NewBodyContent* property value will be ignored

If you provide the *NewBodyContent* property in a *ForwardItem, ReplyToItem,* or *ReplyAllToItem* response object

- The new body content appears before the information header block

It would be good for you to consider the *Body* property and *NewBodyContent* properties as mutually exclusive. If you set both of them, the *NewBodyContent* property value will be ignored. Just to round out your understanding of these body combinations, Figure 7-8 shows a forwarded message with a replaced *Body* while Figure 7-9 shows a forwarded message with a *NewBody* content.

FIGURE 7-8 Forwarded message with a replaced *Body*

FIGURE 7-9 Forwarded message with *NewBodyContent*

The Missing Properties on Response Objects

Response objects are a great concept and simplify common operations such as forwarding a message. However, you saw earlier how the "derivation by restriction" model used for response objects *removes* a number of properties that may be of interest on a forwarded message. For example, you may want to set extended properties on a forwarded message before sending it. However, *ExtendedProperties* is *not* one of the properties that passes through the restriction. There is a work-around, however.

In order to use response objects, you must call the *CreateItem* Web method and pass in the appropriate response object. Do you recall the *MessageDisposition* attribute that is exposed on *CreateItem*? Well, the behavior of *MessageDisposition* does not change just because you are dealing with response objects. As such, you can create a forwarded message without sending it by specifying the *SaveOnly MessageDisposition* as shown in Listing 7-32.

LISTING 7-32 Creating a forwarded message without sending it

```
<CreateItem xmlns=".../messages"
            xmlns:t=".../types"
            MessageDisposition="SaveOnly">
  <Items>
    <t:ForwardItem>
<!-- contents elided -->
    </t:ForwardItem>
  </Items>
</CreateItem>
```

As expected, the response, which is not shown here, contains the *ItemId* of the draft message. You can use *UpdateItem* to make whatever changes are necessary and then send the forwarded item on its merry way by either specifying a *MessageDisposition* of *SendOnly* or *SendAndSaveCopy* as part of the *UpdateItem* call, or by explicitly calling *SendItem*.

Response Object Applicability

Earlier in the chapter, we disussed how you can use only a response object that is applicable to the referenced item. For instance, you cannot create a reply for a draft message, nor can you suppress read receipts on a message that does not have a read receipt request on it.

With this in mind, it might be beneficial to determine whether a given response object action is applicable to a message before trying to perform that action. Since the applicable actions for a message are exposed through the *ResponseObjects* property, you can write code to use the proxy classes and walk through the array of *ResponseObjectType* instances, checking for type equivalence along the way. An example implementation is shown in Listing 7-33.

LISTING 7-33 Determining if a *ResponseObject* action is applicable for an item

```
/// <summary>
/// Determine if the given item supports the templated response object type
/// </summary>
/// <typeparam name="T">Type of response object to check support
/// for</typeparam>
/// <param name="item">Item to check</param>
/// <returns>True if the item supports the supplied response object
/// type</returns>
///
public static bool CanPerformResponseObject<T>(ItemType item)
                where T: ResponseObjectType
{
  foreach (ResponseObjectType responseObject in item.ResponseObjects)
  {
    if (responseObject is T)
    {
      return true;
    }
  }
  return false;
}
```

Let's use the *CanPerformResponseObject* method from Listing 7-33 to see if a *ForwardItemType* response object is available on the supplied message. If applicable, the message is forwarded to a new recipient.

LISTING 7-34 Example scenario using response objects

```
/// <summary>
/// Forward the message if it supports the ForwardItem response object
/// </summary>
/// <param name="binding">Binding to use</param>
/// <param name="message">Message to forward</param>
///
public static void ForwardIfPossible(
            ExchangeServiceBinding binding,
            MessageType message)
{
  if (message.ResponseObjects == null)
  {
    throw new Exception("Item needs ResponseObjects property");
  }

  // For this example, let's forward the message - so go through the
  // available response objects and see if forward is an option
  if (CanPerformResponseObject<ForwardItemType>(message))
  {
    // Let's Forward this email to another recipient
    //
    ForwardItemType forwardItem = new ForwardItemType();
    forwardItem.ReferenceItemId = message.ItemId;

    // Set new body content
    //
    BodyType newContent = new BodyType();
    newContent.Value = "This is the message I said I'd forward";
    newContent.BodyType1 = message.Body.BodyType1;
    forwardItem.NewBodyContent = newContent;

    // Set our recipient
    //
    EmailAddressType toEmail = new
        EmailAddressType("jane.dow@contoso.com");
    EmailAddressType[] recipients = new EmailAddressType[] { toEmail };
    forwardItem.ToRecipients = recipients;

    CreateItemType createItem = new CreateItemType();
    createItem.MessageDisposition =
        MessageDispositionType.SendAndSaveCopy;
    createItem.MessageDispositionSpecified = true;
    createItem.Items = new NonEmptyArrayOfAllItemsType();
    createItem.Items.Items = new ItemType[] { forwardItem };

    // Make our request
    //
    CreateItemResponseType createItemResponse = binding.CreateItem(createItem);

    if (createItemResponse.ResponseMessages.Items[0].ResponseCode !=
        ResponseCodeType.NoError)
    {
      throw new Exception("Failed to forward item. Response code: " +
```

```
            createItemResponse.ResponseMessages.Items[0].ResponseCode.ToString());
      }
   }
   else
   {
      throw new Exception("Can't forward this item");
   }
}
```

Reports

If you send a message with a read and/or delivery receipt, it is reasonable to expect that you will receive some sort of notification that the message has been read and/or delivered. These notifications come in the form of e-mail messages that are delivered to your mailbox, and are better known as *reports*. Although a report is functionally a message, the *ItemClass* property of a report does not follow the IPM.Note prefix pattern that you have seen throughout the book. The *ItemClass* values and the applicable report types are presented in Table 7-6.

TABLE 7-6 *ItemClass* **Values**

ItemClass	Report Type
REPORT.IPM.Note.IPNRN	Read Receipt
REPORT.IPM.Note.IPNNRN	Not Read Receipt (message deleted without reading)
REPORT.IPM.Note.DR	Delivery Receipt
REPORT.IPM.Note.NDR	Non-Delivery Receipt

As an example, Listings 7-35 shows a message created and sent with both a delivery receipt and a read receipt requested.

LISTING 7-35 Creating a message with both read and delivery receipt requests

```
<CreateItem xmlns=".../messages"
            xmlns:t=".../types" MessageDisposition="SendAndSaveCopy">
  <Items>
    <t:Message>
      <t:Subject>Message with delivery receipt</t:Subject>
      <t:ToRecipients>
        <t:Mailbox>
          <t:EmailAddress>ken.malcolmson@contoso.com</t:EmailAddress>
        </t:Mailbox>
      </t:ToRecipients>
      <t:IsReadReceiptRequested>true</t:IsReadReceiptRequested>
      <t:IsDeliveryReceiptRequested>true</t:IsDeliveryReceiptRequested>
    </t:Message>
  </Items>
</CreateItem>
```

After this message is delivered to the recipient's mailbox, the Exchange Store will generate a delivery receipt and send it back to the original sender. Note that the actual time that this report message is generated is a function of when Exchange delivers this message to the recipient's mailbox. It does not depend on the recipient actually reading the message. Figure 7-10 shows a deliver receipt for the message generated in Listing 7-35, while Listing 7-36 shows the Exchange Web Services view of this report.

FIGURE 7-10 Delivery receipt in Outlook Web Access

LISTING 7-36 Partial *GetItem* response for delivery report

```
<!-- xml elided. In addition, other non-pertinent properties were removed -->
    <t:Message>
        <t:ItemId Id="AAAuAHBoeWxs..." ChangeKey="FwAAABYA..."/>
        <t:ItemClass>REPORT.IPM.Note.DR</t:ItemClass>
        <t:Subject>Delivered: Message with delivery receipt</t:Subject>
        <t:InReplyTo>&lt;BD5619DC2027534A...</t:InReplyTo>
        <t:ConversationIndex>A, QHH6+ii/ukc/YC1uU2CzgZpxh/1doxH+XMk</t:
ConversationIndex>
        <t:ConversationTopic>Message with delivery receipt</t:ConversationTopic>
    </t:Message>
<!-- xml elided -->
```

Aside from the *InReplyTo*, *ConversationIndex*, and *ConversationTopic* properties that tied this report back to the original message, it is interesting to notice that the XML element name is indeed a *Message*, yet the *ItemClass* property does not begin with the IPM.Note prefix! Exchange Web Services creates an exception to this rule for report messages.

While a delivery receipt will be generated without any interaction from the recipient, a read receipt will not be generated until the recipient marks the message as being read. Figure 7-11 shows a read receipt for the message generated in Listing 7-35, while Listing 7-37 shows the Exchange Web Services view of this report.

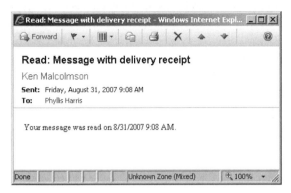

FIGURE 7-11 Read receipt in Outlook Web Access

LISTING 7-37 Partial *GetItem* response for read receipt

```
<!-- xml elided. In addition, other non-pertinent properties were removed -->
  <t:Message>
    <t:ItemId Id="AAAuAHBoeWx..." ChangeKey="FwAAABYA..."/>
    <t:ItemClass>REPORT.IPM.Note.IPNRN</t:ItemClass>
    <t:Subject>Read: Message with delivery receipt</t:Subject>
    <t:ConversationIndex>AQHH6+ii/ukc/YC1uU2CzgZpxh/1doxH+oCM</t:ConversationIndex>
    <t:ConversationTopic>Message with delivery receipt</t:ConversationTopic>
  </t:Message>
<!-- xml elided -->
```

Summary

In this chapter, we introduced *MessageType* and the various behaviors that are specific to messages. While the vending machines were covering Ken, we covered recipient addresses, which provide a way to point to a given endpoint. We then showed you the properties that are exposed on *MessageType* objects and discussed how to use recipient collection and both read and delivery receipts. Delegate access and *SendAs* rights were discussed in the context of Exchange Web Services and how each affects the value of the *Sender* property.

Of course, messages are not any fun if you can't send them, so we covered sending messages using the *SendItem* Web method, although as you have seen before, you can also send messages using *CreateItem* and *UpdateItem* as long as you use an appropriate *MessageDisposition* value. And what fun is receiving a message if you cannot reply to it? We covered the response objects available for messages, which provide a way to reply and forward a message, as well how to suppress read receipts. And lastly, we closed the chapter with a discussion of reports and how to identify them.

Now that you are well-versed in sending and receiving messages, we will turn our attention to calendaring.

Chapter 8
Working with Calendars

For many people, the desire to keep track of time and when events occur is paramount. For these people, the invention of the calendar was truly a remarkable event, and, through the centuries, calendars have sufficed very well as a means of noting important times. Once calendars went digital, things really began to take off. Now, people can enter information about important appointments in an electronic device, and the device will help them remember those appointments. The device can even show them a nice view of their events by day, week, or month. No more bad penmanship, no more endless sticky notes. Our digital lifestyle now includes the ability to note events that will take place next week or years in the future. We also have the ability to record in our digital calendars a particular meeting that will recur every third Tuesday of each month, and when that third Tuesday arrives, our digital assistants are more than happy to remind us.

Despite these wonderful advancements, putting together a well-defined, solid, and reliable calendaring server is no small task. Fortunately, the Microsoft Exchange Server 2007 Web Services (EWS) team has years of calendaring experience and has produced one rock-solid platform for collaboration.

Making the Complex Understandable

At first, calendaring can appear daunting, especially when you consider sending and responding to meeting requests, cancellations and updates, dealing with recurrence patterns, dealing with exceptions to recurrence patterns, time zones, required attendees, optional attendees, resources, free-busy status...whew! Faced with all of this complexity, some programmers cringe at the thought of dealing with calendar programming. Users though, are human, and humans are social creatures who at some point will want to meet with somebody about something. For that reason, the Exchange Web Services development team went to work to put together a set of item types and helpful features to make programming a calendar light work.

The next three chapters will look at the many aspects of calendaring. In this first chapter of the series, we focus on the Calendar folder and the *CalendarItemType* types. We discuss strings for describing dates and times, and start our discussion of time zones. We also examine the *CalendarViewType* type, which is an essential type for finding calendar events that occur within a specific time period. The second chapter in the series looks at recurring calendar items and completes the discussion of time zones, while the third and final chapter in the series focuses on sending meeting requests to others and dealing with their responses.

Creating Your First Calendar Item

Creating a basic appointment on the calendar is a straightforward operation. Like all other item types, you create a calendar item by using the *CreateItem* Web method. Look at Listing 8-1 for the most basic example of creating a calendar item.

LISTING 8-1 Example of creating a calendar item via a *CreateItem* request

```
<CreateItem SendMeetingInvitations="SendToNone"
            xmlns=".../messages"
            xmlns:t=".../types">
  <Items>
    <t:CalendarItem>
      <t:Subject>Write Chapter Explaining Calendar Items</t:Subject>
    </t:CalendarItem>
  </Items>
</CreateItem>
```

As you can see, all you need to do is supply a *CalendarItem* XML node with a child node of *Subject* and set the *SendMeetingInvitations* attribute to *SendToNone*.[1] (We'll discuss the *SendMeetingInvitations* attribute in more depth in Chapter 10, "Scheduling Meetings." For the purposes of this chapter, we will always use the value *SendToNone*.) The same operation via the proxy classes would look something like Listing 8-2.

LISTING 8-2 Creating a new *CalendarItem* via proxy

```
/// <summary>
/// Create a calendar item
/// </summary>
/// <param name="binding">Binding to use for web service call</param>
/// <returns>Id of newly created calendar item</returns>
///
public static ItemIdType CreateCalendarItem(ExchangeServiceBinding binding)
{
  CalendarItemType newCalendarItem = new CalendarItemType();
  newCalendarItem.Subject = "Write Chapter Explaining Calendar Items";
  CreateItemType createItemRequest = new CreateItemType();

  // When using the CreateItem web method to create a CalendarItem, we must
  // specify a value for the SendMeetingInviations attribute
  //
  createItemRequest.SendMeetingInvitations =
          CalendarItemCreateOrDeleteOperationType.SendToNone;
  createItemRequest.SendMeetingInvitationsSpecified = true;

  createItemRequest.Items = new NonEmptyArrayOfAllItemsType();
```

---

[1] In fact, even the *Subject* element is "optional." EWS will honor the request and create a new 30-minute appointment with a start time of when the request was processed and with no specified subject. But that wouldn't make for a very interesting example, would it?

```
createItemRequest.Items.Items = new CalendarItemType[1];
createItemRequest.Items.Items[0] = newCalendarItem;
// Make our request
//
CreateItemResponseType response = binding.CreateItem(createItemRequest);
ItemInfoResponseMessageType responseMessage = response.ResponseMessages.Items[0] as
    ItemInfoResponseMessageType;
if (responseMessage.ResponseCode != ResponseCodeType.NoError)
{
  throw new Exception("CreateCalendarItem failed with response code " +
        responseMessage.ResponseCode.ToString());
}
return responseMessage.Items.Items[0].ItemId;
}
```

If you call the *GetItem* Web method by using the *ItemId* of the calendar item created in the previous example, you'd see something like the response shown in Listing 8-3.

LISTING 8-3 *GetItemResponse* message for a calendar item (*Default* response shape)

```
<GetItemResponse xmlns=".../messages"
                 xmlns:t=".../types">
  <ResponseMessages>
    <GetItemResponseMessage ResponseClass="Success">
      <ResponseCode>NoError</m:ResponseCode>
      <Items>
        <t:CalendarItem>
          <t:ItemId Id="AAAeAGRhdnNOZXJAZX..." ChangeKey="AQAAABYAAAD..."/>
          <t:Subject>Write Chapter Explaining Calendar Items</t:Subject>
          <t:ResponseObjects>
            <t:ForwardItem/>
          </t:ResponseObjects>
          <t:HasAttachments>false</t:HasAttachments>
          <t:Start>2006-11-09T05:30:00Z</t:Start>
          <t:End>2006-11-09T06:00:00Z</t:End>
          <t:LegacyFreeBusyStatus>Busy</t:LegacyFreeBusyStatus>
          <t:CalendarItemType>Single</t:CalendarItemType>
          <t:Organizer>
            <t:Mailbox>
              <t:Name>Andy Jacobs</t:Name>
              <t:EmailAddress>andy@contoso.com</t:EmailAddress>
              <t:RoutingType>SMTP</t:RoutingType>
            </t:Mailbox>
          </t:Organizer>
        </t:CalendarItem>
      </Items>
    </GetItemResponseMessage>
  </ResponseMessages>
</GetItemResponse>
```

Listing 8-3 is your first look at many of the properties present in the *Default* shape of a calendar item. As you can see, this is the most property-filled object type yet. Now, the *CreateItem* Web method in the example above certainly did not have that many properties set, so Exchange Web Services did a lot of work. You can take advantage of the logic that Exchange Web Services uses to set meaningful defaults in the absence of specific property values. That logic also placed the newly created item in the Calendar folder.

Understanding Calendar Items

Soon we are going to take an in depth look at all of the properties on calendar items, but before we get to that, we want to introduce three concepts that are important to understand when working with calendar items. Those concepts are

- Recurrences
- Meetings
- Free/Busy Status

Introducing Recurrences

A sequence of calendar items that follow a distinct pattern and are delimited by a range is called a *recurring series*. A recurring series is created by setting the *Recurrence* property on a new or existing calendar item with a *recurrence pattern* and *recurrence range*. The calendar item that then holds the information in its *Recurrence* property is called the *recurring master*.

When a recurring series is created, calendar items known as *occurrences* are generated, and each occurrence is given an *index* indicating its position within the series. Occurrences that have had a change in one or more of their properties, such that they no longer adhere to the pattern, are called *exceptions*. Finally, a calendar item that is not part of a recurring series is refered to as a *single* calendar item.

Occurrences and exceptions are not actual items in the mailbox; instead they are items that are stored internally as attachments to the recurring master. Occurrences and exceptions do have ids and, for the most part, can be treated just like any other calendar item. Recurring masters also have ids, along with additional property values for assisting developers to maintain a corresponding recurring series.

This chapter will focus on single calendar items. We will discuss the other types of calendar items along with recurrence expansion in detail in Chapter 9, "Recurrences and Time Zones."

Introducing Meetings

Calendar items can be used to represent a meeting between two or more parties. In Exchange Web Services, these parties are called *attendees*. Attendees are stored on a calendar item in one of three different *attendee collections* and are classified based on which collection they are contained in. Any calendar item that has attendees is called a *meeting*, and this designation can be identified by checking the *IsMeeting* property on the calendar item.

The *required attendees* collection is for attendees who must be able to attend the meeting in order for it to occur; the *optional attendees* collection is for attendees who are not required. The *resources attendees* collection is for denoting meeting resources (such as rooms or equipment). Each of these attendee collections are represented on a meeting in the *RequiredAttendees*, *OptionalAttendees*, and *Resources* properties, accordingly.

While meetings are technically just calendar items with attendees, in the real world they are often the result of coordination between all of the attendees trying to find a time to meet together. Meetings have *organizers* who are responsible for sending out *meeting invitations* and coordinating all of the attendees *meeting responses*. Organizers can also send *meeting updates* as well as *meeting cancellations* to any or all attendees. Meeting invitations, responses, updates, and cancellations are collectively referred to as *meeting messages*. The process of organizers and attendees sending meeting messages back and forth to each other is referred to as *meeting workflow*.

A recurring master that is also a meeting is said to be a *recurring meeting*, and all of the attendees are said to be 'taking part in the recurring meeting.'

Chapter 10, "Scheduling Meetings," will cover all of the concepts of meetings in greater detail.

Introducing Free/Busy Status

Every calendar item consumes some amount of time on a user's calendar. Along with a slot of time, there is also a status that is applied to that time called the *free/busy status*. A free/busy status of a calendar item indicates the intention of the calendar item owner with regard to that time slot. For example, you may not wish to be bothered for a certain period of time. You can indicate this by creating a calendar item and marking the free/busy status of that item to "Busy." This means that any other user querying your calendar will see the time slot as busy. Another common use of free/busy status is to indicate to co-workers when you are 'out of the office' (abbreviated OOF.[2]) By creating a calendar item that lasts all day and marking the item's free/busy status with *OOF*, you have effectively told anyone looking at your calendar that you are gone for the day.

---

[2] Yes, we know that technically the acronym should be OOO, but, alas, 'tis not.

Incidentally, the act of querying for the free/busy status of all appointments for a given time period of another user is called "checking that user's availability." Free/busy status and availability are discussed in Chapter 21, "Availability."

CalendarItemType Properties

Now let's talk about the item type for calendar items. The schema type for calendar items is the *CalendarItemType* type. This schema type derives from the *ItemType* type and maintains all of the properties from that type. Naturally, the *CalendarItemType* type has its own set of properties unique to calendar items. Table 8-1 is a listing of all of the properties on a *CalendarItemType* instance. We will explore some of these properties in greater detail later in this chapter.

TABLE 8-1 Properties of *CalendarItemType*

Property name	Type	Comments
Start	*DateTime*	Starting date and time for a calendar item
End	*DateTime*	Ending date and time for a calendar item
OriginalStart	*DateTime*	The original starting time for a calendar item
IsAllDayEvent	Boolean	True if a calendar item is to be interpreted as lasting all day
LegacyFreeBusyStatus	*LegacyFreeBusyType*	Free/busy status for a calendar item
Location	String	Friendly name for where a calendar item pertains to (e.g., a physical address or "My Office")
*When**	String	Description of when a calendar item occurs
IsMeeting	Boolean	True if a calendar item is a meeting
IsCancelled	Boolean	True if a calendar item is a meeting and has been cancelled
IsRecurring	Boolean	True if a calendar item is part of a recurring series**
MeetingRequestWasSent	Boolean	True if a meeting request for a calendar item has been sent to all attendees
IsResponseRequested	Boolean	True if a response to a calendar item is needed

Property name	Type	Comments
CalendarItemType	*CalendarItemTypeType*	The type of calendar item indicating its relationship to a recurrence, if any
MyResponseType	*ResponseTypeType*	The response of the calendar item's owner to the meeting
Organizer	*SingleRecipientType*	For meetings, the party responsible for coordinating attendance
RequiredAttendees	*NonEmptyArrayOfAttendeesType*	Listing of all attendees required to attend a meeting
OptionalAttendees	*NonEmptyArrayOfAttendeesType*	Listing of all attendees not required to attend a meeting
Resources	*NonEmptyArrayOfAttendeesType*	Listing of all scheduled resources for a meeting
ConflictingMeetingCount	Integer	The number of calendar items in conflict with a calendar item
AdjacentMeetingCount	*NonEmptyArrayOfAllItemsType*	The number of calendar items adjacent to a calendar item
ConflictingMeetings	*NonEmptyArrayOfAllItemsType*	A list of calendar items in conflict with a calendar item
AdjacentMeetings	*NonEmptyArrayOfAllItemsType*	A list of calendar items adjacent to a calendar item
Duration	String	Length in time of a calendar item
TimeZone	String	Display name for the time zone associated with a calendar item
AppointmentReplyTime	*DateTime*	Date/time when a calendar item was responded to (applicable to meetings only)
AppointmentSequenceNumber	Integer	The sequence number of a version of a calendar item (applicable to meetings only)
AppointmentState	Integer	Specifies the status of the calendar item (applicable to meetings only)
Recurrence	*RecurrenceType*	Contains the recurrence pattern and range for a recurring series
FirstOccurrence	*OccurrenceInfoType*	Represents the first occurrence of a recurring series
LastOccurrence	*OccurrenceInfoType*	Represents the last occurrence of a recurring series
ModifiedOccurrences	*NonEmptyArrayOfOccurrenceInfoType*	An array of occurrences within a recurring series that have been modified

Property name	Type	Comments
DeletedOccurrences	*NonEmptyArrayOfDeleted OccurrencesType*	An array of deleted occurences from a recurring series
MeetingTimeZone	*TimeZoneType*	The time zone of the location where a meeting is hosted
ConferenceType	Integer	Describes the type of conferencing that is performed with a calendar item
AllowNewTimeProposal	Boolean	True if attendees are allowed to respond to the organizer with new time suggestions
IsOnlineMeeting	Boolean	True if a meeting is to be held online
MeetingWorkspaceUrl	String	A URL for a meeting workspace that is associated with a calendar item
NetShowUrl	String	A URL for a Microsoft NetShow online meeting

*In Exchange Server 2007, there is an issue where the *When* property was improperly implemented and as a result will always return an empty string.

**Note that a recurring master is not considered part of a recurring series, even though it holds the recurrence information.

We will not go into detail for the properties that are inherited from *ItemType* because we talked about them in Chapter 5, "Items."

The *Start* and *End* Properties

The *Start* and *End* properties hold the starting date and time and ending date and time of a calendar item, respectively. The date and time values of these properties are strings in a format called *xs:dateTime*. If you look back at Listing 8-3, you can see an example of the *xs:dateTime* format in the *Start* and *End* elements in the calendar item XML.

We will discuss the *xs:dateTime* format in detail later in this chapter, but we will just briefly mention now that when looking at the XML of a calendar item in a response (from either a *GetItem* or *FindItem* Web method call, for example), the *xs:dateTime* strings in the *Start* and *End* elements will always contain a trailing 'Z' character. This 'Z' character indicates that the date and time represented by the string are in the UTC time zone.

When you set the *Start* and *End* properties on a calendar item via the *CreateItem* Web method, or if you update those properties using the *UpdateItem* Web method, you are not required to specify the *xs:dateTime* strings in UTC. You can choose to express the date and time as UTC time, as a date and time offset from UTC, or as a date and time without any UTC offset.[3]

---

3 When we discuss *xs:datetime* strings in more detail, however, we will explain under what circumstances you would want to include a UTC offset and when you would not.

The *Location* Property

The *Location* property tells any attendees (or reminds the organizer) where a meeting is supposed to take place. Although we aren't covering meeting rooms as resources in this chapter, it is customary for an application to fill in the *Location* property during creation time if a user adds a meeting room as a resource to a new calendar item.

The *CalendarItemType* Property

The *CalendarItemType* property is a read-only property and describes which of the four types the calendar item in question is. The four possible values for *CalendarItemType* are:

- *Single*
- *Occurrence*
- *Exception*
- *RecurringMaster*

By default, all newly created calendar items are of type *Single*. The only way to create a calendar item of type *RecurringMaster* is to set the *Recurrence* property on a calendar item. Calendar items of type *Occurrence* and *Exception* are never directly created by an application; instead, occurrences and exceptions are created as a result of converting a single calendar item into a recurring master by setting the *Recurrence* property.

The Exchange Web Services schema defines a complex type of *CalendarItemType*, along with a property named *CalendarItemType*. Because of this, the proxy will expose the *CalendarItemType* property as *CalendarItemType1*.

```
// Grab the first calendar item from our FindItem web method response.
CalendarItemType currentCalendarItem = (CalendarItemType)findItemResponseItems.Items[0];

// Output to the Console, our current calendar item's CalendarItemType value.
Console.WriteLine("\tCalendar Item Type = " +
    currentCalendarItem.CalendarItemType1 + "\r\n");
```

The *ResponseObjects* Property

Response objects were covered in detail in Chapter 5, "Items," and again in Chapter 7, "Messages." To review, response objects describe a set of actions that are valid to respond to the item in question. When you work with an individually created calendar item, there will be only one such action, namely, *ForwardItem*.[4]

---

4 There are calendar items that can be created as a result of users sending each other meeting requests, a process we will discuss in Chapter 10. There will be more response objects present on calendar items created through this process.

```
<t:CalendarItem>
  <t:ItemId Id="AAAeAGRhdnNOZXJAZX..." ChangeKey="AQAAABYAAAD..."/>
  <t:Subject>Write Chapter Explaining Calendar Items</t:Subject>
  <t:ResponseObjects>
    <t:ForwardItem/>
  </t:ResponseObjects>
</t:CalendarItem>
```

ForwardItem behaves differently with calendar items than it does with messages. You might have assumed that using *ForwardItem* on a *CalendarItem* instance would serve to "invite" a recipient to an event. But instead, when you forward a *CalendarItem* instance, the recipient receives simply a copy of the *CalendarItem* as an attachment to a message.[5]

The *LegacyFreeBusyStatus* Property

LegacyFreeBusyStatus holds the free/busy status of a calendar item.

Don't let the name fool you; there is nothing 'legacy' about this property. This property can be set during item creation to any value from the *LegacyFreeBusyType* enumeration defined in *types.xsd*. The default value is *Busy*.

```
<xs:simpleType name="LegacyFreeBusyType">
  <xs:restriction base="xs:string">
    <xs:enumeration value="Free" />
    <xs:enumeration value="Tentative" />
    <xs:enumeration value="Busy" />
    <xs:enumeration value="OOF" />
    <xs:enumeration value="NoData" />
  </xs:restriction>
</xs:simpleType>
```

Table 8-2 lists possible interpretations for each of the *LegacyFreeBusyType* values. Organizations are free to interpret these values as they see fit, but you should not expect much deviation from these interpretations.

TABLE 8-2 *LegacyFreeBusyType* **Values and Intended Usage Advice**

LegacyFreeBusyType value	Intended usage
Free	Time slot is open for potential meetings. A calendar item marked as *Free* may be a previously scheduled meeting that the owner is no longer planning to attend, but still wants recorded in the calendar.
Tentative	Time slot is potentially filled.
Busy	Time slot is filled and attempts by others to schedule a meeting for this time should be avoided.
OOF	User is out of the office and may not be able to respond to meeting invitations for new meetings that occur in this time slot.
NoData	Applications should avoid explicitly setting this.

---

[5] In Chapter 10, we will explain how to take existing calendar iItems and invite people to attend a meeting through the use of attendee collections.

The *Duration* Property

Duration is a read-only property that uses a string in *xs:duration* format to describe the length of the appointment represented. Refer to the "Understanding *xs:duration*" sidebar later in this chapter for more information on the format of this property value.

Incidentally, *xs:duration* does not translate directly into a .NET Framework structure or class. Therefore, the proxy classes expose the *Duration* property as a string.

The *IsCancelled* Property

The *IsCancelled* property is a read-only Boolean property that indicates a calendar item has been cancelled by the organizer (meaning the calendar item is also a meeting). The *IsCancelled* property is not available from the *FindItem* Web method, a fact that will be important to remember when we cover how to work with meetings in Chapter 10.

The *IsRecurring* Property

The *IsRecurring* property is a read-only Boolean property that indicates that the calendar item is part of a recurring series. Occurrences and exceptions always have the *IsRecurring* property set to true. *IsRecurring* can also be set to true for single calendar items, but this occurs only when an organizer of a recurring meeting invites a new attendee to only one of the series' occurrences. *IsRecurring* is never set to true on a recurring master.

The *IsAllDayEvent* Property

Calendar items with their *IsAllDayEvent* properties set to true are meant to represent 24-hour durations that start at 12:00 A.M. in the calendar item owner's local time zone. As we will discuss, however, calendar items have start and end times specified in UTC, so your application must ensure that this gets translated correctly into the time zone of the user, lest you present an all day meeting that looks like it starts at 9 P.M. one day and ends at 9 P.M. on the next day.

The *TimeZone* Property

> **Warning** There are two properties on a *CalendarItemType* instance that describe time zone information: the *TimeZone* property and the *MeetingTimeZone* property. The *TimeZone* property is a read-only string property and is meant to provide a text-only description of the time zone for a calendar item. The *MeetingTimeZone* property, however, is designed to allow a time zone to actually be set on a new calendar item or updated on an existing item.

There is no solid definition for what a 'text-only description of a time zone' should be. In most cases, however, applications that run on the Microsoft Windows platform will use either a time zone display name from a time zone registry key (Microsoft Office Outlook, for example, uses this approach) or the name of the time zone registry key itself (Outlook Web Access does this). The advantage of using the name of a registry key as the *TimeZone* property value is that client applications can perform their own lookup of the registry key and get a localized version of the display name.[6]

Exchange Web Services, unfortunately, does not allow you to specify the name of a time zone for a calendar item during creation or during update, and as such, any calendar items that are fetched with Exchange Web Services that were also created with Exchange Web Services, will always have an empty *TimeZone* element.[7]

The *MeetingTimeZone* Property

The schema defines the *MeetingTimeZone* property as being of the *TimeZoneType* type.

```
<xs:element name="MeetingTimeZone" type="t:TimeZoneType" minOccurs="0"/>
```

For the purposes of this chapter, we will look only at the one required property on the *TimeZoneType* schema type, and that is the *BaseOffset* property, which is of type *xs:duration*.

```
<xs:complexType name="TimeZoneType">
  <xs:sequence>
    <xs:element name="BaseOffset" type="xs:duration" />
    <xs:sequence minOccurs="0">
      <xs:element name="Standard" type="t:TimeChangeType"/>
      <xs:element name="Daylight" type="t:TimeChangeType"/>
    </xs:sequence>
  </xs:sequence>
  <xs:attribute name="TimeZoneName" type="xs:string" use="optional" />
</xs:complexType>
```

We will discuss the *BaseOffset* property and the *xs:duration* format in more detail later in this chapter. However, this chapter will not cover the *Standard* property, the *Daylight* property, or the *TimeZoneName* attribute on this type. To discuss all of these, we need to first describe the *RelativeYearlyRecurrencePatternType* schema type and discuss how recurrence ranges work.

As mentioned briefly before, a *MeetingTimeZone* is used to assign a time zone to a calendar item. The *MeetingTimeZone* will be returned only on recurring masters, so any call to a *GetItem* Web method asking for the *calendar:MeetingTimeZone* property will return no *MeetingTimeZone* element in the response unless the *CalendarItemType* value on the calendar item being fetched is set to *RecurringMaster*.

---

[6] In Chapter 9, we will cover using the registry to get not only time zone display names, but other time zone information such as base offsets and time change dates as well.

[7] As of this writing, the next service pack of Exchange Server 2007 will include a fix to allow EWS clients to set the name of a time zone; however, this will be done through the *MeetingTimeZone* element and not the *TimeZone* element.

The fact that you can set a time zone on a calendar item using the *MeetingTimeZone* property is important. Having a time zone set on a calendar item is required if that calendar item is a recurring master. As such, if a *MeetingTimeZone* is not provided by the client during item creation, Exchange Web Services will assign a default time zone to the new recurring master. The process of assigning a default time zone to a new recurring master will be explained later in this chapter.

Getting Adjacent and Conflicting Calendar Items

Calendar users are usually looking through their calendars for one of two reasons: 1) to see what is on their schedules for today, or 2) to see if there is some time available on their calendar to squeeze in more appointments. There are four properties on calendar items that can help users in this.

Imagine that your application allows a user to click on any appointement from the day. When your application calls the *GetItem* Web method to get the associated calendar item, it can request additional properties that not only indicate the count of, but also some details about any other calendar items that are adjacent to or in conflict with the calendar item that is being requested.

The *AdjacentMeetingCount* and *ConflictingMeetingCount* Properties

AdjacentMeetingCount and *ConflictingMeetingCount* are two integer properties on the *CalendarItemType* that represent the number of calendar items that are adjacent to or in conflict with a given calendar item, respectively. Adjacent calendar items are those whose time slots immediately precede or immediately follow the calendar item time slot in question. Conflicting calendar items are those whose time slots overlap with the time slot of the calendar item in question.

 Note The use of the word 'meeting' in the names of the properties does not mean that they apply to only adjacent or conflicting meetings. These properties are applicable to all calendar items.

To demonstrate getting conflicting and adjacent meeting counts, let's look at an example.

Consider the appointment entitled "Michael's demo of server deployments" in Figure 8-1. Notice the two adjacent appointments and one conflicting appointment.

FIGURE 8-1 View of conflicting and adjacent meetings in Microsoft Office Outlook Web Access

By requesting the *calendar:AdjacentMeetingCount* and *calendar:ConflictingMeetingCount* in the *AdditionalProperties* element of a *GetItem* Web method request, you can see the number of these adjacent and conflicting meetings represented in the *GetItemResponse*. Listing 8-4 is an example of such a request.

LISTING 8-4 *GetItem* request for the number of conflicting and adjacent meetings to a calendar item

```
<GetItem xmlns=".../messages" xmlns:t=".../types">
  <ItemShape>
    <t:BaseShape>IdOnly</t:BaseShape>
    <t:AdditionalProperties>
      <t:FieldURI FieldURI="item:Subject" />
      <t:FieldURI FieldURI="calendar:ConflictingMeetingCount" />
      <t:FieldURI FieldURI="calendar:AdjacentMeetingCount" />
    </t:AdditionalProperties>
  </ItemShape>
  <ItemIds>
    <t:ItemId Id="AAAoAGV3c3V..." ChangeKey="DwAAABY..."/>
  </ItemIds>
</GetItem>
```

Listing 8-5 is the response from the *GetItem* Web method in Listing 8-4.

LISTING 8-5 *GetItem* response message from a request for conflicting and adjacent meeting counts

```
<m:GetItemResponse xmlns:m=".../messages" xmlns:t=".../types">
  <m:ResponseMessages>
    <m:GetItemResponseMessage ResponseClass="Success">
      <m:ResponseCode>NoError</m:ResponseCode>
      <m:Items>
```

```
    <t:CalendarItem>
      <t:ItemId Id="AAAoAGV3c3VzZX..." ChangeKey="DwAAABYAA..."/>
      <t:Subject>Michael's demo of server deployments</t:Subject>
      <t:ConflictingMeetingCount>1</t:ConflictingMeetingCount>
      <t:AdjacentMeetingCount>2</t:AdjacentMeetingCount>
    </t:CalendarItem>
  </m:Items>
 </m:GetItemResponseMessage>
 </m:ResponseMessages>
</m:GetItemResponse>
```

The *AdjacentMeetings* and *ConflictingMeetings* Properties

In addition to the 'count' properties that we just described, there are two more properties on the *CalendarItemType* that can return a subset of calendar item properties for each of the adjacent and/or conflicting calendar items. The *AdjacentMeetings* and *ConflictingMeetings* properties are defined as being of type *NonEmptyArrayOfAllItemsType* in the schema. This means that these properties could each hold one or more of any type of item that Exchange Web Services supports. In reality though, the arrays for the *AdjacentMeetings* and *ConflictingMeetings* properties will only ever contain *CalendarItemType* objects, and the properties on those objects will be limited to the following set:

- *ItemId*
- *Subject*
- *Start*
- *End*
- *LegacyFreeBusyStatus*
- *Location*

> **Note** The set of properties that is returned on calendar items in the *AdjacentMeetings* and *ConflictingMeetings* array properties is absolute and independent of whatever *BaseShape* element value or *AdditonalProperties* element values are used in the call to the *GetItem* Web method. This is especially important to remember when using the proxy classes, where it is not obvious which properties were present and which were omitted from the *GetItem* Web method response.

Listing 8-6 is an example of calling the *GetItem* Web method adding the *calendar:AdjacentMeetings* and *calendar:ConflictingMeetings* properties to the *AdditonalProperties* element.

LISTING 8-6 *GetItem* request for the information about conflicting and adjacent meetings to a calendar item

```
<GetItem xmlns=".../messages" xmlns:t=".../types">
  <ItemShape>
    <t:BaseShape>IdOnly</t:BaseShape>
    <t:AdditionalProperties>
      <t:FieldURI FieldURI="item:Subject" />
      <t:FieldURI FieldURI="calendar:ConflictingMeetings" />
      <t:FieldURI FieldURI="calendar:AdjacentMeetings" />
    </t:AdditionalProperties>
  </ItemShape>
  <ItemIds>
    <t:ItemId Id="AAAoAGV3c3Vz..." ChangeKey="DwAAABYAAA..."/>
  </ItemIds>
</GetItem>
```

The result, shown in Listing 8-7, is an array of *CalendarItem* instances that are either adjacent or conflicting, respectively.

LISTING 8-7 *GetItem* response message for a request for information about conflicting and adjacent meetings

```
<m:GetItemResponseMessage ResponseClass="Success"
                          xmlns:m=".../messages"
                          xmlns:t=".../types">
  <m:ResponseCode>NoError</m:ResponseCode>
  <m:Items>
    <t:CalendarItem>
      <t:ItemId Id="AAAoAGV3c3VzZX..." ChangeKey="DwAAABYAAA..." />
      <t:Subject>Micheal's demo of server deployments</t:Subject>
      <t:ConflictingMeetings>
        <t:CalendarItem>
          <t:ItemId Id="AAAoAGV3c3VzZ..." ChangeKey="DwAAAB..." />
          <t:Subject>Seminar with Mark on ...</t:Subject>
          <t:Start>2006-11-28T21:30:00Z</t:Start>
          <t:End>2006-11-28T23:00:00Z</t:End>
          <t:LegacyFreeBusyStatus>Busy</t:LegacyFreeBusyStatus>
          <t:Location>Palouse Room 1193/23</t:Location>
        </t:CalendarItem>
      </t:ConflictingMeetings>
      <t:AdjacentMeetings>
        <!-- Array of CalendarItems omitted for simplicity -->
      </t:AdjacentMeetings>
    </t:CalendarItem>
  </m:Items>
</m:GetItemResponseMessage>
```

If you make a request for *AdjacentMeetings* on a calendar item and that calendar item has no adjacent calendar items, then the *AdjacentMeetings* element will not be present in the result. The same is true for *ConflictingMeetings*; if a calendar item has no other items in conflict with it, the *ConflictingMeetings* element will not be returned even if the request specifically asks for it. In the proxy, this means that the *AdjacentMeetings* and *ConflictingMeetings* properties on a *CalendarItemType* instance will be null.

Working with *Date/Time* Strings

When working in the world of Exchange Web Services calendaring, it's important to fully understand how strings representing dates and times are handled. Let's start by looking at the values in the *Start* and *End* properties from Listing 8-3.

```
<t:Start>2006-11-09T05:30:00Z</t:Start>
<t:End>2006-11-09T06:00:00Z</t:End>
```

Start and *End* properties designate the date and time information needed to indicate when the appointment begins and when it ends. This string format is called *xs:dateTime* (or *http:// www.w3.org/2001/XMLSchema:dateTime*). Did you notice the letter 'Z' at the tail end of the strings? This stands for the *Zulu* time zone and is the canonical representation of Coordinated Universal Time (UTC).[8] Essentially, the 'Z' flag indicates that this meeting starts on November 11, 2006, at 5:30 A.M. UTC. Now, you are likely familiar with the notion of time zones and understand that if someone tells you an appointment begins at 5:30 UTC, then you need to account for this in your local time zone. If you live on the East Coast of the United States, then you probably live in the Eastern Time Zone (EST). If you are in the Eastern Time Zone, then for half of the year, your local time zone is said to have a bias of five hours. A bias is used in the following equation to translate between local time and UTC time:[9]

UTC = local time + bias

So a UTC time of 10:30 A.M. minus a bias of five hours is equal to 5:30 A.M. UTC, for one half of the year at least.

10:30 A.M. EST – 5 hours = 5:30 A.M. UTC

Note Many, if not all, recognized time zones in the world have a friendly name associated with them that uses the term GMT, or Greenwich Mean Time. Often, some of these names will include an offset from GMT inside their names (such as "(GMT -08:00) Pacific Time (US & Canada)"). There is a danger in referencing GMT instead of UTC when referring to time zones, and that is the fact that "Greenwich Mean Time" is the name of a time zone that adheres to daylight savings time and therefore changes by one hour twice a year. UTC, on the other hand, is a time zone that does not follow daylight savings time, and therefore serves as an absolute reference point when talking about dates and times. In the interest of keeping things clear, this book will refrain from using the term GMT or making any references to Greenwich Mean Time.

---

[8] Why isn't the acronym CUT? Legend has it one camp wanted CUT, but another camp wanted TUC (from *temps universel coordonné*). UTC was a pleasant compromise.

[9] We discuss the implications of Daylight versus Standard time in Chapter 9.

Understanding *xs:dateTime* and *xs:date*

Exchange Web Services uses the *http://www.w3.org/2001/XMLSchema:dateTime* format (also known as *xs:dateTime*), as described by the W3C in the *"XML Schema Part 2: DataTypes, Second Edition"* recommendation *http://www.w3.org/TR/xmlschema-2/*. According to this recommendation, the format of a *xs:dateTime* string in XML schema is as follows:

'-'? yyyy '-' mm '-' dd 'T' hh ':' mm ':' ss ('.' s+)? (zzzzzz)?

Whereby:[10]

- *'-'? yyyy is a four-or-more digit optionally negative-signed numeral that represents the year; if more than four digits, leading zeros are prohibited, and '0000' is prohibited.*

- *the remaining '-'s are separators between parts of the date portion;*

- *the first mm is a two-digit numeral that represents the month;*

- *dd is a two-digit numeral that represents the day;*

- *'T' is a separator indicating that time-of-day follows;*

- *hh is a two-digit numeral that represents the hour; '24' is permitted if the minutes and seconds represented are zero, and the **dateTime** value so represented is the first instant of the following day (the hour property of a **dateTime** object in the ·value space· cannot have a value greater than 23);*

- *':' is a separator between parts of the time-of-day portion;*

- *the second mm is a two-digit numeral that represents the minute;*

- *ss is a two-integer-digit numeral that represents the whole seconds;*

- *'.' s+ (if present) represents the fractional seconds;*

- *zzzzzz (if present) represents the timezone ([described in a later section...]).*

   For example, 2002-10-10T12:00:00-05:00 (noon on 10 October 2002, Central Daylight Savings Time as well as Eastern Standard Time in the U.S.) is 2002-10-10T17:00:00Z, five hours later than 2002-10-10T12:00:00Z.

This book will use the term *date/time* string to refer to strings that are in the *xs:dateTime* format.

.NET 2.0 Framework/C# developers can take advantage of the *System.Xml.XmlConvert* class to convert a *System.DateTime* object into an *xs:dateTime* formatted string.

---

[10] Taken verbatim from Section 3.2.7.1, "Lexical representation [of dateTime]" source: *"http://www.w3.org/TR/xmlschema-2/"*, August 29, 2007.

```
// Create a DateTime instance representing Now, and get a
// string representation of it valid for xs:dateTime
//
System.DateTime dateTime = System.DateTime.Now;
string xmlDateTime = System.Xml.XmlConvert.ToString(
                    dateTime,
                    System.Xml.XmlDateTimeSerializationMode.RoundtripKind);
```

For more information on the *XmlConvert.ToString* method, including details on the *XmlDateTimeSerializationMode* enumeration, see MSDN: *http://msdn2.microsoft.com/ en-us/library/ms162344.aspx*.

> **Note** If you pass in an invalid string for an *xs:dateTime* property, you will receive an HTTP 500 status code with a SOAP fault message explaining that the request failed schema validation. This will occur in cases where the string is not in the correct format, and also in cases where the string does not represent a valid date, for example, 2006-02-29T06:00:00-08:00 is not a valid date. February 29 is leap-year day and 2006 was not a leap year.

Exchange Web Services also uses the *http://www.w3.org/2001/XMLSchema:date* format (also known as *xs:date*) from the same recommendation that *xs:dateTime* comes from. If you want detail on the *xs:date* format, you can read about it in the Appendix B, "Calendaring Supplementals," on the companion Web page. But simply put, the *xs:date* format is just like the *xs:dateTime* format without the 'Time' portion.

> *Lexical representation of xs:date*
>
> *'-'? yyyy '-' mm '-' dd zzzzzz?*

This book will use the term *date* string when referring to a string that is the *xs:date* format. Some examples of *date* strings are: *02-03-2004Z* and *10-27-2008*.

Understanding Offsets in *Date/Time* Strings

The *xs:dateTime* specification (along with the *xs:date* specification) allows for an optional token, called a 'timezone,' at the end of a string (the token "-07:00" or the special token 'Z' for example). Unfortunately, the idea that these 'timezone' tokens represent an actual time zone is incorrect. The token "-07:00" really just means "seven hours behind UTC;" it has no actual reference to a time zone at all.[11] Therefore, a better term to describe this token is *UTC offset* (or "offset from UTC"). The special 'Z' token at the end of a *date/time* string can also be

---

[11] The designation "-07:00" could represent four different time zones: Pacific Daylight Time, Mountain Standard Time, Arizona Standard Time, or Mexico Standard Time. All four of these time zones have a bias of seven hours at some point during the year.

considered a UTC offset because the 'Z' flag does refer to an offset from UTC. That offset just happens to be zero.

We will refer to tokens on *date* strings as UTC offsets as well, although we won't actually get to talking about properties that use *date* strings until Chapter 9 when we discuss recurrence ranges.

Table 8-3 gives examples of *date/time* strings and *date* strings both with and without UTC offsets.

TABLE 8-3 Strings Representing Times With and Without UTC Offsets

	Without UTC offset	With UTC offset
Date/Time strings	11-15-2007T04:15:00	02-14-2006T08:30:00Z
		04-01-1996T07:45:00-08:00
		12-10-2007T13:45:14+05:30
Date strings	07-02-2015	05-16-1978Z
		06-14-2008+13:00

What is nice about *date/time* strings with UTC offsets is that they are explicit; they identify a specific point in time. Unfortunately, in terms of interpersonal communication, people rarely speak to each other with UTC offsets. Instead, we like to express time by using "local" time statements. For example, you might pass by your co-worker in the hall and ask, "Are you coming to the 3 o'clock meeting?" Both of you inherently understand that 3 o'clock is relative to the time zone that you are in. If you chat with someone long distance, however, or perhaps over the Internet, then you are likely to experience a conversation where the use of local time statements may cause some confusion. The conversation perhaps goes something like this:

"That was a great game—who's up for another round?"

"Not me. I better get to bed."

"What? It's only 10 o'clock. What's wrong with you?"

"Hey, it's 2 A.M. here, I need to go to work in the morning."

The idea of using local time statements as the norm may be a social construct, but it is one that calendaring application developers must deal with. On the one hand, application developers like using strings with UTC offsets because they are explicit, but they also want applications to be user friendly, and users like thinking and communicating in local time statements. Therefore, it's likely you will encounter programming situations where, to avoid inconveniencing users too much, your application must present *date/time* strings to users without UTC offsets.

Note This is the last time you will see the term 'local time' in this book because there is an enumeration in the .NET 2.0 Framework called *DateTimeKind* where one of the values is *Local*. This particular value plays a crucial role in determining how *DateTime* instances are converted to strings during serialization, and as such, we do not want to you to be confused between an enumeration value and the term 'local' time.

So the question naturally arises: How does Exchange Web Services interpret *date/time* strings without UTC offsets? Let's look at that question, and, along the way, talk about some of the best practices that the Exchange Web Services development team recommends regarding the use of UTC offsets.

Exchange Web Services Rules Governing *Date/Time* String Conversion

Important This section is critical to understanding the correct usage of *date/time* strings in your application. It includes best practices that the Exchange Web Services development team highly recommends to ensure that your application uses Exchange Web Services calls with the correct understanding of time zones.

Exchange Web Services stores all date and time values in UTC. Therefore, when it returns any *date/time* strings in calendar items, they will be in UTC, meaning in the XML of the response, all *date/time* strings will contain the Z flag.[12] The fact that Exchange Web Services stores all date and time values in UTC also means that when Exchange Web Services receives a *date/time* string without a UTC offset, it must convert the string to UTC. But what bias should be used? The answer comes from one of two places:

1. If the request contains an explicit time zone definition via a *MeetingTimeZone* element, then all *date/time* strings without UTC offsets are converted using the bias from that definition.

2. If no *MeetingTimeZone* element is included, the bias from the current time zone of the Exchange Client Access Server will be used.

Note As of this writing, the next service pack of Exchange Server 2007 will change the default conversion logic when processing *date/time* strings without UTC offsets. Instead of using the time zone of the Exchange Client Access Server, the UTC time zone will be used.

This means that a *CreateItem* Web method request like this:

---

[12] There are a few exceptions to this rule which are constrained to the *GetUserAvailiability* Web method. We will discuss the *GetUserAvailability* Web method in Chapter 21.

```
<m:CreateItem SendMeetingInvitations="SendToNone"
              xmlns:m=".../messages"
              xmlns:t=".../types">
  <m:Items>
    <t:CalendarItem>
      <t:Subject>My First Meeting using un-timezoned strings</t:Subject>
      <t:Start>2007-01-16T19:00:00</t:Start>
      <t:End>2007-01-16T23:00:00</t:End>
    </t:CalendarItem>
  </m:Items>
</m:CreateItem>
```

would end up with an actual *Start* value based on whatever 19:00:00 was in the time zone of the Exchange Client Access Server itself. Whereas this request:[13]

```
<m:CreateItem SendMeetingInvitations="SendToNone"
              xmlns:m=".../messages"
              xmlns:t=".../types">
  <m:Items>
    <t:CalendarItem>
      <t:Subject>My First Meeting using un-timezoned strings and Meeting Time Zone
      </t:Subject>
      <t:Start>2007-01-16T19:00:00</t:Start>
      <t:End>2007-01-16T23:00:00</t:End>
      <t:MeetingTimeZone>
        <t:BaseOffset>PT8H</t:BaseOffset>
      </t:MeetingTimeZone>
    </t:CalendarItem>
  </m:Items>
</m:CreateItem>
```

will have a start time of 19:00:00-08:00, or 11:00:00Z, specifically.

> **Note** The Exchange Web Services team recommends that all *CalendarItemType* instances using a *MeetingTimeZone* property should be created with *date/time* strings without UTC offsets.
>
> Based on this recommendation, the following is *never* recommended:
>
> ```
> <t:CalendarItem>
>   <t:Start>2007-01-16T19:00:00</t:Start>
>   <t:End>2007-01-16T23:00:00</t:End>
> </t:CalendarItem>
> ```
>
> Instead, the Exchange Web Services team recommends using a *<t:MeetingTimeZone>* element with a base offset:
>
> ```
> <t:CalendarItem>
>   <t:Start>2007-01-16T19:00:00</t:Start>
>   <t:End>2007-01-16T23:00:00</t:End>
>   <t:MeetingTimeZone>
>     <t:BaseOffset>PT8H</t:BaseOffset>
>   </t:MeetingTimeZone>
> </t:CalendarItem>
> ```

---

[13] We will go more into the details of the *MeetingTimeZone* including the format of "PT8H" in a little bit.

There is more to the *MeetingTimeZone* element then just the *BaseOffset* element. Unfortunately, to understand the remaining child elements you need an understanding of relative yearly recurrence patterns. These topics will be covered in Chapter 9.

Working with *DateTime* Structures in the Proxy Classes

> **Note** This section refers to the .NET Framework *DateTimeKind* enumeration, which was a new addition in version 2.0 of the .NET Framework. There is, unfortunately, no equivalent in version 1.0 or 1.1.

Whenever you need to set a property of type *System.DateTime* in the proxy objects, it is important to know how that *DateTime* structure will be serialized into XML for its voyage to Exchange Web Services. The .NET Framework 2.0 *DateTime* class has a *DateTimeKind* enumeration that can be used to define a *DateTime* instance as either *Local*, *UTC*, or *Undefined*. It turns out that this enumeration controls the serialization process and can be used to predict if the seriazlied *date/time* string will contain a UTC offset or not. Table 8-4 shows how *DateTime* instances are serialized.

TABLE 8-4 Mapping .NET *DateTimeKind* to Resulting String Formats

DateTimeKind	Example
Local	04-02-2002T14:31:54+06:00
UTC	01-15-2008T16:01:01Z
Unspecified	11-24-1904T04:15:26

The *DateTime.Kind* property is read-only and, therefore, must be specified during creation via an overloaded constructor.

```
DateTime dateTime = new DateTime(2007, 01, 01, 08, 15, 00, DateTimeKind.Unspecified);
```

Conversion methods on the *DateTime* class allow you to convert to both Local and UTC times (called *ToLocalTime()* and *ToUniversalTime()*, respectively.)

Listing 8-8 demonstrates how the different *DateTimeKind* values can be used to control what XML serialization is going to do. For the example, a series of one-hour duration calendar items is created, and then Listing 8-9 shows what the serialized XML for each of those calendar items would be if the operating system of the machine doing the serialization was set to a time zone with a current bias of eight hours (Pacific Standard Time, for example).

LISTING 8-8 Construction of a *CalendarItemType* using each *DateTimeKind* value

```
/// <summary>
/// Show the result of using various DateTimeKind values
/// </summary>
```

```
public static void FunWithDateTimeKind()
{
  // Create a new DateTime instance, explicitly set it's .Kind value to
  // Unspecified.
  //
  DateTime dateTime = new DateTime(2007, 01, 01, 08, 15, 00,
                                   DateTimeKind.Unspecified);

  // Create a CalendarItem type using the Unspecified DateTime instance to
  // produce an un-timezoned dateTime string.
  //
  CalendarItemType calItemUnspecified = new CalendarItemType();
  calItemUnspecified.Start = dateTime;
  calItemUnspecified.End = calItemUnspecified.Start.AddHours(1);
  calItemUnspecified.StartSpecified = true;
  calItemUnspecified.EndSpecified = true;
  SerializeToConsole("DateTimeKind.Unspecified", calItemUnspecified);

  // Call .ToLocalTime() to produce a timezoned string with an offset matching
  // the time zone of the current operating system. (e.g. PST in this example)
  //
  CalendarItemType calItemLocal = new CalendarItemType();
  calItemLocal.Start = dateTime.ToLocalTime();
  calItemLocal.End = calItemLocal.Start.AddHours(1);
  calItemLocal.StartSpecified = calItemLocal.EndSpecified = true;
  SerializeToConsole("DateTimeKind.Local", calItemLocal);

  // Call .ToUniversalTime() to produce a timezoned string with the canonical
  // 'Z' representation.
  //
  CalendarItemType calItemUTC = new CalendarItemType();
  calItemUTC.Start = dateTime.ToUniversalTime();
  calItemUTC.End = calItemUTC.Start.AddHours(1);
  calItemUTC.StartSpecified = calItemUTC.EndSpecified = true;
  SerializeToConsole("DateTimeKind.UTC", calItemUTC);

}

/// <summary>
/// Serializes the supplied CalendarItemType instance to the Console
/// </summary>
/// <param name="header">Text descriptive header to write out before instance</param>
/// <param name="calendarItem">CalendarItemType to serialize</param>
///
public static void SerializeToConsole(string header, CalendarItemType calendarItem)
{
  XmlSerializer serializer = new XmlSerializer(typeof(CalendarItemType));

  Console.WriteLine(header);
  Console.WriteLine("-------------------------");
  using (Stream outStream = Console.OpenStandardOutput())
  {
    serializer.Serialize(outStream, calendarItem);
  }
  Console.WriteLine();
  Console.WriteLine();
}
```

LISTING 8-9 XML serialized result of each *DateTimeKind* value

```
DateTimeKind.Unspecified
------------------------
<CalendarItemType>
  <Start>2007-01-01T08:15:00</Start>
  <End>2007-01-01T09:15:00</End>
</CalendarItemType>

DateTimeKind.Local
------------------------
<CalendarItemType>
  <Start>2007-01-01T00:15:00-08:00</Start>
  <End>2007-01-01T01:15:00-08:00</End>
</CalendarItemType>

DateTimeKind.UTC
------------------------
<CalendarItemType>
  <Start>2007-01-01T16:15:00Z </Start>
  <End>2007-01-01T17:15:00Z </End>
</CalendarItemType>
```

You can see in Listing 8-9 that XML serialization produced *date/time* strings in three differ-ent *xs:dateTime* formats; however, some implicit conversions also took place. If you convert a *DateTime* instance with a *DateTimeKind* value of *Unspecified* into *Local* time, the .NET Framework treats that *DateTime* instance as if it had a *DateTimeKind* value of *UTC* originally. Similarly, if you convert a *DateTime* instance with a *DateTimeKind* value of *Unspecified* into *UTC* time, the .NET Framework treats that *DateTime* instance as if it had a *DateTimeKind* value of *Local*.

> **More Information** More information on the *System.DateTime* type and its members, as well as additional conversion rules and logic, can be found in the .NET Framework documentation: *http://msdn2.microsoft.com/en-us/library/system.datetime.aspx*.

Working with *Duration* Strings

We have noted that a *MeetingTimeZone* has a property called the *BaseOffset*, the value of which uses a string format that we have not yet explained.

```
<t:MeetingTimeZone>
  <t:BaseOffset>PT8H</t:BaseOffset>
</t:MeetingTimeZone>
```

This string "PT8H" is in a format called *xs:duration*, and you should understand the format of this string before we go into detail about how it is used in the *MeetingTimeZone* element.

Understanding *xs:duration*

Exchange Web Services uses the *http://www.w3.org/2001/XMLSchema:duration* format (also known as *xs:duration*), as described by the W3C in their *"XML Schema Part 2: DataTypes, Second Edition"* recommendation: *http://www.w3.org/TR/xmlschema-2/.*

> *The lexical representation for duration is the [ISO 8601] extended format PnYn MnDTnH nMnS, where nY represents the number of years, nM the number of months, nD the number of days, 'T' is the date/time separator, nH the number of hours, nM the number of minutes and nS the number of seconds. The number of seconds can include decimal digits to arbitrary precision. [...] An optional preceding minus sign ('-') is allowed, to indicate a negative duration.*[14]

The specification format means that the string "PT1H30M" represents a duration of one hour and thirty minutes, whereas the string"-PT20M" represents a duration of negative twenty minutes.

Unlike *xs:dateTime*, there is no .NET Framework type that maps directly to *xs:duration*. Since no direct map exists, you will likely have to write a helper method to convert these strings into an appropriate type (such as a .NET *System.TimeSpan* structure) in your application (see Listing 8-10).

LISTING 8-10 Helper method for converting *System.TimeSpan* into an *xs:duration* formatted string

```
/// <summary>
/// Takes a System.TimeSpan structure and converts it into an xs:duration string as
/// defined by the W3C Recommendation "XML Schema Part 2: Datatypes Second Edition",
/// http://www.w3.org/TR/xmlschema-2/#duration
/// </summary>
/// <param name="timeSpan">TimeSpan structure to convert</param>
/// <returns>xs:duration formatted string</returns>
///
public static string TimeSpanToXSDuration(TimeSpan timeSpan)
{
  // The TimeSpan structure does not have a Year or Month property, therefore we
  // wouldn't be able to return an xs:duration string  containing nY or nM components.
  // This should not be an issue as the xs:duration format places no restriction on
  // the
  // size of the nD component.
  //
  return String.Format("{0}P{1}DT{2}H{3}M{4}S",
      (timeSpan.TotalSeconds < 0) ? "-" : "",  // {0} optional '-' offset
      Math.Abs(timeSpan.Days),
      Math.Abs(timeSpan.Hours),
      Math.Abs(timeSpan.Minutes),
      Math.Abs(timeSpan.Seconds) + "." + Math.Abs(timeSpan.Milliseconds));
}
```

---

[14] Taken verbatim from Section 3.2.6.1, "Lexical representation [of duration]" source: *"http://www.w3.org/TR/xmlschema-2/"*, accessed August 29, 2007.

If you want to create a *TimeSpan* instance that represents a negative duration, the best method is to create a *TimeSpan* instance that represents a positive duration and then subtract the positive instance from an instance that represents a zero-duration.

```
TimeSpan tsPostive = new TimeSpan(5, 20, 34, 53, 83);
TimeSpan tsNegative = (new TimeSpan(0)).Subtract(tsPostive);
```

Getting a *System.TimeSpan* Object from a *Duration* Property

We've demonstrated how to go from a *System.TimeSpan* object to an *xs:duration* string, but not back again. We could show you that now, but a simpler and less error-prone way to get the duration of a calendar item as a *TimeSpan* is to subtract a calendar's *End* value from its *Start* value.

```
// Get a TimeSpan structure of the duration subtracting the calendar
// Start time from the End time.
//
System.TimeSpan duration = calItem.End.Subtract(calItem.Start);
```

Working with *TimeSpan* Structures and the *BaseOffset* Property

Recall that in the *MeetingTimeZone* element there is a child element *BaseOffset*, and that the *BaseOffset* element takes an *xs:duration* formatted string. Recall also that there is no direct .NET Framework type that will serialize into an *xs:duration* formatted string (which was why we had to write a helper method in the"Understanding *xs:duration*" sidebar.)

Recall from the discussion of calendar item properties that the *CalendarItemType* has a *MeetingTimeZone* property that takes an instance of a *TimeZoneType* type.

```
<xs:element name="MeetingTimeZone" type="t:TimeZoneType" minOccurs="0"/>
```

The *TimeZoneType* type has a property called *BaseOffset*, which is of type string. This *BaseOffset* property is the same one that was set when a value on the *BaseOffset* element was set.

Listing 8-11 demonstrates how to create a *TimeZoneType* type and use the *TimeZoneToXSDuration* method (created in Listing 8-10 in the "Understanding *xs:duration*" sidebar) to supply the *BaseOffset* property.

LISTING 8-11 Creating a basic *MeetingTimeZone* type with the proxy classes

```
/// <summary>
/// Creates a calendar item with a meeting time zone
/// </summary>
```

```
/// <returns>New Calendar Item</returns>
///
public static CalendarItemType CreateCalendarItemWithMeetingTimeZone()
{
  // Create a new calendar item
  //
  CalendarItemType newCalendarItem = new CalendarItemType();
  newCalendarItem.MeetingTimeZone = new TimeZoneType();

  // We want to create a MeetingTimeZone for our new calendar item
  // representing a timezone bias of 5 hours, or Eastern Standard Time which
  // is defined as GMT-05:00
  //
  // We will use the TimeSpanToXSDuration method defined in the "Understanding
  // xs:duration sidebar of Chapter 8"
  //
  TimeSpan fiveHourOffset = new TimeSpan(5, 0, 0); // Hours, Minutes, Seconds
  newCalendarItem.MeetingTimeZone.BaseOffset =
              TimeSpanToXSDuration(fiveHourOffset);
  return newCalendarItem;
}
```

Applying Best Practices to New *CalendarItem* Instances with the Proxy Classes

Let's put together all of the knowledge and best practices from this chapter so far and create new calendar items with the proxy classes. Listing 8-12 creates a new appointment for February 26, 2007 at 8 A.M., but in a time zone you may not be familiar with: "Nepal Standard Time," which is defined as UTC+05:45. Listing 8-12 takes advantage of the *TimeSpanToXSDuration* method defined in Listing 8-10. Listing 8-12 also follows the Exchange Web Services team best practice recommendation of using *date/time* strings without UTC offsets when a *MeetingTimeZone* has been provided. The code in Listing 8-12 accomplishes this by using a *DateTimeKind* value of *Unspecified* with all of the *DateTime* instances.

LISTING 8-12 Using a *DateTime* instance with a *DateTimeKind* of *Unspecified* with the proxy classes

```
/// <summary>
/// Create a calendar item in Nepal Standard Time
/// </summary>
/// <param name="binding">Binding to use for call</param>
///
public static void CreateCalendarItemInNepalStandardTime(
                        ExchangeServiceBinding binding)
{
  // Create a new Calendar Item for an appointment to occur on Februrary 26th,
  // 2007 at 8am in Kathmandu, Nepal using DateTime instances with
  // DateTimeKind values of Unspecified, along with a MeetingTimeZone
  //
```

```
CalendarItemType newCalendarItem = new CalendarItemType();
// Create the DateTime instance as Unspecified
//
DateTime startTime = new DateTime(2007, 02, 26, 8, 00, 00,
                DateTimeKind.Unspecified);

newCalendarItem.Start = startTime;
newCalendarItem.End = startTime.AddHours(1);
newCalendarItem.StartSpecified = newCalendarItem.EndSpecified = true;

// Create the MeetingTimeZone with a Time Zone bias of -PT5H45M
//
TimeSpan timeZoneBias = (new TimeSpan(0)).Subtract(new TimeSpan(5, 45, 0));
newCalendarItem.MeetingTimeZone = new TimeZoneType();
newCalendarItem.MeetingTimeZone.BaseOffset =
                TimeSpanToXSDuration(timeZoneBias);
newCalendarItem.Subject = "Feb 26th, 2007 8am meeting in Kathmandu using" +
        "Unspecified DateTime instances (e.g. un-timezoned strings" +
        "w/MeetingTimeZone defining the bias)";

// Format the request and send
//
CreateItemType createItemRequest = new CreateItemType();
createItemRequest.SendMeetingInvitations =
                CalendarItemCreateOrDeleteOperationType.SendToNone;
createItemRequest.SendMeetingInvitationsSpecified = true;
createItemRequest.Items = new NonEmptyArrayOfAllItemsType();
createItemRequest.Items.Items = new CalendarItemType[1];
createItemRequest.Items.Items[0] = newCalendarItem;
//
CreateItemResponseType response = binding.CreateItem(createItemRequest);
ItemInfoResponseMessageType responseMessage = response.ResponseMessages.Items[0] as
        ItemInfoResponseMessageType;
if (responseMessage.ResponseCode != ResponseCodeType.NoError)
{
  throw new Exception("CreateItem failed with response code " +
            responseMessage.ResponseCode.ToString());
}
}
```

Viewing Items on a Calendar

In Chapter 4, "Folders," you learned that each of the specialized folders has a different set of default properties. The *CalendarFolderType* type is used to represent folders that have a *FolderClass* of "IPF.Appointment." The *CalendarFolderType* type derives from the *BaseFolderType* type, which means that it has the properties of *FolderId*, *ParentFolderId*, *FolderClass*, *DisplayName*, *TotalCount*, and *ChildFolderCount*. Each of these properties has been explained before, but there is one property that we will expound on briefly because it segues nicely into a special type that has been created just for calendar folders.

Understanding the *TotalCount* Property on Calendar Folders

As you know, the *TotalCount* property returns the number of items that are contained in a folder, and in this respect, the *TotalCount* property on the *CalendarFolderType* is no different. What is different is that while the *TotalCount* property is counting the number of calendar items in a calendar folder, it is not counting the number of calendar items that are attachments of other calendar items.

At the beginning of this chapter, we briefly introduced recurrences. We said that occurrences and exceptions are not actual items in the mailbox; instead they are items that are stored internally as attachments to a recurring master. This means that occurrences and exceptions are not accounted for in the *TotalCount* property value.[15]

The fact that the *TotalCount* property does not count the number of occurrences or exceptions may not seem like a big deal, but it does highlight that simply thinking of the calendar folder as a bucket of items with start and end times is not the proper perspective. You could, for example, put together a *FindItem* Web method request that places a restriction on the *calendar:Start* and *calendar:End* field URIs, but if you did that, Exchange Web Services would not look through the attachment table of every calendar item looking for exceptions and occurrences. Instead, what you really want to do is something akin to applying a *Dataview* onto a union of two SQL tables, and that is find all calendar items whose *CalendarItemType* is equal to *Single*, *Occurrence*, or *Exception* and whose start and end values are between two *date/time* strings. It turns out there is a special type created to serve that purpose, and it's called the *CalendarViewType* type.

Introducing the *CalendarViewType* Type

Let's begin discussion of the *CalendarViewType* type by looking at its schema as defined in *types.xsd*.

```
<xs:complexType name="CalendarViewType">
  <xs:complexContent>
    <xs:extension base="t:BasePagingType">
      <xs:attribute name="StartDate" type="xs:dateTime" use="required" />
      <xs:attribute name="EndDate" type="xs:dateTime" use="required" />
    </xs:extension>
  </xs:complexContent>
</xs:complexType>
```

As the schema for the *CalendarItemType* type shows, this type derives from the *BasePagingType* schema type and includes two attributes: *StartDate* and *EndDate*, both of

---

[15] It was actually a conscious decision to not have *TotalCount* reflect the number of occurrences and exceptions in the calendar folder. It was for performance reasons, as it does not require EWS to bind to each calendar item looking for attached items to generate the count value.

which are *xs:dateTime*. From the *BasePagingType* schema type, the *CalendarItemType* type inherits one more attribute called *MaxEntriesReturned*.

```
<xs:complexType name="BasePagingType" abstract="true">
  <xs:attribute name="MaxEntriesReturned" type="xs:int" />
</xs:complexType>
```

This allows you to define a window of time, via the *StartDate* and *EndDate* attributes, to apply to a calendar folder to filter in calendar items, including occurrences and exceptions (but not recurring masters, which we will explain in a bit.) You can also control the maximum number of calendar items to filter by setting the *MaxEntriesReturned* value.

But why make the *CalendarViewType* derive from the *BasePagingType* schema type? The reason is ease of use. As you will see in Chapter 14, "Searching the Mailbox," *BasePagingType* instances can be used in *FindItem* Web method calls, and because *CalendarViewType* type is derived from *BasePagingType* type, you can pass it in to the *FindItem* Web method as a paging mechanism.

To demonstrate the use of the *CalendarViewType* type, consider Figure 8-2. In this view, there are seven appointments in this person's work week.

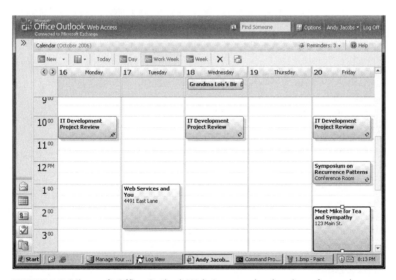

FIGURE 8-2 Microsoft Office Outlook Web Access calendar view of a week

Listing 8-13 demonstrates how to make a request to retrieve all of the occurrences, exceptions, and single calendar items on the work week shown in Figure 8-2 using a *CalendarViewType* instance. Note that the request uses *date/time* strings with UTC offsets, which is recommended when using a calendar view.

LISTING 8-13 Calling the *FindItem* Web method with a *CalendarViewType*

```
<FindItem Traversal="Shallow" xmlns=".../messages" xmlns:t=".../types">
  <ItemShape>
    <t:BaseShape>Default</t:BaseShape>
  </ItemShape>
  <CalendarView StartDate="2006-10-16T08:00:00-07:00"
                EndDate="2006-10-20T18:00:00-07:00" />
  <ParentFolderIds>
    <t:DistinguishedFolderId Id="calendar"/>
  </ParentFolderIds>
</FindItem>
```

Listing 8-13 shows that to use a calendar view, you create the *CalendarView* element, set the *StartDate* and *EndDate* attribute values of the view you want to filter calendar items with, and indicate that you want the view placed on a calendar folder.

A calendar view can be used against any calendar folder, or more specifically, any folder with a *FolderClass* of "IPF.Appointment."[16] Listing 8-14 shows the response with many properties omitted for readability.

LISTING 8-14 *FindItem* response message containing the results of a *CalendarView* paging request

```
<m:FindItemResponse xmlns:m=".../messages" xmlns:t=".../types">
  <m:ResponseMessages>
    <m:FindItemResponseMessage ResponseClass="Success">
      <m:ResponseCode>NoError</m:ResponseCode>
      <m:RootFolder TotalItemsInView="7"
                    IncludesLastItemInRange="true">
        <t:Items>
          <t:CalendarItem>
            <t:ItemId Id="AAAoAGV3c3VzZXIx..." />
            <t:Subject>IT Development Project Review</t:Subject>
            <t:HasAttachments>false</t:HasAttachments>
            <t:Start>2006-10-16T16:00:00Z</t:Start>
            <t:End>2006-10-16T17:00:00Z</t:End>
            <t:LegacyFreeBusyStatus>Busy</t:LegacyFreeBusyStatus>
            <t:Location/>
            <t:CalendarItemType>Occurrence</t:CalendarItemType>
          </t:CalendarItem>
          <t:CalendarItem>
            <t:ItemId Id="AAAoAGV3c3VzZXIx..."/>
            <t:Subject>Web Services and You</t:Subject>
            <t:CalendarItemType>Single</t:CalendarItemType>
            <!-- Start and End Date, and other Properties omitted -->
          </t:CalendarItem>
          <t:CalendarItem>
            <t:ItemId Id="AAAoAGV3c3VzZXI..."/>
```

---

[16] Specifying a non-calendar folder (e.g., one not of type IPF.Appointment) will result in an *ErrorCalendarFolderIsInvalidForCalendarView* response code.

```
                  <t:Subject>Grandma Lois's Birthday</t:Subject>
                  <!-- Additonal Properties snipped -->
                </t:CalendarItem>
                <t:CalendarItem>
                  <t:ItemId Id="AAAoAGV3c3VzZXI..."/>
                  <t:Subject>IT Development Project Review</t:Subject>
                  <t:CalendarItemType>Occurrence</t:CalendarItemType>
                  <!-- Additonal Properties snipped -->
                </t:CalendarItem>
                <t:CalendarItem>
                  <t:ItemId Id="AAAoAGV3c3VzZXIxQGZl... "/>
                  <t:Subject>IT Development Project Review</t:Subject>
                  <t:CalendarItemType>Occurrence</t:CalendarItemType>
                  <!-- Additonal Properties snipped -->
                </t:CalendarItem>
                <t:CalendarItem>
                  <t:ItemId Id="AAAoAGV3c3VzZXIxQGZ..."/>
                  <t:Subject>Symposium on Recurrance Patterns</t:Subject>
                  <!-- Additonal Properties snipped -->
                </t:CalendarItem>
                <t:CalendarItem>
                  <t:ItemId Id="AAAoAGV3c3VzZXIxQ..."/>
                  <t:Subject>Meet Mike for Tea and Sympothy</t:Subject>
                  <!-- Additonal Properties snipped -->
                </t:CalendarItem>
              </t:Items>
            </m:RootFolder>
          </m:FindItemResponseMessage>
        </m:ResponseMessages>
      </m:FindItemResponse>
```

It looks like the calendar view is doing its job. In Figure 8-2 there were seven calendar items present, and in Listing 8-14 we see seven disctinct *CalendarItem* elements. We should call out that the XML for the *FindItem* Web method call in Listing 8-13 uses a *BaseShape* value of *Default*. Even though some of the properties are commented out in Listing 8-14, all of the default properties were returned for each calendar item in the response. Using a calendar view doesn't affect the shape of any of the returned items. Instead, think of a calendar view as the paged view of a calendar, with the ability to move forward and backward through pages by changing the date ranges accordingly.[17]

Note that the date range you specify in a calendar view is inclusive of the *StartDate* specified and exclusive of the *EndDate* specified. This means that a particular item will be returned either if its *End* property value is equal to or after the calendar view's *StartDate* or if its *Start* property value is before, but not equal to, the calendar view's *EndDate*. Table 8-5 demonstrates this concept.

---

[17] You will learn a lot more about indexed paging in Chapter 15, "Advanced Searching."

TABLE 8-5 **Examples of Calendar View Windows and Times That Fall Within**

Given three calendar items with the following *Start* and *End* Times:	
Calendar item A	10:00 A.M.—11:00 A.M.
Calendar item B	11:00 A.M.—12:00 P.M.
Calendar item C	12:00 P.M.—1:00 P.M.
The following views will return these corresponding items:	
View 1: (11:00 A.M. -12:00 P.M.)	A, B
View 2: (11:01 A.M. – 12:00 P.M.)	B
View 2: (11:00 A.M. – 12:01 P.M.)	A, B, C

Using a Calendar View with the Proxy Classes

Creating a calendar view via the proxy classes is simple as well. You need only set the *StartDate* and *EndDate* properties using a .NET *System.DateTime* instance, and optionally set the *MaxChangesReturned* property. However, in an attempt to make the following example useful, Listing 8-15 demonstrates how to create a one-day calendar view for 'today.'

LISTING 8-15 Creating an instance of *CalendarViewType* for viewing 'today's' appointments

```
/// <summary>
/// Create a one day CalendarView starting from 'now'.  'Now' is relative to
/// the current timezone settings of the operating system.
/// </summary>
public static CalendarViewType CreateCalendarViewForToday()
{
    // First create a date time instance which represents "today,
    // 12:00:00am"
    //
    DateTime dtToday12AM =
        new DateTime(DateTime.Now.Year, DateTime.Now.Month,
            DateTime.Now.Day, 0, 0, 0, DateTimeKind.Local);

    CalendarViewType calendarView = new CalendarViewType();
    calendarView.StartDate = dtToday12AM;
    calendarView.EndDate = calendarView.StartDate.AddDays(1);
    calendarView.MaxEntriesReturned = 25;
        // Don't forget to set the specified flag
    calendarView.MaxEntriesReturnedSpecified = true;

    return calendarView;
}
```

Note that the example uses *DateTimeKind.Local*. There are two reasons for this: first, to ensure that the *DateTime* instances are serialized as *date/time* strings with UTC offsets, and second, because the .NET Framework is going to give a UTC offset that is equal to the bias of the time zone of the client machine. This is advantageous because the Exchange Client Access

Server may be in a different time zone then the client, and it is safe to assume that the client would like to view items between 12:00:00 A.M. and 11:59:59 P.M. in the client's time zone.

Ah, but there is a catch here. All those lovely calendar items are going to come back in UTC. Fortunately, you know how to convert between *DateTimeKind.UTC* and *DateTimeKind.Local*, so the rendering viewer (much like the code in Listing 8-16) must convert those times accordingly.[18]

LISTING 8-16 Fetching a *CalendarView* and outputting the result set in local time via the proxy classes

```
/// <summary>
/// This method will walk through the user's (represented by the supplied
/// ExchangeServiceBinding) calendar outputing to the console a rendered
/// view of all appointments found in the supplied CalendarView.
/// </summary>
/// <param name="binding">Fully initialized Exchange Service Binding</param>
/// <param name="calendarView">Calendar view to send as part of the
/// request</param>
public static void RequestAndDisplayCalendarView(
    ExchangeServiceBinding binding,
    CalendarViewType calendarView)
{
    // Prepare the Find Item Request
    //
    FindItemType findItemRequest = new FindItemType();

    // Set the ID(s) of the Find Item Request to be the Distinguished
    // Folder, 'calendar'.
    //
    findItemRequest.ParentFolderIds = new DistinguishedFolderIdType[]
        { new DistinguishedFolderIdType() };
    ((DistinguishedFolderIdType)findItemRequest.ParentFolderIds[0]).Id =
        DistinguishedFolderIdNameType.calendar;
    findItemRequest.Traversal = ItemQueryTraversalType.Shallow;

    // Prepare an Item shape type that defines how the items in view will be
    // returned. This could easily be extended with additional properties to
    // be supplied by the caller
    //
    ItemResponseShapeType itemShapeDefinition = new ItemResponseShapeType();
    itemShapeDefinition.BaseShape = DefaultShapeNamesType.Default;

    // Add our itemShape definition and the caller-supplied calendarView to
    // the FindItem request.  Because CalendarView is a 'paging' type, it is
    // set via the Item property
    //
    findItemRequest.Item = calendarView;
    findItemRequest.ItemShape = itemShapeDefinition;

    // Send the request via the Exchange Service Binding
```

---

[18] As always, your application needs may differ. A Web-based application, for example, may have to prompt the user for a desired time zone view and adjust dates accordingly.

```
FindItemResponseType findItemResponse =
    binding.FindItem(findItemRequest);

// Verify that the FindItem request was successfull
if (findItemResponse.ResponseMessages.Items[0].ResponseClass !=
    ResponseClassType.Success)
{
    // Indicate that we have a problem
    throw new Exception(String.Format(
        "Unable to get calendar view\r\n{0}\r\n{1}",
        findItemResponse.ResponseMessages.Items[0].ResponseCode,
        findItemResponse.ResponseMessages.Items[0].MessageText));
}

// Success, now let's get at the Calendar Items contained in our
// response
//
FindItemResponseMessageType findItemResponseMessage =
    (FindItemResponseMessageType)findItemResponse.
        ResponseMessages.Items[0];
ArrayOfRealItemsType findItemResponseItems =
    (ArrayOfRealItemsType)findItemResponseMessage.RootFolder.Item;

// And print out a nice console-esqe view of our appointments
//
Console.WriteLine(
    "There are {0} appointments between \r\n\t{1} on {2} and\r\n" +
    "\t{3} on {4}\r\n-----------------------------\r\n",
    findItemResponseMessage.RootFolder.TotalItemsInView,
    calendarView.StartDate.ToLongTimeString(),
    calendarView.StartDate.ToLongDateString(),
    calendarView.EndDate.ToLongTimeString(),
    calendarView.EndDate.ToLongDateString());

for (int x = 0;
    x < findItemResponseMessage.RootFolder.TotalItemsInView;
    x++)
{
    // This explicit cast is safe for use because the CalendarView will
    // restrict the result set to CalendarItemTypes only
    //
    CalendarItemType currentCalendarItem =
        (CalendarItemType)findItemResponseItems.Items[x];
    Console.WriteLine(currentCalendarItem.Subject);

    // Exchange stores all calendaring data in UTC time, therefore, out
    // of convenience to the caller, we will convert
    // them to LocalTime before displaying them.
    //
    Console.WriteLine("\tStarts at: {0} on {1}",
        currentCalendarItem.Start.ToLocalTime().ToShortTimeString(),
        currentCalendarItem.Start.ToLocalTime().DayOfWeek);
    Console.WriteLine("\tEnds at:   {0} on {1}",
        currentCalendarItem.End.ToLocalTime().ToShortTimeString(),
```

```
                        currentCalendarItem.End.ToLocalTime().DayOfWeek);
                Console.WriteLine();
        }
    }
```

Let's look at the results from passing in a *StartDate* and *EndDate* matching the calendar display in the chapter's example.

```
Command Prompt
There are 6 appointments between
        12:00:00 AM on Tuesday, November 28, 2006 and
        12:00:00 AM on Wednesday, November 29, 2006


E-Birds Basketball
        Starts at: 5:00 AM on Tuesday
        Ends at:   6:00 AM on Tuesday

Book Review meeting with David
        Starts at: 10:00 AM on Tuesday
        Ends at:   11:00 AM on Tuesday

Lunch with Publisher
        Starts at: 12:00 PM on Tuesday
        Ends at:   1:00 PM on Tuesday

Michael's demo of server deployments
        Starts at: 1:00 PM on Tuesday
        Ends at:   2:30 PM on Tuesday

Seminar with Mark on making contacts
        Starts at: 1:30 PM on Tuesday
        Ends at:   3:00 PM on Tuesday

Huw's dissertation on Complex Search Folder Hierarchies
        Starts at: 2:30 PM on Tuesday
        Ends at:   4:30 PM on Tuesday
```

FIGURE 8-3 Displaying a calendar view result on the console

Note Here is something to keep in mind as an application developer. If users select an occurrence from the rendered calendar view, it is customary to present a dialog box asking them if they want to open the occurrence or the entire recurring series for editing.

CalendarViews and Custom *AppointmentTypes*

Even though Exchange Web Services does not allow you to create non-calendar items in a calendar folder, it will allow you to put a custom *ItemClass* on a calendar item, provided it is just a specialization of "IPM.Appointment" (e.g., "IPM.Appointment.ReallyImportant").[19] A calendar view would then include the specialized calendar item in its result set as well.

Summary

In this chapter, we discussed the nature of calendar items and discussed the various types: single, recurring master, occurrence, and exception. We then took a brief look at all of the properties of calendar items and stopped along the way to discuss several of the more frequently used properties. We discussed how you can get information about conflicting

---

[19] See Chapter 5, "Items," for information on specialized item classes.

and adjacent calendar items. We spent a great deal of time discussing the importance of using *date/time* strings and UTC offsets. We discussed how Exchange Web Services will convert *date/time* strings if it needs to and how you can ensure you are sending the correct strings for *DateTime* instances by using the *DateTimeKind* enumeration. We talked about the importance of setting time zone information correctly and how you should use the *MeetingTimeZone* property and its corresponding *BaseOffset* property to properly assign a time zone to your calendar items. We then ended the chapter by demonstrating the use of a calendar view to get information about calendar items between specified dates.

Chapter 9
Recurring Appointments and Time Zones

Almost everyone has repeating events in their lives that they look forward to: anniversaries, birthdays, or maybe an annual skiing trip to Mt. Whistler in Canada. Unfortunately, almost everyone knows that these fun events too often clash with other, more mundane regular commitments: the daily status meeting with a manager or the weekly crawl through the pile of timecards to complete before 4 P.M. each Friday.

Since single instance appointments are insufficient at representing all of these recurring events in our lives, the Microsoft Exchange Server 2007 Web Services (EWS) team included functionality to make the scheduling of recurring events possible. What you do with those events is up to you, but this chapter is designed to give you all the information you need to create everything from simple yearly recurring series of calendar items, to the biweekly, 'only runs until the last Sunday in June,' recurring series (complete with multiple exceptions of course).

Understanding Recurrences

In the previous chapter, we introduced the concept of a *recurring series*. We said that a recurring series is a sequence of calendar items, known as occurrences, which follow a *recurrence pattern* and are delimited by a *recurrence range*. Every recurring series is anchored by a *recurring master*, which is a calendar item that holds all of the information about the recurrence pattern and range in its *Recurrence* property. We stated that exceptions in a recurring series are calendar items that were once occurrences, but have since been altered in such a way that they no longer adhere to the recurrence pattern. We also stated that all occurrences and exceptions have an *index*, which is a numerical representation of their position in the recurring series.

To illustrate these concepts better, consider Figure 9-1, which is a view of a typical calendar week in Microsoft Outlook Web Access 2007.

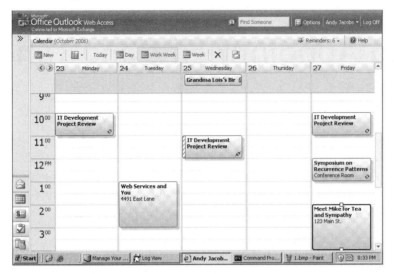

FIGURE 9-1 Calendar display of a fictional work week in Outlook Web Access 2007

Notice the little arrow spinning icons in the lower right corner of Monday's "IT Development Project Review" appointment and on Friday's "IT Development Project Review" and "Symposium on Recurrent Patterns" appointments. This symbol indicates that this calendar item is an occurrence. (See Figure 9-2 for a closer look at the symbol for an occurrence.)

FIGURE 9-2 The icon indicating an occurrence of a recurring series

Notice that the icon for Wednesday's "IT Development Project Review" appointment is slightly different than the others. It is the same icon but with a slash through it. This icon indicates that the calendar item is an exception (see Figure 9-3).

FIGURE 9-3 The icon indicating an exception to a recurring meeting

In Chapter 8, "Working with Calendars" we said that a *FindItem* with a calendar view applied against a calendar folder will return all calendar items that are of type *Single, Occurrence,* and *Exception.* Listing 9-1 shows how you would construct a calendar view for the week in shown in Figure 9-1.

LISTING 9-1 Calling the *FindItem* Web method with a *CalendarView* element

```
<FindItem Traversal="Shallow"
          xmlns=".../messages"
          xmlns:t=".../types">
  <ItemShape>
    <t:BaseShape>IdOnly</t:BaseShape>
    <t:AdditionalProperties>
      <t:FieldURI FieldURI="calendar:Start" />
      <t:FieldURI FieldURI="calendar:CalendarItemType" />
      <t:FieldURI FieldURI="item:Subject" />
    </t:AdditionalProperties>
  </ItemShape>
  <CalendarView StartDate="2006-10-23T00:00:00-07:00"
                EndDate="2006-10-28T00:00:00-07:00"/>
  <ParentFolderIds>
    <t:DistinguishedFolderId Id="calendar"/>
  </ParentFolderIds>
</FindItem>
```

To improve readability, Listing 9-1 requested only the *ItemId, Start, CalendarItemType,* and *Subject* properties be returned for each item. Listing 9-2 shows the *FindItem* Web method response.

LISTING 9-2 *FindItem* response message containing the results of a *CalendarView* paging request

```
<FindItemResponse xmlns:m=".../messages"
                  xmlns:t=".../types"
                  xmlns=".../messages">
  <m:ResponseMessages>
    <m:FindItemResponseMessage ResponseClass="Success">
      <m:ResponseCode>NoError</m:ResponseCode>
      <m:RootFolder TotalItemsInView="7" IncludesLastItemInRange="true">
        <t:Items>
          <t:CalendarItem>
            <t:ItemId Id="AAAeAGRhdnN0..." ChangeKey="AQAAABYAAAD..."/>
            <t:Subject>IT Development Project Review</t:Subject>
            <t:Start>2006-10-23T17:00:00Z</t:Start>
            <t:CalendarItemType>Occurrence</t:CalendarItemType>
          </t:CalendarItem>
          <t:CalendarItem>
            <t:ItemId Id="AAAeAGRhdnN..." ChangeKey="AQAAABYAAAD..."/>
            <t:Subject>Web Services and You</t:Subject>
            <t:Start>2006-10-24T20:00:00Z</t:Start>
            <t:CalendarItemType>Single</t:CalendarItemType>
          </t:CalendarItem>
          <t:CalendarItem>
            <t:ItemId Id="AAAeAGRhdnN0Z..." ChangeKey="AQAAABYA..."/>
            <t:Subject>Grandma Lois's Birthday</t:Subject>
            <t:Start>2006-10-25T07:00:00Z</t:Start>
            <t:CalendarItemType>Single</t:CalendarItemType>
          </t:CalendarItem>
          <t:CalendarItem>
```

```
              <t:ItemId Id="AAAeAGRhdnNOZ..." ChangeKey="AQAAABYAAA..."/>
              <t:Subject>IT Development Project Review</t:Subject>
              <t:Start>2006-10-25T18:00:00Z</t:Start>
              <t:CalendarItemType>Exception</t:CalendarItemType>
            </t:CalendarItem>
            <t:CalendarItem>
              <t:ItemId Id="AAAeAGRhdnN..." ChangeKey="AQAAABY..."/>
              <t:Subject>IT Development Project Review</t:Subject>
              <t:Start>2006-10-27T17:00:00Z</t:Start>
              <t:CalendarItemType>Occurrence</t:CalendarItemType>
            </t:CalendarItem>
            <t:CalendarItem>
              <t:ItemId Id="AAAeAGRhdnN..." ChangeKey="AQAAAB..."/>
              <t:Subject>Symposium on Recurrence Patterns</t:Subject>
              <t:Start>2006-10-27T19:00:00Z</t:Start>
              <t:CalendarItemType>Occurrence</t:CalendarItemType>
            </t:CalendarItem>
            <t:CalendarItem>
              <t:ItemId Id="AAAeAGRhdnN..." ChangeKey="AQAAABY..."/>
              <t:Subject>Meet Mike for Tea and Sympathy</t:Subject>
              <t:Start>2006-10-27T21:00:00Z</t:Start>
              <t:CalendarItemType>Single</t:CalendarItemType>
            </t:CalendarItem>
          </t:Items>
        </m:RootFolder>
      </m:FindItemResponseMessage>
    </m:ResponseMessages>
  </FindItemResponse>
```

The response in Listing 9-2 contains all seven of the calendar items that you saw in Figure 9-1, and each calendar item has a *CalendarItemType* value that agrees with the icon that Outlook Web Access presents for each calendar item in its view.

In Chapter 8, we told you that occurrences and exceptions are stored as attachments on a recurring master. However, as shown in Listing 9-2, Exchange Web Services provides *ItemIds* for occurrences and exceptions. For the most part, Exchange Web Services allows you to treat occurrences and exceptions as any other item. There is one side-effect, however, and that applies to using the *ChangeKey* when performing updates through the *UpdateItem* Web method. This side-effect will be explained later in this chapter.

Mastering the *Occurrence* Relationship

Imagine now, that you would like to find the next occurrence in the "Symposium on Recurrence Patterns" recurring series from Figure 9-1. Accomplishing this task is a three step process:

1. Use the id of an occurrence to look up the corresponding recurring master id for the series.

2. Enumerate through the recurring series to find the index of the current occurrence.

3. Retrieve the next occurrence in the series by requesting the occurrence at the next index.

Getting the Recurring Master of a Series from an Occurrence Id

So how do you find the recurring master of a series when all you have is one or more occurrences? Well, you could try to use the *FindItem* Web method against the calendar folder using restrictions in an attempt to find it, but that solution would be both clumsy (involving string comparisons on the client) and costly (you would potentially have to enumerate through years of items to find the one you are looking for). Rather than perform your own search, Exchange Web Services contains a lookup mechanism for finding the recurring master using the id of any calendar item within the recurring series. This same mechanism can be used to get any occurrence or exception in a recurring series if you have the id of the recurring master and the index of the occurrence or exception that you want. The lookup mechanism between recurring masters and occurrences/exceptions works by using two specific schema types, the *RecurringMasterItemIdType* type and *OccurrenceItemIdType* type.

Look at the schema for the *RecurringMasterItemIdType* type and the *OccurrenceItemIdType* type:

```
<xs:complexType name="RecurringMasterItemIdType">
  <xs:complexContent>
    <xs:extension base="t:BaseItemIdType">
      <xs:attribute name="OccurrenceId"
                    type="t:DerivedItemIdType"
                    use="required" />
      <xs:attribute name="ChangeKey" type="xs:string" use="optional" />
    </xs:extension>
  </xs:complexContent>
</xs:complexType>

<xs:complexType name="OccurrenceItemIdType">
  <xs:complexContent>
    <xs:extension base="t:BaseItemIdType">
      <xs:attribute name="RecurringMasterId"
                    type="t:DerivedItemIdType"
                    use="required" />
      <xs:attribute name="ChangeKey" type="xs:string" use="optional" />
      <xs:attribute name="InstanceIndex" type="xs:int" use="required" />
    </xs:extension>
  </xs:complexContent>
</xs:complexType>
```

Both *RecurringMasterItemIdType* and *OccurrenceItemIdType* extend *BaseItemIdType*, and as such they can be used in any Web method where the *BaseItemIdType* type can be used. For example, there are already a number of ids from the *FindItem* Web method response from Listing 9-2; one of those ids can be used to call *GetItem* using a *RecurringMasterItemId* element instead of an *ItemId* element. To do this, you use the id and change key of any occurrence in the series as the *OccurrenceId* and *ChangeKey* attribute values in the *RecurringMasterItemId* element. Listing 9-3 uses the id and change key from one of the "IT Deployment Project Review" occurrences.

LISTING 9-3   Using the *GetItem* Web method with a *RecurringMasterItemId* element

```
<m:GetItem xmlns:m=".../messages"
           xmlns:t=".../types">
  <m:ItemShape>
    <t:BaseShape>IdOnly</t:BaseShape>
    <t:AdditionalProperties>
      <t:FieldURI FieldURI="calendar:CalendarItemType" />
      <t:FieldURI FieldURI="calendar:Start" />
      <t:FieldURI FieldURI="item:Subject" />
    </t:AdditionalProperties>
  </m:ItemShape>
  <m:ItemIds>
    <t:RecurringMasterItemId OccurrenceId="AAAeAGRhdnNOZX..."
                             ChangeKey="AQAAABYAAAD..."/>
  </m:ItemIds>
</m:GetItem>
```

Listing 9-4 shows the response.

LISTING 9-4   Response to a *GetItem* request with *RecurringMasterItemId*

```
<m:GetItemResponseMessage ResponseClass="Success"
                          xmlns:m=".../messages"
                          xmlns:t=".../types">
  <m:ResponseCode>NoError</m:ResponseCode>
  <m:Items>
    <t:CalendarItem>
      <t:ItemId Id="AAAeAGRhdnNOZ..." ChangeKey="AQAAABYAAAD..."/>
      <t:Subject>IT Development Project Review</t:Subject>
      <t:Start>2006-10-16T16:00:00Z</t:Start>
      <t:CalendarItemType>RecurringMaster</t:CalendarItemType>
    </t:CalendarItem>
  </m:Items>
</m:GetItemResponseMessage>
```

Notice that the calendar item in Listing 9-4 has a subject that matches the subject of the occurrence whose id was passed in and that the calendar item has a *CalendarItemType* value of *RecurringMaster*.

Listing 9-5 demonstrates how to use the proxy classes to find a recurring master for a series using the id of an occurrence.

LISTING 9-5 *GetItem* Web method with the *RecurringMasterItemIdType* type via the proxy classes

```
/// <summary>
/// Get a recurring master for a recurring series from the id
/// of one of the occurrences.
/// </summary>
/// <param name="binding">Binding to use for the web service call</param>
/// <param name="idOfOccurrence">id of an occurence within the series</param>
/// <returns>Id of the recurring master for the series</returns>
///
public static ItemIdType GetRecurringMasterFromOccurrenceId(
    ExchangeServiceBinding binding,
    ItemIdType idOfOccurrence)
{
    // Create the RecurringMasterItemIdType instance that we will pass to GetItem.
    //
    RecurringMasterItemIdType recurringMasterId =
        new RecurringMasterItemIdType();
    recurringMasterId.OccurrenceId = idOfOccurrence.Id;
    recurringMasterId.ChangeKey = idOfOccurrence.ChangeKey;

    GetItemType getItemRequest = new GetItemType();
    getItemRequest.ItemShape = new ItemResponseShapeType();
    getItemRequest.ItemShape.BaseShape = DefaultShapeNamesType.IdOnly;

    getItemRequest.ItemIds = new RecurringMasterItemIdType[] {
        recurringMasterId };

    // Make the call to the GetItem web method, check for success
    // and return the item id accordingly
    //
    GetItemResponseType response = binding.GetItem(getItemRequest);
    ItemInfoResponseMessageType responseMessage =
        response.ResponseMessages.Items[0] as ItemInfoResponseMessageType;

    if (responseMessage.ResponseCode != ResponseCodeType.NoError)
    {
        throw new Exception("GetItem failed with response code " +
                responseMessage.ResponseCode.ToString());
    }

    return responseMessage.Items.Items[0].ItemId;
}
```

So now you have the first piece of the puzzle—the recurring master id. Now you need the second piece—the index of your current occurrence.

Understanding How Occurrences and Exceptions Are Indexed

Before we discuss how you can find an occurrence from a recurring master id, we are going take a moment and talk about how occurrences are indexed in a recurring series.

Each occurrence and exception has an index that represents its location in the recurring series array. The array index starts at one and increases by one for every occurrence in the series. Figure 9-4 provides a pictorial illustration of what a newly created recurrence series might look like.

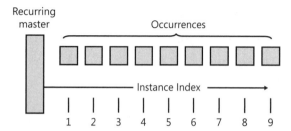

FIGURE 9-4 Newly created recurring series

Any change to an occurrence could cause that occurrence to become an exception. Naturally, changing an occurrence's *Start* or *End* value would be the most obvious reason for the occurrence to become an exception, but even changing a property such as *Location* or *Subject* could cause this transformation as well. In addition to retaining their ids, exceptions also retain their index in the recurring series. This means that the technique used for retrieving an occurrence based on its index will work exactly the same way for an exception.

When an occurrence or an exception is deleted, its position in the recurring series array is still maintained. This means that the indices of all existing occurrences and exceptions are unchanged. If you make a request for a calendar item that has been removed from a series using the *OccurrenceItemIdType* type, Exchange Web Services will respond with a *ErrorCalendarOccurrenceIndexIsOutOfRecurrenceRange* response code.

Finding an Occurrence or Exception by Index

Knowing now about referencing occurrences and exceptions by index, let's continue with step two of our discussion by demonstrating how to use the id of a recurring master and an index to get the id of an occurrence or exception. To get the id of an occurrence or exception, use the *OccurrenceItemId* element instead of the *ItemId* element in your request. Set the *RecurringMasterItemId* and *ChangeKey* attributes to be the id and change key of the recurring master, respectively, and set the value for the *InstanceIndex* attribute to the index of the calendar item that you want to retrieve. Listing 9-6 demonstrates calling the *GetItem* Web method in this way.

LISTING 9-6 *GetItem* with *OccurrenceItemId* element

```
<m:GetItem xmlns:m=".../messages" xmlns:t=".../types">
  <m:ItemShape>
    <t:BaseShape>IdOnly</t:BaseShape>
  </m:ItemShape>
```

```
   <m:ItemIds>
     <t:OccurrenceItemId RecurringMasterId="AAA…" InstanceIndex="1" />
   </m:ItemIds>
 </m:GetItem>
```

In your hunt to find the index of your current occurrence, you can call *GetItem* with a group of *OccurrenceItemId* elements. In that request, use a property path that is unique to each occurrence (such as *calendar:Start*) to serve as a match criteria. Listing 9-7 demonstrates what such a call to the *GetItem* Web method would look like.

LISTING 9-7 *GetItem* with several *OccurrenceItemId* elements

```
<m:GetItem xmlns:m=".../messages" xmlns:t=".../types">
  <m:ItemShape>
    <t:BaseShape>IdOnly</t:BaseShape>
    <t:AdditionalProperties>
      <t:FieldURI FieldURI="calendar:Start" />
    </t:AdditionalProperties>
  </m:ItemShape>
  <m:ItemIds>
    <t:OccurrenceItemId RecurringMasterId="AAA…" InstanceIndex="1" />
    <t:OccurrenceItemId RecurringMasterId="AAA…" InstanceIndex="2" />
    <t:OccurrenceItemId RecurringMasterId="AAA…" InstanceIndex="3" />
  </m:ItemIds>
</m:GetItem>
```

Using this technique, you can put *OccurrenceItemId* elements together in groups of fifteen or so and compare the *Start* value on each one against the *Start* value on the occurrence you have.[1] You can then repeat this until you find a match or until you receive an *ErrorCalendarOccurrenceIndexIsOutOfRecurrenceRange* response code.

We thought it beneficial to provide the code for a method that can find the index of an occurrence using this technique. Therefore, Listing 9-8 not only demonstrates how to use the *OccurrenceItemIdType* type in proxy class code, but also implements the lookup technique for finding an index based on a *Start* property as well.

LISTING 9-8 Find the index of an occurrence using a recurring master id and a *Start* value

```
/// <summary>
/// Get the index of an occurrence by enumerating through a recurring series
/// looking for a matching Start date
/// </summary>
/// <param name="binding">Binding to use for the web service call</param>
/// <param name="idOfRecurringMaster">id of the recurring master</param>
```

---

[1] EWS will maintain order in the response, which means the first item in the response group corresponds to the first *OccurrenceItemId* element in the request.

```
/// <param name="startDate">Date Time value to search with</param>
/// <returns>Index of the occurrence</returns>
///
public static int GetIndexOfOccurrenceFromARecurringSeries(
    ExchangeServiceBinding binding,
    ItemIdType idOfRecurringMaster,
    DateTime startDate)
{
    int currentIndex = 1;
    int idGroupSize = 15;

    // Create a group of OccurrenceItemIdType instances
    // and start enumerating until we find a matching
    // DateTime, or we receive an
    //   ErrorCalendarOccurrenceIndexIsOutOfRecurrenceRange
    // response code.
    //
    OccurrenceItemIdType[] occurrenceItemIds =
        new OccurrenceItemIdType[idGroupSize];

    PathToUnindexedFieldType startDateFieldURI =
        new PathToUnindexedFieldType();
    startDateFieldURI.FieldURI = UnindexedFieldURIType.calendarStart;

    GetItemType getItemRequest = new GetItemType();
    getItemRequest.ItemShape = new ItemResponseShapeType();
    getItemRequest.ItemShape.BaseShape = DefaultShapeNamesType.IdOnly;
    getItemRequest.ItemShape.AdditionalProperties =
        new PathToUnindexedFieldType[] {
            startDateFieldURI };

    while (true)
    {
        for (int x = 0; x < idGroupSize; x++)
        {
            occurrenceItemIds[x] =
                new OccurrenceItemIdType();
            occurrenceItemIds[x].RecurringMasterId = idOfRecurringMaster.Id;
            occurrenceItemIds[x].ChangeKey = idOfRecurringMaster.ChangeKey;
            occurrenceItemIds[x].InstanceIndex = currentIndex++;
        }
        getItemRequest.ItemIds = occurrenceItemIds;

        // Make the call to the GetItem web method, check each response message
        // for success.
        //
        GetItemResponseType response = binding.GetItem(getItemRequest);

        for (int y = 0; y < response.ResponseMessages.Items.Length; y++)
        {
            ResponseMessageType responseMessage =
                response.ResponseMessages.Items[y];
            if (responseMessage.ResponseCode != ResponseCodeType.NoError)
            {
```

```
            throw new Exception(String.Format(
                "GetItem request encountered a failure at InstanceIndex: " +
                "{0}\r\n{1}\r\n{2}",
                    (currentIndex - idGroupSize) + y,
                    responseMessage.ResponseCode,
                    responseMessage.MessageText));
        }

        // Compare the Start value of the item at this index with the
        // value we are looking for
        CalendarItemType occurrenceItem =
            (CalendarItemType)((ItemInfoResponseMessageType)responseMessage)
                .Items.Items[0];

        if (occurrenceItem.Start == startDate)
        {
            return (currentIndex - idGroupSize) + y;
        }
    }
  }
}
```

Note When using a *RecurringMasterItemIdType* instance, you can use the id of an occurrence or exception for the *OccurrenceId* property value. In retrospect, the Exchange Web Services team probably should have called it *OccurrenceOrExceptionIdType*.

Special References to Items in a Recurring Series

To help manage occurrences and to help keep track of exceptions to and deletions from a recurring series, four properties are present on all calendar items. However, these four properties are populated only on a recurring master:

- *FirstOccurrence*

- *LastOccurrence*

- *ModifiedOccurrences*

- *DeletedOccurrences*

FirstOccurrence Property

The *FirstOccurrence* property is an instance of type *OccurrenceInfoType*. The *OccurrenceInfoType* type is designed to hold a subset of properties from an existing calendar item.

```
<xs:complexType name="OccurrenceInfoType">
  <xs:sequence>
    <xs:element name="ItemId" type="t:ItemIdType" />
```

```
        <xs:element name="Start" type="xs:dateTime" />
        <xs:element name="End" type="xs:dateTime" />
        <xs:element name="OriginalStart" type="xs:dateTime" />
    </xs:sequence>
</xs:complexType>
```

The *FirstOccurrence* property on a recurring master will have the same *ItemId, Start, End*, and *OriginalStart* values as the first calendar item in the series.

LastOccurrence Property

The *LastOccurrence* property is also an instance of *OccurrenceInfoType*. The *LastOccurrence* property on a recurring master will have the same *ItemId, Start, End,* and *OriginalStart* values as the last calendar item in the series.

> **Note** The *OccurrenceInfoType* type, like the *OccurrenceItemIdType* type, can refer to either occurrences or exceptions.

ModifiedOccurrences Property

The *ModifiedOccurrences* property is a non-empty array of *OccurrenceInfoType* instances. Just as the *FirstOccurrence* and *LastOccurrence* properties are a subset of properties from existing calendar items, each *OccurrenceInfoType* instance in the *ModifiedOccurrences* array is a subset of properties for all exceptions within the recurring series.

If a recurring series does not contain any exceptions, then the *ModifiedOccurrences* element on the recurring master will be omitted from the XML response, and, if you are working with the proxy, the *ModifiedOccurrences* property will be set to null.

> **Important** Do not assume that the information in the *ModifiedOccurrences* array contains the property that caused a given occurrence to become an exception. Any property change, even one that is not within the subset of properties defined by the *OccurrenceInfoType* type, can cause an occurrence be transformed into an exception.

DeletedOccurrences Property

The *DeletedOccurrences* property is a non-empty array of *DeletedOccurrenceInfoType* instances.

```
<xs:complexType name="DeletedOccurrenceInfoType">
  <xs:sequence>
    <xs:element name="Start" type="xs:dateTime" />
  </xs:sequence>
</xs:complexType>
```

The lone *Start* element holds the *Start* value of a calendar item from the recurring series that has been deleted.

Like the *ModifiedOccurrences* property, if there have been no deleted calendar items from the recurring series, then the *DeletedOccurrences* property will be null.

Example of the Recurring Series Special Reference Properties

Listing 9-9 shows a recurring master that has the *FirstOccurrence*, *LastOccurrence*, *ModifiedOccurences*, and *DeletedOccurrences* elements.

LISTING 9-9 Portion of a *GetItem* Web method response for a recurring master with the *ModifiedOccurrences* and *DeletedOccurrences* properties present

```
<t:CalendarItem xmlns:m=".../messages"
                xmlns:t=".../types">
  <t:Subject>Early Morning Wake-Up Call</t:Subject>
  <t:Recurrence>
    <t:DailyRecurrence>
      <t:Interval>1</t:Interval>
    </t:DailyRecurrence>
    <t:NumberedRecurrence>
      <t:StartDate>2006-12-10Z</t:StartDate>
      <t:NumberOfOccurrences>10</t:NumberOfOccurrences>
    </t:NumberedRecurrence>
  </t:Recurrence>
  <t:FirstOccurrence>
    <t:ItemId Id="AAAoAGV3c3V..." ChangeKey="DKLA..." />
    <t:Start>2006-12-10T13:00:00Z</t:Start>
    <t:End>2006-12-10T13:05:00Z</t:End>
    <t:OriginalStart>2006-12-10T13:00:00Z</t:OriginalStart>
  </t:FirstOccurrence>
  <t:LastOccurrence>
    <t:ItemId Id="AAAoAGV3c3V..." ChangeKey="DKLA..." />
    <t:Start>2006-12-19T13:00:00Z</t:Start>
    <t:End>2006-12-19T13:05:00Z</t:End>
    <t:OriginalStart>2006-12-19T13:00:00Z</t:OriginalStart>
  </t:LastOccurrence>
  <t:ModifiedOccurrences>
    <t:Occurrence>
      <t:ItemId Id="AAAoAGV3c3Vz..." ChangeKey="DKLA..." />
      <t:Start>2006-12-14T12:00:00Z</t:Start>
      <t:End>2006-12-14T12:05:00Z</t:End>
      <t:OriginalStart>2006-12-14T13:00:00Z</t:OriginalStart>
    </t:Occurrence>
    <t:Occurrence>
      <t:ItemId Id="AAAoAGV3c3..." ChangeKey="DKLA..." />
      <t:Start>2006-12-16T15:00:00Z</t:Start>
      <t:End>2006-12-16T15:05:00Z</t:End>
      <t:OriginalStart>2006-12-16T13:00:00Z</t:OriginalStart>
    </t:Occurrence>
  </t:ModifiedOccurrences>
  <t:DeletedOccurrences>
```

```
   <t:DeletedOccurrence>
     <t:Start>2006-12-12T13:00:00Z</t:Start>
   </t:DeletedOccurrence>
   <t:DeletedOccurrence>
     <t:Start>2006-12-17T13:00:00Z</t:Start>
   </t:DeletedOccurrence>
  </t:DeletedOccurrences>
 </t:CalendarItem>
```

Figure 9-5 provides an illustration of how each of the special reference properties map to their respective calendar items.

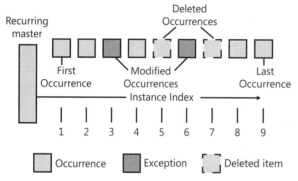

FIGURE 9-5 Illustration of the special reference properties in a recurring series

Creating a Recurring Series

Exchange Web Services gives you a number of types for creating a new recurring series. To create a recurring series, you need to define two pieces of information, the *recurrence pattern* and the *recurrence range*. A recurrence pattern defines the frequency of occurrences within the series. A recurrence range defines the starting date and (optional) ending date of the series.

Before we get into details, let's start with a basic example of a recurring series—a birthday! A birthday follows a recurring pattern—it repeats on the same day of the same month every year. A birthday also has a range—a start date (the year a person was born) and, although depressing to think about, an end date. Allow us to introduce dear Grandma Lois.[2] Grandma Lois was born on a cold wintry night, 70 some years ago. To create a recurring series that represents Grandma Lois' birthday, you call the *CreateItem* Web method to create a new calendar item adding the recurrence information via the *Recurrence* element. See Listing 9-10 for an example.

---

[2] Note: Grandma Lois does not actually exist.

LISTING 9-10 Creating a yearly recurring appointment representing Grandma Lois' birthday

```
<m:CreateItem SendMeetingInvitations="SendToNone"
              xmlns:m=".../messages"
              xmlns:t=".../types">
  <m:Items>
    <t:CalendarItem>
      <t:Subject>Grandma Lois's Birthday</t:Subject>
      <t:IsAllDayEvent>true</t:IsAllDayEvent>
      <t:Recurrence>
        <t:AbsoluteYearlyRecurrence>
          <t:DayOfMonth>15</t:DayOfMonth>
          <t:Month>November</t:Month>
        </t:AbsoluteYearlyRecurrence>
        <t:NoEndRecurrence>
          <t:StartDate>1946-11-15</t:StartDate>
        </t:NoEndRecurrence>
      </t:Recurrence>
      <t:MeetingTimeZone>
        <t:BaseOffset>PT8H</t:BaseOffset>
      </t:MeetingTimeZone>
    </t:CalendarItem>
  </m:Items>
</m:CreateItem>
```

Listing 9-10 uses the *AbsoluteYearlyRecurrence* element to describe the recurrence pattern and the *NoEndRecurrence* element to describe the range. We will describe the child elements of each of these in a moment.

Describing a recurrence pattern and range can essentially be an open-ended task. Instead of providing a syntax that allows unlimited freedom in expressing recurrence information, the Exchange Web Services team instead chose to encapsulate the most common patterns and ranges into distinct types. We will describe each of the different types for defining recurrence patterns and recurrence ranges shortly.

> **Note** Having a finite set of schema types for defining recurrences in Exchange Web Services means that you might not be able to create some of the more exotic patterns that you could with another protocol (e.g., creating a recurring series using an iCal definition over DAV.) Let's say, for example, you wanted to create a recurrence pattern such as "An event that occurs on the 25th of every month, except for those months in which the 25th is a national holiday." In Exchange Web Services, you cannot create a recurring series with these types of exemptions. Instead, you will have to create the series using the supported types, and then perform post-processing on the recurring series to remove any occurrences that you do not want within your series.

Setting the Properties of the *RecurrenceType* Type in Proxy

When creating a recurring series using XML, you create a *Recurrence* element inside a *CalendarItem* element. When using the proxy classes, you set the *Recurrence* property on a *CalendarItemType* instance to a *RecurrenceType* instance. The *RecurrenceType* schema type defines two child elements.

```
<xs:complexType name="RecurrenceType">
  <xs:sequence>
    <xs:group ref="t:RecurrencePatternTypes" />
    <xs:group ref="t:RecurrenceRangeTypes" />
  </xs:sequence>
</xs:complexType>
```

The first element references a group of *RecurrencePatternType* types and the second element references a group of *RecurrenceRangeType* types.

The generated *RecurrenceType* proxy class will have two properties, the first called *Item*, which is of type *RecurrencePatternBaseType*, and the second called *Item1*, which is of type *RecurrenceRangeBaseType*. The fact that the properties are named *Item* and *Item1* can confuse some developers, but if you pay attention to the type of each property, then you can easily determine which one defines the recurrence pattern and which one defines the recurrence range.

```
// The RecurrenceType type has two properties for defining a recurring series:
//  .Item, which defines the recurrence pattern and can be set to an instance of
//         any type deriving from RecurrencePatternBaseType
//  .Item1, which defines the recurrence range and can be set to an instance of
//         any type deriving from RecurrenceRangeBaseType
//
RecurrenceType recurrence = new RecurrenceType();
recurrence.Item = new AbsoluteMonthlyRecurrencePatternType();
recurrence.Item1 = new EndDateRecurrenceRangeType();
```

Understanding Recurrence Patterns

The *BaseRecurrencePatternType* schema type is the base type used for describing a recurrence pattern. In all, there are twelve different schema types that derive from the *BaseRecurrencePatternType* type. However, only six of these types can be used to describe a recurrence pattern for a recurring series, they are:

- *RelativeYearlyRecurrencePatternType*
- *AbsoluteYearlyRecurrencePatternType*
- *RelativeMonthlyRecurrencePatternType*
- *AbsoluteMonthlyRecurrencePatternType*
- *WeeklyRecurrencePatternType*
- *DailyRecurrencePatternType*

These six types can be further grouped into two different groups:

- Fixed Interval Recurrence Pattern Types

- Variable Interval Recurrence Pattern Types

Variable interval recurrence pattern types have an integer *Interval* property that defines the interval between two consecutive occurrences.[3] The type name itself describes how big this interval is; for example, the *Interval* on *AbsoluteMonthlyRecurrenceType* represents the number of months between each occurrence, whereas the *Interval* on *WeeklyRecurrencePatternType* represents the number of weeks between each occurrence. Fixed interval recurrence pattern types still define an interval for a recurrence pattern, but that interval happens to be a fixed value.

Figure 9-6 shows the interval based grouping and the hierarchy of the recurrence pattern types.

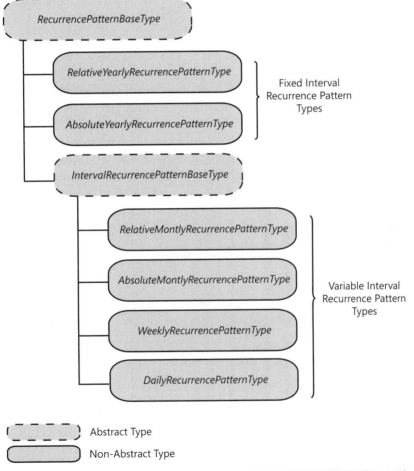

FIGURE 9-6 Grouping and hierarchy of the *RecurrencePatternBaseType* types than can be used to describe a recurrence pattern.

---

3 The *Interval* property is inherited from the *IntervalRecurrencePatternBaseType*.

There is another way of grouping recurrence patterns where one group represents *absolute* recurrence patterns and the other group represents *relative* recurrence patterns. Absolute recurrence patterns are those where each occurrence falls on a specific day of the month such as January 13 or the fifth of each month in a year. In contrast, relative recurrence patterns define their occurrences through an ordinal reference such as the first Tuesday in October or the last Friday of each month in a year. You can tell which group a recurrence pattern type falls into by noting the "Absolute" or "Relative" keyword in the name of the type itself. The two exceptions to this are the *WeeklyRecurrencePatternType* and *DailyRecurrencePatternType* types, in which the recurrence pattern defined by these types does not require an absolute versus relative distinction.

Fixed Interval Recurrence Pattern Types

There are two recurrence pattern types that fall into this group. They are the *AbsoluteYearlyRecurrencePatternType* type and the *RelativeYearlyRecurrencePatternType* type. Each of these types define a recurrence pattern for a calendar item that occurs once every year. Essentially, there is no need to have an *Interval* property on these types because the interval between each occurrence is a fixed value (one year).

Absolute Yearly Recurrence Pattern

Listing 9-10 showed how to create a recurring series for Grandma Lois' birthday. Because her birthday falls on a specific date each year, it is referred to as having an absolute date. Listing 9-11 shows how you can call *CreateItem* with an *AbsoluteYearlyRecurrence* element to indicate that the calendar item occurs on an absolute date, once per year.

 Important In Chapter 8, we told you only enough about the *MeetingTimeZone* property to define a time zone that does not adhere to daylight savings time. We will discuss how to do this later in this chapter. Until then, the examples in this chapter use only time zones that do not have a change in *bias* throughout the year.

LISTING 9-11 Creating a yearly recurring birthday appointment

```
<m:CreateItem SendMeetingInvitations="SendToNone"
              xmlns:m=".../messages"
              xmlns:t=".../types">
  <m:Items>
    <t:CalendarItem>
      <t:Subject>Grandma Lois's Birthday</t:Subject>
      <t:IsAllDayEvent>true</t:IsAllDayEvent>
      <t:Recurrence>
        <t:AbsoluteYearlyRecurrence>
          <t:DayOfMonth>15</t:DayOfMonth>
          <t:Month>November</t:Month>
```

```
        </t:AbsoluteYearlyRecurrence>
        <t:NoEndRecurrence>
          <t:StartDate>1946-11-15</t:StartDate>
        </t:NoEndRecurrence>
      </t:Recurrence>
      <t:MeetingTimeZone>
        <t:BaseOffset>PT7H</t:BaseOffset>
      </t:MeetingTimeZone>
    </t:CalendarItem>
  </m:Items>
</m:CreateItem>
```

As mentioned previously, the recurrence pattern instance encapsulates the definition of the recurrence pattern; your job is to supply the properties. *AbsoluteYearlyRecurrencePatternType* has two properties: *DayOfMonth* and *Month*. You set these two values to be the day and month of any occurrence and let the recurrence range take care of defining the actual year for the first and last occurrences.

Listing 9-12 shows the schema for the *AbsoluteYearlyRecurrencePatternType* type.

LISTING 9-12 Schema definition for *AbosoluteYearlyRecurrencePatternType* type

```
<xs:complexType name="AbsoluteYearlyRecurrencePatternType">
  <xs:complexContent>
    <xs:extension base="t:RecurrencePatternBaseType">
      <xs:sequence>
        <xs:element name="DayOfMonth" type="xs:int" />
        <xs:element name="Month" type="t:MonthNamesType" />
      </xs:sequence>
    </xs:extension>
  </xs:complexContent>
</xs:complexType>
```

The *DayOfMonth* element is an integer with values 1 through 31 being valid. The *Month* element is a string-based enumeration of the standard English month names in the Gregorian calendar as shown in Listing 9-13. If you specify an invalid *DayOfMonth* and *Month* combination, then Exchange Web Services will correct the mismatch by selecting the last available date from the month (for example, the value November 31 will get changed to November 30).

LISTING 9-13 Schema definition listing for *MonthNamesType*

```
<xs:simpleType name="MonthNamesType">
  <xs:restriction base="xs:string">
    <xs:enumeration value="January" />
    <xs:enumeration value="February" />
    <xs:enumeration value="March" />
    <xs:enumeration value="April" />
    <xs:enumeration value="May" />
```

```
        <xs:enumeration value="June" />
        <xs:enumeration value="July" />
        <xs:enumeration value="August" />
        <xs:enumeration value="September" />
        <xs:enumeration value="October" />
        <xs:enumeration value="November" />
        <xs:enumeration value="December" />
    </xs:restriction>
</xs:simpleType>
```

Listing 9-14 shows creation of an *AbsoluteYearlyRecurrencePatternType* instance with the proxy classes.

LISTING 9-14 Creating an *AbsoluteYearlyRecurrencePatternType* instance using the proxy classes

```
// Create a recurrence pattern that represents an annually occurring
// appointment every November 15.
//
AbsoluteYearlyRecurrencePatternType pattern = new
    AbsoluteYearlyRecurrencePatternType();
pattern.Month = MonthNamesType.November;
pattern.DayOfMonth = 15;
```

Relative Yearly Recurrence Pattern

The second kind of yearly recurrence pattern is the relative yearly pattern, and it is defined by using *RelativeYearlyRecurrencePatternType*. The Boston Marathon is an example of a relative yearly recurring event—it occurs annually on the third Monday in April. To create the recurring series for this event, use *RelativeYearlyRecurrencePatternType*, specifying the month, day of the week, and an ordinal reference of the weekday. Listing 9-15 shows an example of creating this type of yearly recurrence pattern.

LISTING 9-15 Use of *RelativeYearlyRecurrencePatternType*

```
<m:CreateItem SendMeetingInvitations="SendToNone"
            xmlns:m=".../messages"
            xmlns:t=".../types">
  <m:Items>
    <t:CalendarItem>
      <t:Subject>See Grandma Lois in the Boston Marathon</t:Subject>
      <t:Start>2007-04-01T06:00:00</t:Start>
      <t:End>2007-04-01T11:00:00</t:End>
      <t:Recurrence>
        <t:RelativeYearlyRecurrence>
          <t:DaysOfWeek>Monday</t:DaysOfWeek>
          <t:DayOfWeekIndex>Third</t:DayOfWeekIndex>
          <t:Month>April</t:Month>
        </t:RelativeYearlyRecurrence>
```

```
          <t:NoEndRecurrence>
            <t:StartDate>2007-04-01</t:StartDate>
          </t:NoEndRecurrence>
        </t:Recurrence>
        <t:MeetingTimeZone>
          <t:BaseOffset>PT7H</t:BaseOffset>
        </t:MeetingTimeZone>
      </t:CalendarItem>
    </m:Items>
  </m:CreateItem>
```

You can see from Listing 9-15 that you set the *Start* and *End* time for the calendar item to be 6 to 11 A.M. on April 1, 2007, and the recurrence range is set to start on April 1, 2007. Despite the reference to April 1 in both places, none of the occurrences will actually occur on April 1 (no fooling!). While the recurrence range says that April 1 is a valid date for the series, the actual dates of the occurrences are dictated by the recurrence pattern you created. Therefore, the first three occurrences of this recurring series would have *Start* values of:

- 6 A.M. on April 16, 2007

- 6 A.M. on April 21, 2008

- 6 A.M. on April 20, 2009

You could have provided March 15, 2007, or even April 30, 2006, as the recurrence range start date and obtained the same results.

The *Start* and *End* properties of the recurring master do not have any effect on the dates of occurrences. The properties are, however, used to determine the start time and duration. For example, if *Start* element in Listing 9-15 was set to "2008-06-28T06:00:00" and the *End* element to "2008-06-29T11:00:00", the result would still be the starting dates you expect as well as the start time of 6 A.M. However, instead of a 5-hour duration, each occurrence would have a 29-hour duration.

Listing 9-16 shows the schema of *RelativeYearlyRecurrencePatternType*.

LISTING 9-16 Schema definition of *RelativeYearlyRecurrencePatternType*

```
<xs:complexType name="RelativeYearlyRecurrencePatternType">
  <xs:complexContent>
    <xs:extension base="t:RecurrencePatternBaseType">
      <xs:sequence>
        <xs:element name="DaysOfWeek" type="t:DayOfWeekType" />
        <xs:element name="DayOfWeekIndex" type="t:DayOfWeekIndexType" />
        <xs:element name="Month" type="t:MonthNamesType" />
      </xs:sequence>
    </xs:extension>
  </xs:complexContent>
</xs:complexType>
```

Similar to the *AbsoluteYearlyRecurrencePatternType*, the *Month* element is a string that maps to the *MonthNamesType* enumeration from Listing 9-13.

The *DaysOfWeek* element is a string that maps to the *DayOfWeekType* enumeration, which is presented in Listing 9-17.

LISTING 9-17 Schema definition of the *DayOfWeekType* enumeration

```
<xs:simpleType name="DayOfWeekType">
  <xs:restriction base="xs:string">
    <xs:enumeration value="Sunday" />
    <xs:enumeration value="Monday" />
    <xs:enumeration value="Tuesday" />
    <xs:enumeration value="Wednesday" />
    <xs:enumeration value="Thursday" />
    <xs:enumeration value="Friday" />
    <xs:enumeration value="Saturday" />
    <xs:enumeration value="Day" />
    <xs:enumeration value="Weekday" />
    <xs:enumeration value="WeekendDay" />
  </xs:restriction>
</xs:simpleType>
```

The *DayOfWeekType* element is the ordinal reference to the day of the month (e.g., first, second, last). It is a string and maps to a value in the *DayOfWeekIndexType* enumeration shown in Listing 9-18.

LISTING 9-18 Schema definition of the *DayOfWeekIndexType* enumeration

```
<xs:simpleType name="DayOfWeekIndexType">
  <xs:restriction base="xs:string">
    <xs:enumeration value="First" />
    <xs:enumeration value="Second" />
    <xs:enumeration value="Third" />
    <xs:enumeration value="Fourth" />
    <xs:enumeration value="Last" />
  </xs:restriction>
</xs:simpleType>
```

Please note that although the element may be named *DaysOfWeek*, it can contain only one day of the week. Trying to include multiple days of the week will result in a schema validation error. For more information, see the sidebar titled "Working with *DaysOfWeek* Properties."

Note Any occurrence in a relative yearly recurring series that falls on February 29 of a non-leap year will instead fall on February 28 of that year.

Listing 9-19 is a proxy class example of creating a *RelativelyYearlyRecurringPatternType* instance for the recurrence pattern in Listing 9-15

LISTING 9-19 Creating a *RelativeYearlyRecurringPatternType* type instance using the proxy classes

```
RelativeYearlyRecurrencePatternType pattern =
    new RelativeYearlyRecurrencePatternType();

pattern.Month = MonthNamesType.April;
pattern.DayOfWeekIndex = DayOfWeekIndexType.Third;

// Although the DaysOfWeek element in the schema is defined
// as being an enumeration, the proxy generator will define
// this property as a string.  To ensure that the correct
// value from the DayOfWeekType enumeration is used, select
// a value from that enumeration and call .ToString() on it.
//
pattern.DaysOfWeek = DayOfWeekType.Monday.ToString();
```

Working with *DaysOfWeek* Properties

Three recurrence pattern schema types specify a string element named *DaysOfWeek*, but use of this element in each type requires special attention.

In *RelativeYearlyRecurrencePatternType* and *RelativeMonthlyRecurrencePatternType*, the *DaysOfWeek* element is meant to take only one *DayOfWeekType* enumeration value. On *WeeklyRecurrencePatternType*, however, the *DaysOfWeek* element can take a space-delimited string of *DayOfWeekType* values.

Table 9-1 describes the three recurrence pattern types that have a *DaysOfWeek* element and gives an explanation of how to properly use each one.

TABLE 9-1 **Mapping of Schema and Proxy Generated Types for Recurrence Patterns That Contain a *DaysOfWeek* Element**

Type Name/Property	Comments
RelativeYearlyRecurrencePatternType	
Schema type	t:DayOfWeekType
XML example	<t:DaysOfWeek>Monday</t:DaysOfWeek>
Proxy type	String
Sample proxy code	DayOfWeekType.Monday.ToString()
RelativeMonthlyRecurrencePatternType	
Schema type	t:DayOfWeekType
XML example	<t:DaysOfWeek>Wednesday</t:DaysOfWeek>
Proxy type	DayOfWeekType
Sample proxy code	DayOfWeekType.Wednesday

Type Name/Property	Comments
WeeklyRecurrencePatternType	
Schema type	t:DaysOfWeekType
XML example	<t:DaysOfWeek>Monday Wednesday Friday</t:DaysOfWeek>
Proxy type	String
Sample proxy code	"Monday Wednesday Friday"

Variable Interval Recurrence Pattern Types

As we mentioned before, all of the variable interval recurrence pattern types require you to define the interval between each occurrence in the series. The size of the interval depends on the recurrence pattern type being used. As such, the interval can represent months (as in every other month), weeks (as in every three weeks), or days (as in every five days).

As Figure 9-6 illustrated, all of the variable interval recurrence pattern types derive from the *IntervalRecurrencePatternBaseType* schema type. It is from this type that all of the recurrence patterns types in this group inherit the *Interval* element.

```
<xs:complexType name="IntervalRecurrencePatternBaseType" abstract="true">
  <xs:complexContent>
    <xs:extension base="t:RecurrencePatternBaseType">
      <xs:sequence>
        <xs:element name="Interval" type="xs:int" />
      </xs:sequence>
    </xs:extension>
  </xs:complexContent>
</xs:complexType>
```

Absolute Monthly Recurrence Pattern

An absolute monthly recurring series is one where the occurrences happen on the same day each month and is represented by *AbsoluteMonthlyRecurrencePatternType*. Listing 9-20 shows the schema for the *AbsoluteMonthlyRecurrencePatternType*.

LISTING 9-20 Schema for *AbsoluteMonthlyRecurrencePatternType*

```
<xs:complexType name="AbsoluteMonthlyRecurrencePatternType">
  <xs:complexContent>
    <xs:extension base="t:IntervalRecurrencePatternBaseType">
      <xs:sequence>
        <xs:element name="DayOfMonth" type="xs:int" />
      </xs:sequence>
    </xs:extension>
  </xs:complexContent>
</xs:complexType>
```

The inherited *Interval* element indicates the interval in months between each occurrence. For example, an *Interval* element value of 1 would yield an appointment occurring twelve times per year, once per month, whereas an *Interval* element value of 3 would produce four occurrences per year, where each occurrence is three months apart.

The *DayOfMonth* element is an integer that represents the day of the month on which each occurrence happens. Values for *DayOfMonth* must be between 0 and 32 or you will receive an *ErrorCalendarOutOfRange* response code. If any occurrences from the series would fall on a date that is not valid for the month (June 31, for example) then the occurrence will be moved to the last available date in that month (June 30).

A good example of an *AbsoluteMonthlyRecurrencePatternType* (albeit a slightly depressing one) is a monthly mortgage payment. Let's say you have a mortgage payment that is due on the fifth of every month and you want to put an item on your calendar to remind you. Listing 9-21 shows how to create a calendar item with such a recurrence pattern.

LISTING 9-21 Creating a calendar item with an *AbsoluteMonthlyRecurrencePatternType* recurrence pattern

```
<m:CreateItem SendMeetingInvitations="SendToNone"
              xmlns:m=".../messages"
              xmlns:t=".../types">
  <m:Items>
    <t:CalendarItem>
      <t:Subject>Monthly Mortgage Payment is due</t:Subject>
      <t:Start>2006-12-01T00:00:00</t:Start>
      <t:End>2006-12-01T00:05:00</t:End>
      <t:Recurrence>
        <t:AbsoluteMonthlyRecurrence>
          <t:Interval>1</t:Interval>
          <t:DayOfMonth>5</t:DayOfMonth>
        </t:AbsoluteMonthlyRecurrence>
        <t:EndDateRecurrence>
          <t:StartDate>2007-01-01</t:StartDate>
          <t:EndDate>2037-01-01</t:EndDate>
        </t:EndDateRecurrence>
      </t:Recurrence>
      <t:MeetingTimeZone>
        <t:BaseOffset>PT7H</t:BaseOffset>
      </t:MeetingTimeZone>
    </t:CalendarItem>
  </m:Items>
</m:CreateItem>
```

You could describe the recurrence pattern in Listing 9-21 as a five-minute appointment that occurs on the fifth of every month at 12:00 A.M., starting on January 1, 2007. To demonstrate the use of the *Interval* property, imagine instead that your mortgage payment was due once every other month. Listing 9-22 demonstrates how you could create a recurring series for such an event.

LISTING 9-22 Using *AbsoluteMonthlyRecurrencePatternType* to create a bi-monthly recurring series

```
<m:CreateItem SendMeetingInvitations="SendToNone"
              xmlns:m=".../messages"
              xmlns:t=".../types">
  <m:Items>
    <t:CalendarItem>
      <t:Subject>Bimonthly Mortgage Payment is due</t:Subject>
      <t:Start>2006-12-01T00:00:00</t:Start>
      <t:End>2006-12-01T00:05:00</t:End>
      <t:Recurrence>
        <t:AbsoluteMonthlyRecurrence>
          <t:Interval>2</t:Interval>
          <t:DayOfMonth>5</t:DayOfMonth>
        </t:AbsoluteMonthlyRecurrence>
        <t:EndDateRecurrence>
          <t:StartDate>2007-01-01</t:StartDate>
          <t:EndDate>2010-01-01</t:EndDate>
        </t:EndDateRecurrence>
      </t:Recurrence>
      <t:MeetingTimeZone>
        <t:BaseOffset>PT7H</t:BaseOffset>
      </t:MeetingTimeZone>
    </t:CalendarItem>
  </m:Items>
</m:CreateItem>
```

Now, how would you describe the recurrence pattern from Listing 9-22? If you're thinking of a five-minute appointment that occurs every two months on the fifth of the month at 12:00 A.M., starting on January 1, 2007, you are correct. Here are the dates and times of the first three instances:

- January 5, 2007, from 12:00 A.M. to 12:05 A.M.

- March 5, 2007, from 12:00 A.M. to 12:05 A.M.

- May 5, 2007, from 12:00 A.M. to 12:05 A.M.

Listing 9-23 creates the same recurring calendar item using the proxy classes.

LISTING 9-23 Creating an *AbsoluteMonthlyRecurringPatternType* instance using the proxy classes

```
// Create an recurrence pattern that represents a bimonthly recurring
// appointment occurring every other month on the fifth of the month.
//
AbsoluteMonthlyRecurrencePatternType pattern = new
    AbsoluteMonthlyRecurrencePatternType();
pattern.DayOfMonth = 5;
pattern.Interval = 2;
```

Relative Monthly Recurrence Pattern

A relative monthly recurring series is one where the occurrences happen on the same ordinal weekday of the month, with a given number of months between each occurrence. Imagine, for example, that you are a member of a book club that decides to meet on the last Wednesday of every month. In that case, you would use *RelativeMonthlyRecurrencePatternType* as shown in Listing 9-24.

LISTING 9-24 Use of *RelativeMonthlyRecurrencePatternType*

```
<m:CreateItem SendMeetingInvitations="SendToNone"
              xmlns:m=".../messages"
              xmlns:t=".../types">
  <m:Items>
    <t:CalendarItem>
      <t:Subject>Book Club at our house</t:Subject>
      <t:Start>2006-12-01T00:00:00</t:Start>
      <t:End>2006-12-01T00:05:00</t:End>
      <t:Recurrence>
        <t:RelativeMonthlyRecurrence>
          <t:Interval>1</t:Interval>
          <t:DaysOfWeek>Wednesday</t:DaysOfWeek>
          <t:DayOfWeekIndex>Last</t:DayOfWeekIndex>
        </t:RelativeMonthlyRecurrence>
        <t:EndDateRecurrence>
          <t:StartDate>2007-01-01</t:StartDate>
          <t:EndDate>2010-01-01</t:EndDate>
        </t:EndDateRecurrence>
      </t:Recurrence>
      <t:MeetingTimeZone>
        <t:BaseOffset>PT7H</t:BaseOffset>
      </t:MeetingTimeZone>
    </t:CalendarItem>
  </m:Items>
</m:CreateItem>
```

Similar to *AbsoluteMonthlyRecurrencePatternType*, the *Interval* element on *RelativeMonthlyRecurrencePatternType* specifies the number of months between each occurrence. The *DaysOfWeek* element takes an English language string for a single day of the week and a *DayOfWeekIndex* string that maps to one of the values in the *DayOfWeekIndexType* enumeration. The schema for *RelativeMonthlyRecurrencePatternType* is in Listing 9-25.

LISTING 9-25 Schema for *RelativeMontlyRecurrencePatternType*

```
<xs:complexType name="RelativeMonthlyRecurrencePatternType">
  <xs:complexContent>
    <xs:extension base="t:IntervalRecurrencePatternBaseType">
      <xs:sequence>
        <xs:element name="DaysOfWeek" type="t:DayOfWeekType" />
        <xs:element name="DayOfWeekIndex" type="t:DayOfWeekIndexType" />
```

```
      </xs:sequence>
    </xs:extension>
  </xs:complexContent>
</xs:complexType>
```

The proxy class example is also similar to the *RelativeYearlyRecurrencePatternType*, with two exceptions. The first exception is that the *Interval* property is present on *RelativeMonthlyRecurrencePatternType* while no such property exists on *RelativeYearlyRecurrencePatternType*. The second exception is that the proxy classes expose the *DaysOfWeek* property as a *DayOfWeekType* as opposed to a string. An example of using the proxy class with the *RelativeYearlyRecurrencePatterType* is shown in Listing 9-26.

LISTING 9-26 Creating a *RelativeMonthlyRecurrencePatternType* type instance using the proxy classes

```
// Create a recurrence pattern that represents a monthly appointment
// occurring on the last Wednesday of each month.
//
RelativeMonthlyRecurrencePatternType pattern = new
    RelativeMonthlyRecurrencePatternType();
pattern.DaysOfWeek = DayOfWeekType.Wednesday;
pattern.DayOfWeekIndex = DayOfWeekIndexType.Last;
pattern.Interval = 1;
```

Weekly Recurrence Pattern

A workweek often contains meetings that recur daily, weekly, or even biweekly. You can use *WeeklyRecurrencePatternType* to create each of these types of series. For example, Listing 9-27 is an example of calling the *CreateItem* Web method to create a weekly recurring series that occurs every Monday.

LISTING 9-27 Use of *WeeklyRecurrencePatternType* type

```
<m:CreateItem SendMeetingInvitations="SendToNone"
              xmlns:m=".../messages"
              xmlns:t=".../types">
  <m:Items>
    <t:CalendarItem>
      <t:Subject>Monday's Morning Meeting</t:Subject>
      <t:Start>2007-05-01T08:00:00</t:Start>
      <t:End>2007-05-01T09:00:00</t:End>
      <t:Recurrence>
        <t:WeeklyRecurrence>
          <t:Interval>1</t:Interval>
          <t:DaysOfWeek>Monday</t:DaysOfWeek>
        </t:WeeklyRecurrence>
        <t:EndDateRecurrence>
          <t:StartDate>2007-05-01</t:StartDate>
          <t:EndDate>2008-04-30</t:EndDate>
```

```
          </t:EndDateRecurrence>
        </t:Recurrence>
        <t:MeetingTimeZone>
          <t:BaseOffset>PT7H</t:BaseOffset>
        </t:MeetingTimeZone>
      </t:CalendarItem>
    </m:Items>
  </m:CreateItem>
```

The weekly recurrence pattern is the most commonly used of all recurrence patterns and can also be used to create the broadest range of recurrence patterns. This is because the *DaysOfWeek* element on the *WeeklyRecurrencePatternType* type can accept a list of days via a space-delimited string rather than just a single day value. This was described in the sidebar titled "Working With *DaysOfWeek* Properties." Listing 9-28 shows the schema for *WeeklyRecurrencePatternType*.

LISTING 9-28 Schema for *WeeklyRecurrencePatternType*

```
<xs:complexType name="WeeklyRecurrencePatternType">
  <xs:complexContent>
    <xs:extension base="t:IntervalRecurrencePatternBaseType">
      <xs:sequence>
        <xs:element name="DaysOfWeek" type="t:DaysOfWeekType"/>
      </xs:sequence>
    </xs:extension>
  </xs:complexContent>
</xs:complexType>
```

For *WeeklyRecurrencePatternType*, the inherited *Interval* element represents the number of weeks between each occurrence, with a value of 1 indicating that occurrences should occur every week.

Before we present an example of creating an instance of *WeeklyRecurrencePatternType* using the proxy classes, let's consider another example of a weekly recurring pattern that is a little more exotic. Imagine that you are in college, and there is a night class that will meet eight times, starting in March, 2007. It is scheduled for Thursday and Friday nights, every other week.

So, the first class is on Thursday, March 1, 2007. The second class is on Friday, March 2, 2007. The third class is on Wednesday, March 14, 2007, and so on. Listing 9-29 is an example of calling the *CreateItem* Web method to create this recurring series. In the example, the *DaysOfWeek* element is set to "Thursday Friday" and the *Interval* is set to 2, meaning every other week.[4]

---

[4] Order is insignificant and duplicates are ignored. Because you have values from an enumeration, however, casing is important.

LISTING 9-29 Using *WeeklyRecurrencePatternType*

```xml
<m:CreateItem SendMeetingInvitations="SendToNone"
               xmlns:m=".../messages"
               xmlns:t=".../types">
  <m:Items>
    <t:CalendarItem>
      <t:Subject>Film Studies class led my Mr. Mainer</t:Subject>
      <t:Start>2007-03-01T19:00:00</t:Start>
      <t:End>2007-03-01T23:00:00</t:End>
      <t:Recurrence>
        <t:WeeklyRecurrence>
          <t:Interval>2</t:Interval>
          <t:DaysOfWeek>Thursday Friday</t:DaysOfWeek>
        </t:WeeklyRecurrence>
        <t:NumberedRecurrence>
          <t:StartDate>2007-03-01</t:StartDate>
          <t:NumberOfOccurrences>8</t:NumberOfOccurrences>
        </t:NumberedRecurrence>
      </t:Recurrence>
      <t:MeetingTimeZone>
        <t:BaseOffset>PT7H</t:BaseOffset>
      </t:MeetingTimeZone>
    </t:CalendarItem>
  </m:Items>
</m:CreateItem>
```

Figure 9-7 illustrates how Outlook Web Access will display the description of the recurring series that was created in Listing 9-29.

FIGURE 9-7 Outlook Web Access description of a semi-monthly, twice per week recurring appointment

Listing 9-30 shows how to create the recurrence pattern for the series from Listing 9-29 using the proxy classes.

LISTING 9-30 Using *WeeklyRecurrencePatternType* via the proxy classes

```csharp
// Create a recurrence pattern that represents a semi-monthly, twice
// a week appointment occurring on Thursday and Friday
//
WeeklyRecurrencePatternType pattern = new WeeklyRecurrencePatternType();
pattern.DaysOfWeek = DayOfWeek.Thursday.ToString() + " " +
    DayOfWeek.Friday.ToString();
pattern.Interval = 2;
```

If you are likely to use the *WeeklyRecurrencePatternType* proxy class frequently, you will want to create an overloaded constructor for the *WeeklyRecurrencePatternType* type that can take an array of *DayOfWeek* enumeration values and parse them accordingly. An example of such an overloaded constructor is shown in Listing 9-29.

LISTING 9-31 Partial class extension of the *WeeklyRecurrencePatternType*

```
/// <summary>
/// Partial class extension of the WeeklyRecurrencePatternType
/// </summary>
public partial class WeeklyRecurrencePatternType
{
    /// <summary>
    /// Default constructor (needed for XML serialization).
    /// </summary>
    public WeeklyRecurrencePatternType() { }

    /// <summary>
    /// Convenience constructor.
    /// </summary>
    /// <param name="interval"> Frequency of the weekly recurring
    /// pattern</param>
    /// <param name="oneOrMoreDaysOfTheWeek"> Group of DayOfWeek values</param>
    ///
    public WeeklyRecurrencePatternType(
        int interval,
        params DayOfWeek[] oneOrMoreDaysOfTheWeek)
    {
        foreach (DayOfWeek dayOfWeek in oneOrMoreDaysOfTheWeek)
        {
            this.DaysOfWeek = this.DaysOfWeek + dayOfWeek.ToString() + " ";
        }
        this.Interval = interval;
    }
}
```

Daily Recurrence Pattern

> **Important** As of this writing, Exchange Web Services has a significant issue that affects the creation of daily recurrence patterns. The issue can cause the start date of the recurrence range to be converted incorrectly, resulting in too many or too few occurrences.[5] Currently, no workaround is available. However, the issue is scheduled to be fixed in the next Service Pack of Exchange Server 2007.

---

[5] We will discuss details of this issue following our discussion of *DailyRecurrencePatternType* in the sidebar titled "Understanding the Issues with Creating Daily Recurrence Patterns."

A daily recurrence pattern is one that repeats a certain number of days. As an example, imagine you would like to get your hands on the newest game for your XBOX 360. The kind-hearted people at your favorite game store, however, refuse to accept pre-orders, and because the new game is so popular, every time they get a shipment, they sell copies in the store only on a first come, first served basis. To make sure that you get up each day in time to be at the front of the line, you decide to create a series of daily recurring calendar items. To create the pattern for this recurring series, you use *DailyRecurrencePatternType*. Listing 9-32 has an example of calling the *CreateItem* Web method to create a daily recurring series.

LISTING 9-32 Use of the *DailyRecurrencePatternType* type

```
<m:CreateItem SendMeetingInvitations="SendToNone"
              xmlns:m=".../messages"
              xmlns:t=".../types">
  <m:Items>
    <t:CalendarItem>
      <t:Subject>Early Morning Wake-Up Call</t:Subject>
      <t:Start>2006-12-10T05:00:00</t:Start>
      <t:End>2006-12-10T05:05:00</t:End>
      <t:Recurrence>
        <t:DailyRecurrence>
          <t:Interval>1</t:Interval>
        </t:DailyRecurrence>
        <t:NumberedRecurrence>
          <t:StartDate>2006-12-10</t:StartDate>
          <t:NumberOfOccurrences>10</t:NumberOfOccurrences>
        </t:NumberedRecurrence>
      </t:Recurrence>
      <t:MeetingTimeZone>
        <t:BaseOffset>PT7H</t:BaseOffset>
      </t:MeetingTimeZone>
    </t:CalendarItem>
  </m:Items>
</m:CreateItem>
```

DailyRecurrencePatternType contains only one child, the *Interval* element, which defines the number of days between each occurrence of the recurring series. Listing 9-33 shows the schema for the *DailyRecurrencePatternType* type.

LISTING 9-33 Schema for the *DailyRecurrencePatternType* type

```
<xs:complexType name="DailyRecurrencePatternType">
  <xs:complexContent>
    <xs:extension base="t:IntervalRecurrencePatternBaseType" />
  </xs:complexContent>
</xs:complexType>
```

Listing 9-34 shows how you would create an instance of *DailyRecurrencePatternType* using the proxy classes.

LISTING 9-34 Creating an instance of *DailyRecurrencePatternType* using the proxy classes

```
// Create a recurrence pattern representing a daily appointment
//
DailyRecurrencePatternType pattern = new DailyRecurrencePatternType();
pattern.Interval = 1;
```

Understanding the Issues with Creating Daily Recurrence Patterns

We mentioned earlier that there is an issue with creating daily recurrence patterns in Exchange Web Services. Imagine you are trying to create a daily recurring series using *DailyRecurrencePatternType*. You set the *Interval* to 1 and define a recurrence range that spans five days (for example, January 10 through January 14). Such a request might look like Listing 9-35.

LISTING 9-35 Creating a recurring series with a daily recurrence pattern and an end date defined recurrence range

```
<m:CreateItem SendMeetingInvitations="SendToNone"
              xmlns:m=".../messages"
              xmlns:t=".../types">
  <m:Items>
    <t:CalendarItem>
      <t:Subject>Should result in five instances</t:Subject>
      <t:Start>2007-01-10T09:00:00</t:Start>
      <t:End>2007-01-10T11:00:00</t:End>
      <t:Recurrence>
        <t:DailyRecurrence>
          <t:Interval>1</t:Interval>
        </t:DailyRecurrence>
        <t:EndDateRecurrence>
          <t:StartDate>2007-01-10</t:StartDate>
          <t:EndDate>2007-01-14</t:EndDate>
        </t:EndDateRecurrence>
      </t:Recurrence>
      <!-- MeetingTimeZone element omitted on purpose. -->
    </t:CalendarItem>
  </m:Items>
</m:CreateItem>
```

Notice that in Listing 9-35, the *MeetingTimeZone* element is omitted. This is because the issue with daily recurrence patterns has to do with the time zone that gets applied to the recurring series.[6] If the series is created with a time zone that is "behind" UTC (such as Pacific Standard Time), then the recurring series would contain only *four* occurrences instead of the expected five, as shown in Listing 9-36.

LISTING 9-36 Enumeration of all occurrences from Listing 9-35 if created using Pacific Standard Time

```
<t:Start>2007-01-10T17:00:00Z</t:Start>
<t:Start>2007-01-11T17:00:00Z</t:Start>
<t:Start>2007-01-12T17:00:00Z</t:Start>
<t:Start>2007-01-13T17:00:00Z</t:Start>
```

However, if a time zone that is "ahead" of UTC (such as India Standard Time) is used instead, then the results are correct, as shown in Listing 9-37.

LISTING 9-37 Enumeration of all occurrences from Listing 9-35 if created using India Standard Time

```
<t:Start>2007-01-10T03:30:00Z</t:Start>
<t:Start>2007-01-11T03:30:00Z</t:Start>
<t:Start>2007-01-12T03:30:00Z</t:Start>
<t:Start>2007-01-13T03:30:00Z</t:Start>
<t:Start>2007-01-14T03:30:00Z</t:Start>
```

So what is happening here? Exchange Web Services is incorrectly assuming that the recurrence range *Start* time is in UTC, but the recurrence range *End* time is in the time zone set on the new recurring master.

Though it might be possible to work around this problem, we would discourage you from doing so. A fix in Exchange Web Services for this issue will likely involve Exchange Web Services correctly treating the *Start* time as being in the time zone of the recurring master. Therefore, if you attempt to work around this issue by offsetting the *StartDate* in your requests, you will end up having to remove this offsetting behavior when this issue is fixed in Exchange Web Services, possibly in the next service pack of Exchange Server 2007. As such, if you must create any daily recurring series prior to the release of Exchange Server 2007 Service Pack 1, then we recommend you do so *without* using *DailyRecurrencePatternType*; instead, create them as a group of single instanced calendar items.

---

[6] Recall from Chapter 8 that in the absence of a time zone defined in a *MeetingTimeZone* property, the time zone of the Exchange Client Access Server processing the *CreateItem* Web method is set on the item.

Summarizing the Use of the *Interval* Property

Now that we've covered all of the different recurrence pattern types, you know that for all of the variable interval recurrence pattern types, the *Interval* property can have different interpretations based on the recurrence pattern in question. Table 9-2 should provide a helpful reminder the next time you are left wondering exactly what that *Interval* property is used for.

TABLE 9-2 Significance of the *Interval* Property on Each Variable Interval Recurrence Pattern Type

Schema Type	Significance of the *Interval* Property
AbsoluteMonthlyRecurrencePatternType	Number of months between occurrences
RelativeMonthlyRecurrencePatternType	Number of months between occurrences
WeeklyRecurrencePatternType	Number of weeks between occurrences
DailyRecurrencePatternType	Number of days between occurrences

Understanding Recurrence Ranges

A recurrence range describes the first valid start date of any occurrence and then optionally defines an end date or a set number of occurrences for the series. There are three schema types that can be used to define a recurrence range:

- *NoEndRecurrenceRangeType*
- *EndDateRecurrenceRangeType*
- *NumberedRecurrenceRangeType*

These types all inherit from the abstract *RecurrenceRangeBaseType*, which holds one child element, *StartDate,* which is an *xs:date*. *EndDateRecurrenceRangeType* adds one additional child element, *EndDate*, which is also an *xs:date*, while *NumberedRecurrenceRangeType* adds a different child element, *NumberOfOccurrences*, which is an integer. Listing 9-38 shows the schema for all of the recurrence range types.

LISTING 9-38 Schema for all of the recurrence range types

```
<!-- Schema for the RecurrenceRangeBaseType type -->
 <xs:complexType name="RecurrenceRangeBaseType" abstract="true">
    <xs:sequence>
      <xs:element name="StartDate" type="xs:date" />
    </xs:sequence>
  </xs:complexType>

 <!-- Schema for the NoEndRecurrenceRangeType -->
   <xs:complexType name="NoEndRecurrenceRangeType">
     <xs:complexContent>
       <xs:extension base="t:RecurrenceRangeBaseType" />
     </xs:complexContent>
   </xs:complexType>
```

```
<xs:complexType name="EndDateRecurrenceRangeType">
  <xs:complexContent>
    <xs:extension base="t:RecurrenceRangeBaseType">
      <xs:sequence>
        <xs:element name="EndDate" type="xs:date" />
      </xs:sequence>
    </xs:extension>
  </xs:complexContent>
</xs:complexType>

<xs:complexType name="NumberedRecurrenceRangeType">
  <xs:complexContent>
    <xs:extension base="t:RecurrenceRangeBaseType">
      <xs:sequence>
        <xs:element name="NumberOfOccurrences" type="xs:int" />
      </xs:sequence>
    </xs:extension>
  </xs:complexContent>
</xs:complexType>
```

To create a recurrence range, you first select your range type depending on whether you need to specify an end date (*EndDateRecurrenceRangeType*), a set number of occurrences (*NumberedRecurrenceRangeType*), or neither (*NoEndRecurrenceRangeType*, implying that your recurrence range has no foreseeable ending date.) Then, specify your start date using the *StartDate* element and set the other element that corresponds with your selection, either your *EndDate* element, *NumberOfOccurrences* element, or neither.

Listing 9-39 shows an XML example of each type of recurrence date range. Listing 9-40 shows those same recurrence ranges using the proxy classes.

LISTING 9-39 Examples of each recurrence range type in XML

```
<!-- Create a recurrence date range that starts on April 1, 2007 and has no end -->

<t:NoEndRecurrence>
  <t:StartDate>2007-04-01</t:StartDate>
</t:NoEndRecurrence>


<!-- Create a recurrence date range that starts on April 1, 2007 and ends on
  April 1, 2008 -->

<t:EndDateRecurrence>
  <t:StartDate>2007-04-01</t:StartDate>
  <t:EndDate>2008-04-01</t:EndDate>
</t:EndDateRecurrence>



<!-- Create a recurrence date range that starts on April 1, 2007 and ends after 12
occurrences -->
```

```
<t:NumberedRecurrence>
  <t:StartDate>2007-04-01</t:StartDate>
  <t:NumberOfOccurrences>12</t:NumberOfOccurrences>
</t:NumberedRecurrence>
```

LISTING 9-40 Examples of an instance of each recurrence range type using the proxy classes

```
// Create three instances of the different recurrence range types, each with a
// starting date of April 1, 2007
//
DateTime april1_07 = new DateTime(
    2007, 04, 01, 00, 00, 00, DateTimeKind.Unspecified);

// Create a recurrence range with no specified end date
//
NoEndRecurrenceRangeType noEndRange = new NoEndRecurrenceRangeType();
noEndRange.StartDate = april1_07;

// Create a recurrence range with an end date one year later then the start date.
//
EndDateRecurrenceRangeType endDateRange = new EndDateRecurrenceRangeType();
endDateRange.StartDate = april1_07;
endDateRange.EndDate = april1_07.AddDays(365);

// Create a recurrence range with a fixed number of occurrences
//
NumberedRecurrenceRangeType numberedRange = new NumberedRecurrenceRangeType();
numberedRange.StartDate = april1_07;
numberedRange.NumberOfOccurrences = 12;
```

Notes on Recurrence Ranges

Important A recurrence range controls only the dates of generated occurrences, not the times. Thus, though the date portions of the *Start* and *End* properties of each calculated occurrence will be different, the times of those properties will be the same as those of the recurring master.

To understand this concept, consider the following recurring series: *"Each calendar item starts at 8 A.M. and lasts until 9 A.M. on the first Thursday of every August in 2007."* Listing 9-41 demonstrates what a *CreateItem* call to create this recurring series would look like.

LISTING 9-41 Creating a recurring series with *Start* and *End* dates outside of the recurrence range

```
<m:CreateItem SendMeetingInvitations="SendToNone"
              xmlns:m=".../messages"
              xmlns:t=".../types">
  <m:Items>
    <t:CalendarItem>
```

```
    <t:Subject>
        From 8am to 9am on the first Thursday of every August
    </t:Subject>
    <t:Start>2007-01-01T08:00:00</t:Start>
    <t:End>2007-01-01T09:00:00</t:End>
    <t:Recurrence>
      <t:RelativeYearlyRecurrence>
        <t:DaysOfWeek>Thursday</t:DaysOfWeek>
        <t:DayOfWeekIndex>First</t:DayOfWeekIndex>
        <t:Month>August</t:Month>
      </t:RelativeYearlyRecurrence>
      <t:NoEndRecurrence>
        <t:StartDate>2007-01-01</t:StartDate>
      </t:NoEndRecurrence>
    </t:Recurrence>
   </t:CalendarItem>
  </m:Items>
</m:CreateItem>
```

Notice that the dates of the *Start*, *End*, and *StartDate* elements are not even in the month of August. This is because the recurrence pattern says that instances can occur only on the first Thursday in August and that none of them should be before January 1, 2007. When occurrences are generated, the date portions of the *Start* and *End* values are dropped and only the times are used. Then the date for each occurrence is calculated based on the recurrence pattern and range.

Establishing Time Zone Information in Recurrence Ranges

In Chapter 8, we discussed *date/time* strings both with and without UTC offsets. This section will explain to you why it is important to use *date/time* strings *without* UTC offsets in recurrence ranges and why it is also important to include a time zone when creating a recurring series. When Exchange Web Services processes a request to create a calendar item, it must associate the calendar item with a time zone so that a *bias* can be used to convert all date and time information to UTC.

When customers began using pre-release versions of Exchange Web Services, one of the most common problems they had was creating recurring meetings in different time zones. This was because developers were under the impression that simply specifying a UTC offset in a recurrence range would set the time zone for the new series. It does not. For example, consider the call to the *CreateItem* Web method in Listing 9-42.

LISTING 9-42 Creating a recurring series with recurrence range date strings containing *UTC offsets*, but without a *MeetingTimeZone*

```
<m:CreateItem SendMeetingInvitations="SendToNone"
              xmlns:m=".../messages"
              xmlns:t=".../types">
  <m:Items>
    <t:CalendarItem>
      <t:Subject>MeetingWithEndDateRecurrance</t:Subject>
      <t:Start>2007-03-05T06:00:00-07:00</t:Start>
      <t:End>2007-03-05T07:00:00-07:00</t:End>
      <t:Recurrence>
        <t:DailyRecurrence>
          <t:Interval>1</t:Interval>
        </t:DailyRecurrence>
        <t:EndDateRecurrence>
          <!-- Important: This Calendar Item is not explicitly
               defining a time zone, so if 3/11 happens to
               fall on a time change boundary for the time zone of
               the server, then the bias of that zone is what
               will determine the time of the 3/11 occurrence. -->
          <t:StartDate>2007-03-05-07:00</t:StartDate>
          <t:EndDate>2007-03-11-07:00</t:EndDate>
        </t:EndDateRecurrence>
      </t:Recurrence>
    </t:CalendarItem>
  </m:Items>
</m:CreateItem>
```

In Listing 9-42, a recurring master is created without a *MeetingTimeZone* element. Unless the caller happens to know the time zone of the Exchange Client Access Server, the time zone that will be applied to this recurring series is essentially an unknown.[7] As a result, the March 11 occurrence from this recurring series could have a start time of 6 A.M. or 7 A.M.

Just specifying the UTC offset "-07:00" in a date string within the *EndDateRecurrence* element is not sufficient for Exchange Web Services to determine if you meant U.S. Mountain Standard Time (Montana), U.S. Pacific Daylight Time (California), or U.S. Mountain Time (Arizona). All three are time zones that use the offset "-07:00" as their bias at some time during the year. The only way you can be sure that you are setting the time zone of a recurring series is to use the *MeetingTimeZone* element.

---

[7] EWS does not provide a way to determine the time zone that a given Client Access Server is configured to use.

Updating a Recurring Series

You can use the *UpdateItem* Web method to make changes to an existing recurring series. However, to do so, you must provide a complete *RecurrenceType* instance. In other words, you cannot change just the recurrence range or just the recurrence pattern of a series; you must provide both in your call to the *UpdateItem* Web method. Listing 9-43 is an example of calling the *UpdateItem* Web method to change a recurring series

LISTING 9-43 Using the *UpdateItem* Web method to change the *Recurrence* on a recurring master

```
<m:UpdateItem ConflictResolution="AutoResolve"
              SendMeetingInvitationsOrCancellations="SendToNone"
              xmlns:m=".../messages"
              xmlns:t=".../types">
  <m:ItemChanges>
    <t:ItemChange>
      <t:ItemId Id="AAAoAGV3c3V..." ChangeKey="DwAA..." />
      <t:Updates>
        <t:SetItemField>
          <t:FieldURI FieldURI="calendar:Recurrence" />
          <t:CalendarItem>
            <t:Recurrence>
              <t:WeeklyRecurrence>
                <t:Interval>1</t:Interval>
                <t:DaysOfWeek>Monday</t:DaysOfWeek>
              </t:WeeklyRecurrence>
              <t:NumberedRecurrence>
                <t:StartDate>2007-02-01-08:00</t:StartDate>
                <t:NumberOfOccurrences>4</t:NumberOfOccurrences>
              </t:NumberedRecurrence>
            </t:Recurrence>
          </t:CalendarItem>
        </t:SetItemField>
      </t:Updates>
    </t:ItemChange>
  </m:ItemChanges>
</m:UpdateItem>
```

When you do this, Exchange Web Services will create all new occurrences. All item ids referencing occurrences prior to the update will become invalid.

> **Note** If you call the *UpdateItem* Web method on a recurring master that has had one or more occurrences turned into meetings, but not the entire series, then you may get an *ErrorIrresolvableConflict* response code indicating that Exchange Web Services will not be able to update the series with the new recurrence. If this happens, your options are probably limited to deleting and re-creating a new recurring series.

Listing 9-44 shows how to use the proxy classes to call the *UpdateItem* Web method to update the recurrence definition.

LISTING 9-44 Using the *UpdateItem* Web method to update the *Recurrence* of a recurring master via the proxy classes

```
/// <summary>
/// Change the recurrence of a recurring series by updating the
/// Recurrence property on a recurring master.  Call will tell
/// EWS to auto-resolve any conflicts and send updates to any
/// and all attendees (if the recurring series is also
/// a recurring meeting)
 /// </summary>
/// <param name="binding">Binding to use for the call</param>
/// <param name="idOfRecurringMaster">id of the recurring master</param>
/// <param name="newRecurrenceInformation">new recurrence information</param>
/// <returns>Updated id of the recurring master</returns>
///
public static ItemIdType ChangeRecurrenceOfARecurringSeries(
    ExchangeServiceBinding binding,
    ItemIdType idOfRecurringMaster,
    RecurrenceType newRecurrenceInformation)
{
    // Verify that the newRecurrenceInformation is complete
    //
    if ((newRecurrenceInformation.Item == null) ||
        (newRecurrenceInformation.Item1 == null))
    {
        throw new ArgumentException("Both the pattern and range of " +
            "the new recurrence must be specified.");
    }

    // Create an empty CalendarItem type to hold the recurrence for the
    // update item call
    //
    CalendarItemType calitem1 = new CalendarItemType();
    calitem1.Recurrence = newRecurrenceInformation;

    // Make the updated recurrence part of a SetItemFieldType instance by
    // specifying both the field we are updating (calendar:Recurrence) and
    // providing our temp calendar item with the recurrence property set.
    //
    SetItemFieldType itemUpdateDescription = new SetItemFieldType();
    itemUpdateDescription.Item = new PathToUnindexedFieldType();

    ((PathToUnindexedFieldType)itemUpdateDescription.Item).FieldURI =
        UnindexedFieldURIType.calendarRecurrence;
    itemUpdateDescription.Item1 = calitem1;

    // Create an UpdateItem requests
    //
    UpdateItemType updateItemRequest = new UpdateItemType();
    updateItemRequest.ConflictResolution = ConflictResolutionType.AutoResolve;
    updateItemRequest.SendMeetingInvitationsOrCancellations =
```

```
        CalendarItemUpdateOperationType.SendOnlyToAll;
    updateItemRequest.SendMeetingInvitationsOrCancellationsSpecified = true;
    updateItemRequest.ItemChanges = new ItemChangeType[] {
        new ItemChangeType() };

    // Set the id of the UpdateItem request to be the id of the
    // recurring master
    //
    updateItemRequest.ItemChanges[0].Item = idOfRecurringMaster;
    updateItemRequest.ItemChanges[0].Updates = new SetItemFieldType[] {
        itemUpdateDescription };

    // Call the UpdateItem web method via the Exchange Service Binding
    UpdateItemResponseType updateItemResponse =
        binding.UpdateItem(updateItemRequest);

    // Verify that the UpdateItem request was successful
    if (updateItemResponse.ResponseMessages.Items[0].ResponseClass !=
        ResponseClassType.Success)
    {
        // Indicate that we have a problem
        throw new Exception(String.Format(
            "Unable to update recurring master\r\n{0}\r\n{1}",
            updateItemResponse.ResponseMessages.Items[0].ResponseCode,
            updateItemResponse.ResponseMessages.Items[0].MessageText));
    }

    // Success, get the new id of the recurring master
    ItemInfoResponseMessageType itemInfoResponseMessage =
        (ItemInfoResponseMessageType)updateItemResponse.
            ResponseMessages.Items[0];

    return itemInfoResponseMessage.Items.Items[0].ItemId;
}
```

Notes on Using Change Keys in a Recurring Series

Although each occurrence and exception in a recurring series has a unique id, they all share a common change key. To better understand why this is the case, recall that all occurrences and exceptions are stored as attachments on a recurring master. Also recall, from Chapter 3, "Property Paths and Response Shapes," that the change key contains information about the type of item. It turns out that when you retrieve an *ItemId* element for an occurrence or exception, the *ChangeKey* attribute on that element is in fact the change key from the recurring master, albeit with extra type information embedded. When a change takes place on an exception or an occurrence, it is actually the change key of the recurring master itself that changes.

Because the type information is embedded, you *cannot* use the change key of a recurring master as the change key for an occurrence or exception in that series. You can, however, freely use the change key from any occurrence or exception in a series for any other occurrence or exception within that series.

The Case of the Missing *When* Element

CalendarItemType has a string element named *When* on it. This element was *supposed* to include a string that describes the recurrence definition in "human-readable" terms (See Figure 9-8).

Appointment	Scheduling Assistant
Subject:	Meeting with Brian
Location:	My Office
Recurrence:	Occurs every Monday, Wednesday, and Friday from 8:00 AM to 9:00 AM effective 10/30/2006 until 12/1/2006.

FIGURE 9-8 Example of a recurrence definition defined as a string

Unfortunately, due to an Exchange Web Service issue, this element is never present, even if a request specifically asks for it via the *calendar:When* property path.[8] The data, however, is still accessible via the extended property with property id 0x8232 (decimal value 33330) in the *Appointment* distinguished property set as is shown in Listing 9-45.

LISTING 9-45 Requesting the recurrence definition string via extended properties

```
<m:GetItem xmlns:m=".../messages"
           xmlns:t=".../types">
  <m:ItemShape>
    <t:BaseShape>IdOnly</t:BaseShape>
    <t:AdditionalProperties>
      <t:ExtendedFieldURI DistinguishedPropertySetId="Appointment"
                          PropertyId="33330"
                          PropertyType="String" />
      <t:FieldURI FieldURI="item:Subject" />
    </t:AdditionalProperties>
  </m:ItemShape>
  <m:ItemIds>
    <t:ItemId Id="AAAnAGN..." ChangeKey="EAAAA..." />
  </m:ItemIds>
</m:GetItem>
```

Listing 9-46 shows an example of the recurrence definition string from the calendar item shown in Figure 9-8.

LISTING 9-46 Response including the recurrence definition string

```
<m:GetItemResponse xmlns:m=".../messages"
                   xmlns:t=".../types">
  <m:ResponseMessages>
    <m:GetItemResponseMessage ResponseClass="Success">
      <m:ResponseCode>NoError</m:ResponseCode>
      <m:Items>
        <t:CalendarItem>
          <t:ItemId Id="AAAnAGNhc..." ChangeKey="EAAA..." />
```

---

[8] As of this writing, the issue of a missing *When* value is expected to be fixed in the next Service Pack of Exchange Server 2007.

```
            <t:Subject>Meeting with Brian</t:Subject>
            <t:ExtendedProperty>
              <t:ExtendedFieldURI DistinguishedPropertySetId="Appointment"
                                  PropertyId="33330"
                                  PropertyType="String" />
              <t:Value>
                  Occurs every Monday, Wednesday, and Friday
                  from 8:00 AM to 9:00 AM effective 10/30/2006 until
                  12/1/2006.
              </t:Value>
            </t:ExtendedProperty>
          </t:CalendarItem>
        </m:Items>
      </m:GetItemResponseMessage>
    </m:ResponseMessages>
  </m:GetItemResponse>
```

Working with Time Zones

In Chapter 8, we presented the rules that apply to a newly created calendar item in order to convert all *date/time* strings without UTC offsets to UTC. We stated that a time zone bias is used to do this conversion, and that this bias can come from one of two places:

1. If the request contains an explicit time zone definition via a *MeetingTimeZone* element, then all *date/time* strings without UTC offsets are converted using the bias from the *MeetingTimeZone*.

2. If no *MeetingTimeZone* element is included, the *bias* from the current time zone of the Exchange Client Access Server will be used.[9]

We also gave you the following equation to explain how the conversion takes place:

UTC = local time + bias

Because Exchange Web Services does not provide a mechanism for you to determine the time zone of the Exchange Client Access Server, we presented the following best practice recommendation:

The Exchange Web Services team recommends that all CalendarItemType *instances that include the* MeetingTimeZone *element should be created with* date/time *strings without UTC offsets.*

So why all the fuss to associate a time zone if the recurring series doesn't span a time change? Two very important reasons: First, recurrence ranges can be updated, and it's easy to forget to consider time change information when you are simply adding to the number

---

[9] As of this writing, the next Service Pack of Exchange Server 2007 will change this behavior to always use the UTC time zone instead of the time zone of the Exchange Client Access Server.

of occurrences in a series. Second, time zones can change the rules regarding when a bias transition from standard time to daylight savings time is made. When this transition happens, all recurring series in a calendar using that time zone must be updated so that occurrences follow the new time change rules—an occurrence that used to be in standard time may now fall into daylight savings time.

Understanding the *MeetingTimeZone* Element

In Chapter 8, we stated that the *MeetingTimeZone* element on the *CalendarItemType* type is of type *TimeZoneType*. You already know that you can use the *BaseOffset* to define a bias for a time zone that does not transition to daylight savings time. Up until now, we were unable to explain time zone transitions in more detail because describing a time zone transition in Exchange Web Services requires an understanding of recurrence patterns. Now that you understand recurrence patterns (the *RelativeYearlyRecurringPatternType,* in particular), we can describe the remaining elements of the *TimeZoneType* type.

This section will now explain the rest of the child elements on the *TimeZoneType* type, starting with schema shown in Listing 9-47.

LISTING 9-47 Schema for *TimeZoneType*

```
<xs:complexType name="TimeZoneType">
  <xs:sequence>
    <xs:element name="BaseOffset" type="xs:duration" />
    <xs:sequence minOccurs="0">
      <xs:element name="Standard" type="t:TimeChangeType"/>
      <xs:element name="Daylight" type="t:TimeChangeType"/>
    </xs:sequence>
  </xs:sequence>
  <xs:attribute name="TimeZoneName" type="xs:string" use="optional" />
</xs:complexType>
```

We already discussed the *BaseOffset* element and the *xs:duration* format in Chapter 8.

TimeZoneName Attribute of the *TimeZoneType* Type

The *TimeZoneName* attribute is a string that describes the name of the time zone. The intended usage of this string is to be the *keyname* from the Windows Registry that matches the time zone being described. These keynames can be found at the following Windows Registry path:

HKEY_LOCAL_MACHINE\Software\Microsoft\Windows NT\CurrentVersion\Time Zones

Although the *TimeZoneName* attribute can be set by the user, the value is ignored by Exchange Web Services. Even so, the *TimeZoneName* attribute will have a value if the calendar item in question has a time zone associated with it. As we will describe later, this occurs when the calendar item is created by means other then through Exchange Web Services.

The fact that Exchange Web Services ignores the *TimeZoneName* attribute during the creation of a calendar item leads to an issue between Exchange Web Services and Outlook Web Access regarding the display of a well-known name for the time zone of a recurring series. This issue is explained in the sidebar titled "Outlook Web Access May Display 'Unknown Time Zone' for a Recurring Series Created by Exchange Web Services."

Standard and *Daylight* Properties

The *Standard* and *Daylight* elements on *MeetingTimeZone* are used to define the date and time of bias transitions for a time zone. The *Standard* element defines the transition from daylight savings time to standard time, and the *Daylight* element defines the transition from standard time to daylight savings time.

Both of these elements are optional, and if omitted, then the *MeetingTimeZone* element represents a time zone that does not use daylight savings time. The Exchange Web Service team recommends that if a time zone does use daylight savings time, then both the *Standard* and *Daylight* elements should always be set.

Both the *Standard* and *Daylight* elements are of the schema type *TimeChangeType*. The *TimeChangeType* is what allows the *Standard* and *Daylight* elements to define a bias transition. The schema for the *TimeChangeType* is shown in Listing 9-48.

LISTING 9-48 Schema for *TimeChangeType*

```
<xs:complexType name="TimeChangeType">
  <xs:sequence>
    <xs:element name="Offset" type="xs:duration" />
      <xs:group ref="t:TimeChangePatternTypes" minOccurs="0"/>
      <xs:element name="Time" type="xs:time" />
    </xs:sequence>
  <xs:attribute name="TimeZoneName" type="xs:string" use="optional" />
</xs:complexType>
```

Offset Element of *TimeChangeType* Type

The *Offset* element on the *TimeChangeType* type is an xs:*duration* that defines how the value of the bias changes during a time change transition for a time zone. When specifying the *Standard* element, this value should always be set to a duration value of zero (e.g., "PT0H"). When specifying the *Daylight* element, the duration value should be one that satisfies the following equation:

Daylight Time Bias = Base Offset Bias + Daylight Offset Duration

For example, during standard time, the bias for Pacific Standard Time is equal to "PT8H"; during daylight savings time, the bias changes to "PT7H", a difference of one hour ("PT1H"). Therefore, when using a *TimeChangeType* instance to define daylight saving time for PST, the value of the *Offset* element should be "-PT1H".

PT7H = PT8H - PT1H

Time Element of the *TimeChangeType*

The *Time* element on the *TimeChangeType* type describes the time of day when a transition from standard time to daylight savings time, and vice versa, is supposed to occur. Pacific Standard Time, for example, changes from standard time to daylight savings time at 2:00 A.M. on whatever day the time change day happens to be for a given year.

The *Time* element is a string in a format called *xs:time*. See the sidebar titled "Understanding *xs:time*" for more detailed information on this format, but here we will just briefly mention that the *xs:time* format is just like the *xs:dateTime* format, but without the date portion.

An example of a *Time* element in XML would be:

```
<t:Time xmlns:t=".../types">02:00:00</t:Time>
```

> **Important** There is an issue regarding XML serialization of the *Time* property that you must be aware of when using the proxy classes. The issue is described in the "Understanding *xs:time* XML Serialization Issues" section later in this chapter.

TimeZoneName Attribute of *TimeChangeType* Type

In addition to the *TimeZoneName* attribute on *TimeZoneType*, there is also a *TimeZoneName* attribute on *TimeChangeType*. While the *TimeZoneName* attribute on a *TimeZoneType* instance is meant to represent the Windows Registry keyname for the time zone, the *TimeZoneName* on a *TimeChangeType* instance is designed to be set to the *Std* or *Dlt* string values from within the time zone registry key.

For example, if you are retrieving a recurring master that has a *MeetingTimeZone* element meant to define Pacific Standard Time, then the *TimeZoneName* on the corresponding *Standard* element would be equal to "Pacific Standard Time." The *TimeZoneName* on the corresponding *Daylight* element would be equal to "Pacific Daylight Time."

As with the *TimeZoneName* attribute on a *TimeZoneType* instance, the *TimeZoneName* attribute on a *TimeChangeType* instance will be ignored by Exchange Web Services. If you retrieve a calendar item that was created via Exchange Web Services, then the *TimeZoneName* values on both the *Standard* and *Daylight* elements will be "Unknown Time Zone."[10] This will not be the case for calendar items created by other clients (Outlook Web Access, for example) where the *TimeZoneName* property on the *Standard* or *Daylight* properties should be set to the display values as present in the *Std* or *Dlt* registry key values accordingly.

Time Change Patterns in the *MeetingTimeZone* Element

The *Standard* and *Daylight* elements of *TimeZoneType* are both *TimeChangeType* elements. The *TimeChangeType* is a reference to a *TimeChangePatternTypes* group. In XML, a *TimeChangeType* reference can be either an *AbsoluteDate* element or a *RelativeYearlyRecurrencePatternType* element. The *TimeChangeType* reference is used to describe the date of a transition from standard time to daylight savings time, and vice versa.

If an *AbsoluteDate* element is used, the value must be an *xs:date* formatted string that represents the date of the transition for the *TimeChangeType* instance. If a *RelativeYearlyRecurrencePattern* element is used, then the element must contain a *RelativelyYearlyRecurrencePatternType* instance that describes the date of the transition using a relative yearly recurrence pattern.

> **Note** As of this writing, nearly all of the time zones defined in the Windows Registry describe the date of the time zone transition as a relative yearly recurrence pattern. Israel Standard Time is one exception, as it uses an absolute date to define its time change transition dates.

For example, in the Eastern Standard Time zone, the transition date can be described using the following relatively yearly recurrence pattern:

"Daylight Savings Time starts on the second Sunday in March at 2:00 A.M."

Listing 9-49 shows how you would use a relative yearly recurrence pattern in a *TimeChangeType* for describing daylight savings time in the Eastern Standard Time Zone.

LISTING 9-49 Use of a *RelativeYearlyRecurrencPatternType* instance to describe a daylight savings time

```
<t:Daylight xmlns:t=".../types">
  <t:Offset>-PT1H</t:Offset>
  <t:RelativeYearlyRecurrence>
    <t:DaysOfWeek>Sunday</t:DaysOfWeek>
    <t:DayOfWeekIndex>Second</t:DayOfWeekIndex>
    <t:Month>March</t:Month>
  </t:RelativeYearlyRecurrence>
  <t:Time>02:00:00</t:Time>
</t:Daylight>
```

---

[10] As of this writing, the next Service Pack of Exchange Server 2007 is expected to allow the proper display names to be set on calendar items created with EWS.

Understanding *xs:time*

Exchange Web Services uses the *http://www.w3.org/2001/XMLSchema:time* format (also known as *xs:time*), as described by the W3C in their *"XML Schema Part 2: DataTypes, Second Edition"* recommendation: *http://www.w3.org/TR/xmlschema-2/*. According to this recommendation, the format of a *xs:time* string in XML schema is as follows:[11]

> *The lexical representation for time is the left truncated lexical representation for [xs:] dateTime: hh:mm:ss.sss with optional [UTC offset]. For example, to indicate 1:20 P.M. for Eastern Standard Time which is 5 hours behind Coordinated Universal Time (UTC), one would write: 13:20:00-05:00.*

Properties defined as *xs:time* will be *System.DateTime* types in the proxy classes. There is only one such element in Exchange Web Services, and that is the *Time* element of the *TimeChangeType* schema type.

More information on the *xs:time* format, including sample code for converting *DateTime* instances to *xs:time* strings can be found in the Appendix B, "Calendaring Supplimentals" available on the companion Web page.

Using the *MeetingTimeZone* to Set a Time Zone with Time Changes on a Calendar Item

Note This section will not give an example of using the *MeetingTimeZone* property to set a time zone with time changes using the proxy classes. This is because there is an issue with the .NET Framework serialization of *DateTime* structures into *xs:time* formatted strings. We will discuss the issue in the section titled "Understanding *xs:time* XML Serialization Issues." Following that discussion, we will re-visit the *MeetingTimeZone* property and describe how to use it via the proxy classes.

Now that we have described all of the child elements that are present on a *MeetingTimeZone*, we can show you an example of creating a new calendar item with a time zone that has a transition to daylight savings time and back again.

Consider the Pacific Standard Time Zone (PST). PST has a standard time bias of eight hours and a daylight savings time bias of seven hours. PST defines daylight savings time as starting on the second Sunday in March at 2:00 A.M. PST and ending on the first Sunday in November at 2:00 A.M. PST. Listing 9-50 is an example of creating a calendar item that runs from 7:00 P.M. to 11:00 P.M. PST.

---

[11] Taken from Section 3.2.8.1, "Lexical representation [of time]" source http://www.w3.org/TR/xmlschema-2/, September 3, 2007

LISTING 9-50 Creating a new calendar item in the Pacific Time Zone

```
<m:CreateItem SendMeetingInvitations="SendToNone"
              xmlns:m=".../messages"
              xmlns:t=".../types">
  <m:Items>
    <t:CalendarItem>
      <t:Subject>Calendar Item in the Pacific Time Zone</t:Subject>
      <t:Start>2007-01-16T19:00:00</t:Start>
      <t:End>2007-01-16T23:00:00</t:End>
      <t:MeetingTimeZone>
        <t:BaseOffset>PT8H</t:BaseOffset>
        <t:Standard>
          <t:Offset>PT0H</t:Offset>
          <t:RelativeYearlyRecurrence>
            <t:DaysOfWeek>Sunday</t:DaysOfWeek>
            <t:DayOfWeekIndex>First</t:DayOfWeekIndex>
            <t:Month>November</t:Month>
          </t:RelativeYearlyRecurrence>
          <t:Time>02:00:00</t:Time>
        </t:Standard>
        <t:Daylight>
          <t:Offset>-PT1H</t:Offset>
          <t:RelativeYearlyRecurrence>
            <t:DaysOfWeek>Sunday</t:DaysOfWeek>
            <t:DayOfWeekIndex>Second</t:DayOfWeekIndex>
            <t:Month>March</t:Month>
          </t:RelativeYearlyRecurrence>
          <t:Time>02:00:00</t:Time>
        </t:Daylight>
      </t:MeetingTimeZone>
    </t:CalendarItem>
  </m:Items>
</m:CreateItem>
```

Updating *MeetingTimeZone*

Updating the time zone of a calendar item can be done via the *UpdateItem* Web method. Unlike updating the *Recurrence* of a recurring master, updating the *MeetingTimeZone* on a recurring master will not cause all the occurrences of a recurring series to be re-generated.

Outlook Web Access May Display "Unknown Time Zone" for a Recurring Series Created by Exchange Web Services

As of this writing, Exchange Web Services ignores any of the *TimeZoneName* properties of a *MeetingTimeZone* that are passed in by the client. This means that the time zone described by a *MeetingTimeZone* element is never associated with a Windows Registry keyname. The result is that any Exchange Web Service calendar items with a defined

MeetingTimeZone will appear in Outlook Web Access as having an "unknown Time Zone" (see Figure 9-9).

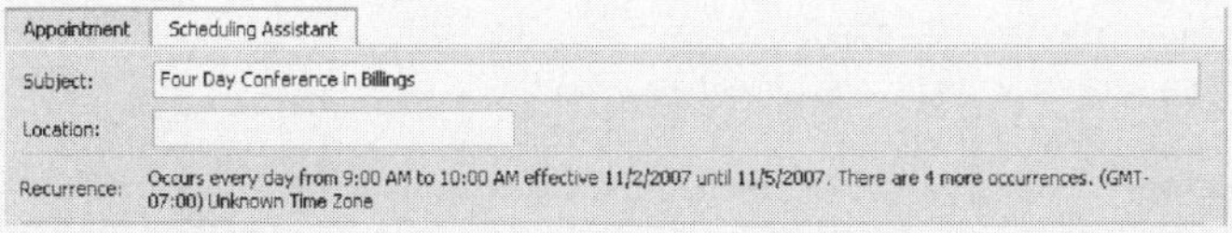

FIGURE 9-9 Example of Outlook Web Access displaying an item with an unknown time zone

The Exchange Web Services team hopes to address this problem in the next service pack of Exchange Server 2007 by analyzing the *TimeZoneName* on the *MeetingTimeZone* element and treating the value as a Windows Registry *keyname* for a time zone. Once this fix is applied, you should not have to supply the *BaseOffset*, *Standard*, or *Daylight* values in the *MeetingTimeZone* element to identify a time zone. Instead, Exchange Web Services will perform a lookup against the Windows Registry for a matching keyname and fill in the remaining pieces of information about the time zone accordingly.

Understanding *xs:time* XML Serialization Issues

As of this writing, there is an issue with XML serialization of *xs:time* in all versions of the .NET Framework. The issue is that when *System.DateTime* structures are serialized into the XML schema data type *xs:time*, the conversion process ignores the *DateTimeKind* value of the *DateTime* instance. The result of this conversion issue is that you may find that all your occurrences of a recurring series have incorrect *Start* and *End* values following a bias transition in the time zone. To understand the issue, look at Listing 9-51, which builds a *TimeChangeType* proxy object for Australian Eastern Daylight Time (AUS) and then creates an *XmlSerializer* to serialize the object into XML.

LISTING 9-51 Demonstration of the XML serialization of a *TimeChangeType* instance

```
/// <summary>
/// This method demonstrates serializing an instance of the
/// TimeChangeType proxy type into XML.  The purpose is to
/// demonstrate the effect of XML serialization on the .Time
/// property.
 /// </summary>
public static void SerializingTimeChangeTypeDemonstration()
{
    RelativeYearlyRecurrencePatternType daylightTimeChangeDay =
        new RelativeYearlyRecurrencePatternType();
    daylightTimeChangeDay.DaysOfWeek =
        DayOfWeekType.Sunday.ToString();
    daylightTimeChangeDay.DayOfWeekIndex = DayOfWeekIndexType.Last;
```

```
    daylightTimeChangeDay.Month = MonthNamesType.October;

    TimeChangeType daylightTimeChange = new TimeChangeType();
    daylightTimeChange.TimeZoneName = "AUS Eastern Standard Time";
    daylightTimeChange.Offset = "-PT60M";
    daylightTimeChange.Item = daylightTimeChangeDay;

    // Define the time change DateTime instance as having a
    // DateTimeKind value of Unspecified.  The expected
    // result here would be an xs:time string without a UTC
    // offset.
    //
    // Remember, the .Time field is a DateTime instance, but the
    // 'date' portion really doesn't matter, just the time.
    //
    daylightTimeChange.Time =
     new DateTime(2007, 11, 28, 03, 00, 00, DateTimeKind.Unspecified);

    // Output to the console the results of serializing our
    // TimeChangeType
    //
    System.Xml.Serialization.XmlSerializer mySerializer =
        new System.Xml.Serialization.XmlSerializer(
            typeof(TimeChangeType));
    mySerializer.Serialize(System.Console.Out, daylightTimeChange);
}
```

Listing 9-52 shows an example of the console output from Listing 9-51.

LISTING 9-52 Results of serializing a *TimeChangeType* proxy object instance

```
<TimeChangeType TimeZoneName="AUS Eastern Standard Time"
                xmlns:t=".../types">
  <Offset>PT60M</Offset>
  <RelativeYearlyRecurrence>
    <DaysOfWeek>Sunday</DaysOfWeek>
    <DayOfWeekIndex>Last</DayOfWeekIndex>
    <Month>October</Month>
  </RelativeYearlyRecurrence>
  <Time>03:00:00.0000000-08:00</Time>
</TimeChangeType>
```

From the proxy code in Listing 9-51, you would expect the *Time* element to *not* contain a UTC offset while Listing 9-52 shows that it is serialized *with* a UTC offset. This particular offset appeared because the operating system (OS) of the machine doing the XML serialization was set to Pacific Standard Time. Even though the proxy code in Listing 9-51 was trying to define the time change information specific to a different time zone, and even though the code was using *DateTimeKind.Unspecified* in the *DateTime* structure, the XML serialization process still appended the UTC offset of the bias of the local OS to the generated *date/time* string.

If you were to set this *TimeChangeType* instance in a *MeetingTimeZone* while trying to create a recurring series, you would in effect be telling Exchange Web Services that the transition from standard to daylight savings time takes place not at 3 A.M. AUS as hoped, but instead at 3 A.M. in a time zone that is seven hours behind UTC. From this, you might expect that the only issue will be that occurrences that end up on the bias transition day will have incorrect times, but this is not so. As an unfortunate result of an issue within Exchange Web Services, a UTC offset in the *Time* element of a *TimeChangeType* instance can effect not only occurrences on the bias transition day, but all occurrences that occur after the bias transition day as well.[12] The size of the impact on occurrence times is related to how different the UTC offset on the *Time* element is from the bias of the zone being described.

This might seem like a "no-win" situation. On the one hand, the best practice recommendation is to always specify a time zone, but on the other hand, there is the issue of the proxy classes serializing that time zone information incorrectly. There is a workaround, however, and it involves a feature in the .NET Framework that grants a developer the ability to "intercept" the XML serialization process for any type and provide a customized implementation of the serialization via the *IXmlSerializable* interface.

Overcoming *xs:time* XML Serialization Issues with *IXmlSerializable*

More Info This section is not intended to be a detailed look at the *IXmlSerializable* interface, but rather a brief explanation for the purposes of describing a workaround necessary for Exchange Web Services applications. For more information on the *IXmlSerializable* interface, see the documentation on the MSDN Web site:

http://msdn2.microsoft.com/en-us/library/system.xml.serialization.ixmlserializable(vs.80).aspx

In order to workaround the *xs:time* XML serialization issue with *TimeChangeType*, you need to create a proxy extension class for the *TimeChangeType* that implements the *IXmlSerializable* interface.

This new implementation comes in two steps. For the first step, search for the *TimeChangeType* class in the file containing your auto-generated proxy classes, then comment out the line containing the *XmlTypeAttribute* attribute. If you forget this first step, you will get an *InvalidOperationException* at run time. Listing 9-53 shows the end result of this action.

---

[12] As of this writing, the EWS team is planning to address this issue in the next service pack of Exchange Server 2007. The current proposal is to correct the issue where a *UTC offset* in the *Time* property impacts generated occurs by always ignoring any *UTC offset* specified.

LISTING 9-53 Commenting out the *XmlTypeAttribute* attribute on the *TimeChangeType* proxy class

```
/// <remarks/>
[System.CodeDom.Compiler.GeneratedCodeAttribute("wsdl", "2.0.50727.42")]
[System.SerializableAttribute()]
[System.Diagnostics.DebuggerStepThroughAttribute()]
[System.ComponentModel.DesignerCategoryAttribute("code")]
//[System.Xml.Serialization.XmlTypeAttribute(…)]
public partial class TimeChangeType {

    private string offsetField;

    private object itemField;

    private System.DateTime timeField;

    ...

}
```

The second step of the fix is to create a proxy class extension that implements the *IXmlSerializable* interface. To implement the *IXmlSerializable* interface, you need to supply implementations for the *GetSchema*, *ReadXml,* and *WriteXml* methods. In the *ReadXml* and *WriteXml* methods, you will be responsible for handling all the XML serialization and deserialization for not only the *TimeChangeType* itself, but for any child elements as well. Fortunately, you can take advantage of the *System.Xml.XmlSerializer* to do some of the heavy lifting for you.

Listing 9-54 is a very large listing of a proxy extension for the *TimeChangeType* type that implements *IXmlSerializable* in order to fix the issue of having a UTC offset in a *Time* element. The fix is implemented in the *WriteXml* method, and involves putting together a custom string using only the hours, minutes, and seconds values from the *DateTime* structure assigned to the *Time* property. The rest of the code is required to satisfy the implementation details of *IXmlSerializable.*

LISTING 9-54 Proxy class extension for the *TimeChangeType* class that implements *IXmlSerializable*

```
///<summary>
/// Proxy extension for TimeChangeType that implements IXmlSerializable.
/// The purpose of this extension is to control the XML for the Time
/// property during serialization due to an issue with the .NET
/// Framework not respecting DateTimeKind during serialization of xs:time-
/// based elements.
///</summary>
///<remarks>
/// For this to work, the XmlTypeAttribute that the proxy generator places on this
/// class in the auto-generated .cs file must be removed
/// E.g.
///<code>
```

```
///      [System.CodeDom.Compiler.GeneratedCodeAttribute("wsdl", "...")]
///      [System.SerializableAttribute()]
///      [System.Diagnostics.DebuggerStepThroughAttribute()]
///      [System.ComponentModel.DesignerCategoryAttribute("code")]
///      //[System.Xml.Serialization.XmlTypeAttribute(Namespace="...")]
///      public partial class TimeChangeType {...}
///</code>
///</remarks>
public partial class TimeChangeType : IXmlSerializable
{
    /// <summary>
    /// Empty constructor, required for partial class implementations
    /// </summary>
    public TimeChangeType()
    { }


    /// <summary>
    /// Returns an XmlSchema for the TimeChangeType that describes the
    /// XML representation of the output that is produced by the WriteXml
    /// method and consumed by the ReadXmlMethod
    /// </summary>
    /// <returns>XmlSchema for the TimeChangeType</returns>
    public System.Xml.Schema.XmlSchema GetSchema()
    {
        // This method must return
        //<xs:schema
        //         id="types"
        //         elementFormDefault="qualified"
        //         version="Exchange2007"
        //         xmlns:t="http://.../types"
        //         targetNamespace="http://.../types"
        //         xmlns:tns="http://.../types"
        //         xmlns:xs="http://www.w3.org/2001/XMLSchema">
        // <xs:complexType name="TimeChangeType">
        //   <xs:sequence>
        //     <xs:element name="Offset" type="xs:duration" />
        //     <xs:group ref="t:TimeChangePatternTypes" minOccurs="0"/>
        //     <xs:element name="Time" type="xs:time" />
        //   </xs:sequence>
        //   <xs:attribute name="TimeZoneName"
        //      type="xs:string" use="optional" />
        //</xs:complexType>
        //</xs:schema>

        string xsTypes =
            "http://schemas.microsoft.com/exchange/services/2006/types";
        string xsSchema = "http://www.w3.org/2001/XMLSchema";

        XmlSchema schema = new XmlSchema();
        schema.Id = "types";
        schema.ElementFormDefault = XmlSchemaForm.Qualified;
        schema.Version = "Exchange2007";
        schema.TargetNamespace = xsTypes;
```

```
        // <xs:complexType ... >
        XmlSchemaComplexType xmlct1 = new XmlSchemaComplexType();
        schema.Items.Add(xmlct1);
        xmlct1.Name = "TimeChangeType";

        // <xs:sequence ... >
        XmlSchemaSequence xmlsq1 = new XmlSchemaSequence();
        xmlct1.Particle = xmlsq1;

        //   <xs:element ... />
        XmlSchemaElement xmle1 = new XmlSchemaElement();
        xmlsq1.Items.Add(xmle1);
        xmle1.Name = "Offset";
        xmle1.SchemaTypeName = new XmlQualifiedName("duration", xsSchema);

        //   <xs:group ... />
        XmlSchemaGroupRef xmlgr1 = new XmlSchemaGroupRef();
        xmlsq1.Items.Add(xmlgr1);
        xmlgr1.RefName =
            new XmlQualifiedName("TimeChangePatternTypes", xsTypes);
        xmlgr1.MinOccurs = 0;

        //   <xs:element ... />
        XmlSchemaElement xmle2 = new XmlSchemaElement();
        xmlsq1.Items.Add(xmle2);
        xmle2.Name = "Time";
        xmle2.SchemaTypeName = new XmlQualifiedName("time", xsSchema);

        // <xs:attribute ... />
        XmlSchemaAttribute xmla1 = new XmlSchemaAttribute();
        xmlct1.Attributes.Add(xmla1);
        xmla1.Name = "TimeZoneName";
        xmla1.Use = XmlSchemaUse.Optional;
        xmla1.SchemaTypeName = new XmlQualifiedName("string", xsSchema);

        return schema;
    }
    /// <summary>
    /// Generates a TimeChangeType object from it's XML representation
    /// </summary>
    /// <param name="reader">XmlReader positioned at the start node
    /// of the TimeChangeType XML
    /// </param>
    public void ReadXml(System.Xml.XmlReader reader)
    {
        // Store the LocalName of the element we are currently at.
        // This should be either "Standard" or "Daylight".
        //
        // This also serves as our key to our position in the stream.
        // Once we reach an EndElement with this name, then we are done
        // with our portion of the XmlStream
        //
        string ruleSetName = reader.LocalName;
```

```
// Value that indicates if the TimeChangePattern for us is a
// RelativeYearlyRecurrence or not.  If not, then it must
// be an AbsoluteDate
//
bool isRelativeYearlyPattern = false;
RelativeYearlyRecurrencePatternType relativeYearlyPattern =
    new RelativeYearlyRecurrencePatternType();
while (true)
{
    // Check to see if we are done processing
    if ((reader.NodeType == XmlNodeType.EndElement) &&
        (0 == String.Compare(reader.LocalName, ruleSetName)))
    {
        // We are done, consume this EndElement and stop processing
        reader.Read();
        break;
    }

    if (reader.NodeType == XmlNodeType.EndElement)
    {
        // This means we are at the closing tag of
        // </RelativeYearlyRecurrence>
        // No data here to process.
        reader.Read();
        continue;
    }

    // Consume TimeZoneName attribute
    // e.g. <Standard|Daylight TimeZoneName="value">
    //
    if ((0 == String.Compare(reader.LocalName, "Standard")) ||
        (0 == String.Compare(reader.LocalName, "Daylight")))
    {
        if (reader.AttributeCount > 0)
        {
            reader.MoveToAttribute("TimeZoneName");
            this.timeZoneNameField = reader.Value;
        }
        // We have consumed what we needed form this element
        reader.Read();
    }

    // Consume Offset
    // e.g <Offset>PT0M</Offset>
    if (0 == String.Compare(reader.LocalName, "Offset"))
    {
        string value = reader.ReadElementContentAsString();
        this.offsetField = value;
    }

    // Consume Time
    // e.g. <Time>02:00:00</Time>
    if (0 == String.Compare(reader.LocalName, "Time"))
    {
```

```
                this.timeField = reader.ReadElementContentAsDateTime();
        }

        // Consume the TimeChangePattern element if it is
        // an AbsoluteDate
        //
        if (0 == String.Compare(reader.LocalName, "AbsoluteDate"))
        {
            isRelativeYearlyPattern = false;
            this.itemField = reader.ReadElementContentAsDateTime();
        }

        // Consume the TimeChangePattern element if it is
        // an RelativeYearlyRecurrence
        //
        if (0 == String.Compare(reader.LocalName,
            "RelativeYearlyRecurrence"))
        {
            isRelativeYearlyPattern = true;
            reader.Read();
        }

        // If the pattern is relative, then the next three checks
        // will get the DayOfWeek, DayOfWeekIndex, and Month values
        // accordingly.
        //
        if (0 == String.Compare(reader.LocalName, "DaysOfWeek"))
        {
            string value = reader.ReadElementContentAsString();
            relativeYearlyPattern.DaysOfWeek = value;
        }

        if (0 == String.Compare(reader.LocalName, "DayOfWeekIndex"))
        {
            string value = reader.ReadElementContentAsString();
            relativeYearlyPattern.DayOfWeekIndex =
                (DayOfWeekIndexType)Enum.Parse(
                    typeof(DayOfWeekIndexType), value);
        }

        if (0 == String.Compare(reader.LocalName, "Month"))
        {
            string value = reader.ReadElementContentAsString();
            relativeYearlyPattern.Month =
                (MonthNamesType)Enum.Parse(
                    typeof(MonthNamesType), value);
        }
    }

    // Before we leave, set the .itemField to our
    // relativeYearlyPattern if necessary
    if (isRelativeYearlyPattern)
        this.itemField = relativeYearlyPattern;
}
```

```
/// <summary>
/// Converts a TimeChangeType object into its XML representation
/// </summary>
/// <param name="writer">XmlWriter positioned at the point
/// to which the XML for this object is to be written to
/// </param>
public void WriteXml(System.Xml.XmlWriter writer)
{
    string xsTypes =
        "http://schemas.microsoft.com/exchange/services/2006/types";

    // Our position in the writer already includes a StartElement
    // for our type, therefore, our job is to pickup writing to the
    // stream all of our content starting with the attributes of
    // the StartElement.

    // Write TimeZoneName attribute
    if (!String.IsNullOrEmpty(this.timeZoneNameField))
    {
        writer.WriteAttributeString("TimeZoneName",
            this.timeZoneNameField);
    }

    // Write Offset
    writer.WriteElementString("Offset", xsTypes, this.offsetField);

    // Write TimeChangeType, which can be either a
    // RelativeYearlyRecurrencePattern or an AbsoluteDate
    //
    if (this.Item is RelativeYearlyRecurrencePatternType)
    {
        string innerNodeValues;

        // For the RelativeYearlyRecurrencePattern portion, we will
        // simply create an XmlSerializer to do the work for us.  We
        // will need a buffer to hold the XML, one 4k buffer should be
        // sufficient.
        //
        using (System.IO.MemoryStream buffer = new
            System.IO.MemoryStream(4096))
        {
            // Create a new Serializer. The .NET Framework internally
            // has a 'cache' of these (each typed XmlSerializer instance lives
            // in a dynamically generated assembly), so even though we
            // are requesting a 'new' one, the .NET Framework is
            // actually reusing an existing assembly for us.
            //
            XmlSerializer xmls = new
                XmlSerializer(typeof(
                    RelativeYearlyRecurrencePatternType));
            xmls.Serialize(buffer, this.Item);

            // Reset the buffer position, and then hookup an XmlReader
            buffer.Seek(0, System.IO.SeekOrigin.Begin);
```

```
            XmlTextReader xmlrdr = new XmlTextReader(buffer);
            xmlrdr.Read();

            // The first node should always be the XmlDeclaration, and
            // we do not want that
            if (xmlrdr.NodeType == XmlNodeType.XmlDeclaration)
            {
                xmlrdr.Read();

                // The XmlSerializer likes to put in some whitespace
                // as well.
                //
                if (xmlrdr.NodeType == XmlNodeType.Whitespace)
                {
                    xmlrdr.Read();
                }
            }

            // Here is the node we are interested in, however, we can't
            // just take the node 'as-is'.  The reason is that the
            // XmlSerializer named the outer node
            // "RelativeYearlyRecurrencePatternType" (the name of the
            // type) but our request must pass this as
            // "RelativeYearlyRecurrence".
            //
            // The InnerXml however, is all valid, so we'll save that
            // information and handle the outer-node part ourselves.
            //
            innerNodeValues = xmlrdr.ReadInnerXml();
        }

        // Write out our recurrence pattern node
        //
        writer.WriteStartElement("RelativeYearlyRecurrence", xsTypes);
        writer.WriteRaw(innerNodeValues);
        writer.WriteEndElement();
    }
    else
    {
        writer.WriteElementString("AbsoluteDate",
            System.Xml.XmlConvert.ToString((DateTime)this.Item,
                XmlDateTimeSerializationMode.RoundtripKind));
    }

    // Write the Time Element
    //
    // This is the primary reason for implementing IXmlSerializable.
    // For it is here where we control the XML output of the Time
    // element of our type to include the 'correct' offset.
    //
    string correctXsTimeString = String.Empty;
    switch (this.timeField.Kind)
    {
        case DateTimeKind.Local:
```

```
                    correctXsTimeString =
                        this.timeField.ToString(@"HH"":"""mm"":"""sszzzzzz");
                    break;
                case DateTimeKind.Utc:
                    correctXsTimeString =
                        this.timeField.ToString(@"HH"":"""mm"":"""ssZ");
                    break;
                case DateTimeKind.Unspecified:
                default:
                    correctXsTimeString =
                        this.timeField.ToString(@"HH"":"""mm"":"""ss");
                    break;
            }

            writer.WriteElementString("Time", xsTypes, correctXsTimeString);

            // No need to write an "EndElement", simply exit.
        }
    }
```

Listing 9-55 shows the new console output you should get from calling the *SerializingTimeChangeTypeDemonstration* (from Listing 9-51) provided the code from Listing 9-53 and Listing 9-54 are all compiled in as well.

LISTING 9-55 Results of serializing a *TimeChangeType* proxy object with an *IXmlSerializable* interface

```
<TimeChangeType TimeZoneName="AUS Eastern Standard Time"
                xmlns="http://.../types">
  <Offset>-PT60M</Offset>
  <RelativeYearlyRecurrence>
    <DaysOfWeek xmlns=".../types">Sunday</DaysOfWeek>
    <DayOfWeekIndex xmlns=".../types">Last</DayOfWeekIndex>
    <Month xmlns=".../types">October</Month>
  </RelativeYearlyRecurrence>
  <Time>03:00:00</Time>
</TimeChangeType>
```

That looks much better! The *Time* element no longer contains a UTC offset.

This code may seem like an extreme way to solve the issue. However, issues with time zones can be very tricky to diagnose. Of course, it's possible that during development of your application you might not encounter this issue at all. Now that you have the code to work around the issue, however, it is our recommendation that you make use of it. Additionally, the technique of implementing the *IXmlSerializable* interface to correct problems in proxy serialization will come up again. In Chapter 21, "Availability," we will explain another issue where Exchange Web Services returns incorrect time offsets for some *date/time* strings, and you will have to use this technique to handle the issue there as well.

Using the *MeetingTimeZone* Property to Set a Time Zone with Time Changes on a Calendar Item via the Proxy

With the proxy extension for the *TimeChangeType* class from Listing 9-53 and Listing 9-54 included, Listing 9-56 shows the creation of a recurring series, complete with a time zone that adheres to daylight savings time.

LISTING 9-56 Creating a recurring series with a time zone that adheres to daylight savings time via the proxy classes

```
/// <summary>
/// Create a daily recurring series with a time zone that adheres to daylight
/// savings time via the proxy
/// </summary>
/// <param name="binding">Binding to use for the web service call</param>
/// <returns>Id of newly created recurring master for the series</returns>
///
public static ItemIdType CreateRecurringSeriesWithChangingTimeZone(
    ExchangeServiceBinding binding)
{
    DateTime nov2nd20078amUnspec = new DateTime(
        2007, 11, 02, 08, 00, 00, DateTimeKind.Unspecified);
    DateTime twoAM = new DateTime(
        DateTime.Now.Year, DateTime.Now.Month,
        DateTime.Now.Day, 02, 00, 00, DateTimeKind.Unspecified);

    // Basic new calendar item information
    //
    CalendarItemType newRecurringMaster = new CalendarItemType();
    newRecurringMaster.Start = nov2nd20078amUnspec;
    newRecurringMaster.StartSpecified = true;
    newRecurringMaster.End = nov2nd20078amUnspec.AddHours(1);
    newRecurringMaster.EndSpecified = true;
    newRecurringMaster.Subject = "Four Day Recurring Series in" +
        "US Mountain Standard Time";

    // Recurrence information for the new series
    //
    DailyRecurrencePatternType recurrencePattern =
        new DailyRecurrencePatternType();
    recurrencePattern.Interval = 1;
    NumberedRecurrenceRangeType recurrenceRange =
        new NumberedRecurrenceRangeType();
    recurrenceRange.StartDate = nov2nd20078amUnspec;
    recurrenceRange.NumberOfOccurrences = 4;

    // We want to create this new series in the "Mountain Time
    // Zone" which is defined as UTC -07:00 and adheres to a
    // Daylight Savings Time.  DLT starts on the second Sunday in
    // March at 2am and ends on the first Sunday in November at 2am.
    // The Daylight Time bias is -06:00
    //
    // We will use two RelativeYearlyRecurrencePatterns to
```

```
// describe the start of Standard and Daylight time
// accordingly
//
RelativeYearlyRecurrencePatternType standardTimeDesc =
    new RelativeYearlyRecurrencePatternType();
standardTimeDesc.DaysOfWeek = DayOfWeekType.Sunday.ToString();
standardTimeDesc.DayOfWeekIndex = DayOfWeekIndexType.First;
standardTimeDesc.Month = MonthNamesType.November;

RelativeYearlyRecurrencePatternType daylightTimeDesc =
    new RelativeYearlyRecurrencePatternType();
daylightTimeDesc.DaysOfWeek = DayOfWeekType.Sunday.ToString();
daylightTimeDesc.DayOfWeekIndex = DayOfWeekIndexType.Second;
daylightTimeDesc.Month = MonthNamesType.March;

// We've defined on what date the time change occurs, but we
// still have to define how far from the base offset the time
// change is, and at what time of day the time change occurs
//
TimeChangeType standardTimeChangeInfo = new TimeChangeType();
standardTimeChangeInfo.Item = standardTimeDesc;
standardTimeChangeInfo.Offset = "PT0H";
standardTimeChangeInfo.Time = twoAM;

TimeChangeType daylightTimeChangeInfo = new TimeChangeType();
daylightTimeChangeInfo.Item = daylightTimeDesc;
daylightTimeChangeInfo.Offset = "-PT1H";
daylightTimeChangeInfo.Time = twoAM;

// Create the meeting time zone object and assign our Daylight
// and Standard time change definitions accordingly
//
TimeZoneType meetingTimeZone = new TimeZoneType();
meetingTimeZone.BaseOffset = "PT7H";
meetingTimeZone.Standard = standardTimeChangeInfo;
meetingTimeZone.Daylight = daylightTimeChangeInfo;

// Assign the Time Zone to our new series
//
newRecurringMaster.MeetingTimeZone = meetingTimeZone;

// Set the Recurring information on our new series
//
newRecurringMaster.Recurrence = new RecurrenceType();
newRecurringMaster.Recurrence.Item = recurrencePattern;
newRecurringMaster.Recurrence.Item1 = recurrenceRange;

// Make our request
//
CreateItemType createItemRequest = new CreateItemType();
createItemRequest.SendMeetingInvitations =
    CalendarItemCreateOrDeleteOperationType.SendToNone;
createItemRequest.SendMeetingInvitationsSpecified = true;
createItemRequest.Items = new NonEmptyArrayOfAllItemsType();
```

```
    createItemRequest.Items.Items = new CalendarItemType[1];
    createItemRequest.Items.Items[0] = newRecurringMaster;

    CreateItemResponseType response = binding.CreateItem(createItemRequest);
    ItemInfoResponseMessageType responseMessage =
        response.ResponseMessages.Items[0] as ItemInfoResponseMessageType;

    if (responseMessage.ResponseCode != ResponseCodeType.NoError)
    {
        throw new Exception("CreateCalendarItem failed with response code " +
                responseMessage.ResponseCode.ToString());
    }
    return responseMessage.Items.Items[0].ItemId;
}
```

Notes on Getting Time Zone Definitions from the Windows Registry

In order for your application to create an Exchange Web Services calendar item in any time zone, your application must be able to construct the definition of each time zone. You might think that having to construct a definition for *every* possible time zone is quite tedious. This can certainly be true, especially when you consider that bias transition rules are always subject to change. Add to this the fact that the .NET Framework *DateTime* structure only has support for *Local* and *UTC* time zones, and you may feel overwhelmed. Fortunately, we've included C# code in Appendix B (available on the companion Web page) for getting time zone information from the Windows Registry and converting that information into a *TimeChangeType* object.

Exchange Web Services has another structure for defining time zone information called the *SerializableTimeZone* type, and its role is almost identical to *MeetingTimeZone* except that it is used exclusively by the *GetUserAvailability* Web method. We will discuss the *SerializableTimeZone* type and the *GetUserAvailability* Web method in Chapter 21. You will need to retrieve Windows Registry time zone information when dealing with *SerializableTimeZone* instances too. As such, the code in Appendix B can be used to create either a *MeetingTimeZone* or a *SerializableTimeZone*, which is precisely why we decided to leave the code in the appendix.

Summary

In this chapter, we discussed how calendar items in a recurring series are indexed and how to use the *RecurringMasterItemIdType* type and the *OccurrenceItemIdType* type to perform lookups between recurring masters and occurrences or exceptions. We looked at a number of special reference properties on a recurring master that can help identify certain occurrences within a recurring series.

This chapter then took a look at creating a recurring series. We talked about how creating a recurring series involves setting two properties on the *Recurrence* of a calendar item. We looked at the different types of recurrence patterns (fixed interval and variable interval) and looked at the three different types of recurrence ranges that can be defined.

The next part of this chapter looked at time zones in great detail. We talked about the *TimeZoneType* and how it can be used in a *MeetingTimeZone* property to describe a time zone that adheres to daylight savings time. We spoke about a few issues that you need to be aware of such as Outlook Web Access displaying an Exchange Web Services-created series with an "Unknown Time Zone" string, as well as how to overcome the XML serialization problem with the *xs:time* format through the use of the *IXmlSerializable* interface.

Finally, we mentioned that Chapter 21 will introduce you to the *SerializableTimeZone* type, and that Appendix B provides C# code that you can use in your applications to query the Windows Registry and fill out not only a *MeetingTimeZone* property, but also a *SerializableTimeZone* instance as well.

Chapter 10
Scheduling Meetings

Calendar items can be used to represent a meeting between two or more parties. In Exchange Web Services (EWS), these parties are called *attendees*. Attendees are stored on a calendar item in one of three different *attendee collections* and are classified based on which collection they are contained in. Any calendar item that has attendees is called a *meeting* and this designation can be identified by checking the *IsMeeting* property on a calendar item.

The *required attendees* collection is for attendees who must be able to attend the meeting in order for it to occur. The *optional attendees* collection is for attendees who are not required. The *resources* attendee collection is for denoting meeting resources (such as rooms or equipment). Each of these attendee collections are represented on a meeting in the *RequiredAttendees*, *OptionalAttendees*, and *Resources* properties respectively.

While meetings are technically just calendar items with attendees, in the real world they are often the result of coordination between all of the attendees trying to find a time to meet together. Meetings have *organizers* who are responsible for sending out *meeting requests* and coordinating all of the attendees *meeting responses*. Organizers can also send *meeting updates* as well as *meeting cancellations* to any or all attendees. Meeting requests, responses, updates, and cancellations are collectively referred to as *meeting messages*. The process of organizers and attendees sending meeting messages back and forth to each other is referred to as *meeting workflow*.

Creating a Meeting and Inviting Attendees

Meetings can be created in two different ways, either via the *CreateItem* Web method to create a calendar item with attendees or via the *UpdateItem* Web method where attendees are added to an already existing calendar item. Regardless of how a meeting is created, during the creation process the meeting organizer is required to indicate to Exchange Web Services how, when, and if meeting requests should be sent to attendees, and thus, starts the meeting workflow process. Before we get into the details of meeting workflow, however, we will start by looking at the two ways of creating a meeting and how you can control the sending of meeting messages.

 Note This chapter will use examples of messages being sent back and forth between parties. In these examples, it is assumed that each party is using Exchange Server 2007 as the messaging server.

Creating a Meeting Using the *CreateItem* Web Method

Often, a meeting organizer creates a meeting from scratch, creating the calendar item that represents the meeting and adding attendees to the attendee collections all at creation time. Consider, for example, three people (Users A, B, and C) and one resource (Room D). User A (call him Andy) wants to create a meeting request and invite User B (Brian) and User C (Carol) to participate. Andy wants the meeting to take place in Room D (Room D331). In this example, then, Andy is the meeting organizer, whereas Brian, Carol, and Room D331 are all attendees.

Andy begins by creating a calendar item for the meeting by calling the *CreateItem* Web method, and he designates Brian as a required attendee, Carol as an optional attendee, and Room D331 as one of the resources for the meeting. Andy does this by creating a *Attendee* element for each attendee, and then creates a *Mailbox* element containing a *Name* and *EmailAddress* element within each *Attendee* element. Andy then places each *Attendee* node inside the *RequiredAttendees, OptionalAttendees*, or *Resources* element as appropriate.

Andy must also set the *SendMeetingInvitations* attribute. So far in this book, all of the examples have used the value *SendToNone* for this attribute. In this example, Andy is going to use the value *SendOnlyToAll*, the significance of which we will explain in a moment. Andy's call to the *CreateItem* Web method would look like Listing 10-1.

LISTING 10-1 Calling the *CreateItem* Web method to create a new meeting

```xml
<m:CreateItem SendMeetingInvitations="SendOnlyToAll"
              xmlns:m=".../messages"
              xmlns:t=".../types">
  <m:Items>
    <t:CalendarItem>
      <t:Subject>Meeting in room D331</t:Subject>
      <t:Start>2007-01-15T19:00:00-08:00</t:Start>
      <t:End>2007-01-15T23:00:00-08:00</t:End>
      <t:Location>Room D331</t:Location>
      <t:RequiredAttendees>
        <t:Attendee>
          <t:Mailbox>
            <t:Name>Brian Smith</t:Name>
            <t:EmailAddress>Brian@contoso.com</t:EmailAddress>
          </t:Mailbox>
        </t:Attendee>
      </t:RequiredAttendees>
      <t:OptionalAttendees>
        <t:Attendee>
          <t:Mailbox>
            <t:Name>Carol Troup</t:Name>
            <t:EmailAddress>carol@contoso.com</t:EmailAddress>
          </t:Mailbox>
        </t:Attendee>
      </t:OptionalAttendees>
      <t:Resources>
```

```
        <t:Attendee>
          <t:Mailbox>
            <t:Name>Meeting Room D331</t:Name>
            <t:EmailAddress>mr_d331@contoso.com</t:EmailAddress>
          </t:Mailbox>
        </t:Attendee>
      </t:Resources>
    </t:CalendarItem>
  </m:Items>
</m:CreateItem>
```

Listing 10-2 demonstrates how to create a meeting with the proxy classes.

Note The method defined in Listing 10-2 requires you to supply *EmailAddressType* type instances for attendees. There are several other examples in this chapter that have the same requirement. You must have valid Exchange Server mailbox accounts that you can test with in order to execute the method with success.

LISTING 10-2 Creating a new meeting with the proxy classes

```
/// <summary>
/// Creates a new meeting and sends invitations to all attendees
/// </summary>
/// <param name="binding">Binding to use for the web service call</param>
/// <param name="meetingStartTime">Start time for the meeting</param>
/// <param name="meetingEndTime">End time for the meeting</param>
/// <param name="meetingTimeZone">Time zone for the meeting</param>
/// <param name="requiredAttendees">All required attendees</param>
/// <param name="optionalAttendees">All optional attendees</param>
/// <param name="meetingRoom">Meeting room location</param>
/// <returns>Id of newly created meeting</returns>
///
public static ItemIdType CreateNewMeetingAndInviteAttendees(
    ExchangeServiceBinding binding,
    DateTime meetingStartTime,
    DateTime meetingEndTime,
    TimeZoneType meetingTimeZone,
    EmailAddressType[] requiredAttendees,
    EmailAddressType[] optionalAttendees,
    EmailAddressType meetingRoom)
{
    // Basic new calendar item information
    //
    CalendarItemType newCalendarItem = new CalendarItemType();
    newCalendarItem.Start = meetingStartTime;
    newCalendarItem.StartSpecified = true;
    newCalendarItem.End = meetingEndTime;
    newCalendarItem.EndSpecified = true;
    newCalendarItem.MeetingTimeZone = meetingTimeZone;
```

```
    // Set the location of the meeting to be the name of the meeting room
    //
    newCalendarItem.Location = meetingRoom.Name;
    newCalendarItem.Subject = "Meeting in room " + meetingRoom.Name;

    // Create an Attendee instance for each EmailAddreesType instance and add
    // is to the appropriate collection
    //
    newCalendarItem.RequiredAttendees = new
        AttendeeType[requiredAttendees.Length];
    for (int x = 0; x < requiredAttendees.Length; x++)
    {
        newCalendarItem.RequiredAttendees[x] = new AttendeeType();
        newCalendarItem.RequiredAttendees[x].Mailbox = requiredAttendees[x];
    }

    newCalendarItem.OptionalAttendees = new
        AttendeeType[optionalAttendees.Length];
    for (int x = 0; x < optionalAttendees.Length; x++)
    {
        newCalendarItem.OptionalAttendees[x] = new AttendeeType();
        newCalendarItem.OptionalAttendees[x].Mailbox = optionalAttendees[x];
    }

    newCalendarItem.Resources = new AttendeeType[1];
    newCalendarItem.Resources[0] = new AttendeeType();
    newCalendarItem.Resources[0].Mailbox = meetingRoom;

    // Prepare the create item request
    //
    CreateItemType createItemRequest = new CreateItemType();
    createItemRequest.SendMeetingInvitations =
        CalendarItemCreateOrDeleteOperationType.SendOnlyToAll;
    createItemRequest.SendMeetingInvitationsSpecified = true;
    createItemRequest.Items = new NonEmptyArrayOfAllItemsType();
    createItemRequest.Items.Items = new CalendarItemType[] { newCalendarItem };

    // Call the CreateItem web method and check for success.
    // If successful, return the id of the new meeting
    //
    CreateItemResponseType response = binding.CreateItem(createItemRequest);
    ItemInfoResponseMessageType responseMessage =
        response.ResponseMessages.Items[0] as
        ItemInfoResponseMessageType;

    if (responseMessage.ResponseCode != ResponseCodeType.NoError)
    {
        throw new Exception(String.Format(
            "Unable to create a new meeting\r\n{0}\r\n{1}",
            responseMessage.ResponseCode,
            responseMessage.MessageText));
    }
    return responseMessage.Items.Items[0].ItemId;
}
```

What Andy might not be able to appreciate is the number of operations that Exchange Web Services is doing in response to his *CreateItem* Web method call. First, a new calendar item with an *IsMeeting* property set to true was created and placed in Andy's calendar folder. Second, meeting requests were created and automatically sent to each attendee. Third, each attendee, upon recieveing the meeting request, will have a corresponding calendar item (also with the *IsMeeting* property set to true) created and placed on their respective calendars. All of the new meetings on the attendees' calendars will have a *free/busy* status of *Tentative*.[1]

What if Andy used the value *SendToAllAndSaveCopy* for *SendMeetingInvitations*? The results would have been the same except that Andy would also have a copy of the meeting request placed in his Sent Items folder.

To help put things in perspective, look at Figure 10-1, which diagrams this process.

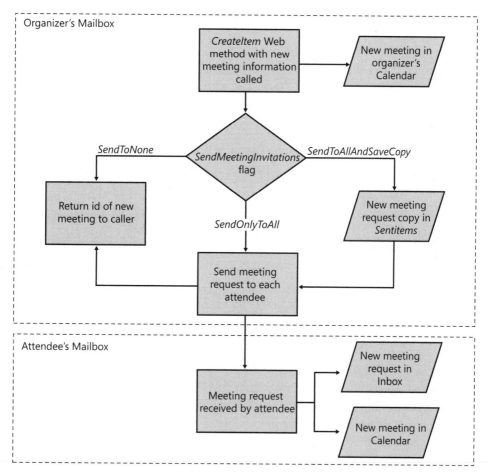

FIGURE 10-1 Process flow diagram for creating a meeting

---

[1] The new meeting on Andy's calendar will have a free/busy status of 'Busy,' which is the default value that has been applied to all other calendar items created in the examples from previous chapters.

You can see that the start of the process diagram Exchange Web Services receives a call to the *CreateItem* Web method and creates a new calendar item in the organizer's calendar folder. Exchange Web Services then processes the *SendMeetingInvitations* value, which can be one of the values from the *CalendarItemCreateOrDeleteOperationType* enumeration shown in Listing 10-3.

LISTING 10-3 Schema for the *CalendarItemCreateOrDeleteOperationType* enumeration

```
<xs:simpleType name="CalendarItemCreateOrDeleteOperationType">
  <xs:restriction base="xs:string">
    <xs:enumeration value="SendToNone" />
    <xs:enumeration value="SendOnlyToAll" />
    <xs:enumeration value="SendToAllAndSaveCopy" />
  </xs:restriction>
</xs:simpleType>
```

Based on the *SendMeetingInvitations* value, Exchange Web Services will create meeting requests for all attendees, optionally place a meeting request copy in the organizer's Sent Items folder, or create no meeting requests. In all cases, the *CreateItem* Web method response will contain the id of the new meeting item. Table 10-1 describes how each value for *SendMeetingInvitations* is processed.

TABLE 10-1 Effects of *SendMeetingInvitations* Values During Meeting Creation

SendMeetingInvitations value	Meeting Requests Sent	Copy of Meeting Request Placed in SentItems
SendToNone	No	No
SendOnlyToAll	Yes	No
SendToAllAndSaveCopy	Yes	Yes

Note The location of meeting request copies cannot be changed when calling the *CreateItem* Web method (for example, by providing a the id of a folder via the *SavedItemFolderId* element). The *SavedItemFolderId* element refers to the saved location of a created calendar item only and does not apply to any meeting request copies that the caller may wish to save. The Exchange Web Services team recommends performing a call to the *MoveItem* Web method in order to place a meeting request copy into a different folder.

In the lower portion of Figure 10-1, the meeting request is received by each attendee. Here the Microsoft Exchange Information Store service (Exchange Store) delivers the meeting request to each attendee's Inbox. The Exchange Store also creates a new meeting and places it on each attendee's calendar.

> **Note** As with all messages sent through Exchange Web Services, any message routing rules that dictate delivery and transportation of messages apply to all meeting messages as well. The Exchange Store will deliver the message via local messaging application programming interface (MAPI) delivery if the attendee's mailbox is located on the local Exchange Mailbox Server, or via Simple Mail Transfer Protocol (SMTP) if delivery requires the message to be transported to a different Exchange Server.

Creating a Meeting Using the *UpdateItem* Web Method

The second way to create a meeting is to call the *UpdateItem* Web method on an existing calendar item and add attendees to any of the *RequiredAttendees*, *OptionalAttendees*, or *Resource* collections. In addition, you must set the *SendMeetingInvitationsOrCancellations* attribute on the *UpdateItem* request to a value indicating to whom and if meeting messages are to be sent.

Consider a second scenario. Andy has already created a calendar item on his calendar and wants to invite Brian, Carol, and set the meeting to occur in Room D331. Andy's call to the *UpdateItem* Web method would look like Listing 10-4.

LISTING 10-4 Updating the attendee list of an existing calendar item and sending invitations

```
<m:UpdateItem ConflictResolution="AutoResolve"
              SendMeetingInvitationsOrCancellations="SendOnlyToAll"
              xmlns:m=".../messages"
              xmlns:t=".../types">
  <m:ItemChanges>
    <t:ItemChange>
      <t:ItemId Id="AAAmAGFsZXh..." ChangeKey="DwAAABY..." />
      <t:Updates>
        <!-- Item Field1 Required Attendees -->
        <t:AppendToItemField>
          <t:FieldURI FieldURI="calendar:RequiredAttendees" />
          <t:CalendarItem>
            <t:RequiredAttendees>
              <t:Attendee>
                <t:Mailbox>
                  <t:Name>Brian Smith</t:Name>
                  <t:EmailAddress>Brian@contoso.com</t:EmailAddress>
                </t:Mailbox>
              </t:Attendee>
            </t:RequiredAttendees>
          </t:CalendarItem>
        </t:AppendToItemField>
        <!-- Item Field2 Optional Attendees -->
        <t:AppendToItemField>
          <t:FieldURI FieldURI="calendar:OptionalAttendees" />
          <t:CalendarItem>
            <t:OptionalAttendees>
```

```
                <t:Attendee>
                  <t:Mailbox>
                    <t:Name>Carol Troup</t:Name>
                    <t:EmailAddress>Carol@contoso.com</t:EmailAddress>
                  </t:Mailbox>
                </t:Attendee>
              </t:OptionalAttendees>
            </t:CalendarItem>
          </t:AppendToItemField>
          <!-- Item Field3 Resources -->
          <t:AppendToItemField>
            <t:FieldURI FieldURI="calendar:Resources" />
            <t:CalendarItem>
              <t:Resources>
                <t:Attendee>
                  <t:Mailbox>
                    <t:Name>Meeting Room D331</t:Name>
                    <t:EmailAddress>mr_d331@contoso.com</t:EmailAddress>
                  </t:Mailbox>
                </t:Attendee>
              </t:Resources>
            </t:CalendarItem>
          </t:AppendToItemField>
        </t:Updates>
      </t:ItemChange>
    </m:ItemChanges>
  </m:UpdateItem>
```

In Listing 10-4, Andy is using the *AppendToItemField* element to add attendees to each of the collections. In this example, Andy could have used the *SetItemField* in his call to the *UpdateItem* Web method as well since the calendar item initially had no attendees. However, if you want to change attendees on an already existing meeting, then your choice of *AppendToItemField* or *SetItemField* will be important. We discuss modifying the attendee collections later in this chapter.

Listing 10-5 shows an example of updating the attendee collections for an existing calendar item, and sending meeting requests to all newly added attendees, via the proxy classes.

LISTING 10-5 Updating the attendee list of an existing calendar item and sending invitations via the proxy classes

```
/// <summary>
/// Updates an existing calendar item, turning it into a meeting
/// and sends invitations to all attendees
/// </summary>
/// <param name="binding">Binding to use for the web service call</param>
/// <param name="existingCalendarItem">Id of the existing calendar item</param>
/// <param name="newRequiredAttendees">All required attendees</param>
/// <param name="newOptionalAttendees">All optional attendees</param>
/// <param name="meetingRoom">Meeting room location</param>
/// <returns>Id of updated meeting</returns>
```

```
///
public static ItemIdType UpdateCalendarItemToMeeting(
    ExchangeServiceBinding binding,
    ItemIdType existingCalendarItem,
    EmailAddressType[] newRequiredAttendees,
    EmailAddressType[] newOptionalAttendees,
    EmailAddressType meetingRoom)
{
    // Create a collection to store all
    // AppendToItemFieldType instances that
    // may be needed.
    //
    List<AppendToItemFieldType> appendToItemObjects =
        new List<AppendToItemFieldType>();

    // Create an AppendToItemFieldType instance for
    // required attendees.
    //
    if (newRequiredAttendees != null &&
        newRequiredAttendees.Length > 0)
    {
        List<AttendeeType> reqAttendees = new List<AttendeeType>();
        foreach (EmailAddressType attendeeEmailInfo in newRequiredAttendees)
        {
            AttendeeType reqAttendee = new AttendeeType();
            reqAttendee.Mailbox = attendeeEmailInfo;
            reqAttendees.Add(reqAttendee);
        }

        CalendarItemType calItemForReqAttendees = new CalendarItemType();
        calItemForReqAttendees.RequiredAttendees =
            reqAttendees.ToArray();

        PathToUnindexedFieldType fieldURI = new PathToUnindexedFieldType();
        fieldURI.FieldURI = UnindexedFieldURIType.calendarRequiredAttendees;

        AppendToItemFieldType reqAttendeesAppend = new AppendToItemFieldType();
        reqAttendeesAppend.Item = fieldURI;
        reqAttendeesAppend.Item1 = calItemForReqAttendees;
        appendToItemObjects.Add(reqAttendeesAppend);
    }

    // Create an AppendToItemFieldType instance for
    // optional attendees.
    //
    if (newOptionalAttendees != null &&
        newOptionalAttendees.Length > 0)
    {
        List<AttendeeType> optAttendees = new List<AttendeeType>();
        foreach (EmailAddressType attendeeEmailInfo in newOptionalAttendees)
        {
            AttendeeType optAttendee = new AttendeeType();
            optAttendee.Mailbox = attendeeEmailInfo;
            optAttendees.Add(optAttendee);
```

```
        }

        CalendarItemType calItemForOptAttendees = new CalendarItemType();
        calItemForOptAttendees.OptionalAttendees =
            optAttendees.ToArray();

        PathToUnindexedFieldType fieldURI = new PathToUnindexedFieldType();
        fieldURI.FieldURI = UnindexedFieldURIType.calendarOptionalAttendees;

        AppendToItemFieldType optAttendeesAppend = new AppendToItemFieldType();
        optAttendeesAppend.Item = fieldURI;
        optAttendeesAppend.Item1 = calItemForOptAttendees;
        appendToItemObjects.Add(optAttendeesAppend);
    }

    // Create an AppendToItemFieldType instance for
    // resources.
    //
    if (meetingRoom != null)
    {
        AttendeeType meetingRoomAttendeeInfo = new AttendeeType();
        meetingRoomAttendeeInfo.Mailbox = meetingRoom;

        CalendarItemType calItemForResources = new CalendarItemType();
        calItemForResources.Resources =
            new AttendeeType[] { meetingRoomAttendeeInfo };

        PathToUnindexedFieldType fieldURI = new PathToUnindexedFieldType();
        fieldURI.FieldURI = UnindexedFieldURIType.calendarResources;

        AppendToItemFieldType resourcesAppend = new AppendToItemFieldType();
        resourcesAppend.Item = fieldURI;
        resourcesAppend.Item1 = calItemForResources;
        appendToItemObjects.Add(resourcesAppend);
    }

    // Throw an exception if there are no changes needed
    //
    if (appendToItemObjects.Count == 0)
    {
        throw new Exception(
            "There were no attendees in any attendee collection.");
    }

    // Create an ItemChangeType instance to hold all the updates
    //
    ItemChangeType itemChangeInfo = new ItemChangeType();
    itemChangeInfo.Item = existingCalendarItem;
    itemChangeInfo.Updates = appendToItemObjects.ToArray();

    // Assemble the UpdateItem request
    //
    UpdateItemType updateItemRequest = new UpdateItemType();
    updateItemRequest.ConflictResolution = ConflictResolutionType.AutoResolve;
```

```
    updateItemRequest.SendMeetingInvitationsOrCancellations =
        CalendarItemUpdateOperationType.SendOnlyToAll;
    updateItemRequest.SendMeetingInvitationsOrCancellationsSpecified = true;
    updateItemRequest.ItemChanges = new ItemChangeType[] { itemChangeInfo };

  // Call the UpdateItem web method via the Exchange Serivce Binding
  UpdateItemResponseType updateItemResponse =
      binding.UpdateItem(updateItemRequest);

  // Verify that the UpdateItem request was successful
  if (updateItemResponse.ResponseMessages.Items[0].ResponseClass !=
      ResponseClassType.Success)
  {
      // Indicate that we have a problem
      throw new Exception(String.Format(
          "Unable to update calendar item\r\n{0}\r\n{1}",
          updateItemResponse.ResponseMessages.Items[0].ResponseCode,
          updateItemResponse.ResponseMessages.Items[0].MessageText));
  }

  // Success, get the updated id of meeting
  ItemInfoResponseMessageType itemInfoResponseMessage =
      (ItemInfoResponseMessageType)updateItemResponse.
          ResponseMessages.Items[0];

  return itemInfoResponseMessage.Items.Items[0].ItemId;
}
```

Similar to the *SendMeetingInvitations* property on the *CreateItem* Web method, the *SendMeetingInvitationsOrCancellations* property on the *UpdateItem* Web method takes values from an enumeration and tells Exchange Web Services to whom to send and if meeting requests should be sent to attendees.

Values for the *SendMeetingInvitationsOrCancellations* property are from the *CalendarItemUpdateOperationType* enumeration, shown in Listing 10-6.

LISTING 10-6 Schema for the *CalendarItemUpdateOperationType* enumeration

```xml
<xs:simpleType name="CalendarItemUpdateOperationType">
  <xs:restriction base="xs:string">
    <xs:enumeration value="SendToNone" />
    <xs:enumeration value="SendOnlyToAll" />
    <xs:enumeration value="SendOnlyToChanged" />
    <xs:enumeration value="SendToAllAndSaveCopy" />
    <xs:enumeration value="SendToChangedAndSaveCopy" />
  </xs:restriction>
</xs:simpleType>
```

The *SendToNone*, *SendOnlyToAll*, and *SendToAllAndSaveCopy* values invoke the same behavior as when using the *SendMeetingInvitations* property on a *CreateItem* Web method call.

The other two values, *SendOnlyToChanged* and *SendToChangedAndSaveCopy*, enable the caller to send meeting messages only to those who need to be informed of the changes (for example, just the newly added or removed attendees). Table 10-2 describes how each value for *SendMeetingInvitationsOrCancellations* is processed.

TABLE 10-2 Effects of *SendMeetingInvitationsOrCancellations* Values During a Meeting Update

SendMeetingInvitationsOrCancellations value	Meeting Messages Sent	Copy of Meeting Message Placed in SentItems
SendToNone	No	No
SendOnlyToAll	Yes, to all attendees	No
SendOnlyToChanged	Yes, to attendees added and/or deleted as a result of the update	No
SendToAllAndSaveCopy	Yes, to all attendees	Yes
SendToChangedAndSaveCopy	Yes, to attendees added and/or deleted as a result of the update	Yes

As an example of using *SendOnlyToChanged* or *SendToChangedAndSaveCopy*, consider the situation where Andy created the meeting with Brian as a required attendee. Later, if Andy decides to add Carol to the required collection, he would probably use *SendOnlyToChanged* or *SendToChangedAndSaveCopy* in his call to the *UpdateItem* Web method. This would result in a meeting request being sent to Carol, and Brian would receive no message indicating this change occurred.

> **Note** A folder id in a *SavedItemFolderId* property on a call to the *UpdateItem* Web method for a meeting item will affect only the location of the meeting item and will not control the location of any meeting message copies. The Exchange Web Services team recommends making a call to the *MoveItem* Web method to place a meeting message copy into a different folder.

Understanding Attendees and Attendee Collections

We have already talked briefly about the three different attendee collections on a calendar item and demonstrated how to add attendees to them. Let's look now at the attendee collections and attendees in some more detail.

Recall from Chapter 8, "Working with Calendars," that each of the attendee collections is represented on the *CalendarItemType* schema type by the *RequiredAttendees*, *OptionalAttendees*, and *Resources* elements. Each of these elements is of the *NonEmptyArrayOfAttendeesType* type. The *NonEmptyArrayOfAttendeesType* type is a simple array type with each element named *Attendee*, each of *AttendeeType* schema type.

```
<xs:complexType name="NonEmptyArrayOfAttendeesType">
  <xs:sequence>
    <xs:element name="Attendee"
                type="t:AttendeeType"
                maxOccurs="unbounded" />
  </xs:sequence>
</xs:complexType>
```

The *AttendeeType* schema type is used to define an attendee.

```
<xs:complexType name="AttendeeType">
  <xs:sequence>
    <xs:element name="Mailbox" type="t:EmailAddressType" />
    <xs:element name="ResponseType" type="t:ResponseTypeType" minOccurs="0" />
    <xs:element name="LastResponseTime" type="xs:dateTime" minOccurs="0" />
  </xs:sequence>
</xs:complexType>
```

So far, all of the examples in this chapter have only demonstrated setting the *Mailbox* property on an *AttendeeType* type instance. The *Mailbox* property is of the *EmailAddressType* schema type, which was covered in detail in Chapter 7, "Messages."

The other two properties, *ResponseType* and *LastResponseTime,* are read-only properties that will be populated by the server and are used for for tracking attendee responses. You can read more about how these properties are used in the "Tracking Meeting Attendance" section of this chapter.

Modifying an Attendee Collection

Recall from Chapter 5, "Items," the difference between using the *SetItemField* and *AppendToItemField* elements when calling the *UpdateItem* Web method. When working to update the attendee list, it is especially important to use caution when using the *SetItemField* element. Using the *SetItemField* on an attendee collection will overwrite the collection with all new attendee values.[2]

> **Note** If you call the *UpdateItem* Web method with the *SetItemField* to update one of the three attendee arrays (*RequiredAttendees, OptionalAttendees,* or *Resources*), and you fail to include all current members of the array, you will receive an *ErrorIrresolvableConflict* response code when using a *ConflictResolution* value of 'NeverOverwrite' or 'AutoResolve'.

---

2   There is a slight caveat to this. If an attendee has responded to a meeting, and that attendee is then included in a *SetItemField* during an update, the *ResponseType* and *LastResponseTime* properties of that attendee will not be overwritten.

Removing Attendees from a Meeting

To remove attendees from an attendee collection, you have to call the *UpdateItem* Web method for the meeting with the *SetItemField* change description to include all current members of the attendee array minus those you want removed. If you try to use a *DeleteItemField* change description, you remove all attendees from the collection. Any attendee who is removed from an attendee list as the result of an update will be sent a meeting cancellation (unless the *SendMeetingInvitationsOrCancellations* value was set to "*SendToNone*").

Any attendee who has been removed from all attendee collections, but has not been sent a meeting cancellation, will still have a copy of the meeting on his calendar. The removed attendee may still register a response even after being removed from the attendee list. If that happens, the removed attendee will be re-added to the optional attendees collection on the meeting in the organizer's calendar.

> **Best Practices** As a general rule, don't use the combination of a *ConflictResolution* value of '*AlwaysOverwrite*' and a *SendMeetingInvitationsOrCancellations* value of '*SendToNone*' in your calls to the *UpdateItem* Web method. The combination of these values will result in any removed attendees not receiving a meeting message indicating they have been removed.

Forwarding Meetings and Meeting Requests

A meeting can be forwarded to others in order to make them an attendee of the meeting. For example, if Andy creates a meeting and invites Brian, Brian can forward his meeting request to Carol and Carol will receive a new meeting request indicating that Brian has invited her to the meeting 'on behalf of' Andy.[3] To forward a meeting request in Exchange Web Services, you call the *CreateItem* Web method and use a *ForwardItem* response object with a reference to the id of either the meeting item or the meeting request. Listing 10-7 is an example.

LISTING 10-7 Using a *ForwardItem* response object on a meeting request

```
<m:CreateItem MessageDisposition="SendOnly"
              xmlns:m=".../messages"
              xmlns:t=".../types">
  <m:Items>
    <t:ForwardItem>
      <t:ToRecipients>
        <t:Mailbox>
          <t:Name>Carol Troup</t:Name>
          <t:EmailAddress>carol@contoso.com</t:EmailAddress>
        </t:Mailbox>
      </t:ToRecipients>
```

---

[3] We will explain the 'on behalf of' reference in a moment.

```
      <!-- Item id of a meeting or a meeting request -->
      <t:ReferenceItemId Id="AAAeAGRhdnNOZXJAZX..." ChangeKey="AQAAABYAAAD..."/>
    </t:ForwardItem>
  </m:Items>
</m:CreateItem>
```

The ability to forward meetings and meeting requests is not limited to attendees; a meeting organizer can also forward meetings as well.

> **Warning** Do not attempt to use the *ForwardItem* response object to try to add attendees to a calendar item that is *not* a meeting. Using *ForwardItem* with a non-meeting only creates and sends a new message with the calendar item as an attachment.

Any recipients of a forwarded meeting request are added to the optional attendee collection of the meeting on the organizer's calendar.

Meeting Forward Notification Messages

When an attendee forwards a meeting request to another attendee, the meeting organizer will receive a *meeting forward notification* message. Exchange Web Services does not have a dedicated type for a meeting forward notification message, and will therefore use the *ItemType* schema type for these messages. Listing 10-8 is an example of a meeting forward notification message in a *GetItem* Web method response.

LISTING 10-8 A meeting forward notification message in a *GetItem* Web method response

```
<m:GetItemResponseMessage ResponseClass="Success"
                          xmlns:m=".../messages"
                          xmlns:t=".../types">
  <m:ResponseCode>NoError</m:ResponseCode>
  <m:Items>
    <t:Item>
      <t:ItemId Id="AAAeAGRhdnNOZXJAZX..." ChangeKey="AQAAABYAAAD..."/>
      <t:ParentFolderId Id="AAAeAGRhdnNOZXJAZX..." ChangeKey="AQAAABYAAAD..."/>
      <t:ItemClass>IPM.Notification.Meeting.Forward</t:ItemClass>
      <t:Subject>Meeting Forward Notification: Meeting for Brian</t:Subject>
      <t:Sensitivity>Normal</t:Sensitivity>
      <t:Body BodyType="HTML">...</t:Body>
      <t:DateTimeReceived>2007-09-08T03:44:52Z</t:DateTimeReceived>
      <t:Size>3067</t:Size>
      <t:Importance>Normal</t:Importance>
      <t:InReplyTo />
      <t:IsSubmitted>false</t:IsSubmitted>
      <t:IsDraft>false</t:IsDraft>
      <t:IsFromMe>false</t:IsFromMe>
      <t:IsResend>false</t:IsResend>
      <t:IsUnmodified>false</t:IsUnmodified>
```

```
        <t:InternetMessageHeaders>
          <!-- Internet Message Headers omitted for brevity -->
        </t:InternetMessageHeaders>
        <t:DateTimeSent>2007-09-08T03:44:52Z</t:DateTimeSent>
        <t:DateTimeCreated>2007-09-08T03:44:52Z</t:DateTimeCreated>
        <t:ResponseObjects>
          <t:ReplyToItem />
          <t:ReplyAllToItem />
          <t:ForwardItem />
        </t:ResponseObjects>
        <t:ReminderDueBy>2007-09-20T19:00:00Z</t:ReminderDueBy>
        <t:DisplayCc />
        <t:DisplayTo>Andy Jacobs</t:DisplayTo>
        <t:HasAttachments>false</t:HasAttachments>
        <t:Culture>en-US</t:Culture>
      </t:Item>
    </m:Items>
  </m:GetItemResponseMessage>
```

A meeting forward notification message has an *ItemClass* of "IPM.Notification.Meeting. Forward". It also has a *Subject* property value prefixed with "Meeting Forward Notification:".[4]

Other than the text of the message itself, there is no property indicating to whom the attendee forwarded the meeting; however, the meeting organizer will receive a meeting response from the new attendee and future meeting updates will be received by the new attendee just as if they were a member of the attendees collection from the beginning.

Recognizing a Meeting Request as 'Sent On Behalf Of'

When a meeting or a meeting request is forwarded to a new attendee, that attendee will receive a meeting request indicating that it was not the organizer who sent the meeting request, but rather another attendee. You can recognize this by comparing the *From* and *Sender* properties of the meeting request. The *From* property will indicate the organizer of the meeting, the *Sender* property will indicate who forwarded the meeting. Listing 10-7 was an example of Brian forwarding a meeting request to Carol. Listing 10-9 is what the *From* and *Sender* properties on Carol's meeting request might look like after making a call to the *FindItem* Web method.

---

[4] The "Meeting Forward Notification:" text will be localized into the language selected by the sender. In Exchange Web Services this is done via the *MailboxCulture* header which was discussed in Chapter 2, "May I See Your Id?"

LISTING 10-9 Example of a forwarded meeting message

```
<m:FindItemResponse xmlns:t=".../types"
                    xmlns:m=".../messages">
  <m:ResponseMessages>
    <m:FindItemResponseMessage ResponseClass="Success">
      <m:ResponseCode>NoError</m:ResponseCode>
      <m:RootFolder TotalItemsInView="1" IncludesLastItemInRange="true">
        <t:Items>
          <t:MeetingRequest>
            <t:ItemId Id="AAAeAGRhdnNOZXJAZX... " ChangeKey="AQAAABYAAAD..."/>
            <t:Subject>FW: Meeting originally for Brian only</t:Subject>
            <t:Sensitivity>Normal</t:Sensitivity>
            <t:HasAttachments>false</t:HasAttachments>
            <t:Sender>
              <t:Mailbox>
                <t:Name>Brian Smith</t:Name>
              </t:Mailbox>
            </t:Sender>
            <t:From>
              <t:Mailbox>
                <t:Name>Andy Jacobs</t:Name>
              </t:Mailbox>
            </t:From>
            <t:IsRead>false</t:IsRead>
            <t:HasBeenProcessed>true</t:HasBeenProcessed>
            <t:ResponseType>NoResponseReceived</t:ResponseType>
            <t:IntendedFreeBusyStatus>Busy</t:IntendedFreeBusyStatus>
            <t:Start>2007-09-20T19:00:00Z</t:Start>
            <t:End>2007-09-20T20:00:00Z</t:End>
            <t:Location>Andy's Office</t:Location>
            <t:Organizer>
              <t:Mailbox>
                <t:Name>Andy Jacobs</t:Name>
              </t:Mailbox>
            </t:Organizer>
          </t:MeetingRequest>
        </t:Items>
      </m:RootFolder>
    </m:FindItemResponseMessage>
  </m:ResponseMessages>
</m:FindItemResponse>
```

The meeting request in Listing 10-9 is considered "From: Brian Smith on behalf of Andy Jacobs." The phrase 'on behalf of' is used to describe this message because of a common practice that other Exchange clients (such as Microsoft Office Outlook and Microsoft Outlook Web Access) have adopted. The Exchange Web Services team recommends that applications follow this practice of reporting messages with differing *From* and *Sender* values as being

From: [Sender value] on behalf of [From value]

Figure 10-2 is the meeting request from Listing 10-9 as seen in Outlook Web Access.

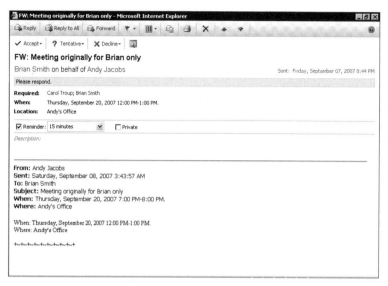

FIGURE 10-2 Example of a forwarded meeting request in Outlook Web Access

Working with Meeting Messages

After a meeting has been created or updated, meeting messages are sent to and from attendees of the meeting to coordinate registration and information about the meeting. A meeting request is just one type of meeting message. In Exchange Web Services, all meeting messages used for meeting workflow share a common base schema type, and that type is the *MeetingMessageType* schema type.

Understanding Meeting Messages

The base schema type used for all meeting messages is the *MeetingMessageType* schema type. Listing 10-10 is the schema for the *MeetingMessageType* type.

LISTING 10-10 Schema for the *MeetingMessageType* type

```
<xs:complexType name="MeetingMessageType">
  <xs:complexContent>
    <xs:extension base="t:MessageType">
      <xs:sequence>
        <xs:element name="AssociatedCalendarItemId"
                    type="t:ItemIdType" minOccurs="0"/>
        <xs:element name="IsDelegated" type="xs:boolean" minOccurs="0" />
        <xs:element name="IsOutOfDate" type="xs:boolean" minOccurs="0" />
        <xs:element name="HasBeenProcessed"
                    type="xs:boolean" minOccurs="0" />
        <xs:element name="ResponseType"
```

```
                    type="t:ResponseTypeType" minOccurs="0" />
        </xs:sequence>
      </xs:extension>
    </xs:complexContent>
  </xs:complexType>
```

The three types that inherit from the *MeetingMessageType* type are
MeetingCancellationMessageType type, *MeetingRequestMessageType* type, and
MeetingResponseMessageType type. Figure 10-3 shows the *MeetingMessageType* hierarchy.

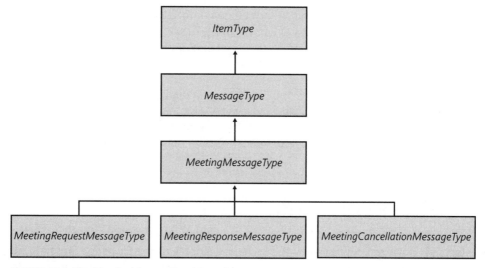

FIGURE 10-3 The *MeetingMessageType* hierarchy

We will begin with the properties of the *MeetingMessageType* base type and then discuss the
properties of the other message types in context as we encounter them in our discussion of
meeting workflow.

AssociatedCalendarItemId Property

The *AssociatedCalendarItemId* property is a read-only property that is set during the creation
of a meeting calendar item by the Exchange Store following the arrival of a meeting request.
This property serves as a link to the meeting and is always in the scope of the current mailbox. A meeting request would not, for example, refer back to the meeting in the organizer's
mailbox. In the case of a new recurring meeting, this id will point to the recurring master.

IsDelegated Property

The *IsDelegated* property indicates if the meeting request was sent by a delegate on behalf
of the organizer or if a meeting response was responded to by a delegate of the attendee.

The *IsDelegated* property will *not* be set to true if the meeting request was forwarded by another attendee.

IsOutOfDate Property

The *IsOutOfDate* property indicates if the current meeting message is up to date. If this property is set to true, the information in this meeting message is no longer up to date, and the meeting itself has been updated with new information. In this situation, none of the information in the meeting message should be trusted.

The Exchange Server will do all it can to prevent attendees from seeing a meeting message that is out of date. However, this cannot be guaranteed because there are multiple ways of accessing a calendar item, some of which can override the logic that tries to delete outdated meeting messages and replace them with updated ones.

> **Best Practices** Exchange Web Services applications should always check the *IsOutOfDate* property on any meeting message before proceeding. It is common practice to inform users when they have selected an item that is out of date, and your application should discourage users from registering any response to a meeting based on out-of-date information. It is customary to allow the user to decide if and when an out-of-date meeting message should be deleted.

HasBeenProcessed Property

The *HasBeenProcessed* property is a read-only Boolean property that indicates if the meeting message has been processed by the Exchange Store (e.g., the Exchange Store has noted the arrival of a meeting request and has created the associated meeting item in the calendar.)

ResponseType Property

The *ResponseType* property is a read-only property that can be one of six possible values from the *ResponseTypeType* enumeration shown in Listing 10-11.

LISTING 10-11 Schema definition of the *ResponseTypeType* enumeration

```
<xs:simpleType name="ResponseTypeType">
  <xs:restriction base="xs:string">
    <xs:enumeration value="Unknown" />
    <xs:enumeration value="Organizer" />
    <xs:enumeration value="Tentative" />
    <xs:enumeration value="Accept" />
    <xs:enumeration value="Decline" />
    <xs:enumeration value="NoResponseReceived" />
  </xs:restriction>
</xs:simpleType>
```

This property is designed to hold the registration response of an attendee for the given meeting. On newly received meeting requests, this property will be set to "*NoResponseReceived.*" This indicates that the attendee has not yet registered a response. On meeting responses, this property will be set to whatever response the attendee has chosen to register.

> **Note** The *ResponseTypeType* enumeration will appear a lot in our discussion of meeting workflow. This enumeration is used in all of the *MeetingMessageType* message types and on instances of the *Attendee* type in the attendee collections.

Understanding Meeting Requests

You have already seen that a meeting request is of type *MeetingRequestMessageType*. Because the number of properties on a *MeetingResponseMessageType* is quite large, many of them have been omitted in Listing 10-12. (We will explain the reason for the omission shortly.)

LISTING 10-12 Partial schema for the *MeetingResponseMessageType* type

```
<xs:complexType name="MeetingRequestMessageType">
  <xs:complexContent>
    <xs:extension base="t:MeetingMessageType">
      <xs:sequence>
        <xs:element name="MeetingRequestType"
          type="t:MeetingRequestTypeType" minOccurs="0" />
        <xs:element name="IntendedFreeBusyStatus"
          type="t:LegacyFreeBusyType" minOccurs="0" />
        <xs:element name="Start" type="xs:dateTime" minOccurs="0" />
        <xs:element name="End" type="xs:dateTime" minOccurs="0" />
        <xs:element name="OriginalStart"
          type="xs:dateTime" minOccurs="0" />
        <xs:element name="IsAllDayEvent"
          type="xs:boolean" minOccurs="0" />
        <xs:element name="LegacyFreeBusyStatus"
          type="t:LegacyFreeBusyType" minOccurs="0" />
        <xs:element name="Location" type="xs:string" minOccurs="0" />
        <xs:element name="When" type="xs:string" minOccurs="0" />
        <xs:element name="IsMeeting" type="xs:boolean" minOccurs="0" />
        <xs:element name="IsCancelled" type="xs:boolean" minOccurs="0" />
        <xs:element name="IsRecurring" type="xs:boolean" minOccurs="0" />
        <xs:element name="MeetingRequestWasSent"
          type="xs:boolean" minOccurs="0" />
        <xs:element name="CalendarItemType"
          type="t:CalendarItemTypeType" minOccurs="0" />
        <xs:element name="MyResponseType"
          type="t:ResponseTypeType" minOccurs="0" />
        <xs:element name="Organizer"
          type="t:SingleRecipientType" minOccurs="0" />
```

```
            <xs:element name="RequiredAttendees"
                type="t:NonEmptyArrayOfAttendeesType" minOccurs="0" />
            <xs:element name="OptionalAttendees"
                type="t:NonEmptyArrayOfAttendeesType" minOccurs="0" />
            <xs:element name="Resources"
                type="t:NonEmptyArrayOfAttendeesType" minOccurs="0" />
          <!-- Additonal schema properties removed -->
          </xs:sequence>
        </xs:extension>
      </xs:complexContent>
    </xs:complexType>
```

As you look through Listing 10-12, you may be thinking, "This type looks a lot like the *CalendarItemType* schema type," and you would be thinking correctly. There is a reason why many of the properties on the *MeetingRequestMessageType* type are duplicates of the *CalendarItemType* type, and the reason has to do with its inheritance model and purpose.

Recall that the *MeetingRequestMessageType* type derives from the *MeetingMessageType* type, which in turn derives from *MessageType* type (see Figure 10-3). The reason that a meeting request ultimately derives from the *MessageType* type is that a meeting request must be able to be transported over SMTP, which means that it must contain all of the properties of a message. However, once it reaches the recipient's mailbox, the Exchange Store must be able to create a new calendar item based on the information in the meeting request, and, therefore, the meeting request must contain all of the properties of a calendar item as well. Since there is no way for a schema type to derive from two different schema types, the Exchange Web Services team had to put many of the properties from the *CalendarItemType* type on the *MeetingRequestMessageType* type as well.

Since many of these properties exist then solely for the purposes of message transport and calendar item creation, this chapter will focus on a subset of properties that you need to build an application that can support meeting workflow.

Properties of a Meeting Request

Recall the first example from the first section of this chapter. User A (Andy) created a new calendar item via the *CreateItem* Web method. He specified User B (Brian) as a required attendee, User C (Carol) as an optional attendee, and Resource D (Room D331) as a resource. He also set the *SendMeetingInvitations* value during his call to the *CreateItem* Web method to *SendOnlyToAll*. From this, you can expect the mailboxes of Brian, Carol, and Room D331 to contain both a new meeting request in the Inbox folder and a new meeting item (marked with a free/busy status of *Tentative*) in the Calendar folder.

Important Meeting requests are not used only for notifying attendees that a new meeting has been created. Meeting requests can also be used to indicate that a change has occurred to the meeting (such as the time has been changed or attendees have been added). For more details see the *MeetingRequestType* property explanation.

Listing 10-13 shows what Brian would see if he called the *GetItem* Web method for the meeting request in his Inbox.

LISTING 10-13 Property listing of a newly received meeting request

```
<m:GetItemResponse xmlns:t=".../types" xmlns:m=".../messages">
  <m:ResponseMessages>
    <m:GetItemResponseMessage ResponseClass="Success">
      <m:ResponseCode>NoError</m:ResponseCode>
      <m:Items>
        <t:MeetingRequest>
          <t:ItemId Id="AAAeAGRhdnN0ZXJAZX..." ChangeKey="AQAAABYAAAD..."/>
          <t:ParentFolderId Id="AAAeAGRhdnN0ZX..." ChangeKey="AQAAABYAAAD..."/>
          <t:ItemClass>IPM.Schedule.Meeting.Request</t:ItemClass>
          <t:Subject>Meeting in room D331</t:Subject>
          <t:Sensitivity>Normal</t:Sensitivity>
          <t:Body BodyType="HTML">...</t:Body>
          <t:DateTimeReceived>2007-09-08T03:43:59Z</t:DateTimeReceived>
          <t:Size>1368</t:Size>
          <t:Importance>Normal</t:Importance>
          <t:IsSubmitted>false</t:IsSubmitted>
          <t:IsDraft>false</t:IsDraft>
          <t:IsFromMe>false</t:IsFromMe>
          <t:IsResend>false</t:IsResend>
          <t:IsUnmodified>false</t:IsUnmodified>
          <t:InternetMessageHeaders>
              <!-- InternetMessageHeaders removed for brevity -->
          </t:InternetMessageHeaders>
          <t:DateTimeSent>2007-09-08T03:43:57Z</t:DateTimeSent>
          <t:DateTimeCreated>2007-09-08T03:43:58Z</t:DateTimeCreated>
          <t:ResponseObjects>
            <t:AcceptItem />
            <t:TentativelyAcceptItem />
            <t:DeclineItem />
            <t:ReplyToItem />
            <t:ReplyAllToItem />
            <t:ForwardItem />
          </t:ResponseObjects>
          <t:ReminderDueBy>2007-09-20T19:00:00Z</t:ReminderDueBy>
          <t:ReminderIsSet>true</t:ReminderIsSet>
          <t:ReminderMinutesBeforeStart>15</t:ReminderMinutesBeforeStart>
          <t:DisplayCc />
          <t:DisplayTo>Brian Smith</t:DisplayTo>
          <t:HasAttachments>false</t:HasAttachments>
          <t:Culture>en-US</t:Culture>
          <t:Sender>
            <t:Mailbox>
```

```
        <t:Name>Andy Jacobs</t:Name>
        <t:EmailAddress>andy@contoso.com</t:EmailAddress>
        <t:RoutingType>SMTP</t:RoutingType>
      </t:Mailbox>
    </t:Sender>
    <t:ToRecipients>
      <t:Mailbox>
        <t:Name>Brian Smith</t:Name>
        <t:EmailAddress>brian@contoso.com</t:EmailAddress>
        <t:RoutingType>SMTP</t:RoutingType>
      </t:Mailbox>
    </t:ToRecipients>
    <t:CcRecipients>
      <t:Mailbox>
        <t:Name>Carol Troup</t:Name>
        <t:EmailAddress>carol@contoso.com</t:EmailAddress>
        <t:RoutingType>SMTP</t:RoutingType>
      </t:Mailbox>
    </t:CcRecipients>
    <t:IsReadReceiptRequested>false</t:IsReadReceiptRequested>
    <t:ConversationIndex>AcfxynyY4XP</t:ConversationIndex>
    <t:ConversationTopic>Meeting in room D331</t:ConversationTopic>
    <t:From>
      <t:Mailbox>
        <t:Name>Andy Jacobs</t:Name>
        <t:EmailAddress>andy@contoso.com</t:EmailAddress>
        <t:RoutingType>SMTP</t:RoutingType>
      </t:Mailbox>
    </t:From>
    <t:InternetMessageId>&lt;99B0D0ACCBBD...</t:InternetMessageId>
    <t:IsRead>true</t:IsRead>
    <t:IsResponseRequested>true</t:IsResponseRequested>
    <t:AssociatedCalendarItemId Id="AAAnN0ZX..." ChangeKey="AQAAAD..."/>
    <t:IsDelegated>false</t:IsDelegated>
    <t:IsOutOfDate>false</t:IsOutOfDate>
    <t:HasBeenProcessed>true</t:HasBeenProcessed>
    <t:ResponseType>NoResponseReceived</t:ResponseType>
    <t:MeetingRequestType>NewMeetingRequest</t:MeetingRequestType>
    <t:IntendedFreeBusyStatus>Busy</t:IntendedFreeBusyStatus>
    <t:Start>2007-09-20T19:00:00Z</t:Start>
    <t:End>2007-09-20T20:00:00Z</t:End>
    <t:IsAllDayEvent>false</t:IsAllDayEvent>
    <t:LegacyFreeBusyStatus>Tentative</t:LegacyFreeBusyStatus>
    <t:Location>Andy's Office</t:Location>
    <t:IsMeeting>true</t:IsMeeting>
    <t:IsCancelled>false</t:IsCancelled>
    <t:IsRecurring>false</t:IsRecurring>
    <t:MeetingRequestWasSent>true</t:MeetingRequestWasSent>
    <t:CalendarItemType>Single</t:CalendarItemType>
    <t:MyResponseType>NoResponseReceived</t:MyResponseType>
    <t:Organizer>
      <t:Mailbox>
        <t:Name>Andy Jacobs</t:Name>
        <t:EmailAddress>andy@contoso.com</t:EmailAddress>
```

```
              <t:RoutingType>SMTP</t:RoutingType>
            </t:Mailbox>
          </t:Organizer>
          <t:RequiredAttendees>
            <t:Attendee>
              <t:Mailbox>
                <t:Name>Brian Smith</t:Name>
                <t:EmailAddress>brian@contoso.com</t:EmailAddress>
                <t:RoutingType>SMTP</t:RoutingType>
              </t:Mailbox>
              <t:ResponseType>Unknown</t:ResponseType>
            </t:Attendee>
          </t:RequiredAttendees>
          <t:OptionalAttendees>
            <t:Attendee>
              <t:Mailbox>
                <t:Name>Carol Troup</t:Name>
                <t:EmailAddress>carol@contoso.com</t:EmailAddress>
                <t:RoutingType>SMTP</t:RoutingType>
              </t:Mailbox>
              <t:ResponseType>Unknown</t:ResponseType>
            </t:Attendee>
          </t:OptionalAttendees>
          <t:ConflictingMeetingCount>0</t:ConflictingMeetingCount>
          <t:AdjacentMeetingCount>0</t:AdjacentMeetingCount>
          <t:Duration>PT1H</t:Duration>
          <t:TimeZone>Pacific Standard Time</t:TimeZone>
          <t:AppointmentSequenceNumber>0</t:AppointmentSequenceNumber>
          <t:AppointmentState>3</t:AppointmentState>
        </t:MeetingRequest>
      </m:Items>
    </m:GetItemResponseMessage>
  </m:ResponseMessages>
</m:GetItemResponse>
```

Listing 10-13 shows that the meeting request is represented by a *t:MeetingRequest* element and that a meeting request has an *ItemClass* of "IPM.Schedule.Meeting.Request." In addition, you see all of the numerous properties that a *MeetingRequestMessageType* type instance has. The properties that we will be discussing in this chapter are in boldface type.

Caution If you intend to display information from a meeting request to a user, the Exchange Web Services team recommends that you should call the a *GetItem* Web method on the *AssociatedCalendarItemId* and display *CalendarItemType* type property values from the associated meeting item instead.

MeetingRequestType Property

The *MeetingRequestType* property is a read-only string property set to a value from the *MeetingRequestTypeType* enumeration shown in Listing 10-14.

LISTING 10-14 Schema for the *MeetingRequestTypeType* enumeration

```
<xs:simpleType name="MeetingRequestTypeType">
  <xs:restriction base="xs:string">
    <xs:enumeration value="FullUpdate" />
    <xs:enumeration value="InformationalUpdate" />
    <xs:enumeration value="NewMeetingRequest" />
    <xs:enumeration value="Outdated" />
    <xs:enumeration value="SilentUpdate" />
  </xs:restriction>
</xs:simpleType>
```

The *MeetingRequestType* property not only indicates to the meeting request recipient what type of meeting request it is, but also serves to provide some information about how a meeting request might have created or updated an existing meeting.

A meeting request of type *NewMeetingRequest* represents a new meeting request and new meeting as well.

Meeting requests of *InformationalUpdate* and *FullUpdate* can both be received when the organizer updates a meeting. What dictates the attendee receiving a *FullUpdate* versus an *InformationalUpdate* has little to do with the properties that are changed as part of the update, but rather the attendees registered response at the time of receiving the meeting request. If a user has either tentatively accepted or accepted a meeting request, then updated meeting requests will come in as *InformationalUpdate*, whereas if the user has not responded to the message at all, the meeting request will come in as a *FullUpdate*.[5]

An *Outdated* meeting request is one that is no longer relevant.

The *SilentUpdate* meeting request type is reserved for internal use.

IntendedFreeBusyStatus Property

The *IntendedFreeBusyStatus* property is a read-only property with a value from the *LegacyFreeBusyType* enumeration shown in Listing 10-15.

---

[5] If the user has declined the meeting, then updates will come as *NewMeetingRequest*, but more on that when we deal with meeting cancellations.

LISTING 10-15 Schema for the *LegacyFreeBusyType* enumeration

```
<xs:simpleType name="LegacyFreeBusyType">
  <xs:restriction base="xs:string">
    <xs:enumeration value="Free" />
    <xs:enumeration value="Tentative" />
    <xs:enumeration value="Busy" />
    <xs:enumeration value="OOF" />
    <xs:enumeration value="NoData" />
  </xs:restriction>
</xs:simpleType>
```

Recall from Chapter 8 that *CalendarItemType* type has a *LegacyFreeBusyStatus* property that uses the *LegacyFreeBusyType* enumeration to indicate the free/busy status of a calendar item. On a meeting request, the *IntendedFreeBusyStatus* property describes the free/busy status that the organizer intended the meeting to have.

This value may not necessarily be the free/busy status of the associated meeting from a meeting request. For example, if the organizer intended the meeting to have a free/busy status of "Busy," then newly created meeting items on an attendee's calendar will start with a free/busy status of "Tentative" until the attendee registers an accept response, at which point the free/busy status of his copy of the meeting changes to "Busy." If the meeting organizer sets the *IntendedFreeBusyStatus* value to "Free," then newly created meeting items on attendee's calendar will have free/busy status of "Free."

The meeting organizer indirectly sets this property by setting the free/busy status of the meeting on her own calendar prior to sending meeting requests.

LegacyFreeBusyStatus Property

The *LegacyFreeBusyStatus* property on a meeting request reflects the free/busy status value of the associated calendar item at the time the meeting request was processed.

MeetingRequestWasSent Property

The *MeetingRequestWasSent* property is a Boolean property that is always set to true on a meeting request. However, this value can be false on the organizer's meeting item if he created the meeting using a call to the *CreateItem* Web method with a *MessageDisposition* value of *SaveOnly* and a *SendMeetingInvitations* value of *SendToNone*. This property's true purpose is to indicate to the meeting organizer if meeting requests have been sent for a meeting.

MyResponseType Property

The *MyResponseType* property is a read-only property of type *LegacyFreeBusyType* that reflects the recipient's registration response at the time the meeting request was processed.

The *RequiredAttendees* and *OptionalAttendees* Properties

These two properties are in fact the same attendee collections we have discussed in this chapter already. They are meant to reflect the contents of the attendee collections on the associated meeting item at the time the meeting request was processed.

While this was not shown in Listing 10-13, the *MeetingRequestMessageType* schema type also has a *Resources* property, which, like the *RequiredAttendees* and *OptionalAttendees* properties, is designed to hold the corresponding attendee collection values on a meeting request. The *Resources* property will only be populated on meeting requests that are sent to the mailbox of the resource itself.

> **Caution** The *RequiredAttendees*, *OptionalAttendees,* and *Resources* properties on both a meeting request and a meeting in a non-organizer's calendar should not be considered the authoritative collections for the meeting. Only the collections as they exist on the organizer's copy of the meeting are authoritative.

You may have noticed from Listing 10-13 that Brian, who is in the *RequiredAttendees* collection, is also in the *ToRecipients* collection. Likewise, Carol, who is in the *OptionalAttendees* collection, is also in the *CcRecipients* collection. While this may seem like a direct correlation, it should not be confused as such. There is no requirement that required attendees be on the *To:* line and optional attendees be on the *CC:* line.

Viewing a Meeting Request via the Proxy Classes

Listing 10-16 shows how to cast an item from a *GetItem* Web method response into a *MeetingRequestMessageType* type using the proxy classes.

LISTING 10-16 Casting a meeting request from a *GetItem* response into a *MeetingRequestMessageType* type instance

```
/// <summary>
/// Gets a MeetingRequestMessageType instance from the id of a
/// meeting request.
/// </summary>
/// <param name="binding">Binding to use for the web service call</param>
/// <param name="meetingRequestItemId">id of the meeting request</param>
/// <returns>Meeting request as a MeetingRequestMessageType instance</returns>
public static MeetingRequestMessageType GetMeetingRequestFromItemId(
    ExchangeServiceBinding binding,
    ItemIdType meetingRequestItemId)
{
    // Create a GetItem request for the default properties of an already
    // known meeting request
    //
    GetItemType getItemRequest = new GetItemType();
    getItemRequest.ItemIds = new ItemIdType[] { meetingRequestItemId };
    getItemRequest.ItemShape = new ItemResponseShapeType();
```

```
            getItemRequest.ItemShape.BaseShape = DefaultShapeNamesType.Default;

            // Call the GetItem web method via the Exchange Serivce Binding
            GetItemResponseType getItemResponse =
                binding.GetItem(getItemRequest);

            // Verify that the GetItem request was successful
            if (getItemResponse.ResponseMessages.Items[0].ResponseClass !=
                ResponseClassType.Success)
            {
                // Indicate that we have a problem
                throw new Exception(String.Format(
                    "Unable to get the meeting request\r\n{0}\r\n{1}",
                    getItemResponse.ResponseMessages.Items[0].ResponseCode,
                    getItemResponse.ResponseMessages.Items[0].MessageText));
            }

            // Verify that the item is indeed a meeting request
            ItemInfoResponseMessageType itemInfoResponseMessage =
                (ItemInfoResponseMessageType)getItemResponse.
                    ResponseMessages.Items[0];

            if (itemInfoResponseMessage.Items.Items[0] is MeetingRequestMessageType)
            {
                // Return the id of the meeting request
                return (MeetingRequestMessageType)itemInfoResponseMessage.
                    Items.Items[0];
            }
            else
            {
                throw new Exception("The id supplied was not for a meeting request.");
            }
        }
```

Registering a Meeting Response

When an attendee receives a meeting request, it serves as an invitation for the attendee to register a response. Attendees do this by selecting one of the registration response options that are available on a meeting request. In Exchange Web Services, an attendee registers a response by creating a response object that represents a registration choice (either accepting, tentatively accepting, or declining the meeting).

While responding to meeting requests with Exchange Web Services is made simple due to the use of response objects provided specifically for meeting workflow, there is an unfortunate side effect to responding to a meeting that you must be prepared for. When a meeting request is responded to, the associated meeting item is deleted and re-created by the Exchange Store. Before we get into the details of this side effect, let's revisit the example that we have been using thus far and explain how to use response objects to allow attendees to respond to a meeting request and register attendance.

User A (Andy) creates a meeting by adding User B (Brian) as a required attendee, User C (Carol) as an optional attendee, and Resource D (Room D331) as a resource. That request, as you recall, was in Listing 10-1. Listing 10-13 showed the XML of a meeting request in the response to a call to the *GetItem* Web method. From Listing 10-13, notice the response objects were present on the meeting request.

```
<t:ResponseObjects>
  <t:AcceptItem/>
  <t:TentativelyAcceptItem/>
  <t:DeclineItem/>
  <t:ReplyToItem/>
  <t:ReplyAllToItem/>
  <t:ForwardItem/>
</t:ResponseObjects>
```

The new response objects are *AcceptItem*, *DeclineItem*, and *TentativelyAcceptItem*, each of which derives from a schema type called *WellKnownResponseObjectType*, but in this chapter we will refer to them as the *meeting registration response objects*. You saw examples of the other three response objects (*ReplyToItem*, *ReplyAllToItem*, and *ForwardItem*) in Chapter 7, so we won't go into detail about those here, other than to suggest that *ReplyToItem* is a good mechanism to use to allow the attendee to reply back to the organizer (for example, to ask a question about the meeting) *without* registering a response.

> **Note** *ResponseObjects* is a calculated property and therefore cannot be requested when calling the *FindItem* Web method. For Exchange Web Services calendaring application developers, this means that when using a *CalendarView* for items, you should not rely on the properties returned from in the *FindItem* Web method response to determine what response objects are valid on a particular item. You can, however, include the *calendar:IsMeeting* property in your *AdditionalProperties* on your *FindItem* request and determine if a subsequent call to the *GetItem* Web method is required to get the list of valid response objects.

The name of each meeting registration response object represents each type of registration an attendee can select when responding to a meeting request. In this way, an attendee can indicate his intention to attend the meeting to the meeting organizer by selecting the corresponding meeting registration response object, rather then setting a property on an item. Table 10-3 lists the attendance registration of each meeting registration response object.

TABLE 10-3 Meeting Registration Response Objects and Associated Attendance Registration

Meeting registration response object type	Associated Attendance Registration
AcceptItem	Attendee will attend the meeting
TentativelyAcceptItem	Attendee may or may not attend the meeting
DeclineItem	Attendee will not attend the meeting

> **Note** When using the meeting registration response objects, Exchange Web Services will apply changes to both the meeting message and the associated meeting item as well; therefore, you do not need to be concerned with changing the *LegacyFreeBusyStatus* property on the associated meeting item after using a meeting registration response object. Exchange Web Services will, however, delete and re-create the associated meeting item in the process, meaning the now new associated meeting item will have a different id.

Understanding the Meeting Registration Response Object Types

Listing 10-17 is the schema for each of the meeting registration response objects.

LISTING 10-17 Schema for the *AcceptItemType*, *TentativelyAcceptItemType*, and *DeclineItemType* types

```
<xs:complexType name="AcceptItemType">
  <xs:complexContent>
    <xs:extension base="t:WellKnownResponseObjectType"/>
  </xs:complexContent>
</xs:complexType>

<xs:complexType name="TentativelyAcceptItemType">
  <xs:complexContent>
    <xs:extension base="t:WellKnownResponseObjectType"/>
  </xs:complexContent>
</xs:complexType>

<xs:complexType name="DeclineItemType">
  <xs:complexContent>
    <xs:extension base="t:WellKnownResponseObjectType"/>
  </xs:complexContent>
</xs:complexType>
```

As you can see from Listing 10-17, each of these schema types differ from each other in name only. This means that the properties that an Exchange Web Services developer needs to be concerned with come from the *WellKnownResponseObjectType* type itself. The schema for the *WellKnownResponseObjectType* type is shown in Listing 10-18

LISTING 10-18 Schema for the *WellKnownResponseObjectType* type

```
<xs:complexType name="WellKnownResponseObjectType">
  <xs:complexContent>
    <xs:restriction base="t:ResponseObjectType">
      <xs:sequence>
        <xs:element name="ItemClass"
                    type="t:ItemClassType" minOccurs="0" />
        <xs:element name="Sensitivity"
                    type="t:SensitivityChoicesType" minOccurs="0" />
```

```
          <xs:element name="Body" type="t:BodyType" minOccurs="0" />
          <xs:element name="Attachments"
                      type="t:NonEmptyArrayOfAttachmentsType" minOccurs="0" />
          <xs:element name="InternetMessageHeaders"
                      type="t:NonEmptyArrayOfInternetHeadersType" minOccurs="0" />
          <xs:element name="Sender"
                      type="t:SingleRecipientType" minOccurs="0" />
          <xs:element name="ToRecipients"
                      type="t:ArrayOfRecipientsType" minOccurs="0" />
          <xs:element name="CcRecipients"
                      type="t:ArrayOfRecipientsType" minOccurs="0" />
          <xs:element name="BccRecipients"
                      type="t:ArrayOfRecipientsType" minOccurs="0" />
          <xs:element name="IsReadReceiptRequested"
                      type="xs:boolean" minOccurs="0" />
          <xs:element name="IsDeliveryReceiptRequested"
                      type="xs:boolean" minOccurs="0" />
          <xs:element name="ReferenceItemId"
                      type="t:ItemIdType" minOccurs="0" />
      </xs:sequence>
      <xs:attribute name="ObjectName" type="xs:string" use="prohibited" />
    </xs:restriction>
  </xs:complexContent>
</xs:complexType>
```

Just as with other response objects that you have seen so far, the meeting registration response objects allow you to set many of the properties of the outgoing meeting message. For more information on each of these properties as applied to response objects, see Chapter 7.

ReferenceItemId Property

Unique to the meeting registration response objects is the fact that you can set the *ReferenceItemId* property on a meeting registration response object to reference a meeting message *or* a meeting calendar item. We will discuss the implications between using a meeting message id or meeting item id in the section titled "Responding to Meetings by Using a *MeetingMessage* Id or a *CalendarItem* Id" later in this chapter.

 Note The *ReferenceItemId* property on the *WellKnownResponseObjectType* type requires an instance of the *ItemIdType* type as opposed to an instance of the *BaseItemIdType* type. This means that you cannot use an *OccurrenceItemIdType* or *RecurringMasterItemIdType* type for the value.[6]

---

[6] These types were discussed in Chapter 9, "Recurring Appointments and Time Zones."

Using the *MessageDisposition* Flag When Creating a Meeting Registration Response Object

When creating any one of the three meeting registration response objects, the *MessageDisposition* flag on the *CreateItem* Web method request is used to indicate if a meeting response message will be sent back to the organizer. Specifying *SaveOnly* will place a meeting response message into the caller's Drafts folder. Specifying *SendAndSaveCopy* will result in a copy of the sent meeting response being placed in the caller's Sent Items folder. These locations *can* be changed by setting the *SavedItemFolderId* property on the request.

Specifying *SaveOnly* will change the registration response of the attendees' meeting item and remove the meeting request; however, since it will not send a meeting response to the meeting organizer, the meeting item on the organizer's calendar will not be updated.

Warning If you use the *SaveOnly* flag to save a meeting response into the Drafts folder and then try to call the *SendItem* Web method with the meeting response, you will receive an *ErrorInvalidItemForOperationSendItem* response code. This issue is intended to be fixed in the next Service Pack of Exchange Server 2007. It is the recommendation of the Exchange Web Services team that you not call the *CreateItem* Web method with a meeting registration response object using the *SaveOnly* flag until after the release of the next Service Pack of Exchange Server 2007.

Accepting a Meeting Request

Returning to the chapter example, imagine that Brian chooses to accept the meeting request from Listing 10-13 as is and simply wants to register his attendance as "will attend." To do this, Brian only needs to call the *CreateItem* Web method with an *AcceptItem* element and set the *ReferenceItemId* to the id of the meeting request that he received in his Inbox. Listing 10-19 shows Brian's call to the *CreateItem* Web method.

LISTING 10-19 Accepting a meeting request

```
<m:CreateItem MessageDisposition="SendOnly"
              xmlns:m=".../messages"
              xmlns:t=".../types">
  <m:Items>
    <t:AcceptItem>
      <t:ReferenceItemId Id="AAAlAGJvYmdz..." />
      <!-- Item Id of the MeetingRequest/CalendarItem -->
    </t:AcceptItem>
  </m:Items>
</m:CreateItem>
```

After processing the *AcceptItem* response object from Listing 10-19, Exchange Web Services will perform the following tasks:

- The meeting request will be moved to Brian's Deleted Items folder

- The associated meeting item will be deleted and re-created with the following property values changed from the original

  - *DateTimeCreated* will now equal the new creation time

  - *LegacyFreeBusyStatus* will equal the value corresponding to the *IntendedFreeBusyStatus* value from the meeting request

  - *MyResponseType* will equal *Accept*

  - *AppointmentReplyTime* will now be set with a value equal to the time the meeting registration response object was processed

- A meeting response will be sent to the meeting organizer indicating the Brian will attend the meeting

Declining a Meeting Request

If Brian needs to indicate to Andy that he will not be attending the meeting, then he does so by calling the *CreateItem* Web method with a *DeclineItem* element rather then an *AcceptItem* element. Listing 10-20 is an example.

LISTING 10-20 Declining a meeting request

```
<m:CreateItem MessageDisposition="SendOnly"
              xmlns:m=".../messages"
              xmlns:t=".../types">
  <m:Items>
    <t:DeclineItem>
      <t:ReferenceItemId Id="AAAlAGJvYmdz..." />
      <!-- Item Id of the MeetingRequest/CalendarItem -->
    </t:DeclineItem>
  </m:Items>
</m:CreateItem>
```

After processing the *DeclineItem* response object from Listing 10-20, Exchange Web Services will perform the following tasks:

- The meeting request will be moved to Brian's Deleted Items folder

- The associated meeting item will be deleted

- A meeting response will be sent to the meeting organizer indicating the Brian will not attend the meeting

Tentatively Accepting a Meeting Request

If Brian was unable to make a firm commitment about the meeting, but wanted to indicate to Andy that he has seen the meeting request, then he does so by calling the *CreateItem* Web method with a *TentativelyAcceptItem* element as shown in Listing 10-21

LISTING 10-21 Tentatively accepting a meeting request

```
<m:CreateItem MessageDisposition="SendOnly"
            xmlns:m=".../messages"
            xmlns:t=".../types">
  <m:Items>
    <t:TentativelyAcceptItem>
      <t:ReferenceItemId Id="AAAlAGJvYmdz..." />
      <!-- Item Id of the MeetingRequest/CalendarItem -->
    </t:TentativelyAcceptItem>
  </m:Items>
</m:CreateItem>
```

After processing the *TentativelyAcceptItem* response object from Listing 10-21, Exchange Web Services will perform the following tasks:

- The meeting request will be moved to Brian's Deleted Items folder
- The associated meeting item will be deleted and re-created with the following property values changed from the original
  - *DateTimeCreated* will now equal the new creation time
  - *LegacyFreeBusyStatus* will be set to *Tentative*
  - *MyResponseType* will equal *Tentative*
  - *AppointmentReplyTime* will now be set with a value equal to the time the meeting registration response object was processed.
- A meeting response will be sent to the meeting organizer indicating the Brian may or may not attend the meeting

Responding to Meetings Using a *MeetingMessage* Id versus Using a *CalendarItem* Id

When users receive a meeting request or cancellation, they have two options for registering their responses.

1. They can respond to the meeting message itself (see Figure 10-4).

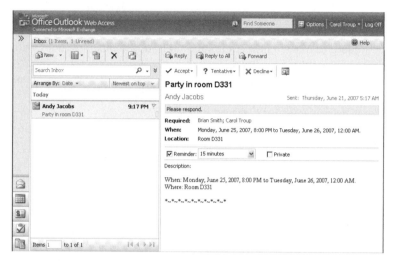

FIGURE 10-4 Register attendance from a Meeting Message

2. They can respond by finding the associated calendar item and registering a response there (see Figure 10-5).

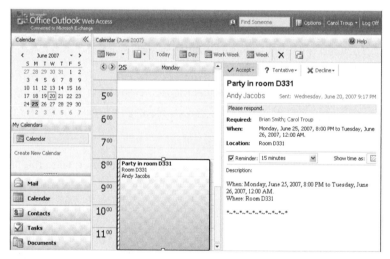

FIGURE 10-5 Register attendance from a Calendar Item

The Exchange Web Services response equivalent to a user choosing the option in Figure 10-4 is shown in Listing 10-22, which is to use a meeting registration response object providing a *ReferenceItemId* value of the meeting message id. The Exchange Web Services response equivalent of Figure 10-5 is shown in Listing 10-23, which is to use a meeting registration response object providing a *ReferenceItemId* value of a meeting calendar item id. Table 10-4 lists the unique side effects of each option.

TABLE 10-4 **Differences in Using a Meeting Message Id Versus a Calendar Item Id in a Meeting Registration Response Object**

Meeting Message Id	Calendar Item Id
CreateItem Web method response *will not* include an item id of the re-created calendar item	*CreateItem* web method response *will* include a new item id for the re-created calendar item
Meeting message *will be* deleted	*No* meeting messages will be deleted

LISTING 10-22 Sample response message from using a calendar item id in a meeting registration response object

```
<m:CreateItemResponseMessage ResponseClass="Success">
  <m:ResponseCode>NoError</m:ResponseCode>
  <m:Items>
    <t:CalendarItem>
      <t:ItemId Id="AAA1AGJvYm..." ChangeKey="DwAAABY..."/>
    </t:CalendarItem>
  </m:Items>
</m:CreateItemResponseMessage>
```

LISTING 10-23 Sample response message from using a meeting message id in an meeting registration response object

```
<m:CreateItemResponseMessage ResponseClass="Success">
  <m:ResponseCode>NoError</m:ResponseCode>
  <m:Items/>
</m:CreateItemResponseMessage>
```

When using a meeting message id in a meeting registration response object, Exchange Web Services will remove the meeting message once the response object is processed. When using a calendar item id, no deleting of meeting messages of any kind will take place.

Users will often respond using the meeting message if they did not need to consult their calendars in order to make a decision. When users do check their calendars (to see if they have any adjacent or conflicting calendar items for example), then they will often register their responses using the calendar item itself. Another common scenario for users using the calendar item to register a response is when the user previously registered a tentative accept, and then later made a determination whether or not they could attend. Since the meeting message was deleted once they made the tentative accept choice, they must use the calendar item to register their new decision.

It is unfortunate that Exchange Web Services is unable to provide the item id of the newly created calendar item in the situation where a meeting message is used. This does mean, however, that as an application developer, you will need to weigh the pros and cons of each option and choose the best for your application's needs. If you do not need to keep a strong reference between meeting messages and the calendar items they represent, then you can use the meeting message id approach. If you need this type of strong reference, then you should use the calendar item id approach, but take precautions to delete the appropriate meeting message yourself.

Including Message Content in a Meeting Response

In the chapter example, Brian has accepted the meeting request as is and simply wants to indicate this to Andy with no additional information. Carol, on the other hand, has chosen to decline the meeting, but in addition to telling Andy she is declining, she also wants to include a message indicating why she cannot attend. Also, to confirm that Andy sees that she is not coming to the meeting, Carol will request both a delivery and read receipt to be sent to her when Andy receives and reads her meeting response, respectively. To do this, Carol will call the *CreateItem* Web method with a *DeclineItem* element and set the *Body*, *IsReadReceiptRequested* and *IsDeliveryReceiptRequested* elements accordingly. Listing 10-24 shows an example of this kind of request.

LISTING 10-24 Declining a meeting request with additional message information

```
<m:CreateItem MessageDisposition="SendAndSaveCopy"
              xmlns:m=".../messages"
              xmlns:t=".../types">
  <m:Items>
    <t:DeclineItem>
      <t:Body BodyType="Text">
          Sorry Andy, must bring pet to the vet
      </t:Body>
      <t:IsReadReceiptRequested>true</t:IsReadReceiptRequested>
      <t:IsDeliveryReceiptRequested>true</t:IsDeliveryReceiptRequested>
      <t:ReferenceItemId Id="AAAnAGNhc3N..." />
    </t:DeclineItem>
  </m:Items>
</m:CreateItem>
```

Responding to a Meeting Request via the Proxy Classes

Listing 10-25 shows a method that encapsulates all of the discussion from this section. It demonstrates creating each of the meeting registration response objects and setting some of the available message properties for the outbound meeting response. The method can re-turn an *ItemIdType* instance; however, it can only do so if the id passed in for reference is for a meeting item and the response to register is not decline.

LISTING 10-25 Method for responding to meeting requests via the proxy

```
/// <summary>
/// Registers a response to a meeting request, allows the caller to
/// request that read and/or delivery receipts be sent.
/// </summary>
/// <remarks>
/// This method will return an id for a new calendar item if
///     1. The meetingMessageOrCalendarItemId represents a calendar item.
///     2. responseToRegister is not set to Decline
/// </remarks>
/// <param name="binding">Binding to use for the web service call</param>
/// <param name="meetingMessageOrCalendarItemId">Id of the meeting request
/// or meeting calendar item to register a response for</param>
/// <param name="responseToRegister">type of response to register</param>
/// <param name="meetingResponseBody">Optional message body to include</param>
/// <param name="requestDeliveryReceipt">Set to true to request a delivery
/// receipt be sent when the organizer receives the meeting response</param>
/// <param name="requestReadReceipt">Set to true to reqest a read receipt
/// be sent when the organizer reads the meeting response</param>
/// <returns>Id of the newly created calendar item if possible
/// (see remarks)</returns>
public static ItemIdType RespondToMeetingRequest(
    ExchangeServiceBinding binding,
    ItemIdType meetingMessageOrCalendarItemId,
    ResponseTypeType responseToRegister,
    string meetingResponseBody,
    bool requestDeliveryReceipt,
    bool requestReadReceipt)
{
    // Determine the type of response object to create
    WellKnownResponseObjectType meetingResponseObject;
    switch (responseToRegister)
    {
        case ResponseTypeType.Accept:
            meetingResponseObject = new AcceptItemType();
            break;
        case ResponseTypeType.Tentative:
            meetingResponseObject = new TentativelyAcceptItemType();
            break;
        case ResponseTypeType.Decline:
            meetingResponseObject = new DeclineItemType();
            break;
        default:
            throw new ArgumentException("ResponseTypeType value of "
                + responseToRegister + " is not a valid meeting " +
                "registration response.");
    }

    meetingResponseObject.ReferenceItemId = meetingMessageOrCalendarItemId;
    meetingResponseObject.IsDeliveryReceiptRequested =
        requestDeliveryReceipt;
    meetingResponseObject.IsDeliveryReceiptRequestedSpecified = true;
    meetingResponseObject.IsReadReceiptRequested =
        requestReadReceipt;
```

```
        meetingResponseObject.IsReadReceiptRequestedSpecified = true;

        // Check and set meeting response body content
        //
        if (!String.IsNullOrEmpty(meetingResponseBody))
        {
            meetingResponseObject.Body = new BodyType();
            meetingResponseObject.Body.BodyType1 = BodyTypeType.Text;
            meetingResponseObject.Body.Value = meetingResponseBody;
        }


        // Assemble our CreateItem request
        //
        CreateItemType createItemRequest = new CreateItemType();
        createItemRequest.MessageDisposition = MessageDispositionType.SendOnly;
        createItemRequest.MessageDispositionSpecified = true;
        createItemRequest.Items = new NonEmptyArrayOfAllItemsType();
        createItemRequest.Items.Items =
            new WellKnownResponseObjectType[] { meetingResponseObject };

        // Call the CreateItem web method and check for success.
        // If successful, see if there is an id that can be returned
        // and do so.
        //
        CreateItemResponseType response = binding.CreateItem(createItemRequest);
        ItemInfoResponseMessageType responseMessage =
            response.ResponseMessages.Items[0] as ItemInfoResponseMessageType;

        if (responseMessage.ResponseCode != ResponseCodeType.NoError)
        {
            throw new Exception(String.Format(
                "Unable to register for meeting\r\n{0}\r\n{1}",
                responseMessage.ResponseCode,
                responseMessage.MessageText));
        }


        // If the id specified was a meeting request, then the Items array
        // in the ItemInfoResponseMesssageType Items array will be
        // null
        //
        if (responseMessage.Items.Items != null)
        {
            // There is an id of a calendar item that can be returned
            return responseMessage.Items.Items[0].ItemId;
        }
        else
        {
            // There is no id to be returned
            return null;
        }
    }
```

Working with Meeting Responses

When meeting attendees respond to a meeting request, they do so by using one of the meeting registration response objects, which generates a meeting response message. When the Exchange Store processes a meeting response message, it notes the attendee's registration response and updates that attendee's registration response status in the attendee collection. Before we explain that process, however, we will first look at the properties of the meeting response message.

Understanding Meeting Response Messages

The schema type for meeting response messages is the *MeetingResponseMessageType* type. As we explained before, *MeetingResponseMessageType* derives from *MeetingMessageType*. Unlike *MeetingRequestMessageType*, however, which must add a large number of additional calendar properties, *MeetingResponseMessageType* adds no additional properties. Therefore, the property set of a meeting response message will look much more like a message then a calendar item. Listing 10-26 is an example of a meeting response message in a *GetItem* Web method response.

LISTING 10-26 *GetItem* Web method response with a meeting response message

```
<m:GetItemResponseMessage ResponseClass="Success"
                          xmlns:m=".../messages"
                          xmlns:t=".../types">
  <m:ResponseCode>NoError</m:ResponseCode>
  <m:Items>
    <t:MeetingResponse>
      <t:ItemId Id="AAAeAGRhdnNOZXJ..." ChangeKey="AQAAABYAAAD..." />
      <t:ParentFolderId Id="AAAeAGRhdnNOZXJAZX..." ChangeKey="AQAAABYAAAD..." />
      <t:ItemClass>IPM.Schedule.Meeting.Resp.Pos</t:ItemClass>
      <t:Subject>Accept: Meeting in Room D331</t:Subject>
      <t:Sensitivity>Normal</t:Sensitivity>
      <t:Body BodyType="Text"/>
      <t:DateTimeReceived>2007-09-11T02:01:54Z</t:DateTimeReceived>
      <t:Size>926</t:Size>
      <t:Importance>Normal</t:Importance>
      <t:IsSubmitted>false</t:IsSubmitted>
      <t:IsDraft>false</t:IsDraft>
      <t:IsFromMe>false</t:IsFromMe>
      <t:IsResend>false</t:IsResend>
      <t:IsUnmodified>false</t:IsUnmodified>
      <t:InternetMessageHeaders>
        <!-- Internet Message Headers omitted for brevity -->
      </t:InternetMessageHeaders>
      <t:DateTimeSent>2007-09-11T02:01:53Z</t:DateTimeSent>
      <t:DateTimeCreated>2007-09-11T02:01:54Z</t:DateTimeCreated>
      <t:ResponseObjects>
        <t:ReplyToItem />
```

```
            <t:ReplyAllToItem />
            <t:ForwardItem />
        </t:ResponseObjects>
        <t:ReminderDueBy>2007-09-10T21:00:00Z</t:ReminderDueBy>
        <t:DisplayCc />
        <t:DisplayTo>Andy Jacobs</t:DisplayTo>
        <t:HasAttachments>false</t:HasAttachments>
        <t:Culture>en-US</t:Culture>
        <t:Sender>
          <t:Mailbox>
            <t:Name>Brian Smith</t:Name>
            <t:EmailAddress>brian@contoso.com</t:EmailAddress>
            <t:RoutingType>SMTP</t:RoutingType>
          </t:Mailbox>
        </t:Sender>
        <t:ToRecipients>
          <t:Mailbox>
            <t:Name>Andy Jacobs</t:Name>
            <t:EmailAddress>andy@contoso.com</t:EmailAddress>
            <t:RoutingType>SMTP</t:RoutingType>
          </t:Mailbox>
        </t:ToRecipients>
        <t:IsReadReceiptRequested>true</t:IsReadReceiptRequested>
        <t:IsDeliveryReceiptRequested>false</t:IsDeliveryReceiptRequested>
        <t:ConversationIndex>AcfOF7mB8...</t:ConversationIndex>
        <t:ConversationTopic>Meeting #1</t:ConversationTopic>
        <t:From>
          <t:Mailbox>
            <t:Name>Brian Smith</t:Name>
            <t:EmailAddress>brian@contoso.com</t:EmailAddress>
            <t:RoutingType>SMTP</t:RoutingType>
          </t:Mailbox>
        </t:From>
        <t:InternetMessageId>99B0D0ACCBBDD24D899...</t:InternetMessageId>
        <t:IsRead>true</t:IsRead>
        <t:AssociatedCalendarItemId Id="AAAeAGR..." ChangeKey="AQAAABYAAAD..." />
        <t:IsDelegated>false</t:IsDelegated>
        <t:IsOutOfDate>false</t:IsOutOfDate>
        <t:HasBeenProcessed>true</t:HasBeenProcessed>
        <t:ResponseType>Accept</t:ResponseType>
      </t:MeetingResponse>
    </m:Items>
  </m:GetItemResponseMessage>
```

Listing 10-26 happens to be a meeting response message for an accept registration. Several of the properties on this message indicate this, including the *ItemClass* of "IPM.Schedule. Meeting.Resp.Pos", a *Subject* property prefixed with "Accept:",[7] and a *ResponseType* property

---

[7] The "Accept:" text will be localized into the language selected by the sender. In Exchange Web Services, this is done via the *MailboxCulture* header, which was discussed in Chapter 2.

value of "Accept." Table 10-5 shows the value of each of these three properties in relation to the type of attendee registration the meeting response message represents.

TABLE 10-5 **Property Values on a Meeting Response Message that Indicate Attendee Registration Choice**

Attendee Registration Choice	*ItemClass*	Localized *Subject* prefix	*ResponseType*
Accept	"IPM.Schedule.Meeting.Resp.Pos"	"Accepted: "	Accept
Tentatively Accept	"IPM.Schedule.Meeting.Resp.Tent"	"Tentative: "	Tentative
Decline	"IPM.Schedule.Meeting.Resp.Neg"	"Declined: "	Decline

Notice in Listing 10-26 that the *Body* element is empty; this is because Brian did not include a message body in his response. As you saw in Listing 10-24, Carol included new body content in her meeting response. In that case, the meeting response from Carol would include *Body* content.

Tracking Meeting Responses

When meeting responses are sent to a meeting organizer, the Exchange Store automatically processes these messages and the registration for each attendee within the attendee collections on the organizer's meeting item.

Once again, consider the chapter example where Andy has sent meeting requests to both Brian and Carol. Brian has accepted, and Carol has declined. Because both Brian and Carol have responded, Andy should have two meeting response messages in his Inbox with their respective registrations. Listing 10-27 shows a request that Andy could make against his Inbox to see these meeting messages. (This assumes that Andy's Inbox was empty prior to sending the meeting request. You will see in Chapter 15, "Advanced Searching," that a better technique for searching for all meeting messages would be to create a Search Folder.)

LISTING 10-27 Call to the *FindItem* Web method for helpful properties of meeting messages

```
<m:FindItem Traversal="Shallow"
            xmlns:m=".../messages"
            xmlns:t=".../types">
  <m:ItemShape>
    <t:BaseShape>IdOnly</t:BaseShape>
    <t:AdditionalProperties>
      <t:FieldURI FieldURI="meeting:ResponseType" />
      <t:FieldURI FieldURI="message:From" />
    </t:AdditionalProperties>
  </m:ItemShape>
  <m:ParentFolderIds>
    <t:DistinguishedFolderId Id="Inbox" />
  </m:ParentFolderIds>
</m:FindItem>
```

Listing 10-28 shows the response from Andy's Inbox.

LISTING 10-28 Response from the *FindItem* Web method with two meeting responses present

```xml
<m:FindItemResponse xmlns:m=".../messages" xmlns:t="http://.../types">
  <m:ResponseMessages>
    <m:FindItemResponseMessage ResponseClass="Success">
      <m:ResponseCode>NoError</m:ResponseCode>
      <m:RootFolder TotalItemsInView="2" IncludesLastItemInRange="true">
        <t:Items>
          <t:MeetingResponse>
            <t:ItemId Id="AAAmAGFsZ..." ChangeKey="DAAAAB... " />
            <t:From>
              <t:Mailbox>
                <t:Name>Carol Troup</t:Name>
              </t:Mailbox>
            </t:From>
            <t:ResponseType>Decline</t:ResponseType>
          </t:MeetingResponse>
          <t:MeetingResponse>
            <t:ItemId Id="AAAmAGFsZ... ChangeKey="DAAAAB..." />
            <t:From>
              <t:Mailbox>
                <t:Name>Brian Smith</t:Name>
              </t:Mailbox>
            </t:From>
            <t:ResponseType>Accept</t:ResponseType>
          </t:MeetingResponse>
        </t:Items>
      </m:RootFolder>
    </m:FindItemResponseMessage>
  </m:ResponseMessages>
</m:FindItemResponse>
```

Listing 10-27 shows you only a subset of the properties on a meeting response. A complete example of a meeting response was shown in Listing 10-26. Once Andy receives an attendee's meeting response, his meeting item is automatically updated. At any time, Andy can look at the attendee collections on his copy of the meeting item and get an accurate picture of who has responded and how they have registered, including those who have declined.

If an attendee has declined, it is up to Andy as the meeting organizer to decide if he or she should be removed from the attendee collections to prevent him or her from receiving future meeting updates.

> **Note** Because Andy called the *FindItem* Web method in Listing 10-27, he is unable to get the attendees' e-mail addresses. To get all the attendee information for attendees, you must use the *GetItem* Web method on the meeting calendar item.

Listing 10-29 shows the attendee collections for the meeting item on Andy's calendar.

LISTING 10-29 Example of the attendee collections from a meeting calendar item with two attendee responses

```
<t:RequiredAttendees>
  <t:Attendee>
    <t:Mailbox>
      <t:Name>Brian Smith</t:Name>
      <t:EmailAddress>brian@contoso.com</t:EmailAddress>
      <t:RoutingType>SMTP</t:RoutingType>
    </t:Mailbox>
    <t:ResponseType>Accept</t:ResponseType>
    <t:LastResponseTime>2007-01-02T18:07:45Z</t:LastResponseTime>
  </t:Attendee>
</t:RequiredAttendees>
<t:OptionalAttendees>
  <t:Attendee>
    <t:Mailbox>
      <t:Name>Carol Troup</t:Name>
      <t:EmailAddress>carol@contoso.com</t:EmailAddress>
      <t:RoutingType>SMTP</t:RoutingType>
    </t:Mailbox>
    <t:ResponseType>Decline</t:ResponseType>
    <t:LastResponseTime>2007-01-02T19:08:17Z</t:LastResponseTime>
  </t:Attendee>
</t:OptionalAttendees>
<t:Resources>
  <t:Attendee>
    <t:Mailbox>
      <t:Name>Meeting Room D331</t:Name>
      <t:EmailAddress>mr_d331@contoso.com</t:EmailAddress>
      <t:RoutingType>SMTP</t:RoutingType>
    </t:Mailbox>
    <t:ResponseType>Unknown</t:ResponseType>
  </t:Attendee>
</t:Resources>
```

Even though Carol declined the meeting, she is still on the attendee list. This means that Carol will still receive any future updates to the meeting as meeting requests of type *NewMeetingRequest*. Also notice that the request for Meeting Room D331 has yet to be processed, and therefore its *ResponseType* is still equal to unknown.

More Info The Exchange Store can be configured to enable resources such as rooms or equipment to auto-accept meeting requests if their schedules so allow. For more information, check out the "Resource Scheduling in Exchange Server 2007" blog post on the Microsoft Exchange Team Blog (*http://msexchangeteam.com/archive/2007/05/14/438944.aspx*).

Cancelling Meetings

Meeting cancellations are sent to each attendee when either

1. The attendee has been removed from the attendee collections of the organizer's meeting item, or

2. The organizer has deleted the meeting item

We have already illustrated how an attendee is removed in the section titled "Removing Attendees from a Meeting," so we shall talk about the other method of sending meeting cancellations, and that is when the organizer deletes the meeting item. Then we will talk about meeting cancellations in more detail.

There are two ways an organizer can delete a meeting. The first is to make a call to the *DeleteItem* Web method with the id of the meeting calendar item. The second is to use the *CancelCalendarItem* response object that is present on a meeting item in the organizer's calendar only.

Removing a Meeting from the Organizer's Calendar Using the *DeleteItem* Web Method

The *DeleteItem* Web method has a *SendMeetingCancellations* flag, which we have not discussed yet in this book. This attribute accepts a value from the *CalendarItemCreateOrDeleteOperationType* enumeration (which was shown in Listing 10-3). The value is used to determine if meeting cancellations should be sent as a result of deleting the meeting calendar item. Copies of meeting cancellations (if requested) will be found in the caller's Sent Items folder. Listing 10-30 shows calling the *DeleteItem* Web method to remove a meeting from the calendar and automatically send meeting cancellations.

LISTING 10-30 Call to the *DeleteItem* Web method to remove a meeting and send meeting cancellations

```
<m:DeleteItem DeleteType="MoveToDeletedItems"
              SendMeetingCancellations="SendToAllAndSaveCopy"
              xmlns:m=".../messages"
              xmlns:t=".../types">
  <m:ItemIds>
    <t:ItemId Id="AAAmAGF..." ChangeKey="DwAAAB..." />
    <!-- Item Id of a meeting calendar item -->
  </m:ItemIds>
</m:DeleteItem>
```

After Exchange Web Services processes the call in Listing 10-30, the result would be a deleted calendar item in the Deleted Items folder, and a copy of the meeting cancellation would be in the Sent Items folder.

> **Note** The *DeleteType* flag on a *DeleteItem* Web method request does not affect the sending of meeting cancellations. It affects only how the meeting item is disposed.

If you try to delete a meeting via the *DeleteItem* Web method without specifying the *SendMeetingCancellations* attribute, you will receive an *ErrorSendMeetingCancellationsRequired* response code.

Using the *DeleteItem* Web method to cancel a meeting can have consequences. For example, if you specify a *SendMeetingCancellations* value of *"SendToNone,"* none of the attendees will receive meeting cancellations. This action will result in the loss of all attendee information from the meeting, and the organizer will lose the ability to send meeting cancellations even if the meeting item is restored.

Another consequence of using the *DeleteItem* Web method to remove a meeting is that you cannot specify any of the message properties for the outbound meeting cancellations. The Exchange Web Services team anticipated the need for organizers wanting to inform attendees of the reason for cancelling the meeting. Therefore, the team created a meeting registration response object specifically for this purpose called the *CancelCalendarItem* response object.

> **Important** The Exchange Web Services team does not recommend calling the *DeleteItem* Web method to remove a meeting from the organizer's calendar. Instead, the team recommends using the *CancelCalendarItem* response object.

Using *CancelCalendarItem* to Cancel a Meeting

The *CancelCalendarItem* response object is the recommended alternative to calling the *DeleteItem* Web method for removing meetings from the organizer's calendar. Using the *CancelCalendarItem* response object will automatically generate meeting cancellations and allow the organizer to set message properties on those cancellations before they are sent. The *CancelCalendarItem* response object is present only on the meeting copy in the organizer's calendar.

```
<t:ResponseObjects>
 <t:CancelCalendarItem />
 <t:ForwardItem />
</t:ResponseObjects>
```

The schema type for the *CancelCalendarItem* response object is the *CancelCalendarItemType* type, which derives from the *SmartResponseType* type. The schema for the *SmartResponseType* type is the same base type for the *ReplyToItemType*, *ReplyAllToItemType*, and *ForwardItemType* types that were discussed in Chapter 7.

> **Note** For all *SmartResponseType* type objects (of which the *CancelCalendarItemType* type is one), you have the ability to set a *Body* property. However, setting this property will have no actual effect on the content of the body sent either in the resulting meeting cancellation or in the associated calendar item. Only the *NewBodyContent* property enables you to change this. Use the *NewBodyContent* property to set the message body of outbound meeting cancellations.

Listing 10-31 is an example of calling the *CreateItem* Web method to create a *CancelCalendarItem* response object and setting the *NewBodyContent* property.

LISTING 10-31 Using the *CancelCalendarItem* response object with updated body content

```
<m:CreateItem MessageDisposition="SendAndSaveCopy"
              xmlns:m="http://.../messages"
              xmlns:t="http://.../types">
  <m:Items>
    <t:CancelCalendarItem>
      <t:ReferenceItemId Id="AAAmAGFs..." ChangeKey="DwAAABYA..."/>
      <t:NewBodyContent BodyType="Text">Sorry folks</t:NewBodyContent>
    </t:CancelCalendarItem>
  </m:Items>
</m:CreateItem>
```

The resulting meeting cancellation item will contain the new body information. When the Exchange Store processes the meeting cancellations, it will overwrite the body information in the attendee's associated meeting item, along with other operations which we will discuss in a moment.

The *MessageDisposition* flag will dictate if meeting cancellations are sent and if a copy of a meeting cancellation is stored in the organizer's Sent Items folder. The meeting calendar item referenced will be moved to the Deleted Items folder, and there is no attribute you can set to change this behavior.

> **Note** If you call the *CreateItem* Web method to use a *CancelCalendarItem* response object referencing a calendar item that is *not* a meeting, you will receive an *ErrorInvalidRecipients* response code. The calendar item that is referenced will not be removed, but will have its *LegacyFreeBusyStatus* value set to *Free*.

Listing 10-32 is an example of a method that uses the *CancelCalendarItem* response object type to cancel a meeting via the proxy classes.

LISTING 10-32 Using the *CancelCalendarItem* response object with updated body content

```
/// <summary>
/// Cancels an exiting meeting on an organizers calendar
/// </summary>
/// <param name="binding">Binding to use for the web service call</param>
/// <param name="meetingCalendarItemId">Id of the meeting to cancel</param>
/// <param name="meetingCancellationBody">Optional message body to include
/// in the resulting meeting cancellations</param>
public static void CancelAnExistingMeeting(
    ExchangeServiceBinding binding,
    ItemIdType meetingCalendarItemId,
    string meetingCancellationBody)
{
    // Create the CancelCalendarItemType instance
    //
    CancelCalendarItemType cancelCalendarItem = new CancelCalendarItemType();
    cancelCalendarItem.ReferenceItemId = meetingCalendarItemId;

    // Set the NewBodyContent property if a meetingCancellationBody
    // was provided.
    //
    if (!String.IsNullOrEmpty(meetingCancellationBody))
    {
        cancelCalendarItem.NewBodyContent = new BodyType();
        cancelCalendarItem.NewBodyContent.BodyType1 = BodyTypeType.Text;
        cancelCalendarItem.NewBodyContent.Value =
            "Sorry folks, my favorite tv series is back!";
    }

    // Assemble our CreateItem request
    //
    CreateItemType createItemRequest = new CreateItemType();
    createItemRequest.MessageDisposition = MessageDispositionType.SendOnly;
    createItemRequest.MessageDispositionSpecified = true;
    createItemRequest.Items = new NonEmptyArrayOfAllItemsType();
    createItemRequest.Items.Items =
        new CancelCalendarItemType[] { cancelCalendarItem };

    // Call the CreateItem web method and check for success.
    //
    CreateItemResponseType response = binding.CreateItem(createItemRequest);
    ItemInfoResponseMessageType responseMessage =
        response.ResponseMessages.Items[0] as ItemInfoResponseMessageType;

    if (responseMessage.ResponseCode != ResponseCodeType.NoError)
    {
        throw new Exception(String.Format(
            "Unable to cancel meeting\r\n{0}\r\n{1}",
            responseMessage.ResponseCode,
            responseMessage.MessageText));
    }
}
```

Understanding Meeting Cancellation Messages

A meeting cancellation is received by an attendee when either the attendee is removed from the attendee collection or the meeting itself has been deleted from the organizer's calendar. There is nothing in a meeting cancellation that indicates which of these two situations caused a meeting cancellation to be sent to the attendee.

The schema type for a meeting cancellation is the *MeetingCancellationMessageType* type, which derives from the *MeetingMessageType* type, and, like the *MeetingResponseMessageType* type, it adds no additional properties.

Listing 10-33 is an example of a meeting cancellation message in a *GetItem* Web method response.

LISTING 10-33 *GetItem* Web method response with a meeting cancellation message

```
<m:GetItemResponseMessage ResponseClass="Success"
                    xmlns:m=".../messages"
                    xmlns:t=".../types">
  <m:ResponseCode>NoError</m:ResponseCode>
  <m:Items>
    <t:MeetingCancellation>
      <t:ItemId Id="AAAeAGRhdnNOZXJAZX..." ChangeKey="AQAAABYAAAD..."/>
      <t:ParentFolderId Id="AAAeAGRhdnNOZXJAZX..." ChangeKey="AQAAABYAAAD..."/>
      <t:ItemClass>IPM.Schedule.Meeting.Canceled</t:ItemClass>
      <t:Subject>Canceled: Meeting in Room D331</t:Subject>
      <t:Sensitivity>Normal</t:Sensitivity>
      <t:Body BodyType="Text">Sorry folks<t:Body>
      <t:DateTimeReceived>2007-09-11T04:01:51Z</t:DateTimeReceived>
      <t:Size>1676</t:Size>
      <t:Importance>Normal</t:Importance>
      <t:IsSubmitted>false</t:IsSubmitted>
      <t:IsDraft>false</t:IsDraft>
      <t:IsFromMe>false</t:IsFromMe>
      <t:IsResend>false</t:IsResend>
      <t:IsUnmodified>false</t:IsUnmodified>
      <t:InternetMessageHeaders>
          <!-- InternetMessageHeaders omitted for brevity -->
      </t:InternetMessageHeaders>
      <t:DateTimeSent>2007-09-11T04:01:49Z</t:DateTimeSent>
      <t:DateTimeCreated>2007-09-11T04:01:51Z</t:DateTimeCreated>
      <t:ResponseObjects>
        <t:RemoveItem />
        <t:ReplyToItem />
        <t:ReplyAllToItem />
        <t:ForwardItem />
      </t:ResponseObjects>
      <t:ReminderDueBy>2007-09-13T14:00:00Z</t:ReminderDueBy>
      <t:DisplayCc>Carol Troup</t:DisplayCc>
      <t:DisplayTo>Brian Smith</t:DisplayTo>
      <t:HasAttachments>false</t:HasAttachments>
      <t:Culture>en-US</t:Culture>
```

```
      <t:Sender>
        <t:Mailbox>
          <t:Name>Andy Jacobs</t:Name>
          <t:EmailAddress>andy@contoso.com</t:EmailAddress>
          <t:RoutingType>SMTP</t:RoutingType>
        </t:Mailbox>
      </t:Sender>
      <t:ToRecipients>
        <t:Mailbox>
          <t:Name>Brian Smith</t:Name>
          <t:EmailAddress>brian@contoso.com</t:EmailAddress>
          <t:RoutingType>SMTP</t:RoutingType>
        </t:Mailbox>
      </t:ToRecipients>
      <t:CcRecipients>
        <t:Mailbox>
          <t:Name>Carol Troup</t:Name>
          <t:EmailAddress>carol@contoso.com</t:EmailAddress>
          <t:RoutingType>SMTP</t:RoutingType>
        </t:Mailbox>
      </t:CcRecipients>
      <t:IsReadReceiptRequested>false</t:IsReadReceiptRequested>
      <t:IsDeliveryReceiptRequested>false</t:IsDeliveryReceiptRequested>
      <t:ConversationIndex>AcfOKHppZ...</t:ConversationIndex>
      <t:ConversationTopic>Meeting In Room D331</t:ConversationTopic>
      <t:From>
        <t:Mailbox>
          <t:Name>Andy Jacobs</t:Name>
          <t:EmailAddress>andy@contoso.com</t:EmailAddress>
          <t:RoutingType>SMTP</t:RoutingType>
        </t:Mailbox>
      </t:From>
      <t:InternetMessageId>99B0D0ACCBBDD2...t:InternetMessageId>
      <t:IsRead>false</t:IsRead>
      <t:IsResponseRequested>true</t:IsResponseRequested>
      <t:AssociatedCalendarItemId Id="AAAeA0ZXJAZX..." ChangeKey="AABYAAAD..."/>
      <t:IsDelegated>false</t:IsDelegated>
      <t:IsOutOfDate>false</t:IsOutOfDate>
      <t:HasBeenProcessed>true</t:HasBeenProcessed>
      <t:ResponseType>NoResponseReceived</t:ResponseType>
    </t:MeetingCancellation>
  </m:Items>
</m:GetItemResponseMessage>
```

A meeting cancellation is represented by a *MeetingCancellation* element and has an
ItemClass of "IPM.Schedule.Meeting.Canceled." The *Subject* property in a meeting cancellation is also prefixed with an appropriately localized version of "Canceled:".

> **Note** When the Exchange Store process a meeting cancellation, it does not automatically re-
> move the associated calendar item from the attendee's calendar. It does, however, change the
> *LegacyFreeBusyStatus* property value to "*Free.*"

Unique to a meeting cancellation is the addition of another response object, this one designed to aid you in removing the associated meeting item from the attendee's calendar.

```
<t:ResponseObjects>
 <t:RemoveItem />
 <t:ReplyToItem />
 <t:ReplyAllToItem />
 <t:ForwardItem />
</t:ResponseObjects>
```

While it is acceptable for you to use the *DeleteItem* Web method to remove the associated calendar item when noticing a meeting cancellation, the *RemoveItem* response object is designed to remove both the meeting cancellation and the associated calendar item in one call.

Removing a Cancelled Meeting with the *RemoveItem* Response Object

The *RemoveItem* response object is an instance of *RemoveItemType* type, which descends directly from *ResponseObjectType*. While *RemoveItem* is still a response object and therefore contains many of the message properties, there is only one property that is actually used by Exchange Web Services, and that is the *ReferenceItemId*. To use a *RemoveItem* response object, call the *CreateItem* Web method and use the id of the meeting cancellation for the *ReferenceItemId* value. Listing 10-34 is an example of calling the *GetItem* Web method to create a *RemoveItem* response object.

LISTING 10-34 Calling the *CreateItem* Web method with the *RemoveItem* response object

```
<m:CreateItem MessageDisposition="SendOnly"
              xmlns:m=".../messages"
              xmlns:t=".../types">
  <m:Items>
    <t:RemoveItem>
      <t:ReferenceItemId Id="AAAlAGJ..." ChangeKey="DQAAA..."/>
      <!-- id of the meeting cancellation item -->
    </t:RemoveItem>
  </m:Items>
</m:CreateItem>
```

When calling the *CreateItem* Web method to create a *RemoveItem* response object, you must provide the *MessageDisposition* attribute. Regardless of which value you use, Exchange Web Services will not send messages of any kind during the creation of a *RemoveItem* response object.

When using a *RemoveItem* response object, you must provide the id of the meeting cancellation and *not* the associated meeting item. If you supply a calendar item id, you will receive a *ErrorInvalidItemForOperationRemoveItem* response code.

When Exchange Web Services processes a *RemoveItem* response object, it will perform the following:

1. Soft-delete the meeting cancellation

2. Soft-delete the associated meeting item

Listing 10-35 is an example of using the *RemoveItem* response object via the proxy classes.

LISTING 10-35 Using the *RemoveItem* response object in the proxy classes

```
/// <summary>
/// Removes a meeting from the calendar that has been cancelled.  Removes the
/// meeting cancellation as well.
/// </summary>
/// <param name="binding">Binding to use for the web service call</param>
/// <param name="meetingCancellationId">Id of the meeting
/// cancellation message</param>
public static void RemoveACancelledMeeting(
    ExchangeServiceBinding binding,
    ItemIdType meetingCancellationId)
{
    // Create the RemoveItemType instance
    //
    RemoveItemType removeItem = new RemoveItemType();
    removeItem.ReferenceItemId = meetingCancellationId;

    // Assemble our CreateItem request
    //
    CreateItemType createItemRequest = new CreateItemType();
    createItemRequest.MessageDisposition = MessageDispositionType.SendOnly;
    createItemRequest.MessageDispositionSpecified = true;
    createItemRequest.Items = new NonEmptyArrayOfAllItemsType();
    createItemRequest.Items.Items =
        new RemoveItemType[] { removeItem };

    // Call the CreateItem web method and check for success.
    //
    CreateItemResponseType response = binding.CreateItem(createItemRequest);
    ItemInfoResponseMessageType responseMessage =
        response.ResponseMessages.Items[0] as ItemInfoResponseMessageType;
    if (responseMessage.ResponseCode != ResponseCodeType.NoError)
    {
        throw new Exception(String.Format(
            "Unable to remove the meeting and/or " +
            "meeting cancellation message\r\n{0}\r\n{1}",
            responseMessage.ResponseCode,
            responseMessage.MessageText));
    }
}
```

Working with Recurring Meetings

When a meeting organizer creates a meeting with recurrences, the Exchange Store will create a recurring master on each attendee's calendar with the same recurrence information. Any updates that the organizer makes to the recurring series are then handled through meeting messages, and the Exchange Store will process these meeting messages to create recurring series exceptions on all attendees' calendars accordingly.

The following example demonstrates some of these concepts in action. Once again, Andy is organizing the meeting. In this case, it will be a meeting with Brian every Monday for 12 weeks starting January 8, 2007. Listing 10-36 is Andy's call to the *CreateItem* Web method.

LISTING 10-36 *CreateItem* Web method call to create a recurring series with attendees

```
<m:CreateItem SendMeetingInvitations="SendOnlyToAll"
              xmlns:m=".../messages"
              xmlns:t=".../types">
  <m:Items>
    <t:CalendarItem>
      <t:Subject>Monday Morning Meeting with Brian</t:Subject>
      <t:Start>2007-01-08T10:00:00</t:Start>
      <t:End>2007-01-08T11:00:00</t:End>
      <t:Location>Andy's Office</t:Location>
      <t:RequiredAttendees>
        <t:Attendee>
          <t:Mailbox>
            <t:Name>Brian Smith</t:Name>
            <t:EmailAddress>Brian@contoso.com</t:EmailAddress>
          </t:Mailbox>
        </t:Attendee>
      </t:RequiredAttendees>
      <t:Recurrence>
        <t:WeeklyRecurrence>
          <t:Interval>1</t:Interval>
          <t:DaysOfWeek>Monday</t:DaysOfWeek>
        </t:WeeklyRecurrence>
        <t:NumberedRecurrence>
          <t:StartDate>2007-01-08</t:StartDate>
          <t:NumberOfOccurrences>12</t:NumberOfOccurrences>
        </t:NumberedRecurrence>
      </t:Recurrence>
      <!-- Meeting TimeZone information omitted -->
    </t:CalendarItem>
  </m:Items>
</m:CreateItem>
```

Brian would respond to the meeting request for this new meeting just as he would one that didn't have a recurrence. He would create the appropriate meeting registration response object either with the meeting request id or with the associated meeting item id, which in this case is pointing to a new recurring master calendar item on his calendar. In this example, he accepts the request. Once he does so, the recurring master *and* each occurrence on his calendar will get marked as with *LegacyFreeBusyStatus* value of *"Busy"* and *MyResponseType* value of *"Accept"* just as it would with a single-instance meeting.[8] Listing 10-37 is a call to the *GetItem* Web method that Brian could make to retrieve the *LegacyFreeBusyStatus*, *CalendarItemType*, and *MyResponseType* properties for the recurring master and the first two occurrences of his copy of the recurring meeting. Listing 10-38 shows the result.

LISTING 10-37 *GetItem* Web method call for properties of a recurring master and the first two occurrences

```
<m:GetItem xmlns:m=".../messages" xmlns:t=".../types">
  <m:ItemShape>
    <t:BaseShape>IdOnly</t:BaseShape>
    <t:AdditionalProperties>
      <t:FieldURI FieldURI="calendar:CalendarItemType" />
      <t:FieldURI FieldURI="calendar:LegacyFreeBusyStatus" />
      <t:FieldURI FieldURI="calendar:MyResponseType" />
    </t:AdditionalProperties>
  </m:ItemShape>
  <m:ItemIds>
    <t:ItemId Id="AAA1AGJvY..." ChangeKey="DwAAABY..." />
    <t:OccurrenceItemId RecurringMasterId="AA..." InstanceIndex="1" />
    <t:OccurrenceItemId RecurringMasterId="AA..." InstanceIndex="2" />
  </m:ItemIds>
</m:GetItem>
```

LISTING 10-38 *GetItem* Web method response for properties of a recurring master and first two occurrences

```
<m:GetItemResponse xmlns:m=".../messages" xmlns:t=".../types">
  <m:ResponseMessages>
    <m:GetItemResponseMessage ResponseClass="Success">
      <m:ResponseCode>NoError</m:ResponseCode>
      <m:Items>
        <t:CalendarItem>
          <t:ItemId Id="AAA1AGJ..." ChangeKey="DwAA..."/>
          <t:LegacyFreeBusyStatus>Busy</t:LegacyFreeBusyStatus>
          <t:CalendarItemType>RecurringMaster</t:CalendarItemType>
          <t:MyResponseType>Accept</t:MyResponseType>
        </t:CalendarItem>
      </m:Items>
    </m:GetItemResponseMessage>
    <m:GetItemResponseMessage ResponseClass="Success">
      <m:ResponseCode>NoError</m:ResponseCode>
      <m:Items>
        <t:CalendarItem>
          <t:ItemId Id="AAA1AGJ..." ChangeKey="EAAAAB..."/>
          <t:LegacyFreeBusyStatus>Busy</t:LegacyFreeBusyStatus>
```

---

[8] Or more accurately, set to the value of the *IntendedFreeBusyStatus* from the meeting request.

```
               <t:CalendarItemType>Occurrence</t:CalendarItemType>
               <t:MyResponseType>Accept</t:MyResponseType>
            </t:CalendarItem>
         </m:Items>
      </m:GetItemResponseMessage>
      <m:GetItemResponseMessage ResponseClass="Success">
         <m:ResponseCode>NoError</m:ResponseCode>
         <m:Items>
            <t:CalendarItem>
               <t:ItemId Id="AAA1AGJ..." ChangeKey="EAAAAB..."/>
               <t:LegacyFreeBusyStatus>Busy</t:LegacyFreeBusyStatus>
               <t:CalendarItemType>Occurrence</t:CalendarItemType>
               <t:MyResponseType>Accept</t:MyResponseType>
            </t:CalendarItem>
         </m:Items>
      </m:GetItemResponseMessage>
   </m:ResponseMessages>
</GetItemResponse>
```

From here on out, both parties will have the opportunity to send and receive meeting messages either on the recurring series as a whole or on individual occurrences.

Changing a Response to One Occurrence of a Recurring Meeting

As it turns out, Brian has a dentist appointment on January 29 and must decline the meeting with Andy on that day, and on that day only. To do this, Brian creates a *DeclineItem* response object providing information in the body as to why he is unable to meet and providing the id of the occurrence that he cannot attend. Listing 10-39 shows Brian's request.

LISTING 10-39 Declining one occurrence of a recurring meeting

```
<m:CreateItem MessageDisposition="SendOnlyToAll"
              xmlns:m=".../messages"
              xmlns:t=".../types">
  <m:Items>
    <t:DeclineItem>
      <t:Body BodyType="Text">
        Can't make it on this day, I have a dentist appointment
      </t:Body>
      <t:ReferenceItemId Id="AAA1AGJv..." />
      <!-- The id above is that of one occurrence -->
    </t:DeclineItem>
  </m:Items>
</m:CreateItem>
```

Exchange Web Services will remove the January 29 occurrence from the recurring series on Brian's calendar. As such, this instance will now appear in the *DeletedOccurrences* array on Brian's recurring master.

```
<t:DeletedOccurrences>
 <t:DeletedOccurrence>
    <t:Start>2007-01-29T10:00:00Z</t:Start>
 </t:DeletedOccurrence>
</t:DeletedOccurrences>
```

Once the meeting response is in Andy's mailbox however, the Exchange Store will update the corresponding occurrence on Andy's calendar changing that occurrence to an exception.

```
<t:CalendarItem>
 <t:ItemId Id="AAAmAGFsZ..." ChangeKey="EAAAA..." />
 <t:Subject>Monday Morning Meeting with Brian</t:Subject>
 <t:Start>2007-01-29T10:00:00Z</t:Start>
 <t:CalendarItemType>Exception</t:CalendarItemType>
 <t:RequiredAttendees>
   <t:Attendee>
     <t:Mailbox>
       <t:Name>Brian Smith</t:Name>
       <t:EmailAddress>Brian@contoso.com</t:EmailAddress>
       <t:RoutingType>SMTP</t:RoutingType>
     </t:Mailbox>
     <t:ResponseType>Decline</t:ResponseType>
     <t:LastResponseTime>2007-01-03T00:30:54Z</t:LastResponseTime>
   </t:Attendee>
 </t:RequiredAttendees>
</t:CalendarItem>
```

Andy is probably unaware that this change has occurred on the recurring meeting series, but he does see Brian's meeting response in his Inbox indicating Brian has declined the January 29 instance. Andy decides that the meeting is important enough to try and schedule it on another day.[9] Andy is able to find out that the following Tuesday would work, so he calls the *UpdateItem* Web method to change the date of the occurrence from January 29 to January 30. Remember that even though Brian has declined his January 29 instance of this meeting, he is still listed on the attendee list and therefore will still receive Andy's updates to the meeting.

Listing 10-40 is Andy's command to update the January 29 instance.

LISTING 10-40 Call to the *UpdateItem* Web method to change the date of an occurrence that has attendees

```
<m:UpdateItem ConflictResolution="AlwaysOverwrite"
              SendMeetingInvitationsOrCancellations="SendOnlyToAll"
              xmlns:m="../messages"
```

---

[9] His efforts will be assisted greatly if he uses the *GetUserAvailability* Web method discussed in Chapter 21, "Availability," to find a new time to meet with Brian.

```
                xmlns:t=".../types">
    <m:ItemChanges>
      <t:ItemChange>
        <t:OccurenceItemId Id="AAAmAGFs..." ChangeKey="EAAAABY..." />
        <!-- This is the item ID of the January 29th Instance -->
        <t:Updates>
          <t:SetItemField>
            <t:FieldURI FieldURI="calendar:Start" />
            <t:CalendarItem>
              <t:Start>2007-01-30T10:00:00</t:Start>
            </t:CalendarItem>
          </t:SetItemField>
          <t:SetItemField>
            <t:FieldURI FieldURI="calendar:End" />
            <t:CalendarItem>
              <t:End>2007-01-30T11:00:00</t:End>
            </t:CalendarItem>
          </t:SetItemField>
        </t:Updates>
      </t:ItemChange>
    </m:ItemChanges>
  </m:UpdateItem>
```

After processing this request, Brian will receive a meeting request of type *FullUpdate* in his Inbox. Listing 10-41 is an example of a *GetItem* Web method response with the new meeting request from Brian's Inbox

LISTING 10-41 Meeting message for an exception to a recurring meeting

```
<m:GetItemResponse xmlns:m=".../messages" xmlns:t=".../types">
  <m:ResponseMessages>
    <m:GetItemResponseMessage ResponseClass="Success">
      <m:ResponseCode>NoError</m:ResponseCode>
      <m:Items>
        <t:MeetingRequest>
          <t:ItemId Id="AAA1AGJvY..." ChangeKey="CwAAAB..."/>
          <t:AssociatedCalendarItemId Id="AAA1A..." ChangeKey="EAA..."/>
          <t:MeetingRequestType>FullUpdate</t:MeetingRequestType>
          <t:Start>2007-01-30T10:00:00Z</t:Start>
          <t:End>2007-01-30T11:00:00Z</t:End>
          <t:LegacyFreeBusyStatus>Tentative</t:LegacyFreeBusyStatus>
          <t:Location>Andy's Office</t:Location>
          <t:IsMeeting>true</t:IsMeeting>
          <t:IsRecurring>true</t:IsRecurring>
          <t:MeetingRequestWasSent>true</t:MeetingRequestWasSent>
          <t:CalendarItemType>Single</t:CalendarItemType>
        </t:MeetingRequest>
      </m:Items>
    </m:GetItemResponseMessage>
  </m:ResponseMessages>
</m:GetItemResponse>
```

Brian received a meeting request of type *FullUpdate* because this occurrence was no longer present on his calendar. Notice also that the *IsRecurring* flag is set to true and the *CalendarItemType* is set to *Single*. This is probably the only time you will encounter these two properties with this combination of values because, as you saw in Chapter 9, this doesn't happen in the course of creating a recurring series within one's own calendar.

But what about the *AssociatedCalendarItemId*—what might that be pointing to? Listing 10-42 is an example of a *GetItem* Web method response that has the answer.

LISTING 10-42 *GetItem* Web method response with an exception created from a meeting message

```xml
<GetItemResponse xmlns:m=".../messages" xmlns:t=".../types">
  <m:ResponseMessages>
    <m:GetItemResponseMessage ResponseClass="Success">
      <m:ResponseCode>NoError</m:ResponseCode>
      <m:Items>
        <t:CalendarItem>
          <t:ItemId Id="AAA1AGJvY..." ChangeKey="EAAAAB..."/>
          <t:Start>2007-01-30T10:00:00Z</t:Start>
          <t:End>2007-01-30T11:00:00Z</t:End>
          <t:OriginalStart>2007-01-29T10:00:00Z</t:OriginalStart>
          <t:LegacyFreeBusyStatus>Tentative</t:LegacyFreeBusyStatus>
          <t:IsMeeting>true</t:IsMeeting>
          <t:IsRecurring>true</t:IsRecurring>
          <t:IsResponseRequested>true</t:IsResponseRequested>
          <t:CalendarItemType>Exception</t:CalendarItemType>
          <t:MyResponseType>NoResponseReceived</t:MyResponseType>
        </t:CalendarItem>
      </m:Items>
    </m:GetItemResponseMessage>
  </m:ResponseMessages>
</m:GetItemResponse>
```

The Exchange Store has re-associated the exception with the original recurring series and labeled it correctly as an exception. You can see from Listing 10-42 that the *OriginalStart* property has a value of January 29, which was the original start time for this occurrence.

From this point, Brian must now register his response for the January 30 instance for Andy to know if the new meeting time will work or not.

Updating the Attendee List for One Occurrence of a Recurring Meeting

Sometimes, a meeting organizer wants to add an attendee to only one occurrence rather than the entire series. The previous example has Andy and Brian meeting every Monday (we are using the recurring meeting created from Listing 10-36). Imagine that Andy wants Carol to be present for the February 5 instance of that meeting. To do this, Andy calls the *UpdateItem* Web method, appending Carol to the optional attendee collection of the February 5 instance. (We won't list that command here because it would be nearly identical to Listing 10-4.) Instead of receiving a meeting request that creates a recurring master as Brian did in Listing 10-38, Carol receives a meeting request where the associated meeting item is of type *Single*.

LISTING 10-43 *GetItem* Web method response with a calendar item created from receiving a meeting request to only one occurrence of a recurring meeting

```
<GetItemResponse xmlns:m=".../messages" xmlns:t="http://.../types">
  <m:ResponseMessages>
    <m:GetItemResponseMessage ResponseClass="Success">
      <m:ResponseCode>NoError</m:ResponseCode>
      <m:Items>
        <t:CalendarItem>
          <t:ItemId Id="AAAnA..." ChangeKey="DwAAA..."/>
          <t:Start>2007-02-05T10:00:00Z</t:Start>
          <t:End>2007-02-05T11:00:00Z</t:End>
          <t:LegacyFreeBusyStatus>Tentative</t:LegacyFreeBusyStatus>
          <t:Location>Andy's Office</t:Location>
          <t:IsMeeting>true</t:IsMeeting>
          <t:IsCancelled>false</t:IsCancelled>
          <t:IsRecurring>true</t:IsRecurring>
          <t:CalendarItemType>Single</t:CalendarItemType>
          <t:MyResponseType>NoResponseReceived</t:MyResponseType>
        </t:CalendarItem>
      </m:Items>
    </m:GetItemResponseMessage>
  </m:ResponseMessages>
</GetItemResponse>
```

Listing 10-43 shows what the meeting item on Carol's calendar looks like. Carol will have a *Single* calendar item, even though the *IsRecurring* flag is set to true. This example shows that the Exchange Store will not go through the overhead of creating a recurring master for attendees who receive one-off meeting requests for individual occurrences, but it will show the recipient that they have been invited to one occurrence of a recurring meeting.

Summary

This chapter began by discussing how to create meetings. We looked at the two ways that meetings are created and how you can control the sending of meeting requests during meeting creation. We then looked closely at attendees and the attendee collections and described how a meeting item on an organizer's calendar serves as the definitive location for where attendees and their registration responses are stored.

This chapter then walked through the process of meeting workflow. We looked at each of the three different meeting message types (the meeting request, the meeting response, and the meeting cancellation). We described that meeting requests, while used to invite attendees to newly created meetings, are also used for meeting informational updates as well. We described that attendees register their responses by using one of the three meeting registration response objects (*AcceptItem*, *TentativelyAcceptItem*, or *DeclineItem*). We discussed how you can use an id of either a meeting message or a meeting item with the meeting registration response objects and described the pros and cons of each.

We described how organizers can cancel meetings and described that the preferred method is to use the *CancelCalendarItem* response object. We also described how recipients of a meeting cancellation can use the *RemoveItem* response object to remove the meeting cancellation and canceled meeting item from their mailboxes.

Finally, this chapter described the meeting workflow process with regard to recurring meetings. We described what type of meeting items are created on attendees' calendars when they are invited to the entire recurring series, as well as individual occurrences.

Chapter 11

Tasks

Everyone has tasks that need to be accomplished. Inherent in the idea of a task is that it is:

- **Actionable** It requires some effort.

- **Measurable** There is a concrete way to measure if the task has been completed, and potentially a way to measure partial completion.

- **Finite** There is an end to the task, typically identified by a due date.

From an Exchange Web Services perspective, a task is simply an item that has an *ItemClass* starting with IPM.Task. A task is exposed in the schema by the *TaskType*, which derives from *ItemType*. As such, *TaskType* inherits all the properties exposed by *ItemType*.

Basic Task Operations

Creating a task is as simple as calling *CreateItem* with a *Task* element containing all the properties that define your new task. For example, Listing 11-1 shows how to create a task and set its subject. Note that it is not necessary to set the *MessageDisposition* attribute on *CreateItem* because a task is not a message.

LISTING 11-1 Creating the first task

```
<CreateItem xmlns=".../messages"
            xmlns:t=".../types">
  <Items>
    <t:Task>
      <t:Subject>My first task</t:Subject>
    </t:Task>
  </Items>
</CreateItem>
```

The response shows that a *Task* element is returned with the id of the newly created task.

```
<CreateItemResponse xmlns:m=".../messages"
                    xmlns:t=".../types"
                    xmlns=".../messages">
  <m:ResponseMessages>
    <m:CreateItemResponseMessage ResponseClass="Success">
      <m:ResponseCode>NoError</m:ResponseCode>
      <m:Items>
        <t:Task>
          <t:ItemId Id="AAAtAEFkbWlua..." ChangeKey="AAAAA..."/>
        </t:Task>
```

```
    </m:Items>
  </m:CreateItemResponseMessage>
 </m:ResponseMessages>
</CreateItemResponse>
```

Listing 11-2 shows what is returned if you call *GetItem* requesting the *AllProperties* response shape on the *ItemId* of the newly created task. You will notice that the response contains properties that we have not yet covered.

LISTING 11-2 Task returned from *GetItem*

```
<t:Task>
    <t:ItemId Id="AAAtAEFkbWlua..." ChangeKey="AAAAA..."/>
    <t:ParentFolderId Id="AAAtAEFklua..." ChangeKey="AAAAA..."/>
    <t:ItemClass>IPM.Task</t:ItemClass>
    <t:Subject>My first task</t:Subject>
    <t:Sensitivity>Normal</t:Sensitivity>
    <t:Body BodyType="Text"/>
    <t:DateTimeReceived>2007-01-29T21:12:59Z</t:DateTimeReceived>
    <t:Size>153</t:Size>
    <t:Importance>Normal</t:Importance>
    <t:IsSubmitted>false</t:IsSubmitted>
    <t:IsDraft>true</t:IsDraft>
    <t:IsFromMe>false</t:IsFromMe>
    <t:IsResend>false</t:IsResend>
    <t:IsUnmodified>false</t:IsUnmodified>
    <t:DateTimeSent>2007-01-29T21:12:59Z</t:DateTimeSent>
    <t:DateTimeCreated>2007-01-29T21:12:59Z</t:DateTimeCreated>
    <t:DisplayCc/>
    <t:DisplayTo/>
    <t:HasAttachments>false</t:HasAttachments>
    <t:Culture>en-US</t:Culture>
    <t:ChangeCount>1</t:ChangeCount>
    <t:IsComplete>false</t:IsComplete>
    <t:IsRecurring>false</t:IsRecurring>
    <t:PercentComplete>0</t:PercentComplete>
    <t:Status>NotStarted</t:Status>
    <t:StatusDescription>Not Started</t:StatusDescription>
</t:Task>
```

Notice that Exchange Web Services did a lot of work behind the scenes by adding values for a number of properties that were not explicitly set.

Just like any other item, *MoveItem*, *CopyItem*, *DeleteItem*, *FindItem*, and *UpdateItem* can all be used to query and manipulate a task. As a result, we will not go over those methods here. What we will do, however, is take a moment to present the properties available on a *Task* item, what they mean, and in some cases, the implications of setting them.

Task Properties

TaskType exposes the properties shown in Table 11-1. In some cases, the comments supplied in the table will be enough to give you an understanding of the property. However, a number of the properties need additional explanation and will be addressed after the table.

TABLE 11-1 Task Specific Properties

Property	Type	Comment
ActualWork	*int*	Represents the actual amount of work expended on the task. Measured in minutes.
AssignedTime	*DateTime*	Time the task was assigned to the current owner.
BillingInformation	String	Billing information associated with this task.
ChangeCount	*int*	How many times this task has been acted upon (sent, accepted, etc.). This is simply a way to resolve conflicts when the delegator sends multiple updates. Also known as *TaskVersion*.
Companies	*ArrayOfStringsType*	A list of company names associated with this task.
CompleteDate	*DateTime*	Time the task was completed.
Contacts	*ArrayOfStringsType*	Contact names associated with this task.
DelegationState	*TaskDelegateStateType*	Enumeration value indicating whether the delegated task was accepted or not.
Delegator	String	Display name of the user that delegated the task.
DueDate	*DateTime*	The date that the task is due.
IsAssignmentEditable	*int*	One of the most confusing property exposed in Exchange Web Services. This is discussed later in this chapter.
IsComplete	*bool*	True if the task is marked as complete.
IsRecurring	*bool*	True if the task is recurring.
IsTeamTask	*bool*	True if the task is a team task.
Mileage	String	Mileage associated with the task, potentially used for reimbursement purposes.

Property	Type	Comment
Owner	String	The name of the user who owns this task.
PercentComplete	*double*	The percentage of the task that has been completed. Valid values are 0-100.
Recurrence	*TaskRecurrenceType*	Used for recurring tasks.
StartDate	*DateTime*	The date that work on the task should start.
Status	*TaskStatusType*	The status of the task.
StatusDescription	String	A localized string version of the status. Useful for display purposes.
TotalWork	*int*	The total amount of work for this task.

Task Delegation and Exchange Web Services

A delegated task is a task that is created by one entity and assigned or *delegated* to another entity. The *AssignedTime, DelegationState, Delegator, IsAssignmentEditable,* and *ChangeCount* properties are all related to task delegation. Exchange Web Services does not support the creation of delegated tasks, although you can retrieve existing ones. How, then, do you create a delegated task? Currently, the best way to create a delegated task is to use Microsoft Office Outlook and create a task request. Doing so creates a task request message, as shown in Figure 11-1.[1]

---

[1] As of this writing Outlook Web Access (OWA) does not support task delegation either.

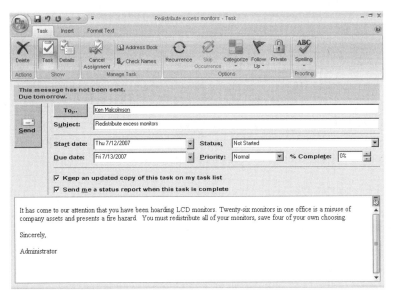

FIGURE 11-1 New task request message in Office Outlook

It should be apparent from Figure 11-1 that delegating a task involves sending a message to the individual that the task is to be assigned to. This is one reason that Exchange Web Services currently cannot support the creation of delegated tasks—Exchange Web Services sends only those items with a message class derived from IPM.Note. Task requests have a message class of IPM.Task. In any case, task requests must be accepted by the assignee before the task is actually assigned. But we digress. Just note that delegation properties are read-only at this point, although this may change in a later version of Exchange Web Services.

AssignedTime Property

The read-only *AssignedTime* is a delegated task property. Its name suggests that it is the instance in time that the task was assigned to the person currently responsible for the task. For purposes of this discussion, we created and sent a delegated task to an assignee using Office Outlook 2007 and then used *FindItem* to retrieve the *ItemId* of the task from the default Tasks folder. Listing 11-3 shows a *GetItem* call and a request for the *ItemId* and the *AssignedTime* property.

LISTING 11-3 Calling *GetItem* to retrieve the *AssignedTime* of a delegated task

```
<GetItem xmlns=".../messages"
         xmlns:t=".../types">
  <ItemShape>
    <t:BaseShape>IdOnly</t:BaseShape>
    <t:AdditionalProperties>
      <t:FieldURI FieldURI="task:AssignedTime"/>
    </t:AdditionalProperties>
```

```
    </ItemShape>
    <ItemIds>
      <t:ItemId Id="AAAtAEFkbWlua..." ChangeKey="AAAAA..."/>
    </ItemIds>
  </GetItem>
```

The response shows the time that the task was assigned to the individual currently responsible for executing the task. Note that this time is in Coordinated Universal Time (UTC) and should be converted to local time if so desired by the caller.

```
<!-- Outer GetItem response elements elided -->
<t:Task>
  <t:ItemId Id="AAAtAEFkbWlua..." ChangeKey="AAAAA..."/>
  <t:AssignedTime>2007-01-30T16:56:00Z</t:AssignedTime>
</t:Task>
```

Of course, if the task in question is not a delegated task, the *GetItem* call in Listing 11-3 returns only the *ItemId* of the task. The *AssignedTime* element will be missing.

DelegationState Property

The *DelegationState* property is another delegated task property and is therefore read-only. This property provides information about the *delegated state* of a given task. Note that this is different from the status of the task in question. We will discuss the possible *DelegationState* values shortly.

It is important to keep in mind that a delegated task has two parts. The first part is represented by the messages that transport the task request and corresponding response. Once the task request is acted upon by the recipient, the actual task is created in the recipient's mailbox by the client application. The resulting task is the second part of a delegated task. Why is this part distinction important? Because the delegated state will never be correct on the request and response messages. The delegated state will be correct on the task creator's task item. The task delegate will never see these values set on their task, only the task creator will.

For instance, when the task creator creates and sends a task, a copy of that task is put in the creator's Tasks folder. A copy of the task request *message* is put into the Sent Items folder. If you look at the delegation state on the sent message, you see it has a value of *NoMatch*. If, however, you look at the delegation state on the task that was placed in the task creator's Tasks folder, you see the delegation state is *OwnNew*. In general, ignore the task request and response messages and concern yourself only with the actual tasks within the task creator's Tasks folder. The values and their meanings are shown in Table 11-2.

TABLE 11-2 *DelegateState* **Values and Meanings**

Enumeration Value	Comments
NoMatch	This is either not a delegated task, or the task request has been created but not sent. This enumeration value is also used for a task request *message* whether in the task creator's Sent Items or the delegate's Inbox.
OwnNew	This is a new task request that has been sent, but the delegate has not yet responded to the task.
Owned	This is a bogus value and should not be in the enumeration. We will discuss this shortly.
Accepted	This is a task that the delegate has accepted.
Declined	This is a task that the delegate has declined.
Max	Ignore this value. It is an internal Outlook engineering detail for bounds checking that should have never been exposed through EWS. You should never see this value.

Unfortunately, the enumeration values are not mapped to the correct values. The Exchange Web Services *DelegationState* property is actually mapped to the wrong Messaging Application Programming Interface (MAPI) property. *DelegationState* is mapped to a MAPI-named property in property set PSETID_Task with a property id of 0x812A but *should* be pulling data from 0x8113. Oddly, both properties are enumerations and have similar values, except that 0x812A has no *Owned* value, and, therefore, the underlying integer values are logically shifted forward by one. What this shift means is that if you call *GetItem* on a delegated task that has been accepted, you get back a delegation state of *Owned*. Worse, if you call *GetItem* on a delegated task that has been declined, you get back a delegation state of *Accepted*. So what can you do about this mapping issue? You should request the actual MAPI property and ignore the current *DelegationState* property.

So how do you ignore the existing property? If you are a proxy class user, you can use a partial class extension, but you must also modify the autogenerated proxy a little bit. The partial class extension is shown in Listing 11-4.

LISTING 11-4 Partial class extension of *TaskType* to fix *DelegationState* enumeration values

```
/// <summary>
/// Partial class extension for TaskType
/// </summary>
public partial class TaskType
{
  /// <summary>
  /// Holds the correct MAPI property we should be getting
  /// </summary>
  public static PathToExtendedFieldType CorrectedDelegationStatePath;

  /// <summary>
  /// Static constructor for initializing our property path
  /// </summary>
  static TaskType()
```

```
{
  CorrectedDelegationStatePath = new PathToExtendedFieldType();
  CorrectedDelegationStatePath.PropertySetId =
      "{00062003-0000-0000-C000-000000000046}";
  CorrectedDelegationStatePath.PropertyId = 0x8113;
  CorrectedDelegationStatePath.PropertyType =
      MapiPropertyTypeType.Integer;
}


/// <summary>
/// Helper to get the corrected enum value and throw if not present
/// </summary>
/// <returns>Delegate state</returns>
///
private TaskDelegateStateType GetCorrectedDelegateState()
{
  TaskDelegateStateType result;
  if (!TryGetCorrectedDelegateState(out result))
  {
    throw new Exception("Corrected delegate state not present");
  }
  return result;
}


/// <summary>
/// Helper to check for the corrected delegate state presence
/// </summary>
///
private bool IsCorrectedDelegateStateSpecified
{
  get
  {
    TaskDelegateStateType state = TaskDelegateStateType.NoMatch;
    return TryGetCorrectedDelegateState(out state);
  }
}


/// <summary>
/// A forgiving method to return the extended prop value if it exists
/// </summary>
/// <param name="state">OUT state</param>
/// <returns>True if it exists, false if not</returns>
///
private bool TryGetCorrectedDelegateState(
                  out TaskDelegateStateType state)
{
  state = TaskDelegateStateType.NoMatch;
  if ((this.ExtendedProperty == null) ||
      (this.ExtendedProperty.Length == 0))
  {
    return false;
  }
  foreach (ExtendedPropertyType prop in this.ExtendedProperty)
  {
```

```
    if ((prop.ExtendedFieldURI.PropertyId ==
            CorrectedDelegationStatePath.PropertyId) &&
        (prop.ExtendedFieldURI.PropertySetId ==
            CorrectedDelegationStatePath.PropertySetId) &&
        (prop.ExtendedFieldURI.PropertyType ==
            CorrectedDelegationStatePath.PropertyType))
    {
      int intValue = Int32.Parse((string)prop.Item);
      state = (TaskDelegateStateType)intValue;
      return true;
    }
  }
  return false;
}


/// <summary>
/// Adds the corrected delegate state property path to our shape for
/// GetItem and FindItem.
/// </summary>
/// <param name="shape">Shape to add to</param>
///
public static void AddCorrectedDelegationStateToShape(
                                ItemResponseShapeType shape)
{
  BasePathToElementType[] additionalProps = shape.AdditionalProperties;
  int existingCount = (additionalProps == null) ? 0 : additionalProps.Length;
  BasePathToElementType[] newAdditionalProps = new
                BasePathToElementType[existingCount + 1];
  if (existingCount > 0)
  {
    Array.Copy(additionalProps, newAdditionalProps, existingCount);
  }

  newAdditionalProps[existingCount] = CorrectedDelegationStatePath;
  shape.AdditionalProperties = newAdditionalProps;
  }
}
```

And of course, you need to call the *GetCorrectedDelegateState* method from somewhere. Here is where you change the autogenerated proxy code(see Listing 11-5).[2]

LISTING 11-5 Autogenerated proxy changes to call new *DelegationState* method

```
/// <remarks/>
public TaskDelegateStateType DelegationState
{
  get
  {
```

---

[2] Changing code directly in the autogenerated proxy is at best a bad idea because any time you regenerate your proxy classes, your modifications will be overwritten. Unfortunately, you don't really have much choice here. Just remember that if you regenerate your proxy classes, you will need to make these modifications again.

```
      return GetCorrectedDelegateState();
    }
    set
    {
      this.delegationStateField = value;
    }
  }

  /// <remarks/>
  [System.Xml.Serialization.XmlIgnoreAttribute()]
  public bool DelegationStateSpecified
  {
    get
    {
      return this.IsCorrectedDelegateStateSpecified;
    }
    set
    {
      this.delegationStateFieldSpecified = value;
    }
  }
}
```

Why were the get property accessors changed but not the set accessors? Since *DelegationState* is read-only, you never expect consumers to set this. They can certainly try, but an *UpdateItem* call will fail if an attempt is made to set this property.

To use the corrected delegated state code, you need to make sure that you call *TaskType. AddCorrectedDelegationStateToShape*() before making a *GetItem* or *FindItem* call so that your item response shape contains the correct property path to retrieve. The corrected delegate state property is not in any of the base shapes (*IdOnly*, *Default*, or *AllProperties*). If you forget to make this call and then try to access the *DelegationState* property on the returned *TaskType* instance, an exception is thrown to remind you of your infraction.

```
ItemResponseShapeType responseShape = new
        ItemResponseShapeType(DefaultShapeNamesType.Default);

TaskType.AddCorrectedDelegationStateToShape(responseShape);
// Now we can make our GetItem or FindItem call...
```

Delegator Property

The read-only *Delegator* property exposes the name of the individual who assigned the task to its current owner. This is present only on the task item in the delegate's Mailbox. The task item in the task creator's Mailbox has an empty *Delegator* property.

IsAssignmentEditable Property

This read-only property is one of the most oddly named properties that you will encounter in Exchange Web Services. Its name suggests that it might be a Boolean, although you can see from the schema that it is actually an integer. Its name also suggests that it has something to do with editing a task assignment. That, too, is wrong. Whereas all of the delegated task properties you have been enjoying are on the task item, this property bucks the trend and is applicable to the task request or response message instead of the task. Simply put, this property tells what type of task request or response message you are dealing with, and it has the values shown in Table 11-3.

TABLE 11-3 *IsAssignmentEditable* **Property Values**

IsAssignmentEditable Value	Comment
0	Not a delegated task message
1	Task request message
2	Task accepted message
3	Task declined message
4	Update to an existing task message

Of course, Exchange Web Services exposes this property as an integer, so you need to do any mapping yourself.

IsComplete and *PercentComplete* Properties

If you have a task, your goal is typically to complete the task. The read-only *IsComplete* property returns true if the task is considered complete. Because *IsComplete* is read-only, how do you mark a task as complete? A task is complete when the writeable *PercentComplete* property is set to 100%, which is done with a simple *UpdateItem* call, as shown in Listing 11-6.

LISTING 11-6 Updating *PercentComplete* to mark a task as complete

```
<UpdateItem ConflictResolution="AutoResolve"
            xmlns=".../messages"
            xmlns:t=".../types">
    <ItemChanges>
        <t:ItemChange>
          <t:ItemId Id="AAAtAEFkbWlua..." ChangeKey="AAAAA..."/>
           <t:Updates>
              <t:SetItemField>
                 <t:FieldURI FieldURI="task:PercentComplete"/>
                 <t:Task>
                     <t:PercentComplete>100</t:PercentComplete>
                 </t:Task>
              </t:SetItemField>
           </t:Updates>
        </t:ItemChange>
    </ItemChanges>
</UpdateItem>
```

If you then call *GetItem* on the modified task, you see that the *IsComplete* and *Status* properties were updated accordingly.[3]

```
<t:Task>
   <t:ItemId Id="AAAoAHNhbmRy...
   <t:IsComplete>true</t:IsComplete>
   <t:PercentComplete>100</t:PercentComplete>
   <t:Status>Completed</t:Status>
</t:Task>
```

You can also mark a task as "complete" by setting the *Status* property to Completed.

IsTeamTask Property

If a task request is sent to more than one individual, then that task is considered a team task. However, *IsTeamTask* is true only on the delegate's view of the task. The creator's task shows *IsTeamTask* as false. This property is read-only.

Owner Property

The value contained in the read-only *Owner* property depends on the type of task you are dealing with. If the task in question is a team task, the *Owner* property shows a semicolon-delimited list of the users responsible for the task. If it is a delegated task, the *Owner* property contains the names of the delegates. If it is a normal task, the *Owner* property contains the name of the task creator.

Status and *StatusDescription* Properties

The *Status* property is exposed as the *TaskStatusType* schema enumeration, indicating the status of the task. The values of the *TaskStatusType* enumeration and their meanings are in Table 11-4.

TABLE 11-4 *TaskStatusType* Values and Meanings

Enumeration Value	Comment
NotStarted	The task has not yet been started. *PercentComplete* is set to zero.
InProgress	The task is in progress.
Completed	The task is complete. *PercentComplete* is set to 100.
WaitingOnOthers	The task is blocked by other individuals.
Deferred	The task has been deferred.

---

[3] We used the *IdOnly* base shape and explicitly requested the additional properties *task:PercentComplete*, *task: IsComplete*, and *task:Status* in our *GetItem* call.

Note that when you set the status to *NotStarted,* Exchange Web Services sets the *PercentComplete* property to zero. When you set the status to *Completed,* Exchange Web Services sets the *PercentComplete* property to 100.

The read-only *StatusDescription* property is interesting. At first glance, you might think the *StatusDescription* property is just the *Status* enumeration value with some embedded spaces. And, if you are using an English-based language, you are correct. The worth of this property is realized when requests come in with a non-English *MailboxCulture* SOAP header. The returned status description is localized based on the value in the *MailboxCulture* SOAP header of the request.[4] For instance, if you call *GetItem* and ask for a Chinese response, you get a Chinese status description. Most of the examples up to this point in the book have omitted the SOAP envelope and header, but they appear here because the *MailboxCulture* must be specified as a SOAP header. The request is shown in Listing 11-7.

LISTING 11-7 Non-English request for task status description

```
<soap:Envelope xmlns:xsi=".../XMLSchema-instance"
               xmlns:xsd=".../XMLSchema"
               xmlns:soap=".../envelope/"
               xmlns:t=".../types">
  <soap:Header>
    <t:MailboxCulture>zh-CN</t:MailboxCulture>
  </soap:Header>
  <soap:Body>
    <GetItem xmlns=".../messages">
      <ItemShape>
        <t:BaseShape>IdOnly</t:BaseShape>
        <t:AdditionalProperties>
          <t:FieldURI FieldURI="task:Status"/>
          <t:FieldURI FieldURI="task:StatusDescription"/>
        </t:AdditionalProperties>
      </ItemShape>
      <ItemIds>
        <t:ItemId Id="AAAtAEFkbWlua..." ChangeKey="AAAAA..."/>
      </ItemIds>
    </GetItem>
  </soap:Body>
</soap:Envelope>
```

As shown in the following code, the *StatusDescription* is localized accordingly.

```
<t:Task>
    <t:ItemId Id="AAAtAEFkbWlua..." ChangeKey="AAAAA..."/>
    <t:Status>NotStarted</t:Status>
    <t:StatusDescription>未始</t:StatusDescription>
</t:Task>
```

---

4 The *MailboxCulture* element was discussed in Chapter 2, "May I See Your Id?"

Task Recurrence

A recurring task is a work item that you enjoyed doing so much the first time you want to do it again and again and again. Okay, maybe that is a slightly inaccurate statement, but the "again and again and again" part isn't. Actually, if you diligently studied calendar item recurrence in Chapter 9, "Recurring Appointments and Time Zones," task recurrence will seem like an old friend to you. However, when considering task recurrence, you need to be aware of some odd behaviors that differ from calendar item recurrence. We will address these shortly.

Creating a Recurring Task

You can create recurring tasks through clients such as Office Outlook or through an application programming interface (API) such as Exchange Web Services. For example, we created a new task in Office Outlook 2007, clicked on the recurrence button, and were presented with the Task Recurrence dialog box shown in Figure 11-2.

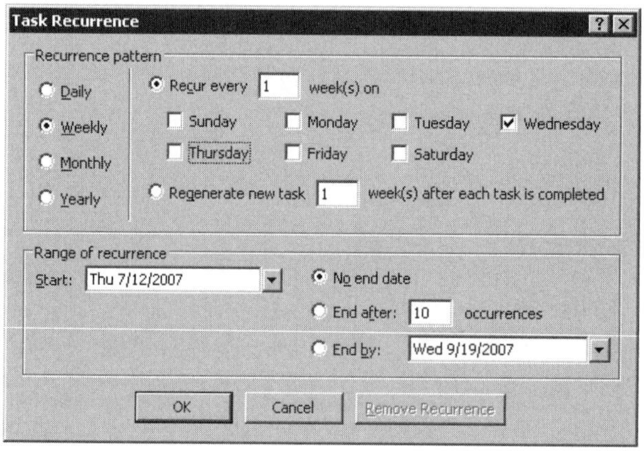

FIGURE 11-2 Outlook 2007 Task Recurrence form

You can see from Figure 11-2 that Office Outlook enables you to specify both a recurrence pattern and a recurrence range. What is interesting is the "Regenerate new task *X* week(s) after each task is completed" option. We will discuss such *regenerating tasks* shortly.

In Exchange Web Services, task recurrence is exposed through the *Recurrence* property on *TaskType* in types.xsd. Listing 11-8 shows the *TaskRecurrenceType,* which is the type of the *Recurrence* property.

LISTING 11-8 *TaskRecurrenceType* schema type

```
<xs:complexType name="TaskRecurrenceType">
  <xs:sequence>
    <xs:group ref="t:TaskRecurrencePatternTypes"/>
    <xs:group ref="t:RecurrenceRangeTypes"/>
  </xs:sequence>
</xs:complexType>
```

A *TaskRecurrenceType* instance has two child elements, each of which is described by a group. Each group is simply a collection of items that can be put in place of the group element. You saw the *RecurrenceRangeTypes* in Chapter 9 when dealing with calendar item recurrence. Recurrence ranges for recurring tasks behave the same way, so we won't cover those here.

The *TaskRecurrencePatternTypes* group represents a choice between several pattern types.

- *RelativelyYearlyRecurrence*
- *AbsoluteYearlyRecurrence*
- *RelativeMonthlyRecurrence*
- *AbsoluteMonthlyRecurrence*
- *WeeklyRecurrence*
- *DailyRecurrence*
- *DailyRegeneration*
- *WeeklyRegeneration*
- *MonthlyRegeneration*
- *YearlyRegeneration*

You saw most of these recurrence patterns in the calendaring chapters. In fact, they are of the same schema types. We should, however, touch on several new ones. The new ones are all suffixed by *Regeneration*.

What Is a Regenerating Recurrence Pattern?

A task with a regenerating recurrence pattern uses the completion date of the current task occurrence as the basis for calculating the due date of the next task occurrence. As an example, let's say that you go grocery shopping every seven days. You could certainly create a weekly recurring pattern for this, but what if you are sick for several days and end up going on the eleventh day instead? Well, you mark your task as complete, but then the next task occurrence is due in four days. It is unlikely that you will need groceries by then. Wouldn't it be better to base the seven days on the completion date of the previous task? Yes, you were late for the last task, but once you pick up groceries, you won't need more for seven days.

This is precisely what regenerating tasks are used for. Now, a mortgage payment is not a good candidate for a regenerating task. Hypothetically, if your mortgage payment is set up as a regenerating task and you are late once, then since the next task occurrence is based on your previous late completion date, all future payments will be late. Therefore, a mortgage payment is clearly a candidate for one of the standard (non-regenerating) recurrence patterns.

Regenerating Recurrence Pattern Types

In the schema, all four regenerating recurrence pattern types derive from the same base *RegeneratingPatternBaseType* and add no additional attributes or elements. As such, the elements and attributes exposed on each are the ones that are exposed through the base type. *RegeneratingPatternBaseType* itself derives from *IntervalRecurrencePatternBaseType*, which comes from *RecurrencePatternBaseType*. This is much too confusing in words. Instead, Figure 11-3 shows the inheritance tree.

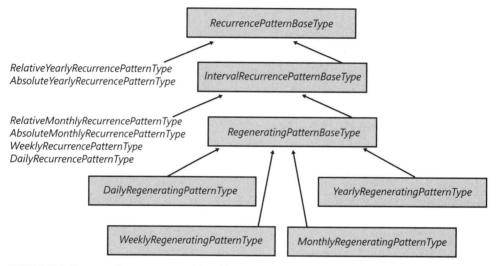

FIGURE 11-3 Regenerating pattern type hierarchy

For reference, Figure 11-3 shows where the standard recurrence patterns fit into the inheritance tree. Listing 11-9 shows a simple regenerating task request.

LISTING 11-9 Creating a daily regenerating task

```
<CreateItem xmlns=".../messages"
            xmlns:t=".../types">
  <Items>
    <t:Task>
      <t:Subject>My Daily recurring task</t:Subject>
      <t:Recurrence>
        <t:DailyRegeneration>
          <t:Interval>2</t:Interval>
        </t:DailyRegeneration>
        <t:NoEndRecurrence>
          <t:StartDate>2007-02-01</t:StartDate>
        </t:NoEndRecurrence>
      </t:Recurrence>
    </t:Task>
  </Items>
</CreateItem>
```

If you check using Office Outlook, you see that the task appears in the Tasks folder. If you double click on the new task, you see how regenerating tasks created through Exchange Web Services are shown in Office Outlook.

In Figure 11-4, Office Outlook adds the notice "Due 2 days after this task is completed effective 7/12/2007." Clicking on the Recurrence button reveals the same task recurrence form you saw in Figure 11-2. This is shown in Figure 11-5.

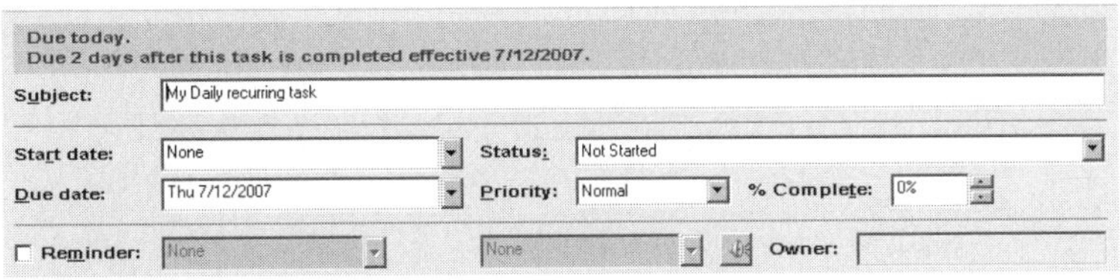

FIGURE 11-4 Daily regenerating task in Outlook 2007

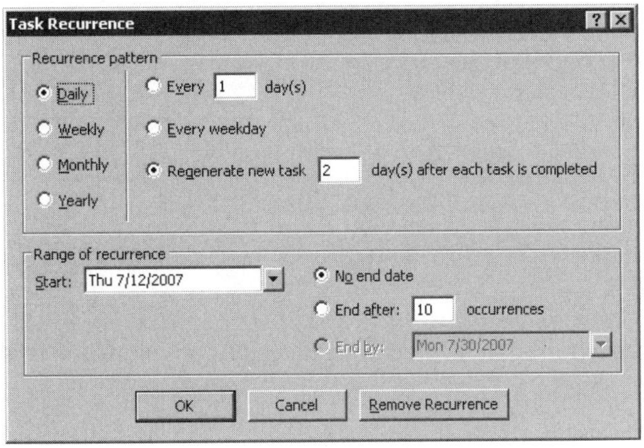

FIGURE 11-5 Daily regenerating task details in Outlook 2007

The next example shows a daily regenerating task with an interval of one day and some instances marked as complete. First, Listing 11-10 shows the request for a daily regenerating task.

LISTING 11-10 Creating a daily regenerating task with an interval of one day

```
<CreateItem xmlns=".../messages"
            xmlns:t=".../types">
  <Items>
    <t:Task>
      <t:Subject>Daily Regenerating Task</t:Subject>
      <t:Recurrence>
        <t:DailyRegeneration>
          <t:Interval>1</t:Interval>
        </t:DailyRegeneration>
        <t:NoEndRecurrence>
          <t:StartDate>2007-02-01</t:StartDate>
```

```
        </t:NoEndRecurrence>
      </t:Recurrence>
    </t:Task>
  </Items>
</CreateItem>
```

Next, Listing 11-11 shows a simple *GetItem* call that will reveal some of the initial values of the new task.

LISTING 11-11 Retrieving the first regenerating task instance

```
<GetItem xmlns=".../messages"
         xmlns:t=".../types">
  <ItemShape>
    <t:BaseShape>IdOnly</t:BaseShape>
    <t:AdditionalProperties>
      <t:FieldURI FieldURI="task:DueDate"/>
      <t:FieldURI FieldURI="task:IsComplete"/>
      <t:FieldURI FieldURI="task:ChangeCount"/>
      <t:FieldURI FieldURI="task:Status"/>
    </t:AdditionalProperties>
  </ItemShape>
  <ItemIds>
    <t:ItemId Id="AAAtAEFkbWlua..." ChangeKey="AAAAA..."/>
  </ItemdIds>
</GetItem>
```

Looking at the *GetItemResponse*, you see that the task instance has an initial due date of February 1, 2007 at 8 A.M.

```
<!-- Outer elements elided -->
<t:Task>
    <t:ItemId Id="AAAtAEFkbWlua...
    <t:ChangeCount>1</t:ChangeCount>
    <t:DueDate>2007-02-01T08:00:00Z</t:DueDate>
    <t:IsComplete>false</t:IsComplete>
    <t:Status>NotStarted</t:Status>
</t:Task>
```

Eh? Where did the 8 A.M. come from? It looks like when the task was created, it assumed that you were passing in local time (T-08:00) and converted it to UTC. In this case, the call was made in Pacific Standard Time, hence the 8 hour offset from UTC.

Now, Listing 11-12 shows how the instance is marked complete by setting the *PercentComplete* property to 100. This call is made at 3:45 AM Pacific Standard Time (PST).

LISTING 11-12 Marking the regenerating task as complete

```
<UpdateItem ConflictResolution="AutoResolve"
            xmlns=".../messages"
            xmlns:t=".../types">
    <ItemChanges>
        <t:ItemChange>
            <t:ItemId Id="AAAtAEFkbWlua..." ChangeKey="AAAAA..."/>
            <t:Updates>
              <t:SetItemField>
                <t:FieldURI FieldURI="task:PercentComplete"/>
                <t:Task>
                    <t:PercentComplete>100</t:PercentComplete>
                </t:Task>
              </t:SetItemField>
            </t:Updates>
        </t:ItemChange>
    </ItemChanges>
</UpdateItem>
```

Great, so the task is marked as complete. Now what is returned if a *FindItem* request is issued on the default Tasks folder? Take a look at the results in Listing 11-13.

```
<FindItem xmlns=".../messages"
          xmlns:t=".../types"
          Traversal="Shallow">
  <ItemShape>
    <t:BaseShape>Default</t:BaseShape>
    <t:AdditionalProperties>
      <t:FieldURI FieldURI="task:CompleteDate"/>
      <t:FieldURI FieldURI="task:IsRecurring"/>
    </t:AdditionalProperties>
  </ItemShape>
  <ParentFolderIds>
    <t:DistinguishedFolderId Id="tasks"/>
  </ParentFolderIds>
</FindItem>
```

LISTING 11-13 *FindItem* task results

```
<!-- outer elements elided -->
<m:RootFolder TotalItemsInView="2" IncludesLastItemInRange="true">
   <t:Items>
      <t:Task>
         <t:ItemId Id="AAAtAEFkbWlua..." ChangeKey="AAAAA..."/>
         <t:Subject>Daily Regenerating Task</t:Subject>
         <t:HasAttachments>false</t:HasAttachments>
         <t:DueDate>2007-02-16T08:00:00Z</t:DueDate>
         <t:IsRecurring>true</t:IsRecurring>
            <t:PercentComplete>0</t:PercentComplete>
         <t:Status>NotStarted</t:Status>
      </t:Task>
      <t:Task>
```

```
                <t:ItemId Id="AAAtAEFWl..." ChangeKey="AAAAA..."/>
                <t:Subject>Daily Regenerating Task</t:Subject>
                <t:HasAttachments>false</t:HasAttachments>
                <t:CompleteDate>2007-02-15T08:00:00Z</t:CompleteDate>
                <t:IsRecurring>false</t:IsRecurring>
                <t:DueDate>2007-02-01T08:00:00Z</t:DueDate>
                <t:PercentComplete>100</t:PercentComplete>
                <t:Status>Completed</t:Status>
            </t:Task>
        </t:Items>
    </m:RootFolder>
```

Listing 11-13 provides some insight as to what is going on. There are two tasks in the response and the second one is marked as complete, although the *CompleteDate* time is incorrect. Remember, the task was "completed" around 3:45 A.M. PST, yet it is marked as being complete at midnight PST.[5]

Looking a little further, notice that *IsRecurring* is false. That might seem a bit odd. This is a recurring task! In contrast, *IsRecurring* is true for the other occurrence in the response. What is going on? When the recurring task is marked as complete through *UpdateItem*, the id that is returned is different than the id passed in. This isn't just a change key difference—the id part is different. Why is that? Because the id that *UpdateItem* returns in this case refers to a *different item* than the one that was passed in. When a recurring task is marked as complete, the existing recurring instance is *updated* to reflect the next instance. A shiny, new, non-recurring task is created and marked as complete. *UpdateItem* returns the id of this shiny new task. So how do you get the id of the updated recurring task? Well, it's already there—it was passed into *UpdateItem* in the first place. Of course, the change key is now stale, so to make further updates to the recurring task, you would need to call *GetItem* to retrieve the updated change key.

To consider this *CompleteDate* strangeness a little further, look at Listing 11-14 where the new instance is marked as complete, but the *CompleteDate* property is set to something other than midnight Pacific Standard Time.

LISTING 11-14 Marking the task as complete via the *CompleteDate*

```
<!-- Outer elements elided -->
<t:SetItemField>
    <t:FieldURI FieldURI="task:CompleteDate"/>
    <t:Task>
        <t:CompleteDate>2007-02-15T12:06:00Z</t:CompleteDate>
    </t:Task>
</t:SetItemField>
```

---

[5] Or 8 A.M. Greenwich Mean Time.

In Listing 11-14, the *CompleteDate* is set to 12:06 P.M. UTC (4:06 A.M. PST). Calling *GetItem* on the completed task shows something interesting.

```
<t:CompleteDate>2007-02-15T08:00:00Z</t:CompleteDate>
```

The *CompleteDate* that was set on the task did not reflect the time value specified in the *UpdateItem* call. So, it is best to view *CompleteDate* as simply a date value rather than as a date + time value.

Note that when a regenerating task is marked as complete, clients such as Office Outlook and Outlook Web Access will show only the updated task occurrence. They will not show the completed task occurrences, although those occurrences are still there.

Task Properties and Restrictions

We will cover restrictions in depth in Chapter 14, "Searching the Mailbox." but since tasks are the current topic of discussion, it seems prudent to let you in on a little secret related to tasks and restrictions. None of the task-specific properties can be used within *FindItem* restrictions, which is an unfortunate omission that may be rectified in a future release of Exchange Web Services. Of course, you can work around this issue by using extended properties. To pay penance for this omission, we offer up Table 11-5, which shows you the extended property information for each of the properties.[6] These properties are defined within the PSETID_Task namespace: {00062003-0000-0000-C000-000000000046}. Note that *IsRecurring*, *Recurrence*, *StartDate*, and *StatusDescription* are calculated properties and are therefore unusable in restrictions. As such, they are omitted from Table 11-5.

TABLE 11-5 Task Extended Property Information

Task Property	MAPI Property Type Enumeration	Property Set Id	Property Id
ActualWork	Integer	Task	0x8110
AssignedTime	SystemTime	Task	0x8115
BillingInformation	String	Common	0x8535
ChangeCount	Integer	Task	0x8112
Companies	StringArray	Common	0x8539
CompleteDate	SystemTime	Task	0x810F
Contacts	StringArray	Common	0x853A
DelegationState	Integer	Task	0x812A
Delegator	String	Task	0x8121
DueDate	String (surprise!)	Common	0x8105
IsAssignmentEditable	Integer	Common	0x8518

---

[6] Extended properties are covered in Chapter 13, "Extended Properties."

Task Property	MAPI Property Type Enumeration	Property Set Id	Property Id
IsComplete	Boolean	Task	0x811C
IsTeamTask	Boolean	Task	0x8103
Mileage	String	Common	0x8534
Owner	String	Task	0x811F
*PercentComplete**	Double	Task	0x8102
Status	Integer	Task	0x8101
TotalWork	Integer	Task	0x8111

* When dealing with the raw MAPI property for *PercentComplete*, note that the value will be returned in the range of 0-1 rather than 0-100.

Overdue Regenerating Tasks

Let's say you have a daily recurring task and a daily regenerating task that are five days overdue. This means that in both cases you have several occurrences that are all overdue, not just the current occurrence. How do these intervening overdue occurrences behave in the recurring and regenerating task cases? Just for fun, let's illustrate this by using a proxy class example. First, create a daily recurring task for five days ago. Then start marking instances complete until you no longer have instances due today. You then do the same thing with a daily regenerating task. We will also provide another version of *SimpleGetItem* that takes the response shape of the item to return.

LISTING 11-15 Proxy example for recurring tasks

```
/// <summary>
/// Creates an overdue task and marks instances as complete until we are no
/// longer overdue.
/// </summary>
/// <param name="binding">Binding to use</param>
/// <param name="recurrencePattern">Recurrence pattern</param>
/// <param name="subject">Subject</param>
///
public static void CreateOverdueTaskAndComplete(
                ExchangeServiceBinding binding,
                RecurrencePatternBaseType recurrencePattern,
                string subject)
{
    // First create our recurring task
    //
    ItemIdType id = CreateRecurringTask(
                    binding,
                    subject,
                    recurrencePattern);

    ItemResponseShapeType getItemResponseShape =
            new ItemResponseShapeType(
                    DefaultShapeNamesType.IdOnly,
                    new PathToUnindexedFieldType(
```

```
                            UnindexedFieldURIType.taskDueDate));

    // Retrieve the recurring task just to get the original due date
    //
    TaskType recurringTask = (TaskType)SimpleGetItem(
                                    binding,
                                    id,
                                    getItemResponseShape);
    Console.WriteLine("Original Due Date: " +
              recurringTask.DueDate.ToString());

    while (true)
    {
      // On each iteration, mark the recurring task as complete
      //
      ItemIdType oneOffId = MarkTaskAsComplete(binding, id);

      // Retrieve the updated Id and the next due date
      //
      recurringTask = (TaskType)SimpleGetItem(
                                    binding,
                                    id,
                                    getItemResponseShape);

      // Grab our updated id with change key.  Remember this is the id of
      // the recurring task, NOT the one off.
      //
      id = recurringTask.ItemId;

      DateTime newTaskDueDate = recurringTask.DueDate;
      Console.WriteLine("\tNext Due Date: " + newTaskDueDate.ToString());
      if (newTaskDueDate.DayOfYear > DateTime.Now.DayOfYear)
      {
        Console.WriteLine("We are now up to date!");
        break;
      }
    }
  }
}


/// <summary>
/// Creates a recurring task given the recurrence pattern
/// </summary>
/// <param name="binding">Binding to use</param>
/// <param name="subject">Subject for task</param>
/// <param name="recurrencePattern">Recurrence pattern</param>
/// <returns>Id of newly created task</returns>
///
public static ItemIdType CreateRecurringTask(
                            ExchangeServiceBinding binding,
                            string subject,
                            RecurrencePatternBaseType recurrencePattern)
{
  CreateItemType request = new CreateItemType();
  TaskType task = new TaskType();
```

```
TaskRecurrenceType taskRecurrence = new TaskRecurrenceType();
taskRecurrence.Item = recurrencePattern;

// We will just use a no end recurrence here
//
NoEndRecurrenceRangeType noEnd = new NoEndRecurrenceRangeType();

// Even though we are setting this as a full DateTime, the XML
// serializer is smart enough to only send across the date part.
// Otherwise it would be a schema violation.
//
task.StartDate = DateTime.Now.AddDays(-5d); // move back 5 days
task.StartDateSpecified = true;
noEnd.StartDate = task.StartDate;
taskRecurrence.Item1 = noEnd;

task.Recurrence = taskRecurrence;
task.Subject = subject;
task.StartDate = noEnd.StartDate;

request.Items = new NonEmptyArrayOfAllItemsType();
request.Items.Items = new ItemType[] { task };

// Make our CreateItem call
//
CreateItemResponseType response = binding.CreateItem(request);
ItemInfoResponseMessageType responseMessage =
        response.ResponseMessages.Items[0] as
                    ItemInfoResponseMessageType;
if (responseMessage.ResponseCode != ResponseCodeType.NoError)
{
    throw new Exception(
            "Failed to create recurring task.  Response Code: " +
            responseMessage.ResponseCode.ToString());
}
    return responseMessage.Items.Items[0].ItemId;
}


/// <summary>
/// Marks a task as complete by setting the percent complete property to
/// 100
/// </summary>
/// <param name="binding">Binding to use</param>
/// <param name="taskId">Id of the task to complete</param>
/// <returns>Id of the one-off generated task (in the case of recurring
/// tasks)</returns>
///
public static ItemIdType MarkTaskAsComplete(
                    ExchangeServiceBinding binding,
                    ItemIdType taskId)
{
    Console.WriteLine("Marking task as complete...");
    UpdateItemType updateRequest = new UpdateItemType();
    updateRequest.ConflictResolution =
```

```
                    ConflictResolutionType.AlwaysOverwrite;
    ItemChangeType itemChange = new ItemChangeType();
    itemChange.Item = taskId;

    TaskType newTask = new TaskType();
    newTask.PercentComplete = 100d;

    // Remember that PercentComplete is an optional value type, so set the
    // specified flag.
    //
    newTask.PercentCompleteSpecified = true;

    SetItemFieldType set = new SetItemFieldType(
                new PathToUnindexedFieldType(
                        UnindexedFieldURIType.taskPercentComplete),
                newTask);

    itemChange.Updates = new ItemChangeDescriptionType[] { set };
    updateRequest.ItemChanges = new ItemChangeType[] { itemChange };

    UpdateItemResponseType response = binding.UpdateItem(updateRequest);
    ItemInfoResponseMessageType responseMessage =
            response.ResponseMessages.Items[0] as
                        ItemInfoResponseMessageType;

    if (responseMessage.ResponseCode != ResponseCodeType.NoError)
    {
        throw new Exception(
                "Failed to mark the task as complete.  Response Code: " +
                responseMessage.ResponseCode.ToString());
    }
    return responseMessage.Items.Items[0].ItemId;
}


/// <summary>
/// Binds to an item and returns the item with the supplied response shape
/// </summary>
/// <param name="binding">Binding to use</param>
/// <param name="id">Id of item to bind to</param>
/// <returns>ItemType instance or null if error</returns>
///
public static ItemType SimpleGetItem(
                        ExchangeServiceBinding binding,
                        ItemIdType id,
                        ItemResponseShapeType responseShape)
{
    // Create our request type
    //
    GetItemType getItemRequest = new GetItemType();
    getItemRequest.ItemIds = new ItemIdType[] { id };
    getItemRequest.ItemShape = responseShape;

    // Now make the call
    //
```

```
GetItemResponseType getItemResponse = binding.GetItem(getItemRequest);

// GetItem returns ItemInfoResponseMessages.  Since we only requested one
// item, we should only get back one response message.
//
ItemInfoResponseMessageType getItemResponseMessage =
        getItemResponse.ResponseMessages.Items[0] as
            ItemInfoResponseMessageType;

// Like all good, happy and compliant developers, we should check our
// response code...
//
if (getItemResponseMessage.ResponseCode == ResponseCodeType.NoError)
{
  return getItemResponseMessage.Items.Items[0];
}
else
{
  throw new Exception("Failed to retrieve item.  Response Code: " +
      getItemResponseMessage.ResponseCode.ToString());
}
}
```

Listing 11-14 contains several helper methods, but the main method of interest is *CreateOver dueTaskAndComplete*. This method performs the following steps:

1. Creates the task with the specific recurrent pattern.

2. In a loop, does the following:

   a. Marks the task as complete

   b. Grabs the updated change key of the recurring task

   c. Checks to see if the new due date indicates that the task is no longer overdue.

And, of course, you need something to call *CreateOverdueTaskAndComplete*.

LISTING 11-16 Proxy class test harness

```
/// <summary>
/// Test our CreateOverdueTaskAndComplete method
/// </summary>
/// <param name="binding">Binding to use for our call</param>
///
public static void TestOverdueTaskCompletion(ExchangeServiceBinding binding)
{
  Console.WriteLine("Daily Recurrence");
  Console.WriteLine("===========================");
  DailyRecurrencePatternType dailyRecurrence = new DailyRecurrencePatternType();
  dailyRecurrence.Interval = 1;
  string subject = "Clean your room " + Environment.TickCount.ToString();
```

```
    CreateOverdueTaskAndComplete(binding, dailyRecurrence, subject);
    Console.WriteLine("\r\n\r\n");

    Console.WriteLine("Daily Regenerating");
    Console.WriteLine("=========================");
    DailyRegeneratingPatternType dailyRegenerating =
                         new DailyRegeneratingPatternType();
    dailyRegenerating.Interval = 1; // 1 day
    subject = "Clean your room " + Environment.TickCount.ToString();
    CreateOverdueTaskAndComplete(binding, dailyRegenerating, subject);
}
```

Listing 11-16 shows that you call *CreateOverdueTaskAndComplete* twice—once for daily recurring tasks and once for daily regenerating tasks. Figure 11-6 shows the results of executing this method.

FIGURE 11-6 Results of overdue recurring tasks proxy example

As you can see from Figure 11-6, you had to "catch up" on all overdue instances of your daily recurring task, whereas you only needed to mark the single instance of your daily regenerating task as complete.[7]

Modifying Recurrence Patterns

Given that you can create a recurring task by setting the recurrence pattern, it is reasonable to conclude that you can change a recurring task by updating the recurrence pattern. This is accomplished by using the *UpdateItem* Web method just as it was with calendar item recurrence patterns.

---

[7] If you haven't figured it out, we ran this on July 7, 2007.

How Are Recurring Task Instances Related?

You have seen how marking a recurring task as complete creates a non-recurring task instance to represent the completed task and then updates the existing recurring task instance to represent the next, uncompleted instance. It would be nice to be able to relate completed instances with the current recurring task instance. Unfortunately, there is no simple way to do this. Certainly, using Exchange Web Services, you can stamp new recurring tasks with your very own extended property that can be used to find related items, but clients such as Office Outlook do not do this. So, you might end up with a mix of stamped and unstamped tasks within a Mailbox. As such, you have to find related task occurrences using restrictions. The code shown in Listing 11-17 finds related task occurrences using the PR_INTERNET_MESSAGE_ID MAPI property (property tag 0x1035). The cloned one-off tasks have the same internet message id value as the original recurring task.

LISTING 11-17 Finding related tasks via the proxy

```
/// <summary>
/// Finds the related tasks for a given task
/// </summary>
/// <param name="binding">Binding to use for EWS calls</param>
/// <param name="taskId">The Id of the task to find</param>
/// <returns>The matching items</returns>
///
public static ItemType[] FindRelatedTasks(
                    ExchangeServiceBinding binding,
                    ItemIdType taskId)
{
    // First, retrieve the internet message id (0x1035) for the supplied task
    // by supplying the extended field property path in the response shape
    //
    PathToExtendedFieldType messageIdProp = new PathToExtendedFieldType();
    messageIdProp.PropertyTag = "0x1035";
    messageIdProp.PropertyType = MapiPropertyTypeType.String;

    ItemResponseShapeType responseShape = new ItemResponseShapeType(
                    DefaultShapeNamesType.IdOnly,
                    messageIdProp);

    // Retrieve the task item and read off the internet message id which is the
    // only extended property that we requested, so it will be the first item
    // in the array.
    //
    ItemType taskItem = SimpleGetItem(binding, taskId, responseShape);
    string messageId = (string)taskItem.ExtendedProperty[0].Item;

    // Now perpare our FindItem call and restrict on the internet message id
    // value...
    //
    RestrictionType restriction = new RestrictionType();
    IsEqualToType equalsMessageId = new IsEqualToType();
    equalsMessageId.Item = messageIdProp;
```

```
equalsMessageId.FieldURIOrConstant = new FieldURIOrConstantType();
ConstantValueType messageIdConstantValue = new ConstantValueType();
messageIdConstantValue.Value = messageId;
equalsMessageId.FieldURIOrConstant.Item = messageIdConstantValue;

restriction.Item = equalsMessageId;
FindItemType findRequest = new FindItemType();
findRequest.ItemShape = new
        ItemResponseShapeType(DefaultShapeNamesType.Default);

// Look in the default tasks folder.
//
findRequest.ParentFolderIds = new BaseFolderIdType[] { new
        DistinguishedFolderIdType(DistinguishedFolderIdNameType.tasks) };
findRequest.Restriction = restriction;
findRequest.Traversal = ItemQueryTraversalType.Shallow;

// Make the actual FindItem call
//
FindItemResponseType findResponse = binding.FindItem(findRequest);
FindItemResponseMessageType findMessage =
        findResponse.ResponseMessages.Items[0] as FindItemResponseMessageType;

if (findMessage.ResponseCode != ResponseCodeType.NoError)
{
    throw new Exception("Find failed with response code: " +
            findMessage.ResponseCode.ToString());
}
ItemType[] items = (findMessage.RootFolder.Item as
            ArrayOfRealItemsType).Items;
    return items;
}
```

Summary

Tasks are items that are actionable, measurable, and finite. They are actionable because they require some effort on the task owner's part to complete them. They are measurable because they can be completed. They are finite because there is a date when they are considered complete. In this chapter, we discussed the various task properties. We discussed recurring tasks, which are tasks that repeat based on a user-defined recurrence pattern. We explained the difference between normal recurring tasks and regenerating tasks, when to use each, and how overdue instances of these types of tasks behave when you mark them as complete.

Now, we can mark the task of writing this chapter as complete. Thankfully, writing the chapter isn't a recurring task.

Chapter 12
Attachments

Users are quite familiar with e-mail attachments. Attachments can be the source of much joy (pictures of the grandchildren), or much pain (XYZVirus.exe). Microsoft Exchange Server 2007 Web Services (EWS) supports the creation and retrieval of attachments. In this chapter, we will discuss item and file attachments, their structure, and best practices when dealing with them.

What Are Attachments?

A given item within a Mailbox can have zero or more attachments associated with it. When an item has attachments, the data about these attachments will be stored within the Exchange Store attachments table. Using Outlook Spy, you can easily see attachment information for a given item. For example, we sent a simple e-mail with an image attachment and then used Outlook Spy to look at the received message. Indeed, the message has a single item in the attachment table, as shown in Figure 12-1.

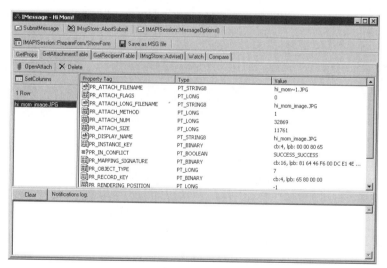

FIGURE 12-1 Outlook Spy Attachment Table view

Notice that Outlook Spy shows that attachments have properties just like items do. (We will get to that shortly.)

A file attached to a message is aptly called a file attachment. Attaching the file to a message imports its contents into the Exchange Store database. You can determine if a given message has a file attachment by looking at the *PR_ATTACH_METHOD* property in Outlook Spy, as shown in Figure 12-2. Notice in this example that the symbol value for this property is

ATTACH_BY_VALUE. The entire contents of the file have been copied into the Store, hence *by value*. ATTACH_BY_VALUE also implies that changes to the original file will not be reflected in the file attachment after the attachment has been created.

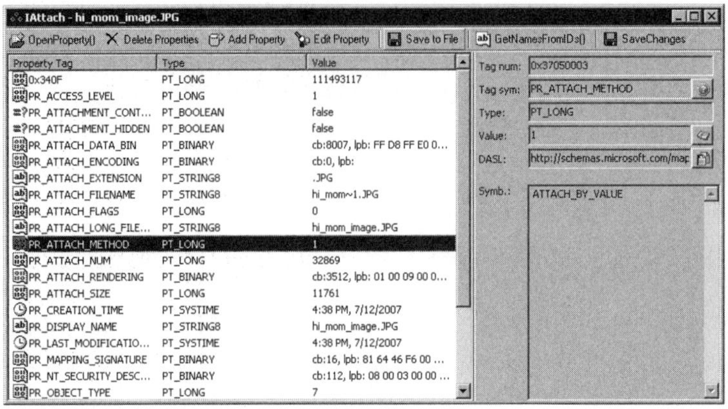

FIGURE 12-2 Outlook Spy view of *PR_ATTACH_METHOD* for a file attachment

In contrast, you can also attach items to other items. This type of attachment is called an item attachment. To determine if an attachment is an item attachment, you can look at the *PR_ATTACH_METHOD* property in Outlook Spy, as shown in Figure 12-3. Notice in this example that its symbol value is *ATTACH_EMBEDDED_MSG*.

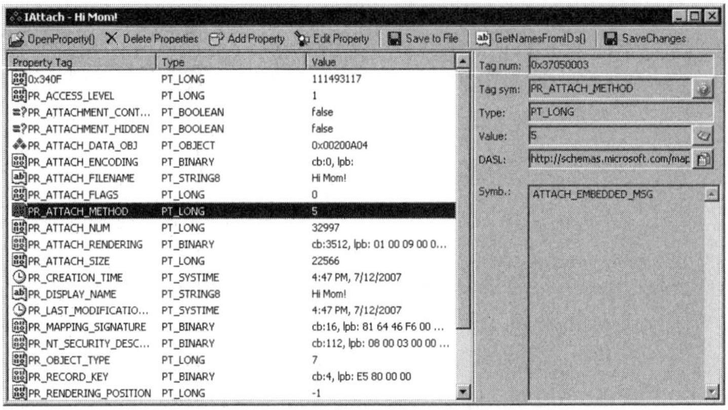

FIGURE 12-3 Outlook Spy view of *PR_ATTACH_METHOD* for an item attachment

Item attachments can form hierarchies. For instance, you can have an item attachment that has its own item attachment that has its own attachment, and so forth. Of course, any of those item attachments can also have file attachments on them, too. We will discuss such attachment hierarchies later in this chapter.

Attachments, Property Paths, and Item Shapes

Attachments are details of a given item, and therefore it is reasonable to assume that an item property path identifies them. And indeed it does. The property path *item:Attachments* can be used within a *GetItem* call to retrieve attachment *metadata* information for an item. Attachment *metadata*?[1] Yes, *GetItem* will return only information about the attachments. We will introduce another Web method shortly that can be used to retrieve the actual attachment contents. The attachment metadata collection is also included in the default shape for *ItemType* and all *ItemType* descendants.

So if the attachment collection is part of the default shape, why hasn't that element shown up in any of the responses before this chapter? If a given item has no attachments, the attachment collection will not be emitted into the resulting XML. If you are dealing with the proxy classes the *Attachments* property will be null in such cases. In earlier chapters, all the example items were "attachment-less."

Another property path of interest when dealing with attachments is *item:HasAttachments*, which is associated with the *HasAttachments* property on *ItemType*. Can't you tell if an item has attachments by simply looking for the presence of the attachment collection? The answer is yes and no. An attachment can be visible or invisible. A *visible* attachment is meant to be seen as an attachment by the user. In other words, Microsoft Office Outlook and Outlook Web Access (OWA) should show the paper clip icon beside the message when you view the contents of a folder. An *invisible* attachment is not intended to be seen as an attachment by the user. An example of an invisible attachment is an inline image within the Hypertext Markup Language (HTML) body content of a message. The user will see the image in the body of the e-mail, but the image shouldn't show up as an attachment (that is, there should be no paper clip).

With this in mind, an item is considered to have attachments if it has one or more visible attachments, and the *HasAttachments* property takes this into account.[2] In contrast, the attachments collection will return all attachments regardless of their visibility. Unfortunately, Exchange Web Services does not yet expose a way to determine the visibility of a particular attachment. This visibility information is stored as a Messaging Application Programming Interface (MAPI) property in the attachment table, but Exchange Web Services does not provide a way to retrieve arbitrary MAPI properties from the attachments table.[3]

Attachments are exposed in the schema through *AttachmentType*. Both *FileAttachmentType* and *ItemAttachmentType* derive from *AttachmentType*. These two descendants are the only

---

[1] Note that *item:Attachments* is only accessible via *GetItem*. Because this property refers to the attachments table, *FindItem* is not able to return attachment information. Therefore, *item:Attachments* is not permitted in the response shape of a *FindItem* call.

[2] Because of this "intelligence," *item:HasAttachments* is only accessible via *GetItem*.

[3] This may be fixed in a future release.

attachment types you will encounter. As such, you should treat *AttachmentType* as if it were abstract, even though it is not marked as such in the schema. We will first look at file attachments and basic attachment functionality and then discuss item attachments.

File Attachments

Let's assume that you have an item in your Mailbox that already has a visible file attachment on it. Call *GetItem* on this item and see what data is returned. Although you could just use the *Default* base shape, you should always request only the information that you need. So instead, use the *IdOnly* base shape and request both the *item:Attachments* and *item:HasAttachments* property paths via the *AdditionalProperties* element. This is shown in Listing 12-1.

LISTING 12-1 *GetItem* with attachments

```
<GetItem xmlns=".../messages"
         xmlns:t=".../types">
  <ItemShape>
    <t:BaseShape>IdOnly</t:BaseShape>
    <t:AdditionalProperties>
      <t:FieldURI FieldURI="item:Attachments"/>
      <t:FieldURI FieldURI="item:HasAttachments"/>
    </t:AdditionalProperties>
  </ItemShape>
  <ItemIds>
    <t:ItemId Id="AAAtAEFkbWlua..." ChangeKey="AAAAA..."/>
  </ItemIds>
</GetItem>
```

The message portion of the response is shown in Listing 12-2.

LISTING 12-2 Partial *GetItemResponse* for an item with file attachment

```
<!-- xml elided -->
<t:Message>
  <t:ItemId Id="AAAtAEFkbWlua..." ChangeKey="AAAAA..."/>
  <t:Attachments>
    <t:FileAttachment>
      <t:AttachmentId Id="AAAtAE..."/>
      <t:Name>hi_mom_image.JPG</t:Name>
    </t:FileAttachment>
  </t:Attachments>
  <t:HasAttachments>true</t:HasAttachments>
</t:Message>
<!-- xml elided -->
```

The returned message contains an *Attachments* element that holds a single *FileAttachment*. As mentioned earlier, the attachments collection returned by *GetItem* is a metadata *only* collection, meaning that it contains information *about* the attachments, but it will *never* contain the actual attachment contents. The actual contents are retrieved via the *GetAttachment* Web method call, which we will discuss shortly. Also note that the message contains the *HasAttachments* element, which is true because there is a visible attachment.

Retrieving Attachment Content

Retrieving the actual content of an attachment is the realm of the *GetAttachment* Web method.

The basic structure of the *GetAttachment* Web method is shown in Listing 12-3.

LISTING 12-3 Basic structure of the *GetAttachment* Web method

```
<GetAttachment xmlns=".../messages"
               xmlns:t=".../types">
  <AttachmentShape/>
  <AttachmentIds>
    <t:AttachmentId …
    <t:AttachmentId …
  </AttachmentIds>
</GetAttachment>
```

AttachmentShape Element

The first child element in *GetAttachment* is *AttachmentShape*, which is defined by *AttachmentResponseShapeType* in the schema.

```
<xs:complexType name="AttachmentResponseShapeType">
  <xs:sequence>
    <xs:element name="IncludeMimeContent" type="xs:boolean" minOccurs="0" />
    <xs:element name="BodyType" type="t:BodyTypeResponseType" minOccurs="0" />
    <xs:element name="AdditionalProperties"
                type="t:NonEmptyArrayOfPathsToElementType"
                minOccurs="0" />
  </xs:sequence>
</xs:complexType>
```

AttachmentShape looks quite promising from the schema, but is useless when dealing with file attachments. Why? Well, the *IncludeMimeContent* and *BodyType* elements have nothing to do with file attachments. The *AdditionalProperties* element gives some hope. We mentioned earlier that the Exchange Store holds MAPI properties for each attachment in the Store attachments table. It would be reasonable to assume that you could use the *AdditionalProperties* element to specify which attachment related properties you would like returned for your attachment.

Unfortunately, the *AdditionalProperties* element is completely ignored by Exchange Web Services when dealing with file attachments.[4] Hopefully, Exchange Web Services will expose more complete access to properties contained in the attachment table in a future release. As you will see later in this chapter, when dealing with item attachments, the *AttachmentShape* element is respected in a *GetItem* call.

In contrast to *GetItem* and the *ItemShape* element, for *GetAttachment*, the *AttachmentShape* element is optional.

AttachmentIds Element

In the schema, the *AttachmentIds* element is an instance of type *NonEmptyArrayOfRequestAttachmentIdsType*. As its name implies, you must specify at least one attachment id. Of course, these ids had to come from somewhere, most likely from the attachment collection in the *GetItem* response.

Listing 12-4 shows a call to retrieve a single file attachment. Note that the optional *AttachmentShape* element is omitted. You are free to include it if it makes you feel better.

LISTING 12-4 Calling *GetAttachment*

```
<GetAttachment xmlns=".../messages"
               xmlns:t=".../types">
  <AttachmentIds>
    <t:AttachmentId Id="AAAtAEFkbWlua..."/>
  </AttachmentIds>
</GetAttachment>
```

Listing 12-5 shows the response.

LISTING 12-5 *GetAttachment* response

```
<GetAttachmentResponse xmlns:m=".../messages"
                       xmlns:t=".../types"
                       xmlns=".../messages">
  <m:ResponseMessages>
    <m:GetAttachmentResponseMessage ResponseClass="Success">
      <m:ResponseCode>NoError</m:ResponseCode>
      <m:Attachments>
        <t:FileAttachment>
          <t:AttachmentId Id="AAAtAEFkbWlua..."/>
          <t:Name>hi_mom_image.JPG</t:Name>
          <t:Content>/9j/4AAQSkZJRgAB...</t:Content>
        </t:FileAttachment>
```

---

[4] Even if the *AdditionalProperties* element was not ignored by Exchange Web Services, *FileAttachmentType* does not expose an *ExtendedProperty* array element, so there would be no way to return extended property data even if you could request it.

```
        </m:Attachments>
      </m:GetAttachmentResponseMessage>
    </m:ResponseMessages>
  </GetAttachmentResponse>
```

As expected, the call returned a file attachment. It would make sense that given such an attachment, you should be able to recreate the file, right? Absolutely. The *Content* element is the Base64-encoded binary data of the file. Keep in mind that although it is Base64 encoded when you look at the raw XML, the proxy classes see that the *Content* element is of type xs:base64Binary in the schema. As a result, the proxy classes intelligently expose this as a *byte[]* rather than as a *string*. In other words, you don't have to call *System.Convert. FromBase64String* when using the proxy classes. Listing 12-6 shows an example of retrieving the file attachment content from an item and saving the content off to a directory of your choosing.

LISTING 12-6 Proxy class example of retrieving file attachments and saving them to a file

```
/// <summary>
/// Gets the file attachments and saves them to a directory.
/// </summary>
/// <param name="binding">Binding to use for the call</param>
/// <param name="destinationPath">Destination directory to save the
/// attachments to</param>
/// <param name="attachmentIds">Array of attachment Ids to retrieve</param>
///
public static void GetFileAttachmentAndSave(
                          ExchangeServiceBinding binding,
                          string destinationPath,
                          params AttachmentIdType[] attachmentIds)
{
  GetAttachmentType getAttachmentRequest = new GetAttachmentType();

  // Note that AttachmentIdType derives from RequestAttachmentIdType, so
  // we can directly assign here.
  //
  getAttachmentRequest.AttachmentIds = attachmentIds;

  // Remember, we don't even need to set the attachment shape.
  //
  GetAttachmentResponseType getAttachmentResponse =
                  binding.GetAttachment(getAttachmentRequest);

  // Now, here we might have asked for multiple attachments. If so, we will
  // get back multiple response messages.

  foreach (AttachmentInfoResponseMessageType attachmentResponseMessage in
            getAttachmentResponse.ResponseMessages.Items)
```

```
{
   if (attachmentResponseMessage.ResponseCode ==
                             ResponseCodeType.NoError)
   {
      FileAttachmentType fileAttachment =
          attachmentResponseMessage.Attachments[0] as FileAttachmentType;

      // If fileAttachment is null, then it must be an item attachment
      // which we will not save out.
      //
      if (fileAttachment != null)
      {
         // Now, just save out the file contents
         //
         using (FileStream file = File.Create(
               Path.Combine(destinationPath, fileAttachment.Name)))
         {
            file.Write(
                 fileAttachment.Content,
                 0,
                 fileAttachment.Content.Length);
            file.Close();
         }
      }
   }
}
```

Creating File Attachments

Given that *ItemType* exposes an *Attachments* element, you might think that you can add attachments when you create an item by filling in the attachment information. Although reasonable, the Exchange Web Services team decided to separate item and attachment creation, making a two-step process. As such, the *Attachments* element on *ItemType* is read-only. You must first create the item that the attachment will attach to. Of course, if you already have the parent item of interest, the first step can be omitted. Second, you add the attachment to that item via the *CreateAttachment* method.

Assume here that the first step has been executed, so you already have the item that you want to add an attachment to. The next step is to create the attachment via the *CreateAttachment* Web method. *CreateAttachment* has a simple structure, as shown in Listing 12-7.

LISTING 12-7 Basic structure of *CreateAttachment*

```
<CreateAttachment xmlns=".../messages">
  <ParentItemId/>
  <Attachments/>
</CreateAttachment>
```

The first element, *ParentItemId*, is the id of the item that you want to add the attachment to. It is of type *ItemIdType* and is required. Up to this point in the book, you are probably used to seeing item ids with a *t:ItemId* local name. This is one of the rare deviations in Exchange Web Services. Here, the local name is *ParentItemId*.

The second element, *Attachments*, holds a collection of *Attachment* elements. The collection itself is a *NonEmptyArrayOfAttachmentsType*, which is the same type as the *Attachments* element on *ItemType*. You can use *CreateAttachment* to create one or more attachments and attach them to a single item. If you want to create attachments for multiple items, you will need to call *CreateAttachment* several times—one for each item that you want to add attachments to.

So far, so good. How do you define your *Attachment* element? What do you put in there? Well, because we are talking about file attachments, let's look at the properties exposed by the *FileAttachmentType*, what they mean, and how to use them.

FileAttachmentType derives from *AttachmentType* in the schema, and therefore inherits all the elements that are exposed on *AttachmentType*. Table 12-1 shows the properties exposed by *AttachmentType*, their types, and their purposes.

TABLE 12-1 *AttachmentType* **Properties**

Property Name	Type	Comments
AttachmentId	*AttachmentIdType*	The id of the attachment. This property is read-only and therefore cannot be set when calling *CreateAttachment*.
Name	String	The name of the attachment. Multiple attachments on a given item can have the same name, although doing so has questionable value.
ContentType	String	The Multipurpose Internet Mail Extensions (MIME) content type of the attachment. Defined in RFC 2046.
ContentId	String	An identifier for the attachment. This is primarily used for inline attachments so that rendering code can identify an attachment. *ContentId* is optional.
ContentLocation	*xs:string*	A location identifier for the attachment. This is used primarily for inline attachments so that rendering code can determine where to render the attachment within the body of the document. *ContentLocation* is optional.

FileAttachmentType adds a single element, *Content*, to those shown in Table 12-1. You have already seen the *Content* element in action when you retrieved the contents of an existing *FileAttachment*. Now, it is your turn to fill in this information. As mentioned earlier, the *Content* element is of type *xs:base64Binary*. When dealing with raw XML, you must set the *Content* element to be the Base64-encoded string content of the file. When dealing with the proxy classes, you set the *Content* property as a byte[].

Listing 12-8 shows a basic *CreateAttachment* call to add a *FileAttachment* to an existing item. Note that this is a simple file attachment; therefore, no content id or content location is added in this call. Although not recommended, the *ContentType* element is also omitted. We will see how to correctly identify the *ContentType* shortly.

LISTING 12-8 *CreateAttachment* call with *FileAttachment*

```
<CreateAttachment xmlns=".../messages"
                  xmlns:t=".../types">
  <t:ParentItemId Id="AAAtAEFkbWlua..." ChangeKey="AAAAA..."/>
  <Attachments>
    <t:FileAttachment>
      <t:Name>hi_mom_image.jpg</t:Name>
      <t:Content>/9j/4AAQSkZJRgABAQEA...
    </t:FileAttachment>
  </Attachments>
</CreateAttachment>
```

Now, to be a good Exchange Web Services citizen, you *should* set the *ContentType* for the attachment, which was not done in Listing 12-8. Determining the content type can be painful if you need to accept arbitrary file types. Fortunately, Windows stores file extension to content type mappings in the registry. Listing 12-9 offers a method to perform this lookup. Note that the account that this code runs under must have rights to read the HKEY_CLASSES_ROOT registry hive.

LISTING 12-9 Looking up MIME content type in the registry

```
/// <summary>
/// Returns the Content type for the passed file based on the extension
/// </summary>
/// <param name="filename">Filename to determine mime type for</param>
/// <returns>Content type string</returns>
///
public static string GetMimeTypeForFile(string filename)
{
    // There are two places in the registry where we might be able to find
    // content type information for a given extension.  The first, and definitely
    // the quickest, is to look in the HKEY_CLASSES_ROOT hive. Each registered
    // extension is supposed to have its own subkey under HKCR.
    // If we don't find our extension using the first approach, we can look at
    // the registered MIME types.  Unfortunately there, we have to walk through
    // all of those keys and see if that MIME type is associated with our
    // extension of interest.
    //
    // First try to retrieve the content type via the extension directly.
    //
    string extension = Path.GetExtension(filename);
    using (RegistryKey extensionKey =
                Registry.ClassesRoot.OpenSubKey(
                          extension,
```

```
                            false /* need writable */))
   {
     if (extensionKey != null)
     {
       string contentType = (string)extensionKey.GetValue(
                   "Content Type");
       if (!String.IsNullOrEmpty(contentType))
       {
         return contentType;
       }
     }
   }

   // If we are here, then we couldn't find the content type value using the
   // extension name. So, as a fallback, look at the
   // HKEY_CLASSES_ROOT\MIME\Database\Content Type key
   // and look at the Extension key for the correct file extension
   //
   using (RegistryKey mimeDatabaseKey =
             Registry.ClassesRoot.OpenSubKey(
                 @"MIME\Database\Content Type",
                 false /* need writable */))
   {
     if (mimeDatabaseKey != null)
     {
       string[] subkeys = mimeDatabaseKey.GetSubKeyNames();
       // Enuemrate across all of the registered MIME types.
       //
       foreach (string subkey in subkeys)
       {
         using (RegistryKey contentTypeKey =
                   mimeDatabaseKey.OpenSubKey(subkey))
         {
           string contentTypeValue =
                   (string)contentTypeKey.GetValue("Content Type");
           if (contentTypeValue == extension)
           {
             return subkey;
           }
         }
       }
     }
   }

   // We didn't find it.
   //
   return String.Empty;
}
```

The static method in Listing 12-10 creates an attachment and sets the content type via the proxy class. Note that this method calls the *GetMimeTypeForFile* helper method from Listing 12-9.

LISTING 12-10 Creating and adding an attachment by using the proxy

```csharp
/// <summary>
/// Creates and adds an attachment to the parent item specified
/// </summary>
/// <param name="binding">Binding to use for Web method call</param>
/// <param name="parentId">Id of parent item to attach to</param>
/// <param name="fullFilePath">Full path (including file name) of
/// attachment</param>
/// <returns>Id of attachment</returns>
///
public static AttachmentIdType CreateAndAddAttachment(
                        ExchangeServiceBinding binding,
                        ItemIdType parentId,
                        string fullFilePath)
{
  FileAttachmentType attachment = new FileAttachmentType();

  // Read the content of the file.  Remember the Content property is
  // byte[], so no need to call System.Convert.ToBase64String().
  //
  attachment.Content = File.ReadAllBytes(fullFilePath);

  // Set the name to be the filename (minus the path)
  //
  attachment.Name = Path.GetFileName(fullFilePath);

  // Retrieve the content type
  //
  string contentType = GetMimeTypeForFile(fullFilePath);
  if (!String.IsNullOrEmpty(contentType))
  {
    attachment.ContentType = contentType;
  }

  // Make our request and examine the result
  //
  CreateAttachmentType request = new CreateAttachmentType();
  request.ParentItemId = parentId;
  request.Attachments = new AttachmentType[] { attachment };

  CreateAttachmentResponseType response =
            binding.CreateAttachment(request);

  AttachmentInfoResponseMessageType responseMessage =
          response.ResponseMessages.Items[0] as
                    AttachmentInfoResponseMessageType;

  if (responseMessage.ResponseCode == ResponseCodeType.NoError)
  {
    return responseMessage.Attachments[0].AttachmentId;
  }
  else
  {
    throw new Exception("Error trying to create attachment.  " +
          "Response code: " + responseMessage.ResponseCode.ToString());
  }
}
```

Note that both *GetAttachment* and *CreateAttachment* return *AttachmentInfoResponseMessageType* response messages. This follows the pattern of *GetItem* returning *ItemInfoResponseMessageType* response messages.

Attachment Ids

Just like items and folders, attachments have their own id type. Unlike items and folders, the id type used for requests is different from the id type used for responses. Of course, this warrants explanation. The attachment id type used for requests is called *RequestAttachmentIdType*. It exposes a single attribute called Id, which is the opaque identifier for that attachment. Note that there is no concept of a change key for an attachment and therefore no *ChangeKey* element.[5] When you make either a *GetAttachment* or *DeleteAttachment*[6] request, you use a *RequestAttachmentIdType* for the id. Of course, you don't specify an attachment id in *CreateAttachment* because the attachment doesn't yet exist. Simple enough.

Both *CreateAttachment* and *GetAttachment* return *AttachmentInfoResponseMessageType* response messages. These response messages in turn hold an array of *AttachmentType* instances called *Attachments*. A given *AttachmentType* instance exposes an *AttachmentId* element, but its type is not *RequestAttachmentIdType*, but rather *AttachmentIdType*. How do these differ? Well, *AttachmentIdType* derives from *RequestAttachmentIdType*, so it inherits the *Id* attribute. It also, however, adds two additional attributes.

The basic structure of *AttachmentIdType* is shown in Listing 12-11.

LISTING 12-11 Basic structure of *AttachmentIdType*

```
<t:AttachmentId Id="<id of the attachment>"
                RootItemId="<id of parent item>"
                RootItemChangeKey="<new parent item change key>">
```

Remember that an attachment does not exist on its own. Changes to an attachment on an item affect the item. For example, if you create a new attachment on an item, you need the id of the new attachment to be returned to you. But adding the attachment modifies the item that the attachment was added to. As such, the change key of the parent item has changed. Therefore, *CreateAttachment* always returns the *RootItemId* and *RootItemChangeKey* attributes. If it didn't return these attributes, you would need to call *GetItem* with the id of the parent item to get the up-to-date change key. It is important to note here that the change key is the change key of the parent (or "root") item. Remember, attachments don't have change keys.

---

[5] We are going to throw a wrench into this in a minute.

[6] *DeleteAttachment* will be discussed shortly.

Where things get a bit weird is that although *GetAttachment* also returns *AttachmentIdType* instances, these new attributes are omitted. Why? Because *GetAttachment* doesn't modify the parent item, so there is no need to return these attributes. The moral of the story here is that when you have an *AttachmentIdType* instance, don't assume that the *RootItemId* and *RootItemChangeKey* will be filled in unless you know that the id was returned by *CreateAttachment*.

One side effect of this disparity between request and response attachment ids is that when dealing with raw XML, you cannot simply take an *AttachmentId* element returned by *CreateAttachment* and pass it to *GetAttachment*. Why? Because the *RootItemId* and *RootItemChangeKey* attributes do not exist on *RequestAttachmentIdType,* and therefore the request will be schema invalid. You need to create a new element and copy the *Id* attribute over. When dealing with the proxy classes, you have better luck. Because *AttachmentIdType* derives from *RequestAttachmentIdType*, you can pass an *AttachmentIdType* instance to *GetAttachment*. The instance is treated polymorphically as the base class, and therefore the derived properties are ignored.

Deleting File Attachments

To delete an existing attachment, you make a call to the *DeleteAttachment* Web method. *DeleteAttachment* is a very simple Web method and has the basic structure shown in Listing 12-12.

LISTING 12-12 Basic structure of *DeleteAttachment*

```
<DeleteAttachment>
  <AttachmentIds>
    <t:AttachmentId/>
    <!-- more if necessary -->
  </AttachmentIds>
</DeleteAttachment>
```

DeleteAttachment has a single child element, *AttachmentIds*, that holds the ids of the attachments to delete. Don't be fooled by the fact that the local name is *AttachmentId*—these are *RequestAttachmentIdType* instances, not *AttachmentIdType* instances.

Deleting an attachment from an item changes that item, and therefore the change key of that item changes. *DeleteAttachment* is kind in this regard and returns *DeleteAttachmentResponseMessageType* instances for each deleted attachment. These specialized response messages expose a *RootItemId* element that is of type *RootItemIdType*. A *RootItemId* element is on the *AttachmentIdType* too, but in that case it is an *xs:string*. In *AttachmentIdType*, the change key is in a separate attribute, *RootItemChangeKey*. This inconsistency is easily worked around, but it can be a minor annoyance. Just remember that when dealing with *DeleteAttachmentResponseMessageType* instances, the change key for the parent item is contained as a child attribute on the *RootItemId* element. Listing 12-13 shows a *DeleteAttachment* request.

LISTING 12-13 *DeleteAttachment* request

```
<DeleteAttachment xmlns=".../messages"
                  xmlns:t=".../types">
  <AttachmentIds>
    <t:AttachmentId Id="AAAtAE..."/>
  </AttachmentIds>
</DeleteAttachment>
```

Listing 12-14 shows us the response.

LISTING 12-14 *DeleteAttachment* response

```
<DeleteAttachmentResponse xmlns:m=".../messages"
                          xmlns:t=".../types"
                          xmlns=".../messages">
  <m:ResponseMessages>
    <m:DeleteAttachmentResponseMessage
        xsi:type="m:DeleteAttachmentResponseMessageType"
        ResponseClass="Success">
      <m:ResponseCode>NoError</m:ResponseCode>
      <m:RootItemId RootItemId="AAAtAEF..."
                RootItemChangeKey="AAAAABYA..."/>
    </m:DeleteAttachmentResponseMessage>
  </m:ResponseMessages>
</DeleteAttachmentResponse>
```

So, the response message includes the *RootItemId* element that contains both the *RootItemId* and *RootChangeKey* attributes. Listing 12-15 uses proxy classes to delete an attachment, but it also calls *GetItem* on the returned root item id. Why? To illustrate another issue. Let's look.

LISTING 12-15 *DeleteAttachment* and *GetItem* via the proxy (look for the bug)

```
/// <summary>
/// Deletes an attachment and returned the Id and updated change key of the
/// parent item
/// </summary>
/// <param name="binding">Exchange binding to use</param>
/// <param name="attachmentId">Attachment id to delete</param>
/// <returns>Id and updated change key of the parent item</returns>
///
public static ItemIdType DeleteAttachmentAndGetItem(
                ExchangeServiceBinding binding,
                RequestAttachmentIdType attachmentId)
{
  DeleteAttachmentType request = new DeleteAttachmentType();
  request.AttachmentIds = new RequestAttachmentIdType[] { attachmentId };
```

```
DeleteAttachmentResponseType response =
            binding.DeleteAttachment(request);
DeleteAttachmentResponseMessageType responseMessage =
            response.ResponseMessages.Items[0] as
                DeleteAttachmentResponseMessageType;
if (responseMessage.ResponseCode != ResponseCodeType.NoError)
{
  throw new Exception("Delete attachment failed.  Response code: " +
            responseMessage.ResponseCode.ToString());
}
else
{
  // Normally, we could just return the root item id from our Delete
  // Attachment response.  But I want to prove a point here, so we will
  // call GetItem and see what happens.

  // There is a bug here....
  //
  GetItemType getRequest = new GetItemType();
  getRequest.ItemIds = new BaseItemIdType[] {
                     responseMessage.RootItemId };
  getRequest.ItemShape = new ItemResponseShapeType(
                     DefaultShapeNamesType.IdOnly);
  GetItemResponseType getResponse = binding.GetItem(getRequest);
  ItemInfoResponseMessageType getResponseMessage =
          getResponse.ResponseMessages.Items[0] as
                ItemInfoResponseMessageType;

  if (getResponseMessage.ResponseCode != ResponseCodeType.NoError)
  {
    throw new Exception("GetItem failed.  Response code: " +
            getResponseMessage.ResponseCode.ToString());
  }
  else
  {
    return getResponseMessage.Items.Items[0].ItemId;
  }
}
}
```

When this code is called, the *DeleteAttachment* call works just fine. Then the *RootItemId* from the response is passed into the *GetItem* call. Because *RootItemId* is a *BaseItemIdType* descendant, the proxy happily complies. But when the call is made, an *InvalidOperationException* is returned. The inner exception message is as follows:

```
The type ProxyHelpers.EWS.RootItemIdType was not expected. Use the XmlInclude or SoapInclude
attribute to specify types that are not known statically.
```

What is going on here? Well, *GetItem* expects a *NonEmptyArrayOfBaseItemIdsType* (as defined in the schema). Only three valid types are there: *ItemIdType*, *OccurrenceItemIdType*, and

RecurringMasterItemIdType. Notice that *RootItemIdType* is *not* among them. Unfortunately, C# is not capable of limiting arguments to a subset of *BaseItemIdType* derived types, though this is perfectly acceptable in the schema. So, the proxy "allows" you to set up a call that the *XmlSerializer* will choke on when it tries to create the request XML, hence the *InvalidOperationException*.

What can you do about this? Well, the easiest workaround is to create a new *ItemIdType* instance and fill in the information from the returned *RootItemId*. Then this *ItemIdType* instance can be used in the *GetItem* call. The updated code is shown in bold in Listing 12-16.

LISTING 12-16 Corrected code for calling *GetItem* with the *RootItemId* from *DeleteAttachment*

```
// previous code elided…

// Normally, we could just return the root item id from our
// DeleteAttachment response.  But I want to prove a point here, so we will
// call GetItem and see what happens.

GetItemType getRequest = new GetItemType();

// This is what we should have done - copy the id information into an
// ItemIdType instance.
//
ItemIdType idForGetItem = new ItemIdType();
idForGetItem.Id = responseMessage.RootItemId.RootItemId;
idForGetItem.ChangeKey = responseMessage.RootItemId.RootItemChangeKey;

// Now this should work fine...
//
getRequest.ItemIds = new BaseItemIdType[] { idForGetItem };
getRequest.ItemShape = new ItemResponseShapeType(
                              DefaultShapeNamesType.IdOnly);
GetItemResponseType getResponse = binding.GetItem(getRequest);

// remaining code stays the same…
```

When you think about it, *RootItemIdType* looks just like *ItemIdType*, so *RootItemIdType* really isn't needed at all. *DeleteAttachmentResponseMessageType* could just expose an *ItemIdType* instance with a local name of *RootItemId*. But, alas, it is there and you must contend with it.

If you find that you need *ItemId* values for the updated parent ids returned by *DeleteAttachment*, it would be worthwhile to provide a conversion method on *RootItemIdType* via a partial class extension. Listing 12-17 provides two different approaches. The first is simply a new *ItemIdType* constructor that takes a *RootItemIdType* argument. The second, which actually uses the first, is a *ToItemId()* instance method on *RootItemIdType*. In the example implementation, *ToItemId()* calls the overloaded constructor. Feel free to go whichever direction you want with this.

LISTING 12-17 Partial class extensions to deal with the *ItemId/RootItemId* inconsistency

```
/// <summary>
/// Partial class extension to ItemIdType
/// </summary>
public partial class ItemIdType
{
  /// <summary>
  /// Default constructor needed for xml serialization (since we are
  /// defining a non default constructor)
  /// </summary>
  ///
  public ItemIdType()
  { }


  /// <summary>
  /// Constructor
  /// </summary>
  /// <param name="rootItemId">RootItemId instance to initialize
  /// from</param>
  ///
  public ItemIdType(RootItemIdType rootItemId)
  {
    this.Id = rootItemId.RootItemId;
    this.ChangeKey = rootItemId.RootItemChangeKey;
  }
}

/// <summary>
/// Partial class extension to RootItemIdType
/// </summary>
public partial class RootItemIdType
{
  /// <summary>
  /// Converts this instance to an ItemIdType
  /// </summary>
  /// <returns>ItemIdType containing data from this instance</returns>
  ///
  public ItemIdType ToItemId()
  {
    return new ItemIdType(this);
  }
}
```

Hidden/Inline Attachments

Table 12-1 introduced two attributes. *ContentId* and *ContentLocation* are associated with in-line attachments. Consider an e-mail created in Office Outlook 2007 with an image pasted somewhere in the middle of the message text. *ContentId* and *ContentLocation* preserve the position of the image relative to the text in the message body when the e-mail is sent. Figure 12-4 shows a received message with an inline attachment.

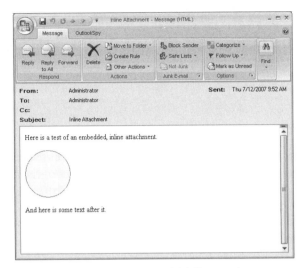

FIGURE 12-4 Received message with inline attachment

To obtain information about an inline attachment, you can call *GetItem* on the message and ask for two properties of interest: *item:Attachments* and *item:HasAttachments*. We will also need the body shortly, so we request *item:Body* as well. You saw this form of *GetItem* earlier in the chapter.

```
<GetItem xmlns=".../messages"
         xmlns:t=".../types">
  <ItemShape>
    <t:BaseShape>IdOnly</t:BaseShape>
    <t:AdditionalProperties>
      <t:FieldURI FieldURI="item:Attachments"/>
      <t:FieldURI FieldURI="item:HasAttachments"/>
      <t:FieldURI FieldURI="item:Body"/>
    </t:AdditionalProperties>
  </ItemShape>
  <ItemIds>
    <t:ItemId Id="AAAtAEFkbWlua..." ChangeKey="AAAAA.../>
  </ItemIds>
</GetItem>
```

Now, the message part of the response is shown in Listing 12-18.

LISTING 12-18 Message from the *GetItem* response with an inline attachment

```
<!-- xml elided -->
<t:Message>
  <t:ItemId Id="AAAtAEFkbWlua..." ChangeKey="AAAAA..."/>
  <t:Body.../> <!-- body elided here, will be shown shortly -->
  <t:Attachments>
    <t:FileAttachment>
      <t:AttachmentId Id="AAAtAEFkbWlua..."/>
      <t:Name>hi_mom_image.jpg</t:Name>
```

```
      <t:ContentType>image/jpeg</t:ContentType>
      <t:ContentId>hi_mom_image.jpg@01C759A2.4FFCA580</t:ContentId>
    </t:FileAttachment>
  </t:Attachments>
  <t:HasAttachments>false</t:HasAttachments>
</t:Message>
<!-- xml elided-->
```

Notice in Listing 12-18 that Outlook gave the inline image a unique name, set the content type, and the *ContentId* value. The name, content type and content id properties come to life when you look at the body of the message. If you skip to the *Body* property that we elided in Listing 12-18, you see the actual HTML content there.

```
<body lang="EN-US" link="blue" vlink="purple">
   <div class="Section1">
      <p class="MsoNormal">Here is a test of an embedded, inline attachment.
         <o:p></o:p>
      </p>
      <p class="MsoNormal">
         <o:p> </o:p>
      </p>
      <p class="MsoNormal">
         <img width="100" height="100" id="Picture_x0020_1"
                 src="cid:hi_mom_image.jpg@01C759A2.4FFCA580">
         <o:p></o:p>
      </p>
      <p class="MsoNormal">
         <o:p> </o:p>
      </p>
      <p class="MsoNormal">And here is some text after it
         <o:p></o:p>
      </p>
   </div>
</body>
```

Do you notice, right in the middle of the body an <img> tag with a source that just happens to match the *ContentId* of the attachment? Coincidence? We think not.

Furthermore, in Listing 12-18, the *HasAttachments* property is false. This is because the only attachment is a "hidden" attachment, meaning that it does not show up as a normal attachment on the item, but rather is exposed as an inline attachment. You can confirm this by looking at the attachment table through Outlook Spy, as shown in Figure 12-5.

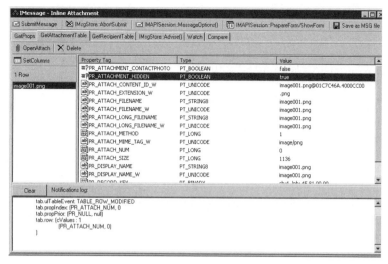

FIGURE 12-5 Hidden attachments seen in Outlook Spy

So we have seen that Office Outlook 2007 uses the content id to maintain all of its embedded attachment information while *ContentLocation* is ignored. However, other e-mail clients do use *ContentLocation* when creating inline attachments. Just know that you may encounter either or both when dealing with arbitrary messages with attachments.

Updating Attachments

So, now you know how to retrieve, create, and delete file attachments. How do you update an existing attachment? No *UpdateAttachment* method is available. If you want to update information about an attachment, you need to retrieve the attachment, delete it, and then recreate the attachment with the updated information.

Finding Attachments

Although *FindItem* does not return the *Attachments* property for each returned item, you can do some limited filtering based on the content in the attachments table. Implicit subfilters are discussed at length in Chapter 14, "Searching the Mailbox." For now, we will just give you an example. Let's say you wanted to find messages that have attachments where the attachment name starts with *image*. Listing 12-19 shows the *FindItem* call.

LISTING 12-19 Finding items based on attachment table information

```
<FindItem xmlns=".../messages"
          xmlns:t=".../types"
          Traversal="Shallow">
  <ItemShape>
    <t:BaseShape>IdOnly</t:BaseShape>
  </ItemShape>
```

```
<Restriction>
  <t:Contains ContainmentComparison="IgnoreCase"
              ContainmentMode="Prefixed">
    <t:FieldURI FieldURI="item:Attachments"/>
    <t:Constant Value="image"/>
  </t:Contains>
</Restriction>
<ParentFolderIds>
  <t:DistinguishedFolderId Id="inbox"/>
</ParentFolderIds>
</FindItem>
```

To filter on the attachments table, you must use the *Contains* filter expression with the *item:Attachments* property path. Only the attachment display name is considered when performing the filter.

Item Attachments

Now that you have a handle on file attachments, it is time to consider the second type of attachment that you will encounter on items: item attachments. As defined earlier in the chapter, an item attachment is an attachment that is itself an item. An e-mail attached to another e-mail is an item attachment. So, for example, say you created an e-mail message with a single file attachment. For this discussion, let's call this original message *Inner*. Then you created a second message and attach message *Inner* to it. Let's call this second message *Outer*. Figure 12-6 illustrates how message *Inner* is contained—or nested—within message *Outer*. Message *Inner* is an item attachment.

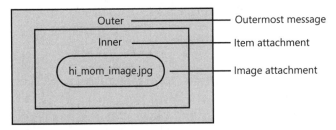

FIGURE 12-6 Nested attachments

Calling *GetItem* on message *Outer* and asking for *item:Attachments* and *item:HasAttachments* gives us the message shown in Listing 12-20.

LISTING 12-20 Message with an item attachment

```
<!-- xml elided -->
<t:Message>
  <t:ItemId Id="AAAeAGRhdnN...
```

```
  <t:Attachments>
    <t:ItemAttachment>
      <t:AttachmentId Id="AAAeAGRhdnNOZX...
      <t:Name>Inner</t:Name>
    </t:ItemAttachment>
  </t:Attachments>
  <t:HasAttachments>true</t:HasAttachments>
</t:Message>
```

Just like file attachments, the item attachment information returned by *GetItem* provides metadata about the attachments. The attachment content must be retrieved by calling *GetAttachment* on each *AttachmentId*. The *GetAttachment* call for item attachments looks just like the call for file attachments.

```
<GetAttachment xmlns=".../messages"
               xmlns:t=".../types">
  <AttachmentIds>
    <t:AttachmentId Id="AAAeAGRhd...
  </AttachmentIds>
</GetAttachment>
```

Listing 12-21 shows the response.

LISTING 12-21 *GetAttachmentResponse* for *ItemAttachment*

```
<GetAttachmentResponse xmlns:m=".../messages"
                       xmlns:t=".../types"
                       xmlns=".../messages">
  <m:ResponseMessages>
    <m:GetAttachmentResponseMessage ResponseClass="Success">
      <m:ResponseCode>NoError</m:ResponseCode>
      <m:Attachments>
        <t:ItemAttachment>
          <t:AttachmentId Id="AAAeAGRhd...
          <t:Name>Inner</t:Name>
          <t:Message>
            <t:ItemClass>IPM.Note</t:ItemClass>
            <t:Subject>Inner</t:Subject>
<!-- content elided -->
            <t:Attachments>
              <t:FileAttachment>
                <t:AttachmentId Id="AAAeAGRh...
                <t:Name>hi_mom_image.jpg</t:Name>
                <t:ContentType>image/jpeg</t:ContentType>
                <t:ContentId>hi_mom_image.jpg@01C759A2.4FFCA580</t:ContentId>
              </t:FileAttachment>
            </t:Attachments>
<!-- content elided -->
          </t:Message>
        </t:ItemAttachment>
      </m:Attachments>
    </m:GetAttachmentResponseMessage>
  </m:ResponseMessages>
</GetAttachmentResponse>
```

There are several things to note about Listing 12-21. First, the attachment is indeed an item attachment. Also, the *Message* is a child of *ItemAttachment*. This *Message* element represents the embedded item, which is the *Inner* message. Even though this is a *MessageType* instance, it does not have an *ItemId* element of its own. Finally, the *Inner* message has its own attachment collection with one inline *FileAttachment*.

In the schema, *ItemAttachmentType* derives from *AttachmentType* and therefore inherits all the elements from the base class. In addition, *ItemAttachmentType* exposes a single choice element. This choice can be an *Item, Message, CalendarItem, Contact, MeetingMessage, MeetingRequest, MeetingResponse, MeetingCancellation,* or *Task*. These possible choices are the essence of what an item attachment is. With file attachments, the content is the actual binary content of the file. With item attachments, the content is an actual item instance that derives from *ItemType*.

Reintroducing the *AttachmentShape*

When dealing with item attachments, *GetAttachment* is quite similar in structure and behavior to *GetItem*. *GetItem* returns the actual item, and *GetAttachment* returns the item attachment. One of the best things about *GetItem* is that through judicious use of the *ItemShape* element, you have control over the properties that are returned. When you consider something like a *MessageType* instance, you may not be interested in many of the instance's properties. As you have seen in the examples throughout this book, you can include the *AdditionalProperties* element in the response shape of a *GetItem* call and use the *IdOnly* base shape to limit the properties that are returned to those that are of interest.

GetAttachment also provides a shape element called *AttachmentShape*. You saw that this element is ignored when dealing with file attachments. However, it does come to life when dealing with item attachments, although it limps a little. Listing 12-22 shows us the basic structure of the *AttachmentResponseShapeType*.

LISTING 12-22 Basic structure of *AttachmentResponseShapeType*

```
<AttachmentShape>
  <t:IncludeMimeContent>true | false</t:IncludeMimeContent>
  <t:BodyType>Best | HTML | Text</t:BodyType>
  <t:AdditionalProperties/>
</AttachmentShape>
```

There is a noteworthy and slightly painful omission from this type. Can you spot it? There is no *BaseShape* element in *AttachmentResponseShapeType*. This implies that Exchange Web Services chooses a base shape for you. And what shape does it choose? *AllProperties*. What this means is that the item attachments that come back from a *GetAttachment* call have all their available properties returned. There is nothing that you can do about the omission of the base shape in *AttachmentResponseShapeType*. Of course, you can request additional properties to be returned using the *AdditionalProperties* element, but as you know, that simply adds to the already bulky set of properties returned by *AllProperties*.

Both the *IncludeMimeContent* and *BodyType* elements behave in the same manner as *GetItem* and the *ItemShape* element. Refer to Chapter 5, "Items," if you would like more information on those elements.

Listing 12-23 shows the code to retrieve an item attachment using the proxy classes. The listing also uses the attachment response shape just to show that it indeed works.

LISTING 12-23 Retrieving an *ItemAttachment* through the proxy classes

```
/// <summary>
/// Return the embedded item within an item attachment
/// </summary>
/// <param name="binding">binding to use for EWS calls</param>
/// <param name="attachmentId">Id of the item attachment</param>
/// <returns>Embedded ItemType from attachment</returns>
///
public static ItemType GetItemAttachment(
                        ExchangeServiceBinding binding,
                        RequestAttachmentIdType attachmentId)
{
    GetAttachmentType getAttachmentRequest = new GetAttachmentType();

    // Just for fun, let's request the mime content and text body on our
    // attachment.
    AttachmentResponseShapeType responseShape = new AttachmentResponseShapeType();
    responseShape.BodyType = BodyTypeResponseType.Text;
    responseShape.BodyTypeSpecified = true;
    responseShape.IncludeMimeContent = true;
    responseShape.IncludeMimeContentSpecified = true;

    // Also, let's grab an extended property just to show that we can do that
    // with our response shape.
    //
    PathToExtendedFieldType useTNEFPath = new PathToExtendedFieldType();
    useTNEFPath.PropertySetId = "{00062008-0000-0000-C000-000000000046}";
    useTNEFPath.PropertyId = 0x8582;
    useTNEFPath.PropertyIdSpecified = true;
    useTNEFPath.PropertyType = MapiPropertyTypeType.Boolean;

    responseShape.AdditionalProperties = new BasePathToElementType[] {
                                    useTNEFPath };
    getAttachmentRequest.AttachmentShape = responseShape;
    getAttachmentRequest.AttachmentIds = new RequestAttachmentIdType[] {
                                    attachmentId };

    // Now make the actual call.
    //
    GetAttachmentResponseType response =
                binding.GetAttachment(getAttachmentRequest);
    AttachmentInfoResponseMessageType responseMessage =
```

```
            response.ResponseMessages.Items[0] as
                    AttachmentInfoResponseMessageType;

    if (responseMessage.ResponseCode == ResponseCodeType.NoError)
    {
      ItemAttachmentType itemAttachment = responseMessage.Attachments[0] as
              ItemAttachmentType;
      // Make sure we are dealing with an item attachment
      //
      if (itemAttachment == null)
      {
        throw new ArgumentException("Attachment Id must refer to an item " +
                "attachment", "attachmentId");
      }
      ItemType item = itemAttachment.Item;

      // Now show the subject and the userTNEF prop
      //
      Console.WriteLine("Subject: " + item.Subject == null ? "<NULL>" :
                        item.Subject);

      if (item.ExtendedProperty.Length > 0)
      {
        Console.WriteLine("UseTNEF? " + (string)item.ExtendedProperty[0].Item);
      }
      return item;
    }
    else
    {
      throw new Exception("Failed to get item attachment.  Response code: " +
          responseMessage.ResponseCode.ToString());
    }
  }
}
```

When the code in Listing 12-23 is run against an item attachment, the subject of the *item attachment* will be written to the console along with an indication of whether the attachment is TNEF encoded.

Creating an Item Attachment

You create an item attachment by using the *CreateAttachment* Web method, in the same manner you did when creating a file attachment. However, instead of passing in a *FileAttachment* element, you need to specify an *ItemAttachment* element. You saw earlier that *ItemAttachment* derives from *AttachmentType* and includes the definition of the item that is to make up the attachment. What this implies is that there is no way to pass an item id into *CreateAttachment* to attach an *existing* item to a message. The only way to create an item attachment is create the item at the same time that it is attached. Listing 12-24 shows how to create a simple item attachment. Notice that we specify the item attachment with all the properties that we want to set. It looks eerily similar to a *CreateItem* call.

LISTING 12-24 Creating a new item attachment

```
<CreateAttachment xmlns=".../messages"
                  xmlns:t=".../types">
  <ParentItemId Id="AAAeAGRh..." ChangeKey="CQAAABYA..."/>
  <Attachments>
    <t:ItemAttachment>
      <t:Name>Attached Message</t:Name>
      <t:Message>
        <t:Subject>Attached message</t:Subject>
        <t:Body BodyType="Text">Body of the attached message</t:Body>
      </t:Message>
    </t:ItemAttachment>
  </Attachments>
</CreateAttachment>
```

Although creating item attachments out of thin air is interesting, many times you will want to attach an *existing* item as an item attachment. In such cases, you need to call *GetItem* with the *AllProperties* base shape and request any extended properties that are of interest. Then you need to call *CreateAttachment* and pass in the information returned by *GetItem*. Is there an easier way? Somewhat. In Chapter 5, you saw that one of the properties you can request in *GetItem* is the MIME content of the item (property path *item:MimeContent*).[7] Listing 12-25 shows the *GetItem* call to retrieve the message along with its MIME content.

LISTING 12-25 *GetItem* with MIME content

```
<GetItem xmlns=".../messages"
         xmlns:t=".../types">
  <ItemShape>
    <t:BaseShape>IdOnly</t:BaseShape>
    <t:AdditionalProperties>
      <t:FieldURI FieldURI="item:MimeContent"/>
    </t:AdditionalProperties>
  </ItemShape>
  <ItemIds>
    <t:ItemId Id="AAAeAG...
  </ItemIds>
</GetItem>
```

The response contains the *Message* with just the MIME content and the item id.

---

[7] As mentioned in Chapter 5, retrieving the MIME content will only work for messages, posts (IPM.Post), and calendar items. You cannot get the MIME content for other item types. For other item types, you must grab the entire Item with all the properties of interest and attach it that way.

```
<t:Message>
  <t:MimeContent CharacterSet="UTF-8">UmVjZW12ZW...</t:MimeContent>
  <t:ItemId Id="AAAtAEFkbWlua..." ChangeKey="AAAAA..."/>
</t:Message>
```

Now, you should be able to call *CreateAttachment* with this message. Listing 12-26 shows this call.

LISTING 12-26 Creating an *ItemAttachment* by using MIME content

```
<CreateAttachment xmlns=".../messages"
                  xmlns:t=".../types">
  <ParentItemId Id="AAAtAEFkbWlua..." ChangeKey="AAAAA..."/>
  <Attachments>
    <t:ItemAttachment>
      <t:Name>ItemAttachemnt via Mime</t:Name>
      <t:Message>
        <t:MimeContent CharacterSet="UTF-8">UmVjZW12Zb2EYtR...</t:MimeContent>
      </t:Message>
    </t:ItemAttachment>
  </Attachments>
</CreateAttachment>
```

Note that the *MessageType* instance that *GetItem* returns will always have an *ItemId* element. Of course, *ItemId* is read-only, so before you pass the *MessageType* instance to *CreateAttachment*, you must remove the *ItemId* element. If you neglect this, you will get an *ErrorInvalidPropertyForSet* response code indicating that you cannot set the *ItemId*.

If you call *GetAttachment* on the attachment id returned by Listing 12-26, you will see that the MIME content was indeed processed and all of the item properties set correctly. This includes any custom MAPI properties that were set on the message.

With this in mind, it makes sense to add a proxy method to "attach" an existing item as an item attachment. Internally it will get the MIME content of the item to be attached. This is shown in Listing 12-27.

LISTING 12-27 Attaching an existing item as an *ItemAttachment*

```
/// <summary>
/// Attach an existing item to another message
/// </summary>
/// <param name="binding">binding to use</param>
/// <param name="itemIdToAttach">Id of existing item to attach</param>
/// <param name="parentItemToAttachTo">Parent item to attach to</param>
/// <returns>Id of new attachment</returns>
///
public static AttachmentIdType AttachExistingItemToMessage(
                  ExchangeServiceBinding binding,
                  ItemIdType itemIdToAttach,
                  ItemIdType parentItemToAttachTo)
```

```
{
  // First, get the MIME content of the message to be attached.
  //
  GetItemType getItemRequest = new GetItemType();

  // We will also grab the subject so that we can name our attachment.
  //
  getItemRequest.ItemShape = new ItemResponseShapeType(
            DefaultShapeNamesType.IdOnly,
            new PathToUnindexedFieldType(
                UnindexedFieldURIType.itemMimeContent),
            new PathToUnindexedFieldType(
                UnindexedFieldURIType.itemSubject));

  getItemRequest.ItemIds = new BaseItemIdType[] { itemIdToAttach };
  // make the GetItem call
  //
  GetItemResponseType getItemResponse = binding.GetItem(getItemRequest);
  ItemInfoResponseMessageType getItemResponseMessage =
            getItemResponse.ResponseMessages.Items[0]
                        as ItemInfoResponseMessageType;
  if (getItemResponseMessage.ResponseCode != ResponseCodeType.NoError)
  {
    throw new Exception("Failed to retrieve MIME content for item. " +
        "Response code: " + getItemResponseMessage.ResponseCode.ToString());
  }
  else
  {
    // Retrieve the item to attach
    //
    ItemType itemToAttach = getItemResponseMessage.Items.Items[0];

    // Now we MUST null out the ItemId element.  Otherwise our
    // CreateAttachment call will fail.  ItemId is read only and we are
    // "creating" an attachment item here.  We can't set the ItemId.
    //
    itemToAttach.ItemId = null;

    // Set up our CreateAttachment request
    //
    CreateAttachmentType createAttachRequest = new
            CreateAttachmentType();
    createAttachRequest.ParentItemId = parentItemToAttachTo;
    ItemAttachmentType itemAttachment = new ItemAttachmentType();
    itemAttachment.Name = itemToAttach.Subject;

    // Now null out the subject.  All that info is contained in the MIME
    // content.  We don't want contention between the mime content and
    // the explicit properties.
    //
    itemToAttach.Subject = null;

    itemAttachment.Item = itemToAttach;
    createAttachRequest.Attachments = new AttachmentType[] {
```

```
            itemAttachment };

    // make the CreateAttachment call
    //
    CreateAttachmentResponseType createAttachResponse =
            binding.CreateAttachment(createAttachRequest);
    AttachmentInfoResponseMessageType attachInfo =
            createAttachResponse.ResponseMessages.Items[0]
                    as AttachmentInfoResponseMessageType;
    if (attachInfo.ResponseCode != ResponseCodeType.NoError)
    {
        throw new Exception("Failed to create item attachment. " +
            "Response code: " +
            attachInfo.ResponseCode.ToString());
    }
    else
    {
        return attachInfo.Attachments[0].AttachmentId;
    }
  }
}
```

Deleting Item Attachments

You delete an item attachment in the same way that you delete a file attachment. Just call *DeleteAttachment* and pass in the id of the item attachment that you want to delete.

Attachment Hierarchies

As a parting example, the following code follows or *walks* the attachment hierarchy of an item and displays it in the console window. If items could have only file attachments, there would be no concept of an attachment hierarchy. But because items can have item attachments, and those item attachments can have their own attachments, a nesting or hierarchy of attachments can indeed be realized. What is important to note is that each attachment has its own attachment id, and if you have the attachment id, you can retrieve any attachment regardless of how deep within an attachment hierarchy it is. Listing 12-28 shows us how to walk the attachment hierarchy for any given item.

LISTING 12-28 Walking attachment hierarchies

```
/// <summary>
/// Takes an item and displays its attachment hierarchy (deep
/// traversal).  This is the main entry point for this functionality.
/// </summary>
/// <param name="binding">Binding to use for EWS calls</param>
/// <param name="parentId">Id of parent item to walk</param>
```

```
///
public static void WalkAttachmentHierarchy(
           ExchangeServiceBinding binding,
           ItemIdType parentId)
{
  // First, retrieve the item with its attachments.  We will also get the
  // subject for display purposes
  //
  GetItemType getItemRequest = new GetItemType();
  getItemRequest.ItemShape = new ItemResponseShapeType(
      DefaultShapeNamesType.IdOnly,
     new PathToUnindexedFieldType(UnindexedFieldURIType.itemAttachments),
     new PathToUnindexedFieldType(UnindexedFieldURIType.itemSubject));

  getItemRequest.ItemIds = new BaseItemIdType[] { parentId };
  GetItemResponseType getItemResponse = binding.GetItem(getItemRequest);
  ItemInfoResponseMessageType getItemResponseMessage =
             getItemResponse.ResponseMessages.Items[0]
                   as ItemInfoResponseMessageType;

  if (getItemResponseMessage.ResponseCode != ResponseCodeType.NoError)
  {
    throw new Exception("GetItem failed.  Response Code: " +
                getItemResponseMessage.ResponseCode.ToString());
  }
  ItemType item = getItemResponseMessage.Items.Items[0];

  Console.WriteLine("ParentItem subject: {0}", item.Subject);

  // Now, walk the attachments
  //
  WalkAttachmentHierarchyByItemType(binding, item, 0 /* initial offset*/);
}

/// <summary>
/// Given an ItemType instance, walk the attachments and display metadata
/// about them
/// </summary>
/// <param name="binding">Binding to use for EWS calls</param>
/// <param name="item">The ItemType instance to walk</param>
/// <param name="offset">Offset used for display purposes</param>
///
public static void WalkAttachmentHierarchyByItemType(
           ExchangeServiceBinding binding,
           ItemType item,
           int offset)
{
  // Build up a prefix tab to show our heirarchy
  //
  StringBuilder builder = new StringBuilder();
  for (int i = 0; i < offset; i++)
  {
    builder.Append("\t");
  }
```

```
string prefixTabs = builder.ToString();

// If there are no attachments, say so.  Nothing to walk.
//
if (item.Attachments == null)
{
  Console.WriteLine("{0} -- <No Attachments>", prefixTabs);
}
else
{
  // Cycle through each attachment on the passed item
  //
  foreach (AttachmentType attachment in item.Attachments)
  {
    FileAttachmentType fileAttachment = attachment as
              FileAttachmentType;
    if (fileAttachment != null)
    {
      // If it is a file attachment, the "walk" stops here.  File
      // attachments do not have attachments of their own.
      //
      Console.WriteLine("{0} -- FileAttachment: {1}",
                  prefixTabs, fileAttachment.Name);
    }
    else
    {
      // If it is an item attachment, we need to grab the actual
      // attachment using GetAttachment so that we get the embedded
      // item
      //
      ItemAttachmentType itemAttachment = attachment as
              ItemAttachmentType;
      Console.WriteLine("{0} -- ItemAttachment: {1}",
              prefixTabs, itemAttachment.Name);

      GetAttachmentType getAttachmentRequest =
              new GetAttachmentType();
      getAttachmentRequest.AttachmentIds = new
              RequestAttachmentIdType[] { itemAttachment.AttachmentId };
      GetAttachmentResponseType getAttachmentResponse =
              binding.GetAttachment(getAttachmentRequest);
      AttachmentInfoResponseMessageType attachInfo =
              getAttachmentResponse.ResponseMessages.Items[0]
                  as AttachmentInfoResponseMessageType;

      if (attachInfo.ResponseCode != ResponseCodeType.NoError)
      {
        Console.WriteLine("{0} -- ERROR calling GetAttachment.  " +
              "Response Code: {1}",
              prefixTabs,
              attachInfo.ResponseCode.ToString());
      }
      else
      {
```

```
// If sucessfully retrieve the item attachment, we want
// to recursively walk its attachments.  So increment our
// "tab offset" and call ourselves again.
//
ItemType embeddedItem = (attachInfo.Attachments[0] as
            ItemAttachmentType).Item;
WalkAttachmentHierarchyByItemType(
            binding,
            embeddedItem,
            offset+1);
      }
    }
  }
}
}
```

Running the code in Listing 12-28 against the item introduced in Figure 12-6 is shown in Figure 12-7.

FIGURE 12-7 Output of walking the attachment hierarchy

Summary

Exchange Web Services supports two types of attachments. File attachments contain the binary content of the attached file while Item attachments are *ItemType* descendants in and of themselves, and they can have their own attachments, thus creating an attachment hierarchy. The *GetItem* Web method can return metadata about an item's attachments. But to retrieve the actual content of the embedded attachment, you must call the *GetAttachment* Web method. Creating an attachment is handled by the *CreateAttachment* Web method. As you saw, to attach an existing Store item to another item, you must retrieve the pertinent properties for the item to be attached and then create the new item attachment from those properties. You also saw how you can delete file and item attachments by using the *DeleteAttachment* method.

Chapter 13
Extended Properties

Although there are a large number of useful properties exposed on the item and folders types that you have seen so far, there are times where you need to access properties that Exchange Web Services did not expose. That is precisely why extended properties were added to Exchange Web Services. So, just what *is* an extended property? Considering the name, it would be reasonable to conclude that such properties are in addition to some set of "common" accessible properties. That is partially correct. Or it may be reasonable to deduce that extended properties are an extension of existing properties. Maybe.

When the Exchange Web Services team first started writing specification documents for extended properties, they called the feature Extended *MAPI* Properties. As the feature progressed through documentation and development, they dropped the *MAPI* name because they didn't want to tie the Exchange Web Service schema directly to the Messaging Application Programming Interface (MAPI). Regardless of the absence of MAPI from the feature title, extended properties are all about accessing native MAPI properties, and nothing more. To appreciate the need for extended properties, let's look at the system that sits beneath Microsoft Exchange Server 2007 Web Services (EWS). Note that it is not necessary to understand the following background section. However, doing so will give you a better grasp of why extended properties work the way that they do.

A Little Background

Messages, items, folders, and the like are stored within an Exchange 2007 Store Mailbox. A Mailbox is contained within a Mailbox database. Now, if you have had any experience with databases, you may know that a table within a database has an associated schema that describes each of the data columns and their types. Interestingly enough, whereas most relational databases have fixed schemas, the schema within Exchange Store databases can be dynamically extended.

Each item or folder *property* within the database is assigned an identifier called a property tag (*proptag*, for short), which uniquely identifies that column within that *specific* database. Think of this as the property's name within the Mailbox database. In a relational database, you ask for properties by column name, for example, CUSTOMER_ID, whereas properties within the Mailbox database are referenced by proptag. A proptag is represented as an unsigned 32-bit integer. The low 16 bits contain the type for the proptag, and the high 16 bits represent the actual identifier for the property. The layout of a proptag is shown in Figure 13-1.

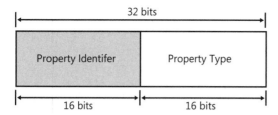

FIGURE 13-1 Property tag layout

Property Type

As shown in Figure 13-1, the lower 16 bits of a proptag (the section to the right) specify the data type for the property. A given property can have one and only one type. Table 13-1 shows the common MAPI property types and the support that Exchange Web Services provides for each.

TABLE 13-1 Support for MAPI Property Types

MAPI Property Type	Lower 16 bits	Extended Property Type	.NET Type
PT_UNSPECIFIED	0	Unsupported	Unsupported
PT_NULL	1	Null	Unsupported
PT_SHORT (PT_I2)	2	Short	Short
PT_LONG (PT_I4)	3	Integer	Int32
PT_FLOAT	4	Float	float
PT_DOUBLE	5	Double	double
PT_CURRENCY	6	Currency	Int64
PT_APPTIME	7	ApplicationTime	double
PT_ERROR	0xA	Error	Unsupported
PT_BOOLEAN	0xB	Boolean	bool
PT_OBJECT	0xD	Object	Unsupported
PT_LONGLONG (PT_I8)	0x14	Long	Int64
PT_STRING8	0x1E	String	string
PT_UNICODE	0x1F	String	string
PT_SYSTIME	0x40	SystemTime	DateTime
PT_CLSID	0x48	CLSID	Guid
PT_BINARY	0x102	Binary	Byte[]
PT_MV_SHORT	0x1002	ShortArray	Short[]
PT_MV_LONG (PT_MV_I4)	0x1003	IntegerArray	Int[]
PT_MV_FLOAT	0x1004	FloatArray	Float[]
PT_MV_DOUBLE	0x1005	DoubleArray	Double[]
PT_MV_CURRENCY	0x1006	CurrencyArray	Int64[]

MAPI Property Type	Lower 16 bits	Extended Property Type	.NET Type
PT_MV_APPTIME	0x1007	ApplicationTimeArray	Double[]
PT_MV_OBJECT	0x100D	ObjectArray	Unsupported
PT_MV_LONGLONG (PT_MV_I8)	0x1014	LongArray	Int64[]
PT_MV_STRING8	0x101E	StringArray	String[]
PT_MV_UNICODE	0x101F	StringArray	String[]
PT_MV_SYSTIME	0x1040	SystemTimeArray	DateTime[]
PT_MV_CLSID	0x1048	CLSIDArray	Guid[]
PT_MV_BINARY	0x1102	BinaryArray	Byte[][]

More information about MAPI property types can be found in MSDN at *http://msdn.microsoft.com/library/default.asp?url=/library/en-us/mapi/html/bc517300-98db-4d3e-8303-557e18b5e71f.asp.*

There are several points regarding Table 13-1 that we need to talk briefly about. First, extended property types *Null, Error, Object,* and *ObjectArray* will be encountered only in Exchange Web Service responses. You are not allowed to specify those property types in requests. Second, the *Currency* property type is a monetary value that represents the number of cents. Third, the *ApplicationTime* property type is exposed as a double where the integer part of the number represents the number of days since midnight on December 30, 1899, while the fractional part of the number represents the time.

The fourth one may take a little getting used to. The PT_LONGLONG value, which represents a 64-bit integer, is mapped to property type *Long* while the PT_LONG value, which represents a 32-bit integer, is mapped to property type *Integer*. The reason for this confusing relationship is that in the Microsoft .NET framework, a *long* value represents a 64-bit signed integer. The Exchange Web Services team decided that it would be more confusing if there was a discrepancy between the .NET framework and Exchange Web Services property types.

The fifth, and last piece of information regarding property types in Table 13-1 deals with the PT_STRING8 and PT_UNICODE types. Prior to Exchange Web Services, you had the ability to use both ASCII string values (PT_STRING) as well as Unicode string values (PT_UNICODE). However, in the .NET framework all strings are Unicode values. As such, Exchange Web Services exposes both property types as Unicode strings.

PropTag Ranges

Using what you have learned so far, you could take a proptag such as 0x0037001E and break the value into a property identifier of 0x0037 and a property type of 0x001E (PT_STRING8, which maps to the *System.String* type).[1]

The possible 16-bit property identifier values are broken into a standard range (0x0000 to 0x7FFF) and a custom range (0x8000 to 0xFFFE). The definition of property identifiers within the *standard* range will be the same across Mailbox databases.[2] Using the example from the preceding paragraph, 0x0037 will refer to PT_SUBJECT property on any Mailbox database that you encounter.

Now, the *custom* range is a different story. As was mentioned earlier, the "schema" for a Mailbox database can be extended. Let's say that you create a message and give it a custom *Boolean* property called *BookWorthy*, which is used to indicate whether you feel your message is good enough to publish. When you create the message, the Mailbox database determines that it has never seen *BookWorthy* before and extends the schema to include *BookWorthy*. During that process, it gives *BookWorthy* a proptag with a unique property id in the custom property range. Now, the e-mail is shipped along the wire until it ultimately arrives at its destination on another Exchange Server. The receiving Exchange Server saves the message in the database containing the destination Mailbox, and in the process of doing so, notices that it has never seen the *BookWorthy* custom property either. It also extends its schema to include *BookWorthy* and assigns the property a proptag value with a unique property id value in the custom prop range. What are the chances that the two assigned proptag values are the same? Don't count on it. With this in mind, you can hopefully see that making assumptions about the proptag value of a custom property is not necessarily a good thing.

Identifying Extended Properties

"But how do you specify a custom property if the proptag value isn't assigned until after the Exchange Store sees it?" We're glad you asked. While both standard and custom extended properties can be identified by a proptag, there is a second way to identify *custom* extended properties. Actually, to be more accurate, the proptag should be considered the second way to identify the custom property—at least when you consider the timeline of events.

The first (and proper) way a custom extended property is identified is with either a Globally Unique Identifier (GUID)+ name or GUID + dispatch id pair. We will refer to these as GUID+Name and GUID+Id respectively. In the case of GUID+Name, the name is a *string* and must be unique within the namespace defined by the GUID. In the case of GUID+Id, the dispatch id is a 32-bit *integer* and must be unique within the namespace defined by the GUID.

---

[1]   For the curious, this proptag represents the subject (PT_SUBJECT) of an item.

[2]   Note that not all property identifier values within the standard range are documented, nor are all of them used. You should assume, however, that all of them are reserved for one purpose or another.

A given custom property can be identified by *either* a GUID+Name or GUID+Id. It cannot, however, be identified by both. When you create the custom property, you must choose how it should be represented.

Going back to our *BookWorthy* custom property example, when you create the *BookWorthy* property, what you are really doing is creating a GUID+Name custom property with a property name of *BookWorthy* that is defined within some namespace. For the purposes of this discussion, we will use the following GUIDs.[3]

- MySpecialGuid = 24040483-cda4-4521-bb5f-a83fac4d19a4
- YourSpecialGuid = 3cd40456-6991-4ebb-a01a-d4bc711b301f

MySpecialGuid holds a GUID that defines my namespace. It is not sufficient to just say that you are dealing with custom property *BookWorthy* because there could also be a custom property *BookWorthy* within the namespace defined by *YourSpecialGuid*. In fact, the *BookWorthy* custom property defined in *MySpecialGuid* is completely different from the *BookWorthy* custom property defined in *YourSpecialGuid*. So when setting the *BookWorthy* custom property on a message, you must fully qualify the property name by including the *MySpecialGuid* namespace. The Store looks to see if it has already encountered this GUID+Name pair and if not, it assigns a proptag (with an unused property identifier) value to the custom property and creates a mapping from the GUID+Name pair to the new proptag value.

But how does this help? Well, you see, although the proptag value assigned to a given custom property may be different from one Mailbox database to the next, *the GUID+Name pair will always be the same*. So rather than requesting the custom property by proptag through Exchange Web Services, you request it by GUID+Name. The Store *still* thinks in terms of proptags, so it converts the GUID+Name pair into the corresponding proptag. The Store then uses the proptag to manipulate the property within the Store database.

GUID+Id custom properties work in exactly the same manner.

Extended Properties in Exchange Web Services

So how does this all tie into Exchange Web Services? Exchange Web Services exposes property paths for extended properties through the *PathToExtendedFieldType* schema type, shown in Listing 13-1.

---

[3] You can generate your own GUIDs using *System.Guid.NewGuid()*.

LISTING 13-1 *PathToExtendedFieldType* schema type

```
<xs:complexType name="PathToExtendedFieldType">
  <xs:complexContent>
    <xs:extension base="t:BasePathToElementType">
      <xs:attribute name="DistinguishedPropertySetId"
                    type="t:DistinguishedPropertySetType"
                    use="optional" />
      <xs:attribute name="PropertySetId" type="t:GuidType"
                    use="optional" />
      <xs:attribute name="PropertyTag" type="t:PropertyTagType"
                    use="optional" />
      <xs:attribute name="PropertyName" type="xs:string"
                    use="optional" />
      <xs:attribute name="PropertyId" type="xs:int"
                    use="optional" />
      <xs:attribute name="PropertyType" type="t:MapiPropertyTypeType"
                    use="required" />
    </xs:extension>
  </xs:complexContent>
</xs:complexType>
```

PathToExtendedFieldType can represent paths to extended properties by proptag, GUID+Name, or GUID+Id. The Exchange Web Services team strongly considered whether the three extended property naming approaches should be broken into three different extended property path types or whether they should all be represented by a single type such as *PathToExtendedFieldType*. For better or worse, they kept the single type. Although the type is called *PathToExtendedFieldType*, you will encounter it in XML instance documents by the local name of *ExtendedFieldURI*.

Property Type

All *PathToExtendedFieldType* instances must have the *PropertyType* attribute set. The *PropertyType* attribute dictates the data type for the custom property. As noted in the schema in Listing 13-1, this is a *MapiPropertyTypeType* and can contain any of the supported values shown in Table 13-1. Rendered in XML, this would look as follows:

```
<t:ExtendedFieldURI PropertyType="Integer" ...more.../>
```

If you are using the proxy classes, you would use the following code:

```
PathToExtendedFieldType myCustomPropPath = new PathToExtendedFieldType();

// Set the property type
//
myCustomPropPath.PropertyType = MapiPropertyTypeType.Integer;
```

Notice that when you are using the proxy classes, the *PropertyType* property does not have an associated *PropertyTypeSpecified* property. Can you guess why? Because the schema requires that property to be there (use="required"), and therefore the proxy class generator does not create the extra property.

Property Tags

Although many MAPI properties are available as item and folder properties in the Exchange Web Services schema, a number of MAPI properties are not exposed and therefore can only be accessed by their proptags. You express a proptag extended property by a combination of the *PropertyTag* attribute and the required *PropertyType* attribute. No other attributes are permitted.

```
<t:ExtendedFieldURI PropertyTag="0x1234" PropertyType="String"/>
```

One thing that should be noticeably different between the MAPI and Exchange Web Services representation of proptags is that in Exchange Web Services, the property identifier and property type are broken into separate attributes. There are two main reasons for this. First, it is much easier to see what type a given proptag is referring to when dealing with enumeration values rather than hexadecimal identifiers. Second, by restricting the property type to an enumeration that is schema validated, you remove the possibility of encountering a unknown type within a *PathToExtendedFieldType* instance.

What this means, however, is that if you have a MAPI proptag that you want to reference using an extended property path, you will need break apart the MAPI proptag into its property identifier and property type parts and then map the MAPI property type integer value to the correct *MapiPropertyTypeType* enumeration value. To assist in this separation, we offer a partial class extension to *PathToExtendedFieldType* in Listing 13-2 for breaking MAPI proptag values into their property id and *MapiPropertyTypeType* values. The method of interest is *ParsePropertyTag*.

LISTING 13-2 Partial class extension for parsing MAPI proptags

```
/// <summary>
/// Extension of PathToExtendedFieldType to add some helpful overloads
/// and methods
/// </summary>
public partial class PathToExtendedFieldType
{
    private static Dictionary<int, SingleAndArrayPair> mapping =
                new Dictionary<int, SingleAndArrayPair>();

    /// <summary>
    /// Static constructor.  Used to fill up our dictionary
    /// </summary>
    static PathToExtendedFieldType()
    {
```

```
        // The low word of a MAPI property tag contains the property type.
        // We want to create a mapping of MAPI property type value (short) to
        // MapiPropertyTypeType enumeration value. Note that array types in MAPI
        // have the value of their non-array counterparts bitwise AND'd with 0xF000
        //
        mapping.Add(2, new SingleAndArrayPair(
            MapiPropertyTypeType.Short, MapiPropertyTypeType.ShortArray));
        mapping.Add(3, new SingleAndArrayPair(
            MapiPropertyTypeType.Integer, MapiPropertyTypeType.IntegerArray));
        mapping.Add(4, new SingleAndArrayPair(
            MapiPropertyTypeType.Float, MapiPropertyTypeType.FloatArray));
        mapping.Add(5, new SingleAndArrayPair(
            MapiPropertyTypeType.Double, MapiPropertyTypeType.DoubleArray));
        mapping.Add(6, new SingleAndArrayPair(
            MapiPropertyTypeType.Currency, MapiPropertyTypeType.CurrencyArray));
        mapping.Add(7, new SingleAndArrayPair(
            MapiPropertyTypeType.ApplicationTime,
            MapiPropertyTypeType.ApplicationTimeArray));
        mapping.Add(0xB, new SingleAndArrayPair(MapiPropertyTypeType.Boolean));
        mapping.Add(0x14, new SingleAndArrayPair(
            MapiPropertyTypeType.Long, MapiPropertyTypeType.LongArray));
        mapping.Add(0x1E, new SingleAndArrayPair(
            MapiPropertyTypeType.String, MapiPropertyTypeType.StringArray));
        mapping.Add(0x1F, new SingleAndArrayPair(
            MapiPropertyTypeType.String, MapiPropertyTypeType.StringArray));
        mapping.Add(0x40, new SingleAndArrayPair(
            MapiPropertyTypeType.SystemTime, MapiPropertyTypeType.SystemTimeArray));
        mapping.Add(0x48, new SingleAndArrayPair(
            MapiPropertyTypeType.CLSID, MapiPropertyTypeType.CLSIDArray));
        mapping.Add(0x102, new SingleAndArrayPair(
            MapiPropertyTypeType.Binary, MapiPropertyTypeType.BinaryArray));
    }


    /// <summary>
    /// Parses a full MAPI proptag and extracts the property identifier and
    /// property type
    /// </summary>
    /// <param name="fullPropertyTag">Full MAPI proptag to parse</param>
    /// <param name="propertyId">OUT property identifier</param>
    /// <param name="propertyType">OUT property type</param>
    ///
    public static void ParsePropertyTag(
                        int fullPropertyTag,
                        out string propertyId,
                        out MapiPropertyTypeType propertyType)
    {
        // The property id is contained in the high word. As such, mask off the
        // low word and then shift the result down 16 bits to get the short
        // equivalent. Then convert it to a hex string since that is how the proxy
        // classes surface the property identifier.
        //
        ushort propertyIdValue = (ushort)((fullPropertyTag & 0xFFFF0000) >> 16);
        propertyId = string.Format("0x{0:x}", propertyIdValue);
```

```csharp
        // The type is in the low word.  Mask it off and look it up in our mapping.
        //
        ushort type = (ushort)(fullPropertyTag & 0xFFFF);
        ushort rawType = ExtractTypeFromArrayType(type);
        SingleAndArrayPair pair;
        if (!mapping.TryGetValue(rawType, out pair))
        {
          throw new ArgumentException("Unsupported property type: " + type);
        }
        if (IsArrayType(type))
        {
          if (pair.ArrayValueType.HasValue)
          {
            propertyType = pair.ArrayValueType.Value;
          }
          else
          {
            throw new ArgumentException(
                "No array type provided for type: " + type);
          }
        }
        else
        {
          propertyType = pair.SingleValueType;
        }
      }


      /// <summary>
      /// Returns true if the prop tag type passed in represents an array
      /// type</summary>
      /// <param name="propTagType">Property tag type</param>
      /// <returns>True if array type</returns>
      ///
      private static bool IsArrayType(ushort propTagType)
      {
        // MAPI array types have the 0xF000 flag set.  Check for it.
        //
        return (propTagType & 0xF000) !=0;
      }


      /// <summary>
      /// Extracts the raw type from the prop tag.  Will be the same for
      /// single and multivalued types </summary>
      /// <param name="propTagType">Type to examine</param>
      /// <returns>Raw type</returns>
      ///
      private static ushort ExtractTypeFromArrayType(ushort propTagType)
      {
        return (ushort)(propTagType & 0x0FFF);
      }


      /// <summary>
      /// Nested class for holding MapiPropertyTypeType values that are
      /// related</summary>
```

```
private class SingleAndArrayPair
{
  private MapiPropertyTypeType singleValue;
  private MapiPropertyTypeType? arrayValue;

  /// <summary>
  /// Constructor
  /// </summary>
  /// <param name="singleValue">Type for single valued items</param>
  /// <param name="arrayValue">OPTIONAL type for multi-valued items.  There
  /// is no bool[] for instance</param>
  ///
  public SingleAndArrayPair(
                MapiPropertyTypeType singleValue,
                MapiPropertyTypeType arrayValue)
  {
    this.singleValue = singleValue;
    this.arrayValue = arrayValue;
  }

  /// <summary>
  /// Constructor to use for single valued items only
  /// </summary>
  /// <param name="singleValue">Type for single valued
  /// items</param>
  ///
  public SingleAndArrayPair(MapiPropertyTypeType singleValue)
  {
    this.singleValue = singleValue;
    this.arrayValue = null;
  }

  /// <summary>
  /// Accessor for the single value type
  /// </summary>
  public MapiPropertyTypeType SingleValueType
  {
    get { return this.singleValue; }
  }

  /// <summary>
  /// Accessor for the array value type
  /// </summary>
  public MapiPropertyTypeType? ArrayValueType
  {
    get { return this.arrayValue; }
  }
}
}
```

Using the new methods from Listing 13-2, you can simplify your proxy coding experience when dealing with MAPI proptags by adding two factory methods for creating extended property paths to *PathToExtendedFieldType* as shown in Listing 13-3.

LISTING 13-3 Factory methods for building extended property paths from MAPI proptags

```
/// <summary>
/// Extension of PathToExtendedFieldType to add some helpful overloads
/// and methods
/// </summary>
public partial class PathToExtendedFieldType
{
  // .. methods from Listing 13-2 omitted ...
  //

  /// <summary>
  /// Creates a prop tag extended field uri
  /// </summary>
  /// <param name="propId">16-bit Id of property tag</param>
  /// <param name="propType">property type</param>
  /// <returns>PathToExtendedFieldType</returns>
  ///
  public static PathToExtendedFieldType BuildPropertyTag(
                                      ushort propId,
                                      MapiPropertyTypeType propType)
  {
    PathToExtendedFieldType result = new PathToExtendedFieldType();
    result.PropertyTag = string.Format("0x{0:x}", propId);
    result.PropertyType = propType;
    return result;
  }

  /// <summary>
  /// Creates a prop tag extended field uri from a full MAPI proptag
  /// </summary>
  /// <param name="propertyTag">Full MAPI proptag</param>
  /// <returns>PathToExtendedFieldType</returns>
  ///
  public static PathToExtendedFieldType BuildPropertyTag(int propertyTag)
  {
    string tempPropertyId;
    MapiPropertyTypeType tempPropertyType;
    PathToExtendedFieldType.ParsePropertyTag(
                                propertyTag,
                                out tempPropertyId,
                                out tempPropertyType);

    PathToExtendedFieldType result = new PathToExtendedFieldType();
    result.PropertyTag = tempPropertyId;
    result.PropertyType = tempPropertyType;
    return result;
  }
}
```

Earlier in the chapter, we discussed how proptag property identifiers for custom properties are not guaranteed to be the same across Mailbox databases. As a result, Exchange Web Services does *not* support referencing custom properties with proptags in the custom range 0x8000 to 0xFFFE) by their proptag value. You must reference such properties by their GUID+Name or GUID+Id pair. Of course, all extended properties in the standard property identifier range (0x0000 to 0x7FFF) can be accessed via proptag.

Custom Properties by Name

While proptag extended properties are identified using the *PropertyTag* attribute, Guid+Name custom properties are identified using three other attributes on *PathToExtendedFieldType*. The first of these attributes defines the namespace or scope for your property name. There are several well-known custom namespaces exposed through the *DistinguishedPropertySetType* enumeration that are used by various client applications such as Microsoft Office Outlook to identify custom properties that are important to them. To use these well-known namespaces, you must set the *DistinguishedPropertySetId* attribute.

```
<t:ExtendedFieldURI DistinguishedPropertySetId="PublicStrings" ..more../>
```

And in proxy class code:

```
PathToExtendedFieldType fieldUri = new PathToExtendedFieldType();
fieldUri.DistinguishedPropertySetId =
                DistinguishedPropertySetType.PublicStrings;

// Don't forget to set the specified property for optional value type
// properties
//
fieldUri.DistinguishedPropertySetIdSpecified = true;
```

For all other namespaces, the *PropertySetId* attribute is available. The *PropertySetId* attribute is exposed as a string in the schema and must be set to the GUID value of the namespace without the enclosing braces. The *MySpecialGuid* and *YourSpecialGuid* values we defined earlier in this chapter are precisely the kind of namespaces that *PropertySetId* uses. Capitalization of the *PropertySetId* GUID string does not matter. The following code shows the GUID format of the well-known *PublicStrings* namespace.[4]

```
<t:ExtendedFieldURI PropertySetId="00020329-0000-0000-C000-000000000046" more… />
```

When using the proxy classes, the *PropertySetId* property is exposed as a string and must be the GUID value of the namespace without the enclosing braces. Because strings are reference types, there is no need for the **Specified* property, even though the attribute is optional in the schema. Reference types use null to indicate that no value has been set.

```
PathToExtendedFieldType fieldUri = new PathToExtendedFieldType();
fieldUri.PropertySetId = "00020329-0000-0000-C000-000000000046";
```

---

[4] One extended property path specifying the *PublicStrings DistinguishedPropertySetId* and another extended property path specifying the corresponding *PropertySetId* GUID will point to the same underlying MAPI property.

Of course, namespaces wouldn't be too useful if you didn't have a way to dictate which property you were referring to within the namespace. That is the job of the aptly named *PropertyName* attribute. This attribute takes a *case-sensitive* string.

```
PathToExtendedFieldType fieldUri = new PathToExtendedFieldType();
fieldUri.PropertySetId = "00020329-0000-0000-C000-000000000046";
fieldUri.PropertyName = "BookWorthy";
fieldUri.PropertyType = MapiPropertyTypeType.Boolean;
```

Custom Properties by Id

We have talked about identifying extended properties by proptag and GUID+Name. The third and final way to identify an extended property is to use a GUID with a dispatch identifier (GUID+Id)

Just as with GUID+Name custom properties, you use the *PropertySetId* (or *DistinguishedPropertySetId*) to identify your namespace scope. The difference is that instead of specifying the *PropertyName* attribute, you use the *PropertyId* attribute, which is an integer. Now, the naming of the *PropertyId* attribute is a little unfortunate. When talking about MAPI proptags, we mentioned how the most significant word is the property identifier for the proptag in question. Such is the *proper* use of the term *property identifier*. When considering GUID+ID custom properties, the integer identifier is known as a *dispatch identifier*. However, that distinction did not end up in the product, so just realize that when you see the term *PropertyId*, it is referring to the dispatch identifier of a GUID+Id custom property and not the property identifier part of a MAPI proptag.

```
<t:ExtendedFieldURI
    PropertySetId="00020329-0000-0000-C000-000000000046"
    PropertyId="2"
    PropertyType="Integer"/>
```

Because *PropertyId* is an optional value type, the proxy class exposes the *PropertyIdSpecified Boolean* property that must be set to true if you are going to supply a value for the *PropertyId*.

```
PathToExtendedFieldType fieldUri = new PathToExtendedFieldType();
fieldUri.PropertySetId = "00020329-0000-0000-C000-000000000046";
fieldUri.PropertyId = 2;
fieldUri.PropertyIdSpecified = true;
fieldUri.PropertyType = MapiPropertyTypeType.Integer;
```

Earlier, an added factory method created a *PathToExtendedFieldType* instance from a MAPI proptag value. It seems prudent to do the same for both GUID+Name and GUID+Id custom properties too. These factory methods are shown in Listing 13-4.

LISTING 13-4 Custom property factory methods for *PathToExtendedFieldType*

```
/// <summary>
/// Extension of PathToExtendedFieldType to add some helpful overloads
/// and methods
/// </summary>
public partial class PathToExtendedFieldType
{
  // .. methods from Listing 13-2 and 13-3 omitted ...
  //

  /// <summary>
  /// Creates a GuidId extended field uri
  /// </summary>
  /// <param name="guid">Guid representing the property set</param>
  /// <param name="propId">Property id of the named property</param>
  /// <param name="propType">Property type</param>
  /// <returns>PathToExtendedFieldType proxy object</returns>
  ///
  public static PathToExtendedFieldType BuildGuidId(
                                          Guid guid,
                                          int propId,
                                          MapiPropertyTypeType propType)
  {
    PathToExtendedFieldType result = new PathToExtendedFieldType();
    result.PropertyId = propId;
    // Don't forget to set the specified property to true for optional value
    // types!!
    //
    result.PropertyIdSpecified = true;
    result.PropertySetId = guid.ToString("D");
    result.PropertyType = propType;
    return result;
  }


  /// <summary>
  /// Creates a GuidId extended field URI for a distinguished property set id
  /// </summary>
  /// <param name="propertySet">DistinguishedPropertySetId</param>
  /// <param name="propId">dispatch Id</param>
  /// <param name="propType">Property type</param>
  /// <returns>PathToExtendedFieldType</returns>
  ///
  public static PathToExtendedFieldType BuildGuidId(
                  DistinguishedPropertySetType propertySet,
                  int propId,
                  MapiPropertyTypeType propType)
  {
    PathToExtendedFieldType result = new PathToExtendedFieldType();
    result.PropertyId = propId;
    result.PropertyIdSpecified = true;
    result.DistinguishedPropertySetId = propertySet;
    result.DistinguishedPropertySetIdSpecified = true;
    result.PropertyType = propType;
    return result;
```

```
    }

    /// <summary>
    /// Builds a guid/name extended property
    /// </summary>
    /// <param name="guid">Property set guid</param>
    /// <param name="propertyName">Property name</param>
    /// <param name="propType">Property type</param>
    /// <returns>Guid/Name extended property</returns>
    ///
    public static PathToExtendedFieldType BuildGuidName(
                                    Guid guid,
                                    string propertyName,
                                    MapiPropertyTypeType propType)
    {
      PathToExtendedFieldType result = new PathToExtendedFieldType();?
      result.PropertySetId = guid.ToString("D");
      result.PropertyName = propertyName;
      result.PropertyType = propType;
      return result;
    }

    /// <summary>
    /// Build a guid/name extended property path with DisinguishedPropertySetId
    /// </summary>
    /// <param name="propertySetId">DistinguishedPropertySetId</param>
    /// <param name="propertyName">Property Name</param>
    /// <param name="propertyType">Property Type</param>
    /// <returns>PathToExtendedFieldType</returns>
    ///
    public static PathToExtendedFieldType BuildGuidName(
                        DistinguishedPropertySetType propertySetId,
                        string propertyName,
                        MapiPropertyTypeType propertyType)
    {
      PathToExtendedFieldType result = new PathToExtendedFieldType();
      result.DistinguishedPropertySetId = propertySetId;
      result.DistinguishedPropertySetIdSpecified = true;
      result.PropertyName = propertyName;
      result.PropertyType = propertyType;
      return result;
    }
}
```

Extended Property Metadata and Data

So far in this chapter, we have been talking about how extended property paths are represented in XML and proxy class code. However, a property path is simply metadata about the
property of interest. When you encounter the actual data value for that property on an item
you will be presented with both *which* extended property (metadata) you are talking about

and *what* (data) its value is. The combination of the extended property path and the actual extended property data is expressed in the *ExtendedPropertyType* schema type. Table 13-1 showed that Exchange Web Services supports both single-valued as well as multi-valued data types. As such, there are two basic representations of *ExtendedPropertyType*. For single-valued extended properties, the property value is exposed through a single *Value* element.

```
<t:ExtendedProperty>
  <t:ExtendedFieldURI .../>
  <t:Value>some string value</t:Value>
</t:ExtendedProperty>
```

For multi-valued properties, the property values are exposed as children of a *Values* (notice the plural) element.

```
<t:ExtendedProperty>
  <t:ExtendedFieldURI .../>
  <t:Values>
    <t:Value>value 1</t:Value>
    <t:Value>value 2</t:Value>
    <!-- more values if necessary -->
  </t:Values>
</t:ExtendedProperty>
```

Figure 13-2 shows how *ExtendedPropertyType* acts as a container for both the extended property path as well as the property data.

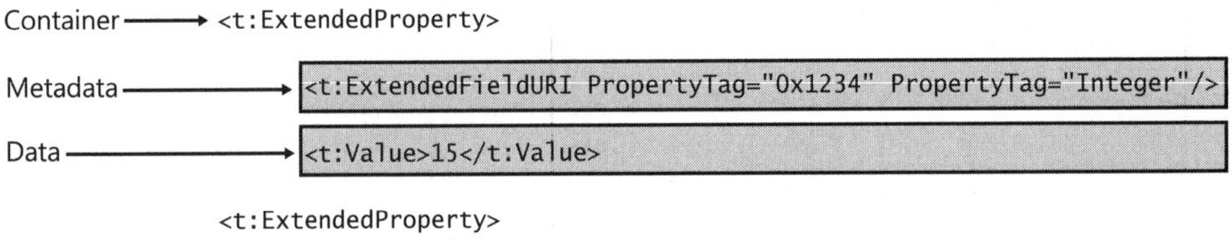

```
Container ─────▶ <t:ExtendedProperty>

Metadata ──────────────▶ <t:ExtendedFieldURI PropertyTag="0x1234" PropertyTag="Integer"/>

Data ──────────────────▶ <t:Value>15</t:Value>

                  <t:ExtendedProperty>
```

FIGURE 13-2 Extended property structure

Since the property path describes both the identity as well as the type of the data, it follows that the property type indicated within the metadata must agree with the type of the data. So the following would result in an error:

```
<!-- This won't work since the types don't match -->
<t:ExtendedProperty>
  <t:ExtendedFieldURI PropertyTag="0x0036" PropertyType="Integer"/>
  <t:Value>This is a string</t:Value>
</t:ExtendedProperty>
```

Since the *Value* elements within *ExtendedPropertyType* are represented as strings, how do you encode the various types within each *Value* element? Table 13-2 shows examples for each *MapiPropertyTypeType* enumeration value.

TABLE 13-2 **String Representation of Property Types**

MapiPropertyTypeType	Comments	Example
ApplicationTime	A double value.	1234.12
Binary	Base-64 encoded string. Use System.Convert.ToBase64String().	BAUGBw==
Boolean	For False, use false or 0. For True, use true or 1.	true
CLSID	A GUID string without the enclosing brackets. If using a GUID type, use myGuid.ToString("D").	24040483-cda4-4521-bb5f-a83fac4d19a4
Currency	Monetary value in units of cents	1234
Double	A double value	1234.45
Float	A float value	1234.45
Integer	An integer value	1234
Long	A 64 bit integer value	1234
Short	A 16 bit signed integer value	1234
SystemTime	Internally, Exchange Web Services represents this as a *DateTime* and parses it using *DateTime.TryParse*. It assumes Coordinated Universal Time (UTC) if no time zone is specified.	5/6/2005 8:30am
String	A string value	"I like extended properties"

Listing 13-5 shows an example of using the proxy classes to create an extended property with a *SystemTime* type.

LISTING 13-5 Using the proxy classes to create a *SystemTime* extended property

```
// Set up the metadata (which property we are referring to)
//
PathToExtendedFieldType metadata = new PathToExtendedFieldType();
metadata.PropertyTag = "0x0039";
metadata.PropertyType = MapiPropertyTypeType.SystemTime;

// Now create the container and set the value
//
ExtendedPropertyType extendedProperty = new ExtendedPropertyType();
extendedProperty.ExtendedFieldURI = metadata;

// For single valued extended properties, Item must be a string
//
extendedProperty.Item = DateTime.UtcNow.ToString();
```

Properties with Multiple Values

As mentioned earlier, multi-valued extended properties require a slight modification of the data section of an extended property, as shown in Listing 13-6.

LISTING 13-6 Extended property with multiple values

```
<t:ExtendedProperty>
  <t:ExtendedFieldURI
        PropertySetId= "24040483-cda4-4521-bb5f-a83fac4d19a4"
        PropertyId="3"
        PropertyType="IntegerArray"/>
  <t:Values>
    <t:Value>1</t:Value>
    <t:Value>2</t:Value>
    <t:Value>3</t:Value>
  </t:Values>
</t:ExtendedProperty>
```

Now, let's do the same thing with the proxy classes. This is shown in Listing 13-7.

LISTING 13-7 Multi-valued extended properties using proxy classes.

```
// Set up the metadata (which property we are referring to)
//
PathToExtendedFieldType metadata =
        PathToExtendedFieldType.BuildGuidId(
                new Guid("24040483-cda4-4521-bb5f-a83fac4d19a4"),
                3, /* dispatch id */
                MapiPropertyTypeType.IntegerArray);

// Now create the container and set the value
//
ExtendedPropertyType extendedProperty = new ExtendedPropertyType();
extendedProperty.ExtendedFieldURI = metadata;

// For multi-valued properties, Item must be an instance of
// NonEmptyArrayOfPropertyValuesType
//
NonEmptyArrayOfPropertyValuesType arrayValues = new
                NonEmptyArrayOfPropertyValuesType();
arrayValues.Items = new string[3];
for (int index = 1; index <= 3; index++)
{
  arrayValues.Items[index - 1] = index.ToString();
}
extendedProperty.Item = arrayValues;
```

Now that you know about the *ExtendedPropertyType* container class, you can add two overloaded constructors to *ExtendedPropertyType* via partial class extension as shown in Listing 13-8.

LISTING 13-8 Partial class extension of *ExtendedPropertyType*

```
/// <summary>
/// Extension of the ExtendedPropertyType
/// </summary>
public partial class ExtendedPropertyType
{
  /// <summary>
  /// Constructor needed for xml serialization since we are providing overloads.
  /// </summary>
  public ExtendedPropertyType()
  {}

  /// <summary>
  /// Constructor
  /// </summary>
  /// <param name="fieldURI">FieldURI representing metadata about the
  /// property</param>
  /// <param name="value">Value for the property</param>
  ///
  public ExtendedPropertyType(PathToExtendedFieldType fieldURI, string value)
  {
    this.ExtendedFieldURI = fieldURI;
    this.Item = value;
  }

  /// <summary>
  /// Constructor
  /// </summary>
  /// <param name="fieldURI">FieldURI representing metadata about the
  /// property</param>
  /// <param name="values">PARAMS array of values for multivalued
  /// property</param>
  ///
  public ExtendedPropertyType(
              PathToExtendedFieldType fieldURI,
              params string[] values)
  {
    this.ExtendedFieldURI = fieldURI;
    NonEmptyArrayOfPropertyValuesType array =
          new NonEmptyArrayOfPropertyValuesType();
    array.Items = new string[values.Length];

    int index = 0;
    foreach (string value in values)
    {
      array.Items[index++] = value;
    }
    this.Item = array;
  }
}
```

If Listing 13-7 is rewritten using the new overloaded *ExtendedPropertyType* constructor, the code is reduced to two lines (ignoring line breaks).

```
PathToExtendedFieldType metadata =
        PathToExtendedFieldType.BuildGuidId(
                new Guid("24040483-cda4-4521-bb5f-a83fac4d19a4"),
                3, /* dispatch id */
                MapiPropertyTypeType.IntegerArray);

ExtendedPropertyType extendedProperty =
                new ExtendedPropertyType(metadata, "1", "2", "3");
```

Using Extended Properties

Now that you know what extended properties are and how they are declared, let's look at how you use these extended properties with Exchange Web Services methods.

First, we show how to create a message with extended properties by using *CreateItem* from Chapter 5, "Items." We will use this message in our ongoing extended property discussions. Because you are setting the *values* for these properties, you need to use the *ExtendedProperty* container element that contains both the metadata (the property in question) and the data that you wish to set. Listing 13-9 sets two different properties.

LISTING 13-9 Creating an item with two extended properties

```
<CreateItem xmlns=".../messages"
            xmlns:t=".../types"
            MessageDisposition="SaveOnly">
  <Items>
    <t:Message>
      <t:Subject>Test27</t:Subject>
      <t:ExtendedProperty>
        <t:ExtendedFieldURI PropertySetId="24040483-cda4-4521-bb5f-a83fac4d19a4"
                            PropertyId="2"
                            PropertyType="StringArray"/>
        <t:Values>
          <t:Value>Fee</t:Value>
          <t:Value>Fi</t:Value>
        </t:Values>
      </t:ExtendedProperty>
      <t:ExtendedProperty>
        <t:ExtendedFieldURI DistinguishedPropertySetId="PublicStrings"
                            PropertyName="ShoeSize"
                            PropertyType="Float"/>
        <t:Value>12</t:Value>
      </t:ExtendedProperty>
    </t:Message>
  </Items>
</CreateItem>
```

Specifying Extended Properties in Shapes

After successful creation, you will be able to retrieve the message from Listing 13-9 with a *GetItem* call. *GetItem* will return the properties that are applicable to the message you just created, but that certainly won't include your custom properties unless you explicitly ask for those custom properties. So how do you indicate your desire to retrieve those properties? You need to explicitly ask for them within the *AdditionalProperties* child element of the item response shape, as shown in Listing 13-10.

LISTING 13-10 Retrieving a message with extended properties

```
<GetItem xmlns=".../messages"
         xmlns:t=".../types">
  <ItemShape>
    <t:BaseShape>IdOnly</t:BaseShape>
    <t:AdditionalProperties>
      <t:ExtendedFieldURI
            PropertySetId="24040483-cda4-4521-bb5f-a83fac4d19a4"
            PropertyId="2"
            PropertyType="StringArray"/>
      <t:ExtendedFieldURI
            DistinguishedPropertySetId="PublicStrings"
            PropertyName="ShoeSize"
            PropertyType="Float"/>
    </t:AdditionalProperties>
  </ItemShape>
  <ItemIds>
    <t:ItemId Id="AAAtAEFkbWluaXN..." ChangeKey="CQAAs8A6QI2x..."/>
  </ItemIds>
</GetItem>
```

In the *AdditionalProperties* element of the *GetItem* call, you use only the metadata format (the property path) of the extended properties that you wish to request. That should make sense because you are *requesting* the data and therefore would have no data values to put there.

And the response in Listing 13-11 shows that everything went as planned.

LISTING 13-11 *GetItemResponse* with extended properties

```
<GetItemResponse xmlns:m=".../messages"
                 xmlns:t=".../types"
                 xmlns=".../messages">
  <m:ResponseMessages>
    <m:GetItemResponseMessage ResponseClass="Success">
      <m:ResponseCode>NoError</m:ResponseCode>
      <m:Items>
        <t:Message>
          <t:ItemId Id="AAAtAEFkbWluaXN..." ChangeKey="CQAAs8A6QI2x..."/>
          <t:ExtendedProperty>
```

```
                <t:ExtendedFieldURI
                    PropertySetId="24040483-cda4-4521-bb5f-a83fac4d19a4"
                    PropertyId="2"
                    PropertyType="StringArray"/>
                <t:Values>
                    <t:Value>Fee</t:Value>
                    <t:Value>Fi</t:Value>
                </t:Values>
            </t:ExtendedProperty>
            <t:ExtendedProperty>
                <t:ExtendedFieldURI
                    DistinguishedPropertySetId="PublicStrings"
                    PropertyName="ShoeSize"
                    PropertyType="Float"/>
                <t:Value>12</t:Value>
            </t:ExtendedProperty>
          </t:Message>
        </m:Items>
      </m:GetItemResponseMessage>
    </m:ResponseMessages>
</GetItemResponse>
```

Listing 13-12 shows how to add extended property paths to the response shape of a *GetItem* or *FindItem* call when using the proxy classes. Note that several of the partial class extension methods that we have introduced are used.

LISTING 13-12 Requesting extended properties by using the proxy

```
PathToExtendedFieldType extendedPropPath1 =
            PathToExtendedFieldType.BuildGuidId(
                new Guid("24040483-cda4-4521-bb5f-a83fac4d19a4"),
                2,
                MapiPropertyTypeType.StringArray);

PathToExtendedFieldType extendedPropPath2 =
            PathToExtendedFieldType.BuildGuidName(
                DistinguishedPropertySetType.PublicStrings,
                "ShoeSize",
                MapiPropertyTypeType.Float);

// Use our ItemResponseShapeType overloaded constructor
//
ItemResponseShapeType responseShape = new ItemResponseShapeType(
                                DefaultShapeNamesType.IdOnly,
                                extendedPropPath1,
                                extendedPropPath2);
```

Updating Extended Properties

Updating extended properties on an item follows the same pattern as updating any other property. Simply specify the property path that you wish to change using the metadata format and then embed the extended property (both metadata and data) as a child element of the item in the *UpdateItem* call. This is shown in Listing 13-13.

LISTING 13-13 Updating extended properties on a message

```
<UpdateItem MessageDisposition="SaveOnly"
            ConflictResolution="AutoResolve"
            xmlns=".../messages"
            xmlns:t=".../types">
   <ItemChanges>
     <t:ItemChange>
       <t:ItemId Id="AAAtAEFkbWluaXN..." ChangeKey="CQAAABYAA..."/>
       <t:Updates>
         <t:SetItemField>
           <t:ExtendedFieldURI
               PropertySetId="24040483-cda4-4521-bb5f-a83fac4d19a4"
               PropertyId="2"
               PropertyType="StringArray"/>
           <t:Message>
             <t:ExtendedProperty>
               <t:ExtendedFieldURI
                   PropertySetId="24040483-cda4-4521-bb5f-a83fac4d19a4"
                   PropertyId="2"
                   PropertyType="StringArray"/>
               <t:Values>
                 <t:Value>Foe</t:Value>
                 <t:Value>Fum</t:Value>
               </t:Values>
             </t:ExtendedProperty>
           </t:Message>
         </t:SetItemField>
       </t:Updates>
     </t:ItemChange>
   </ItemChanges>
</UpdateItem>
```

Note that appending to extended properties is not supported, so trying to use an *AppendToItemField* element within an *UpdateItem* call on an extended property results in an *ErrorInvalidPropertyAppend* response code. To mimic an append, you must first retrieve the extended property value using *GetItem*, manually append the new value to the retrieve property value, and then call *UpdateItem* with a *SetItemField* action to overwrite the old property value with the concatenated data.

Overriding Exchange Web Services Business Logic

The Exchange Web Services business logic layer tries to make sense of MAPI by restricting which properties you can set on a given item type. For instance, most people don't need to get or set a start date on a message. That is typically used only by calendar items and tasks. What if you do *really* need to set the start date on a message? You can look up the MAPI information for the property in question in Appendix C (available on the companion Web page) and access it using the extended property path syntax.

Exchange Web Services validates certain property relationships when saving changes to an item or folder. For instance, a calendar item must have both a start date and an end date, and the start date must be less than or equal to the end date. It will do you no good to try to set the start date to be greater than the end date via extended properties since the validation checks are performed against the item *after* the properties have been set but *before* the item is saved to the Exchange Store.

Managed Folders

Way back in Chapter 4, we discussed the concept of managed folders. At that point, we hadn't delved into the world of extended properties, so you had to fetch all of the subfolders of the root folder and look for the *ManagedFolderInformation* property on each subfolder. Though that approach does work, there is a more efficient way to do this.

As discussed in Chapter 4, the *ManagedFolderInformation* property can be used to determine which folders are managed and which are not. You can perform a *FindFolder* operation with a restriction and ask it to return only those folders that have managed folder information.[5] Here is the request:

```
<FindFolder xmlns=".../messages"
            xmlns:t=".../types"
            Traversal="Deep">
  <FolderShape>
    <t:BaseShape>Default</t:BaseShape>
  </FolderShape>
  <Restriction>
    <t:Exists>
      <t:FieldURI FieldURI="folder:ManagedFolderInformation"/>
    </t:Exists>
  </Restriction>
  <ParentFolderIds>
    <t:DistinguishedFolderId Id="root"/>
  </ParentFolderIds>
</FindFolder>
```

---

[5] *FindFolder* and restrictions are discussed in detail in Chapter 14, "Searching the Mailbox."

And the response.

```
<FindFolderResponse xmlns:m=".../messages"
                    xmlns:t=".../types"
                    xmlns=".../messages">
  <m:ResponseMessages>
    <m:FindFolderResponseMessage ResponseClass="Error">
      <m:MessageText>The property can not be used with this type of
             restriction.</m:MessageText>
      <m:ResponseCode>ErrorUnsupportedPathForQuery</m:ResponseCode>
      <m:DescriptiveLinkKey>0</m:DescriptiveLinkKey>
      <m:MessageXml>
        <t:FieldURI FieldURI="folder:ManagedFolderInformation"/>
      </m:MessageXml>
    </m:FindFolderResponseMessage>
  </m:ResponseMessages>
</FindFolderResponse>
```

There is a problem—you can't create a restriction on the *folder:ManagedFolderInformation* property path. Don't lose hope, however. Situations like these often require you to roll up your sleeves and deal with the MAPI properties directly. Managed folders have a MAPI property with proptag 0x672D0003 set on them that identifies them as managed folders. The value of this MAPI property is not important here.[6] However, the *existence* of this property is important. You can issue a *FindFolder* call and use the *Exists* restriction type to return only the folders that have the special MAPI property set on them. Listing 13-14 shows the request.

LISTING 13-14 Finding managed folders by using extended properties

```
<FindFolder xmlns=".../messages"
            xmlns:t=".../types"
            Traversal="Deep">
  <FolderShape>
    <t:BaseShape>IdOnly</t:BaseShape>
    <t:AdditionalProperties>
      <t:FieldURI FieldURI="folder:DisplayName"/>
      <t:FieldURI FieldURI="folder:ManagedFolderInformation"/>
    </t:AdditionalProperties>
  </FolderShape>
  <Restriction>
    <t:Exists>
      <t:ExtendedFieldURI PropertyTag="0x672D"
                          PropertyType="Integer"/>
    </t:Exists>
  </Restriction>
  <ParentFolderIds>
    <t:DistinguishedFolderId Id="root"/>
  </ParentFolderIds>
</FindFolder>
```

---

[6] Nor should you rely on a specific value for this property, because it is undocumented. The probability of the data format for these properties changing is directly proportional to how much of your code depends on these values not changing.

Now, you get a successful response back.

```
<FindFolderResponse xmlns:m=".../messages"
                    xmlns:t=".../types"
                    xmlns=".../messages">
  <m:ResponseMessages>
    <m:FindFolderResponseMessage ResponseClass="Success">
      <m:ResponseCode>NoError</m:ResponseCode>
      <m:RootFolder TotalItemsInView="3"
                    IncludesLastItemInRange="true">
        <t:Folders>
          <t:Folder>
            <t:FolderId Id="AQAtAEFkbWl..." ChangeKey="AQ..."/>
            <t:DisplayName>Managed Folders</t:DisplayName>
            <t:ManagedFolderInformation>
              <t:CanDelete>false</t:CanDelete>
              <t:CanRenameOrMove>false</t:CanRenameOrMove>
              <t:MustDisplayComment>false</t:MustDisplayComment>
              <t:HasQuota>false</t:HasQuota>
              <t:IsManagedFoldersRoot>true</t:IsManagedFoldersRoot>
            </t:ManagedFolderInformation>
          </t:Folder>
          <t:Folder>
            <t:FolderId Id="AQAtAEX..." ChangeKey="AQAAABYAAAB…"/>
            <t:DisplayName>Case 123 Infringement</t:DisplayName>
            <t:ManagedFolderInformation>
              <t:CanDelete>false</t:CanDelete>
              <t:CanRenameOrMove>true</t:CanRenameOrMove>
              <t:MustDisplayComment>false</t:MustDisplayComment>
              <t:HasQuota>false</t:HasQuota>
              <t:IsManagedFoldersRoot>false</t:IsManagedFoldersRoot>
              <t:ManagedFolderId>0944fd0e-8a36-4dc7-9788-dbec80e06bd4
              </t:ManagedFolderId>
              <t:Comment>All items related to the 123 infringement
                  case</t:Comment>
            </t:ManagedFolderInformation>
          </t:Folder>
          <t:Folder>
            <t:FolderId Id="AQAtAEFkbWl..." ChangeKey="AQAAABY..."/>
            <t:DisplayName>Patent Filings</t:DisplayName>
            <t:ManagedFolderInformation>
              <t:CanDelete>false</t:CanDelete>
              <t:CanRenameOrMove>true</t:CanRenameOrMove>
              <t:MustDisplayComment>false</t:MustDisplayComment>
              <t:HasQuota>false</t:HasQuota>
              <t:IsManagedFoldersRoot>false</t:IsManagedFoldersRoot>
              <t:ManagedFolderId>bdc01af2-502b-44d2-9ad2-
                  70f8d340669e</t:ManagedFolderId>
              <t:Comment>Patent filing related information</t:Comment>
            </t:ManagedFolderInformation>
          </t:Folder>
        </t:Folders>
      </m:RootFolder>
    </m:FindFolderResponseMessage>
  </m:ResponseMessages>
</FindFolderResponse>
```

MAPI Entry Ids

Many current MAPI-based applications may be migrated to Exchange Web Services. MAPI identifies items and folders in a mailbox using an *entry id* (PR_ENTRYID). However, an entry id is not the same thing as an Exchange Web Services *ItemId* (or *FolderId* for that matter). So, what if you have an existing MAPI application that uses entry id values in some places and you want to supply these entry id values to Exchange Web Services? This could occur in a couple of cases.

- You may have a local database of items that you would like to access, but the only identifier that you have is the entry id because the local database was populated using a legacy application.

- You may be upgrading a legacy application piece-by-piece and have some legacy components that process entry ids, and you need to provide these entry id values to your new Exchange Web Service code.

Let's look at how you would use the entry id to access an item using Exchange Web Services. Note that the following discussion uses concepts from Chapter 14, "Searching the Mailbox."

Retrieving an Entry Id by Using OutlookSpy

While you will already have the entry id value that you would like to use with Exchange Web Services, we do not have one for the example, so let's retrieve one using the OutlookSpy plugin for Microsoft Office Outlook (*http://www.dimastr.com/outspy*).

Using OutlookSpy, you can determine the property tag information for *PR_ENTRYID* as shown in Figure 13-3.

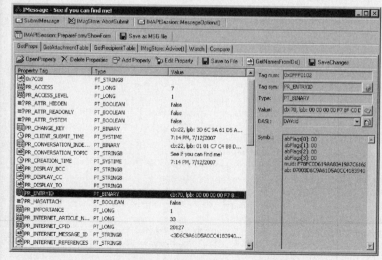

FIGURE 13-3 *PR_ENTRYID* in OutlookSpy

After selecting the PR_ENTRYID property in the list of properties, you can click on the little icon next to the *value* text box on the right hand side of the OutlookSpy dialog box to be presented with the HexView Editor dialog. Using the HexView Editor dialog, you can save the binary entry id data into a file using the File|Save menu option. For our example, we will use a filename of *c:\MyEntryId.dat*.

OutlookSpy shows that the property tag for *PR_ENTRYID* is 0x0FFF0102 and its type is a byte[], so all you need to be concerned with is the most significant word (0x0FFF). You can then perform a shallow traversal *FindItem* request and search for the item that has the entry id in question.

All binary properties must be Base64 encoded when dealing with Exchange Web Services. The *System.Convert* class exposes the *ToBase64String* method, which converts a byte array into a Base64-encoded string and the *FromBase64String* method does just the opposite. The following code takes the binary entry Id saved out to the file MyEntryId.dat, reads it in, and converts it into a Base64-encoded string.

```
string base64;
using (FileStream fs = File.OpenRead(@"c:\MyEntryId.dat"))
{
  BinaryReader reader = new BinaryReader(fs);
  byte[] bytes = reader.ReadBytes((int)fs.Length);
  base64 = System.Convert.ToBase64String(bytes);
}
```

If you run the preceding code, you get the following Base64-encoded entry id.

```
AAAAAIUnJ7skJWxMk4SkP5mmyOgHAIeKIfEv1k9KqJx6faPnw54AAACiQdwAANw+LZ+k1ONBpOrzVAeB39s
AO7niICgAAA==
```

Using the Base64-encoded entry id, you can build a *FindItem* request with a restriction (filter), as shown in Listing 13-15.

LISTING 13-15 Finding an item by using *PR_ENTRYID*

```
<FindItem xmlns=".../messages"
          xmlns:t=".../types"
          Traversal="Shallow">
  <ItemShape>
     <t:BaseShape>Default</t:BaseShape>
  </ItemShape>
  <Restriction>
    <t:IsEqualTo>
       <t:ExtendedFieldURI PropertyTag="0x0FFF" PropertyType="Binary"/>
       <t:FieldURIOrConstant>
         <t:Constant Value="AAAAAIUnJ7skJWxMk4SkP5mmyOgHAIeKIfEv1k9KqJ
                x6faPnw54AAACiQdwAANw+LZ+k1ONBpOrzVAeB39sAO7niICgAAA=="/>
       </t:FieldURIOrConstant>
    </t:IsEqualTo>
```

```
    </Restriction>
    <ParentFolderIds>
      <t:DistinguishedFolderId Id="inbox"/>
    </ParentFolderIds>
  </FindItem>
```

The request in Listing 13-15 says, "Give me all the items (*FindItem*) that are direct children of the Inbox (*ParentFolderIds*) that have the PR_ENTRYID property set to this binary value (*Restriction*)." Let's look at the response to see if our item has been found.

```
<FindItemResponse xmlns:m=".../messages"
                  xmlns:t=".../types"
                  xmlns=".../messages">
  <m:ResponseMessages>
    <m:FindItemResponseMessage ResponseClass="Success">
      <m:ResponseCode>NoError</m:ResponseCode>
      <m:RootFolder TotalItemsInView="1" IncludesLastItemInRange="true">
        <t:Items>
          <t:Message>
            <t:ItemId Id="AAAeAGRdnX..." ChangeKey="CQAAABYAA..."/>
            <t:Subject>See if you can find me!</t:Subject>
            <t:Sensitivity>Normal</t:Sensitivity>
            <t:Size>2598</t:Size>
            <t:DateTimeSent>2006-09-21T17:13:19Z</t:DateTimeSent>
            <t:DateTimeCreated>2006-09-21T17:13:35Z</t:DateTimeCreated>
            <t:HasAttachments>false</t:HasAttachments>
            <t:From>
              <t:Mailbox>
                <t:Name>Ken Malcolmson/t:Name>
              </t:Mailbox>
            </t:From>
            <t:IsRead>false</t:IsRead>
          </t:Message>
        </t:Items>
      </m:RootFolder>
    </m:FindItemResponseMessage>
  </m:ResponseMessages>
</FindItemResponse>
```

Now, you can extract the *ItemId* of the message from this response. It is important to note that retrieving an item by issuing a *FindItem* request with a restriction on the entry id is *much* slower and more demanding on the Exchange Server than using the *ItemId* in a *GetItem* call. But, given an entry id, using *FindItem* is your only option for retrieving that item through Exchange Web Services.

Summary

When using Exchange Web Services, you can reference MAPI properties using extended properties. In this chapter, we discussed the three categories of extended properties—proptag, Guid+Id, and Guid+Name. Extended properties in the standard property identifier range can use only the proptag extended property representation while extended properties in the custom range must use either the Guid+Id or Guid+Name representation.

Next we discussed the difference between the metadata (*PathToExtendedFieldUriType*) and data representations of extended properties and how these two concepts are wrapped by the *ExtendedPropertyType* container. Using this, we saw how we could retrieve and set extended property values on items. We revisited managed folders from Chapter 4 and saw how you can call *FindFolder* with a restriction on an extended property path to return only managed folders. We concluded the chapter by discussing how to retrieve an item from Exchange Web Services using a MAPI entry id.

Part III
Searching

Chapter 14
Searching the Mailbox

There are a number of features in the computer realm that would be nice to have in real life. At the top of that list is undo. With a real-life undo, a woodworker wouldn't have to be precise in his measurements. He could simply cut a piece of lumber, and if the resulting piece is too short, he could just press Ctrl+Z and do it again. Can you imagine the arguments that could be avoided? "Oops, I didn't mean to say that." Ctrl+Z! Ah, what a day that would be!

The second feature that would be nice to have in real life is search. Ken Malcolmson has a son with built-in search capabilities. No joke. If there is anything that Ken misplaced, his son can find it. "Andrew," he says, "have you seen my keys?" That is sufficient to get his son's search engine up and running. Invariably, Andrew finds the item of interest and presents it to his father. Ken's wife claims that Andrew is just more observant than Ken. But Ken knows that his son is quietly building an index of all things in the house and registering for change notifications so that he can keep that index up to date. This symbiotic relationship works quite well. Ken always misplaces things, and Andrew always finds them. Ken's lack of organizational skills is a built-in unit test for his son's index. You see, this is part of Ken's plan to contribute to the future success of his child.

Back in world of writing code, Microsoft Exchange Server 2007 Web Services also provides a way to search for items and folders within a Mailbox. In Chapter 4, "Folders," you saw that you can use the *FindFolder* and *FindItem* Web methods to return all the children of a given folder. But there is much more to search than simplistic enumeration. Exchange Web Services also exposes the ability to:

- Define a filter (restriction) that determines which folders or items get returned.

- Group related items together in a response.

- Create paged responses so that data can be processed in manageable chunks rather than as a single large result set.

- Create a search folder that acts as a virtual folder containing those items that pass the search folder restriction.

These features are exposed through the *FindFolder* and *FindItem* Web methods and also through the *SearchFolder* folder type. In this chapter, we will limit ourselves to discussing the restriction syntax in Exchange Web Services. The next chapter will discuss grouping, paging, and search folders.

Restrictions

There are many, many objects in Ken's house. But at any given time, Ken is looking for a specific item. Rarely is Ken interested in looking through every item in the house. When Ken asks his son if he has seen the keys, Ken is indicating his interest in a specific item—keys. In the database world, this can be represented as a SQL statement such as

`SELECT Location FROM House WHERE Item_Of_Interest = 'keys'.`

This statement has significantly reduced the number of items that could possibly be returned by Ken's son, Andrew. Now, of course, Andrew could turn around and return his mother's keys, but that could be easily rectified by further filtering the results:

`SELECT Location FROM House`

`WHERE Item_Of_Interest = 'keys' AND Owner = 'daddy'.`

Exchange Web Services exposes such conditional expressions as *restrictions*. A restriction determines which items or folders appear in the response. In the database world, this would equate to the *WHERE* clause of a SQL query. Because Exchange Web Services is built indirectly on top of the Messaging Application Programming Interface (MAPI), an Exchange Web Services restriction gets turned into a MAPI restriction (hence the name). Both *FindFolder* and *FindItem* surface an optional *Restriction* element.[1] Listing 14-1 presents an example to whet your appetites.[2]

LISTING 14-1 The first *FindFolder* restriction

```
<FindFolder xmlns=".../messages"
            xmlns:t=".../types"
            Traversal="Shallow">
  <FolderShape>
    <t:BaseShape>Default</t:BaseShape>
  </FolderShape>
  <Restriction>
    <t:IsEqualTo>
      <t:FieldURI FieldURI="folder:DisplayName"/>
      <t:FieldURIOrConstant>
        <t:Constant Value="Inbox"/>
      </t:FieldURIOrConstant>
    </t:IsEqualTo>
  </Restriction>
  <ParentFolderIds>
    <t:DistinguishedFolderId Id="msgfolderroot"/>
  </ParentFolderIds>
</FindFolder>
```

---

1 Search folders also surface restrictions, but in that case they are mandatory.

2 Listing 14-1 does something that we explicitly forbade you to do in Chapter 2, "May I See Your Id?" But, as an introduction to restrictions, nothing works better than doing simple comparisons against the names of the distinguished folders. So forgive our inconsistency here—just remember that you shouldn't do this in your code.

Listing 14-1 can be read as follows: "Give me all of the folders [*FindFolder*] that are found direct children [*Traversal*] of msgfolderroot [*ParentFolderIds*] and have a display name that is equal to 'Inbox' [*Restriction*]." The call in Listing 14-1 returns the following response:

```
<FindFolderResponse xmlns:m=".../messages"
                    xmlns:t=".../types"
                    xmlns=".../messages">

  <m:ResponseMessages>
    <m:FindFolderResponseMessage ResponseClass="Success">
      <m:ResponseCode>NoError</m:ResponseCode>
      <m:RootFolder TotalItemsInView="1"
                    IncludesLastItemInRange="true">
        <t:Folders>
          <t:Folder>
            <t:FolderId Id="AQAtAEFk..." ChangeKey="AQAAABYAA…"/>
            <t:DisplayName>Inbox</t:DisplayName>
            <t:TotalCount>1</t:TotalCount>
            <t:ChildFolderCount>0</t:ChildFolderCount>
            <t:UnreadCount>0</t:UnreadCount>
          </t:Folder>
        </t:Folders>
      </m:RootFolder>
    </m:FindFolderResponseMessage>
  </m:ResponseMessages>
</FindFolderResponse>
```

There is much more to restrictions than just simple property equality. You can change Listing 14-1 a bit to find all of the folders that have the substring "box" as part of their display name. Such a request should at least return the In*box* and Out*box*.

```
<FindFolder xmlns=".../messages"
            xmlns:t=".../types"
            Traversal="Shallow">
  <FolderShape>
    <t:BaseShape>Default</t:BaseShape>
  </FolderShape>
  <Restriction>
    <t:Contains ContainmentMode="Substring"
                ContainmentComparison="IgnoreCase">
      <t:FieldURI FieldURI="folder:DisplayName"/>
      <t:Constant Value="box/>
    </t:Contains>
  </Restriction>
  <ParentFolderIds>
    <t:DistinguishedFolderId Id="msgfolderroot"/>
  </ParentFolderIds>
</FindFolder>
```

Here the *Contains* expression uses a *ContainmentMode* of *Substring* to checks for partial word matches. This restriction can be read "Give me all of the folders [*FindFolder*] that are the direct children of msgfolderroot [*Traversal*] that have a display name that contains the character sequence *box*, case insensitive [*Contains* with *ContainmentComparison*]." And the response:

```
<FindFolderResponse xmlns:m=".../messages"
                    xmlns:t=".../types"
                    xmlns=".../messages">
  <m:ResponseMessages>
    <m:FindFolderResponseMessage ResponseClass="Success">
      <m:ResponseCode>NoError</m:ResponseCode>
      <m:RootFolder TotalItemsInView="2"
                    IncludesLastItemInRange="true">
        <t:Folders>
          <t:Folder>
            <t:FolderId Id="AQAtAEFkbWl…"
            <t:DisplayName>Inbox</t:DisplayName>
            <t:TotalCount>2</t:TotalCount>
            <t:ChildFolderCount>0</t:ChildFolderCount>
            <t:UnreadCount>0</t:UnreadCount>
          </t:Folder>
          <t:Folder>
            <t:FolderId Id="AQAtAEFkbW..."
            <t:DisplayName>Outbox</t:DisplayName>
            <t:TotalCount>0</t:TotalCount>
            <t:ChildFolderCount>0</t:ChildFolderCount>
            <t:UnreadCount>0</t:UnreadCount>
          </t:Folder>
        </t:Folders>
      </m:RootFolder>
    </m:FindFolderResponseMessage>
  </m:ResponseMessages>
</FindFolderResponse>
```

Now that we have introduced you to restrictions, let's look at the various pieces that you can use to create a restriction. These pieces are called *search expressions*, although we often refer to them as *filters* for the sake of brevity.

Search Expressions

All search expressions (filters) in Exchange Web Services are exposed as descendants of the *SearchExpressionType* schema type. *SearchExpressionType* is an abstract type, meaning that you will never encounter one in an instance document. Figure 14-1 shows the search expression class hierarchy exposed by Exchange Web Services.

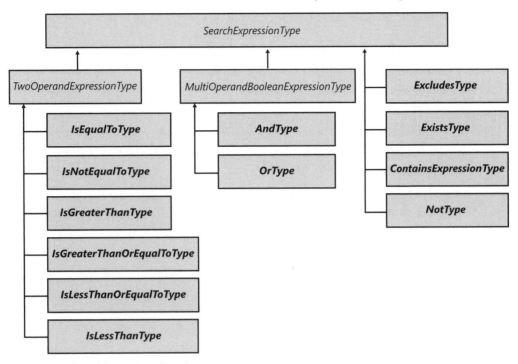

FIGURE 14-1 *SearchExpression* Hierarchy

A restriction has a tree structure. The *Restriction* element is always the root node of this tree. From there, the tree expands out based on the various filters contained within the restriction. Following the nature of a tree, you have branches and you have leaves. A branch is often called a *non-leaf.* Anyway, non-leaf filters must have other filters as children.[3] The name *non-leaf* implies that you are not at the end of the tree yet. If you start at the *Restriction* element and walk down all the branches (non-leaf filters) of your restriction, you will always end at a leaf filter. Leaf filters never have children. They are always the end. We will now discuss each filter type and how each falls into this leaf and non-leaf distinction.

TwoOperandExpressionType

TwoOperandExpressionType descends from *SearchExpressionType*. It is an abstract type, meaning that you will never encounter one of these in an instance document. *TwoOperandExpressionType* does, however, serve as the base class of all leaf filters that compare two values against each other. Listing 14-2 shows the general structure of *TwoOperandExpressionType*.

---

[3] In Exchange Web Services, there is no concept of dead or leafless branches. Analogies between computers and real life only go so far

LISTING 14-2 *TwoOperandExpressionType* structure

```
<TwoOperandExpressionType>4
  <t:FieldURI> | <t:IndexedFieldURI> | <t:ExtendedFieldURI>
  <t:FieldURIOrConstant/>
</TwoOperandExpressionType>
```

Listing 14-2 shows that the first child element is a property path. You always compare a given property on each item or folder to something. That "something" is exposed through the next child element—*FieldURIOrConstant*.

FieldURIOrConstant represents a choice of either a constant value or a property path. The unfortunate name *FieldURIOrConstant* implies that you can use only *FieldURI* property paths or constant values. Thankfully, you can use any property path type here (*FieldURI*, *IndexedFieldURI*, or *ExtendedFieldURI*). It should have been called *PropertyPathOrConstant*.

If you want to compare the first property path against the value of another property path, you use the appropriate property path child element of *FieldURIOrConstant* as follows:[5]

```
<t:FieldURIOrConstant>
  <t:FieldURI FieldURI="item:Subject"/>
</t:FieldURIOrConstant>
```

If you want to compare the first property path against a constant value, you use the *Constant* child element of *FieldURIOrConstant* as follows:

```
<t:FieldURIOrConstant>
  <t:Constant Value="some value"/>
</t:FieldURIOrConstant>
```

Table 14-1 shows the six concrete leaf expression classes derive from *TwoOperandExpressionType*.

TABLE 14-1 *TwoOperandExpressionType* **Descendants**

Filter	Description
IsEqualToType	Evaluates to true if the two arguments are exactly equal
IsNotEqualToType	Evaluates to true if the two arguments are not equal
IsGreaterThanType	Evaluates to true if the first property path has a value that is greater than the value of the second argument

---

[4] Although the general structure has a *TwoOperandExpressionType* element, this is just for illustration. *TwoOperandExpressionType* is abstract and therefore cannot appear in instance documents. In its place, you will use one of its descendant types such as *IsEqualTo*.

[5] To be exact, you are comparing the value of the property that is pointed to by the first property path in *TwoOperandSearchExpression* against a constant value, but that requires far too many words.

Filter	Description
IsGreaterThanOrEqualToType	Evaluates to true if the first property path has a value that is greater than or equal to the value of the second argument
IsLessThanType	Evaluates to true if the first property path has a value that is less than the value of the second argument
IsLessThanOrEqualToType	Evaluates to true if the first property path has a value that is less than or equal to the value of the second argument

Why *FieldURIOrConstant?*

FieldURIOrConstant is somewhat like an embarrassing relative that you hope doesn't show up at the next family gathering. This type is the result of limitations of the .NET Framework 1.1 proxy generator. When the Exchange Web Services team first designed *TwoOperandExpressionType*, they wanted to be able to compare a given item or folder property against *either* a constant value (for example, *DateTimeCreated* == "11/1/2006") or against another property (for example, *DateTimeCreated* != *DateTimeSent*). This desire implied the following XML schema:

```
<xs:complexType name="TwoOperandExpressionType" abstract="true">
  <xs:complexContent>
    <xs:extension base="t:SearchExpressionType">
      <xs:sequence>
        <xs:element ref="t:Path"/>
        <xs:choice>
          <xs:element name="Constant" type="t:ConstantValueType"/>
          <xs:element ref="t:Path"/>
        </xs:choice>
      </xs:sequence>
    </xs:extension>
  </xs:complexContent>
</xs:complexType>
```

Notice in this schema that there will always be a property path and then either a constant value or another property path. Now, when the .NET Framework 1.1 proxy generator processes this schema, it builds the proxy class for *TwoOperandExpressionType* just fine. So what is the problem? Well, when code that uses the generated proxy classes is *run*, the .NET Framework 1.1 fails when processing the *TwoOperandExpressionType* class. It returns the following error:

```
The XML element 'FieldURI' from namespace
'http://schemas.microsoft.com/exchange/services/2006/types' is already present in
the current scope. Use XML attributes to specify another XML name or namespace for
the element.
```

The issue with the XML schema for *TwoOperandExpressionType* above is that the proxy classes *could* encounter an instance document with two elements that have the same name. For example, the following instance document complies with the schema suggested above:

```
<IsEqualTo>
  <t:FieldURI FieldURI="item:Subject"/>
  <t:FieldURI FieldURI="item:DateTimeCreated"/>
</IsEqualTo>
```

The .NET Framework 1.1 proxy generator has no idea which *FieldURI* element from the preceding XML fragment to map to which property on the generated class. Does the first element go to the first property or the second property? In the .NET Framework 2.0, a new *order* .NET property attribute was created to handle this situation such that each property in the proxy class could indicate its position in the instance document. Of course, Exchange Web Services couldn't refuse to work with .NET Framwork 1.1 generated proxies, so the schema had to be modified.

As the error message indicates, the Exchange Web Services team had to remove the possibility of encountering two elements in the same scope (parent element) with the same name. To do this, a new complex type was created to represent the choice of a property path or constant value. *FieldURIOrConstantType* was born.

For instance, you could use the *IsGreaterThanType* type with a *FieldURIOrConstant* element, which looks for all items that have a *Size* property that is greater than 100,000 bytes:

```
<t:IsGreaterThan>
  <t:FieldURI FieldURI="item:Size"/>
  <t:FieldURIOrConstant>
    <t:Constant Value="100000"/>
  </t:FieldURIOrConstant>
</t:IsGreaterThan>
```

Listing 14-3 shows how this looks using the proxy classes.

LISTING 14-3 *IsGreaterThan* via the proxy classes

```
// build up our IsGreaterThan leaf filter
//
IsGreaterThanType greaterThan = new IsGreaterThanType();
PathToUnindexedFieldType sizePath = new PathToUnindexedFieldType();
sizePath.FieldURI = UnindexedFieldURIType.itemSize;
greaterThan.Item = sizePath;
FieldURIOrConstantType constant = new FieldURIOrConstantType();
ConstantValueType constantValue = new ConstantValueType();
constantValue.Value = "100000";

// Note that FieldURIOrConstantType.Item is of type object.  This is
// because it can take either a ConstantValueType instance or a property
// path such as PathToUnindexedFieldType.
//
constant.Item = constantValue;
greaterThan.FieldURIOrConstant = constant;
```

```
RestrictionType restriction = new RestrictionType();
// Set our IsGreaterThan instance to be the filter associated with our
// restriction element
//
restriction.Item = greaterThan;
```

Of course, you can also compare properties to other properties as follows:

```
<t:IsEqualTo>
  <t:FieldURI FieldURI="item:DateTimeCreated"/>
  <t:FieldURIOrConstant>
    <t:FieldURI FieldURI="item:DateTimeSent"/>
  </t:FieldURIOrConstant>
</t:IsEqualTo>
```

And the proxy class representation is as follows:

```
IsEqualToType isEqualTo = new IsEqualToType();
isEqualTo.Item = new PathToUnindexedFieldType(UnindexedFieldURIType.itemDateTimeCreated);
FieldURIOrConstantType dateTimeSent = new FieldURIOrConstantType();

// Now we will set the Item property to a property path instance
//
dateTimeSent.Item = new PathToUnindexedFieldType(UnindexedFieldURIType.itemDateTimeSent);
isEqualTo.FieldURIOrConstant = dateTimeSent;
```

What if you wanted to find all items that were sent more than a day after they were created? This would imply something like *item:DateTimeSent > item:DateTimeCreated + OneDay*. Unfortunately you can't express this using the Exchange Web Services restriction syntax To *manually* support such functionality, you would first need to create a restriction such as *item:DateTimeSent > item:DateTimeCreated*. Then you would need to manually look at each item returned by Exchange Web Services and remove the item if the difference between the created date and the sent date is less than one day.

We mentioned previously that *TwoOperandExpressionType* descendants are leaf filters. Leaf filters cannot contain other filters. It wouldn't make sense for them to do so. For instance, the following doesn't make much sense:

```
IsEqualTo(IsGreaterThan(a, 15), true).
```

IsGreaterThan evaluates to a Boolean. That means that the preceding code is the same as

```
IsGreaterThan(a, 15).
```

How about this one?

```
IsEqualTo(IsGreaterThan(a,15), false)
```

Well, that is the same as either of the following:

```
IsLessThanOrEqualTo(a, 15)
```

```
Not(IsGreaterThan(a, 15)).⁶
```

Regardless of how you approach it, it never makes sense for leaf filters to contain other filters. And, of course, the schema doesn't enable you to, so that removes the possibility. *TwoOperandExpressionType* leaf filters can contain only a property path and either another property path or a constant value.

Now that you know how to create create a single filter clause, what if you wanted to add more clauses? Suppose you wanted to find all the items with a *Size* greater than 100,000 bytes that were also sent more than a week ago? Well, you would need two leaf filters to do that— *IsGreaterThan*(size, 100000) and *IsLessThan*(sent date, a week ago). But the *Restriction* element provides for only a single child element. You must therefore combine the results of these two filters. Doing so requires a non-leaf filter element that can combine the two filters into a single result. There are three such non-leaf filters. We will discuss the simplest of these first.

NotType Search Expression

The *NotType* search expression implements a *Not* filter. To be clear, by "*Not* filter" we are not saying that it is *not* a filter. We are saying that the filter performs a logical *not* operation.⁷ Have you ever encountered someone who can take what you say and turn it completely up-side down? That person is a *Not* filter. Up is down, down is up. Now, Exchange Web Service *Not* filters are not quite so nefarious. The *Not* filter contains a single child filter element which can be either a leaf or a non-leaf filter. A *Not* filter simply takes the results from its contained filter and flips it. For instance:

```
Not(IsEqualTo(x, y))⁸ == IsNotEqualTo(x,y)
Not(IsNotEqualTo(x,y)) == IsEqualTo(x,y)
Not(IsLessThan(x,y)) == IsGreaterThanOrEqualTo(x,y)
```

And so on. Here is an example:

```
<t:Not>
  <t:IsGreaterThan>
    <t:FieldURI FieldURI="item:Size"/>
    <t:FieldURIOrConstant>
      <t:Constant Value="100000"/>
    </t:FieldURIOrConstant>
  </t:IsGreaterThan>
</t:Not>
```

---

⁶ *Not* is a unary non-leaf filter that we will discuss shortly.

⁷ By *Not operation*, we are not saying here that it isn't an operation. The operation it performs is a *NOT*. We could go on with this digression for quite a while, you know.

⁸ This is also the same as Not(Not(Not(IsEqualTo)))..

Creating the same *Not* filter using the proxy classes is as simple as wrapping the code in Listing 14-3 with a new *NotType* instance. This is shown in Listing 14-4. The new and modified lines are boldfaced.

LISTING 14-4 *Not(IsGreaterThan)* via the proxy

```
// Create our Not type
//
NotType not = new NotType();

// build up our IsGreaterThan leaf filter
//
IsGreaterThanType greaterThan = new IsGreaterThanType();
PathToUnindexedFieldType sizePath = new PathToUnindexedFieldType();
sizePath.FieldURI = UnindexedFieldURIType.itemSize;
greaterThan.Item = sizePath;
FieldURIOrConstantType constant = new FieldURIOrConstantType();
ConstantValueType constantValue = new ConstantValueType();
constantValue.Value = "100000";

// Note that FieldURIOrConstantType.Item is of type object.  This is
// because it can take either a ConstantValueType instance or a property
// path such as PathToUnindexedFieldType.
//
constant.Item = constantValue;
greaterThan.FieldURIOrConstant = constant;
not.Item = greaterThan;

RestrictionType restriction = new RestrictionType();
// Set our Not instance to be the filter associated with our restriction
// element
//
restriction.Item = not;
```

Of course, this is really the same thing as

```
<t:IsLessThanOrEqualTo>
  <t:FieldURI FieldURI="item:Size"/>
  <t:FieldURIOrConstant>
    <t:Constant Value="100000"/>
  </t:FieldURIOrConstant>
</t:IsLessThanOrEqualTo>
```

The *Not* filter seems pretty useless then, doesn't it? Well, if there were no other filter types, it would be. Fortunately, there are. We will now discuss the other two non-leaf filters, both of which work nicely with the *Not* filter.

And and *Or* Filters

Exchange Web Services exposes two more non-leaf filters. Both of these derive from the *MultipleOperandBooleanExpressionType* type. The name *MultipleOperandBooleanExpressionType* implies that these non-leaf filters can contain more than one operand. In fact, they require at least two operands to be schema valid. The *And* filter evaluates to true if and only if all of its child filter elements evaluate to true. As presented earlier, what if you wanted to find all items with a size greater than 100,000 bytes that were also sent more than a week ago? Two conditions must be true for an item to pass the filter which makes it a great candidate for the *And* filter. Let's take a look at Listing 14-5.[9]

LISTING 14-5 The *And* filter

```
<t:And>
  <t:IsGreaterThan>
    <t:FieldURI FieldURI="item:Size"/>
    <t:FieldURIOrConstant>
      <t:Constant Value="100000"/>
    </t:FieldURIOrConstant>
  </t:IsGreaterThan>
  <t:IsLessThan>
    <t:FieldURI FieldURI="item:DateTimeSent"/>
    <t:FieldURIOrConstant>
      <t:Constant Value="2006-11-03T12:00:00Z"/>
    </t:FieldURIOrConstant>
  </t:IsLessThan>
</t:And>
```

Notice that the *And* filter in Listing 14-5 contains two leaf filters, an *IsGreaterThan* filter and an *IsLessThan* filter. It would be just as valid for the *And* filter to contain non-leaf filters. For instance, notice that the *IsGreaterThan* filter is negated in Listing 14-6. Also, an additional filter element (*IsEqualTo*) is added to show that *And* can contain more than two children.

LISTING 14-6 *And* filter with more than two children

```
<t:And>
  <t:Not>
    <t:IsGreaterThan>
      <t:FieldURI FieldURI="item:Size"/>
      <t:FieldURIOrConstant>
        <t:Constant Value="100000"/>
      </t:FieldURIOrConstant>
    </t:IsGreaterThan>
  </t:Not>
  <t:IsLessThan>
    <t:FieldURI FieldURI="item:DateTimeSent"/>
    <t:FieldURIOrConstant>
```

---

[9] Note that November 3 *was* a week ago when the chapter was being written.

```
      <t:Constant Value="2006-11-03T12:00:00Z"/>
    </t:FieldURIOrConstant>
  </t:IsLessThan>
  <t:IsEqualTo>
    <t:FieldURI FieldURI="item:ItemClass"/>
    <t:Constant Value="IPM.Note"/>
  </t:IsEqualTo>
</t:And>
```

The filter in Listing 14-6 can now be read as follows: "Give me all the items where the Size is not greater than 100,000 bytes [*Not(IsGreaterThan)*] that were sent more than a week ago [*IsLessThan*] and have an *ItemClass* of IPM.Note [*IsEqualTo*]."

Listing 14-7 shows how this would look using the proxy classes.

LISTING 14-7 Proxy class example of *And* filter with more than two children

```
// first child of And --> Not(IsGreaterThan(itemSize, 100000))
//
NotType not = new NotType();

// build up our IsGreaterThan leaf filter
//
IsGreaterThanType greaterThan = new IsGreaterThanType();
PathToUnindexedFieldType sizePath = new PathToUnindexedFieldType();
sizePath.FieldURI = UnindexedFieldURIType.itemSize;
greaterThan.Item = sizePath;
FieldURIOrConstantType constant = new FieldURIOrConstantType();
ConstantValueType constantValue = new ConstantValueType();
constantValue.Value = "100000";

// Note that FieldURIOrConstantType.Item is of type object.  This is
// because it can take either a ConstantValueType instance or a property
// path such as PathToUnindexedFieldType.
//
constant.Item = constantValue;
greaterThan.FieldURIOrConstant = constant;
not.Item = greaterThan;

// second child of And --> IsLessThan(datesent, 2006-11-03T12:00:00Z)

IsLessThanType lessThan = new IsLessThanType();
PathToUnindexedFieldType dateSentPath = new PathToUnindexedFieldType();
dateSentPath.FieldURI = UnindexedFieldURIType.itemDateTimeSent;
lessThan.Item = dateSentPath;
FieldURIOrConstantType dateConstant = new FieldURIOrConstantType();
ConstantValueType dateConstantValue = new ConstantValueType();
dateConstantValue.Value = "2006-11-03T12:00:00Z";

dateConstant.Item = dateConstantValue;
lessThan.FieldURIOrConstant = dateConstant;
```

```
// last child of And --> IsEqualTo(itemClass, "IPM.Note")
//
IsEqualToType isEqualTo = new IsEqualToType();
PathToUnindexedFieldType itemClassPath = new PathToUnindexedFieldType();
itemClassPath.FieldURI = UnindexedFieldURIType.itemItemClass;
isEqualTo.Item = itemClassPath;
FieldURIOrConstantType itemClassConstant = new FieldURIOrConstantType();
ConstantValueType itemClassConstantValue = new ConstantValueType();
itemClassConstantValue.Value = "IPM.Note";

itemClassConstant.Item = itemClassConstantValue;
isEqualTo.FieldURIOrConstant = itemClassConstant;

// now, create our and.  It has three child filters
//
AndType and = new AndType();
and.Items = new SearchExpressionType[] {greaterThan, lessThan, isEqualTo };

RestrictionType restriction = new RestrictionType();
// Set our And instance to be the filter associated with our restriction
// element

restriction.Item = and;
```

Wow, that was quite a bit of code! Can you make this cleaner? Of course! Just extend the *TwoOperandExpressionType* class to include factory methods for creating both constant comparisons as well as property path comparisons. The proxy class extension is shown in Listing 14-8.

LISTING 14-8 Extension of *TwoOperandExpressionType*

```
/// <summary>
/// Extension of the TwoOperandExpressionType
/// </summary>
public partial class TwoOperandExpressionType
{
  /// <summary>
  /// Initialization method for constant value comparison
  /// </summary>
  /// <param name="path">Property path to check</param>
  /// <param name="constantValue">Constant value to check against</param>
  ///
  protected virtual void Initialize(
                    BasePathToElementType path,
                    string constantValue)
  {
    this.FieldURIOrConstant = new FieldURIOrConstantType();
    ConstantValueType constantWrapper = new ConstantValueType();
    constantWrapper.Value = constantValue;
    this.FieldURIOrConstant.Item = constantWrapper;
    this.Item = path;
  }
```

```csharp
/// <summary>
/// Initialization method for property comparison
/// </summary>
/// <param name="pathA">First property path to check</param>
/// <param name="pathB">Property path to check it against</param>
///
protected virtual void Initialize(
                    BasePathToElementType pathA,
                    BasePathToElementType pathB)
{
  this.FieldURIOrConstant = new FieldURIOrConstantType();
  this.FieldURIOrConstant.Item = pathB;
  this.itemField = pathA;
}


/// <summary>
/// Factory method for creating constant comparisons
/// </summary>
/// <typeparam name="T">Type of comparison.  Must be a
/// TwoOperandExpressionType descendant</typeparam>
/// <param name="path">Property path to check</param>
/// <param name="constantValue">Constant value to check against</param>
/// <returns>Newly constructed comparison of type T</returns>
///
public static T CreateConstantComparison<T>(
                        BasePathToElementType path,
                        string constantValue)
                            where T: TwoOperandExpressionType, new()
{
  T result = new T();
  result.Initialize(path, constantValue);
  return result;
}


/// <summary>
/// Factory method for creating comparisons of two properties
/// </summary>
/// <typeparam name="T">Type of comparison.  Must be a
/// TwoOperandExpressionType descendant</typeparam>
/// <param name="pathA">First property path to check</param>
/// <param name="pathB">Second property path to check it against</param>
/// <returns>Newly constructed comparison of type T</returns>
///
public static T CreateConstantComparison<T>(
                    BasePathToElementType pathA,
                    BasePathToElementType pathB)
                        where T : TwoOperandExpressionType, new()
{
  T result = new T();
  result.Initialize(pathA, pathB);
  return result;
}
}
```

Now, this code is a little bit unconventional, but there is a method to the madness. These factory methods were originally written as normal overloaded constructors on the *TwoOperandExpressionType* class. Of course, you can't instantiate *TwoOperandExpressionType*, you need to instantiate one of its descendants. To call the new constructor overloads, however, you must introduce those new constructors into the descendant classes just so that you can call the constructor on the base class. That means you need 12 "do-nothing" constructors (two for each descendant). Instead of going down that path, for our example we decided to create two factory methods on the base class that use C# generics to indicate which comparison class we really want to use. We use the *where* clause to restrict the specialized type to a descendant of *TwoOperandExpressionType*. Adding the *new()* constraint allows you to create an instance of the specialized type in the factory method. Of course, it also means that the specialized type must also surface a default constructor. Fortunately, since all XML serializable types must have default constructors in order to function properly, you are all set there.

We moved the initialization code into two virtual *Initialize()* methods. Should a descendant class need to do additional work, it can override either method. Otherwise, it inherits the default behavior. So, how does this partial class extension reduce the code? Compare Listing 14-7 to the updated Listing 14-9. Also, note the use of the *PathToUnindexedFieldType* extensions that were introduced in Chapter 3, "Property Paths and Response Shapes."

LISTING 14-9 Updated code using the new extensions

```
// first child of And --> Not(IsGreaterThan(itemSize, 100000))
//
NotType not = new NotType();

// build up our IsGreaterThan leaf filter
//
IsGreaterThanType greaterThan =
  TwoOperandExpressionType.CreateConstantComparison<IsGreaterThanType>(
          new PathToUnindexedFieldType(
              UnindexedFieldURIType.itemSize),
              "100000");

not.Item = greaterThan;

// second child of And --> IsLessThan(datesent, 2006-11-03T12:00:00Z)
//
IsLessThanType lessThan =
  TwoOperandExpressionType.CreateConstantComparison<IsLessThanType>(
        new PathToUnindexedFieldType(
              UnindexedFieldURIType.itemDateTimeSent),
              "2006-11-03T12:00:00Z");

// last child of And --> IsEqualTo(itemClass, "IPM.Note")
//
IsEqualToType isEqualTo =
    TwoOperandExpressionType.CreateConstantComparison<IsEqualToType>(
          new PathToUnindexedFieldType(
```

```
                    UnindexedFieldURIType.itemItemClass),
                    "IPM.Note");

// now, create our and.  It has three child filters
//
AndType and = new AndType();
and.Items = new SearchExpressionType[] {
            greaterThan, lessThan, isEqualTo };

RestrictionType restriction = new RestrictionType();
// Set our Not instance to be the filter associated with our restriction
// element
restriction.Item = and;
```

What a breath of fresh air clean and compact code can be! Of course, you could further sim-plify things by adding overloaded constructors for *AndType, NotType,* and *RestrictionType.* With a little work, you can move a lot of the boilerplate code to the partial class extensions so that you have to write the code only once.

The last of the non-leaf filters is the *Or* filter. The *Or* filter returns true if any of its child filter elements return true. For instance, if you wanted to find all items that had a subject of either *Happy* or *Sad,* you could do the following:

```
<t:Or>
  <t:IsEqualTo>
    <t:FieldURI FieldURI="item:Subject"/>
    <t:FieldURIOrConstant>
      <t:Constant Value="Happy"/>
    </t:FieldURIOrConstant>
  </t:IsEqualTo>
  <t:IsEqualTo>
    <t:FieldURI FieldURI="item:Subject "/>
    <t:FieldURIOrConstant>
      <t:Constant Value="Sad"/>
    </t:FieldURIOrConstant>
  </t:IsEqualTo>
</t:Or>
```

And of course, as with *And,* the *Or* filter can contain more than two child elements, but must not contain less. The NAND (Not And) and NOR (Not Or) Boolean operations can be achieved by wrapping *And* and *Or* in a *Not* filter respectively.

We have three more filter types to talk about, so let's keep moving.

Exists Filter

The *Exists* filter returns true if the property referenced by the property path in the filter *exists* on the item or folder in question. The structure of *Exists* is shown in Listing 14-10.

LISTING 14-10 *Exists* filter structure

```
<t:Exists>
  <t:FieldURI> | <t:IndexedFieldURI> | <t:ExtendedFieldURI>
</t:Exists>
```

Let's say there is a custom extended property called *ShoeSize* which is set on some contacts and not on others. If you wanted to determine all of the contacts that you had a shoe size for, you could use the *Exists* clause as follows:

```
<t:Exists>
  <t:ExtendedFieldURI DistinguishedPropertySetId="PublicStrings"
                      PropertyName="ShoeSize"
                      PropertyType="Double"/>
</t:Exists>
```

Or course, if you want to determine all of the contacts that you did *not* have a shoe size for, you would wrap the *Exists* filter in a *Not* filter like this:

```
<t:Not>
  <t:Exists>
    <t:ExtendedFieldURI DistinguishedPropertySetId="PublicStrings"
                        PropertyName="ShoeSize"
                        PropertyType="Double"/>
  </t:Exists>
</t:Not>
```

Now, there is a difference between a property being empty and the property not actually being there. Think of it like a post office box. You may have a post office box at the local post office, but it may not have any mail in it. However, having an empty post office box is significantly different than not having a post office box at all. The *Exists* filter checks to see if the specified property exists on an item. It doesn't care whether the property contains a value or not.

Contains Filter

The *Contains* filter enables you to perform text searches on string properties. Take a look at the structure of *Contains* in Listing 14-11.

LISTING 14-11 *Contains* structure

```
<t:Contains ContainmentMode="[mode enumeration value]"
            ContainmentComparison="[comparison enumeration value]">
  <t:FieldURI> | <t:IndexedFieldURI> | <t:ExtendedFieldURI>
  <t:Constant Value="string to search for"/>
</t:Contains>
```

The *Contains* expression exposes two required attributes. Their names are not terribly indicative of the actions that they perform, so some discussion is necessary.

ContainmentMode Attribute

The first of these attributes is the optional *ContainmentMode,* which indicates which parts of the property text value are compared to the supplied constant value. We'll admit, that description is quite vague. Looking at the possible enumeration values in Table 14-2 will hopefully clear things up.

TABLE 14-2 *ContainmentMode* **Enumeration Values**

Enumeration value	Description
FullString	Evaluates to true if the property value on the item/folder exactly matches the supplied query value
Prefixed	Evaluates to true if the property text begins with the supplied constant value
Substring	Evaluates to true if the supplied constant value appears anywhere in the property text value.
PrefixOnWords	Evaluates to true if the supplied constant value appears at the beginning of any word in the property text value.
ExactPhrase	Evaluates to true if the entire supplied query value is found within the property value; word order is preserved

Okay, so the table leaves a little to be desired too. How about some examples?

Let's say that you have a message subject of *This is an e-mail message for our Contains query.* Table 14-3 shows a couple of constant values for the Contains filter and how the *ContainmentMode* affects each.

TABLE 14-3 **Contrasting *ContainmentMode* values for (Subject: This is an e-mail message for our Contains query)**

Constant	FullString	Prefixed	Substring	ExactPhrase	PrefixOnWords
e-mail message	No	No	Yes	Yes	Yes
This is an e-mail message for our Contains query	Yes	Yes	Yes	Yes	Yes
message e-mail	No	No	No	No	No
e-ma	No	No	Yes	Yes	Yes
Thi	No	Yes	Yes	Yes	Yes
ess	No	No	Yes	Yes	Yes

It would seem reasonable to think that since Exchange Web Services exposes an *ExactPhrase ContainmentMode, Substring* would look for each word regardless of position. But because *Substring* did not match *message e-mail,* it looks like *ExactPhrase* and *Substring* do the same thing. In addition, *PrefixOnWords* should not be matching "ess" as there are no words in our supplied string that being with that character sequence. These two behaviors require some explanation.

A *FindItem* or *FindFolder* call with a restriction creates a MAPI restriction under the covers to perform the actual search. Exchange supports two different search mechanisms. The first we like to call "store" search and the second is known as content indexing (CI). The strange *ContainmentMode* behavior that we have been discussing is a result of the fact that some of the *ContainmentMode* enumeration values are applicable for store search and others are applicable for CI. To make matters worse, if the supplied *ContainmentMode* value is *not* applicable to the search technology being used to perform the search, Exchange will effectively use another *ContainmentMode* value that *is* applicable to the search technology being used.

Exchange Web Services uses store search in all of its restrictions. It just so happens that *ExactPhrase* and *PrefixOnWords* are only applicable to CI searches. Therefore, *ExactPhrase* and *PrefixOnWords* are being converted to *Substring* silently, which results in the strange behavior we have observed. As a result, you can safely ignore *ExactPhrase* and *PrefixOnWords*.

If you omit the *ContainmentMode* attribute, the containment mode will default to *FullString*.

ContainmentComparison Attribute

The second attribute of the *Contains* search expression type determines how case and non-spacing characters are considered when evaluating the filter. The available values are shown in Table 14-4.

TABLE 14-4 *ContainmentComparison* **Enumeration Values**

Enumeration Value	Description
Exact	Property value must match supplied value in case, non-spacing characters, and so on
IgnoreCase	Perform a case insensitive match
IgnoreNonSpacingCharacters	Ignore non-spacing unicode characters such as diacritical marks (accents and the like)
Loose	*IgnoreCase* and *IgnoreNonSpacingCharacters*
IgnoreCaseAndNonSpacingCharacters	Do not use
LooseAndIgnoreCase	Do not use
LooseAndIgnoreNonSpace	Do not use
LooseAndIgnoreCaseAndIgnoreNonSpace	Do not use

The enumeration values *Exact*, *IgnoreCase*, *IgnoreNonSpacingCharacters* and *Loose* are loosely related to similar values from MAPI. The cooresponding MAPI enumeration is defined as a set of flags such that you can combine the various enumeration values together to create a composite value. However, XML schema does not support flags enumerations directly. So, when the Exchange Web Services team designed the schema, they created each sensible combination of these flags. In the flags enumeration, *Exact* has a value of *0*, *IgnoreCase* a value of *1*, *IgnoreNonSpacingCharacters* a value of *2*, and *Loose* a value of *4*. But the way that it is implemented in Exchange Web Services, *Loose* is *treated* as *IgnoreCase | IgnoreNonSpacingCharacters*. As a result, the last four enumeration values in Table 14-4 above have the same meaning as *Loose*. So, use the first four enumeration values and ignore the others.

If you omit the *ContainmentComparison* attribute, the comparison will default to *Default*.

Excludes Filter

The *Excludes* filter is a bitmask operator with a twist. It returns true if the property path value in question does *not* contain any of the set bits of the user-supplied value. If any of the set bits match, *Excludes* will return false. You can see the structure of *Excludes* in Listing 14-12

LISTING 14-12 *Excludes* structure

```
<t:Excludes>
   <t:FieldURI> | <t:IndexedFieldURI> | <t:ExtendedFieldURI>
   <t:Bitmask Value="bitmask value"/>
</t:Excludes>
```

Let's consider the *Bitmask* element a bit more. When you think in terms of a bitmask, you consider values in either binary (Base-2) or hexadecimal (Base-16) format. Bitmasks just don't work well in decimal (Base-10) format. Nevertheless, Exchange Web Services does allow you to specify the *Bitmask* value in Base-10. You are also permitted to use Base-16, but unfortunately not Base-2. To specify Base-10 values, just use the value directly. For instance, here are some Base-10 values.

```
<t:Bitmask Value="2"/>
<t:Bitmask Value="125"/>
<t:Bitmask Value="111"/>
```

To specify Base-16 values, prefix your value with either *0x* or *0X*. Here are some Base-16 values.[10]

```
<t:Bitmask Value="0x2"/>
<t:Bitmask Value="0x125"/>
<t:Bitmask Value="0X111"/>
```

Now create an message that has an custom extended property called *MyFlags* of type *Integer* and give it a value of *0*.

---

[10] Of course, 111 is not the same value as 0x111. But you already knew that. We are just trying to reach our footnote quota.

```
<CreateItem xmlns=".../messages"
            xmlns:t=".../types"
            MessageDisposition="SaveOnly">
  <Items>
    <t:Message>
      <t:Subject>Message with MyFlags as Zero</t:Subject>
      <t:ExtendedProperty>
        <t:ExtendedFieldURI
              DistinguishedPropertySetId="PublicStrings"
              PropertyName="MyFlags"
              PropertyType="Integer"/>
        <t:Value>0</t:Value>
      </t:ExtendedProperty>
    </t:Message>
  </Items>
</CreateItem>
```

Now that you have created this message, you can try a couple of values in the *Excludes* filter
to see what happens. First, Listing 14-13 shows what the *FindItem* request looks like.

LISTING 14-13 *FindItem* with *Excludes*

```
<FindItem xmlns=".../messages"
          xmlns:t=".../types"
          Traversal="Shallow">
  <ItemShape>
    <t:BaseShape>IdOnly</t:BaseShape>
    <t:AdditionalProperties>
      <t:FieldURI FieldURI="item:Subject"/>
    </t:AdditionalProperties>
  </ItemShape>
  <Restriction>
    <t:Excludes>
      <t:ExtendedFieldURI
            DistinguishedPropertySetId="PublicStrings"
            PropertyName="MyFlags"
            PropertyType="Integer"/>
<!-- we will be replacing the Value of the bitmask shortly
      <t:Bitmask Value="supplied value"/>
    </t:Excludes>
  </Restriction>
  <ParentFolderIds>
    <t:DistinguishedFolderId Id="drafts"/>
  </ParentFolderIds>
</FindItem>
```

You can read this query as "Find all the items [*FindItem*] in the drafts folder [*ParentFolderIds*]
that have a *MyFlags* property that excludes the value *supplied value* represented as a bitmask.
[*Excludes*]." Now, replace *supplied value* with several valid bitmask values and see what the
results are.

Supplied Value	Result
0 or 0x0	Match
1 or 0x1	Match
156748 (or 0x2644C)	Match

What is going on here? Well, because the message has a *MyFlags* value of zero, no bits are set. Remember, *Excludes* only considers those bits that are set. So, the message in question will always pass the *Excludes* test. Now, what if you were to create another message that did *not* have the *MyFlags* property at all?

```
<CreateItem xmlns=".../messages"
            xmlns:t=".../types"
            MessageDisposition="SaveOnly">
  <Items>
    <t:Message>
      <t:Subject>Message without MyFlags</t:Subject>
    </t:Message>
  </Items>
</CreateItem>
```

What do you expect should happen? If you reissue the *FindItem* request from Listing 14-13 with a supplied value of zero, you get the following:

```
<FindItemResponse xmlns:m=".../messages"
                  xmlns:t=".../types"
                  xmlns=".../messages">
  <m:ResponseMessages>
    <m:FindItemResponseMessage ResponseClass="Success">
      <m:ResponseCode>NoError</m:ResponseCode>
      <m:RootFolder TotalItemsInView="1"
                    IncludesLastItemInRange="true">
        <t:Items>
          <t:Message>
            <t:ItemId Id="AQAtAEFkbWlu..." ChangeKey="CQAAABY..."/>
            <t:Subject>Message with MyFlags as Zero</t:Subject>
          </t:Message>
        </t:Items>
      </m:RootFolder>
    </m:FindItemResponseMessage>
  </m:ResponseMessages>
</FindItemResponse>
```

The only message that was returned was the one that had the *MyFlags* property set to zero.

Let's examine a fictitious scenario to get a better understanding of the *Excludes* filter. Imagine that you are writing a custom application using the proxy classes. Each message that comes into a shared Mailbox must be examined by inspectors 1, 2, and 3. When all of the inspectors have examined and approved the message, it can move on in the process (whatever process that is). In addition, you will add a flag to indicate how urgent the inspecting process is for this e-mail. So, to assist you, you need to define a flags enumeration as shown in Listing 14-14.

LISTING 14-14 *InspectionState* flags

```
[Flags]
public enum InspectionState
{
  None = 0,
  Inspector1 = 1,
  Inspector2 = 2,
  Inspector3 = 4,
  Urgent = 8,
}
```

So, if you have a message that has the *Inspector1* and *Urgent* flags both set, it means that the message is urgent and that Inspector1 has seen the message. As part of the custom application, you have an e-mail processing engine that uses Exchange Web Services Notifications to receive information regarding new e-mails.[11] These new e-mails are processed (somehow) and stamped with the *InspectionState* extended property. You define your own property set globally unique identifier (GUID) because this is a real-world application. The inspection state extended property path looks like this:

```
<t:ExtendedFieldURI
        PropertySetId="a879806c-03df-4750-a2b1-85ef625f959b"
        PropertyName="InspectionState"
        PropertyType="Integer"/>
```

You can use the method shown in Listing 14-15 in your email processing engine to stamp then new e-mail with the inspection state flags.

LISTING 14-15 Stamping an item with the inspection state

```
// Declare our Guid
public static readonly Guid InspectionGuid =
    new Guid("{a879806c-03df-4750-a2b1-85ef625f959b}");
public static readonly String InspectionStatePropertyName = "Inspection State";
/// <summary>
/// Stamp an existing item with our InspectionState
/// </summary>
/// <param name="binding">Service binding to use for the UpdateItem
/// call</param>
/// <param name="id">Id of existing item to stamp</param>
/// <param name="inspectionState">Inspection state</param>
///
public static void StampItemWithInspectionState(
                    ExchangeServiceBinding binding,
                    ItemIdType id,
                    InspectionState inspectionState)
{
  UpdateItemType updateRequest = new UpdateItemType();
```

---

[11] Notifications are covered in Chapter 17.

```
updateRequest.ConflictResolution = ConflictResolutionType.AutoResolve;
updateRequest.MessageDisposition = MessageDispositionType.SaveOnly;
updateRequest.MessageDispositionSpecified = true;
SetItemFieldType setItemField = new SetItemFieldType();

// Notice that we are using the ExtendedProperty extensions that we wrote
// in Chapter 13
//
PathToExtendedFieldType inspectionStatePath =
        PathToExtendedFieldType.BuildGuidName(
                InspectionGuid,
                InspectionStatePropertyName,
                MapiPropertyTypeType.Integer);

// We want to get the numeric value for this flags combination
//
ExtendedPropertyType inspectionStateProperty =
        new ExtendedPropertyType(
                inspectionStatePath,
                ((int)inspectionState).ToString());
MessageType updateMessage = new MessageType();
updateMessage.ExtendedProperty = new ExtendedPropertyType[] {
        inspectionStateProperty };

setItemField.Item = inspectionStatePath;
setItemField.Item1 = updateMessage;
ItemChangeType itemChange = new ItemChangeType();
itemChange.Item = id;
itemChange.Updates = new ItemChangeDescriptionType[] { setItemField };
updateRequest.ItemChanges = new ItemChangeType[] { itemChange };
UpdateItemResponseType response = binding.UpdateItem(updateRequest);

if (response.ResponseMessages.Items[0].ResponseCode != ResponseCodeType.NoError)
{
    throw new Exception("Stamping operation failed with response code: " +
        response.ResponseMessages.Items[0].ResponseCode.ToString());
}
}
```

So for each message that comes in, you determine how it needs to be stamped and stamp it using the *StampItemWithInspectionState* method from Listing 14-15. Each morning, a special process runs in the background and builds up a list of the messages that each inspector needs to examine during that day. Of course, urgent messages need to appear first. You identify which items are of interest by using the *Excludes* filter element. To determine the messages of interest to Inspector1, you need to find all messages that do not have the *Inspector1* flag set in the extended property, which implies the following:

```
<t:Excludes>
  <our property>
  <Bitmask Value="Inspector1's flag value"/>
</t:Excludes>
```

Or in real markup

```
<t:Excludes>
  <t:ExtendedFieldURI
        PropertySetId="a879806c-03df-4750-a2b1-85ef625f959b"
        PropertyName="InspectionState"
        PropertyType="Integer"/>
  <t:Bitmask Value="1"/>
</t:Excludes>
```

To aid in the discussion, create one message that no one has examined and one urgent one that Inspector2 has examined. Note that the first of these messages will not be stamped at all. In other words, the extended property will not be present. You have seen a number of *CreateItem* examples, so we won't show that here. The code for determining which messages are applicable to a given inspector is shown in Listing 14-16.

LISTING 14-16 Finding items for a given inspector

```
static List<ItemIdType> FindItemsForInspector(
                        ExchangeServiceBinding binding,
                        InspectionState inspector)
{
  FindItemType request = new FindItemType();
  PathToExtendedFieldType inspectionStatePath =
          PathToExtendedFieldType.BuildGuidName(
                  InspectionGuid,
                  InspectionStatePropertyName,
                  MapiPropertyTypeType.Integer);
  ExcludesType excludes = new ExcludesType();
  excludes.Item = inspectionStatePath;
  excludes.Bitmask = new ExcludesValueType();
  excludes.Bitmask.Value = ((int)inspector).ToString();

  request.Restriction = new RestrictionType();
  request.Restriction.Item = excludes;
  request.ItemShape = new ItemResponseShapeType();
  request.ItemShape.BaseShape = DefaultShapeNamesType.Default;
  request.Traversal = ItemQueryTraversalType.Shallow;
  DistinguishedFolderIdType drafts = new DistinguishedFolderIdType();

  drafts.Id = DistinguishedFolderIdNameType.drafts;
  request.ParentFolderIds = new BaseFolderIdType[] { drafts };
  FindItemResponseType response = binding.FindItem(request);
  FindItemResponseMessageType responseMessage =
  response.ResponseMessages.Items[0] as FindItemResponseMessageType;
  if (responseMessage.ResponseCode != ResponseCodeType.NoError)
  {
    throw new Exception("FindItemsForInspector failed with response code: " +
        responseMessage.ResponseCode.ToString());
  }
  List<ItemIdType> result = new List<ItemIdType>();

  // We did a normal find item (not grouped), so we should expect an array
```

```
    // of real items back
    //
    ArrayOfRealItemsType realItems = (responseMessage.RootFolder.Item as
            ArrayOfRealItemsType);
    foreach (ItemType item in realItems.Items)
    {
      result.Add(item.ItemId);
    }
    return result;
  }
```

The *Excludes* filter is used to retrieve all items that have not been processed by Inspector 1. In other words, all items where the *Inspector1* flag has not been set. Running this method returns only a single message. Can you guess why? We probably gave the answer away before, but the message that has not been inspected does not include the extended property at all and therefore will not pass the filter. In practice, this would likely indicate a bug in the custom application stamping code, but for a moment, assume that this condition is okay and that you really want to return "unstamped" messages too. Just add a *Not(Exists)* clause to the restriction. So, conceptually the new query will be "Find me all of the items that have an *InspectorState* extended property that excludes the inspector I am interested in *or* do not have an *InspectorState* extended property at all." Listing 14-17 shows how the new restriction looks for *Inspector1*.

LISTING 14-17 Adding the *Not(Exists)* clause for unstamped messages

```
<Restriction>
  <t:Or>
    <t:Excludes>
      <t:ExtendedFieldURI
        PropertySetId="a879806c-03df-4750-a2b1-85ef625f959b"
        PropertyName="InspectionState"
        PropertyType="Integer"/>
      <t:Bitmask Value="1"/>
    </t:Excludes>
    <t:Not>
      <t:Exists>
        <t:ExtendedFieldURI
          PropertySetId="a879806c-03df-4750-a2b1-85ef625f959b"
          PropertyName="InspectionState"
          PropertyType="Integer"/>
      </t:Exists>
    </t:Not>
  </t:Or>
</Restriction>
```

Calling *FindItem* with the restriction shown in Listing 14-17 returns the two records that you expect.

Special Considerations

All of the property paths that we have been using in our examples refer to properties that are stored directly on the items being filtered (for instance, the subject of a message). However as you saw in Chapter 6, "Messages," and Chapter 12, "Attachments," data about an item can also be stored within the recipient and attachment tables within the mailbox. We will now discuss the limited support for creating restrictions that consider the property values within these two tables.

Recipient Subfilters

Each message recipient in the *To, Cc, and Bcc* lines of a message will appear in the recipient table. MAPI surfaces the concept of a *subfilter*, which enables you to apply MAPI restrictions to records in the recipient table. Exchange Web Services does not allow you to create your own subfilter restrictions explicitly. Instead, you can use one of the special recipient property paths listed below within a restriction, and it will be implicitly translated into a subfilter.

- item:ToRecipients
- item:CcRecipients
- item:BccRecipients.
- calendar:RequiredAttendees
- calendar:OptionalAttendees
- calendar:Resources

These six property paths can only appear within a *Contains* filter.

When Exchange Web Services encounters a *Contains* filter with one of the six special recipient subfilter property paths, it takes the text value specified in the *Contains* filter and compares it against the Simple Mail Transfer Protocol (SMTP) address (PR_SMTP_ADDRESS) and the e-mail address (PR_EMAIL_ADDRESS) on each entry of the recipient table.[12] No other recipient properties are considered when performing implicit subfilter restrictions. Exchange Web Services does not support full MAPI subfilter restriction functionality.

You may encounter another limitation when dealing with existing search folders. Because there is no Exchange Web Services representation for subfilters (in XML), if you have an existing search folder that contains a MAPI recipient subfilter restriction that does not conform to the narrow requirements mentioned previously, Exchange Web Services will not be able to return the *syntax* of that search folder restriction. It will certainly be able to return items that the Store linked into the search folder, but if you ask Exchange Web Services to give you back

---

[12] PR_EMAIL_ADDRESS will contain the Exchange Legacy Distinguished Name (LegDN) if the recipient is in the Active Directory. If it is an external recipient, PR_EMAIL_ADDRESS will contain the SMTP address of the recipient.

the actual restriction text, you will receive an *ErrorUnsupportedTypeForConversion* response code. This may be rectified in a future release of Exchange.

So, what does a recipient subfilter query in Exchange Web Services look like? Just so that you have a better understanding of what is going on, let's create a meeting request and invite a couple of attendees, then search for messages that were sent to a particular attendee. Listing 14-18 shows the meeting request that is created and sent.

LISTING 14-18 The meeting request

```
<CreateItem xmlns=".../messages"
            xmlns:t=".../types"
            MessageDisposition="SendAndSaveCopy"
            SendMeetingInvitations="SendToAllAndSaveCopy">
  <Items>
    <t:CalendarItem>
      <t:Subject>Some Meeting Request</t:Subject>
      <t:Body BodyType="Text">Meet to discuss purchasing better
          coffee for the kitchen</t:Body>
      <t:Start>2006-12-12T17:00:00Z</t:Start>
      <t:End>2006-12-12T18:00:00Z</t:End>
      <t:RequiredAttendees>
        <t:Attendee>
          <t:Mailbox>
            <t:EmailAddress>tina.makovec@contoso.com</t:EmailAddress>
          </t:Mailbox>
        </t:Attendee>
      </t:RequiredAttendees>
      <t:OptionalAttendees>
        <t:Attendee>
          <t:Mailbox>
            <t:EmailAddress>ken.malcolmson@contoso.com</t:EmailAddress>
          </t:Mailbox>
        </t:Attendee>
      </t:OptionalAttendees>
    </t:CalendarItem>
  </Items>
</CreateItem>
```

Once the meeting request is created, you can query the Sent Items folder of the organizer to find all calendar items in which Ken is an optional attendee.

```
<FindItem xmlns=".../messages"
          xmlns:t=".../types"
          Traversal="Shallow">
  <ItemShape>
    <t:BaseShape>Default</t:BaseShape>
  </ItemShape>
  <Restriction>
    <t:Contains ContainmentMode="Substring"
                ContainmentComparison="Loose">
      <t:FieldURI FieldURI="calendar:OptionalAttendees"/>
      <t:Constant Value="ken.malcolmson"/>
```

```
      </t:Contains>
    </Restriction>
    <ParentFolderIds>
      <t:DistinguishedFolderId Id="sentitems"/>
    </ParentFolderIds>
  </FindItem>
```

Do you see the subfilter? Well, not really. A subfilter is *implied* by the fact that you are using the *calendar:OptionalAttendees* property path within a *Contains* filter element. The *Substring ContainmentMode* eliminates the need to specify the entire primary SMTP address. Because both PR_SMTP_ADDRESS and PR_EMAIL_ADDRESS are checked, using the Legacy Exchange Distinguished Name (DN) format for the *Constant* value nets the same result. If you wanted to query based on Legacy Exchange DNs, you would just change the constant value as shown here:

```
<Restriction>
  <t:Contains ContainmentMode="Substring"
              ContainmentComparison="Loose">
    <t:FieldURI FieldURI="calendar:OptionalAttendees"/>
    <t:Constant Value="/cn=Recipients/cn=Ken"/>
  </t:Contains>
</Restriction>
```

Attachment Subfilters

Attachment subfilters query the attachment table of an item in the Store. Similar to recipient subfilters, Exchange Web Services hides attachment subfilters behind the *item:Attachments* property path. For attachment subfilters, you specify a *Contains* filter with *item:Attachments* as the property path to examine, and the *display name* of the attachment as the value to compare against. Note that the display name property that is examined is the display name (proptag 0x3001001F) of the attachment in the attachments table. The structure of the restriction is exactly like the recipient subfilter example with the exception of the property path:

```
<Restriction>
  <t:Contains ContainmentMode="Substring"
              ContainmentComparison="Loose">
    <t:FieldURI FieldURI="item:Attachments"/>
    <t:Constant Value="MyAttachment.doc"/>
  </t:Contains>
</Restriction>
```

Summary

Restrictions enable you to limit the folders and items returned from *FindFolder* and *FindItem* calls, respectively. We covered all of the search expression types, how to use each of them, and how they interact with each other. We also discussed subfilters, how they are transparently represented in Exchange Web Services, and the limitations surrounding them. In the next chapter, we will discuss some of the other interesting features of *FindItem* and *FindFolder* and finally meet the Search folder.

Chapter 15
Advanced Searching

The previous chapter covered restrictions in detail. *Restrictions* are great for retrieving only those records that are interesting to you. However, other features of *FindItem* and *FindFolder* might also be of interest to you. In addition to these other features, this chapter covers search folders.

Paging

Let's say that you are writing an application with a user interface, and you want to display a list of subfolders within a given folder. Let's also assume that there are no bounds to how many folders can be contained within a given folder. How are you going to display all of those folders? What if you happen to have 10,000 subfolders? Would you like to wait for that request to come back? Most likely, you would not try to display such a large number of folders on the screen at one time. For one thing, you are limited by screen real estate. In addition, there is a really good chance that the user will not scroll through all 10,000 folders. It would be really nice to find a way to request only the data that you want to display and then make additional requests as needed for the remaining items. Welcome to paging.

If you were to take the text of this entire book and print it out on one continuous sheet of paper, you would find it quite unwieldy to deal with. Can't you imagine a professor saying, "Please roll to line number 157,203," and the despondent students unrolling their scrolls at blinding speeds to get there before the end of class? It makes much more sense to break the book into reasonably sized pages. As in the scroll example, turning to page 324 in a discretely paged book is much more feasible than trying to find that particular spot on one continuous sheet. Now, back to the folder example. What if you downloaded all 10,000 folders, and the user wanted to skip to the middle of the collection? Certainly you can do this programmatically, but you just pulled down 5,000 folders that you didn't need.

Paging enables you to pull down parts of a *FindItem/FindFolder* response that are of interest to you. *FindFolder* supports two kinds of paging via the *IndexedPageFolderView* and *FractionalPageFolderView* optional elements. *FindItem* supports four kinds of paging via the *IndexedPageItemView*, *FractionalPageItemView*, *CalendarView*, and *ContactsView* optional elements. In both *FindItem* and *FindFolder*, only one paging mechanism can be specified. *CalendarView* was discussed in Chapter 8, "Working with Calendars," and *ContactsView* was discussed in Chapter 6, "Contacts and Distribution Lists."

Indexed Paging

IndexedPageFolderView and *IndexedPageItemView* are both instances of
IndexedPageViewType. As such, we will use *FindFolder* in our examples. Just note that the construct is exactly the same when dealing with *FindItem*.

Indexed paging enables you to specify a starting point and the maximum number of folders
or items to be returned. Let's look at the structure of *IndexedPageFolderView*, which exposes
all of its settings through attributes.

```
<IndexedPageFolderView MaxEntriesReturned="100"
                       Offset="0"
                       BasePoint="[Beginning | End]"/>
```

The optional *MaxEntriesReturned* attribute indicates the maximum number of folders to
return, regardless of the number that could be returned. If the number of available folders is less than *MaxEntriesReturned*, *FindFolder* will return all available folders. Setting
MaxEntriesReturned to zero or a negative number is invalid and will result in a response code
of *ErrorInvalidPagingMaxRows*. If you do not specify *MaxEntriesReturned*, all available records
starting at the offset will be returned.

The required *Offset* attribute indicates which index to start at when returning data. The offset
is inextricably tied to the required *BasePoint* attribute. The offset indicates the index, whereas
the *BasePoint* indicates the origin of that index. With *Offset=0* and *BasePoint=Beginning*,
you are starting at the beginning of the result set. If you instead provide *Offset=0* and
BasePoint=End, then you are starting from the end of the result set.

The *BasePoint* value also suggests the direction of navigation. If you indicate a *BasePoint* of
Beginning, an *Offset* of *0*, and a *MaxEntriesReturned* of *100*, then your client will grab the first
folder and the following 99 folders. You are moving from the beginning to the end. If, however, you indicate a *BasePoint* of *End*, an *Offset* of *0*, and a *MaxEntriesReturned* of *100*, then
your client will grab the last folder and the preceding 99 folders.

It is wonderful that you can specify where you want to start and the number of rows to be
returned, but after you get your first response, how do you continue your paging? What is
the next index that you should use? When do you know that you are done? All good questions. Let's look at forward navigation in detail to see if we can answer some of them.

Forward Navigation

We have been talking about folders with 10,000 subfolders, but frankly, you probably don't
want to create that many right now. For the examples below, let's assume a folder with 100
subfolders. Just for kicks, we show this programmatically in Listing 15-1.

LISTING 15-1 Creating 100 folders via the proxy

```
public static void CreateOneHundredFolders(
                    ExchangeServiceBinding binding)
{
  CreateFolderType request = new CreateFolderType();
  DistinguishedFolderIdType inbox = new DistinguishedFolderIdType();
  inbox.Id = DistinguishedFolderIdNameType.inbox;
  request.ParentFolderId = new TargetFolderIdType();
  request.ParentFolderId.Item = inbox;
  BaseFolderType[] foldersToCreate = new BaseFolderType[100];
  for (int folderIndex = 0; folderIndex < 100; folderIndex++)
  {
    FolderType folder = new FolderType();
    folder.DisplayName = "Folder_" + folderIndex.ToString();
    foldersToCreate[folderIndex] = folder;
  }
  request.Folders = foldersToCreate;
  binding.CreateFolder(request);
}
```

Great—now there are 100 folders in the Inbox. Did you notice that was done in a single *CreateFolder* call?

With forward navigation, you can start anywhere in the result set, but you will always be moving forward. You specify forward navigation by supplying *BasePoint* of *Beginning*. Let's start at the beginning and request 10 records. To save on space, the following request receives just the id and the display name.

```
<FindFolder xmlns=".../messages"
            xmlns:t=".../types"
            Traversal="Shallow">
  <FolderShape>
    <t:BaseShape>IdOnly</t:BaseShape>
    <t:AdditionalProperties>
      <t:FieldURI FieldURI="folder:DisplayName"/>
    </t:AdditionalProperties>
  </FolderShape>
  <IndexedPageFolderView MaxEntriesReturned="10"
                         Offset="0"
                         BasePoint="Beginning"/>
  <ParentFolderIds>
    <t:DistinguishedFolderId Id="inbox"/>
  </ParentFolderIds>
</FindFolder>
```

You expect to get folder_0 through folder_9 back, based on insertion order. Figure 15-1 shows this graphically.

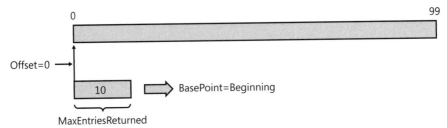

FIGURE 15-1 Forward navigation

The response shows something peculiar.

```
<FindFolderResponse xmlns:m=".../messages"
                    xmlns:t=".../types"
                    xmlns=".../messages">
  <m:ResponseMessages>
    <m:FindFolderResponseMessage ResponseClass="Success">
      <m:ResponseCode>NoError</m:ResponseCode>
      <m:RootFolder IndexedPagingOffset="10"
                    TotalItemsInView="100"
                    IncludesLastItemInRange="false">
        <t:Folders>
          <t:Folder>
            <t:FolderId Id="AQAtAEFkbWluaXNOcm…
            <t:DisplayName>Folder_0</t:DisplayName>
          </t:Folder>
          <t:Folder>
            <t:FolderId Id="AQAtAEFkbWluaXNOcmF0b3…
            <t:DisplayName>Folder_1</t:DisplayName>
          </t:Folder>
          <t:Folder>
            <t:FolderId Id="AQAtAEFkbWluaXNOcm…
            <t:DisplayName>Folder_10</t:DisplayName>
          </t:Folder>
          <t:Folder>
            <t:FolderId Id="AQAtAEFkbWluaXNOcmFtc…
            <t:DisplayName>Folder_11</t:DisplayName>
          </t:Folder>
          <t:Folder>
            <t:FolderId Id="AQAtAEFkbWluaXNOcmF0…
            <t:DisplayName>Folder_12</t:DisplayName>
          </t:Folder>
          <t:Folder>
            <t:FolderId Id="AQAtAEFkcmF0b3JAdWJtc…
            <t:DisplayName>Folder_13</t:DisplayName>
          </t:Folder>
          <t:Folder>
            <t:FolderId Id="AQAtAEFkbWluaXNOcmF0b3…
            <t:DisplayName>Folder_14</t:DisplayName>
          </t:Folder>
          <t:Folder>
            <t:FolderId Id="AQAtAEFkbWluaXNOcmF0b3JA…
            <t:DisplayName>Folder_15</t:DisplayName>
```

```
      </t:Folder>
      <t:Folder>
        <t:FolderId Id="AQAtAEFkbWluaXN0c…
        <t:DisplayName>Folder_16</t:DisplayName>
      </t:Folder>
      <t:Folder>
        <t:FolderId Id="AQAtAEFkbWluaXN0c…
        <t:DisplayName>Folder_17</t:DisplayName>
      </t:Folder>
     </t:Folders>
    </m:RootFolder>
   </m:FindFolderResponseMessage>
  </m:ResponseMessages>
</FindFolderResponse>
```

Okay, maybe not that peculiar, but the folders came back in alphabetical order by display name. Can you get this back in any other order? Nope—not for folders.[1] Alphabetical sort is your only option at this point for *FindFolder*. Any other sorting needs to occur on the client.

There is more to the response structure. Of particular interest is the *RootFolder* element.

```
<m:RootFolder IndexedPagingOffset="10"
              TotalItemsInView="100"
              IncludesLastItemInRange="false">
```

The attributes of the *RootFolder* element tell you three things. First, they tell you the next index that you should request if you want the next page. This is represented by the *IndexPagingOffset* attribute. The first request retrieved 10 items starting at index 0, so a next index of 10 makes sense. The *TotalItemsInView* attribute tells how many folders there are to retrieve in total. If you were to make a *FindFolder* request and omit the paging element, you would get this many folders in the response. The last attribute in the *RootFolder* element is *IncludesLastItemInRange*. This attribute tells whether there are more folders you need to retrieve. Once you have retrieved the very last folder from the server, *IncludesLastItemInRange* will be set to true. Because you are performing forward navigation here, the "last item" is the last folder (alphabetically). For backward navigation, the "last item" is the first folder (alphabetically).

Let's trust these attributes and make the next request using them. We are still performing forward navigation, so *BasePoint* stays the same. We don't really want to change our page size midstream, so we keep that at 10. The only thing changed is the offset.

Alphabetically, you should expect that the next folder returned is folder_18 because the last call ended with folder_17. Here is that request:

```
<FindFolder xmlns=".../messages"
            xmlns:t=".../types"
            Traversal="Shallow">
```

---

[1] You can, however, specify sorting for items (*FindItem*). This was discussed in Chapter 5, "Items."

```
<FolderShape>
  <t:BaseShape>IdOnly</t:BaseShape>
  <t:AdditionalProperties>
    <t:FieldURI FieldURI="folder:DisplayName"/>
  </t:AdditionalProperties>
</FolderShape>
<IndexedPageFolderView MaxEntriesReturned="10"
                       Offset="10"
                       BasePoint="Beginning"/>
<ParentFolderIds>
  <t:DistinguishedFolderId Id="inbox"/>
</ParentFolderIds>
</FindFolder>
```

Figure 15-2 gives a visual representation of what is going on.

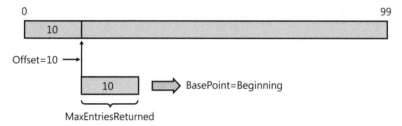

FIGURE 15-2 The second forward navigation request

The response agrees with our assumptions.

```
<FindFolderResponse xmlns:m=".../messages"
                    xmlns:t=".../types"
                    xmlns=".../messages">
  <m:ResponseMessages>
    <m:FindFolderResponseMessage ResponseClass="Success">
      <m:ResponseCode>NoError</m:ResponseCode>
      <m:RootFolder IndexedPagingOffset="20"
                    TotalItemsInView="100"
                    IncludesLastItemInRange="false">
        <t:Folders>
          <t:Folder>
            <t:FolderId Id="AQAtAEFkbWluaXN0cmF0...
            <t:DisplayName>Folder_18</t:DisplayName>
          </t:Folder>
          <t:Folder>
            <t:FolderId Id="AQAtAEFkbWluaXN0cmF0b3J...
            <t:DisplayName>Folder_19</t:DisplayName>
          </t:Folder>
          <t:Folder>
            <t:FolderId Id="AQAtAEFkbWluaXN0cmF0...
            <t:DisplayName>Folder_2</t:DisplayName>
          </t:Folder>
<!-- intervening folder element removed for brevity's sake -->
          <t:Folder>
            <t:FolderId Id="AQAtAEFkbWluaXN0cmF0b3...
```

```
         <t:DisplayName>Folder_26</t:DisplayName>
        </t:Folder>
       </t:Folders>
     </m:RootFolder>
    </m:FindFolderResponseMessage>
  </m:ResponseMessages>
</FindFolderResponse>
```

At the end of the list, the *IncludesLastItemInRange* attribute is set to true, indicating that it is done. Asking for more items than there are remaining, will return what is left. The following requests 10 records at an offset of 97 to confirm this.

```
<FindFolder xmlns=".../messages"
            xmlns:t=".../types"
            Traversal="Shallow">
  <FolderShape>
    <t:BaseShape>IdOnly</t:BaseShape>
    <t:AdditionalProperties>
      <t:FieldURI FieldURI="folder:DisplayName"/>
    </t:AdditionalProperties>
  </FolderShape>
  <IndexedPageFolderView MaxEntriesReturned="10"
                         Offset="97"
                         BasePoint="Beginning"/>
  <ParentFolderIds>
    <t:DistinguishedFolderId Id="inbox"/>
  </ParentFolderIds>
</FindFolder>
```

The response contains the three remaining folders.

```
<FindFolderResponse xmlns:m=".../messages"
                    xmlns:t=".../types"
                    xmlns=".../messages">
  <m:ResponseMessages>
    <m:FindFolderResponseMessage ResponseClass="Success">
      <m:ResponseCode>NoError</m:ResponseCode>
      <m:RootFolder IndexedPagingOffset="100"
                    TotalItemsInView="100"
                    IncludesLastItemInRange="true">
        <t:Folders>
          <t:Folder>
            <t:FolderId Id="AQAtAEFkbWluaXN0cmF0b…
            <t:DisplayName>Folder_97</t:DisplayName>
          </t:Folder>
          <t:Folder>
            <t:FolderId Id="AQAtAEFkbWluaXN0cmF0b3JA…
            <t:DisplayName>Folder_98</t:DisplayName>
          </t:Folder>
          <t:Folder>
            <t:FolderId Id="AQAtAEFkbWluaXN0cmF0b3…
            <t:DisplayName>Folder_99</t:DisplayName>
          </t:Folder>
        </t:Folders>
```

```
        </m:RootFolder>
      </m:FindFolderResponseMessage>
    </m:ResponseMessages>
</FindFolderResponse>
```

If the *Offset* is set to be greater than the total number of folders, the response has an empty
RootFolder element.

Indexed Paging Using The Proxy   We haven't forgotten about our proxy friends. Listing
15-2 shows how to issue a forward navigation, indexed page view in C# by using the proxy
objects.

LISTING 15-2 Indexed page views using the proxy

```csharp
public static void IndexedPageView(ExchangeServiceBinding binding)
{
  FindFolderType request = new FindFolderType();
  request.FolderShape = new FolderResponseShapeType();
  request.FolderShape.BaseShape = DefaultShapeNamesType.IdOnly;

  // add the additional property
  //
  PathToUnindexedFieldType displayNamePath = new PathToUnindexedFieldType();
  displayNamePath.FieldURI = UnindexedFieldURIType.folderDisplayName;
  request.FolderShape.AdditionalProperties = new BasePathToElementType[]
          { displayNamePath };

  // Set up the paging
  //
  IndexedPageViewType paging = new IndexedPageViewType();
  paging.BasePoint = IndexBasePointType.Beginning;
  paging.MaxEntriesReturned = 10;
  paging.MaxEntriesReturnedSpecified = true;
  paging.Offset = 10;

  // Yes, this is weird.  Set the paging on the Item property.
  //
  request.Item = paging;

  // Parent folders to search from
  //
  DistinguishedFolderIdType inboxId = new DistinguishedFolderIdType();
  inboxId.Id = DistinguishedFolderIdNameType.inbox;
  request.ParentFolderIds = new BaseFolderIdType[] { inboxId };
  request.Traversal = FolderQueryTraversalType.Shallow;

  FindFolderResponseType response = binding.FindFolder(request);
  FindFolderResponseMessageType responseMessage =
     response.ResponseMessages.Items[0] as FindFolderResponseMessageType;

  Console.WriteLine("Our paging results:");
  Console.WriteLine("Included last item: {0}",
      responseMessage.RootFolder.IncludesLastItemInRange);
  Console.WriteLine("Next index to fetch: {0}",
```

```
            responseMessage.RootFolder.IndexedPagingOffset);
    Console.WriteLine("Total items that can be returned: {0}",
            responseMessage.RootFolder.TotalItemsInView);
    Console.WriteLine("Items returned in THIS page: {0}",
            responseMessage.RootFolder.Folders.Length);
}
```

As shown in Figure 15-3, you get the same results that you received when posting the XML directly.

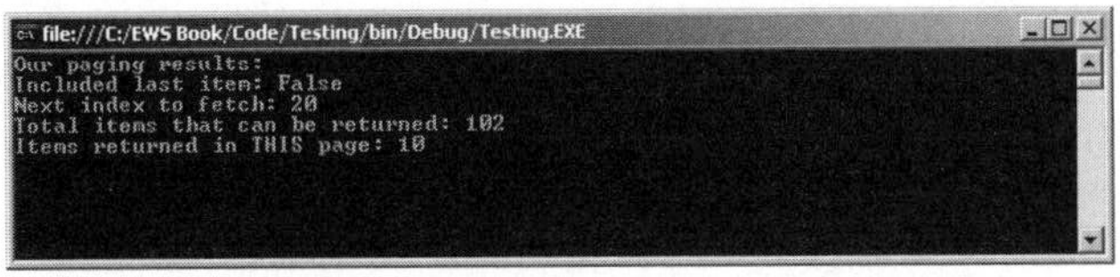

FIGURE 15-3 Running the indexed paging proxy example

Watch out for two things when doing indexed paging through the proxy objects. First, on the *FindFolder* request, the paging property is called *Item*. This has to do with how the proxy generator deals with *xs:choice* structures in a schema. If you look at the schema (messages. xsd), *FindFolderType* declares the paging element as a choice as shown here:

```
<xs:choice maxOccurs="1" minOccurs="0">
  <xs:element name="IndexedPageFolderView" type="t:IndexedPageViewType"/>
  <xs:element name="FractionalPageFolderView"
            type="t:FractionalPageViewType"/>
</xs:choice>
```

So, the schema enables you to use either an *IndexedPageFolderView* or a *FractionalPageFolderView* element. So what should the proxy class call this property? It certainly can't name the property both of these. Choosing the first one wouldn't be a good idea either. In reality, the proxy generator has no idea what to name the property. So it chooses *Item*. Unfortunately, the term *Item* has special significance in Microsoft Exchange Server 2007 Web Services (EWS). So, you are left with a confusing proxy. We discussed this all in Chapter 1, "Welcome to Exchange Web Services." In cases like these, Microsoft Visual Studio IntelliSense is your friend. Placing your cursor over the *Item* property in the drop-down list, as demonstrated in Figure 15-4, shows you that its type is *BasePagingType*.

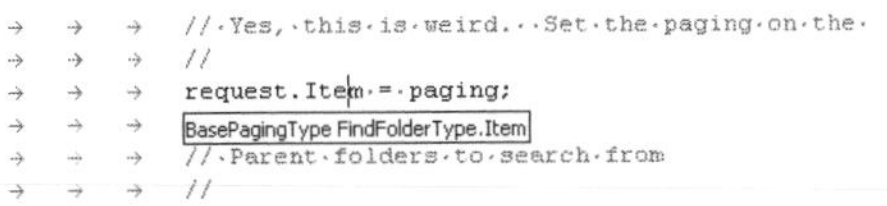

```
→    →    →    //·Yes,·this·is·weird.··Set·the·paging·on·the·
→    →    →    //
→    →    →    request.Item·=·paging;
→    →    →    │BasePagingType FindFolderType.Item│
→    →    →    //·Parent·folders·to·search·from
→    →    →    //
```

FIGURE 15-4 Visual Studio IntelliSense and the proxy

You should be able to determine from the ToolTip what property *Item* is actually referring to.

Backward Navigation

Most of the time, forward navigation meets your needs. Other times, however, you just don't feel well, and you have a strong desire to page backward through the result set. Or possibly, you have a compelling business need to do so. Regardless, you specify backward paging by setting the *BasePoint* attribute to *End*.

With backward navigation, Exchange Web Services truly turns forward navigation on its head. The *Offset* attribute indicates the number of items to move in from the end of the result set. So, an offset of 0 would start with the last item. *MaxEntriesReturned* does indicate the total number of items to return per page, but they are counted backward from the origin point. This is represented in Figure 15-5.

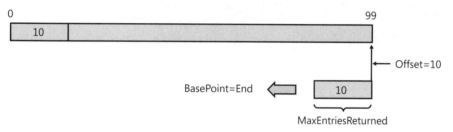

FIGURE 15-5 Backward navigation

Because you specified *BasePoint=End*, *Offset*=0 means an offset from the end. When you request records, you are moving backward through the result set. Here is that request:

```
<FindFolder xmlns=".../messages"
            xmlns:t=".../types"
            Traversal="Shallow">
  <FolderShape>
    <t:BaseShape>IdOnly</t:BaseShape>
    <t:AdditionalProperties>
      <t:FieldURI FieldURI="folder:DisplayName"/>
    </t:AdditionalProperties>
  </FolderShape>
  <IndexedPageFolderView MaxEntriesReturned="10"
                         Offset="0"
                         BasePoint="End"/>
  <ParentFolderIds>
    <t:DistinguishedFolderId Id="inbox"/>
  </ParentFolderIds>
</FindFolder>
```

Does the response match your expectation?

```
<FindFolderResponse xmlns:m=".../messages"
                    xmlns:t=".../types"
                    xmlns=".../messages">
  <m:ResponseMessages>
    <m:FindFolderResponseMessage ResponseClass="Success">
```

```
        <m:ResponseCode>NoError</m:ResponseCode>
        <m:RootFolder IndexedPagingOffset="10"
                      TotalItemsInView="100"
                      IncludesLastItemInRange="false">
          <t:Folders>
            <t:Folder>
              <t:FolderId Id="AQAtAEFkbWluaXN0cmF0b3...
              <t:DisplayName>Folder_90</t:DisplayName>
            </t:Folder>
            <t:Folder>
              <t:FolderId Id="AQAtAEFkbWluaXN0cm...
              <t:DisplayName>Folder_91</t:DisplayName>
            </t:Folder>
<!-- intervening folders omitted in the name of common decency -->
            <t:Folder>
              <t:FolderId Id="AQAtAEFkbWluaXN0cmF0b3JAdWJtcGJ...
              <t:DisplayName>Folder_99</t:DisplayName>
            </t:Folder>
          </t:Folders>
        </m:RootFolder>
      </m:FindFolderResponseMessage>
    </m:ResponseMessages>
  </FindFolderResponse>
```

Notice that the results are still returned in alphabetical order. Also, looking at the response, nothing indicates in which direction (*BasePoint*) the next indexed paging request should go. You will need to keep that straight in your own code.

Now, let's look at how the attributes from the *RootFolder* element are used in the next request.

```
<FindFolder xmlns=".../messages"
            xmlns:t=".../types"
            Traversal="Shallow">
  <FolderShape>
    <t:BaseShape>IdOnly</t:BaseShape>
    <t:AdditionalProperties>
      <t:FieldURI FieldURI="folder:DisplayName"/>
    </t:AdditionalProperties>
  </FolderShape>
  <IndexedPageFolderView MaxEntriesReturned="10"
                         Offset="10"
                         BasePoint="End"/>
  <ParentFolderIds>
    <t:DistinguishedFolderId Id="inbox"/>
  </ParentFolderIds>
</FindFolder>
```

If you continue paging until the beginning of the result set, *IncludesLastItemInRange* returns true, indicating that the traversal is completed.

Paging is an optional element. If it is not supplied, then all matching folders are returned.

Fractional Paging

With all the fun you have been having with indexed paging, it is hard to believe that there is more fun to come. With fractional paging, the origin point is determined by a numerator and denominator. Divide those values, and you will get a decimal representation of a fraction. You can go only forward with fractional paging. Of course, the introduction of a numerator and denominator means that you need to set different attributes. Let's look at those.

```
<FractionalPageFolderView MaxEntriesReturned="10"
                          Numerator="0"
                          Denominator="5"/>
```

The *MaxEntriesReturned* attribute behaves exactly as it did in indexed paging. The *Numerator* and *Denominator* together determine the offset point that is used when returning data for this page. Exchange Web Services takes the *Numerator* and *Denominator* and does the following:

```
int offset = (numerator / denominator) * TotalItemsInView;
```

Then, using that calculated offset, Exchange Web Services does indexed paging. No joke. So why would you use fractional paging? Well, when the first request comes in, you don't know the value of *TotalItemsInView*. Fractional paging enables you to index into your result set by percentage rather than using a hard offset value. Listing 15-3 shows a fractional paging request.

LISTING 15-3 Fractional paging request

```
<FindFolder xmlns=".../messages"
            xmlns:t=".../types"
            Traversal="Shallow">
  <FolderShape>
    <t:BaseShape>IdOnly</t:BaseShape>
    <t:AdditionalProperties>
      <t:FieldURI FieldURI="folder:DisplayName"/>
    </t:AdditionalProperties>
  </FolderShape>
  <FractionalPageFolderView MaxEntriesReturned="10"
                            Numerator="0"
                            Denominator="5"/>
  <ParentFolderIds>
    <t:DistinguishedFolderId Id="inbox"/>
  </ParentFolderIds>
</FindFolder>
```

The response is shown in Listing 15-4.

LISTING 15-4 Fractional paging response

```
<FindFolderResponse xmlns:m=".../messages"
                    xmlns:t=".../types"
                    xmlns=".../messages">
  <m:ResponseMessages>
    <m:FindFolderResponseMessage ResponseClass="Success">
      <m:ResponseCode>NoError</m:ResponseCode>
      <m:RootFolder NumeratorOffset="10"
                    AbsoluteDenominator="100"
                    TotalItemsInView="100"
                    IncludesLastItemInRange="false">
        <t:Folders>
          <t:Folder>
            <t:FolderId Id="AQAtAEFkbWluaXN0cmF0b3JA…
            <t:DisplayName>Folder_0</t:DisplayName>
          </t:Folder>
          <t:Folder>
            <t:FolderId Id="AQAtAEFkbWluaXN0cmF0b3JJAdW…
            <t:DisplayName>Folder_1</t:DisplayName>
          </t:Folder>
<!-- intervening folder elements were removed for brevity's sake -->
          <t:Folder>
            <t:FolderId Id="AQAtAEFkbWluaXN0cmF0b3JJAdWJtcGJ…
            <t:DisplayName>Folder_17</t:DisplayName>
          </t:Folder>
        </t:Folders>
      </m:RootFolder>
    </m:FindFolderResponseMessage>
  </m:ResponseMessages>
</FindFolderResponse>
```

Look at the *RootFolder* response element from Listing 15-4.

```
<m:RootFolder NumeratorOffset="10"
              AbsoluteDenominator="100"
              TotalItemsInView="100"
              IncludesLastItemInRange="false">
```

It has changed! Yes, it has returned and now has a new set of friends. Two of them are familiar and have the same meaning as they do for indexed paging—*TotalItemsInView* and *IncludesLastItemInRange*. The two new guests are *NumeratorOffset* and *AbsoluteDenominator*. Just like *IndexedPagingOffset*, these two values indicate the next values you should specify to continue your paging. What is interesting is that the denominator has changed. Why is that? Well, consider that the original request came in with a numerator of 0 and denominator of 5. Using the handy fractional to offset conversion provides an offset of 0.

```
0/5 * TotalItems = 0 * TotalItems = 0
```

So Exchange Web Services grabs 10 items and returns them to the caller. We are physically at an offset of 10 into our result set. Let's see how that could be expressed using 5 as a denominator.

0.5/5

Hmmm. The schema defines the numerator as an integer. No luck there. But you do know that 0.5/5 is the same thing as 10/100, right? In fact, you can always express the next integer offset to use if you make the denominator be the total number of items in the view. And that is exactly what you do.

Just to show you that fractional and indexed paging are truly related, the next request is made using fractional paging, then the fractional to indexed conversion is made. Does an indexed request give the same data? Listing 15-5 shows the next fractional request.

LISTING 15-5 The next fractional paging request

```
<FindFolder xmlns=".../messages"
            xmlns:t=".../types"
            Traversal="Shallow">
  <FolderShape>
    <t:BaseShape>IdOnly</t:BaseShape>
    <t:AdditionalProperties>
      <t:FieldURI FieldURI="folder:DisplayName"/>
    </t:AdditionalProperties>
  </FolderShape>
  <FractionalPageFolderView MaxEntriesReturned="10"
                            Numerator="10"
                            Denominator="100"/>
  <ParentFolderIds>
    <t:DistinguishedFolderId Id="inbox"/>
  </ParentFolderIds>
</FindFolder>
```

Here is the response:

```
<FindFolderResponse xmlns:m=".../messages"
                    xmlns:t=".../types"
                    xmlns=".../messages">
  <m:ResponseMessages>
    <m:FindFolderResponseMessage ResponseClass="Success">
      <m:ResponseCode>NoError</m:ResponseCode>
      <m:RootFolder NumeratorOffset="20"
                    AbsoluteDenominator="100"
                    TotalItemsInView="100"
                    IncludesLastItemInRange="false">
        <t:Folders>
          <t:Folder>
            <t:FolderId Id="AQAtAEFkbWluaXN0cmF0b3JAdWJtc…
            <t:DisplayName>Folder_18</t:DisplayName>
          </t:Folder>
```

```
      <t:Folder>
        <t:FolderId Id="AQAtAEFkbWluaXNOcmFOb3JAdW…
        <t:DisplayName>Folder_19</t:DisplayName>
      </t:Folder>
<!-- Intervening folders removed -->
      <t:Folder>
        <t:FolderId Id="AQAtAEFkbWluaXNOcmF…
        <t:DisplayName>Folder_26</t:DisplayName>
      </t:Folder>
    </t:Folders>
  </m:RootFolder>
    </m:FindFolderResponseMessage>
  </m:ResponseMessages>
</FindFolderResponse>
```

And the conversion gives an offset of 10.

```
Numerator / Denomimator * TotalItemsInView = (10/100) * 100 = 10
```

Listing 15-6 shows that value used in the following indexed paging request.

LISTING 15-6 Indexed paging request after offset conversion

```
<FindFolder xmlns=".../messages"
            xmlns:t=".../types"
            Traversal="Shallow">
  <FolderShape>
    <t:BaseShape>IdOnly</t:BaseShape>
    <t:AdditionalProperties>
      <t:FieldURI FieldURI="folder:DisplayName"/>
    </t:AdditionalProperties>
  </FolderShape>
  <IndexedPageFolderView MaxEntriesReturned="10"
                         Offset="10"
                         BasePoint="Beginning"/>
  <ParentFolderIds>
    <t:DistinguishedFolderId Id="inbox"/>
  </ParentFolderIds>
</FindFolder>
```

The response is as expected.

```
<FindFolderResponse xmlns:m=".../messages"
                    xmlns:t=".../types"
                    xmlns=".../messages">
  <m:ResponseMessages>
    <m:FindFolderResponseMessage ResponseClass="Success">
      <m:ResponseCode>NoError</m:ResponseCode>
      <m:RootFolder IndexedPagingOffset="20"
                    TotalItemsInView="100"
                    IncludesLastItemInRange="false">
        <t:Folders>
          <t:Folder>
```

```
            <t:FolderId Id="AQAtAEFkbWluaXN0cmF…
            <t:DisplayName>Folder_18</t:DisplayName>
          </t:Folder>
          <t:Folder>
            <t:FolderId Id="AQAtAEFkbWluaXNOcmFOb3…
            <t:DisplayName>Folder_19</t:DisplayName>
          </t:Folder>
<!-- Intervening folders removed -->
          <t:Folder>
            <t:FolderId Id="AQAtAEFkbWluaXNOcmFOb…
            <t:DisplayName>Folder_26</t:DisplayName>
          </t:Folder>
        </t:Folders>
      </m:RootFolder>
    </m:FindFolderResponseMessage>
  </m:ResponseMessages>
</FindFolderResponse>
```

It is interesting to note that the *NumeratorOffset* that is returned in fractional paging is always the offset that should be requested in indexed paging. Why? Because *AbsoluteDenominator* is equal to the total items in view, and the fractional part of the conversion equation is always 1, which leaves only *NumeratorOffset*.

```
Offset = (NumeratorOffset/Absolute Denominator) * TotalItemsInView

Offset = (NumeratorOffset/TotalItemsInView) * TotalItemsInView

Offset = NumeratorOffset * 1 = NumeratorOffset
```

You should know about a couple of constraints.

- Numerator must be greater than or equal to zero.

- Numerator must be less than or equal to Denominator.

- Denominator must be greater than zero.

Of course, you are by all means free to start a fractional paging request and then convert to indexed paging. For example, you could use fractional paging to start in the middle of the result set, but then use indexed to page on to the end of the result set. And the reverse is also true.

Paging and Stale Data

So, what happens if someone adds, deletes, or modifies data that should affect your query while you are in the middle of paging? That completely depends on where the item falls in the result set. If folders are added such that they fall into data you have already processed, everything shifts by the number of added folders, and your next paging request will start with the folders that the previous request ended with. If the folders are added such that they fall into data you have not yet processed, there are no negative impacts, although the *TotalItemsInView* will have increased.

If, on the other hand, folders are deleted, things shift in the other direction. So, if a folder you already processed disappears, then everything conceptually shifts to the left, and you might end up missing a folder during paging. It is good to remember that the response indexing attributes such as *IndexedPagingOffset* and *TotalItemsInView* are snapshots in time and might just change beneath you.

Of course, this can be disconcerting if you are trying to process data that is contained in a Mailbox. Let's say that your inbox has 100 items. You grab the first 10 items and process them, as in Figure 15-6.

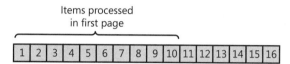

FIGURE 15-6 Grabbing the first 10 items

Unfortunately, while that is occurring, someone deletes an item from the 10 that you were looking at. As a result, all of the items after the deleted item conceptually shifted to the left by one. Note that your local copy isn't affected, but the item in the Exchange Store no longer exists. Assuming that item 10 was deleted, old item 11 has now become item 10 and so on, as you can see in Figure 15-7.

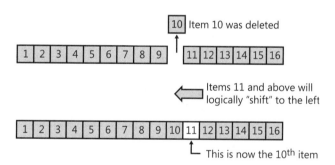

FIGURE 15-7 Deleting an item and the resulting shift

When you try to fetch the next 10 items, you will get old item 12 and so on. The result is that you missed old item 11! Nothing has happened to item 11, it was just shuffled around in the result set. Figure 15-8 shows how the items are paged after the deleting item 10.

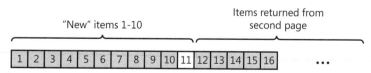

FIGURE 15-8 Grabbing the next page

That is an ugly problem. Can you do anything about this problem? Well, you can at least detect it.

As before, you want to fetch items by using pages of 10 items each. Instead of fetching 10 items though, you fetch 11. Now, you are not going to process that eleventh item, but it does tell you which item you should *expect* to be at the front of the next page. Figure 15-9 shows the item that should act as the indicator for the start of the next page.

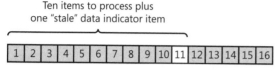

FIGURE 15-9 Fetching the page with extra indicator item

So, after processing the first 10 items, you fetch another 11 starting at an offset of 10, as shown in Figure 15-10.

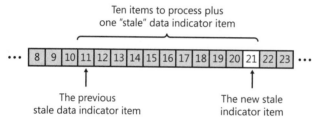

FIGURE 15-10 Fetching the next page with overlap

Then you can compare the *ItemId* of the first item in this new page with the id that you expected to start the page (your previous stale data indicator). If they do not match, then something changed beneath you, and you can start the processing again, or potentially do some backtracking to figure out what changed.

Grouped Item Queries

FindItem surfaces two mutually exclusive elements that we have deftly passed over until now. These elements enable you to indicate that the results of a *FindItem* operation should be returned in groups rather than as a flat list of items. The group that a given item will be returned in is dictated by the attributes in the grouping element. For instance, if you perform a *FindItem* against your Mailbox and group the results by sender, you should expect to get a group back for each unique sender in your Mailbox. Each group would contain the items sent by the sender represented by that group. Listing 15-7 shows the structure of the grouping elements within the *FindItem* request type as defined in messages.xsd.

LISTING 15-7 Grouping elements within *FindItem*

```
<xs:complexType name="FindItemType">
  <!-- Intervening elements removed for brevity's sake -->
  <xs:choice minOccurs="0">
    <xs:element name="GroupBy" type="t:GroupByType"/>
    <xs:element name="DistinguishedGroupBy"
                type="t:DistinguishedGroupByType"/>
  </xs:choice>
  <!-- Intervening elements removed for brevity's sake -->
</xs:complexType>
```

The schema fragment in Listing 15-7 shows that you can have zero or one instances of either (*xs:choice*) a *GroupBy* element or a *DistinguishedGroupBy* element. Let's discuss the *GroupBy* element first. It will be easier to then explain *DistinguishedGroupBy*.

GroupBy Element

The *GroupBy* element describes a user-defined grouping mechanism to apply to the results of a *FindItem* operation. Listing 15-8 shows the structure of *GroupByType* as defined in types.xsd.

LISTING 15-8 *GroupByType* basic structure

```
<GroupBy Order="Asending or Descending"
        xmlns=".../messages">
        xmlns=".../types"
  <t:FieldURI> | <t:IndexedFieldURI> | <t:ExtendedFieldURI>
  <t:AggregateOn Aggregate="Minimum or Maximum">
    <t:FieldURI> | <t:IndexedFieldURI> | <t:ExtendedFieldURI>
  </t:AggregateOn>
</GroupBy>
```

The first child element of *GroupBy* is a property path that tells which property defines the resulting groups. If you choose a property such as *item:Size*, then you will get a group for each unique item size in the folder, and all items within each group will be of that size. The *Order* attribute determines the ordering of the groups (more on this in a minute). Let's try this just for kicks. Because we haven't talked about the *AggregateOn* element, we will just throw something in there right now. Listing 15-9 shows the structure of the *GroupBy* element. To reduce the size of the response just the id, subject, and size are requested.

LISTING 15-9 Grouping by size

```
<FindItem xmlns=".../messages"
        xmlns:t=".../types"
        Traversal="Shallow">
  <ItemShape>
    <t:BaseShape>IdOnly</t:BaseShape>
    <t:AdditionalProperties>
```

```
      <t:FieldURI FieldURI="item:Subject"/>
      <t:FieldURI FieldURI="item:Size"/>
    </t:AdditionalProperties>
  </ItemShape>
  <GroupBy Order="Ascending">
    <t:FieldURI FieldURI="item:Size"/>
    <t:AggregateOn Aggregate="Maximum">
      <t:FieldURI FieldURI="item:DateTimeCreated"/>
    </t:AggregateOn>
  </GroupBy>
  <ParentFolderIds>
    <t:DistinguishedFolderId Id="drafts"/>
  </ParentFolderIds>
</FindItem>
```

The *GroupBy* element can be read as "Group the results of the *FindItem* operation so that each item is placed in a group according to the size of the item [*item:Size*]. Return the groups in ascending order [*Order* attribute]." Again, we will touch on aggregation shortly. Listing 15-10 shows the response.

LISTING 15-10 Grouped *FindItem* response

```
<FindItemResponse xmlns:m=".../messages"
                  xmlns:t=".../types"
                  xmlns=".../messages">
  <m:ResponseMessages>
    <m:FindItemResponseMessage ResponseClass="Success">
      <m:ResponseCode>NoError</m:ResponseCode>
      <m:RootFolder TotalItemsInView="6"
                    IncludesLastItemInRange="true">
        <t:Groups>
          <t:GroupedItems>
            <t:GroupIndex>138</t:GroupIndex>
            <t:Items>
              <t:Message>
                <t:ItemId Id="AAAtAEFkbWluaX...
                <t:Subject>Urgent and Inspector 2</t:Subject>
                <t:Size>138</t:Size>
                <t:DateTimeCreated>
                     2006-11-24T16:51:35Z</t:DateTimeCreated>
              </t:Message>
            </t:Items>
          </t:GroupedItems>
          <t:GroupedItems>
            <t:GroupIndex>220</t:GroupIndex>
            <t:Items>
              <t:Message>
                <t:ItemId Id="AAAtAEFkbWluaXN0...
                <t:Subject>Test27</t:Subject>
                <t:Size>220</t:Size>
                <t:DateTimeCreated>
```

```
                    2006-11-29T15:02:41Z</t:DateTimeCreated>
          </t:Message>
        </t:Items>
      </t:GroupedItems>
      <t:GroupedItems>
        <t:GroupIndex>134</t:GroupIndex>
        <t:Items>
          <t:Message>
            <t:ItemId Id="AAAtAEFkbWlu...
            <t:Subject>I am the latest one!</t:Subject>
            <t:Size>134</t:Size>
            <t:DateTimeCreated>
                    2006-11-30T20:06:53Z</t:DateTimeCreated>
          </t:Message>
        </t:Items>
      </t:GroupedItems>
      </t:Groups>
    </m:RootFolder>
  </m:FindItemResponseMessage>
 </m:ResponseMessages>
</FindItemResponse>
```

Note that the ordering is a bit weird. We will get to that shortly. You may also notice that the
TotalItemsInView is double what you might expect. We will also touch on that shortly. For
now, notice that the response is the same as a normal *FindItem* operation up to and including
the *RootFolder* element. *FindItem* operations return *FindItemResponseMessageType* instances.
Within this response message, the *RootFolder* element is of type *FindItemParentType* (defined
in types.xsd). Listing 15-11 shows that *FindItemParentType* can expose either an *Items* element or a *Groups* element.

LISTING 15-11 *FindItemParentType* schema type

```
<xs:complexType name="FindItemParentType">
  <xs:choice>
    <xs:element name="Items" type="t:ArrayOfRealItemsType"/>
    <xs:element name="Groups" type="t:ArrayOfGroupedItemsType"/>
  </xs:choice>
  <xs:attributeGroup ref="t:FindResponsePagingAttributes"/>
</xs:complexType>
```

So, what determines which of these elements will show up in the response? Well, the format
of the request does. If you make a *FindItem* call and omit the *GroupBy* element, then the returned *RootFolder* element will contain an *Item* child element (of type *ArrayOfRealItemsType*).
If you make a *FindItem* call and *include* a grouping mechanism, then the returned *RootFolder*
element will contain a *Groups* child element (of type *ArrayOfGroupedItemsType*).

Order Attribute

The request in Listing 15-9 specified an order attribute of *Ascending*. What exactly is it sorting by? Unless Exchange Web Services developers don't know how to count, it must be considering something other than the item size. Let's see if this has anything to do with aggregation.

Aggregation

This is somewhat strange, but the position of a group in the response has nothing to do with the group identifier. It actually has everything to do with aggregation. Aggregation is the process by which the items within a group are examined to determine the ordering of the group itself. Let's look at the *GroupBy* element once again in Listing 15-12.

LISTING 15-12 Examining the *GroupBy* element

```
<GroupBy Order="Descending">
  <t:FieldURI FieldURI="item:Size"/>
  <t:AggregateOn Aggregate="Maximum">
    <t:FieldURI FieldURI="item:DateTimeCreated"/>
  </t:AggregateOn>
</GroupBy>
```

When the grouping is evaluated, each *item* within a given group is examined for the value of the aggregate property path. In this case, that property is *item:DateTimeCreated*. Then *one* item from that group is nominated to represent that group. Which one? That depends on the value of the *Aggregate* attribute. In Listing 15-12, the aggregation mode is set to *"Maximum"*. This means that Exchange Web Services will look at the creation date for each item within a group and nominate the item that has the most recent (or maximum) creation date as the item to represent the group. If an *Aggregate* value of *"Minimum"* was used, then the oldest item would be used to represent the group.

Let's create some custom properties to better show this. The "group by" property is defined like this:

```
<t:ExtendedFieldURI PropertySetId="a879806c-03df-4750-a2b1-85ef625f959b"
                    PropertyName="MyGroupingProperty"
                    PropertyType="String"/>
```

The "aggregate on" property is defined like this:

```
<t:ExtendedFieldURI PropertySetId="a879806c-03df-4750-a2b1-85ef625f959b"
                    PropertyName="MyAggregateIndicator"
                    PropertyType="Integer"/>
```

Using these properties, the values in Table 15-1 can be used to create six new messages.

TABLE 15-1 **Grouping Items**

Subject	*GroupBy* Value	*AggregateOn* Value
B1	Blue	1
B2	Blue	2
B3	Blue	8
R1	Red	4
R2	Red	5
R3	Red	6

Next, the request shown in Listing 15-13 is issued.

LISTING 15-13 Grouping the response and aggregate on a custom property

```
<FindItem xmlns=".../messages"
          xmlns:t=".../types"
          Traversal="Shallow">
  <ItemShape>
    <t:BaseShape>IdOnly</t:BaseShape>
    <t:AdditionalProperties>
      <t:FieldURI FieldURI="item:Subject"/>
    </t:AdditionalProperties>
  </ItemShape>
  <GroupBy Order="Ascending">
    <t:ExtendedFieldURI
        PropertySetId="a879806c-03df-4750-a2b1-85ef625f959b"
        PropertyName="MyGroupingProperty"
        PropertyType="String"/>
    <t:AggregateOn Aggregate="Maximum">
      <t:ExtendedFieldURI
          PropertySetId="a879806c-03df-4750-a2b1-85ef625f959b"
          PropertyName="MyAggregateIndicator"
          PropertyType="Integer"/>
    </t:AggregateOn>
  </GroupBy>
  <ParentFolderIds>
    <t:DistinguishedFolderId Id="drafts"/>
  </ParentFolderIds>
</FindItem>
```

What should you expect given your understanding of aggregation? Figure 15-11 should help you through this.

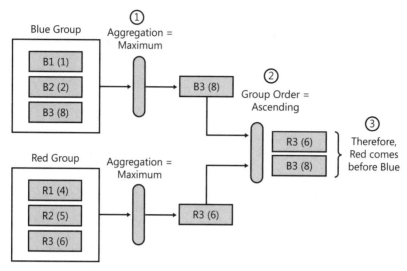

FIGURE 15-11 Maximum aggregation in action

First, you know that messages R1, R2, and R3 will end up in the Red group. Messages B1, B2, and B3 will end up in the Blue group. Because *"MyAggregateIndicator"* is used as the *aggregation* property, let's first take one of the groups (doesn't matter which) and look at the items in it. In the Blue group, B1 has an aggregate property value of 1, B2 of 2, and B3 of 8. The aggregation mode is *Maximum*, so B3 will end up representing the group because 8 is greater than 1 and 2. This is shown in step 1 in Figure 15-11.

Looking at the Red group, R1 has an aggregate property value of 4, R2 of 5, and R3 of 6. As a result, R3 will end up representing the Red group because 6 is greater than 4 and 5. So, the Red group's value is 6 and the Blue group's value is 8 (again, step 1).

Now that each group has elected a representative, how the groups themselves are ordered must be determined. The *Order* attribute (from the *GroupBy* element) indicates that the groups should be *ascending* (step 2). This implies that the Red group should come first (value of 6) and the Blue group should come second (value of 8). This is shown in step 3 in Figure 15-11. Let's see if that is the case.

```
<FindItemResponse xmlns:m=".../messages"
                  xmlns:t=".../types"
                  xmlns=".../messages">
  <m:ResponseMessages>
    <m:FindItemResponseMessage ResponseClass="Success">
      <m:ResponseCode>NoError</m:ResponseCode>
      <m:RootFolder TotalItemsInView="8" IncludesLastItemInRange="true">
        <t:Groups>
          <t:GroupedItems>
            <t:GroupIndex>Red</t:GroupIndex>
            <!-- Items omitted for brevity's sake -->
          </t:GroupedItems>
```

```
        <t:GroupedItems>
          <t:GroupIndex>Blue</t:GroupIndex>
          <!-- Items omitted for brevity's sake -->
        </t:GroupedItems>
      </t:Groups>
    </m:RootFolder>
  </m:FindItemResponseMessage>
 </m:ResponseMessages>
</FindItemResponse>
```

The results agree. If you change the *Aggregate* mode to *Minimum*, the Blue group would be represented by B1 with a value of 1 (smallest value in the group), and the Red group would be represented by R1 with a value of 4. This is still, however, performing an *Ascending Order*, so in this case the Blue group would come first (because 1 is less than 4). This is shown in Figure 15-12.

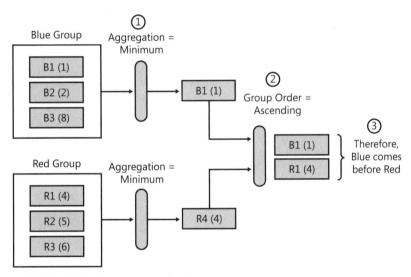

FIGURE 15-12 Minimum aggregation in action

Changing the *Order* attribute to descending turns all of the results around.

So, now you know how to deal with aggregation. Of course, we haven't really shown *why* you would want to use aggregation. To do so, we will introduce the second grouping mechanism that can be used in *FindItem* calls.

DistinguishedGroupBy Element

In Chapter 4, "Folders," we discussed distinguished folders, which are simply "well-known" folders. Distinguished folder ids provide a quick way to identify such folders. In the same way, you will use common grouping scenarios time and time again. Rather than requiring the caller to specify the grouping and aggregation values, these common scenarios are packaged as distinguished groupings. The basic structure of the element is shown in Listing 15-14.

LISTING 15-14 *DistinguishedGroupBy* structure

```
<t:DistinguishedGroupBy Order="Ascending or Descending">
  <t:StandardGroupBy>ConversationTopic</t:StandardGroupBy>
</t:DistinguishedGroupBy>
```

DistinguishedGroupByType derives from *BaseGroupByType,* which means that it inherits the *Order* attribute just like *GroupByType* does. In addition, *DistinguishedGroupByType* exposes the *StandardGroupBy* child element, which is of the enumeration type *StandardGroupByType.* Currently only one value is available in the enumeration. This value is *ConversationTopic.*

When it encounters a request with a *DistinguishedGroupBy* element, Exchange Web Services transforms it into a *GroupBy.* The *DistinguishedGroupBy* in Listing 15-14 gets turned into the *GroupBy* in Listing 15-15.

LISTING 15-15 *GroupBy* equivalent of *DistinguishedGroupBy*

```
<GroupBy Order="Ascending or Descending">
  <t:FieldURI FieldURI="message:ConversationTopic"/>
  <t:AggregateOn Aggregate="Maximum">
    <t:FieldURI FieldURI="item:DateTimeReceived"/>
  </t:AggregateOn>
</GroupBy>
```

What if you wanted to change the *Aggregate* type from *Maximum* to *Minimum*? Well, then you just need to provide your own *GroupBy* with the appropriate values. The aggregation mode is fixed in the *DistinguishedGroupBy* element.

So what exactly does this *DistinguishedGroupBy* element give you? Well, the *FindItem* response comes back in "thread" view. You have a group for each new e-mail. All the replies to that e-mail appear as children of this group. Of course, the original e-mail is also in the group. The groups themselves are sorted such that the group that has the most recently received item will appear at the top.

Aggregation is useful, although sometimes you really just want to sort the groups by the group identifiers themselves. In that case, just use the same property path for both the grouping property and the aggregation property. All items in the group will have the same value for the aggregation property so that group will be represented by the group id.

Grouped Results and *TotalItemsInView*

You may have noticed that the *TotalItemsInView* attribute that comes back does not agree with the number of items that actually match the restriction. Unfortunately, the value of that attribute is the combination of the total number of items *and* the number of groups. For instance, if you perform a grouped *FindItem* call and group by a *Boolean* property, the *TotalItemsInView* will equal the total number of items plus two. Why two? Because there are two possible groups for a *Boolean* value: *true* and *false*. Of course, if you group by something like *item:DateTimeReceived*, the number of groups is not so easily calculated. If you are not using paging, you can just look at the count of groups in your response and manually determine the number of items by subtracting the group count from *TotalItemsInView*. If, however, you are using paging, you won't know how many groups are there because you haven't fetched everything yet.

As a result, when doing grouped *FindItem* queries that are also paged, you can either ignore the *TotalItemsInView* attribute, or if you really need to know, you can do the following.

1. Perform an ungrouped *FindItem* query with indexed paging and a maximum number of records set to 1.

2. Grab the *TotalItemsInView* from that response.

3. Issue your grouped *FindItem* query and use the *TotalItemsInView* from step 1 instead of the one from step 3.

Dealing with the Results

When you use the proxy classes to process the response of a *FindItem* call, you are left bewildered by the plethora of properties named *Item*. Let's simplify this a little bit by extending the *FindItemParentType* proxy class as shown in Listing 15-16.

LISTING 15-16 Partial class extension of *FindItemParentType*

```
/// <summary>
/// Partial class extension of FindItemParentType proxy class
/// </summary>
public partial class FindItemParentType
{
  /// <summary>
  /// Returns the normal (non-grouped) results from a FindItem query for
  /// this RootFolder
  /// </summary>
  /// <returns>Array of items</returns>
  ///
  public ItemType[] GetNormalResults()
  {
    ArrayOfRealItemsType realItems = this.Item as ArrayOfRealItemsType;
```

```
    //
    return realItems.Items;
  }

  /// <summary>
  /// Returns the grouped result from a FindItem query for this RootFolder
  /// </summary>
  /// <returns>Array of groups</returns>
  ///
  public GroupedItemsType[] GetGroupedResults()
  {
    ArrayOfGroupedItemsType groupedItems = this.Item as
            ArrayOfGroupedItemsType;
    return groupedItems.Items;
  }
}
```

Now that you have these handy helper methods, Listing 15-17 shows a grouped *FindItem* query via the proxy classes using the same *item:Size* grouping from earlier in the chapter.

LISTING 15-17 Grouped *FindItem* via the proxy

```
/// <summary>
/// Grouped FindItem call using the proxy
/// </summary>
/// <param name="binding">Binding used for the call</param>
///
static void GroupedFindItemUsingProxy(ExchangeServiceBinding binding)
{
  FindItemType request = new FindItemType();
  // Set up our grouping
  //
  GroupByType grouping = new GroupByType();
  grouping.AggregateOn = new AggregateOnType();
  grouping.AggregateOn.Item = new
    PathToUnindexedFieldType(
            UnindexedFieldURIType.itemDateTimeCreated);
  grouping.AggregateOn.Aggregate = AggregateType.Maximum;
  grouping.Item = new
    PathToUnindexedFieldType(UnindexedFieldURIType.itemSize);
  grouping.Order = SortDirectionType.Ascending;

  // How intuitive!  Well, of course Item1 would be the grouping type. What
  // else could it be? :)
  request.Item1 = grouping;
  request.ItemShape = new ItemResponseShapeType();
  request.ItemShape.BaseShape = DefaultShapeNamesType.IdOnly;
  PathToUnindexedFieldType subjectPath = new
      PathToUnindexedFieldType(UnindexedFieldURIType.itemSubject);
  PathToUnindexedFieldType sizePath = new
      PathToUnindexedFieldType(UnindexedFieldURIType.itemSize);
```

```
request.ItemShape.AdditionalProperties = new
    BasePathToElementType[] { subjectPath, sizePath };

request.Traversal = ItemQueryTraversalType.Shallow;
DistinguishedFolderIdType drafts = new DistinguishedFolderIdType();
drafts.Id = DistinguishedFolderIdNameType.drafts;

request.ParentFolderIds = new BaseFolderIdType[] { drafts };
// issue our request
FindItemResponseType response = binding.FindItem(request);
FindItemResponseMessageType responseMessage =
    response.ResponseMessages.Items[0] as FindItemResponseMessageType;

// Since we did a grouped find item, we can expect to get our grouping
// response
if (responseMessage.ResponseCode == ResponseCodeType.NoError)
{
  // use our new helper method to get the grouped results out
  GroupedItemsType[] groups =
    responseMessage.RootFolder.GetGroupedResults();
  foreach (GroupedItemsType group in groups)
  {
    Console.WriteLine("Group ID: {0}", group.GroupIndex);
    foreach (ItemType item in group.Items.Items)
    {
      Console.WriteLine("        Subject: {0}, Size: {1}",
          item.Subject, item.Size);
    }
  }
}
```

The *GetGroupedResults* helper method returns an array of *GroupedItemsType* instances. Each instance represents a single group. Figure 15-13 shows the results of running the example. You will notice that there are three such groups and therefore three *GroupedItemsType* instances.

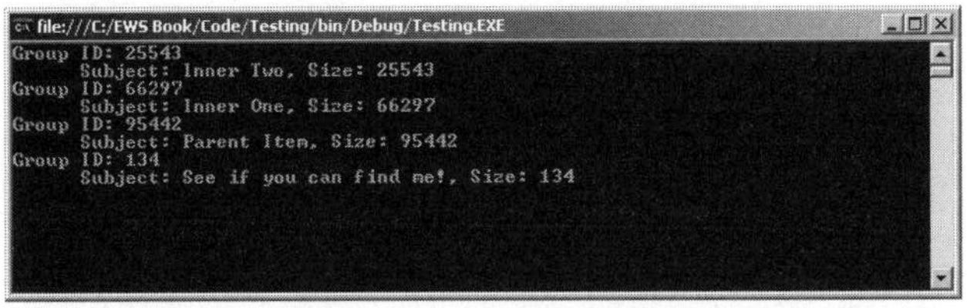

FIGURE 15-13 Results of the grouped *FindItem* example

More on the Group Identifier

Let us examine some finer points of performing a grouped query.

Grouping by a Property that Doesn't Exist for an Item

What happens if you try to group by a property that does not exist for an item? Well, it actually works just fine. The items that don't have the property set all fall into one *"NotFound"* category, although the group name is a bit odd. For example, look at this *FindItem* with the following *GroupBy* element:

```
<GroupBy Order="Descending">
  <t:ExtendedFieldURI DistinguishedPropertySetId="PublicStrings"
                      PropertyName="I Dont Exist"
                      PropertyType="String"/>
  <t:AggregateOn Aggregate="Maximum">
    <t:FieldURI FieldURI="item:DateTimeReceived"/>
  </t:AggregateOn>
</GroupBy>
```

A response comes back, but the group identifier is a bit weird.

```
<t:GroupIndex>Property = [{00020329-0000-0000-c000-000000000046}:'I Dont Exist'] GuidName_I
Dont Exist, PropertyErrorCode = NotFound, PropertyErrorCode = -2147221233</t:GroupIndex>
```

Where did this name come from? The query requested the group id property along with a bunch of other properties. Unfortunately, the group id property didn't exist on the item, so internally an error code is returned indicating that the property wasn't found. Trying to render a string version of this identifier just spills out the error information. Not pretty, but it is correct.

Acceptable Group by Properties

Which properties are acceptable for grouping? Knowing how *FindItem* works, you can expect that calculated properties are not permissible. But are all other properties acceptable? You could dig around in the code to determine this, but why put all that effort into it when you can write code to do it for you?

LISTING 15-18 Determining unacceptable *FieldURI* elements

```
/// <summary>
/// Determine which FieldURIs are unacceptable for grouping.
/// </summary>
/// <param name="binding">Binding to use</param>
///
static void DetermineUnacceptableGroupingProperties(
                ExchangeServiceBinding binding)
{
  FindItemType request = new FindItemType();

  // Set up our grouping
  //
  GroupByType grouping = new GroupByType();
```

```
grouping.AggregateOn = new AggregateOnType();
grouping.AggregateOn.Item = new
    PathToUnindexedFieldType(UnindexedFieldURIType.itemDateTimeCreated);

grouping.AggregateOn.Aggregate = AggregateType.Maximum;
grouping.Order = SortDirectionType.Ascending;
request.Item1 = grouping;

request.ItemShape = new ItemResponseShapeType();
request.ItemShape.BaseShape = DefaultShapeNamesType.IdOnly;
request.Traversal = ItemQueryTraversalType.Shallow;
DistinguishedFolderIdType drafts = new DistinguishedFolderIdType();
drafts.Id = DistinguishedFolderIdNameType.drafts;
request.ParentFolderIds = new BaseFolderIdType[] { drafts };

// Create a dictionary to hold all the invalid URIs.  Map FieldURI to
// error code.
//
Dictionary<UnindexedFieldURIType, ResponseCodeType> invalidURIs = new
        Dictionary<UnindexedFieldURIType,ResponseCodeType>();
// Grab all of the FieldURIs...
//
Array fieldURIValues = Enum.GetValues(typeof(UnindexedFieldURIType));

// Iterate across each field URI and make the call.  If we get back an
// error, add it to the dictionary
//
foreach (object value in fieldURIValues)
{
  int fieldURIInt = (int)value;
  grouping.Item = new
      PathToUnindexedFieldType((UnindexedFieldURIType)fieldURIInt);
  FindItemResponseType response = binding.FindItem(request);
  FindItemResponseMessageType responseMessage =
      response.ResponseMessages.Items[0] as FindItemResponseMessageType;
  if (responseMessage.ResponseCode != ResponseCodeType.NoError)
  {
    invalidURIs.Add(
            (UnindexedFieldURIType)fieldURIInt,
            responseMessage.ResponseCode);
  }
}
// now dump out the bad ones....
using (StreamWriter writer =
        File.CreateText(@"c:\unsupportedURIsForGrouping.txt"))
{
  writer.WriteLine("Unsupported FieldURIs for grouping");
  writer.WriteLine("===================================");
  foreach (KeyValuePair<UnindexedFieldURIType, ResponseCodeType> pair
          in invalidURIs)
  {
    writer.WriteLine("URI: {0}, Error: {1}", pair.Key, pair.Value);
  }
  writer.Flush();
}
}
```

Running this returns 82 items. The error code that comes back is
ErrorUnsupportedPathForSortGroup. The other 68 FieldURIs are therefore acceptable. Because
the acceptable list is shorter, it is presented in Table 15-2.

TABLE 15-2 Acceptable *FieldURIs* for Grouping

folderDisplayName	calendarMeetingRequestWasSent
folderUnreadCount	calendarOrganizer
folderTotalCount	calendarTimeZone
folderChildFolderCount	calendarAppointmentReplyTime
folderFolderClass	calendarAppointmentSequenceNumber
itemItemId	calendarAppointmentState
itemItemClass	calendarConferenceType
itemSubject	calendarAllowNewTimeProposal
itemDateTimeReceived	calendarIsOnlineMeeting
itemSize	calendarMeetingWorkspaceUrl
itemCategories	calendarNetShowUrl
itemImportance	contactsAssistantName
itemInReplyTo	contactsBirthday
itemInternetMessageHeaders	contactsBusinessHomePage
itemDateTimeSent	contactsChildren
itemDateTimeCreated	contactsCompanyName
itemBody	contactsDepartment
itemSensitivity	contactsDisplayName
messageConversationIndex	contactsFileAs
messageConversationTopic	contactsFileAsMapping
messageInternetMessageId	contactsGeneration
messageIsResponseRequested	contactsGivenName
messageReferences	contactsInitials
messageFrom	contactsJobTitle
messageSender	contactsManager
meetingHasBeenProcessed	contactsMiddleName
meetingRequestIntendedFreeBusyStatus	contactsMileage
calendarStart	contactsNickname
calendarEnd	contactsOfficeLocation
calendarIsAllDayEvent	contactsPostalAddressIndex
calendarLegacyFreeBusyStatus	contactsProfession
calendarLocation	contactsSpouseName
calendarWhen	contactsSurname
calendarIsRecurring	contactsWeddingAnniversary

Are you surprised to see the folder properties in this list? Can you really group messages by *folder:UnreadCount*? Well, you can try, but the response returns nothing. The ability to group by folder properties will likely go away, and because you don't get anything out of it, we suggest ignoring the fact that you can use folder properties in groups.

Grouping by Attachments

Noticeably absent from Table 15-2 is *item:HasAttachments*. Why is this? Well, the *item:HasAttachments* property is actually a calculated property. It takes into consideration whether the attachments are hidden. If an item has only hidden attachments, then *HasAttachments* will be false. You could use the *HasAttach* messaging application programming interface (MAPI) property (proptag 0x0E1B000B), although this will return true even if all the attachments are hidden. A better way to do this is to use a combination of the *HasAttach* MAPI property and another MAPI property that indicates if all attachments are hidden (Common namespace, PropertyId = 0x8514 [decimal 34068], PropertyType = Boolean). If *AllAttachmentsHidden* is true, then act as though the item has no attachments. If *AllAttachmentsHidden* is false, then you know that it does have attachments. If *AllAttachmentsHidden* is missing, but *HasAttach* is true, then treat it like there are attachments.

One downside of this is that you cannot do this simply by using grouping. Why? Because the determination of whether something has attachments is a function of *two* properties rather than one. You could use grouping, although you would end up with data that needs a little more processing before you can proceed.

If you group by *AllAttachmentsHidden*, then you can ignore the true group because it has no attachments. You would, of course, treat the false group as containing items that have attachments. Unfortunately, the group that has no *AllAttachmentsHidden* property needs to be manually examined. Treat items where *HasAttach* is true like they have an attachment. Treat items where *HasAttach* is false like they have no attachments. In other words, you have to iterate across this third group and divvy up its contents into the first two groups based on the value of *HasAttach*.

If you group by *HasAttach*, you have the same issue. If *HasAttach* is false, then you certainly don't have any attachments. If *HasAttach* is true, then you don't really know if the item has attachments. Why? Because all the attachments might be hidden. So, you really need to iterate across those items and check their *AllAttachmentsHidden* value. If the value is true, the item doesn't have any attachments. If it is false or missing, it does.

Grouping by *AllAttachmentsHidden* requires iteration across a potentially smaller fraction than *HasAttach* grouping requires. One problem with either approach is that you lose the sorting information when you redistribute items. Also, because group ordering is based on aggregation, you could potentially move an item that was chosen as the representative during aggregation from one group to another.

So what is our suggestion? If you *really* need to group by attachments, your best bet is to avoid grouping altogether and just use a standard *FindItem*, building your groups based on the response. Let's give this a shot.

LISTING 15-19 Mimicking *HasAttachments* grouping

```
/// <summary>
/// Simulates grouping by attachment
/// </summary>
/// <param name="binding">ExchangeServiceBinding to use for the
/// call</param>
/// <param name="itemsWithAttachments">OUT list of items with
/// attachments</param>
/// <param name="itemsWithNoAttachments">OUT list of items without
/// attachments</param>
///
static void GroupByHasAttachments(
            ExchangeServiceBinding binding,
            out List<ItemType> itemsWithAttachments,
            out List<ItemType> itemsWithNoAttachments)
{
    // We will perform a FindItem request and get our two "attachment"
    // related properties
    // No need to do any grouping here as we will redistribute things
    // anyways.
    //
    FindItemType request = new FindItemType();
    request.ItemShape = new ItemResponseShapeType();

    // For this example, we will get the subject and PR_HASATTACH and the
    // all attachments hidden MAPI prop
    //
    request.ItemShape.BaseShape = DefaultShapeNamesType.IdOnly;
    PathToUnindexedFieldType subjectPath = new
            PathToUnindexedFieldType(UnindexedFieldURIType.itemSubject);
    PathToExtendedFieldType hasAttachPath =
            PathToExtendedFieldType.BuildPropertyTag(
                    0x0E1B,
                    MapiPropertyTypeType.Boolean);
    PathToExtendedFieldType allAttachHiddenPath =
            PathToExtendedFieldType.BuildGuidId(
                new Guid("{00062008-0000-0000-c000-000000000046}"),
                34068,
                MapiPropertyTypeType.Boolean);

    request.ItemShape.AdditionalProperties = new BasePathToElementType[] {
                subjectPath, hasAttachPath, allAttachHiddenPath};

    request.Traversal = ItemQueryTraversalType.Shallow;
    DistinguishedFolderIdType inbox = new DistinguishedFolderIdType();
    inbox.Id = DistinguishedFolderIdNameType.inbox;
```

```
request.ParentFolderIds = new BaseFolderIdType[] { inbox };

// Issue the query
//
FindItemResponseType response = binding.FindItem(request);

// Use our handy extractor to get our ItemType array (since it was
// ungrouped)
//

ItemType[] results = ((FindItemResponseMessageType)
    response.ResponseMessages.Items[0]).RootFolder.GetNormalResults();

itemsWithAttachments = new List<ItemType>();
itemsWithNoAttachments = new List<ItemType>();

// iterate through the results and figure out which have attachments and
// which do not...
foreach (ItemType item in results)
{
  ExtendedPropertyType hasAttachProp = item.ExtendedProperty[0];
  // AllAttachHidden can be missing.  If it is, treat it as if it is
  // false.
  //
  ExtendedPropertyType allAttachHiddenProp =
      (item.ExtendedProperty.Length > 1) ?
          item.ExtendedProperty[1] : null;
  bool hasAttach = bool.Parse((string)hasAttachProp.Item);
  bool allAttachHidden = (allAttachHiddenProp == null) ?
          false : bool.Parse((string)allAttachHiddenProp.Item);

  // so if it doesn't have an attachment (hasAttach == false) then it
  // definitely is "attachment-less".
  //
  if (hasAttach)
  {
    // we need to check to see if allAttachmentsHidden is true;
    if (allAttachHidden)
    {
      itemsWithNoAttachments.Add(item);
    }
    else
    {
      itemsWithAttachments.Add(item);
    }
  }
  else
  {
    itemsWithNoAttachments.Add(item);
  }
}
Console.WriteLine("Items with attachments: " +
        itemsWithAttachments.Count);
Console.WriteLine("Items with no attachments: " +
        itemsWithNoAttachments.Count);
}
```

Search Folders

Each day, a massive amount of information moves across the globe. And some of that information reaches your Exchange Web Services Mailbox. Information workers can be inundated with an overwhelming load of items in their Mailboxes. Search folders help users easily find important information located in their Exchange Mailboxes.

Users can create search folders to help organize piles of information into custom views. This is particularly useful for those who prefer to keep their Exchange data in fewer folders holding larger amounts of information, as opposed to those who like to actively file items into custom folders. For example, users can create search folders that search for items sent by their managers so that they can easily recall that information. This type of functionality makes search folders a powerful tool for organizing views of Exchange information.

What Are Search Folders?

Search folders are "always on" searches of the Exchange database. You create them just like a custom folder, along with an additional property that contains a set of restrictions used to limit the search results for the folder. These restrictions reside in the Exchange database and are run when changes are made to the folders targeted by the search folder. Search folders can be created using an application programming interface (API) such as Exchange Web Services, or they can be added to a Mailbox by using client applications such as Microsoft Office Outlook.

Search folders can reside in any folder in the Exchange database. However, for a search folder to appear in the Search Folders folder in Outlook, the search folder must be created in the Finder folder off the Exchange Mailbox root.[2] See Chapter 4 for information about the structure of the folder hierarchy in the Exchange database.

Search folders are defined by the *SearchFolderType* schema type. *SearchFolderType* is a descendent of *FolderType,* which is a decendent of *BaseFolderType*. Figure 15-14 shows the properties inherited by *SearchFolderType*.

---

[2] Search folders outside the Finder folder appear as regular folders in Office Outlook 2007 when the application uses online mode. If Office Outlook 2007 uses cached mode, search folders do not appear in the folder hierarachy.

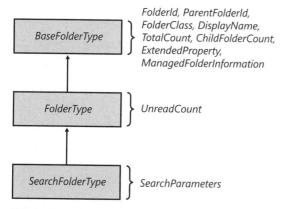

FIGURE 15-14 *SearchFolderType* hierarchy and properties

We will discuss the *SearchParameters* property shortly.

If you remember from Chapter 4, folder types can typically be determined by the folder class (*PR_CONTAINER_CLASS*) property stamped on the folder. Well, that technique falls flat when dealing with search folders. In fact, most search folders we have seen have a folder class of *IPF.Note*. Thankfully, Exchange Web Services is able to look at additional MAPI properties to determine whether a given folder is a search folder.

How Are Search Folders Created?

Search folders are created in much the same way as regular folders. The distinguishing difference between search folders and regular folders is that search folders have a property that defines the restriction used by the search folder, the traversal scope for that restriction, and the root folders to apply that restriction to. The *SearchFolderType* introduces the *SearchParameters* property, which describes how the search folder searches the Mailbox.

SearchParametersType

The *SearchParameters* property is defined by the *SearchParametersType* in types.xsd, as shown in Listing 15-20.

LISTING 15-20 *SearchParametersType* as defined in types.xsd

```
<xs:complexType name="SearchParametersType">
  <xs:sequence>
    <xs:element name="Restriction" type="t:RestrictionType"/>
    <xs:element name="BaseFolderIds"
                type="t:NonEmptyArrayOfBaseFoldersIdType"/>
  </xs:sequence>
  <xs:attribute name="Traversal" type="t:SearchFolderTraversalType"/>
</xs:complexType>
```

The *SearchParametersType* contains the following required information:

1. The *Restriction* that describes the filter. Thankfully, all the restriction nuances that you learned in Chapter 14, "Searching the Mailbox," are applicable here.

2. The folders searched by the search folder. This is identified by the *BaseFolderIds* property. This property is set with an array of *BaseFolderIdType* descendents. The array can contain *FolderIdType* and *DistinguishedFolderIdType* instances.

3. The *Traversal* of the searched folders. This describes whether the search traverses just the folders identified by the *BaseFolderIds* property (shallow), or if the traversal searches all the folders contained in the folders identified by the *BaseFolderIds* property (deep).

Now that you know what makes a search folder different from a regular folder, let's create a search folder. First, take a look at a simple request for creating a search folder (see Listing 15-21).

LISTING 15-21 Creating a search folder

```
<CreateFolder xmlns=".../messages"
              xmlns:t=".../types">
  <ParentFolderId>
    <t:DistinguishedFolderId Id="searchfolders"/>
  </ParentFolderId>
  <Folders>
    <t:SearchFolder>
      <t:DisplayName>MySearchFolder</t:DisplayName>
      <t:SearchParameters Traversal="Deep">
        <t:Restriction>
          <t:Contains ContainmentComparison="Exact"
                      ContainmentMode="Substring">
            <t:FieldURI FieldURI="item:Subject"/>
            <t:Constant Value="Status"/>
          </t:Contains>
        </t:Restriction>
        <t:BaseFolderIds>
          <t:DistinguishedFolderId Id="inbox"/>
        </t:BaseFolderIds>
      </t:SearchParameters>
    </t:SearchFolder>
  </Folders>
</CreateFolder>
```

You create the *CreateFolder* request in much the same way for search folders as for other folder types. Let's dissect the request from Listing 15-21 and examine each component in turn.[3] The following list describes each part of this XML request that defines the search folder.

- The *ParentFolderId* element contains a *DistinguishedFolderId*, which describes where the search folder should be created. Because the search folder is created in the *searchfolders* distinguished folder, it will be visible to clients such as Office Outlook in the folder named Search Folders.[4] This is because the *searchfolders* distinguished folder is an alias for the Finder folder used by clients such as Office Outlook for displaying the search folders in a user interface.

The search folder could have been created in any other folder, either a distinguished folder or a folder identified by the *FolderIdType*. The *DisplayName* element states the name of the new search folder as MySearchFolder. This is the same *DisplayName* property that is exposed on standard folders.

- The *SearchParameters* element contains the restriction, the targeted folders, and the traversal of the targeted folders as being a deep traversal.

    - The *Contains* element describes the single restriction in the request. The Restriction describes a filter on the *Subject* property for an exact comparison of any substring that equals *Status*.

    - The *DistinguishedFolderId* element in the *BaseFolderIds* element describes the folder searched by the Restriction. In this example, the targeted folder is the Inbox. This value can be either a distinguished folder or a folder identified by the *FolderIdType*. As suggested by the nature of the element name, *BaseFolderIds* can contain a plurarlity of target or root folders from which to perform the search.[5]

As you would expect, the *CreateFolder* call from Listing 15-21 returns the *FolderId* for the newly created search folder. Listing 15-22, shows this response. Notice how the local name of the returned folder element is indeed *SearchFolder*.

LISTING 15-22 *CreateFolder* (*SearchFolder*) response

```
<CreateFolderResponse xmlns:m=".../messages"
                      xmlns:t=".../types"
                      xmlns=".../messages">
  <m:ResponseMessages>
    <m:CreateFolderResponseMessage ResponseClass="Success">
      <m:ResponseCode>NoError</m:ResponseCode>
```

---

[3] Although this request creates a single search folder, you can create multiple search folders in a single *CreateFolder* request by specifying multiple *SearchFolder* elements.

[4] Note that you could have specified the *FolderId* for the Finder folder with the same effect. The distinguished folder id just makes life a little easier for such well-known folders.

[5] Note, however, that the results of the search folder are squished together into a single result set. This is in contrast to *FindItem/FindFolder*, which return a distinct array of items for each root folder passed in.

```
    <m:Folders>
      <t:SearchFolder>
        <t:FolderId Id="AAAtAEFkbWl...
      </t:SearchFolder>
    </m:Folders>
  </m:CreateFolderResponseMessage>
 </m:ResponseMessages>
</CreateFolderResponse>
```

Let's take a look at Listing 15-23 to see how this request is constructed using the proxy objects.

LISTING 15-23 Creating the first search folder by using the proxy classes

```
/// <summary>
/// Creates a search folder
/// </summary>
/// <param name="binding">binding to use</param>
///
public static void FirstProxySearchFolder(ExchangeServiceBinding binding)
{
  // Create the request.
  //
  CreateFolderType request = new CreateFolderType();
  // Identify the parent folder.
  //
  request.ParentFolderId = new TargetFolderIdType();
  DistinguishedFolderIdType searchFolders = new
                DistinguishedFolderIdType();
  searchFolders.Id = DistinguishedFolderIdNameType.searchfolders;
  request.ParentFolderId.Item = searchFolders;

  // Identify a single folder to create.
  SearchFolderType mySearchFolder = new SearchFolderType();
  mySearchFolder.DisplayName = "MySearchFolder";

  // Identify the search parameter information.
  //
  mySearchFolder.SearchParameters = new SearchParametersType();
  mySearchFolder.SearchParameters.Traversal =
                    SearchFolderTraversalType.Deep;
  mySearchFolder.SearchParameters.TraversalSpecified = true;

  // Identify the folders to search.  Use just the inbox for right now.
  //
  DistinguishedFolderIdType[] folders = new DistinguishedFolderIdType[1];
  folders[0] = new DistinguishedFolderIdType();
  folders[0].Id = DistinguishedFolderIdNameType.inbox;
  mySearchFolder.SearchParameters.BaseFolderIds = folders;

  // Identify the restriction to filter the inbox items.
  //
```

```
RestrictionType restriction = new RestrictionType();
PathToUnindexedFieldType itemSubject = new PathToUnindexedFieldType();
itemSubject.FieldURI = UnindexedFieldURIType.itemSubject;
ContainsExpressionType contains = new ContainsExpressionType();
contains.Item = itemSubject;
ConstantValueType constant = new ConstantValueType();
constant.Value = "Status";
contains.Constant = constant;
contains.ContainmentComparison = ContainmentComparisonType.Exact;
contains.ContainmentComparisonSpecified = true;
contains.ContainmentMode = ContainmentModeType.Substring;
contains.ContainmentModeSpecified = true;
restriction.Item = contains;

// Set the restriction on our search parameters.
//
mySearchFolder.SearchParameters.Restriction = restriction;

// Add the search folder to the request.
//
request.Folders = new BaseFolderType[1];
request.Folders[0] = mySearchFolder;

// Send the request and get the response.
CreateFolderResponseType response = binding.CreateFolder(request);

// Cast to the appropriate response type. We assume only a single
// response message since a single search folder is created.
FolderInfoResponseMessageType firmt = response.ResponseMessages.Items[0]
            as FolderInfoResponseMessageType;
if (firmt.ResponseCode == ResponseCodeType.NoError)
{
    Console.WriteLine("New folder id is :" +
                firmt.Folders[0].FolderId.Id);
}
else
{
    Console.WriteLine("Folder not created. Error code: " +
                firmt.ResponseCode.ToString());
}
}
```

Retrieving Your Search Folder

Now, given that you know how to create a search folder, it seems reasonable that you should be able to retrieve the search folder along with the restriction that you originally set. Before you get too far, however, let's get something straight. There are two ways to look at a search folder. First, you can look at the search folder definition itself. Just like a normal folder, a search folder has the standard *DisplayName*, *ParentFolderId*, and other properties. In addition, you have seen that *SearchFolderType* exposes this nifty *SearchParameters* property. When you retrieve the search folder via *GetFolder* or find the search folder via *FindFolder*, all you are doing is returning the *folder definition itself*.

This needs to be contrasted with the second way of looking at a search folder, which is looking at the "contents" of a given search folder. You can think of this second way as the *effects* of applying the search folder criteria to the Mailbox. We will get to this second view shortly.

In the meantime, what does the search folder *itself* look like (that is, the first view of the search folder)? The best way to see it is to call *GetFolder* on the returned *FolderId* from Listing 15-23. Note that you specify the *AllProperties* response shape because the *SearchParameters* property does not exist in the *Default* response shape for *SearchFolders*. Alternatively, you could specify the *searchfolder:SearchParameters* property path in the *AdditionalProperties* node of the response shape. By now, the *GetFolder* request should look quite familiar.

```
<GetFolder xmlns=".../messages"
           xmlns:t=".../types">
  <FolderShape>
    <t:BaseShape>AllProperties</t:BaseShape>
  </FolderShape>
  <FolderIds>
    <t:FolderId Id="AAAtAEFk…
  </FolderIds>
</GetFolder>
```

What is interesting is the response, which is shown in Listing 15-24.

LISTING 15-24 *GetFolder* response for the search folder

```
<GetFolderResponse xmlns:m=".../messages"
                   xmlns:t=".../types"
                   xmlns=".../messages">
  <m:ResponseMessages>
    <m:GetFolderResponseMessage ResponseClass="Success">
      <m:ResponseCode>NoError</m:ResponseCode>
      <m:Folders>
        <t:SearchFolder>
          <t:FolderId Id="AAAtAEFkbWl...
          <t:ParentFolderId Id="AQAtAEFkbWl...
          <t:FolderClass>IPF.Note</t:FolderClass>
          <t:DisplayName>MySearchFolder</t:DisplayName>
          <t:TotalCount>0</t:TotalCount>
          <t:ChildFolderCount>0</t:ChildFolderCount>
          <t:UnreadCount>0</t:UnreadCount>
          <t:SearchParameters Traversal="Deep">
            <t:Restriction>
              <t:Contains ContainmentMode="Substring"
                          ContainmentComparison="Exact">
                <t:FieldURI FieldURI="item:Subject"/>
                <t:Constant Value="Status"/>
              </t:Contains>
```

```
            </t:Restriction>
            <t:BaseFolderIds>
             <t:FolderId Id="AQAtAEFkbWlu...
            </t:BaseFolderIds>
          </t:SearchParameters>
        </t:SearchFolder>
      </m:Folders>
    </m:GetFolderResponseMessage>
  </m:ResponseMessages>
</GetFolderResponse>
```

Hey—that kind of looks like the search folder that was created earlier! Here are a couple of noteworthy things before we move ahead.

- The *FolderClass* is set to IPF.Note. You can just ignore this for search folders. The matching items are a function of the restriction (search criteria) stamped on the search folder. The *FolderClass* has nothing to do with it.

- *TotalCount* truly reflects the number of matching items that pass the restriction stamped on the search folder.

- *ChildFolderCount* is always zero. Why? Because a search folder cannot contain other folders. Go ahead—try it and see. If you try to create a subfolder within a search folder, you are greeted by the *ErrorInvalidParentFolder* response code.

- The Inbox *BaseFolderId* changed from a distinguished folder id into a folder id. Yes, that's right. Note that it is indeed the same folder—the restriction parser just did not map the folder id back to its distinguished counterpart. That shouldn't be a problem, though. If you really need to see whether the base folder id is a distinguished folder id, use the *GetAllDistinguishedFolderIds* method defined in Chapter 2, "May I See Your Id?" to get the FolderId for the Inbox and compare it with the FolderId from your restriction.

Updating Your Search Folder

So you have created your handy search folder that will save you hours of time wading through old e-mails. But, oh! You didn't mean to look for *status* in your subject line! You meant to look for *statii*.[6] Of course, you could delete the folder and create a new one with your updated search criteria. Instead, it's best to simply update your existing search folder and set the new search criteria as shown in Listing 15-25.

---

[6] Which is the unofficial plural form of *status*.

LISTING 15-25 *UpdateFolder* call to change the search folder restriction

```
<UpdateFolder xmlns=".../messages"
              xmlns:t=".../types">
  <FolderChanges>
    <t:FolderChange>
      <t:FolderId Id="AAAtAEFkbWl...
      <t:Updates>
        <t:SetFolderField>
          <t:FieldURI FieldURI="folder:SearchParameters"/>
          <t:SearchFolder>
            <t:SearchParameters Traversal="Deep">
              <t:Restriction>
                <t:Contains ContainmentMode="Substring"
                            ContainmentComparison="Exact">
                  <t:FieldURI FieldURI="item:Subject" />
                  <t:Constant Value="statii" />
                </t:Contains>
              </t:Restriction>
              <t:BaseFolderIds>
                <t:DistinguishedFolderId Id="inbox" />
              </t:BaseFolderIds>
            </t:SearchParameters>
          </t:SearchFolder>
        </t:SetFolderField>
      </t:Updates>
    </t:FolderChange>
  </FolderChanges>
</UpdateFolder>
```

Following the pattern of the other *UpdateFolder* calls you saw in Chapter 4, you simply set the property path that you want to update (*folder:SearchParameters* in this case) and then define the content of the actual property via the *SearchParameters* element. Notice how the *SearchParameters* element is contained in the *SearchFolder* element. That should make sense because the *SearchParameter* element appears only once in the schema—as a child of the *SearchFolderType*.

After making the *UpdateFolder* call from Listing 15-25, Exchange Web Services responds with the folder id and updated change key for the modified search folder.

What Else Can Be Done Once Search Folders Are Created?

Search folders are handled in much the same way as other Exchange Web Services folders. Aside from the *GetFolder* and *UpdateFolder* operations you have already seen in this chapter, you can perform the following operations on search folders.

- *CopyFolder/MoveFolder* Search folders can be moved just like other folders. Copying and moving search folders does not change the contents of the search folder.

- *DeleteFolder* Search folders are deleted just like other folders.

Refer to Chapter 4 for more information about operations that can be performed on folders.

Search Folders and the *FindItem* Operations

We mentioned earlier that there are two ways to "look" at a search folder. The first is looking at the search folder definition (the metadata, if you will) of the folder itself. That is fine and dandy for certain purposes, but it is likely that the reason you created the search folder in the first place is that you *wanted the filtered data!* However, search folders are strange beasts because they offer up a collection of items that passes the search folder's search criteria, yet those items don't actually *live* in the search folder. Want proof? Create a search folder that matches all items in your Inbox with an *item:Size* that is greater than zero. Then delete the search folder.[7] Phew! Deleting the search folder does *not* delete the items that match the search folder.

Given that a search folder does not actually contain the items that match the query, how do you retrieve the list of matching items? Thankfully, *FindItem* is smart enough to know that it is dealing with a search folder, and it acts as if the search folder does indeed house those items.

```
<FindItem xmlns=".../messages"
          xmlns:t=".../types"
          Traversal="Shallow">
  <ItemShape>
    <t:BaseShape>IdOnly</t:BaseShape>
  </ItemShape>
  <ParentFolderIds>
    <t:FolderId Id="AAAtAEFkbWluaX...
  </ParentFolderIds>
</FindItem>
```

Hey, that looks just like any other *FindItem* call! Yes, indeed it does. In fact, all of the facilities of *FindItem* are available to you. Did you notice that the *SearchParameters* property defined for the search folder did not have any information about sorting, grouping, or paged views? Have no fear—you can specify those in your call to *FindItem*.

Remember that *FindItem* also surfaces a *Restriction*. You can apply a restriction in your *FindItem* call that will further filter the items surfaced by your search folder. However, don't re-apply the same filter that you defined when you created your search folder. That is simply a waste of resources. In addition, if you find yourself repeatedly calling *FindItem* with a certain restriction on an existing search folder, you should probably consider whether the two restrictions should be combined into one and simply set on your search folder. Then you can call *FindItem* without any restriction element.

---

[7] Note that deleting items found using a search folder will truly delete them.

The *FindItem/SearchFolder* Balancing Act

In Chapters 4 and 14, you saw how you can query a Mailbox by using the *FindItem* call. In this chapter, you have seen how you can create a *SearchFolder* to define a virtual folder and then get its contents by using the *FindItem* call. Well, if both of these end up with a *FindItem* call, where would you ever use search folders?

Table 15-3 compares the functionality provided by search folders and the *FindItem* operation.

TABLE 15-3 Comparing *SearchFolders* and *FindItem*

Functionality/Property	Search Folders	*FindItem* Operation
Search multiple folders	X	X
Soft-deleted traversal		X
Deep traversal	X	
Support restrictions	X	X

So, why should you use search folders? They are useful for creating views that client applications often reference. So if a client application often uses a specific *FindItem* operation, you should consider the query a candidate for creating a search folder. The following list describes the differences between search folders and *FindItem* calls.

- One difference between search folders and a *FindItem* query is the permanence of the search. A *FindItem* call with a Restriction causes a dynamic restriction to be created. This restriction will "expire" after three days, or potentially earlier if it gets bumped due to other restrictions being created. In contrast, a search folder restriction lives as long as the search folder does.

- Another difference is that search folders support deep traversal searches, whereas *FindItem* with Restrictions does not.

- A third difference is that search folders combine the results from the *BaseFolderIds* that the search is run against, whereas *FindItem* keeps the results for each parent folder id separate.

Note *FindItem* queries are more appropriate than search folders for queries constructed from user input and queries that change often. However, we do not recommend using Exchange Web Services as an ad-hoc query tool due to the performance implications of dynamic filters.

Exchange Web Services Search Folder Quirks

Search folders are a great feature, and it is exciting that Exchange Web Services provides support for them. That said, Exchange Web Services isn't a model player in a couple cases that you should be aware of. Note that these are active issues that the Exchange Web Services design team is looking into addressing in a future release of Exchange Web Services.

Partial Support for MAPI Restrictions

The Exchange Web Services restriction syntax is a large subset of the restriction syntax supported by MAPI. Exchange Web Services is particularly weak when it comes to subfilter queries. MAPI supports complex queries against both the recipient and attachment tables. Now, when you looked at the *GetFolder* Web method earlier in this chapter, you saw that you can retrieve the actual restriction clause stamped on the search folder by using the *AllProperties* base shape or by specifying the *folder:SearchParameters* additional property in the response shape.

What do you think will happen when you try to retrieve the search parameters for an existing folder when the associated MAPI restriction contains clauses that are unsupported by Exchange Web Services? Ah, yes, it dies—albeit in a calm and gentle way. In such a case, it will return a response code such as *ErrorUnsupportedQueryFilter*. Now, this does not mean that anything is wrong with your search folder. It just means that Exchange Web Services cannot render the restriction clause. Before you get all up in arms, note that Exchange Web Services is able to use that search folder in a *FindItem* call just fine. You can get all the matching items. It is only the rendering of the actual restriction clause in XML that is limited at this point.

If you want to see this in action, try to call *GetFolder* with *AllProperties* against one of the standard Outlook search folders such as Large Mail.

Subfilters Not Supported for Office Outlook Search Folders

When you create a search folder under the Finder folder, something special happens. Exchange Web Services internally creates the search folder as an Office Outlook-visible folder, which means that the folder is stamped with all sorts of wonderful MAPI properties and gets associated with a Folder Associated Item (FAI) message that convinces Office Outlook to display the search folder. Part of that process is writing the restriction information to the associated FAI message. Unfortunately, any subfilter restrictions are not written to the information correctly. As such, you cannot create any Office Outlook-visible search folders that use the following property paths within the restriction.

- item:Attachments

- message:ToRecipients

- message:CcRecipients

- message:BccRecipients

- calendar:RequiredAttendees

- calendar:OptionalAttendees

- calendar:Resources

If you are willing to live with a search folder that is not visible to Office Outlook, you can certainly create such search folders outside of the Finder folder. Such search folders do not have the FAI messages, and so the whole restriction information generation code is skipped. This may be fixed in a future release of Exchange.

Summary

This chapter discussed using *FindItem* and *FindFolder* to search folder items and folders in your Mailbox. Aside from *Restrictions,* which were discussed in the previous chapter, you can further control the data that your request returns via paging and grouping. Paging plays a big part in responsive applications—only get the data you need! We then took an in-depth look at grouped queries. Grouping applies only to *FindItem* but gives you extensive control over how groups are formed and the order in which they are returned. We had a discussion of the *HasAttachments* property and how we can work around the fact that it is a calculated property.

You can use search folders to create custom views on one or more folders based on a specific restriction (filter). Items that are within the folder scope and that pass the filter defined by the search folder criteria are viewed as if they are actually "in" the search folder. These persistent views make running *common* queries against your Mailbox an easy endeavor because the Mailbox server maintains the index for you, thus paving the way for a responsive, snappy system. However, this snappiness comes at a price. Search folders can be a heavy load on the Mailbox server if not used in moderation. Use search folders for frequently used, unchanging queries (think *Unread items*) and use *FindItem* with restrictions for less frequent queries so that such restrictions can be timed out by the server to free up resources.[8]

---

[8] More than three days between invocations.

Part IV
Keeping You in the Loop

Chapter 16
Synchronization

What Is Synchonization?

Synchronization, also known as Sync, has become an increasingly important technology over the past few years. Sync helps solve the problem of maintaining up-to-date information on multiple devices. These days, people can have computers at work, computers at home, PDAs, and Smart phones. Inevitably, users want to be able to

- Work on the latest versions of documents, whether at work or at home.

- Transfer files between their work computers and their PDAs.

- Have their calendars, contacts, and e-mail available and up to date on their mobile devices.

Because of this great interest in keeping everything up-to-date, Microsoft Exchange Server 2007 Web Services (EWS) includes Sync functionality.

If you are writing an application that needs to keep an offline copy of some or all data in an Exchange mailbox, then Sync is a valuable tool.[1]

Exchange Web Services Sync enables you to retrieve an initial copy of the folders and items within an Exchange mailbox and then keep that copy up-to-date. Both the initial copy as well as the ongoing synchronization are performed using the *SyncFolderHierarchy* Web method (for folders) and *SyncFolderItems* Web method (for items). It is important to keep in mind that Exchange Web Services Sync is one-way, meaning that data comes from Exchange Web Services to your client application. Exchange Web Services Sync does not provide a mechanism for propagating local changes back to Exchange Web Services. If you need to make changes to data contained within an Exchange mailbox, you must use the other Exchange Web Services methods described in previous chapters, such as *CreateFolder/CreateItem*, *UpdateFolder/UpdateItem*, and *DeleteFolder/DeleteItem*.

---

[1] Notifications also help you to maintain synchronized copies of Exchange mailbox data and will be discussed in Chapter 17, "Notification."

Syncing the Folder Hierarchy

Maintaining an accurate copy (or snapshot) of the folder hierarchy contained within an Exchange mailbox is the realm of the aptly named *SyncFolderHierarchy* Web method. Listing 16-1 shows the basic structure of a *SyncFolderHierarchy* request.

LISTING 16-1 Basic structure of a *SyncFolderHierarchy* request

```
<SyncFolderHierarchy xmlns=".../messages">
  <FolderShape/>
  <SyncState/>
</SyncFolderHierarchy>
```

As shown in Listing 16-1, *SyncFolderHierarchy* is a relatively simple operation consisting of two child elements, *FolderShape* and *SyncState*.

FolderShape Element

The required *FolderShape* element is an instance of *FolderResponseShapeType*, which you became familiar with in Chapter 3, "Property Paths and Response Shapes." Syncing the folder hierarchy is a data retrieval operation, and therefore you must tell Exchange Web Services which properties should be returned for folders contained in the response. The *FolderShape* element behaves in the same manner as it does in *GetFolder* with one somewhat significant limitation.

In Chapter 3, we mentioned that when making a *GetItem* or *GetFolder* call, any additional properties that are requested must be applicable for the folder or item type whose id you are requesting. So, if you call *GetFolder* on the Inbox folder and request the *folder:SearchParameters* property path, you should expect to get back an error response code (*ErrorInvalidPropertyRequest* to be exact). Of course, since you know which folder you are requesting, you will likely know the type of the folder and therefore you will know which additional properties you are allowed to request.

In contrast to *GetFolder*, *SyncFolderHierarchy* returns a *set* of folders, *not* in response to a corresponding set of requested ids, but as a result of the folder modifications that have occurred in the Exchange mailbox. As such, you will likely have no idea what folder types will be returned by *SyncFolderHierarchy*, which also means that you will likely have no idea which additional properties are applicable to the folders that will be returned. Whether *SyncFolderHierarchy* succeeds or fails with *ErrorInvalidPropertyRequest* depends on the additional properties that are requested and the actual folder types that are returned.

With this limitation in mind, if you are going to specify additional properties within the *FolderShape* of a *SyncFolderHierarchy* request, make sure that they are either extended property paths or that the property paths are applicable to *BaseFolderType* so that they make sense for all possible folder types.[2] Thankfully, there are only two folder property paths that fall into the "don't use" camp: *folder:UnreadCount* and *folder:SearchParameters*. If you want the folder unread count to be returned, you must specify a base shape of either *Default* or *AllProperties* since *folder:UnreadCount* is included in both of these base shapes for folders. If you want the search folder parameters to be returned, you must specify a base shape of *AllProperties* since *folder:SearchParameters* is included in the *AllProperties* base shape for search folders. You should not specify either *folder:UnreadCount* or *folder:SearchParameters* in the *AdditionalProperties* element of the *FolderShape* for *SyncFolderHierarchy*. Doing so will lead to intermittent failures depending on the folder types that *SyncFolderHierarchy* returns.

> **Important** As a rule of thumb, for *SyncFolderHierarchy* requests, use the *AdditionalProperties* element of *FolderShape* only for extended property paths or property paths that are applicable to *BaseFolderType*.

Listing 16-2 shows a request that would return the *SearchParameters* property on any applicable search folders.

LISTING 16-2 *SyncFolderHierarchy* request for returning *SearchParameters* on modified *SearchFolders*

```
<SyncFolderHierarchy xmlns=".../messages">
  <FolderShape>
    <t:BaseShape>AllProperties</t:BaseShape>
  </FolderShape>
</SyncFolderHierarchy>
```

SyncState Element

The second and last element in a *SyncFolderHierarchy* request is the optional *SyncState* element. If the *SyncFolderHierarchy* Web method returns changes that have occurred to the folder and folder hierarchy within a mailbox, the *SyncState* answers the question "since when?" If Exchange Web Services did not expose the ability to answer the *SyncState* question, then *SyncFolderHierarchy* would behave like *FindFolder* and would be superfluous. The *SyncState* element is defined in the schema as a string. Just like folder ids and change keys, the contents of the *SyncState* should be considered opaque.

Of course, the first time you call *SyncFolderHierarchy*, you don't have a *SyncState* that you can supply, which is precisely why the element is optional. Listing 16-2 showed a *SyncFolderHierarchy* request. Listing 16-3 shows the response.

---

2 See Chapter 3, Table 3-3 for the property paths that are applicable to *BaseFolderType*.

LISTING 16-3 Initial *SyncFolderHierarchy* response

```
<m:SyncFolderHierarchyResponse xmlns:t=".../types"
                               xmlns:m=".../messages">
  <m:ResponseMessages>
    <m:SyncFolderHierarchyResponseMessage ResponseClass="Success">
      <m:ResponseCode>NoError</m:ResponseCode>
      <m:SyncState>H4sIAAAAAAAEAO29B2A...</m:SyncState>
      <m:IncludesLastFolderInRange>true</m:IncludesLastFolderInRange>
      <m:Changes>
        <!-- Contents elided for brevity -->
      </m:Changes>
    </m:SyncFolderHierarchyResponseMessage>
  </m:ResponseMessages>
</m:SyncFolderHierarchyResponse>
```

There are several elements of interest in Listing 16-3, but for right now, we want to draw your attention to the *SyncState* element. Remember the question that *SyncState* answers. The response in Listing 16-3 can be thought of as, "Here are the changes that occurred to the mailbox in question up to this *SyncState* value." While the *SyncState* that is passed in with the request answers the question, "Since *when?*", the response *SyncState* sets the boundary for the changes returned in the response. The *SyncFolderHierarchy* response then makes the claim, "Here are the changes up to this new *SyncState* value."

To explore this boundary further, look at Listing 16-4 where the *SyncFolderHierarchy* is requested again, but this time with the *SyncState* from Listing 16-3 included in the request.

LISTING 16-4 *SyncFolderHierarchy* request with a *SyncState*

```
<SyncFolderHierarchy xmlns=".../messages">
  <FolderShape>
    <t:BaseShape>AllProperties</t:BaseShape>
  </FolderShape>
  <SyncState>H4sIAAAAAAAEAO29B2A...</SyncState>
</SyncFolderHierarchy>
```

The response is shown in Listing 16-5.

LISTING 16-5 *SyncFolderHierarchy* response with no changes

```
<m:SyncFolderHierarchyResponse xmlns:t=".../types"
                               xmlns:m=".../messages">
  <m:ResponseMessages>
    <m:SyncFolderHierarchyResponseMessage ResponseClass="Success">
      <m:ResponseCode>NoError</m:ResponseCode>
      <m:SyncState>H4sIAAAAAAAEAO29B2A...</m:SyncState>
      <m:IncludesLastFolderInRange>true</m:IncludesLastFolderInRange>
      <m:Changes/>
    </m:SyncFolderHierarchyResponseMessage>
  </m:ResponseMessages>
</m:SyncFolderHierarchyResponse>
```

If you look at Listing 16-5, you will notice that the *Changes* element is empty, indicating that no changes have occurred to the folder hierarchy since the point in time that the *SyncState* supplied in the request represents. Also notice that the response includes the *SyncState* element. It is reasonable to assume that a response with no changes would also give back the same *SyncState* that was passed into the request. In fact, Listing 16-6 verifies this assumption.

LISTING 16-6 Verification that *SyncState* changes correspond with actual folder modifications

```
/// <summary>
/// Compares the passed in sync state with the current sync state on the server
/// </summary>
/// <param name="binding">Binding to use for call</param>
/// <param name="sinceSyncState">"lower" bounds of change</param>
///
static bool FolderChangesExist(
    ExchangeServiceBinding binding,
    string sinceSyncState)
{
  SyncFolderHierarchyType request = new SyncFolderHierarchyType();
  request.FolderShape = new FolderResponseShapeType(DefaultShapeNamesType.IdOnly);
  request.SyncState = sinceSyncState;

  SyncFolderHierarchyResponseType response = binding.SyncFolderHierarchy(request);
  SyncFolderHierarchyResponseMessageType responseMessage =
        response.ResponseMessages.Items[0] as
          SyncFolderHierarchyResponseMessageType;

  if (responseMessage.ResponseCode != ResponseCodeType.NoError)
  {
    throw new Exception("SyncFolderHierarchy failed with response code: " +
        responseMessage.ResponseCode.ToString());
  }

  if (responseMessage.SyncState == sinceSyncState)
  {
    // If the sync state is the same, there are NO changes.  Assert this as
    // EWS should be consistent.
    //
    Debug.Assert(responseMessage.Changes.Items == null);
    return false;
  }
  else
  {
    // If the sync state is different, then there should be changes.
    //
    Debug.Assert(responseMessage.Changes.Items != null);
    return true;
  }
}
```

In Listing 16-6, notice the assertion that if the *sinceSyncState* argument matches the *SyncState* returned by *SyncFolderHierarchy* then there must be no changes (the *Changes* array is empty). Of course, in practice it makes more sense to simply check the contents of the *Changes* array in order to determine whether there are folder changes or not.

Notable Omissions

Looking back at Listing 16-1, you might notice that there are no elements available for indicating the root folder where the folder sync operation should begin. This implies two points. First, Exchange Web Services must use some default folder as the root folder for synchronization. Second, the actual mailbox that is synchronized must be determined by something outside of the *SyncFolderHierarchy* request.

Regarding the first point, Exchange Web Services does indeed choose a root folder for synchronization for a *SyncFolderHierarchy* request—the IPM Subtree, which is exposed as the *msgfolderroot* distinguished folder in Exchange Web Services. You cannot change the root folder to use for folder synchronization. Regarding the second point, Exchange Web Services uses the mailbox of the *caller* when executing a *SyncFolderHierarchy* request. The only way to sync the contents of a mailbox other than your own is to either issue the *SyncFolderHierarchy* request using the credentials of the mailbox owner or to use *Exchange Impersonation*, which is covered in Chapter 21, "Server-To-Server Authentication."

In addition to the omission of a root folder for synchronization, *SyncFolderHierarchy* does not allow you to control the depth of the sync operation. Folder sync is always a deep traversal operation and you will receive changes for any folder that is a direct or indirect child of *msgfolderroot*.

SyncFolderHierarchy Responses

Now that you know how to build a *SyncFolderHierarchy* request, we will turn our attention to the response returned by *SyncFolderHierarchy*. First, let's make the initial *SyncFolderHierarchy* call again. Remember, to make this initial call, you simply omit the *SyncState* element. We won't show the request here—you can refer to Listing 16-2 if you want to see how it is structured. Listing 16-7 shows the response.

LISTING 16-7 Initial *SyncFolderHierarchy* response

```
<m:SyncFolderHierarchyResponse xmlns:t=".../types"
                               xmlns:m=".../messages">
  <m:ResponseMessages>
    <m:SyncFolderHierarchyResponseMessage ResponseClass="Success">
      <m:ResponseCode>NoError</m:ResponseCode>
      <m:SyncState>...</m:SyncState>
      <m:IncludesLastFolderInRange>true</m:IncludesLastFolderInRange>
      <m:Changes>
        <t:Create>
          <t:CalendarFolder>
```

```
        <t:FolderId Id="AQAsAHRpbm..." ChangeKey="AgAAABQAA..."/>
        <t:ParentFolderId Id="AQAsAHRpbmE..." ChangeKey="AQAAAA=="/>
        <t:FolderClass>IPF.Appointment</t:FolderClass>
        <t:DisplayName>Calendar</t:DisplayName>
        <t:TotalCount>0</t:TotalCount>
        <t:ChildFolderCount>0</t:ChildFolderCount>
      </t:CalendarFolder>
    /t:Create>
    <t:Create>
      <t:ContactsFolder>
        <t:FolderId Id="AQAsAHRpbmEubWF..." ChangeKey="AwAAABQA..."/>
        <t:ParentFolderId Id="AQAsAHRpbmEubWF..." ChangeKey="AQAAAA=="/>
        <t:FolderClass>IPF.Contact</t:FolderClass>
        <t:DisplayName>Contacts</t:DisplayName>
        <t:TotalCount>1</t:TotalCount>
        <t:ChildFolderCount>0</t:ChildFolderCount>
      </t:ContactsFolder>
    </t:Create>
    <!-- remaining Create elements omitted for brevity -->
  </m:Changes>
 </m:SyncFolderHierarchyResponseMessage>
 </m:ResponseMessages>
</m:SyncFolderHierarchyResponse>
```

You have already seen the *ResponseCode* and *SyncState* elements, so we will skip over to the two elements that we have not talked about yet.

IncludesLastFolderInRange Element

The *IncludesLastFolderInRange* element was originally intended to indicate whether the *SyncFolderHierarchy* response represented a complete set of folder changes or not. If false, *IncludesLastFolderInRange* would suggest that there would be a way to retrieve the rest of the folders. You saw such a construct when dealing with paging in Chapter 15, "Advanced Searching." However, *IncludesLastFolderInRange* will always be true and therefore should be ignored. All applicable folder modifications will be returned in a *SyncFolderHierarchy* response.

Changes Element

The *Changes* element contains the actual folder changes that have occurred since the point in time suggested by the supplied *SyncState* from the request. The *Changes* element itself is an instance of type *SyncFolderHierarchyChangesType*, which is an unbounded sequence of *Create*, *Update*, or *Delete* changes as shown in Listing 16-8.

LISTING 16-8 *SyncFolderHierarchyChangesType* from the schema

```
<xs:complexType name="SyncFolderHierarchyChangesType">
  <xs:sequence>
    <xs:choice maxOccurs="unbounded" minOccurs="0">
      <xs:element name="Create" type="t:SyncFolderHierarchyCreateOrUpdateType"/>
      <xs:element name="Update" type="t:SyncFolderHierarchyCreateOrUpdateType"/>
      <xs:element name="Delete" type="t:SyncFolderHierarchyDeleteType"/>
    </xs:choice>
  </xs:sequence>
</xs:complexType>
```

The *Create*, *Update*, and *Delete* changes represent the modification actions that you will be notified of. Notice the absence of actions such as *Move* and *Copy*. You will certainly be notified of such actions, but they will be exposed as a combination of *Create, Update*, and *Delete* changes. We will discuss these combinations shortly.

The response from Listing 16-7 contains a collection of *Create* changes. Since the corresponding request did not specify a *SyncState,* all change entries will be *Create* changes. Let's look at the structure of the *Create* change entry.

Create Change Entries

Create change entries are instances of *SyncFolderHierarchyCreateOrUpdateType* which is shown in Listing 16-9

LISTING 16-9 *SyncFolderHierarchyCreateOrUpdateType* schema structure

```
<xs:complexType name="SyncFolderHierarchyCreateOrUpdateType">
  <xs:choice>
    <xs:element name="Folder" type="t:FolderType"/>
    <xs:element name="CalendarFolder" type="t:CalendarFolderType"/>
    <xs:element name="ContactsFolder" type="t:ContactsFolderType"/>
    <xs:element name="SearchFolder" type="t:SearchFolderType"/>
    <xs:element name="TasksFolder" type="t:TasksFolderType"/>
  </xs:choice>
</xs:complexType>
```

From Listing 16-9, you see that *SyncFolderHierarchyCreateOrUpdateType* is simply a choice of the various folder types that Exchange Web Services supports. In fact, if you examine one of the *Create* elements from Listing 16-7, you will see that indeed the *Create* element simply wraps a folder instance.

```
<t:Create>
  <t:CalendarFolder>
    <t:FolderId Id="AQAsAHRpbm..." ChangeKey="AgAAABQAA..."/>
    <t:ParentFolderId Id="AQAsAHRpbmE..." ChangeKey="AQAAAA=="/>
    <t:FolderClass>IPF.Appointment</t:FolderClass>
    <t:DisplayName>Calendar</t:DisplayName>
```

```
            <t:TotalCount>0</t:TotalCount>
            <t:ChildFolderCount>0</t:ChildFolderCount>
        </t:CalendarFolder>
      </t:Create>
```

The properties returned for each folder are governed by the *FolderShape* that was specified in the *SyncFolderHierarchy* request.

Now, let's create a new folder under the inbox.

```
<CreateFolder xmlns=".../messages"
              xmlns:t=".../types">
  <ParentFolderId>
    <t:DistinguishedFolderId Id="inbox"/>
  </ParentFolderId>
  <Folders>
    <t:Folder>
      <t:DisplayName>Folder Under Inbox</t:DisplayName>
    </t:Folder>
  </Folders>
</CreateFolder>
```

Next, the *SyncFolderHierarchy* call is reissued but now includes the *SyncState* that was returned in Listing 16-7. Note that the *Default* base shape is requested in the interest of space.

```
<SyncFolderHierarchy xmlns=".../messages">
  <FolderShape>
    <t:BaseShape>Default</t:BaseShape>
  </FolderShape>
  <SyncState>H4sIAAAAAAAEA029B...</SyncState>
</SyncFolderHierarchy>
```

The response is shown in Listing 16-10.

LISTING 16-10 *SyncFolderHierarchy* response after creating a single folder

```
<m:SyncFolderHierarchyResponse xmlns:t=".../types" xmlns:m=".../messages">
  <m:ResponseMessages>
    <m:SyncFolderHierarchyResponseMessage ResponseClass="Success">
      <m:ResponseCode>NoError</m:ResponseCode>
      <m:SyncState>H4sIAAAAAAAEA029B...</m:SyncState>
      <m:IncludesLastFolderInRange>true</m:IncludesLastFolderInRange>
      <m:Changes>
        <t:Create>
          <t:Folder>
            <t:FolderId Id="AQAsAHRpbmEubWFrb3..." ChangeKey="AQAAABYAAA..."/>
            <t:DisplayName>Folder Under Inbox</t:DisplayName>
            <t:TotalCount>0</t:TotalCount>
            <t:ChildFolderCount>0</t:ChildFolderCount>
            <t:UnreadCount>0</t:UnreadCount>
          </t:Folder>
        </t:Create>
      </m:Changes>
    </m:SyncFolderHierarchyResponseMessage>
  </m:ResponseMessages>
</m:SyncFolderHierarchyResponse>
```

Listing 16-10 contains a single folder. Why? Because the only change to the folder hierarchy since the *SyncState* passed into the *SyncFolderHierarchy* call was the addition of the "Folder Under Inbox" folder.

Update Change Entries

What do you think will happen if *UpdateFolder* is called on the new folder and the display name is changed? Let's find out.

```
<UpdateFolder xmlns=".../messages"
              xmlns:t=".../types">
  <FolderChanges>
    <t:FolderChange>
      <t:FolderId Id="AQAsAHRpbm..." ChangeKey="AQAAABYAAA..."/>
      <t:Updates>
        <t:SetFolderField>
          <t:FieldURI FieldURI="folder:DisplayName"/>
          <t:Folder>
            <t:DisplayName>Folder Under Inbox (Modified)</t:DisplayName>
          </t:Folder>
        </t:SetFolderField>
      </t:Updates>
    </t:FolderChange>
  </FolderChanges>
</UpdateFolder>
```

Listing 16-11 shows the response when the *SyncFolderHierarchy* request is reissued with the updated *SyncState* from Listing 16-10.

LISTING 16-11 *SyncFolderHierarchy* response after updating a folder display name

```
<m:SyncFolderHierarchyResponse xmlns:t=".../types"
                               xmlns:m=".../messages">
  <m:ResponseMessages>
    <m:SyncFolderHierarchyResponseMessage ResponseClass="Success">
      <m:ResponseCode>NoError</m:ResponseCode>
      <m:SyncState>H4sIAAAAAAAEAO...</m:SyncState>
      <m:IncludesLastFolderInRange>true</m:IncludesLastFolderInRange>
      <m:Changes>
        <t:Update>
          <t:Folder>
            <t:FolderId Id="AQAsAHRpbmEubWF..." ChangeKey="AQAAABYA..."/>
            <t:DisplayName>Folder Under Inbox (Modified)</t:DisplayName>
            <t:TotalCount>0</t:TotalCount>
            <t:ChildFolderCount>0</t:ChildFolderCount>
            <t:UnreadCount>0</t:UnreadCount>
          </t:Folder>
        </t:Update>
      </m:Changes>
    </m:SyncFolderHierarchyResponseMessage>
  </m:ResponseMessages>
</m:SyncFolderHierarchyResponse>
```

Notice that the response in Listing 16-11 now includes a single *Update* change element. And what does it contain? Why, the folder that was changed of course. You may have been able to deduce that based on the type that we introduced when talking about *Create* changes: *SyncFolderHierarchyCreateOrUpdateType*. The name suggests that this type is used for both *Create* and *Update* change entries, which indeed it is.

Looking at Listing 16-11, can you tell *what* changed about the folder? No, you cannot. All you know is that *something* on that folder was updated. In fact, the update does not even have to be to a property that is contained in the *Update* element. Remember, the properties that are returned in a *SyncFolderHierarchy* call are a function of the *FolderShape* that was specified in the request. As such, it is prudent for you to retrieve all of the properties that are of interest to you in order to determine if the change to the folder is noteworthy.

There is an issue with *SyncFolderHierarchy* and extended property modifications.[3] If you update a folder by either setting or deleting an extended property, a subsequent call to *SyncFolderHierarchy* will *not* include an *Update* entry for the extended property change. In fact, if you run the *FolderChangesExist* method from Listing 16-6 after updating an extended property and pass in the *SyncState* value from before the extended property was updated, the *FolderChangesExist* method will assert! Why? Because the *SyncState* has indeed changed, but Exchange Web Services does not indicate which folders have changed. The only option in this situation is to perform an initial *SyncFolderHierarchy*, requesting the properties that are of interest to you, and then do a manual comparison between the retrieved folders and your local folders to determine which folder has changed.

In fact, the only property changes that *will* cause a folder change entry to be generated for *SyncFolderHierarchy* are *DisplayName*, *ParentFolderId*, and *FolderClass*. Changes in the *TotalCount* and *UnreadCount* for a folder will not generate update changes; however, the *SyncState* will not change in that case either.

Delete Change Entries

If you delete a folder from the mailbox and then reissue your *SyncFolderHierarchy* call, you should expect to see the third and final change entry, which is *Delete*. First, the *DeleteFolder* call is issued as shown in Listing 16-12.

LISTING 16-12 Deleting a folder

```
<DeleteFolder xmlns=".../messages"
              xmlns:t=".../types"
              DeleteType="HardDelete">
  <FolderIds>
    <t:FolderId Id="AQAsAHRpbmEu..." ChangeKey="AQAAABY..."/>
  </FolderIds>
</DeleteFolder>
```

---

[3] This issue may be addressed in a future release of Exchange Web Services.

And then the *SyncFolderHierarchy* call is reissued. The response is shown in Listing 16-13.

LISTING 16-13 *SyncFolderHierarchy* response for deleted folder

```
<m:SyncFolderHierarchyResponse xmlns:t=".../types"
                               xmlns:m=".../messages">
  <m:ResponseMessages>
    <m:SyncFolderHierarchyResponseMessage ResponseClass="Success">
      <m:ResponseCode>NoError</m:ResponseCode>
      <m:SyncState>H4sIAAAAAAAEAO29B2A...</m:SyncState>
      <m:IncludesLastFolderInRange>true</m:IncludesLastFolderInRange>
      <m:Changes>
        <t:Delete>
          <t:FolderId Id="AQAsAHRpbmEubWF..." ChangeKey="AQAAAA=="/>
        </t:Delete>
      </m:Changes>
    </m:SyncFolderHierarchyResponseMessage>
  </m:ResponseMessages>
</m:SyncFolderHierarchyResponse>
```

Now, the *Delete* change entry has its own type since it has no need to represent the entire folder. Listing 16-14 shows the *SyncFolderHierarchyDeleteType*, which is the type for the *Delete* change entry.

LISTING 16-14 *SyncFolderHierarchyDeleteType* schema type

```
<xs:complexType name="SyncFolderHierarchyDeleteType">
  <xs:sequence>
    <xs:element name="FolderId" type="t:FolderIdType"/>
  </xs:sequence>
</xs:complexType>
```

SyncFolderHierarchyDeleteType exposes a single child element called *FolderId* that contains the *FolderId* of the folder that was deleted.

The "Other" Delete

Listing 16-12 specified a *DeleteType* of *HardDelete* when deleting the folder. Chapter 4 explained how calling *DeleteFolder* with a *DeleteType* of *MoveToDeletedItems* was actually not a *delete* at all, but rather a *move* operation. To appreciate what this "move to the Deleted Items folder" means, let's create another folder in the inbox.

```
<CreateFolder xmlns=".../messages"
              xmlns:t=".../types">
  <ParentFolderId>
    <t:DistinguishedFolderId Id="inbox"/>
  </ParentFolderId>
  <Folders>
```

```
   <t:Folder>
      <t:DisplayName>Folder to move to DeletedItems</t:DisplayName>
   </t:Folder>
  </Folders>
</CreateFolder>
```

Although we will not show the request, we will show a *SyncFolderHierarchy* call to get the updated *SyncState*. The *SyncFolderHierarchy* call is followed with a *DeleteFolder* call whose *DeleteType* is *MoveToDeletedItems*.

```
<DeleteFolder xmlns=".../messages"
              xmlns:t=".../types"
              DeleteType="MoveToDeletedItems">
  <FolderIds>
    <t:FolderId Id="AQAsAHRpbmEub..." ChangeKey="AQAAABYAAAC..."/>
  </FolderIds>
</DeleteFolder>
```

And finally, *SyncFolderHierarchy* is called once again with the most recent *SyncState*. Listing 16-15 shows the response.

LISTING 16-15 How *MoveToDeletedItems* affects *SyncFolderHierarchy* responses

```
  <m:SyncFolderHierarchyResponse xmlns:t=".../types"
                                 xmlns:m=".../messages">
    <m:ResponseMessages>
      <m:SyncFolderHierarchyResponseMessage ResponseClass="Success">
        <m:ResponseCode>NoError</m:ResponseCode>
        <m:SyncState>H4sIAAAAAAAE...</m:SyncState>
        <m:IncludesLastFolderInRange>true</m:IncludesLastFolderInRange>
        <m:Changes>
          <t:Update>
            <t:Folder>
              <t:FolderId Id="AQAsAHRpbmEubWFr..." ChangeKey="AQAAABYAAAC..."/>
              <t:ParentFolderId Id="AQAsAHRpbmEubWFrb..." ChangeKey="AQAAAA=="/>
              <t:DisplayName>Folder to move to DeletedItems</t:DisplayName>
              <t:TotalCount>0</t:TotalCount>
              <t:ChildFolderCount>0</t:ChildFolderCount>
              <t:UnreadCount>0</t:UnreadCount>
            </t:Folder>
          </t:Update>
        </m:Changes>
      </m:SyncFolderHierarchyResponseMessage>
    </m:ResponseMessages>
  </m:SyncFolderHierarchyResponse>
```

The response in Listing 16-15 contains an *Update* change instead of a *Delete* change. Can you guess which property has changed? The *ParentFolderId* changed because the parent folder is no longer the Inbox, but rather it is the Deleted Items folder. Calling *GetFolder* on the *ParentFolderId* value from Listing 16-15 confirms this. The response is shown in Listing 16-16 and confirms that the *ParentFolderId* does indeed refer to the Deleted Items folder.

LISTING 16-16 *GetFolder* response for folder deleted with *MoveToDeletedItems*

```
<m:GetFolderResponse xmlns:t=".../types"
                     xmlns:m=".../messages">
  <m:ResponseMessages>
    <m:GetFolderResponseMessage ResponseClass="Success">
      <m:ResponseCode>NoError</m:ResponseCode>
      <m:Folders>
        <t:Folder>
          <t:FolderId Id="AQAsAHRpbmEubWF..." ChangeKey="AQAAAB..."/>
          <t:DisplayName>Deleted Items</t:DisplayName>
          <t:TotalCount>0</t:TotalCount>
          <t:ChildFolderCount>2</t:ChildFolderCount>
          <t:UnreadCount>0</t:UnreadCount>
        </t:Folder>
      </m:Folders>
    </m:GetFolderResponseMessage>
  </m:ResponseMessages>
</m:GetFolderResponse>
```

Moving and Copying Folders

When you move a folder using *MoveFolder* and then call *SyncFolderHierarchy,* an *Update* change entry will be returned in the *SyncFolderHierarchy* response just as in the *DeleteItem* with *MoveToDeletedItems* case above.

In contrast, when you copy a folder, you are not changing the existing folder, but you are rather creating a *clone* of the original folder. To see the results of copying a folder on the *SyncFolderHierarchy* response, let's create...another folder!

```
<CreateFolder xmlns=".../messages"
              xmlns:t=".../types">
  <ParentFolderId>
    <t:DistinguishedFolderId Id="inbox"/>
  </ParentFolderId>
  <Folders>
    <t:Folder>
      <t:DisplayName>Folder To Copy</t:DisplayName>
    </t:Folder>
  </Folders>
</CreateFolder>
```

A call to *SyncFolderHierarchy* to get the latest *SyncState* is followed by a *CopyFolder* call, which will copy the new folder into the Sent Items folder.

```
<CopyFolder xmlns=".../messages"
            xmlns:t=".../types">
  <ToFolderId>
    <t:DistinguishedFolderId Id="sentitems"/>
  </ToFolderId>
```

```
    <FolderIds>
      <t:FolderId Id="AQAsAHRpbmEubW..." ChangeKey="AQAAABYAAA..."/>
    </FolderIds>
  </CopyFolder>
```

Listing 16-17 shows the response when *SyncFolderHierarchy* is called again with the latest *SyncState*.

LISTING 16-17 *SyncFolderHierarchy* response for copied folder

```
  <m:SyncFolderHierarchyResponse xmlns:t=".../types" xmlns:m=".../messages">
    <m:ResponseMessages>
      <m:SyncFolderHierarchyResponseMessage ResponseClass="Success">
        <m:ResponseCode>NoError</m:ResponseCode>
        <m:SyncState>H4sIAAAAAAAEA...</m:SyncState>
        <m:IncludesLastFolderInRange>true</m:IncludesLastFolderInRange>
        <m:Changes>
          <t:Create>
            <t:Folder>
              <t:FolderId Id="AQAsAHRpbmE..." ChangeKey="AQAAABYAAA..."/>
              <t:ParentFolderId Id="AQAsAHRpbmEubWF..." ChangeKey="AQAAAA=="/>
              <t:DisplayName>Folder To Copy</t:DisplayName>
              <t:TotalCount>0</t:TotalCount>
              <t:ChildFolderCount>0</t:ChildFolderCount>
              <t:UnreadCount>0</t:UnreadCount>
            </t:Folder>
          </t:Create>
        </m:Changes>
      </m:SyncFolderHierarchyResponseMessage>
    </m:ResponseMessages>
  </m:SyncFolderHierarchyResponse>
```

The response in Listing 16-17 agrees with the assumption that *CopyFolder* does not modify the original folder, but rather *creates* a copy of the folder in the new location.

Dealing with the Response

In response to an initial *SyncFolderHierarchy* call, Exchange Web Services returns a flat and potentially long list of *Create* change entries to represent the folders within your mailbox. By *flat* we mean that the *Create* entries in the response are all direct children of the *Changes* element rather than being children of their parent folder's *Create* entry. Depending on your needs, you may need to take the returned flat list and expand the contents into the hierarchy that represents your mailbox. Thankfully, *SyncFolderHierarchy* can return the *ParentFolderId* of each returned folder, which can be used to generate this hierarchy. Listing 16-18 demonstrates how building this hierarchy can be accomplished using the proxy classes.

LISTING 16-18 Proxy class method for build tree representation of initial folder sync

```
/// <summary>
/// Represents the type of change
/// </summary>
public enum FolderSyncChangeType
{
  Create,
  Update,
  Delete,
}

/// <summary>
/// Wrapper class to hold the folder and its list of children
/// </summary>
public class FolderSyncChange
{
  private BaseFolderType folder;
  private FolderSyncChangeType changeType;
  private List<FolderSyncChange> children;

  /// <summary>
  /// Constructor
  /// </summary>
  /// <param name="folder">The folder</param>
  /// <param name="changeType">Type of change (create, update)</param>
  ///
  public FolderSyncChange(BaseFolderType folder, FolderSyncChangeType changeType)
  {
    this.folder = folder;
    this.changeType = changeType;
    this.children = new List<FolderSyncChange>();
  }

  /// <summary>
  /// Accessor for folder
  /// </summary>
  ///
  public BaseFolderType Folder
  {
    get { return this.folder; }
  }

  /// <summary>
  /// Accessor for change type
  /// </summary>
  ///
  public FolderSyncChangeType ChangeType
  {
    get { return this.changeType; }
  }

  /// <summary>
  /// Accessor for children
  /// </summary>
```

```
  ///
  public List<FolderSyncChange> Children
  {
    get { return this.children; }
  }

  /// <summary>
  /// Returns true if there are any children for this folder
  /// </summary>
  ///
  public bool HasChildren
  {
    get { return this.children.Count > 0; }
  }
}


/// <summary>
/// Calls SyncFolderHierarchy and the converts the response into a tree structure
/// </summary>
/// <param name="binding">Binding to use for call</param>
/// <param name="responseShape">Response shape</param>
/// <param name="newSyncState">New sync state</param>
/// <returns>List of top level changes (immediate children of IPM
/// Subtree)</returns>
///
public static List<FolderSyncChange> SyncFolderHierarchyWithExpansion(
  ExchangeServiceBinding binding,
  FolderResponseShapeType responseShape,
  out string newSyncState)
{
  // First make our SyncFolderHierarchy call.
  //
  SyncFolderHierarchyType request = new SyncFolderHierarchyType();
  request.FolderShape = responseShape;
  SyncFolderHierarchyResponseType response = binding.SyncFolderHierarchy(request);
  SyncFolderHierarchyResponseMessageType responseMessage =
    response.ResponseMessages.Items[0] as
      SyncFolderHierarchyResponseMessageType;

  if (responseMessage.ResponseCode != ResponseCodeType.NoError)
  {
    throw new Exception("SyncFolderHierarchy failed with response code: " +
      responseMessage.ResponseCode.ToString());
  }

  Dictionary<string, FolderSyncChange> parentFolderMap =
      new Dictionary<string, FolderSyncChange>();

  // set the sync state
  //
  newSyncState = responseMessage.SyncState;
  List<FolderSyncChange> result = new List<FolderSyncChange>();

  // Unfortunately, Changes is exposed as an object array since there is no other
```

```
// common base class between the various change types. Since this is an initial
// sync, we will have no delete changes.
//
for (int index = 0; index < responseMessage.Changes.Items.Length; index++)
{
  SyncFolderHierarchyCreateOrUpdateType change =
   responseMessage.Changes.Items[index] as
     SyncFolderHierarchyCreateOrUpdateType;
  if (change == null)
    continue;

  // We need the parent folder id to build our hierarchy, so make sure the
  // response shape they supplied retrieved the parent folder id.
  //
  if (change.Item.ParentFolderId == null)
  {
    throw new ArgumentException("ResponseShape must include the ParentFolderId",
      "responseShape");
  }

  FolderSyncChange folderChange;

  // we have either a create or update change.  Need to look at the
  // ItemsElementName to determine which it is.
  switch (responseMessage.Changes.ItemsElementName[index])
  {
    case ItemsChoiceType1.Create:
      folderChange = new FolderSyncChange(
        change.Item,
        FolderSyncChangeType.Create);
      break;

    case ItemsChoiceType1.Update:
      folderChange = new FolderSyncChange(
        change.Item,
        FolderSyncChangeType.Update);
      break;

    default:
      Debug.Assert(
          false,
          "We should not hit this since we have an instance of " +
          "SyncFolderHierarchyCreateOrUpdateType.");
      return null;
  }

  // Now, figure out which parent to put the folder change under.
  //
  FolderSyncChange parent;
  if (parentFolderMap.TryGetValue(
    folderChange.Folder.ParentFolderId.Id,
    out parent))
  {
    parent.Children.Add(folderChange);
```

```
      }
      else
      {
        // this is contained in the root, so therefore it goes into the response list
        // directly.
        //
        result.Add(folderChange);
      }

      // Now, add this to the dictionary as this folder could have its own
      // subfolders.
      //
      parentFolderMap.Add(folderChange.Folder.FolderId.Id, folderChange);
  }

  return result;
}
```

At the top of Listing 16-18, the *FolderSyncChangeType* enumeration is defined with three values: *Create*, *Update*, and *Delete*. These values correspond to the three *Change* entry types that you can encounter in a *SyncFolderHierarchy* response. *Create* and *Update* change entries have an interesting representation when dealing with the proxy classes. Earlier in the chapter, Listing 16-8 showed that both the *Create* and the *Update* changes share a common type *SyncFolderHierarchyCreateOrUpdateType*. When the proxy classes deserialize a *SyncFolderHierarchy* response, the local XML element names are discarded and both *Create* and *Update* changes are deserialized into instances of *SyncFolderHierarchyCreateOrUpdateType*. If you were to place a deserialized *Create* right next to a deserialized *Update*, you would not be able to tell the difference because, in fact, there *is* no difference. Of course, you *must* be able to distinguish between *Create* changes and *Update* changes, and thankfully, the proxy generator has preserved this distinction. Listing 16-19 shows how the proxy generator accomplishes this.

LISTING 16-19 *SyncFolderHierarchyChangesType* proxy class

```
public partial class SyncFolderHierarchyChangesType {

  private object[] itemsField;
  private ItemsChoiceType1[] itemsElementNameField;

  /// <remarks/>
  [System.Xml.Serialization.XmlElementAttribute(
    "Create",
    typeof(SyncFolderHierarchyCreateOrUpdateType))]
  [System.Xml.Serialization.XmlElementAttribute(
    "Delete",
    typeof(SyncFolderHierarchyDeleteType))]
  [System.Xml.Serialization.XmlElementAttribute(
    "Update",
```

```
       typeof(SyncFolderHierarchyCreateOrUpdateType))]
    [System.Xml.Serialization.XmlChoiceIdentifierAttribute("ItemsElementName")]
    public object[] Items {
      get {
        return this.itemsField;
      }
      set {
        this.itemsField = value;
      }
    }

    /// <remarks/>
    [System.Xml.Serialization.XmlElementAttribute("ItemsElementName")]
    [System.Xml.Serialization.XmlIgnoreAttribute()]
    public ItemsChoiceType1[] ItemsElementName {
      get {
        return this.itemsElementNameField;
      }
      set {
        this.itemsElementNameField = value;
      }
    }
  }

  public enum ItemsChoiceType1 {
    Create,
    Delete,
    Update,
  }
```

The important lines to note in Listing 16-19 are in bold. Notice first that the *Items* property that holds the actual *Create*, *Update*, and *Delete* changes has been decorated with an
XmlChoiceIdentifierAttribute attribute. Also notice that the name supplied in the attribute's
constructor is the same name that decorates the *ItemsElementName* property below (also in
bold). By decorating the *Items* property as such, the XML serializer takes the XML local name
of each change and places the corresponding *ItemChoicesType1* enumeration value into the
ItemsElementName array. The array index of the change in the *Items* property will correspond
with the array index of the change type in the *ItemsElementName* property.

Given that the proxy generator already created an enumeration to represent the type of
change, why did we introduce the *FolderSyncChangeType* in Listing 16-18? Although we could
have reused *ItemChoicesType1*, the name is not very indicative of what it represents, so our
developer conscience required us to create a more friendly enumeration name.

The *FolderSyncChange* class is also defined in Listing 16-18 and wraps the folder definition, the *FolderSyncChangeType* that occurred, and a list of children under that folder,
if any. Given the relationship between the *Items* and *ItemsElementName* properties of
SyncFolderHierarchyChangesType, Listing 16-18 creates an instance of *FolderSyncChange* for

each *SyncFolderHierarchyCreateOrUpdateType* instance in the response. The pertinent code from Listing 16-18 is repeated here.

```
for (int index = 0; index < responseMessage.Changes.Items.Length; index++)
{
  SyncFolderHierarchyCreateOrUpdateType change =
   responseMessage.Changes.Items[index] as
     SyncFolderHierarchyCreateOrUpdateType;

  // code elided...
  FolderSyncChange folderChange;

  // we have either a create or update change.  Need to look at the
  // ItemsElementName to determine which it is.
  switch (responseMessage.Changes.ItemsElementName[index])
  {
    case ItemsChoiceType1.Create:
      folderChange = new FolderSyncChange(
        change.Item,
        FolderSyncChangeType.Create);
      break;

    case ItemsChoiceType1.Update:
      folderChange = new FolderSyncChange(
        change.Item,
        FolderSyncChangeType.Update);
      break;

    default:
      Debug.Assert(
          false,
          "We should not hit this since we have an instance of " +
          "SyncFolderHierarchyCreateOrUpdateType.");
      return null;
  }

  // code elided...
}
```

SyncFolderHierarchyWithExpansion returns a list of *FolderSyncChange* instances that represent the folders directly contained within the IPM subtree (msgfolderroot). Each *FolderSyncChange* instance also exposes a list of its own child folders, so we have effectively created a tree structure to represent the folder hierarchy.

The method in Listing 16-20 adds a way to display this tree structure.

LISTING 16-20 Displaying the tree structure returned by *SyncFolderHierarchyWithExpansion*

```
/// <summary>
/// Writes the tree structure of a given FolderSyncChange to the console
/// </summary>
/// <param name="toDraw">FolderSyncChange to draw including its children</param>
/// <param name="offset">Current tab offset</param>
```

```
///
public static void DrawFolderSyncHierarchy(FolderSyncChange toDraw, int offset)
{
  StringBuilder builder = new StringBuilder();
  for (int i = 0; i < offset; i++)
  {
    builder.Append("\t");
  }
  string prefixTabs = builder.ToString();

  // Draw this folder
  Console.WriteLine("{0}{1} ({2})",
          prefixTabs,
          toDraw.Folder.DisplayName,
          toDraw.Children.Count);

  // If the folder has children, recursively call DrawFolderSyncHierarchy
  //
  if (toDraw.HasChildren)
  {
    offset++;
    foreach (FolderSyncChange child in toDraw.Children)
    {
      DrawFolderSyncHierarchy(child, offset);
    }
  }
}
```

Listing 16-21 shows a way to call *SyncFolderHierarchyWithExpansion* and *DrawFolderSyncHierarchy*.

LISTING 16-21 Drawing the full hierarchy

```
/// <summary>
/// Draw the full sync folder hierarchy
/// </summary>
/// <param name="binding">Binding to use for the call</param>
///
public static void DrawFullHierarchy(ExchangeServiceBinding binding)
{
  string syncState;
  List<FolderSyncChange> result = SyncFolderHierarchyWithExpansion(
                    binding,
                    new FolderResponseShapeType(
                            DefaultShapeNamesType.AllProperties),
                    out syncState);

  Console.WriteLine("IPM Subtree (msgfolderroot)");
  foreach (FolderSyncChange change in result)
  {
    DrawFolderSyncHierarchy(change, 1 /*offset*/);
  }
}
```

The results of running the code in Listing 16-21 against an example mailbox are shown in Figure 16-1.

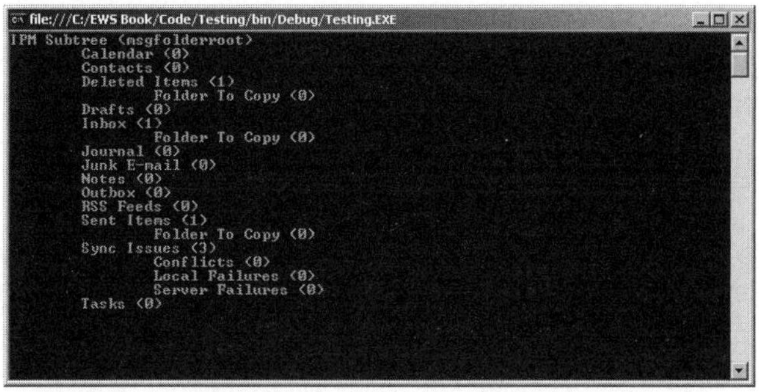

FIGURE 16-1 Running *DrawFullHierarchy* against a mailbox

Syncing Items Within a Folder

Now that we have exhausted the topic of syncing the folder hierarchy, we will turn our attention to syncing items within the mailbox. Syncing the items contained within a mailbox is accomplished using the *SyncFolderItems* Web method. While *SyncFolderHierarchy* performs a deep traversal sync of all folders that have changed since the point in time suggested by the supplied *SyncState, SyncFolderItems* will sync only those items contained within the folder that you specify. Listing 16-22 shows the basic structure of a *SyncFolderItems* request.

LISTING 16-22 Basic structure of a *SyncFolderItems* request

```
<SyncFolderItems xmlns=".../messages"
                 xmlns:t=".../types">
  <ItemShape/>
  <SyncFolderId/>
  <SyncState/>
  <Ignore/>
  <MaxChangesReturned/>
</SyncFolderItems>
```

ItemShape Element

The first child element of *SyncFolderItems* is the required *ItemShape*. In the same way that the *FolderShape* is used in *SyncFolderHierarchy* to determine which properties are returned in a response, the *ItemShape* is used by *SyncFolderItems* to determine which properties are returned in a *SyncFolderItems* response. *ItemShape* is an instance of *ItemResponseShapeType* and was covered in detail in Chapter 3.

However, the additional properties limitation encountered with *SyncFolderHierarchy* is not present on *SyncFolderItems*. As such, you can specify any additional property of interest in the *ItemShape* of a *SyncFolderItems* request and rest assured that you will not encounter a response code of *ErrorInvalidPropertyRequest*. That being said, the properties that can be requested are limited to those supported in the *FindItem* Web method.[4]

SyncFolderId Element

As mentioned above, *SyncFolderItems* will sync only those items within the folder that you specify, and the required *SyncFolderId* element is how you specify which folder to consider. *SyncFolderId* is an instance of *TargetFolderIdType*, which means that the actual folder id is contained as a child of *SyncFolderId*. You can use either a *DistinguishedFolderId* or a *FolderId*. For instance, both of the following are valid *SyncFolderId* elements:

```
<SyncFolderId>
  <DistinguishedFolderId Id="drafts"/>
</SyncFolderId>

<SyncFolderId>
  <FolderId Id="AQAsAHRpbmEub..." ChangeKey="AQAAAA=="/>
</SyncFolderId>
```

When using the proxy classes, you must create an instance of *TargetFolderIdType* as shown here for *DistinguishedFolderId*:

```
SyncFolderItemsType request = new SyncFolderItemsType();
request.SyncFolderId = new TargetFolderIdType();
request.SyncFolderId.Item =
    new DistinguishedFolderIdType(DistinguishedFolderIdNameType.drafts);
```

And for *FolderId*:

```
SyncFolderItemsType request = new SyncFolderItemsType();
request.SyncFolderId = new TargetFolderIdType();
FolderIdType folderId = new FolderIdType();
folderId.Id = "AQAsAHRpbmEub...";
folderId.ChangeKey = "AQAAAA==";
request.SyncFolderId.Item = folderId;
```

Hey! If you can specify a *FolderId* or *DistinguishedFolderId*, does that mean that you can sync items from a mailbox other than your own? Assuming that you have the appropriate delegate rights to the *folder* specified in *SyncFolderId* on the mailbox in question, the answer is yes. You can simply add the *Mailbox* child element to the *DistinguishedFolderId* element as shown here:

```
<SyncFolderId>
```

---

[4] Refer to Appendix C on the companion Web page for the properties that are available in *FindItem* requests.

```
<t:DistinguishedFolderId Id="inbox">
  <t:Mailbox>
    <t:EmailAddress>ken.malcolmson@contoso.com</t:EmailAddress>
  </t:Mailbox>
</t:DistinguishedFolderId>
</SyncFolderId>
```

Or, if you have a *FolderId* that corresponds to a folder in another mailbox, you can use that in place of the *DistinguishedFolderId* and achieve the same results.

SyncState Element

The optional *SyncState* element allows you to indicate the starting point in time after which changes should be reported. *SyncState* within *SyncFolderItems* has the same structure as it does in a *SyncFolderHierarchy* request. In *SyncFolderHierarchy*, the *SyncState* was tied to a given mailbox. You could not, for instance, take the *SyncState* obtained from a *SyncFolderHierarchy* call on Ken Malcolmson's mailbox and use it in a *SyncFolderHierarchy* request on Tina Makovec's mailbox. In contrast, the *SyncState* of a *SyncFolderItems* request is tied to the *folder* identified by the *SyncFolderId* element. The end result of this folder association is that you must store the latest *SyncState* value for *each* folder that you wish to maintain a local copy of.

Omitting the *SyncState* element will cause *SyncFolderItems* to return all the items that are present within the folder.

As an example, let's make a *SyncFolderItems* request against the inbox using the elements that we have described so far. Note that the request must include the *MaxChangesReturned* element—we will discuss this element shortly. For brevity's sake, the example specifies an *IdOnly* base shape and the *item:Subject* is added as an additional property path. The request is shown in Listing 16-23.

LISTING 16-23 The first *SyncFolderItems* request

```
<SyncFolderItems xmlns=".../messages" xmlns:t=".../types">
  <ItemShape>
    <t:BaseShape>IdOnly</t:BaseShape>
    <t:AdditionalProperties>
      <t:FieldURI FieldURI="item:Subject"/>
    </t:AdditionalProperties>
  </ItemShape>
  <SyncFolderId>
    <t:DistinguishedFolderId Id="inbox"/>
  </SyncFolderId>
  <MaxChangesReturned>512</MaxChangesReturned>
</SyncFolderItems>
```

The response is shown in Listing 16-24.

LISTING 16-24 Response to the first *SyncFolderItems* request

```
<m:SyncFolderItemsResponse xmlns:t=".../types"
                           xmlns:m=".../messages">
  <m:ResponseMessages>
    <m:SyncFolderItemsResponseMessage ResponseClass="Success">
      <m:ResponseCode>NoError</m:ResponseCode>
      <m:SyncState>H4sIAAAAAAAEA...</m:SyncState>
      <m:IncludesLastItemInRange>true</m:IncludesLastItemInRange>
      <m:Changes>
        <t:Create>
          <t:Message>
            <t:ItemId Id="AAAuAHBoeWxsaXMua..." ChangeKey="CQAAABYAAAC9V..."/>
            <t:Subject>You have been designated as a delegate for Tina
                    Makovec</t:Subject>
          </t:Message>
        </t:Create>
        <t:Create>
          <t:Message>
            <t:ItemId Id="AAAuAHBoeWxsaXMuaGFy..." ChangeKey="CQAAAB..."/>
            <t:Subject>Message to send to DL</t:Subject>
          </t:Message>
        </t:Create>
  <!-- additional Create elements elided -->
      </m:Changes>
    </m:SyncFolderItemsResponseMessage>
  </m:ResponseMessages>
</m:SyncFolderItemsResponse>
```

As you can see from Listing 16-24, the structure of a *SyncFolderItems* response is quite similar to the structure of a *SyncFolderHierarchy* response. In fact, an initial item sync contains *Create* change entries just like the ones encountered when you request an initial folder sync. We will examine the structure of the response in more detail shortly.

Ignore Element

The optional *Ignore* element allows you to indicate that there are items in the folder to sync that you are not interested in receiving change entries for. So, why would you ever want to ignore changes to an item in a folder? Imagine that you have a local copy of your Inbox folder that you keep up to date using *SyncFolderItems*. If *you* explicitly make a *DeleteItem* request to remove an item from the Inbox, then you don't really need to wait for the next *SyncFolderItems* response to tell you that you need to delete the item from your local copy of the Inbox—you can just delete the item yourself. However, when you next call *SyncFolderItems*, you will be told about this delete, unless you tell *SyncFolderItems* to ignore changes to the item in question.

The *Ignore* element is an instance of *ArrayOfBaseItemIdsType*, which is simply an unbounded sequence of *ItemIdType* instances. When using the proxy classes, *Ignore* is exposed as an *ItemIdType[]*.

The next example begins by retrieving the latest *SyncState* on the Drafts folder. The initial changes aren't of interest right now, so the request specifies a *BaseShape* of *IdOnly* to reduce network traffic.

```
<SyncFolderItems xmlns=".../messages"
                 xmlns:t=".../types">
  <ItemShape>
    <t:BaseShape>IdOnly</t:BaseShape>
  </ItemShape>
  <SyncFolderId>
    <t:DistinguishedFolderId Id="drafts"/>
  </SyncFolderId>
  <MaxChangesReturned>512</MaxChangesReturned>
</SyncFolderItems>
```

Next, Listing 16-25 shows a *CreateItem* request to create two messages in the Drafts folder.

LISTING 16-25 Creating two messages in the Drafts folder

```
<CreateItem xmlns=".../messages"
            xmlns:t=".../types"
            MessageDisposition="SaveOnly">
  <Items>
    <t:Message>
      <t:Subject>Message that we want to ignore changes to</t:Subject>
    </t:Message>
    <t:Message>
      <t:Subject>Message that we do NOT want to ignore changes to</t:Subject>
    </t:Message>
  </Items>
</CreateItem>
```

Now, Listing 16-26 shows a *SyncFolderItems* request with the latest *SyncState*, and this time, the request includes the *ItemId* of the message to be ignored.

LISTING 16-26 *SyncFolderItems* with *Ignore*

```
<SyncFolderItems xmlns=".../messages"
                 xmlns:t=".../types">
  <ItemShape>
    <t:BaseShape>Default</t:BaseShape>
  </ItemShape>
  <SyncFolderId>
    <t:DistinguishedFolderId Id="drafts"/>
  </SyncFolderId>
  <SyncState>H4sIAAAAAAAEA029...</SyncState>
  <Ignore>
```

```
    <t:ItemId Id="AAAuAHBoeWxsaXM..." ChangeKey="CQAAABYAAAC9..."/>
  </Ignore>
  <MaxChangesReturned>512</MaxChangesReturned>
</SyncFolderItems>
```

Due to the *Ignore* element, you would expect the response to contain a single *Create* change entry corresponding to the message with subject "Message that we do NOT want to ignore changes to." Listing 16-27 shows that the response does indeed meet this expectation.

LISTING 16-27 *SyncFolderItems* response with *Ignore*

```
<m:SyncFolderItemsResponse xmlns:t=".../types"
                           xmlns:m=".../messages">
  <m:ResponseMessages>
    <m:SyncFolderItemsResponseMessage ResponseClass="Success">
      <m:ResponseCode>NoError</m:ResponseCode>
      <m:SyncState>H4sIAAAAAAAEAO29B...</m:SyncState>
      <m:IncludesLastItemInRange>true</m:IncludesLastItemInRange>
      <m:Changes>
        <t:Create>
          <t:Message>
            <t:ItemId Id="AAAuAHBoeWxs..." ChangeKey="CQAAABYAAAC..."/>
            <t:Subject>Message that we do NOT want to ignore changes to</t:Subject>
            <t:Sensitivity>Normal</t:Sensitivity>
            <t:Size>134</t:Size>
            <t:DateTimeSent>2007-09-21T15:11:37Z</t:DateTimeSent>
            <t:DateTimeCreated>2007-09-21T15:11:37Z</t:DateTimeCreated>
            <t:HasAttachments>false</t:HasAttachments>
            <t:IsRead>true</t:IsRead>
          </t:Message>
        </t:Create>
      </m:Changes>
    </m:SyncFolderItemsResponseMessage>
  </m:ResponseMessages>
</m:SyncFolderItemsResponse>
```

It is important to note that the presence of the *Ignore* element does not change the *SyncState* value that is returned. If the request from Listing 16-26 is reissued, but the *Ignore* element is *omitted*, then the response will contain the two messages that were created rather than the single message returned in Listing 16-27. Exchange Web Services effectively retrieves all of the changes since the supplied *SyncState* and then removes those items referenced in the *Ignore* element before sending the response.

If an *ItemId* supplied in the *Ignore* element contains a *ChangeKey* that is not current, and a change occurs to the item in question, *SyncFolderItems* will include the "ignored" item in the response.

MaxChangesReturned Element

The required *MaxChangesReturned* element indicates the maximum number of entries that you would like to receive in the *Changes* element of a *SyncFolderItems* response. *MaxChangesReturned* must be an integer value between 1 and 512 (inclusive). Note that the proxy classes expose *MaxChangesReturned* as an integer, meaning that you can set the value to an integer outside of the allowed range. However, doing so will cause a SOAP exception to be thrown when the request is processed by Exchange Web Services due to a schema validation error.

So what happens if the number of actual changes exceeds the value listed in *MaxChangesReturned*? After calling *SyncFolderItems* to retrieve the latest *SyncState*, let's create ten messages in the drafts folder.

```
<CreateItem xmlns=".../messages"
            xmlns:t=".../types"
            MessageDisposition="SaveOnly">
  <Items>
    <t:Message><t:Subject>Message1</t:Subject></t:Message>
    <t:Message><t:Subject>Message2</t:Subject></t:Message>
    <t:Message><t:Subject>Message3</t:Subject></t:Message>
    <t:Message><t:Subject>Message4</t:Subject></t:Message>
    <t:Message><t:Subject>Message5</t:Subject></t:Message>
    <t:Message><t:Subject>Message6</t:Subject></t:Message>
    <t:Message><t:Subject>Message7</t:Subject></t:Message>
    <t:Message><t:Subject>Message8</t:Subject></t:Message>
    <t:Message><t:Subject>Message9</t:Subject></t:Message>
    <t:Message><t:Subject>Message10</t:Subject></t:Message>
  </Items>
</CreateItem>
```

Now, Listing 16-28 shows a *SyncFolderItems* request using the latest *SyncState* but the *MaxChangesReturned* element is set to 5.

LISTING 16-28 *SyncFolderItems* with a small *MaxChangesReturned* value

```
<SyncFolderItems xmlns=".../messages"
                 xmlnst:=".../messages">
  <ItemShape>
    <t:BaseShape>IdOnly</t:BaseShape>
  </ItemShape>
  <SyncFolderId>
    <t:DistinguishedFolderId Id="drafts"/>
  </SyncFolderId>
  <SyncState>H4sIAAAAAAAEA...</SyncState>
  <MaxChangesReturned>5</MaxChangesReturned>
</SyncFolderItems>
```

The response is shown in Listing 16-29.

LISTING 16-29 *SyncFolderItems* response when more changes are available

```xml
<m:SyncFolderItemsResponse xmlns:t=".../types"
                           xmlns:m=".../messages">
  <m:ResponseMessages>
    <m:SyncFolderItemsResponseMessage ResponseClass="Success">
      <m:ResponseCode>NoError</m:ResponseCode>
      <m:SyncState>H4sIAAAAAAAEAO29...</m:SyncState>
      <m:IncludesLastItemInRange>false</m:IncludesLastItemInRange>
      <m:Changes>
        <t:Create>
          <t:Message>
            <t:ItemId Id="AAAuAHBoeWxsaXM..." ChangeKey="CQAAABYAAAC9Vh..."/>
            <t:Subject>Message1</t:Subject>
          </t:Message>
        </t:Create>
        <t:Create>
          <t:Message>
            <t:ItemId Id="AAAuAHBoeWxsaX..." ChangeKey="CQAAABYAAAC9..."/>
            <t:Subject>Message2</t:Subject>
          </t:Message>
        </t:Create>
        <t:Create>
          <t:Message>
            <t:ItemId Id="AAAuAHBoeWxsaXMua..." ChangeKey="CQAAABYAAAC9Vhn..."/>
            <t:Subject>Message3</t:Subject>
          </t:Message>
        </t:Create>
        <t:Create>
          <t:Message>
            <t:ItemId Id="AAAuAHBoeWxsaXMua..." ChangeKey="CQAAABYAAAC..."/>
            <t:Subject>Message4</t:Subject>
          </t:Message>
        </t:Create>
        <t:Create>
          <t:Message>
            <t:ItemId Id="AAAuAHBoeWxsaXMu..." ChangeKey="CQAAABYAAAC9Vhnc..."/>
            <t:Subject>Message5</t:Subject>
          </t:Message>
        </t:Create>
      </m:Changes>
    </m:SyncFolderItemsResponseMessage>
  </m:ResponseMessages>
</m:SyncFolderItemsResponse>
```

The response in Listing 16-29 contains five changes as expected, but what is really note-worthy is that the *IncludesLastItemInRange* element is set to false, indicating that there are more changes available. You may recall from Chapter 15, "Advanced Searching," that paged *FindItem* and *FindFolder* calls exposed a similar construct for indicating that more results were available; however, in the *FindItem* and *FindFolder* case, the response provided an index that could be passed to a subsequent call to retrieve the remaining data. Nothing from the re-sponse in Listing 16-29 appears to offer such an index for *SyncFolderItems*. And yet, such an index *is* there, hiding inside the returned *SyncState* value! Indeed, if the request from Listing 16-28 is reissued using the *SyncState* returned in Listing 16-29, you will see that the remaining five messages are returned and that the *IncludesLastItemInRange* is set to true. The response is shown in Listing 16-30.

LISTING 16-30 The remaining changes in the *SyncFolderItems* response

```
<m:SyncFolderItemsResponse xmlns:t=".../types"
                           xmlns:m=".../messages">
  <m:ResponseMessages>
    <m:SyncFolderItemsResponseMessage ResponseClass="Success">
      <m:ResponseCode>NoError</m:ResponseCode>
        <m:SyncState>H4sIAAAAAAAEAO29B2A...</m:SyncState>
        <m:IncludesLastItemInRange>true</m:IncludesLastItemInRange>
        <m:Changes>
          <t:Create>
            <t:Message>
              <t:ItemId Id="AAAuAHBoeWxsaX..." ChangeKey="CQAAABYAAAC9..."/>
              <t:Subject>Message6</t:Subject>
            </t:Message>
          </t:Create>
          <t:Create>
            <t:Message>
              <t:ItemId Id="AAAuAHBoeWaGFycm..." ChangeKey="CQAAABYAAAC9Vhn..."/>
              <t:Subject>Message7</t:Subject>
            </t:Message>
          </t:Create>
          <t:Create>
            <t:Message>
              <t:ItemId Id="AAAuAHBoeWxsaXM..." ChangeKey="CQAAABYAAAC9Vh..."/>
              <t:Subject>Message8</t:Subject>
            </t:Message>
          </t:Create>
          <t:Create>
            <t:Message>
              <t:ItemId Id="AAAuAHBoeWxsaXMu..." ChangeKey="CQAAABYAAAC9..."/>
              <t:Subject>Message9</t:Subject>
            </t:Message>
          </t:Create>
          <t:Create>
            <t:Message>
              <t:ItemId Id="AAAuAHBoeWxsaXMu..." ChangeKey="CQAAABYAAAC9..."/>
              <t:Subject>Message10</t:Subject>
            </t:Message>
          </t:Create>
        </m:Changes>
    </m:SyncFolderItemsResponseMessage>
  </m:ResponseMessages>
</m:SyncFolderItemsResponse>
```

SyncFolderItems Responses

You have seen much of the *SyncFolderItems* response structure so far, but there is more to be covered. *SyncFolderItems* returns a single response message of type *SyncFolderItemsResponseMessageType*, whose basic structure is shown in Listing 16-31.

LISTING 16-31 Basic structure of *SyncFolderItemsResponseMessageType*

```
<m:SyncFolderItemsResponseMessage ResponseClass="Success|Error">
  <m:ResponseCode/>
  <m:SyncState/>
  <m:IncludesLastItemInRange/>
  <m:Changes/>
</m:SyncFolderItemsResponseMessage>
```

All of the elements in Listing 16-31 have been addressed with the exception of the *Changes* element.

Changes Element

The *Changes* element contains the actual item changes that have occurred in the folder since the point in time suggested by the supplied *SyncState* from the request. The *Changes* element is an instance of *SyncFolderItemsChangesType* and is an unbounded sequence of *Create*, *Update*, or *Delete* changes as shown in Listing 16-32.

LISTING 16-32 *SyncFolderItemsChangesType* schema

```
<xs:complexType name="SyncFolderItemsChangesType">
  <xs:sequence>
    <xs:choice maxOccurs="unbounded" minOccurs="0">
      <xs:element name="Create" type="t:SyncFolderItemsCreateOrUpdateType"/>
      <xs:element name="Update" type="t:SyncFolderItemsCreateOrUpdateType"/>
      <xs:element name="Delete" type="t:SyncFolderItemsDeleteType"/>
    </xs:choice>
  </xs:sequence>
</xs:complexType>
```

The schema in Listing 16-32 should look quite similar to the schema type used for representing folder changes in a *SyncFolderHierarchy* response.

Create and *Update* **Change Entries**   As with *SyncFolderHierarchy*, there is a single type, *SyncFolderItemsCreateOrUpdateType*, representing *Create* and *Update* changes on an item. *SyncFolderItemsCreateOrUpdateType* is a simple wrapper around the single item that has changed.

```
<xs:complexType name="SyncFolderItemsCreateOrUpdateType">
  <xs:choice>
    <xs:element name="Item" type="t:ItemType"/>
    <xs:element name="Message" type="t:MessageType"/>
    <xs:element name="CalendarItem" type="t:CalendarItemType"/>
    <xs:element name="Contact" type="t:ContactItemType"/>
    <xs:element name="DistributionList" type="t:DistributionListType"/>
    <xs:element name="MeetingMessage" type="t:MeetingMessageType"/>
    <xs:element name="MeetingRequest" type="t:MeetingRequestMessageType"/>
    <xs:element name="MeetingResponse" type="t:MeetingResponseMessageType"/>
    <xs:element name="MeetingCancellation" type="t:MeetingCancellationMessageType"/>
    <xs:element name="Task" type="t:TaskType"/>
  </xs:choice>
</xs:complexType>
```

You will encounter a *Create* change entry as the result of an initial sync or as the result of an item being created after the boundary indicated by the *SyncState* passed into the *SyncFolderItems* request.

You will encounter an *Update* change entry as the result of changes to an item that occurred after the boundary indicated by the *SyncState* passed into the *SyncFolderItems* request.

While *SyncFolderHierarchy* considers only changes to the *DisplayName*, *ParentFolderId*, or *FolderClass* to be sufficient enough to generate an update change entry, *any* property change to an item is sufficient to generate an update change entry for a *SyncFolderItems* response.

When the item is returned within an *Update* change entry, can you tell *what* changed about the item? No, you cannot. All you know is that *something* on that item was updated. In fact, the update does not even have to be to a property that is contained on the item in the *Update* element. Remember, the properties that are returned in a *SyncFolderItems* response are a function of the *ItemShape* that was specified in the request. As such, it is prudent for you to retrieve all of the properties that are of interest to you so that you can determine if the change is noteworthy..

Delete **Change Entries**   A *Delete* change returned in a *SyncFolderItems* response contains the *ItemId* of the item that was deleted. Listing 16-33 shows an example *SyncFolderItems* response after an item is deleted from the Drafts folder.

LISTING 16-33 *SyncFolderItems* response with *Delete* change entry

```
<m:SyncFolderItemsResponse xmlns:t=".../types"
                           xmlns:m=".../messages">
  <m:ResponseMessages>
    <m:SyncFolderItemsResponseMessage ResponseClass="Success">
      <m:ResponseCode>NoError</m:ResponseCode>
      <m:SyncState>H4sIAAAAAAAE...</m:SyncState>
      <m:IncludesLastItemInRange>true</m:IncludesLastItemInRange>
      <m:Changes>
        <t:Delete>
```

```
            <t:ItemId Id="AAAuAHBoeWxs..." ChangeKey="AAAAAA=="/>
        </t:Delete>
      </m:Changes>
    </m:SyncFolderItemsResponseMessage>
  </m:ResponseMessages>
</m:SyncFolderItemsResponse>
```

SyncFolderItems Responses and the Proxy Classes

When examining *SyncFolderItems* responses using the proxy classes, you encounter the same situation that you do with *SyncFolderHierarchy,* namely that it is not possible to determine whether a given change entry is a *Create* or an *Update.* In order to determine the actual change type, you must examine the corresponding entry in the *ItemsElementName* array on the *Changes* property. Listing 16-33 provides a method that performs a *SyncFolderItems* call and then places the *Create, Update,* and *Delete* changes into separate lists.

LISTING 16-33 Method to separate *Create, Update,* and *Delete* changes

```
/// <summary>
/// SyncFolderItems and separate the create, update and delete changes
/// </summary>
/// <param name="binding">Binding to use for call</param>
/// <param name="syncFolderId">Folder to sync from</param>
/// <param name="syncState">REF sync state to use (and update outbound)</param>
/// <param name="responseShape">Response shape</param>
/// <param name="createdItems">OUT list of create items. Could be null.</param>
/// <param name="updatedItems">OUT list of updated items. Could be null.</param>
/// <param name="deletedItems">OUT list of deleted items. Could be null.</param>
///
public static void SyncFolderItemsWithChange(
                        ExchangeServiceBinding binding,
                        BaseFolderIdType syncFolderId,
                        ref string syncState,
                        ItemResponseShapeType responseShape,
                        out List<ItemType> createdItems,
                        out List<ItemType> updatedItems,
                        out List<ItemIdType> deletedItems)
{
    SyncFolderItemsType request = new SyncFolderItemsType();
    request.ItemShape = responseShape;
    request.MaxChangesReturned = 512;
    request.SyncFolderId = new TargetFolderIdType();
    request.SyncFolderId.Item = syncFolderId;

    request.SyncState = syncState;
    SyncFolderItemsResponseType response = binding.SyncFolderItems(request);
    SyncFolderItemsResponseMessageType responseMessage =
            response.ResponseMessages.Items[0] as SyncFolderItemsResponseMessageType;

    if (responseMessage.ResponseCode != ResponseCodeType.NoError)
```

```
  {
    throw new Exception("SyncFolderItems failed with response code: " +
              responseMessage.ResponseCode.ToString());
  }

  createdItems = null;
  updatedItems = null;
  deletedItems = null;

  if (responseMessage.Changes.Items == null)
  {
    // No changes!
    //
    return;
  }

  for (int index = 0; index < responseMessage.Changes.Items.Length; index++)
  {
    switch (responseMessage.Changes.ItemsElementName[index])
    {
      case ItemsChoiceType2.Create:
        if (createdItems == null)
        {
          createdItems = new List<ItemType>();
        }
        SyncFolderItemsCreateOrUpdateType create =
          responseMessage.Changes.Items[index] as SyncFolderItemsCreateOrUpdateType;
        createdItems.Add(create.Item);
        break;

      case ItemsChoiceType2.Update:
        if (updatedItems == null)
        {
          updatedItems = new List<ItemType>();
        }
        SyncFolderItemsCreateOrUpdateType update =
          responseMessage.Changes.Items[index] as SyncFolderItemsCreateOrUpdateType;
        updatedItems.Add(update.Item);
        break;

      case ItemsChoiceType2.Delete:
        if (deletedItems == null)
        {
          deletedItems = new List<ItemIdType>();
        }
        SyncFolderItemsDeleteType delete =
            responseMessage.Changes.Items[index] as SyncFolderItemsDeleteType;
        deletedItems.Add(delete.ItemId);
        break;
    }
  }
  syncState = responseMessage.SyncState;
}
```

Syncing Items Outside of the IPM Subtree

SyncFolderHierarchy is limited to sync folder data for folders contained in the IPM Subtree (*msgfolderroot*) and its subfolders. *SyncFolderItems* has no such limitation. You are free to specify any folder in the mailbox as the *SyncFolderId*. For instance, Listing 16-34 shows a request that will perform an initial sync of the Non IPM Subtree (*root*) folder.

LISTING 16-34 *SyncFolderItems* on the Non IPM Subtree

```
<SyncFolderItems xmlns=".../messages"
                 xmlns=".../types">
  <ItemShape>
    <t:BaseShape>IdOnly</t:BaseShape>
    <t:AdditionalProperties>
      <t:FieldURI FieldURI="item:Subject"/>
    </t:AdditionalProperties>
  </ItemShape>
  <SyncFolderId>
    <t:DistinguishedFolderId Id="root"/>
  </SyncFolderId>
  <MaxChangesReturned>512</MaxChangesReturned>
</SyncFolderItems>
```

Summary

Exchange Web Services provides two methods to allow you to discover changes that have occurred to your mailbox from some starting point (indicated by the *SyncState*) until the time that the request is made. *SyncFolderHierarchy* allows you to determine changes that have occurred to the folder hierarchy. *SyncFolderHierarchy* calls always start in the IPM subtree (*msgfolderroot*) and consider all changes within the folder hierarchy (deep traversal). In addition, there is no way to limit the number of changes returned by *SyncFolderHierarchy*—all changes since the point in time suggested by the supplied *SyncState* will be returned.

SyncFolderItems allows you to determine changes that have occurred to the contents of a single folder since the point in time suggested by the supplied *SyncState*. *SyncFolderItems* allows you to *ignore* changes to certain items within a folder by providing the *ItemIds* for the items to ignore within the *Ignore* element. We discussed how the *MaxChangesReturned* element controls the maximum number of changes that are returned within a single *SyncFolderItems* response and how to retrieve the additional data by passing in the updated *SyncState*.

Chapter 17
Notification

What Is a Notification?

So you've just bought a brand new car, and it is the first year the model has been out. The dealership sends you a letter several weeks later thanking you for choosing them and telling you all about the servicing options. You are having fun driving around in your new car. You've been washing it every weekend and checking that you don't have that first stone chip or door ding. Then *it* arrives—the notification of a recall on your car. Apparently your brand new car has been known to explode when it's being filled up at the gas station.

The recall takes the shine off your new car a little bit, but you received the notification so you take the car back to the dealership to get it fixed. And everything is great again—that is, until the next recall. Yes, that is one of the downsides to buying a new car, but at least you were notified of the problems so that you were able to take prompt, corrective action.

Notification in Microsoft Exchange Server 2007 Web Services (EWS) works in a similar manner, only instead of notifying you of recalls on your brand new car, Notification informs you about events such as new e-mail messages in your Inbox or changes to appointments in your Calendar.

The new car scenario describes what is equivalent to an Exchange Web Services *push notification* mechanism—the notifications are sent to you as they occur without you actively having to do anything other than provide a channel for the notifications to be sent to (that is, your address). Then you sit and wait for them to turn up.[1] Push notifications are passive for the client—the server initiates them.

In contrast, imagine a scenario where you have to periodically go to a Web site and see if any recalls have been made for your car model. In Exchange Web Services, such a proactive check like that would be considered a *pull notification* mechanism—you repeatedly ask the server for the information you are interested in, and the system returns such information if any is available at the time of the request. In contrast to push notifications, pull notifications are active for the client.

---

[1] Or rather in this new car case, you hoped the recall notices would never show up!

How Do Sync and Notification Differ?

In Chapter 16, "Synchronization," we discussed the *SyncFolderHierarchy* and *SyncFolderItems* Web methods. Though Sync and Notification share a common goal of providing you with a way to keep an up-to-date copy of Mailbox data, there are some differences between the two.

Weight

The first difference between Sync and Notification is the amount of information each returns. Notification is lightweight and returns just the id of the affected item or folder along with the type of event that has occurred. You use a subsequent *GetItem* or *GetFolder* call with the id returned by the notification to retrieve the item or folder properties. In contrast, Sync allows you to specify the response shape, or list of properties, that should be returned for each item or folder in the response. As such, with Sync, there is no need for the additional *GetItem* or *GetFolder* call. In a very loose sense, you can consider it like this:

Sync = Pull Notification + *GetItem/GetFolder*.

Folders versus Items

Sync has separate methods for retrieving changes on items (*SyncFolderItems*) and folders (*SyncFolderHierarchy*). With Notification, you get folder and item change information together.

Server versus Client Held State

With Notification, the Client Access Server (CAS) maintains all state data for your Notification subscription. With Sync, the state data for the subscription is passed back and forth in the *SyncState* parameter, which can actually get quite large.

Information Richness

Notification provides richer information on what is happening to the Mailbox contents. As well as telling you about the creation, modification, and deletion of Mailbox items, Notification also tells you if items have been moved or copied and can tell you about new mail arrival.

Control Over Information Received

Notification provides you with more control over what changes you hear about. You can opt into only those types of changes you are interested in. On the other hand, with Sync, all changes are returned.[2] For example, imagine that you want to set some special property on all items as they are created. With Notification, you can register your interest in item creation alone. With Sync, you would receive information about item creation, deletion, and modification, and would therefore have to filter the information returned to get to just the creation changes.

Other Mailboxes

SyncFolderItems allows you to sync against another user's Mailbox. However, Notification works only for the caller's Mailbox.

Pull Notifications

Several weeks prior to Ken Malcolmson's failure to order the supplies for the company meeting,[3] Ken and his manager, Tina Makovec, were waiting for a table at the Contoso Fine Dining restaurant. The restaurant did not yet have those fancy beepers that flash and vibrate in order to alert you that your table is ready. Instead, the hostess added Ken's name to the waiting list and suggested that they wait in the lobby. Five minutes later, Ken walked up to the hostess stand and asked if their table was ready. "Not yet," came the reply. Three minutes later, Ken returned to the hostess stand and asked once again, "Is our table ready? It should be listed under 'Malcolmson.' That's M-A-L-C-O-L-M..." "Not yet," the hostess replied, interrupting him. Two minutes later, Ken returned and asked the same question. This time, the hostess responded in the affirmative, and Ken and Tina were led to their table.

This restaurant scenario is very similar to how pull notifications work. First, Ken had to register his interest in being notified, which he did by supplying his name. He also provided another qualifier for his notification—he requested a table for two. At any given time during Ken and Tina's wait, the hostess knew whether Ken's table for two was available, yet the information was relayed to Ken only when he presented himself and requested the status of his table. Ken had to *pull* the information from the hostess. With Exchange Web Services pull notifications, the CAS (hostess) holds the information about what has changed (event), but it is up to you (Ken) to check the status.

So what is a pull notification in Exchange Web Services? First, let's explain the basic process involved in pull notifications.[4] As stated earlier, the process of retrieving information from a pull subscription is client-initiated.

---

[2] With the exception of those items listed in *SyncFolderItem Ignore* property.

[3] See chapter 6 for the first part of this story.

[4] This explanation is not intended to be a complete explanation of how the Notification mechanism works in Exchange Web Services. We took some liberties with the architecture where necessary to simplify this discussion.

The following table includes a few definitions to help clarify the discussion.

TABLE 17-1 Some Useful Terminology

Term	Description
event	A Mailbox action that occurs on the server.
notification	The message sent to the client; contains the list of events that the client registered an interest in.
Event Queue	Maintains the list of events that the user registered interest in and that have occurred since the last notification was sent out. Each subscription has a corresponding Event Queue on the server.
Subscribe	The Exchange Web Services Web method used to register your interest in a certain set of events. This method creates the Event Queue and returns the id of your subscription.

You register your interest in the pull notifications process by issuing a *Subscribe* Web request. This request contains the folder for which you wish to receive events as well as the type of events you want to know about. See the following list of events you can receive information about. A single subscription can request that one, some, or all of these events be returned by Notification.

- New mail arrival
- Item creation
- Item deletion
- Item move
- Item copy
- Item modification

In response to the *Subscribe* request, the server returns a subscription id to the client.[5] Events occur on the server, and if these events match the criteria specified in the *Subscribe* request, they will be added to the Event Queue for that subscription. The client then periodically issues a *GetEvents* request using the subscription id. In response to the *GetEvents* request, the server takes all events from the Event Queue for that subscription—identified by the subscription id provided in the *GetEvents* request—and sends them back in a Notification response.

If no events have occurred since the last Notification response was sent out (that is, if the Event Queue is empty), a status event is returned to the client. This basically means the server is acknowledging the request from the client but is stating that it has no new information to return. Now that you have a high-level understanding of what is going on, let's dig deeper into pull notification subscriptions and how they work.

---

5 A watermark is also returned, but we're going to leave this out of the description for now to keep the discussion simple.

Creating a Pull Notification Subscription

First, let's look in more detail at how you go about creating a subscription for pull notifications. The XML request for creating a pull notifications subscription (we will use the term *pull subscription* from now on) is shown in Listing 17-1.

LISTING 17-1 Pull subscription request

```
<Subscribe xmlns=".../messages"
           xmlns:t=".../types">
  <PullSubscriptionRequest>
    <t:FolderIds>
      <t:DistinguishedFolderId Id="inbox"/>
      <t:DistinguishedFolderId Id="calendar"/>
    </t:FolderIds>
    <t:EventTypes>
      <t:EventType>CreatedEvent</t:EventType>
      <t:EventType>ModifiedEvent</t:EventType>
    </t:EventTypes>
    <t:Timeout>30</t:Timeout>
  </PullSubscriptionRequest>
</Subscribe>
```

The *FolderIds* Element

The required *FolderIds* element contains a list of one or more folders that the subscription should monitor. You can use either *DistinguishedFolderId* elements, as is shown in Listing 17-1, or *FolderId* elements. Events that occur on a folder of interest and events that occur directly on subfolders of a folder of interest will be returned. For the subscription in Listing 17-1, if a folder is created in the Inbox, then a *Create* event will be added to the Event Queue for the subscription. However, events that occur to items or folders contained within a subfolder are not considered applicable events for the subscription. For example, items created in a sub-folder of the Inbox will not trigger a *Create* event to be added to the Event Queue for your subscription. To register your interest in events that occur on items and folders within a sub-folder, you must create a separate subscription for that specific folder. Of course, you are free to create a single subscription that monitors a folder as well as its subfolders.

The *Timeout* Element

The required *Timeout* element value is measured in minutes and indicates how long a pull subscription will remain active if the client does not access that subscription. A client accesses the subscription by sending a *GetEvents* request that returns all events currently queued for that subscription in a Notification response. In Listing 17-1, the *Timeout* is set to 30 minutes, which means that if more than 30 minutes elapses between calls from the client, the sub-scription on the server will expire and be deleted. To prevent a subscription from expiring, you therefore want your application to call *GetEvents* at an interval slightly shorter than the *Timeout* value specified when creating the subscription.

Listing 17-2 provides the response to the request from Listing 17-1.

LISTING 17-2 Pull subscription response

```
<SubscribeResponse xmlns:m="...messages"
                   xmlns:t=".../types"
                   xmlns=".../messages">
  <m:ResponseMessages>
    <m:SubscribeResponseMessage ResponseClass="Success">
      <m:ResponseCode>NoError</m:ResponseCode>
      <m:SubscriptionId>5f023ab6-...-ed3728fc44fe</m:SubscriptionId>
      <m:Watermark>AQAAAHpbMtN3AjZMsSnFCPBLszoTBQAAAAAAAE=</m:Watermark>
    </m:SubscribeResponseMessage>
  </m:ResponseMessages>
</SubscribeResponse>
```

SubscriptionId and *Watermark* Response Elements

In the response shown in Listing 17-2, the *SubscriptionId* uniquely identifies the pull subscription you have just created. Similar to the *SyncState* value used in *SyncFolderHierarchy* and *SyncFolderItems*, the *Watermark* element ensures that you receive only the new events that have occurred. If you lose either value, you need to recreate the subscription. You should treat the returned *Watermark* value with the same reverence you gave *SyncState* in Sync. Both the *SubscriptionId* and *Watermark* must be passed into *GetEvents* requests.

Using the Proxy Classes

So you've seen how to create a pull subscription via XML, but how do you do the same using the proxy classes? Listing 17-1 shows that, unlike other Exchange Web Services methods, the *Subscribe* request element does not directly contain the subscription details. Rather, it includes a *PullSubscriptionRequest* element that contains all the properties necessary for creating the request. The *Subscribe* method is actually used to create a subscription for both pull and push notifications, and as such, it can contain either a *PullSubscriptionRequest* element or a *PushSubscriptionRequest* element.[6]

Let's provide a constructor to help create the *PullSubscriptionRequest*. The *PullSubscriptionRequest* element maps to an instance of type *PullSubscriptionRequestType* in the proxy classes, and as previously stated takes the following parameters:

- One or more folders to subscribe to

---

6 Push subscriptions will be discussed shortly.

- One or more event types to listen for

- A timeout value (in minutes)

- Optionally, a watermark if you are recreating a previous subscription

The constructor is shown in Listing 17-3.

LISTING 17-3 Overloaded constructor for a pull subscription request

```
/// <summary>
/// Partial class extension of the PullSubscriptionRequestType
/// </summary>
public partial class PullSubscriptionRequestType
{
  /// <summary>
  /// Default constructor needed for XML serialization
  /// </summary>
  public PullSubscriptionRequestType()
  {}


  /// <summary>
  /// Overloaded constructor which helps in the creation of the Subscribe
  /// request for a Pull Subscription
  /// </summary>
  /// <param name="subscriptionFolders">The Distinguished folders
  /// you wish to subscribe to</param>
  /// <param name="eventTypes">The events to subscribe for</param>
  /// <param name="watermark">Watermark for recreating a previous
  /// Subscription</param>
  /// <param name="timeout">Timeout for Subscription in minutes</param>
  ///
  public PullSubscriptionRequestType(
              BaseFolderIdType[] subscriptionFolders,
              NotificationEventTypeType[] eventTypes,
              string watermark,
              int timeout)
  {
    this.FolderIds = subscriptionFolders;
    this.EventTypes = eventTypes;

    // If we have a Watermark then set it on the Subscribe request
    //
    if (!string.IsNullOrEmpty(watermark))
    {
      this.Watermark = watermark;
    }

    this.Timeout = timeout;
  }
}
```

Using this overloaded constructor, the code to create a new subscription is shown in Listing 17-4.

LISTING 17-4 Create a pull subscription by using the constructor from Listing 17-3

```csharp
/// <summary>
/// Create a new Pull Notifications Subscription
/// </summary>
/// <param name="binding">Binding to use for call</param>
/// <param name="eventTypes">Events for which to Subscribe</param>
/// <param name="subscriptionFolders">Folders for which to Subscribe</param>
/// <param name="subscriptionId">Returned id for the Subscription created</param>
/// <param name="watermark">Returned watermark for the Subscription created</param>
///
public static void CreatePullSubscription(
                        ExchangeServiceBinding binding,
                        NotificationEventTypeType[] eventTypes,
                        BaseFolderIdType[] subscriptionFolders,
                        out string subscriptionId,
                        out string watermark)
{
  subscriptionId = string.Empty;
  watermark = string.Empty;

  // Call the overloaded constructor
  //
  PullSubscriptionRequestType pullSubscription =
          new PullSubscriptionRequestType(
                  subscriptionFolders,
                  eventTypes,
                  string.Empty, /* New Subscription so pass in empty Watermark */
                  30 /* 30 minute timeout */);

  // Create the Subscribe request and submit the request to the server
  //
  SubscribeType subscribeRequest = new SubscribeType();
  subscribeRequest.Item = pullSubscription;
  SubscribeResponseType subscribeResponse = binding.Subscribe(subscribeRequest);

  // We have a response. Now we need to parse it to get the SubscriptionId and the
  // Watermark
  //
  SubscribeResponseMessageType subscribeResponseMessage =
        subscribeResponse.ResponseMessages.Items[0] as
            SubscribeResponseMessageType;

  if (subscribeResponseMessage.ResponseCode == ResponseCodeType.NoError)
  {
    subscriptionId = subscribeResponseMessage.SubscriptionId;
    watermark = subscribeResponseMessage.Watermark;
  }
  else
  {
    // We received an error in the response
    throw new Exception(subscribeResponseMessage.MessageText);
  }
}
```

And using the *CreatePullSubscription* method from Listing 17-4 is straightforward:

```
string subscriptionId;
string watermark;

CreatePullSubscription(
            binding, /* ExchangeServiceBinding to use for call */
            new NotificationEventTypeType[] {
                  NotificationEventTypeType.CreatedEvent },
            new BaseFolderIdType[] {
                  new DistinguishedFolderIdType(DistinguishedFolderIdNameType.inbox) },
            out subscriptionId,
            out watermark);

Console.WriteLine("Subscription Id: {0}, \r\n Watermark: {1}", subscriptionId, watermark);
```

Re-Creating a Subscription

So if your subscription expires or you're careless with your latest watermark, how do you re-create the subscription without missing any events?[7] You send a *Subscribe* request that contains the same information as the expired subscription (that is, the same folder ids and the same events of interest). In addition, you pass in the last valid watermark that you have. The request XML is shown in Listing 17-5 with the *Watermark* element in bold.

LISTING 17-5 Request to re-create a pull subscription

```xml
<Subscribe xmlns=".../messages"
           xmlns:t=".../types">
  <PullSubscriptionRequest>
    <t:FolderIds>
      <t:DistinguishedFolderId Id="inbox"/>
      <t:DistinguishedFolderId Id="calendar"/>
    </t:FolderIds>
    <t:EventTypes>
      <t:EventType>CreatedEvent</t:EventType>
      <t:EventType>ModifiedEvent</t:EventType>
    </t:EventTypes>
    <t:Watermark>AQAAAH...AAAAE=</t:Watermark>
    <t:Timeout>30</t:Timeout>
  </PullSubscriptionRequest>
</Subscribe>
```

If you don't have a watermark, you can create a new subscription with the same event[s] and folder[s]. However, you will have lost all events that occurred between your last *GetEvents* call and your *Subscribe* call to create the new subscription.

---

[7] Which you really have no excuse for, given that we have told you to take good care of the watermark!

So, now you can create and re-create your pull subscriptions as necessary. The next step is to retrieve the events that will be generated for that subscription.

Retrieving and Interpreting Events

Events are retrieved from a pull subscription via the *GetEvents* Web method. *GetEvents* retrieves all events that have occurred on a pull subscription since the point in time indicated by the supplied *Watermark* value. You can think of the watermark as a timestamp that basically says, "I have all events up to this point, so give me only events later than this."[8] The request XML is shown in Listing 17-6.

LISTING 17-6 *GetEvents* request XML

```
<GetEvents xmlns=".../messages">
  <SubscriptionId>5e0fe1f2-...-bb74bf84b5d7</SubscriptionId>
  <Watermark>AQAAAG...AAAAE=</Watermark>
</GetEvents>
```

And the response XML is shown in Listing 17-7. In this example, a single *CreatedEvent* is returned.

LISTING 17-7 *GetEvents* response

```
<GetEventsResponse xmlns:m=".../messages"
                   xmlns:t=".../types"
                   xmlns=".../messages">
  <m:ResponseMessages>
    <m:GetEventsResponseMessage ResponseClass="Success">
      <m:ResponseCode>NoError</m:ResponseCode>
      <m:Notification>
        <t:SubscriptionId>5e0fe1f2-...-bb74bf84b5d7</t:SubscriptionId>
        <t:PreviousWatermark>AQAAAG...AAAAE=</t:PreviousWatermark>
        <t:MoreEvents>false</t:MoreEvents>
        <t:CreatedEvent>
          <t:Watermark>AQAAAG...AAAAE=</t:Watermark>
          <t:TimeStamp>2007-01-11T23:24:03Z</t:TimeStamp>
          <t:ItemId Id="AQAtA..." ChangeKey="CQAAAA=="/>
          <t:ParentFolderId Id="AQAtA..." ChangeKey="AQAAAA=="/>
        </t:CreatedEvent>
      </m:Notification>
    </m:GetEventsResponseMessage>
  </m:ResponseMessages>
</GetEventsResponse>
```

---

8 It isn't actually a timestamp, but that description will suffice for this discussion. A more detailed description would require more information on the exact workings of the Microsoft Exchange events table, and that certainly isn't in the scope of this book!

SubscriptionId and *PreviousWatermark* Elements in Response

GetEvents echoes back the *SubscriptionId* that was sent in the request. The *Watermark* element that was passed in with the request is returned back in the *PreviousWatermark* element. Note that the new *Watermark* value is included as a child of the *CreatedEvent* element in Listing 17-7.

MoreEvents Element in Response

An Event Queue cannot hold an infinite number of events. Once the Event Queue is full, Exchange Web Services stops adding events to the Event Queue. When *GetEvents* is called, all the events in the Event Queue are returned and the queue is refilled. When *GetEvents* encounters an Event Queue that is full, the *MoreEvents* element is set to true in the response to indicate that more events exist for you to retrieve.[9]

To retrieve the remaining events, *GetEvents* must be called again with the last watermark returned. However, it may take Exchange Web Services several seconds to refill the Event Queue with the remaining events, which makes it possible for a subsequent *GetEvents* request to return no events or only a few events with *MoreEvents* still set to true. As a general rule, you should keep calling *GetEvents* until *MoreEvents* is false.

Watermark Element in Response

You may be wondering what we meant by the term *last watermark returned* in the preceding paragraph. Events are returned in the order in which they occurred, and, as shown in Listing 17-7, each returned event contains its own watermark. As you are iterating through events in the response, you should update the watermark you have stored with the one for that event. This means that if at any point you are forced to stop iterating through the response (maybe your code throws an exception, for example), you can pick up again where you left off by re-subscribing using the last watermark you saw (as demonstrated in Listing 17-5).

ItemId or *FolderId* in Response

The *ItemId* or *FolderId* in each event element is the id of the item or folder affected by the event.

Timestamp Element in Response

The *Timestamp* indicates the date and time the event occurred in the Coordinated Universal Time (UTC) time zone.

---

9   This flag serves a purpose similar to the *IncludesLastItemInRange* flag returned by *SyncFolderItems*.

ParentFolderId Element in Response

The final piece of information all event types return is the *ParentFolderId,* which is the *FolderId* of the folder that contains the item or folder affected by the event.

Figure 17-1 shows the inheritance hierarchy for the event types that can be returned.

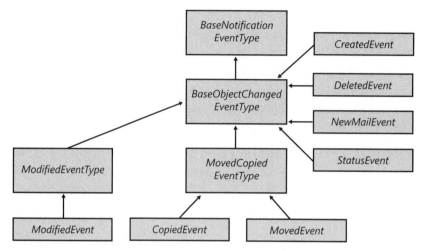

FIGURE 17-1 Inheritance hierarchy of event types

StatusEvent

The *StatusEvent* event derives from *BaseNotificationEventType* and returns just a *Watermark* element.

```
<t:StatusEvent>
  <t:Watermark>AQAAAI85jUceTjJLtPBtBnGseAt2CgAAAAAAAE=</t:Watermark>
</t:StatusEvent>
```

CreatedEvent, *DeletedEvent*, and *NewMailEvent*

These three events are instances of *BaseObjectChangedEventType* and return the following child elements.

- *Watermark*
- *Timestamp*
- *ItemId/FolderId*
- *ParentFolderId*

```
<t:CreatedEvent xmlns:t=".../types">
  <t:Watermark>AQAAAI85jUceTjJLtPBtBnGseAt2CgAAAAAAAE=</t:Watermark>
  <t:TimeStamp>2007-08-24T22:33:51Z</t:TimeStamp>
  <t:ItemId Id="AAAtA..." ChangeKey="CQ..."/>
  <t:ParentFolderId Id="AQAtA..." ChangeKey="AQ..."/>
</t:CreatedEvent>
```

CopiedEvent and MovedEvent

CopiedEvent and *MovedEvent* are instances of *MovedCopiedEventType* that itself derives from *BaseObjectChangedEventType*. So in addition to the elements returned by the above event types, these events also provide two extra child elements.

- **OldItemId/OldFolderId** The id of the item or folder as it was in its previous location

- **OldParentFolderId** The parent folder id of the folder that previously contained the item or folder in question.

CopiedEvent and *MovedEvent* events are triggered when items or folders are copied or moved into or from the folder to which you hold a subscription.

```
<t:MovedEvent xmlns:t=".../types">
  <t:Watermark>AQAAAI85jUceTjJLtPBtBnGseAuBCgAAAAAAAE=</t:Watermark>
  <t:TimeStamp>2007-08-25T03:07:48Z</t:TimeStamp>
  <t:ItemId Id="AAAtA..." ChangeKey="CQ..."/>
  <t:ParentFolderId Id="AQAtA..." ChangeKey="AQ..."/>
  <t:OldItemId Id="AAAtA..." ChangeKey="AA..."/>
  <t:OldParentFolderId Id="AAAAf..." ChangeKey="AQ..."/>
</t:MovedEvent>
```

ModifiedEvent

ModifiedEvent is an instance of *ModifiedEventType*, which again derives from *BaseObjectChangedEventType*. In addition to the four elements returned for this base type, *ModifiedEvent* can also return *UnreadCount*. The *UnreadCount* element is returned only for modify events on a folder, and then only if the *UnreadCount* has changed. For example, *UnreadCount* is returned if an item in the folder is read (or marked as read), or if a new unread message arrives in the folder.

```
<t:ModifiedEvent xmlns:t=".../types">
  <t:Watermark>AQAAAI85jUceTjJLtPBtBnGseAujCgAAAAAAAE=</t:Watermark>
  <t:TimeStamp>2007-09-25T03:18:50Z</t:TimeStamp>
  <t:FolderId Id="eHFqL..." ChangeKey="AQ..."/>
  <t:ParentFolderId Id="cmFOb..." ChangeKey="AQ..."/>
  <t:UnreadCount>1</t:UnreadCount>
</t:ModifiedEvent>
```

One additional point to note here is that notifications (pull and push) do not return complete *ChangeKeys* for items or folders. If you intend to call *UpdateItem* or *UpdateFolder* on an item of folder returned in a notification, you must retrieve an up-to-date and full change key for the item (using *GetItem*) or folder (using *GetFolder*) in question.

> **Note** At this point, we would like to explain a behavior you see if you subscribe to
> *ModifiedEvents*. Unlike other event types, you get *ModifiedEvents* from the Subscription folder
> itself as well as from items and folders directly contained within the Subscription folder.
> *ModifiedEvents* from the Subscription folder can be quite frequent because almost any change to
> an item or subfolder triggers a *ModifiedEvent* on the parent folder to which you are subscribed.
> In most cases, you won't care about these *ModifiedEvents* on the Subscription folder because
> nothing on the folder has really changed. But they do generate a lot of extra noise in the system.
>
> We can't offer one hard and fast rule for how to deal with these additional *ModifiedEvents*.
> However, one method we have found useful is as follows.
>
> For each *ModifiedEvent,* see if the event is for a folder (it will contain a *FolderId* rather than an
> *ItemId*). If the event is for an item, then you will likely want to process the event.
>
> If it is for a folder, compare the *FolderId* with the *FolderId* of the folder to which you are sub-
> scribed. If it matches, you know it is an event on one of your Subscription folders, which you can
> choose to ignore.
>
> If you care about the Unread Count on the folders you are subscribed to, you may want to do a
> further check of any *ModifiedEvent* to see that it doesn't contain an *UnreadCount* node.

Using the Proxy Classes

It is time to see some more proxy class code. You can add an overloaded constructor to help
in creating the *GetEvents* request. *GetEvents* takes the *SubscriptionId* and *Watermark* returned
in the *Subscribe* response. Both of these are string values, so the constructor is simple (as
shown in Listing 17-8).

LISTING 17-8 Overloaded constructor for *GetEvents*

```
/// <summary>
/// Extension of GetEventsType to add some helpful overloads and methods
/// </summary>
public partial class GetEventsType
{
    /// <summary>
    /// Constructor
    /// </summary>
    public GetEventsType()
    {}

    /// <summary>
    /// Overloaded constructor for creating GetEvents request
    /// </summary>
    /// <param name="subscriptionId">ID of Subscription</param>
    /// <param name="watermark">Subscription watermark</param>
    public GetEventsType(string subscriptionId, string watermark)
    {
        this.SubscriptionId = subscriptionId;
        this.Watermark = watermark;
    }
}
```

As with the Sync Web method responses, a *GetEvents* response contains two different array properties. The first array, which is exposed on *GetEventsResponseMessageType. Notification.Items*, contains the actual events, and the second array, which is exposed on *GetEventsResponseMessageType.Notification.ItemsElementName*, indicates the corresponding type of each event. The type of each event in the *ItemsElementName* array property is taken from the *ItemsChoiceType* enumeration, which is shown in Listing 17-9.[10]

LISTING 17-9 *ItemsChoiceType* enumeration used in the *GetEvents* response to show event type

```
public enum ItemsChoiceType
{
    CopiedEvent,
    CreatedEvent,
    DeletedEvent,
    ModifiedEvent,
    MovedEvent,
    NewMailEvent,
    StatusEvent,
}
```

Listing 17-10 demonstrates code for a call to *GetEvents* by using the *GetEventsType* constructor created in Listing 17-8. This code also shows how you might parse the response and extract the data from each event once you have a response from *GetEvents*.

LISTING 17-10 Code for calling *GetEvents* and parsing the response

```
/// <summary>
/// Call GetEvents and parse the results
/// </summary>
/// <param name="binding">Binding to use for the call</param>
/// <param name="subscriptionId">Id of subscription to retrieve events for</param>
/// <param name="watermark">REF Watermark - will be updated on return</param>
/// <param name="newMailEvents">OUT List of new mail events</param>
/// <param name="createdEvents">OUT List of created events</param>
/// <param name="deletedEvents">OUT List of deleted events</param>
/// <param name="movedEvents">OUT List of moved events</param>
/// <param name="copiedEvents">OUT List of copied events</param>
/// <param name="modifiedEvents">OUT List of modified events</param>
///
public static void CallGetEvents(
                    ExchangeServiceBinding binding,
                    string subscriptionId,
                    ref string watermark,
                    out List<BaseObjectChangedEventType> newMailEvents,
                    out List<BaseObjectChangedEventType> createdEvents,
                    out List<BaseObjectChangedEventType> deletedEvents,
                    out List<MovedCopiedEventType> movedEvents,
```

---

[10] For those of you who have read the Sync chapter, this type name will look familiar. For *SyncFolderHierarchy*, you had *ItemsChoiceType1*. For *SyncFolderItems*, you had *ItemsChoiceType2*.

```
                            out List<MovedCopiedEventType> copiedEvents,
                            out List<ModifiedEventType> modifiedEvents)
{
  // Create the OUT lists
  //
  newMailEvents = new List<BaseObjectChangedEventType>();
  createdEvents = new List<BaseObjectChangedEventType>();
  deletedEvents = new List<BaseObjectChangedEventType>();
  movedEvents = new List<MovedCopiedEventType>();
  copiedEvents = new List<MovedCopiedEventType>();
  modifiedEvents = new List<ModifiedEventType>();

  // We want to deal with the case where GetEvents indicates that there are more
  // events available in the Event Queue, so call this in a loop until moreEvents
  // is false
  //
  bool moreEvents = true;
  while (moreEvents)
  {
    // Create the GetEvents request using the overloaded constructor
    //
    GetEventsType getEventsRequest = new GetEventsType(subscriptionId, watermark);

    // Now call GetEvents
    //
    GetEventsResponseType getEventsResponse = binding.GetEvents(getEventsRequest);
    GetEventsResponseMessageType getEventsResponseMessage =
        getEventsResponse.ResponseMessages.Items[0] as GetEventsResponseMessageType;
    if (getEventsResponseMessage.ResponseCode != ResponseCodeType.NoError)
    {
      throw new Exception("GetEvents failed with response code: " +
              getEventsResponseMessage.ResponseCode.ToString());
    }

    NotificationType notifications = getEventsResponseMessage.Notification;
    for (int count = 0; count < notifications.Items.Length; count++)
    {
      BaseNotificationEventType actualEvent = notifications.Items[count];
      // Update the Watermark
      //
      watermark = notifications.Items[count].Watermark;
      // Now parse the response and save off the events to
      // the appropriate List variable
      //
      switch (notifications.ItemsElementName[count])
      {
        case ItemsChoiceType.NewMailEvent:
          newMailEvents.Add(actualEvent as BaseObjectChangedEventType);
          break;
        case ItemsChoiceType.CreatedEvent:
          createdEvents.Add(actualEvent as BaseObjectChangedEventType);
          break;
        case ItemsChoiceType.DeletedEvent:
          deletedEvents.Add(actualEvent as BaseObjectChangedEventType);
```

```
        break;
      case ItemsChoiceType.CopiedEvent:
        copiedEvents.Add(actualEvent as MovedCopiedEventType);
        break;
      case ItemsChoiceType.MovedEvent:
        movedEvents.Add(actualEvent as MovedCopiedEventType);
        break;
      case ItemsChoiceType.ModifiedEvent:
        modifiedEvents.Add(actualEvent as ModifiedEventType);
        break;
      case ItemsChoiceType.StatusEvent:
        // Don't need to do anything here. This is just a status event
        //
        break;
    }
  }
 }
}
}
```

Unsubscribing

Though subscriptions tidy themselves up via timeouts, you will want to be nice to your under-appreciated Exchange Server and tidy up the subscriptions yourself when you are done with them given that subscriptions consume resources on the Client Access Server. For pull notifications, you can delete a subscription using the *Unsubscribe* request, the XML for which is shown in Listing 17-11. Note that the *Unsubscribe* Web method is *not* allowed for push subscriptions. We will discuss unsubscribing from push subscriptions later in this chapter.

LISTING 17-11 *Unsubscribe* request and response

```
<Unsubscribe xmlns=".../messages">
  <SubscriptionId>577f5f3-...-6aca72b2edbc</SubscriptionId>
</Unsubscribe>
```

And the response from *Unsubscribe* is shown in Listing 17-12

LISTING 17-12 *Unsubscribe* response

```
<UnsubscribeResponse xmlns:m=".../messages"
                     xmlns:t="...types"
                     xmlns=".../messages">
  <m:ResponseMessages>
    <m:UnsubscribeResponseMessage ResponseClass="Success">
      <m:ResponseCode>NoError</m:ResponseCode>
    </m:UnsubscribeResponseMessage>
  </m:ResponseMessages>
</UnsubscribeResponse>
```

As you can see, *Unsubscribe* is a simple request and requires just the *SubscriptionId* of the pull notifications subscription you wish to unsubscribe from. Because *Unsubscribe* takes only one element, and that element is compulsory, *Unsubscribe* is a prime candidate for a proxy class constructor overload. Listing 17-13 shows how to extend the *UnsubscribeType* class to include the overloaded constructor.

LISTING 17-13 Overloaded constructor for an *Unsubscribe* request

```
/// <summary>
/// Extension of UnsubscribeType to add some helpful overloads and methods
/// </summary>
public partial class UnsubscribeType
{
    /// <summary>
    /// Constructor required for XML serialization
    /// </summary>
    public UnsubscribeType()
    {}

    /// <summary>
    /// Overloaded constructor which takes the Subscription ID you wish
    /// to unsubscribe from
    /// </summary>
    /// <param name="subscriptionId">Subscription ID</param>
    public UnsubscribeType(string subscriptionId)
    {
        this.SubscriptionId = subscriptionId;
    }
}
```

The method you would then write to unsubscribe from a pull notification subscription would look something like what is shown in Listing 17-14.

LISTING 17-14 Method for calling *Unsubscribe* on a pull notification subscription

```
/// <summary>
/// Unsubscribe from a Pull Notification Subscription
/// </summary>
/// <param name="binding">EWS binding</param>
/// <param name="subscriptionId">Subscription ID</param>
private static void Unsubscribe(ExchangeServiceBinding binding,
                               string subscriptionId)
{
    // Call the overloaded constructor to create the Unsubscribe request
    UnsubscribeType unsubscribeRequest = new UnsubscribeType(subscriptionId);

    // Call the Unsubscribe method and check that the call succeeds
    UnsubscribeResponseType unsubscribeResponse =
        binding.Unsubscribe(unsubscribeRequest);
    if (unsubscribeResponse.ResponseMessages.Items[0].ResponseCode !=
        ResponseCodeType.NoError)
```

```
    {
        throw new Exception("Unsubscribe failed for subscription: " +
            subscriptionId);
    }
}
```

Push Notifications

One problem with pull subscriptions is determining when and how often to poll the server using *GetEvents*. If you poll too frequently, you may receive many *StatusEvent* responses basically stating that there is nothing to return. This is wasted effort on the part of the client, and it causes the server to do unnecessary work. In fact, if you recall the earlier example of Ken at the restaurant, Ken's frequent and fruitless trips to the hostess station before his table was ready is a great example of polling too frequently. If you poll too *in*frequently then there is a delay between an event occurring on the server and the client being aware of that event.

Let's revisit Ken Malcolmson and Tina Makovec at the world famous Contoso Fine Dining restaurant. If we rewind the story a bit, Ken and Tina enter the restaurant and Ken walks up to the hostess station to add his name to the waiting list. Rather than the unrefined paper and pencil method of writing down names for those parties waiting to be seated, Contoso Fine Dining has a number of fancy flashing and vibrating devices (FFVDs) that can be used to notify diners that their table is ready. The hostess enters Ken's information, including his "table for two" seating requirements into the system, registers one of the FFVDs accordingly, and hands the device to Ken. Ken now holds in his hands a mechanism through which the hostess can alert him when their table is ready.

There is no need for Ken to return to the hostess station every few minutes to check the status of his table. In fact, doing so may irritate the hostess. Ken can rest assured that once his table is ready the FFVD will notify him of the event that he is interested in—the availability of his table. The hostess, through the FFVD, is *pushing* information about the availability of his table to Ken.

If you need to passively receive notification of server events, you need push notifications. With a push subscription, Exchange Web Services sends notification of events as soon as they occur—without waiting for the client to request them. The tradeoff is that the client application becomes more complicated because it must be able to "listen" for the server sending out these notifications. We will examine this complexity shortly, but first you need to be able to create a push subscription.

Creating a Push Notification Subscription

Creating a push subscription is similar to creating a pull subscription. You create a push subscription by using the same *Subscribe* Web method used for pull subscriptions. However, instead of passing in a *PullSubscriptionRequest* element, you pass in a *PushSubscriptionRequest* element. The XML request for creating a push subscription is shown in Listing 17-15.

LISTING 17-15 Push subscription request

```
<Subscribe xmlns=".../messages"
           xmlns:t=".../types>
  <PushSubscriptionRequest>
    <t:FolderIds>
      <t:DistinguishedFolderId Id="drafts"/>
      <t:DistinguishedFolderId Id="calendar"/>
    </t:FolderIds>
    <t:EventTypes>
      <t:EventType>CreatedEvent</t:EventType>
      <t:EventType>DeletedEvent</t:EventType>
    </t:EventTypes>
    <t:StatusFrequency>10</t:StatusFrequency>
    <t:URL>http://myClientMachine:1234</t:URL>
  </PushSubscriptionRequest>
</Subscribe>
```

And the response is shown in Listing 17-16.

LISTING 17-16 Push subscription response

```
<SubscribeResponse xmlns:m=".../messages"
                   xmlns:t=".../types"
                   xmlns=".../messages">
  <m:ResponseMessages>
    <m:SubscribeResponseMessage ResponseClass="Success">
      <m:ResponseCode>NoError</m:ResponseCode>
      <m:SubscriptionId>8fcd3dab-...-b0288637e521</m:SubscriptionId>
      <m:Watermark>AQAAAGAyh4eh9F9Nq37f+1jtSAYqXAAAAAAAAAE=</m:Watermark>
    </m:SubscribeResponseMessage>
  </m:ResponseMessages>
</SubscribeResponse>
```

As with a pull subscription, a push subscription can be created for multiple folders and for multiple events on those folders. The types of events you can receive notification of are the same as those for pull subscriptions. Also, the *Subscribe* response is identical for both push and pull subscriptions. The differences lie in the two other pieces of information included in the *PushSubscriptionRequest* element.

StatusFrequency Element in Request

The *StatusFrequency* element indicates how often, measured in minutes, notification mes-sages are sent to the client, even if there are no events to send. This way, the client can know that the subscription is still alive. If the client doesn't hear from the server for longer than the time period specified in the *StatusFrequency*, the client can take action such as re-creating the subscription or pinging the server to make sure it is still available.[11]

URL Element in Request

Since push notifications are server initiated, Exchange Web Services must have the informa-tion necessary to get in contact with the client application. The *URL* element provides this contact information, which happens to be the location at which a *client-side* Web service is running and listening for the server notifications. The server communicates with the client by sending an HTTP POST to the URL provided. In other words, your client application becomes an HTTP server.

Push Subscription Lifetime

Wait. There is no timeout value. Does that mean push subscriptions never time out and re-main around forever? Not necessarily. So how do push subscriptions time out? The answer is that the client-side Web service has to respond to every notification or status ping that the Client Access Server sends out.[12] If the server does not get a response, it will go into what we call *retry mode*. In retry mode the Client Access Server attempts to send the same notification to the client several times before it gives up on the subscription.

- The first retry is attempted 30 seconds after the initial attempt to communicate with the client failed. It is possible that this initial failure was the result of a request time out. As such, this first retry attempt may occur after a period longer than 30 seconds.

- Subsequent retries are made at a growing interval of two times the previous interval (second attempt one minute after first retry is determined to be invalid, third attempt at two minutes, and so on.)

- Retries are attempted until the next retry interval will exceed the *StatusFrequency* value for the subscription.

For example, if the *StatusFrequency* is 5 minutes then the behavior will be as follows:

- Retry after 30 seconds

- Second retry after an additional 1 minute (1 minute 30 seconds after initial failure)

---

[11] Load on the Client Access Server can mean that the poll from the server can be delayed beyond the time limit specified in *StatusFrequency*. A good rule of thumb is to wait twice as long as the *StatusFrequency*. If you still don't hear from the server, then you can assume the Subscription is gone and re-create as necessary.

[12] Just as the server responds to every request you send to EWS.

- Third retry after an additional 2 minutes (3 minutes 30 seconds after initial failure)

- Fourth and final retry after an additional 4 minutes (7 minutes 30 seconds after initial failure). This is the final retry because the next interval will be 4 x 2 = 8 minutes which is longer than the *StatusFrequency* of 5 minutes.

If Exchange Web Services still doesn't get a response from the retries, the server assumes the client is no longer interested in the subscription. The subscription is then removed. By using the *StatusFrequency* as part of the algorithm and encouraging push subscription clients to be coded to recreate subscriptions after a period of time that is twice the *StatusFrequency*, it is reasonable to expect both sides will give up on a subscription in roughly the same timeframe.

Using the Proxy Classes

The proxy class code for creating a push subscription is similar to the code for creating a pull subscription. The *PushSubscriptionRequest* element maps to an instance of type *PushSubscriptionRequestType*, and, as previously stated, takes the following child elements:

- One or more folders to which to subscribe

- One or more event types to listen for

- A status frequency value (in minutes)

- URL location of the client-side application Web service

- An optional watermark if you are re-creating a previous subscription

As with *PullSubscriptionRequestType*, you can create an overloaded constructor for *PushSubscriptionRequestType* that takes the above list of parameters. The constructor is shown in Listing 17-17.

LISTING 17-17 Overloaded constructor for a push subscription request

```
/// <summary>
/// Extension of PullSubscriptionRequestType to add some helpful overloads
/// and methods
/// </summary>
public partial class PushSubscriptionRequestType
{
    /// <summary>
    /// Constructor required for XML Serialization
    /// </summary>
    public PushSubscriptionRequestType()
    {}

    /// Overloaded constructor which helps in the creation of the Subscribe
    /// request for a Push Subscription
    /// </summary>
    /// <param name="subscriptionFolders">The folders you wish to subscribe to</param>
    /// <param name="eventTypes">The events to subscribe for</param>
    /// <param name="statusFrequency">Frequency in minutes of server ping</param>
```

```
/// <param name="url">URL for client Notifications web service</param>
/// <param name="watermark">Watermark for recreating a previous Subscription</
param>
///
public PushSubscriptionRequestType(
                BaseFolderIdType[] subscriptionFolders,
                NotificationEventTypeType[] eventTypes,
                int statusFrequency,
                string url,
                string watermark)
{
    this.FolderIds = subscriptionFolders;
    this.EventTypes = eventTypes;
    this.StatusFrequency = statusFrequency;
    this.URL = url;

    // If we have a Watermark then set it on the Subscribe request
    //
    if (!string.IsNullOrEmpty(watermark))
    {
        this.Watermark = watermark;
    }
}
}
```

Using this overloaded constructor, the code to create a new subscription is shown in Listing 17-18.

LISTING 17-18 Code to create a new push subscription by using overloaded constructor

```
/// <summary>
/// Create a push subscription
/// </summary>
/// <param name="binding">ExchangeServiceBinding to use for the call</param>
/// <param name="eventTypes">Event types to subscribe to</param>
/// <param name="subscriptionFolders">Folder to look for changes in</param>
/// <param name="clientURL">URL of the client-side web service</param>
/// <param name="statusFrequencyInMinutes">Status frequency</param>
/// <param name="subscriptionId">OUT new subscription Id</param>
/// <param name="watermark">OUT new watermark</param>
///
public static void CreatePushSubscription(
                ExchangeServiceBinding binding,
                NotificationEventTypeType[] eventTypes,
                BaseFolderIdType[] subscriptionFolders,
                string clientURL,
                int statusFrequencyInMinutes,
                out string subscriptionId,
                out string watermark)
{
    // Call the overloaded constructor
    //
```

```
PushSubscriptionRequestType pushSubscription =
        new PushSubscriptionRequestType(
                    subscriptionFolders,
                    eventTypes,
                    statusFrequencyInMinutes,
                    clientURL,
                    null /* A new Subscription so no watermark */);

SubscribeType subscribeRequest = new SubscribeType();
subscribeRequest.Item = pushSubscription;
SubscribeResponseType subscribeResponse = binding.Subscribe(subscribeRequest);

// We have a response. Now we need to parse it to get the SubscriptionId and
// the Watermark
//
SubscribeResponseMessageType subscribeResponseMessage =
        subscribeResponse.ResponseMessages.Items[0] as
            SubscribeResponseMessageType;

if (subscribeResponseMessage.ResponseCode == ResponseCodeType.NoError)
{
    subscriptionId = subscribeResponseMessage.SubscriptionId;
    watermark = subscribeResponseMessage.Watermark;
}
else
{
    // We received an error in the response
    throw new Exception(subscribeResponseMessage.MessageText);
}
}
```

Push Notification Requests and Responses

Listing 17-19 shows an example of the request that Exchange Web Services sends out to
your client-side Web service. Remember that in this case, Exchange Web Services is the client making a request against your application. Your application has become the server in this
communication.

LISTING 17-19 *SendNotification* request from the Exchange server

```
<SendNotification xmlns:m=".../messages"
                  xmlns:t=".../types"
                  xmlns=".../messages">
  <m:ResponseMessages>
    <m:SendNotificationResponseMessage ResponseClass="Success">
      <m:ResponseCode>NoError</m:ResponseCode>
      <m:Notification>
        <t:SubscriptionId>ded2678b-...572c5</t:SubscriptionId>
        <t:PreviousWatermark>AQAAA...AAAE=</t:PreviousWatermark>
        <t:MoreEvents>false</t:MoreEvents>
```

```
      <t:CreatedEvent>
        <t:Watermark>AQAAA...AAAE=</t:Watermark>
        <t:TimeStamp>2007-02-01T00:05:08Z</t:TimeStamp>
        <t:ItemId Id="AAAtA...nAAA=" ChangeKey="CQAAAA=="/>
        <t:ParentFolderId Id="AQ...AA==" ChangeKey="AQAAAA=="/>
      </t:CreatedEvent>
    </m:Notification>
  </m:SendNotificationResponseMessage>
  </m:ResponseMessages>
</SendNotification>
```

Interestingly, the contents of the *SendNotification* request look quite similar to the contents in *GetEventsResponse*, with the exception that *SendNotification* contains a *SendNotificationResponseMessage* while *GetEventsResponse* contains a *GetEventsResponseMessage*.

SendNotification can be confusing due to the presence of the *SendNotification**Response**Message* element. Remember, *SendNotification* is a request. You must ignore the term *response* contained therein.

MoreEvents Element in *SendNotification*

With pull subscriptions, the *MoreEvents* element tells you—the client—if you need to poll the server again because more information is available in the Event Queue. With push subscriptions, you aren't in control of the communication of events. Therefore, all that the *MoreEvents* element really tells you is that you should expect another communication from the server soon. It is therefore safe to ignore *MoreEvents* when dealing with push notifications.

Responding to *SendNotification*

The client Web service response to the *SendNotification* request is shown in Listing 17-20.

LISTING 17-20 *SendNotificationResult* sent from the client

```
<SendNotificationResult xmlns=".../messages">
  <SubscriptionStatus>OK</SubscriptionStatus>
</SendNotificationResult>
```

SendNotificationResult contains a single child element called *SubscriptionStatus* that can contain one of two possible values. A value of *OK* indicates that your client Web service received the notification and is interested in continuing the subscription. A value of *Unsubscribe* tells Exchange Web Services that you no longer want to receive push notifications for this subscription. In fact, aside from allowing push subscriptions to time-out, responding with a *SubscriptionStatus* of *Unsubscribe* is the only way to gracefully unsubscribe from a push subscription. You cannot call the *Unsubscribe* Web method for push subscriptions as it is only applicable to pull subscriptions.

Listing 17-22 shows the structure of a *SendNotificationResult* response indicating a desire to unsubscribe to a push subscription.

LISTING 17-22 Unsubscribe response from a push subscription client Web service

```
<SendNotificationResult xmlns=".../messages">
  <SubscriptionStatus>Unsubscribe</SubscriptionStatus>
</SendNotificationResult>
```

The Art of Listening: The Push Subscription Client

So you've created your pull subscription and know the structure of both the notification request sent by Exchange Web Services and the response you are to send back, but this information isn't very useful without a client to receive the notifications. As we already mentioned, the client is actually a Web service. This client Web service will receive a request called *SendNotification* as defined in the NotificationService.wsdl file.[13]

> **Note** Due to an issue with Exchange Web Services, the client-side Web service must support anonymous access when you are outside of the corporate network. This is because Exchange Web Services does not impersonate the user when making the *SendNotification* request. Instead, Exchange Web Services makes the request as the Local System account of the Client Access Server. When Local System fails to authenticate to the client machine using Kerberos due to a firewall or misconfiguration of the Service Principal Name (SPN), Windows falls back to NT Lan Manager (NTLM) authentication, which sends out the request anonymously. This issue should be rectified in the next release of Exchange 2007. If enabling anonymous access on your client-side Web service is not an option for your solution, you should use pull notifications instead.[14]

There are a number of ways that you could create your own client-side Web service to receive push notification requests from Exchange Web Services. The most common approach would be to create a set of server interface proxy classes using the NotificationService.wsdl file, implement the resulting *INotificationServiceBinding* interface and then host the Web Service within IIS.[15] But then, how does your client application deal with incoming push notifications? Does your entire application need to reside within the client-side Web service? Do

---

[13] The NotificationService.wsdl file is part of the Exchange 2007 Server SDK which can be obtained from http://www.microsoft.com/downloads/details.aspx?FamilyID=5c11fa93-13c5-49f7-bf3c-3e9fcb2b9707&DisplayLang=en. After installation, the WSDL can be found at c:\ Program Files\Microsoft\Exchange Server 2007 SDK*[SDK release date]*\ Libraries\PushNotificationClient\NotificationService.wsdl.

[14] And we wouldn't blame you at all.

[15] Run wsdl.exe /? From the command line for more information about the serverInterface flag.

you need to implement some cross-process remoting solution so that the client application can be alerted to notifications received by the Web service within IIS?

Since challenges make us better developers, we decided to take a different approach in this book that allows you to host the client Web service *outside* of IIS. In fact, you can host your Web service within a console application, WinForms application, Windows NT Service, and so on. The end result of our work will be a C# class that you instantiate and pass a single delegate that will be called whenever a valid notification request is received. Does this sound too good to be true? Read on.

In the .NET 2.0 framework, a new set of classes were introduced in the *System.Net* namespace that interacts with http.sys, which is the kernel component that handles HTTP requests. By using the *HttpListener* class, you can open an endpoint without having to deal with Internet Information Server (IIS) configuration and receive requests on that endpoint. To make the class more usable, all dealings with the *HttpListener* class happen on background threads.[16] This keeps the main thread of execution unblocked. Listing 17-21 shows the *PushNotificationClient* class. We recommend that you compile this class into its own class library so that it can be reused in multiple applications.

The *PushNotificationClient* class uses the normal autogenerated proxy classes we have used throughout this book.

LISTING 17-21 *PushNotificationClient* class

```
// PushNotificationClient.cs
//
// Copyright (c) 2007 Grandma Lois who doesn't exist
//

using System;
using System.Collections.Generic;
using System.Text;
using System.Net;
using System.Threading;
using System.Xml;
using System.IO;
using ProxyHelpers.EWS;
using System.Xml.Serialization;

namespace PushNotificationClient
{
    /// <summary>
    /// Enumeration indicating possible response values
    /// </summary>
    public enum NotificationResponse
    {
```

---

[16] Note that as a result, events will be fired on background threads. As such, if you are using the PushNotificationClient class, make sure that your delegate method is thread safe.

```
  OK,
  Unsubscribe,
}


/// <summary>
/// Delegate to be called when notifications are received
/// </summary>
/// <param name="sender">Sender (PushNotificationClient in this case)</param>
/// <param name="notification">Actual Notification received from server</param>
/// <returns>Response to send back to server</returns>
///
public delegate NotificationResponse NotificationEventsReceived(
                object sender,
                SendNotificationResponseMessageType notification);

/// <summary>
/// Exception thrown when client is in wrong state for method call.
/// </summary>
public class PushNotificationStateException : Exception
{
  public PushNotificationStateException(string message) : base(message) { }
}


/// <summary>
/// Client implementation
/// </summary>
public class PushNotificationClient
{
  private uint portNumber;
  private NotificationEventsReceived eventHandler;
  private bool isListening = false;
  private ManualResetEvent stopEvent = new ManualResetEvent(false);
  private bool shouldStop = false;
  private XmlNamespaceManager mgr;
  private XmlSerializer ser;

  /// <summary>
  /// Constructor
  /// </summary>
  /// <param name="portNumber">Port number to listen on</param>
  /// <param name="eventHandler">delegate to call when notifications are
  /// received</param>
  ///
  public PushNotificationClient(
                uint portNumber,
                NotificationEventsReceived eventHandler)
  {
    this.portNumber = portNumber;
    if (eventHandler == null)
    {
      throw new ArgumentNullException("eventHandler");
    }
    this.eventHandler = eventHandler;
```

```
    // namespace manager is used for XPath queries when parsing the request
    //
    this.mgr = new XmlNamespaceManager(new NameTable());
    this.mgr.AddNamespace("t",
        "http://schemas.microsoft.com/exchange/services/2006/types");
    this.mgr.AddNamespace("m",
        "http://schemas.microsoft.com/exchange/services/2006/messages");

    // XmlSerializer is used to convert SendNotification elements into proxy
    // class instances
    //
    this.ser = new XmlSerializer(typeof(SendNotificationResponseType));
}

/// <summary>
/// Start Listening
/// </summary>
public void StartListening()
{
  VerifyNotListening();

  this.stopEvent.Reset();
  this.shouldStop = false;

  // Run the listener on a background thread so we are not blocked
  //
  ThreadPool.QueueUserWorkItem(new WaitCallback(ListenOnThread));
}

/// <summary>
/// Stop Listening
/// </summary>
public void StopListening()
{
  VerifyListening();

  // Set the stopEvent. This will cause the worker thread to close our and
  // dispose of the HttpListener and exit the thread
  //
  this.stopEvent.Set();
}

/// <summary>
/// Thread pool method to start listening on the background thread
/// </summary>
/// <param name="state">State - ignore</param>
///
private void ListenOnThread(object state)
{
  using (HttpListener listener = new HttpListener())
  {
    listener.Prefixes.Add(
        String.Format(
          "http://+:{0}/PushNotificationsClient/",
```

```
                    this.portNumber.ToString()));
    listener.Start();
    this.isListening = true;
    while (!shouldStop)
    {
      IAsyncResult asyncResult = listener.BeginGetContext(
            AsyncCallbackMethod, listener);

      // Wait on either the listener or the stop event
      //
      int index = WaitHandle.WaitAny(
        new WaitHandle[] { stopEvent, asyncResult.AsyncWaitHandle });
      switch (index)
      {
        case 0:
          // Stop event was triggered.
          //
          shouldStop = true;
          break;

        case 1:
          // Notification was received. Just loop around so we can call
          // BeginGetContext again
          //
          break;
      }
    }
    listener.Stop();
  }
  this.isListening = false;
}


/// <summary>
/// Async method called once we receive a request
/// </summary>
/// <param name="result">Async result containing our HttpListener</param>
///
private void AsyncCallbackMethod(IAsyncResult result)
{
  HttpListener listener = result.AsyncState as HttpListener;
  if (!this.isListening)
  {
    // Our callback gets fired when we stop the listener too.  If it is not
    // listening, just return.
    //
    return;
  }
  HttpListenerContext context = listener.EndGetContext(result);
  SendNotificationResponseType request;

  // Now use the XML serializer to turn the XML into a notification
  // serialization type...
  //
  XmlDocument doc = new XmlDocument();
```

```csharp
try
{
  doc.LoadXml(
      new StreamReader(
          context.Request.InputStream).ReadToEnd());

  // retrieve the first SendNotification element (there should be only one).
  //
  XmlNodeList nodes = doc.SelectNodes("//m:SendNotification[1]", this.mgr);
  if (nodes.Count == 0)
  {
    // this wasn't a SendNotification request or it was malformed or
    // something like that.
    //
    FailRequest(context);
    return;
  }

  string sendNotification = nodes[0].OuterXml;
  using (MemoryStream ms = new MemoryStream())
  {
    byte[] bytes = Encoding.UTF8.GetBytes(sendNotification);
    ms.Write(bytes, 0, bytes.Length);
    ms.Flush();
    ms.Position = 0L;
    request = (SendNotificationResponseType)this.ser.Deserialize(ms);
  }
}
catch (XmlException)
{
  // Failed to deserialize request.
  //
  FailRequest(context);
  return;
}

// Fire the delegate
//
NotificationResponse response = eventHandler(
                    this, /* sender */
                    request.ResponseMessages.Items[0]
                            as SendNotificationResponseMessageType);

GenerateResponseXML(context, response);
}

/// <summary>
/// Fail the request. Right now we don't differentiate between reasons why it
/// failed.
/// </summary>
/// <param name="context">Request context</param>
///
private void FailRequest(HttpListenerContext context)
{
```

```
        context.Response.ContentEncoding = Encoding.UTF8;
        context.Response.ContentType = "text/xml; charset=utf-8";
        context.Response.ProtocolVersion = new Version(1, 1, 0, 0);
        context.Response.StatusCode = 400;
        string response = "<?xml version=\"1.0\"?>" +
                          "<Error>Bad Request</Error>";
        byte[] responseBytes = Encoding.UTF8.GetBytes(response);
        context.Response.ContentLength64 = responseBytes.Length;
        context.Response.OutputStream.Write(
                responseBytes, 0, responseBytes.Length);
        context.Response.OutputStream.Flush();
    }


    /// <summary>
    /// Generate the response xml
    /// </summary>
    /// <param name="context">call context</param>
    /// <param name="response">The response enum value</param>
    ///
    private void GenerateResponseXML(
                    HttpListenerContext context,
                    NotificationResponse response)
    {
      StringBuilder builder = new StringBuilder();
      builder.AppendLine("<?xml version=\"1.0\"?>");
      builder.AppendLine("<s:Envelope xmlns:s= " +
                "\"http://schemas.xmlsoap.org/soap/envelope/\">");
      builder.AppendLine("<s:Body>");
      builder.AppendLine("  <SendNotificationResult " +
          "xmlns=\"http://schemas.microsoft.com/exchange/services/2006/messages\">");
      builder.AppendFormat("  <SubscriptionStatus>{0}</SubscriptionStatus>\r\n",
          response.ToString());
      builder.AppendLine("  </SendNotificationResult>");
      builder.AppendLine("</s:Body>");
      builder.AppendLine("</s:Envelope>");

      context.Response.ContentEncoding = Encoding.UTF8;
      context.Response.ContentType = "text/xml; charset=utf-8";
      context.Response.ProtocolVersion = new Version(1, 1, 0, 0);
      context.Response.StatusCode = 200;
      byte[] responseBytes = Encoding.UTF8.GetBytes(builder.ToString());
      context.Response.ContentLength64 = responseBytes.Length;
      context.Response.OutputStream.Write(
                responseBytes, 0, responseBytes.Length);
      context.Response.OutputStream.Flush();
    }

    /// <summary>
    /// Returns true if the listener is listening
    /// </summary>
    public bool IsListening
    {
      get
      {
```

```
        return isListening;
    }
}

/// <summary>
/// Verifies that the listener isn't listening
/// </summary>
private void VerifyNotListening()
{
  if (isListening)
  {
    throw new PushNotificationStateException("Cannot perform this operation " +
              "when listening");
  }
}

/// <summary>
/// Verifies that the listener is listening
/// </summary>
private void VerifyListening()
{
  if (!isListening)
  {
    throw new PushNotificationStateException("Cannot perform this operation " +
          "when not listening");
  }
  }
 }
}
```

In addition to the code in Listing 17-21, you must add a single attribute to the *SendNotificationResponseType* proxy class. When Exchange Web Services sends the listener a notification, the element name of the *SendNotificationResponseType* instance is *SendNotificationResponse*. As such, in order for the *XmlSerializer* to properly deserialize the XML for the *SendNotificationResponse* element, the corresponding XML serializable type must be decorated with the *XmlRoot* attribute indicating the element name that should be expected. If this attribute is omitted, then deserialization of the request will fail since the *XmlSerializer* expects an element name to be the same as the class name by default.

Thankfully, you do not need to modify the auto-generate proxy class file itself, but can add this attribute using a partial class extension as shown in Listing 17-22. The *XmlRoot* attribute is shown in bold. Also note the added convenience method for returning the strongly-typed response message.

LISTING 17-22 Partial class extension of *SendNotificationResponseType*

```
/// <summary>
/// Partial class extension of SendNotificationResponseType so that we can add the
/// XmlRoot attribute used during Push Notification deserialization
/// </summary>
[XmlRoot(ElementName = "SendNotification",
    Namespace = "http://schemas.microsoft.com/exchange/services/2006/messages")]
public partial class SendNotificationResponseType : BaseResponseMessageType
{
  /// <summary>
  /// Return the single response message cast to the proper type
  /// </summary>
  /// <returns>SendNotificationResponseMessageType</returns>
  ///
  public SendNotificationResponseMessageType GetResponseMessage()
  {
    return this.ResponseMessages.Items[0] as SendNotificationResponseMessageType;
  }
}
```

Using the *PushNotificationClient* class is quite easy. Simply create an instance of the class and pass in the port you wish to listen on and a delegate that should be called when notifications come in. To start listening on the port call *StartListening*, and to stop listening call *StopListening*. Listing 17-23 provides code that performs the following steps, just to provide you with a more complete picture of push notifications using the *PushNotificationsClient*.

1. Create a binding.

2. Create a push subscription.

3. Create a PushNotificationClient and begin listening.

4. Create a message in the folder the subscription is monitoring.

5. When the notification is received, retrieve the message using GetItem and write out the message subject to the console.

6. Unsubscribe from the push subscription.

7. Close the PushNotificationClient.

LISTING 17-23 Using the *PushNotificationClient* class

```
// Using Push Notifications and the PushNotificationClient
//
class Program
{
  private static ExchangeServiceBinding binding;

  /// <summary>
  /// Main entry point
```

```
/// </summary>
/// <param name="args">args</param>
///
static void Main(string[] args)
{
  // STEP 1: Create our binding
  //
  binding = new ExchangeServiceBinding();
  binding.Url = "https://contoso.com/ews/Exchange.asmx";
  binding.UseDefaultCredentials = true;

  // STEP 2: Create our Push subscription. Note that the PushNotificationsClient
  // listens on http://{host:port}/PushNotificationsClient
  //
  string subscriptionId;
  string watermark;
  CreatePushSubscription(
              binding,
              new NotificationEventTypeType[] {
                      NotificationEventTypeType.CreatedEvent },
              new BaseFolderIdType[] {
                      new DistinguishedFolderIdType(
                          DistinguishedFolderIdNameType.drafts) },
              @"http://yourClient:8081/PushNotificationsClient",
              5,
              out subscriptionId,
              out watermark);

  // STEP 3: Create the listener and begin listening
  //
  PushNotificationClient.PushNotificationClient c = new
        PushNotificationClient.PushNotificationClient(
              8081, /* port */
              HandleNotificationReceived /* delegate */);
  c.StartListening();
  Console.WriteLine("Listening");

  // STEP 4: Create a message in the drafts folder
  //
  CreateItemType createItemRequest = new CreateItemType();
  createItemRequest.MessageDisposition = MessageDispositionType.SaveOnly;
  createItemRequest.MessageDispositionSpecified = true;
  MessageType message = new MessageType();
  message.Subject = "Testing Push Notifications";
  createItemRequest.Items = new NonEmptyArrayOfAllItemsType();
  createItemRequest.Items.Items = new ItemType[] { message };
  binding.CreateItem(createItemRequest);

  // STEP 7: Close the push notifications client. See delegate below for steps
  // 5 and 6.
  //
  Console.WriteLine("Press any key to stop listening");
  Console.ReadLine();
  c.StopListening();
```

```
    }

    /// <summary>
    /// Delegate for handling notifications from EWS
    /// </summary>
    /// <param name="sender">PushNotificationsClient</param>
    /// <param name="eventData">Notification</param>
    /// <returns>Notification response (ok or unsubscribe)</returns>
    ///
    private static PushNotificationClient.NotificationResponse
HandleNotificationReceived(
            object sender,
            SendNotificationResponseMessageType eventData)
    {
        // Write out the watermark for fun
        //
        Console.WriteLine(eventData.Notification.Items[0].Watermark);

        // STEP 5: Call GetItem and write out the subject of the created message
        //
        BaseObjectChangedEventType createdEvent = eventData.Notification.Items[0] as
                BaseObjectChangedEventType;
        ItemIdType modifiedItemId = createdEvent.Item as ItemIdType;

        GetItemType getItemRequest = new GetItemType();
        getItemRequest.ItemShape = new ItemResponseShapeType(
                DefaultShapeNamesType.Default);
        getItemRequest.ItemIds = new BaseItemIdType[]{modifiedItemId};
        GetItemResponseType getItemResponse = binding.GetItem(getItemRequest);
        ItemInfoResponseMessageType responseMessage =
            getItemResponse.ResponseMessages.Items[0] as ItemInfoResponseMessageType;

        Console.WriteLine("Item created in drafts folder: " +
            responseMessage.Items.Items[0].Subject);

        // STEP 6: Unsubscribe
        //
        return PushNotificationClient.NotificationResponse.Unsubscribe;
    }
}
```

What Happens When Things Go Wrong?

With most Exchange Web Services Web methods, erroneous conditions are usually immediately apparent—you issue a request and you receive an error response. However, with push subscriptions, erroneous conditions are not always immediately apparent since the client is not in control of the communication.

As mentioned earlier, the *StatusFrequency* value sent in the request gives a client some control over how long it waits to hear from the push subscription. If the client doesn't hear from the server for a period (in minutes) longer than the specified *StatusFrequency,* the client can attempt to create a new subscription using the last successfully received watermark without losing any events that occur. If you don't have the last watermark, you can still recreate the subscription. However, you will have lost any events that occurred between the last successful push notification from the server and the time you re-subscribed.

In addition, you can use the Exchange Web Services performance counters to track some basic subscription statistics. You can find these performance counters under the *MSExchangeWS* Performance Object and they are listed in Table 17-2.

TABLE 17-2 Useful Performance Counters for Notifications

Performance counter name	Description
Active Subscriptions	The number of active subscriptions in all mailboxes on the server. Includes push and pull subscriptions.
Push Notifications Failed	The total number of push notifications for which the server has not successfully received an OK response from the client.
Push Notifications Succeeded	The total number of push notifications for which the server has successfully received an OK response.
Subscribe Requests	The total number of *Subscribe* requests made to the server. Includes push and pull subscriptions.
Unsubscribe Requests	The total number of *Unsubscribe* requests made to the server. This includes *Unsubscribe* requests sent from a pull notifications client and *Unsubscribe* responses sent from a push notifications client.

Summary

In this chapter, we've shown you how Notification can keep you abreast of changes in a mailbox. We've shown that with pull notifications, the client can take charge of when to receive the events on a mailbox. We also examined push notifications where the server drives the communication with the client, and the client listens for the server via a client-side Web service.

Part V
Advanced Topics

Chapter 18
Errors Never Happen

How much easier our lives as developers would be if we never encountered erroneous conditions! Bad or missing input, data, hardware, assumptions, and a myriad of other conditions can cause untold grief. This is especially true if your code is not designed to handle such conditions properly. Microsoft Exchange Server 2007 Web Services (EWS) must also deal with error conditions. Being an application programming interface (API), in most cases Exchange Web Services reports these conditions to you, the caller. This chapter is all about how these conditions are reported and what you can do about them.

SOAP and Batch Processing

Because Exchange Web Services is a standards-based Web service, all Exchange Web Services requests and responses are packaged as Simple Object Access Protocol (SOAP) messages. The SOAP 1.1 and 1.2 specifications expose the concept of a SOAP "fault," which is used to convey error conditions to the caller. Such faults are returned as XML within the SOAP body of a response and indicate whether the client or the server was responsible for the error condition. In addition, a SOAP fault exposes an optional *detail* element that can hold additional information regarding the failure. When a .NET proxy client makes a call that results in a SOAP fault being returned by the Web service, a *SoapException* containing information about the SOAP fault is thrown on the client and provides access to this *detail* element.

SOAP faults work great in principle, although the Exchange Web Services designers decided to put SOAP faults in the "Camp of Little Favor."

Most developers who have dealt with distributed systems know that a local call is much cheaper than a remote call. The more boundaries you put between the caller and the callee, the more overhead is involved in the ensuing communication. As such, when creating distributed systems, the more information that can be fit into a single request, the better.[1]

When Exchange Web Services was designed, the team decided to allow reasonable batching within the scope of a single Web method. Take almost any Exchange Web Services Web method, and you can perform actions against multiple items or folders in a single call.[2] Do you need to create ten messages? You can do that in a single *CreateItem* Web method call.

---

[1] Of course, you should be sensible about this. There is a balance between performance, usability, and complexity. If you tip the scales too far in one direction, someone is going to suffer as a result whether it be the end user, the support engineer, the network administrator, or yourself when you try to debug such a beastly code base.

[2] *GetEvents* is one exception.

This is great from a performance standpoint, but it does complicate the proxy classes. And it definitely complicates error handling.

Let's say that you make your *CreateItem* call to create ten messages. And let's further say that the fifth item in the batch fails to be created because the data you sent for that item is invalid. Exchange Web Services has several options. It could

1. Fail the entire request. This involves rolling back the previous four message creations.

2. Fail the rest of the request, but leave the changes up to the fifth item as is.

3. Leave the previous changes as is, fail this single item, and continue processing the rest of the batch.

The Exchange Web Services team chose option 3 above when designing the API. In many cases, a given operation within a batch is distinct from the other operations in that batch so that a failure in one does not imply that the entire batch should fail. In some cases, however, you would like for a batched operation to be an "all or nothing" proposition. Although Exchange Web Services typically ensures that a *single item* within a batch is an all or nothing operation, there is no transactional support *across* items within a batched operation. If you need transaction support, you need to roll your own log-and-rollback mechanism. Exchange Web Services does not support this.

Now, given that Exchange Web Services processes as much of a batched request as it can, how does it report partial failures to you? The Exchange Web Services team could have chosen the SOAP fault route, but it would be a little strange for two reasons.

- When you encounter exceptions, it is natural to assume that the operation that was just tried failed completely. It is unusual to expect partial success.

- When dealing with the proxy classes and SOAP exceptions, parsing the SOAP fault detail element is a less than ideal proposition.[3]

Having said all of this, Exchange Web Services returns SOAP faults for very limited and specific situations, which we will discuss shortly, but the normal error reporting mechanism does not use SOAP faults.

The Normal Mechanism

So how does Exchange Web Services report errors back to you, the ever vigilant developer? Exchange Web Services uses *response messages* to marry the results of a given batched operation with the status of that operation. Figure 18-1 shows the general structure of a response message.[4]

---

[3] We do this later in the chapter.

[4] This is an over-simplification but will serve our purposes until we dig into response messages in more detail.

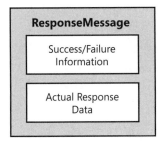

FIGURE 18-1 Response message makeup

Before we dig in too far, take a look at an example. Let's successfully create an item by using the *CreateItem* Web method and see what comes back. Listing 18-1 shows the response.

LISTING 18-1 Successful *CreateItem* response

```
<CreateItemResponse xmlns:m=".../messages"
                    xmlns:t=".../types"
                    xmlns=".../messages">
  <m:ResponseMessages>
    <m:CreateItemResponseMessage ResponseClass="Success">
      <m:ResponseCode>NoError</m:ResponseCode>
      <m:Items>
        <t:Message>
          <t:ItemId Id="AAAtAEFkbWlua..." ChangeKey="AAAAA..."/>
        </t:Message>
      </m:Items>
    </m:CreateItemResponseMessage>
  </m:ResponseMessages>
</CreateItemResponse>
```

Notice in Listing 18-1 that the response came back with a *ResponseMessages* element. This container element is on every single Exchange Web Services Web method response.[5] Contained therein is a response message for each batched operation specified in the request.

We can map the response from Listing 18-1 onto the response message structure from Figure 18-1. This is shown in Figure 18-2.[6]

---

[5] With the exception of Autodiscover responses (Chapter 20), but AutoDiscover does not support batching either.

[6] To be fair, the *ResponseClass* attribute on the *ResponseMessage* should probably be included in the success/failure box, but that made the diagram far too ugly for print.

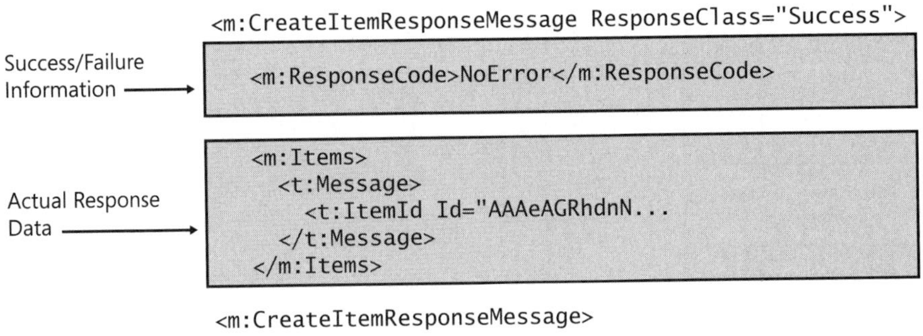

```
                          <m:CreateItemResponseMessage ResponseClass="Success">
Success/Failure
Information ───────→        <m:ResponseCode>NoError</m:ResponseCode>


                          <m:Items>
                            <t:Message>
Actual Response             <t:ItemId Id="AAAeAGRhdnN...
Data ──────────→            </t:Message>
                          </m:Items>

                          <m:CreateItemResponseMessage>
```

FIGURE 18-2 Breaking up the *CreateItem* response message

The *CreateItem* call requested a single item, and therefore Listing 18-1 shows that the response came back with a single *CreateItemResponseMessage* instance. If the *CreateItem* call requested two messages, the response would contain two response messages. A batched request is shown in Listing 18-2.

LISTING 18-2 Creating two messages in one call

```
<CreateItem xmlns=".../messages"
            xmlns:t=".../types"
            MessageDisposition="SaveOnly">
  <Items>
    <t:Message>
      <t:Subject>I am batched message #1</t:Subject>
    </t:Message>
    <t:Message>
      <t:Subject>I am batched message #2</t:Subject>
    </t:Message>
  </Items>
</CreateItem>
```

And the response in Listing 18-3 confirms two response messages.

LISTING 18-3 *CreateItem* response with two response messages

```
<CreateItemResponse xmlns:m=".../messages"
                    xmlns:t=".../types"
                    xmlns=".../messages">
  <m:ResponseMessages>
    <m:CreateItemResponseMessage ResponseClass="Success">
      <m:ResponseCode>NoError</m:ResponseCode>
      <m:Items>
        <t:Message>
          <t:ItemId Id="AAAtAEFkbWlua..." ChangeKey="AAAAA..."/>
        </t:Message>
      </m:Items>
    </m:CreateItemResponseMessage>
```

```
    <m:CreateItemResponseMessage ResponseClass="Success">
      <m:ResponseCode>NoError</m:ResponseCode>
      <m:Items>
        <t:Message>
          <t:ItemId Id="AAAtAEFkbWlaba..." ChangeKey="AAAAA..."/>
        </t:Message>
      </m:Items>
    </m:CreateItemResponseMessage>
  </m:ResponseMessages>
</CreateItemResponse>
```

But what happens if one of them fails? Let's try to create a message but set its *ItemClass* to an invalid value. This request is shown in Listing 18-4.

LISTING 18-4 Batched *CreateItem* with a single failure

```
<CreateItem xmlns=".../messages"
            xmlns:t=".../types"
            MessageDisposition="SaveOnly">
  <Items>
    <t:Message>
      <t:Subject>I am batched message #1</t:Subject>
    </t:Message>
    <t:Message>
      <t:ItemClass>I should not work</t:ItemClass>
      <t:Subject>Watch me fail!</t:Subject>
    </t:Message>
  </Items>
</CreateItem>
```

When this request is issued, the response shown in Listing 18-5 is returned.

LISTING 18-5 Batched *CreateItem* response with single failure

```
<CreateItemResponse xmlns:m=".../messages"
                    xmlns:t=".../types"
                    xmlns=".../messages">
  <m:ResponseMessages>
    <m:CreateItemResponseMessage ResponseClass="Success">
      <m:ResponseCode>NoError</m:ResponseCode>
      <m:Items>
        <t:Message>
          <t:ItemId Id="AAAtAEFkbWlua..." ChangeKey="AAAAA..."/>
        </t:Message>
      </m:Items>
    </m:CreateItemResponseMessage>
    <m:CreateItemResponseMessage ResponseClass="Error">
      <m:MessageText>Operation would change object type, which is not
                     permitted.</m:MessageText>
      <m:ResponseCode>ErrorObjectTypeChanged</m:ResponseCode>
```

```
      <m:DescriptiveLinkKey>0</m:DescriptiveLinkKey>
      <m:Items/>
    </m:CreateItemResponseMessage>
  </m:ResponseMessages>
</CreateItemResponse>
```

As expected, the first item was successfully created (as can be seen by the response code of *NoError* and the returned *ItemId*). In contrast, the second item failed. Notice several things about the second response message.

1. The *ResponseClass* attribute is *"Error"* rather than *"Success."*

2. There is a new *MessageText* element that provides textual information about what failed.

3. The *ResponseCode* element is *ErrorObjectTypeChanged* rather than *NoError*.

4. The *Items* array is empty.

Another noteworthy thing is that the response came back with an HTTP response code of 200 (OK). In fact, the vast majority of error responses that you do receive come back with an HTTP status code of 200. As you will see later in this chapter, several conditions cause the HTTP 500 status code to be returned.

Typically, when you receive a response message that has error information in it, the data part of the response message will be empty.[7]

Given that all of the responses come back within these *ResponseMessage* container elements, it is worthwhile to examine the *ResponseMessage* element in more detail.

Response Messages

All response messages that you encounter derive from *ResponseMessageType* in messages.xsd. The basic structure of *ResponseMessageType* is shown in Listing 18-6.

LISTING 18-6 Basic structure of *ResponseMessageType*

```
<ResponseMessage ResponseClass="Success | Warning | Error">
  <MessageText/>
  <ResponseCode/>
  <DescriptiveLinkKey/>
  <MessageXml/>
</ResponseMessage>
```

---

[7] We say typically because there is a case with *ResolveNames* in which an error response code is returned but actual data is also returned.

ResponseClass Attribute

The *ResponseClass* attribute is an enumeration of type *ResponseClassType* and has three possible values: *Success, Warning,* or *Error. Success* means that the operation was success-ful. It will always be coupled with a *ResponseCode* of *NoError. Warning* is encountered in a *ResolveNames* Web method response only when multiple matches are found for a given ambiguous name. *Warning* is significant in that actual data can still be returned inside a response message descendant, just like a *Success* response class. *Error* is encountered when the request cannot be processed for one reason or another. You need to refer to the *ResponseCode* and/or *MessageText* to determine what went wrong.

MessageText Element

The *MessageText* element appears in the response message only when the *ResponseClass* is either *Warning* or *Error.* The *MessageText* element contains a human-readable description of what went wrong with the request. This description is localized based on the *MailboxCulture* specified in the SOAP header (discussed in Chapter 2, "May I See Your Id?"). So, if you were to repeat your request but pass in zh-CN for the *MailboxCulture,* you would get back the failure message in Chinese (mainland), as shown in Listing 18-7.

LISTING 18-7 Mainland China *MessageText*

```
<m:CreateItemResponseMessage ResponseClass="Error">
  <m:MessageText>操作将更改⊠象类型 ， 不允⊠⊠⊠做。</m:MessageText>
  <m:ResponseCode>ErrorObjectTypeChanged</m:ResponseCode>
  <m:DescriptiveLinkKey>0</m:DescriptiveLinkKey>
  <m:Items/>
</m:CreateItemResponseMessage>
```

Localized *MessageText* content can be used for user interface (UI) display, logging, or simply to help developers who are working with Exchange Web Services. However, we do not suggest that you make any programmatic decisions based on the content of the *MessageText* element.

ResponseCode Element

The *ResponseCode* element appears in all response messages regardless of the *ResponseClass* value. One thing you can count on is that when the *ResponseClass* attribute is *Success, ResponseCode* will be set to *NoError. ResponseCode* is an enumeration of type *ResponseCodeType* and is defined in messages.xsd. In Exchange Web Services there are 275 response code values. Appendix A, "Error Codes," (available on the companion Web page) contains a table of the response code values and includes brief commentary about the con-ditions surrounding each.

DescriptiveLinkKey Element

DescriptiveLinkKey is currently unused and always comes back as zero if present. It was originally intended to be some sort of lookup value into the Microsoft Developer Network (MSDN) online library to enable you to get more information about a given error condition, but the lookup values never made it into the code. So, now the *DescriptiveLinkKey* is just a reliable way for you to know what the true value of zero is.

MessageXml Element

The *MessageXml* element is emitted when a given error condition has additional information that it needs to convey. As you saw in the first erroneous condition in Listing 18-5, *ErrorObjectTypeChanged* didn't come with any additional information, but other response codes do. For the most part, error response codes that fill in *MessageXml* information give back a property path that indicates which property was in error. The response codes that do so are listed in Table 18-1.

TABLE 18-1 Response Codes That Emit Property Paths in *MessageXml*

ErrorCalendarInvalidAttributeValue	*ErrorInvalidPropertyRequest*
ErrorCalendarInvalidDayForTimeChangePattern	*ErrorInvalidPropertySet*
ErrorCalendarInvalidDayForWeeklyRecurrence	*ErrorInvalidPropertyUpdateSentMessage*
ErrorCalendarInvalidPropertyState	*ErrorInvalidRoutingType*
ErrorCalendarInvalidPropertyValue	*ErrorInvalidValueForProperty*
ErrorCalendarOutOfRange	*ErrorItemPropertyRequestFailed*
ErrorDataSizeLimitExceeded	*ErrorItemSavePropertyError (plurality of PropertyPaths)*
ErrorFolderPropertyRequestFailed	*ErrorPropertyUpdate (plurality of PropertyPaths)*
ErrorFolderSavePropertyError (plurality of PropertyPaths)	*ErrorRequiredPropertyMissing*
ErrorInvalidExtendedProperty	*ErrorUnsupportedPathForQuery*
ErrorInvalidExtendedPropertyValue	*ErrorUnsupportedPathForQuery*
ErrorInvalidPropertyAppend	*ErrorUnsupportedPathForSortGroup*
ErrorInvalidPropertyDelete	*ErrorUnsupportedPathForSortGroup*
ErrorInvalidPropertyForExists	*ErrorUpdatePropertyMismatch*
ErrorInvalidPropertyForOperation	

As an example, if you try to create a message by using *CreateItem* and set the read-only *ItemId* property, you get back a *ErrorInvalidPropertySet* response code, as shown in Listing 18-8.

LISTING 18-8 *MessageXml* for *ErrorInvalidPropertySet*

```
<CreateItemResponse xmlns:m=".../messages"
                    xmlns:t=".../types"
                    xmlns=".../messages">
  <m:ResponseMessages>
    <m:CreateItemResponseMessage ResponseClass="Error">
      <m:MessageText>Set action is invalid for property.</m:MessageText>
      <m:ResponseCode>ErrorInvalidPropertySet</m:ResponseCode>
      <m:DescriptiveLinkKey>0</m:DescriptiveLinkKey>
      <m:MessageXml>
        <t:FieldURI FieldURI="item:ItemId"/>
      </m:MessageXml>
      <m:Items/>
    </m:CreateItemResponseMessage>
  </m:ResponseMessages>
</CreateItemResponse>
```

A few response codes give back other information, as shown in Table 18-2.

TABLE 18-2 **Non-Standard Usage of the *MessageXml* Element**

Response Code	*MessageXml* contains...
ErrorNonPrimarySmtpAddress	Primary Simple Mail Transfer Protocol (SMTP) address to use in element *Primary*
ErrorNonExistentMailbox	The invalid SMTP address from the request in element *SmtpAddress*
ErrorOccurrenceCrossingBoundary	Includes the following elements: *AdjacentOccurrenceOriginalStartTime* *AdjacentOccurrenceStartTime* *AdjacentOccurrenceEndTime* *ModifiedOccurrenceOriginalStartTime* *ModifiedOccurrenceStartTime* *ModifiedOccurrenceEndTime*
ErrorRecurrenceHasNoOccurrence	Includes the following elements: *EffectiveStartDate* *EffectiveEndDate*

Errors and the Proxy Classes

Now that you know what a response message is and how error information is embedded in it, how do you deal with response message errors when you are using the proxy classes? First, the response class and response code are exposed as properties on *ResponseMessageType*, so accessing those is quite easy. You can check the *ResponseClass* property if you like.

```
if (myResponseMessage.ResponseClass != ResponseClassType.Success)
{
  // Either an error or a warning...
  //
}
```

Or you can check the *ResponseCode* property.

```
if (myResponseMessage.ResponseCode != ResponseCodeType.NoError)
{
  // Either an error or a warning...
  //
}
```

You could also check *ResponseClass* for a value of *Warning*. However, the only warning Exchange Web Services exposes is returned by *ResolveNames*. Therefore, you can safely ignore the *Warning ResponseClass* value when calling the other Web methods.

Of course, once things go wrong, you might want to do something with the information. The example code in Listing 18-9, tries to create an item, set the read-only *ItemId*, and then parse out the failure information from the response message.

LISTING 18-9 Parsing property paths from response messages (first attempt)

```
/// <summary>
/// Tries to create an invalid item and then parses out the property path
/// from the response message
/// </summary>
/// <param name="binding">Binding to use for the call</param>
///
public static void CreateItemSetItemIdAndFail(
                    ExchangeServiceBinding binding)
{
  // Create our request
  //
  CreateItemType request = new CreateItemType();
  request.Items = new NonEmptyArrayOfAllItemsType();
  ItemType itemToCreate = new ItemType();
  itemToCreate.ItemId = new ItemIdType();
  itemToCreate.ItemId.Id = "This is a bad Id";
  itemToCreate.Subject = "I cannot succeed";

  request.Items.Items = new ItemType[] { itemToCreate };
  // Make the call...
  //
  CreateItemResponseType response = binding.CreateItem(request);

  // Remember, all of the success/failure information is on the base type.
  // No need to cast when checking this information.
  //
  ResponseMessageType responseMessage =
                response.ResponseMessages.Items[0];
  if (responseMessage.ResponseCode != ResponseCodeType.NoError)
```

```
    {
      // we want to look at the offending property here...
      //
      XmlElement[] messageXmlElements = responseMessage.MessageXml.Any;
      foreach (XmlElement messageXmlElement in messageXmlElements)
      {
        if ((messageXmlElement.LocalName == "FieldURI") &&
            (messageXmlElement.NamespaceURI ==
             "http://schemas.microsoft.com/exchange/services/2006/types"))
        {
          // Ah! an offending item...
          //
          XmlAttribute fieldURIAttribute =
              messageXmlElement.Attributes["FieldURI"] as XmlAttribute;
          UnindexedFieldURIType path =
              (UnindexedFieldURIType) Enum.Parse(
               typeof(UnindexedFieldURIType),
               fieldURIAttribute.Value.Replace(":",String.Empty));
          Console.WriteLine(path.ToString());
        }
      }
    }
  }
}
```

This particularly ugly piece of code in Listing 18-9 shows something interesting. The *MessageXml* element contains an *Any* property that is an array of *XmlElement*. This is because *MessageXml* is specified as an *xs:any* element in the schema. So really, any valid XML can occur as a child of *MessageXml*. Arbitrary XML is bad for developers because it provides nothing concrete to hold onto. Thankfully, while the schema allows any XML to be contained within the *MessageXml* element, in practice, there is a finite list of child elements that actually occur therein.

Given the array of *XmlElements*, you can do some basic manipulation by using the classes in the *System.Xml* namespace to get the information that you want. The code in Listing 18-9 does something interesting with the *FieldURI* attribute value. If you look at the XML response from Listing 18-8, you'll notice that there is a property path with a colon in the middle.

```
<m:MessageXml>
  <t:FieldURI FieldURI="item:ItemId"/>
</m:MessageXml>
```

Of course, *"item:ItemId"* is not a valid .NET identifier. So, we simply removed the colon from the attribute value and parse the string into the enumeration type.

```
UnindexedFieldURIType path =
            (UnindexedFieldURIType) Enum.Parse(
              typeof(UnindexedFieldURIType),
              fieldURIAttribute.Value.Replace(":",String.Empty));
```

String manipulation of this type is not the best programming practice you can get into. Can you do anything about it?

When you use the proxy classes, you deal with enumeration values such as *itemItemId*. However, the XML that is sent to Exchange Web Services must use *item:ItemId* instead. The proxy classes must therefore do some sort of mapping. If you take a look at the *UnindexedFieldURIType* in the auto-generated proxy classes, you see something interesting.

```
public enum UnindexedFieldURIType
{
  // code elided...
  /// <remarks/>
  [System.Xml.Serialization.XmlEnumAttribute("item:ItemId")]
  itemItemId,

  // code elided
```

The *XmlEnumAttribute* attribute tags each of the *UnindexedFieldURIType* enumeration values with the correct "colon-ized" name. The presence of this attribute is relatively easy to take advantage of. Listing 18-10 shows the *FieldURIMapper* class that uses reflection to build a map of *UnindexedFieldURI* enumeration values to their corresponding XML string representations. We also do this for *DictionaryFieldURIs*.

LISTING 18-10 *FieldURIMapper* class

```
/// <summary>
/// Holds maps of UnindexedFieldURI and DictionaryURI values to XML strings
/// for those values
/// </summary>
public static class FieldURIMapper
{
  private static Dictionary<string, UnindexedFieldURIType>
    stringToFieldURIMap = new Dictionary<string, UnindexedFieldURIType>();
  private static Dictionary<UnindexedFieldURIType, string>
    fieldURIToStringMap = new Dictionary<UnindexedFieldURIType,string>();
  private static Dictionary<string, DictionaryURIType>
    stringToIndexedMap = new Dictionary<string, DictionaryURIType>();
  private static Dictionary<DictionaryURIType, string>
    indexedToStringMap = new Dictionary<DictionaryURIType, string>();


  /// <summary>
  /// Static constructor used to fill our maps.  This isn't cheap, so we
  /// only want to do it once.
  /// </summary>
  static FieldURIMapper()
  {
    CreateMapping<UnindexedFieldURIType>(
                        stringToFieldURIMap,
                        fieldURIToStringMap);
    CreateMapping<DictionaryURIType>(
                        stringToIndexedMap,
                        indexedToStringMap);
```

```
}

/// <summary>
/// Generic method for reflecting the XmlEnum attributes on a given
/// type's fields and mapping those to the actual field value.
/// </summary>
/// <typeparam name="T">Enum type</typeparam>
/// <param name="stringToMap">Dictionary holding string to T mappings</param>
/// <param name="toStringMap">Dictionary holding T to string mappings</param>
///
private static void CreateMapping<T>(
                Dictionary<string, T> stringToMap,
                Dictionary<T, string> toStringMap)
{
  Type type = typeof(T);
  FieldInfo[] fields = type.GetFields();
  foreach (FieldInfo field in fields)
  {
    // we are only interested in the fields with XmlEnum attributes
    //
    object[] attributes =
              field.GetCustomAttributes(
                      typeof(XmlEnumAttribute), false);
    if (attributes.Length == 1)
    {
      XmlEnumAttribute enumAttribute = attributes[0] as XmlEnumAttribute;
      T enumValue = (T)field.GetRawConstantValue();
      // Add to both the lookup and reverse map
      //
      stringToMap.Add(enumAttribute.Name, enumValue);
      toStringMap.Add(enumValue, enumAttribute.Name);
    }
  }
}


/// <summary>
/// Returns the xml string value for a given UnindexedFieldUri
/// </summary>
/// <param name="fieldUri">FieldURI to look up</param>
/// <returns>xml string for the enum value</returns>
///
public static string FieldUriToString(UnindexedFieldURIType fieldUri)
{
  return fieldURIToStringMap[fieldUri];
}


/// <summary>
/// Returns the UnindexedFieldURI value for a given xml string.  Note
/// that if it is not found, an exception will be thrown.
/// </summary>
/// <param name="fieldUriString">string to look up</param>
/// <returns>UnindexedFieldURIValue</returns>
///
public static UnindexedFieldURIType StringToFieldUri(string fieldUriString)
```

```
  {
    return stringToFieldURIMap[fieldUriString];
  }


  /// <summary>
  /// Returns the xml string for a given DictionaryURI value
  /// </summary>
  /// <param name="fieldUri">Dictionary URI value</param>
  /// <returns>xml string</returns>
  ///
  public static string IndexedFieldUriToString(DictionaryURIType fieldUri)
  {
    return indexedToStringMap[fieldUri];
  }


  /// <summary>
  /// Returns the DictionaryURI value for a given xml string.  Note that
  /// if it is not found, an exception will be thrown by the dictionary.
  /// </summary>
  /// <param name="fieldUriString">String to look up</param>
  /// <returns>DictionaryURI</returns>
  ///
  public static DictionaryURIType StringToIndexedFieldUri(string fieldUriString)
  {
    return stringToIndexedMap[fieldUriString];
  }


  /// <summary>
  /// Tries to get unindexed and indexed field URIs from a response
  /// message
  /// </summary>
  /// <param name="responseMessage">Response message to examine</param>
  /// <param name="paths">OUT property paths</param>
  /// <returns>True if it found property paths</returns>
  ///
  public static bool TryExtractFieldURIsFromResponseMessage(
                  ResponseMessageType responseMessage,
                  out BasePathToElementType[] paths)
  {
    List<BasePathToElementType> pathsList = new List<BasePathToElementType>();
    if ((responseMessage.ResponseCode == ResponseCodeType.NoError) ||
        (responseMessage.MessageXml == null))
    {
      paths = null;
      return false;
    }
    XmlElement[] elements = responseMessage.MessageXml.Any;
    foreach (XmlElement element in elements)
    {
      switch (element.LocalName)
      {
        case "FieldURI":
          XmlAttribute fieldURIAttribute =
                element.Attributes["FieldURI"] as XmlAttribute;
```

```
            UnindexedFieldURIType fieldURI =
                StringToFieldUri(fieldURIAttribute.Value);
            PathToUnindexedFieldType propertyPath =
                new PathToUnindexedFieldType();
            propertyPath.FieldURI = fieldURI;
            pathsList.Add(propertyPath);
            break;

        case "IndexedFieldURI":
            XmlAttribute indexedFieldURIAttribute =
                element.Attributes["FieldURI"] as XmlAttribute;
            XmlAttribute fieldIndexAttribute =
                element.Attributes["FieldIndex"] as XmlAttribute;
            PathToIndexedFieldType indexedPropertyPath = new
                PathToIndexedFieldType();
            indexedPropertyPath.FieldURI =
                StringToIndexedFieldUri(indexedFieldURIAttribute.Value);
            indexedPropertyPath.FieldIndex = fieldIndexAttribute.Value;
            pathsList.Add(indexedPropertyPath);
            break;

        case "ExtendedFieldURI":
            // Homework...
            //
            throw new NotImplementedException();
        }
    }
    paths = (pathsList.Count == 0) ? null : pathsList.ToArray();
    return paths != null;
    }
}
```

Aside from maintaining the maps, the *FieldURIMapper* class also offers the *TryExtractFieldURIsFromResponseMessage* method. If a given failure response message includes embedded property paths, this method extracts them and returns true. Note that you need to implement the *ExtendedFieldURI* case if you want to use this for your own purposes. With this new class, the example from Listing 18-9 becomes a lot cleaner, as shown in Listing 18-11.

LISTING 18-11 Parsing property paths from response messages (second attempt)

```
// previous code elided...
//
if (responseMessage.ResponseCode != ResponseCodeType.NoError)
{
    // we want to look at the offending property here...
    //
    BasePathToElementType[] paths = null;
    if (FieldURIMapper.TryExtractFieldURIsFromResponseMessage(
                    responseMessage,
                    out paths))
    {
```

```
    foreach (BasePathToElementType path in paths)
    {
      // do something with the paths.
    }
  }
}
```

This is quite a bit cleaner than before, although it still is a bit of a special case that would be better to avoid. We will provide a slightly better approach shortly.

HTTP 500 Status Codes

As mentioned earlier in the chapter, you will sometimes encounter HTTP 500 status codes. You encounter these errors when something about your request causes the entire request to fail. Typically, such erroneous conditions occur before the first item in the request is processed. For instance, if you pass in a request that is not schema-compliant, you receive an HTTP 500 status code, and the response code of *ErrorSchemaValidation* is embedded in the *detail* node of the SOAP fault. Let's see that in action. The invalid request is shown in Listing 18-12.

LISTING 18-12 Schema invalid request

```
<CreateItem xmlns=".../messages"
            xmlns:t=".../types"
            MessageDisposition="SaveOnly">
  <Items>
    <t:Messagez>
      <t:Subject>I am batched message #1</t:Subject>
    </t:Messagez>
  </Items>
</CreateItem>
```

Note that the request in Listing 18-12 misspelled the *Message* element by including a *z* at the end. As a result of this lexical *faux pas*, you are greeted with an HTTP 500 response, as shown in Listing 18-13.

LISTING 18-13 HTTP 500 response due to schema violation

```
HTTP/1.1 500 Internal Server Error
Date: Fri, 23 Mar 2007 01:33:41 GMT
Server: Microsoft-IIS/6.0
X-Powered-By: ASP.NET
X-AspNet-Version: 2.0.50727
Content-Length: 1471
Cache-Control: private
Content-Type: text/xml; charset=utf-8
```

```
<?xml version="1.0"?>
<soap:Envelope xmlns:soap="http://schemas.xmlsoap.org/soap/envelope/">
  <soap:Header>
    <t:ServerVersionInfo …
  </soap:Header>
  <soap:Body>
    <soap:Fault>
      <soap:faultcode>Client</soap:faultcode>
      <soap:faultstring>The request failed schema validation.</soap:faultstring>
      <detail>
        <e:ResponseCode xmlns:e=".../errors">ErrorSchemaValidation</e:ResponseCode>
        <e:Message xmlns:e=".../errors">The element 'Items' in namespace 'http://
schemas.microsoft.com/exchange/services/2006/messages' has invalid child element
'Messagez' in namespace 'http://schemas.microsoft.com/exchange/services/2006/
types'. List of possible elements expected: 'Item, Message, CalendarItem, Contact,
DistributionList, MeetingMessage, MeetingRequest, MeetingResponse, MeetingCancellation,
Task, ReplyToItem, ForwardItem, ReplyAllToItem, AcceptItem, TentativelyAcceptItem,
DeclineItem, CancelCalendarItem, RemoveItem, SuppressReadReceipt' in namespace
'http://schemas.microsoft.com/exchange/services/2006/types'.</e:Message>
        <e:Line xmlns:e=".../errors">6</e:Line>
        <e:Position xmlns:e=".../errors">6</e:Position>
      </detail>
    </soap:Fault>
  </soap:Body>
</soap:Envelope>
```

Notice a couple of things from the response in Listing 18-13.

First, there is indeed a *soap:fault* element, and the *soap:faultCode* is marked as *Client*, indicating that the caller was responsible for this failure.

Second, notice that the *soap:faultString* contains the textual string indicating what went wrong. This corresponds to the *MessageText* element within the *ResponseMessage*. Note, however, that although the *ResponseMessage MessageText* element respects the *MailboxCulture* SOAP header when localizing the failure message, fault strings within the SOAP faults do not. This is not a limitation of SOAP faults; instead, it is because requests are schema validated by Exchange Web Services before anything else is done. Therefore, the *MailboxCulture* SOAP header has not yet been parsed by the time this failure is generated.

Third, notice that the *detail* element contains the trusty *ResponseCode* element, which in this case is *ErrorSchemaValidation*.

Now, trying to generate a schema validation error when using the proxy is more difficult because the proxy classes were created from the schema. However, it is not impossible. Take Listing 18-14, which shows the *PropertyTagType* in types.xsd.

LISTING 18-14 *PropertyTagType* in types.xsd

```xml
<xs:simpleType name="PropertyTagType">
  <!-- annotation elided -->
  <xs:union memberTypes ="xs:unsignedShort">
    <xs:simpleType id="HexPropertyTagType">
      <xs:restriction base="xs:string">
        <xs:pattern value="(0x|0X)[0-9A-Fa-f]{1,4}"/>
      </xs:restriction>
    </xs:simpleType>
  </xs:union>
</xs:simpleType>
```

As you saw in Chapter 13, you use the *PropertyTagType* when defining MAPI extended properties. Since *PropertyTagType* is a restriction on a string type, for it be schema valid the property tag must be in a hexidecimal format, such as 0x1234. If you were to specify five hex digits (0x12345), the request would be schema invalid due to the {1,4} length restriction in the pattern. Interestingly enough, the schema exposes property tags as *strings* with no reference to these restrictions. As such, you can set values within a proxy class request that will be schema invalid. What happens in that case? Listing 18-15 shows code that causes such a schema violation.

LISTING 18-15 Causing a schema violation by using the proxy

```csharp
/// <summary>
/// Causes a SoapException to be thrown due to schema violation
/// </summary>
/// <param name="binding">Binding to use</param>
///
public static void CauseSchemaViolationThroughProxy(ExchangeServiceBinding binding)
{
    PathToExtendedFieldType badProp = new PathToExtendedFieldType();

    // PropertyTagType is limited in the schema to 4 digits.  Use 5 instead...
    //
    badProp.PropertyTag = "0x12345";
    badProp.PropertyType = MapiPropertyTypeType.String;

    // Issue a FindItem request and ask for our "bad" extended property
    //
    FindItemType findItem = new FindItemType();

    // Use our partial class extension overloads to reduce typing...
    //
    findItem.ItemShape = new ItemResponseShapeType(
                        DefaultShapeNamesType.IdOnly,
                        badProp);
    findItem.ParentFolderIds = new BaseFolderIdType[] {
                        new DistinguishedFolderIdType(
                                DistinguishedFolderIdNameType.inbox) };
```

```
    // Our SoapException will be thrown when we call this line...
    //
    FindItemResponseType response = binding.FindItem(findItem);
}
```

If you run the code from Listing 18-15 in the Microsoft Visual Studio debugger, you get an
unhandled exception, as shown in Figure 18-3.

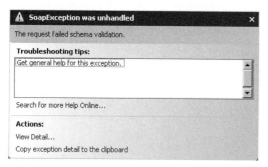

FIGURE 18-3 *SoapException* due to schema violation

Other than schema violation errors, several other error conditions cause SOAP faults to
be returned. First, if something unexpected happens on the server, you may encounter an
ErrorInternalServerError. This is typically returned if there is an unhandled exception within
the Exchange Web Services code. Second, when performing Server to Server (S2S) authentication calls, malformed headers, insufficient permissions, and so on all cause SOAP faults to
be returned.[8] Why? Because S2S authentication is a call-wide feature and is processed before
any of the items within the SOAP body are processed.

So, given that you encounter SOAP faults in certain circumstances, how do you deal with
them? Thankfully, *SoapException* instances expose a *Detail* element that is of type *System.Xml.
XmlNode*. Knowing that Exchange Web Services embeds the response code within the *details*
element, you can write a method to extract that information, as shown in Listing 18-16.

LISTING 18-16 Extracting the *ResponseCode* from a SOAP exception

```
/// <summary>
/// Grab the response code from within a soap exception
/// </summary>
/// <param name="soapException">Soap Exception to examine</param>
/// <returns>True if parse was successful</returns>
///
public static bool TryGetResponseCodeFromSoapException(
                            SoapException soapException,
                            out ResponseCodeType responseCode)
```

---

[8]   Server to Server authentication is discussed in Chapter 19.

```
{
  responseCode = ResponseCodeType.NoError;
  XmlElement detailElement = (XmlElement)soapException.Detail;
  if (detailElement == null)
  {
    return false;
  }
  XmlElement responseCodeElement = detailElement[
            "ResponseCode",
            "http://schemas.microsoft.com/exchange/services/2006/errors"];
  if (responseCodeElement == null)
  {
    return false;
  }
  responseCode = (ResponseCodeType)Enum.Parse(
                typeof(ResponseCodeType),
                responseCodeElement.InnerText);
  return true;
}
```

With such a method in your arsenal, you can wrap your calls in a try catch block and parse the response code out if necessary. Taking the invalid *PropertyTagType* example from Listing 18-15, you can wrap the call as shown in Listing 18-17.

LISTING 18-17 Using the *TryGetResponseCodeFromSoapException* method

```
// previous code elided
try
{
  // Our SoapException will be thrown when we call this line...
  //
  FindItemResponseType response = binding.FindItem(findItem);
}
catch (SoapException soapException)
{
  ResponseCodeType responseCode;
  if (TryGetResponseCodeFromSoapException(
                    soapException,
                    out responseCode))
  {
    Console.WriteLine(responseCode.ToString());
  }
  else
  {
    throw;
  }
}
```

Programming Consistency

Programmers using a .NET language are comfortable with errors being reported by exceptions. Component Object Model (COM) and Win32 API programmers from yesteryear are comfortable with HRESULTs and response code values coming back from their calls. As you have seen in this chapter, Exchange Web Services programmers have to contend with a mixture of response values (response codes) and exceptions (SOAP faults). So now that you are here, is there anything that you can do to unify these two error-reporting mechanisms? That all depends on how much of an investment you want to put into extending the auto-generated proxy classes. For instance, if you are writing a simple component that needs to make one call using Exchange Web Services, it might be okay to just deal with this inconsistency. If, however, you are writing an application that relies on Exchange Web Services as a primary API and makes all sorts of interesting Exchange Web Services calls, you are well served by adding functionality to the auto-generated proxy classes.

You can take one of two approaches. First, if you never see yourself using batching, we recommend moving to the exception approach. With this non-batched approach, you create your own class that wraps the *ExchangeServiceBinding* and exposes the Web methods you are interested in as wrapper methods. These wrapper Web methods take a single item (instead of a batch of items), make the call, and then translate any failures into an exception. As an example, let's look at how this would be done using the *GetItem* Web method.

The Non-Batched, Exception Approach

First, let's create the exception class. For simplicity, we will create a single exception class that exposes the response message details as properties. In addition, we will allow this exception to be created using a *ResponseMessageType* instance or a *SoapException* instance. We will also use the handy *FieldURIMapper* class to parse out any offending property paths from the response message XML. The resulting *EWSException* class is shown in Listing 18-18.

LISTING 18-18 The *EWSException* class

```
/// <summary>
/// Exception class thrown when we encounter either a failure response
/// message or a soap exception
/// </summary>
///
[Serializable]
public class EWSException: Exception
{
  private ResponseMessageType responseMessage;
  private bool fromSoapFault;
  private BasePathToElementType[] propertyPaths = null;

  /// <summary>
  /// Constructor
  /// </summary>
```

```
/// <param name="responseMessage">ResponseMessage to build it
/// from</param>
///
public EWSException(ResponseMessageType responseMessage) :
                base(responseMessage.MessageText)
{
  this.responseMessage = responseMessage;
  this.fromSoapFault = false;
  // Look at the MessageXml and see if there are any property paths
  //
  FieldURIMapper.TryExtractFieldURIsFromResponseMessage(
                        responseMessage,
                        out this.propertyPaths);
}


/// <summary>
/// Constructor
/// </summary>
/// <param name="soapException">SoapException to build it from</param>
///
public EWSException(SoapException soapException) :
                base(soapException.Message, soapException)
{
  this.responseMessage =
          BuildResponseMessageFromSoapFault(soapException);
  this.fromSoapFault = true;
}


/// <summary>
/// Accessor for the contained response message
/// </summary>
///
public ResponseMessageType ResponseMessage
{
  get
  {
    return this.responseMessage;
  }
}


/// <summary>
/// Returns true if this was generated from a soap fault
/// </summary>
///
public bool FromSoapFault
{
  get
  {
    return this.fromSoapFault;
  }
}


/// <summary>
/// Accessor for any offending property paths
```

```
    /// </summary>
    public BasePathToElementType[] PropertyPaths
    {
      get
      {
        return this.propertyPaths;
      }
    }


    /// <summary>
    /// Helper method for building a ResponseMessageType instance from a
    /// soap fault
    /// </summary>
    /// <param name="soapException">Soap exception</param>
    /// <returns>ResponseMessage</returns>
    ///
    private ResponseMessageType BuildResponseMessageFromSoapFault(
                      SoapException soapException)
    {
      ResponseMessageType result = new ResponseMessageType();
      result.DescriptiveLinkKey = 0;
      result.DescriptiveLinkKeySpecified = true;

      result.MessageText = soapException.Message;
      XmlElement detailElement = soapException.Detail as XmlElement;
      XmlElement responseCodeElement = detailElement[
          "ResponseCode",
          "http://schemas.microsoft.com/exchange/services/2006/errors"];

      result.ResponseCode = (ResponseCodeType)Enum.Parse(
                                typeof(ResponseCodeType),
                                responseCodeElement.InnerText);
      result.ResponseCodeSpecified = true;
      result.ResponseClass = ResponseClassType.Error;
      result.MessageXml = null;
      return result;
    }


    /// <summary>
    /// Helper method for examining a response message and throwing an
    /// exception if it is an error
    /// </summary>
    /// <param name="responseMessage">ResponseMessage to examine</param>
    ///
    public static void ThrowIfError(ResponseMessageType responseMessage)
    {
      // NOTE:  You will need to change this if you want to fail on
      // warnings.
      //
      if (responseMessage.ResponseClass == ResponseClassType.Error)
      {
        throw new EWSException(responseMessage);
      }
    }
  }
}
```

Now that we have the exception type, let's create a *GetItem* proxy method wrapper and call it *GetSingleItem*. This is shown in Listing 18-19.

LISTING 18-19 *GetSingleItem* Web method (partial class extension of *ExchangeServiceBinding*)

```
/// <summary>
/// Gets a single item and uses the new EWSException class to report errors
/// </summary>
/// <param name="responseShape">response shape to use</param>
/// <param name="itemId">Id of item to get</param>
/// <returns>Retrieved ItemType instance</returns>
///
public ItemType GetSingleItem(
            ItemResponseShapeType responseShape,
            ItemIdType itemId)
{
  GetItemType getItemRequest = new GetItemType();
  getItemRequest.ItemShape = responseShape;
  getItemRequest.ItemIds = new BaseItemIdType[] { itemId };
  GetItemResponseType response = null;
  try
  {
    response = this.GetItem(getItemRequest);
  }
  catch (SoapException soapException)
  {
    throw new EWSException(soapException);
  }

  // if the call was an error, throw.
  //
  ItemInfoResponseMessageType itemResponseMessage =
        response.ResponseMessages.Items[0] as
            ItemInfoResponseMessageType;
  EWSException.ThrowIfError(itemResponseMessage);

  // return our single item
  //
  return itemResponseMessage.Items.Items[0];
}
```

Listing 18-19 adds some very simple, yet very useful features.

1. The method takes individual parameters rather than requiring you to create a *GetItemType* wrapper request.

2. The method uses the *EWSException* to map *SoapExceptions* into usable exceptions.

3. The method examines the response message and throws an *EWSException* if the response is an error.

4. The method parses out the resulting *ItemType* instance and does away with the thick *Response/ResponseMessage* wrapper around it.

This wrapper approach can be used for the other Web methods of interest as well. It doesn't take much to do so, and the end result is quite pleasing.

The Batched Approach

The batched approach isn't quite as easy. We can throw *EWSException* when SOAP faults are encountered. The entire request failed anyway. Otherwise, we would really need to create "fake" response messages for each batched item so that we would have something to iterate through when examining your response.

One thing that would help is to get rid of the outer response wrapper and base types that cause us to do unwieldy casts. Listing 18-20 shows the *GetBatchedItems* method, again created via partial class extension of *ExchangeServiceBinding*.

LISTING 18-20 *GetBatchedItems* method (via partial class extension of *ExchangeServiceBinding*)

```
/// <summary>
/// Helper method for performing batched GetItem calls
/// </summary>
/// <param name="responseShape">ResponseShape to return</param>
/// <param name="itemIds">params array of itemIds</param>
/// <returns>ItemInfoResponseMessageType array</returns>
///
public ItemInfoResponseMessageType[] GetBatchedItems(
          ItemResponseShapeType responseShape,
          params ItemIdType[] itemIds)
{
  GetItemType getItemRequest = new GetItemType();
  getItemRequest.ItemShape = responseShape;
  getItemRequest.ItemIds = itemIds;
  GetItemResponseType response = null;
  try
  {
    response = this.GetItem(getItemRequest);
  }
  catch (SoapException soapException)
  {
    // if we encounter a soap exception, throw an EWS exception
    // instead
    //
    throw new EWSException(soapException);
  }

  ItemInfoResponseMessageType[] results = new
      ItemInfoResponseMessageType[response.ResponseMessages.Items.Length];
  int index = 0;
  foreach (ItemInfoResponseMessageType responseMessage in
                  response.ResponseMessages.Items)
  {
    results[index++] = responseMessage;
  }
  return results;
}
```

Listing 18-20 is certainly not as significant an improvement as the non-batched *GetItem* call from Listing 18-19, but it does make life easier.

Of course, numerous other improvements could be made. For instance, rather than having a single *EWSException* class, you could derive a new *EWSExceptionWithProperties* class from the base *EWSException* and have the offending properties exposed there. In addition, you could add another descendant *EWSNonPrimarySmtpException* that parses out and exposes the correct primary SMTP address to use. Think of the auto-generated proxy classes as a starting point for your Exchange Web Services class library, not the ending point. Institute whatever improvements will make your life easier.

Batch Stop Processing Errors

As a general rule, Exchange Web Services tries to fulfill as much of a batched request as possible. Of course, schema invalid requests and requests that fail SOAP header parsing result in SOAP faults being returned. You may encounter another class of conditions that cause a given batch to stop processing. They are called *batch stop processing errors*.

Batch stop processing errors occur while an item within a given batch is being operated on. This means that the request has already been schema validated and the contents of the SOAP headers have been accepted, but conditions arise such that Exchange Web Services realizes that it cannot continue processing the other items within the batch. When an item fails due to a batch stopping condition, all other items within that request are failed without Exchange Web Services even trying to process them. Each corresponding response message is marked with an *ErrorBatchProcessingStopped* response code.

As an example, let's stop the Microsoft Exchange Information Store service to simulate the store being down and make a simple *GetFolder* request on multiple folders. The response is shown in Listing 18-21.

LISTING 18-21 Batch stop response code

```
<GetFolderResponse xmlns:m=".../messages"
                   xmlns:t=".../types"
                   xmlns=".../messages">
  <m:ResponseMessages>
    <m:GetFolderResponseMessage ResponseClass="Error">
      <m:MessageText>The mailbox database is temporarily
                 unavailable.</m:MessageText>
      <m:ResponseCode>ErrorMailboxStoreUnavailable</m:ResponseCode>
      <m:DescriptiveLinkKey>0</m:DescriptiveLinkKey>
      <m:Folders/>
    </m:GetFolderResponseMessage>
    <m:GetFolderResponseMessage ResponseClass="Warning">
      <m:MessageText>Item was not processed as a result of a previous
                 error.</m:MessageText>
```

```
      <m:ResponseCode>ErrorBatchProcessingStopped</m:ResponseCode>
      <m:DescriptiveLinkKey>0</m:DescriptiveLinkKey>
      <m:Folders/>
    </m:GetFolderResponseMessage>
  </m:ResponseMessages>
</GetFolderResponse>
```

The first response item in Listing 18-21 shows the error condition that was encountered, *ErrorMailboxStoreUnavailable*. Because this was a batch stop condition, the next item indicates that Exchange Web Services didn't even attempt to process this item, *ErrorBatchProcessingStopped*.

The following response codes are all considered batch stop errors, meaning that if your response contains one of these, all subsequent operations within that batched call will be marked as *ErrorBatchProcessingStopped*.

- *ErrorAccessDenied*
- *ErrorAccountDisabled*
- *ErrorADUnavailable*
- *ErrorADOperation*
- *ErrorConnectionFailed*
- *ErrorMailboxStoreUnavailable*
- *ErrorMailboxMoveInProgress*
- *ErrorPasswordChangeRequired*
- *ErrorPasswordExpired*
- *ErrorQuotaExceeded*
- *ErrorInsufficientResources*

Summary

Typical Web services return failures using SOAP faults. However, because Exchange Web Services makes heavy use of batched operations, SOAP faults are not the primary mechanism for reporting error conditions due to their "whole call" affinity. Response messages are used instead, which provide for item-by-item success or failure information. That being said, SOAP faults are used in a certain cases, such as when a schema invalid request is passed in or when a failure occurs while the SOAP headers are being processed. After we discussed error information within response messages, we attempted to simplify error handling by writing some additional classes and methods to wrap error conditions and report errors in a uniform way.

This works well for non-batched requests. We were able to simplify error handling in batched requests by turning *SoapException* instances into *EWSException* instances, but you still have to deal with errors contained within response messages. We concluded the chapter by discussing batch stop processing errors.

Chapter 19
Server to Server Authentication

Knock! Knock! Knock!

Phyllis Harris stands impatiently outside the Contoso Ltd. office supply room, the door to which is locked. Tina Makovec sent her to retrieve a box of black pens.

"Open up!" she demands.

Among his many other duties, Ken Malcolmson controls the dissemination of office supplies and is often overzealous in his duties.

"Who is it? What's the password?" comes a voice from inside.

"It's Phyllis. Come on, Ken, open the door. I need a box of black pens!" she implores.

Being that Phyllis has no jurisdiction over Ken, and being that Ken is in a particularly over-zealous mood, Ken pays her no heed.

"Come on, Ken. Tina sent me to get some pens!"

Upon hearing this, Ken unlocks the door and lets the flustered Phyllis through the door. You see, although Phyllis does not have the authority to require Ken to open the door, Tina certainly has such authority. Phyllis did not come in her own name, but rather in the name of Tina. And since Phyllis has the rights to wield the name of Tina, additional privileges follow, including banging Ken on the head with the box of pens as she exits the supply room.

Microsoft Exchange Server 2007 works great as a standalone messaging and collaboration server. However, application developers often find that they want to include Exchange Server as part of a more elaborate work process (or system). In such a work process, it is often necessary for the system to perform work on behalf of another account, in much the same way as Phyllis was retrieving the box of pens for Tina. Phyllis's work on behalf of Tina gave Phyllis certain rights that she would not have under her own authority. In the same manner, when the system performs work on behalf of another account, that work is done with the same rights (and restrictions) that apply to the other account. The system may create and send e-mail messages and meeting requests, yet a user expects such e-mail messages and meeting requests to appear as if they were initiated by the account that the system is working on be-half of, rather than being initiated by the system itself.

Microsoft Exchange Server 2007 Web Services (EWS) exposes the ability to perform work on behalf of another account using a feature known as *Server To Server (S2S) authentication*. To assist in our discussion of S2S authentication, we will consider a fictitious interconnected pro-curement system for Contoso Ltd. called the "Interconnected Procurement System," or IPS for short.

An IPS procurement specialist pushes some buttons and twirls some widgets on a secure IPS Web site to submit an asynchronous request for a purchase and then breaks for coffee.[1] Behind the scenes, the IPS submits price requests to several vendors, finds the best combination of price and quality, and submits the suggested invoice to another part of the system for approval. At some point, the invoice is approved by an invoice manager and the purchase is made by the IPS. Once the product vendor confirms that the transaction was successful, the IPS uses Exchange Web Services to send a message to the client from the procurement specialist's account and then schedules a meeting three days after the promised delivery date so that the procurement specialist and the client can meet to discuss the received product. This system could involve several servers on different operating system platforms.

The Two Hop Problem

Now, when considering how Exchange Server fits into the IPS system, there are a number of ways to make it look like the e-mail to come *from* the procurement specialist:

- Grant SendAs rights on the procurement specialist's Mailbox to the account that will make calls to Exchange Web Services (the service account).[2]

- Require the procurement specialist to give his or her credentials to the IPS so that the IPS service account can explicitly authenticate against any server that IPS needs to communicate with as if it were the specialist.

- Grant the service account that calls Exchange Web Services Exchange Administrator rights and have Exchange Web Services perform an administrative logon to the procurement specialist's Mailbox.[3]

- Configure Windows Kerberos Constrained Delegation (KCD) so that the service account can work on behalf of the initial caller (solving the two hop problem).

- Purchase and configure some kind of single sign-on (SSO) solution.

Don't be offended if we left out your favorite two hop solution. This isn't intended to be a survey of all possible methods for solving this problem. Such a survey is outside of the scope of this book.

So what is this two hop problem? Once the procurement specialist has authenticated against the initial IPS Web site, the Web site has the specialist's user token. When the IPS Web application starts to fulfill the request, which account is the Web application running under? It is running under the account that the IPS Web site application pool was configured to run un-

---

[1] Cream, no sugar please.

[2] SendAs rights were discussed in Chapter 7, "Messages"

[3] Note that Exchange Web Services does not expose the ability to perform administrative logons to any mailbox, regardless of the rights the caller has been granted.

der (Network Service, Local System, or some other custom account). To execute the request under the procurement specialist's account, the IPS Web application will need to impersonate the caller. Then, further actions are restricted based on the caller's rights, not the rights that the Web application is running under.

Now, when the IPS Web application makes a call to another Web application (outside of the current application pool), who is actually making the call? You might think that it depends on whether you impersonated the caller, but you would be mistaken. Why? Because when a user authenticates against a Web application, the Web application is not permitted to "hop" to another server as if it actually is that user.

So what solution does Exchange Web Services provide for the two hop problem and why should you care?

The Exchange Two Hop Solution

First of all, Exchange Web Services S2S authentication is completely administered by Exchange Server administrators. This may not seem like a big deal, but Exchange Server administrators are not always Active Directory domain administrators. Windows KCD is under the control of a Microsoft Active Directory domain administrator, *not* an Exchange Server administrator.[4] Unfortunately (or fortunately, depending on your view), Exchange Server administrators don't always call the shots, and requests to configure KCD to be used solely by Exchange Web Services might be ignored, scoffed at, mocked, and so on. In contrast, Exchange Server administrators can easily administer S2S authentication from the Exchange Management Shell.

Some other dependencies surrounding Windows KCD make it more difficult to configure.

- The server initiating KCD and the destination server must be in the same Active Directory domain.

- The domain's Active Directory must be running at the Windows 2003 forest functional level.

- The user who work is being done on behalf of must be located in a Windows 2003 domain in the same Active Directory forest or be in a forest that has a two-way trust with the Active Directory forest that contains the server performing KCD.

The Principle of Least Privilege

It is a good security practice to give accounts only the limited set of rights that they need to accomplish a task. As an example, should every Contoso Ltd. employee have the rights to

---

4   Kerberos Constrained Delegation is a Windows feature that enables administrators to configure accounts (machine or otherwise) to delegate an authenticated session to a service on another machine.

wield Tina's name whenever they need to obtain office supplies from the supply room? No, only those employees who Tina has explicitly sent should be able to invoke her name. And consider a bank—should every bank employee have keys to the vault? No, only those employees who *must* have keys to accomplish their job should have them.

The principle of *least privilege* was one of the primary reasons why S2S was created. Of course, the Exchange Web Services team could have required that any service account wanting to perform work on behalf of another user be given Exchange Server administrator rights so that Exchange Web Services could perform an administrative logon to the Mailbox. However, in addition to sending mail, Exchange Server administrators can change Exchange attributes in the the Active Directory, add and remove Mailboxes, and access any Mailbox they want. Such unbridled access is not good. If Phyllis only needs to get a box of black pens from the supply room, why give her access to browse through the employee data in the Human Resources department? In our IPS scenario from above, if the IPS service account really just needs to send an e-mail and meeting invitation as the procurement specialist, why give the service account full administrative access? S2S authentication exposes three new extended rights in the Active Directory so that service accounts that need to perform work on behalf of other accounts do not need extensive control of the system.

More Account Control

Both administrative access and Windows KCD give access to all accounts. By this, we mean that if any domain user authenticates against your service, KCD enables you to work on behalf of that user, regardless of who that user is. There are no per-user settings. For instance, in the IPS procurement example, it would be reasonable if the service account could send e-mail and schedule meetings for procurement specialists, but why should it have those rights for users on the sales, research and development, and executive teams? In contrast, S2S authentication can be configured on a Mailbox-by-Mailbox, contact-by-contact basis so that only those accounts that you want to allow impersonation for can be impersonated.

The Basic Principle

Let's start with a basic walk-through of how S2S authentication works. You might consider the starting point to be the point at which the user accesses some portal server or Web application. From a work process perspective, you would be correct. However, for S2S authentication, whether the work process is initiated by the actual user or not is an external detail.

The starting point for S2S authentication is when a service account makes an Exchange Web Services request, such as *GetItem*, with additional information indicating which user the work should be performed on behalf of. Sure, this *typically* occurs as a result of direct user access, but such user involvement isn't necessary.[5] In the IPS scenario, the service account wants to perform work on behalf of, or in the name of, the procurement specialist. It is important to note that the account that is authenticated against Exchange Web Services is the *service account* that is making the call, not the user to perform work for. If you are calling Exchange Web Services from an ASP.NET application, the service account will be the identity that your application pool is set up to run under. If your application pool is configured to run as the NetworkService account, such a request will appear to come from the machine account of the computer that the application is running on. When Exchange Web Services receives this request, it will verify that the calling service account has the appropriate rights to perform work on behalf of the user specified in the request. Assuming that such rights have been granted, the request goes forward *as if the user to perform work for made the request.* The service account is out of the picture for all intents and purposes.

Meet the Cast

Before we get too far, let's agree on some terminology. Two or more identities are involved in S2S authentication requests.

The Service Account

The *Service account* is the account that actually makes the Exchange Web Services S2S request. It's called a Service account because typically it is the account that another application, sometimes known as a service, is running under. In reality, the Service account can be any domain account. In the Contoso Ltd. office supply example, Phyllis represents the Service account.

Now, there is no need for the Service account to have a Mailbox on the system. Nor does the Service account need delegate or owner rights to any of the Mailboxes on the system. All the Service account needs are the appropriate S2S authentication rights, which will be discussed shortly. Once authorization against these S2S authentication rights is made, the request is treated as if it came directly from the user to be impersonated. In the same manner, Phyllis needs to have the rights to invoke Tina's name in order to retrieve the pens from the office supply room.[6]

---

[5] In fact, you could have a service account that makes EWS calls on behalf of an account based on a schedule rather than as a result of direct user involvement.

[6] Our office supply room example isn't a perfect match as Ken has no way to ensure that Tina really did send Phyllis short of calling Tina on the phone. Hopefully the analogy will serve its purpose and help you understand S2S authentication, and possibly amuse you in the process.

The Act As Account

There really isn't a good name for this account. We could use the term *impersonated* account, but that can easily be confused with Windows Impersonation (think *WindowsIdentity.Impersonate*), which is not what we mean. We could use *in the name of* account, but that is too long. So, we will use the term *Act As* account because the call will be processed as if the Act As account made the request. In our Contoso Ltd. office supply example, Tina represents the Act As account. Phyllis is acting on behalf of Tina.

Just like the service account, the Act As account does not necessarily need to have a Mailbox on the system. It does, however, need to have rights to *access* a Mailbox on the system and must be located in the current Active Directory forest or in an Active Directory forest that has a two-way trust established with the current forest. You could certainly make an Exchange Web Services request using S2S authentication and act as an account that doesn't have rights to any Mailbox in the system, but such a request would be pointless because you couldn't access anything.

The Mailbox Account

The Mailbox account is the actual Mailbox resource that you are trying to access. In the Contoso Ltd. office supply scenario, the office supply room represents (in a very loose sense) the resource that Phyllis was trying to access on behalf of Tina. In many cases, the Mailbox account is implied by the Act As account. In Chapter 2, "May I See Your Id?" we discussed how Exchange Web Services knows the identity of the caller and his or her corresponding Mailbox. With S2S authentication, Exchange Web Services assumes that a request is accessing the Act As account's Mailbox unless another Mailbox account is specifically listed in the request (via a *Mailbox* element or embedded within an item or folder id). If a destination Mailbox is not specifically listed, the Act As account *must* have a Mailbox on the system. Otherwise, Exchange Web Services has no idea what Mailbox the caller is trying to access, and it fails the call.

Types of S2S Authentication Requests

There are two types of S2S authentication requests. *Exchange Impersonation* is the publicly supported S2S authentication mechanism and is geared toward third-party applications that need to perform work on behalf of other accounts. *Token Serialization* is intended for use only in Exchange Server to Exchange Server communication and is not publicly supported by Microsoft. Given that, we could just gloss over Token Serialization and cover Exchange Impersonation in great depth. You are not going to use Token Serialization, right? However, this approach has several problems.

- First, many developers have a voracious appetite for figuring out undocumented features, and the very fact that we have indicated that Token Serialization is not publicly supported by Microsoft is enough to push a swath of developers to dig in and try to figure it out. Being that Token Serialization is a security feature, there is a danger in making the wrong assumptions or in blindly assigning the rights to perform Token Serialization to various accounts.

- Second, Exchange Server administrators will want to know why these insatiably curious developers want to have Token Serialization rights given to their personal user accounts.

- Third, the Exchange Server administrators will need to know that they shouldn't give such rights to these curious developers and probably shouldn't let their children play together either.

As a result, and probably against our better judgment, we *will* explain the basics of how Token Serialization works and why it is there. Maybe after that explanation, you will see that there is nothing you can do with Token Serialization that you cannot do with Exchange Impersonation, and the curiosity of the developer world will be satiated. If this new information emboldens you to go ahead with Token Serialization, do note that such use in third-party applications is not supported by Microsoft, and that Microsoft reserves the right to change the behavior of Token Serialization in the future.

Exchange Impersonation

So, without further ado, let's dig into Exchange Impersonation. Now, *Exchange Impersonation* is quite an unfortunate name. Why? Because consumers quickly think that Exchange Web Services is impersonating an account by using something like *WindowsIdentity.Impersonate*, which isn't the case. However, the name is what it is, and you must live with it. Exchange Impersonation is specified in an Exchange Web Services request by an element named *ExchangeImpersonation* in the SOAP header. This element enables you to specify who the Act As account is going to be. The *ExchangeImpersonation* global element is defined within types.xsd and is an instance of *ExchangeImpersonationType*. Its basic structure is shown in Listing 19-1.

LISTING 19-1 Basic structure of the *ExchangeImpersonation* type

```
<t:ExchangeImpersonation>
  <t:ConnectingSID>
    <t:PrincipalName/>
    <t:SID/>
    <t:PrimarySmtpAddress/>
  </t:ConnectingSID>
</t:ExchangeImpersonation>
```

The *ExchangeImpersonation* element has a single required child element with a local name of *ConnectingSID*. This is a slightly strange name in that a security identifier (SID) is only one of the identifiers you can use within a *ConnectingSID* element. Really, it should have been named something like *Identity* or *InTheNameOf* or *ActAs*, but alas, it was not.

The *ConnectingSID* element contains a sequence of three optional child elements, which implies that you can fill in zero or more of these elements. Although the schema enables you to specify a *ConnectingSID* element with no children, Exchange Web Services fails the request with a response code of *ErrorInvalidExchangeImpersonationHeaderData* if no child elements are supplied. Let's first visit each of these elements and then discuss the interaction between them.

PrincipalName

The user principal name (UPN) is a way to uniquely identify a user by an alias and a domain name system (DNS) fully qualified domain name (FQDN). The UPN typically takes the form of an e-mail address such as ActAsUser@contoso.com. When you create accounts through the Exchange Management Console, the UPN is typically filled in for you, although you have the opportunity to override this value with one of your own choosing.[7]

Note that an Act As account that is specified via *PrincipalName* in an *ExchangeImpersonation* header does not have to have a Mailbox on the system.

Listing 19-2 shows an example of an *ExchangeImpersonation* header with the *PrincipalName* filled in.

LISTING 19-2 *ExchangeImpersonation* header with *PrincipalName*

```
<t:ExchangeImpersonation>
  <t:ConnectingSID>
    <t:PrincipalName>procurementSpecialist@contoso.com</t:PrincipalName>
  </t:ConnectingSID>
</t:ExchangeImpersonation>
```

SID

When a domain user account is created, the Active Directory assigns a unique, read-only SID to the new account. Exchange Web Services can therefore resolve a SID to a user account in the Active Directory. Aside from Active Directory user objects, you can also specify what are known as cross-forest contact objects via SID.[8] We will explore this more advanced topic later in the chapter.

---

[7] It is implicitly calculated from the user's sAMAccountName + "@" + the domain's FQDN.

[8] Of course, contact objects don't have an *objectSid* attribute in the Directory. In resource forest deployment scenarios, a contact object in the Exchange Server resource forest is mapped to a user object in another forest

If specified, the value in the *SID* element must be in the Security Definition Description Language (SDDL) string format. An example *ExchangeImpersonation* element containing a *SID* element in SDDL string format is shown in Listing 19-3.

LISTING 19-3 *ExchangeImpersonation* header with *SID*

```
<t:ExchangeImpersonation>
  <t:ConnectingSID>
    <t:SID>S-1-5-21-435198278-499628651-2752260815-500</t:SID>
  </t:ConnectingSID>
</t:ExchangeImpersonation>
```

In code, generating the SDDL form of a SID is quite easy. Just call *ToString*() on the *System. Security.Principal.SecurityIdentifer* instance. For example, the code shown in Listing 19-4 shows how to get the SID of the account that the current thread is running under.

LISTING 19-4 Getting the current user's SID

```
using System.Security.Principal;
...
/// <summary>
/// Get the current user's sid
/// </summary>
/// <returns>Sid</returns>
///
public static SecurityIdentifier GetCurrentUsersSid()
{
  AppDomain.CurrentDomain.SetPrincipalPolicy(
                 PrincipalPolicy.WindowsPrincipal);
  WindowsIdentity currentUser = Thread.CurrentPrincipal.Identity as
                 WindowsIdentity;
  SecurityIdentifier sid = currentUser.User;
  Console.WriteLine("The current user's sid in SDDL format is: " +
             sid.ToString());
  return sid;
}
```

Now, if you are writing an ASP.Net Web application, the code in Listing 19-4 returns the identity of the account that the application pool is running under.[9] However, you typically want to identify the account that made the call to your Web application. This information is exposed on the *HttpContext* class, as shown in Listing 19-5.

---

via an Exchange Server-specific attribute called *msExchMasterAccountSid*. It is also possible to map Exchange Server resource forest *user* objects in this manner. Either way, you identify them using the *SID* element in an *ExchangeImpersonation* header.

[9] Unless of course you have impersonation turned on in the web.config file. In that case, the thread will be running under the caller's account.

LISTING 19-5 Getting the SID of the current ASP.Net caller account

```
/// <summary>
/// Get the sid of the current authenticated ASP.Net caller
/// </summary>
/// <returns>Sid of current caller</returns>
///
public static SecurityIdentifier GetCurrentCallersSid()
{
  WindowsIdentity caller = HttpContext.Current.User.Identity as
                            WindowsIdentity;

  return caller.User;
}
```

One concept that is important to understand is that, although Listings 19-4 and 19-5 dealt with an account that was already authenticated, it is also acceptable to pull *valid* SIDs out of thin air for use with *ExchangeImpersonation*. For instance, you could have a list of procurement specialist account SIDs stored in a SQL database. Then your client application could start up, read the procurement specialist SIDs from the database, and start making Exchange Impersonation calls using the retrieved SIDs, assuming of course that your client application has the rights to perform Exchange Impersonation with those SIDs. The users associated with those SIDs did *not* need to log on, make a call, or in any way authenticate for your client application to use those SIDs. The fact that the owner of the Act As account does not have to initiate such actions implies that the account that has Exchange Impersonation rights is a powerful account, and such rights should not be given out without fully examining the security implications.

PrimarySmtpAddress

Last, and probably least, you can identity an Act As account using its primary Simple Mail Transfer Protocol (SMTP) address. As with the UPN, the primary SMTP address is filled in by the Exchange Server 2007 administrative tools when user accounts are created. However, users and contacts created through the Active Directory Users and Computers Microsoft Management Console (MMC) snap-in will not have this attribute set.[10] The Active Directory does not guarantee the uniqueness of the primary SMTP address throughout an Active Directory forest.[11] Certainly, when creating or modifying a user account, the Exchange Server 2007 administrative tools verify that both primary and non-primary proxy addresses are unique, but there is nothing stopping you from using your favorite Active Directory editing tool such as LDP or ADSIEdit to create users with duplicate primary SMTP addresses.[12] The fact that you may encounter duplicate primary SMTP addresses within the Active Directory

---

[10] To be more precise, Exchange Server adds a multi-valued proxy addresses attribute on Active Directory user objects. The primary SMTP address is the proxy address with the capital SMTP: prefix.

[11] Of course, if the attribute is not unique, mail routing won't work either.

[12] Proxy addresses are discussed in Chapter 7.

is also one of the reasons that using the *PrimarySmtpAddress* element to specify the Act As account is discouraged. When an Act As account is specified using the *PrimarySmtpAddress* element, Exchange Web Services must first verify that there is only one such account in the Active Directory. After performing that check, Exchange Web Services then retrieves the user SID of the corresponding Act As account so that it can continue on with S2S Authentication. In other words, a significant amount of work within Exchange Web Services can be bypassed by simply supplying the user *SID* element in the first place. However, if all you have is the primary SMTP address of the account you wish to act as, feel free to use it instead of performing the Active Directory lookup yourself.

Although any proxy address should be able to uniquely identify a user in the Active Directory (assuming no duplicates), Exchange Web Services does not allow you to specify a non-primary SMTP proxy address in the *PrimarySMTPAddress* element of an *ExchangeImpersonation* SOAP header. Listing 19-6 shows how to specify the *PrimarySmtpAddress* in the *ExchangeImpersonation* header. Note that the value for the *PrimarySmtpAddress* is case-insensitive.

LISTING 19-6 Specifying an Act As account by using the *PrimarySmtpAddress*

```
<soap:Header>
  <t:ExchangeImpersonation>
    <t:ConnectingSID>
      <t:PrimarySmtpAddress>procurementSpecialist@contoso.com
      </t:PrimarySmtpAddress>
    </t:ConnectingSID>
  </t:ExchangeImpersonation>
</soap:Header>
```

Using the Proxy Classes

Given that the *ExchangeImpersonation* SOAP header is specified outside of the actual Web method that you are invoking, where do you specify it when making a proxy class call? Thankfully, the proxy generator considers the SOAP headers when proxy classes are generated against the Web Services Description Language (WSDL) document. When you run wsdl.exe (or add a Visual Studio Web Reference), it adds all SOAP headers specified in the WSDL file as properties of the *ExchangeServiceBinding* class. In fact, if you look at the autogenerated code, you see that each SOAP header has a public property to access the value for each corresponding header, as shown in Listing 19-7.

LISTING 19-7 *ExchangeServiceBinding* and the exposed SOAP header properties

```
public partial class ExchangeServiceBinding :
        System.Web.Services.Protocols.SoapHttpClientProtocol
{
  // code elided...  Also, getter and setter code removed for brevity
  //
```

```
public ExchangeImpersonationType ExchangeImpersonation
{ get; set; }

public SerializedSecurityContextType SerializedSecurityContext
{ get; set; }

public language MailboxCulture
{ get; set; }

public ServerVersionInfo ServerVersionInfoValue
{ get; set; }

public AvailabilityProxyRequestType ProxyRequestTypeHeader
{ get; set; }

    // code elided…
}
```

Now, what is lost is the direction of the SOAP headers. For instance, all of the SOAP headers shown in Listing 19-7 are for the request (inbound) only except for *ServerVersionInfoValue*, which is set on each response (outbound) to show the version of Exchange Web Services that serviced the request.

Ignoring the other SOAP headers for a moment, how do you set the *ExchangeImpersonation* header on a proxy class request? Simply create an instance of *ExchangeImpersonationType*, fill in the relevant information, set it on the *ExchangeServiceBinding* instance, and make your request. Doing so using the *SID* of the Act As account is shown in Listing 19-8.

LISTING 19-8 Setting the *ExchangeImpersonation* SOAP header via the proxy classes

```
/// <summary>
/// Sets the ExchangeImpersonation soap header on the binding prior to a
/// call
/// </summary>
/// <param name="binding">Binding to configure for
/// ExchangeImpersonation</param>
/// <param name="sid">SID of user to "Act As"</param>
///
public static void SetExchangeImpersonation(
                ExchangeServiceBinding binding,
                SecurityIdentifier sid)
{
  ExchangeImpersonationType header = new ExchangeImpersonationType();
  header.ConnectingSID = new ConnectingSIDType();
  header.ConnectingSID.SID = sid.ToString();
  binding.ExchangeImpersonation = header;
}
```

Of course, identifying the Act As account via *PrincipalName* or *PrimarySmtpAddress* is just as simple—just set the appropriate properties on the *ExchangeImpersonationType* instance.

Exchange Impersonation and Windows Logon

When a user walks up to a Windows machine and logs on interactively with a user name and password, the operation system must resolve the supplied user name and password into a user *token* which includes not only the user's SID, but also an expanded list of the groups that the user is a member of. Using that token, Windows can determine if the user has the rights to log into the machine, and, if so, the operating system can start up a new desktop for the user, load user settings, and so forth. For the life of that session, actions performed by the user are evaluated against the user's token to see if the user has the proper permissions to perform that action such as deleting files, accessing printers, and so on. Such rights might be granted directly to the user, but often they are granted to a group that the user is a member of.

Now, when a caller makes an Exchange Web Services request with an *ExchangeImpersonation* SOAP header, Exchange Web Services doesn't need to create a Windows desktop for the Act As account, but it certainly must convert the Act As user identifier into a corresponding user token. This is because Exchange Web Services uses the Act As user's token for checking rights in the same manner as Windows. This means that when Exchange Web Services resolves a given user identifier, Active Directory must be consulted so that group membership for the Act As user account can be expanded. This implies three points:

1. The account that the Exchange Web Services application pool is currently running under must have rights to read group membership (*tokenGroupsGlobalAndUniversal* attribute) from the Active Directory. This should be taken care of already since the default account that Exchange Web Services is running under is a member of the Windows Authorization Access Group.[13] However, we have encountered several cases where this group membership was inadvertently removed and had to be added once again.

2. If the Act As account resides in another Active Directory forest, a trust between forests must be in place so that a domain controller in the current Active Directory forest can contact the Act As account's Active Directory forest to expand group membership.

3. If any of the accounts to be acted as were created prior to Windows 2003, the account that the Exchange Web Services application pool is currently running under must be a member of the Pre-Windows 2000 Compatibility Access group. If this group membership is missing, Exchange Impersonation calls using an Act As account that was created prior to Windows 2003 will fail.

---

[13] For more information, refer to the Microsoft Knowledge Base (KB) article "Some applications and APIs require access to authorization information on account objects" at *http://support.microsoft.com/kb/331951*.

It would be quite unpalatable if any user could act like any other user by default. By default, no account can perform Exchange Impersonation. In fact, during installation of Exchange Server 2007, all administrative groups such as Exchange administrators, domain administrators, enterprise administrators, and so on are explicitly denied the various S2S authentication rights because the administrative groups are typically given all rights when the groups are first created.[14] The S2S authentication rights should not be granted to anyone by default.

The ms-Exch-EPI-Impersonation Right

There are two Active Directory extended rights related to *ExchangeImpersonation*. The first of these rights is called ms-Exch-EPI-Impersonation and has a rights globally unique identifier (GUID) of {8DB0795C-DF3A-4ACA-A97D-100162998DFA}.[15] Its friendly name, or the name you see in tools such as the Active Directory Users and Computers MMC snap-in, is *Exchange Web Services Impersonation*. This right is applicable to the security descriptor on Exchange Server objects. What we mean by this is that user interface (UI) tools such as Active Directory Users and Computers do not show this right as settable on any object type other than an Exchange Server.

Rights are granted to a given account SID or group SID from the Active Directory. The combination of a right, the SID the right is considering, and whether the consideration is to allow the right or deny the right for that SID is represented by an Access Control Entry (ACE). An ACE indicates that the group or account with the given SID is either allowed or denied the specified right—but to what? Well, that depends on the object that the ACE is set, or *stamped* on.[16] Because an ACE with the ms-Exch-EPI-Impersonation right is stamped *on* an Exchange Server object in the Active Directory, it implies that the resource that you are either allowing or denying rights to is the Exchange Server itself.[17] This may seem a little strange, but this ACE either allows or denies the caller the right to make *ExchangeImpersonation* calls *through* the Client Access Server (CAS) in question.

We like to think of it this way: You may have the keys that unlock a given post office box at the local post office, but if the post office doors are locked, you are denied access. In the same way, you may have rights to impersonate a given Mailbox (post office box) in the system, but if you do not have rights to send a request through the Client Access Server (the front doors of the post office), your request is denied with a SOAP fault containing the response code *ErrorImpersonationDenied* and the error message "The server to which the application is connected cannot impersonate the requested user due to insufficient permission."

---

[14] Of course, domain administrators can simply go in and remove this restriction, but at least then it is a conscious effort rather than being allowed by default.

[15] *EPI* stands for *Exchange Programming Interface*. It was one of the acronyms that the EWS team was originally considering before settling on EWS. They never updated the rights name. A little piece of trivia for you.

[16] In reality, ACEs exist in the Access Control List (ACL) of the Security Descriptor on the object in question. However, it is sometimes easier to talk about a right being set on the resource being controlled.

[17] The Client Access Server, to be exact.

The error message is a bit misleading because it isn't that the Client Access Server doesn't have the permission, it is the caller ("application," in this context). Really, it should say "The caller does not have permission to make impersonation calls through this Client Access Server." Regardless, this error is propagated back as a SOAP fault, and therefore proxy clients must catch a *SoapException* to deal with this condition.[18]

There are two main ways to stamp a Client Access Server with an ms-Exch-EPI-Impersonation ACE. The first way is to use the Active Directory Sites and Services MMC snap-in.

When you first bring up Active Directory Sites and Services, the Services node is missing. If you click the root node of the tree view and then check View | Show Services Node from the main menu, your tree view is updated to include the Services node. Expand the Services node until you get to the Servers container. The path typically matches the following format:

```
Services\Microsoft Exchange\[Your Org Name]\Administrative Groups\[Your Administrative
Group]\Servers\[Your CAS Server Name]
```

The tree on our Exchange Server 2007 machine is shown in Figure 19-1.

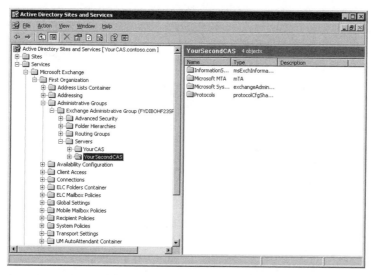

FIGURE 19-1 Server object shown in Active Directory Sites and Services

Now, right-click the Server object that you want to allow the Exchange Impersonation call to go through and choose Properties from the pop-up menu. Next, choose the Security tab from the page control. You are then presented with a view of the security descriptor for the selected Server object. On top of the property page is a list of the security principals (users and groups) that are explicitly listed in the Server's security descriptor. Below the list of security principals is a list of the permissions (allows and denies) that are assigned to the currently selected principal.

---

[18] Refer to Chapter 18, "Errors Never Happen," for dealing with *SoapExceptions*.

Let's say that you have created a service account called My Service Account that will make Exchange Impersonation calls through your server (YourSecondCAS, in this case). From the Security property page, click Add to add an ACE in the Server's ACL, type in the name of My Service Account, and click Check Names. It should resolve to your service account, as shown in Figure 19-2.

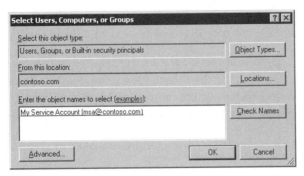

FIGURE 19-2 Selecting My Service Account for ACL inclusion

Click OK to add My Service Account to the list of user/group security principals in your server's security descriptor. Of course, you haven't given the service account any rights at this point. In other words, your Server object does not yet have any ACEs that relate to the My Service Account.

Now, making sure that My Service Account is selected, scroll down the list of permissions until you get to Exchange Web Services Impersonation. This is the ms-Exch-EPI-Impersonation right, as shown in Figure 19-3.

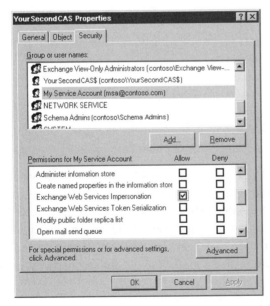

FIGURE 19-3 Exchange Web Services Impersonation right

Simply check the Allow box beside the right and click OK. Close out the remaining property pages. You just stamped the YourSecondCAS object with an allow ACE giving My Service Account the ms-Exch-EPI-Impersonation right. Note that if you had instead checked the *Deny* box beside the right, you would have also stamped the YourSecondCAS object with an ACE, but it would have added a *deny* ACE instead of an *allow* ACE.

The second way to set the ms-Exch-EPI-Impersonation right is to use the Exchange Management Shell. The *Add-ADPermission* cmdlet can be used to give My Service Account the right to make *ExchangeImpersonation* calls through YourSecondCAS. You can use the call in Listing 19-9 to add the permission.

LISTING 19-9 Using the *Add-ADPermission* cmdlet to assign the ms-Exch-EPI-Impersonation right

```
Add-ADPermission
-Identity (Get-ExchangeServer -Identity YourSecondCAS).DistinguishedName
-User (Get-User -Identity "My Service Account").identity
-extendedRight ms-Exch-EPI-Impersonation
```

The first *Identity* parameter passed to the *Add-ADPermission* cmdlet represents the object whose security descriptor you are adding an ACE to. Because you have multiple CAS servers in the topology, you specified the YourSecondCAS machine by using the *-Identity* parameter of the *Get-ExchangeServer* cmdlet. The *User* parameter indicates the account that you are giving the rights to, in this case My Service Account. And the *extendedRight* parameter indicates the named right that you wish to give to My Service Account.

Whether you choose to use the Active Directory Sites and Services MMC snap-in or the Exchange Management Shell is up to you. Either way, what you just did is give the My Service Account account the right to make Exchange Impersonation calls through the YourSecondCAS Exchange Client Access Server. Looking back at Figure 19-1, notice that there are two front-end CAS servers listed in the topology. After our *Add-ADPermission* cmdlet call, My Service Account can make *only* Exchange Impersonation calls through YourSecondCAS. Attempts to make Exchange Impersonation calls through YourCAS fail with the *ErrorImpersonationDenied* response code in a SOAP fault. However, if you make the call through YourSecondCAS, a different error response code is returned—*ErrorImpersonateUserDenied*. This error says that "the account does not have permission to impersonate the requested user." Ah, that message is a little clearer.

Moving back to the post office example, you now have access to get in through the front doors of the post office, but you don't have rights to get into any of the post office boxes at this point. You tried to open a box, but you were rejected. Alas, what are you to do? Enter the second Exchange Impersonation right.

The ms-Exch-EPI-May-Impersonate Right

The second Exchange Impersonation right is called ms-Exch-EPI-May-Impersonate and has a rights GUID of {BC39105D-9BAA-477C-A34A-997CC25E3D60}. Its friendly name, or the name you will see it in tools such as the Active Directory Users and Computers Microsoft Management Console (MMC) snap-in is *Allow Impersonation to Personal Exchange Information*. This right is applicable to the security descriptor on Active Directory *User* and *msExchPrivateMDB* objects.

Granting the ms-Exch-EPI-May-Impersonate Right on the User Object   Before we go any further, we want to reiterate something regarding the Act As account. Although the account you act as will *usually* have a Mailbox on the system, this is not a requirement. It is entirely acceptable to act as an account that doesn't have a Mailbox on the system, but that may have rights to a Mailbox on the system. The Act As account can be any account in the Active Directory forest, even ones created outside of the Exchange Management Console.

Because the ms-Exch-EPI-May-Impersonate right is stamped *on* an Active Directory *user* object in the directory, it implies that the resource that you are either allowing or denying rights to *is* the Active Directory *user* object itself. Yes, that is correct—the resource is *not* the Mailbox that the Active Directory user owns, for indeed the Active Directory user may not have a Mailbox on the system at all. The ms-Exch-EPI-May-Impersonate right simply gives the caller the right to impersonate the Active Directory user in question. To stress this *no Mailbox* point a little more, we used the Active Directory Users and Computers MMC snap-in to create a normal Active Directory User called *No Mailbox*. You can create the No Mailbox account if you want to—the following prose will assume that the account is there. Let's now give My Service Account the right to impersonate the No Mailbox user.

As you saw with the ms-Exch-EPI-Impersonation right, there are two main ways to set the ms-Exch-EPI-May-Impersonate right on the Active Directory User. First, using the Active Directory Users and Computers MMC snap-in, you need to turn on the Advanced Features to get access to the security descriptor for the Active Directory user object. You do this by clicking on View on the main menu and making sure that the Advanced Features menu option is checked. Once that is done, you simply select the applicable *Users* tree node and look on the right-hand side to find the No Mailbox user that was created. Once found, you right-click the user, choose Properties, and go to the Security tab.[19] This property page should look like the one shown in Figure 19-3.

As before, we want to stamp No Mailbox's security descriptor with an allow ACE giving My Service Account the ms-Exch-EPI-May-Impersonate right. To do so, you click Add and enter My Service Account just like when dealing with the ms-Exch-EPI-Impersonation right. Once the account is added, you simply check Allow on the Allow Impersonation To Personal Exchange Information right, click OK, and close out the property pages.

---

[19] If there is no Security tab, then you likely didn't turn on the Advanced Features menu option under View.

You can also use the Add-ADPermission cmdlet in the Exchange Management Shell to assign the ms-Exch-EPI-May-Impersonate right. In fact, the structure of the command is quite like what you saw for assigning the ms-Exch-EPI-Impersonation right except that the you are no longer stamping the right on the Client Access Server, but rather on the Active Directory user object for the No Mailbox account. This command is shown in Listing 19-10.

LISTING 19-10 Adding the ms-Exch-EPI-May-Impersonate right using *Add-ADPermission*

```
Add-ADPermission
   -Identity (Get-User -Identity "No Mailbox").DistinguishedName
   -User (Get-User -Identity "My Service Account").identity
   -extendedRight ms-Exch-EPI-May-Impersonate
```

Now, because we created No Mailbox by using Active Directory Users and Computers, it won't have a primary SMTP address. However, it *will* have a SID and an implied UPN. To get the SID, you can use the handy *Get-User* cmdlet in the Exchange Management Shell.

```
(get-user -identity "No Mailbox").SID.Value
```

The *Get-User* cmdlet above gives back the SID, which is actually an instance of the *System. Security.Principal.SecurityIdentifier* class. We are really only interested in the SDDL string representation. Therefore, we access the *Value* property on the *SecurityIdentifier* instance instead. And the resulting SID is

S-1-5-21-435198278-499628651-2752260815-1136.

Remember, this SID represents the No Mailbox user. Now, you can use this SID string representation in an Exchange Impersonation request as shown in Listing 19-11.

LISTING 19-11 Making the *ExchangeImpersonation* call with proper rights configured

```
<?xml version="1.0" encoding="utf-8"?>
<soap:Envelope xmlns:xsi="http://www.w3.org/2001/XMLSchema-instance"
               xmlns:xsd="http://www.w3.org/2001/XMLSchema"
               xmlns:soap="http://schemas.xmlsoap.org/soap/envelope/"
               xmlns:t=".../types">
  <soap:Header>
    <t:ExchangeImpersonation>
      <t:ConnectingSID>
        <t:SID>S-1-5-21-435198278-499628651-2752260815-1136</t:SID>
      </t:ConnectingSID>
    </t:ExchangeImpersonation>
  </soap:Header>
  <soap:Body>
    <GetFolder xmlns=".../messages"
               xmlns:t=".../types">
    <FolderShape>
      <t:BaseShape>AllProperties</t:BaseShape>
    </FolderShape>
```

```
    <FolderIds>
      <t:DistinguishedFolderId Id="inbox"/>
    </FolderIds>
  </GetFolder>
 </soap:Body>
</soap:Envelope>
```

Now, assuming that you have all the correct Exchange Impersonation rights in place, what do you think the response to this call should be? An error, actually (*ErrorMissingEmailAddress*). Why? Because we want to once again point out that the Act As account *does not represent a Mailbox*. It is simply an account. As such, when the *GetFolder* call was made for the Inbox, Exchange Web Services had no idea which Inbox to access. Since the No Mailbox account doesn't have a Mailbox on the system, there is no implied Mailbox in the request. Since there is no *Mailbox* child element under *DistinguishedFolderId,* there is no explicit Mailbox in the request. And since Exchange Web Services needs to know which Mailbox to access, it returns an error. Remember, once the two Exchange Impersonation rights are validated, the calling account (My Service Account in this case) is completely out of the picture, and it is as if No Mailbox made the Exchange Web Services call.

Now, let's take a real Mailbox user—Mr Mailbox—and stamp the user object with an allow ACE giving My Service Account the ms-Exch-EPI-May-Impersonate right. Of course,the SID of Mr Mailbox is available to set the Act As account SID in the SOAP header. Because this account is a real, *bona fide* Mailbox user, you can also get the UPN and e-mail address.

```
(get-user -identity "Mr Mailbox") | format-list
        SID,WindowsEmailAddress,UserPrincipalName

Sid                  : S-1-5-21-435198278-499628651-2752260815-1137
WindowsEmailAddress : mrmailbox@contoso.com
UserPrincipalName    : mrmailbox@contoso.com
```

For consistency's sake, let's use the *SID* in the *ExchangeImpersonation* header as with No Mailbox. The call is made with the new header, and—behold—success. The Inbox for Mr. Mailbox is indeed returned!

Granting ms-Exch-EPI-May-Impersonate to the Mailbox Database   Now that you have seen how to stamp Active Directory *user* objects with the ms-Exch-EPI-May-Impersonate right, you must do this for every single user account that you want to impersonate, and you will be set, right? What if you have an application that needs to impersonate a whole bunch of accounts? There is an ongoing management issue here. An administrator should not have to worry about whether each and every new user has the correct rights stamped on his or her user object in Active Directory. There must be a better way.

We mentioned earlier that the ms-Exch-EPI-May-Impersonate right is applicable to Active Directory user objects as well as msExchPrivateMDB objects. So what is this msExchPrivateM-DB? It is a Mailbox database, simply put. This is in contrast to a public folder database. A Mailbox database holds Mailboxes for a number of users. Because the ms-Exch-EPI-May-Impersonate right is applicable to a Mailbox database, it is reasonable to conclude that applying the right to an msExchPrivateMDB object allows access to all Mailboxes contained inside that database. That, indeed, is correct.

Notice the following subtle shift, though. A Mailbox database is a collection of *Mailboxes*. It is *not* a collection of arbitrary accounts. Therefore, if you have any non-Mailbox Active Directory user accounts that you need to impersonate (like the No Mailbox account), you need to stamp each account individually with the ms-Exch-EPI-May-Impersonate right. Let's first look at stamping the msExchPrivateMDB security descriptor with the ms-Exch-EPI-May-Impersonate right, and then let's look at the finer nuances of this arrangement.

You can stamp the Mailbox database by using either the Active Directory Sites and Services MMC snap-in or the Exchange Management Shell. After bringing up the Active Directory Sites and Services MMC snap-in, make sure the View Services Node menu option is checked under the View menu. Follow the same path that you took to get to your *Server* object for the ms-Exch-EPI-Impersonation right (Figure 19-1), but continue from there along the following path: .\Information Store\[Your Storage Group Name]\[Your Mailbox Database Name]. Figure 19-4 shows what this path looks like in our test domain.

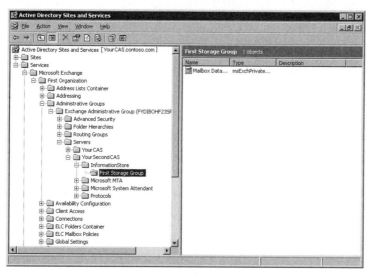

FIGURE 19-4 Stamping the Mailbox database through Active Directory Site and Services

Right-click the database object, choose Properties from the pop-up menu, and then go to the Security tab. Add the My Service Account principal by using the Add button. Then, scroll down to the *Allow Impersonation to Personal Exchange Information* right and check Allow to create the allow ACE. This is shown in Figure 19-5.

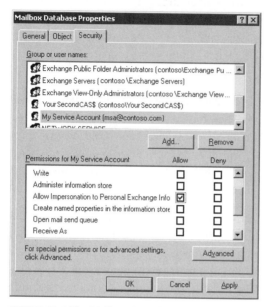

FIGURE 19-5 The Mailbox database security descriptor

Can you do this using the *Add-ADPermission* cmdlet in the Exchange Management Shell? Of course.

```
Add-ADPermission
    -Identity
      (Get-MailboxDatabase
          -Identity "Mailbox Database").DistinguishedName
    -User (Get-User -Identity "My Service Account").identity
    -extendedRight ms-Exch-EPI-May-Impersonate
```

Notice, however, that instead of stamping the Active Directory user object, you are using the *Get-MailboxDatabase* cmdlet to retrieve the msExchPrivateMDB that you want to stamp. Of course, you would change the Mailbox Database name to be the name of your Mailbox database. If you have only one Mailbox database, you can omit the *Identity* parameter passed to *Get-MailboxDatabase*.

Given the ms-Exch-EPI-May-Impersonate right, the My Service Account principal can now impersonate any Mailbox contained in the Mailbox database in question. If there are other Mailbox databases on the system, and you want My Service Account to be able to impersonate Mailboxes on those other Mailbox databases, you need to stamp the associated Mailbox databases accordingly.

An obvious follow-up question is, "Is there any way to allow a service account to impersonate all Mailboxes regardless of which Mailbox database they reside in?" The answer to that question is no. As of this writing, each Mailbox database of interest must be stamped with the ms-Exch-EPI-May-Impersonate right.

Resolving Rights Discrepancies   Given that you can stamp both the Mailbox database and individual user accounts within that Mailbox database with the ms-Exch-EPI-May-Impersonate right, what happens if you have conflicting rights? Rather than combining rights, Exchange Web Services uses a *user trumps all* approach. When an Exchange Impersonation call comes in, Exchange Web Services performs the following actions:

1. Perform a rights check against the Act As account to see if the caller has the ms-Exch-EPI-May-Impersonate right.

   a. If so, allow the request to continue.

   b. If not, check to see if the access check failure was due to an *explicit* deny ACE or simply because there was not an allow ACE in the ACL. If it was an explicit deny, fail the request with *ErrorImpersonateUserDenied*. If not, continue to step 2.

2. Check to see if the account in question represents a Mailbox on the system.

   a. If it does, retrieve the database identifier associated with that Mailbox and continue to step 3.

   b. If not, then fail the request with *ErrorImpersonateUserDenied*—the implicit deny is good enough.

3. Perform an access check against the Act As account's Mailbox database to see if the caller has the ms-Exch-EPI-May-Impersonate right.

   a. If so, allow the request to continue.

   b. If not, fail the request with *ErrorImpersonateUserDenied*.

So, if Exchange Web Services finds either an allow ACE or an *explicit* deny ACE on the user object, it doesn't even check the settings on the Mailbox database. Table 19-1 summarizes how the ms-Exch-EPI-May-Impersonate right is resolved for the various permutations. A value of *Missing* in the first two columns indicates that the ms-Exch-EPI-May-Impersonate right is not present in any of the ACEs in the object's security descriptor. A value of *Allow* in the first two columns indicates that the ms-Exch-EPI-May-Impersonate right is present in an allow ACE in the object's security descriptor (the user has been granted rights). A value of *Deny* in the first two columns indicates that the ms-Exch-EPI-May-Impersonate right is present in a deny ACE in the object's security descriptor. The third column indicates the result of the combination of the first two columns.

TABLE 19-1 Mixing May Impersonate Rights

Mailbox Database	User Object	Result
Missing	Missing	Deny
Missing	Allow	Allow
Missing	Deny	Deny
Allow	Missing	Allow
Allow	Allow	Allow
Allow	Deny	Deny
Deny	Missing	Deny
Deny	Allow	Allow
Deny	Deny	Deny

Exchange Impersonation and Cross-Forest Contacts

You have seen how Active Directory user objects and Mailbox databases can be stamped with the ms-Exch-EPI-May-Impersonate right. In addition, an Active Directory *contact* object can also be stamped. This may not sound very exciting, but when dealing with an organization that shares resources across Active Directory forests, cross-forest contacts are often the way to go. Let's assume for a moment that two companies merge (company A and company B). Rather than combine their existing Active Directory forests into a single new combined forest, each division decides to manage its own forest and create a two-way trust between the forests. Now, there are a number of ways these forests could be configured, but for the moment, let's assume that Exchange Server 2007 is installed in both forests. Users in Forest A (company A) have a Mailbox in Exchange A, and users in Forest B (company B) have a Mailbox in Exchange B.

Now, what happens if you want a user in Forest A to have rights to Active Directory objects in Forest B? Well, one reasonable way to do this is to create a contact in Forest B that represents the user from Forest A. We'll call this contact Cross-Forest Contact AB. The *AB* represents that the *user* exists in Forest A but is represented as a *contact* in Forest B. Now, how is this contact in Forest B tied to the user in Forest A? Normally, an Active Directory contact is not too interesting, but Exchange Server 2007 adds two Active Directory attributes that enable you to change this simple looking contact into a cross-forest contact that is tied to a user object in another forest.

The first of these attributes is called *msExchMasterAccountSid,* and it contains the SID of the user's account in Forest A. So if User A's SID is S-1-5-21-435198278-499628651-2752260815-1137, then Cross-Forest Contact AB's *msExchMasterAccountSid* must be set to the same value. Next, the contact object must have its *legacyExchangeDN* attribute properly set to the same value as the *legacyExchangeDN* in the user's forest. Why are both attributes necessary? Because the Active Directory uses SIDs, whereas the Exchange Store uses both Legacy Exchange DNs as well as SIDs. If either is missing, Exchange Impersonation will fail.

Now, making calls while acting as a cross-forest contact is exactly the same as making calls while acting as a user account. You simply specify the SID of the cross-forest contact in the *ExchangeImpersonation* header. Of course, you must use the SID contained in the *msExch-MasterAccountSid* attribute because contact objects in the Active Directory are not security principals (and therefore do not have their own SID assigned by the Active Directory). Exchange Web Services resolves the *msExchMasterAccountSid* to the cross-forest contact object in question (in Forest B) and asks Forest A to resolve group membership for it. Once Exchange Web Services has the token that represents the Act As account, the call continues as before.

Looking at the Security Descriptor

Of course, you may also be interested in looking at the security descriptor for a given object to see which rights are stamped on it. This is the realm of the *Get-ADPermission* Exchange Management Shell cmdlet.

```
Get-ADPermission -Identity ((Get-User -Identity "Mr Mailbox").Identity)
```

This command returns a list of all of the principals contained in Mr Mailbox's security descriptor, their rights, and whether each is an allow or deny ACE. You can get a little fancier by using a PowerShell script, as shown in Listing 19-12. Note that you can also use the script to look for the ms-Exch-EPI-Impersonation right simply by changing the name of the right to check against.

LISTING 19-12 PowerShell script for finding extended rights

```
# First get all of the ACEs on our user object
#
$aces = Get-ADPermission
    -Identity ((Get-User -Identity "Mr Mailbox").Identity)

foreach ($ace in $aces){
  # Look to see if there are extended rights associated with this ace
  #
  if ($ace.ExtendedRights -ne $null){
    # if so, then look at each extended right and see if it is our
    # right in question
    #
    foreach ($extendedRight in $ace.ExtendedRights)
    {
      if ($extendedRight.ToString() -eq "ms-Exch-EPI-May-Impersonate")
      {
        # display the ace
        #
```

```
        $ace
      }
    }
  }
}
```

Token Serialization

The second method of S2S authentication is called Token Serialization. Before beginning here, let us once again reiterate that Token Serialization is unsupported by Microsoft for use in third-party applications, and the Exchange Web Services team included it simply as a way for Exchange Servers to talk to each other. However, because the associated types were exposed in the schema files, and the SOAP header was exposed in the WSDL file, we feel it is prudent to cover the basics here so that you understand what Token Serialization is and why you shouldn't use it.

Why Two Formats for S2S Authentication?

So, if Exchange Impersonation works, why would the Exchange Web Services team create a second method for S2S authentication? Good question. There are really three main reasons.

Performance   When a caller authenticates against Exchange Web Services, Active Directory is consulted to expand the caller's group membership, and a token is created to represent that user. If the CAS needs to send a request to a second CAS to perform work on behalf of the caller, it seems somewhat wasteful to have the second CAS query the Active Directory once again to expand group membership and create yet another token. Why not simply take the token from the first CAS and pass it to the second CAS? Now, of course, this token passing arrangement assumes that the second CAS trusts that the first CAS is indeed getting a valid token for the user in question and passing its contents properly. As such, when the second CAS receives this token, it can simply use it for access checks against Store resources.

Now, an interesting point here is that although the second CAS now has this token representing the original caller, it cannot use that token to access files on the network, log onto SQL databases, access bank accounts, and so on. This token is used simply to identify the original caller in question for Exchange Server-related resources. Here is the principle of least privilege at work.

Configuration   In Exchange Impersonation calls, Exchange Web Services is given a single identifier that it uses to create a token for the Act As account. This token generation requires Active Directory lookups and Services For You (S4U) logon privileges. But what if the CAS that needs to expand the token doesn't have the rights to access the Active Directory containing the user account, or what if S4U is not configured? Well, in that case, the Exchange

Impersonation call fails. However, if the CAS box in question already has all the user information that it needs, there is no need for a Active Directory lookup, and therefore configuration issues do not cause call failure.

Wider-Scoped Privileges   As you saw with Exchange Impersonation, you must set the ms-Exch-May-Impersonate right on each user or contact object or Mailbox database that contains Mailbox accounts that you intend the service account to be able to impersonate. Having to set rights on each Mailbox database can be an issue when Exchange Client Access Servers need to talk to each other. So, instead of having two rights, there is a single right for Token Serialization that is stamped on the *Server* object. If the caller has this right, then it can serialize tokens for anyone in the organization.

Token Serialization in the Schema

The Services.wsdl file defines a SOAP header called *SerializedSecurityContext* for most Web methods in the service. The corresponding type is defined in types.xsd. The basic structure is shown in Listing 19-13.

LISTING 19-13 Basic structure of the *SerializedSecurityContext* SOAP header

```
<t:SerializedSecurityContext>
  <t:UserSid/>
  <t:GroupSids/>
  <t:RestrictedGroupSids/>
  <t:PrimarySmtpAddress/>
</t:SerializedSecurityContext>
```

UserSid **Element**[20]   The *UserSid* element is required and contains the SDDL string format of the Act As account SID.

GroupsSids **Element**   The *GroupSids* element is indicated as optional in the schema and is of type *NonEmptyArrayOfGroupIdentifiersType*, which is a fancy way of saying that it is an array of group SIDs. To be precise, it is a sequence of *SidAndAttributesType* elements with each element named *GroupIdentifier.* So, for instance

```
<t:GroupSids>
  <t:GroupIdentifier/>
  <t:GroupIdentifier/>
  <t:GroupIdentifier/>
  <!-- more -->
</t:GroupSids>
```

---

[20] You may have noticed that when designing the schema, the Exchange Web Services team ran into a capitalization identity crisis here. For *ExchangeImpersonation,* you have all capital letters (*SID*). With *SerializedSecurityContext,* you have camel-casing (Sid).

Each group has a SID that represents the group itself, but it also includes an attribute named *Attributes*, which describes how the group SID is to be used. The valid group attributes are described at *http://msdn2.microsoft.com/en-us/library/aa379624.aspx*.

Although the schema indicates that this element is optional, failing to include it will result in an error being returned by Exchange Web Services. The reason for this requirement is that a given token must have at least one group, often called the primary group, for Portable Operating System Interface (POSIX) compatibility. Of course, because clients should *never* create tokens out of thin air, any valid token you receive will at least include the Domain Users group, so this shouldn't be an issue.

RestrictedGroupSids **Element**   The *RestrictedGroupSids* element has the same structure as the *GroupSids* element with the exception that its children have a local name of *RestrictedGroupIdentifier* instead of *GroupIdentifier*. A discussion of restricted group SIDs is outside of the scope of this book.

PrimarySmtpAddress **Element**   The *PrimarySmtpAddress* element was intended as a shortcut so that if the caller knew the primary SMTP address of the user, he or she could supply it in a Token Serialization call so that the second CAS would not have to look it up. But, alas, for various reasons, this element is ignored.

Creating the *SerializedSecurityContext*

To create a *SerializedSecurityContext*, you need to extract the user SID, group SIDs, and restricted group SIDs, along with their attributes, from a valid user token. This is a non-trivial process and involves the AuthZ Win32 API calls. Because this is an unsupported feature and is a significant amount of code, we will not provide code for doing so in this book.

Token Serialization Right

Token Serialization is governed by a single right in the directory lovingly known as the ms-Exch-EPI-Token-Serialization right, and it has a rights GUID of {06386F89-BEFB4-E48-BAA1-559FD9221F78}. The friendly name of this right is *Exchange Web Services Token Serialization*.

> **Important**   Administrators, if anyone sends you an e-mail and requests that you give them the Exchange Web Services Token Serialization right or ms-Exch-EPI-Token-Serialization, be forewarned that this is both unsupported by Microsoft and allows the caller to make Exchange Web Services calls as if they were anyone in the organization.

The ms-Exch-EPI-Token-Serialization right is stamped on the Exchange Client Access Server object just like the ms-Exch-EPI-Impersonation right is. In fact, you can simply take the exact same *Add-ADPermission* cmdlet example from Listing 19-12 and change the name of the right, as shown in Listing 19-14.

LISTING 19-14 Adding the token serialization right by using Add-ADPermission

```
Add-ADPermission
  -Identity (Get-ExchangeServer -Identity YourSecondCAS).DistinguishedName
  -User (Get-User -Identity "My Service Account").identity
  -extendedRight ms-Exch-EPI-Token-Serialization
```

Of course, you can also do this through the Active Directory Sites and Services MMC snap-in just like you can for the ms-Exch-EPI-Impersonation right. Follow the same steps but select the Exchange Web Services Token Serialization right instead.

Oh, How I Trust Thee!

Given that the caller is passing the serialized token to the CAS, Exchange Web Services places a significant amount of trust in the caller. Exchange Web Services assumes that the token that is being passed is a valid token with all valid group SIDs and restricted group SIDs present. Of course, there is a potential for abusing the ms-Exch-EPI-Token-Serialization right. For instance, given the token for a normal user such as Mr Mailbox, the caller could simply add a group SID to the serialized token for Exchange Administrators, and then the destination CAS assumes that Mr Mailbox is indeed an Exchange Administrator. Before you get all excited, however, realize that a domain administrator could just go in and add Mr Mailbox to the Exchange Administrator group to have the same effect.

In fact, you could create tokens on the fly to represent any collection of groups you want, but doing so is a grave misuse of the technology. You should use the following three rules when determining whether you should assign the ms-Exch-EPI-Token-Serialization right to an account.

1. Don't give the ms-Exch-EPI-Token-Serialization right out to anyone.

2. If you do give out the right, make sure you understand the implications of doing so and that you trust the account that will be assigned the ms-Exch-EPI-Token-Serialization right.

3. Don't give the ms-Exch-EPI-Token-Serialization right out to anyone.[21]

---

[21] Yes, we are fully aware that we said that twice.

Not All Methods Are Created Equal

For the most part, all Exchange Web Services methods respect the *ExchangeImpersonation* and *SerializedSecurityContext* SOAP headers. However, the Availability Web methods referred to in Chapter 21 and Chapter 22 do not honor the *ExchangeImpersonation* SOAP header, but instead rely solely on the *SerializedSecurityContext* SOAP header. If you make an Availability Web method call such as *GetUserOofSettings* and pass in an *ExchangeImpersonation* SOAP header, the header is ignored, and the call will be associated with the actual calling account rather than the Act As account in the *ExchangeImpersonation* header. The Availability Web methods use Token Serialization for internal purposes. It doesn't make sense for you as a consumer to use Token Serialization when making Availability method requests.

Going Back to IPS

At the beginning of the chapter, we discussed a fictitious distributed application called IPS that uses Exchange Web Services at two points during the work process. You should now be able to see that Exchange Web Services can send out e-mails on behalf of the procurement specialist as well as schedule meetings. First, the IPS service account that makes requests to Exchange Web Services must be given the ms-Exch-EPI-Impersonation right against the Exchange CAS and the ms-Exch-EPI-May-Impersonate right against all Mailbox databases that contain users to be impersonated. Second, to fill in the *ExchangeImpersonation* header, the IPS service account must know the user principle name, the SID, or the primary SMTP address of the procurement specialist so that the Act As identifier can be used in the *ExchangeImpersonation* SOAP header of the Exchange Web Services request. That is all there is to it. No need to set up a complicated single sign-on solution or configure KCD.

Summary

To be part of a larger composite work process, Exchange Web Services exposes the idea of Server to Server (S2S) authentication, which enables service accounts to act on behalf of a user as if the user is actually making the request. There are several benefits to S2S authentication, including the principle of least privilege and the ability to configure the various rights as an Exchange Administrator. Exchange Impersonation is the publicly supported way for third-party developers to use S2S authentication. After the proper rights are configured, you simply add the *ExchangeImpersonation* SOAP header to indicate who the call should act as, and then you make your call. Token Serialization is an S2S authentication feature that Microsoft does not support for use in third-party application. It enables the caller to act as any account in the organization, but it is intended for Exchange Client Access Servers to use when talking to each other. Avoid the use of Token Serialization in your code.

Chapter 20
Autodiscover

Configuring client applications to communicate with an Exchange Server can be a daunting task when thousands of users exist in an organization. Up until Exchange Server 2007, users have been required to manually configure their individual client applications such as Microsoft Office Outlook. Manual configuration can introduce errors that may result in extra help desk calls for such reasons as input errors or incomplete user instructions. To complicate matters, when user mailboxes are moved from one mailbox server to another, which is sometimes done to balance the load between servers, all client applications that connect to the moved mailboxes must be reconfigured.

Exchange Server 2007 introduces a new Web service named *Autodiscover*, which is installed with the Client Access Server role right along with Exchange Web Services (EWS). As its name implies, Autodiscover allows callers of the Web service to *automatically discover* the client configuration values that a given mailbox user needs in order to communicate with various Exchange components. For example, Autodiscover provides Office Outlook 2007 with configuration information for the Unified Messaging service, the Availability service, and the Offline Address Book.

Although Autodiscover is indeed a Web service, we use the term in a broad sense, for Autodiscover is not a SOAP-based Web service, nor does it provide a WSDL file or schema. Rather than wrapping requests and responses in SOAP envelopes, Autodiscover uses Plain Old XML (POX), which is essentially a SOAP message with all the SOAP "rinsed" off.

Talking to Autodiscover

As Autodiscover is a POX-based rather than a SOAP-based Web service, it is reasonable to assume that it is exposed at a different URL than the rest of the Exchange Web Services. Indeed it is. The Autodiscover URL follows the following basic structure:

```
https://<smtp-address-domain>/autodiscover/autodiscover.xml
```

The *smtp-address-domain* is the fully qualified domain name (FQDN) of the primary SMTP address for the account you need to look up configuration information for. As an example, imagine that Ken Malcolmson needs to look up his Exchange configuration information. Since Ken's primary SMTP address is ken.malcolmson@contoso.com, he would use the following URL to access Autodiscover:

```
https://contoso.com/autodiscover/autodiscover.xml
```

Oddly enough, although the web.config file for Autodiscover indicates that it supports HTTP GET requests, attempting to issue a GET request against Autodiscover fails because Autodiscover expects the request to be contained in the body of the HTTP request, not as a query string contained in the URL.

Of course, since Autodiscover is a Web service you need to add information to the body of an HTTP POST request to indicate the operation you want Autodiscover to perform. However, before we can talk about the Autodiscover operation, we need to discuss the role of Autodiscover *providers*.

Autodiscover Providers

For a given mailbox user account, there is a plethora of information available in Active Directory. However, it is unlikely that a client application that needs configuration information will require all of the data from Active Directory. In fact, different client applications will require different data. These differing requirements are embodied in Autodiscover *providers*. Different providers will return different data for an equivalent request. In Exchange Server 2007, there are two different providers available: the Outlook provider and the MobileSync provider.

The Outlook Provider

The Outlook provider was originally developed to allow Office Outlook 2007 to retrieve information for configuring e-mail accounts that communicate with Exchange Server 2007, hence the name. However, as we will see shortly, the Outlook provider returns additional information that is outside of the scope of Office Outlook but quite interesting to other client applications.

Autodiscover exposes a single operation regardless of the provider you want to generate your data. You indicate the provider you are interested in *not* by the operation name, but rather by the namespace that the Autodiscover request is in.[1] In the same way that *System. String* is a different type than *FicticiousUtilities.String*, changing the namespace of the Autodiscover request makes the request a different operation.

Listing 20-1 shows the basic structure of an Outlook provider Autodiscover request.

LISTING 20-1 The basic structure of an Outlook provider Autodiscover request

```
<Autodiscover
    xmlns="http://schemas.microsoft.com/exchange/autodiscover/outlook/
requestschema/2006">
  <Request>
    <EMailAddress/> | <LegacyDN/>
    <AcceptableResponseSchema/>
  </Request>
</Autodiscover>
```

---

[1] An additional piece of information must be supplied to choose the correct provider for fulfilling the Autodiscover request. We will discuss this additional information shortly.

Notice that the *Autodiscover* element is defined in XML namespace:

`http://schemas.microsoft.com/exchange/autodiscover/`**`outlook/requestschema/2006`**

In this chapter, we will shorten this namespace to the following in the interest of brevity:

`xmlns="`.../`outlook/requestschema/2006"`

In Listing 20-1, the Outlook provider *Autodiscover* element has a single child element called *Request* that contains two optional elements, *EMailAddress* and *LegacyDN*, and one required element, *AcceptableResponseSchema*.

EMailAddress Element

The optional *EMailAddress* element contains the e-mail address of the account that you want to retrieve configuration information for. The e-mail address that you supply can be any valid SMTP proxy address for the account. You cannot use proxy addresses with other routing types such as X500 in the *EMailAddress* element. Should you supply an invalid value for the *EMailAddress*, or a value that does not resolve to a valid Exchange mailbox, you will receive an HTTP 200 response with an error, as shown in Listing 20-2.

LISTING 20-2 Autodiscover error when supplied with an invalid SMTP address

```
<?xml version="1.0" encoding="utf-8"?>
<Autodiscover xmlns="http://schemas.microsoft.com/exchange/autodiscover/
responseschema/2006">
  <Response>
    <Error Time="03:52:10.9173306" Id="4130155074">
      <ErrorCode>500</ErrorCode>
      <Message>The e-mail address cannot be found.</Message>
      <DebugData/>
    </Error>
  </Response>
</Autodiscover>
```

Knowing that Autodiscover is not a SOAP-based Web service, it should come as no surprise that it does not return SOAP faults to indicate erroneous conditions.

It is worth noting that the casing of the element name *EMailAddress* is slightly different than how it is presented in other places within Exchange Web Services. With Autodiscover, the *M* is capitalized. If you make an Autodiscover request and supply an *EmailAddress* element (lowercase M), you will receive an error response with a message of *Invalid Request*.

LegacyDN Element

In lieu of the *EMailAddress* element, you can use the Legacy Exchange Distinguished Name (LegacyDN) of the user that you want Outlook Autodiscover configuration data returned for.

The *LegacyDN* element is where you supply this information. For example, you could use Ken's LegacyDN address as follows:

```
<?xml version="1.0" encoding="utf-8"?>
<Autodiscover xmlns=".../outlook/requestschema/2006">
  <Request>
    <LegacyDN>/O=CONTOSO/OU=FIRST ADMINISTRATIVE GROUP/CN=RECIPIENTS/CN=KEN.MALCOLMSON</
LegacyDN>
    <AcceptableResponseSchema>http://schemas.microsoft.com/exchange/autodiscover/outlook/
        responseschema/2006a</AcceptableResponseSchema>
  </Request>
</Autodiscover>
```

Note that when requesting information from the Outlook provider, you must supply either an *EMailAddress* element or a *LegacyDN* element. Oddly enough, Autodiscover does not complain if you supply *both* elements in a single request. What Autodiscover does, however, is ignore the value in the *EMailAddress* element and uses the address in the *LegacyDN* element. We recommend that you stay away from such practices.

AcceptableResponseSchema Element

The required *AcceptableResponseSchema* element allows client applications to indicate the version of Autodiscover responses that the client supports. By supplying a value for *AcceptableResponseSchema*, you will receive a response that is in agreement with the response format of the supplied *AcceptableResponseSchema*, even if Autodiscover changes in the future to return information in a different format.

Earlier, we mentioned that the provider that is chosen to fulfill an Autodiscover request is determined by the namespace of the *Autodiscover* element. However, the *Autodiscover* element namespace is only half of the provider-determining information. The second piece of information that is used to determine the provider that will service the request is the value of the *AcceptableResponseSchema* element. In Exchange Server 2007, the only valid Outlook provider value for *AcceptableResponseSchema* is

```
http://schemas.microsoft.com/exchange/autodiscover/outlook/responseschema/2006a
```

In this book, we will shorten this value to ".../outlook/responseschema/2006a" in the interest of brevity.

It is very important that both the namespace of the *Autodiscover* element and the value of the *AcceptableResponseSchema* element are correct. The Autodiscover provider that services your request is matched based on the value of *both* of these. Therefore if one of these values is incorrect, or inconsistent with the other value, Autodiscover will return a "Provider is not available" error as shown here:

```
<?xml version="1.0" encoding="utf-8"?>
<Autodiscover xmlns="http://schemas.microsoft.com/exchange/autodiscover/
responseschema/2006">
  <Response>
    <Error Time="05:18:05.6846959" Id="4130155074">
      <ErrorCode>601</ErrorCode>
      <Message>Provider is not available</Message>
      <DebugData/>
    </Error>
  </Response>
</Autodiscover>
```

Table 20-1 provides the namespace of the *Autodiscover* element, as well as the value of the *AcceptableResponseSchema* element, that is necessary to use the Outlook provider to fulfill an Autodiscover request.

TABLE 20-1 *Autodiscover* **Element Namespace and** *AcceptableResponseSchema* **Value for Outlook Provider**

Autodiscover element namespace	*http://schemas.microsoft.com/exchange/autodiscover/outlook/ requestschema/2006*
AcceptableResponseSchema value	*http://schemas.microsoft.com/exchange/autodiscover/outlook/ responseschema/2006a*

The Outlook Provider Autodiscover Response

Now that we have covered all the elements within an Autodiscover request for the Outlook provider, Listing 20-3 shows a request to retrieve Ken Malcolmson's information.

LISTING 20-3 Outlook Provider Autodiscover request for Ken Malcolmson's configuration

```
<Autodiscover xmlns=".../outlook/requestschema/2006">
  <Request>
    <EMailAddress>ken.malcolmson@contoso.com</EMailAddress>
    <AcceptableResponseSchema>.../outlook/responseschema/2006a
  </AcceptableResponseSchema>
  </Request>
</Autodiscover>
```

The Autodiscover response to the request is shown in Listing 20-4.

LISTING 20-4 Outlook Provider Autodiscover response for Ken Malcolmson

```
<Autodiscover
xmlns="http://schemas.microsoft.com/exchange/autodiscover/responseschema/2006">
  <Response xmlns=".../outlook/responseschema/2006a">
    <User>
      <DisplayName>Ken Malcolmson</DisplayName>
      <LegacyDN>/O=CONTOSO/OU=FIRST ADMINISTRATIVE
GROUP/CN=RECIPIENTS/CN=KEN.MALCOLMSON
```

```
      </LegacyDN>
      <DeploymentId>66971497-b785-4592-a192-30fd7215875a</DeploymentId>
    </User>
    <Account>
      <AccountType>email</AccountType>
      <Action>settings</Action>
      <Protocol>
        <Type>EXCH</Type>
        <Server>contosoMailServer.contoso.com</Server>
        <ServerDN>/o=Contoso/ou=Exchange Administrative Group

(FYDIBOHF23SPDLT)/cn=Configuration/cn=Servers/cn=contosoMailServer</ServerDN>
        <ServerVersion>720082AD</ServerVersion>
        <MdbDN>/o=Contoso/ou=Exchange Administrative Group
            (FYDIBOHF23SPDLT)/cn=Configuration/cn=Servers/cn=contosoMailServer/
            cn=Microsoft PrivateMDB</MdbDN>
        <ASUrl>https://contosoCAS.contoso.com/EWS/Exchange.asmx</ASUrl>
        <OOFUrl>https://contosoCAS.contoso.com/EWS/Exchange.asmx</OOFUrl>
        <UMUrl>https://contosoCAS.contoso.com/UnifiedMessaging/Service.asmx</UMUrl>
        <OABUrl>http://contosoCAS.contoso.com/OAB/e2cfe9eb-03a2-4c13-83b2-
            e17ee86b0987/</OABUrl>
      </Protocol>
      <Protocol>
        <Type>WEB</Type>
        <Internal>
          <OWAUrl AuthenticationMethod="Basic,
              Fba">https://contosoCAS.contoso.com/owa</OWAUrl>
          <Protocol>
            <Type>EXCH</Type>
            <ASUrl>https://contosoCAS.contoso.com/EWS/Exchange.asmx</ASUrl>
          </Protocol>
        </Internal>
      </Protocol>
    </Account>
  </Response>
</Autodiscover>
```

There is a lot of information in the Listing 20-4 response, so let's break this down into manageable chunks. If we collapse the XML structure of the *Response* element, we get the basic structure shown in Listing 20-5.

LISTING 20-5 Basic structure of an Outlook provider Autodiscover response

```
<Autodiscover xmlns="http://schemas.microsoft.com/exchange/autodiscover/
responseschema/2006">
  <Response xmlns=".../outlook/responseschema/2006a">
    <User/>
    <Account/>
  </Response>
</Autodiscover>
```

The *Response* element in Listing 20-5 contains two child elements, *User* and *Account*.

The *User* Element   The User element contains three child elements: *DisplayName*, *LegacyDN*, and *DeploymentId*. The *DisplayName* element is simply the display name of the mailbox user that the Autodiscover request was issued for. The *LegacyDN* element contains the LegacyDN value for the mailbox user. The *DeploymentId* returns the GUID identifier of the Active Directory forest that the mailbox user account is contained in. In Listing 20-4 you saw that Ken Malcolmson had the following values:

```
<User>
  <DisplayName>Ken Malcolmson</DisplayName>
  <LegacyDN>/O=CONTOSO/OU=FIRST ADMINISTRATIVE GROUP/CN=RECIPIENTS/CN=KEN.MALCOLMSON
  </LegacyDN>
  <DeploymentId>66971497-b785-4592-a192-30fd7215875a</DeploymentId>
</User>
```

The *Account* Element   The *Account* element is where most of the interesting Autodiscover information resides. Since the *Account* element contains a lot of information, Listing 20-6 shows the basic structure of the *Account* element.

LISTING 20-6 Basic structure of the *Account* element in an Outlook provider Autodiscover response

```
<Account>
  <AccountType>email</AccountType>
  <Action>settings</Action>
  <Protocol/>
  <Protocol/>
  <Protocol/>
</Account>
```

There are three basic child elements within an *Account* element. The *AccountType* element is hardcoded to "email" and the *Action* element is hardcoded to "settings." As such, don't expect other values from these elements for the current Outlook provider namespaces. After these first two elements, *Account* can contain up to three *Protocol* elements (EXCH, EXPR, WEB).

The *EXCH* Protocol   The *EXCH* protocol gets its name from "EXCHange" and indicates access to the Exchange system from within the corporate firewall. This is often referred to as internal access. The basic structure of the *EXCH* protocol is shown in Listing 20-7.

LISTING 20-7 Basic structure of the *EXCH* protocol element

```
<Protocol>
  <Type>EXCH</Type>
  <Server>mailbox FQDN</Server>
  <ServerDN>mailbox LegacyDN</ServerDN>
  <ServerVersion>mailbox server version</ServerVersion>
  <MdbDN>mailbox database LegacyDN</MdbDN>
  <ASUrl>internal URL for Availability Service if available</ASUrl>
  <OOFUrl>internal URL for user OOF Web methods if available </OOFUrl>
  <UMUrl>internal URL for the Unified Messaging web service if available </UMUrl>
  <OABUrl>internal URL for the Offline Address book if available </OABUrl>
</Protocol>
```

From Listing 20-4, you saw that Ken Malcolmson had the EXCH protocol shown here:

```
<Protocol>
  <Type>EXCH</Type>
  <Server>contosoMailServer.contoso.com</Server>
  <ServerDN>/o=Contoso/ou=Exchange Administrative Group(FYDIBOHF23SPDLT)/cn=Configuration/
            cn=Servers/cn=contosoMailServer</ServerDN>
  <ServerVersion>720082AD</ServerVersion>
  <MdbDN>/o=Contoso/ou=Exchange Administrative Group(FYDIBOHF23SPDLT)/cn=Configuration/
            cn=Servers/cn=contosoMailServer/cn=Microsoft PrivateMDB</MdbDN>
  <ASUrl>https://contosoCAS.contoso.com/EWS/Exchange.asmx</ASUrl>
  <OOFUrl>https://contosoCAS.contoso.com/EWS/Exchange.asmx</OOFUrl>
  <UMUrl>https://contosoCAS.contoso.com/UnifiedMessaging/Service.asmx</UMUrl>
  <OABUrl>http://contosoCAS.contoso.com/OAB/e2cfe9eb-03a2-4c13-83b2-e17ee86b0987/</OABUrl>
</Protocol>
```

If you look closely at the EXCH protocol fragment above, you will notice that there is no element that suggests a URL for Exchange Web Services. However, as you will see in Chapter 21, "Availability," the *GetUserAvailability*, *GetUserOofSettings*, and *SetUserOofSettings* Web methods are actually a part of Exchange Web Services. As such, the *ASUrl* element (which stands for Availability Service URL) actually points to Exchange Web Services. So why isn't the element called *EWSUrl* instead? Simply because the Availability Service was originally a separate Web service and in fact predates Exchange Web Services. Once the Exchange Web Services team was assembled, the Availability service became part of Exchange Web Services, but not before the Autodiscover service was set in stone for compatibility with Office Outlook 2007. As an additional aside, the *OOFUrl* refers to the Web service that exposes the *GetUserOofSettings* and *SetUserOofSettings* Web methods, which just so happens to be Exchange Web Services too.[2]

Note that the *ASUrl*, *OOFUrl*, *UMUrl*, and *OABUrl* will be present in a response only if the IIS virtual directory for the corresponding component has a URL for internal access.

The *EXPR* Protocol   The *EXPR* protocol gets its name from "EXchange PRoxy" and indicates access to the Exchange system from outside of the corporate firewall. This is often referred to as external access. The basic structure of the *EXPR* protocol element is shown in Listing 20-8.

LISTING 20-8 Basic structure of the *EXPR* Protocol element

```
<Protocol>
  <Type>EXPR</Type>
  <Server>FQDN of the mailbox server used for RPC/HTTP</Server>
  <SSL>On | Off (based on the presence of http/https in the RPC/HTTP URL)</SSL>
  <AuthPackage>Basic | Ntlm</AuthPackage>
  <ASUrl>external URL for Availability Service if available</ASUrl>
  <OOFUrl>external URL for user OOF Web methods if available </OOFUrl>
  <UMUrl>external URL for the Unified Messaging web service if available </UMUrl>
  <OABUrl>external URL for the Offline Address book if available </OABUrl>
</Protocol>
```

---

2   Although this has not been proven, it have been stated that the importance of a client access mechanism is determined by the number of times it appears within the Autodiscover response.

As with the *EXCH* protocol, the *ASUrl, OOFUrl, UMUrl,* and *OABUrl* will be present in a response only if the IIS virtual directory for the corresponding component has a URL for external access.

The *WEB* Protocol   The last supported protocol, *WEB,* exposes information about Exchange components that are accessible over the Web. However, that is a strange designation since several such components are also in both the *EXCH* and *EXPR* protocol sections. What is unique about the *WEB* protocol is that the internal and external Outlook Web Access URLs are listed therein. The basic structure of the *WEB* protocol is shown in Listing 20-9.

LISTING 20-9 Basic structure of the *WEB* protocol

```
<Protocol>
  <Type>WEB</Type>
  <External>
    <OWAUrl
      AuthenticationMethod="None &| Basic &| Ntlm &| Fba &| Digest &|
WindowsIntegrated">
        External URL for OWA access</OWAUrl>
    <Protocol>
      <Type>EXPR</Type>
      <ASUrl>external URL for Exchange Web Services if available</ASUrl>
    </Protocol>
  </External>
  <Internal>
      AuthenticationMethod="None &| Basic &| Ntlm &| Fba &| Digest &|
WindowsIntegrated">
        Internal URL for OWA access</OWAUrl>
    <Protocol>
      <Type>EXCH</Type>
      <ASUrl>internal URL for Exchange Web Services if available</ASUrl>
    </Protocol>
  </Internal>
</Protocol>
```

If either internal or external access is not available for Exchange Web Services, the *WEB* protocol will omit the corresponding *Protocol* element within either the *External* or *Internal* element.

Note that it is possible to have more than one *OWAUrl* listed for internal access. This will typically occur when there are several Client Access Servers available within the Active Directory site containing the user's mailbox.

Outlook Provider Redirections

If the user account specified in an Outlook provider Autodiscover request corresponds to a mail-enabled user or contact whose mailbox resides in another forest, the Outlook provider will return a redirect response like the one shown in Listing 20-10.

LISTING 20-10 Outlook Provider redirect response

```
<Response>
  <Account>
    <Action>redirectAddr</Action>
    <RedirectAddr>External email address of user or contact</RedirectAddr>
  </Account>
</Response>
```

When a redirect response is encountered, you can simply call Autodiscover again using the SMTP address specified in the *RedirectAddr* element as the *EMailAddress* in the request.

The MobileSync Provider

The MobileSync provider was developed to allow the retrieval of information for configuring mobile devices that communicate with Exchange Server 2007 over the MobileSync protocol. Knowing that the Autodiscover provider is determined by the namespace of the *Autodiscover* request element and the value of the *AcceptableResponseSchema* element, examine Table 20-2, which shows the two values that cause an Autodiscover request to be serviced by the MobileSync provider.

TABLE 20-2 *Autodiscover* **Element Namespace and** *AcceptableResponseSchema* **Value for MobileSync Provider**

Autodiscover element namespace	*http://schemas.microsoft.com/exchange/autodiscover/mobilesync/ requestschema/2006*
AcceptableResponseSchema value	*http://schemas.microsoft.com/exchange/autodiscover/mobilesync/ responseschema/2006*

As with the Outlook provider namespaces, we will shorten the Autodiscover element namespace to

```
../mobilesync/requestschema/2006
```

We'll shorten the *AcceptableResponseSchema* value to

```
../mobilesync/responseschema/2006
```

For a successful response from the MobileSync provider, the Active Sync virtual directory must have an externally facing URL. If an external URL is not set on the Active Sync virtual directory, an Autodiscover request for the MobileSync provider will return the highly informative "Active Directory not available" error.

A MobileSync provider Autodiscovery request has the same structure as an Outlook provider Autodiscovery request with the exception that the MobileSync provider does not allow you to specify the *LegacyDN* element. You must use the *EMailAddress* element to indicate which account you wish to retrieve configuration information for. Since the structures are basically the same, we will show an example request and then move on to discuss the MobileSync provider response. The example is shown in Listing 20-11.

LISTING 20-11 Example MobileSync provider Autodiscovery request

```
<?xml version="1.0" encoding="utf-8"?>
<Autodiscover xmlns=".../mobilesync/requestschema/2006">
  <Request>
    <EMailAddress>ken.malcolmson@contoso.com</EMailAddress>
    <AcceptableResponseSchema>.../mobilesync/responseschema/2006
    </AcceptableResponseSchema>
  </Request>
</Autodiscover>
```

Listing 20-12 shows the response.

LISTING 20-12 MobileSync provider Autodiscover response for Ken Malcolmson

```
<?xml version="1.0" encoding="utf-8"?>
<Autodiscover xmlns="http://schemas.microsoft.com/exchange/autodiscover/
responseschema/2006">
  <Response xmlns=".../mobilesync/responseschema/2006">
    <Culture>en:en</Culture>
    <User>
      <DisplayName>Ken Malcolmson</DisplayName>
      <EMailAddress>ken.malcolmson@contoso.com</EMailAddress>
    </User>
    <Action>
      <Settings>
        <Server>
          <Type>MobileSync</Type>
          <Url>https://contoso.com/Microsoft-Server-ActiveSync</Url>
          <Name>https://contoso.com/Microsoft-Server-ActiveSync</Name>
        </Server>
      </Settings>
    </Action>
  </Response>
</Autodiscover>
```

MobileSync Provider for Autodiscover Response

The Autodiscover response in Listing 20-11 has three child elements within the MobileSync provider *Response* element—*Culture, User,* and *Action.*

The *Culture* Element   The *Culture* element is currently hardcoded to en:en. Likely this should have been "en-US", or better yet, the preferred culture of the mailbox user.

The *User* Element As with the Outlook provider for Autodiscover response, the *User* element contains basic information about the user account in question. However, instead of the LegacyDN for the user account, the primary SMTP address is emitted instead. Also, the *DeploymentId* element that was returned by the Outlook provider is not returned by the MobileSync provider.

The *Action* Element The *Action* element contains the information of interest for mobile devices, namely the *Url* element, which is a child of the *Server* element as seen here:

```
<Action>
  <Settings>
    <Server>
      <Type>MobileSync</Type>
      <Url>https://contoso.com/Microsoft-Server-ActiveSync</Url>
      <Name>https://contoso.com/Microsoft-Server-ActiveSync</Name>
    </Server>
  </Settings>
</Action>
```

Incorporating Autodiscover into Your Client Application

Now that we have covered the two Autodiscover providers in depth, how do you use Autodiscover in your client applications to make them more resilient to changes in the server topology of Exchange? Let's first examine Figure 20-1, which shows the typical flow of information between a client application and a client access component that the application desires to communicate with such as Exchange Web Services.

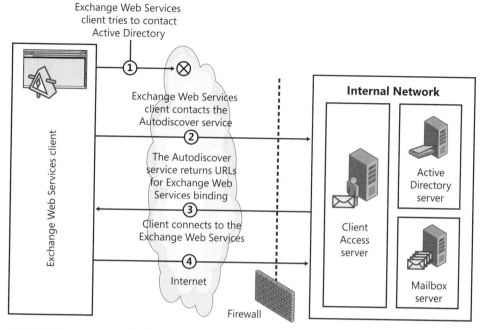

FIGURE 20-1 Information flow between a client application and Exchange Web Services

Figure 20-1 shows the following steps:

1. The client sends an Outlook provider Autodiscover request and specifies the mailbox user whose configuration information should be returned.

2. The Autodiscover service returns a response containing the Exchange Web Services URL for accessing the user's mailbox specified in step 1.

3. The client application uses the URL for creating a connection to Exchange Web Services.

All of our examples up to this point in the chapter have been in XML. However, you will likely want a proxy class to simplify calling Autodiscover. However, as mentioned earlier, Autodiscover does not have a WSDL document nor does it expose XML schemas. As a result, you must hand craft your XML requests and manually parse the XML responses to retrieve the information of interest.

To keep the example in Listing 20-13 small, we will consider only the Outlook provider and will parse some basic information out the response such as the display name for the user as well as the external Exchange Web Services URL to use when communicating with Exchange Web Services. This example also handles redirections returned by the Outlook provider.

LISTING 20-13 An Autodiscover proxy method

```csharp
/// <summary>
/// Enumeration allowing us to indicate whether we want internal or external URLs
/// </summary>
public enum AutodiscoverProtocol
{
  Internal,
  External,
}


/// <summary>Access the Autodiscover service to configure client application.
  </summary>
/// <param name="userSMTPAddress">User's primary SMTP</param>
/// <param name="redirections">Redirections to Autodiscover service. Use zero as the
/// initial value</param>
/// <returns>The Exchange Web Services URL.</returns>
///
public static string GetExchangeWebServicesURL(
                        string userSMTPAddress,
                        AutodiscoverProtocol autodiscoverProtocol,
                        int redirections)
{
  // Check redirection counter. We don't want to get in an endless loop.
  //
  if (redirections > 2)
  {
    throw new Exception("Maximum of 2 redirections.");
  }

  // Check the SMTP address.
  //
  if (userSMTPAddress == string.Empty)
  {
    throw new Exception("Provide an SMTP address.");
  }


  // Get the username and domain from the SMTP address.
  //
  string[] smtpParts = userSMTPAddress.Split('@');
  if (smtpParts.Length != 2)
  {
    throw new Exception("Invalid Smtp address format");
  }
  string username = smtpParts[0];
  string domain = smtpParts[1];

  // Construct the Autodiscover URL if it was not passed in.
  //
  string autoDiscoverURL =
        @"https://" + domain + @"/autodiscover/autodiscover.xml";

  // Create the Outlook provider Autodiscover request.
  //
  StringBuilder request = new StringBuilder();
```

```
request.Append("<?xml version=\"1.0\" encoding=\"utf-8\" ?>");
request.Append(
    "<Autodiscover xmlns=\"http://schemas.microsoft.com/exchange/autodiscover/" +
    "outlook/requestschema/2006\">");
  request.Append("  <Request>");
  request.Append("    <EMailAddress>" + userSMTPAddress + "</EMailAddress>");
  request.Append(
      "<AcceptableResponseSchema>http://schemas.microsoft.com/exchange/" +
      "autodiscover/outlook/responseschema/2006a</AcceptableResponseSchema>");
  request.Append("  </Request>");
  request.Append("</Autodiscover>");

  string requestString = request.ToString();
  // Create a WebRequest object to send our request to the server.
  // Add a password and domain for the user.
  //
  HttpWebRequest webRequest = (HttpWebRequest)WebRequest.Create(autoDiscoverURL);
  webRequest.Credentials = new NetworkCredential("username", "password", "domain");
  webRequest.Method = "POST";
  webRequest.ContentType = "text/xml; charset=utf-8";
  webRequest.ContentLength = requestString.Length;

  using (Stream requestStream = webRequest.GetRequestStream())
  {
    byte[] requestBytes = Encoding.ASCII.GetBytes(requestString);
    // Write the request to the output stream.
    //
    requestStream.Write(requestBytes, 0, requestBytes.Length);
    requestStream.Close();
  }

  // Get the response
  //
  HttpWebResponse response = (HttpWebResponse)webRequest.GetResponse();

  // Throw exception if the request failed.
  //
  if (HttpStatusCode.OK != response.StatusCode)
  {
    throw new InvalidOperationException(response.StatusDescription);
  }

  string responseXML;
  // Otherwise, read the content of the response and return it.
  //
  using (StreamReader sr = new StreamReader(response.GetResponseStream()))
  {
    responseXML = sr.ReadToEnd();
  }

  XmlDocument xmlDoc = new XmlDocument();
  xmlDoc.LoadXml(responseXML);
  XmlNamespaceManager namespaceManager = new XmlNamespaceManager(xmlDoc.NameTable);
  namespaceManager.AddNamespace(
```

```
        "r",
        @"http://schemas.microsoft.com/exchange/autodiscover/" +
        "outlook/responseschema/2006a");

    // Get the EWS URL if it is available.
    //
    string protocolString = (autodiscoverProtocol == AutodiscoverProtocol.Internal) ?
            "EXCH" :
            "EXPR";

    XmlNodeList ewsProtocolNodes =
            xmlDoc.SelectNodes(@"//r:Protocol", namespaceManager);

    // For each protocol in the response, look for the appropriate protocol type
    // (internal/external)
    // and then look for the corresponding ASUrl element.
    //
    foreach (XmlNode node in ewsProtocolNodes)
    {
      string type = node.SelectSingleNode(@"r:Type", namespaceManager).InnerText;
      if (type == protocolString)
      {
        XmlNodeList nodes = node.SelectNodes(@"r:ASUrl[1]", namespaceManager);
        if ((nodes != null) || (nodes.Count > 0))
        {
          return nodes[0].InnerText;
        }
      }
    }

    // If we are here, then either Autodiscovery returned an error or there is a
    // redirect address to retry the Autodiscover lookup.
    //
    XmlNodeList redirectAddr =
          xmlDoc.SelectNodes(@"//r:RedirectAddr[1]", namespaceManager);

    // Check if redirect URL or redirect address is in response.
    if ((redirectAddr != null) && (redirectAddr.Count > 0))
    {
      redirections++;
      // Retry with the redirect address.
      //
      return GetExchangeWebServicesURL(
                  redirectAddr[0].InnerText,
                  autodiscoverProtocol,
                  redirections);
    }
    else
    {
      throw new Exception("Autodiscovery call failed unexpectedly");
    }
}
```

Using the *GetExchangeWebServicesURL* method is simple. Listing 20-14 shows how to properly set up an ExchangeServiceBinding for a mailbox you want to access.

LISTING 20-14 Using Autodiscover to configure the ExchangeServiceBinding

```
// Create the binding
//
ExchangeServiceBinding binding = new ExchangeServiceBinding();

// Retrieve the correct URL for Ken Malcolmson
//
binding.Url = GetExchangeWebServicesURL(
            "ken.malcolmson@contoso.com",
            AutodiscoverProtocol.Internal,
            2 /*redirections allowed*/);
```

Summary

This chapter introduced the Autodiscover service and the two Autodiscover providers, Outlook and MobileSync. Although we discussed both providers, the Outlook provider offers the configuration information that is of interest when determining which Client Access Server a client application should use for sending Exchange Web Service requests. We discussed the various protocols exposed in an Outlook provider Autodiscover response and which protocol is used for internal as compared to external access. Outlook provider redirections were also covered. We concluded the chapter by providing a C# method that issues the Autodiscover request for you and extracts the Exchange Web Services URL from the response.

Chapter 21
Availability

The telephone was a magnificent invention, and though it still excels for such scenarios as carrying on a conversation, confirming appointments with people, or sending informational updates, let's face it, when it comes to scheduling, the telephone just doesn't cut it. We've all been in that situation where we try to assemble a group of friends for something as simple as a movie night, only to have our conversations bounce back and forth between all the interested parties.

"How about Friday night, Brian?"

"Not good; I have practice until 8:30. How about Saturday evening?"

"That works for me, but I'll have to check with Andy." [click]

"Andy, it's Carol. Brian can't do Friday night. Would Saturday work?"

"Sorry, going to be out of town that night. Are you sure Brian can't make Thursday?"

You get the picture.

It would be nice if the telephone had a display hooked up to it that could at least show you the schedule of the person you are talking to. It wouldn't have to show you the details about their schedules, but just enough information to allow you to find a free slot of time that works for whatever you are organizing. What would be even better is if that display could show multiple people's schedules and maybe even do intelligent searching across those schedules to find time slots that would work for everyone. Well don't blink, because that future device is coming really soon, and though we can't provide you the LCD and the hardware interface, we can provide you the tools for getting just such information from Microsoft Exchange Server 2007 Web Services (Exchange Web Services) through a concept called User Availability.

What Is User Availability?

The concept of Availability may seem straightforward ("Is User A busy at this time, or is she free?"), but as relatively simple as this concept may be, finding a workable meeting time amongst several participants and booking a room and resources can be difficult. Exchange Web Services simplifies this process by not only providing access to attendees' free/busy status, but also by providing meeting suggestion times that would allows as many of the participants as possible to attend.[1]

---

[1] Those who have had experience with previous versions of Exchange Server may know that replication of free/busy information across multiple Exchange servers is not always up to date.

The term *Availability* in Exchange Web Services is used to encompass five different concepts:

- **Attendees**   Any person, room, or resource that is having their free/busy information retrieved. Attendees are listed individually in an array of the request and are each assigned a role via an enumeration.

- **Working Hours**   Times of the day that are valid for meetings to be considered for an attendee. Working Hours are defined on a per-attendee basis outside of Exchange Web Services (for example, via the Microsoft Office Outlook calendar options menu).

- **Free/busy information**   The Busy, Tentative, Free, or OOF status of an attendee for a given point in time. Free/busy information can also include details about different calendar appointments that the attendee may have. Free/busy information is only included in the response if the request specifically calls for it.

- **Timezone**   A time zone structure that serves to scope all of the *date/time* strings present in the request and response. All Availability requests require a time zone.

- **Suggestions**   A list of potential meeting times, each with its own quality level (Excellent, Good, Fair, or Poor). Suggestions will be returned in the response only if the request specifically calls for it.

A great way to illustrate the different terms and concepts related to Availability is to look at how Microsoft Office Outlook Web Access presents them through the Scheduling Assistant in Exchange Server 2007. An example of the Scheduling Assistant is shown in Figure 21-1.

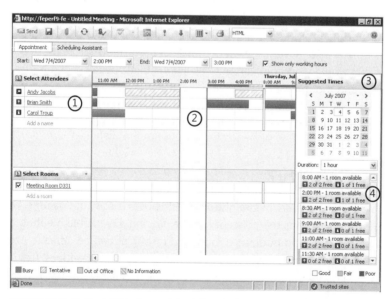

FIGURE 21-1 Outlook Web Access Scheduling Assistant

We have numbered a few things in Figure 21-1 to enable an in-depth discussion. What is happening in this figure is that Andy wants to schedule a one hour meeting with both Brian and Carol. On the left side of the display (1), we can see that Andy, Brian, and Carol are listed. Because Andy is organizing the meeting, he is listed as the Organizer (which is what the icon to the left of his name indicates). Andy has added Brian as a required attendee and Carol as an optional attendee. You can also see (below the name listing) that Andy has selected a meeting room to hold the meeting in.

In the middle of the Scheduling Assistant display (2), is the free/busy status of all attendees. Different shades are used to distinguish different free/busy status information for each attendee. Andy can use this information to find a slot of time that is free for all the attendees he wishes to invite to his new meeting. Andy can see from the display that both he, Brian, and Carol are all free at 2 P.M. If Andy then needed to schedule a meeting for this time using Exchange Web Services, he would call the *CreateItem* Web method to create a new calendar item with Brian, Carol, and the e-mail address of his chosen meeting room as attendees and send meeting invitations. The process of creating a new calendar item and sending meeting invitations was described in Chapter 10, "Scheduling Meetings."

Imagine now that Andy feels that the 2 P.M. time slot will not work and wishes to find a different potential meeting time. Andy could scroll through the display—left or right—to try to find a new time; however, in the right side of the display in Figure 21-1, the Scheduling Assistant is already displaying a number of suggested meeting times. In the right-most portion of the display, there is a date picker control labeled "Suggested Times" with various dates color coded to indicate other potential dates for the meeting. Once again, shading is used to indicate the potential for meetings on that day. Days that are not shaded are rated *Good*, meaning that there is a time slot on that day open for many if not all attendees. Partially shaded days are *Fair*, meaning there may be a few potential time slots that are acceptable for most attendees. Fully shaded days are *Poor*, meaning there is likely no time slots on that day that are acceptable.

Below the "Suggested Times" date picker control is a "Duration" value, indicating the current proposed meeting length, and a list of suggested meeting times for the currently selected day (4). The suggestions are ranked in order from *Good* to *Fair* to *Poor*. Each suggested time also includes the number of rooms available, as well as the number of required and optional participants who are listed as free for the given time slot.

Exchange Web Services allows you to get all of the information about meeting attendees and resources that you see in Figure 21-1 using the *GetUserAvailability* Web method.

History of the *GetUserAvailability* Web Method

You are going to see as we explore the *GetUserAvailability* Web method that some of the functionality of this method has overlap with the *CalendarView* type that we talked about in Chapter 8, "Working with Calendars." Therefore, we want you to be prepared because our discussion may cause you to have a sense of déjà vu. Where possible, we will highlight many of the similarities and differences between these two methods and explain why one may be better suited for a particular task than the other.

Just to give you a brief bit of trivia, the *GetUserAvailability*, *GetUserOofSettings*, and *SetUserOofSettings* methods were all part of what was originally called the Availability Service (or AS). During the early stages of development of Exchange Server 2007, it was the intent that the AS would be run on the Exchange Mailbox server role and not the Exchange Client Access Server (CAS) role. Later in the ship cycle of Exchange Server 2007, it was determined that these methods should exist on the CAS, and therefore be in Exchange Web Services. Unfortunately, this decision was made too late to afford the time to go back and revise the schema for the AS methods. As such, the decision was made to keep the *AS* Web method interfaces intact.

Understanding the *GetUserAvailabilityRequest*

To call the *GetUserAvailability* Web method, you supply a *GetUserAvailabilityRequest* element in your call. The schema type for a *GetUserAvailabilityRequest* is the *GetUserAvailabilityRequestType*, which is shown in Listing 21-1.

LISTING 21-1 Schema for *GetUserAvailabilityRequestType*

```
<xs:complexType name="GetUserAvailabilityRequestType">
 <xs:complexContent mixed="false">
  <xs:extension base="m:BaseRequestType">
   <xs:sequence>
    <xs:element ref="t:TimeZone" />
    <xs:element name="MailboxDataArray" type="t:ArrayOfMailboxData" />
    <xs:element minOccurs="0" maxOccurs="1"
                ref="t:FreeBusyViewOptions" />
    <xs:element minOccurs="0" maxOccurs="1"
                ref="t:SuggestionsViewOptions" />
   </xs:sequence>
  </xs:extension>
 </xs:complexContent>
</xs:complexType>
```

There are two required elements in a *GetUserAvailabilityRequest,* the *TimeZone* and *MailboxDataArray* elements. And there are two optional elements, the *FreeBusyViewOptions* and *SuggestionsViewOptions* elements. Although listed as optional, a *GetUserAvailabiltyRequest* must include *FreeBusyViewOptions* and/or a *SuggestionsViewOptions.* This requirement is not enforced in schema, but rather in server-side processing of the request itself. If you do not supply one of these arguments, Exchange Web Services will return a SOAP fault with an embedded *Microsoft.Exchange.InfoWorker.Common. Availability.MissingArgumentException.*

LISTING 21-2 Example of a *MissingArgumentException* in a SOAP fault

```
<soap:Fault>
  <faultcode>soap:Client</faultcode>
   <faultstring>Microsoft.Exchange.InfoWorker.Common.
      Availability.MissingArgumentException:
      RequestedFreeBusyView and requestedSuggestionsView
      cannot both be null. ---&gt; RequestedFreeBusyView and
      requestedSuggestionsView cannot both be null.
   </faultstring>
   <faultactor>http://.../ews/Exchange.asmx</faultactor>
   <detail>
     <ErrorCode xmlns="http://schemas.microsoft.com/
         exchange/services/2006/messages">5028</ErrorCode>
   </detail>
</soap:Fault>
```

Listing 21-3 is an example of a *GetUserAvailabilityRequest* with *FreeBusyOptions.*

LISTING 21-3 A *GetUserAvailabilityRequest* with *FreeBusyOptions*

```
<m:GetUserAvailabilityRequest xmlns:m=".../messages" xmlns:t=".../types">
  <t:TimeZone>
    <t:Bias>480</t:Bias>
    <t:StandardTime>
      <t:Bias>0</t:Bias>
      <t:Time>02:00:00</t:Time>
      <t:DayOrder>1</t:DayOrder>
      <t:Month>11</t:Month>
      <t:DayOfWeek>Sunday</t:DayOfWeek>
    </t:StandardTime>
    <t:DaylightTime>
      <t:Bias>-60</t:Bias>
      <t:Time>02:00:00</t:Time>
      <t:DayOrder>2</t:DayOrder>
      <t:Month>3</t:Month>
      <t:DayOfWeek>Sunday</t:DayOfWeek>
    </t:DaylightTime>
  </t:TimeZone>
  <m:MailboxDataArray>
```

```
    <t:MailboxData>
      <t:Email>
        <t:Address>Andy@contoso.com</t:Address>
      </t:Email>
      <t:AttendeeType>Organizer</t:AttendeeType>
    </t:MailboxData>
  </m:MailboxDataArray>
  <t:FreeBusyViewOptions>
    <t:TimeWindow>
      <t:StartTime>2007-04-21T00:00:00</t:StartTime>
      <t:EndTime>2007-04-21T23:59:00</t:EndTime>
    </t:TimeWindow>
    <t:MergedFreeBusyIntervalInMinutes>30</t:MergedFreeBusyIntervalInMinutes>
    <t:RequestedView>DetailedMerged</t:RequestedView>
  </t:FreeBusyViewOptions>
</m:GetUserAvailabilityRequest>
```

The request in Listing 21-3 is asking for the free/busy information of one attendee. Unlike other methods that you've seen that use the calling user context to scope the request (for example, a *FindItem* with no *Mailbox*-specified acts on the mailbox of the caller), a *GetUserAvailabilityRequest* requires an e-mail address to be supplied in the *MailboxDataArray*, even if the request is only for data about the caller.

> **Important** It is important to note that the *GetUserAvailability* Web method uses the calling credentials to determine what kind and how much free/busy information the caller is allowed to see for each attendee. Additionally, the Exchange Server enterprise configuration (organizations, for example, that have Exchange Server 2003 servers) can also affect the amount of free/busy information that Exchange Web Services is able to return.

The *AttendeeType* value of *Organizer* holds little value in this request, but because it is a required field, we have chosen the default value for it.[2]

Listing 21-4 shows a *GetUserAvailabilityRequest* but this time with *SuggestionsViewOptions* instead of *FreeBusyViewOptions*.

LISTING 21-4 *GetUserAvailabilityRequest* with *SuggestionsViewOptions* element

```
<m:GetUserAvailabilityRequest xmlns:m=".../messages" xmlns:t=".../types">
  <t:TimeZone>
    <!-- Omitted for brevity -->
  </t:TimeZone>
  <m:MailboxDataArray>
    <t:MailboxData>
      <t:Email>
        <t:Address>Andy@contoso.com</t:Address>
```

---

[2] *Default* meaning the value that the auto-generated proxy class code supplies if not specified.

```
          </t:Email>
          <t:AttendeeType>Organizer</t:AttendeeType>
          <t:ExcludeConflicts>false</t:ExcludeConflicts>
        </t:MailboxData>
        <t:MailboxData>
          <t:Email>
            <t:Address>Brian@contoso.com</t:Address>
          </t:Email>
          <t:AttendeeType>Required</t:AttendeeType>
          <t:ExcludeConflicts>false</t:ExcludeConflicts>
        </t:MailboxData>
      </m:MailboxDataArray>
      <t:SuggestionsViewOptions>
        <t:MeetingDurationInMinutes>60</t:MeetingDurationInMinutes>
        <t:MinimumSuggestionQuality>Good</t:MinimumSuggestionQuality>
        <t:DetailedSuggestionsWindow>
          <t:StartTime>2007-05-09T00:00:00</t:StartTime>
          <t:EndTime>2007-05-10T00:00:00</t:EndTime>
        </t:DetailedSuggestionsWindow>
      </t:SuggestionsViewOptions>
    </m:GetUserAvailabilityRequest>
```

Listing 21-5 is an example of using the proxy classes to create a *GetUserAvailabilityRequestType* instance with both *FreeBusyViewOptions* and a *SuggestionsViewOptions*. We will explain how to call the *GetUserAvailability* Web method via the proxy classes later in this chapter.

LISTING 21-5 Creating a *GetUserAvailabilityRequestType* instance with *SuggestionsViewOptions* and *FreeBusyView* via the proxy classes.

```
/// <summary>
/// Creates a GetUserAvailabilityRequest instance for an organizer
/// and attendees, getting both Free/Busy informaiton and Suggestions for
/// the entire meeting day.
/// </summary>
/// <param name="organizer">Email address of the organizer</param>
/// <param name="attendees">Array of email addresses for attendees</param>
/// <returns>GetUserAvailabilityRequest instance.</returns>
public static GetUserAvailabilityRequestType CreateGetUserAvailRequest(
    DateTime meetingDayAndTime,
    EmailAddress organizer,
    EmailAddress[] attendees)
{
    // Create a TimeZone structure representing Pacific Standard Time.
    //
    SerializableTimeZone timeZone = new SerializableTimeZone();
    timeZone.Bias = 480;
    timeZone.StandardTime = new SerializableTimeZoneTime();
    timeZone.StandardTime.Bias = 0;
    timeZone.StandardTime.Time = "02:00:00";
    timeZone.StandardTime.DayOrder = 1;
    timeZone.StandardTime.DayOfWeek = DayOfWeekType.Sunday.ToString();
    timeZone.StandardTime.Month = 11;
```

```
timeZone.DaylightTime = new SerializableTimeZoneTime();
timeZone.DaylightTime.Bias = -60;
timeZone.DaylightTime.Time = "02:00:00";
timeZone.DaylightTime.DayOrder = 2;
timeZone.DaylightTime.DayOfWeek = DayOfWeekType.Sunday.ToString();
timeZone.DaylightTime.Month = 3;

// Create the Mailbox array for all attendees
//
MailboxData[] mailboxes = new MailboxData[attendees.Length + 1];
for (int x = 0; x < mailboxes.Length; x++)
{
    mailboxes[x] = new MailboxData();

    if (x == 0)
    {
        mailboxes[x].Email = organizer;
        mailboxes[x].AttendeeType = MeetingAttendeeType.Organizer;
    }
    else
    {
        mailboxes[x].Email = attendees[x-1];
        mailboxes[x].AttendeeType = MeetingAttendeeType.Required;
    }
}

// Configure the 24-hour window and details for Free/Busy
// information.
//
Duration duration = new Duration();
duration.StartTime = new DateTime(
    meetingDayAndTime.Year,
    meetingDayAndTime.Month,
    meetingDayAndTime.Day,
    0,
    0,
    0,
    DateTimeKind.Unspecified);
duration.EndTime = duration.StartTime.AddDays(1);

FreeBusyViewOptionsType freeBusyViewOpts =
    new FreeBusyViewOptionsType();
freeBusyViewOpts.TimeWindow = duration;
freeBusyViewOpts.RequestedView = FreeBusyViewType.DetailedMerged;
freeBusyViewOpts.RequestedViewSpecified = true;
freeBusyViewOpts.MergedFreeBusyIntervalInMinutes = 30;
freeBusyViewOpts.MergedFreeBusyIntervalInMinutesSpecified = true;

// Configure the suggestions view options.
//
SuggestionsViewOptionsType suggestionsViewOpts =
    new SuggestionsViewOptionsType();
suggestionsViewOpts.CurrentMeetingTime = meetingDayAndTime;
suggestionsViewOpts.CurrentMeetingTimeSpecified = true;
```

```
suggestionsViewOpts.MeetingDurationInMinutes = 60;
suggestionsViewOpts.MeetingDurationInMinutesSpecified = true;
suggestionsViewOpts.MaximumResultsByDay = 3;
suggestionsViewOpts.MaximumResultsByDaySpecified = true;

// The server enforces that the time window for suggestions must be
// less than or equal to the time window for free/busy information.
// Therefore, setting both time windows to be the same duration
// makes sense.
//
suggestionsViewOpts.DetailedSuggestionsWindow = duration;

// Prepare the request
//
GetUserAvailabilityRequestType getUserAvailRequest =
    new GetUserAvailabilityRequestType();
getUserAvailRequest.TimeZone = timeZone;
getUserAvailRequest.FreeBusyViewOptions = freeBusyViewOpts;
getUserAvailRequest.MailboxDataArray = mailboxes;
getUserAvailRequest.SuggestionsViewOptions = suggestionsViewOpts;

return getUserAvailRequest;
}
```

You can see from Listing 21-5 that there are a large number of properties on the *GetUserAvailabilityRequestType*, and this brief look did not cover all of them. We'll get into the details of each property after we look at the *GetUserAvailability* Web method response type (the *GetUserAvailabilityResponseType*). For now, just understand that the properties serve to scope the free/busy information, indicate the level of detail, and influence suggestions that are returned in the response.

Understanding the *GetUserAvailabilityResponse*

Listing 21-6 shows what a response from a *GetUserAvailability* Web method call using a request that contained both *FreeBusyViewOptions* and *SuggestionsViewOptions* might look like.

LISTING 21-6 *GetUserAvailabilityResponse* with *FreeBusy* and *Suggestions* information

```
<m:GetUserAvailabilityResponse xmlns:m=".../messages" xmlns:t=".../types">
  <m:FreeBusyResponseArray>
    <m:FreeBusyResponse>
      <m:ResponseMessage ResponseClass="Success">
        <m:ResponseCode>NoError</m:ResponseCode>
      </m:ResponseMessage>
      <m:FreeBusyView>
        <t:FreeBusyViewType>DetailedMerged</t:FreeBusyViewType>
        <t:MergedFreeBusy>0223</t:MergedFreeBusy>
        <t:CalendarEventArray>
```

```
    <t:CalendarEvent>
      <t:StartTime>2007-05-11T09:00:00-07:00</t:StartTime>
      <t:EndTime>2007-05-11T10:00:00-07:00</t:EndTime>
      <t:BusyType>Busy</t:BusyType>
      <t:CalendarEventDetails>
        <t:ID>00AB4E9A...</t:ID>
        <t:Subject>Office Hours</t:Subject>
        <t:Location>TBD</t:Location>
        <t:IsMeeting>false</t:IsMeeting>
        <t:IsRecurring>true</t:IsRecurring>
        <t:IsException>false</t:IsException>
        <t:IsReminderSet>true</t:IsReminderSet>
        <t:IsPrivate>false</t:IsPrivate>
      </t:CalendarEventDetails>
    </t:CalendarEvent>
    <!-- Additional CalendarEvents -->
  </t:CalendarEventArray>
  <t:WorkingHours>
  <!-- This time zone is for Eastern Standard Time -->
    <t:TimeZone>
      <t:Bias>300</t:Bias>
      <t:StandardTime>
        <t:Bias>0</t:Bias>
        <t:Time>02:00:00</t:Time>
        <t:DayOrder>1</t:DayOrder>
        <t:Month>11</t:Month>
        <t:DayOfWeek>Sunday</t:DayOfWeek>
      </t:StandardTime>
      <t:DaylightTime>
        <t:Bias>-60</t:Bias>
        <t:Time>02:00:00</t:Time>
        <t:DayOrder>2</t:DayOrder>
        <t:Month>3</t:Month>
        <t:DayOfWeek>Sunday</t:DayOfWeek>
      </t:DaylightTime>
    </t:TimeZone>
    <t:WorkingPeriodArray>
      <t:WorkingPeriod>
        <t:DayOfWeek>
            Monday Tuesday Wednesday Thursday Friday
        </t:DayOfWeek>
        <t:StartTimeInMinutes>480</t:StartTimeInMinutes>
        <t:EndTimeInMinutes>1020</t:EndTimeInMinutes>
      </t:WorkingPeriod>
    </t:WorkingPeriodArray>
  </t:WorkingHours>
 </m:FreeBusyView>
 </m:FreeBusyResponse>
 <!-- Any additional FreeBusyResponses-->
</m:FreeBusyResponseArray>
<m:SuggestionsResponse>
  <m:ResponseMessage ResponseClass="Success">
    <m:ResponseCode>NoError</m:ResponseCode>
  </m:ResponseMessage>
```

```
    <m:SuggestionDayResultArray>
      <t:SuggestionDayResult>
        <t:Date>2007-05-11T00:00:00</t:Date>
        <t:DayQuality>Excellent</t:DayQuality>
        <t:SuggestionArray>
          <t:Suggestion>
            <t:MeetingTime>2007-05-11T10:00:00-07:00</t:MeetingTime>
            <t:IsWorkTime>true</t:IsWorkTime>
            <t:SuggestionQuality>Excellent</t:SuggestionQuality>
            <t:AttendeeConflictDataArray>
              <t:IndividualAttendeeConflictData>
                <t:BusyType>Free</t:BusyType>
              </t:IndividualAttendeeConflictData>
              <t:IndividualAttendeeConflictData>
                <t:BusyType>Free</t:BusyType>
              </t:IndividualAttendeeConflictData>
            </t:AttendeeConflictDataArray>
          </t:Suggestion>
          <!-- Any additional Suggestions for this Day -->
        </t:SuggestionArray>
      </t:SuggestionDayResult>
      <!-- Any additional SuggestionDayResults -->
    </m:SuggestionDayResultArray>
  </m:SuggestionsResponse>
</m:GetUserAvailabilityResponse>
```

This is quite a lengthy response, and we've gone ahead and removed several elements where they tend to repeat. We will begin our discussion of the response with the *GetUserAvailabilityResponseType* itself, and how we can check the various elements in the response for success.

GetUserAvailabilityResponseType

Unlike other response types in Exchange Web Services, the *GetUserAvailiabilityResponseType* does not extend the *BaseResponseMessageType*. This means that it does not have an *ArrayOfResponseMessages*; rather, it contains two elements, an array of type *ArrayOfFreeBusyResponse* called *FreeBusyResponseArray* and a *SuggestionsResponse* element of *SuggestionsResponseType*. Listing 21-7 shows the schema for the *GetUserAvailabilityResponseType*.

LISTING 21-7 Schema definition for *GetUserAvailabilityResponseType*

```
<xs:complexType name="GetUserAvailabilityResponseType">
  <xs:sequence>
    <xs:element minOccurs="0"
                maxOccurs="1"
                name="FreeBusyResponseArray"
                type="m:ArrayOfFreeBusyResponse" />
```

```
    <xs:element minOccurs="0"
                maxOccurs="1"
                name="SuggestionsResponse"
                type="m:SuggestionsResponseType" />
  </xs:sequence>
</xs:complexType>
```

A *GetUserAvailiabilityResponse* will contain a *FreeBusyResponseArray* only if the corresponding request included a *FreeBusyViewOptions*. Likewise, a *GetUserAvailiabilityResponse* will contain a *SuggestionsResponse* only if the request included a *SuggestionsViewOptions*.

Caution The fact that the *GetUserAvailiabilityResponseType* does not inherit from the *BaseResponseMessageType* also means that you cannot check for the *ResponseCode* by simply looking at the first Item in the *ResponseMessages* array.

Listing 21-8 is a portion of the *GetUserAvailiabilityResponse* from Listing 21-6. Notice that the response contains *Success* responses scattered throughout the response.

LISTING 21-8 *GetUserAvailiabilityResponse* detailing the different locations of *ResponseClass="Success"*

```
<GetUserAvailabilityResponse xmlns=".../messages">
  <FreeBusyResponseArray>
    <FreeBusyResponse>
      <!-- For attendee 0 -->
      <ResponseMessage ResponseClass="Success">
        <ResponseCode>NoError</ResponseCode>
      </ResponseMessage>
      <FreeBusyView ... />
    </FreeBusyResponse>
    <FreeBusyResponse>
      <!-- For attendee 1 -->
      <ResponseMessage ResponseClass="Success">
        <ResponseCode>NoError</ResponseCode>
      </ResponseMessage>
      <FreeBusyView ... />
    </FreeBusyResponse>
  </FreeBusyResponseArray>
  <SuggestionsResponse>
    <ResponseMessage ResponseClass="Success">
      <ResponseCode>NoError</ResponseCode>
    </ResponseMessage>
    <SuggestionDayResultArray ... />
  </SuggestionsResponse>
</GetUserAvailabilityResponse>
```

Introducing the *FreeBusyResponseArray* and *FreeBusyView*

The *FreeBusyResponseArray* in a *GetUserAvailabilityResponse* contains a *FreeBusyResponse* for each attendee that was part of the *MailboxDataArray* from the request. Order is preserved such that *MailboxDataArray[x]* = *FreeBusyResponseArray[x]*. Each *FreeBusyResponse* is of the *FreeBusyResponseType* schema type, which contains only two elements, a *ResponseMessage* (that is of type *ResponseMessageType* that you know well) and the *FreeBusyView* element. Listing 21-9 shows the schema for the *FreeBusyResponseType*.

LISTING 21-9 Schema definition for *FreeBusyResponseType*

```
<xs:complexType name="FreeBusyResponseType">
  <xs:sequence>
    <xs:element minOccurs="0"
                maxOccurs="1"
                name="ResponseMessage"
                type="m:ResponseMessageType" />
    <xs:element minOccurs="0"
                maxOccurs="1"
                name="FreeBusyView"
                type="t:FreeBusyView" />
  </xs:sequence>
</xs:complexType>
```

The *FreeBusyView* property will be discussed later in the chapter. The focus right now is on the *ResponseMessage* property.

A response class of *Success* in a *FreeBusyResponse* typically indicates that Exchange Web Services did not encounter any issues in getting free/busy information for the attendee. A response class of *Error* can occur for a number of reasons such as an invalid SMTP address, or the caller did not have permissions to access the attendee's free/busy information. Listing 21-10 is an example of a *FreeBusyResponse* with a *ResponseClass* of *Error* because the e-mail address of the attendee was incorrect.

LISTING 21-10 Example of a *FreeBusyResponse* with an *Error*

```
<FreeBusyResponse xmlns=".../messages">
  <ResponseMessage ResponseClass="Error">
    <MessageText>
      Unable to resolve e-mail address david@contoso.com to an Active Directory
      object.
    </MessageText>
    <ResponseCode>ErrorMailRecipientNotFound</ResponseCode>
    <DescriptiveLinkKey>0</DescriptiveLinkKey>
    <MessageXml>
      <ExceptionType xmlns=".../services/2006/errors">
```

```
            Microsoft.Exchange.InfoWorker.Common.Availability.
            MailRecipientNotFoundException
        </ExceptionType>
        <ExceptionCode xmlns=".../services/2006/errors">5009</ExceptionCode>
      </MessageXml>
    </ResponseMessage>
    <FreeBusyView>
      <FreeBusyViewType xmlns=".../types">None</FreeBusyViewType>
    </FreeBusyView>
  </FreeBusyResponse>
```

Introducting the *SuggestionsResponse*

The *SuggestionsResponse* in a *GetUserAvailabilityResponse* is of the *SuggestionsResponseType* schema type and contains the *ResponseMessage* as one of its properties. Unlike the *FreeBusyResponse* where there is one per attendee, there is only ever one *SuggestionsResponse*, and, therefore, only one *ResponseMessage* that you need to be concerned with. Listing 21-11 shows the schema for the *SuggestionsResponseType*.

LISTING 21-11 Schema definition for *SuggestionsResponseType*

```
<xs:complexType name="SuggestionsResponseType">
  <xs:sequence>
    <xs:element minOccurs="0"
                maxOccurs="1"
                name="ResponseMessage"
                type="m:ResponseMessageType" />
    <xs:element minOccurs="0"
                maxOccurs="1"
                name="SuggestionDayResultArray"
                type="t:ArrayOfSuggestionDayResult" />
  </xs:sequence>
</xs:complexType>
```

The *SuggestionDayResultArray* property will be discussed later in this chapter.

> **Note** You are unlikely to encounter an *Error* in a *SuggestionsResponse*. Even in situations where the Microsoft Exchange Information Store service itself is offline, the *SuggestionsResponse* will still report *Success*, although there will be no usable suggestions in the response. Despite this, the Exchange Web Services team still recommends checking the *ResponseMessage* for *Success* before acting on any suggestions that may be contained within a *SuggestionsResponse*.

Checking for Success in a *GetUserAvailabilityResponse* via the Proxy Classes

Checking for success in a *GetUserAvailabilityResponse* with the proxy classes requires more code then with other response types. Recall in Listing 21-5 that you have a method called *CreateUserAvailRequest* that returns an instance of a *GetUserAvailabilityRequestType*. Listing 21-12 provides a method that can use the output of the *CreateUserAvailRequest* method to call the *GetUserAvailability* Web method and check for success amongst all elements of a *GetUserAvailabiltyResponse* via the proxy classes.

LISTING 21-12 Calling the *GetUserAvailabilityRequest* Web method and checking for *Success* in the response via the proxy classes

```
/// <summary>
/// Calls the GetUserAvailability Web method and parses the response for
/// any errors.
/// </summary>
/// <param name="binding">Binding to use for the call</param>
/// <param name="request">request with all relivant properties defined</param>
/// <param name="didErrorsOccur">true if any errors were present in the response
/// </param>
/// <param name="allErrors">StringBuilder of all errors that were
/// present</param>
/// <returns>The server response</returns>
public static GetUserAvailabilityResponseType CallGetUserAvailAndCheckResponse(
    ExchangeServiceBinding binding,
    GetUserAvailabilityRequestType request,
    out bool didErrorsOccur,
    out StringBuilder allErrors)
{
    // Call the GetUserAvailability Web method
    //
    GetUserAvailabilityResponseType response =
        binding.GetUserAvailability(request);

    // A GetUserAvailiability response can contain lots of error response codes,
    // but still contain usefull information, therefore this method will not
    // throw an exception when it detects an error, but rather store that error
    // in a string buffer and return it to the caller.
    //
    allErrors = new StringBuilder();

    // Our response will have one FreeBusyResponseType for each participant, and
    // only if the request included FreeBusyViewOptions. Therefore, when
    // checking for success, first check that the array is populated, and then
    // check that each element has a success response message attached to it.
    //
    FreeBusyResponseType[] fbResponseArray = response.FreeBusyResponseArray;
    if (fbResponseArray != null)
    {
        for (int x = 0; x < fbResponseArray.Length; x++)
        {
            if (fbResponseArray[x].ResponseMessage.ResponseClass !=
                ResponseClassType.Success)
```

```
            {
                allErrors.AppendLine("There was a problem with particpant #" + x
                    + "\r\n" + fbResponseArray[x].ResponseMessage.ResponseCode +
                    "\r\n" + fbResponseArray[x].ResponseMessage.MessageText);
            }
            else
            {
                // Hint: You could put a call to the PrintFreeBusyInformation
                // method from Listing 21-37 right here
            }
        }
    }

    // Unlike the FreeBusyResponseArray which includes one per participant,
    // there is only going to be one SuggesstionsResponse with a response
    // message.
    //
    SuggestionsResponseType sgResponse = response.SuggestionsResponse;
    if (sgResponse != null)
    {
        if (sgResponse.ResponseMessage.ResponseClass !=
            ResponseClassType.Success)
        {
            allErrors.AppendLine("There was a problem with the suggestions " +
                "response.\r\n" + sgResponse.ResponseMessage.ResponseCode +
                "\r\n" + sgResponse.ResponseMessage.MessageText);
        }
        else
        {
            // Hint: You could put a call to the PrintSuggestionsInformation
            // method from Listing 21-54 right here
        }
    }

    didErrorsOccur = (allErrors.Length > 0);

    return response;
}
```

Working with *TimeZone* and *MailboxData* Properties in a *GetUserAvailabilityRequest*

This section will cover the *TimeZone* and *MailboxData* properties of the *GetUserAvailabilityRequest*. The other two properties (the *FreeBusyViewOptions* and *SuggestionsViewOptions*) have their own section because they require you to look at a lot of properties of both the request and response to fully understand how they work.

> **Important** When working with the *GetUserAvailability* Web method, you should use the bias in the *TimeZone* from the *GetUserAvailabilityRequest* to scope any *date/time* strings that are returned from the server. However, with Exchange Server 2007 there is an issue where a UTC offset is incorrectly appended to *date/time* strings in *CalendarEvents* and *Suggestions* in a *GetUserAvailabilityResponse*. We will explain in detail how to work around this issue for each of these types.

TimeZone Element

The *GetUserAvailability* Web method requires a time zone be defined in every request. You may recall from Chapter 8, "Working with Calendars," that we introduced the *MeetingTimeZone* element, which uses the *TimeZoneType* schema type to set the time zone on calendar items. In much the same way, you use the *SerializableTimeZone* type to set the *TimeZone* property in a *GetUserAvailabilityRequest*. The *TimeZoneType* and *SerializableTimeZone* are similar in the way they describe a time zone semantically, but they differ in syntax. Listing 21-13 shows the schema for the *SerializableTimeZone* type.

LISTING 21-13 Schema definition for *SerializableTimeZone*

```
<xs:complexType name="SerializableTimeZone">
 <xs:sequence>
  <xs:element minOccurs="1" maxOccurs="1" name="Bias"
              type="xs:int" />
  <xs:element minOccurs="1" maxOccurs="1" name="StandardTime"
              type="t:SerializableTimeZoneTime" />
  <xs:element minOccurs="1" maxOccurs="1" name="DaylightTime"
              type="t:SerializableTimeZoneTime" />
 </xs:sequence>
</xs:complexType>
```

Listing 21-14 is an example of a *SerializableTimeZone*, representing Australian Eastern Standard Time or the Sydney, Australia time zone (GMT +10:00).

LISTING 21-14 Example of a *SerializableTimeZone*

```
<SerializableTimeZone xmlns=".../types">
  <Bias>-600</Bias>
  <StandardTime>
    <Bias>0</Bias>
    <Time>03:00:00</Time>
    <DayOrder>5</DayOrder>
    <Month>3</Month>
    <DayOfWeek>Sunday</DayOfWeek>
  </StandardTime>
  <DaylightTime>
    <Bias>-60</Bias>
    <Time>02:00:00</Time>
```

```
    <DayOrder>5</DayOrder>
    <Month>10</Month>
    <DayOfWeek>Sunday</DayOfWeek>
  </DaylightTime>
</SerializableTimeZone>
```

Bias Element of the SerializableTimeZone

The *Bias* element represents the base offset of the time zone, and it is similar to the *BaseOffset* property of the *TimeZoneType*. Unlike the *BaseOffset* element on the *TimeZoneType*, which is of type *xs:duration*, the *Bias* is an integer value that represents the time zone bias in minutes.[3] For example, a time zone with a bias of eight hours (Pacific Standard Time for example), would have a *Bias* value of 480, whereas a time zone with a bias of negative ten hours (Australian Eastern Standard Time, for example) would have a *Bias* value of -600.[4]

> **More Info** If you have questions about what the bias of a time zone is, then you should consult the "Working with Time Zones" section in Chapter 9, "Recurring Appointments and Time Zones."

StandardTime and DaylightTime Properties

Like the *TimeZoneType*, the *SerializableTimeZone* uses two instances of another type, in this case the *SerializableTimeZoneTime* type, to represent the start and ending dates of daylight savings time. The *StandardTime* element defines the transition from daylight savings time to standard time, and the *DaylightTime* element defines the transition from standard time to daylight savings time.

Both of these elements are required, even when defining a zone that does not use daylight savings time. If you need to define a time zone that does not use daylight savings time, set the *Bias* in both your *Standard* and *Daylight* elements to "0", and then provide values for the remaining elements to reference any date and time you choose.[5] When that is the case, you should provide values for all of the *SerializableTimeZoneTime* properties, ensuring that the *Bias* property on each is set to "0".

The schema for the *SerializableTimeZoneTime* type is shown in Listing 21-15.

---

3 Remember that the *bias* must satisfy the formula UTC = local time + bias.

4 The same time zones would be represented as PT480M and –PT600M respectively if used in a *BaseOffset* element of a *TimeZoneType*.

5 The Exchange Web Services team recommends using a time zone that does use daylight savings time as a 'template' in this situation (PST for example) to fill the remaining elements of the *SerializableTimeZone*.

LISTING 21-15 Schema definition for *SerializableTimeZoneTime*

```
<xs:complexType name="SerializableTimeZoneTime">
  <xs:sequence>
    <xs:element minOccurs="1" maxOccurs="1"
                name="Bias" type="xs:int" />
    <xs:element minOccurs="1" maxOccurs="1"
                name="Time" type="xs:string" />
    <xs:element minOccurs="1" maxOccurs="1"
                name="DayOrder" type="xs:short" />
    <xs:element minOccurs="1" maxOccurs="1"
                name="Month" type="xs:short" />
    <xs:element minOccurs="1" maxOccurs="1"
                name="DayOfWeek" type="t:DayOfWeekType" />
  </xs:sequence>
</xs:complexType>
```

The *SerializableTimeZoneTime* type is essentially a combined version of the *TimeChangeType* and *RelativeYearlyRecurrencePattern* whereby it takes the properties of both and combines them into one type.[6]

Bias Element of *SerializableTimeZoneTime*

The *Bias* value of a *SerializableTimeZoneTime* defines by how many minutes the bias of the time zone changes during a transition. When specifying the *DaylightTime* element, the *Bias* value should be one that satisfies the following equation:

Daylight Time Zone Bias = Bias + SerializableTimeZoneTime Bias

For example, during standard time, the bias for Pacific Standard Time in minutes is 480, during daylight savings time, the bias changes to 420, a difference of sixty minutes. Therefore, when using a *SerializableTimeZoneTime* to define daylight savings time for PST, the *Bias* element should be -60.

$420 = 480 - 60$

The *Bias* value in a *Standard* element should always be "0".

Time Element of *SerializableTimeZoneTime*

The *Time* element describes time of day when a transition from standard time to daylight savings time, and vice versa, is supposed to occur. The value is a string in the format *hh:mm:ss*. Pacific Standard Time, for example, changes from standard time to daylight savings time at 2:00 A.M. A *Time* element indicating a time change at 2:00 A.M. would be 02:00:00.

---

[6] *RelativeYearlyRecurrencePattern* is a type used to define a day that occurs on a specific index of a month every *n* number of years. The *RelativeYearlyRecurrencePattern* type was discussed in Chapter 9, "Recurring Appointments and Time Zones."

> **Important** The format of the *Time* element on the *SerializableTimeZoneTime* closely resembles the *xs:time* format that is used by the *Time* element on the *TimeChangeType*. However, the *Time* element on the *SerializableTimeZoneTime* is a string property, and therefore, cannot be set using a *System.DateTime* structure in the proxy classes unless converted to a string.

The *DayOrder, Month,* and *DayOfWeek* Elements of *SerializableTimeZoneTime*

The *DayOrder, Month,* and *DayOfWeek* elements represent the date of a time zone transition defined as a relative day of the month (just like the *RelativeYearlyRecurrencePatternType*).

The *DayOrder* element is an integer with values 1 through 5 corresponding to the ordinal reference to the day of the month of the time change. Table 21-1 shows this mapping.

TABLE 21-1 Mapping the *DayOrder* Integer Value to the Ordinal Reference

DayOrder value	Ordinal Reference
1	First
2	Second
3	Third
4	Fourth
5	Last

The *Month* element is an integer with values 1 through 12 corresponding to the month of the year of the time change. Table 21-2 shows this mapping.

TABLE 21-2 Mapping the *Month* Integer Value to the Corresponding Calendar Month

DayOrder value	Month
1	January
2	February
3	March
4	April
5	May
6	June
7	July
8	August
9	September
10	October
11	November
12	December

The *DayOfWeek* element is a string that maps to the *DayOfWeekType* enumeration, which is shown in Listing 21-16

LISTING 21-16 Schema definition of the *DayOfWeekType* enumeration

```
<xs:simpleType name="DayOfWeekType">
  <xs:restriction base="xs:string">
    <xs:enumeration value="Sunday" />
    <xs:enumeration value="Monday" />
    <xs:enumeration value="Tuesday" />
    <xs:enumeration value="Wednesday" />
    <xs:enumeration value="Thursday" />
    <xs:enumeration value="Friday" />
    <xs:enumeration value="Saturday" />
    <xs:enumeration value="Day" />
    <xs:enumeration value="Weekday" />
    <xs:enumeration value="WeekendDay" />
  </xs:restriction>
</xs:simpleType>
```

Comparison of *RelativeYearlyRecurrencePatternType* and *SerializableTimeZoneTime*

Both the *RelativeYearlyRecurrencePatternType* and the *SerializableTimeZoneTime* are used to define the date of a time zone transition. Table 21-3 illustrates the similarities of these two types and their property values.

TABLE 21-3 Comparison of Property Names and Types in the Two Time Zone Definition Structures

Parent Type	Property Name	Property Type	Example Values
For Representing the Month of the Time Change			
RelativeYearlyRecurrencePattern	*Month*	t:MonthNamesType	*April, October*
SerializableTimeZoneTime	*Month*	xs:short (1-12)	*4, 10*
For Representing the Day of the Time Change			
RelativeYearlyRecurrencePattern	*DaysOfWeek*	t:DayOfWeekType	*Sunday, Friday*
SerializableTimeZoneTime	*DayOfWeek*	t:DayOfWeekType	*(same as above)*
For Representing the Ordinal Day of the Month			
RelativeYearlyRecurrencePattern	*DayOfWeekIndex*	t:DayOfWeekIndexType	*First, Third, Last*
SerializableTimeZoneTime	*DayOrder*	xs:short (1-5)	*1, 3, 5*

> **Note** Appendix B, "Calendaring Supplementals," (available on the companion Web page) contains code that you can use to extract time zone information from the Windows registry and construct not only a *SerializableTimeZone*, but also the *TimeZoneType* from Chapter 9, "Recurring Appointments and Time Zones."

MailboxDataArray Element

The *MailboxDataArray* element on the *GetUserAvailabilityRequest* is a required element of type *ArrayOfMailboxData*, which itself is an array of *MailboxData* elements. Each *MailboxData* element represents one attendee (person or resource) via an e-mail address. Each *MailboxData* element must also include an *AttendeeType* value as well as an optional *ExcludeConflicts* flag. Listing 21-17 shows the schema for the *MailboxData* type.

LISTING 21-17 Schema definition for *MailboxData*

```
<xs:complexType name="MailboxData">
  <xs:sequence>
    <xs:element minOccurs="1" maxOccurs="1"
                name="Email" type="t:EmailAddress" />
    <xs:element minOccurs="1" maxOccurs="1"
                name="AttendeeType"
                type="t:MeetingAttendeeType" />
    <xs:element minOccurs="0" maxOccurs="1"
                name="ExcludeConflicts" type="xs:boolean" />
  </xs:sequence>
</xs:complexType>
```

Listing 21-18 is an example of a *MailboxDataArray* with two participants, one marked as *Organizer* and the second as *Required*.

LISTING 21-18 Example of using a *MailboxDataArray* in a request

```
<m:MailboxDataArray xmlns:m=".../messages" xmlns:t=".../types">
  <t:MailboxData>
    <t:Email>
      <t:Address>Andy@contoso.com</t:Address>
    </t:Email>
    <t:AttendeeType>Organizer</t:AttendeeType>
    <t:ExcludeConflicts>false</t:ExcludeConflicts>
  </t:MailboxData>
  <t:MailboxData>
    <t:Email>
      <t:Address>Brian@contoso.com</t:Address>
    </t:Email>
    <t:AttendeeType>Required</t:AttendeeType>
    <t:ExcludeConflicts>false</t:ExcludeConflicts>
  </t:MailboxData>
</m:MailboxDataArray>
```

Email Element of *MailboxData*

The *Email* element is of the schema type *EmailAddress* shown in Listing 21-19.

LISTING 21-19 Schema for the *EmailAddress* type

```
<xs:complexType name="EmailAddress">
  <xs:sequence>
    <xs:element minOccurs="0" maxOccurs="1"
                name="Name" type="xs:string" />
    <xs:element minOccurs="1" maxOccurs="1"
                name="Address" type="xs:string" />
    <xs:element minOccurs="0" maxOccurs="1"
                name="RoutingType" type="xs:string" />
  </xs:sequence>
</xs:complexType>
```

When using an *EmailAddress* in a *MailboxData* element in a *GetUserAvailabilityRequest*, you need not be concerned with the *Name* and *RoutingType* elements. You need to provide only the *Address* element where the value is the primary SMTP address of the mailbox of the user that you are representing in the *MailboxData* element.

> **Note** Exchange Web Services will also allow you to specify the e-mail address of a distribution list (DL) instead of an individual's e-mail address.

When you provide a DL address, the amount of free/busy information and suggestion information that Exchange Web Services will return will be different. Throughout this chapter, we will highlight when and where these differences occur, but the section titled "Getting Free/Busy Information from a Distribution List" includes most of the information about the differences you will encounter.

AttendeeType

The *AttendeeType* element is a required element that takes a value from the *MeetingAttendeeType* enumeration shown in Listing 21-20.

LISTING 21-20 Schema definition of the *MeetingAttendeeType* enumeration

```
<xs:simpleType name="MeetingAttendeeType">
  <xs:restriction base="xs:string">
    <xs:enumeration value="Organizer"/>
    <xs:enumeration value="Required"/>
    <xs:enumeration value="Optional"/>
    <xs:enumeration value="Room"/>
    <xs:enumeration value="Resource"/>
  </xs:restriction>
</xs:simpleType>
```

Although a required element, this value is used by Exchange Web Services only when you provide a *SuggestionsViewOptions* element in your *GetUserAvailabilityRequest*. It is used to designate roles for each of the attendees. The role of an attendee impacts the quality level for each suggestion that is returned by Exchange Web Services. For more information on suggestion quality level, see the description of the *SuggestionQuality* element later in this chapter.

The proxy classes default this value to *Organizer*, which is acceptable if you have only one attendee. If you have multiple attendees, you should only set one to be the organizer, and the remaining attendees should be designated with some other role.

ExcludeConflicts

The *ExcludeConflicts* element is an optional Boolean and is used by Exchange Web Services only when you provide a *SuggestionsViewOptions* in your *GetUserAvailabilityRequest*. This value is *false* by default, and a value of *true* is meaningful only if the attendee has an *AttendeeType* value of *Organizer* or *Required*. When you set this value to true, you are indicating in your *GetUserAvailiabilityRequest* that only suggestion times that are free for this attendee should be returned.

In some ways, this element can be thought of as indicating that an attendee is *really required*, which might seem to diminish an *AttendeeType* value of *Required*. When trying to find suggestions for a large number of attendees, however, Exchange Web Services may not be able to come up with a suggestion time that is free for all required attendees. Even so, Exchange Web Services will return these suggestion times, just with a lower quality level. The *ExcludeConflicts* element, then, allows you to filter the suggestions even more by telling Exchange Web Services to eliminate suggestion times that are not free for certain attendees.

> **Tip** If your intent is to ensure that all suggestions work for every required attendee, then you'll find that an element on *SuggestionViewOptions*, called *MinimumSuggestionQuality*, is more effective at excluding any suggestions that are not free for all required attendees. Setting the *MiminumSuggestionQuality* value to *Excellent,* for example, has essentially the same effect as setting *ExcludeConflicts* to true for all required attendees.

Working with Free/Busy Information

Free/busy information that is returned in a *GetUserAvailiabilityResponse* can come in various levels of detail. The most basic level of detail is free/busy status only (indicates if the attendee is busy, tentatively busy, free, or out of the office for a given time slot.) Higher levels of detailed free/busy information include details about calendar items that attendees have on their calendar, such as the calendar item subject and location.

The amount of free/busy information that a caller is allowed to see for an attendee depends on the permission level the caller has against the attendee's primary calendar folder. Microsoft Office Outlook 2007, for example, allows anyone to set this level of permission by selecting the Permissions tab on the properties of the Calendar folder (See Figure 21-2).

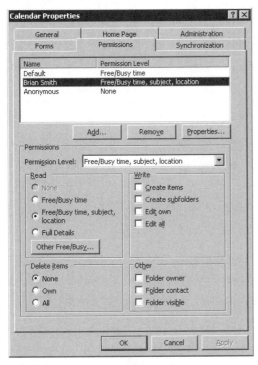

FIGURE 21-2 Setting free/busy permissions on a Calendar folder in Office Outlook 2007

You request the amount of free/busy detail that you would like for all attendees in the *FreeBusyViewOptions* element of your *GetUserAvailiabilityRequest*. Exchange Web Services will then return as much of this detail that you are allowed to see based on your effective permissions on the attendee's primary Calendar folder.

More Info Exchange Web Services in Exchange Server 2007 does not allow users to alter the permission level of other users on a Calendar folder. As of this writing, the next Service Pack of Exchange Server 2007 will allow these permissions to be set using Exchange Web Services.

Introducing the Merged Free/Busy Information Stream

In earlier versions of Microsoft Exchange, free/busy information was provided to application developers in a sequence of digits known as a *merged free/busy stream*. In Exchange Web Services, merged free/busy streams can be returned in a *FreeBusyView* as a string in a *MergedFreeBusy* element. Listing 21-21 is an example of a *FreeBusyView* that contains a merged free/busy stream.

LISTING 21-21 Schema definition for *FreeBusyViewOptionsType*

```
<m:GetUserAvailabilityResponse xmlns:m=".../messages" xmlns:t=".../types">
  <m:FreeBusyResponseArray>
    <m:FreeBusyResponse>
      <m:ResponseMessage ResponseClass="Success">
        <m:ResponseCode>NoError</m:ResponseCode>
      </m:ResponseMessage>
      <m:FreeBusyView>
        <t:FreeBusyViewType>DetailedMerged</t:FreeBusyViewType>
        <t:MergedFreeBusy>002211333000</t:MergedFreeBusy>
        <t:CalendarEventArray ... />
        <t:WorkingHours ... />
      </m:FreeBusyView>
    </m:FreeBusyResponse>
  </m:FreeBusyResponseArray>
</m:GetUserAvailabilityResponse>
```

In a merged free/busy stream, each digit is a value from 0 through 4, with each digit representing a fixed length of time and each value mapping to a corresponding *LegacyFreeBusyType* value. The value mapping is shown in Table 21-4.

TABLE 21-4 *MergedFreeBusy* Digit Value and Its Corresponding *LegacyFreeBusyType* Value

MergedFreeBusy digit value	*LegacyFreeBusyType* value
0	Free
1	Tentative
2	Busy
3	OOF
4	NoData

The default length of time represented by each digit in a merged free/busy stream is 30 minutes. In Exchange Web Services, this length can be set using the *MergedFreeBusyIntervalInMinutes* element in *FreeBusyViewOptions*.

As an example of a merged free/busy stream, consider Figure 21-3, which is a view of a calendar day in Outlook Web Access.

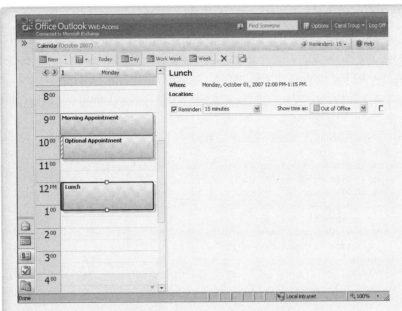

FIGURE 21-3 View of a calendar day in Outlook Web Access

A merged free/busy stream for the period from 8 A.M. to 3.P.M would be

00221100333000

Notice the digit representing 1 P.M. to 1:30 P.M. is 3. This is because a merged free/busy stream digit is always the highest free/busy status value of any period of time within the segment. If Carol's lunch appointment in Figure 21-3 ended at 1:01 P.M. instead, the result would be the same.

The following merged free/busy stream represents the same length of time only with each digit representing 15 minutes instead of 30.

000022221111000033333000000000

It is important to understand and code your application to handle merged free/busy streams. Exchange Web Services may not be able to return the amount of free/busy detail that you request in a *FreeBusyView* and, as such, may end up returning a merged free/busy stream only. A common reason for Exchange Web Services to return a merged free/busy stream only is when you use a Distribution List (DL) address as an attendee. When a DL is used as an attendee, Exchange Web Services will collect all of the free/busy information for each DL member and *merge* it together in one merged free/busy stream. For more information, see the section titled "Getting Free/Busy Information from a Distribution List" later in this chapter.

FreeBusyViewOptions in an Availability Request

Getting free/busy information for participants starts with *FreeBusyOptions*. Use it to specify a time window, and desired level of free/busy detail for each attendee. A *FreeBusyOptions* element is defined by the *FreeBusyViewOptionsType* schema type shown in Listing 21-22.

LISTING 21-22 Schema definition for *FreeBusyViewOptionsType*

```
<xs:complexType name="FreeBusyViewOptionsType">
  <xs:sequence>
    <xs:element minOccurs="1" maxOccurs="1" name="TimeWindow"
                type="t:Duration" />
    <xs:element minOccurs="0" maxOccurs="1"
                name="MergedFreeBusyIntervalInMinutes"
                type="xs:int" />
    <xs:element minOccurs="0" maxOccurs="1" name="RequestedView"
                type="t:FreeBusyViewType" />
  </xs:sequence>
</xs:complexType>
```

Listing 21-23 is an example of a *FreeBusyViewOptions* element being used to request detailed free/busy information for each attendee for May 9, 2007.

LISTING 21-23 Example of using a *FreeBusyViewOptions* element in a request

```
<m:GetUserAvailabilityRequest xmlns:m="../messages" xmlns:t="../types">
  <t:TimeZone>
    <!-- TimeZone contents omitted for clarity -->
  </t:TimeZone>
  <m:MailboxDataArray>
    <!-- MailboxDataArray contents omitted for clarity -->
  </m:MailboxDataArray>
  <t:FreeBusyViewOptions>
    <t:TimeWindow>
      <t:StartTime>2007-05-09T08:00:00</t:StartTime>
      <t:EndTime>2007-05-09T12:00:00</t:EndTime>
    </t:TimeWindow>
    <t:MergedFreeBusyIntervalInMinutes>30</t:MergedFreeBusyIntervalInMinutes>
    <t:RequestedView>Detailed</t:RequestedView>
  </t:FreeBusyViewOptions>
</m:GetUserAvailabilityRequest>
```

Free/busy information is returned to the caller in the form of a *FreeBusyResponse*. As was describe earlier in this chapter, each attendee in the request is represented by an individual *FreeBusyResponse* with order being maintained such that *MailboxDataArray[x]* = *FreeBusyResponseArray[x]*. The *FreeBusyResponse* has a *ResponseMessage* and a *FreeBusyView*. Listing 21-24 shows an example of a *FreeBusyView* element within a *FreeBusyResponse*.

LISTING 21-24 Example of a *FreeBusyView* element in a *FreeBusyResponse*

```
<m:FreeBusyResponse xmlns:m=".../messages" xmlns:t=".../types">
  <m:ResponseMessage ResponseClass="Success">
    <m:ResponseCode>NoError</m:ResponseCode>
  </m:ResponseMessage>
  <m:FreeBusyView>
    <t:FreeBusyViewType>FreeBusy</t:FreeBusyViewType>
    <t:CalendarEventArray>
      <t:CalendarEvent>
        <t:StartTime>2007-05-09T10:00:00-07:00</t:StartTime>
        <t:EndTime>2007-05-09T11:00:00-07:00</t:EndTime>
        <t:BusyType>Busy</t:BusyType>
      </t:CalendarEvent>
    </t:CalendarEventArray>
    <t:WorkingHours>
      <t:TimeZone>
        <!-- Time Zone detail omitted for brevity -->
      </t:TimeZone>
      <t:WorkingPeriodArray>
        <t:WorkingPeriod>
          <t:DayOfWeek>Monday Tuesday Wednesday Thursday Friday</t:DayOfWeek>
          <t:StartTimeInMinutes>480</t:StartTimeInMinutes>
          <t:EndTimeInMinutes>1020</t:EndTimeInMinutes>
        </t:WorkingPeriod>
      </t:WorkingPeriodArray>
    </t:WorkingHours>
  </m:FreeBusyView>
</m:FreeBusyResponse>
```

We will discuss all of the elements of the *FreeBusyViewOptions* and *FreeBusyView* in more detail in a moment. For now we want to point out that a *FreeBusyView* contains a *FreeBusyViewType* indicating the level of free/busy detail that Exchange Web Services was able to return for an attendee: a *CalendarEventArray* with *CalendarEvents* (each of which represents a different calendar item for that attendee) and a *WorkingHours* property that describes valid working hours for an attendee.

FreeBusyViewOptions Elements

This section will look at each of the elements of the *FreeBusyViewOptions* before moving on to the *FreeBusyView*. When we discuss the *FreeBusyView* we will refer back to many of the elements in this section to describe in more detail how these elements effect the free/busy information represented in the *FreeBusyView*.

TimeWindow

The *TimeWindow* element of the *FreeBusyViewOptions* defines the range of time to request free/busy details for. Essentially, you can think of it as a calendar view scoping the number and date range of all *CalendarEvents* that will be returned. It is of type *Duration*, which is an Exchange Web Services schema type shown in Listing 21-25.

LISTING 21-25 Schema for the *Duration* type

```
<xs:complexType name="Duration">
  <xs:sequence>
    <xs:element minOccurs="1" maxOccurs="1"
                name="StartTime" type="xs:dateTime" />
    <xs:element minOccurs="1" maxOccurs="1"
                name="EndTime" type="xs:dateTime" />
  </xs:sequence>
</xs:complexType>
```

Important Do not confuse the *Duration* schema type with the XML schema type *xs:duration*.

Duration has two elements, *StartTime* and *EndTime*. Both of these elements are of type *xs:dateTime*. In a *TimeWindow*, it is the *StartTime* and *EndTime* values that set the range of time for free/busy details. Listing 21-26 is an example of a *TimeWindow* element.

LISTING 21-26 Example of a *TimeWindow* with *StartTime* and *EndTime* properties set

```
<t:TimeWindow xmlns:t=".../types">
  <t:StartTime>2007-05-09T08:00:00</t:StartTime>
  <t:EndTime>2007-05-09T12:00:00</t:EndTime>
</t:TimeWindow>
```

Note Because all *GetUserAvailiabity* Web method requests require a time zone definition via the *TimeZone* element, you should use *date/time* string without UTC offsets for the *StartTime* and *EndTime* elements. Exchange Web Services will use the time zone information defined in the *TimeZone* element from your *GetUserAvailiabilityRequest* to determine the bias of these strings accordingly.

MergedFreeBusyIntervalInMinutes

The *MergedFreeBusyIntervalInMinutes* element is an integer value that sets the length of time that each digit in a merged free/busy stream represents. Exchange Web Services will return a merged free/busy stream for each attendee in the *MergedFreeBusy* element in the *FreeBusyView*. See the sidebar titled "Introducing the Merged Free/Busy Information Stream" for more information on merged free/busy streams.

RequestedView

RequestedView is an optional string element where values map to the *FreeBusyViewType* enumeration shown in Listing 21-27.

LISTING 21-27 Schema definition of the *FreeBusyViewType* enumeration

```
<xs:simpleType name="FreeBusyViewType">
  <xs:list>
    <xs:simpleType>
      <xs:restriction base="xs:string">
        <xs:enumeration value="None" />
        <xs:enumeration value="MergedOnly" />
        <xs:enumeration value="FreeBusy" />
        <xs:enumeration value="FreeBusyMerged" />
        <xs:enumeration value="Detailed" />
        <xs:enumeration value="DetailedMerged" />
      </xs:restriction>
    </xs:simpleType>
  </xs:list>
</xs:simpleType>
```

Each of these values represents a desired level of free/busy detail to return for all attendees. For the most part, a *RequestView* value of *MergedOnly* indicates your need to have free/busy information as a merged free/busy stream only, and a value of *Detailed* indicates you wish to have calendar item details from all attendee calendars. If Exchange Web Services is unable to provide the desired level of free/busy detail for an attendee, then a fallback hierarchy is used. For example, if you are not allowed to see detailed information for an attendee, then the resulting level of detail may be reduced to *FreeBusy* or *MergedOnly*. Figure 21-4 shows this hierarchy.

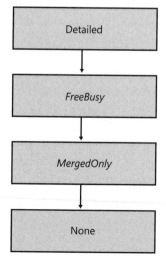

FIGURE 21-4 *FreeBusyType* fallback hierarchy

You will notice that Figure 21-4 does not contain the *FreeBusyMerged* or *DetailedMerged* values. This is because these are special enumeration values that indicate that, along with the specified level of detail, Exchange Web Services should also return a merged free/busy stream for each attendee in the response.[7]

The default value for *RequestedView* is *FreeBusy*.

FreeBusyView in an Availability Response

This section will explain how the elements of *FreeBusyViewOptions* affect the resulting free/busy information in a *FreeBusyView*.

Recall that there is one *FreeBusyResponse* element in the *FreeBusyResponseArray* for each attendee in a *GetUserAvailabilityRequest* and that order is maintained such that *FreeBusyResponseArray[x]* = *MailboxData[x]*. Also recall that each *FreeBusyResponse* contains two elements: the *ResponseCode* and the *FreeBusyView*. A *FreeBusyView* is defined by the *FreeBusyViewType* schema type, which is shown in Listing 21-28.

LISTING 21-28 Schema for the *FreeBusyView* type

```
<xs:complexType name="FreeBusyView">
  <xs:sequence>
    <xs:element minOccurs="1" maxOccurs="1"
                name="FreeBusyViewType" type="t:FreeBusyViewType" />
    <xs:element minOccurs="0" maxOccurs="1"
                name="MergedFreeBusy" type="xs:string" />
    <xs:element minOccurs="0" maxOccurs="1"
                name="CalendarEventArray"
                type="t:ArrayOfCalendarEvent" />
    <xs:element minOccurs="0" maxOccurs="1"
                name="WorkingHours" type="t:WorkingHours" />
  </xs:sequence>
</xs:complexType>
```

The schema defines that only the *FreeBusyViewType* property is required, but in practical application, a *FreeBusyView* always contains at least one of the other three elements as well.

An example of a *FreeBusyView* in a *GetUserAvailabilityResponse* was shown in Listing 21-24.

FreeBusyViewType

The *FreeBusyViewType* element is a string that maps to the *FreeBusyViewType* enumeration. This is the same enumeration that the *RequestedView* element from *FreeBusyViewOptions* uses. It is shown in Listing 21-27.

---

[7] Think of them as additional flags.

As we have already mentioned, the *RequestedView* value is not necessarily the resulting level of free/busy detail that the caller will receive. The *FreeBusyViewType* element in a *FreeBusyView* is the actual level of detail of free/busy information that Exchange Web Services was able to retrieve for the corresponding attendee.

MergedFreeBusy

The *MergedFreeBusy* element is a string, the value of which is a merged free/busy stream for the corresponding attendee. See the sidebar titled "Introducing the Merged Free/Busy Stream" for details.

CalendarEventArray and CalendarEvents

The *CalendarEventArray* element is an optional array of *CalendarEvent* elements. A *FreeBusyView* may not contain a *CalendarEventArray* if:

- If the *FreeBusyViewType* in your *FreeBusyViewOptions* is *MergedOnly* or *None*

- If the attendee has no calendar items within the *TimeWindow* of your *FreeBusyViewOptions*

A *CalendarEvent* can be thought of as mini version of a *CalendarItem*. The *CalendarEvent* type contains many similar properties, albeit with different name and type conventions. Each *CalendarEvent* element in a *CalendarEventsArray* represents an existing calendar item on the attendee's calendar and contains different levels of detail based on the *FreeBusyViewType* of your *FreeBusyView*.

Listing 21-29 shows the schema for the *CalenderEvent* type.

LISTING 21-29 Schema of the *CalendarEvent* type

```
<xs:complexType name="CalendarEvent">
  <xs:sequence>
    <xs:element minOccurs="1" maxOccurs="1" name="StartTime"
                type="xs:dateTime" />
    <xs:element minOccurs="1" maxOccurs="1" name="EndTime"
                type="xs:dateTime" />
    <xs:element minOccurs="1" maxOccurs="1" name="BusyType"
                type="t:LegacyFreeBusyType" />
    <xs:element minOccurs="0" maxOccurs="1"
                name="CalendarEventDetails"
                type="t:CalendarEventDetails" />
  </xs:sequence>
</xs:complexType>
```

The *StartTime* and *EndTime* elements, both of type *xs:dateTime*, should be familiar to you by now (these elements were discussed in Chapter 8). Likewise, *BusyType*—being of type *LegacyFreeBusyType*—should be no surprise at this point. We will discuss *CalendarEventDetails* shortly.

Listing 21-30 is an example of a *CalendarEvent* returned in a *FreeBusyView,* where the *CalendarEvent* does not have *CalendarEventDetails.*

LISTING 21-30 Example of a *CalendarEvent* in a *FreeBusyView* without *CalendarEventDetails*

```
<m:FreeBusyView xmlns:m=".../messages" xmlns:t=".../types">
  <t:FreeBusyViewType>FreeBusy</t:FreeBusyViewType>
  <t:CalendarEventArray>
    <t:CalendarEvent>
      <t:StartTime>2007-05-09T10:00:00-07:00</t:StartTime>
      <t:EndTime>2007-05-09T11:00:00-07:00</t:EndTime>
      <t:BusyType>Busy</t:BusyType>
    </t:CalendarEvent>
  </t:CalendarEventArray>
  <t:WorkingHours ... />
</m:FreeBusyView>
```

Important The *StartTime* and *EndTime date/time* strings in a *CalendarEvent* incorrectly contain UTC offsets. The Exchange Web Services team recommends that you **ignore** any UTC offsets that are present in *StartTime* and *EndTime* elements. For more information, see the section titled "Understanding Time Zone Issues with *CalendarEvents*" later in this chapter.

CalendarEventDetails

CalendarEventDetails is an optional element on a *CalendarEvent.* It is a grouping of additional elements that are returned by Exchange Web Services when Exchange Web Services was able to get detailed free/busy information for an attendee. The presence of *CalendarEventDetails* is dependent on the *FreeBusyViewType* value. Table 21-5 describes which enumeration values in the *FreeBusyViewType* indicate the presence of *CalendarEventDetails.*

TABLE 21-5 *FreeBusyViewType* **Values and the Corresponding Presence of** *CalendarEventDetails*

FreeBusyViewType value	*CalendarEventDetails* present
Detailed, DetailedMerged	Yes
FreeBusy, FreeBusyMerged	No
MergedOnly, None	Not applicable; there are no *CalendarEvent* parent elements in this case

Listing 21-30 showed that when the *FreeBusyType* of a *FreeBusyView* is set to *FreeBusy,* then *CalendarEventDetails* are not present. Listing 21-31 shows the same *CalendarEvent,* but this time with *CalendarEventDetails.*

LISTING 21-31 Example of a *CalendarEvent* in a *FreeBusyView* with *CalendarEventDetails*

```
<m:FreeBusyView xmlns:m=".../messages" xmlns:t=".../types">
  <t:FreeBusyViewType>Detailed</t:FreeBusyViewType>
  <tCalendarEventArray>
    <t:CalendarEvent>
      <t:StartTime>2007-05-09T10:00:00-07:00</t:StartTime>
      <t:EndTime>2007-05-09T11:00:00-07:00</t:EndTime>
      <t:BusyType>Busy</t:BusyType>
      <t:CalendarEventDetails>
        <t:ID>4DD858D...</t:ID>
        <t:Subject>Status Meeting</t:Subject>
        <t:Location>Conf Room 34/3301</t:Location>
        <t:IsMeeting>true</t:IsMeeting>
        <t:IsRecurring>true</t:IsRecurring>
        <t:IsException>false</t:IsException>
        <t:IsReminderSet>true</t:IsReminderSet>
        <t:IsPrivate>false</t:IsPrivate>
      </t:CalendarEventDetails>
    </t:CalendarEvent>
  </t:CalendarEventArray>
</m:FreeBusyView>
```

Note By default, the permission level of calendar folders provided to other users inside an organization is "Free/Busy time only." At this permission level, most *CalendarEvent* elements will not contain *CalendarEventDetails*. See the section titled "Working with Free/Busy Information" earlier in this chapter for information on how users can grant additional permissions to other users within an organization.

Table 21-6 includes a brief description of each of the properties defined in the *CalendarEventDetails* type.

TABLE 21-6 Properties of *CalendarEventDetails*

Property Name	Type	Description
ID	String	A unique ID for the event
Subject	String	Subject of the calendar event.; not present if *IsPrivate* is true
Location	String	Location of the calendar event.; not present if *IsPrivate* is true
IsMeeting	String	Is the event a meeting
IsRecurring	Boolean	Is the event part of a recurrence set
IsException	Boolean	Is the event an exception from a recurrence set
IsReminderSet	Boolean	Does the event have an associated reminder set with it?
IsPrivate	Boolean	Has this calendar event been marked as private by the owner?

Unlike with *CalendarItem* elements returned via the *GetItem* or *FindItem* Web methods, you cannot request additional properties for *CalendarEvent* elements via the *GetUserAvailability* Web method beyond those defined in the *CalendarEvent* and *CalendarEventDetails* schema.

The *ID* property of a *CalendarEventDetails* is a string whose value is significant. Though it does not represent a standard Exchange Web Services *ItemId*, it is, in fact, a hexadecimal *PR_ENTRY_ID*. Those with previous programming experience using the message application programming interface (MAPI) are familiar with the concept of the *PR_ENTRY_ID* and know that it can be obtained in a number of ways. You will see how a *PR_ENTRY_ID* can be used in Exchange Web Services when we discuss the *GlobalObjectId* element in *SuggestionViewOptions* later in this chapter.

Appendix B, "Calendaring Supplementals," (available on the companion Web page) has a section titled "Getting a *CalendarItem* from *CalendarEvents*." There we will provide you with a method to convert the *ID* from a *CalendarEvent* into an Exchange Web Services *ItemId*.

> **More Info** The next Service Pack of Exchange Server 2007 will have an additional Web method to enable you to convert this Entry ID into an Exchange Web Services *ItemId*.[8]

WorkingHours

The *WorkingHours* element is an optional element in the *FreeBusyView* response. It represents the valid working times for an attendee. You can then consider this information when making scheduling decisions or if you are designing an application to display attendee free/busy information (for example, graying out the non-working hours of an attendee in a calendar display).

Honoring an attendee's working hours is your responsibility. Exchange Web Services does not reject out-of-hand any meeting requests that fall outside an attendee's working hours. In fact, if Exchange Web Services must query the free/busy information for a large number of attendees when processing your *GetUserAvailabilityRequest*, it is likely to return suggestion times that conflict with some of the attendees' defined working hours.

The schema for the *WorkingHours* element is shown in Listing 21-32.

LISTING 21-32 Schema for *WorkingHours*

```
<xs:complexType name="WorkingHours">
  <xs:sequence>
    <xs:element minOccurs="1" maxOccurs="1" name="TimeZone"
                type="t:SerializableTimeZone" />
    <xs:element minOccurs="1" maxOccurs="1" name="WorkingPeriodArray"
                type="t:ArrayOfWorkingPeriod" />
  </xs:sequence>
</xs:complexType>
```

An example of *WorkingHours* in a *GetUserAvailabilityResponse* is shown in Listing 21-33.

---

8 See Appendix A on the companion Web page for information about new Web methods that will be present in Exchange 2007 SP1.

LISTING 21-33 Example of *WorkingHours* in a *GetUserAvailabilityResponse*

```
<m:GetUserAvailabilityResponse xmlns:m=".../messages" xmlns:t=".../types">
  <m:FreeBusyResponseArray>
    <m:FreeBusyResponse>
      <m:ResponseMessage ResponseClass="Success">
        <m:ResponseCode>NoError</m:ResponseCode>
      </m:ResponseMessage>
      <m:FreeBusyView>
        <t:FreeBusyViewType>DetailedMerged</t:FreeBusyViewType>
        <t:MergedFreeBusy>0223</t:MergedFreeBusy>
        <t:CalendarEventArray ... />
        <t:WorkingHours>
        <!-- This time zone is for Eastern Standard Time -->
          <t:TimeZone>
            <t:Bias>300</t:Bias>
            <t:StandardTime>
              <t:Bias>0</t:Bias>
              <t:Time>02:00:00</t:Time>
              <t:DayOrder>1</t:DayOrder>
              <t:Month>11</t:Month>
              <t:DayOfWeek>Sunday</t:DayOfWeek>
            </t:StandardTime>
            <t:DaylightTime>
              <t:Bias>-60</t:Bias>
              <t:Time>02:00:00</t:Time>
              <t:DayOrder>2</t:DayOrder>
              <t:Month>3</t:Month>
              <t:DayOfWeek>Sunday</t:DayOfWeek>
            </t:DaylightTime>
          </t:TimeZone>
          <t:WorkingPeriodArray>
            <t:WorkingPeriod>
              <t:DayOfWeek>
                 Monday Tuesday Wednesday Thursday Friday
              </t:DayOfWeek>
              <t:StartTimeInMinutes>480</t:StartTimeInMinutes>
              <t:EndTimeInMinutes>1020</t:EndTimeInMinutes>
            </t:WorkingPeriod>
          </t:WorkingPeriodArray>
        </t:WorkingHours>
      </m:FreeBusyView>
    </m:FreeBusyResponse>
  </m:FreeBusyResponseArray>
  </m:SuggestionsResponse>
</m:GetUserAvailabilityResponse>
```

TimeZone Element of *WorkingHours*

The *TimeZone* element on *WorkingHours* is of type *SerializableTimeZone,* which we have discussed at length already. Therefore, we won't go into that particular property here.

> **Important** The *TimeZone* element in *WorkingHours* applies *only* to the working hours of the attendee. It does not apply to any of the *date/time* strings in a *CalendarEvent* element, nor does it apply to *date/time* strings in a *Suggestion* element.

WorkingPeriodArray and *WorkingPeriod*

The *WorkingPeriodArray* is an array of *WorkingPeriod* elements. A *WorkingPeriod* has three values that define the days, start time, and end time that an attendee has defined as working hours. The schema for *WorkingPeriod* is shown in Listing 21-34.

LISTING 21-34 Schema of the *WorkingPeriod* type

```
<xs:complexType name="WorkingPeriod">
  <xs:sequence>
    <xs:element minOccurs="1" maxOccurs="1" name="DayOfWeek"
              type="t:DaysOfWeekType" />
    <xs:element minOccurs="1" maxOccurs="1"
              name="StartTimeInMinutes" type="xs:int" />
    <xs:element minOccurs="1" maxOccurs="1"
              name="EndTimeInMinutes" type="xs:int" />
  </xs:sequence>
</xs:complexType>
```

Despite *WorkingPeriodArray* being an array, an attendee is allowed to define only one working period.

DayOfWeek Element on of *WorkingPeriod*

The *DayOfWeek* element uses the familiar *DaysOfWeekType*, which, as you may recall, is a list of *DayOfWeekType* values. This means that the *DayOfWeek* property has a misleading name because it truly is the days of the week that this attendee considers workdays. As such, the value is a space delimited string of *DayOfWeekType* values. Listing 21-35 is an example of a *WorkingPeriod* with a *DayOfWeek* element defined as multiple days.

LISTING 21-35 Example of *WorkingPeriod* with multiple days defined as working days

```
<WorkingPeriod>
  <DayOfWeek>Monday Tuesday Wednesday Thursday Friday</DayOfWeek>
  <StartTimeInMinutes>480</StartTimeInMinutes>
  <EndTimeInMinutes>1020</EndTimeInMinutes>
</WorkingPeriod>
```

In proxy code, this property is cast as a string as well.

StartTimeInMinutes and *EndTimeInMinutes*

The *StartTimeInMinutes* and *EndTimeInMinutes* elements are integers that indicate when work begins and ends for this attendee. Each value is an offset in minutes from 12 A.M. in the time zone defined by the *TimeZone* element in the *WorkingHours* on each attendee defined working day. For example, if the *TimeZone* element in the *WorkingHours* defines a current bias of 300, and you have a *StartTimeInMinutes* value of 480, then your attendee's starting work time is 08:00:00–05:00:00 on each working day.

Understanding Time Zone Issues with *CalendarEvents*

When Exchange Web Services returns *CalendarEvent* elements in a *FreeBusyView*, all *date/time* strings in each *CalendarEvent* will contain a UTC offset. Unfortunately, while the *time* portion of the *date/time* strings is correct with regards to the time zone information defined in the *TimeZone* element in your *GetUserAvailabilityRequest*, the UTC offset in *every date/time* string is incorrect.

To illustrate this problem, look at Figure 21-5, which shows a calendar view of a day with two appointments, one in the morning that starts at 8:00 A.M. Pacific Daylight Time (PDT) and one that starts in the afternoon at 1:00 P.M. PDT.

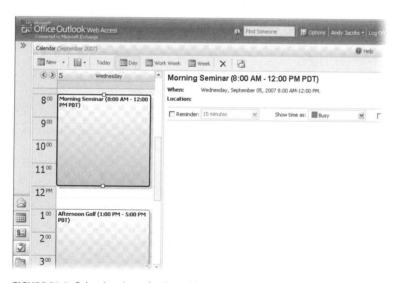

FIGURE 21-5 Calendar view of a day with two appointments in PDT

Assume that the Exchange Client Access Server (CAS) that is processing the *GetUserAvailabilityRequest* is in the same time zone as your client (that is, both are in the PDT time zone). Each of these calendar items then would be presented by the *CalendarEvent* elements shown in Listing 21-36.

LISTING 21-36 Two *CalendarEvent* elements from a PDT server

```
    </CalendarEventArray>
      <CalendarEvent>
        <StartTime>2007-08-01T08:00:00-07:00</StartTime>
        <EndTime>2007-08-01T12:00:00-07:00</EndTime>
        <BusyType>Busy</BusyType>
      </CalendarEvent>
      <CalendarEvent>
        <StartTime>2007-08-01T13:00:00-07:00</StartTime>
        <EndTime>2007-08-01T17:00:00-07:00</EndTime>
        <BusyType>Busy</BusyType>
      </CalendarEvent>
    </CalendarEventArray>
```

In Listing 21-36 there is no indication of any issue. The *StartTime* and *EndTime* of both *CalendarEvent* elements appears to have the correct start and end time, along with the correct UTC offset. But then consider what happens if the CAS is in a different time zone, say, Eastern Daylight Time (EDT) instead. Listing 21-37 shows how the same calendar items (with the same start times and end times) would be returned as *CalendarEvent* elements if a CAS in EDT is processing your *GetUserAvailabilityRequest*.

LISTING 21-37 Two *CalendarEvent* elements from an EDT server

```
    </CalendarEventArray>
      <CalendarEvent>
        <StartTime>2007-08-01T08:00:00-04:00</StartTime>
        <EndTime>2007-08-01T12:00:00-04:00</EndTime>
        <BusyType>Busy</BusyType>
      </CalendarEvent>
      <CalendarEvent>
        <StartTime>2007-08-01T13:00:00-04:00</StartTime>
        <EndTime>2007-08-01T17:00:00-04:00</EndTime>
        <BusyType>Busy</BusyType>
      </CalendarEvent>
    </CalendarEventArray>
```

Notice that while the *time* portion of the *date/time* strings are still correct, the UTC offsets are not. If you were to strip the offset from these strings, you would have a set of *date/time* strings without UTC offsets. And in that situation, you would use the time zone information in the *TimeZone* from your *GetUserAvailabiltyRequest* to serve as the bias for those *date/time* strings. Table 21-7 lists the steps needed to correctly calculate *StartTime* and *EndTime* for *CalendarEvent* elements that are returned by Exchange Web Services.

TABLE 21-7 **Steps to Correctly Calculate *StartTime* and *EndTime* from a *CalendarEvent***

1. Compute current bias from *TimeZone* in *GetUserAvailabilityRequest*	-07:00
2. Observe the current *StartTime* from *CalendarEvent*	2007-08-01T08:00:00-04:00
3. Remove the UTC offset from the current *StartTime*	2007-08-01T08:00:00
4. Calculate the correct *StartTime* by applying the bias from step 1.	2007-08-01T08:00:00-07:00

> **More Info** As of this writing, Exchange Server 2007 Service Pack 1 (SP1) will include a fix to correctly emit the *StartTime* and *EndTime* of a *CalendarEvent* as *date/time* strings without UTC offsets. The string values will be correct with regard to the time zone information from the *TimeZone* element of your *GetUserAvailabilityRequest*.

Applications that work directly with the XML should ignore UTC offsets in *StartTime* and *EndTime* elements of a *CalendarEvent*, and should be designed to not expect UTC offsets in future versions of Exchange Web Services. Designing an application to ignore these UTC offsets with the proxy classes, however, requires the use of a proxy extension class for the *CalendarEvent* that implements the *IXmlSerializable* interface.

Overcomming Incorrect *CalendarEvent* Time Values with *IXmlSerializable*

> **More Info** This section is not intended to be a detailed look at the *IXmlSerializable* interface, but rather a brief explanation for the purposes of describing a workaround necessary for Exchange Web Services applications. For more information on the *IXmlSerializable* interface, see the documenatation on the MSDN Website:
>
> *http://msdn2.microsoft.com/en-us/library/system.xml.serialization.ixmlserializable(vs.80).aspx*

In order to work around the incorrect *CalendarEvent* time issue with the proxy classes, you need to create a proxy extension class for the *CalendarEvent* type that implements the *IXmlSerializable* interface. You may recall from our discussion of *IXmlSerializable* in Chapter 9 that this implementation requires two steps. For the first step, search for the *CalendarEvent* class in the file containing your auto-generated proxy classes, then comment out the line containing the *XmlTypeAttribute* attribute. If you forget this first step, you will get an *InvalidOperationException* at run time. Listing 21-38 shows the end result of this action.

LISTING 21-38 Commenting out the *XmlTypeAttribute* on the *CalendarEvent* proxy class

```
/// <remarks/>
[System.CodeDom.Compiler.GeneratedCodeAttribute("wsdl", "2.0.50727.42")]
[System.SerializableAttribute()]
[System.Diagnostics.DebuggerStepThroughAttribute()]
[System.ComponentModel.DesignerCategoryAttribute("code")]
//[System.Xml.Serialization.XmlTypeAttribute(...)]
```

```
public partial class CalendarEvent {

    private System.DateTime startTimeField;

    private System.DateTime endTimeField;

    private LegacyFreeBusyType busyTypeField;

    ...

}
```

The second step of the fix is to create a proxy class extension that implements the *IXmlSerializable* interface. To implement the *IXmlSerializable* interface, you need to supply implementations for the *GetSchema, ReadXml,* and *WriteXml* methods. In the *ReadXml* and *WriteXml* methods, you will be responsible for handling all the XML serialization and deserialization for not only the *StartTime* and *EndTime* elements, but for the *BusyType* and *CalendarEventDetails* as well. Fortunately, you can take advantage of the *System.Xml. XmlSerializer* to write the XML for *CalendarEventDetails*.

Listing 21-39 is a very large listing of a proxy extension for the *CalendarEvent* class that implements *IXmlSerializable* in order to fix the issue of Exchange Web Services returning an incorrect UTC offset in the *StartTime* and *EndTime* elements of a *CalendarEvent*. The fix is implemented in the *ReadXml* method and involves using a regular expression to parse *date/ time strings* for date and time information only. The rest of the code is required to satisfy the implementation details of *IXmlSerialiazble*.

LISTING 21-39 Proxy extension for *CalendarEvent* that implements *IXmlSerializable*

```
///<summary>
/// Proxy extension for CalendarEvent that implements IXmlSerializable.
/// The purpose of this extension is to control the XML for the StartTime
/// and EndTime properties during de-serialization due to an issue in the
/// Exchange Server where the date/time strings in these properties
/// incorrect contains the UTC offset of the Client Access Server
/// processing the GetUserAvailabilityRequest.
///</summary>
///<remarks>
/// For this to work, the XmlTypeAttribute that the proxy generator places on
/// this class in the auto-generated .cs file must be removed
/// E.g.
///<code>
///     [System.CodeDom.Compiler.GeneratedCodeAttribute("wsdl", "2.0.50727.42")]
///     [System.SerializableAttribute()]
///     [System.Diagnostics.DebuggerStepThroughAttribute()]
///     [System.ComponentModel.DesignerCategoryAttribute("code")]
///     //[System.Xml.Serialization.XmlTypeAttribute(Namespace="...")]
///     public partial class CalendarEvent {...}
///</code>
```

```csharp
///</remarks>
public partial class CalendarEvent : IXmlSerializable
{
    /// <summary>
    /// Empty constructor, required for partial class implementations
    /// </summary>
    public CalendarEvent()
    { }

    /// <summary>
    /// Returns an XmlSchema for the CalendarEvent that describes the
    /// XML representation of the output that is produced by the WriteXml
    /// method and consumed by the ReadXmlMethod
    /// </summary>
    /// <returns>XmlSchema for the CalendarEvent</returns>
    public System.Xml.Schema.XmlSchema GetSchema()
    {
        // This method must return
        //<xs:schema
        //          id="types"
        //          elementFormDefault="qualified"
        //          version="Exchange2007"
        //          xmlns:t=".../types"
        //          targetNamespace=".../types"
        //          xmlns:tns=".../types"
        //          xmlns:xs="http://www.w3.org/2001/XMLSchema">
        //   <xs:complexType name="CalendarEvent">
        //     <xs:sequence>
        //       <xs:element minOccurs="1" maxOccurs="1" name="StartTime"
        //                 type="xs:dateTime" />
        //       <xs:element minOccurs="1" maxOccurs="1" name="EndTime"
        //                 type="xs:dateTime" />
        //       <xs:element minOccurs="1" maxOccurs="1" name="BusyType"
        //                 type="t:LegacyFreeBusyType" />
        //       <xs:element minOccurs="0" maxOccurs="1"
        //                 name="CalendarEventDetails"
        //                 type="t:CalendarEventDetails" />
        //     </xs:sequence>
        //   </xs:complexType>
        string xsTypes =
            "http://schemas.microsoft.com/exchange/services/2006/types";
        string xsSchema = "http://www.w3.org/2001/XMLSchema";

        XmlSchema schema = new XmlSchema();
        schema.Id = "types";
        schema.ElementFormDefault = XmlSchemaForm.Qualified;
        schema.Version = "Exchange2007";
        schema.TargetNamespace = xsTypes;

        // <xs:complexType ... >
        XmlSchemaComplexType xmlct1 = new XmlSchemaComplexType();
        schema.Items.Add(xmlct1);
        xmlct1.Name = "CalendarEvent";
```

```
       // <xs:sequence ... >
       XmlSchemaSequence xmlsq1 = new XmlSchemaSequence();
       xmlct1.Particle = xmlsq1;

       //   <xs:element ... name="StartTime" ... />
       XmlSchemaElement xmle1 = new XmlSchemaElement();
       xmlsq1.Items.Add(xmle1);
       xmle1.Name = "StartTime";
       xmle1.MinOccurs = 1;
       xmle1.MaxOccurs = 1;
       xmle1.SchemaTypeName = new XmlQualifiedName("dateTime", xsSchema);

       //   <xs:element ... name="EndTime" ... />
       XmlSchemaElement xmle2 = new XmlSchemaElement();
       xmlsq1.Items.Add(xmle2);
       xmle2.Name = "EndTime";
       xmle2.MinOccurs = 1;
       xmle2.MaxOccurs = 1;
       xmle2.SchemaTypeName = new XmlQualifiedName("dateTime", xsSchema);

       //   <xs:element ... name="BusyType" ... />
       XmlSchemaElement xmle3 = new XmlSchemaElement();
       xmlsq1.Items.Add(xmle3);
       xmle3.Name = "BusyType";
       xmle3.MinOccurs = 1;
       xmle3.MaxOccurs = 1;
       xmle3.SchemaTypeName = new XmlQualifiedName(
           "LegacyFreeBusyType", xsTypes);

       //   <xs:element ... name="CalendarEventDetails" ... />
       XmlSchemaElement xmle4 = new XmlSchemaElement();
       xmlsq1.Items.Add(xmle4);
       xmle4.Name = "CalendarEventDetails";
       xmle4.MinOccurs = 0;
       xmle4.MaxOccurs = 1;
       xmle4.SchemaTypeName = new XmlQualifiedName(
           "CalendarEventDetails", xsTypes);

       return schema;
    }


    /// <summary>
    /// Generates a CalendarEvent object from it's XML representation
    /// </summary>
    /// <param name="reader">XmlReader posistioned at the start node
    /// of the CalendarEvent XML</param>
    public void ReadXml(System.Xml.XmlReader reader)
    {
        string xsTypes =
            "http://schemas.microsoft.com/exchange/services/2006/types";

        // Store the LocalName of the element we are currently at.
        // This should be "CalendarEvent".
        //
```

```
// This also serves as our key to our position in the stream.
// Once we reach an EndElement with this name, then we
// are done with our portion of the XmlStream.
//
string toplevelElementName = reader.LocalName;
reader.Read();

while (true)
{
    // Check to see if we are done processing
    if ((reader.NodeType == XmlNodeType.EndElement) &&
        (0 == String.Compare(reader.LocalName, toplevelElementName)))
    {
        // We are done, consume this EndElement and stop processing
        reader.Read();
        break;
    }

    if (reader.NodeType == XmlNodeType.EndElement)
    {
        // This means we are at the closing tag of
        // </CalendarEventDetails>
        // No data here to process.
        reader.Read();
        continue;
    }

    // Consume StartTime or EndTime
    if ((0 == String.Compare(reader.LocalName, "StartTime")) ||
        (0 == String.Compare(reader.LocalName, "EndTime")))
    {
        // Store the localName, we'll need this to determine if this is
        // the StartTime or EndTime field later.
        string localName = reader.LocalName;

        // StartTime or EndTime is the reason we needed to implement
        // IXmlSerializable, the server will always append a UTC offset
        // to the CalendarEvent date/time strings, and this offset
        // can not be trusted.  The 'time' of the event is
        // always valid if treated as Local time.
        //
        // We will use a Regular Expression to extract whatever was
        // supplied as a local time only
        //
        string timeValue = reader.ReadElementContentAsString();
        System.Text.RegularExpressions.Regex regex =
            new System.Text.RegularExpressions.Regex(
                @"(?<datetime>\d{4}-\d{2}-\d{2}T\d{2}:\d{2}:\d{2})",
                System.Text.RegularExpressions.RegexOptions.Compiled);

        string nonUTCOffsettedString =
            regex.Match(timeValue).Result("${datetime}");
        DateTime parsedDateTime = DateTime.Parse(nonUTCOffsettedString);
```

```
                    // Set to the appropriate field
                    if (0 == String.Compare(localName, "StartTime"))
                    {
                        this.startTimeField = parsedDateTime;
                    }
                    else
                    {
                        this.endTimeField = parsedDateTime;
                    }
                }

                // Consume BusyType
                if (0 == String.Compare(reader.LocalName, "BusyType"))
                {
                    string value = reader.ReadElementContentAsString();
                    this.busyTypeField =
                        (LegacyFreeBusyType)Enum.Parse(
                            typeof(LegacyFreeBusyType), value);
                }

                // Consume CalendarEventDetails, we are going to create an
                // XmlSerializer for this to allow that type's default
                // serialization process to occur.
                if (0 == String.Compare(reader.LocalName,
                    "CalendarEventDetails"))
                {
                    using (System.IO.StringReader strdr =
                        new System.IO.StringReader(reader.ReadOuterXml()))
                    {
                        XmlSerializer xmls =
                            new XmlSerializer(
                                typeof(CalendarEventDetails), xsTypes);

                        this.calendarEventDetailsField =
                            (CalendarEventDetails)xmls.Deserialize(strdr);
                    }
                }
            }
        }
    }

    /// <summary>
    /// Converts a CalendarEvent object into its XML representation
    /// </summary>
    /// <param name="writer">XmlWriter positioned at the point
    /// to which the XML for this object is to be written to</param>
    public void WriteXml(System.Xml.XmlWriter writer)
    {
        string xsTypes =
            "http://schemas.microsoft.com/exchange/services/2006/types";

        // Our position in the writer already includes a StartElement
        // for our type, therefore, our job is to pickup writing to the
        // stream all of our properties.
```

```
                    // Write StartTime
                    writer.WriteElementString("StartTime",
                        System.Xml.XmlConvert.ToString((DateTime)this.startTimeField,
                            XmlDateTimeSerializationMode.RoundtripKind));

                    // Write EndTime
                    writer.WriteElementString("EndTime",
                        System.Xml.XmlConvert.ToString((DateTime)this.endTimeField,
                            XmlDateTimeSerializationMode.RoundtripKind));

                    // Write BusyType
                    writer.WriteElementString("BusyType", xsTypes,
                        this.busyTypeField.ToString());

                    // Write CalendarEventDetails
                    XmlSerializer xmls =
                        new XmlSerializer(typeof(CalendarEventDetails), xsTypes);
                    xmls.Serialize(writer, this.calendarEventDetailsField);
            }
    }
```

Once the code is commented out as in Listing 21-38 and the class in Listing 21-39 is compiled in with your proxy code, the .NET Framework calls these methods during serialization/deserialization of any *CalenderEvent* elements.

Getting Free/Busy Information from the Proxy Classes

With the proxy extension for the *CalendarEvent* class from Listing 21-38 and Listing 21-39 included, Listing 21-40 shows how to extract the *FreeBusyView* property from the *FreeBusyResponseArray* and parse it for relevant information. (Hint: You could take advantage of this method from inside the code in Listing 21-12 while you are parsing a *GetUserAvailabilityResponse*.)

LISTING 21-40 Example of displaying free/busy information from a *FreeBusyResponseType* via the proxy classes

```
/// <summary>
/// Takes a FreeBusyResponseType instance along with a friendly name to
/// associate with it, and prints to the Console the free/busy information.
/// </summary>
/// <param name="fbResponse">Instance of a FreeBusy response</param>
/// <param name="participantName">Name to associate with the FreeBusy
/// information</param>
public static void PrintFreeBusyInformation(
    FreeBusyResponseType freeBusyResponse,
    string attendeeName)
{
    // Extract the FreeBusyView from the response
    //
    FreeBusyView freeBusyView = freeBusyResponse.FreeBusyView;
```

```
// Determine what type of information the freeBusyView contains based
// on the FreeBusyViewType value
//
bool containsMergedData =
    (freeBusyView.FreeBusyViewType == FreeBusyViewType.MergedOnly ||
    freeBusyView.FreeBusyViewType == FreeBusyViewType.DetailedMerged ||
    freeBusyView.FreeBusyViewType == FreeBusyViewType.FreeBusyMerged);

bool containsCalendarEvents =
    (freeBusyView.FreeBusyViewType != FreeBusyViewType.MergedOnly &&
    freeBusyView.FreeBusyViewType != FreeBusyViewType.None);

bool containsCalendarEventDetails =
    (freeBusyView.FreeBusyViewType == FreeBusyViewType.Detailed ||
    freeBusyView.FreeBusyViewType == FreeBusyViewType.DetailedMerged);

Console.WriteLine("FreeBusy view for [ " + attendeeName + " ]:");
Console.WriteLine("\tHas Merged Data: " + containsMergedData);
Console.WriteLine("\tHas Calendar Events: " + containsCalendarEvents);
Console.WriteLine("\tHas Calendar Event Details: " +
    containsCalendarEventDetails);

// Display Merged Free Busy data if we have it.
if (containsMergedData)
{
    Console.WriteLine("Merged Free Busy: " +
        freeBusyView.MergedFreeBusy);
}

// Display Calendar Events if they are present, (and
// CalendarEventDetails as well.)
//
// Why the check for freeBusyView.CalendarEventArray == null?  Because,
// even though the view type is FreeBusy or Detailed, this user
// may have no events on this day, in which case the event array
// will be null.
//
if (containsCalendarEvents && freeBusyView.CalendarEventArray != null)
{
    Console.WriteLine("Listing of Calendar Events:");

    foreach (CalendarEvent calendarEvent in freeBusyView.CalendarEventArray)
    {
```

```
Console.WriteLine(String.Format("Event ({0}) {1} - {2}",
    calendarEvent.BusyType,
    calendarEvent.StartTime,
    calendarEvent.EndTime));

if (containsCalendarEventDetails)
{
    // Do not attempt to print Subject and Location if the event is
    // private.  The properties will have null values in the
    // CalendarEventDetails anyway.
    //
    if(calendarEvent.CalendarEventDetails.IsPrivate)
    {
        Console.WriteLine("\tDetails: <Private Details Omitted>");
    }
    else
    {
        Console.WriteLine("\tDetails:");
        Console.WriteLine("\t\tSubject: " +
            calendarEvent.CalendarEventDetails.Subject);
        Console.WriteLine("\t\tLocation: " +
            calendarEvent.CalendarEventDetails.Location);
    }

    // The rest of the details, always present reguarless of
    // IsPrivate flag
    //
    Console.WriteLine("\t\tMeeting: {0}, Recurring {1}\r\n" +
        "\t\tException {2}, ReminderSet {3}",
        calendarEvent.CalendarEventDetails.IsMeeting,
        calendarEvent.CalendarEventDetails.IsRecurring,
        calendarEvent.CalendarEventDetails.IsException,
        calendarEvent.CalendarEventDetails.IsReminderSet);
    }
  }
}
// Final trailing line for nice formatting
Console.WriteLine();
}
```

Figure 21-6 shows an example of console output from the *PrintFreeBusyInformation* method from Listing 21-39.

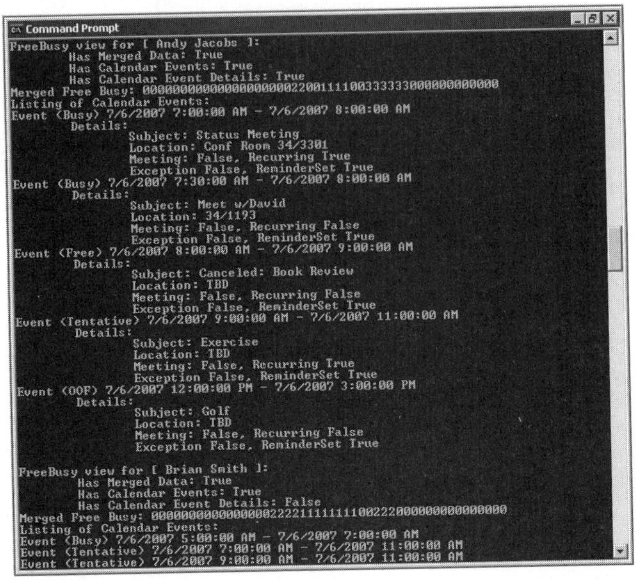

FIGURE 21-6 Sample output from the *PrintFreeBusyInformation* method

Getting Free/Busy Information from a Distribution List

One feature of the *GetUserAvailability* Web method is that you can get free/busy information for all of the members of a distribution list (DL) by supplying the e-mail address of the
distribution list as an attendee. Listing 21-41 shows using an e-mail address of a DL in a
MailboxData element.

LISTING 21-41 *GetUserAvailabilityRequest* with a distribution list in a *MailboxData* element

```xml
<m:GetUserAvailabilityRequest xmlns:m=".../messages" xmlns:t=".../types">
  <t:TimeZone ... />
  <m:MailboxDataArray>
    <t:MailboxData>
      <t:Email>
        <t:Address>DistributionList@contoso.com</t:Address>
      </t:Email>
      <t:AttendeeType>Required</t:AttendeeType>
      <t:ExcludeConflicts>false</t:ExcludeConflicts>
    </t:MailboxData>
  </m:MailboxDataArray>
  <t:FreeBusyViewOptions ... />
</m:GetUserAvailabilityRequest>
```

When Exchange Web Services processes a *MailboxData* element with a DL as the attendee,
the following two things happen to the associated *FreeBusyResponse*:

1. There will be only one *FreeBusyResponse* element for the entry. In other words, there will *not* be one *FreeBusyResponse* element for each member of the DL.

2. The free/busy data detail will be reduced to *MergedOnly*.

Listing 21-42 shows an example of a *FreeBusyResponseArray* with free/busy information for a DL.

LISTING 21-42 Sample of a *GetUserAvailabilityResponse* with *MergedOnly* data

```
<m:FreeBusyResponseArray xmlns:m=".../messages" xmlns:t=".../types">
  <m:FreeBusyResponse>
    <m:ResponseMessage ResponseClass="Success">
      <m:ResponseCode>NoError</m:ResponseCode>
    </m:ResponseMessage>
    <m:FreeBusyView>
      <t:FreeBusyViewType>MergedOnly</t:FreeBusyViewType>
      <t:MergedFreeBusy>00113333</t:MergedFreeBusy>
    </m:FreeBusyView>
  </m:FreeBusyResponse>
</m:FreeBusyResponseArray>
```

The merged free/busy stream that is returned represents the free/busy status of all DL members in a combined view. A merged free/busy digit of 0 means that all DL members are free at that time segment, while a merged free/busy digit of 3 means that at least one member of the DL is busy during that time segment. You cannot request that multiple *MailboxData* elements be combined into one merged free/busy stream. Exchange Web Services will return only a merged free/busy stream that contains multiple attendees free/busy information through the use of a DL address as an attendee.

Working with Suggestions

When you provide a *SuggestionsViewOptions* element in your *GetUserAvailabilityRequest*, Exchange Web Services compiles all attendees' free/busy information and assembles a list of potential meeting times ranked in quality order from best (*Excellent*) to worst (*Poor*). You can use these suggestion times to determine a meeting time that works well for many or all attendees.

A suggestion includes a suggestion time and a quality level, as well as a flag indicating if the suggestion time is within the organizer's working hours. A suggestion also includes information about any conflicts that attendees may have with the suggestion time.

Exchange Web Services uses a suggestion generation algorithm that is optimized for working with free/busy data for a large number of attendees. For the most part, you have very little input as to the parameters of this algorithm. Therefore, we won't be discussing the details of this algorithm in this book.

While you cannot influence the suggestion generation algorithm that much, Exchange Web Services does provide you a number of element values that serve to filter certain suggestion times from the result set. Each of these elements is found in the *SuggestionViewOptions* in your *GetUserAvailabilityRequest*.

SuggestionsViewOptions in an Availability Request

You have seen some examples of the *SuggestionsViewOptions* element already, in Listing 21-6 for example. The schema type for *SuggestionsViewOptions* is the *SuggestionsViewOptionsType* type shown in Listing 21-43.

LISTING 21-43 Schema for the *SuggestionsViewOptionsType*

```
<xs:complexType name="SuggestionsViewOptionsType">
  <xs:sequence>
    <xs:element minOccurs="0" maxOccurs="1"
                name="GoodThreshold" type="xs:int" />
    <xs:element minOccurs="0" maxOccurs="1"
                name="MaximumResultsByDay" type="xs:int" />
    <xs:element minOccurs="0" maxOccurs="1"
                name="MaximumNonWorkHourResultsByDay"
                type="xs:int" />
    <xs:element minOccurs="0" maxOccurs="1"
                name="MeetingDurationInMinutes" type="xs:int" />
    <xs:element minOccurs="0" maxOccurs="1"
                name="MinimumSuggestionQuality"
                type="t:SuggestionQuality" />
    <xs:element minOccurs="1" maxOccurs="1"
                name="DetailedSuggestionsWindow"
                type="t:Duration" />
    <xs:element minOccurs="0" maxOccurs="1"
                name="CurrentMeetingTime" type="xs:dateTime" />
    <xs:element minOccurs="0" maxOccurs="1"
                name="GlobalObjectId" type="xs:string" />
  </xs:sequence>
</xs:complexType>
```

Previous examples in this chapter have shown using the *DetailedSuggestionsWindow* and *CurrentMeetingTime*. We've also mentioned that you can use the *MinimumSuggestionQuality* as an alternative to setting the *ExcludeConflicts* element on the *MailboxData* element of each attendee. As another example, though, Listing 21-44 shows a *GetUserAvailabilityRequest* that contains *SuggestionsViewOptions* with all of the child elements, including those we have not discussed yet.

LISTING 21-44 Example of using a *SuggestionsViewOptions* element in a *GetUserAvailabilityRequest*

```
<m:GetUserAvailabilityRequest xmlns:m=".../messages" xmlns:t=".../types">
  <t:TimeZone ... />
  <m:MailboxDataArray ... />
```

```
  <t:SuggestionsViewOptions>
    <t:GoodThreshold>49</t:GoodThreshold>
    <t:MaximumResultsByDay>2</t:MaximumResultsByDay>
    <t:MaximumNonWorkHourResultsByDay>1</t:MaximumNonWorkHourResultsByDay>
    <t:MeetingDurationInMinutes>180</t:MeetingDurationInMinutes>
    <t:MinimumSuggestionQuality>Good</t:MinimumSuggestionQuality>
    <t:DetailedSuggestionsWindow>
      <t:StartTime>2007-05-11T00:00:00</t:StartTime>
      <t:EndTime>2007-05-12T00:00:00</t:EndTime>
    </t:DetailedSuggestionsWindow>
    <t:CurrentMeetingTime>2007-05-11T08:00:00</t:CurrentMeetingTime>
    <!-- t:GlobalObjectId>00AB0</t:GlobalObjectId -->
  </t:SuggestionsViewOptions>
</m:GetUserAvailabilityRequest>
```

In Listing 21-44, the *GlobalObjectId* element is purposely commented out. We did this to illustrate that although it is an element of *SuggestionsViewOptions*, including it in the request in Listing 21-44 would not be prudent with some of the other elements that were used.

Listing 21-45 is an example of a *GetUserAvailiabiltyResponse* that contains a *Suggestion* element.

LISTING 21-45 Example of a suggestion in a *GetUserAvailabilityResponse*

```
<m:GetUserAvailabilityResponse xmlns:m=".../messages" xmlns:t=".../types">
  <m:SuggestionsResponse>
    <m:ResponseMessage ResponseClass="Success">
      <m:ResponseCode>NoError</m:ResponseCode>
    </m:ResponseMessage>
    <m:SuggestionDayResultArray>
      <t:SuggestionDayResult>
        <t:Date>2007-05-11T00:00:00</t:Date>
        <t:DayQuality>Good</t:DayQuality>
        <t:SuggestionArray>
          <t:Suggestion>
            <t:MeetingTime>2007-05-11T08:00:00-07:00</t:MeetingTime>
            <t:IsWorkTime>true</t:IsWorkTime>
            <t:SuggestionQuality>Poor</t:SuggestionQuality>
            <t:AttendeeConflictDataArray>
              <t:IndividualAttendeeConflictData>
                <t:BusyType>Busy</t:BusyType>
              </t:IndividualAttendeeConflictData>
              <t:IndividualAttendeeConflictData>
                <t:BusyType>Free</t:BusyType>
              </t:IndividualAttendeeConflictData>
            </t:AttendeeConflictDataArray>
          </t:Suggestion>
        </t:SuggestionArray>
      </t:SuggestionDayResult>
    </m:SuggestionDayResultArray>
  </m:SuggestionsResponse>
</m:GetUserAvailabilityResponse>
```

> **Note** If you look at the *MeetingTime* element in Listing 21-43, you see the *date/time* string contains a UTC offset. This is because the issue that affects *date/time* strings in *CalendarEvent* elements also effects *MeetingTime* elements as well. As with *CalendarEvents*, the Exchange Web Services team recommends that you always *ignore* the UTC offset and use the time zone information from the *TimeZone* element in your *GetUserAvailabilityRequest* to provide the bias for the *date/time* strings.

We won't dig into the elements of the response until after we look at the elements of the request in more detail, but at this point we will point out that the response has a *SuggestionDayResultsArray,* which is an array that contains an element for each day that has a potential suggestion time. Inside each *SuggestionDayResult* is another array that contains each suggestion time for the corresponding day.

SuggestionsViewOptions Elements

This section will look at each of the elements of the *SuggestionViewOptions* before moving on to the *SuggestionsResponse*. When we discuss the *SuggestionsResponse,* we will refer back to many of the elements in this section to describe in more detail how these elements affect the suggestions represented in the *SuggestionsResponse*.

An example of *SuggestionsViewOptions* in a *GetUserAvailabilityRequest* was shown in Listing 21-44.

GoodThreshold

The *GoodThreshold* element is an integer value and represents the percentage of *required* attendees that must be free before a suggestion time can be considered of good quality. Valid values range from 1 to 49, and the default value is 25.

MaximumResultsByDay

The *MaximumResultsByDay* element is an integer value that limits the maximum number of suggestion times for any given day. Valid values range from 1 to 48, with the default being 10.

MaximumNonWorkHourResultsByDay

The *MaximumNonWorkHourResultsByDay* element is an integer value that controls how many suggestion times are allowed outside the *organizer's* working hours. By default, this value is 0. Valid values range from 0 to 48.

Working hours of attendees are not considered by Exchange Web Services when generating suggestion times.

MeetingDurationInMinutes

The *MeetingDurationInMinutes* element is an integer value and represents the proposed meeting time. Values between 1 and 1440 are acceptable, with 60 being the default value.

All suggestion times that Exchange Web Services returns will represent slots of time equal to the *MeetingDurationInMinutes* value.

MinimumSuggestionQuality

The *MinimumSuggestionQuality* element is a string that maps to the *SuggestionQuality* enumeration shown in Listing 21-46.

LISTING 21-46 Schema definition of the *SuggestionQuality* enumeration

```xml
<xs:simpleType name="SuggestionQuality">
  <xs:restriction base="xs:string">
    <xs:enumeration value="Excellent" />
    <xs:enumeration value="Good" />
    <xs:enumeration value="Fair" />
    <xs:enumeration value="Poor" />
  </xs:restriction>
</xs:simpleType>
```

MinimumSuggestionQuality determines the lowest level of quality for suggestion times that Exchange Web Services will return. By default, this quality value is *Fair*.

As you will see later, every day that contains suggestions is also given a quality ranking via a *DayQuality* element; however, while the *MinimumSuggestionQuality* value does determine the minimum quality level for all suggested times, it does not directly determine the quality of suggestion days that are returned by Exchange Web Services.[9] The *DayQuality* element will be discussed later.

DetailedSuggestionsWindow

The *DetailedSuggestionsWindow* element defines the range of potential suggestion times. It is of the schema type *Duration,* which was shown in Listing 21-25. Being of type *Duration,* a *DetailedSuggestionsWindow* element has both *StartTime* and *EndTime* values. These values set the range for all potential suggestion times.

```xml
<DetailedSuggestionsWindow>
  <StartTime>2007-05-09T00:00:00</StartTime>
  <EndTime>2007-05-10T00:00:00</EndTime>
</DetailedSuggestionsWindow>
```

---

[9] There is a situation where Exchange Web Services will return a suggestion time with a quality level less than *MinimumSuggestionQuality.* See the sidebar titled "Forcing Evaluation of a Proposed Meeting Time" for details.

The *StartTime* and *EndTime* values in a *DetailedSuggestionsWindows* must represent whole days without any hour, minute, or second values. Because the schema for *Duration* does not make this requirement, Exchange Web Services enforces it by returning an *InvalidParameterException* SOAP fault in the event that the *StartTime* and *EndTime* values are invalid.

```
System.Web.Services.Protocols.SoapException: Microsoft.Exchange.InfoWorker.Common.
InvalidParameterException: SuggestionsViewOptions.DetailedSuggestionsWindow.StartDate: Date
must have zero hours, minutes and seconds.
```

Best Practices   The Exchange Web Services team recommends using *date/time* strings without *UTC* offsets for the *StartTime* and *EndTime* values in a *DetailedSuggestionsWindow*. Exchange Web Services will use the time zone bias defined in the *TimeZone* element of your *GetUserAvailabilityRequest* to scope these strings.

Note   If a *GetUserAvailabilityRequest* includes both a *FreeBusyViewOptions* element and a *SuggestionsViewOptions* element, then the *DetailedSuggestionsWindow* of the *SuggestionsViewOptions* element *must* fall within the *TimeWindow* of the *FreeBusyViewOptions* element. If your request does not meet this requirement, Exchange Web Services will return an *InvalidParameterException* SOAP fault.

CurrentMeetingTime

The *CurrentMeetingTime* element is a string in the *xs:dateTime* format. The value of a *CurrentMeetingTime* element represents the proposed meeting start time, whereby the proposed meeting duration is defined by the *MeetingDurationInMinutes* element.

Supplying a *CurrentMeetingTime* value in *SuggestionsViewOptions* is akin to sending in your own suggestion time to Exchange Web Services that you would like evaluated. Exchange Web Services is not required to return the quality of this suggestion time, however. See the sidebar titled "Forcing Evaluation of a Proposed Meeting Time" later in this chapter for more information.

Best Practices   The Exchange Web Services team recommends using *date/time* strings without UTC offsets for the *CurrentMeetingTime* element. Exchange Web Services will use the time zone bias defined in the *TimeZone* element of the *GetUserAvailabilityRequest* to scope these strings.

GlobalObjectId

The *GlobalObjectId* element is a string whose value represents the id of another calendar event in the organizer's calendar. Using a *GlobalObjectId* can be thought of as an alternative to using *CurrentMeetingTime* and *MeetingDurationInMinutes*. Exchange Web Services will use the start time and duration of the calendar event represented by the *GlobalObjectId* as a proposed meeting time. Calendar event ids are found in the *ID* element of a *CalendarEvent*.

```
<CalendarEvent>
  <StartTime>2007-05-09T10:00:00</StartTime>
  <EndTime>2007-05-09T11:00:00</EndTime>
  <BusyType>Busy</BusyType>
  <CalendarEventDetails>
    <ID>A994636C00...</ID>
    <Subject>Status Meeting</Subject>
    <...>
  </CalendarEventDetails>
</CalendarEvent>
```

As you saw in our discussion of *CalendarEventDetails,* this *ID* value is a hexadecimal *PR_ENTRY_ID* and can be used as a *GlobalObjectId* element value in a *SuggestionsViewOptions*.

```
<SuggestionsViewOptions xmlns=".../types">
 <DetailedSuggestionsWindow>
  <StartTime>2007-05-10T00:00:00</StartTime>
  <EndTime>2007-05-11T00:00:00</EndTime>
 </DetailedSuggestionsWindow>
 <GlobalObjectId>A994636C00...</GlobalObjectId>
</SuggestionsViewOptions>
```

The purpose of allowing the *ID* value from a *CalendarEvent* to be an element value in *SuggestionsViewOptions* is to save you from having to perform a lookup for start time and duration of an existing calendar item if you already have the PR_ENTRY_ID.

> **Warning** The server will not reject a request that has both a *GlobalObjectId* and a *CurrentMeetingTime* element. However, the Exchange Web Services team does not recommend including both a *GlobalObjectId* and a *CurrentMeetingTime* in a *GetUserAvailabilityRequest*.

Forcing Evaluation of a Proposed Meeting Time

Normally, a list of suggestion times would all have a minimum quality level based on the *MinimumSuggestionsQuality* value in your *GetUserAvailabilityRequest*. However, if you were to experiment with the *GetUserAvailiability* Web method, you might likely find a situation in which you have set the *MimimumSuggestionsQuality* to *Excellent* but received a suggestion time of *Fair* quality or *Good* quality. This would occur when your *GetUserAvailabilityRequest* includes either a *CurrentMeetingTime* element or a *GlobalObjectId* element.

When Exchange Web Services process a *GetUserAvailabilityRequest* with a *CurrentMeetingTime* or a *GlobalObjectId*, it considers the time slot represented as a proposed suggestion time. Exchange Web Services will evaluate and return your suggestion time as a suggestion in the *GetUserAvailabilityResponse* unless it fails any of the following criteria:

- Your suggestion time is outside of the *DetailedSuggestionsWindow*

- Your suggestion time falls outside the *WorkingHours* of the organizer and the *MaximumNonWorkHourResultsByDay* value is 0

It is not possible to call the *GetUserAvailability* Web method for a suggested time list that includes *only* your suggestion time, unless of course that time happens to be the only valid suggestion time that meets all of the criteria of your *SuggestionsViewOptions*.

SuggestionsResponse in an Availability Response

This section will examine how Exchange Web Services returns suggestions in a *GetUserAvailabilityResponse*. Suggestions are returned within an array for each suggestion day in a *SuggestionResponse* element.

You first saw a *SuggestionsResponse* in Listing 21-6, after which we discussed how to check for a response class of *Success*. You saw another example in Listing 21-45 where we talked about how suggestions are returned in individual suggestion days and how each suggestion day is represented by a *SuggestionDayResult* inside a *SuggestionDayResultArray* element.

Listing 21-47 is an example of a *GetUserAvailabilityResponse* highlighting the location of the *SuggestionDayResultArray*.

LISTING 21-47 Sample *GetUserAvailabilityResponse* with a *SuggestionDayResultArray*

```
<m:GetUserAvailabilityResponse xmlns:m=".../messages" xmlns:t=".../types">
  <m:SuggestionsResponse>
    <m:ResponseMessage ResponseClass="Success">
      <m:ResponseCode>NoError</m:ResponseCode>
    </m:ResponseMessage>
    <m:SuggestionDayResultArray>
      <t:SuggestionDayResult>
        <t:Date>2007-05-09T00:00:00</t:Date>
        <t:DayQuality>Poor</t:DayQuality>
        <t:SuggestionArray />
      </t:SuggestionDayResult>
    </m:SuggestionDayResultArray>
  </m:SuggestionsResponse>
</m:GetUserAvailabilityResponse>
```

SuggestionDayResult

The *SuggestionDayResultArray* of a *SuggestionsResponse* contains one or more *SuggestionDayResult* elements, each one representing a suggestion day. The schema for the *SuggestionDayResult* is shown in Listing 21-48.

LISTING 21-48 Schema of the *SuggestionDayResult* type

```
<xs:complexType name="SuggestionDayResult">
  <xs:sequence>
    <xs:element minOccurs="1" maxOccurs="1" name="Date"
                type="xs:dateTime" />
    <xs:element minOccurs="1" maxOccurs="1" name="DayQuality"
                type="t:SuggestionQuality" />
    <xs:element minOccurs="0" maxOccurs="1" name="SuggestionArray"
                type="t:ArrayOfSuggestion" />
  </xs:sequence>
</xs:complexType>
```

Date Element of *SuggestionDayResult*

The *Date* element in a *SuggestionDayResult* should be pretty self-explanatory. We'll note just two points here. First, even though it is *xs:dateTime*, it is essentially only a date with a time portion equal to 00:00:00. Second, the value is returned as a *date/time* string without a UTC offset; therefore, you should use the bias of the time zone information from the *TimeZone* element of your *GetUserAvailabilityRequest* to scope this value.

DayQuality Element

The *DayQuality* element is a string that maps to the *SuggestionQuality* enumeration shown in Listing 21-46. The value of *DayQuality* represents the quality level of a suggestion day. The quality of a day is determined by Exchange Web Services and is influenced by the number of suggestions within that day that achieve a certain quality level. For example, a day that has five suggestion times, four of them with *Good* quality and one with *Poor* quality, is likely to be given a *DayQuality* value of *Good*.

The purpose of this chapter is not to explain the number of suggestions that must be of a certain quality level for Exchange Web Services to consider a suggestion day to be of a particular quality. Exchange Web Services could conceivably return a suggestion day with a quality value of of *Poor* when the day has one or more suggestions of quality *Excellent*.[10]

One example of using the quality level represented by the *DayQuality* element is in Outlook Web Access, which shades suggestion days in its day-picker user interface (UI) to assist the

---

[10] Conceivably, but quite unlikely.

user in finding good days. Figure 21-7 is an example of the day-picker UI in Outlook Web Access.

FIGURE 21-7 Example of the Outlook Web Access Day-Picker UI with day quality color coding

SuggestionArray

The *SuggestionArray* element is an array of *Suggestion* elements where each *Suggestion* element represents a suggestion for the associated day. Although the *SuggestionArray* element is optional, Exchange Web Services always returns the element. But if there are no suggestions for that day, the element will be empty. An empty *SuggestionArray* could result if you call the *GetUserAvailiabilityRequest* Web method with a *DetailedSuggestionsWindow* that spans several days and a *MiminumSuggestionQuality* equal to *Excellent*. In this case, Exchange Web Services may return a *SuggestionDayResult* with a *DayQuality* of *Poor* and an empty *SuggestionArray* (because none of the potential suggestion times on that day met the criteria). Listing 21-49 is an example of a *SuggestionDayResult* with an empty *SuggestionArray* element.

LISTING 21-49 Example of a *SuggestionDayResult* with an empty *SuggestionArray*

```
<m:SuggestionDayResultArray xmlns:m=".../types" xmlns:t=".../types">
  <t:SuggestionDayResult >
    <t:Date>2007-05-12T00:00:00</t:Date>
    <t:DayQuality>Poor</t:DayQuality>
    <t:SuggestionArray />
  </t:SuggestionDayResult>
</m:SuggestionDayResultArray>
```

Suggestions

When Exchange Web Services returns a suggestion, it is represented by a *Suggestion* element inside the *SuggestionArray* of a *SuggestionDayResult*. The schema for the *Suggestion* type is shown in Listing 21-50.

LISTING 21-50 Schema of the *Suggestion* type

```
<xs:complexType name="Suggestion">
  <xs:sequence>
    <xs:element minOccurs="1" maxOccurs="1"
                name="MeetingTime" type="xs:dateTime" />
    <xs:element minOccurs="1" maxOccurs="1"
                name="IsWorkTime" type="xs:boolean" />
    <xs:element minOccurs="1" maxOccurs="1"
                name="SuggestionQuality"
                type="t:SuggestionQuality" />
    <xs:element minOccurs="0" maxOccurs="1"
                name="AttendeeConflictDataArray"
                type="t:ArrayOfAttendeeConflictData" />
  </xs:sequence>
</xs:complexType>
```

MeetingTime Element of *Suggestion*

The *MeetingTime* element is a string in the *xs:dateTime* format whose value represents the time of the suggestion.

```
<Suggestion>
  <MeetingTime>2007-05-09T14:00:00-07:00</MeetingTime>
  <IsWorkTime>true</IsWorkTime>
  <SuggestionQuality>Excellent</SuggestionQuality>
  <!-- AttendeeConflictDataArray omitted for brevity -->
</Suggestion>
```

> **Important** The *date/time* string in a *MeetingTime* element of a *Suggestion* incorrectly contains a UTC offset. The Exchange Web Services team recommends that you *ignore* the UTC offset that is present in the *MeetingTime* element. For more information, see the section titled "Understanding Time Zone Issues with *Suggestions*" later in this chapter.

IsWorkTime

The *IsWorkTime* element is a Boolean value that indicates if the suggestion time falls outside of the working hours of the organizer. Recall that by default the *MaximumNonWorkHourResultsByDay* value of the *SuggestionsViewOptions* is 0, meaning you will not see this value ever returned as false unless the you set *MaximumNonWorkHourResultsByDay* in your *SuggestionsViewOptions* to be greater then 0.

SuggestionQuality

The *SuggestionQuality* element is a string that maps to the *SuggestionQuality* enumeration shown in Listing 21-46. The value of *SuggestionQuality* represents the quality level of a suggestion time. The quality of a suggestion time is determined by Exchange Web Services; however, the criteria for setting a quality value of *Good* versus *Fair* can be impacted by setting the *GoodThreshold* value in your *SuggestionsViewOptions*.

An attendee's role is used by Exchange Web Services to influence the quality level of each suggested time that will be returned. For example, consider a meeting with three required attendees and three optional attendees. A suggestion time where one of the three required attendees and three of the optional attendees can attend will be given a lower quality level than a suggestion time where two of the three required and three of the three optional can attend. While the purpose of this chapter is not to go into detail about how the quality level for a suggestion time is determined, Table 21-8 gives you the general description of what a quality level on a suggestion means.

TABLE 21-8 Explanation of a *SuggestionQuality* value

SuggestionQuality value	Explanation
Excellent	All required attendees and nearly all optional attendees have this suggestion time free, and many resources are available
Good	The percentage of required attendees that have this suggestion time free is greater than the *GoodThreshold* value, and many resources are available.
Fair	The percentage of required attendees that have this suggestion time free is less than the *GoodThreshold* value, and some resources are available.
Poor	Few required attendees have this suggestion time free.

Attendee Conflict Data

Each suggestion includes information about any attendees that may have a conflict with the suggestion time. This information is returned in the *AttendeeConflictDataArray* element of a *Suggestion*. Attendee conflict data can appear in one of four different formats: as *individual* conflict data, as *group* conflict data, as *unknown attendee* conflict data, or as the absence of conflict data if an attendee group is too large.

The *AttendeeConflistDataArray* is of the *ArrayOfAttendeeConflictData* schema type, which is shown in Listing 21-51.

LISTING 21-51 Schema of the *ArrayOfAttendeeConflictData* type

```
<xs:complexType name="ArrayOfAttendeeConflictData" xmlns:xs="t">
  <xs:choice minOccurs="0" maxOccurs="unbounded">
    <xs:element minOccurs="1" maxOccurs="1"
                name="UnknownAttendeeConflictData" nillable="true"
                type="t:UnknownAttendeeConflictData" />
    <xs:element minOccurs="1" maxOccurs="1"
                name="IndividualAttendeeConflictData"
                nillable="true"
                type="t:IndividualAttendeeConflictData" />
    <xs:element minOccurs="1" maxOccurs="1"
                name="TooBigGroupAttendeeConflictData"
                nillable="true"
                type="t:TooBigGroupAttendeeConflictData" />
    <xs:element minOccurs="1" maxOccurs="1"
                name="GroupAttendeeConflictData" nillable="true"
                type="t:GroupAttendeeConflictData" />
  </xs:choice>
</xs:complexType>
```

The *AttendeeConflictDataArray* element will always be present on a *Suggestion*; however, this does not necessarily mean that any of the attendees have a conflict with the suggestion time represented by the *Suggestion*. If each attendee has no conflict with the suggestion time, then the *AttendeeConflictDataArray* will contain *IndividualAttendeeConflictData* elements, each with its own *BusyType* value of *Free*.

```
<Suggestion>
  <MeetingTime>2007-09-26T14:00:00-07:00</MeetingTime>
  <IsWorkTime>true</IsWorkTime>
  <SuggestionQuality>Excellent</SuggestionQuality>
  <AttendeeConflictDataArray>
    <IndividualAttendeeConflictData>
      <BusyType>Free</BusyType>
    </IndividualAttendeeConflictData>
    <IndividualAttendeeConflictData>
      <BusyType>Free</BusyType>
    </IndividualAttendeeConflictData>
  </AttendeeConflictDataArray>
</Suggestion>
```

We will discuss the *IndividualAttendeeConflictData* element and the *BusyType* element shortly.

An *AttendeeConflictDataArray* will always have at least one of the child elements shown in the schema in Listing 21-51 for each attendee represented by a *MailboxData* element in your *GetUserAvailabilityRequest*. Like the *FreeBusyResponseArray*, every element in the *AttendeeConflictDataArray* corresponds to a *MailboxData* element such that *MailboxDataArray[x] = AttendeeConflictDataArray[x]*.

UnknownAttendeeConflictData

The presence of an *UnknownAttendeeConflictData* element in an *AttendeeConflictDataArray* indicates that Exchange Web Services was *unable* to retrieve free/busy information for an attendee (for example, an incorrect e-mail address was supplied or the Client Access Server was unable to communicate with the attendee's Mailbox Server).

An *UnknownAttendeeConflictData* element will contain no additional information. However, you can take advantage of its location in the *AttendeeConflictDataArray* to find the corresponding *MailboxData* element for the attendee in question.

IndividualAttendeeConflictData

The presence of an *IndividualAttendeeConflictData* element indicates that Exchange Web Services was able to retrieve the free/busy status of an attendee for the suggestion time. An *IndividualAttendeeConflictData* element contains one child element, *BusyType*. The *BusyType* element is a string that maps to the *LegacyFreeBusyType* enumeration. The value is simply the free/busy status of the attendee for the suggestion time. Listing 21-52 is an example of an *AttendeeConflictDataArray* with two *IndividualAttendeeConflictData* elements.

LISTING 21-52 Example of *AttendeeConflictDataArray* for two individual participants

```
<t:AttendeeConflictDataArray xmlns:t=".../types">
  <t:IndividualAttendeeConflictData>
    <t:BusyType>Busy</t:BusyType>
  </t:IndividualAttendeeConflictData>
  <t:IndividualAttendeeConflictData>
    <t:BusyType>Free</t:BusyType>
  </t:IndividualAttendeeConflictData>
</t:AttendeeConflictDataArray>
```

TooBigGroupAttendeeConflictData

The presence of a *TooBigGroupAttendeeConflictData* element in an *AttendeeConflictDataArray* indicates that Exchange Web Services was unable to obtain free/busy information for members of a DL due to the size of the DL itself.[11] No additional information will be contained in a *TooBigGroupAttendeeConflictData* element.

GroupAttendeeConflictData

The presence of a *GroupAttendeeConflictData* element indicates that Exchange Web Services was able to retrieve free/busy information for some, if not all, of the members of a DL. The

---

[11] How big is too big? Because Exchange Web Services might have to request free/busy information from multiple servers, an internal algorithm determines—based on the predicted number of hops—if it should return this element. As such, there really is no set value. We have it on good authority though that it is "large enough."

GroupAttendeeConflictData element will use four child elements to return information about how much free busy information Exchange Web Services was able to return. Those four elements and the information they report is shown in Table 21-9

TABLE 21-9 Information About a DL Returned by Each Element of *GroupAttendeeConflictData*

Element name	Information described
NumberOfMembers	The total number of members in the DL
NumberOfMembersAvailable	The number of members in the DL that are free during the suggestion time
NumberOfMembersWithConflict	The number of members in the DL that are *not* free during the suggestion time
NumberOfMembersWithNoData	The number of members in the DL for which Exchange Web Services was unable to determine free/busy status for the suggestion time

Listing 21-53 shows an example of a result for a *Suggestion* with a *GroupAttendeeConflictData* element.

LISTING 21-53 *Suggestion* with *GroupAttendeeConflictData*

```
<Suggestion>
  <MeetingTime>2007-05-11T08:00:00-07:00</MeetingTime>
  <IsWorkTime>true</IsWorkTime>
  <SuggestionQuality>Poor</SuggestionQuality>
  <AttendeeConflictDataArray>
    <GroupAttendeeConflictData>
      <NumberOfMembers>2</NumberOfMembers>
      <NumberOfMembersAvailable>0</NumberOfMembersAvailable>
      <NumberOfMembersWithConflict>2</NumberOfMembersWithConflict>
      <NumberOfMembersWithNoData>0</NumberOfMembersWithNoData>
    </GroupAttendeeConflictData>
  </AttendeeConflictDataArray>
</Suggestion>
```

Understanding Time Zone Issues with *Suggestions*

When Exchange Web Services returns *Suggestion* elements in a *SuggestionsResponse*, the *date/time* strings in each *MeetingTime* element will contain a UTC offset. Similar to the *StartTime* and *EndTime* on a *CalendarEvent* element, the *time* portion of the *date/time* string in a *MeetingTime* element is correct with regard to the time zone information defined in the *TimeZone* element of your *GetUserAvailabilityRequest*. The UTC offset, however, will always be that of the current time zone bias of the Client Access Server that is processing the request. Listing 21-54 highlights the UTC offset that is present in the *MeetingTime* element of a *Suggestion*.

LISTING 21-54 Example of a *Suggestion* highlighting the UTC offset present in the *MeetingTime* element

```
<Suggestion>
  <MeetingTime>2007-05-09T14:00:00-07:00</MeetingTime>
  <IsWorkTime>true</IsWorkTime>
  <SuggestionQuality>Excellent</SuggestionQuality>
  <!-- AttendeeConflictDataArray omitted for brevity -->
</Suggestion>
```

We explained the details of this issue when we discussed *CalendarEvents* in the "Understanding Time Zone Issues with *CalendarEvents*" section earlier in this chapter. Therefore, we will not look into details of the issue here since the recommended steps to work around this issue with regards to *MeetingTime* elements is the same.

Important Unlike *date/time* strings in *CalendarEvent* elements, the UTC offset issue in *MeetingTime* elements is *not* scheduled to be fixed in the next service pack of Exchange Server 2007.

Applications that work directly with XML should ignore UTC offsets in the *MeetingTime* element of a *Suggestion*. Applications that use the proxy classes will require a proxy extension class for the *Suggestion* type that implements the *IXmlSerializable* interface in order to work around the issue.

Overcoming Incorrect *Suggestion MeetingTime* Values with *IXmlSerializable*

More Info This section is not intended to be a detailed look at the *IXmlSerializable* interface, but rather a brief explanation for the purposes of describing a workaround necessary for Exchange Web Services applications. For more information on the *IXmlSerializable* interface, see the documenatation on the MSDN Website:

http://msdn2.microsoft.com/en-us/library/system.xml.serialization.ixmlserializable(vs.80).aspx

To work around the incorrect *Suggestion* time issue with the proxy classes, you need to create a proxy extension class for the *Suggestion* type that implements the *IXmlSerializable* interface. Begin by locating the *XmlTypeAttribute* for the *Suggestion* class in the file containing your auto-generated proxy classes, then comment out the line containing the *XmlTypeAttribute* attribute. Listing 21-55 shows the end result of this action.

LISTING 21-55 Commenting out the *XmlTypeAttribute* on the *Suggestion* proxy class

```
/// <remarks/>
[System.CodeDom.Compiler.GeneratedCodeAttribute("wsdl", "2.0.50727.42")]
```

```
[System.SerializableAttribute()]
[System.Diagnostics.DebuggerStepThroughAttribute()] [System.ComponentModel.DesignerCat
egoryAttribute("code")]
//[System.Xml.Serialization.XmlTypeAttribute(...)]
public partial class Suggestion {

        private System.DateTime meetingTimeField;

        private bool isWorkTimeField;

        private SuggestionQuality suggestionQualityField;

        ...
}
```

Next, supply implementations for the *GetSchema, ReadXml,* and *WriteXml* methods. In the *ReadXml* and *WriteXml* methods, you will be responsible for handling all the XML serialization and deserialization for the *MeetingTime, IsWorkTime, SuggestionQuality,* and *AttendeeConflictDataArray* elements.

Listing 21-56 is a very large listing of a proxy extension for the *Suggestion* class that implements *IXmlSerializable* in order to fix the issue of Exchange Web Services returning an incorrect UTC offset in the *MeetingTime* element of a *Suggestion.* The fix is implemented in the *ReadXml* method and involves using a regular expression to parse the *date/time* string for date and time information only.

LISTING 21-56 Proxy extension for *Suggestion* that implements *IXmlSerializable*

```
///<summary>
/// Proxy extension for Suggestion that implements IXmlSerializable.
/// The purpose of this extension is to control the XML for the MeetingTime
/// propery during de-serialization due to a problem in the Exchange Server
/// where the date/time string in this property incorrectly contains the UTC
/// offset of the Client Access Server processing the
/// GetUserAvailabilityRequest.
///</summary>
///<remarks>
/// For this to work, the XmlTypeAttribute that the proxy generator places on
/// this class in the auto-generated .cs file must be removed
/// E.g.
///<code>
///      [System.CodeDom.Compiler.GeneratedCodeAttribute("wsdl", "2.0.50727.42")]
///      [System.SerializableAttribute()]
///      [System.Diagnostics.DebuggerStepThroughAttribute()]
///      [System.ComponentModel.DesignerCategoryAttribute("code")]
///      //[System.Xml.Serialization.XmlTypeAttribute(Namespace="...")]
///      public partial class Suggestion {...}
///</code>
///</remarks>
public partial class Suggestion : IXmlSerializable
```

```
{
    /// <summary>
    /// Empty constructor, required for partial class implementations
    /// </summary>
    public Suggestion()
    { }


    /// <summary>
    /// Returns an XmlSchema for the Suggestion that describes the
    /// XML representation of the output that is produced by the WriteXml
    /// method and consumed by the ReadXmlMethod
    /// </summary>
    /// <returns>XmlSchema for the Suggestion</returns>
    public System.Xml.Schema.XmlSchema GetSchema()
    {
        // This method must return
        //<xs:schema
        //        id="types"
        //        elementFormDefault="qualified"
        //        version="Exchange2007"
        //        xmlns:t=".../types"
        //        targetNamespace=".../types"
        //        xmlns:tns=".../types"
        //        xmlns:xs="http://www.w3.org/2001/XMLSchema">
        // <xs:complexType name="Suggestion">
        //  <xs:sequence>
        //    <xs:element minOccurs="1" maxOccurs="1" name="MeetingTime"
        //              type="xs:dateTime" />
        //    <xs:element minOccurs="1" maxOccurs="1" name="IsWorkTime"
        //              type="xs:boolean" />
        //    <xs:element minOccurs="1" maxOccurs="1"
        //              name="SuggestionQuality"
        //              type="t:SuggestionQuality" />
        //    <xs:element minOccurs="0" maxOccurs="1"
        //              name="AttendeeConflictDataArray"
        //              type="t:ArrayOfAttendeeConflictData" />
        //  </xs:sequence>
        // </xs:complexType>

        string xsTypes =
            "http://schemas.microsoft.com/exchange/services/2006/types";
        string xsSchema = "http://www.w3.org/2001/XMLSchema";

        XmlSchema schema = new XmlSchema();
        schema.Id = "types";
        schema.ElementFormDefault = XmlSchemaForm.Qualified;
        schema.Version = "Exchange2007";
        schema.TargetNamespace = xsTypes;

        // <xs:complexType ... >
        XmlSchemaComplexType xmlct1 = new XmlSchemaComplexType();
        schema.Items.Add(xmlct1);
        xmlct1.Name = "Suggestion";
```

```csharp
    //   <xs:sequence ... >
    XmlSchemaSequence xmlsq1 = new XmlSchemaSequence();
    xmlct1.Particle = xmlsq1;

    //    <xs:element ... name="MeetingTime" ... />
    XmlSchemaElement xmle1 = new XmlSchemaElement();
    xmlsq1.Items.Add(xmle1);
    xmle1.Name = "MeetingTime";
    xmle1.MinOccurs = 1;
    xmle1.MaxOccurs = 1;
    xmle1.SchemaTypeName = new XmlQualifiedName("dateTime", xsSchema);

    //    <xs:element ... name="IsWorkTime" ... />
    XmlSchemaElement xmle2 = new XmlSchemaElement();
    xmlsq1.Items.Add(xmle2);
    xmle2.Name = "IsWorkTime";
    xmle2.MinOccurs = 1;
    xmle2.MaxOccurs = 1;
    xmle2.SchemaTypeName = new XmlQualifiedName("boolean", xsSchema);

    //    <xs:element ... name="SuggestionQuality" ... />
    XmlSchemaElement xmle3 = new XmlSchemaElement();
    xmlsq1.Items.Add(xmle3);
    xmle3.Name = "SuggestionQuality";
    xmle3.MinOccurs = 1;
    xmle3.MaxOccurs = 1;
    xmle3.SchemaTypeName = new XmlQualifiedName(
        "SuggestionQuality", xsTypes);

    //    <xs:element ... name="AttendeeConflictDataArray" ... />
    XmlSchemaElement xmle4 = new XmlSchemaElement();
    xmlsq1.Items.Add(xmle4);
    xmle4.Name = "AttendeeConflictDataArray";
    xmle4.MinOccurs = 0;
    xmle4.MaxOccurs = 1;
    xmle4.SchemaTypeName = new XmlQualifiedName(
        "ArrayOfAttendeeConflictData", xsTypes);

    return schema;
}


/// <summary>
/// Generates a Suggestion object from it's XML representation
/// </summary>
/// <param name="reader">XmlReader posistioned at the start node
/// of the Suggestion XML</param>
public void ReadXml(System.Xml.XmlReader reader)
{
    string xsTypes =
        "http://schemas.microsoft.com/exchange/services/2006/types";

    // Store the LocalName of the element we are currently at.
    // This should be "Suggestion".
    //
```

```
        // This also serves as our key to our position in the stream.
        // Once we reach an EndElement with this name, then we
        // are done with our portion of the XmlStream.
        //
        string toplevelElementName = reader.LocalName;
        reader.Read();

        while (true)
        {
            // Check to see if we are done processing
            if ((reader.NodeType == XmlNodeType.EndElement) &&
                (0 == String.Compare(reader.LocalName, toplevelElementName)))
            {
                // We are done, consume this EndElement and stop processing
                reader.Read();
                break;
            }

            if (reader.NodeType == XmlNodeType.EndElement)
            {
                // This likely means we are at the closing tag of
                // </AttendeeConflictDataArray>
                // No data here to process.
                reader.Read();
                continue;
            }

            // Consume MeetingTime
            if (0 == String.Compare(reader.LocalName, "MeetingTime"))
            {
                // MeetingTime is the primary reason we needed to implement
                // IXmlSerializable, the server will always append a UTC offset
                // to the date/time string in the MeetingTime element.  This
                // offset can not be trusted.  The 'time' of the suggestion is
                // always valid if treated as Local time.
                //
                // We will use a Regular Expression to extract whatever was
                // supplied as a local time only
                //
                string meetingTimeValue = reader.ReadElementContentAsString();
                System.Text.RegularExpressions.Regex regex =
                    new System.Text.RegularExpressions.Regex(
                        @"(?<datetime>\d{4}-\d{2}-\d{2}T\d{2}:\d{2}:\d{2})",
                        System.Text.RegularExpressions.RegexOptions.Compiled);

                string nonUTCOffsettingString =
                    regex.Match(meetingTimeValue).Result("${datetime}");
                this.meetingTimeField = DateTime.Parse(nonUTCOffsettingString);
            }

            // Consume IsWorkTime
            if (0 == String.Compare(reader.LocalName, "IsWorkTime"))
            {
                this.isWorkTimeField = reader.ReadElementContentAsBoolean();
```

```
        }

        // Consume SuggestionQuality
        if (0 == String.Compare(reader.LocalName, "SuggestionQuality"))
        {
            string value = reader.ReadElementContentAsString();
            this.suggestionQualityField =
                (SuggestionQuality)Enum.Parse(typeof
                    (SuggestionQuality), value);
        }

        // Consume AttendeeConflictDataArray
        if (0 == String.Compare(reader.LocalName,
            "AttendeeConflictDataArray"))
        {
            // Unfortunately, the XmlSerializer can't just de-serialize an
            // array of items, therefore we need to look at the types of
            // each indivudal elements of the array and de-serialize them
            // based on their type.
            XmlDocument xmld = new XmlDocument();
            string outerXml = reader.ReadOuterXml();
            xmld.LoadXml(outerXml);

            if (!xmld.HasChildNodes)
            {
                // This an an empty AttendeeConflictDataArray, so were done.
                this.attendeeConflictDataArrayField =
                    new AttendeeConflictData[0];
                continue;
            }

            XmlNodeList attendeeConflictNodes = xmld.FirstChild.ChildNodes;
            List<AttendeeConflictData> attendeeConflictDataList =
                new List<AttendeeConflictData>(attendeeConflictNodes.Count);

            foreach (XmlNode xmln in attendeeConflictNodes)
            {
                if (0 == String.Compare(xmln.Name,
                    "IndividualAttendeeConflictData"))
                {
                    using (System.IO.StringReader strdr =
                        new System.IO.StringReader(xmln.OuterXml))
                    {
                        XmlSerializer xmls =
                            new XmlSerializer(
                                typeof(IndividualAttendeeConflictData),
                                xsTypes);

                        attendeeConflictDataList.Add(
                            (IndividualAttendeeConflictData)
                            xmls.Deserialize(strdr));
                    }
                }
                if (0 == String.Compare(xmln.Name,
```

```
                        "GroupAttendeeConflictData"))
        {
            using (System.IO.StringReader strdr =
                new System.IO.StringReader(xmln.OuterXml))
            {
                XmlSerializer xmls =
                    new XmlSerializer(
                        typeof(GroupAttendeeConflictData),
                        xsTypes);

                attendeeConflictDataList.Add(
                    (GroupAttendeeConflictData)
                    xmls.Deserialize(strdr));
            }
        }
        if (0 == String.Compare(xmln.Name,
            "UnknownAttendeeConflictData"))
        {
            using (System.IO.StringReader strdr =
                new System.IO.StringReader(xmln.OuterXml))
            {
                XmlSerializer xmls =
                    new XmlSerializer(
                        typeof(UnknownAttendeeConflictData),
                        xsTypes);

                attendeeConflictDataList.Add(
                    (UnknownAttendeeConflictData)
                    xmls.Deserialize(strdr));
            }
        }
        if (0 == String.Compare(xmln.Name,
            "TooBigGroupAttendeeConflictData"))
        {
            using (System.IO.StringReader strdr =
                new System.IO.StringReader(xmln.OuterXml))
            {
                XmlSerializer xmls =
                    new XmlSerializer(
                        typeof(TooBigGroupAttendeeConflictData),
                        xsTypes);

                attendeeConflictDataList.Add(
                    (TooBigGroupAttendeeConflictData)
                    xmls.Deserialize(strdr));
            }
        }
    }

    // Convert our list of AttendeeConflictData to an array
    this.attendeeConflictDataArrayField =
        attendeeConflictDataList.ToArray();
    }
}
```

```
    }

    /// <summary>
    /// Converts a Suggestion object into its XML representation
    /// </summary>
    /// <param name="writer">XmlWriter positioned at the point
    /// to which the XML for this object is to be written to</param>
    public void WriteXml(System.Xml.XmlWriter writer)
    {
        string xsTypes =
            "http://schemas.microsoft.com/exchange/services/2006/types";

        // Our position in the writer already includes a StartElement
        // for our type, therefore, our job is to pickup writing to the
        // stream all of our properties.

        // Write Meeting Time
        writer.WriteElementString("MeetingTime",
            System.Xml.XmlConvert.ToString(
                (DateTime)this.meetingTimeField,
                XmlDateTimeSerializationMode.RoundtripKind));

        // Write IsWorkTime
        writer.WriteElementString("IsWorkTime", xsTypes,
            this.isWorkTimeField.ToString());

        // Write Suggestion Quality
        writer.WriteElementString("SuggestionQuality", xsTypes,
            this.suggestionQualityField.ToString());

        // Write AttendeeConflictDataArray
        XmlSerializer xmls = new XmlSerializer(
            typeof(AttendeeConflictData[]), xsTypes);
        xmls.Serialize(writer, this.attendeeConflictDataArrayField);
    }
}
```

Once the code is commented out as in Listing 21-55 and the class in Listing 21-56 is compiled in with your proxy code, the .NET Framework will call these methods during serialization/deserialization of any *Suggestion* instances. Like you did for *CalendarEvent* class in the *ReadXml()* method for the *Suggestion* class, you use a *RegularExpression* to parse the *date/ time* string, meaning your code is forward compatible if/when a fix is released for Exchange Server 2007 in the future.

Getting Suggestion Information with the Proxy Classes

With the proxy extension for the *Suggestion* class from Listing 21-55 and Listing 21-56 included, Listing 21-57 shows how to enumerate through a *SuggestionsDayResult* array and display each *Suggestion* instance, associating the attendee conflict data with the corresponding *MailboxData* entry from the request. (Hint: You could take advantage of this method from inside the code in Listing 21-12 while you are parsing a *GetUserAvailabilityResponse*.)

LISTING 21-57 Example of displaying suggestion information from a *FreeBusyResponseType* via the proxy classes

```
/// <summary>
/// Displays to the console each of the suggestions that are included in the
/// provided SuggestionDayResult array.
/// </summary>
/// <param name="suggestionDays">Array of SuggestedDayResults</param>
/// <param name="participants">MailboxData array that was used in the
/// GetUserAvailabilityRequest instance.</param>
public static void PrintSuggestionsInformation(
    SuggestionDayResult[] suggestionDays,
    MailboxData[] attendees)
{
    foreach (SuggestionDayResult suggestionDay in suggestionDays)
    {
        Console.WriteLine("Suggestion Day ({0}): {1}",
            suggestionDay.DayQuality,
            suggestionDay.Date);

        foreach (Suggestion suggestion in suggestionDay.SuggestionArray)
        {
            Console.WriteLine("Time ({0}): {1}",
                suggestion.SuggestionQuality,
                suggestion.MeetingTime);

            // Display conflict information, there should be an entry
            // in the AttendeeConflictDataArray for each attendee.
            int numberOfUnknownOrTooBigParticipants = 0;
            for (int x = 0;
                x < suggestion.AttendeeConflictDataArray.Length;
                x++)
            {
                string participantName = attendees[x].Email.Name;
                if (String.IsNullOrEmpty(participantName))
                    participantName = attendees[x].Email.Address;

                AttendeeConflictData attendeeConflictData =
                    suggestion.AttendeeConflictDataArray[x];
                if (attendeeConflictData is IndividualAttendeeConflictData)
                {
                    IndividualAttendeeConflictData individualConflictData =
                        (IndividualAttendeeConflictData)attendeeConflictData;

                    Console.WriteLine("{0} is {1}",
                        participantName,
                        individualConflictData.BusyType);
                }
                if (attendeeConflictData is GroupAttendeeConflictData)
                {
                    GroupAttendeeConflictData groupConflictData =
                        (GroupAttendeeConflictData)attendeeConflictData;

                    Console.WriteLine("The \"{0}\" group has:" +
```

```
                        "\r\n\t{1} Available" +
                        "\r\n\t{2} Conflicting" +
                        "\r\n\t{3} With No Data Available",
                    participantName,
                    groupConflictData.NumberOfMembersAvailable,
                    groupConflictData.NumberOfMembersWithConflict,
                    groupConflictData.NumberOfMembersWithNoData);
            }
            if (attendeeConflictData is UnknownAttendeeConflictData ||
                attendeeConflictData is TooBigGroupAttendeeConflictData)
            {
                numberOfUnknownOrTooBigParticipants++;
            }
        }

        if (numberOfUnknownOrTooBigParticipants > 0)
        {
            Console.WriteLine("You have {0} participant(s) that are " +
                "invalid.",
                numberOfUnknownOrTooBigParticipants);
        }
    }
    Console.WriteLine();
}
}
```

Figure 21-8 is an example of the console output from the *PrintSuggestionsInformation* method from Listing 21-57.

FIGURE 21-8 Sample output from the *PrintSuggestionsInformation* method

Summary

This chapter covered getting availability of users using the *GetUserAvailability* Web method. We explained that the term Availability involves five concepts: Attendees, Working Hours, Time zones, Free/Busy Information, and Suggestions. We began by looking at the *GetUserAvailiabilityRequest* and how to check for success in all of the various elements of the *GetUserAvailabilityResponse*.

We then described how time zone information is defined for a *GetUserAvailabilityRequest* via the *TimeZone* element. We also described how attendees are represented by *MailboxData* elements in the *MailboxDataArray*. We explained that Exchange Web Services will attempt to retrieve the free/busy information from each attendee and will use that information to generate suggested meeting times for each attendee if your request asks for them.

We then described the *FreeBusyViewOptions* and how all of its elements can affect the free/busy information for each attendee that is returned in a *FreeBusyView*. We looked at the *SuggestionViewOptions* and likewise described how all of its elements can affect suggestions that are returned in a *SuggestionsResponse*.

This chapter also included two large proxy class extensions for the *CalendarEvent* type and *Suggestion* type to work around issues with Exchange Web Services returning UTC offsets in the *date/time* strings of these elements that may be incorrect.

Chapter 22
Out Of Office Settings

In Chapter 21, "Availability," we talked about the telephone, espousing its usefulness in multi-party communication but lamenting its flaws when it comes to multi-party coordination. Well, nearly every telephone in the home today has a companion device. Often these devices are so integrated that we rarely think of them as ever having been separate. These devices are answering machines. These excellent telephone companion devices come in all shapes and sizes, but all are designed to deliver on essentially the same two features.

1. Play a recorded message informing those trying to reach you that you are currently unavailable.

2. Allow those trying to reach you to leave a message indicating their desire to reach you and their reason for calling.

In the digital messaging world, there is also a need for a mechanism that delivers on these two features. The second feature, where people can leave a message for you, is covered by the e-mail features in Microsoft Exchange Server 2007 Web Services (EWS). The first feature, which can be thought of as automatically sending an e-mail message to someone who just sent an e-mail message to you, is accomplished though Out Of Office (OOF) reply messages. Microsoft Exchange Server 2007 can be configured, through the use of Out Of Office settings (or OOF settings), to automatically reply to new e-mail messages in your mailbox with an OOF reply message on your behalf. The Exchange Server will use the OOF settings that you establish to determine which e-mail addresses should receive OOF reply messages and can determine the message body of those OOF reply messages. Figure 22-1 shows an example via Microsoft Office Outlook Web Access (OWA) of what an OOF reply message might look like to a message recipient.

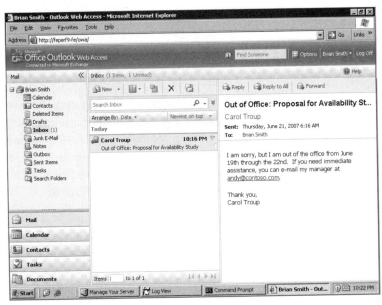

FIGURE 22-1 Example of a received Out Of Office reply message

You have a number of options available to you when setting your OOF settings. For example, you can configure the Exchange Server to send OOF reply messages only to internal e-mail addresses (members of your organization, for example) or to include external e-mail addresses as well. Another option allows you to configure the Exchange Server to send to an external e-mail address only if that e-mail address is a *known* e-mail address. The Exchange Server considers a *known* e-mail address to be one that is present on any of the contact items in your Contacts folder

Note Microsoft Exchange Server 2007 allows administrators to set an organizational policy that can restrict the sending of OOF messages. This policy can prevent the Exchange Server from sending OOF reply messages to any and all external e-mail addresses, or to allow OOF reply messages to be sent to external e-mail addresses only if they are *known* e-mail addresses. This chapter will not go into how this OOF reply message policy is defined, but we will explain how you can find out what the policy setting is.

Another option you have with OOF settings is to configure the Exchange Server to send OOF reply messages only during a specified date range. This is known as a *scheduled* OOF.

Important When you set your OOF settings via Exchange Web Services, Exchange Web Services will not automatically set the free/busy status on your calendar to OOF. In other words, setting your OOF settings via Exchange Web Services will inform people who send you an e-mail message that you are out of the office based on the OOF reply message they get back. However, people who ask for your availability (via the *GetUserAvailability* Web method, for example) would not see that you are OOF unless you also have a calendar item in your Calendar folder with a free/busy status of *OOF* for the duration of time you are gone.

Introducing the *SetUserOofSettings* Web Method

You can set your OOF settings with Exchange Web Services by calling the *SetUserOofSettings* Web method. To call the *SetUserOofSettings* Web method via XML, you supply a *SetUserOofSettingsRequest* element in your call. The schema type for a *SetUserOofSettingsRequest* element is also named *SetUserOofSettingsRequest*, and is shown in Listing 22-1

LISTING 22-1 Schema for the *SetUserOofSettingsRequest* type

```
<xs:complexType name="SetUserOofSettingsRequest">
  <xs:complexContent mixed="false">
    <xs:extension base="m:BaseRequestType">
      <xs:sequence>
        <xs:element minOccurs="1" maxOccurs="1" ref="t:Mailbox" />
        <xs:element minOccurs="1" maxOccurs="1" ref="t:UserOofSettings" />
      </xs:sequence>
    </xs:extension>
  </xs:complexContent>
</xs:complexType>
```

Note In the proxy classes, the *SetUserOofSettings* Web method is called with the *SetUserOofSettings* method on your *ExchangeServiceBinding* instance. Note that the naming is slightly different. When using XML, you supply a *SetUserOofSettings**Request*** element as opposed to a *SetUserOofSettings* element. The same applies to the *GetUserOofSettings* Web method where the proxy class method is *GetUserOofSettings* but the XML request element is named *GetUserOofSettings**Request***.

There are three flags that can be used to configure when and if the Exchange Server should send OOF reply messages on your behalf. One flag configures the Exchange Server to begin sending OOF reply messages on your behalf instantly, while a second flag stops OOF reply messages being sent on your behalf immediately (for example, when you are back in the office). A third flag allows you to define a window of time when OOF reply messages should be sent.

Important Like the *GetUserAvailability* Web method, the *SetUserOofSettings* Web method (and the *GetUserOofSettings* Web method as well) requires that you specify the primary SMTP address of your mailbox in your *Mailbox* element even if you are trying to set or get your own OOF settings. While you are allowed to specify the primary SMTP address of another mailbox, Exchange Web Services will return a *Microsoft.Exchange.Data.Storage.AccessDeniedException* in a SOAP fault unless you have owner-level access to that mailbox as well.

Listing 22-2 is an example of calling the *SetUserOofSettings* Web method with a *SetUserOofSettingsRequest* element to configure the Exchange Server to start sending OOF reply messages immediately. The example also shows how to specify the OOF reply message body that should be sent to all internal e-mail addresses, and a second OOF reply message body that should be sent to external e-mail addresses only if they are *known* e-mail addresses.

LISTING 22-2 Example call to the *SetUserOofSettings* Web method

```
<m:SetUserOofSettingsRequest xmlns:m=".../messages"
                             xmlns:t=".../types">
  <t:Mailbox>
    <t:Address>carol@contoso.com</t:Address>
  </t:Mailbox>
  <t:UserOofSettings>
    <t:OofState>Enabled</t:OofState>
    <t:ExternalAudience>Known</t:ExternalAudience>
    <t:InternalReply>
      <t:Message>
        My internal OOF message.  This message will be sent to all e-mail
        recipients within my organizations e-mail system.
      </t:Message>
    </t:InternalReply>
    <t:ExternalReply>
      <t:Message>
        My external OOF message.  This message will be sent only to external
        e-mail addresses if the e-mail address happens to be in my Contacts
        folder.  This is because the ExternalAudience element in my request is
        set to Known.
      </t:Message>
    </t:ExternalReply>
  </t:UserOofSettings>
</m:SetUserOofSettingsRequest>
```

Mailbox Element in *SetUserOofSettingsRequest*

The *Mailbox* element in a *SetUserOofSettingsRequest* is of the schema type *EmailAddress* shown in Listing 22-3.[1]

LISTING 22-3 Schema for the *EmailAddress* type

```
<xs:complexType name="EmailAddress">
  <xs:sequence>
    <xs:element minOccurs="0" maxOccurs="1" name="Name" type="xs:string" />
    <xs:element minOccurs="1" maxOccurs="1" name="Address" type="xs:string" />
    <xs:element minOccurs="0" maxOccurs="1" name="RoutingType" type="xs:string" />
  </xs:sequence>
</xs:complexType>
```

---

1 Not to be confused with the *EmailAddressType* schema type, which has been used extensively in this book already.

When using an *EmailAddress* in a *Mailbox* element in a *SetUserOofSettingsRequest*, you need not be concerned with the *Name* and *RoutingType* elements. You need to provide only the *Address* element where the value is the primary SMTP address of the mailbox you are setting OOF settings for.

UserOofSettings Element in *SetUserOofSettingsRequest*

The *UserOofSettings* element in *SetUserOofSettingsRequest* defines all of the OOF settings options that are available to you. The *UserOofSettings* element is defined by the schema type of the same name, which is shown in Listing 22-4

LISTING 22-4 Schema for the *UserOofSettings* element

```
<xs:complexType name="UserOofSettings">
  <xs:sequence>
    <xs:element minOccurs="1" maxOccurs="1"
                name="OofState" type="t:OofState" />
    <xs:element minOccurs="1" maxOccurs="1"
                name="ExternalAudience"
                type="t:ExternalAudience" />
    <xs:element minOccurs="0" maxOccurs="1"
                name="Duration" type="t:Duration" />
    <xs:element minOccurs="0" maxOccurs="1"
                name="InternalReply" type="t:ReplyBody" />
    <xs:element minOccurs="0" maxOccurs="1"
                name="ExternalReply" type="t:ReplyBody" />
  </xs:sequence>
</xs:complexType>
```

OofState Element in *UserOofSettings*

The *OofState* element is a required string that maps to a value from the *OofState* enumeration shown in Listing 22-5

LISTING 22-5 Schema for the *OofState* enumeration

```
<xs:simpleType name="OofState">
  <xs:restriction base="xs:string">
    <xs:enumeration value="Disabled" />
    <xs:enumeration value="Enabled" />
    <xs:enumeration value="Scheduled" />
  </xs:restriction>
</xs:simpleType>
```

Setting the *OofState* value to *Enabled* will tell the Exchange Server to start sending OOF reply messages on your behalf immediately. Setting the *OofState* value to *Disabled* will tell the Exchange Server to stop sending OOF reply messages on your behalf immediately. Setting the *OofState* value to *Scheduled* will tell the Exchange Server to start sending OOF reply messages at a specific date and to stop sending them at another specific date. The start date and end date for sending OOF reply messages in scheduled OOF settings is defined in the *Duration* element of *UserOofSettings*, which we will explain shortly.

ExternalAudience Element in *UserOofSettings*

The *ExternalAudience* element is a string that maps to a value from the *ExternalAudience* enumeration shown in Listing 22-6.

LISTING 22-6 Schema for the *ExternalAudience* enumeration

```
<xs:simpleType name="ExternalAudience">
 <xs:restriction base="xs:string">
  <xs:enumeration value="None" />
  <xs:enumeration value="Known" />
  <xs:enumeration value="All" />
 </xs:restriction>
</xs:simpleType>
```

If you set the *ExternalAudience* in the *UserOofSettings* element of your request to *None*, you are telling the Exchange Server to not send OOF reply messages to any external e-mail addresses. A setting value of *All* indicates that OOF reply messages should be sent to all external e-mail addresses. Setting the *ExternalAudience* value to *Known* tells the Exchange Server to send OOF reply messages only to *known* external e-mail addresses.

All of the *ExternalAudience* values are subject to the organization's OOF reply message policy that we have been discussing in this chapter. For more information on the specifics of how the OOF reply message policy can overrule your *ExternalAudience* value, see the sidebar titled "Determining the Effective *ExternalAudience* Value in a *GetUserOofSettingsResponse*."

The *ExternalAudience* element is required, even when your request sets the *OofState* value to *Disabled*.

Duration Element in *UserOofSettings*

The *Duration* element is of schema type *Duration*, which, as discussed previously, has a required *StartTime* element and a required *EndTime* element, both of type *xs:dateTime*. The *StartTime* and *EndTime* elements of a *Duration* element in *UserOofSettings* tells the Exchange Server when to start and stop sending OOF reply messages on your behalf during a *scheduled* OOF.

Listing 22-7 shows an example of a *SetUserOofSettingsRequest* with an *OofState* value of *Scheduled* and a *Duration* element.

LISTING 22-7 Example call to the *SetUserOofSettings* Web method with scheduled OOF settings

```
<m:SetUserOofSettingsRequest xmlns:m=".../messages"
                             xmlns:t=".../types">
  <t:Mailbox>
    <t:Address>carol@contoso.com</t:Address>
  </t:Mailbox>
  <t:UserOofSettings>
    <t:OofState>Scheduled</t:OofState>
    <t:ExternalAudience>None</t:ExternalAudience>
    <t:Duration>
      <t:StartTime>2007-07-21T08:00:00-05:00</t:StartTime>
      <t:EndTime>2007-08-01T17:00:00-05:00</t:EndTime>
    </t:Duration>
    <t:InternalReply>
      <t:Message>
        I am sorry, but I am out of the office from June 15th through the 22nd.
        If you need immediate assistance, you can e-mail my manager at
        andy@contoso.com
      </t:Message>
    </t:InternalReply>
    <t:ExternalReply />
  </t:UserOofSettings>
</m:SetUserOofSettingsRequest>
```

Exchange Web Services requires the *Duration* element only if the *OofState* property is set to *Scheduled*. Exchange Web Services will return an *InvalidScheduledOofDuration* response code if your request has an *OofState* of *Scheduled* and does not include a *Duration* property. Exchange Web Services will also return an *InvalidScheduledOofDuration* message if your *Duration* property is invalid, for example, if it has a *StartTime* that is greater than the *EndTime* or if it has an *EndTime* value that occurs in the past.

> **Important** The *SetUserOofSettings* Web method does not have a property for describing the request's time zone information for the *Duration*. This means that you should always specify the *StartTime* and *EndTime* date/time strings with UTC offsets. The Exchange Web Services team recommends always using UTC time for *date/time* strings in *Duration* elements in a call to the *SetUserOofSettings* Web method.

InternalReply and *ExternalReply* Elements in *UserOofSettings*

The *InternalReply* and *ExternalReply* elements are both of the *ReplyBody* schema type, which is shown in Listing 22-8

LISTING 22-8 Schema for the *ReplyBody* type

```
<xs:complexType name="ReplyBody">
  <xs:sequence>
    <xs:element minOccurs="0" maxOccurs="1" name="Message" type="xs:string" />
  </xs:sequence>
  <xs:attribute ref="xml:lang" use="optional" />
</xs:complexType>
```

A *ReplyBody* contains only one element, called *Message,* which is a string. When used in an *InternalReply* element, the *Message* value is the message body that will be used for OOF reply messages destined for internal e-mail addresses. When used in an *ExternalReply* element, the *Message* value is the message body that will be used for OOF reply messages destined for external e-mail addresses.

The *ReplyBody* schema type will allow you to specify the language of the OOF reply message body by including the *xml:lang* attribute. In *InternalReply* or *ExternalReply* elements, you would place this attribute directly within the element itself. Listing 22-9 is an example of using an *InternalReply* element with an *xml:lang* attribute.

LISTING 22-9 Example of an *InternalReply* with an *xml:lang* attribute.

```
<m:SetUserOofSettingsRequest xmlns:m=".../messages" xmlns:t=".../types">
  <t:Mailbox>
    <t:Address>carol@contoso.com</t:Address>
  </t:Mailbox>
  <t:UserOofSettings>
    <t:OofState>Enabled</t:OofState>
    <t:ExternalAudience>None</t:ExternalAudience>
    <t:InternalReply xml:lang="es-ES">
      <t:Message>No estoy trabajando hoy.</t:Message>
    </t:InternalReply>
    <t:ExternalReply />
  </t:UserOofSettings>
</m:SetUserOofSettingsRequest>
```

Although *InternalReply* and *ExternalReply* are listed as optional in the schema, Exchange Web Services requires you to provide both of these elements in your request, even if your *OofState* value is *Disabled.* You can, however, provide the elements without a value and Exchange Web Services will accept them. Listing 22-10 is an example of a *SetUserOofSettingsRequest* with empty *InternalReply* and *ExternalReply* elements.

LISTING 22-10 Example call to the *SetUserOofSettings* Web method disabling OOF reply message sending

```
<m:SetUserOofSettingsRequest xmlns:m=".../messages" xmlns:t="http://.../types">
  <t:Mailbox>
    <t:Address>carol@contoso.com</t:Address>
  </t:Mailbox>
  <t:UserOofSettings>
    <t:OofState>Disabled</t:OofState>
    <t:ExternalAudience>None</t:ExternalAudience>
    <t:InternalReply />
    <t:ExternalReply />
  </t:UserOofSettings>
</m:SetUserOofSettingsRequest>
```

Understanding the *SetUserOofSettingsResponse*

The *SetUserOofSettings* Web method returns a *SetUserOofSettingsResponse*. The *SetUserOofSettingsResponse* is of the schema type of the same name shown in Listing 22-11

LISTING 22-11 Schema for the *SetUserOofSettingsResponse* type

```
<xs:complexType name="SetUserOofSettingsResponse">
  <xs:sequence>
    <xs:element minOccurs="0"
                maxOccurs="1"
                name="ResponseMessage"
                type="m:ResponseMessageType" />
  </xs:sequence>
</xs:complexType>
```

A *SetUserOofSettingsResponse* contains one element, and that element is the *ResponseMessage*. This makes working with a *SetUserOofSettingsResponse* easier then working with many of the other Exchange Web Services Web method responses. This is because there can be only one *ResponseMessage* that you need to check for a *ResponseClass* of *Success*.

```
<SetUserOofSettingsResponse xmlns=".../messages">
  <ResponseMessage ResponseClass="Success">
    <ResponseCode>NoError</ResponseCode>
  </ResponseMessage>
</SetUserOofSettingsResponse>
```

Setting User OOF Settings via the Proxy Classes

Listing 22-12 is a method that shows how to call the *SetUserOofSettings* Web method via the proxy classes to set scheduled OOF settings.

LISTING 22-12 Example of calling the a *SetUserOofSettings* Web method via the proxy classes

```
/// <summary>
/// Example of calling the SetUserOofSettingsRequest Web method to
/// create a scheduled OOF
/// </summary>
/// <param name="binding">Binding to make the call with</param>
/// <param name="userToSetOofFor">EmailAddress of the user
/// to set the OOF settings for.</param>
public static void SetUserOofSettings(
    ExchangeServiceBinding binding,
    EmailAddress userToSetOofFor)
{
    // Assemble the user OOF options, this example will set
    // a scheduled OOF for October 15th, 2007, through October 22nd, 2007,
    // and set an ExternalReply to be sent to all external recipients
    //
    Duration oofDuration = new Duration();
    oofDuration.StartTime =
        new DateTime(2007, 10, 15, 8, 0, 0, DateTimeKind.Utc);
    oofDuration.EndTime =
        new DateTime(2007, 10, 22, 17, 0, 0, DateTimeKind.Utc);

    ReplyBody internalReply = new ReplyBody();
    internalReply.Message = "I am sorry, but I am out of the office " +
        "from October 15th through the 22nd.  If you need immediate " +
        "assistance, you can e-mail my manager at andy@contoso.com" +
        "\r\n" +
        "Thank you, " +
        "Carol";

    ReplyBody externalReply = new ReplyBody();
    externalReply.Message = "I am sorry, but I am out of the office " +
        "at this time.  I shall attempt to respond to your e-mail " +
        "as soon as I possibly can." +
        "\r\n" +
        "Sincerely, " +
        "Carol Troup";

    UserOofSettings userOofSettings = new UserOofSettings();
    userOofSettings.OofState = OofState.Scheduled;
    userOofSettings.Duration = oofDuration;
    userOofSettings.ExternalAudience = ExternalAudience.All;
    userOofSettings.InternalReply = internalReply;
    userOofSettings.ExternalReply = externalReply;

    // Put together the SetUserOofSettingsRequest
    //
    SetUserOofSettingsRequest setUserOofReq = new
```

```
      SetUserOofSettingsRequest();
  setUserOofReq.Mailbox = userToSetOofFor;
  setUserOofReq.UserOofSettings = userOofSettings;

  // Send the request and check for any errors.  In the
  // SetUserOofSettingsResponse, there is one and only
  // one ResponseMessage.
  //
  SetUserOofSettingsResponse setUserOofResponse =
      binding.SetUserOofSettings(setUserOofReq);
  if (setUserOofResponse.ResponseMessage.ResponseClass !=
      ResponseClassType.Success)
  {
      // Indicate that we have a problem
      throw new Exception(String.Format(
          "Error in setting OOF settings.\r\n{0}\r\n{1}",
          setUserOofResponse.ResponseMessage.ResponseCode,
          setUserOofResponse.ResponseMessage.MessageText));
  }
}
```

Introducing the *GetUserOofSettings* Method

You can get your OOF settings with Exchange Web Services by calling the *GetUserOofSettings* Web method. To call the *GetUserOofSettings* Web method via XML, you supply a *GetUserOofSettingsRequest* element in your call. The schema type for a *GetUserOofSettingsRequest* element is also named *GetUserOofSettingsRequest* and is shown in Listing 22-13.

LISTING 22-13 Schema for the *GetUserOofSettingsRequest* type

```
<xs:complexType name="GetUserOofSettingsRequest">
  <xs:complexContent mixed="false">
    <xs:extension base="m:BaseRequestType">
      <xs:sequence>
        <xs:element minOccurs="1" maxOccurs="1" ref="t:Mailbox" />
      </xs:sequence>
    </xs:extension>
  </xs:complexContent>
</xs:complexType>
```

The *Mailbox* element in your *GetUserOofSettingsRequest* element defines which mailbox you want to get OOF settings for. Just as in a *SetUserOofSettingsRequest* element, Exchange Web Services requires you to provide the *Mailbox* element in your *GetUserOofSettingsRequest* element, even if you are requesting the OOF settings for your own mailbox. Also like a *SetUserOofSettingsRequest* element, you only need to provide the primary SMTP address of the mailbox in the *Address* element of the *Mailbox* in your request.

Listing 22-14 is an example of a call to the *GetUserOofSettings* Web method using a *GetUserOofSettingsRequest* element.

LISTING 22-14 Example of calling the *GetUserOofSettings* Web method.

```
<m:GetUserOofSettingsRequest xmlns:m="../messages"
                             xmlns:t="../types">
  <t:Mailbox>
    <t:Address>carol@contoso.com</t:Address>
  </t:Mailbox>
</m:GetUserOofSettingsRequest>
```

Understanding the *GetUserOofSettingsResponse*

The *GetUserOofSettings* Web method will return a *GetUserOofSettingsResponse*. The schema type for *GetUserOofSettingsResponse* is of the same name and is shown in Listing 22-15

LISTING 22-15 Schema for the *GetUserOofSettingsResponse* type

```
<xs:complexType name="GetUserOofSettingsResponse>
  <xs:sequence>
    <xs:element minOccurs="1" maxOccurs="1"
                name="ResponseMessage" type="m:ResponseMessageType" />
    <xs:element minOccurs="0" maxOccurs="1" ref="t:OofSettings" />
    <xs:element minOccurs="0" maxOccurs="1"
                name="AllowExternalOof" type="t:ExternalAudience" />
  </xs:sequence>
</xs:complexType>
```

A *GetUserOofSettingsResponse* includes the response class and response code in a single *ResponseMessage* as an element.

The *OofSettings* element in a *GetUserOofSettingsResponse* is of the schema *UserOofSettings*, which was shown in Listing 22-4. The *OofSettings* element contains all of the current OOF settings for mailbox.

Listing 22-17 shows an example of a *GetUserOofSettingsResponse*.

LISTING 22-17 Example of a *GetUserOofSettingsResponse*

```
<GetUserOofSettingsResponse xmlns=".../messages">
  <ResponseMessage ResponseClass="Success">
    <ResponseCode>NoError</ResponseCode>
  </ResponseMessage>
  <OofSettings xmlns=".../types">
    <OofState>Scheduled</OofState>
    <ExternalAudience>All</ExternalAudience>
    <Duration>
      <StartTime>2007-10-15T08:00:00Z</StartTime>
      <EndTime>2007-10-22T17:00:00Z</EndTime>
    </Duration>
    <InternalReply>
      <Message>
        I am sorry, but I am out of the office from October 15th through the
        22nd.  If you need immediate assistance, you can e-mail my manager at
        andy@contoso.com. Thank you, Carol
      </Message>
    </InternalReply>
    <ExternalReply>
      <Message>
        I am sorry, but I am out of the office at this time.  I shall attempt
        to respond to your e-mail as soon as I possibly can.
        Sincerely, Carol Troup
      </Message>
    </ExternalReply>
  </OofSettings>
  <AllowExternalOof>All</AllowExternalOof>
</GetUserOofSettingsResponse>
```

Important Although the *OofSettings* element in a *GetUserOofSettingsResponse* has all of the same elements as the *UserOofSettings* element in a *SetUserOofSettingsRequest*, it does not necessarily have the same values. For example, when you call the *SetUserOofSettings* Web method, and then call the *GetUserOofSettings* Web method, you may not get the same OOF settings every time. Between your two calls, the user may have set his/her OOF settings using some other client (such as Outlook Web Access), or the effective OOF settings may have been changed to adhere to organizational policy. See the description of each element in *OofSettings* below for details on how element values in a response may be different than in a request.

OofState Element in *OofSettings*

The *OofState* element in *OofSettings* is a string that maps to a value in the *OofState* enumeration (which was shown in Listing 22-5). The *OofState* element value reflects the value set by the user the last time he/she set the OOF settings.

The *OofState* value in a *GetUserOofSettingsResponse* does not change from *Scheduled* to *Enabled* or *Disabled* once the scheduled start and end times of the OOF settings have been reached. For example, imagine that you used Exchange Web Services to set your OOF settings. You defined the *OofState* in your *SetUserOofSettingsRequest* to *Scheduled* and set the *StartTime* to a value of 2007-10-01T01:00:00Z and the *EndTime* to a value of 2007-11-01T01:00:00Z. If you used the *GetUserOofSettings* Web method on October 15, 2007, then the *OofState* value in your *GetUserOofSettingsResponse* will be *Scheduled* even though the Exchange Server is actively sending OOF reply messages on your behalf. Likewise, if you called the *GetUserOofSettings* Web method on November 15, 2007, the *OofState* value would still be *Scheduled* even though your scheduled OOF is now complete, and the Exchange Server is no longer sending OOF reply messages on your behalf.

ExternalAudience Element in *OofSettings*

The *ExternalAudience* element in *OofSettings* reflects the value last set by the user. The *ExternalAudience* value *may not* represent the current effective setting that the Exchange Server is using with regard to sending external OOF reply messages on behalf of the user. Organizations are allowed to establish a policy that restricts the sending of external OOF reply messages, and that policy may be overriding the value chosen by the user.

For more information about the policy value and rules of enforcement regarding the sending of external OOF reply messages, see the sidebar entitled "Determining the Effective *ExternalAudience* Value in a *GetUserOofSettingsResponse*."

Duration Element in *OofSettings*

The *Duration* element in *OofSettings* will contain the last set scheduled OOF duration set by the user. The presence of *Duration* values should not be used to conclude that the user currently has a scheduled OOF in progress. Exchange Web Services will always return the user's last specified scheduled OOF duration, even if the current *OofState* value is *Enabled* or *Disabled*.

InternalReply and *ExternalReply* Elements in *OofSettings*

The *InternalReply* and *ExternalReply* elements in *OofSettings* will contain the last internal and external OOF message bodies set by the user. The presence of these values should not be used to conclude that that OOF reply messages are actively being sent by the Exchange Server on behalf of the mailbox owner.

Note If you are developing an application that allows a user to set his or her OOF settings, then it is customary to allow the user to edit his or her last set internal and external OOF message rather than require them to re-define the messages each time.

AllowExternalOof in *GetUserOofSettingsResponse*

The *AllowExternalOof* element is a string that maps to the *ExternalAudience* enumeration that was shown in Listing 22-6. The value reflects the minimum *ExternalAudience* value currently allowed by the organization's OOF reply message policy.

Determining the Effective *ExternalAudience* Value in a *GetUserOofSettingsResponse*

In the discussion above of the *ExternalAudience* element in *OofSettings*, it was noted that the value of the *ExternalAudience* element may not be the effective setting that is being used by the Exchange Server to determine whether or not external OOF reply messages are to be sent on behalf of mailbox owner. The actual setting that is being used by the Exchange Server to determine if external OOF reply messages are to be sent is the more restrictive of the *AllowExternalOof* and *ExternalAudience* elements in the *GetUserOofSettingsResponse*. The restrictive ranking of each of the *ExternalAudience* enumeration values is shown in Table 22-1

TABLE 22-1 Restrictive Value of Each *ExternalAudience* Enumeration Value

ExternalAudience enumeration value	Restrictive value
None	Most
Known	More
All	Least

For example, if you receive *OofSettings* in your *GetUserOofSettingsResponse* with an *ExternalAudience* value of *Known* and an *AllowExternalOof* value of *None*, then the effective value that the Exchange Server is using with regard to sending external OOF reply messages is *None*.

> **Note** Exchange Web Services does not reject calls to the *SetUserOofSettings* Web method containing *UserOofSettings* with an *ExternalAudience* value that is less restrictive then the organization's allowed external OOF reply message policy. For example, if your organization has a policy that states that OOF messages can be sent only to *known* e-mail addresses, and you call the *SetUserOofSettings* Web method setting a value of *All*, Exchange Web Services will accept your request without returning an error, but your *ExternalAudience* setting will be ignored because the organization's policy is more restrictive.

For more information on configuring the OOF reply message organizational policy, see the article titled "Managing the Out of Office Feature" on Microsoft TechNet at *http://technet.microsoft.com/en-us/library/aa998593.aspx*.

Getting User OOF Settings via the Proxy Classes

Listing 22-16 is an example of calling the *GetUserOofSettings* Web method via the proxy classes.

LISTING 22-16 Example of calling the *GetUserOofSettings* Web method and working with the *GetUserOofSettingsResponse* via the proxy classes

```
/// <summary>
/// Example of using the GetUserOofSettings method to get OOF
/// settings for a user.
/// </summary>
/// <param name="binding">Binding to make the call with</param>
/// <param name="userToSetOofFor">EmailAddress of the user
/// to get  OOF settings for.</param>
public static void GetUserOofSettings(
    ExchangeServiceBinding binding,
    EmailAddress userToGetOofFor)
{
    GetUserOofSettingsRequest getUserOofRequest =
        new GetUserOofSettingsRequest();
    getUserOofRequest.Mailbox = userToGetOofFor;

    // Set the request and check for any errors
    //
    GetUserOofSettingsResponse getUserOofResponse =
        binding.GetUserOofSettings(getUserOofRequest);
    if (getUserOofResponse.ResponseMessage.ResponseClass !=
        ResponseClassType.Success)
    {
        Console.WriteLine(String.Format(
            "Error in getting OOF settings.\r\n{0}\r\n{1}",
            getUserOofResponse.ResponseMessage.ResponseCode,
            getUserOofResponse.ResponseMessage.MessageText));
        return;
    }

    // Display the OOF settings we received
    //
    Console.WriteLine("User OOF Settings for {0}",
        (String.IsNullOrEmpty(getUserOofRequest.Mailbox.Name) ?
            getUserOofRequest.Mailbox.Address :
            getUserOofRequest.Mailbox.Name));

    Console.WriteLine("OOF State: " +
        getUserOofResponse.OofSettings.OofState);
    if (getUserOofResponse.OofSettings.OofState == OofState.Scheduled)
    {
        Console.WriteLine("\tDuration: {0} - {1}",
            getUserOofResponse.OofSettings.Duration.StartTime,
            getUserOofResponse.OofSettings.Duration.EndTime);
    }
    Console.WriteLine("Internal Reply:\r\n\t" +
        getUserOofResponse.OofSettings.InternalReply.Message);
```

```
    Console.WriteLine("External Audience: " +
        getUserOofResponse.OofSettings.ExternalAudience);
    if (getUserOofResponse.OofSettings.ExternalAudience !=
        ExternalAudience.None)
    {
        Console.WriteLine("External Reply:\r\n\t" +
            getUserOofResponse.OofSettings.ExternalReply.Message);
    }
}
```

Summary

This chapter discussed what Out Of Office (OOF) reply messages are and how you can call the *GetUserOofSettings* and *SetUserOofSettings* Web methods to get and set the criteria that the Exchange Server will use to send OOF reply messages on your behalf. We discussed the differences between internal and external e-mail addresses, as well as how OOF reply message bodies can be customized for each.

We stated that organizations can implement a policy that restricts the sending of OOF reply messages to external recipients, and how you can determine the effective setting from the values in a *GetUserOofSettingsResponse*.

David Sterling

David Sterling is a software developer on the Microsoft Exchange Web Services team and a skilled coffee drinker. Before joining Microsoft, David developed software in various industries such as electronic voting, CRM, and pharmaceuticals. When he is not writing software, he and his wife can be found taking a perfectly good room in a house and tearing it apart to build another, slightly different, perfectly good room in the same house. Then David can be found cleaning up the aforementioned perfectly good room. He lives in North Carolina with his wife, five children, one dog, and four cats.

Benjamin Spain

Benjamin Spain has been a Software Tester at Microsoft for seven years. In that time, he has worked on a variety of third party messaging protocols such as SMTP, POP3, IMAP4, DAV, and NNTP. Prior to working at Microsoft, Ben attended Minnesota State University, Mankato, where he received a Bachelors Degree in 2000 in Computer and Information Sciences.

When not at work, Ben enjoys either a rousing game of Ultimate Frisbee using only high-quality Discraft 175g Ultra-Star™ discs, charging down the snowy caps of the cascades on his 155cm snowboard, or smacking a 1.6 oz golf ball over 100 meters to the left with his 7-iron. Recently, though, Ben has discovered that rolling around on the floor with his 20 pound 2-year old son, Isaiah, is just as exciting as all of his other activities combined. Ben, his wife Stacey, and their son Isaiah live in Bothell, WA.

Michael Mainer

Michael Mainer has been in the computer industry for nearly a decade and has participated in the development of a few SDKs for Visual Studio and Exchange Server. He currently works at Microsoft on the Exchange Server SDK team, where his focus is primarily on Exchange Web Services. He brings to Microsoft experience working with GIS technology and B2B sales experience for the geo-spatial and IT value-added reseller industries.

Mark Taylor

Mark Taylor was born in a village in the North West of England called Hadfield. It is only 15 miles from Manchester and so he has been a big Manchester United fan since going to his first game when he was 5 years old. Mark came over to the U.S. to work for Microsoft after meeting a very special girl, whom he recently married. He's been at Microsoft for almost five years, all of them spent working on Exchange Server. He loves the Seattle area, especially the mountains, which are short in both height and supply back in the UK. His wife is fond of saying that if Mount Rainier were a woman she would be very worried about the way Mark's head automatically turns towards it whenever it is in view!

Huw Upshall

For more than nine years, Huw Upshall has worked in the test org of Microsoft Exchange Server. During that time, he has contributed to numerous projects including WebDav for both Windows and Exchange, ActiveSync, and Web Services. He is currently the test architect for the Exchange Client Access Server product. During his free time, Huw enjoys working on his house and restoring classic British sports cars.

Index

A

What do you think of this book?

We want to hear from you!

Do you have a few minutes to participate in a brief online survey?

Microsoft is interested in hearing your feedback so we can continually improve our books and learning resources for you.

To participate in our survey, please visit:

www.microsoft.com/learning/booksurvey/

...and enter this book's ISBN-10 or ISBN-13 number (located above barcode on back cover*). As a thank-you to survey participants in the United States and Canada, each month we'll randomly select five respondents to win one of five $100 gift certificates from a leading online merchant. At the conclusion of the survey, you can enter the drawing by providing your e-mail address, which will be used for prize notification only.

Thanks in advance for your input. Your opinion counts!

* Where to find the ISBN on back cover

ISBN-13: 000-0-0000-0000-0
ISBN-10: 0-0000-0000-0

Example only. Each book has unique ISBN.

Microsoft®
Press